Dictionary of English Words in Context

von
Wolf Friederich
unter Mitwirkung von
John Canavan

VERLAG LAMBERT LENSING · DORTMUND

ISBN 3-559-**22638**-4

Satz: Satz-Rechen-Zentrum Hartmann + Heenemann KG, Berlin
Druck: Lensingdruck, Dortmund

VORWORT

Das vorliegende Wörterbuch will ein Hilfsmittel sein, das heute mehr denn je von Lehrenden und Lernenden als notwendig empfunden wird: Wir wissen, daß der schwierigste Baustein zusammenhängender Texte nicht die Einzelwörter oder die Regeln der Grammatik sind, sondern die Redewendungen oder Kollokationen – die Verbindungen, die Wörter miteinander eingehen. Die häufige Frage „Kann man das im Englischen sagen?" bezieht sich zumeist darauf. Die Verbindungen, die Substantive, Verben, Adjektive und Adverbien miteinander eingehen, sind nicht frei, sondern liegen fest; sie unterliegen keinen Regeln oder Gesetzmäßigkeiten. Die Frage „Falsch oder Richtig?" ist aber eine Frage des individuellen, historisch gewachsenen Sprachgebrauchs. Hier größere Sicherheit zu verschaffen ist das Ziel dieses Wörterbuchs.

Es ist natürlich nicht möglich, den gesamten Sprachschatz in seinen Wortverbindungen zu erfassen. Das Selbstverständliche wurde ebenso fortgelassen wie das Seltenere, Veraltende, wenig Geläufige. Aber auch bei dieser Grenzziehung würde eine vollständige Erfassung des Nötigen ein mehrbändiges Werk erfordern, wodurch Handlichkeit und häufige Benutzung stark eingeschränkt wären. Es wurde deshalb den Stichwörtern der Vorzug gegeben, die für den praktischen Sprachgebrauch besonders wichtig sind und sich durch Häufigkeit des Vorkommens oder besondere Schwierigkeiten auszeichnen.

Was die Stilebene der Wörter und ihrer Bedeutungen betrifft, so wurde die neutrale Ebene unbezeichnet gelassen, die gehobene als ‚literarisch' und die umgangssprachliche als ‚informell' gekennzeichnet.

Zur Schwierigkeit der Auswahl kommt das Problem, wie man Wendungen anführen soll: *to lead s.o. up the garden path* unter *lead, garden, path*? Der Benutzer möge, wenn er einen Ausdruck an mehr als einer Stelle nachschlagen muß, bis er ihn findet, nicht entmutigt sein. Der folgende Abschnitt „Zur Benutzung des Wörterbuchs" sollte aber unbedingt gelesen werden.

Selbstverständlich entsteht ein so umfangreiches Werk nicht von heute auf morgen. Nach dem Abschluß der Arbeiten am Manuskript nimmt auch die technische Vorbereitung viel Zeit in Anspruch. Während der letzten Phasen der Fertigstellung dieses Werkes erschienen zwei Lexika, die leider nicht mehr berücksichtigt werden konnten, und zwar die 6. Auflage des *Concise Oxford Dictionary of Current English* und *Longman's Dictionary of Contemporary English*.

Für Anregungen zur Verbesserung des Buches sind Verlag und Verfasser dankbar.

Wolf Friederich

ZUR BENUTZUNG DES WÖRTERBUCHS

Anordnung der Stichwörter

Die Stichwörter sind alphabetisch angeordnet. Die *phrasal verbs* (Verben + Partikel) sowie die Verbindungen „Verb + Präposition" sind, soweit sie als eigene Stichwörter erscheinen, unmittelbar an das betreffende Verb angeschlossen: auf *do* folgen *do about, do at, do by, do down, do for, do in . . . do without*, dann *dog, dominate, door, double* usw. Gelegentlich sind Ausdrücke wie *at length, at liberty* eigene Stichwörter; sie erscheinen nach ihren Substantiven (*length, liberty*).
Mit hochgestellten Ziffern sind Probleme unterschieden, wie sie etwa bei *bank*[1], *bank*[2] oder *lie*[1], *lie*[2] etc. auftauchen.

Auswahl der Stichwörter

Als Stichwörter erscheinen Substantive, Verben, Adjektive und Adverbien (zumeist soweit sie ohne *-ly* gebildet sind). Hierbei ist folgende Einschränkung zu machen: wenn alles, was zum Gebrauch eines Wortes zu sagen ist, rein syntaktischer Natur ist und daher im *Grammatischen Wörterbuch – Englisch* von Leonhardi/Welsh (Verlag Lambert Lensing, Best.-Nr. 22617) voll erfaßt ist, dann ist dieses Stichwort hier nicht berücksichtigt. Daher fehlen z.B. *to congratulate*, während *congratulation* mit seinen Verbindungen erscheint; *to consent*, während *the consent* aufgeführt ist, *to denounce, to deny, to depart, to esteem* (*the esteem* ist gegeben), *to forget, to prohibit, to protest* u.a.

Aufbau der Stichwortartikel

Jedes Stichwort ist mit *n, v, vt (vi), adj, adv* als Substantiv, Verb, Adjektiv oder Adverb gekennzeichnet (Liste der Abkürzungen s. Seite 7). Die einzelnen Bedeutungen des Stichworts sind durch Ziffern (1), (2), (3) usw. geschieden.
Den Ziffern sind Erläuterungen beigefügt, wenn die Beispiele selbst nicht ausreichen, um die jeweilige Bedeutung des Stichworts klar zu zeigen. Diese Erläuterungen sind keine erschöpfenden Definitionen, sondern sollen nur den Bedeutungsbereich anzeigen, in dem das Stichwort hier gemeint ist; sie sollen also helfen zu differenzieren. Die Erläuterungen enthalten, wenn nötig, den Hinweis auf britisches bzw. amerikanisches Englisch (s. Seite 6).
Bei den Verben wurden transitive bzw. intransitive Bedeutungen jeweils zusammengefaßt und durch *vt* oder *vi* gekennzeichnet. Wenn diese Gliederung ungeeignet erschien, den Gebrauch des Verbs zu veranschaulichen, wurden beide Gruppen zusammen behandelt und mit *vt/i* gekennzeichnet.
Syntaktische Besonderheiten der Stichwörter sind nicht besonders formuliert, sondern den Beispielen zu entnehmen. Wenn z.B. bei *compare* (1) alle Beispiele mit *to*, bei den Bedeutungen (3), (4), (5) dagegen alle Beispiele mit *with* erscheinen, bei *compare* (2) aber das Partizip *compared* mit *with* oder *to*, dann sind das syntaktische Eigenheiten, die mit den jeweiligen Bedeutungen parallel laufen. Ebenso sind z.B. die Beispiele von *defend* (1) mit *against*, die von *defend* (2) mit *from* gebildet.

Einordnung der Wendungen (Kollokationen)

In der Regel wurde bei der Einordnung der Wendungen wie folgt verfahren:
Adjektiv + Substantiv erscheint unter dem Substantiv;
Adverb + Verb erscheint unter dem Verb;
Substantiv + Verb (Subjekt + Verb, Verb + Objekt) erscheint unter dem Verb;
Verb + Adjektiv (Prädikativum, z.B. *to drive s.o. mad*) steht unter dem Verb.

Eine Anzahl Verben, die besonders häufig vorkommen und deren Bedeutungen oft hinter der des dazugehörigen Substantivs verblassen, wurden anders behandelt: sie erscheinen vielfach bei den Substantiven. Es sind die Verben:

be	*give*	*hold*	*put*	*turn*
do	*go*	*keep*	*set*	*use*
get	*have*	*make*	*take*	

Um die Benutzung des Buches zu erleichtern, wurde hier und sonst von Verweisen (→) reichlich Gebrauch gemacht.

Beispiele

Die im Wörterbuch zu den Stichwörtern gegebenen Beispiele sind von dreierlei Art:

1) Beispiele, die keinen sinnvollen Beschränkungen unterliegen.
   to put s. th. on the table besagt, daß man *something* auf den Tisch legen kann: alles was sinnvoll ist, ist hier auch richtig.
2) Beispiele, bei denen gewisse Auswahlmöglichkeiten bestehen.
   Hier bedeuten senkrechte Striche (/) Austauschbares, die Klammern ( ) dagegen enthalten Wörter, die ergänzt oder weggelassen werden können. (Was in Klammern kursiv gedruckt erscheint, ist immer eine Erläuterung.) Also:
   distance *n* (1) . . . the station is no ~
   (away) *(quite near)* / is a great ~ off; . . .
   Dies bedeutet (zur Tilde s. unten): man kann sagen *the station is no distance* oder *no distance away* oder *is a great distance off*. Der Hinweis *quite near* soll helfen, die beiden ersten Beispiele genau zu verstehen.
3) Beispiele, die eine ganz feste Form haben (und oft auch idiomatisch sind). Sie sind durch das Zeichen □ kenntlich gemacht.

Tilde

Die Tilde (~) ersetzt das Stichwort, 2 Tilden ein aus 2 Wörtern bestehendes Stichwort (**do about** we cannot ~ anything ~ it = we cannot do anything about it), 3 Tilden ein aus 3 Wörtern bestehendes Stichwort (**do away with** let's ~~~ these old newspapers = let's do away with these old newspapers; aber: they did ~~ this law in 1949 = they did away with this law in 1949).
Partikeln und Präpositionen, die nur aus 2 Buchstaben bestehen (*at*, *by*, *in* usw.) wurden nicht durch die Tilde ersetzt.
Orthographische Veränderungen bleiben teilweise unberücksichtigt: change: ~ing = changing; marry: ~ed = married usw.

Stilebenen

Der gehobene literarische Gebrauch mancher Ausdrücke ist ebenso gekennzeichnet wie der informelle, ungezwungene Sprachgebrauch (*lit*, *inform*). Slang-Ausdrücke oder -bedeutungen, die der Nichtengländer durchaus verstehen, aber nicht so ohne weiteres verwenden sollte, haben *slang* (*sl*) als Hinweis.

Britisches und Amerikanisches Englisch

Die Varianten des britischen und amerikanischen Englisch sind durch *BE* und *AE* kenntlich gemacht. Der Zusatz BE bzw. AE bedeutet, daß die betreffende Bedeutung des Stichworts oder die betreffende einzelne Wendung im britischen (bzw. amerikanischen) Englisch zu Hause ist und außerhalb dieses Bereichs unbekannt oder zumindest unüblich ist. Da das britische Englisch in dieser Hinsicht laufend starken Veränderungen unterworfen ist, sollte man in der Anerkennung von „Amerikanismen" im britischen Englisch großzügig sein.

ABKÜRZUNGSVERZEICHNIS

adj	adjective
adv	adverb
AE	American English
BE	British English
dir	direct
eg	exempli gratia (for example)
esp	especially
etc	et cetera
fig	figurative
form	formal
ft	foot / feet
indef	indefinite
indir	indirect
inf	infinitive
inform	informal
kg	kilogram
lit	literary
milit	military
n	noun
neg	negative
obj	object
o. s.	oneself
part	participle
pass	passive
pl	plural
predic	predicative
prepos	preposition
sg	singular
sl	slang
s. o.	someone
s. th.	something
syn	synonym(ous)
usu.	usually
v	verb
vi	verb intransitive
vt	verb transitive
vt/i	verb transitive or intransitive
yd	yard

A

abandon *vt* (1) ~ ship / the sinking ship; the regiment ~ed the position; ~ a scheme; ~ the attempt (in despair) / all hope (2) it's wrong for a man to ~ his wife / family; an ~ed wife (3) the army ~ed the city to the enemy; ~ s.o. to his fate; ~ o.s. to the waves; ~ o.s. to one's work / to despair - *adj* an ~ed *(immoral)* woman.

abate *vi* (1) the wind / storm / pain / popular rage / fear of immediate war / epidemic ~d; his fury / anger ~d; the floods ~, - *vt* (2) some medicine to ~ the pain; ~ the horrors of war / the anger of the mob; the tax was ~d. (3 *put an end to*; *legal use*) we must ~ the smoke nuisance in our big cities; ~ abuses.

abbreviate *vt* 'Mister' is ~d 'Mr' or 'Mr.'; 'January' is often ~d to 'Jan.'; I have read only an ~d version of *Moby Dick*.

abide *vt* (1) she can't ~ him / his rudeness / wasps; I can't ~ to live in poverty. - *vi* (2) the players must ~ by the ruling; ~ by a contract / one's promises / a statement (3 *continue, endure*) even after disappointment, hope still ~s; the sailors abode / ~d in spite of the sea's fury.

ability *n* the ~ to reason makes man different from the animals; all men are not equal in ~; s.o.'s native ~; show outstanding / natural / *etc* ~ (in painting / *etc*); he has considerable ~, but he is lazy; a man of great ~ / ~ies; he has no organizing / artistic / *etc* ~ whatsoever; have / possess the ~ to (design beautiful buildings / *etc*); the ~ to be expert in doing s.th.; lose the ~ to concentrate; do s.th. to the best of one's ~.

able *adj* (1) when I'm not tired I am ~ to work faster; a mouse is ~ to run up smooth walls; a machine (which is) ~ to lift 10 tons; owls are ~ to see in the dark; I was ~ to put it on the top shelf; he was only ~ to swim halfway before he collapsed; American women are ~ to vote. (2) the lawyer was a very ~ man; an ~ worker / teacher / leader; he is the ~st man I know; he has an ~ mind; an ~ speech (3 *be ~ + pass inform*) he is ~ to be seen; a hill ~ to be climbed.

abolish *vt* ~ war / slavery / capital punishment / intemperance / poverty / old customs / privileges; ~ a law / regulation / tax / fee / office / institution / usage.

abound *vi* (1) deer ~ in these woods. (2 *be rich in*) these lakes ~ in trout; forests ~ing in game; the town ~s in historic remains; he ~s in courage. (3 *be infested with*) the hut ~ed with vermin; the fields ~ with stones.

abridge *vt* (1) ~ a book for magazine publication / a speech (2) all laws ~ liberty; Congress shall make no law ~ing the freedom of speech or of the press. - *adj* (3) the ~d edition of a book; the ~d version of a film; an ~d visit.

absence *n* (1) his ~ (from school) was immediately noted; in his father's ~ ; numerous ~s from school; be conspicuous by one's ~ (2) cold is the ~ of heat; the ~ of evidence / proof; □ ~ of mind *(inattention)*.

absent *adj* (1) ~ from school / work; who is ~ ? the ~ are always in the wrong. (2) look at s.o. / answer in an ~ manner / way; an ~-minded person; he has an ~ look in his eyes; react ~ly / ~-mindedly.

absorb *vt* (1) blotting-paper ~s ink; ~ water like a sponge; ~ immigrants / refugees into the local population; fees and taxation ~ed £600. (2) a bright child ~s knowledge easily; his mind could not ~ so many details. - *adj* (3) be ~ed in play / (reading) a book / the study of Latin; an ~ing book.

abstain *vi* ~ from alcohol / smoking / drink(ing) / women / (eating) meat / comment / voting.

abundance *n* there was food in ~ / an ~ of food; live in ~ ; illustrated with an ~ of figures and diagrams.

abundant *adj* (1) they found ~ game in the forests; we have ~ proof of his guilt; it is / should be made ~ly clear that we . . . (2) a land ~ in minerals.

abuse *n* (1) do you understand this ~ against a harmless opponent? a shower of ~ ; heap / shower ~ on s.o. (2) the ~ of power / authority; put an end to all ~s; the system is open to ~ by unscrupulous people. (3) the fine yarns can't take the same ~ as the heavier ones *(are more easily worn out)*.

abuse *vt* (1) ~ one's talents; the stomach will cause serious trouble only if grossly ~d. (2) ~ one's authority / position; ~ s.o.'s confidence / good nature / hospitality; ~ a privilege (3) the candidates ~d each other during the campaign; he ~d me with his / in obscene language.

abusive *adj* ~ language; an ~ tone of voice; ~ treatment (of a person).

academic *adj* (1) ~ freedom / studies / training; an ~ career / degree / subject / year; ~ matters (2) a (merely / purely) ~ method / discussion / question / point.

accelerate *vt* (1) ~ the motor by stepping on the pedal; ~ (the) speed / one's pace; ~ proceedings / technological progress / production (2) these measures ~d the dictator's fall. - *vi* (3) do not ~ when being overtaken (by another vehicle).

accept *vt* (1) ~ an offer / gift / present / invitation (to dinner) / proposal / challenge / bet / condition; ~ an offer of s.th. / to do s.th.; ~ s.o.'s apology / the terms of a contract (2) ~ an applicant / s.o. as one's assistant; the children immediately ~ed their new classmate. (3 *recognize as true*) ~ a statement / an explanation / s.o.'s view(s) / s.o.'s innocence; the jury ~ed his story; an ~ed truth (4 *agree to do what is required*) ~ an obligation / bill of exchange; ~ an office. - *vi* (5) he ~ed with thanks.

acceptance *n* (1) his ~ of his fate / position / role (2) his (full) ~ into the club was a long time in coming. (3) an ~ speech.

access *n* (1) ~ to the building from two roads / through the park; gain / obtain / allow s.o. / have ~ to the files / records / safes of a bank / Prime Minister; s.th. is easy / difficult of ~ (2 *form: outburst*) (have) an ~ of anger / fury / rage / despair / pessimism / fever / paralysis.

accident *n* (1) be involved / injured / killed in an (air / aircraft / railway / road / motor(ing) / car) ~; a serious / tragic / dreadful / ghastly / fatal / freak ~ ; our flat tyre was an unlucky ~ ; he has had / met with an ~ . (2) we met by ~ ; he did it by ~; discover s.th. by ~; be privileged / rich by ~ of birth.

accommodate *vt* (1) this bus / room / hotel will, can ~ 40 people; we were ~d at the Grosvenor Hotel / in a small room. (2) ~ s.o. with a loan / the use of one's car / lodgings; he did it to ~ *(oblige)* you. (3) the (pupil of the) eye ~s itself to light; in a strange country, we have to ~ ourselves to new ways of living; ~ o.s. to (the) circumstances (4) ~ a difference / quarrel.

accommodation *n* (1 *BE sg, AE pl lodging*) they finally found ~(s) at a motel; hotel ~ was / ~s were scarce during the Olympic Games; the town has excellent ~(s); give / offer s.o. ~(s); provide ~(s) for s.o.; supply s.o. with ~(s) (2) the ~ of the eye to light; the ~ of one's plans to those of another (3) that £1,000 loan was an ~ *(s.th. done to oblige)*. (4) the trend towards an ~ with Russia.

accompany *vt* (1) ~ s.o. on a walk / journey; father will ~ us to the concert. (2) wind ~ied the rain; heavy rain, ~ied with / by thunder; ~ one's words with lively gestures; ~ words with actions; ~ requests with threats; beauty is often ~ied by arrogance; pneumonia ~ied by high temperature / fever (3) ~ a song / singer on / at the piano.

accomplish *vt* (1) ~ a design / task (ingeniously / by collective action); he works hard but ~es nothing. - *adj* (2) be an ~ed musician / dancer / linguist / young lady.

accord *n* (1) I am in ~ *(agreement)* with your plans: we shall attack at dawn; his account of the matter is not in ~ with the facts; the costumes in the play were in ~ with the setting; all with one ~ refused; → own *adj.* (2) make an ~ with a country / between two countries.

accord *vt* (1) they ~ed him a hero's welcome; ~ dignity / praise / indulgence / a request to s.o.; words can ~ no comfort / consolation in this situation; children will readily ~ to others what others ~ to them. - *vi* (2) his evidence does not ~ with the policeman's; his actions ~ with his principles; this interpretation does not ~ with the spirit of the treaty; his ideas ~ with theirs.

accordance *n* in ~ with your plans, we attacked at dawn; his actions are in ~ with his principles; everything was carried out in ~ with instructions; in ~ with custom / regulations / your wishes.

account *n* (1) he gave us his ~ of the accident; a credible / detailed / accurate / one-sided / first-hand / exciting / *etc* ~; □ call / bring s.o. to ~ *(make him justify his conduct)*; □ give a good ~ of o.s. *(justify o.s.; perform well)*; he is, by all ~s *(as most people believe)*, a very rich man. (2)

a bank(ing) ~; I have an ~ with / at the Midland Bank; I have 500 marks in my ~; credit / charge it to my ~; open an ~ with / at a bank / the Post Office / a shop; pay £5 on ~ *(in part payment)*; please send in / render your ~ *(tell me what is owing)*; settle one's ~ *(pay)*; balance / settle ~s (with s.o.) *(pay what is owing)*; *(fig)* have an ~ to settle with s.o.; *(fig)* settle / square ~s with s.o. (3) be quick at ~s *(at calculating)* (4 *importance, value, valuation)* s.th. is of no / little / some ~ ; make much / little ~ of s.th.; leave s.th. out of ~; take no ~ *(notice)* of s.th.; you must take his family / past into ~; in judging the results, we must take ~ of the fact / take into ~ the fact that he is ...; turn / put s.th. to ~ *(make it profitable)* (5 *cause, reason*) I have gone to all this trouble on your ~; on no ~ are you to let anyone into the building; you must on no ~ repeat it! don't leave the baby alone on any ~; → own *adj.*

account *vt* Einstein is often ~ed the greatest of modern scientists; I ~ it a piece of good fortune (that we ...).

account for (1 *furnish reckoning*) she must ~ (to him) ~ every penny she spends. (2 *make amends*) he will ~ ~ his crime in jail / with a heavy fine. (3 *explain, give account for*) how would you ~ ~ the accident? the victim's disappearance has never been satisfactorily ~ed ~; the headmaster asked him to ~ ~ his absence / conduct / tardiness; everyone is present or ~ed ~ ; the prisoner-of-war list ~ed ~ 20 of the missing soldiers. (4 *be answerable for*) a dry spell ~ed ~ the poor crops; faulty tyres ~ed ~ the accident (5 *capture, put out of action*) the patrol ~ed ~ five of the enemy *(prisoners / losses)* (6 *kill*) our dog ~ed ~ two of the rabbits; the patrol ~ed ~ five of the enemy (dead).

accountable *adj* (1 *responsible*) hold / consider s.o. ~ for his actions / deeds; small children cannot be held ~ for outbursts of temper; stress is ~ for many a hasty decision; he is directly ~ to the children's parents for their safety. (2 *explicable*) his was an ~ action in view of the circumstances.

accumulate *vt* (1) ~ wealth / treasure(s) / capital / goods / a fortune / a collection of s.th. / papers on the table; ~ wisdom / ill will; boys ~ many things in their pockets. - *vi* (2) dust ~ed in every corner / on the unused books.

accurate *adj* an ~ measuring instrument / clock / weight; ~ scales; an ~ report / statement / translation / measurement; ~ reckoning; an ~ copy of the statue; they couldn't give us any ~ information; make an ~ assessment of the situation; he is very ~ in his work / extremely ~ in all matters.

accusation *n* bring / raise an ~ of theft / *etc* against s.o.; be under an ~ ; a false / unjust / unfounded / well-founded / *etc* ~; I refuse to put up with these / your ~s any longer.

accuse *vt* ~ s.o. of cowardice / a crime / an offence; ~ s.o. falsely / wrongfully / maliciously.

accustom *vt* ~ s.o. to order / heat / hard work / getting up early / sleeping alone; ~ o.s. to heat / *etc*; he cannot ~ himself to their diet.

accustomed *adj* at the ~ time; he misses his ~ surroundings; be / become / get ~ to heavy work / doing s.th.; in those days I was ~ to take a short walk before breakfast; we are ~ to think of Britain as ...; were you ~ to do that in your last post? I'm not ~ to walking long distances.

ache *vi* (1) my head / tooth ~s; the fever caused her body to ~; after climbing the mountain, he ~ed all over. (2) I am ~ing to see the new car; it makes my heart ~ *(sad).*

achieve *vt* (1) ~ a task / feat / journey (2) ~ (a great) success / glory / an honour / a reputation / a victory / one's end / a brilliant record in the sciences; I've already ~d quite a lot; I went to the consulate today but ~d nothing; we ~d good results with the experiment.

acknowledge *vt* (1) ~ a fact / a fault / (having made) a mistake; he ~d himself to be wrong / firing the shot / himself beaten. (2) ~ s.o. / s.o.'s authority / a child; ~ a claim / truth / debt to s.o.; ~ s.o. as / s.o. to be king; ~ a work to be excellent; he is ~d as the leader of his party. (3) ~ a gift / letter / receipt of s.th. / greeting / nod. - *adj* (4) an ~d authority / doctrine / custom / usage.

acquaint *vt* (1) I ~ed the new clerk with his duties / myself with my new duties. - *adj* (2) be / become ~ed with s.o./ s.th.; we are ~ed; make o.s. ~ed with s.th.

acquaintance *n* (1) his ~ with the language will be useful to him; he had a close

~ with the facts of the case; make s.o.'s ~; he improves upon closer ~. (2) he is not a friend of mine, merely an ~ ; we are old ~s; a casual / passing ~.

acquiesce *vi* ~ in a proposal / arrangement / opinion; ~ in s.o.'s plans / request.

acquire *vt* (1) ~ money / fortune / property / land / German citizenship; ~ s.th. by purchase / work (2) ~ a position / rights / the copyright / skill (in doing s.th.) / knowledge / fluency (in a language) / respect for s.th.; ~ an interest in s.th. / taste for s.th. / (particular) importance / significance / inclination (for s.th.). - *adj* (3) innate and ~d characteristics; an ~d taste.

acquit *vt* (1) the jury ~ted the man (on two of the charges); I cannot ~ him of negligence; ~ s.o. of blame / a crime (2) ~ o.s. (of a task / duty) well / admirably / creditably / with credit / with distinction / ill / poorly.

act *vt* (1) ~ Othello / a part / a play / a role (2) stop ~ing the ass / fool / goat / idiot; ~ your age *(don't be foolish)*. - *vi* (2) he ~s well; she loves to ~ in amateur productions; do you forget yourself when you are ~ing? (3) his plays / this role won't ~; → read *vi* 17. (4) ~ like an amateur; she ~s as if she were about to cry / be sick; you're ~ing like a baby! the dog ~s friendly. (5) ~ from fear / love / a sense of duty; ~ out of regard for s.o.; ~ on an impulse / impulsively; ~ (un)fairly to(wards) s.o. / foolishly / generously / promptly / wisely; ~ according to one's convictions / principles / profession / reputation; ~ up to one's engagements *(fulfil them)*; ~ up to one's principles; the police ~ed quickly; it's time to ~; we shall ~ as directed; ~ under compulsion / a misapprehension / orders; ~ (up)on s.o.'s advice / instruction / suggestions; ~ upon the information one receives (6) ~ as counsellor / go-between / interpreter; he ~ed for Ann while she was ill. (7) the acid ~ed on the metal; alcohol ~s on the nervous system; this medicine ~s on the brain / glands / *etc*; how does the chemical ~ when mixed with water?; the car's brakes refused to / wouldn't ~ (so there was an accident). (8) he isn't serious, he's just ~ing.

act up (1 *behave different from normal*) occasionally the river ~s up; I'd advise you not to ~ up with me. (2 *function badly*) this typewriter is ~ing up again; my car has been ~ing up recently. (3) → act *vi* 5.

act *n* (1) perform an ~ ; (it was) a cruel / kind / foolish / noble / base / mean / valiant / heroic / good / voluntary / lawful / criminal / belated doubtful / *etc* ~; it was a virtuous ~; an ~ of folly / madness / cruelty / faith / will / mercy / kindness / heroism / self-defence; an ~ of a fool; put on an ~ *(pose insincerely)*; an Act of God; in the case of Acts of God; judge s.o. by his ~s; faithful in word and ~; innocent in thought and ~ (2) he was (caught / surprised) in the (very) ~ of stealing / taking the money / escaping; in the ~ of jumping / diving (3) an Act of Parliament / Congress (4) a play in five ~s (5) a circus / music-hall ~.

action *n* (1) a man of ~; a virtuous course of ~; suit the ~ to the words (→ word *n* *2*); faithful in speech and ~; effective / prompt / quick ~; put a plan / *etc* into ~ (→ put *vt* 6a); set / bring / call s.th. into ~; accomplish s.th. by collective / joint ~; it's time to take ~ (2) judge s.o. by his ~s; everyone is responsible for his own ~s; history is the account of the ~s of men; the ~s of a fool cannot be foreseen; by judicious ~s he avoided war; a good / mean / cruel / kind / foolish / noble / base / ill-advised / premeditated ~ (3 *effect*) the ~ of the rain washed away the soil; the ~ of light on s.th. (4) the ~ of a machine; put a machine out of ~ (5 *legal process*) bring / enter an ~ against s.o.; dismiss an ~; an ~ for damages; can the county courts try any ~? (6 *battle*) go into ~; open / break off the ~; put a gun / a ship / the enemy out of ~; killed in ~; two small ~s for control of the hill.

active *adj* (1) an ~ supporter / helper / reformer / partner / member (of a club / party); ~ in local politics; children are ~ in the morning. (2) an ~ drug / disease / occupation / mind / brain; have an ~ imagination; take an ~ interest / part in s.th.; ~ life / measures / resistance / co-operation; an ~ volcano (3) ~ assets *(bearing interest)* (4) be on ~ duty in the military.

actual *adj* was Robinson Crusoe an ~ person? I cannot give you the ~ figures; what is the ~ position of affairs?

actually *adv* (1 *really*) he pretended to be deaf, but ~ he was not; did you ~ build this model aeroplane? he was there, but I didn't ~ see him. (2 *strange as it may* *seem*) he ~ sells those terrible paintings; he ~ thought that I was a thief. (3 *at this moment*) the goverment ~ in office.

acute *adj* (1) ~ hearing / perception; dogs have an ~ sense of hearing / smell; an ~ observer / critic; an ~ suggestion *(shrewd)* (2) ~ pain; an ~ (labour) shortage; an ~ attack of (a disease); s.th. reaches its ~ stage (3) ~ sounds *(shrill)*.

adapt *vt* (1) ~ a novel / play for broadcasting / the stage; ~ a garage for use as a workshop; a system which can be ~ed for use in the home; ~ a book for beginners / to the needs of beginners (2) ~ o.s. to (new) circumstances / one's environment - *vi* (3) the trouble with John is that he doesn't ~ easily / well.

add *vt* (1) ~ a figure; if you ~ 3 to 4 you get 7; ~ 6, carry 3. (2) ~ eggs to the batter / some wine (to the gravy); ~ your letters to mine / these items to my order / your signature (to a document / list) / (a few) marginal notes; suspense ~s interest to a story; the book ~s nothing to what is already known; ~ dimensions of enjoyment to life; □ ~ insult to injury (3) ~ a new storey to a house (4) 'And don't be late,' he ~ed. - *vi* (5) ~ in one's head / on paper / on an ~ing machine / on a calculator; you don't know how to ~. (6) the house has been ~ed to from time to time. (7) losing the rope ~ed to our difficulties; this ~ed to our joy.

add in ~ this in with the rest.

add up (1) ~ up figures / expenses / *etc*; you haven't ~ed the figures up right. (2) the figures ~ up to 283. (3) what do his remarks ~ up to *(mean)*? (4) his story doesn't ~ up *(inform: make sense)*.

addicted *adj* be / become ~ to drink / gambling / betting / lying / drugs / the bottle / gossip; be ~ to meringues / baseball / study.

address *n* (1) what is your ~? a permanent / forwarding ~; give exact postal ~! change one's ~ (2) he is at his old ~; a good ~ *(house in a fashionable district)* (3 *speech*) deliver / give an ~ (of congratulation / condolence / *etc*); an opening / inaugural ~ (4) a man of pleasing / winning ~; a good ~ *(pleasant manner)*; her ~ in rendering her guests easy with one another.

address *vt* (1) ~ a letter / parcel; this letter is ~ed to you. (2) ~ a meeting / audience; never ~ an unmarried lady by 'Miss' only; she ~ed the stranger politely. (3) ~ remarks / protest / a petition to the Minister; a book ~ed to the teenager; we are ~ing ourselves primarily to teachers, but ...; ~ o.s. to other tasks; ~ o.s. to theory.

adjust *vt* (1) ~ a tool / instrument (to s.th.); the mechanic ~ed the fuel pump in the engine; a piano stool may be ~ed to suit the height of the player; ~ the length of a coat (2) ~ o.s. to new circumstances / the wilderness; ~ means to ends (3) ~ differences of opinion; ~ a claim *(settle it)*.

administer *vt*(1) ~ s.o.'s affairs / an estate / the affairs of the country (2) ~ justice / punishment / the laws / the sacraments (3) ~ (s.o.) a medicine / dose of s.th. / *(inform)* a box on the ear; an anaesthetist ~s anaesthetics; the drug should be ~ed in the early stages of the disease. (4) the bailiff ~ed the oath to the witness. - *vi* (5) ~ to s.o.'s comfort / pleasure *(care for)*.

admiration *n* (1) feel / be filled with / be full of / ~ for s.o./ s.th.; stand / be lost in ~ of the beauty of the scene; look at s.o. / s.th. with ~ (2) she was the ~ of all (the young men in the village); the team was the ~ of all the school.

admire *vt* (1) ~ a picture / the nobility of s.o.'s aims / s.o. for his courage; we ~d her handling of the younger children; a much-~d actor (2) don't forget to ~ the baby.

admission *n* (1) ~ (to the theatre) by ticket only; gain ~; ~ free; free ~ is limited to certain days; apply for ~ to an exam (2) ~ two dollars; we paid 3 marks ~; (3) he signed an ~ of his guilt. A (reluctant / damaging / *etc*) ~ (of a mistake).

admit *vt* (1) this ticket will ~ you to the concert; the child was ~ted to school; children not ~ted; children are ~ted free; my friend got me ~ted to the embassy; ~ s.o. into a club / to an examination; ~ sad thoughts (2) this hall ~s a thousand people. (3 *recognize as true*) ~ a claim / assumption (4) I ~ my mistake / the theft / that you are right; ~ the truth / one's hatred of s.th. / one's liking for s.th. / one's guilt; he ~s himself guilty; he ~s (to) stealing it; I must ~ to feeling ashamed; I have to ~ my ignorance; one must ~ one's faults to oneself. - *vi* (5) this door ~s to the concert hall.

admit of the emergency ~s of no delay; such conduct ~s of no excuse; this passage ~s of two interpretations; many crucial dilemmas simply do not ~ of analysis on one page.

admittance *n* no ~ (except on business); a stranger asked for ~; my friend gained me ~ to the embassy.

adopt *vt* (1) ~ a child / s.o. as (an) heir; the ~ing parents; an ~ed child (2) the Normans ~ed the French language; ~ a name / idea / opinion / view / point of view / attitude / outlook / policy / recommendation / (new) method / system; ~ the decimal system; ~ a particular mode of living / a custom (3 *vote to accept*) the committee ~ed the chairman's plan; ~ the minutes; ~ a motion / bill / resolution / report; ~ a measure *(take it)*; ~ a candidate *(BE appoint him)*.

adorn *vt* (1) the hat was ~ed with roses; ~ o.s. / s.o. with jewels / *etc* (2) virtue ~s the mind; great men ~ their country; we hope you will ~ our rural rectory with your presence.

adult *adj* (1) an ~ man / animal / plant; the standards of the ~ world; you are too ~ly serious. (2) ~ education / baptism; an ~ residential college; behave in an ~ fashion.

advance *n* (1) nothing could stop the ~ of the enemy. (2) send your luggage in ~; pay rent in ~; spend one's income in ~. (3) the ~ of science; science has made great ~s; the new process is a significant ~ on earlier methods; ~(s) (made) in medicine; the social ~s of the last hundred years (4) an ~ in the cost of living / petrol taxes; the average ~ in prices (5) banks make ~s to business firms; ask for an ~ on one's salary (6) when the family moved to the new house, their neighbours made the first ~s; encourage / repel s.o.'s ~s. - *adj* (7) procure ~ information about s.th.; an ~ copy of a book; the ~ booking office; ... if ~ notice is given.

advance *vt* (1) ~ a pawn *(in chess)*; ~ the film *(in a camera)* (2) the general ~d three officers to colonel. (3) ~ prices / one's charges (by 20%) (4) the date of the meeting was ~d from May 8 to May 5. (5) his employer ~d him a month's salary; my father ~d me my next week's allowance. (6) ~ a claim / an objection / one's opinion (on a matter) / a theory (7) ~ science / peace / the cause of freedom; this will never ~ the interests of the workers; ~ s.o. in his career / profession. - *vi* (8) the army ~d (against / on / towards the enemy); our troops have ~d two miles (9) he ~d to colonel / the position of manager. (10) prices continue to ~; coal ~d 50p a ton. (11) his work ~d rapidly.

advanced *adj* (1) he's ~ in years; at an ~ age; we are well ~ in the development of this model; the disease is already so far ~ that an operation is unavoidable. (2) ~ ideas / thinkers / studies / students; an ~ course / textbook.

advancement *n* his ~ to such a high position has been rapid; have hopes of ~; contribute to the ~ of science.

advantage *n* (1) there are few / many ~s in that method; the ~s outweigh the disadvantages; this school offers valuable educational ~s; have / gain / win / give s.o. an ~ (over s.o.) (2) get / have the ~ of s.o. *(get / be in an advantageous position)*; he had the ~ of good training; find some ~ in even the worst circumstances; he gained little ~ from his visit to London; take (unfair) ~ of s.o. / s.o.'s weaknesses / his ignorance / *etc*; he always takes full ~ of the mistakes made by his rivals; spend one's money to the best ~; it is to his (best) ~ that he ...; (don't let him) take ~ of you *(deceive)*; turn s.th. to (good) ~ *(use it profitably)*; the decision was / proved to (be to) John's ~ / to the ~ of John; → show *vi* 7a.

adventure *n* (1) meet with (an) / have an ~; the great ~; an amorous ~; incredible / uncommon / singular / strange / amusing / *etc* ~s; an ~ / ~s in outer space (2) go / set out in quest / search of ~; life is full of ~ for the young; a story of ~.

advertise *vt* (1) ~ a meeting / reward / change of schedule; he does it to ~ himself; the firm ~d that it was opening a new branch office. (2) shopkeepers ~ the goods they want to sell; - *vi* (3) do you never ~?; he ~s for a house to rent; people often ~ for servants in the papers.

advertisement *n* small / classified ~s; (an) ~ helps to sell goods; insert / put an ~ in the paper (for s.th.)

advice *n* ask for / seek / request ~ from s.o. (on s.th.); give s.o. good ~; follow / take s.o.'s ~; take legal ~ *(consult a lawyer)*; take medical ~; to give ~ is easy, to take ~ is often difficult; well-meant / wise / worthless / fatherly / paternal ~; a piece / bit / word of ~; I'm sure that's good ~, but ...; the book offers a fund of sound ~; ~ to students on ... is given by...

advise *vt* (1 *give advice*) I would ~ you to save your money / be cautious; I did not ~ his doing it; he ~d me on / about the best way of conduct; I ~d that he (should) avoid the stock market for a while. (2 *to inform*) the campers were ~d about the danger of snakes; I will ~ you in due course (of my decision); we have pleasure in ~ing you that our products ... - *vi* (3 *consult*) ~ with one's associates / colleagues / partners / *etc.* - *adj* (4) he would be badly / ill / soundly / well-~d to continue in this way; he is a poorly / well- / *etc* ~d executive.

advocate *vt* ~ a cause / the paying of close attention to any experiments / that the refugees should be taken in / rationing the use of cars; he ~s careful spending of our country's money.

affair *n* (1) the railway accident was a terrible ~; a sinister / hit-and-miss ~ (2) ~s of state; internal ~s; life is a monotonous ~ to many people; I don't want to be mixed up with this ~; that's my ~, not yours; this is a nice state of ~s! private ~s (3) an ~ of honour *(duel)*; keep one's (love) ~ secret (4) the cab was a ramshackle ~; her hat is a wonderful ~; the concert was rather an amateurish ~.

affect *vt* (1) the climate ~ed our health; flood damage adversely ~ed the crops; oxygen ~s nearly everything. (2) ~ s.o.'s civil rights / property; does this change ~ your plans / the results? a number of factories were not ~ed by the strike at all; the districts worst ~ed by the fire (3) strong coffee ~s the heart; the swelling ~ed the entire leg; whooping-cough mainly ~s children under 5; this small type ~s the eyes. (4) the news of Jim's death ~ed him deeply; his fate ~s all of us; this kind of music ~s my feelings; I was strangely ~ed by his words. (5 *pretend*) ~ indifference / interest / ignorance / sincerity / conscientiousness / *etc*; although Mary hoped John would win, she ~ed a nonchalant manner; she ~ed not to care. (6 *show off*) ~ airs / a grand manner; she ~s a hyper-correct pronunciation and a pseudo-educated vocabulary. - *adj* (7) the lung is already ~ed; a badly ~ed liver (8) she was too ~ed to say anything. (9 *pretentious*) an ~ed attitude / nonchalance / indifference / interest / ignorance / sincerity / conscientiousness (10 *artificial*) an ~ way of behaving / speaking.

affection *n* (1) s.o.'s genuine / deep / tender / fraternal / sisterly / parental / *etc* ~; have ~ for s.o.; feel ~ towards s.o.; he hopes to win her ~(s); who is the object of his ~s *(the one he loves)*? (2) an ~ of the right lung / the liver / *etc.*

afford *vt* (1) the tower ~s a fine view; swimming ~s enjoyment and muscular training; history ~s several examples of it; his son's success ~ed him great pleasure; ~ s.o. satisfaction; ~ an opportunity / occasion (to do s.th.) (2) can you ~ (to take) a taxi? ; I cannot ~ (the time) to go out; I cannot ~ (to buy) that / (to pay for) such expensive books; I cannot ~ to be critical / to be seen in places like that; we cannot ~ private music lessons for our son.

afraid *adj* nothing can make me ~; some women are ~ of mice; she was ~ of wakening the sleeper *(by closing the door noisily)*; I'm ~ of going home by myself; you have nothing to be ~ of; the boy was ~ to go near the dog *(didn't want to)*; she was ~ to waken the sleeper *(dared not wake him)*; I'm not ~ to stress the need for discipline; he was ~ to seem ungrateful if he refused; he was ~ (that) the dog would bite him; I'm ~ it's too late; she was ~ for her son's life.

age *n* (1) what's your ~? he is my ~; he is twice my ~; he does not look his ~; he is five years of ~ (now); his ~ is now five years; at the ~ of ten; a ten years of ~; at my ~ you just don't take up skiing; he is tall for his ~; what's the ~ of that old castle? (2) reach school ~; a boy of primary-school ~; the ~ of reason / discretion; be under / over (the required ~ (3) be of (full) ~ *(be 18 or 21)*; come of ~; be under ~; the legal ~ (4) a man of middle ~; attain old ~; live to a (ripe) old / a great ~; die at a good old ~; grey with old ~; weak and feeble from ~; eyes dim with ~; the wisdom / ripeness of ~ (5) the Stone / Bronze / ice- / Elizabethan / *etc* ~; the Middle Ages; the ~ of chivalry / Pericles / *etc*; a new / the atomic ~; the ~ of space travel; ~s yet unborn; in ~s to come; I haven't seen him for ~s *(a long time)*; it has taken me ~s to do it; that happened ~s ago; it's an ~ since we last met.

age *vt* (1) fear and worry / his illness ~d him. (2) ~ wine / cheese - *vi* (3) she has ~d (overnight); she hasn't ~d a bit. (4) this whisky hasn't ~d (long) enough.

aged *adj* (1) a boy ~ ten (2) an ~ man; the poor and the ~; ~ relics / ruins / times; an ~ city / forest / tree; ~ wrinkles; (properly) ~ wine / cheese.

aggravate *vt* (1) ~ a wound / disease / grievance / sorrow / offence / situation; scratching a mosquito bite ~s it. (2 *inform*) he ~d *(annoyed)* his parents by staying out late at night; how ~ing!

agitate *vt* (1) the wind ~d the lake. (2) the bad news ~d him. (3) the paper ~d for better housing; the workers ~ for higher wages / a reform of . . .; the report ~d interest in social reform. - *adj* (4) she'll get very ~d *(upset)* if she hears you're coming; he was ~d about his wife's health; speak in an ~d voice.

agony *n* (1) the wounded shark thrashed about in mortal ~; be in ~ies of pain; I've suffered ~ies / been in ~ies with toothache (2) be in an ~ of remorse; an ~ of joy; ~ies of delight; (an) ~ / ~ies of doubt (3) go through ~ies *(try very hard)* to get s.th.

agree *vi* (1 *say yes, consent*) I asked him to come with us and he ~d; I (fully) ~ that your plan is better; she ~d to try out the scheme / let me have her car; the Americans have at last ~d to remove this restriction; he ~d to pay the sum; let's ~ to differ; ~ to s.o.'s conditions / terms / proposals (under protest); ~ to a plan; the terms have now been ~d to; father ~d to my becoming an engineer; I certainly could not ~ to parting with him. (2 *have the same opinion as s.o.*) I quite ~ with you on that point / about his stinginess / that it is too late; ~ with s.o. in an opinion; I ~ in what you say; no two scholars would ~ in the selection of pertinent examples. (3 *get along together*) the two managed to ~ fairly well; the children can't ~, they're always quarrelling. (4 *think the same about s.th., consider right*) s.o. ~s with an opinion / suggestion / proposal / statement / practice; I hope you ~ with what I have said; I don't ~ with buying children expensive presents. (5 *correspond, of things*) the copies ~ exactly with the originals; their findings ~ with mine; his report does not ~ with the facts. (6 *reach a harmonious understanding*) we couldn't even ~ among ourselves; I have ~d on the price with her; we ought to ~ on some plan of action; they couldn't ~ on the policy to be adopted; we eventually ~d on the best plan / on a fair division of the profits; we ~d on (making) an early start / to start early / that we should start early; we could not ~ (as to) how it should be done; they could never ~ about the merits of Picasso as a painter; we don't ~ about the dog; have you ~d about the price yet? (7 *be fitting, healthful*) a dry climate will ~ with the patient; this damp weather doesn't ~ with my rheumatism; onions don't ~ with everyone. (8 *correspond, in grammar*) the German verb ~s with its subject in person and number. *vt* (9 *consent*) I (fully) ~ (that your plan is better). (10 *BE approve, settle*) the following articles were ~d; has the Office now ~d the plans? neither the site nor the financial problems involved have been ~d; they have ~d their quarrel; did you ~ *(confirm)* the bill? I ~ the claim for damages; please ~ *(check)* my total. - *adj* (11 → 10) an ~d price; an ~d policy, clearly stated, will mean less trouble. (12 → 2) scholars are not ~d on that point; they are all ~d in finding him guilty.

agreeable *adj* (1) an ~ manner / voice / smell / taste / conversation; ~ behaviour / company; make o.s. ~ to s.o.; ~ly surprised (2) are you ~ to this plan? I'm quite ~ to your having Wednesday afternoon off; I'm ~ to do what you suggest; if that is ~ to you.

agreement *n* (1) be in (complete / full / partial / satisfactory) ~ with a measure / in, about a matter / on the conditions, a price, *etc*; they were in substantial ~; come to ~ on the terms of a treaty; by tacit ~ (2) there was complete ~ between the stories of the two witnesses; be in ~ with the facts (3) an ~ to buy s.th. / to rent a house; a verbal / oral / written / international / trade / *etc* ~; make / arrive at / enter into / conclude / come to an ~ with s.o. in, about a matter / on the price of s.th. / *etc*; to bring two parties to an ~.

aid *n* (1) give / render s.o. ~; he came to my ~; a bazaar will be held in ~ of church funds; what is the collection in ~ of? he opened the lock with the ~ of a hairpin; invaluable ~ to their further progress (2) they reconstructed their economy with American ~; the country has cut down its ~ to India; ~ for refugees / orphans / *etc*; first ~ (3) books are an ~ to learning; ~s to memory; a deaf-~; visual ~s; ~s and appliances.

aid *vt* he ~ed me in my work; a glass of wine ~s digestion; this method ~s the memory.

ail *vt/ i* what ~s him? does anything ~ him? he is ~ing.

aim *n* (1) take (careful / good) ~ (at / towards s.th.); miss one's ~ (2) have an ~ in life; the main ~ is to finish (the work) quickly.

aim *vt* (1) he ~ed (his gun) at the lion and fired. (2) he ~ed the stone at the dog / the blows at his chin. (3) those insults were ~ed at you; realize who that remark was ~ed at. - *vi* (4) ~ at / towards a target; you are ~ing too low; ~ high *(also fig)* (5) he was ~ing for (the) directorship; ~ at perfection; what are you ~ing at? he ~s at becoming a doctor; we're ~ing to find a house in N.; we ~ to please.

air *n* (1) let's go out and get / have some fresh ~; wholesome / salubrious / crisp / salutary mountain ~; □ (our plans are still) in the ~ *(unsettled)*; □ (there are rumours) in the ~ *(spreading)*; □ clear the ~ *(in a room; also fig. get rid of doubt by giving facts)*; □ (build) castles in the ~; □ walk on ~ *(feel elated)* (2) go by ~; send letters by ~ (3) be on the ~ *(broadcast)*; what's on the ~ this evening? go on the ~ *(begin broadcasting)*; go off the ~ (4 *tune*) sing an ~; she played some of the old ~s; hum the ~ of the Blue Danube (5 *manner*) have a nonchalant / confident / dignified / innocent / jaunty ~; have an ~ of nonchalance / confidence / dignity / innocence / importance / superiority; her city ~s annoyed her friends at home; the house has an ~ of comfort; give o.s. / put on ~s *(have an affected attitude)* (6 *aura*) the room has an ~ of mystery.

air *vt* (1) ~ a room / the beds / freshly ironed clothes (2) ~ one's grievances (to everyone); ~ one's view / opinion / a theory; he likes to ~ his knowledge; (3 *BE*) ~ one's fine clothes *(show off)*.

alarm *n* (1) everyone rushed out in ~ when the fire started; he jumped up in ~; → take *vt* 17; ~ spread among the people. (2) give the ~ to s.o.; sound / ring the ~; false ~ (3) a burglar / fire ~ *(device)*; set the ~(-clock) for six o'clock.

alarm *vt* (1) he was ~ed at her appearance; my mother, ~ed by the cries, came running ... - *adj* (2) ~ing news; she was ~ingly ugly.

alert *vt* we ~ed them to the dangers / consequences of their doings; be ~ed to danger; he was ~ed by the flight of the geese.

alert *adj* (1) ~ to danger(s); an ~ intellect / mind. - *n* (2) be on the ~ (3 *signal*) the ~ flashed / sounded / warned of danger.

alight *vi* (1) ~ from a vehicle / bicycle / horse; ~ on water / the ground / the pavement; ~ (up)on the top branch; ~ at the church / Trafalgar Square.

allay *vt* (1) ~ tumult / disturbances / the tempest (2) ~ pain / trouble / excitement / fears / anxieties.

alleviate *vt* (1) ~ pain / suffering / the itching / (the discomfort of) a disease / s.o.'s sorrow (2) ~ problems / the labour shortage / the causes of conflicts among nations / the tax burden.

allow *vt* (1) the hospital ~s no visitors; I am ~ed wine; ~ me one word! ~ o.s. another cigar / insolent remarks / *etc*; ~ me to remark that he ...; I was ~ed / they ~ed me (to do s.th.) (2 *give*) the class was ~ed one hour to finish the test; ~ a discount / privilege / rebate to s.o.; he ~s his son £500 a year; she ~ed her imagination full play. (3 *accept as true, admit*) his claim was ~ed; we must ~ him to be a genius; I ~ that to be true; ~ that he is a genius; I ~ that I have made a mistake. - *vi* (4 *with non-personal subjects*) if the weather ~s; as soon as circumstances ~; the decision / matter ~s of no delay; in a tone which ~ed of no reply; the passage ~s of several interpretations; his condition would not ~ of his going out.

allow for ~ ~ unexpected expenses; ~ ~ extra time to travel, because of the icy streets; ~ extra time ~ s.th.; we must ~ ~ his being ill / the youth of the accused; ~ing ~ exceptions, the rule may stand.

allowance *n* (1) an ~ of pocket money / food / wine / petrol / *etc*; a family / travelling ~ (2) an ~ for wear and tear / used goods traded in (3) he left early to make ~ for bad road conditions; we must make ~(s) for the youth of the accused / his lack of experience (→ make *vt* 16).

allure *vt* (1) ~ s.o. with promises / by the promise of pleasure; ~ customers (into bars / shops). - *adj* (2) an ~ing woman; circuses are very ~ing to children.

alone *adj* (1) he's going ~; he likes living ~; I'm all ~ today; she's ~ in the world; I did it ~; his house stands ~ on the hillside; → leave *vt* 6, let alone. (2) he ~ has the answer / knows why; he ~ can do it; God ~ can help us; courage ~ is not enough; we are not ~ in thinking that we...

alter *vt* (1) he ~ed the 6 into an 8; the tailor ~ed the suit to fit the boy; the bike is all right - you won't even need to ~ the height of the saddle; the ship ~ed course; ~ a word / a sentence (in a text) / the sense; ~ one's opinion / plans / tone; I must have this dress ~ed; that ~s matters / the case; it won't ~ matters in any way; ~ s.th. for the better / worse; you will find him greatly ~ed. - *vi* (2) he has ~ed a great deal; my opinion ~ed when I learned the facts.

alteration *n* (1) there isn't much ~ in the village. (2) an ~ of plans / opinions / *etc*; make an ~ to a dress (→ make *vt* 16); prices / times / service / *etc* subject to ~; we reserve the right to make ~s.

alternate *vt* (1) ~ red and blue lines / red lines with blue; she ~d bullying and cajoling / kindness with severity. - *vi* (2) my sister and I ~ in cleaning our room. (3) white and black tiles ~d; white tiles ~d with black; day ~s with night; optimism ~d with pessimism; her mood ~s between happy and euphoric. - *adj* (4) the pattern consists of ~ reds and blacks.

amass *vt* ~ money / riches / great wealth / a fortune / a treasure / scientific knowledge.

amazement *n* fill s.o. / be filled with ~; I heard with ~ that he ...; look at s.o. in ~; stand in (speechless) ~; to my great ~.

ambition *n* (1) healthy / morbid ~; eaten up with ~; he lacks / has no ~; it is my ~ (to visit Asia) (2) he had an ~ (to fly round the world); he has great ~s. (3) he attained his ~ (to become a reporter); achieve one of childhood's greatest ~s.

ameliorate *vt* ~ conditions (in the slums) / the condition of the working classes / poverty and misery; my misery cannot be ~d.

amenable *adj* (1) we are all ~ to the law. (2) s.o. has an ~ disposition; be ~ to reason / suggestion / advice / argument / kindness / discipline (3) the case / this situation is not ~ to ordinary rules; s.th. is ~ to a test / very high temperatures.

amenity *n* (1) the ~ of the Californian climate / the countryside; his ~ of temper (2) the ~ies of literature (3) ~ies like shops and community centres; a town with many ~ies *(parks, sports facilities, public libraries, etc)*; the houses have all the ~ies usually found only in cities - electricity, stainless steel sinks, a bathroom and so on; ~ies will be provided for all sports including athletics, gymnastics, indoor bowls, swimming and tennis. (4 *BE*) a small house in a choice ~; they preserved the region and developed it as an ~; this small forest, a favourite week-end spot for the nearby town of H., was classed as a local ~.

amount *n* a (large / great / enormous / huge / *etc*) ~ of material / rubbish / money / work / *etc*; an unprecedented ~ of snow; a surprising ~ of patience; the total ~; he paid the full ~; a bill / cheque for / to / in the ~ of £ 12.

amount *vi* (1) the bill ~s to £ 12; his fortune ~ed to £1,000,000; the total ~s to 83. (2) what he says ~s to a refusal; a statement ~ing to libel; that ~s to the same thing; what, after all, does it ~ to? his arguments do not ~ to much.

ample *adj* (1) the ~ rooms held all of the furniture. (2) we have an ~ supply of / ~ drinking water; there is ~ coal to carry us through the winter; our coal is ~; they will start housekeeping with ~ linen, plate and crockery; he has ~ courage; there is ~ time; ~ opportunities were given; he has given ~ proof of ...

amplify *vt* (1) ~ radio signals / sound / the voltage / the current (2) will you ~ that statement so that we can understand it? ~ an account / a story / one's remarks; don't ~ (on) the story, just tell me the facts.

amuse *vt* (1) the story / conjurer ~d the children; ~ the child with a story; I was greatly ~d by the play; he ~d himself (by) throwing pebbles into the water. - *adj* (2) keep the baby ~d with these toys; they were ~d at / by the jokes; were ~d to hear that he ...; an ~d smile; an ~ing story / book / person.

analysis *n* (1) an ~ of water; make an ~; a quantitative / chemical / wet / dry / *etc* ~ (2) the ~ of a sentence (3) an ~ of a plan; this problem depends in the last ~ on the willingness of Egypt to let it be solved. (4) submit to / undergo ~ *(psychoanalysis).*

anchor *n* (1) let go / drop the ~; cast / drop ~; weigh *(raise)* ~; be / lie / ride / at ~; bring a ship to ~ (2) he relied on the ~ of his faith *(fig).*

anchor *vt* (1) ~ a buoy / mine / ship; it was hard to ~ the ship in the swift current; heavy bolts ~ed the sign securely to the post. - *vi* (2) the ship ~ed at noon / off Cuxhaven.

ancient *adj* (1) the ~ Romans / Britons; the remains of the ~ city walls, erected by William the Conqueror; ~ times / coins / civilizations (2 *inform*) she isn't old - she's positively ~; an ~ car / hat / dress.

anger *n* an outburst of (violent) ~ (over s.th.); be filled / bursting / seething with ~ (at s.o. / s.th.); easily aroused to ~; all this roused sudden ~ in him, but he subdued it; conceal / swallow one's ~; do s.th. in (a moment of) ~; she sat in mute ~.

angry *adj* (1) your father is very ~ about your / with you for staying out so late; he became ~ at the mere suggestion of such a thing; he was very ~ at being confronted with a bill for over ten pounds; answer ~ily; behave ~ily towards s.o. (2) an ~ *(inflamed)* wound; the ~ flesh round the wound (3) an ~ river / sea / sky.

annex *vt* (1) ~ a territory (to one's state) (2) the company ~ed two smaller shops to its national chain.

announce *vt* ~ news / plans / an engagement (officially); ~ one's intention to do s.th.; he ~d the meeting opened; the book was ~d as in preparation; he ~d her to the audience as 'the world's greatest singer'.

answer *n* (1) an ~ to a letter / invitation / question / problem / puzzle; an ~ by return (of post); an ~ is requested; verbal and written ~s; an intelligent / exact / detailed / definite / direct / positive / polite / politic / chill / blunt / sharp / biting / curt / bitter / (un)satisfactory / evasive / ignorant / silly / saucy / impudent / cheeky / mild / soft / prompt / reluctant ~; an affirmative / negative ~; give / make an ~; have / find an ~ for everything; write s.o. an ~; he's always ready with an ~; in ~ to this remark he ...; in ~ to your letter; he nodded in ~; his ~ was to slam the door. (2) the ~ to a sum; the ~ to 3 x 11 is 33; the ~ is to try harder.

answer *vt* (1) ~ an invitation / letter / question / telephone ring (promptly / readily / reluctantly / *etc)*; ~ the telephone; ~ the door / (door-)bell *(go to the door)*; he ~ed (me) that he ...; ~ me this question; ~ yes / no (2) ~ the enemy's fire (3) can you ~ the charges? *(defend yourself)* (4) this apartment ~s all our needs at present; that did not ~ my hopes; ~ the purpose; he ~s (to) the description; does this ~ (to) your requirements? - *vi* (5) ~ with (complete) assurance / with a mumble (6) you will have to ~ to the committee for your conduct of the affair; they shall ~ to me for it; I'll ~ for his safety if he goes with us. (7 *be effective)* we have tried every known method, but none of them will ~; methods that ~ with one person will not ~ with another; I doubt its ~ing in this case. (8 *respond*) the car would not ~ to the steering-wheel; the ship no longer ~s (to) the helm. - *adj* (9) he gave an ~ing nod.

answer back he has an unfortunate habit of ~ing ~; I'm not going to have her ~ing me ~; don't ~ ~ to your elders.

anticipate *vt* (1 *look forward to; expect*) I don't ~ meeting any opposition; she ~d great pleasure from her visit to Italy; we ~d a good time on the picnic; I ~ being in hospital about ten days; they ~d that all would be well; I ~ (that there will be) trouble; a riot is ~d. (2 *see what needs doing, will happen, etc, and do what is necessary; deal with beforehand*) he tries to ~ all my needs / wishes; ~ the enemy's movements; I ~d her design by placing myself between her and the door; he neither felt guilt nor ~d disaster; we ~d the crisis; in this old book there are statements that seem to ~ the opinions of modern philosophers. (3 *use in advance*) a man who always ~s his income can never save; ~ an inheritance (4 *do s.th. before s.o. else does it*) the Vikings ~d Columbus in the discovery of America; he ~d the vengeance of heaven. - *vi* (5 → 2) the result was - but I will not ~.

anxious *adj* (1 *worried*) she is very ~ about her husband's health. (2 *eager*) he is ~ for his son to succeed / that his son should succeed; he is ~ to help / to do the right thing; be ~ for s.o. ('s safety); they were ~ for him to receive a good education. (3 *full of worry*) an ~ night / moment / look / thought / feeling / father; we have had an ~ time; running a small workshop can be an ~ business.

apology *n* (1) offer s.o. an ~ / one's ~ies; make an ~ / one's ~ies (to s.o.) (for doing s.th.); demand an ~; accept s.o.'s ~ (2 *an unworthy substitute; inform*) an ~ for champagne / a meal / *etc*; a bar of chocolate is only an ~ for a lunch.

appal (*AE* appall) *vt* (1) the town was ~led by the number of traffic accidents; we were quite ~led when we heard the story; the sight / thought ~led him; he was ~led at the sight / thought. - *adj* (2) the election revealed an ~ling lack of interest in national affairs.

appeal *n* (1) an ~ went out from the flooded town; make an ~ to s.o.; an ~ to reason / arms; he stared at us in mute ~. (2 *legal use*) an ~ from / against a decision / judgement / sentence; file / set down / lodge an ~ with a higher court; an ~ lies *(is permissible)* direct to the Court of A~; allow / dismiss the ~ (3 *attraction*) the life of a policeman has no ~ for me; the picture has a wide ~ because of its soft colours; sex ~; mass ~; poems selected for their imaginative ~ to young people.

appeal *vi* (1) he ~ed to his friends for support / to support him; I ~ to you to vote against it; ~ to s.o.'s benevolence / pity / sense of right; I ~ to you: was it unreasonable? the committee ~ed for funds on behalf of the blind. (2 *legal use*) ~ to a higher court / against a decision; ~ from / against a judgement / sentence / conviction (3) ~ to the country *(hold a general election)*; ~ to the sword *(let war decide)* (4) the life of a policeman does not ~ to me; these pictures ~ to the eye; the idea ~s to me. - *vt* (5 *legal use*) ~ a case / decision / fine / judgement.

appear *vi* (1 *come into view*) a sail ~ed on the horizon; the first flowers ~ed above the snow; suddenly the peak ~ed before us; a rash ~ed on her arm; the Lord ~ed to him in a dream. (2 *present o.s. formally*) the policeman ~ed on the scene at the right moment; ~ before a judge / court of justice; ~ as a witness (3 *present o.s. before public*) ~ as an actor / as a singer / in public / on the stage; will she ~ in the new play? (4 *be published*) the new book / edition will ~ soon; ~ in print / in a magazine; these ideas ~ again and again in his books; the name ~s several times in the document. (5 *seem*) the book ~s to have been used many times; you ~ to forget things; it ~s to me that he ...; strange as it may ~; he is quite well as it ~s; the place ~ed familiar to him; the matter thus ~s in a different light; it ~s extremely unlikely that he ...

appearance *n* (1) the ~ of a ghost / of a book; an ~ in court; daily / weekly ~; make one's first ~ on the stage / in society / as an orator; the ~ of an actor in a play; the first violets had already made their ~; a rash made its (unwelcome) ~ on her arm; → put in 3. (2) a man of pleasant ~; a manly / (un)healthy / unkempt / varied / whimsical / *etc* ~; be much concerned with outward ~s; if you judge him by his ~; by all ~s the strike will go on for a long time; the dog was to all ~s (*also* ~) dead; → keep up 6. (3) it has every ~ of being fine tomorrow; it had all the ~ of being true; he had the ~ of being quite well.

appease *vt* (1) the angry crowd was ~ed by his gentle words; ~ an aggressor (2) ~ (one's / s.o.'s) hunger / appetite; ~ s.o.'s curiosity / anger / rage / temper / scruples.

appetite *n* (1) have a good / hearty / healthy / keen / voracious / wolfish / poor ~; go for a walk to get up an ~; the walk gave him a good ~; lose one's ~; spoil / take away s.o.'s ~; have an ~ for s.th. (*also fig*); the ~ grows with eating *(also fig)*. (2) an ~ for reading / power / *etc*; intellectual / natural / carnal / sexual ~(s).

applaud *vt* (1) ~ s.o. (loudly / enthusiastically / *etc*) (for several minutes) (2) I ~ your courage / decision. - *vi* (3) the audience ~ed for a full five minutes.

applause *n* (1) greet s.o. with (loud / thunderous / vociferous / lukewarm / *etc*) ~; with a storm / tempest of ~; thunder(s) of ~; receive / meet with / win (the) ~ (of the audience); the audience broke into ~. (2) courage worthy of ~.

application *n* (1) make an ~ (to s.o.) (for s.th.); put in / send (in) a written ~; a letter of ~; all ~s are to be made in writing; invite ~s for a vacancy; rates / prices (will be sent) on ~; (further) information on ~ (2) the medicine is for external / outward ~ only; ~ of ice to the forehead made me feel better; the ~ of a poultice / a coating / paint (3) hot and cold ~s (4) the ~ of astronomy to navigation; this testimony has no ~ to the case; this rule is of general ~ *(applies to all cases)*; the ~ of a discovery to industry; his speech had both bearing and ~ (up)on the problem at hand. (5) the student shows ~ in his work; my work demands close ~.

apply *vt* (1) ~ the brakes (of a car); ~ a match to the fire (2) ~ a plaster (to a wound) / a poultice / a remedy; we must ~ ice to relieve the swelling on his leg; ~ (a coating of) paint (to a surface); ~ polish to brasswork; ~ pressure to s.th. (3) ~ a law / principle / rule (to s.th.); ~ one's attention / energies / mind to one's work; ~ one's experience to a situation; ~ money towards a purchase; ~ money for the benefit of homeless children; the profits are ~ied to the building fund (4) ~ o.s. to one's work / the study of a problem / a task (with diligence); ~ yourself to your books. - *vi* (5) this rule ~ies to beginners / all cases; what I'm saying does not ~ to you (6) ~ to a banker for a loan; ~ for leave / permission / a job / a position / a post; for further particulars / information ~ to the secretary; you must ~ (to the Town Hall) in person / by letter / in writing; ~ at the booking office / Town Hall *(personally)*. - *adj* (7) ~ied arts / linguistics / science(s); an ~ied linguist / scientist.

appoint *vt* (1) we ~ed an agent / him agent / him to act / him to the post; ~ a new librarian / a committee; ~ s.o. to the Chair of (Linguistics); he was ~ed captain of the team; we ~ed him as our representative. (2) we must ~ the time and place for the next meeting; at the time ~ed. - *adj* (3) each of the boys had his ~ed task; our ~ed lot (4) a well ~ed fleet; magnificently ~ed buildings; an elegantly ~ed flat.

appointment ~ *n* (1) meet s.o. by ~; arrange / make / fix an ~ with s.o. (at / for 3 o'clock); can you give me an ~ for tomorrow? I have an ~ with my doctor this afternoon; keep / break an / one's ~ (2) after his ~ as headmaster / to a headmastership, he ...; receive one's ~ as minister; certificate of ~ (to an office) (3) obtain a good ~ in a business firm; applications are invited for the following ~s (4 *pl furnishings*) luxurious / magnificent ~s bore witness to the architect's good taste.

appraise *vt* (1) ~ goods / property (for taxation) / a diamond / a fire loss (2) ~ an achievement / a country's strength / the full value of s.o.'s influence; this difficulty of ~ing literature absolutely; their tactics on every question must be ~d in the light of their ideology.

appreciate *vt*(1) ~ artistic quality / music / poetry / the difference between right and wrong; he ~d (the fact) that a new era was beginning; such things must be experienced to be ~d; regular study of it will help you to ~ industry's problems and prospects; H-bombs have made us ~ the full horror of war; ~ a military situation (2) I ~ your kindness; a hungry man ~s a good dinner; we ~ your help / handling the case; we all ~ your wanting to help us in our difficulties. - *vi* (3 *increase in value*) apples ~d 2 to 5 cents per box; shares / investments ~; capital / land ~s.

apprehension *n* (1) be full of / filled with ~; nerves taut with ~; s.th. gives cause for ~ ; I entertain / feel (no) ~ for his safety; I have certain ~s; be under some ~(s) about s.th.; be a prey to the most fearful ~s (2) he's a boy of weak ~ ; be quick / slow of ~ (3 *capture*) the ~ of a thief.

approach *n* (1) they fled at our ~; the place is easy / difficult of ~ *(also fig., of a person)*; we started for home at the ~ of night. (2) the ~es to the town; a path is the only ~ (to the castle). (3) a new ~ to the study of language; a sane ~ to a problem; have the right ~ to one's work; it is true to say of such readers that their ~ is from the particular to the general; he argues for a flexible ~ towards the problem. (4) that's his nearest ~ to a smile; an ~ to perfection.

approach *vt* (1) ~ a town / position; the stream ~es the village through the forest; the castle is ~ed by a path; we are ~ing summer; they were ~ing the hour of departing / the time of decision; the play now ~es its climax. (2) I am ~ing the Secretary with a suggestion / on this matter; when is the best time to ~ him? ~ the bank for a loan (3) ~ a problem; they ~ed the matter / question (of ...) with due care (4) the figure now ~es 500; our annual steel production ~es 30 million tons; leather now ~es (the) plastics for / in cheapness; ~ perfection; his passion for collecting ~es madness; Marlowe ~es Shakespeare in poetic power. - *vi* (5) winter / the procession is ~ing. - *adj* (6) for your ~ing wedding I send you...

approval *n* (1) give one's (qualified / grudging / *etc*) ~ to s.th.; your plans have my ~; the budget has been submitted to Parliament for ~; have / take / buy goods on ~ (2) his behaviour does not meet with my ~; meet with / receive (warm / hearty / enthusiastic / *etc*) ~; he nodded in / his ~.

approve *vt* (1) ~ a plan / a scheme / the balance sheet / the budget; the plans for ... have been officially ~d. - *vi* (2) he may only eat meat if the doctor ~s. (3) I can't ~ of your going there / Ann's marriage / men drinking; does his mother ~ of his new friends? grandfather doesn't ~ of modern gadgets.

apt *adj* (1) he is ~ at learning / that kind of work; one of my ~est pupils (2) an ~ remark / retort; an ~ quotation for the occasion; the 'space age' is an ~ name for the period we are living in. (3) when in a hurry, anyone is ~ to be careless; damage is ~ to be done; difficulties are ~ to occur; lovers' vows are ~ to be broken; matinée hats are ~ to cause ill temper (→ liable 3); he is ~ to promise more than he can perform (*the fault suggested is his unrealiability*; → liable 3).

argue *vi* (1) ~ with s.o. about s.th.; he can be ~d with; the matter is not worth ~ing about; we ~d with him over philosophical matters; he ~s soundly; ~ against / for / in favour of s.th.; ~ for ~ing's sake / for the sake of argument - *vt* (2) he ~d that to do that would be to invite disaster. (3) ~ a subject (hotly / *etc*); let's ~ the matter out; you can't ~ it away; at first he was opposed to the scheme, but I managed to ~ him round; when I left they were still ~ing the point *(suggests useless, interminable ~ing)* (4) ~ s.o. into / out of doing s.th.; ~ s.o. out of a belief / position; he was ~d into it by his wife (5 *be a sign of*) his behaviour ~s lack of will power; his accent ~ s him to be / that he is a foreigner.

argument *n* (1) put forward / advance a (biting / convincing / effective / weighty / indisputable / devastating / irrelevant / shaky / unsound / ill-founded / misleading / well-founded / sound / watertight / cogent) ~; the clinching ~; a good ~ can be made for the position that we ... (2) the ~ about / over whether the films should be censored or not; they spent hours in (an) ~ about how to do it; be engaged in an ~ with s.o.; it is beyond ~ that he... *(quite certain)*; the ~ of philosophers over the precise meaning of words (3) they had a violent ~ (about money) last night; a heated / fierce ~.

arise *vi* (1) ~ and take me to your leader; he arose (as) from a trance; he arose, took two steps forward and collapsed. (2) a mist suddenly arose and enveloped the hills; a storm arose; clouds of smoke ~ from a forest fire; there arose a great cry / loud shouting; everywhere new buildings arose. (3) illnesses that ~ from a wrong diet; the costs ~ing from it; her discontent arose from her slow progress; if an argument should ~, try to keep your temper; how have these differences between British and American English ~n? faith / a doubt / a rumour / suspicion / hatred / an awkward situation / a question / a difficulty / a quarrel / a friendship ~s; difficulties / thoughts / results / effects / uncertainties ~ (4) new prophets ~ from time to time; two men of genius arose among them.

arm[1] *n* (1) the upper ~; the fore~; lift / raise / lower / cross / bend / stretch one's ~s; have a basket on one's ~; carry a child on one's ~ / in one's ~s; carry s.th. under one's ~; hold / carry s.th. at ~'s length; □ keep s.o. at ~'s length *(avoid becoming familiar with him)*; lead s.o. by the ~; give / offer one's ~ to s.o.; take s.o.'s ~; walk ~ in ~; put one's ~ round s.o.; fold / take s.o. in one's ~s; she ran into my ~s; receive / greet / welcome s.o. with open ~s / open-~ed; look on with folded ~s (2) the ~ of a chair / anchor / balance / lever / signal; the ~s of a coat / *etc* (3) an ~ of the sea / a river (4) the (long) ~ of the law (5 *fig*) he is my right ~.

arm[2] *n* (1) fire-~s; small ~s *(rifles, revolvers, etc)*; Germany had more than half a million men under ~s; up in ~s (against s.o.) *(also fig)*; the whole town was up in ~s about the proposal to demolish this historic building; receive a call to ~s *(military service)*; → bear *vt* 1, lay down 3, rise up 2, take up 2a (2 *branch of military service*) the infantry / air ~; a fighting ~; all ~s of the fighting forces.

arm *vt* (1) ~ a country / a regiment / s.o.; ~ o.s. against an attack with a gun / stick (2) ~ o.s. with patience. - *adj* (3) ~ed with a gun / stick; offer ~ed resistance; ~ed neutrality / peace; an ~ed attack / raid; men ~ed to the hilt / teeth; a heavily ~ed knight; an animal ~ed with teeth / unusual cunning (4) ~ed with patience; ~ed with evidence of one's adversary's guilt; ~ed with unassailable arguments.

arouse *vt* (1) ~ comment / public opinion / criticism / opposition / curiosity / interest / confidence / hope / pity / compassion / sympathy / emotion / passion / indignation / anger / mistrust / suspicion / fear / resentment / envy / animosity hatred; ~ a violent desire in s.o.; his remark ~d great mirth / loud laughter; he could ~ a man's worst instincts. (2) ~ s.o. from sleep / his lethargy; one who requires ~ing is a lazy person.

arrange *vt* (1) ~ words alphabetically; ~ books on a shelf; ~ the furniture in a room; ~ fruit in a dish; ~ one's hair (carefully); he made his bed and ~d his room. (2) ~ one's business affairs; the difficult task of ~ing a peaceful world; we ~d things so that Father could go to N.; let me know the time of your arrival so that I can ~ matters accordingly; I so ~d it that nobody knew of his departure; ~ one's plans according to s.o.'s suggestions; ~ the details of a conference; ~ the date / time for a meeting; ~ a picnic / feast / party / wedding; the meeting ~d for tomorrow has been postponed; the conference was held as ~d; ~ a divorce; a marriage has been ~d between A and B; I'm sure we can ~ a compromise; I want the bank to ~ a loan for me. (3) ~ disputes / differences (between persons) (4) ~ a tune for a dance band; ~ a flute sonata for the violin; ~ a folk melody *(orchestrate)* - *vi* (5) can you ~ (for John) to be here at two o'clock? The band ~d for a series of concerts; we have ~d for Mr X to give a lecture on May 3; I will ~ for a taxi to meet you at the station. (6) ~ with the grocer for regular deliveries; we ~d with the travel agent for a June passage.

arrears *n* (1) ~ of rent / wages; be in ~ with the rent (2) ~ of work / correspondence; ~ of industrial replacements *(old machines to be replaced);* be in ~ with work; I am working off ~.

arrest *n* put / place / hold / keep s.o. under ~; be under ~; under house ~.

arrest *vt* (1) ~ s.o. for stealing / for theft / on a charge of theft / on political grounds / as an undesirable alien (2) spot cancer in time to ~ it; poor food ~s the natural growth of children; ~ the flow of water; measures to ~ inflation (3) ~ s.o.'s attention. - *adj* (4) these questions are sufficiently ~ing to challenge consideration.

arrive *vi* (1) ~ at / in a place / from Paris / at a port / in harbour / at one's destination / at the end of one's journey; ~ home; he'll ~ here / there tomorrow; ~ in time (→ time *n* 3a) / on time (→ time *n* 4b) / next week / safely / early / (un)punctually / at the appointed hour (2) at last the day ~d; he ~d with his relatives in tow. (3) ~ at a decision / conclusion / solution / result; ~ at manhood / the age of 50; ~ at a price; a peace ~d at this way cannot last. (4 *establish one's position*) he is a man who will ~; he has ~d.

art *n* (1) Greek / German / primitive / prehistoric / Romanesque / Gothic / impressionist / abstract / non-objective / non-representational / dramatic / 20th-century / applied ~; history / science / theory / work of ~; ~ history / theory / critic(ism); ~(s) and science(s); ~ dealer / student / collection / gallery / exhibition; these reliefs are not great ~, but ...; life is sombre, ~ serene; ~ is long and life is fleeting. (2) the creative / fine / graphic / performing / static / dynamic / industrial ~s; ~s and crafts; the liberal ~s (3) the ~ of reading / writing / riding / *etc*; the ~ of building / printing / healing / living / medicine / war / cooking / sewing / lying; the healing ~; the noble ~ of self-defence; well versed in the ~ of politics; the ~ of love; black ~; a design carried out with exquisite ~ (4 *trick*) he employed all his ~s; he gained his ends by ~; the witch doctor used strange ~s to cast a spell. (5) her complexion owes more to ~ than to nature.

ascertain *vt* ~ the truth / the facts / s.o.'s name / s.o.'s whereabouts / the number of those present / what really happened / whether the train stops at X.

ask *vt* (1 *put a question to*) ~ s.o. a question; ~ a question (of s.o.); she ~ed the same question of everyone in turn; may I ~ (you) a question? I ~ myself why this happened; really! I ~ you! I'm afraid I must ~ (you) a few personal questions. (2 *seek information, inquire about s.th.*) ~ s.o. his opinion / the time / the way; ~ (him) how he's getting on / where he lives / whether he wants to come; they ~ed (us) our names; I have ~ed Mr. X about this matter / about his intentions; he ~ed me about my work; may I ~ your name? do you mind my ~ing your age? (3 *make a request*) ~ (s.o.) for bread / a loan / money; ~ a lady for her hand; ~ (s.o.) for advice / help / information / justice / mercy / permission to do s.th.; ~ s.o.'s leave / permission to do s.th.; ~ s.o.'s advice; I ~ed her forgiveness / pardon; I ~ed that she forgive me; we ~ed them to forgive us; I ~ed to see him; he ~ed to get up / that he might get up; I must ~ to be excused; she ~ed to leave the room; ~ s.o. (for) a favour; I have a favour to ~ (of) you. (4 *require, expect, demand*) ~ (for) s.o.'s passport; what price are you ~ing for it? he is ~ ing more than is due to him / more than is his due; he first ~ed £50, but ...; what I ~ is only just; it is ~ing too much of him to expect ...; he didn't comply with my request, though I did not ~ a great deal of him. (5 *invite*) ~ s.o. down for the weekend / round for the evening / to tea; ~ s.o. out (to dinner / lunch / tea / a dance); you must ~ her to our party; N is at the door - shall I ~ him in? she is always being ~ed out *(to parties etc)*; ~ a lady to dance; ~ s.o. at a meeting to say a few words. - *vi* (6 *inquire*) this gentleman is ~ing for the manager; the motorist was ~ed for his name and address; has anyone ~ed for me?; he ~s about / after you in every letter; ~ after s.o.'s health; how old are you, if I / one may ~? ... if you don't mind my ~ing (→ 2) (7 *make a request*) you can have it / it's yours for the ~ing. (8 *require*) it ~s for attention; this ~s for great prudence (9 *bring about unintentionally*) to do that is ~ing for disaster / trouble; to go about without a coat in this weather is ~ing for pneumonia / for it *(inform: trouble)*; you ~ed for it, now you're going to get it *(inform: threat of ensuing unpleasantness)*.

ask off if it's necessary for me to be present at the meeting I shall have to ~ ~ *(ask for time off from work / one's job)*.

assail *vt* (1) ~ a castle; ~ a place with artillery; ~ s.o. with blows (2) ~ s.o. with questions / arguments / appeals / reproaches / insults; be ~ed with / by fear / doubt(s) / temptation(s).

assemble *vt* (1) the king ~d his men; ~ members of the party; the second state of planning is ~ing the necessary facts and forecasts. (2) ~ the parts of a radio / a motor / a watch. - *vi* (3) a crowd ~d; the students ~d in the hall.

assert *vt* (1) he ~ed his innocence and pleaded not guilty; the lawyer ~ed that his client was innocent; one should never ~ anything that one cannot prove; usage is not, as it is often ~ed to be, the absolute law of language. (2) they ~ed their rights against the unjust claims of ...; ~ a claim; the tyrant ~ed his authority over most of Europe; human nature ~ed its rights, and she fell asleep. (3) in adolescence a boy is interested primarily in ~ing himself in action; in times of crisis Parliament can always ~ itself and ...

assess *vt* (1 *determine the amount of*) ~ a tax / fine (at a certain amount); the damage has been ~ed at 500 marks (2 *make an official valuation of*) ~ property (for taxation); his fortune is ~ed at £90,000. (3 *judge definitively*) ~ a speech at its true worth; ~ the impact of advertisements on the public; market research ~es smoking habits; painstakingly ~ing consumer requirements; ~ men as leaders.

assign *vt* (1) ~ s.o. a share / part / portion / place; ~ a share / *etc* to s.o.; ~ s.o. rooms at a hotel; an attic was ~ed to me as a temporary office; your teacher ~s you work to do at home; ~ property / a right / a position to s.o. (2) ~ s.o. to a position (3) has a day been ~ed for the exam? (4) ~ a picture to a painter / period / century; ~ a book to an author.

assignment *n* (1) receive an ~ from s.o. to do s.th.; an easy / exciting / dangerous ~; what is today's ~ *(task, homework)*? (2) the ~ of seats in a classroom; he was pleased at his ~ to such an important position.

assimilate *vt* (1) we ~ some kinds of food easily; plants ~ nourishment through their roots. (2) ~ knowledge / ideas; the book can be ~d easily by the educated layman; he ~d the customs of his new country. (3) the old Russian Empire ~d many smaller states. (4) ~ one's pronunciation to that of one's neighbours; ~ o.s. to new surroundings. - *vi* (5) this food does not ~ easily; not all immigrants ~ easily / well.

assist *vt* (1) ~ s.o. in his work / in doing s.th. / with a task / with the housework; can I ~ you with those parcels? ~ a blind man across a road; he was ~ed home drunk. (2) a glass of wine ~s digestion; this method ~s the memory. - *vi* (3) four acolytes ~ed at / during the communion service; the surgeon let his associate take over but remained to ~.

assist *n* (1 *AE*) Jones scored a goal with an ~ from Smith *(in soccer, ice hockey).* (2 *AE fig*) the new ballet was produced with a (financial) ~ from an unnamed beneficiary.

assistance *n* give / render / lend ~ to s.o.; give / *etc* (s.o.) (willing / unselfish / occasional) ~; offer / refuse / reject ~; receive ~ from s.o.; he won't accept any ~; come / rush to s.o.'s ~; with financial ~ from the government; can I be of any ~ (to you)? go on national ~ *(BE draw unemployment benefit).*

associate *vt* (1) we ~ war with misery; he ~s wooden houses with his childhood; he wished to forget everything ~d with his former life; I don't wish to ~ myself with what has been said. - *vi* (2) they ~d / he ~d with him in publishing the book; John was forbidden to ~ with the boy next door. (3) he likes ~ing with such people; he ~s chiefly with people in his own profession.

associate *n* (1) a business ~; ~s in a business firm (*partners*); Smith, Jones und A~s *(minor partners).* - *adj* (2) an ~ editor (*second to editor*); ~ professor (AE: *rank below full professor*); an ~ member of a club (*having only limited privileges*) (3) ~ circumstances (*following or accompanying*).

assume *vt* (1) an appearance / (threatening / haughty / hostile) attitude / (casual / graceful / stiff) pose / tone (of severity); ~ a mask of indifference / festive look / solemn expression / disguise / foreign accent; the disease ~s many forms. (2) he ~d the president's duties during his chief's absence; ~ (the) control of s.th. / a responsibility / the direction of a business / the reins of government (3) ~ a statement to be true; ~ s.o.'s guilt / him (to be) guilty / that he is guilty; it is ~d that he won't come back; let us ~ that it ...; ~ing he is / him to be the heir. - *adj* (4) appear on the stage / write under an ~d name; an ~d *(false)* title / friendliness.

assurance *n* (1) we had every ~ our team would win; there is no ~ of success; shake s.o.'s ~ (2) answer all the questions with ~; assert / maintain s.th. with ~; the actor played the part with complete ~. (3) he had the ~ (*impudence*) to say that he could speak 30 foreign languages fluently. (4) he gave me his / a definite ~ that he ...; we had his ~ that he ... (5 *BE*) life ~ (policy); ~ company.

assure *vt* (1) he ~d me that all would be well; I ~d the old lady that her son was safe; I can ~ you of his reliability / that he is reliable; I was able to ~ them of the accuracy of the report. (2) hard work will ~ success; we are trying to ~ our kids a better world; an international organization capable of ~ing the security of all nations (3 *BE*) ~ one's life *(AE: insure).* - *adj* (4) you can / may rest ~d that I ...; an ~d income; an ~d way to do s.th.

atone *vi* (1) ~ for a sin / for one's sins (2) you cannot / nothing can ~ for your negligence; how can I ~ for hurting your feelings? ~ for an omission / fault / wrong (by doing s.th.); colourful description ~s for the story's lack of cohesion.

attach *vt* (1) ~ a hook to the line / labels to the luggage; ~ a document / sample to a letter; the written directions are ~ed to the tool; a house with a garage ~ed (2) two conditions are ~ed to his offer; ~ importance to s.th.; I ~ed no meaning to his words; ~ a penalty to an act; ~ blame to s.o.; no liability is ~ed. (3) ~ o.s. to a political party / an expedition (4) she is deeply ~ed to her father; he is foolishly ~ed to old customs / his prejudices; he has the gift of ~ing people to him. (5) he is ~ed to the commission as an observer; ~ an officer to the General Staff (6) his salary was ~ed *(seized)* by his creditors. - *vi* (7) certain duties ~ to this position; no blame / suspicion ~ed to him / his act.

attack *n* follow through / lead / order an ~; leave o.s. open to ~.

attack *vt* (1) the enemy ~ed (us from the rear / at dawn); we were ~ed by a pack of wolves. (2) the newspaper ~ed the senator's speech; ~ one's adversary / a doctrine / a religion / an interest (3) some insects ~ our gardens; a disease ~s an organ; mumps is a disease that ~s children; ~ed by gout; water / rust ~s iron. (4) ~ a job with vigour; they next ~ed the problem of ...; he ~ed his dinner at once. - *vi* (5) the best way to defend is to ~.

attain *vt* (1 *succeed in getting*) he has ~ed great skill in playing chess; to make a thing desirable it is only necessary to make it difficult to ~; ~ a(n academic) degree / a high position / a rank / great honours; ~ power / fame / wealth; territories that have ~ed their independence. (2 *reach, arrive at*) ~ the summit of a mountain / a high speed / old age / one's majority; men had ~ed the stratosphere; ~ one's aim / goal / purpose / end(s) / object / hopes (3) ~ to: *→2, emphasizing motion, growth, effort*) this plant ~s to a height of 10 feet; he has achieved heights that I can never hope to ~ to; ~ to clarity / perfection / power / prosperity / riches / fame; ~ to full maturity.

attempt *n* (1) make an (un)successful / futile / vain / frenzied / faint / touching / concerted / *etc* ~ (to do s.th.); they made no ~ to escape / at escaping; his second ~ at skating was successful; he failed in / at all his ~s (to do s.th.); the task is difficult, but I shall make an ~ at it. (2) her ~ at a Christmas cake had to be thrown away. (3) make an ~ on s.o.'s life / the speed record; an ~ upon / against the liberty of our people.

attempt *vt* (1) you have ~ed a difficult task; do not ~ more than three questions; don't ~ impossibilities; ~ a rescue; he ~ed (to commit) suicide; she must at least ~ to be worthy of him; I am ~ing to answer you. (2) ~ the life of (the king).

attend *vt* (1 *be present at*) ~ church / school; ~ a meeting / concert / wedding / funeral; all children over five must ~ school; the ball was well ~ed by the social elite; a huge crowd ~ed the game (2 *be present as circumstance or result*) many infirmities ~ old age; success ~ed his final effort(s); our best wishes ~ you; pain ~ed with fever; a royal visit ~ed by much shouting and flag-waving; an action / plan / situation / task ~ed with great difficulties; a scheme ~ed with grave consequences should it fail (3 *accompany, wait upon*) ~ an ambassador / bishop / minister; a priest ~ed by two deacons; a maid ~s her mistress; four bridesmaids ~ed the bride. (4 *minister to*) ~ a patient (*pay constant visits to, etc→* attend to); in his last illness he was ~ed by Dr. C; our doctor has ~ed our family these 20 years; which doctor is ~ing you? (5 *form: listen to, heed*) ~ my commands / instructions / words; ~ s.o.'s (good) advice. - *vi* (6 *be present*) there is a dance next Friday - will you ~? Committee meetings are every Wednesday - we ~ but our hearts aren't in it. (7 *pay attention, heed*) sit up and listen to me, you are not ~ing. (8 *serve; escort; accompany;* '~ on' *suggests royal personages or pomp*) a company of nobles ~ed (on) the king; the honour of ~ing (upon) the prince; ~ (up)on a bride.

attend to (1 *deal with*) I still have some things to ~ to; ~ to one's business / s.o.'s car / a matter / the wants of the customers / one's work (2 *listen carefully*) ~ to the instructions / the lesson / the teacher / what I am saying (3 *treat*) a doctor ~s ~ a patient / wound (*renders help on a particular occasion →* attend *vt* 4).

attendance *n* (1) the ~ of several students has been sporadic; the ~ of meetings takes up a great deal of my time; ~ at church / meetings / lectures / school (is compulsory); the boy was given a prize for regular ~. (2) the servants' ~ on the Emperor; → dance *vt* 3 (3) the doctor in ~ is Dr. C.; Dr. C. is in ~. (4) the ~ at the game was very small; ~s at the professional theatre have dropped very sharply.

attention *n* (1) listen with (half-hearted / undivided / constant / *etc*) ~; with close / studious ~ to detail; pay ~ to s.o. / s.th.; give one's (whole / best / full) ~ to s.o. / s.th.; give s.o. / s.th. one's ~; direct / turn one's ~ to s.th.; call / attract / draw s.o.'s ~ to s.th.; ask for / solicit s.o.'s ~ ; engage / arrest / catch / hold / win / secure s.o.'s ~; call ~ to (an error); attract ~; draw ~ to o.s. (by s.th.); escape s.o.'s ~ ; divert / distract / draw away s.o.'s ~ (from s.th.); he falls short in ~ to his work; a letter for the ~ of Mr X (2) the matter will receive immediate ~; the brakes need ~; it's time we had some repairs done - there's quite a lot that wants ~; (3) you must have medical ~; he needs ~; the injured man received ~ at the nearest hospital. (4 *polite act*) pay one's ~s to s.o.; shower ~(s) on s.o.; be all ~(s) to s.o.; his constant ~s annoyed her. (5) stand at ~; come to ~.

attitude *n* (1) what ~ was the body in? in a relaxed ~ (2) assume / adopt / take up / maintain / preserve a (firm / broad-minded / liberal / casual / disdainful / haughty / belligerent / threatening / defiant / strictly impartial / *etc*) ~; an ~ of disobedience / deference / humility / pride / grief / despair; his political / religious ~; a positive / negative / scientific ~; I can't understand his ~ in this matter; what's his ~ to(wards) life / this question / his parents? □ strike an ~ *(assume a theatrical pose).*

attract *vt* (1) a magnet ~s iron; jam ~s wasps; water ~s midges. (2) shout to ~ attention; the play ~ed a lot of notice / a large audience. (3) do you feel / are you ~ed to her? she doesn't ~ him; a courteous man ~s friends easily; the plan does not ~ him. - *vi* (4) opposites ~.

attractive *adj* an exceptionally / highly / very ~ idea / offer / person / prospect; an ~ location / site for a business / house; she was ~ly dressed in an otherwise simple dress.

attribute *vt* (1) ~ one's success to hard work / an accident to bad luck / unfavourable circumstances; she ~s their losses to her husband's gross carelessness. (2) he ~s to him a power he does not possess; he ~s wisdom to his teachers; ~ a motive to s.o. (3) well-known quotations are often ~d to Shakespeare.

author *n* (1) a celebrated / *etc* ~; s.o.'s favourite ~; this ~ *(his books)* is often asked for in the library. (2) the ~ of a plan / an ingenious scheme; the ~ of the universe.

authority *n* (1) the general had ~ to start the attack; give s.o. ~ to do s.th.; published by ~ of Parliament; this letter is my ~ to inspect the accounts. (2) an officer has / exercises ~ over the soldiers under him; maintain one's ~; do s.th. on one's own ~; parental / priestly / royal ~; the highest ~ in the state; a ruling on this matter from someone in ~; speak with ~. (3) local / municipal / county / public ~ies; the Port of London A~ (4) he is an ~ on this subject / in this field; on each occasion an ~ will give an introductory talk; the Oxford English Dictionary is the best ~ on English words; what is your ~ for that statement? I have it on good ~ / on the ~ of a Councillor that we ...; on the ~ of an eyewitness (5) the ~ of long experience.

avail *vt* (1) ~ o.s. of an opportunity; I shall ~ myself of your kind offer; he ~ed himself of a holiday to visit the seaside. (2) all his efforts ~ed him little / ~ed him nothing / did not ~ him; his pleas for leniency did not ~ the prisoner.

avenge *vt* I will ~ the death of my brother (upon his murderer); he swore to ~ the insult / his father's death; ~ o.s. (upon one's enemies).

average *n* (1) find the ~ (of several numbers); take an ~ of the results; strike a rough ~; my income was never more than ~; we sell on an ~ a thousand copies a year; he works eight hours on (the) ~; be up to / above / below the ~; his height is above ~. - *adj* (2) a man of ~ height / intelligence.

average *vt* (1) if you ~ 2, 3 and 7, you get 4; ~ the results (2) our sales ~ a thousand copies a year; he ~s 3 dollars an hour; their profits ~ up to £3,000 a year; during our motor trip we ~d 200 miles a day; suicides ~ two a week; in five years at the factory she ~d (having) 16 accidents a year (3) these problems will probably ~ out to be less serious than they seem at the moment.

averse *adj* he is ~ to fish / rice / *etc*; I am quite ~ to / towards climbing that mountain; any person ~ to / towards this plan should leave immediately.

aversion *n* he has a (distinct / strong / unsurmountable / *etc*) ~ to fish at dinnertime; feel an ~ for / to / towards s.o.; he took an ~ to me; there exists a mutual ~ between them; I have a marked ~ to witnessing such subservience as his. (2) one of her pet ~s was mosquitoes; he is my pet ~.

avert *vt* (1) ~ one's eyes / face / gaze (from a terrible sight / out of embarrassment); ~ a blow / thrust (2) ~ failure / (a) danger / one's mind (from s.th.); ~ an accident / strike / war.

avoid *vt* ~ s.o. / a house / the ditch / s.o.'s company / a pitfall / an accident / collision; ~ evil / hard drinks; he ~ed making any promise; we could not ~ seeing him.

await *vt* (1) ~ an event / happening / occurrence / development; ~ the results / end / outcome / upshot (of s.th.); ~ death; I ~ / am ~ing your reply / instructions; I am ~ing the arrival of the train; ~ me here at four o'clock; he can hardly ~ her return. (2) a surprise / disappointment / hearty welcome ~s him; death ~s us all; a letter ~ed me.

awake *vi* (1) she awoke to the danger / to the unpleasant facts / from her day-dream / from her illusion / from her apathy; his conscience awoke; fatherly feelings awoke in him; the woman in her awoke; all nature ~s; the national spirit awoke (2) what time did you ~? ~ from a troubled sleep (3) he awoke the fury of the mob; the wonders of the New World awoke a burst of extravagant fancy in the Old World.

awaken *vt* (1) ~ emotion / passion / antagonism / fear / anxiety / suspicion / curiosity / interest / attention / memories / hope; ~ a violent desire in s.o.; the national spirit was ~ed; he has ~ed the public to the importance of the Commonwealth. (2) ~ s.o. from sleep; what time shall we ~ him? - *adj* (3) these ~ing cultural interests; the newly ~ing national life.

award *vt* ~ s.o. a prize / scholarship / medal; ~ a medal / *etc* to s.o.; the judge ~ed her (£50 as) damages; ~ a firm a contract (to build s.th.); ~ a penalty / payment to s.o.

awe *n* (1) the priests endeavoured to hold the crowd in ~ of their deities; in holy ~; the sight of the altar filled them with ~; savages often live in ~ of nature. (2) stand in ~ of s.o. / s.th.; every pupil held his teacher in ~; she goes in ~ of the manager.

awkward *adj* (1) this is an ~ door to open; an ~ staircase; there have been several bad accidents here - it's a very ~ corner; an ~ turn in the road; the handle of this teapot is an ~ shape; ~ tools (2 *embarrassing, difficult to deal with*) an ~ situation / affair / job / problem; the meeting was at nine o'clock, which was an ~ time for many people; he spared her from explanations which it was ~ to give; □ an ~ customer *(person / animal difficult or dangerous to deal with)*; □ the ~ age *(when adolescents lack self-confidence)* (3) an ~ workman; he is ~ at handling such tools; he is rather ~ in his movements / gait (4) I felt ~ when I went into the room and saw that everyone except me was in evening dress.

B

back *n* (1) a round / bent / crooked / lame ~; lie / sleep / swim on one's ~; carry s.th. / s.o. on one's ~; lean one's ~ against a wall; stand with one's ~ to the wall; say / do s.th. behind s.o.'s ~; be / lie (flat) on one's ~ *(be ill in bed)*; □ be glad to see the ~ of s.o.; have s.o. / s.th. at one's ~ / at the ~ of s.th. *(as support)*; have one's ~ to the wall *(defend o.s. in a desperate situation; also fig)*; a stab in the ~ *(a treacherous act)*; → put *vt* 7a, turn *vt* 1b (2) the ~ of a chair / seat; the chairs were arranged ~ to ~. (3) the ~ of one's hand / the head / a knife / a book / an envelope; she put her dress on ~ to front; □ (it is a story of one calamity) on the ~ of another; the business failed, and on the ~ of that his wife died. (4) a garden at the ~ of a house; a room in / at the ~ of a house; □ (I have an idea / I have had it) at the ~ of my mind; □ (he lives somewhere) at the ~ of beyond.

back *vt* (1) ~ a curtain with heavy material (2) ~ a car (into / out of the garage) (3) ~ a plan / campaign / venture / political movement / colleague / politician (4) ~ a horse *(bet on its success)*; □ ~ the wrong horse *(misplace one's trust)*; □ ~ a winner *(undertake s.th. very successful)*. - *vi* (5) the house ~s on (to) the river.

back away the two robbers ~ed ~ when they saw the fierce dog.

back down he claimed he could juggle, but he ~ed ~ when asked to; threatened, he ~ed ~.

background *n* (1) ~ of a picture; in the ~; red flowers against / on a black ~; ~ music / noise / effects; serve as a ~ (to s.th.); form the ~ of s.th.; keep (o.s.) / remain / stay / be in the ~; push s.o. into the ~ (2) this question has receded completely into the ~; the murder has a political ~; the ~ of the present tension; he has no ~ for the job; the listeners' occupations and ~s may be as far apart as (those of) labourer and lawyer; they fear his lack of understanding of the wider ~.

back out at first he said he would go, but then he ~ed ~; ~ ~ of an agreement / contract / deal.

back up (1) they ~ed up their friend in what he said; evidence to ~ up his story (2) he ~ed up the car a foot or two / somewhat.

bad *adj* (1 *not good, not as it should be*) a ~ habit / example / bargain; ~ company; → debt *n* 1; a ~ business / job *(unfortunate affair)*; □ make the best of a ~ job / bargain; he will come to a ~ end (yet); be in a ~ way *(very ill, unfortunate, in trouble)*; he / his business is in a ~ way; a ~ light for reading; the film was not (so) ~ / not half ~ *(inform: quite good)*; that's not a ~ idea. (2 *evil, wicked*) it is ~ to lie; he is a ~ man; lead a ~ life; John's been a ~ (*naughty*) boy today; ~ language *(swear words)*; → egg 2, faith 5, lot 3, name 2. (3 *incorrect*) his English is very ~; he speaks ~ English; a ~ translation (4 *of poor quality*) there is ~ housing in the slums; ~ food; a ~ specimen; write ~ verses; he took the photographs when the light was ~; a ~ carpenter / *etc* (5 *rotten)* a ~ egg; ~ apples / meat / fish / food / water; → go 20a. (6 *unpleasant*) a ~ taste / smell / dream; ~ weather; a ~ thunderstorm; a ~ time with the dentist; we've had ~ news; he's in a ~ temper; things look ~ for him. (7 *of things that are never good*) a ~ accident / illness / wound / headache / cold / pain; a ~ mistake / blunder (8 *harmful*) spices are ~ for him; ~ habits; smoking is ~ for the health; very small print is ~ for the eyes; ~ air (9 *ill*) feel ~; she was taken ~ during the night; a ~ hand / leg / tooth; he is very ~ today. (10 *inform: distressed*) feel ~ about s.th. (11 *not clever*) he is ~ at arithmetic.

bad *n* (1) go from ~ to worse *(get worse every day)*; □ take the ~ with the good; the ~ in him comes from his background; □ go to the ~ *(become criminal)* (2) £1,000 to the ~ *(debit side)*; we were several pounds to the ~ *(lost them)* over the transaction.

bake *vt* (1) ~ bread in an oven; she ~d her own birthday cake. (2) ~ bricks, cups, plates in a kiln (3) the sun ~d the muddy river banks *(hardened them)*. - *vi* (4) the bread is ~ing. (5) we were ~ing in the sun.

balance *n* (1) spring-~; letter-~; siding-weight ~; weigh s.th. in / with a ~; turn / tip the ~ *(also fig: be decisive)*; his fate was (hanging) in the ~ *(was undecided)*; □ tremble in the ~ *(be in a crititcal condition)* (2) keep one's ~ (on the deck of a ship); don't get excited - keep your ~; he lost his ~ and fell (over); recover one's ~; the news threw him off (his) ~; ~ of mind; after this failure his emotional ~ was completely upset; disturb the ~ of power in Europe; □ hold the ~ *(have the power to decide)* (3) establish an acceptable ~ between satisfactions and frustrations; □ on ~ *(considering every aspect)*: on ~ I should think we should benefit by the scheme. (4 *greater amount*) the ~ of advantage / opinion is on our side. (5) strike the ~ *(find the difference between credit und debit sides; also fig)* (6 *remainder; inform*) ~ to be paid within one week; play the ~ of the afternoon; the answer will be given in the ~ of this chapter.

balance *vt* (1) ~ a stick on (the end of) one's nose; ~ (o.s.) on one foot / one's toes (2) ~ weights; ~ two things *(weigh them)* (3 *compare*) ~ the chances of the two groups; ~ two things against one another; ~ arguments / facts / values / *etc* against other arguments / *etc* (4 *make the same*) ~ a disadvantage by / with an advantage; ~ forces (5 *be the same*) the votes 'for' exactly ~ the votes 'against'; his prudence ~s her ardour. (6) ~ income and expenditure; ~ exports and imports; ~ the accounts / budget *(arrange for credit and debit sides to be equal)* - *vi* (7) ~ on a rail / tightrope / one's toes / *etc* (8) my accounts ~; income and expenditure ~ out. - *adj* (9) a ~d diet.

ball[1] *n* (1) play ~; have a game of ~; □ start / set / get the ~ rolling *(start s.th., esp. conversation)*; □ keep the ~ rolling (→ keep *vt* 8c); the ~ is with you *(it's your turn)* (2) a ~ of snow / paper / wool / string; a meat- / snow-~.

ball[2] *n* give a / go to a ~; open the ~; a charity / social ~; have a ~ (*inform: have a good time*).

ballot *n* (1) take a ~ *(decide by voting)* (2) have the ~ *(right to vote)*.

ban *n* put s.o. / s.th. under a ~; impose a ~ on s.o. / s.th.; be under a ~; a Church ~; New York's parking ~ on numerous crosstown streets.

ban *vt* the play was ~ned by the censor; ~ profane language / (all) obscene magazines; authorities ~ned the building of wooden houses in that area; ~ s.o. from driving / the club.

band *n* (1) a ~ of musicians / fugitives / outlaws / robbers / soldiers / wild dogs; a ~ of scientists made the discovery that... (2) a dance ~; a brass ~.

band *vt* (1) ~ people together. - *vi* (2) the states ~ed together to form a union; the outlaws ~ed together against the sheriff; ~ with others to do s.th.

bank[1] *n* (1) have an account with a (leading) ~; have money in the ~ ; draft a cheque on a ~; instruct one's ~; a run on the ~(s) (2) hold / break the ~ *(in gaming)* (3) a blood / bone / eye / *etc* ~.

bank[2] *n* river ~; ~ of snow / sand; get stuck on a mud- / sand-bank; on the ~(s) of a / the river; they stood on the ~ and watched the boat.

bank[1] *vi* (1) clouds are ~ing up; the snow has ~ed up. - *vt* (2) ~ up a river; ~ up earth against the wall / around a building.

bank[2] *vt* (1) he ~s part of his salary every month. - *vi* (2) who do you ~ with? ~ downtown (3) ~ on s.o.('s support / help); you can ~ on his honesty; today, as hitherto, we ~ on war.

bar *n* (1) a ~ of soap / chocolate / wood / iron; a chocolate / iron ~ (2) (he ought to) be behind ~s *(in prison)*; place s.o. behind (prison) ~s (3) poor reading is a ~ to success in school work; deafness is a ~ to many careers; ~s against immigration (4) be tried at (the) Bar *(in open court)*; the prisoner at the ~ *(the accused)* (5) be called to the Bar *(become a barrister)*; read for the Bar *(study to become a barrister)*; a member of the Bar; take / pass one's ~-examination(s) (6) have a drink at the ~; a milk- / quick-lunch / snack-~ (7) he played a few ~s of the sonata; the opening ~s of Beethoven's Fifth.

bar *vt* (1) I locked and ~red the door; we ~red the ground-floor windows. (2 *fig*) the sky was ~red with black clouds. (3) if Tom doesn't get home before 10 o'clock, I'll ~ him out; he ~red himself in. (4) snow / soldiers ~red the way through the pass; ~ a passage; a long train ~red the passage along the road. (5) fresh reserves to ~ the enemy's advance; poor health ~red his chances of success. (6) ~ a topic from discussion / s.o. from a competition; nothing ~red them from meeting together; the club ~s playing cards for money; ~ s.o. (from) attending political meetings.

bargain *n* (1) a sharp / hard ~; a sorry ~ *(one to be regretted)*; close / conclude / settle a ~; drive a (hard) ~; he made a ~ to deliver the coal weekly; they struck a ~ to sell only to each other; meet one's part of the ~; □ into the ~ *(in addition)*; John boxed his ears into the ~ *(besides refusing the request)*; → bad *adj* 1; a ~'s a ~. (2) at that price the house is a ~ ; a good / bad / real ~ ; get a ~.

bargain *vi* (1) ~ with s.o. for / over s.th. (2) more guests arrived than she had ~ed for *(expected)*; I didn't ~ for all this trouble. - *vt* Tom ~ed his fish-hooks for a bullfrog.

barometer *n* tap the ~; the ~ rises in fine weather / is falling; what does the ~ say? the ~ is at change / set fair; the ~ is holding steady / remains unchanged.

barter *vt* (1) ~ s.th. for / against s.th. else. - *vi* (2) ~ with s.o. for s.th.; ~ away one's freedom / rights / honour.

base *n* (1) the ~ of a pillar / column / wall / cup / wine-glass / table-lamp; the ~ of the skull (2) a naval / air / supply / rocket / agrarian ~; the ~ of operations / an expedition (3) the Great War shook civilization to its ~; he tried to furnish criticism with a psychological ~.

base *vt* what do you ~ your suspicions on? an opinion / story ~d on fact(s); he ~d his researches on the work of ...; this rule is ~d on mathematical laws; his suspicion is ~d on an unpleasant experience.

basis *n* the ~ of a theory / calculation / discussion / constitution / democratic state; (on) a firm / secure / sound / broad / shaky / questionable ~; serve as / form the ~ for / of s.th.; put s.th. on a better financial ~; implicit trust is the ~ of a lasting friendship; build up a business on a sound ~ (of customer satisfaction / service / *etc*).

bath *n* (1) have / take a (hot / cold) ~; draw / run the / a ~ *(let water run into the tub)*; your ~ is ready; give a child a ~; an air / sun / mud ~ (2) public / medicinal / Turkish / steam ~s (3) two rooms, kitchen and ~ *(bathroom)* (4) I was (sitting) in the ~ *(bathtub)* when the telephone rang.

bath (*BE only; AE* bathe *vt*) *vt* (1) ~ a baby / child / invalid. (2) do you ~ every day?

bathe (*BE only*; *AE* bath *n*) *n* a ~ in the sea / waves; a ~ in a lake / river / swimming-pool; have a / go for a ~.

bathe *vt* (1) ~ a wound / one's eyes / one's feet (in a river) / *(AE)* a baby; ~ in a *(BE)* bath / *(AE)* bathtub. - *vi* (2) ~ in the sea / *etc*; go ~ing; can we ~, Mummy? - *adj* (3) be ~ed in tears / perspiration (4) ~d in sunlight; the stage was ~d in light.

batter *vt* (1) the police ~ed down the door; the heavy waves ~ed the ship to pieces. (2) the boys soon ~ed all the new furniture *(by misuse)*. (3) few nations were so ~ed by the war as Finland. - *vi* (4) someone was ~ing at the door; waves ~ed (on) the cliff. - *adj* (5) a ~ed old car / hat.

battle *n* the ~ of Waterloo / for Stalingrad; join ~ *(begin to fight)*; go into ~; die in ~; win / lose a ~; a hard-fought / critical / crucial / decisive / *etc* ~ *(also fig)* (2) a ~ between the two gangs; the ~ against cancer; he had to fight a painful ~ with himself; the ~ of life; the advocates of classical education have been fighting a losing ~ for over half a century. (3 *victory*) the ~ is to the strong *(they win)*; youth is half the ~; (4) give / offer ~ *(show readiness to fight)*; accept / refuse ~.

battle *vt* (1) ~ a hurricane / one's way. - *vi* (2) ~ against, with an emotion / s.o. / a task; ~ against, with the current / fire / wind; ~ for freedom.

bay *n* keep / hold at ~ *(prevent from coming too near)*; bring an animal / enemy to ~ *(corner and force to fight)*; the bear stood at ~ as the dogs attacked from all sides.

beam *n* (1) a ~ of sunlight; the ~ of a searchlight (2) a ~ of joy lighted her face; with a ~ of delight / pleasure (3) a radio / guiding ~; fly / ride the ~ *(fly a plane following a radio ~)*; on the ~ *(on course; fig: functioning well)*; off the ~.

beam *vi* (1) the moon / sun ~ed (brightly). (2) she ~ed with happiness / satisfaction; he ~ed on his friends. - *vt* (3) ~ a broadcast to / at Russia; ~ a programme across the iron curtain / via satellite (4) a sales campaign ~ed at sportsmen; a programme ~ed at women.

bear *vt* (1 *support, carry physically*) the table ~s my weight; the ice won't ~ you(r weight); ~ a load / burden *(also fig)*; the cheering masses bore the players to the dressing room; the glider was borne aloft by an upward draught; □ ~ arms *(serve in the military)* (2 *carry mentally, maintain*) ~ s.o. a grudge / a grudge towards s.o. (for s.th.); I ~ him no ill will; ~ (no) malice towards s.o.; they bore a lifelong affection for each other; the love / hatred she bore him; I'll ~ it in mind *(not forget it)*. (3 *transmit, relate*) ~ glad tidings; he ~s a letter of introduction from Mr X. (4 *have as characteristic, quality or form*) ~ an inscription / motto / name / seal / sign / stamp; ~ scars; ~ the marks / signs / traces of (punishment / wounds / *etc*); he ~s no likeness at all / a strong resemblance to his father; he / his face bore a haughty expression; the cheque bore the drawer's signature; the product ~s our trademark; ~ a sense; the word ~s several meanings; this question ~s a / some / no relation to the larger matter of import policy; this crime ~s a striking similarity to his previous crime. (5 *carry, conduct o.s.*) he ~s himself like a soldier / nobly / proudly / regally / with dignity / well; they ~ themselves like grown-ups. (6 *be accountable for, assume*) ~ liability / responsibility for s.th.; the officer ~s the burden of command / leadership; he ~s the blame for the decision; ~ a part in s.th. *(have a share in it)*; ~ the (entire) expense of s.th.; all (additional) costs must be borne by the traveller; who ~s the handling / transport charges? (7 *have a tolerance for, endure*) she can't ~ that colour / the sight of blood; ~ pain / hardship / stress / the suspense / one's fate; paper won't ~ pressure; these shoes won't ~ hard wear; ~ a difficult situation / loss / strain; I cannot ~ the heat / cold (weather) / it here any longer; □ ~ the brunt of an attack *(bear the chief strain)*; she can't ~ being with him any more / travelling with her back to the engine / his gossiping / being laughed at; how can you ~ to read that? (8 *have susceptibility to; admit to*) such weak claims will not ~ much probing; his story ~s looking into; his language won't ~ repeating; this plan will not ~ analysis / discussion / study; these two reports will not ~ comparison (to any other) / looking into. (9 *give birth to*) ~ a baby / a child / children; she bore him two sons; of all the children borne by her / born to them only one survives. → born; (10 *produce, yield*) a tree ~s fruit; barren soil ~s no grain; the savings account ~s 5% interest; I hope your efforts / work will ~ fruit. (11 *offer, render*) ~ (false) witness to (having seen) s.th. / that ...; his writings ~ witness to his industry; ~ a hand with s.th. / in doing s.th. *(help)*; ~ s.o. company (→ company 1) (12 *move by steady pressure, push*) the gale bore the ship into iceberg-infested waters; we were borne backwards by the crowd. - *vi* (13 *yield a product; produce*) his apple trees ~ abundantly / poorly / well (14 *be relevant to*) the fact does not ~ on the subject we are talking about; your remarks do not ~ on the matter at / in hand (15 *move in a given direction*) the ship bore westward; when you come to the church, ~ (to the) right. (16 *press*) don't ~ on that handle so much; the old man was ~ing heavily on his stick; taxation ~s hard on everybody; it was gradually borne upon me that he is dishonest; → bring to bear.

bear away he bore ~ the palm / several prizes (at the sports meeting).

bear down (1 *press*) you must not ~ ~ so hard on the crayon (2 *overcome*) he has been able to ~ ~ all opposition / resistance; ~ ~ the enemy (3 *move menacingly*) the frigate bore ~ upon our ship; the cavalry bore ~ upon the enemy's right flank; the master bore ~ on Smith as he was entering the school.

bear in it was borne in on me how the weeds of one country are the flowers of another; he must have had borne in on him the immense gulf between all-round American and European achievement.

bear off John bore ~ the prize.

bear out the experiment ~s ~ *(confirms)* his theory; he will ~ me ~ in all that I have said; history will ~ his prediction ~.

bear up (1) water ~s up a ship; the bridge cannot long ~ up against the force of the current (2) ~ up after one's mother's death *(not show despair)*; tell her to ~ up *(be brave)*; come on, ~ up! things are not so bad; ~ up against / under misfortunes.

bear with if you can ~ ~ me for a few minutes, I can explain everything; I could not ~ ~ his violent temper.

bearing *n* (1) have a proud ~; he has the ~ of a gentleman; a man of noble / soldierly / dignified ~ (2) your remarks have no ~ on the question; apart from its direct ~ on British problems, the book will be invaluable to students everywhere; consider s.th. in all its ~s (3) take a compass ~; take one's ~s *(find one's position)*; the boy lost his ~s in the forest; be out of one's ~s; would you like me to give you some idea of your ~s *(of where you are)*? (4) his conduct was beyond (all) ~. (5) in full ~ *(producing fruit well)*; if trees are well cared for, they can be kept in ~ for many years.

beat *vt* (1) ~ the dust out of a carpet; ~ a carpet / drum; ~ the ground (with one's feet); ~ one's breast (in anguish); ~ one's head against the wall; ~ a retreat *(give such a signal; fig: go back)*; ~ a way through the undergrowth; □ ~ the air *(strive in vain)*; □ ~ about the bush *(approach a subject indirectly)*; → brain 3. (2) ~ a child / donkey / s.o. black and blue (3) he was soundly / has never been ~en at tennis; the boxer was ~en on points; ~ a competitor / rival / team; Russia is always defeated but never ~en; ~ a record (4) ~ an egg / egg whites (with a rotary beater); ~ the eggs into the mixture (one at a time); ~ flour and eggs to a paste / to creamy smoothness / together (5) a bird ~s its wings. (6) ~ time *(in music)* (7) that problem has ~en me / has me ~(en) *(puzzled)*; it ~s me (how you solve this problem / how he can do such a thing). - *vi* (8) somebody was ~ing at / upon the door; the rain was ~ing against the windows; waves ~ against the shore. (9) his heart ~ violently; fear makes the heart ~ faster. (10) we heard the drums ~ing.

beat about ~ ~ *(search)* for an excuse; he is ~ing ~ for an answer to the problem of how ...

beat back ~ ~ an attacker / the enemy; the flames ~ ~ the firemen.

beat down (1) the sun ~s ~ on the roof / the waiting crowd. (2) the rain ~ ~ *(fell heavily)*. (3) the wheat was ~en ~ by the rain. (3) at first he asked £50, but I ~ ~ the price to £45 / I ~ him ~ to £45.

beat in that's why we ~ the door in.

beat off he ~ ~ his attackers / a swarm of wasps.

beat up (1) she ~ up the eggs for the cake / the ingredients and ... (2) ~ s.o. up *(thrash him severely)* (3) the hunter ~ up the quarry *(disturbed it)*.

become *vi* (1a) a lamb ~s a sheep; he became a doctor / famous man / grandfather; the custom has now ~ a rule; after the death of Charles I England became a republic. (1 b *become + adj*) ~ indignant / angry / wistful / sentimental / melancholy / overjoyed / happy / silent / thoughtful / eloquent / mad / insane; ~

blue / red / cold / sour / thin / pale / ill; the iron is fast ~ing hot; the animal became nasty; the river became dry; the sky became cloudy; it gradually / suddenly became obvious. (1c *become + part*) he became bent and wrinkled; ~ accustomed to s.th.; at last the truth became known; the carpet became torn through the maid's carelessness. (2) what will ~ of me if you go? what is to ~ of that young man? what has ~ of John / those papers I left on my desk? - *vt* (3) the colour / new dress ~s her; everything ~s a pretty face. (4) modesty ~s a woman; it ~s children to be respectful; it would ill ~ you to praise yourself; it would not ~ the Government to perpetuate this situation.

bed *n* (1) a single / double ~; a room with twin *(two single)* ~s; be / lie / stay in ~; be (lying) ill in ~; lie / sit on a ~; go to ~; get / climb into ~; take to one's ~ *(because of illness)*; make a ~ / the ~s (in the morning); put a child to ~; send the children off to ~; climb / get / leap / jump / slip / fall out of ~; □ get out of ~ on the wrong side *(be in a bad mood)*; a ~ of straw (2) a ~ of roses / tulips / onions / *etc*; a seed / flower / vegetable ~; life's not all a ~ of roses; a ~ of thorns (3) a ~ of gravel / sand / coal (4) the concrete ~ of a machine (5) a lake / river / ocean ~.

bee *n* ~s hum / buzz / swarm / fly from blossom to blossom / suck honey / sting; keep ~s; be as busy as a ~; have a ~ in one's bonnet *(be obsessed by an idea)*.

beer *n* pale / dark / small ~; ~ on draught; draught / bottled ~; ~ barrel; sit over one's ~; go and have a ~; □ think no small ~ of s.o. *(have a high opinion of him)*.

beg *vt* (1) ~ a few pence (of us); ~ a meal / money (from s.o.) (2) ~ s.o.'s forgiveness / pardon; ~ a favour (of s.o.); they ~ged (of) him to stay / not to do it; the children ~ged (permission) to stay up late; I ~ leave to disagree; I ~ to differ (from you) / to disagree; □ ~ the question *(found a conclusion on s.th. that needs to be proved)*: 'fox hunting is not cruel since the fox enjoys fun' - saying this is ~ging the question. - *vi* (3) ~ for alms / food / money (from s.o.); ~ in the streets; a dog ~s for food; live by ~ging; go ~ging; offers / things go ~ging *(fig: are unwanted)* (4) ~ for mercy.

beg off (1) he promised to come and help but has since ~ged ~. (2) ~ s.o. ~ *(get him excused from a penalty)*.

begin *vt* (1a) ~ one's work; ~ a task / correspondence (with s.o.) / letter / day / speech (with a quotation); when did you ~ school? (1b *begin + inf, gerund*) don't ~ writing until I tell you; I ~ to see your point; I can see you ~ning to smile; the cherry blossom has begun to drop; he saw the lorry ~ to slide / sliding. - *vi* (2) the performance ~s at 7 o'clock; the play began with a prologue; dinner ~s with soup; let us ~ with Ann; he began by writing the address / saying that he...; (we haven't got enough money), to ~ with *(in the first place)*. (3) the brook ~s in the hills.

behave *vi* (1) ~ well / properly / wisely / badly / *etc*; ~ like a fool / lunatic / *etc*; don't ~ like that; he knows how to ~ in company. (2) please let me go and I'll ~ *(properly)*. (3) study how steel ~s under stress; how does the car ~ on long trips? - *vt* (4) ~ yourself! I told them to ~ themselves; she knows that she has got to ~ herself.

behaviour *n* (1) have, show good / bad ~ (towards s.o.); s.o.'s gentlemanlike / blameless / prudent / intelligent / acceptable / childish / foolish / furtive / lax / cheap / impudent / aggressive / dubious / ambiguous / disgraceful / unheard-of / *etc* ~; be on one's good / best ~; put s.o. on his best ~ *(warn him to behave himself)* (2) s.o.'s adult / social / individual ~; his ~ under the impress of loneliness (3) the ~ of a new car / dyes in certain weathers / a kite in the wind.

belief *n* (1) nothing will shake my ~ in his honesty; ~ in God / eternal life / fate / miracles / ghosts / dreams / the supernatural; it is my firm ~ that he...; I have no(t much) ~ in quack medicine; he had no great ~ in his doctor; to the best of my (knowledge and) ~ (this is correct). (2) hold / have religious ~s; his ~ rests / relies / is founded on the Bible; a firm / secure / fundamental / accepted ~; pagan ~s (3) the erroneous ~ that (the earth was flat); argue s.o. out of the ~ that (war is inevitable).

believe *vt* (1 *take as true, honest; trust*) ~ s.o.; ~ a story / statement; I don't ~ a word you say; ~ me, I didn't do it on purpose; she could not ~ her ears / eyes. (2 *be convinced*) he firmly ~s his theory to be correct; I ~ that he means well. (3 *suppose*) ~ o.s. (to be) alone / ill; you wouldn't ~ it possible (for people to be so stupid); do you ~ (that) it will rain tomorrow? I ~d her to be in Paris; he is ~d to be in Rome. - *vi* (4 *be convinced*) I used to ~ otherwise, but now ...; a story that divided the audience into those who ~d and those who didn't (5 *suppose*) he lives abroad, I ~; Mr. Brown, I ~. (6 *have faith in*) ~ in fairies / ghosts / God / the supernatural / *etc*; ~ in the forgiveness of sins (7 *think much of*) ~ in freedom / human equality / one's friends; ~ in old-fashioned remedies / buying cheap goods; I've never ~d in saving on the wrong things; he ~s in getting plenty of exercise. (8 *judge, evaluate*) ~ badly / ill / well of s.o.

bell *n* a ~ rings / sounds / tolls / chimes / peals / tinkles; ring / sound / toll / chime / tinkle a ~; the ~ goes / rings / sounds *(at school)*; has the ~ gone / *etc* yet?

belong *vi* (1) does the chair ~ here? shoes ~ in the cupboard; the vase ~s on the table; this book ~s with the works of reference; do you ~ *(live)* here? he ~s in jail / the hospital; his ideas about politics ~ among his more bizarre inventions. (2) this dog ~s to Ann; the house ~s to him (by right). (3 *be a member of*) do you ~ to the choir? which club does he ~ to? (4 *be classified as*) the whale ~s to the class of / ~s among the mammals; do mice and squirrels ~ to the same family? (5 *be part of a whole*) South Tyrol no longer ~s to Austria; this tube ~s to the vacuum cleaner; buttons that ~ to a dress; concepts that ~ to geometry; she ~s to him body and soul.

bend *vt* (1) ~ a piece of metal / wire; ~ bamboo / a bow / a rod; ~ the elbow / knee (before the altar) / the, one's neck; ~ one's body backward / forward; ~ s.th. down / up / crooked / straight / to one side; don't ~ these photos; ~ one's steps *(turn)* towards home (2) the tyrant bent everyone to his will; ~ the law (3) he couldn't ~ his mind to his studies; ~ one's energies to a task / towards solving a problem. - *vi* (4) he bent down to pick up the papers; he bent over the child; he bent forward to listen to her; the tree bent to / in / before the wind; ~ under a load. (5) the twig / *etc* ~s easily. (6) the river / road ~s (slightly) to the left. (7) I ~ to your wishes; ~ to s.o.'s will; he's obstinate - he will not ~. (8) □ ~ over backwards (to please s.o. / to do s.th.) *(go to extremes)*. - *adj* (9) bent with age / grief / sorrow / troubles (10) all eyes were bent on him. (11) be bent on (mastering French / passing the exam / world conquest).

benefit *n* (1) did you get much ~ from your holiday? he gave us the ~ of his advice; derive ~ from s.th.; confer a ~ on s.o.; do s.th. for the ~ of (the poor); the dictionary wasn't of much ~ to me; it would not be to my ~ to do that; □ give s.o. the ~ of the doubt *(decide in his favour in case of doubt)* (2) the ~s of good education; the ~s we receive from our parents and teachers (3) unemployment / sickness / medical / maternity ~(s) (4) a ~ ball *(charity ball)*; N's ~ match.

benefit *vt* (1) exercise will ~ her; the rest ~ed his health; the new factory will ~ the household with a variety of articles. - *vi* (2) ~ from s.o.'s advice / one's past experience; ~ by paying close attention to s.o.; when you help others, you ~, too.

bereave *vt* (1) an accident ~d him of his father; be ~d of one's friend / parents / wife (2) nothing can ~ me of my memories; indignation had bereft him of (all) speech. - *adj* are you bereft of your senses? a ~d husband / mother / *etc*; bereft of reason / (all) hope.

berth *n* □ give s.o. / s.th. a wide ~ *(avoid)*.

bespeak *vt* (1 *BE*) ~ a room in a hotel / a table in a restaurant (2 *BE, AE*) his good manners ~ a fine upbringing; his arrogance ~s his youth. - *adj* (3 *BE*) bespoke boots *(made to order)*; bespoke bootmaker / tailor.

best *adj* the ~ man on earth; the ~ thing to do / she could do was (to stay at home); which is the ~ way to (go from here to) the station?; (wait) the ~ part of an hour; the job took the ~ part of a week to finish.

best *adv* I can work ~ after a good night's sleep; do as you think ~; do it as ~ you can; you had ~ go at once; which do you like ~ (of all)? you know ~; the ~ dressed woman; the ~ looking girl; the ~ hated man.

best *n* (1) he is the ~ of men; the ~ of men (may err); we are the ~ of friends; give your wife my ~ *(greet her from me)*; all the actors gave of their ~ *(talent, effort)*; the ~ of the (recruits / class); you deserve the ~; the ~ isn't good enough (for her); do / try one's ~; look one's ~;

get / have the ~ of it *(win in a contest)*; make the ~ of things / one's time; make the ~ of a bad job / bargain / business (→ make *vt* 1d, bad *adj* 1); make the ~ of one's way home *(return as quickly as possible)*; enjoy / get / have / want the ~ of both / two worlds *(of two rather different situations, etc)* (→ world 7). (2 *with prepos*) I am at my ~ early in the morning; he was at his ~ in comedy; the roses are at their ~ now; the book, at ~, may sell 1,000 copies; at ~ we can only hope to finish third; (his health was never very good,) (even) at the ~ of times; I did it for the ~ *(with the ~ intentions)*; ..., but it turned out for the ~ (in the end); it's all for the ~; I am in the ~ of health; (appear / be dressed) in one's (Sunday) ~; to the ~ of one's ability / belief / knowledge / recollection; he can climb / dance / sing / *etc* with the ~ *(as well as anyone else)*.

bestow *vt* (1) ~ a title / medal / award / honour (up)on s.o. (2) ~ great attention on one's garden; ~ much thought / time on a plan; her parents ~ed on her all their care and affection. (3) ~ a son / daughter in marriage to s.o.

bet *n* (1) make / accept / take up / win / lose a ~; lay a ~ on a horse (2) my ~ was £1 / a bottle of champagne (3) that horse is a sure / poor ~ (to win / place / lose).

bet *vt* (1) he ~ me five pounds / a bottle of wine I could not do it; I have ~ £10 against it; I ~ you can't do this puzzle; he ~ me that I couldn't do it; I'll ~ my bottom dollar / you can ~ your life he finds some excuse ...; the money was all ~ted away. - *vi* (2) and did you accept the offer? - you ~ *(inform: most certainly)* I did.

betray *vt* (1) ~ one's country; a disloyal soldier ~ed the army. (2) ~ information / a secret / a friend (3) his confusion ~s his nervousness; the gleam in his eye ~ed his interest; ~ one's ignorance / o.s. (4) ~ the trust put in one *(not justify)*.

better *adj* (1) he is a ~ man than you; she is a much ~ cook than I (am); you will find no ~ / not find a ~ hotel than this (one); I have a ~ opinion of him; this material is of a much ~ quality; she has seen ~ days; to walk to town takes the ~ part of an hour; □ my ~ half *(spouse)* (2) that's ~; it / things couldn't be ~; it is ~ than nothing; he is little / no ~ than a thief; you look (ever so much) ~ today; his work is getting ~; □ be ~ than one's word *(do more than one promised)* (3) feel / look ~; I have been ill, but I am ~ now; are you any ~? is your mother ~ *(recovering)*? (4) I have something ~ to do than (wait hours for him); do you know of anything ~? (5) be ~ off *(richer; in a better position)*.

better *adv* she cooks much ~ than I (do); I know that ~ than you; it works ~ that way; I am ~ paid here; I like him ~ than I used to; think ~ of (doing) s.th. *(decide not to do it)*; think (all) the ~ of s.o. *(have a higher opinion of him)*; I thought you knew ~ than to (quarrel with him); he says he didn't cheat but I know ~; I can understand it all the ~ because ...; he is none the ~ for it; the ~ I know him, the more I ...; you had ~ go now / write it; what had I ~ do? hadn't you ~ make haste? □ go s.o. one ~ *(AE outwit, outdo)* □ go one ~ than s.o.

better *n* get the ~ of one's opponent; his shyness got the ~ of him; one's ~s *(those who are wiser, higher in rank)*; a change for the ~; things are taking a turn for the ~.

better *vt* (1) ~ the conditions of the peasants; he took some courses to ~ himself. (2) this record has never been ~ed; try to ~ one's opponent's achievement (3) leave a firm to ~ o.s. / one's circumstances.

beware *vi* one should ~ of strange dogs; ~ of frivolous women / forming bad habits / the fallacy that ...; ~ (of) what you do.

bewilder *vt* (1) the noise and crowds of the town ~ed him; be ~ed by contradictory orders. - *adj* (2) (textbooks) in ~ing variety; the traffic system here is ~ing. (3) a completely ~ed man came up to me and asked the way; he had a (totally) ~ed look on his face.

bias *n* (1) the article shows a ~ against the U.S.A.; he has a ~ towards / against the plan. (2) cut (cloth / a skirt) on the ~ *(diagonally)*.

bias *vt* ~ the opinions of people; this newspaper is ~ed in favour of Labour; loyalty to the team ~ed us against the umpire.

bid *n* (1) make the first / opening / starting ~; make a higher / further ~ (2) make a ~ for fame / popular support.

bid *vt* (1) I ~ £ 2 for the bicycle; the goods were ~ up beyond their real value. (2) ~ s.o. good-bye / farewell / welcome / good night (3) ~ defiance to (the enemy) (4 *archaic*) he bade me help him; do as you are ~; all the peasants were ~den to the feast. - *vi* (5) did you ~ for the house? a rich man ~ against me *(more than I).* (6) this method ~s fair to achieve good results *(is likely).*

big *adj* (1) a ~ man is heavy and bulky, a large man tall and broad; a ~ house / building / ship / car; a ~ apple / box / parcel / stone / hole; the ~ toe; you're rather ~ for your age; a small boy with ~ eyes; what do you want to do when you are ~? ~ boys don't cry; ~ game; a ~-game hunter; ~ with child *(pregnant)*; the ~ Dipper; □ get / grow too ~ for one's boots *(become conceited)* (2) a ~ income / fortune / sum of money / profit / transaction / loss; ~ business; a ~ size / difference. (3) a ~ voice; saying this he got a ~ laugh; thunder makes a ~ noise; □ he's a ~ noise in the banking world *(inform: prominent man)*; (4) it was a ~ success; a ~ affair; ~ news; a ~ idea; have ~ ideas *(be ambitious)*; think ~; a ~ man *(great)*; the ~ men of the town; be conscientious about little things as well as ~ ones; he has a ~ heart *(generous).* (5) several ~ mistakes in his work; you are the ~gest fool of the lot. (6 *boastful*) ~ words; have a ~ mouth *(inform: boast)* (7) be ~ on s.th. *(AE like it very much).* - *adv* (8 *AE largely*) pay ~ for a privilege; I eat ~ in the mornings. (9 *boastfully*) talk ~; act ~.

bill *n* (1) have you paid the hotel ~? ask for the ~; may I have the ~? present one's ~; run up a ~; foot the ~ *(pay it)* (2 *placard*) a theatre / concert ~; post a ~; stick no ~s!; the ~ says that the circus comes in August; head / top the ~ *(in large letters, etc)*; ~ of fare *(menu)* (3 *certificate*) (clean) ~ of health; ~ of lading *(receipt for goods shipped)* (4 *proposed law*) draft / bring in / introduce / present / pass / approve / reject a ~.

bill *vt* (1) he used to ~ his customers monthly; the shop will ~ me for these things later. (2) the actor is ~ed to appear next week.

bind *vt* (1) ~ s.o. (to a tree with a rope); ~ a prisoner (tight / hand and foot); lie bound in chains; ~ a package with twine; ~ (up) corn / wheat into sheaves (2) ~ a wound with bandages → bind up 1 (3) ~ a book (in boards / cloth / leather / linson (4) cement ~s bricks together in a wall; frost ~s the ground in winter. (5) ~ the cuffs of a jacket / the edge of a carpet / a seam (6) ~ paint witl oil. ~ a mixture with eggs / flour (7 *link*) friendship ~s them together; they are (eternally) bound by ties of friendship; commerce ~s nations together; (the power of) gravity ~s the planets to the sun. (8 *oblige*) s.th. ~s the conscience; ~ s.o. to pay a debt; we do not ~ you to these prices; ~ s.o. to secrecy in a matter; ~ o.s. to s.th.; be bound by contract / an oath; am I bound by this promise? feel bound to s.th.; the boy was bound (out / over) (as an) apprentice to a (tailor). (9) cocoa ~s the bowels *(constipates).* (10) the book / new impression is ~ing *(being bound).* (11) clay ~s when it is baked. - *adj* (12) a ~ing agreement; regard an agreement as ~ing (on all parties); → bound[1] *adj.*

bind down we mustn't ~ ~ the architect too much - he will want to develop his own ideas; the young scientist felt bound ~ by all the rules and regulations.

bind up (1) ~ up a wound (tight) / a sprained ankle / *etc*; ~ up one's hair (before sweeping the room) (2) be bound up in one's work *(be very busy)*; be bound up with s.th. *(closely connected).*

bird *n* migratory ~; ~s of prey / passage; □ a ~ in the hand *(s.th. known)*; □ a ~ in the bush *(s.th. uncertain)*; □ kill two ~s with one stone; □ ~s of a feather *(people of similar character)*; give s.o. the ~ *(hiss him)*; get the ~.

birth *n* (1) an easy / difficult ~; die at ~; dumb from ~; give ~ to a son / idea / plan / poem (2) the ~ of surrealism / a nation (3) be of French ~; be French by ~; of high / low / humble ~.

bit *n* (1) a (little) ~ of bread / sugar; a few ~s of paper; eat every ~ of one's meal; he has saved a nice ~ of money; cut / pull / tear s.th. to ~s; go / come to ~s (2) wait a ~; let's rest for a ~; I'll be ready in a ~; after a ~ he came ...; restrictions will be lifted ~ by ~; a ~ at a time (3) he knows a ~ of English; we had a ~ of trouble getting / to get the car started; I have a ~ of a headache / cold; he's a ~ of a fool / dandy / coward; he's a ~ silly / *etc*; the exam was a ~ difficult; it's a ~ cold today;

that coat is a ~ too dear; I'm not a ~ tired; it's not a ~ of use trying to help him; do you think he'll do it? not a ~ of it! he doesn't care a ~; you're every ~ as good as he is; □ to do one's ~ *(share of work)*; □ give s.o. a ~ of one's mind *(scold him)*.

bite *vt* (1) ~ one's tongue / lips *(also fig)*; ~ one's (finger)nails; □ ~ the dust *(fall dead / wounded)* (2) a dog bit him in the leg; badly bitten by fleas (3) the icy wind bit my face; pepper ~s the tongue. (4) his fingers / the dahlias were bitten by frost. (5) acids ~ (into) metals. - *vi* (6) ~ into an apple / on s.th. hard; ~ at s.o. / s.th. *(try to ~)* (7) be careful, that dog ~s; a mosquito ~s. (8) the fish are ~ing today *(taking the bait)*; I made him several tempting offers, but he wouldn't ~ *(fig)*. (9 *grip*) the rails were slippery with ice and the wheels of the engine would not ~; the spurs bit into the horse's side. - *adj* (10) a ~ing wind; ~ing cold *(also adv)*; the ~ing taste of vinegar (11) ~ing irony / remorse / wit; her ~ing words; make a ~ing remark; give a ~ing answer (12) get one's feet / nose frost-bitten; have frost-bitten feet.

bite off ~ ~ a large piece of the cake; it was a stupid thing to say - I could ~ my tongue ~ whenever I think of it; □ ~ ~ more than one can chew *(attempt too much)*; □ ~ s.o.'s head ~ *(scold him severely for a trivial fault)*; ~ s.o.'s nose ~ *(speak angrily to him)*.

black *adj* (1) ~ colour / cloud(s) / *etc*; a ~ night / sky / *etc*; paint s.th. ~ ; be ~ and blue *(covered with bruises)*; ~ in the face *(flushed with anger or effort)* (2) a ~ day for our team; the prospects look ~ ; look ~ at s.o. *(look angrily)*; not so ~ as he is painted *(not so bad as he is said to be)* (3) a ~ deed; a soul ~ as night.

black *n* (1) be dressed in ~ ; put down in / have s.th. down in ~ and white *(written, printed)* (2) you have some ~ on your hand; there is too much ~ in the picture. (3) be in the ~ *(be solvent)* (4) he hates the ~s *(Negroes)*.

black *vt* (1) ~ shoes / leather / grates / a face (2) ~ s.o.'s eyes.

blacken *vt* (1) soot ~s kettles; the ceiling is ~ed with smoke. (2) ~ s.o.'s reputation / character (to s.o. else). - *vi* (3) the sky ~ed; silver ~s with age.

blame *n* (1) where does the ~ lie for our failure? bear the ~ ; lay / put the ~ (for s.th.) on s.o. / s.th.; shift the ~ on to s.o. for s.th.; take on o.s. all the ~ for the project's failure (2) she must take the ~ for her children's bad manners; if you don't work well, you'll incur ~ .

blame *vt* he ~d the weather for his poor crops; he ~d his poor crops on the weather; ~ s.o. for an accident; ~ an accident on s.o.; who is to ~ for (the mistake)? (2) his behaviour was not to ~ ; his conduct is to ~; I don't ~ you for (leaving him); I am in no way to ~ ; I have nothing to ~ myself for.

blank *n* (1) leave ~s for the words you don't know. (2) my mind / memory was / became a (complete) ~ when I heard the question; for me the time after the accident was a total ~.

blank *adj* (1) a ~ page / questionnaire (2) a ~ look (on one's face); a (perfectly) ~ personality (3) a ~ key *(unfinished)* (4) to give / receive a ~ refusal (from s.o.).

blast *n* (1) a ~ of hot air from a furnace; an icy ~ came in when I opened the window. (2) a ~ of dynamite; an atomic ~ (3) the ~ of a car horn; blow a ~ on a trumpet / horn (4) the scheme is running / going (at) full ~.

blast *vt* (1) ~ rocks in a quarry; ~ a tunnel; danger, ~ing in progress! (2 *ruin*) the cherry blossoms were ~ed by frost; the tree was ~ed by lightning; his hopes were ~ed; time had ~ed his ambition. (3 *attack*) ~ the opposition / s.o.'s reputation.

bleed *vt* (1) doctors used to ~ people when they were ill; ~ a tree (2 *fig*) that swindler ~s his victims white; the blackmailer bled him for $500.- *vi* (3) ~ freely / heavily / to death / like a pig; his finger bled from the cut; he is ~ing at the nose; his nose is ~ing; the tree is ~ing where the branch was cut off. (4) during the war men bled and died for their country. (5) my heart ~s for her; his heart bled at the sight (6) wash this garment separately: this colour ~s *(is not fast)*; the red bled into the yellow and now the dress is ruined. - *adj* (7) a ~ing wound (8) a ~ing colour / dye *(one that is not fast)*.

blend *vt* (1) ~ flour with broth to thicken a gravy; ~ the eggs into the batter; carefully ~ed teas / tobaccoes. (2) he successfully ~ed amusement with instruction; ~ the cultures of East and West; - *vi* (3) oil and water do not ~. (4) these colours ~ well; how well the new curtains ~ with the carpet; pick a colour that will ~ with your skin. (5) the immigrants ~ed with the natives.

bless *vt* (1) ~ an altar /new church; ~ the worshippers (in a church); ~ the fields / relics (2) fortune ~ed him with a good disposition. - *adj* (3) be ~ed with good health / a good digestion / ignorance; what a ~ed thing is sleep; such ~ed gifts as peace and quiet.

blind *adj* (1) ~ in one eye; ~ from birth (2) ~ flying / guessing; a ~ flight (3) be ~ to danger / s.o.'s faults / one's own weakness; love made him ~ to her faults. (4 *unthinking*) in ~ haste; ~ panic / rage / enthusiasm / faith / obedience / stupidity / carelessness; a ~ decision; trust s.o. ~ly; the world is not governed by ~ forces. (5 *difficult to see*) slow down before a ~ or sharp bend; a ~ curve / turning / corner (6 *without opening, outlet*) a ~ wall; a ~ door / window; a ~ passage / alley.

blind *vt* (1) be ~ed in the war; be ~ed by tears / dust / a bomb (2) love has ~ed him to her faults; superstitions which ~ men to the facts.

block *n* (1) cement ~s are used in building; a ~ of soap / paper / wood; a statue cut out of a ~ of marble (2) a ~ of houses / *(BE)* flats; *(BE)* an office ~; *(AE)* he walked five ~s *(as far as the fifth cross-road).* (3) a ~ in a pipe; *(BE)* a traffic ~; the police set up road-~s around the prison. (4) a butcher's ~ (5) on the ~ *(up for auction)* (6) have a mental ~ (towards s.th.) *(be unable to recall or learn s.th.).*

block *vt* (1) ~ (up) traffic; the ambulance was ~ed by traffic; a piece of rock is ~ing (up) the path; the entrance to the cave had been ~ed up. (2) ~ an opponent('s plans); try to ~ s.o.'s election; his brother ~ed him at every turn. - *adj* (3) I thought the pipe might be ~ed.

blood *n* (1) spit ~; staunch / stop ~; give / donate ~; give one's ~ for one's country; shed / spill ~; covered / steeped in ~; ~ pressure; a ~ test / donor / *etc*; the ~ rushed to her face; all the ~ (was) drained from her face. (2) the ~ curdled in my veins *(I was filled with fear)*; my ~ ran cold; his ~ boiled / was up *(he was angry)*; the sight made his ~ boil; kill s.o. in cold ~ (3) the ~ of the grape (4) ~-ties; ties of ~; children of the same ~; □ ~ is thicker than water; (acting) is in his ~. (5) blue ~; of noble / royal ~; (a person) of the ~ *(of royal lineage)* (6) the country lost over 40 per cent of its youngest and strongest ~; new ~ (in the company) (7) s.th. causes / makes bad ~ (between two persons) *(disharmony).*

bloom *n* (1) the roses are in ~; the trees have come / burst into ~; (2) the violet has a delicate ~; fragrant ~s (3) the ~ of wine (4) a girl in the (full) ~ of youth / her beauty / her loveliness; the ~(ing-time) of a period of art *(period of full development).*

bloom *vi* (1) that bush will ~ soon; in our climate the roses ~ in June. (2) the arts ~ed in this stimulating environment. - *adj* (3) she looks ~ing.

blossom *n* (1) the apple-trees are in ~; Kent is a land of orchards and of ~. (2) fragrant ~s; cut a branch of cherry- / apple-~. (3) the ~(ing-time) of a period of art *(the beginning of that period).*

blossom *vi* the apple-trees are ~ing; the ~ing-time of a tree; this lily ~s very early.

blot *n* (1) a ~ of ink; you've made an ugly ink-~ in your letter (2) a ~ on s.o.'s character / reputation; this ugly building is a ~ on the landscape; slavery has been called 'human nature's broadest, foulest ~'.

blot *vt* (1) ~ paper (with ink); □ ~ one's copy-book *(spoil one's good reputation)* (2) ~ ink; ~ting-paper; ~ up a stain (3) the dark clouds ~ted out the sun; that species was ~ted out by ruthless hunters. - *vi* (4) cheap paper ~s easily.

blow *vt* (1) the wind blew dust in his face; the wind blew the papers all over the lawn / out of my hand. (2) it was ~ing a gale. (3) ~ the dust off the furniture; ~ an egg *(hollow)*; ~ one's nose with / on a handkerchief (4) ~ a trumpet / whistle; □ ~ one's own trumpet *(proclaim one's merits)* (5) ~ soap bubbles; ~ glass (6) don't ~ the fuse. - *vi* (7) the wind is ~ing (harder than before); it is ~ing outside; it was ~ing hard; □ (find out) how / which way the wind ~s / is ~ing (8) ~ on the soup / one's (burned) fingers (9) the door blew open; the dust has ~n into the house. (10) the fuse has ~n. (11) stop work when the whistle ~s. (12) the old man was puffing and ~ing when he got to the top of the hill.

blow away (1) the wind blew his paper ~. (2) his papers were ~n ~.

blow down the storm blew several trees ~.
blow in (1) a lot of dust has ~n in. (2) an old friend blew in last night *(inform).*
blow off (1) the wind blew my hat ~. (2) ~ ~ steam *(also fig)* (3) my hat blew ~.
blow out (1) ~ ~ a match / candle / flame; ~ ~ a paper bag; don't ~ ~ the fuse. (2) sit tight until the storm has ~n itself ~. (3) ~ s.o.'s brains ~; ~ one's (own) brains ~ (4) suddenly one of our tyres blew ~. (5) the candles blew ~; the fuse blew ~ and the house was in darkness.
blow over (1) the wind is almost strong enough to ~ you ~. (2) the storm / those clouds will soon ~ ~. (3) the disagreement / scandal / quarrel / fuss will soon ~ ~; the opposition to this reform will (gradually) ~ ~.
blow up (1) ~ up a balloon / tyre; ~up the fire *(make it burn better)*; up a photograph *(enlarge it greatly)* (2) ~ up a bridge / the railway track / a train / the door of the safe (3) a bad storm blew up *(arose)* over the mountain; a gale blew up suddenly; it is ~ing up for rain *(the wind will bring rain).* (4) the boiler blew up because of too much steam pressure; the barrel of gunpowder blew up with a terrific noise. (5) ~ s.o. up for lateness / idling his time away *(inform: criticize severely)* (6) remember how I blew up *(became angry)* about David's teacher?
blow[1] *n* (1) give your nose a good ~. (2 *breathing*) go for / have a ~ *(go outdoors for fresh air).*
blow[2] *n* (1) aim a ~ at s.o; strike / deal s.o. a (violent / hard / fatal / vital / terrific / *etc*) ~; deal out ~s; ward off / avert / avoid / dodge / parry a ~; come to ~s *(begin fighting)*; exchange ~s; ~s hailed / rained / showered down on him; that ~ struck home. (2) the bad news was quite a / a great ~ (to him / our hopes).
blue *adj* (1) her nose was ~ with cold; dye s.th. ~; □ once in a ~ moon *(very rarely)* (2) ~ blood (3 *sad*) he was lonely and ~; she looked ~; things are looking ~.
blue *n* (1) these two ~s are quite different; Prussian / navy / French ~; a midnight ~; there isn't enough ~ in it; the ~ of the sky; dressed in ~ (2 *unknown*) a trip into the ~; (appear / come) out of the ~ *(unexpected)*; □ a bolt from / out of the ~ *(s.th. quite unexpected).*
blunder *vi* (1) John ~ed about as if drunk; he ~ed through school, career and indeed his whole life; he ~ed into a good job. (2) he only ~ed once during the quiz: when he cited the wrong date. - *vt* (3) he ~s every job he takes on. (4) he ~ed out the secret and that was the end of the surprise.
board *n* (1) a loose ~; the floor consisted merely of rough ~s; □ above ~ *(honest)* (2) a *(BE)* notice- / *(AE)* bulletin / chess- / draught-~; a diving-~ (3) full ~ (and lodging); partial ~; how much do you pay for (room and) ~? (4) the ship had 100 passengers on ~; she wrote the letter on ~ ship; come / go / be / stay on ~ (a liner / the Bremen / *etc*); cargo / a mast went by the ~; this tradition went quietly by the ~; all our plans have gone by the ~. (5) a book in (cloth)~s; card~ (6) on the ~s *(stage)*; tread the ~s *(perform).*
board *vt* (1) ~ up a door / window (2 *give lodging to*) ~ students (3) ~ a plane / ship / train. - *vi* (4) he ~s at the YMCA (hostel) / with his aunt; he ~s out *(elsewhere).* - *adj* (5) the floor was ~ed.
boast *n* (1) it was his proud ~ that he had always paid his own way. (2) the new hospital was the ~ of the town.
boast *vi* (1) he ~ed of the success of his team; you may be the best cricketer in the school, but you needn't ~ about it (2) the city of York can ~ of many historic buildings; I have never been able to ~ of good health. - *vt* (3) he ~ed that no one could beat him in a race. (4) the health resort ~ed a fifteen-story hotel; Germany can ~ excellent roads.
boat *n* a rowing- / sailing- / ferry- / mail / life / *etc* ~; a leaky ~; lower / launch / row / sail / steer a ~; cross a river in a ~; go in a / by ~; carry s.th. ashore by ~; take to the ~s *(when the ship sinks)*; he came from England in the last ~; the night-~ took us across the Channel; □ we are (all) in the same ~ *(face the same risks)*; □ burn one's ~s *(make return impossible).*
boat *vi* (1) we ~ed down the river; go ~ing. - *vt* (2) this is where they ~ the cargo *(load).* (3 *AE*) the cargo is ~ed through / along this canal *(transported).*
body *n* (1) the human / animal ~; an animal's ~; an athletic / muscular / slim ~; harden / toughen (up) one's ~; (be healthy in) ~ and mind; (give o.s.) ~ and soul (to s.th.); he earns scarcely enough to

keep ~ and soul together. (2) he had a rash on the arms and ~; he pushed his head and ~ through the hole. (3) they found the victim's ~ in the river; a lifeless ~; his ~ was brought back to England for burial. (4) solid / liquid / gaseous ~ies; a hollow ~; a foreign ~ (in the eye) (5) heavenly / celestial ~ies (6) the ~ of a tool / stringed instrument / motor-car / aeroplane / building; the ~ of colour / wine; wine of good ~; the ~ of a letter / book / *etc (main portion)* (7) a ~ of men / soldiers; a legislative / corporate / non-profit-making ~; the ~ medical *(the doctors)*; (they went to him) in a ~ *(all together)*; the staff resigned in a ~. (8) a lake is a ~ of water; he had a large ~ of facts to prove his statements; a ~ of doctrine; there is no well-defined ~ of public conviction on such questions; the research yielded a valuable ~ of knowledge about pollution; the overwhelming ~ of advertisements is addressed to women.

boil *vt* (1) ~ fish / meat / milk / potatoes / rice / vegetables / water / *etc*; ~ an egg (hard / soft); ~ the kettle / pan (2) ~ linen / rags / soap / the washing. - *vi* (3) the water / *etc* is ~ing; the water should ~ briskly; the water (in the radiator) / the car is ~ing; the radiator is ~ing (over). (4) the water ~ed through the canyon. (5) he was ~ing with rage; → blood 2. - *adj* (6) a ~ing hot day; → keep *vt* 8c; the boat was swallowed up by the ~ing waves; reach the ~ing point (7) ~ed ham / potatoes / *etc*; *(BE)* ~ed sweets.

boil away (1) I heated the water till it ~ed ~. (2) the kettle was ~ing ~ merrily on the fire.

boil down (1) the water has ~ed ~ and now there is not enough to make tea. (2) ~ this passage ~ to about a hundred words. (3) his statement ~s ~ to one simple fact; it all ~s ~ to the fact that he is lazy.

boil over (1) the kettle / pan / pot / milk is ~ing ~ - turn the gas down. (2) the newspaper ~ed ~ with indignation; suddenly she ~ed ~ and told us what she really thought of him.

boil up (1) ~ milk / *etc* up (2) the milk is ~ing up *(rising)*.

boil *n* bring s.th. to the / a rapid ~; come to the ~; the water is near / at / on the ~; hold s.th. at a vigorous ~; *(BE)* the soup has gone off the ~.

bond *n* (1) enter into a ~ with s.o.; his word is as good as his ~ *(he never breaks a verbal promise)*. (2) a ~ of friendship; a close ~ of affection between A and B; ~s of matrimony; matrimonial ~s; the ~(s) between mother and child is / are immensely powerful; the ~s which unite Goethe to his time (3) be in ~s *(as a slave, prisoner)*; the ~s of superstition / passion; break / burst the ~s of slavery; take off / remove s.o.'s ~s; break one's ~ asunder; burst one's ~s; tear one's ~s apart / asunder; throw off / cast off one's ~s.

bone *n* (1) ~ is a hard living tissue which forms the framework of the body; some buttons are made of ~; → skin. (2) every ~ in his body ached; he has no flesh on his ~s *(is thin)*; rest one's (old / weary) ~s; my old ~s are not what they used to be; I've still got flu in my ~s; his ~s *(corpse)* were laid to rest; □ feel in one's ~s *(know intuitively)*; you'll never cure him of his meanness - it's in his ~s; □ have a ~ to pick with s.o. *(s.th. to complain about)*; I'm afraid he won't make old ~s *(live long)*; he made no ~s about the fact that he was suffering from incurable cancer; they dismissed him and made no ~s about it; frozen to the ~ *(completely)* (3) a fish full of ~s.

bone *vt* (1) ~ boiled fish / a chicken - *vi* (2) for the exam I've got to ~ up on all kinds of learned publications *(inform: study hard)*.

book *n* (1) an (un)bound / paper-back(ed) ~; a note~; an exercise ~; a classic / delightful / exciting / absorbing / dry / worthless / *etc* ~; a learned / scientific / reference / *etc* ~; write / print / produce / publish / bring out a ~ (under one's own name / a pseudonym / a pen-name); a ~ comes out / is out *(published; lent by a library)* / is published / appears / is out of print / is reprinting / is binding; this ~ deals with / is about / treats of / has to do with (science); read s.th. (aloud) from a ~; he sounds / talks / speaks like a ~; read s.o. like a ~ *(know what he is thinking)*; □ go by the ~ *(follow regulations blindly)*; I can't speak by the ~ *(with authority)*, but I know this is wrong; □ a sealed ~ *(s.th. unknown, difficult to understand)* (2) a ~ of tram / bus tickets; a 50p. ~ of stamps; a cheque-~ (3 *a record of bets at a race*) make a ~ *(BE)* / make ~

(AE) (4) enter s.th. in the *(business)* ~s; bring (the) ~s up to date; □ be in s.o.'s good / bad ~s *(in / out of favour with s.o.)*; on the ~s *(in a list of members)*; take s.o.'s name off the ~s; □ throw the ~ at s.o. *(inform: bring all possible charges against s.o. in a court of law)* → bring 9.

book *vt* (1) ~ an item / order / sum (2) ~ a ticket (in advance); ~ a berth / flight / passage / room (in a hotel) / seat / table (in a restaurant) / trunk-call; ~ seats for the theatre by phone (3) can I ~ you to lecture to the Society on May 5? we have ~ed speakers for all the meetings; are you ~ed for this evening? I'll ~ Friday for you *(reserve)*. (4) ~ a motorist for failing to stop / exceeding the speed limit; most policemen would have ~ed you for that. - *vi* (5) can I ~ through to Berlin?

book down (1) ~ ~ every sum of money received (2) are you paying now, or shall we ~ it ~ to you?

book in on arrival at the office all employees have to ~ in; he ~ed in at the Berlin Hilton *(registered)*.

book up I am ~ed up for May, but I could come in June; I'm afraid I can't see you this week - I'm ~ed up every evening; the theatre is ~ed up for every evening this week; we'll have to decide soon where we're going for our summer holidays, or everywhere will be ~ed up.

boom *vi* (1) the cannons ~ed; thunder ~ed across the valley (2) business ~ed; steel is ~ing again; California began to ~ when gold was dicovered there; he is ~ing as a novelist *(becoming famous)*. - *adj* (3) a ~ing voice (4) what saved the Finns was a ~ing world market for wood and paper.

boom *n* (1) the ~ of the guns; a ~ of thunder (2) the business / an $8,000,000 building ~; the manufacturing ~ of the reconstruction period following the war.

boost *vt* (1) if you ~ me I can climb that tree. (2) ~ sales / profits / production (by 20 percent); an advertising programme to ~ local products abroad; ~ s.o. into a good job *(by praising him)*; they began to ~ him for the presidency early. (3) ~ a candidate's chances; an extra holiday to ~ morale.

boost *n* (1 *AE*) give s.o. a ~ over a wall (2) a ~ *(increase)* in potato acreage; a ~ in salary; the Government's latest measures should give a much-needed ~ to the industry.

border *n* (1) (on) the ~ of a lake / stream / forest / flower bed; a ~ of flowers along a path; the ~ of a carpet / rug / handkerchief; the ~ of wallpaper; a blue table-cloth with a red ~; a lace ~ (2) the ~ of a country / district; a ~ town / dispute / incident / *etc*; ~ police; cross / go across / go beyond the ~; patrol the ~.

border *vt* (1) his estate / field of research ~s mine; our garden is ~ed by a stream. (2) ~ a path with flowers / a road with poplars; ~ s.th. with lace / ribbon. - *vi* (3) Burma ~s on India. (4) his excuse ~s on the ridiculous; his conduct ~ed on impertinence / insanity.

borderline *n* (1) the ~ between religion and philosophy / imagination and reality. - *adj* (2) a ~ case (of madness / schizophrenia / manslaughter / *etc*).

bore[1] *vt* (1) ~ a hole (in / through s.th.); ~ a tunnel (through a mountain / under a river); ~ a shaft / well; the water ~s (its way) through the rocks. - *vi* (2) ~ for minerals / oil / water; the oil drill ~s into the ground.

bore[2] *vt* (1) dancing / his old jokes ~ed me; I have never been so ~d by a book in my life. - *adj* (2) were you ~d reading this book? be ~d to death / distraction / tears; he got ~d, so he left; a ~d countenance / glance / look / *etc* (3) I found the speaker / talk ~ing; a ~ing evening / speech / *etc*.

bore *n* that tune is a ~ when it is played over and over again; I found his friend a ~; it will be a great ~ to the public; he is a colossal ~.

born *part, adj* (1) be ~ blind / rich / to a large fortune / to sorrows; ~ of poor but honest parents; a ~ poet / actor / orator / teacher / fool; ~ to be a poet / ruler / *etc*; the man who (really understands women) is / has yet to be ~; be ~ under a lucky / evil star; he was not ~ yesterday *(is not naive)*. (2) an idea / plan / story is ~; courage ~ of despair; → bear *vt* 9.

borrow *vt* (1) pupils are allowed to ~ two books a week from the library; can I ~ your typewriter for a couple of hours? ~ money from / of s.o. (2) many English words are ~ed from the French; this expression is ~ed from Shakespeare; ~ ideas from s.o. else.

boss *n* (1) why don't you ask your ~ about it? I'm having to run the office while my ~

is on holiday. (2) little Ann is a real ~ *(domineering child).* (3) is the ~ in *(the head of the household at home)*? (4 *AE*) a political ~; the ~ of a political machine.

boss *vt* (1) the narcotics trade is ~ed from Italy by X. (2) he ~es his little sister; □ ~ the show *(assume authority)*; no matter what she is concerned in, she always wants to ~ the show.

boss about she ~ed all the younger children ~ / around.

bother *vt* (1) be ~ed by mosquitoes; the ringing telephone ~ed him; is the cough ~ing you? I hope my smoking doesn't ~ you; don't ~ me with foolish questions; he is always ~ing me to lend him money; his conscience ~ed him; □ ~ o.s. / one's head about s.th. *(feel anxious).* - *vi* (2) don't ~ about getting / to get supper for me; please don't ~ (to come to the door - I can let myself out); you need not ~ about me any longer; I said I was interested, but he didn't even ~ writing / to write my name down. (3) don't ~ about Jack - he is always late; there is no point in ~ing about that now; I have no time to ~ with your small worries.

bother *n* (1) did you have much ~ (in) finding our house? (2) the broken zipper is a ~; the child's constant questions are a ~.

bottom *n* (1) the ~ of a box / bag / bottle / barrel / well; a suitcase with a double / false ~; the ~ *(underside)* of a plate; drain one's glass to the ~; some tea-leaves in the ~ of the cup; the ~ of a pie (2) the ~ of a ship *(underwater hull)*; a boat floating ~ upwards; the sailors scrubbed the ship from top to ~. (3) the chair needs a new ~; I'll smack your ~ if you're naughty; as smooth as a baby's ~ (4) the ~ of a lake / river / swimming-pool; a river ~; the ~ of the sea / ocean; the ship went to the ~ of the sea; a German U-boat sent the ship to the ~. (5) the ~ of a mountain / hill; at the ~ *(far end)* of the garden; the shop is at the ~ of King Street; (see the notes) at the ~ of page 7. (6) get to the ~ of a / the matter / mystery; now we touch ~ at last; who is at the ~ of this *(caused it)*? can't you see what lies at the ~ of his intentions? John is at the ~ of the class; he's a good man at ~ *(essentially)*; (I wish you luck) from the ~ of my heart; □ knock the ~ out of an argument *(prove it wrong)*; □ scrape the ~ of the barrel.

bottom *adj* (1) the book is on the ~ shelf. (2) what's your ~ price? the ~ boy of a class; → bet *vt* 1.

bound[1] *n* the ultimate ~s of space; the origin of life is beyond the ~s of human knowledge; keep (s.th.) / remain within (certain, definite, established, reasonable) ~s; you must keep / remain within the ~s of propriety / reason; set ~s to s.o.'s ambition / authority / power / rights; she set ~s to her passion; exceed the ~s of possibility; pass all / go beyond all ~s (of reason / decency / *etc*); human vanity knows no / is without ~s; his passion broke the narrow ~s of convention; □ out of ~s *(not to be entered)*: this café has been placed out of ~s to / for schoolboys; the town is out of ~s to our troops; the ball went out of ~s *(outside the playing area)*; his conduct is out of all ~s *(intolerable).*

bound[1] *vt* (1) Canada ~s the United States on the north; Italy is ~ed to the north by the Alps; a garden ~ed by a stream; lines ~ a surface; surfaces ~ a solid. (2) one should ~ one's desires.

bound[2] *n* with one ~ he made the distance from boat to shore; □ by leaps and ~s *(very rapidly).*

bound[2] *vi* the dancer ~ed on to the stage; the ship ~ed along against the soft south wind; the chamois ~ed from rock to rock; the ball ~ed off the fence; his dog went ~ing after the ball.

bound[1] *adj* (1) he was ~ to admit he was wrong; you are ~ to obey; are you ~ to go yet? (2) he's ~ to see you there; you're ~ to be tired if you hike all day; that's what he told me, but it's not ~ to be true.

bound[2] *adj* they were ~ for South America; a ship ~ for Rio; homeward / outward ~; a train ~ from Edinburgh to London.

boundary *n* (1) the ~ of a territory / estate; a natural / artificial ~; a ~ stone / wall; the Rhine is part of the ~ of Germany; the Alps form the northern ~ of Italy; mark out / determine / draw a ~ (line) (2) Ireland lies on the ~ of Europe.

bow[1] *n* (1) an archer's ~; ~ and arrow; draw / bend / overbend the ~; □ draw the long ~ *(exaggerate)*; □ have two strings to one's ~ *(have more than one plan, idea)* (2) a violin is played with a ~. (3) tie (a shoe lace in) a ~; she had a ~ of red ribbon in her hair.

bow[2] *n* make a / one's ~ to s.o.: he answered with a ~; he gave me a ~.

bow *vt* (1) ~ the / one's knee (before the altar); ~ one's head (in prayer); ~ one's appreciation / thanks (2) care and age have ~ed him. - *vi* (3) the singer ~ed in response to the applause; the minister ~s and scrapes as if he were a lowly servant. (4) ~ to s.o.'s judgment / wishes; ~ to circumstances / a decision / the inevitable / the law / public opinion (5 *bow + out of: withdraw from a contest*) he ~ed out of the race for governor; he ~ed out of the argument. - *adj* (6) their hearts were ~ed with grief; his head was ~ed in prayer.

bow down (1) care and age have ~ed him ~; ~ed ~ by age; the branches were ~ed ~ with the weight of the snow. (2) refuse to ~ ~ to tyranny / wealth / power.

bow out he ~ed ~ before the going got tough; he ~ed ~ after 40 years of teaching.

brain *n* (1) the ~ has many parts with different functions; his ~ was hurt. (2) ~s with browned butter; ~s and tongue of ox, sheep and pig are generally regarded as delicacies. (3) work with one's ~(s); be a ~-worker; have a good / fine / teeming / sluggish / *etc* ~; make use of one's ~(s); he has ~s, but he won't use them; he has no / not much ~s; □ rack / cudgel / beat one's ~s about s.th. / over s.th. / for an explanation; □ have s.th. on the ~ *(think of nothing else)*; that fellow has (nothing but) football on the ~; □ turn s.o.'s ~ *(make him vain)*; → blow out 3; some say that ~s and womanly charm seldom go together; the West has the ~s, the technological knowhow. (4) the professor, who is the ~s of the gang, tells her ...; a small committee, including some of the ablest ~s in the party, ...

brake *n* (1) ~ lever / pedal; air / disc / hydraulic ~; apply / put on / step on / take off the ~(s); pull the emergency ~; the ~s worked / failed / screamed / were jammed. (2) you should put a firm ~ on him; act as a ~ upon s.o. ('s activities).

brake *vt* (1) ~ a car. - *vi* (2) the driver ~d suddenly; ~ing distance.

branch *n* (1) saw through a ~; □ saw off the ~ one is sitting on; □ saw the ~ / limb out from under you (2) the ~ of a river / road / railway / line of mountains / nerve (3) the ~ of a club / association / chain store / firm; a ~ of the armed services; a ~ office / establishment / post-office; the three ~es of government; the legislative ~ of government; the Swiss ~ of the family; Russian is a ~ of the Indo-European family of languages; a ~ of learning / knowledge.

branch *vi* (1) the tree ~es (out) over the river; the road ~es here (in three directions); many minor roads ~ from / off (from) the main road. (2) starting as a grocer, he ~ed out into drapery; if you take up the study of history you can always ~ out into other subjects.

brand *n* (1) the farmer put his ~ on the cattle. (2) the best ~s of cigars; an excellent / popular ~ of coffee (3) America's own ~ of humour.

brand *v* (1) ~ an animal / slave (2) ~ s.o. as a spy / traitor / liar; ~ s.o. with infamy (3) these frightful experiences are ~ed on his memory.

breach *n* (1) a ~ of promise *(esp to marry)* / faith / duty / contract / manners; a ~ of the peace *(BE a riot; AE disorderly conduct)* (2) make a ~ in (the enemy's lines); throw / fling o.s. into the ~ *(help those who are in trouble)*; stand in the ~ *(do most of the hard work)*; fill the ~ for s.o.; step into a ~ (at short notice) (3) a ~ in a dyke / hedge.

bread *n* (1) a loaf / slice / piece of (white / brown / *(AE)* graham / rye / wheat) ~; fresh / new / stale / old / mouldy / light ~; bake / cut / slice ~; (cut) ~ and butter; send s.o. a ~-and-butter letter *(one of thanks for hospitality)*; a ~-and-butter job *(one taken out of necessity)* (2) the / one's daily ~; earn one's ~ (and butter) (by hard work); □ know which side one's ~ is buttered (on) *(where one's interest lies)*; → quarrel *vi* 2; □ take the ~ out of s.o.'s mouth *(take away his means of living by competition)*.

break *vt* (1) ~ a chain / chair / dish / link / lock / rope / seal / stick (in half, through the middle) / thread / window(-pane); ~ ice; she dropped her doll and broke it; he broke a branch from a tree; ~ bread into pieces; ~ a bone; he fell and broke his leg / collar-bone / *etc*; ~ s.o.'s back / neck / nose; ~ one's neck; ~ one's head / crown; he broke a tooth on the cherry-stone; □ ~ the ice *(overcome initial shyness or awkwardness)*: he broke the ice by offering her a cigarette; □ ~ one's chains *(throw them off)*; □ ~ the back of a job *(do the hardest part)*; ~ s.o.'s back *(give* *him too much to do)* (2 *make useless*) ~ a clock / sewing-machine / *etc* (3 *dig up*) ~ the ground / soil (with a hoe / rake / spade) (4 *cut open*) ~ the skin; he hurt his arm but didn't ~ the skin; he broke *(the skin of)* his knee on a sharp rock. (5 *destroy, ruin*) great losses broke the bank; every shopping-trip nearly ~s me; ~ a monopoly (6 *demote*) ~ an officer; the major was broken to lieutenant / sergeant. (7 *make known*) ~ the news; ~ the (startling or bad) news to s.o. *(say it gently)* (8 *decipher*) ~ a code (9 *tame*) ~ a horse (to the saddle / to reins) (10 *surpass*) ~ a record; he broke the record for the 100 yd dash; ~ the sound barrier (11 *escape*) ~ (out of) jail / prison; then I saw a fox ~ cover and run across the field. (12 *make different, worse*) the unhappy love affair broke his heart; it almost broke her heart to leave ...; sorrow is ~ing my heart; business worries (eventually / gradually / rapidly) broke his health. (13 *interrupt*) ~ an electric circuit; telephone communications with Berlin have been broken; this device ~s contact when the set temperature is exceeded; ~ one's journey (at N.); ~ one's fast; the noise of the storm broke my rest; the firemen's net will ~ his fall. (14 *interrupt the continuation of*) ~ the gloom / a habit / the silence; thus the spell was broken; there was nothing to ~ the monotony of the landscape. (15 *violate, not keep*) ~ the law / peace / rules; ~ an agreement / appointment / contract / engagement / promise / resolution / treaty / vow; ~ one's word / oath; ~ faith with s.o. *(deceive him)* (16 *render ineffective)* ~ s.o.'s opposition / power / pride / resistance / spirit / will; ~ a rebellion / strike; the dike ~s the force of the waves; the hedge ~s the force of the wind; he broke the force of the blow with his forearm. (17 *cut, sever*) at 18, he broke the ties which bound him to his family; divorce ~s the bond of matrimony; ~ a relation(ship) / link (18 *end relations, practices*) ~ s.o. of a (bad) habit; ~ o.s. of a habit; she broke him of smoking. (19 *disrupt order, completeness of*) when the alarm sounded the soldiers broke formation and scattered; ~ (up) a set of books *(sell books of a series individually)* (20 *exchange, change into smaller units*) can you ~ this $5 bill for me? I need some coins for the telephone. - *vi* (21) the glass broke (into pieces / in two); a chain / rope / stick / *etc* ~s; the branch bent but didn't ~; the iron bar broke in half / through the middle; the dam had broken in several places; the ice broke under him; in spring the ice ~s; the clouds broke and the sun came out; huge waves are ~ing against / on / over the rocks; the sea was ~ing on the beach; an abscess / blister / boil / bubble ~s; □ ~ even *(emerge with neither loss nor gain)* (22 *break + through: move, get beyond s.th.*) the prisoners broke through the wall; the excited crowd broke through the police cordon; I broke through the ice yesterday; the sun ~s through the clouds; ~ through the enemy lines; he ~s through all obstacles; ~ through *(overcome)* s.o.'s reserve (23 *escape*) ~ free (frons clutches / handcuffs / *etc*); ~ loose from s.o. / s.th. ; some of the animals broke loose; ~ loose and run; he broke out of my grasp and ran off; break out of jail / prison / a cage (24 *begin*) day / dawn is ~ing; the storm is ~ing over the mountains; suddenly a storm broke (with great fury); his anger broke loose; the weather is ~ing *(changing)*; the frost has broken; the drought broke at last. (25 *become known*) the scandal / news / story broke / began to break when ... (26 *become different, worse*) his voice broke at the age of 14; her voice broke with emotion; his health broke under the strain; my heart is ~ing with sorrow. (27 *discontinue s.th.*) he broke with his former associates; they broke with one another; ~ with old habits / tradition(s) / a certain practice (28 *be ruined*) when the bank broke, many people were ruined. - *adj.* (29) a broken clock / glass / machine / *etc*; a broken limb (of a tree); broken type *(in printing)*; broken ground *(uneven)* → ground *n* 3. (30 broken hopes / rest / sleep; a broken home / marriage (31) a broken voice; speak broken English *(imperfect)* (32) in broken health; she looked completely broken (in health / spirit). (33) Napoleon was a broken man after his defeat at Waterloo; he was completely broken as the result of the failure of his business.

break away (1) a great piece broke ~. (2) the horse reared and broke ~; the prisoner broke ~ from his guards.

break down (1) they broke the door ~; the mob broke ~ the barriers. (2) ~ ~

s.o.'s resistance / opposition (3) they broke ~ the total cost into its separate items of expenditure; ~ ~ population figures; proteins are broken ~ by enzymes into amino acids. (4) the bridge broke ~. (5) his car broke ~ in remote countryside. (6) a plan / system / scheme ~s ~; the negotiations broke ~. (7) his health broke ~; her resistance broke ~; he broke ~ in the middle of his speech; she broke ~ and cried; he broke ~ and had to take a complete rest.

break forth his anger / indignation broke ~.

break in (1) can we ~ the door in? (2) ~ in the recruits; ~ s.o. in to control / a habit; *(AE)* a new car has to be broken in. (3) ~ in a horse / bullock (4) he broke in as she was speaking; ~ in (up)on a conversation; the police broke in (up)on the robbers. (5) he was arrested for attempting to ~ in.

break into (1) ~ ~ s.o.'s conversation; social duties ~ ~ my time / leisure; an evening already broken ~ (2) ~ ~ a bank; the house had been broken ~. (3) ~ ~ laughter / tears / (loud) sobs / sobbing / swearing / lamentation; ~ ~ a song; ~ ~ a run *(start running)*; the horse broke ~ a gallop / trot. (4) ~ ~ a five-pound note *(pay a sum smaller than £5)*.

break off (1) ~ the handle ~; ~ the point ~ a pencil; he broke ~ a piece of toffee; don't ~ the branch ~; the mast was broken ~. (2) the door-handle has broken ~; the mast broke ~. (3) ~ ~ relations (with s.o.) / all dealings with s.o. / negotiations; ~ ~ an engagement / battle / conversation; they broke ~ their engagement; ~ ~ with s.o. (5) let's ~ ~ for half an hour and have some tea.

break open (1) ~ ~ a box / door / safe / lid of a desk / seal; ~ ~ a new deck *(AE)* / pack of (playing) cards; ~ ~ a blister / wound (2) during the earthquake the tomb broke ~ and revealed unheard-of riches. (3) the (murder) case broke wide ~ when the reporter found out that ...

break out (1) a great piece broke ~. (2) the sun broke ~ (from behind the clouds). (3) six criminals have just broken ~ (of prison); → break *vt* 11, *vi* 23. (4) a fire / war / rebellion / quarrel / epidemic ~s ~; cholera broke ~; his pent-up fury / anger broke ~. (5) ~ ~ in(to) spots / a rash / boils; the boy broke ~ in(to) red spots; a rash has broken ~ on her hands; she / her hand has broken ~ into a rash; his face broke ~ into pimples; he broke ~ into (a) sweat; sweat broke ~ on his brow. (6) 'I hate you', she broke ~. (7) ~ ~ into loud sobs / sobbing / abuse / curses / a laugh.

break through the defence was strong, but our soldiers broke ~ (in several places); the sun broke ~; → break *vi* 22.

break up (1) ~ up a box (for firewood); ~ up an old ship (for scrap) (2) ~ up a word into syllables; ~ up a long translation among several persons (3) the police broke up the crowd / meeting / traffic jam; ~ up a fight; ~ up the feudal system (4) the ice ~s up; the ship was ~ing up on the rocks. (5) the meeting broke up quietly; Parliament ~s up. (6) we ~ up (school) on July 25th *(finish school)*; the school ~s up on July 25th; when do you ~ up (school) for Easter? the college ~s up on Tuesday. (7) he's over 90 and is ~ing up *(becoming weak)*. (8) the weather is ~ing up *(changing after being fine)*.

break *n* (1) a ~ in a pipe / wiring circuit; through a ~ in the hedge (2) a ~ in the clouds / skin (3) at ~ of day; at day~ (4 *change*) there has been a ~ in the weather *(change for the better)*; a ~ in one's way of living (5) a ~ in the conversation; a coffee / tea ~; I travelled to Brussels without a ~; the rain has brought no lasting ~ in the heat; you ought to make more ~s in your reading. (6) □ make a ~ for it *(try to run away)* (7) give s.o. a ~ *(opportunity)*; he has had a bad ~ *(bad luck)*; that investment was a lucky ~ for him; he has not had a fair ~ in years.

breakfast *n* have (one's) ~; eat ~ (regularly); we had ~ late / a late ~ today; have you had your ~ yet? have an egg for (one's) ~; he hasn't eaten much ~; they were at ~ when I got down; room with ~; bed and ~; the President gave a ~ for his guest.

breakfast *vi* we ~ed late today; we ~ed on eggs, toast and ...

breath *n* (1) have sweet / odourless / bad ~; draw / take ~; take a deep ~; give s.o. time to take ~; hold / catch one's ~ (from fear / excitement); run o.s. out of ~; wait until I get my ~; our ~ was beginning to fail; he soon gets out of / loses his ~; be out of / short of ~; recover one's ~; listen with bated ~; □ draw one's last ~ *(die)*; □ speak / say s.th./ mutter s.th under /

below one's ~ *(in a whisper)*; □ waste one's ~ *(talk without result)*; □ save / spare one's ~ *(keep quiet because argument is useless)*; □ take s.o.'s ~ away *(surprise him greatly)*; in the same ~ *(at the same moment)*: he said 'yes' and 'no' almost in the same ~; Byron would certainly not be spoken of in the same ~ as Shakespeare and Milton; (he will resist) to his last ~. (2) there's not a ~ of air in the room; the sun's really hot and there isn't a ~ of wind; a ~ of spring (3) a ~ of scandal / suspicion.

breathe *vt* (1) ~ one's native air; ~ a sigh of relief; □ ~ one's last *(die)*; □ ~ new life into s.o. / s.th. (2) here everything ~s peace; the flowers ~d forth perfume; her bearing ~s simplicity; every blade of grass ~s Indian culture. (3) don't ~ a word to anyone about this; ~ threats / vengeance. - *vi* (4) ~ deeply / freely / gently / softly / hard / heavily / with difficulty; give s.o. time to ~; □ ~ again / freely *(recover from exertion, fear, etc)*.

breed *vt* (1) ~ cattle / sheep (for the market) (2) dirt ~s disease; slums ~ crime; war ~s violence; cold weather ~s colds / flu; ~ discontent / hatred / individualism; □ what is bred in the bone *(hereditary traits)* (3 *educate*) he was bred a lawyer / to the law / in the tradition of liberalism. - *vi* (4) guinea pigs ~ rapidly; llamas ~ well in this country. - *adj* (5) an Englishman born and bred; a well-bred man.

brew *vt* (1) ~ beer / ale (2) ~ tea / punch / a (strange / terrible / *etc*) concoction (3) ~ mischief / trouble / a rebellion. - *vi* (4) tea is ~ing. (5) a storm is ~ing. (6) mischief / trouble / a quarrel is ~ing.

bribe *vt* (1) ~ s.o. (to keep quiet); he had been ~d into silence; a ~d witness; he knew how to ~ his way. (2) we ~d the child / the child was ~d to take the nasty medicine.

brief *adj* a ~ moment / stay; a ~ nod / glance / gesture / answer; a ~ announcement / statement / explanation / report / reference / description / prayer; make ~ notes; he recounted ~ly / gave a ~ account of (what had happened); he glanced at her ~ly; he paid us a ~ visit; after a ~ rest they went on; life is so ~; please be ~, I haven't got much time.

bright *adj* (1) ~ light / days; a ~ moon / star / flame / colour; she wears ~ colours; ~ sunlight; rub the silver to a ~ polish; the fire was burning ~ly. (2) ~ faces; a ~ smile; they tried to be ~ and gay; she smiled at me with her ~ eyes. (3) a ~ child / pupil / chap; a ~ remark / idea (4) a ~ outlook / prospect / future; the future looks ~; the picture is generally ~: no serious accidents ...

bring *vt* (1) ~ s.o. a glass of water / present / *etc*; take this magazine away and ~ me another one (from the living-room); has the postman brought the letters yet? you cannot ~ plants into England without a permit; the children ~ plenty of life into the house; ~ discord into a family; ~ the ship into port; ~ s.o./ s.th. ashore; ~ s.o. to one's home; ~ a friend home (to dinner); ~ your friend with you; what has brought you to me? the stork has brought a baby; □ ~ s.o./ s.th. low *(make low in health, wealth, position)* (2) the remark brought a smile to her face; the sad news brought tears to her eyes. (3) ~ s.o. help / comfort / greetings from s.o. / bad luck / news / honour; broken dishes ~ good luck. (4) the wind has brought the rain; springtime ~s flowers; old age ~s white hair. (5) your jewellery will ~ a good price; his writings ~ him £400 a year. (6) ~ s.o. before the judge / law; ~ s.o. (in)to court; ~ s.o. to trial (for s.th.); ~ an action / charge (against s.o.) (7 *bring + obj + inf*) I could not ~ him to see the wisdom of my plan; she could not ~ herself to believe it / to ask; try to ~ him to accept; he may be brought to forgive (8 *bring + obj + into / on / under + n*) ~ money into circulation; ~ s.th. into fashion; ~ s.th. into play *(make use of it)*; ~ s.o. into line *(persuade him to conform)*; ~ trouble / infamy on o.s.; ~ discredit / misfortune on s.o.; ~ the fire / the children / *etc* under control (9 *bring + obj + to + n*) ~ s.o. to beggary / the gallows / perdition / safety; ~ s.o. to his senses *(make him see reason)*; ~ s.o. (back) to reason; ~ s.o. (back) to life *(from fainting, death)*; ~ s.o. to book for s.th. *(require him to explain his conduct)*; ~ a mistake / *etc* to light; ~ s.th. to a close / end / stop / halt / successful conclusion; ~ s.th. to s.o.'s knowledge / notice; ~ s.th. to mind *(remind one)*; ~ things to a head *(climax)*; ~ s.th. to the boil.

bring about ~ ~ a change / ruin / war / loss / fall / misunderstanding / reconciliation between A and B; ~ ~ price control / the downfall of the government; a quarrel brought ~ the break; the big fire was brought ~ by a cigarette thrown away carelessly.

bring along he brought ~ his guitar / wife / *etc.*

bring back (1) ~ ~ the library books / an escaped prisoner (2) that music ~s ~ many happy memories. (3) her stay in the mountains brought her ~ to health; → bring 9.

bring down (1) I brought my trunk ~ from the attic. (2) ~ ~ enemy aircraft; he aimed, fired and brought ~ the antelope. (3) ~ ~ the government / a tyrant (4) this cloth is expensive - will you ~ ~ the price (to £8 or so)? if you grow too many apples you'll ~ ~ the price. (5) □ ~ ~ the house *(win great applause)*; the comedian's jokes brought the house ~. (6) ~ ~ a curse on s.o.; ~ ~ a penalty / s.o.'s anger on o.s.

bring forth (1) animals ~ ~ young. (2) what will the future ~ ~? the evidence brought ~ in the case proved his guilt.

bring forward (1) the rain will ~ ~ the young crops. (2) ~ ~ a question / topic / proposal (at a meeting / for discussion).

bring home ~ ~ to s.o. the need for reform; you must try to ~ it ~ to your son that he must work harder; a visit to the slums brought ~ to me what poverty means.

bring in (1) ~ in the washing with you; may I ~ my friend in? (2) ~ in the corn; the soldiers brought in ten prisoners; after the battle many wounded were brought in. (3) the new tax will ~ in 50 million pounds a year; this investment should ~ (you) in a good sum; ~ in profit / interest; that doesn't ~ much in. (4) ~ in new ideas / many changes; ~ in a topic / quotation / new fashion; don't ~ in things that are irrelevant. (5) this radio set ~s in the whole of Europe. (6) ~ in a bill / law / verdict of not guilty; ~ s.o. in not guilty.

bring off (1) they brought ~ *(rescued)* the passengers on the wrecked ship. (2 *do successfully*) ~ ~ a plan / business deal (over a bottle of wine); he is trying to get a scholarship, but he doesn't think he will ~ it ~; she is a good actress - she played Ophelia yesterday and brought it ~ very well.

bring on (1) heat brought on the fever; gout is often brought on by high living; what brought on the indisposition / fainting attack? several causes operated to ~ on the war. (2) the fine weather is ~ing the crops on nicely.

bring out (1) she brought the tea ~ to us in the garden. (2) the rain brought ~ thousands of insects; the sunshine will ~ ~ the apple blossom; how can I ~ ~ the grain of this wood? (3) ~ ~ a (new edition of a) dictionary / catalogue / new product (4) ~ ~ the truth of a matter; examples intended to ~ ~ the meanings of words; ~ ~ some surprising facts / the best in s.o.; John is a very quiet man - it is difficult to ~ him ~ *(make him talk)*.

bring round (1) ~ your friend ~ tonight. (2) I managed to ~ him ~ *(persuade)*; he can usually be brought ~ by tactful handling; he brought me ~ to his way of thinking. (3) they brought her ~ (with brandy / smelling salts) *(back to consciousness)*.

bring through careful nursing brought him ~.

bring to (1) the ship was brought to *(forced to stop)*. (2) a bucket of water was used to ~ him to.

bring to bear (1 *direct*) our guns were brought to bear upon the enemy's batteries; raise the lamp - now ~ it to bear on the picture. (2 *concentrate*) ~ one's mind to bear on a problem (3 *make effective*) ~ pressure to bear on s.o.; ~ one's influence / authority to bear (on s.o./ s.th.).

bring under William the Conqueror soon brought the English ~; the rebels were quickly brought ~ .

bring up (1) ~ up a subject / question / topic (for discussion); the point can be brought up at the next meeting. (2) ~ up children / a family; this cat has been well brought up *(behaves itself)*. (3) ~ up the poison one has swallowed; he brought up his dinner. (4) that statement brought me up (short / with a jerk); I was suddenly brought up by a notice in a shop window; he brought up the horse suddenly; the ship brought up at a port in Greece *(ended its voyage there)*.

bristle *vi* (1) the cat's hair ~d when the dog barked; the dog was angry and ~d (up). (2) the witness ~d at the rude question *(showed signs of anger)*. (3) a fortress ~ing with guns (4) the book ~d with mistakes; a subject ~ing with difficulties.

broad *adj* (1) a ~ door / road / river / expanse (of ocean) / valley; the ~ ocean / sea; a river 50 feet ~; ~ acres / lands / estates / fields / blades / leaves / spearheads / beans; a ~ nib / penstroke / brim; a ~-brimmed hat / brow / forehead / back / chest / bosom; ~ shoulders *(also fig)*; a page with a ~ margin; he is as ~ as he is tall; s.th. is as ~ as it is long *(also fig: all the same)*. (2 *full, manifest*) in ~ daylight; ~ distinctions / differences; give s.o. a ~ hint; a ~ grin; grin ~ly (3 *general*) the ~ mass of the people; ~ facts; a ~ rule / distinction; he gave his views in ~ outline; ~ly speaking (it is true); a ~ style *(not subtle)*; in the ~est sense; a ~ generalization *(disregarding unimportant exceptions)*; achieve ~ agreement on an issue; there are three ~ problems during a polling enquiry. (4 *not narrow, liberal*) a man of ~ views *(implying tolerance)*; a ~ mind / outlook; a ~ discussion *(not keeping within severe limits of propriety, orthodoxy, etc)*; a ~ range of subjects *(implying weight, generosity)*; a ~ly-based investigation; a ~ story / jest / joke / farce *(not avoiding indecency)*; ~ humour (5 *marked*) a ~ accent / dialect; ~ Scots.

brush *vt* (1) ~ one's hair / teeth / clothes / shoes; ~ s.th. clean; ~ up the dust; ~ the dirt off / away (2 *touch*) the leaves of the trees ~ed my face as I ran through the forest; he ~ed my shoulders on the way out; he ~ed past / against / by me in a rude way; ~ over a problem *(treat it lightly)*.

brush aside / off ~ ~ objections / all opposition / the subject / a suggestion / an amendment.

brush up (1) → brush *vt* 1 (2) ~ up one's English / mathematics / *etc.*

build *vt* (1) ~ a house / fence / machine / organ / railway / road / ship; birds ~ their nests in spring / with hay and moss; our house is built of stone; ~ a cupboard / safe / pipe into a wall; an argument built on solid facts; □ ~ castles in the air / in Spain. – *vi* (2) we're going to ~ next year; they don't want to ~ too near the road; ~ on sand *(also fig)*; do not ~ on her assistance / promises. – *adj* (3) built-in cupboards; a bicycle with a built-in speedometer.

build up (1) ~ up a door / window *(fill it with bricks)* (2) the fields where we played are all built up now; this area has been built up very recently; a built-up area (3) ~ up a business / organization / practice; ~ up a reserve fund; they are ~ing up their military forces; spoken words are built up of sounds; ~ up atoms artificially; ~ up evidence against s.o.; he has built up a good name for himself. (4) ~ up one's health; the doctor prescribed nourishing food to ~ her up. (5) they built him up with a series of articles and broadcasts *(by means of extravagant publicity)*; they built him up to be a hero. (6) our pressure on the enemy is ~ing up; in narrow streets the traffic ~s up and great congestion is created.

bump *vt* (1) the boy ~ed his head when he fell; I ~ed (my head) against the door. – *vi* (2) the lorry ~ed into a car / against the kerb; ~ into s.o. *(also fig: meet accidentally)*; □ ~ s.o. off *(inform: murder)* (3) the wagon ~ed along the rough road.

bunch *n* a ~ of flowers / grapes / bananas / asparagus / radishes / keys; a ~ of students *(inform)*.

bundle *n* a ~ of hay / straw / sticks / clothes / rags / wires / thread / wool / asparagus; a ~ of nerves *(also fig)*; make a ~ of s.th.; make / tie s.th. up into a ~.

bundle *vt* (1) ~ wood / straw / *etc*; ~ up things / the washing; will you please ~ these shirts together? we ~d everything into a drawer *(put it away without order)*. (2 *send, go in a hurry*) they ~d him into a taxi; his mother ~d him off to school; why did you ~ him out? – *vi* (3) then they all ~d off / away.

burden *n* (1) a beast of ~; take up / put down / throw off a ~ (2) be a ~ to (one's parents / family / *etc*); we won't take the child with us – he will only be a ~; a ~ of responsibility / sorrow / care / grief / sin / taxation / debts; great wealth can be a heavy ~; the ~ of proof lies / rests with the plaintiff. (3 *chief theme*) that is the ~ of what Mr K. has been saying at Geneva; the ~ of his remarks / this study is that we …

burden *vt* (1) ~ o.s. with a heavy overcoat (2) ~ a country with taxes; be ~ed with debts; I will not ~ you with my troubles; ~ one's memory with unnecessary dates. – *adj* (3) a ~ed estate.

burn *vt* (1) this furnace ~s oil, coal, wood or peat; ~ s.th. to ashes; ~ s.o. alive / to death; people used to ~ candles to get light; ~ gas, electricity; □ ~ the candle at both ends *(work too hard)*; □ ~ the midnight oil *(study at night)*; □ (they) have money to ~ *(more than enough)*; → boat *n* (2 *make by burning*) ~ a mark into an animal's skin; she / acid ~t a hole in her dress; ~ bricks / charcoal / lime; □ money ~s a hole in s.o.'s pocket *(makes him want to spend it)*. (3) I / the match ~t my fingers; the coffee is hot - don't ~ your mouth; the sun ~t and blistered her back; pepper ~s the tongue; the ground was ~t hard by the hot sun; □ ~ one's fingers *(because of rash behaviour)*. - *vi* (4) a log ~ed in the fireplace; the wood / stove ~s well; the fire / light ~ed all night / for several days; the whole village was ~ing. (5 *be spoilt by fire, heat*) don't let the roast ~; the meat is ~ing; the milk / sauce has ~t; she has a skin that ~s easily; acid ~s into copper. (6 *be painful*) the wound ~ed; my ears are ~ing. (7) what he saw ~ed into his mind / memory. (8 *feel hot*) her face / cheeks ~ed with embarrassment / shame. (9) the / a desire for freedom / revenge ~ed within him / in his heart; ~ with indignation / anger / envy / hatred / love / passion; they were ~ing to avenge the death of their leader. - *adj* (10) ~ing sands; the ~ing desert; ~ing thirst; a ~ing desire / question (11) all the buildings are ~t to the ground; the milk pudding is ~t again - we shall have to have fruit.

burn away (1) ~ ~ metal / rust / weeds (2) half the candle had ~t ~; the fire ~ed ~. (3) the fire was ~ing ~ merrily.

burn down (1) the rebels ~t ~ all the barns in the district; the hotel was ~t ~ over night. (2) the fire was ~ing ~; let a match ~ ~; the house ~t ~.

burn off ~ ~ metal / rust / weeds; ~ ~ paint with a blow-torch.

burn out (1) they / the acid ~t his eyes ~. (2) the fire / candle has ~t (itself) ~. (3) two rooms were completely ~t ~; our house has / we have been ~t ~ twice. (4) our motor ~t ~; we ~t the motor ~ *(by overwork)*. (5) he ~ed himself ~ in a very short time *(by overwork, dissipation)*; her burst of energy soon ~t ~ *(came to nothing)*.

burn up (1) we ~t up all the dead leaves. (2) all the grass had been ~t up during the hot summer. (3) put some wood on the fire and make it ~ up.

burst *vi* (1) bombs / shells / soap bubbles ~; a boiler / balloon / belt / door / lock / blood-vessel can ~; the cask ~ asunder / into pieces; the bag was so full that it ~; the dam / river bank had ~ in several places; the seam has ~; if you eat much more, you'll ~. (2) the leaves / buds will be ~ing soon; an abscess / boil ~s. (3 *be very full*) storehouses ~ing with grain; the bag was ~ing with apples; the train was full to ~ing; schools are crammed to ~ing. (4) be ~ing with anger / fury / impatience / excitement / pride / laughter / happiness / health; he was laughing fit to ~; he was ~ing to tell us the news. (5) the storm ~ without any warning; he ~ / came ~ing into the room; the enemy ~ out of an ambush; the oil ~ out of the ground; the sun ~ through the clouds. (6 *burst + into: start suddenly*) the shrubs / trees ~ into flower / bloom / blossom; the house ~ into flame(s); the horse ~ into a gallop; the birds ~ into song; ~ into tears / (a fit of) laughter / a loud laugh / a fit of passion / activity; he ~ into angry words. (7 *burst + upon: become visible, audible suddenly*) the sea ~ upon our view; the view ~ upon our sight; the truth ~ upon him *(he suddenly realized it)*; the news ~ upon him like an earthquake; the cries of the mob ~ upon our ears. - *vt* (8) blow up a paper bag and ~ it; ~ a tyre / balloon; he ~ a blood-vessel *(one of his blood-vessels ~)*; the river will ~ its banks; the prisoners ~ their bonds / chains;she is so fat - she'll soon ~ her clothes; □ ~ one's sides with laughing / laughter (9) ~ a hole in a canoe; ~ open a door.

burst in (1) we must ~ the door in. (2) we were just discussing the matter when you ~ in. (3) ~ in upon a conversation; he likes to ~ in on a party three hours late.

burst out (1) the sun ~ ~ from behind the clouds. (2) his pent-up fury / anger ~ ~; an uproar / war / disease ~ ~. (3) suddenly he ~ ~ with it; ~ ~ laughing / crying; ~ ~ into threats / explanations / a tirade (4) 'Give me back my money!' he ~ ~.

bury *vt* (1) ~ a corpse in a grave; ~ s.o. in his native earth / soil; ~ s.o. with military / all due honours; be ~ied in the cemetery at N.; he was ~ied at sea; ~ied alive *(also fig: living in a remote place)* (2) the dog ~ied its bone; squirrels ~ nuts in the ground; ~ treasure in the ground; □ ~ the hatchet *(stop quarrelling)* (3) the house was half ~ied under snow; the village lay ~ied under an avalanche; he ~ied his head / face in his hands; ~ one's hands in one's pockets; I found it ~ied under my papers; □ ~ o.s. in the country *(stay in a remote place)*; □ ~ one's head in the sand *(refuse to face a difficulty)* (4) ~ a plan in oblivion; she wishes the whole thing ~ied and forgotten; ~ all one's hopes. - *adj* (4) long ~ied feelings; be ~ied in thought / memories of the past; he lives very quietly, ~ied in his books / research.

bus *n* go / travel by ~; catch a / the ~; take the ~; be on a / the ~; miss the ~ *(also fig: lose an opportunity).*

business *n* (1 *buying and selling*) our firm is engaged in overseas ~; he did ~ in France; we do ~ with France / a French firm; our firm did such little ~ that it...; ~ is good / brisk / booming / bad / slack / stagnating / improving everywhere / expanding; big ~; transact ~ for one's own account; conclude / settle a ~ deal; do a good piece of ~; my father is in the clothing ~; he has set up in ~ as a (grocer); we shall put the boy into ~; go into ~ *(become a ~man)*; go out of ~; he is in ~ for himself *(independent)*; a ~ address / agreement; ~ hours; I have come on a matter of ~; are you here on ~ or (for) pleasure? ~ before pleasure (2 *shop*) a solid / substantial / sound / crooked / *etc* ~; open / manage / carry on / close down a ~; put all one's money into one's ~; I have no time - the ~ comes first. (3 *affairs*) the ~ before a committee; manage a club's / company's ~; the ~ of the day / meeting *(agenda)*; I have some urgent ~ to attend to; let's get (down) to ~; we'll deal with ~ (matters) later; no admittance except on ~; □ mean ~ *(be in earnest)* (4 *occupation*) what's his ~ *(how does he earn a living)*? (5) the ~ of doctors is to prevent and cure diseases; it is a teacher's ~ to help his pupils; I will make it my ~ to see that you get your money; mind your own ~; that's no ~ of yours; that is none of your ~, is it? you have no ~ (to be) here; he has no ~ to do that; □ send s.o. about his ~ *(tell him not to interfere)*; go about your ~; □ make a ~ of s.th. *(consider important)*; many firms make a ~ of rendering special services to...; life is a sorry ~; I am sick of the whole ~; what a ~ it is getting the children off to school.

busy *adj* (1) he was usually ~ with his stamps; I am ~ at the moment; I shall keep him ~; I'm ~ writing down examples. (2) a ~ street / crossing / railway station / seaport / shop / office; a ~ day; ~ fingers; the telephone was ~. (3) a ~ design *(cluttered with detail)*; a ~ floral wallpaper.

busy *vt* he usually ~ied himself with his stamps; he ~ied himself about the room.

butter *n* sweet / new / fresh / salt(ed) / rancid ~; peanut / cocoa ~; spread a piece of bread with ~; make ~; the cream has turned to ~; → bread 1,2.

butter *v* (1) ~ a piece of bread; → bread 2. (2) I detest being ~ed up *(flattered)* by people who I know have no real regard for me.

buy *vt* (1) ~ s.th. at a shop / from a firm / from s.o.; I would like to ~ myself a new shirt; ~ one for me; ~ me one; ~ a ticket; where did you ~ it? ~ s.th. at a high / low / reasonable / reduced price; ~ s.th. cheap(ly) / new / secondhand; I bought this house for £15,000; ~ s.th. on account / on credit / by instalments / on hire-purchase / on H.P. / on deferred terms / *(BE inform)* on the never-never; □ ~ a pig in a poke *(fig: without seeing the goods)* (2 *bribe*) ~ an official / witness / *etc* (3) ~ honour with flattery; ~ freedom with one's blood; she bought her success at a high price; her success has been dearly bought; money cannot ~ happiness. (4) £120 will ~ the machine; the dollar ~s less than it used to. (5) he tried to get me interested in that scheme but I wasn't ~ing it (*inform: wasn't deceived*). - *vi* (6) ~ wholesale; ~ low - sell high; ~ now - pay later; you may be selling, but I'm not ~ing. - *adj* (7) a dear(ly) bought experience / victory; (shop- / *AE* store-) bought clothes *(not hand-made).*

buy in (1) hearing of the likelihood of a typhoon, she bought in as many tins of food as possible. (2) why did you ~ in these paintings? *(buy for yourself what you have offered for sale at auction).*

buy off (1) ~ ~ a blackmailer / claimant *(get rid of him by payment)* (2) ~ ~ those who oppose the plan; they bought

~ the only person who intended to contest the legality of the will. (3) ~ s.o. / o.s. ~ *(free from an obligation by payment).*

buy out (1) the firm gradually eliminated its competitors by ~ing them ~; it's no use trying to ~ him ~ - he'll never sell. (2) ~ o.s. / one's son ~ *(of military service).*

buy over he tried to ~ ~ the customs officer.

buy up they bought up all the oil shares available / the entire stock of ...; ~ up land / a firm.

C

calculate *vt* (1) ~ the cost / price / value of s.th.; ~ the amount / quantity of s.th.; ~ the distance between two points; ~ the area of a triangle / the size of the moon / the speed, velocity of light; the ~d sum is wrong; a ~ting machine (2) ~ the effect(s) of a manoeuvre / speech / *etc*; he ~d all his moves with the deliberation of a chess-player; a promise ~d to win votes. - *vi* (3) he can't ~. (4) he ~d on darkness making escape easy; he ~d on s.o.('s aid). - *adj* (5) a ~d risk; ~d politeness / rudeness; do s.th. / act in a ~ing manner.

call *n* (1) the (harsh / lyrical / typical / *etc*) ~ of a bird; a bugle ~; the ~ of animals to their young; a ~ for help; the dog immediately came at the hunter's ~; be within ~(ing distance) (2 *visit*) pay a ~ (up)on s.o.; I have several ~s to make. (3 *demand*) there are / he has many ~s on his time/ money; the ~(s) of justice demanded his punishment; the ~ of humanity; the aircraft industry continues to have first ~ on aluminium production; there isn't much ~ for horsefeed nowadays; there have been no ~s for ploughshares for five or six years. (4 *summons, invitation*) he answered the ~ of his country; the ~ of duty; a ~ to arms / to war; the government issued a ~ for voluntary wage controls; be on ~; is there a doctor / an ambulance on ~? (5 *vocation*) feel / follow a ~ to the priesthood / Church / teaching profession; he became a monk without having the ~. (6 *telephone*) (here is) your ~ to Nottingham 2264; your ~ has come through; give s.o. / get a ~ (7 *need, occasion*) you have no ~ to complain; there's no ~ for you to blush / worry / be upset.

call *vt* (1) what's this thing ~ed? what are you going to ~ the baby? he ~s himself a linguist; ~ s.o. a liar / fool / *etc*; it is rude to ~ (s.o.) names; stop ~ing your brother names; he ~ed him all the names he could lay his tongue to; □ ~ a spade a spade *(speak plainly)*; □ ~ it a day *(finish for the day)* (2) the principal ~ed me to his office; ~ the police / a doctor / *etc*; will you ~ a taxi (for me) / me a taxi? God has ~ed him home *(he has died)*; ~ a meeting (at short notice); ~ the witnesses / s.o. as a witness / the next case; □ ~ the roll *(read names to see who is present)*; □ ~ a strike *(order workers to go on strike)*; □ ~ s.o. to account *(demand an explanation from him)*; □ ~ s.o. to attention *(tell him to pay attention)*; □ ~ s.o. to order (in a meeting); □ ~ s.o. over the coals (about his carelessness) *(scold him)*; → bar *n* 5, tune *n* 1. (3 *wake up*) please ~ me at 6 a.m.; do you want to be ~ed in the morning? (4 *speak to by phone, wireless*) ~ him on the phone; my brother ~ed (me) from Rome last night; the aircraft was ~ing (to) the control tower at the airport. (5 *declare*) ~ a foul; ~ a halt (to nuclear armament / *etc*) (6 *consider*) I ~ that dishonest / a shame; would you ~ Russian a difficult language? shall we ~ it a pound *(settle at £1)*? how far would you ~ it to town? I ~ that a good 20 miles. (7) be ~ed to the teaching profession / priesthood / Church *(feel a vocation)*; many are ~ed but few are chosen. (8 *bring direct*) the Accession of Elizabeth II naturally ~s to mind England's first Elizabethan period; ~ (s.o.'s) attention to s.th.; ~ an organization / *etc* into being; ~ s.th. in question *(cast doubt on it)*. - *vi* (9) Mother ~ed, but I didn't hear (her); I ~ed to him, but ...; the dove ~s to her mate; ~ for help (10 *come to s.o., a place briefly*) I'm sorry I was out when you ~ed; has the milkman ~ed yet? the grocer's boy ~s (on us) every Monday for orders / has ~ed to know whether you want anything; ~ at a shop / the library / the bank; ~ on a friend / the Joneses / the people next door; the trains

~ at the station when required; does the ship ~ at Portsmouth?

call away her husband has been ~ed ~ on urgent business.

call by Mr. Smith is ~ing by at 5.

call down (1) ~ ~ a blessing on the crops; ~ ~ curses on s.o.'s head (2 *AE inform: scold*) the principal ~ed him ~ severely for making so much trouble.

call for (1) → call *vi* 9. (2) ~ ~ an actor (after a performance); ~ ~ an encore (3) shall we send the goods or will you ~ ~ them? we can ~ ~ the tickets ten minutes before the play begins; my driver will ~ ~ you at two; (letter) to be ~ed ~ (4) the Opposition ~ed ~ the minister's resignation / an investigation of the facts; he ~ed ~ a round of drinks. (5 *require*) boxing ~s ~ quick reactions; skating ~s ~ good balance; this news ~s ~ a celebration; his crimes ~ ~ punishment; marriage ~s ~ much mutual understanding.

call forth ~ ~ admiration / enthusiasm / criticism / protest; this task will ~ ~ all his energies; the job ~ed ~ unsuspected talents.

call in (1) ~ in an old coinage / all gold coins / passports / *etc* (to replace them by other coins, *etc*); the librarian has ~d in all the books. (2) ~ in debts / one's accounts *(demand payment)* (3) ~ in medical aid / professional advice / a doctor / the police / an expert.

call off (1) ~ ~ a row of figures (2) ~ ~ your dog at once *(call him away from s.o.)*; her attention was ~ed ~ by a new arrival. (3) because of the rain the game / meeting was ~ed ~; ~ ~ a visit / trip.

call on / upon (1) → call *vi* 10. (2) ~ on s.o.'s help / skill / knowledge / services; ~ upon the Lord; I ~ upon you to witness that I am innocent; I felt myself ~ed upon to help (him) / warn him; ~ on the public to return to work; my friend was ~ed upon to make a speech.

call out (1) ~ ~ the bus stops / s.o.'s name (in a restaurant); an auctioneer ~s ~ the lots; put your hand up if you know the answer - don't ~ ~. (2) ~ ~ the doctor *(for emergency service)*; the police were ~ed ~ to help in the evacuation of the villagers; the union ~ed the men ~ *(on strike)*.

call over (1) ~ ~ the pupils' names / the articles on the list (2) ~ your friend ~ to our table so I can meet him.

call together ~ ~ an assembly.

call up (1) he asked to be ~ed up at half past six *(waked; → call vt 3)*; what time shall I ~ you up? (2) my brother ~ed me up from Rome last night. (3) the government has ~ed up the reserves; be ~ed up into / for the army / navy; extra police were ~ed up to protect the meeting. (4) ~ up the spirit of (a dead person) (5) ~ up memories of (a holiday / old times); the song ~ed up the old days when ...; can't you ~ up the situation of that day?

calm *n* (1) ~ and quiet are characteristic of this remote wood; the ~ was shattered by the screech of an owl. (2) a ~ usually precedes a storm; □ this was the ~ before the storm.

calm *adj* (1) a ~ lake / sea / day / passage; ~ weather (2) be / remain / keep ~ (in a crisis); the consciousness of innocence makes any man ~; left to herself, she grew quieter, and at last ~.

cancel *vt* (1) ~ a word / figure / line / section in a contract; ~ a stamp (2) ~ an appointment / engagement / date / order for goods; ~ permission / (military) leave; (the rest of) your debt is ~led; this order will be in force until ~led. (3) mathematical terms (in an equation, fraction) may ~ one another / ~ out; ~ three out of a fraction.

cancel down ~ a fraction ~.

cancel out (1) → cancel 3. (2) two things may ~ one another ~; the likes are ~led ~ by the dislikes.

candle *n* cast / mould / draw ~s; light / blow out / extinguish / snuff out a ~; the ~ is lit / burning (smokily) / dripping / dying down / going out; → burn *vt* 1, game *n* 1, hold *vt* 1.

cap *vt* (1) ~ a bottle (2) mountains ~ped with snow (3) can you ~ this story / joke *(tell a better one)*? first the lights fused, next a water pipe burst, and then, to ~ it all, part of the ceiling fell down; □ ~ the climax *(beat everything)*.

capability *n* no one doubts his ~; intellectual ~ies; make the most of one's ~ies; they participated in sports according to their ~ies.

capable *adj* (1) a (very) ~ man / instructor / lawyer / stenographer / *etc*; he is very / highly ~ in his field. (2) be ~ of work / movement / concentration / expression / enthusiasm; be ~ of anything / any crime; be ~ of walking / seeing / driving / answering a question / pulling o.s. together / changing one's mind at the last moment / lying on, under oath / *etc*; few people are ~ of judging modern art. (3) the aeroplane is ~ of supersonic speeds; the situation is ~ of improvement; a port ~ of containing 500 ships; a computer ~ of storing millions of bits of information.

capacity *n* (1) the hall has a seating ~ of 2,000 people; be filled to ~ *(completely full)*; the cafés are always packed to ~; a ~ of a million gallons; the working ~ of an industrial plant; this factory is working to ~ *(to the fullest possible extent)*; a mind of great ~ (2) a teacher who serves in the ~ of coach; in his ~ as chairman / critic / *etc* (3) a student of great (mental / intellectual) ~; his ~ for mathematics; he has a natural ~ for enjoying life / an amazing ~ for concentration / little ~ for organization; young people's ~ to read continuously / for grasping abstract ideas is limited; this book is within the ~ of young readers *(can be understood by them)*. - *adj* (4 → 1) a ~ crowd attended the premiere.

car *n* drive (s.o. in) a ~ (to a place); can you drive a / the ~? go / travel by ~; we'll come by ~; I came by ~ / in the ~; I think I'll take the ~ this morning; I wish my father would let me drive the ~; he drove / ran his ~ into a wall; ride in a ~; → order *n* 2, repair *n* 3.

card *n* (1) a birthday / Christmas / visiting / invitation / membership / business / index / filing / *etc* ~; announce one's engagement by sending out ~s; punch one's (time-)~ (when entering a factory *etc*) (2) playing-~; a pack / *(AE)* deck / game of ~s; a high / low ~; play ~s; shuffle / cut / deal / distribute the ~s; hold good / bad ~s; play a game with exposed ~s / with ~s face up, down; draw / take / pick / choose a ~; fortune-telling / fortune teller's ~s; □ put (all) one's ~s on the table *(make one's plans known)*; □ play one's ~s well; □ have a ~ up one's sleeve *(have a secret plan in reserve)*; □ (play) one's best ~; a sure / safe / doubtful ~ *(such a plan)*; □ a house of ~s *(s.th. impracticable)*; tell s.o.'s fortune from the ~s; consult the ~s for s.o.; it is on the ~s *(likely)* that (my cousin will be the next Lord Mayor).

care *n* (1) perform one's duties / handle fragile objects with ~; give little / more ~ to one's work; do one's work with much / more ~; (this work) needs great / the utmost ~; → bestow 2, done with particular / painstaking / infinite ~; take ~ not to break the vase; did you take ~ to lock the door? take ~ (of yourself)! her mother takes ~ of *(looks after)* the children; she takes ~ of a ten-room house without help; each operator can take ~ of three machines; if I lend you my typewriter you must promise to take ~ of it *(handle it with care)*; take ~ of your bicycle or it will soon be useless; a mother's ~; individual / medical / tender ~. (2 *charge, task*) leave documents / children in s.o.'s ~; under a doctor's / nurse's ~; the library is under the ~ of N.; that will be my ~; entrust / commit / consign s.o. / s.th. to s.o.'s ~; entrust s.o. with the ~ of s.th.; have the ~ of s.o./ s.th. (3 *worry*) full of ~; worn with ~s; be harassed by the ~s of a large family; ~ made him look ten years older; I haven't a ~ in the world; be free from ~(s).

care *vi* (1) I don't ~ much about music *(am not interested)*; I don't ~ about him; who ~s what happens now? why should I ~ what he said? he doesn't ~ about politics / anything; he ~s about nothing but himself; I don't ~ about the price, so long as the car is in good condition; □ I don't ~; □ I couldn't ~ less *(inform: it doesn't matter at all)*. - *vt* (2) □ I don't ~ what you say *(whatever you may say)* (you won't find a pleasanter spot than this); he doesn't ~ a damn / pin / farthing / fig / hoot / straw (what happens) *(inform)*. (3 *care + inf: like*) would you ~ to try it on? would you ~ (to go) for a walk?; would you ~ to lock the door for me? I should not ~ to be seen with him; I don't ~ to be famous.

care for (1) I don't ~ for jazz / this cheese / dry sherry; would you ~ ~ another cup of tea / a lift to town? I don't ~ ~ fame; we don't ~ a rap ~ him *(inform)*. (2) my sister ~d ~ me while I was ill; who ~s ~ your cat and the plants during your absence? (3) he ~s ~ neither God nor devil; she ~s only ~ herself and her family.

career *n* (1) enter upon a promising / challenging / *etc* ~; a varied / checkered / downward ~; make a ~ of (science / *etc*); he has a brilliant ~ before him; his ~ (as a lawyer / physician / *etc*) was highly successful / (truly) meteoric / *etc*; he had a successful / meteoric / *etc* ~. (2) Shakespeare's professional and literary ~ is not known in all its details; the ~s of Jefferson and Lincoln still influence American history.

carry *vt* (1) he was ~ing the chair across the room when ...; ~ the coal to the cellar; ~ a burden on one's shoulders / the head; ~ an umbrella (in one's hand); he ~ied the child gently in his arms; can you ~ the weight?; ~ it carefully. (2 *have with one*) do you ~ your purse / wallet in your hip pocket? ~ a coat / stick / knife / watch; I never ~ much money with / about / on me; ~ one's identity card / passport on / with one; the police in Britain don't ~ fire-arms. (3 *transport*) how many passengers does this bus ~? the ship ~ies cargo from New York to London; ~ goods to the station; aeroplanes ~ mail; ... and a bus ~ied him to Fleet Street; he ran as fast as his legs could / would ~ him; ~ war into a country; □ ~ the can (back) *(answer for others' misdeeds)*; □ ~ coals to Newcastle *(do s.th. unnecessary)*; □ ~ all before one *(go from success to success)*; □ ~ the war into the enemy's country *(bring countercharges)* (4a *take*) ~ this letter to the post; ~ the news / message / information to s.o.; the old man ~ied his secret to the grave; how far will five gallons of petrol ~ me? (4b *fig*) he ~ied his complaint to the president; the children ~ied their woes to their mother; the boy ~ied tales to his teacher. (5) flies ~ germs; mosquitoes ~ malaria; this water is polluted and is ~ing dysentery; the breath ~ies this infection. (6 *publish*) today's paper ~ies the story of a murder on the front page; it ~ies the foreign news on the middle pages; the 'Times' ~ies fuller parliamentary reports than any other paper. (7) this job ~ies (a salary of) £1,000 a year / a pension / the right to ... / an entitlement to a house; all the positions ~ high salaries and excellent opportunities for the right men; the loan ~ies interest; these investments ~ a dividend of ... / a yield of ...; this product ~ies a two-year guarantee; the crime ~ied a three-year sentence. (8) this pipe ~ies water to the basin; the main road ~ies six lanes of traffic; the new bridge ~ies a great deal of traffic; the Kiel Canal ~ies ships to the Baltic; this wire ~ies the electric current for the lighting of this room; the new generators ~ the peak load with ease; copper is a good conductor and ~ies heat well; a gale ~ied the fire through the town; the wind ~ied the sound of the orchestra far over the lake. (9 *conquer, defeat*) a flank attack ~ied the town / hill; the tanks ~ied the first line of defence; our troops ~ied the day *(won victory)* at Waterloo after heavy fighting. (10 *extend*) the wall is ~ied to the end of the street; we must ~ the tower 10 feet higher; ~ a fence round a field / pipes under a street (11) the Government ~ied the Bill through Parliament by a narrow margin; the committee ~ied the resolution / motion / vote of thanks (unanimously); the motion / resolution was ~ied; ~ a resolution into effect; which party will ~ *(win)* the election? ~ one's point (→ point *n* 11) (12) this fine speaker ~ied the meeting with him; I hope I shall be able to ~ the members with me on this proposal; the film ~ies us to 16th-century Venice / Roman Britain; they are ~ing the affair too far in taking it to court; ~ one's arguments to extremes; that argument ~ies us too far; ~ the matter into the realm of pure speculation; in his book he ~ies logic to extremes; don't ~ modesty to excess; ~ s.o. off his feet *(fill with strong enthusiasm)* (13) her enthusiasm / enormous energy ~ied her through the first difficult year; his faith / dogged perseverance / careful planning ~ied him to success / victory. (14 *support s.th. static*) four piers ~ the dome; beams ~ the (weight of the) roof; the matchbox will not ~ the weight of the table; this bridge ~ies loads up to 200 tons; this tree ~ies a heavy crop of fruit. (15) he ~ies himself like a soldier; ~ one's head high; ~ one's body / head proudly (16 *bear, fig*) the job ~ies great responsibility; the captain of the team / the captaincy ~ies the burden of leadership; the accountant ~ies all the financial responsibility; her tone / the last paragraph ~ied a note of displeasure; the joke ~ies a note of cynicism; his tone / sincerity / reasoning ~ies conviction; the speech ~ies indications of a change of policy; a statement / report / *etc* ~ies a hint / implications / a reminder / no allusion to ... / a recommendation / an appeal for help; his statements / these figures ~ considerable weight with (the committee); a word / sentence ~ies (no / little / some) meaning; he ~ies the seal of a gentleman in all he says and does; we all ~ the stamp of our upbringing all our lives. - *vi* (17 → 11) unless illegally suppressed, the motion will ~; the motion to adjourn ~ied easily. (18 *have range*) my voice ~ies to the back of the room; ... he said in a ~ing voice; the light from this torch ~ies to the ceiling; the sound of the explosion ~ied ten miles; this rifle ~ies half a mile; our guns did not ~ far enough; if I throw this piece of chalk, it will not ~ across the playground.

carry about he ~ies ~ toys and books for sale; ~ a loaded pistol ~ (in one's pocket).

carry along his speech ~ied everyone ~ and we all volunteered for the dangerous task.

carry away (1) the ambulance ~ied ~ the injured man / ~ied him ~; the raven ~ied ~ a silver ring; the ship's masts were ~ied ~ during the storm. (2) they were ~ied ~ by the music / the speech / his enthusiasm; be ~ied ~ with emotion.

carry back an incident that ~ied me ~ to my schooldays.

carry off (1) be ~ied ~ by the current (2) the police seized the spy and ~ied him ~ to prison; looters ~ied ~ goods from the damaged shops. (3) ~ ~ *(win)* an award / a medal / a prize (4) cholera has ~ied ~ *(killed)* half the people of the village. (5) although she had only rehearsed the part a few times, she ~ied it ~ beyond all expectation; ~ ~ a situation (successfully / well).

carry on (1) ~ on one's husband's business; the loyal workers ~ied on (with their work / with the job / building the house); ~ on until I tell you to stop; ~ on with what you are doing. (2) for the next ten years he ~ied on the business of a bookseller; ~ on a conversation / correspondence (3) if you ~ on *(behave)* in that way, you'll get the club a bad name; she ~ied on like a child; he was ~ing on *(flirting)* with his wife's sister. (4) he ~ies on at the children until they have come to dislike him; she ~ied on about the next-door neighbours / cost of living until I was tired of listening to her.

carry out ~ ~ a promise / threat / plan / design / programme / scheme / policy / proposal / order / instruction / task / operation / analysis / investigation / experiment / reform / search / conquest; ~ ~ work / measures / orders / one's duties / one's, the daily cleaning (properly); ~ ~ a raid in broad daylight; I hope to ~ ~ my intention in a few days.

carry through (1) he ~ied ~ most of his reforms. (2) Churchill's determination ~ied him ~; perseverance will ~ a man ~ (many difficulties).

case *n* (1 *set of facts, circumstances having to do with a particular person, thing*) investigate the ~ of a missing person; an individual / isolated / concrete / interesting / minor / *etc* ~; circumstances alter ~s; it would be excusable for a starving man, but that was not your ~ / the ~ with you; that is my ~ exactly; in your ~ I would not hesitate; what succeeds in one ~ may fail in another; in many / some / certain / rare / doubtful / similar ~s; in such a ~; in one such ~; in such ~s; in ~s such as these; in that ~ you should sue; in no ~ are you to leave your post; too much sun is harmful in each of these ~s / in every ~; great care is necessary in each / every ~; in three ~s out of four ... (2 *s.th. that has happened, an occurrence*) four ~s of fire; several cases of hijacking; a ~ of careless work / bad temper; a bad ~ of blackmailing; a clear ~ of cheating / wishful thinking; a typical ~ of jealousy, if that / this / such is the ~; is it the ~ *(true)* that you ...? no, that's not the ~; previously the cost of living was lower than is now the ~ *(it is now)*; we thought him reliable, but just the opposite is the ~. (3) a medical / welfare ~; there are several ~s of polio; a bad ~ of tb; a classic ~ of typhoid; the Smith ~; Smith's ~; the ~ of Smith; famous/notorious ~s; an obstinate/difficult/hopeless ~ (4 *patient*) the doctor saw ten ~s today; three of the five ~s died; the ~ will come to surgery / be dismissed tomorrow. (5 *lawsuit*) a legal ~; famous / notorious ~s; the Smith / *etc* ~ (→ case 3); a civil / criminal ~; a ~ of fraud / *etc*; who will try that ~? his ~ has been reviewed. (6 *facts, arguments for or against s.o., s.th.*) the ~ for completing the scheme is powerful: further delays would be wasteful; and there is some ~ for ...; the ~ for the defence / defendant; state one's ~; never overstate your ~; let's put the ~ *(suppose)* that (he won't return); I am only putting a ~; he had a good / a strong / no ~; → make out 3; a ~ in point *(an illustrative example)*.

in case (1) take a map in ~ you get lost; you had better take your umbrella, in ~ it rains; I will take my umbrella, just in ~. (2) in ~ of fire *(if fire should occur)*, summon the fire brigade; in ~ of danger (3) we shall call on him in any ~, though we may not be able to stay long; bring the book in any ~; he should get more sleep in any ~; you need not apologize - I could not have come in any ~. (4) you say your father might object - in that ~ *(since / if that is so)* I will not press the matter: the man cannot have come across the garden, for in that ~ we should see his footprints.

cash *n* (1) ready / hard ~; ~ in hand *(available)*; a ~ price / sale / transaction / *etc*; I have no ~ on / with me - may I pay by cheque? sell goods for ~; pay ~ (down) / in ~; pay £20 in ~; the car costs £6000 ~ down; ~ on delivery (C.O.D.); buy on a ~-and-carry basis (2 *money*) be in ~; run out of ~; be short of ~; be out of ~; be rolling in ~; turn / convert s.th. into ~.

cash *vt* can I ~ this traveller's cheque here?

cash in (1) the gambler ~ed his chips in and left the casino. (2) the Opposition were not slow to ~ in on the unpopularity of the measures announced by the Government *(inform: take advantage of it)*.

cash up if he wants a job done, it's always urgent, but he's not in such a hurry when it comes to ~ing up for it.

cast *vt* (1a) ~ stones; fishermen ~ their nets; ~ the line; ~ for fish; ~ seed; a ship ~s anchor; ~ s.o. into prison; ~ s.o. out of one's home / presence / thoughts; deer ~ their horns / antlers; a snake ~s its skin / slough; my horse ~ its shoe; birds in moulting ~ their feathers. (1b) ~ a ballot / vote; the ~ing vote *(the decisive one)*; the number of votes ~; ~ lots / dice; □ the die is ~ *(the decision is irrevocably made)*; □ ~ pearls before swine; □ ~ a mistake / s.o.'s shortcomings in his teeth *(reprimand him)*; □ ~ prudence / a warning / *etc* to the winds (2 *turn, direct*) ~ a glance / look / eye at / on / over s.th.; the tower ~ a long shadow; coming events ~ their shadows before them; □ ~ light on (a problem); □ ~ a spell on s.o.; □ ~ a chill over s.o. ('s spirits); ~ suspicion on s.o.; ~ a slur on s.o.'s reputation; if you fear ~ all your cares on God. (3) ~ a bronze statue; ~ a statue in bronze; ~ a bell / gun / *etc*; ~ lead into bullets; ~ iron (4) let us ~ John as the hero of the new play; ~ an actor for a part; ~ a part to an actor; ~ a play (5 *reckon*) ~ (up) an account / row of figures; ~ the page of entries in an account book; ~ s.o.'s horoscope *(calculate it)*.

cast about ~ ~ for a solution / explanation / excuse / way of escape / chance to make some money / opportunity (to do s.th.).

cast aside ~ ~ all, one's reserve / all self-control / the love of truth; ~ care ~ and enjoy yourself.

cast down (1) ~ the eyes ~; the boy ~ ~ his book in despair. (2) be ~ ~ (by bad news / one's failure / one's dismissal).

cast in □ ~ in one's lot with s.o *(be ready to share his fortunes)*.

cast off (1) ~ ~ the yoke / one's fetters / one's winter clothing; he has at last ~ ~ his old suit and bought a new one. (2) ~ ~ one's former friends / associates (3) ~ ~ a manuscript *(estimate its printed space)*; the sailors ~ ~ (the ropes holding the boat) and we proceeded up the river.

cast out the medicine man's dance was supposed to ~ ~ evil spirits.

cast up ~ up figures rapidly; the accounts have to be ~ up at the end of each day; → cast *vt* 5.

cast *n* (1) the ~ of a fishing line / net; the fisherman made a ~ of 40 feet; the ~ of dice (2) what was the ~ *(number thrown in a game of dice)*? (3) the sculptor made a ~ of his clay model. (4) John had to wear a (plaster) ~ for six weeks when he broke his arm. (5) a ~ of actors; a good / all-star / star-studded ~; the ~ and credits of a film (6 *type, characteristic*) the sad ~ of s.o.'s countenance; his countenance was of the true Scottish ~; a strongly individual ~ of character; reflections of a moral ~; s.o.'s ~ of mind; my mind has a melancholy ~. (7 *tinge*) a rosy ~; his teeth have a yellowish ~. (8) a ~ in the / one eye *(a squint)*.

cat *n* have as many lives as a ~; □ when the ~'s away the mice will play; in the dark / when candles are away all ~s are grey; □ a ~ may look at a king; □ bell the ~ *(do s.th. dangerous to save others)*; □ lead a ~ and dog life (→ lead *vt* 6); play (at) ~ and mouse with s.o.; wait for the ~ to jump / see which way the ~ jumps *(what turn events will take)*; → let *vt* 3, rain *vt* 4.

catch *vt* (1a) ~ a fish / insect / thief / *etc*; an animal ~es its prey; cats ~ mice; the dog caught the ball in its mouth; a fresh-caught / freshly caught trout; be caught in one's own trap *(also fig)* (1b) ~ a ball / falling object; the path is very steep and slippery. - I'll ~ you if you fall, Mum. (2) what train are you ~ing? you ~ the bus just opposite the Town Hall; ~ the post *(put a letter in the box in time)* (3a *surprise*) ~ s.o. stealing apples / napping; we caught the dog scratching up the seeds; be caught in the act / red-handed / on the hop; I had better get changed - I don't want to be caught in these dirty clothes; the police caught them at their little game; be caught between two fires / the devil and the deep blue sea *(in a dilemma)* (3b) he caught all of us on the riddle; that question has caught a good many people. (4 *hit*) the stone caught him on the shin; he was caught on the hand by a piece of flying glass; he caught it *(was hit)* right on the forehead; ~ him one in the eye *(inform)*; she caught him one on the cheek *(inform)*. (5) I'll try to ~ him for a minute after the meeting; you might ~ him if you call about 9.30. (6) the milk nearly boiled over - I caught it just in time; dry rot can be stopped from spreading if it is caught in its early stages. (7) this side of the house ~es the east wind; her arms were red where they had been caught by the sun / where the sun had caught them; the wind caught his hat and ...; before we were out of the woods, night caught us; the boat / swimmer was caught by the current; the flames / fire caught the church. (8) the edges of the carpet are curling up and I caught my foot in it; I caught my fingers / coat in the door; I got my fingers / coat caught in the door; he caught his toe against the leg of a chair; I caught the cup with my elbow *(and broke it)*; → breath *n* 1; a nail caught her dress; she caught her stocking on a rough fingernail; the car caught the pedestrian. (9) ~ (a) cold; ~ an infection / sore throat / sunstroke; ~ diphtheria / measles / *etc*; you will ~ your death (of cold) if you go out without a coat; you'll ~ it *(inform: be punished)*; the house / vehicle caught fire; her dress caught alight; ~ s.o.'s enthusiasm; we were caught by the spirit of the crowd. (10 *understand*) I didn't ~ his name; I don't ~ your meaning; I could only ~ a few words of the conversation. (11 + *abstract objects*) I caught sight / a glimpse of him in the crowd; he tried to ~ a glance from her eye / ~ her eye; her eyes / glance caught mine; s.o.'s eye / attention is caught by s.th.; that colour ~es the eye; ~ s.o.'s attention / fancy; ~ the popular fancy; ~ hold of s.o./ s.th. *(seize)*; yawning / a disease / laughter / good humour is often ~ing. (12) in this description the peaceful mood of the evening is effectively caught; ~ an expression / likeness / tune. - *vi* (13) the bolt does not ~; the lock finally caught. (14) the kite caught in the tree; her dress caught on a nail / the door-knob; his voice caught *(broke with emotion)*.

catch at he caught at a rope but missed it and sank; a drowning man will ~ at a straw; she caught at the chance to go abroad; ~ at an opportunity (to make money).

catch on (1) a new idea / song / habit / custom / new style ~es on; the film gradually caught on; s.o. ~es on to a new idea (2) they didn't ~ on *(inform: understand)*.

catch out he was caught ~ by a question which caused him to contradict himself; the lawyer caught ~ the witness.

catch up (1) he caught up a stick and ...; the dead leaves were caught up by a gust of wind. (2) his clothing was caught up in the machine. (3) I'll ~ you up in a few minutes; we can't hope to ~ up (with) that car in front of us; I couldn't ~ up with him / ~ him up. (4) I have neglected my work for so long that I'll never ~ up (with it); I've so much work to ~ up (with); I have got very much behind-hand with my reading: I must try and ~ up on it; reality was never able to ~ up with the American Dream.

catch *n* (1) that was a good ~ *(the ball was caught expertly)*. (2) a fine ~ of fish; make a good ~ (3) a ~ in the voice (→ catch *vi* (14) (4) there's a ~ in this contract *(a complication, trap)*.

cause *n* (1) carelessness is a major ~ of road accidents; a direct / indirect ~; what was the ~ of his rapid rise to fame? God is the ~ of all things. (2) I have no / he has given me no ~ to complain / for complaint; the situation gives ~ for apprehension; he had good ~ to repent his bargain; there's no ~ for alarm. (3) work for the ~ of peace; fight for a good / just

~; defend the ~ of the working classes; a lost *(hopeless)* ~; the customs officers made common ~ with the smugglers.

cause *vt* (1) speeding ~s many accidents; the floods have ~d great distress; the hurricane ~d (the) destruction of many homes on the coast; a burn frequently ~s blisters; the accident ~d a short delay; reading in a dim light may ~ injury to the eyes; something has happened which ~s me some anxiety; ~ (s.o.) trouble / discomfort; ~ (much) damage (to s.o.) (2) a noise ~d me to jump back; what ~d the trees and plants to die thousands of years ago? what ~d him to change his mind? the mistakes of others ~ one to be wary; circumstances over which I had no control ~d my being late. (3) Caesar ~d a bridge to be built.

celebrate *vt* (1) ~ an event / anniversary / victory / feast / festival / wedding; ~ Christmas / New Year / Mass / the Lord's Supper; ~ one's birthday / engagement / (silver / *etc*) wedding / promotion (2) her book ~s a forgotten hero. - *vi* (3) let's ~; one must ~ when the occasion presents itself.

celebrated *adj* a ~ actor / musician / author / painter / personality; a woman (much) ~ for her beauty; Mozart was the most ~ composer of his time.

celebration *n* the ~ of a religious holiday / the Mass; hold a ~; a joyous / picturesque / solemn ~; have a birthday / engagement / wedding ~ (at the Park Hotel); on the occasion of such ~s the wine flowed like water.

centre *n* (1) the ~ of a circle / a wheel / the road / *etc*; the ~ of a town (2) a shopping / business / trading ~; an arts ~; the N.Y. C~ of (the) Performing Arts; a ~ of commerce / trade / government (3) she is the ~ of attention; he is the ~ of everything.

centre *vt* (1) we ~d the picture over the sofa. (2) the American motor industry is ~d around / in / on Detroit. (3) the crowd's attention was ~d on the fire engine; all her attention was ~d on her family. - *vi* (4) the conversation ~d on tennis; the whole of his argument ~s / is ~d on the assumption that we ...

certain *adj* (1) it is ~ that (the earth turns round the sun); I think it is ~ that (he will get the job); nothing ~ is known; we all face ~ death; there is no ~ cure for this disease; one thing is ~, I shan't lend him money again; you are ~ to need help; the attempt is ~ to fail; he is ~ to come. (2) I am (quite / absolutely) ~ I never said that; are you ~ of what you say? no one can be ~ of living till seventy; you can be ~ of success / being rewarded; no one was ~ about his qualifications for the job; as long as I'm not ~ about it, I cannot comment on it; he is more ~ about this matter than about others; I am fairly / reasonably / most ~ that ...; the child was ~ to be punished; → make *vt* 21. (3 *not stated, but statable*) there are ~ things that we ...; ~ conditions in the contract are superfluous; the museum is open only on ~ days; a ~ Mr Mill; at a ~ time; for a ~ reason; on ~ conditions; in a ~ sense (4 *some, not much*) I agree with you to a ~ extent; you must show a ~ amount of tact; he had a ~ coldness of manner; there has been a ~ improvement in the patient's condition; accept s.th. with a ~ reluctance; to a ~ degree.

for certain know s.th. ~ ~; know ~ ~ that he ...; he will come ~ ~; I must find out ~ ~ whether he ...; I cannot say ~ ~ when he will start.

certainly *adv* I ~ like to read detective stories; you will ~ get there too late; they will ~ try their best; this film is ~ worth seeing; I would ~ have come if ...; I most ~ won't go there; there is ~ some cause for anxiety.

certainty *n* (1) achieve / attain ~; a feeling of ~; it cannot be said with ~ whether he ...; some philosophies tend to destroy man's ~ of his own existence. (2) a dead / moral ~ *(an absolute one)*; it is a ~ that the sun will rise tomorrow; I know for a ~ that he ...

certify *vt* (1) ~ a document / copy / signature; a ~ied cheque; I ~ this a true copy; this is to ~ that Mr John Smith ...; the doctor ~ied that the man had been ill for three weeks; I shall be pleased to ~ that you have worked for me for nine months; the accounts were ~ied (as) correct; he was ~ied insane; (AE) a ~ied public accountant / midwife *(holding a professional certificate)*; ~ied milk *(guaranteed free from tubercle bacilli)* (2) a ~ied patient / inmate (*one officially declared insane)*.

chair *n* (1) a wooden / wicker / upholstered / *etc* ~; a folding / rocking / garden / deck / *etc* ~; won't you take a

~ *(sit down)*? sit (down) on a (dining-room) ~; be curled up in an arm ~ / easy ~ (2) be offered / accept / obtain / get / refuse a ~ (at N. university); he resigned to take the ~ of Economics at B.; he was appointed to the ~ of History. (3 *office*) take the ~ *(act as chairman)*; leave the ~ *(end proceedings)*; be in the ~ (4 *person*) appeal to the ~ *(chairman)*; address your questions to the ~ during the meeting.

chalk *n* (1) ~ hills / cliffs; the colour of ~ (2) write with ~; mark a line with ~; draw in / with ~; a drawing in ~(s) / ~ drawing; I've got ~ all over my fingers / myself; □ (this house is the better of the two) by a long ~ *(by far)*.

chalk *vt* ~ a line on the pavement; they ~ed slogans on walls; ~ (up) a billiard cue *(cover the tip with chalk)*.

chalk out ~ ~ a plan *(sketch it roughly)*.

chalk up (1) ~ up the drinks *(inform: give credit)*; have one's drinks/ meal ~ed up to one (2) ~ up points / a good deed / s.o.'s mistakes; the offence will be ~ed up against you; ~ that up to experience.

challenge *n* (1) send s.o. a ~ (by one's seconds); the chief sent a warlike ~ to the neighbouring tribe. (2) 'who goes there?' is the ~ *(demand for identification)*. (3 *a serious problem to be solved*) the industrial ~ of nuclear energy; the professional men who serve a university are not shielded from the ~s of citizenship.

challenge *vt* (1) ~ s.o. to a duel; ~ s.o. to (a) fight; he ~d me to run a race; ~ fate; his attitude ~s one to contradict him. (2) the sentry ~d him at the gate *(demanded identification)*. (3 *dispute, question*) ~ (the truth of) a statement / a hasty remark; we ~ the argument that...; people realized that the atomic bomb brutally ~d their security; in those years England ~d the maritime supremacy of Spain; the opposition ~d the election results. (4 *be extremely difficult for*) whooping-cough still ~s medicine; the problem was so ~ing that he ...; the game of Scrabble ~s the most astute gamester. (5 *claim superiority to*) the Eskimo's scenting powers ~ the polar bear's; the scenery of the Lake District cannot ~ the magnificence of the Alps; we are about to ~ interplanetary distances.

chance *n* (1) your future should not be decided by ~ but by choice; let's leave it to ~ *(trust to luck)*; let ~ decide; a game of ~ *(not skill)*; meet s.o. by ~; ~ made me go there. (2 *opportunity*) give me another ~ to show I can work hard; you have not given me a ~ of defence; he never lets a ~ go by; you will never find a better ~; he had no ~ to escape / of escaping; he has long hoped for a ~ of promotion; miss a / one's ~; wait for a ~; it's the ~ of a lifetime; □ have an eye for the main ~ *(an opportunity of making money)*; → dog *n* 1. (3 *possibility*) there is a ~ that he may live; have a fair ~ of winning; you stand a (good / fair / reasonable) ~ of success (with him); I have no earthly ~ of success; he has a sporting *(50 : 50)* ~ of getting the post; is there any ~ of that happening / catching the train? there is not much ~ of rain today; I came on the ~ of finding you; Britain would have had little ~ of resisting an invasion. (4 *risk*) in such a situation one must take one's ~(s); good drivers don't take ~s; → run *vt* 66.

chance *vi* (1) it ~d that I was away the day you dropped by; it so ~d that we met again; it ~d that Sleeping Beauty found an old woman ... - *vt* (2) I ~d to overhear a remark which ...; he ~d to see me in town. (3 *risk*) it is a dangerous enterprise but I will ~ it; it was decided to withdraw rather than ~ defeat; we may be too late, but let's ~ it; I'll do it and ~ the consequences; I'll ~ being punished; at two o'clock in the morning, we can ~ taking this road, although it's closed to traffic; □ ~ one's arm *(take a great risk)*.

chance (up)on he ~d (up)on the very thing he had been looking for.

change *n* (1) need / want / undergo a (complete / radical / slight / sudden / striking / welcome / *etc*) ~; their ~ of tactics (is amazing); as we had usually taken a seaside holiday we decided that we would go into the country for a ~; you've been out every night this last fortnight - why can't you spend an evening at home for a ~? (2) many ~s have taken place since I was in the village twenty years ago; there's going to be a ~ in the weather; you need a ~ (of air); there has been a ~ for the better / worse in his condition; a ~ of mind / meaning / topic / scene; make a ~ in a programme / design / plan (3) take a ~ of clothes / underwear with you. (4) 100p are ~ for a pound; have you got ~ for a pound? I have no (small) ~ on me; his ~ jingled in his pocket. (5) if you buy something that costs 20p and pay for it with a pound note, you'll get 80p change; see that you get the right ~; (don't forget to) count your ~; he left his ~ on the shop counter.

change *vt* (1a) ~ one's coat / tie / clothes / *etc*; ~ one's name / address / position / hairdresser; ~ a battery / bulb; ~ the (bed-)linen; they ~d places with each other; shall we ~ seats? we have to ~ (trains) at Crewe; a shop / farm / picture / *etc* ~s hands *(passes to another owner)*; ~ the subject (of a conversation); can you ~ (me) a pound note (to 100p)?; I'm afraid I can't ~ that; I don't care for this red tie - could you ~ it for a green one? (1b) ~ a bed *(put fresh sheets on it)*; ~ a baby *(put a clean napkin on it)* (2 *alter*) the ring can be ~d to fit your finger; he ~d the 3 to an 8; when she marries, a woman ~s her surname to that of her husband; leaves ~ their colour in the autumn; □ ~ colour *(turn pale or blush from sudden emotion)*; ~ one's plans / opinion / view / tone; □ ~ one's note / tune *(adopt a humbler attitude)*; □ ~ one's mind *(come to a new opinion, decision)*; □ ~ one's ground *(viewpoint)*; ~ s.th. for the better / worse; a man's character cannot be ~d; the appearance of the town is quite ~d. (3) the conjurer ~d the handkerchief into a white rabbit; ~ water into wine. - *vi* (4) a caterpillar ~s into a butterfly; the snake ~d into a beautiful lady. (5) the character of the country ~d as we flew south; he has greatly ~d; how much ~d did he appear to you after those long years? times / things have ~d; time ~s and we ~ with it; the weather will ~ to rain; we have recently ~d to central heating; he ~d from his bad habits; at Rugby we must ~ for Manchester; he has ~d for the better / worse; ~ overnight; he ~d into evening dress / a shirt and shorts; it won't take me five minutes to ~; ~ into second (gear) (→ gear *n* 2).

change round ~ machine parts / tyres ~ (to avoid uneven wear).

character *n* (1) a man / woman of good / bad / strong / weak / fine / noble / generous / miserly / cheerful / melancholy / (in)sensitive / excitable / stern / cruel / *etc* ~; he revealed his true ~ thereby; that is part of his ~; (he has / lacks) strength of ~; build / form / mould the ~; the way you tell me he has acted towards you is quite in ~ *(in keeping with his character)*; be out of ~ (2 *moral strength*) he is a man of ~; he has / lacks ~. (3) he is a bad / weird / odd / worthy / *etc* ~; a public ~ *(well-known person)*; he's quite a ~ *(not average, peculiar)*. (4) the ~s in a play; Shakespeare's ~s are true to nature; all the ~s in this book are fictitious; he scored a great success in the ~ of a Cockney workman; I went to see him in the ~ of a friend, not in that of a lawyer. (5) a region with a ~ of its own; the house is not in keeping with the ~ of the landscape; the English national ~ (6 *reputation*) he has an excellent ~ for honesty; he has gained the ~ of a miser; his association with evil companions detracted from his ~. (7 *certificate*) your ~ seems quite satisfactory; my chauffeur came to me with a good ~ / with good ~ references. (8 *letter, symbol*) Greek / Chinese / Sanskrit ~s.

charge *n* (1) legal / postal / telephone / railway / hotel / warehouse / hairdresser / *etc* ~s; the ~s of a lawyer / doctor; the ~s for trunk calls / trunk ~s have gone up; reverse the ~(s) *(of a telephone call)*; reversed ~ (call); free of ~; a ~ of 50p is made for the certificate; the ~ for parking is . . .; the papers are handed over on payment of the ~s; forward (newspapers etc.) at reduced ~s; no ~ for admittance; is there any ~? living at the ~ of his brother (2) he became a ~ upon the parish; I hope you will never become a ~ on the public *(to be supported at public expense)*; I have many ~s on my income; the babysitter read her ~s a bedtime story. (3 *attack*) make a ~ (on the fort) (4 *accusation*) bring a ~ (of theft / murder / *etc*) against s.o.; arrest s.o. on a ~ of theft; lay s.th. to s.o.'s ~ *(accuse him of it)* (5) the judge's ~ *(instructions)* to the jury (6) the nurse was left in ~ of the children *(supervised them)*; the children were left in the ~ of the nurse; the bank manager is in ~ of the bank; I have placed the documents in the ~ of my bank manager; put s.o. in ~ of s.o. / s.th.; who is in ~ here? John is in ~ of the business; her child is in my ~ this afternoon; the nurse has the ~ of watching the children; take ~ of s.th. *(be responsible for it)*; five detectives, under the ~ of an Inspector, are inquiring into the crime; □ give s.o. in ~ *(to the police)* (7) a ~ of six volts; the battery is on ~ *(being charged).*

charge *vt* (1 *attack*) the cavalry ~d a marching column; the bull ~d (towards) the campers. (3 *accuse*) ~ s.o. with a crime / offence; ~ a crime / offence to s.o.; ~ s.o. with unkindness / neglect / cowardice (4 *instruct*) the judge ~d the jury to weigh all the evidence; Gustavus considered himself ~d by God with the defence of the true Lutheran faith; Mother has ~d me to take care of you; he was ~d with an important mission; the Commission is ~d with seeing that (the wild animals are preserved). (5) ~ s.o. a sum for goods / services / doing s.th; the goods / services are ~d to s.o.; the shopkeeper ~d me a dollar for it; he ~d 3 dollars to repair my shoes; how much did they ~ you? a fee of 50p is ~d for the certificate; ~ s.o.'s account (with a sum); please ~ it to my account / these goods to me. (6) ~ a gun (with an explosive) / the magazine of a machine-gun (with bullets); ~ a battery; a cable is ~d with electricity; ~ a furnace; ~ one's memory with many details. - *vi* (7) he ~d sword in hand; the men ~d with bayonets; the wounded lion suddenly ~d at me. (8 *hurry, rush; inform*) he ~d off down the road; one morning he ~d into my studio.

charity *n* (1) and now abideth faith, hope, ~, these three, but the greatest of these is ~; he exhibited a rare example of Christian ~; with malice toward none, with ~ for all; □ ~ begins at home *(is due first to one's own people)*; practise ~ towards s.o.; do s.th. (for s.o.) in / out of ~ (2 *alms*) live / depend on ~ (3 *welfare organization*) leave all one's money to ~ies; ~ work / worker / bazaar / ball; collect (money) for (a children's) ~.

chase *vt* (1) ~ s.o. / an animal; dogs ~ rabbits; ~ a butterfly; ~ the dog out (of the garden); the children ~d (one another) about in the schoolyard; the wind ~d dark clouds across the sky. (2) ~ (after) wealth / happiness (3) how can we ~ these fears from her mind? ... and a radiant smile ~d away sorrow.

chatter *vi* (1) sparrows / magpies / monkeys / streams / typewriter keys / tools / machine parts ~; the two boys went ~ing down the road; he came ~ing after me as fast as he could; his teeth ~ed with the / from cold, with fear. - *vt* (2) ~ a lot of nonsense.

cheap *adj* ~ goods; buy ~(ly); one lives in Berlin more ~ly than in London; it looks a ~ dress; it is too ~ to be good; a ~ shop; I got it (on the) ~ *(inform)*; travel on the ~ *(inform)*; a ~ *(easy)* victory; they won the victory ~ly. (2 *worthy of scorn*) a ~ trick; (AE) a real ~ guy; a ~ girl; ~ jokes / flattery; s.o.'s ~ behaviour; hold s.th. ~ *(despise it)*; make o.s. ~ *(so that one's reputation goes down)* (3) he felt ~ *(ashamed)* about his bad behaviour.

cheat *vt* (1) ~ s.o. (out) of s.th.; ~ s.o. out of his savings / inheritance; ~ the customs / fate / death; ~ s.o. into a belief; we have been ~ed of our best years; I am not so easily ~ed. - *vi* (2) ~ at play / cards / school; ~ in an examination / on a test.

check *n* (1 *esp AE*) mark s.th. with a ~; put a ~ against (a name/ figure/ *etc*) (2) a ~ for coats / hats / *etc*; a hat ~ (for coats, hats, *etc*); a luggage ~; I've lost the ~ for my suitcase. (3) the machines are subjected to a regular ~ (-up); a thorough ~ on all instruments; keep a ~ on (s.o. 's movements / all the instruments (4 *AE*) → cheque. (5 *AE bill*) after lunch he signalled the waiter for his ~. (6) wind acts as a ~ on speed; Tom's illness gave a ~ to our plans; our soldiers met with a slight ~ *(had to stop)*; keep a ~ on one's temper; keep / hold the enemy in ~; put an opponent's king in ~ *(chess).*

check *vt* (1) ~ a paper / list / invoice / statement / account; ~ information / results / figures / one's watch; we must ~ his story / the authenticity of the document. (2) the rope ~ed his fall; ~ motion / movement / flow; she ~ed her horse's speed; ~ the advance of the enemy; ~ the working of a machine; he started to speak but then he ~ed himself; he couldn't ~ his anger; ~ extravagant spending; ~ a tendency (3 *AE leave in temporary custody*) ~ your umbrellas at the door. (4 *AE accept for temporary custody*) we accept responsibility for any article we ~ here. (5 *AE send to a destination under the privilege of a passenger ticket*) we ~ed two trunks to Paris. (6 *AE accept for conveyance under the privilege of a passenger ticket*) please, ~ this trunk to Paris. (7 *AE inform*) ~! *(agreed! correct!).*

check in ~ ~ *(register)* at a convention / hotel / hospital; ~ ~ for a flight.

check off ~ ~ a paper / name *(mark as verified)*; ~ ~ (items in) a list.

check out (1 *AE withdraw by cheque*) he ~ed ~ all his money. (2) when did he ~ ~ (of the hotel)?

check up the police are ~ing ~ on the suspect / alleged theft.

checkup *n* (1) the police requested a ~ of the suspect's tax returns. (2) a (thorough) medical ~.

cheek *n* (1) full / fat / chubby / plump / hollow / bloodless / shrunken ~s; a swollen ~; her ~s glowed; a blush rose to her ~s; shame flushed his ~s. (2 *impudence*) what (a) ~! I have had enough of your ~; he has enough ~ for anything; he had the ~ to ask me to lend him ...; he gave me a (whole) lot of ~ *(said cheeky things).*

cheek *vt* (BE) he ~s his parents in front of other people; if you're going to ~ me, I'll ~ you back.

cheer *n* (1) the crowd gave a ~ / three ~s for our team. (2) words of ~ (3 *gaiety*) an evening of ~; Christmas ~ *(also fig, alcoholic beverages:* a cup / glass of Christmas ~).

cheer *vt* (1) we ~ed the winning runner. (2) he tried to ~ his sad friend; a ~ing letter (3) the speaker was ~ed loudly.

cheer on we went to the match to ~ our team on.

cheer up (1) she wants s.o. to ~ her up; she was ~ed up by the news that she ... (2) she ~ed up at the good news; ~ up - everything will be all right!

cheque *n (BE)* a ~ for £12 / on a bank; a traveller's ~; a cashier's / certified ~; make out / issue / write (out) / fill in / sign a ~; pay by ~; cash a ~.

cherish *vt* (1) ~ an illusion / ideal / belief / tradition; ~ hatred against s.o. / memories / hopes; a ~ed possession; ~ one's friends; he ~ed a few books for the pleasure they had given him; something the heart must have to ~; husband and wife should love, honour and ~ each other. (2) a mother ~es her children.

child *n* (1) a newborn / stillborn ~; an only ~; an (il)legitimate / natural ~; a normal / model / (dis)obedient/ precocious / intelligent / curious / frail / delicate / sickly / fretful / troublesome / naughty / trying / unruly / wayward / *etc* ~; noisy ~ren; bring a ~ into the world; give birth to a ~; any ~ knows that; he's still / just a big ~; behave like a ~; you are no longer a ~ / not a ~ any more; □ be with ~ *(pregnant)*; a ~'s / ~ren's game *(not fig)*; that's ~'s play *(very easy)*; I have known her from a ~ *(since childhood).* (2) be a ~ of one's time / the 18th century; ~ren of light / darkness; a ~ of the devil; this poem is a ~ of his muse; a ~ of the imagination.

chill *n* (1) there is a(n autumn) ~ in the air; take the ~ off (the wine / claret) *(warm it slightly)* (2) put on your coat - I don't want you to get a ~; take / catch a ~; have a ~ on the kidneys (3) → cast *vt* 2.

chill *vt* (1) ~ the fruit juice / wine / champagne; ~ meat / *etc (refrigerate, but not freeze)*; be ~ed to the bone (2) ~ s.o.'s enthusiasm. - *vi* (3) do you ~ easily *(feel cold)*?

chill *adj* (1) a ~ night / wind / breeze (2) a ~ reception / welcome / answer.

chilly *adj* (1) ~ wind / weather / rooms; it was wet and ~. (2) feel ~; I'm getting quite ~. (3) a ~ reception / welcome; a ~ manner / personality; greet s.o. with ~ reserve / politeness.

choice *n* (1 *act of choosing*) a judicious ~; make a careful ~; I'll leave the ~ of a film to you; such abundance makes ~ difficult; who is the girl of his ~? most working-class wives work rather from ~ than from actual necessity. (2 *possibility of choosing*) have a free ~; we had a ~ between the mountains and the seaside for our holiday; there is / I have no ~ left to me but to (accept his conditions); *(BE)* I should take this one for ~ *(preferably).* (3 *what is chosen*) take your ~; which is your ~? (4 *number of persons, things from which to choose*) there is a ~ of colours among these hats; the shop has a wide ~ of (wines); we keep a great ~ of ...; you have a ~ of questions in the examination. - *adj* (4) a ~ wine / cut of meat.

choke *vt* (1) the smoke ~d the firemen; the piece of food nearly ~d him; ~ s.o. to death (2) mud and leaves ~d the drain. (3) weeds ~d the flowers / lake / river; ~ a fire. - *vi* (4) the boy ~d after taking a big swallow of water; he nearly ~d to death with coughing / laughter; she was almost ~ing with tears. - *adj* (5) her voice was ~d with tears; a ~d drain / pump.

choke back ~ ~ one's anger / emotion / tears; ~ ~ a sob.

choke down (1) ~ ~ food (2) ~ ~ one's anger / emotion / tears; ~ ~ a sob.

choke off he wanted to join the mountaineering party but the leader ~d him ~ *(dissuaded him)*; a clever bit of propaganda enabled the politician to ~ ~ all opposition.

choke up the chimney is ~d (up) with soot; the garden is ~d (up) with weeds; the room was ~d up with useless old furniture.

choose *vt* (1) you may ~ whatever you like; ~ s.o. for a friend; there's not much / nothing / little to ~ between them *(they are about equal)*; send s.o. patterns to ~ from; he was chosen from hundreds of applicants; ~ writing as a career / law as a profession (2) he ~s not to answer; I do not ~ to enter into particulars; I would not ~ to live in Alaska; the leader chose me to go with him; if I have to ~ between going and remaining, I ~ remaining. - *vi* (3) ~ between two / among several things. (4 *form*) I cannot ~ but *(must)* do it; I could not ~ but laugh.

chop *vt* ~ (up) vegetables / herbs / meat (finely); ~ped ham, kidney, tomatoes, mushrooms etc may be spread on an omelette before it is folded; ~ (up) wood; ~ down a tree; ~ a branch off a tree; don't ~ your finger off; ~ a way through the undergrowth.

church *n* (1 *building*) a Byzantine / Romanesque / Gothic *etc* ~; consecrate / dedicate a ~; they are in the ~(→ 3). (2 *institution*) the Protestant / (Roman) Catholic / Anglican / Methodist / *etc* C~; the C ~ of England; C ~ and State; in the bosom of the C ~; leave the C ~; enter the C~ *(become a priest)*; are you ~ or chapel *(BE member of the Church of England or of one of the Free Churches)*? (3 *service*) go to / attend ~ (regularly); the bells were ringing for ~; what time does ~ begin? they are in / at ~ *(attending a service)*; we'll meet after ~.

cinema *n* (1 *BE*) go to the ~; were you at the ~ last night? have you been to the ~ this week? (2) the official birth-date of the modern ~ is 1895; in 1928 the Russian ~ had reached a high artistic level; in the years after the Second World War the ~ enjoyed its period of greatest popularity; the cultural potential of the ~.

circle *n* (1) draw / describe a ~ (about a polygon) (with a pair of compasses); calculate (the area of) a ~; the radius / diameter / circumference of a ~ (2) place / arrange chairs in a ~; they made a ~ for a folk dance; they sat / stood / walked (round) in a ~; in the dense fog we had gone round / described a ~; the path describes a ~ round the hill; □ come full ~ *(end at the starting-point)*; □ run round in ~s *(be fussily busy with little result)* (3 *series*) a year is made up of a ~ of 12 months; the ~ of the seasons; □ argue in a ~; □ vicious ~ (4) in diplomatic / (well-) informed ~s it is thought ...; court / business / literary / theatrical / social / fashion(able) ~s; this young poet is already well known to a wide ~ of people; musical evenings in the family ~; a ~ of friends.

circle *vt* (1) please ~ the right answers. (2) Drake ~d the globe; the satellite ~d the earth ten times; the plane / eagle ~d (above / over) the field. (3) the guards ~d the prison. - *vi* (4) the sheepdog ~d slowly round the flock; vultures ~d overhead; ~ with one's arm / leg *(in gymnastics)* (5) the news ~d round.

circulate *vi* (1) hot water ~s in a heating-system; blood ~s in the body / veins and arteries. (2) the news ~d quickly; money ~s freely / quickly / slowly / *etc*; nearly 300 religious papers ~ in Britain; in which area does this newspaper ~? - *vt* (3) he ~d the cigars / wine; ~ a report / a lie / rumours; the letter has been ~d among all the relatives.

circulation *n* (1) the heart keeps the blood in ~; the free ~ of air; he has a good / bad ~. (2) the ~ of news / rumours; traffic ~ (3 *distribution*) the ~ of a leaflet; are there any forged bank-notes in ~? this book has been withdrawn from ~; put new coins into ~; national ~ (4 *number of copies*) a magazine of large ~; Paris Match, with a ~ of two million, is ...; this paper has a ~ of more than a million.

circumstance *n* (1) the time, place, and other ~s of an action; ~s alter cases; depend on ~s; aggravating / extenuating / attendant / accompanying / incidental / *etc* ~s; there are unusual / special ~s attached to this ring; struggle against adverse ~s; under suspicious ~s; under existing ~s, the only way to get there is by bus; in these / such / particular / *etc* ~s; in / under the ~s *(things being as they are)*, I think it is advisable ...; under / in no ~s must you go to see this film; I will not play such a trick on him under / in any

~s. (2 *fact, detail*) the happy ~ of his arrival; I was ignorant of one important ~; he has plenty of money, which is a fortunate ~; a story told with much ~ (3 ~s: *financial condition*) (live) in easy / good / flourishing / bad / poor / reduced / straitened ~s (4 *ceremony, pomp*) too much pomp and ~; the great inequalities of wealth and ~ in Britain today.

claim *n* (1) a legal / lawful / justified / well-founded / *etc* ~ to s.th.; wage ~(s); ~s to quality; a fictitious ~; establish / substantiate a ~; assert / waive / renounce one's ~ (to s.th.); we still have a ~ for a sum of £200 on your firm; he made a ~ against the other driver; make a ~ for damages (→ make *vt* 7); put in a ~ for damages; lay ~ to s.th. (→ lay *vt* 9); I do not lay ~ to learning; set up a ~ for s.th.; make ~s on s.o./ s.th.; have a ~ on s.o.; I have some ~s on his friendship; I have many ~s on my time. (2 *assertion*) the ~s of a company about its products (3 *tract of land*) the miner staked his ~ and registered it with the state authorities; work a ~; jump *(take illegal possession of)* a / s.o. else's ~ (→ jump *vt* 5).

claim *vt* (1) she ~ed her purse at the lost-property office; ~ a right / honour / privilege; ~ the right to do s.th.; we ~ no more than (is) our due; ~ damages / compensation (from / against s.o.) (2) important matters ~ed his attention; the work on this dictionary ~s all my spare time; last month road accidents ~ed 50 lives. (3 *state*) the customer ~ed that he had already paid; he ~s that he has broken the record for long-distance flying; it is ~ed that this discovery will revolutionize surgery; the witness ~ed to have seen the accused / a flying saucer; he ~s to be the heir / have told the truth; both sides ~ed the victory; he has a quality that few of us can ~; he ~s *(professes)* peaceful intentions.

class *n* (1) the junior / senior ~es of the school; be in the second-year ~; in which ~ is he? which ~ is he in? be at the top of one's ~; stay down in a ~ for a second year; jump/ miss a ~ (2 *lesson, esp outside school*) what time does the ~ begin? history ~ starts at nine; outdoor ~es; she is taking ~es in cookery; who is taking this ~ today *(teaching it)*? (3 *group of pupils*) my ~ is in Room 6. (4) social ~es; upper / lower / working ~es; the middle / propertied / moneyed / managerial / ruling ~ (5) a ~ of product; a first-~ artist / hotel / liar / *etc*; first-~ products; second-~ mail; travel first ~; as an actor he is not in the same ~ with N. *(is not so good)* / in a ~ all by himself *(the best)*; he is several ~es better than his opponent.

class *vt* ~ an animal as a mammal; do you ~ a bat as a bird? ~ a book as a novel.

classify *vt* (1) please ~ these specimens as A, B or C; these words are ~ied according to their inflectional endings; the books on this shelf are ~ied by subject. (2 *AE assign a degree of secrecy*) the F.B.I. ~ied the information 'top secret'; this is ~ied (information); the ~ied documents were finally recovered intact.

clean *adj* (1) ~ hands / clothes / shoes / *etc*; a ~ room / street / *etc*; scrub the floor ~; brush a coat ~; → make *vt* 1e. (2 *not used*) ~ linen; a ~ plate / sheet of paper; put on a ~ shirt / collar; put ~ sheets on the bed (3) lead a ~ life; have a ~ (police) record *(one without faults)*; a ~ bill of health; make a ~ *(new)* start (4 *simple, even*) a sharp knife makes a ~ cut; ~ timber *(without knots)*; a car with ~ lines (5 *skilful*) a ~ blow / stroke.

clean *adv* (1) the bullet went ~ through his shoulder; he threw the ball ~ over the roof; the island had been blown ~ out of the water. (2) I ~ forgot to ask him about it; the prisoner got ~ away.

clean *vt* (1) ~ one's hands / nails / shoes / *etc*; have a suit (dry) ~ed *(chemically)*; □ ~ one's plate (up) *(eat everything)* (2) modern sinks ~ easily *(can easily be cleaned)*.

clean down ~ ~ the walls / a car.

clean out (1) ~ ~ a box / drawer / cupboard / room / attic / one's pockets; ~ ~ a ditch; ~ ~ a womb *(medically)* (2) be ~ed ~ *(inform: have no money)*.

clean up ~ up an attic / desk *(tidy it)*; ~ up after a picnic; ~ up one's homework *(AE finish it)* (2) ~ up a town *(end corruption)* (3 *inform*) they ~ed up a tidy sum by selling their tickets at a high price just before the concert.

clear *adj* (1 *free from what is unwanted*) the air and the water were ~; crystal-~ water(s) / air / sky, skies; ~ eyes; a ~ skin / complexion *(no blemishes)*; a ~ sky / day; ~ weather; a ~ flame / fire (without smoke) / light; shine / burn ~ly; a ~ view; a ~ path; is the road ~ *(no obstacles)*? keep the road ~ (of snow); the roads were ~ of traffic; ~ glass / crystals; hang / stand ~; □ the coast is ~ *(there's no problem)*; a ~ conscience; he remained ~ of any suspicion; in the ~ *(innocent)* (2 *distinct, pure*) a ~ voice; the ~ note of a bell / trumpet; a ~ pronunciation; speak loud and ~; speak ~ly *(also fig: on difficult topics)*; ~ly visible / audible; sing ~ly; ~ hearing / sight; see / hear (s.th.) ~ly; a ~ reflection in the water; a ~ photograph / mirror; ~ handwriting / print; write ~ly; in ~ *(not in code)*; the outlines of the ship were ~ against the sky; it was dark but I could distinguish the house ~ly. (3 *entire, with nothing taken away*) three ~ days; a ~ month; a ~ (profit of) £80; a ~ majority of ten votes; gain a ~ win/ victory (over an opponent) (4 *at a safe distance*) get ~ of a danger; stand ~ of the gates; keep ~ of the machinery / another ship / the coast / that fellow / difficulties; he works hard, but he can't get ~ of debt. (5 *free from doubt, difficulty*) a ~ statement / explanation / definition / indication / proof / decision; ~ provisions of a contract; a ~ idea / thought; a ~ recollection of s.th.; have a ~ conception / notion / idea of s.th.; give a ~ answer; expressed in ~ terms; state / express / prove s.th. ~ly; express o.s. (more) ~ly; tell me ~ly what you want; the case still isn't ~; a ~ case of bribery; make one's meaning / o.s. ~; make s.th. ~ to s.o.; I made it quite ~ to her that she ...; get s.th. ~ in one's own mind; a ~ mind / head; a ~ style; it is ~ that (he is lying); is that ~ (to you)? it became ~ to him that (he was wrong); see one's way ~ (6 *certain*) he is not ~ about it himself / on this point; I am not quite ~ what you mean / as to what you expect me to do; he was quite ~ that (it should not have happened).

clear *adv* the bullet went ~ through the door; the prisoner got ~ away; cut s.th. ~ off.

clear *vt* (1) ~ a liquid; the storm ~ed the air; the wind ~ed the landing-field (of fog); ~ a street / entrance (of snow); ~ a desk; ~ the table (of dirty dishes); ~ a letter-box several times a day; ~ a room of furniture (→ clear out 1, 2); they ~ed the field of stumps; ~ a canal of / from obstruction; ~ the ground *(cut down trees etc)*; ~ a country of bandits; the judge gave orders to ~ the court; ~ port *(leave it)*; □ ~ the decks (for action) *(get a ship ready for a fight; get ready for any struggle, activity)*; ~ cargo / a ship / luggage *(get free by payment of dues)*; ~ luggage through customs; ~ one's throat (2) ~ snow from the streets; ~ things out of a room / attic / cupboard / *etc*; ~ the furniture out of a room; ~ all that rubbish out of the greenhouse. (3 *pass without touching*) he can ~ (a height of) 6 feet; ~ a hurdle / hedge / fence / gatepost; our car just managed to ~ the truck. (4) ~ five dollars (on s.th.); ~ expenses *(make enough money to pay expenses)*; ~ a debt *(settle it)* (5) ~ one's reputation; the President's decision ~ed the air / atmosphere; the evidence ~ed him; ~ s.o. of blame / guilt / an accusation / a murder charge; ~ one's mind of doubt / cant. – *vi* (6) the liquid has ~ed; the clouds ~ed; the sky / it / the weather is ~ing; the channel ~ed when the ice melted. (7) → clear out 3. (8) the situation has ~ed.

clear away (1) ~ ~ snow (from roads); ~ ~ the dirty plates / tea-things (2) the clouds / mist soon ~ed ~; the thunder has ~ed ~. (3) ~ ~ doubts / suspicions / difficulties.

clear off (1) ~ ~ litter (2) ~ ~ a debt (3) ~ s.o. ~ *(send away)* (4) the clouds have ~ed ~. (5) the boys ~ed ~ when they saw the farmer; now then, ~ ~!

clear out (1) ~ ~ a desk / cupboard / wardrobe / room / stable / drain; be ~ed ~ *(have no money left)* (2) ~ ~ the furniture (→ clear *vt* 2); some boys were ~ed ~ by an attendant. (3) the gang ~ed ~ fast; they told her to ~ ~; now then, ~ ~ (of here) quickly.

clear up (1) the wind has ~ed up the sky / weather. (2) it / the weather is going to ~ up; the sky has ~ed up; it may ~ up by morning. (3) ~ up a room / attic / one's desk (4) ~ up the rubbish / litter; ~ up after the children; we need a few volunteers to ~ up after the fête; I have some unfinished work to ~ up before I ... (5) her face ~ed up as she read the letter. (6) ~ up a mystery / problem / mistake / questions / matter / case; ~ up difficulties / all doubts; the case / situation has ~ed (itself) up.

clever *adj* (1) a ~ workman; he was ~ with his fingers / a saw / his pen; he is ~ at drawing animals / making model aeroplanes / handicrafts / making excuses. (2)

be ~ at one's lessons / mathematics; a ~ salesman (3) a ~ book / speech / solution / excuse / trick.

climate *n* (1) a marine / maritime / mediterranean / temperate / tropical / subtropical / extreme / continental ~; a mild / genial / moderate / agreeable / even / equable / curative / healthful / (un)healthy / (un)wholesome / (un)favourable / unfriendly / sickly ~; a wet / rainy / damp / cold / frigid / severe / rigorous / rough / harsh / inclement / trying / warm / hot / torrid / *etc* ~; the ~ does not suit / is not good for his health; the ~ does not agree with his health. (2) the intellectual ~ of the Enlightenment; a ~ of opinion; the political ~.

climb *vt* (1) ~ the stairs / steps / mountain; have you ~ed the Zugspitze? (2) ~ (up) a tree / rope / ladder / wall (3) roses / ivy ~ed (up) the wall. - *vi* (4) ~ on all fours (5) ~ out of / into bed; ~ over obstacles / through a window / into the chest / *etc* (6) the road ~ed steadily; mercury ~s in a thermometer; the needle of the speedometer ~ed to 90 miles an hour; the aircraft ~ed to (a height of) 40,000 feet. (7) ~ to fame / success; ~ to the head of the class.

climb down (1) ~ ~ (a ladder / mountain / *etc*) (2) ~ ~ in one's demands.

climb off ~ ~ a horse / *etc.*

climb up → climb *vt* 2, 3; ~ up to the summit; ~ up on to a wall.

cling *v* (1) patches of mould clung on the wall; dew drops were still ~ing on the trees; mud ~s to our shoes; wet clothes ~ to the body; the vine ~s to the wall; the monkey clung to the branch. (2) the boat clung to the coast *(did not go far from it).* (3) they saw someone ~ing on to the chimney; a boy clung on to the back of the carriage; the child clung weeping to its mother. (4) ~ to old ideas / traditions / superstitions / memories / hope / a straw; the party will ~ to their leader.

clock *n* (1) an eight-day / church / grandfather('s) / alarm / time ~; wind (up) / set (right) / regulate a ~; set a ~ going that ~ is (five minutes) fast / slow - I'd better put it back / forward; put the ~ on / ahead one hour (for Summer Time); put the ~ back *(also fig: take reactionary measures)*; the ~ won't go / stops / has run down / wants winding (up) / keeps time / is slow / is quite right / strikes the (full) hour / is out of order. (2) it's five o'~ (a.m. / p.m.); what o'~ is it? □ work round the ~ *(all day and night)*; □ work against the ~ *(work fast to finish before a certain time).*

clock *vt* ~ a race / s.o.'s time (in a race); he ~ed an average of 110 mph.

clock in / out what time did you ~ in / out today *(on a time clock)*?

close *vt* (1) ~ the window / door / box; when I came near, he ~d the door on me; ~ the door on (further negotations / *etc*); fallen rocks had ~d the old mine opening; ~ a gap (2) ~ a road to motor traffic; ~ a park / a church to the public (3 *bring to an end*) ~ a letter; ~ a discussion / debate / speech / meeting / chapter / list / book; the Peace of Westphalia ~d the Thirty Years' War; he apologized - the incident was ~d; ~ a bargain; ~ an account *(pay what one owes and cease buying)*; ~ the books (4 *bring together*) the troops ~d their ranks *(also fig).* - *vi* (5) many flowers ~ at night; the door ~s easily; the (lid of the) suitcase won't ~. (6) the theatres have ~d for the summer; when do the bars ~? (7 *come to an end*) I ~ with best wishes for your health; the meeting ~d at 5 o'clock; the financial year ~s on April 1; his career ~d with this incident. (8 *come together*) the wound has not yet ~d; the curtains ~d at the end of the play; the grave has ~d over him; at last the water ~d over the sinking ship / her head. - *adj* (9) his fists were ~d; ~d circuit *(in TV / electronics)* (10) the conference took place behind ~d doors; most of the shops are ~d on Sundays. (11) the ~ing days of the year.

close about darkness / the mists ~d ~ *(surrounded)* us.

close down (1) the works have been ~d ~ for two months. (2) the shop ~d ~ after a week (through lack of business); the newspaper ~d ~; the radio station ~s ~ at midnight.

close in (1) the days ~ in *(become shorter)* in winter. (2) the enemy / mist ~d in on us *(came nearer)*; the police are ~ing in on the criminal.

close up (1) the house has been ~d up for several years; he ~d up shop and retired. (2) can you ~ up a bit *(sit / stand closer)*?

close with (1) ~ ~ *(accept)* an offer; he made me quite a reasonable offer, so I ~d ~ him. (2) ~ ~ an opponent *(come within striking distance).*

close *n* at the ~ of (the) day / the year / the season / the century; towards / by the ~ of the 19th century; bring an undertaking / war / speech to a ~; the year / his life is drawing to a ~; day had reached its ~.

close *adj* (1) there's a bus-stop ~ to the school; the ship keeps ~ to the coast; an ibis is very colourful at ~ range; fire at ~ range; as ~ together as bungalows in a suburb; in ~ combat; in ~ proximity *(almost touching)*; a ~ view; they are ~ on us *(will catch us soon)*; cut the lawn ~; a ~ shave (→ 6); run s.o. ~ *(be nearly equal to him)* (2) the end is now ~; he is ~ (up)on sixty; it was ~ (up)on midnight; one calamity followed ~ on another. (3) a ~ weave / piece of cloth; cloth of ~ texture; ~ writing; ten ~ly written pages; a ~ thicket; live in ~ quarters *(crowded space)*; draw the curtain ~! (4) plants in ~ rows; a ~ly fitting / ~-fitting jumper; ~ly fitting windows; a ~ lid; she drew her coat more ~ly about her; he held her ~ly, kissing her tenderly. (5 *stuffy, oppressive*) it's rather ~ in here, let's open the window; the air / this room is ~; ~ weather (6 *fig, esp: intimate*) ~ friends / relatives / colleagues / friendship / co-operation / connection / relationship; a ~ resemblance / correspondence between them; resemble one's father ~ly; these incidents are ~ly connected; entertain ~ relations with s.o.; come into / keep (in) ~ contact with s.o.; it cost me ~ *(BE)* on / *(AE)* to £100; □ a ~ thing / call *(almost an accident / failure)*; □ a ~ shave *(narrow escape)* (7) it was a ~ finish / race / *(the runners were nearly equal)*; a ~ contest / game / match / election; a ~ly contested election (8 *strict*) the prisoner was under ~ guard / ~ly guarded; keep s.o. a ~ prisoner; keep a ~ watch on s.o.; watch s.o. ~ly; ~ confinement; a ~ blockade / siege; a ~ *(strictly guarded)* secret (9 *thorough, precise*) ~ examination of s.th.; examine s.th. ~ly; make a ~ study / investigation of s.th.; after ~ consideration; (make) a ~ analysis / translation of s.th.; give s.o. one's ~ attention; a ~ reading; listen ~ly; a ~ observer; I am following the matter ~ly; her belongings were ~ly inspected; a argument; ~ reasoning (10) keep / lie ~ *(hide)*; keep s.th. ~ *(keep it secret)*; s.o.'s ~ *(secretive)* habits / disposition; be ~ about s.th. (11) be ~ *(stingy)* with one's money (12) a ~ scholarship *(restricted to certain candidates)*; ~ season *(when certain animals may not be shot, etc)*.

close *adv* (1) he parked ~ to the kerb; he stood ~ to the door; we sat / stood ~ together / against the wall; a man was standing ~ by; he lives ~ to / by the river; he came ~ up to me; follow ~ behind; sail ~ to the wind *(almost against it; fig: almost break a law)*; shave ~; the lid fits ~; ~ shut (2) the elections are ~ at hand. (3) keep ~ to the original; this success brings us ~r to final victory.

cloud *n* (1) the top of the mountain was covered with / hidden under ~; it will be rather warm with variable ~; ~s drift / sail / fleet / chase / gather / thicken / tower; the sky is overcast with low ~s; the ~s are lifting / high; a fluffy / fleecy / filmy ~; black / dark / heavy / ominous / rainy ~s; □ have one's head in the ~s *(be a dreamer)* (2) a ~ of insects / flies / gnats / locusts / mosquitoes / arrows / horsemen; a ~ of dust / sand / smoke / steam (3) a ~ of grief / hate / suspicion; □ be under a ~ *(under suspicion, in disgrace)*; □ have a ~ on one's brow *(look worried)*.

cloud *vt* (1) the sun was ~ed; smoke ~ed the air; mud ~ed the water; her eyes were ~ed with tears. (2) grief ~ed his mind; anger ~ed his face. - *vi* (3) the sky / it is ~ing over. (4) his brow ~ed (over). - *adj* his mind became ~ed; a ~ed look (on one's face).

coal *n* natural / fat / lean ~; white ~; live ~s; a live / hot ~ fell on the carpet; haul / mine / extract / produce ~; put more ~ on the fire; □ haul / rake / call / drag s.o. over the ~s *(scold severely)*; □ heap ~s of fire on s.o.'s head *(return good for evil)*; □ carry ~s to Newcastle *(do s.th. superfluous)*.

coarse *adj* (1) ~ cloth(ing) / material / fabric / paper / stockings / (kinds of) pottery / wire; a ~ thread / yarn / bristle / wire / needle; a ~ sieve / brush; ~ skin / complexion / features / hands (2) a ~ grain / particle; ~ gravel / sand / sugar; grind s.th. ~(ly) (3) ~ food / fare / fish / bread; a ~ meal (4) ~ language / words / speech / jokes / laughter / manner / tastes; a ~ man / fellow; be ~ of speech.

coax *vt* (1) ~ a baby to eat / a child to take its medicine; ~ s.o. into / out of doing s.th. (2) ~ a smile from the baby; ~

money / a secret out of s.o.; she could not ~ the keys out of him / him out of the keys. (3) ~ a fire to burn; ~ (up) the fire; ~ a key into a lock; ~ a kitten down a tree; ~ smouldering twigs into flame.

coffee *n* (1) ground / roasted / weak / strong / black ~; ~ with milk / cream; a cup / pot of ~; (double-)filtered ~; make / brew some ~; make (o.s. a cup of) ~; have / drink a cup of ~ (2) three black and two white ~s, please! (3) morning ~; have / ask s.o. in for (afternoon) ~.

coin *n* gold / silver / copper ~s (fresh from the mint); current / ancient ~(s); a heap of ~(s); souvenir ~s; false / counterfeit ~; change this pound note for ~; □ pay s.o. back in his own ~.

coin *vt* (1) ~ money / medals / gold; □ be (virtually) ~ing money *(make money fast)* (2) ~ a (new) word / phrase / expression.

coincide *v* (1) this carriageway has two different numbers for the stretch where two roads ~. (2) their holidays ~ this year; his holiday ~s with hers. (3) your interest and mine ~; the story ~s with the facts; his tastes and habits ~ with those of his wife; your statement does not ~ with his; the judges did not ~ in opinion.

cold *adj* (1) ~ weather / water; a ~ day / night / climate; a ~ meal / dishes; feel ~; I am ~; my hands are ~; it is getting ~er; it was bitter(ly) ~; the weather is still / remains ~; don't let the soup get / go ~; a ~ shiver ran down my spine; he was seized / filled with ~ dread; knock s.o. ~ *(unconscious)*; break out in a ~ sweat (2) a ~ reception / welcome / greeting / look; have a ~ heart; a ~ beauty; the ~ splendour of the palace; ~ colours; look ~ly at s.o.; a ~ly calculating person; that idea / person leaves me ~; he refused with a ~ smile; be ~ towards s.o. / to an appeal; → blood 2.

cold *adv* (1 *AE inform: totally*) be turned down ~; he was ~ sober. (2 *AE inform: abruptly*) he quit the job ~.

cold *n* (1) damp / dry / icy / severe / intense / biting / piercing / nipping / pinching ~; the (mid)winter ~; in the bitter ~; I mind the ~ less than the heat; feel the ~; he left me standing in the ~; be shivering with ~; ten degrees of ~; produce ~; □ be / feel left out in the ~ *(ignored)* (2) have a ~; catch (a) cold; you may catch (your death of) ~ if you go out without a coat; a bothersome ~; catch ~ from the draught; he caught a bad ~ yesterday; → take *vt* 13; a cold in the nose / head; a head-/ chest-cold; protect o.s. from ~s.

coldness *n* (1) the ~ of the day / winter / climate / room (2) the ~ of s.o.'s manner / tone / smile; there was a certain ~ in his manner; the ~ of my reception.

collapse *vi* (1) the roof ~d under the weight of the snow; a blood vessel that ~d (2) some tables and chairs ~ / can be ~d; a telescope that ~s (3) the negotiations ~d before a settlement was reached; she ~d into tears; if you work too hard, you(r health) may ~; his plans ~d; the price of silver ~d. – *vt* (4) the explosion ~d several buildings.

collect *vt* (1) ~ the papers / the exercise-books / money (from the class); ~ one's letters from the post office; luggage is ~ed from the station; he went to ~ his suitcase; ~ a child from school / one's car from the garage (2) ~ stamps / coins / shells / *etc* (3) ~ taxes / rent / contributions; ~ votes / news / statistics / data / facts (4) ~ an army / all the pupils (in the hall) (5) ~ one's thoughts / ideas / courage / energies; it was good to have an hour to ~ oneself. – *vi* (6) a crowd ~ed at the corner; water ~s in ditches; dust ~ed on the shelf; flies ~ on food. – *adj* (7) the ~ed works of T. S. Eliot (8) he was calm and ~ed when he entered.

collect in the teacher ~ed in the exercise-books.

collect up two pupils ~ed up all the exercise-books.

collide *vi* (1) while trying to overtake, the lorry ~d with a sports car; cars are likely to ~ on that turn. (2) your ideas ~ with his; if the aims of two countries ~, there may be war.

colour *n* (1) a warm / cold / pure / broken / deep / rich / gay / cheerful / lively / glowing / bright / strident / violent / dirty / muddy / dead *(no gloss)* / neutral / pale / dull / dark / light / loud / luminous / gaudy / garish ~; harmonious ~s; a reddish-brown / horrible greenish / *etc* ~; what ~ is (his car)? it is an unusual ~; the apples were a beautiful ~; a fast *(not fading)* colour; obtainable in all ~s; sparkle / flash / shine all ~s (2) there isn't enough ~ in the picture; a film / magazine in ~; photograph in ~; her dress resembles yours in ~. (3) water-~s; oil-~s; mix / blend ~s; □ paint the future in glowing / bright / dark ~s *(make it appear (un)favourable)*; □ see s.th. in its true ~(s) *(as it really is)*; □ see everything in rosy ~s (4) have a good / healthy ~; be / look a bad ~; have a high ~ *(red cheeks)*; she has very little ~ *(is pale)*; lose ~ *(become pale)*; change ~; regain ~; indignation / the walk brought the ~ to his cheeks; be / feel off ~ *(not very well)* (5 *a certain appearance*) his story has some ~ of truth; give / lend ~ to (a story); his absence gave ~ to the rumours of his disgrace; I don't like the ~ of those remarks; newspapers often give a false ~ to the news they report; a novel with a local ~; a local-~ novel / short story; he stole money under ~ *(with the pretext)* of making investments for clients. (6 *~s: flag; armed forces*) the ~s of a regiment / political party; captured ~s; a salute to the ~s; serve with / join the ~s; rally / hasten / hurry to the ~s; follow the ~(s); with ~s flying; (pass an exam) with flying ~s; → come off 7, through 3; □ sail under false ~s *(be an impostor)*; □ desert one's ~s; □ show one's true ~s; □ stick to one's ~s *(not change one's opinion, party)*.

colour *v* (1) ~ a picture / wall / *etc* green / brown / *etc*; ~ metal / glass / food; water ~ed with a purple dye; ~ed by hand (2) the leaves have begun to ~; he ~ed (with embarrassment). (3) ~ a story (to make it more exciting); views ~ed by prejudice.

colour up her face / her cheeks / she ~ed up.

comb *vt* (1) ~ one's hair; ~ hair / a dog (through) (2) ~ an area (for a missing person / *etc*).

comb out ~ ~ the weaker applicants; ~ ~ a government department *(get rid of inefficient personnel)*.

combat *vt* (1) ~ the enemy / an opponent / disease / an epidemic / evil / error; ~ a proposal / principle. *-vi* (2) the ship ~ed with the wind and waves.

combine *vt* (1) ~ colours / systems / processes / qualities; a ~d radio and TV set; ~ one's efforts (to solve a problem); ~ forces (to defeat the enemy); ~ work with pleasure. - *vi* (2) oil and water do not ~; hydrogen and oxygen ~ / hydrogen ~s with oxygen to form water; the two businesses have ~d; many factors ~d to produce that result; everything ~d against him.

come *vi* 1 - 10; 12 - 14; *vt* 11
The patterns are grouped as follows: personal subjects: 1, 7; non-personal subjects; 2, 4, 5, 6, 7; *fig* use: 3; ~ + *adj*: 9; ~ + *n*: 10; ~ + *inf*: → come to do; ~ + *part*: 12; ~ = that has come, when ... has come: 13; ~ + *prepos*: after 4, 5; from 2, 3, 7; of 7, 8; out of 8; ~ across / at / before / by / down / for / into / off / on / over / through / to / under / upon: → separate entries.

(1 *used of persons, not fig*)
he will ~ tomorrow; ~ late / early / home; will you be ~ing home soon? ~ this way! they came with him part of the way; I saw him ~ing along the road; ~ by car / train / bus / tram; the postman has ~ for his Christmas box; they came for help; what has he ~ here for? as we rounded the bend we came in (full) view of the lake; ~ into a room / the garden; I came *(fell)* on my head / feet; ~ out of a building; ~ out of prison / hiding; he came round the corner / across the field; will you ~ / be ~ing to Paris on your trip? I can't ~ to your lecture; will you ~ to the cinema with me? ~ with me! I'll ~ and see you next week; ~ and show me what you have done.

(2 *used of things, not fig*)
has the post ~ yet? this letter came yesterday; the train will ~ in 20 minutes; the wind ~s from the west; cold weather / a thunderstorm is ~ing; the coat / dress ~s in all sizes.

(3 *approach, happen, fig*)
a noise came from the next room; the news came as a surprise to me; all things ~ to those who wait; a new idea came to me; it came to me that he was unwell; the answer came to him in the bath; his answers came softly / hesitantly; when temptation ~s; such opportunities never ~ my way: if failure ~s your way be a man and show that you can take it (→ way *n* 11); take life as it ~s; when the time / hour ~s; the years ~ and go; and then the war came; this event came later; this has ~ at just the right moment (for me); □ ~ home to s.o. *(affect him closely)*; the arguments ~ home forcibly; lies / follies / curses ~ home to roost *(will take effect on the liar etc)*; □ (the invitation) came out of the blue *(was unexpected)*; □ he came out of the clouds *(was surprised)*.

(4 *expressing sequence*)
first ~s a flower shop and then a bank;

first ~s a violin concert and then ...; what ~s first? thunder ~s after lightning; the time will ~ when ...; joy will ~ after sorrow; the speaker then came to the problem of ...; when your turn ~s, do your best; the family must ~ first; for many people money ~s before honour; baronets ~ before knights; the best is yet to ~; in years to ~ *(future years)*; the life to ~ *(in the next world)*.
(5 *have its place*)
Tuesday ~s after Monday; May ~s between April and June; on what page does that ~? the explanation ~s at the end; it ~s under another heading; this book ~s under Non-Fiction; this department will now ~ under the Research Unit; that doesn't ~ within my province / responsibility / jurisdiction.
(6 *reach, extend*)
her hair ~s (down) to her shoulders; windows ~ing right down to the floor; the water ~s up to my chin; a bullet came within a foot of my head.
(7 *originate*)
this wine ~s from Spain; the only light came from a small candle; he ~s from Kent; she ~s of / from a good family / of mixed blood; geniuses can ~ from the most ordinary families; the word ~s from (the) Latin; all these rumours ~ from the same source.
(8 *be the result of*)
what has ~ of your application? this accident ~s of your carelessness; that ~s of being lazy; that's what ~s of trusting people; if anything is to ~ of the plan, we ...; nothing is likely to ~ of it; nothing ~s of nothing; nothing came out of all his talk; what will ~ out of the committee's discussions, no-one can say; □ ~ of age *(reach legal age)*.
(9 *come + adjective*)
the liquid is ~ing green; the handle has ~ loose; a garment / envelope ~s open; the sewing came apart; the boat came adrift; ~ clean *(also fig: reveal the facts, inform)*; the prisoner did not ~ clean; it all came right eventually; things ~ cheap / expensive; it ~s dear to buy things in small quantities; it ~s cheaper if you have a season ticket; the dead things seemed to ~ alive; his dreams came true; that sort of thing ~s natural to her; it ~s natural to birds to fly; it ~s easy with practice; his payments came short of *(were less than)* my expectations.
(10 *come + noun: pretend to be, give the impression of*)
amongst strangers she always tried to ~ the fine lady; he'd better not try and ~ the schoolmaster with me; don't ~ the young innocent / old soldier / heavy father; don't ~ the bully over me; he tried to ~ the virtuous over me.
(11 *come vt: try, act, do; inform*)
don't ~ that game / those tricks! he won't ~ any of his nonsense here; don't ~ it *(put on airs, boast)*; that's ~ing it a bit strong *(is going too far)*.
(12 *come + present / past participles*)
he came running / walking / stumbling (along); the arrow came flying through the air; the train came roaring along; a dress / knot / string / packet ~s undone; your shoe-lace / the sewing has ~ undone; the flap of the envelope has ~ unstuck; the seam came unstitched; □ our plans have ~ unstuck *(inform: failed)*.
(13 *that has come, when ... has come*)
this castle is a child's dream of fairyland ~ true; Kuwait - this is the never-never land ~ true; we shall have lived here ten years ~ Christmas; "how old are you?" "forty-five ~ Saturday"; she can be a tomboy in shorts on the tennis court in the afternoon and a siren in tulle ~ nightfall; its aim is to wash 63 million Americans into the polling booths, ~ next November 4.
(14 *come + infinitive:* →come to do *below*).

come about how did that ~ ~ *(happen)*? a situation / quarrel / war ~s ~; how does it ~ ~ that he ...?

come across (1) we came ~ the Alps by car. (2) the thought came ~ my mind that he ... (3) in the library I came ~ / upon an old manuscript *(by chance)*; ~ ~ a friend (4 *come across with: inform: pay money owing; give information; give what is wanted*) let's go out to dinner - John came ~ with the $30 he owed me; the suspect came ~ with the names of three accomplices; Jim came ~ with the tools I needed to fix the car.

come after → come 4, 5.

come along (1) ~ ~ (with me / us)! we're having a party next week - you'll ~ ~ to that, won't you? (2) her business is ~ing ~ very well; "how's the novel?" "it's ~ing ~ slowly." (3) ~ ~ *(hurry up)*!

come around *(AE)* → come round.
come at (1) it was too high for me to ~ at. (2) the thieves came at him *(attacked)* from the shadows. (3) the truth is often difficult to ~ at.
come away (1) you're too near the stove – ~ ~! ~ ~ from the stove. (2) the knob of the wireless set came ~ in my hands.
come back (1) when will he ~ ~? ~ ~ from the war; he came ~ a changed man. (2) ankle-length skirts have ~ ~. (3) he came ~ with a stinging reply. (4) now that you mention his name, the whole story ~s ~ to me; his name will ~ ~ to me soon.
comeback *n* (1 *return to former success*) make / try / attempt a ~; the singer tried a ~ after 5 years of retirement. (2 *retort, repartee*) the comedian is known for his fast / snappy / biting / *etc* ~s.
come before (1) → come 4. (2) the complaint will ~ ~ the United Nations Assembly next week; ~ ~ a judge.
come by (1) → come 1. (2) did you see anyone ~ by? (3) his paintings are hard to ~ by *(obtain)*; he came by a few thousand through his uncle; money that is easily ~ by is lightly valued. (4) how did you ~ by that scar on your arm? how did he ~ by his death *(what caused it)*? ~ by one's death through taking foolish risks.
come down (1) ~ ~ the mountain / river / stairs; ~ ~ from the tree / a ladder; she came ~ (the stairs) to greet us; just look at the rain ~ing ~; □ (when he was given the bill) he came ~ to earth with a bang / bump; → come 6. (2) this custom ~s ~ from our ancestors; the only manuscript of this author that has ~ ~ to us; ~ ~ to modern times (3) cotton came ~ yesterday *(became cheaper)*; I hope they will soon ~ ~ in price. (4) the quality of that firm's goods has ~ ~ in recent years. (5) when did he ~ ~ from Oxford *(graduate, leave)*? (6) ~ ~ from generalities to particularities (7) ~ ~ in the world *(lose social position)*; he had ~ ~ to begging. (8 *inform*) my uncle came ~ handsomely *(made a generous gift of money to me)*; I had to ~ ~ with £5 to her favourite charity. (9) ~ ~ with the measles / a bad cold / *etc* (10) you will have to ~ ~ on one side or the other – you can't just sit on the fence; ultimately, the Lord Chancellor came ~ heavily on Lord N.'s side. (11) ~ ~ on s.o. for the slightest fault *(criticize severely)*; examiners ~ ~ pretty heavily on mistakes in spelling. (12) the authorities have ~ ~ on me for the payment of £20 income tax.
comedown *n* the politician's sudden ~ was a shock to the voters; he experienced one ~ after another.
come for (1) → come 1. (2) a dog dashed out of the gate and came ~ *(attacked)* us.
come forward will no one ~ ~ as a candidate? the police asked witnesses of the accident to ~ ~; no one came ~ to give evidence.
come from → come 2, 3, 7.
come in (1) please ~ in and sit down; the train came in early; the rain came (in) through the window; the tide is ~ing in; the trumpet came in on the wrong note / at the wrong time. (2) the slowest runner ~s in last in a race; which horse came in first? (3) Saturday came in wet; the New Year came in with heavy snow storms; summer came in early last year; it is ~ing in foggy; it's ~ing in quite chilly now. (4) law and order came in with the new sheriff; nylon stockings came in soon after the end of the war; beards are ~ing in again. (5) if the Democrats ~ in *(are elected)*, we … (6) they have £40 ~ing in monthly; are your royalties still ~ing in well? (7) where do I ~ in *(what's my share, duty, advantage)*? that's where you ~ in. (8) that suit will ~ in *(be useful)* for the school play; those old dusters may ~ in for polishing the car; don't throw it away – it may ~ ~ useful / handy for something or other. (9) he came in for *(inherited)* several thousand through an uncle; ~ in for a fortune (10) the system came in for some criticism; when she opens the letter and reads it, she'll ~ in for a shock.
come into (1) → come 1; □ ~ ~ the world *(be born)*; tears came (in)to the child's eyes; an idea suddenly came ~ my head. (2) ~ ~ bud / leaf / blossom / flower *(begin to bud, etc)* (3) ~ ~ collision *(collide)*; ~ ~ contact (with s.o.); ~ ~ possession (of a large estate) (4) ~ ~ existence; the aeroplane did not ~ ~ being until gasoline engines were invented; ~ ~ fashion / vogue / (general) use / usage / prominence *(become prominent)*; ~ ~ effect / force / power; ~ ~ play *(become active)*; ~ ~ question *(be discussed)*; ~ ~ sight; as we rounded the bend the lake came ~ view; ~ ~ the picture *(fig: appear)* (5) when

her uncle died, she came ~ a fortune / a lot of money. (6) □ ~ ~ one's own *(get the recognition, prosperity one deserves)*; when Father is tired of entertaining his guests the film projector ~s ~ its own – it cannot tire; it was not until the mid-twentieth century that psychology really came ~ its own.

come near (1) when I came ~ (to) him, I ... (2) the army came ~ obtaining a complete victory; she had ~ very ~ hating him; I had ~ ~ to forgetting; this came ~ convincing him.

come of → come 7, 8.

come off (1) this button has just ~ ~ (my coat); paint / dirt / a wheel / a stain ~s ~ (2) ~ ~ a bicycle / horse *(fall)* (3) now, you boys, ~ ~ it *(stop it)*! (4) ~ ~ it *(stop pretending)*, darling - you can't mean that! now, ~ ~ it, Harry - we've heard that tale before. (5 *take place*) in the not too distant future a general election is ~ing ~ in Germany; the concert ~s ~ next week; this journey never came ~. (6 *emerge*) you came ~ lightly in the accident; in an interview for a post it is often the person who knows how to set out his stall that ~s ~ best; how did you ~ ~ under your uncle's will? the concert came ~ well; who came ~ best *(won)*? you have ~ ~ much better than I have in this deal. (7 *succeed*) the experiment did not ~ ~; the plan was a gamble but it came ~; if all his ideas had ~ ~, he...; ~ ~ with flying colours *(achieve great success)* (8) that comedy ~s ~ tomorrow *(is taken off)*.

come on (1) → come 1. (2) he came (up)on the cabin while wandering through the woods; I came (up)on the missing portrait quite by chance. (3) you go first – I'll ~ on later; the actress came on (the stage), dressed as a queen. (4) ~ on, help me! ~ on, don't be angry! ~ ~ (hurry up), I'm tired of waiting. (5 *make progress*) how is your garden ~ing on? the strawberries are ~ing on; the students have ~ on well this term; how are you ~ing on at your new job? (6 *start*) night came on; it came on to rain; the rain came on worse than ever; he said he felt a cold ~ing on. (7) 'Macbeth' is ~ing on again next month. (8) the light will not ~ on - the bulb has gone. (9) when does the case ~ on for trial *(will the court deal with it)*?

come-on *(AE inducement)* the company offered a set of teaspoons as a ~ to anyone who bought a new set of dishes; that gift is just a ~ to get you to spend a lot of money.

come out (1) can you ~ ~ for a walk? (2) the sun / stars came ~; the buds came ~ in spring; most spring flowers came ~ later than usual this year. (3) he came ~ third in the final test; John came ~ top of his form in his examination. (4) she came ~ when she was 17 *(was presented in society)*. (5) the miners came ~ in sympathy *(went on strike)*; ~ ~ in rebellion against s.o. (6) when did the book / the new edition ~ ~? new films ~ ~ every year. (7) your photos always ~ ~ better than mine; you have ~ ~ well in / on that photograph; he always ~s ~ well *(photographs well)*. (8) these ink stains won't ~ ~ *(be removed)*; the stains will ~ ~ in the next wash. (9) will the colour ~ ~ *(fade)* if the material is washed? (10) her hands came ~ in a rash; she came ~ in a rash / in spots. (11) her foul temper came ~ again in her child; his arrogance ~s ~ in every speech he makes. (12) the total ~s ~ at 97 *(is 97)*; the totals came ~ (in)correctly; the equation wouldn't ~ ~; I can't make this sum / equation ~ ~. (13) if the truth ever ~s ~ ...; the matter would never have ~ ~ if he had not been so careless; it came ~ they had been secretly married for years; everything ~s ~ in time. (14) ~ ~ with a new model / a statement / a question / a suggestion; he came ~ with the information that her brother was in prison; he came ~ with some vile oaths; if anything bothers you ~ ~ with it; he came ~ with the most extraodinary ideas.

come over (1) could I ~ ~ and see you for a few minutes? he came ~ to England for the summer. (2) John came ~ to our side during the debate. (3) a change suddenly came ~ him; a look of terror came ~ his face; suddenly a great weakness came ~ him; it came ~ me that he was unwell. (4) the sky came ~ cloudy; soon after midday it came ~ very dull; as we were crossing the moors it came ~ misty / chilly / dark. (5 *inform*) as I was walking along the street, I came ~ dizzy; ~ ~ sleepy / drowsy / faint / queer / feverish.

come round *(AE: around)* (1) → come 1; the road was blocked so we had to ~ ~ by the fields. (2) the two of them came ~ to see me yesterday; I shall be free to see you if you ~ ~ about 7 clock; could I ~ ~ and see you for a few minutes? how early does the paper boy ~ ~ in the morning? (3) I am always glad when pay-day ~s ~; well, the holidays have ~ ~ again; late duty for each member of the staff ~s ~ every ten days. (4) ..., but now I've ~ ~ to your point of view; they finally came ~ to my way of thinking; he has ~ ~ *(accepted).* (5) she fainted but soon came ~ / to; we waited for her to ~ ~ / to(→ come to 8).

come through (1) the carnival procession will ~ ~ here. (2) the rain is ~ing ~ (the roof) in my room. (3) we thought he would die of this disease, but he came ~ it; she has just ~ ~ a serious illness; he has ~ ~ two world wars; he came safely ~ the war; ~ ~ with flying colours (→ come off 7). (4) for all his city manners the farmer in him is always ~ing ~.

come to (1) → come 1, 3, 4. (2) the title came *(fell)* to the younger son. (3) that ~s nearest / closest to the correct solution; ~ to completion / an end / a bad end / a standstill; he has ~ to the end of his money; ~ to an agreement / understanding (with s.o.) / decision; ~ to terms; to ~ to the point: what do they want? (4) the bill ~s to 15 dollars; his earnings ~ to £1,000 a year. (5) the thing came to pieces *(brokc)* in his hand; he will ~ to grief with that motor bike of his; the children had ~ to no harm; no harm will ~ to you; ~ to blows *(begin fighting)*; he will ~ to heel *(will obey)* if tackled in the right way; ~ to power; ~ to one's senses / to oneself *(become conscious, sensible)*; ten minutes after the accident he came to his senses; I hope he will soon ~ to his senses and behave more wisely; he will never ~ to *(attain)* much; ~ to little / nothing (6) ~ to s.o.'s ears / knowledge / notice; new evidence has ~ to light; he just grabbed the first thing that came to hand and ...; as soon as any information ~s to hand we will pass it on to you. (7) it won't ~ to that; we hope it will not ~ to war; if it / the worst ~s to the worst, we ...; when it ~s to a pinch he lets you down; ~ to a head (→ head *n* 5); what will all this agitation ~ to? what his explanation ~s to is that we can expect no further help from him; when it ~s to mathematics, I'm completely at sea; if it ~s to building, Austins are the firm you should consult; when it ~s to your turn, do your best; when it ~s to telling others about it, she is silent; when it ~s to paying he usually disappears; when it ~s to the weekend I am tired out. (8) when he came to, he found himself in the ward of a hospital (→ come round 5).

come to do (1 *inf expresses purpose*) I only came to say hallo; he often ~s to see me; she is ~ing to dine with us tonight. (2 *come in simple tenses: happen*) ... and that is how the calf came to be named Nora; how did you ~ to hear the news? now that I ~ to think of it, ...; it came to pass at that time that ... (3 *come in simple or continuous tenses; gradually*) when I came to know them better, ...; they came to have a real affection for him; he came to be a famous man; two new forms of entertainment were ~ing to occupy the Englishman's spare time. (4 *come in perfect tenses: now*) the Smiths have ~ to live in the house opposite; the word has ~ to be used *(is now used)* that way; I have come to believe that we ...; I have ~ to see the problem in another light; he had ~ to be a good violinist; the jet airliner has ~ to stay *(will not disappear).*

come under (1) → come 5. (2) ~ ~ s.o.'s notice / influence.

come up (1) ~ up and take a look at the bedroom. (2) an attendant came up and offered us a catalogue of the exhibition; a beggar came up to us and asked for money; s.o. ~s up to the counter / table / *etc*; I can see Ann ~ing up the path; a signpost / the station should be ~ing up *(~ into sight)* soon; ~ up to town *(travel to town)*; in this way the enemy came up on us from the rear. (3) the daffodils will be ~ing up soon; the seed never came up at all. (4) a matter / question ~s up (at a meeting); the case ~s up tomorrow; when they first ~ up *(go to university)*, most students are impressed by the freedom of university life. (5) ~ up against *(meet)* difficulties / opposition (6) the snow came up to the roof (→ come 6). (7) no other dramatist ~s up to Shakespeare; his second novel did not ~ up to his first / to our expectations; ~ up to scratch *(inform: reach the required standard)*; this book ~s up to my idea of ...; these goods do not ~ up to the mark *(are inferior to the samples).*

come upon (1) he came ~ the announcement in the newspaper; in digging a well he came ~ a vessel with old coins; →

come on 2, come across 3. (2) I came ~ him as he was stealing the eggs; the natives came ~ us in the night. (3) fear came ~ us; the disaster that came ~ them.

comeuppance *(inform: deserved punishment)* she gave him his ~ by refusing to see him again; just wait and see - you'll get your ~!

comfort *n* (1) sympathy from friends is a real ~ to anyone in trouble; that news brought great ~ to her; I have found ~ in doing my duty; seek ~ (in s.th.); □ (take) cold ~ *(poor consolation)* (in / from s.th.) (2) ointment on a burn gives some ~; it's a ~ to know that she is safe. (3) an open fire gives a feeling of ~; although they are not rich, they live in (comparative) ~; look after the ~ of one's guests (4) the pioneers had few of the ~s of life; the hotel has every modern ~ / all modern ~s; do / go without one's accustomed ~s.

command *n* (1) give / issue / carry out / obey / follow a ~; do s.th. at/by s.o.'s ~; ~s rang out across the parade-ground; on the ~ 'go!' the runners shot away from their marks; your wish is my ~. (2) be in / take over / hand over / assume / take ~ (of an army); the army is under the ~ of General X; he has a hundred men under his ~; the Minister of Defence has supreme ~ over the armed forces; exercise ~ over s.o.; I am at your ~. (3 *troops*) the officer inspected his ~. (4) have a good ~ of French; have ~ of one's temper; he has no ~ over himself; he offered me all the money at his ~.

command *vt* (1) he ~ed the troops to march forward; he did what / as I ~ed him (to do); ~ silence (2) a captain ~s his ship and men; ~ an army (3) the vast manpower which the Soviets can ~; ~ unlimited capital (4) ~ one's temper / passions / emotions / o.s. (5) integrity ~s respect; in his office Sir Douglas ~s great loyalty; his sufferings ~ sympathy. (6) rare books often ~ a high price; no other singer ~s her huge fees; ~ a high salary (7) the fort ~s the town / the entrance to the harbour; this window ~s a fine view; the house ~s the whole bay. - *vi* (8) God ~s and man obeys.

comment *n* (1) ~ on the day's / week's events / on the week; have you any ~s (to make) on the proposal? no ~ (required); you can keep your ~s to yourself. (2) there was much ~ about the plans for a new church; her strange behaviour caused a good deal of ~.

comment *vi* (1) ~ on political / economic / *etc* events; ~ on a proposal / a plan / *etc*; ~ on a literary text / the Bible / *etc*; everyone ~ed on the good food. - *vt* (2 *AE annotate*) ~ a poem / novel / *etc*; he ~ed the new edition of N's works.

commit *vt* (1) ~ a blunder / (grave / unforgivable) error (of judgment) / sin; ~ a crime / offence (against s.o.); ~ murder / suicide / adultery / frightful atrocities (2) ~ a patient to a hospital; ~ a man to prison (for an offence) (3) ~ s.o./ s.th. to s.o.'s care; ~ the management of an estate to an agent; when one is ill, one has to ~ o.s. to doctors and nurses; ~ one's soul to God; ~ s.th. to memory *(learn by heart)*; ~ s.th. to writing / paper; ~ to the flames *(burn, cremate)* (4) ~ s.o. / o.s. to an undertaking / proposal / scheme / course of action; if you have the goods on approval, it does not ~ you to buying them; we cannot ~ ourselves to paying whatever he may ask; he ~ted himself to support his brother's children. (5) don't ~ yourself (by saying something rash).

common *adj* (1 *belonging to many*) parks in a town are ~ property; the ~ land; ~ pasture; these characteristics are ~ to all mammals; the C~ Market; be on ~ ground with s.o. *(in a dispute)*; make ~ cause with s.o.; have ~ interests / ideas (2 *wide-spread, general*) daisies are ~ / the daisy is a ~ flower in England; the ~ violet / nightingale / house-fly / *etc*; ~ salt; it is a ~ thing for families to have a TV set; a ~ practice; a ~ expression / belief; it is a ~ error to think that man ...; it is ~ knowledge that he ...; → sense *n* 4; our party wants ~ welfare; labour for the ~ good; the ~ weal; by ~ consent; a ~ nuisance *(a nuisance to everybody)* (3 *frequent*) motor accidents are becoming more and more ~; political disturbances have been ~ in Europe during recent years; a ~ saying / phrase; that is ~ly said. (4 *average, ordinary*) the ~ man / people / spectator; a ~ sailor / beggar / thief / criminal; ~ phenomena / ideas; ~ courtesy; a ~ make of goods; he is a man of no ~ mind / ability. (5 *vulgar, bad*) ~ manners / behaviour / speech; a ~ accent / appearance; her way of speaking is so ~ / downright ~; he looks rather ~; behave / dress ~ly.

common *n* all mammals have these characteristics in ~; have interests in ~; all that we own in ~; they have nothing in ~ with one another; in ~ with most Bavarians he is very fond of beer; out of the ~ *(unusual).*

company *n* (1 *being together with others*) I shall be glad of your ~ on the journey; she was shy in the ~ of strangers; keep / bear s.o. ~ (→ bear *vt* 11, keep *vt* 8d); seek s.o.'s ~; she is always seen in his ~; I travelled in very pleasant ~; I gave her a dog for ~; he also took a piece of cake, just for the ~; I was sorry to part ~ with him; plague, in ~ with famine, killed almost half the population. (2 *guests*) we're expecting ~; my ~ came for dinner; I saw some more ~ *(visitors)* arriving; we do not see much ~. (3 *persons with whom one spends one's time*) know / judge s.o. by the ~ he keeps; the trapper lived alone and had little ~; be in / keep good, bad ~; get into bad ~; he soon found suitable ~; he is good / excellent / poor / bad ~ *(a good etc companion).* (4 *group of people*) he addressed the assembled ~; a ~ of players / actors; a ~ (of soldiers) (6) a railway / insurance / limited liability ~; a theatrical / repertory ~.

compare *vt* (1 *state the resemblances of*) he ~d life to a game of skill; ~ a girl to a rose / s.o.'s teeth to pearls / sleep to death; Shakespeare ~d the world to a stage. (2 *examine to find out the similarities and / or differences between*) ~ this cloth with that, and it will be obvious which is the better quality; ~ your solution with the equation on the blackboard; ~ Homer with Virgil; ~d with / to him I am a bungler; most working people are well off ~d with what they were in the 1930's; in a nation where conditions, ~d to those of most European countries, are decent ... (3 *admit of comparison with*) 5 billion for public education ~s rather poorly with the 18 billion spent on automobiles; how does your new car ~ with your old one for petrol consumption? there is no publication with a circulation-density to ~ with that of the Radio Times. (4 *consider as good as*) this one is not to be ~d with the other where quality is concerned; this wine can be ~d with the best claret; as an actor he cannot be ~d with his brother. *-vi* (5 *be considered as good as*) this wine can't ~ with last year's; art cannot ~ with nature; his house ~s (favourably) with the best in town.

comparison *n* make / draw a ~ between two things; the ~ of the heart to a pump / between the heart and a pump, though wrong, is a very common one; a ~ of one car with another; we mustn't carry this ~ too far; there is no ~ between (a hi-fi and an ordinary gramophone); an ordinary gramophone won't / can't stand / bear ~ with a hi-fi one; this one costs more, but is really cheaper by ~; the tallest buildings in London are small in ~ with the skyscrapers of New York.

compensate *vt* (1) ~ s.o. for an injury / damage / loss; the firm will ~ them for working overtime; ~ evil with good. - *vi* (2) nothing can ~ for the loss of one's health; glasses ~ for weaknesses of the eye; his good qualities ~ for his shortcomings. (3 *psychol: counterbalance a weakness or unwanted characteristic*) small men sometimes ~ by being especially agressive; tall women may ~ by stooping slightly.

compete *vi* (1) ~ (hotly) in a race / contest; ~ with others / against an opponent for a prize / award / position; ~ for export markets (2) we cannot hope to ~ with *(equal)* so experienced a team; we cannot ~ with such prices.

complain *vi* (1) bear one's pain without ~ing; ~ of nausea / a headache / a pain; ~ of ill treatment / the cold; the customer ~ed to the manager of the discourtesy of an assistant; she is continually ~ing about the neighbours; ~ about the bad weather; she ~ed to me about this injustice; I have nothing to ~ of; I can't ~. (2 *report*) ~ to the police / *etc* against / about s.th. - *vt* (3) he ~ed that he never had enough money; "you're always watching soccer games on the telly," she ~ed.

complaint *n* (1) be full of ~s about s.th.; bear one's pain without ~; I have no ~s to make; I have no cause / grounds for ~; he has never given me the slightest cause / grounds for ~; her eternal ~s; lodge / make a ~ (against s.o. / with s.o.) (2) my chief ~ is the high cost of living; its poor light was their only ~ against the office. (3 *illness*) he is suffering from a heart / liver / stomach ~; general ~s.

complete *vt* (1) ~ one's work; ~ a task / book / investigation; every year the earth

~s its circuit of the sun. (2) buy stamps to ~ one's collection; travel ~s an education; this ~s my happiness.

compliment *n* (1) a polite / nice / sincere / dubious / clumsy / left-handed / idle / empty / hollow ~; pay s.o. a ~; the guests paid the hostess many ~s on her cooking; fish for ~s; that's the greatest ~ I have ever been paid; may I return the ~? my ~s! (2 *~s: greetings*) (give) my ~s to your wife! with the ~s of the season *(at Christmas).*

comply *vi* ~ with (s.o.'s) request / orders / instructions / demands; ~ with the rules / regulations; he asked us to be quiet and we ~ied.

compose *vt* (1) ~ a song / symphony / opera / sentence / letter / essay / speech / *etc*; ~ a painting / menu / dish (2) ~ type / copy / an article (3) ~ a quarrel / dispute / difference (4 *calm*) ~ s.o.'s fears / mind / passions / thoughts; ~ yourself! the girl ~d herself before she spoke; ~ one's features / face *(make them look calm)* (5) a machine is ~d of many parts; the parts that ~ the whole; bronze is ~d of copper and tin; our party was ~d of teachers and parents. – *vi* (6) he is a writer and also ~s. (7) ~ing machine / room.

comprehend *vt* (1) I heard his speech but did not ~ his meaning; a child can apprehend the distinction between right and wrong, yet a philosopher cannot ~ it in its fullness. (2) education ~s the training of many kinds of ability; science ~s the study of chemistry, physics and biology; it is the aim of science to find universal law, to ~ all experience in a closed system; Webster's Dictionary had to be brought up to date to ~ these vast changes.

comprise *vt* the house ~s a living-room, a kitchen, a bathroom and two bedrooms; these two books ~ all the best poems by that author; his course of study ~s English, French, European history and mathematics; his philosophy ~s all the various trends of thought current in his time; what is ~d in the collection? this month's figures are ~d in the total.

compromise *vi* (1) we cannot ~ with such people; I can't ~ on fundamentals / in matters of faith and conscience. – *vt* (2) ~ one's reputation / good name / o.s.; several leading politicians could be ~d by the publication of these photos; she ~d herself publicly by this affair. (3 *endanger*) the position of the army was seriously ~d by the general's mistake.

conceal *vt* a house is hidden by foliage – the bird's nest is artfully ~ed; he held a telegram ~ed in his hand; ~ a book / scar / bad odour / *etc*; ~ one's intentions from s.o.; language was given to men to ~ their thoughts; there was no ~ing from herself the fact that she loved Jim; people often laugh to ~ their shame or shyness.

concede *vt* (1) ~ a point in a debate; ~ s.th. as true; everyone will ~ that 2 and 2 make 4; he was unwilling to ~ the supremacy of any group; I ~ that I have made a mistake. (2) ~ a right / privilege / advantage to s.o.; ~ s.o. access / free passage / a right / *etc*; ~ a rise in wages (3) we cannot ~ any of our territory. – *vi* (4) after evaluating his poor defences the chess player ~d (defeat) to his opponent.

conceive *vt* (1) ~ an idea / plan / scheme / trick / purpose / plot (against the king) / wicked trap / *etc*; he was the first man to ~ the idea of jet-propelled rockets; a building badly ~d and carelessly constructed (2) ~ a liking / dislike for s.o.; ~ a profound prejudice against s.th./ an aversion to s.o. (3) I can't ~ why you allowed / of your allowing the child to travel alone; I can't ~ where he has gone / that this course is expedient now; I ~d that there must be some difficulties; he cannot ~ that anyone would have stolen his painting. – *vi* (4) can you ~ of such a situation? I can't ~ of his ever agreeing to come along; he could never even ~ of such a bizarre plan / scheme / *etc.*

concentrate *vt* (1 *direct towards a common centre*) ~ troops in an area / along the banks of a river / at a seaport; ~ gunfire on a town; the general ordered the bombing (to be) ~d on the industrial areas; ~d fire; the American motor industry is ~d around Detroit. (2) ~ (one's attention) on a problem / one's work; ~ (all) one's efforts / thoughts / energies on doing s.th. (3) ~ a liquid / juice (by removing excess water); ~d orange / grape / *etc* juice. – *vi* (4 → 1) the troops ~d near the station / port / *etc.* (5) he ~d on studying for his examinations; ~ (up)on the work at hand; ~ upon the magician's hands and you will see how ...

concern *n* (1 *matter*) this is no ~ of yours; what ~ is it of yours? mind your own ~s; he is always meddling in my ~s; you should drop the whole ~; the switchboard and the motorcar, the building of a crèche and a reactor are our daily ~s - by these we act and live. (2 *deep interest, worry*) the health of our children, their education and upbringing are our constant ~; he did not show much ~ in it; ... institutions whose fortunes he follows with close ~; my chief ~ is his refusal to work; the mother's ~ over her sick child kept her awake all night; feel / express ~ about, for s.o.'s safety; be filled with ~; look at s.o. in ~; express ~ at s.o.'s absence (3) he has a ~ *(share)* in the business / industry. (4 *firm*) invest one's money in a promising / flourishing / rising ~; the shop is now a paying ~ *(one that makes profits)*; a going ~ *(one successfully in operation, not merely planned)*.

concern *vt* (1) this matter does not ~ you; the question ~s you closely; To Whom It May C~; the persons / parties ~ed; there was hearty applause for all ~ed; those ~ed personally must...; as ~s (the price / this question / me)...; as far as (the price / this question) is ~ed; as far as I am ~ed; where the law is ~ed, you cannot plead ignorance in excuse of your conduct; you are in no way ~ed in the business; the business does not ~ you in any way; a question in which the whole world is ~ed / which ~s the whole world; we are all ~ed in his fate. (2 *involve*) he is said to have been ~ed in the crime / riot / conspiracy. (3) don't ~ yourself with other people's affairs / such trivial matters; he is ~ed with the discovery of a new drug. (4 *worry*) his unhappy fate ~ed me a great deal; please don't let my illness ~ you; be ~ed about the future / s.o.'s health / s.o.'s safety / *etc*; the doctor is very ~ed about him; his father was very ~ed about his poor behaviour; be ~ed at s.o.'s absence / a sign of danger; everybody was ~ed at the news; I am ~ed at his delay - I hope he has not met with an accident; politicians seem ~ed over the possibilities of a Conservative failure. (5 *take care of the welfare of, be anxious to secure*) all the political parties keep on saying how deeply ~ed they are for the housewife; wildfowl are an economic asset, so that Governments are ~ed for their numbers and conservation; be ~ed for s.o.'s safety; a good employer should be ~ed for the welfare of his workers.

conclude *vt* (1) ~ a speech / lecture / sermon / meeting / conference / session (2) ~ a purchase / sale; ~ a peace treaty / an agreement (with s.o.) (3) the jury ~d from the evidence that the accused man was not guilty; ~ s.th. from s.th. - *vi* (4) he ~d by saying that he .../ with a prayer; the meeting will probably ~ without any solution of the problem.

conclusion *n* (1) bring a matter to a satisfactory / happy ~; at the ~ of the winter term; the ~ of the concert / trial / evidence; write a ~ to an unfinished novel; in ~, I should like to thank... (2) ~ of a treaty / agreement (3) draw a ~ from evidence / data; I have come to the ~ that he ...; what ~ did you reach in your discussion? arrive at a ~; □ a foregone ~ *(s.th. already settled)*; → jump *vi* 1.

concur *vi* (1 *agree*) ~ with a person in his opinion / view; ~ with a person's opinion / plan / view (2 *approve jointly*) ~ in a plan; both firms ~red in raising the prices of their products; they ~red to raise the prices of ... (3 *occur at the same time*) unfortunate coincidences ~red to keep the lovers apart.

condemn *vt* (1) ~ s.o.('s conduct) / an act / a method / *etc*; we all ~ cruelty to children. (2) ~ s.o. to imprisonment / prison (for robbery); he was ~ed to death for murder. (3) by his sickness he was ~ed to (complete) inactivity; the millions are ~ed to toil with their hands. (4 *declare unusable*) the house was ~ed as unfit for habitation; ~ meat as unfit for consumption; this old bridge ought to be ~ed; the road was ~ed and closed to travel. (5 *declare hopelessly ill*) he got well again, although the doctors had ~ed him. (6 *show s.o.'s guilt*) his looks / words ~ him. (7 *declare public property*) ~ smuggled goods; merchant ships captured in war are often ~ed.

condition *n* (1) the hurricane left the town in a chaotic ~; butter in a liquid ~; be in good / excellent / poor ~; all these cars are in good / running ~; he is in good / healthy ~; he's in no ~ to travel; get in *(good)* ~ for an athletic event; have a car put in *(good)* ~; the living ~s of the people; unable to come under existing ~s; under those ~s, I'm in favour of going. (2) agree to / accept / reject s.o.'s ~s; on what ~ will you agree? you must on no ~ tell him what has happened; I will go, on one ~; I will go on ~ that you ...;

they said they would not go back under any ~(s); mother made it a ~ that we should finish our homework before we could watch TV; healthy sleep is a prime ~ of good health. (3 *ailment*) a skin / eye / pathological / ulcerous / *etc* ~ (4 *social rank*) medieval serfs were of low ~; persons of every ~ / all ~s.

condole *vi* I ~ with you upon the loss of your mother; he ~d with me in my loss; the play seems a waste of N's acting talents - one ~s with him.

condolence *n* a letter / visit / expression of ~; please accept my ~s; offer s.o. one's (sincere) ~s.

conduct *vt* (1) ~ s.o. round / through a museum; ~ed tours; ~ s.o. to his seat / room; ~ s.o. in / out (2) ~ business / public affairs; ~ an expedition / campaign / business; ~ an orchestra / choir; who is ~ing (the orchestra)? (3) gutters ~ rainwater; these wires / cables ~ electricity / a current of 20,000 volts; ~ heat / light / sound (4) he ~ed himself well / with patience and tact; he knew how to ~ himself in an emergency.

confer *vi* (1) mother ~red with the teacher about my stuttering; ~ with one's lawyer. - *vt* (2) ~ a title / knighthood / honour / medal / (academic) degree / right / privilege (up)on s.o.; ~ benefits (up)on s.o. (3) carbon ~s hardness upon steel; the only thing that ~s stability on the earth is the fact that it is not quite spherical; the National Health Service has ~red tremendous benefits.

confide *vt* (1) she ~d her problems to her sister; she ~d to me that she ... (2) ~ a secret / valuables / documents to s.o. - *vi* (3) ~ in God / a friend; the safest way to keep a secret is to ~ in no one; is there nobody he ~s in? you can ~ in his honesty.

confidence *n* (1) place entire / the utmost / every ~ in s.o.'s honesty / skill / judgment; I have ~ in your ability to pass the test; enjoy / share the ~ of s.o.; I'm telling you this in (strict / the strictest) ~; take s.o. into one's ~; I don't put much ~ in what he says. (2) although he is poor, he is full of ~; his ~ makes him a fine actor; he answered all the questions with ~; no one can say with ~ what the outcome will be. (3 *secret*) the two girls sat in a corner exchanging ~s.

confine *vt* (1) ~ one's studies to one field; ~ s.o.'s authority (to) within certain limits; we are ~d to our senses for perceiving the world; ~ your remarks to the main issue; I shall ~ myself to saying that we ...; ~ o.s. (strictly) to the subject (2) a cold ~d her to her bed; she was ~d to bed with a cold. (3) it is cruel to ~ a lark in a cage; be ~d within the four walls of an office all day.

confirm *vt* (1) ~ a report / rumour / suspicion; ~ news / s.o.'s fears; his answer ~ed my opinion of him; this information ~s my belief that (he is to blame); experience has ~ed his theory; he will ~ that I have spoken the truth; this is to ~ that Mr N ... (2 *make definite, legal*) ~ an appointment / nomination / decision / deed / contract; the court of appeal has ~ed the judgment. (3) ~ a (customer's) order; I ~ with thanks your order; I herewith ~ my telephone order for ... (4) ~ s.o. in a resolution / desire / opinion; this information ~s me in the belief that (he is to blame).

confront *vt* (1) ~ s.o. with a letter / document / witness / demand / *etc*; ~ s.o. with facts / reality; ~ the accused with the witness; ~ two witnesses; when ~ed with the evidence he admitted his guilt; he found himself ~ed with an unexpected difficulty. (2) ~ the enemy boldly; a soldier has to ~ danger. (3) my house ~s his. (4) the difficulties that ~ us seem insuperable; the problems and hardships ~ing the pioneers; he entered the room, to be ~ed by a scene of confusion.

congest *vt* (1) holiday traffic ~ed the roads; ~ed streets, corridors; streets ~ed with traffic. - *vi* (2) his lungs are ~ed (with blood).

congratulation *n* offer / send / express one's (sincere / hearty / cordial / heartfelt) ~s (on s.th.); please accept my (belated) ~s.

connect *vt* (1) ~ a railway coach to a train; ~ a lamp to a battery (2) a bus line ~s the two towns / town A with town B; the towns are ~ed by a railway; ~ me with number 255, please; ~ telephone subscribers (3) he is ~ed with the Smiths by marriage; he is well ~ed *(has important relatives)*. (4) ~ names with faces; ~ several things in one's mind; the police do not ~ the knife with the murder; do people still ~ America with 'unlimited possibilities'? he is ~ed with the textile industry. - *vi* (5) the two parts do not ~ properly; this pipe ~s with the sewer; two ~ing rooms; this train ~s at L. with the steamship; does this train ~ for Leeds?

connection *n* (1) how long will the ~ of the new telephone take *(joining the house to the exchange)*? (2) a broken ~ in a pipe; the ~ between the radio and the battery (is broken) (3) have good / no ~s (with s.o.); make use of one's ~s; enter into ~s with s.o.; family ~s; establish business ~s; open up a business ~ with a firm; break off all ~s (with s.o./ a firm) (4) a bus ~ ; a train runs in ~ with another train; this train has a ~ with / to Bern; I only just got my ~ at Munich; get one's *(telephone)* ~ (with s.o.) (5) the ~ between two ideas / cause and effect / French and German literature; a close ~ between two facts; Goethe's ~s with Italy; in this / that ~; there are difficulties in ~ with the text. (6) the major is a distant ~ of the Millers. (7 *customers*) he set up in business and soon had / established a good ~; that dressmaker has a good ~ among the well-to-do women of the town.

conquer *vt* (1) ~ an adversary / enemy / country; ~ new territory / the world; the conquerors and the ~ed (2) ~ one's temper / feelings / passions / will; ~ a bad habit / s.o.'s will / difficulties. - *vi* (3) I came, I saw, I ~ed; ultimately one or the other must ~.

conscience *n* have a clear / good / tender / guilty / bad ~ (about s.th.); his ~ bothers / troubles / torments / worries him; my ~ pricked me; pangs / pricks / doubts / the voice of ~; follow the prompting of one's ~; act according to / against one's ~; have s.th. on one's ~; that takes a weight / load off my ~; I cannot reconcile this with my ~; in (all) ~ *(truth)* I must admit ...

consent *n* (1) give / refuse / withhold one's ~ (to s.th.); he gave his ~ for the marriage to take place; get / obtain s.o.'s ~ (to do s.th.) (2) be chosen / elected by common / general ~; with one ~ *(unanimously)*; silence gives ~.

consequence *n* (1) inevitable / unpleasant / serious / grave / far-reaching ~s; face / bear / accept / take the ~s; suffer the ~s of one's carelessness; the (immediate / direct) ~ of this was that he ...; that will not be without ~s; her decision is bound to have its ~s; we hadn't enough money to pay our bus fare, and in ~ we had to walk; in ~ of his illness / her father's death (2 *importance*) a man of ~; a matter of no ~; is it of any / much ~? (3) it follows as a *(logical)* ~ that A equals B.

consider *vt* (1) ~ a matter / offer / *etc*; we have ~ed all the possibilities carefully; the company is ~ing his claim; ~ the risk (of doing s.th.); ~ how difficult it is to ...; I have seriously ~ed accepting the offer; a ~ed reply / statemant / proposal / judgement (2) you must ~ his youth / that the child is only ten years old; ~ the expense / the risk / s.o.'s feelings; late applications cannot be ~ed. (3) they ~ him / he is ~ed innocent; I ~ this matter settled; he ~s himself lucky; ~ yourself at home / under arrest.

consideration *n* (1) after much ~ he decided which car to buy; careful ~ of (a proposal); this problem needs (serious) ~; (an offer) worth(y of) ~; read a book with ~; take circumstances / conditions / facts / *etc* into ~; we must take into ~ that he ...; his application cannot be given ~; ~ of his application is out of the question; the matter is at present under ~; leave s.th. out of ~ *(neglect it)*; after / in ~ of his blameless past we forgive him; he agreed to turn witness for the prosecution in ~ of some very favourable guarantees. (2) he turned down the radio out of ~ for his neighbours; he had no ~ for anyone's feelings; show ~ for others / s.o.'s old age; treat s.o. with ~ (3) weigh all ~s; several ~s have influenced me in coming to a decision; time is an important ~ in this case; their welfare is his first ~ (4 *reward*) do s.th. for a ~.

consist *vi* (1) his meal ~ed of bread and cheese; his fortune ~s mainly of shares; the programme ~ed of three plays. (2) the difficulty ~s in the fact that we ...; true happiness ~s in making others happy; what does beauty ~ in?

constitute *vt* (1) twelve things ~ a dozen; the parts that ~ the whole; his house and factory ~ his entire estate; enough players to ~ a team (2) the child ~s her whole happiness; the murder ~d our main topic of conversation; we must first decide what ~s nationality; the qualities that ~ a hero; that ~s a precedent; ~ an obstacle (3) the meeting ~d him chairman; the will ~d him guardian of the estate; ~ o.s. a judge of s.th. (4) ~ a public body /

committee / *etc* (5) he is so ~d that he needs very little sleep / can accept insults without getting angry.

construct *vt* (1) ~ a building (of wood, stone, concrete) / bridge / machine / aeroplane / ship / factory / road / barometer / *etc*; a model ~ed from odds and ends of metal (2) ~ a phrase / sentence / argument / plan / triangle (on base AB) / theory / drama; a well-~ed novel.

construction *n* (1) the ~ of a bridge / *etc*; several roads are under / in the course of ~. (2) the department store is a huge ~ of steel and glass. (3) the new factory is of very solid ~. (4 *interpretation*) don't put a wrong ~ on his statement / action; he always puts a bad ~ on my remarks; he denied that his broadcast could bear any such ~. (5) his alibi is a carefully wrought ~, but not a word of it is true.

consult *vt* (1) ~ a lawyer (on a point of law) / a doctor (about one's health) / one's friends / one's bankers; ~ a map / dictionary / time-table / oracle; ~ one's conscience (2 *consider*) I always try to ~ my mother's wishes; we must ~ his convenience *(not inconvenience him)*. - *vi* (3) the doctors ~ed before operating; ~ with one's colleagues.

consume *vt* (1) ~ provisions / ammunition / food / fuel; ~ one's time / life / fortune; ~ all one's energies (2) he ~d everything we put before him. (3) the flames / fire ~d the old barn. (4) ~d with envy / hatred / jealousy / curiosity / ambition / desire / grief. - *vi* (5) ~ away with grief (6) a ~ing desire for s.th.

contact *n* (1) be / get / keep / remain in (close) ~ (with s.o./ s.th.); come / bring into ~ (with s.o./ s.th.); lose / establish ~ with s.o.; make ~ with a firm / one's neighbours (2) he has good ~s (in the food trade); he made many useful social ~s while he was in Canada; a ~(-man); Mr. Jones is your ~ in Rio. (3) make / establish ~ between two conductors of electricity; diseases transferred by immediate ~.

contain *vt* (1) this cupboard ~s books; the book ~s illustrations; that bottle only ~s water; some paints ~ lead; a substance ~ing arsenic (2) a book that ~s many truths / a good deal of information; 14 ~s 2 and 7; 5 is ~ed in 30 6 times. (3 *equal*) a quart ~s 2 pints; a yard ~s 3 feet; that bottle ~s a pint. (4) the crowd could scarcely ~ their excitement; he could not ~ his enthusiasm / indignation / anger; he could not ~ himself for joy.

contempt *n* (1) have / feel / show / display ~ for s.o./ s.th.; hold s.o. in ~; his foolish behaviour will bring him into ~; he fell into ~ as the result of his foolish behaviour; his action is beneath ~. (2) in ~ of all rules and regulations; ~ of court; do s.th. in ~ of death / danger.

contend *vi* (1) ~ with an opponent / obstacle / impediment / *etc*; ~ with ill health / adverse circumstances / hostile criticism; ~ with others for a prize / a lady's favours / *etc*; ~ for a seat in Parliament; in the war, the North ~ed against the South; ~ against vastly superior numbers (2) he ~ed that gambling was a far worse evil than drunkenness; English, she ~s, is the universal language; he is fond of ~ing about everything.

content *vt* (1) it was a dull job and did not ~ him; there's no ~ing some people. (2) ~ o.s. with a frugal meal; ~ o.s. with doing s.th.

content *n* (1) the gold ~ of a ring; the sulphur ~ of air; the fat ~ of milk (2 *capacity*) cubic ~; the ~ of a barrel / cask; a ~ of 40 gallons (3 *substance, gist*) the speech was well delivered, but had little ~; the ~ of a book / poem / report / article / speech / proposal; the play lacks ~; the inner / intellectual ~ (of a doctrine / literary work).

contents *n* (1) the ~ of a bottle / case / pocket / room / *etc* (2) the ~ of a book; the table of ~s. (3 *table of contents*) I cannot find his name in the ~.

contest *vt* (1) ~ a statement / point / will; ~ s.o.'s right to do s.th. (2 *try to win*) ~ an election / seat *(in Parliament)*; ~ a race / (sports) event; troops ~ed every foot of the battlefield. - *vi* (3) ~ with / against s.o./ s.th. for s.th.; New York was ~ing with New Orleans for first place among American ports.

continue *vi* (1) the forest ~s for miles; the desert ~d as far as the eye could reach; how far does the road ~? (2) the rain ~d all day / well into the night; I hope this wet weather will not ~; his speech ~d for another half hour; ~ on one's way; ... but then she ~d; he ~d calm during the trouble; ~ to be in poor health; ~ to be chairman; he hopes to ~ at school for two more years; prices ~d to rise; the illusion ~s that we ... - *vt* (3) we will ~ the game after dinner; ~ one's work / study / speech / journey / *etc*; ~ payments / negotiations / *etc*; ~ working / reading / *etc*; they ~d eating until they could eat no more; ~d effort / interest (4) a palisade ~s the wall; we ~d the hedge beyond the gateway. (5) "well," he ~d, "we can't. . .". (6) the town clerk was ~d in office.

contract *n* a ~ of purchase / sale / insurance; make / enter into / sign a ~ (with s.o. for s.th.); draw up / accept / approve / break / annul a ~; a ~ was signed between them; be engaged on a ~ (to supply s.th.); the ~ is null and void / has expired; bind o.s. by ~; work is done on ~; breach of ~; conditions of ~; the builders are under ~ to finish the work by the end of June.

contract[1] *vi* (1) ~ with s.o. to do s.th.; ~ to build a house; ~ with a firm for 1,000 tons of cement. - *vt* (2) ~ a marriage (with s.o.); ~ an alliance with a foreign country; ~ a friendship (3 *form, catch*) ~ bad habits / debts / a disease / an illness.

contract[2] *vt* (1) ~ a muscle / the brows / the forehead; ~ 'do not' to 'don't' (2 *reduce*) ~ expenses / efforts; his mind / faculties had become ~ed by disuse. - *vi* (3) metals ~ in cold weather; a rubber band ~s after it has been stretched; the chest expands and ~s. (4) the valley ~ed to a gorge.

contrast *n* (1) ~ often makes a thing seem more beautiful than it is when seen alone; colours / a picture lacking (in) ~ / full of ~ / rich in ~; his behaviour is in sharp ~ with his principles; the white figure stood out plainly in ~ with the dark background; in (marked) ~ to his brother, he was always very friendly. (2) what a ~ between them! a light / slight / striking / sharp / harsh / strange ~; the (direct) ~ of virtue and vice; form a (direct) ~ with s.th.; offer / present a ~; point out / notice a ~ between two things (3) she is a ~ to her shy husband; he was a great ~ to his predecessor.

contrast *vt* (1) ~ one thing with another / two things (with one another); the buyer ~ed the price of the two lamps; ~ his record with his promises. - *vi* (2) her black hair ~s (beautifully / strongly) with her white skin; these two colours ~ sharply with one another; his elegant clothes ~ed with his rough speech. (3) his actions ~ badly with his promises.

contribute *vt* (1) ~ money / one's share; ~ food and clothing for the refugees / the relief of the poor; ~ suggestions to a committee; ~ new information on a scientific problem (2) ~ articles / poems to a magazine; he ~d (feature articles) to the newspaper for several years. - *vi* (3) ~ to the Red Cross / the blood bank; ~ to a discussion; all the girls ~d towards a wedding present for Ann. (4) sunshine ~s to the health of the body; drink ~d to his ruin; good health ~d to his success; his war injuries ~d to his early death; everything ~d to make him happy.

contrive *vt* (1) ~ a scheme / means of escape / way to help / *etc* (2) ~ a new aircraft model; he ~d a unique safety device which can be installed in any kind of automobile. (3) ~ to live on a small income / to make ends meet; can you ~ to be here earlier? you must ~ to get over this difficulty; despite all the injuries on their team they ~d to win; he ~d to make matters worse *(unintentionally)*. - *vi* (4 *BE*) she finds it difficult to ~ *(manage her household)* when prices rise every month. - adj (5) the plots in X's novels are unnatural and ~d.

control *n* (1) get / gain / lose ~ over / of o.s./ s.th; exercise ~ over s.o./ s.th.; have / lose ~ of one's car; he has ~ / is in ~ of the stores; → take *vt* 17; he is under the ~ of a woman; children who lack parental ~; a teacher who has no ~ over his class; get / gain ~ over a horse; lose ~ of one's temper; keep one's temper / feelings under ~; ~ of one's emotions / passions; this dancer's ~ during his pirouettes is amazing; get flood waters under ~; the children were beyond ~ *(did not obey)*; circumstances beyond our ~; birth / wage / price / rent / foreign-exchange / traffic / weed / pest / air-pollution ~; thought ~ (2) (operate) the ~s of an aeroplane / car; at the ~s; the ~s of a wireless set.

control *vt* (1 *direct, command*) he knows how to ~ his horse; the coach ~s the health habits of the football team. (2) ~ one's temper / anger / passions / emotions; ~ yourself! (3 *regulate*) ~ prices; houses let at ~led rents; a crossing ~led by traffic lights; on a zebra crossing you have the right of way unless a police officer is ~ling traffic over it. (4 *verify*) ~ expenditure / payments / the accounts; ~ an experiment (5 *fight against*) ~ air pollution / pests / flies / *etc.*

convert *vt* (1) ~ water into steam / cream into butter / rags into paper / a bedroom into a sitting-room / securities into cash / pounds into francs; an old mansion ~ed for use as a guest house; monkeys in a roomy ~ed chicken house (2) missionaries ~ed everyone in the village; ~ s.o. to Christianity / Socialism; he became ~ed; this book ~ed him from pacifism. - *vi* (3) ~ to Christianity / Islam / *etc*; not until he was eighty did he ~.

convey *vt* (1) some trains ~ both passengers and goods; pipes ~ hot water from a boiler to all parts of a building; ~ equipment somewhere by truck (2) ~ an idea (through a gesture); ~ information / news / greetings / a message (to s.o.); words fail to ~ my feelings; her expression ~ed her disappointment; this statement / word / gesture / fact ~ed little / nothing / a great deal / an idea / an impression to him, his mind; what did his speech ~ to you? (3) air ~s sound and smell. (4 *transfer legally*) the estate was ~ed to his brother.

cook *vt* (1) ~ one's dinner; ~ a steak / joint / goose / *etc*; be ~ed alive in the tropics (2 *falsify*) ~ accounts / statistics / the evidence. - *vi* (3) the ham ~ed for an hour; these apples don't ~ well.

cook up *(inform)* ~ up a story / excuse / alibi / scheme; ~ up charges (against s.o.).

cool *adj* (1) a ~ day / evening / wind / summer; a ~ breeze blowing off the lake; ~ autumn weather; let's sit in the shade and get ~; keep ~ on a hot summer day; put something warm on, it has got ~er; the coffee isn't ~ enough to drink yet. (2 *providing a cool feeling*) a ~ dress / summer suit / room (3) give s.o. a ~ reception; his manner is very ~; she is ~ and reserved; her ~ manner made him suddenly insecure. (4) he remained ~ in the confusion; be ~ in the face of danger; he was very ~ outwardly; keep ~ / a ~ head in a crisis; keep a ~ head; weigh s.th. up ~ly; after ~ consideration; upon ~er reflection I think I could have done it alone. (5 *calmly impudent*) a ~ stare; ~ behaviour; □ a ~ customer (6 *inform: entire, full*) he lost a ~ million in that (business) deal.

cool *n* (1) the ~ of early morning / the evening (2) the ~ in her eyes was always disconcerting.

cool *vt* (1) ~ wine / the air / a wound; ~ the dessert in the fridge; ~ s.o.'s brow; eau de Cologne ~s and refreshes; ~ hot metal down / off (2) ~ s.o.'s love / zeal / friendship / enthusiasm / passion. (3 *inform*) ~ one's heels *(be kept waiting for a long time)*. - *vi* (4) the pies ~ed on the window sill; the wine / day / *etc* ~ed; the hot metal ~ed (down / off). (5) his love / zeal / friendship / enthusiasm / passion ~ed.

cooperate *vi* (1) ~ with friends in starting a newspaper; ~ with s.o. for a purpose; the two firms are ~ing in an / the attempt to find a cure for the common cold; if everyone ~s, the job will be finished sooner. (2 *contribute*) everything ~d to make our holiday a success.

cope *vi* ~ with (the burden of) one's work / difficulties / (the difficulties of) one's job; ~ with a situation (efficiently); ~ with danger / a problem / *etc*; he is too skilful, you can't ~ with him; the task looks a formidable one, but I think we can ~ (with it).

copy *n* (1) a (faithful / unfaithful) ~ of a picture / statue / dress / piece of furniture; a ~ of jewellery; a first / rough / fair ~ (of a letter / *etc*); the (hectographic) ~ of a drawing / *etc*; take / make a (true) ~ of a document; make two carbon ~ies of this letter. (2) a (new / second-hand) ~ of a book; he has two ~ies of that dictionary; an edition of 5,000 ~ies (3 *material to be printed*) the printers demand ~ at once; this news will make good ~ *(be an exciting story)*.

copy *vt* (1) ~ a letter / document / report / *etc*; ~ a design / drawing on to s.th.; ~ a text fair; ~ notes (out of a book) into a notebook; ~ s.th. down (from the blackboard); ~ out a letter *(copy it completely)* (2) ~ the answer / exercise (from another pupil); be punished for ~ing (3) ~ a painting / statue / (model) dress / design / invention; often ~ied, but never equalled (4) ~ the movements of a dancer; ~ s.o.('s style / manner); she tried to ~ the famous actress; you should ~ his good points, not his bad points.

corner *n* (1) a cozy / quiet / dark ~; look for s.th. in every ~; s.th. stands in the ~ of a room. (2) the ~ of a table / page / picture / box / field; the address is in the top left-hand ~ of the letter; the ~s of the book are worn; meet me at the ~ of the street; a shop situated on / at the corner;

he lives round the ~; go round / turn the ~; □ turn the ~ *(pass the critical stage)*; cut off a ~ *(take a short cut)* (3 *hidden place*) let's find a quiet ~ where we can talk; have a ~ in s.o.'s heart; hidden in odd ~s (4 *faraway place*) he has stamps from every ~ of the earth; the four ~s of the earth (5 *difficult situation*) the lawyer's question put the witness in a ~; in a tight ~; drive / put s.o. in(to) a ~.

corner *vt* (1) the cat ~ed the mouse. (2 *put into a difficult position*) when ~ed, he will fight; that question ~ed me; the escaped prisoner was ~ed at last. - *vi* (3 *turn a corner*) the car is sprung to ride smoothly and ~ safely.

correct *vt* (1) ~ a mistake / error / figures / statement / invoice / misconception / speech defect; ~ s.o.; ~ evils / abuses / s.o.'s pronunciation; ~ a watch by a radio time signal (2) ~ a test / exercise / translation; ~ the proofs (3) ~ a child for lying / disobedience / rudeness.

correspond *vi* (1 *be the same, be in harmony*) the prices quoted in your letter do not ~ with those given in the catalogue; his report does not ~ with the facts; the house exactly ~s with my needs; this interpretation does not ~ with the spirit of the treaty; his job ~s with his interests. (2 *be similar, adequate, equivalent*) the bird's wing ~s to the human arm; the French Sureté ~s to the British Scotland Yard; red lines on the map ~ to major roads; his expenses do not ~ to his income; fulfilment seldom ~s to anticipation; not all of these roads ~ to the needs of modern traffic. (3) we have ~ed (with one another) for three years.

cost *n* (1) the ~(s) of goods / transport / repairs / the damage; living ~s; the ~ of living (is continually rising); the ~ of houses has gone up; ~s are increasing all the time; production ~s; sell s.th. at ~ (price) *(at production cost)*; I'll let you have it below ~; he built his house without regard to ~. (2) the court ordered him to pay the ~s; the ~s of the action are met/ borne by the unsuccessful litigant; he had to pay a £20 fine and £5 ~s. (3) he got rich at the ~ of his health; he saved her from drowning, but only at the ~ of his own life; the battle was won at great ~ of life; (determined to win) at all ~s / any ~ *(whatever it may cost)*; know / have learned s.th. to one's ~ *(from bitter experience)*; □ count the ~ *(consider the risks involved)*.

cost *vt* (1) a car ~s a great deal of money; the books ~ 20 marks; these apples ~ (me) a dollar; smoking ~s him a lot of money; how much did it ~ (you)? we must manage it, ~ what it may / whatever it may ~. (2) making a dictionary ~s much time and care; s.th. ~s s.o. time / sweat / tears / no slight effort; it ~ her a lot to give in. (3) his negligence ~ him his job / life / reputation; the forest fire ~ the life of many animals; ~ s.o. dearly (4) the lawsuit / John's foolish behaviour ~ us many a sleepless night. (5 *estimate the cost of*) she ~ed the items and found that the total was within her means.

count *n* (1) a ~ showed that one boy was missing; the final ~ was 50 dollars; four ~s were necessary before we were certain of the total; keep / lose ~ of s.th. *(know / not know how many there are)* (2) take no / some / not much ~ of what people say; do you take ~ of such things? (3) he was found guilty on all ~s.

count *vt* (1) ~ 20; ~ eggs / marbles / *etc*; ~ days on one's fingers (2) he was ~ing his money / change; have the votes been ~ed yet? ~ heads / noses *(those present)*; □ ~ one's chickens before they're hatched *(be too hopeful of one's success)* (3) there were 50 people, (not) ~ing the children; I no longer ~ him among my friends; in this case anyone over 18 is ~ed as an adult. (4) I ~ myself fortunate in being here with you; I'm afraid we must ~ him as dead; I ~ it folly / a great honour (to do that); he is young and inexperienced, but do not ~ that against him. - *vi* (5) ~ from 1 to 10; ~ (up) to 10; he can't ~ yet. (6) money ~s with him more than anything; you ~ among my best friends; every minute ~s *(is important)*; that doesn't ~; in this case anyone over 18 ~s as an adult; that point ~s to me; the fact that he has admitted his mistakes ~s to his credit; his age ~ed against him. (7) titles ~ for little / much / nothing there; in early Victorian England, family ~ed for a good deal, wealth for very little; in soccer a goal ~s (for) one point. (8) can I ~ on all of you to help / on your help / the help of all of you? may I ~ on your coming? ~ on s.o.('s cooperation / sympathy / support / honesty / *etc*).

count in ~ me in if you decide to go on a picnic; go and see how many plates we have, but don't ~ in the cracked ones.

count out (1) ~ ~ the money for s.th. (2) the boxer was ~ed ~. (3) ~ me ~ if you're going swimming; we have ten applicants, but two of them are foreigners, so we can ~ them ~ / so they can be ~ed ~.

country *n* (1) a free / (in)dependent / newly liberated / industrial / backward / savage / lawless / *etc* ~; an imaginary ~; the mother ~; England is his native ~; European ~ies (2) hilly / mountainous / flat / level / sandy / desert / barren / fertile ~; miles of densely wooded ~; Switzerland is a mountainous ~; live / spend a day in the ~; the ~ of origin *(country from which s.th. comes)*; this is unknown ~ to me *(also fig: an unfamiliar branch of learning, etc)*. (3 *the people of a country*) the ~ is opposed to war; go / appeal to the ~ *(BE hold a general election)*.

couple *n* (1 *two*) a ~ of houses / birds / apples / rabbits / *etc*; can you lend me a ~ of pounds? she had a ~ of eggs with her tea. (2) a loving / engaged / married / old ~; a ~ of lovers / newly-weds; the newly wedded / married ~; ten ~s took the floor *(began dancing)*; not every ~ is a pair. (3 *inform: a few*) I had a ~ of drinks after dinner; spend a ~ of hours reading; he put me off with a ~ of words.

couple *vt* (1) ~ dogs / railway carriages; the dining-car was ~d to the train / ~d on at Crewe. (2) her name was ~d with his; we ~ the name of Oxford with the idea of learning; ~ justice and / with mercy.

courage *n* have / show / display (dauntless / unfaltering / indomitable / dogged) ~; it requires ~ to tell the truth; take (→ take *vt* 17) / pluck up / muster up ~ *(be brave)*; lose ~; he lacks the ~ to do it / the necessary ~; □ take one's ~ in both hands *(summon up all one's courage)*; □ have the ~ of one's convictions *(be brave enough to do what one knows is right)*.

course *n* (1) the ~ of a ship; the ship is on / off her right ~; because of fog the pilot went off ~; stay / keep on ~; our ~ was due north; your best ~ is London, Dover, Calais, Marseilles; the ship set ~ for America; steer / hold / pursue / follow a (straight) ~; change / alter the, one's ~; he took a diagonal ~ across the field; the ~ of a river; a river in its ~ to the sea (2) the ~ of history / events / nature / business; the ~ of life from the cradle to the grave; the ordinary ~ of this disease; the disease / year ran / took its ~; we let things run their ~; justice / the law must take its ~; the ~ of the argument suddenly changed; □ in due ~ *(at the proper time)*; we shall get to know the results of the examination in due ~; I will consider the matter and let you know my answer in due ~; sow the seed now and in due ~ you will have the flowers; in ~ of *(in process of)*; the new railway is in ~ of construction; all the old houses here are in ~ of demolition; in ~ of time *(after an unspecified time has passed)*; everything wears in ~ of time; in ~ of time I got to know him better; in the ~ of time *(while time passes)* many empires have risen and fallen; in the ~ of their investigations they made a discovery which ...; did you ever visit Egypt in the ~ of your travels? (3) a ~ of lectures / study / instruction; a study ~; a three-year ~ in nursing; an English / lifesaving / *etc* ~; attend a ~ in Russian; take part in a ~ for advanced students / in an advanced ~; a ~ of X-ray treatments / mud-baths / *etc* (4) a golf ~; a racing / race ~ (5) they discussed several possible ~s and decided to follow a middle ~; your only proper ~ is to rewrite the paper; the best ~ is to keep quiet until the trouble has blown over ; (the suggested) ~ of action; he took to evil ~s *(bad ways of living)*. (6) a dinner of five ~s; a four-~ meal; the fish ~.

court *n* (1) a ~ of law / justice; a law ~; a juvenile ~; the prisoner was brought to ~ for trial; take s.o. / a matter to ~; s.o. appears / comes before a ~ / in ~; a matter comes to / is brought before ~; settle a case / dispute out of ~ *(without it)*; the ~ meets / sits / holds a sitting / hears the accused / witness; the ~ gives / passes / pronounces judgement (up)on s.o.; the ~ sentences s.o.; s.o. gives evidence / testifies to a fact in ~; be ruled / be put / put o.s. out of ~ *(do s.th. so that one is not entitled to be heard)*; the case will be heard at the next ~ *(sitting)*. (2) a tennis / basketball / volleyball / badminton ~; a grass / asphalt / hard ~ (3) the ~ of a king / *etc*; the royal / imperial ~; the king and his ~; hold a large ~; at ~; pay ~ to a king; pay (one's) ~ to a woman.

cover *n* (1) the ~ of a box / pot / pan; some chairs are fitted with loose ~s. (2) the ~ of a book, a book-~ ; read a book from ~ to ~ (3 *envelope*) send s.th. under separate / the same ~ ; first-day ~, FDC *(envelope with new stamp cancelled on day of issue)* (4) the treeless land provided no ~ for our troops; run for ~; take ~ (from the enemy / rain / *etc*); it's raining - get under ~ quickly; attack under ~ of darkness / of heavy artillery fire; under the ~ of fog, the smugglers' boat slipped off to sea. (5 *pretence*) do s.th. under of friendship / religion / patriotism / *etc* (6) ~s were laid for six people; a dinner of 50 ~s.

cover *vt* (1) ~ s.th. with earth / dust / snow; use this cloth to ~ the table; on country roads cars ~ us with dust / mud; the furniture was ~ed with dust; his shoes were ~ed with / in mud; remain ~ed *(keep one's hat on)*; ~ one's head; ~ one's face in / with one's hands (2) snow ~ed the ground; the floods ~ a large area; the wood ~s 20 acres; mist ~s the valley; a wall ~ed with ivy; an ivy-~ed wall; a lid ~s a box / pot / pan; paint that ~s well (3) cats are ~ed with fur and dogs are ~ed with hair; the bush was ~ed with blossom; hills densely ~ed with forest; be ~ed with *(overcome by)* shame / confusion (4) ~ upholstered furniture / eiderdown / buttons (with material); ~ a cushion with silk; ~ chairs with leather / walls with wall-paper / a roof with tiles (5) our war-ships ~ed the landing of the troops; ~ the army's retreat; the frontier is ~ed by a chain of forts; enemy guns ~ed the valley; the enemy were ~ed from our sight by woods; ~ s.o. with a gun / revolver *(aim it at him)* (6) she laughed to ~ her nervousness; he tried to ~ his mistake; ~ one's confusion / annoyance / anxiety / shame / embarrassment (7) ~ o.s. with glory / honour; ~ o.s. / s.o. with shame / disgrace (8) he ~ed 50 yards in six seconds; the bus has ~ed 30 miles since leaving N. (9) his lectures / researches ~ a wide field; this book ~s the whole subject; in his report the President ~ed all aspects of national policy; we have ~ed a great deal of ground in our discussion; these figures ~ all available statistical data over the period 1950–65; volume II ~s methods of testing. (10 *apply to, include*) the new regulation ~s the matter you have raised; this clause ~s those who failed to register within the time limit; the new restrictions ~ all forms of transport; the register ~s all who graduated; the invoice ~s the goods delivered this week; the definition does not ~ this type of machine; the word 'set' ~s a great variety of meanings; the resolution in its present form ~s divergent points of view. (11) I am well ~ed by insurance: my policy ~s illness as well as accident / me against loss from fire; ~ the expenses / a deficit; ~ s.o.'s / one's needs / requirements; the cheque is ~ed; the selling-price barely ~s the cost; the new price ~s our probable losses on the old price; these measures ~ every foreseeable eventuality; supplies of tin easily ~ the present demand. (12 *report*) ~ events / proceedings; 4000 journalists ~ed the Olympic Games in 1972.

cover in (1 *put a roof on*) ~ in a barn / house / garage / *etc* (2 *fill in, esp with earth*) the grave was quickly ~ed in.

cover over (1) ~ ~ a hole in the roof (2) ~ ~ a mistake / one's (sinful) past.

cover up (1) only one blanket to ~ oneself up with; ~ the baby up carefully when you put her to bed; it's cold out - you must ~ yourself up warmly. (2) he tried to ~ his mistake up by tearing a page out of the register; □ ~ (up) one's tracks *(hide one's deeds)*.

crash *vi* (1) the tree ~ed through the window; the dishes ~ed to the floor; the aeroplane ~ed on a hillside; the car ~ed into the gate; our train ~ed into a goods train. (2) the elephant ~ed through the jungle; the search party ~ed through the underbrush. (3 *collide*) two cars ~ed on that curve. (4) the whole financial scheme ~ed disastrously; the national economy ~ed. - *vt* (5) what ~ed the aircraft? (6) he ~ed the glass against the wall. (7) ~ a dance / party / executive's office *(inform: come uninvited)*.

create *vt* (1) God ~d heaven and earth; ~ a drama / theory / system of philosophy; ~ an army / powerful industry / insurance company / new tyranny; the fashion house of X has ~d a startling new line; ~ a character in a novel (2) peers are ~d by the Sovereign; ~ a man a baron; ~ a cardinal (3) ~ trouble / delay / difficulties / illusions / opposition; ~ a disturbance / precedent / difficulty; her appearance ~d a sensation; this gas ~s a painful feeling in the throat.

credit *n* (1 *belief, trust*) they deserve some degree of ~; this tale / man deserves no ~; do you give ~ to his account of what happened? it's unwise to place / put too much ~ in hearsay; the rumour is gaining ~ that he ...; the latest news lends ~ to the earlier reports. (2 *good reputation*) he is a man of (the highest) ~; his ~ has suffered as a result of his action; an effort to restore his ~; he added greatly to his ~ by being very modest about his discoveries; this new book won't add to his ~. (3 *acknowledgment, recognition*) to whom should we give the ~ of having invented the radio? count s.th. to s.o.'s ~; give s.o. ~ for s.th.; he did not actually write the book, but he got / was given ~ for it; → take *vt* 17; he's cleverer than I gave him ~ for *(than I thought he was)*; I gave him ~ for being a more sensible fellow; the offer does you ~; do ~ to one's country; his smart appearance does ~ to his tailors; his fluency in Russian reflects great ~ on him / his teacher; it must be said to his ~ that he ...; it is greatly to your ~ that you have passed such a difficult examination; to N. goes ~ for first discovering ...; she is in high ~ with her colleagues. (4) he is a ~ to his parents / school / country; he is not much of a ~ either to himself or his family. (5 *money owned*) how much have I standing to my ~? debit and ~; be entered on the ~ side; place / put / enter a sum to s.o.'s ~ (6 *money lent*) a short-term / medium-term / long-term / (un)covered / (un)secured ~; apply for / raise / take up / draw upon a ~; give / grant / allow s.o. a ~ (of up to 2,000 marks); I shall have to raise (a) ~ from the bank to buy the house; the bank refused further ~s to the firm. (7 *power to obtain goods without immediate payment*) purchase / sale on ~; he bought / took / sold it on ~; our ~ with the bank / him is good; he will get no more ~ from me; his ~ is good for £1,000; no ~ is given at this shop.

credit *vt* (1) who would ~ that ridiculous story? nobody would ~ this piece of news. (2) until now I have always ~ed him with some sense; you would hardly ~ him with having acted so foolishly; these relics are ~ed with miraculous powers *(people believe they have them)*. (3) ~ s.o. with a sum; ~ a sum to s.o.; ~ s.o.('s account) with an amount; the amount has been ~ed to him / his account; ~ s.o. for returned goods.

creep *vi* (1) the snail crept across the path; the cat crept quietly nearer to the bird; we will ~ up on them from behind and surprise them. (2) he's very old, but he can still ~ about the house. (3) ivy had crept over the ruins. (4) various errors have crept into the book; anxiety crept into their hearts; old age ~s upon one unawares; ~ing inflation; time crept on. (5) it makes my flesh ~ to see some of the things that appear on television nowadays; it made me ~ all over. (6) ~ after s.o. *(be obsequious)*; Jones would never have been promoted if he hadn't crept after the boss so much.

crime *n* (1) commit / perpetrate a (horrible / hideous / outrageous / fiendish / monstrous / atrocious / abominable) ~ (against s.o.); a capital ~; war ~s; a ~ against society; ~s against humanity (2) an increase in ~; it is the business of the police to detect ~ and of the law-courts to punish ~; ~ doesn't pay. (3) it's a ~ to waste that whisky.

critic *n* (1) an (un)fair / (im)partial / severe / loud / vociferous / *etc* ~ (of s.o./ s.th.); he is his own worst ~; his ~s attack him at every chance; the government's ~s (have taken up the battle). (2) an art / book / music / motion picture / drama / television / *etc* ~; a literary ~; a professional / newspaper ~; to act as ~; to assume the role of ~.

critical *adj* (1) be ~ of s.o. / s.th.; ~ remarks; a ~ look / glance / gesture / tone of voice / word; a ~ person; a ~ opinion; she is very ~; she is ~ of his every move; why are you so ~? (2) a ~ essay / study / edition (of a book / play / *etc*); ~ opinions on / judgements of a work of art / literature / *etc* (3 *of a crisis: dangerous*) a ~ moment / situation / development / state of affairs; the ~ point (in the battle / *etc*) has been overcome; there is a ~ shortage of ammunition / blood reserves / fire-fighters. (4) the patient remains in a ~ condition; his condition remains ~; fever becomes ~ when it cannot be reduced.

criticism *n* (1) (un)fair / (im)partial / severe / devastating / bitter / undue / loud / vociferous ~; ~ of government policies / the Vietnam War / atomic tests / *etc* (2) art / literary / *etc* ~; → critic *n* 2.

criticize *vt* (1) ~ s.o./ s.th. (fairly / severely / *etc*); he ~d her for not showing enough interest; they ~ their children constantly; he was ~d for failing to foresee the problems. (2) the reviewer ~d the book's lack of originality; the actor was virtually ~d out of the part *(forced by criticism to leave the role)*. - *vi* (3) you may disagree with me but don't ~!

cross *n* (1) put a ~ at the end of a document; make a / one's ~ (2) death on the ~; nail s.o. to the ~ *(also fig: sacrifice)* (3 *Christian cross*) follow the C~; make the sign of the C~ (over s.o.); preach the C~ (4 *suffering*) bear one's (heavy) ~ (with patience); take up one's ~; God has given me a heavy ~ to bear / laid a heavy ~ upon me. (5) this rose is a ~ between two well-known varieties; a mule is a ~ between a mare and a donkey.

cross *vt* (1) ~ the street (without looking); ~ a road / river / bridge / field; ~ the sea / English Channel / Sahara Desert / mountains; we ~ed the water by ferry; ~ the frontier; ~ party lines *(join another party)*; no ~ing of the rails! ~ s.o.'s path (2) ~ one's legs / arms; sit with one's legs ~ed; ~ one's fingers / keep one's fingers ~ed for s.o. *(hope thus to avert bad luck)* (3) a bridge ~es the river. (4) my letter must have ~ed yours (in the post); the mechanic ~ed the ignition wires and got the motor started; the wires are ~d (and have caused a short circuit); you've got your wires ~ed *(inform: you are confused)*. (5 *oppose*) don't ~ him when he is angry; ~ s.o.'s plan / intentions; he ~es me in everything; he has been ~ed in love *(has failed to win the love of the woman he was in love with)*. (6) this possibility never ~ed my mind; it never ~ed my mind that he might refuse the request. (7) ~ animals / plants; different breeds of sheep were ~ed to achieve this kind of wool. - *vi* (8) our letters have ~ed in the post / mail; the lines / roads ~ there (at an angle of 45 degrees).

cross off ~ ~ a word / a line / s.o.'s name; I ~ed his name ~ the list.

cross out ~ ~ a word / a line / s.o.'s name.

crowd *n* (1) there were ~s of people when I arrived; a (large / huge) ~ gathered / collected (in the street) / streamed out / gushed forth (from the hall) / circulated / flowed (through the streets); an enthusiastic ~ lined the streets / burst into cheers (when ...) / cheered frantically; make / work / force / push / elbow one's way through a (noisy / riotous / tumultuous) ~; □ go with / follow the ~ *(do what most other people do)*; (the new book) would / might pass in a ~ *(is not obviously unsatisfactory)*. (2 *set, clique*) she came in with all her ~; the college ~; a rough ~ (3 *the common people*) that speech was aimed at the ~. (4) a desk covered with a ~ of papers and books; a ~ of things to do.

crowd *vi* (1) the visitors ~ed through the gates; the people are ~ing to the theatre; the pupils ~ed round the teacher; people quickly ~ round when there is a street accident; hundreds of people ~ed in (to see ...) (2 *press forward*) he ~ed into the lift; ~ on one's way; his heart ~ed up into his breast. (3) memories ~ed in upon me; suspicions and alarms ~ed upon him. - *vt* (4) ~ a building with people; people ~ the beaches; the streets were ~ed with people; they were ~ed (together) in the small space; ~ a room with furniture (5) ~ people into a building; the cattle were ~ed into the barn; ~ books into a box.

crowd out we tried to get in but were ~ed ~; the room was ~ed ~ and we could not even find a place to stand; your article was ~ed ~ *(not printed because of lack of space)*; we allowed a false creed to ~ ~ the true American tradition.

crown *vt* (1) ~ a / s.o. king; ~ed heads (2) ~ s.o. with a wreath; ~ s.o. victor / with the victor's laurels (3) ~ a building with a cupola / statue (4) ~ an occasion with a speech / banquet; the acrobat ~ed his performance with a triple somersault; be ~ed with victory / glory; his efforts were ~ed with success. (5) a wreath of laurels ~s the victor's head; a castle ~s the mountain peak; a statue ~s the dome; the hill is ~ed with a wood. (6) a firework display ~ed the evening; the ~ing achievement of s.o.'s career; the ~ing event / moment of a celebration / s.o.'s life; open a bottle of champagne to ~ a feast; □ *(BE)* to ~ all / *(BE, AE)* to ~ it all *(as climax)*: it rained, we had no umbrellas, and, to ~ (it) all, we missed the last bus. (7) ~ a tooth.

crush *vt* (1) wine is made by ~ ing grapes; don't ~ this box, it has flowers in it; ~ ice; a child was ~ed to death in the crowd. (2) the hat was ~ed when he sat on it; if the case is too full, the clothes will be ~ed. (3) we can't ~ more people into the hall - it's crowded already; we had to ~ our way through the crowd. (4 *destroy, overwhelm*) the government ~ed the rebellion; our hopes have been ~ed; he was quite ~ed by all these misfortunes; she ~ed him *(made him feel very embarrassed)* with a haughty look; provincial differences were ~ed into national unity by the pressure of the conqueror. - *vi* (5) this (textile) material ~es very easily. (6) hundreds ~ed into the hall / the front seats. - *adj* (7) a ~ing defeat; a ~ing retort; ~ing grief.

crush down (1) make cement by ~ing ~ stone; ~ ~ plants (2) ~ ~ opposition; be ~ed ~ by grief.

crush out (1) ~ ~ the juice from tomatoes / oranges; ~ ~ one's cigarette (2) ~ ~ a rebellion.

crush up a device to ~ up nuts / sugar; he ~ed up the letter in his hand.

cry *n* (1 *shout*) utter / give a (low / weak / feeble / loud / piercing / unearthly / dismal / *etc*) ~; a ~ of pain / distress / fear / joy / triumph; a ~ for help; the ~ of battle; a battle-~; a war-~; the happy ~ies of children; (suppress) an involuntary ~; they raised a great ~; there arose a great ~; there were angry ~ies from the mob; a (shrill / sharp / *etc*) ~ rent the air / broke the silence of the night; are miniskirts still the last ~? □ a far ~; it's a far ~ *(long way)* to that place; it's a far ~ from *(great contrast to)* the first draft. (2 *words / spoken loudly*) the ~ of a nightwatchman / pedlar (3) hearing the news she went to her room and had a good ~; let her have her ~ out.

cry *vi* (1 *call loudly*) a baby can ~ as soon as it is born; men / wild beasts / swans ~; he ~ied with pain. (2) why did he ~ to you? the flamingo ~ies to its mate; the starving men ~ied for bread / help. (3 *weep*) stop ~ing and wipe away your tears; she was ~ing for joy / pain; ~ wildly / bitterly; the child is ~ing for its toy *(wants to get it by crying)*; what's the child ~ing about? it's no use ~ing over it / spilt milk - it's too late now; □ ~ for the moon *(demand s.th. impossible)* (4) evils that ~ for redress; the situation ~ies for a remedy; the blood of the murdered ~ied for vengeance. - *vt* (5) "what a pity," he ~ied; □ ~ halves *(demand a share)*; □ ~ quits *(agree to stop a quarrel)*; □ ~ shame on s.o. *(say he ought to be ashamed of himself)*; □ ~ wolf *(raise a false alarm)* (6 *make known*) ~ the news / one's wares (7 *weep*) ~ o.s. to sleep; she ~ied hot tears. - *adj* (8) a ~ing evil / shame / *(urgent)* need.

cry down she was constantly ~ing ~ her son's ability as an artist *(saying it was worth little)*.

cry off he was going to join our society but he ~ied ~ *(withdrew from that agreement)*; the team that was to have opposed us has ~ied ~.

cry out (1) they ~ied ~ when the bus passed them; she was badly hurt but didn't ~ ~; he ~ied ~ with pain. (2) ~ ~ against the tyranny of ...; the people ~ ~ against the high taxes. (3) ~ one's heart / eyes ~.

cry up these pills are ~ied up *(praised highly)* as a remedy for all ailments.

cultivate *vt* (1) ~ land / the soil; ~ a field / garden; ~ crops / plants / roses / *etc*; ~ bacteria (2) ~ the mind (by study); ~ one's talents / taste / style; a ~d man (3) ~ a / s.o.'s friendship / acquaintance; why does he ~ the acquaintance of Mr N.? (4) he ~s only rich and important people *(tries to win their friendship)*.

cure *n* (1 *remedy*) an efficacious ~ (for a cold); quinine is a ~ for malaria; there is no certain ~ for cancer; a rest-~; a water-~; a drinking-~; a bathing-~ (2 *fact of being cured, succesful treatment*) a complete ~ after a long illness; seek a ~ (at a spa); to travel to a spa to take a ~; undergo a ~; effect a ~; miraculous ~s; his ~ took six weeks; can you guarantee a ~? (3) find a ~ for unemployment / social unrest / *etc*.

cure *vt* (1) ~ a disease / illness / evil / *etc.* (2) ~ s.o. of a disease / illness / headache / bad habit; she is completely ~d; this medicine ~d me; that has ~d him of his credulity / superstition / vanity / mistrust / *etc*; we must ~ his laziness / drunkenness; ~ poverty (3 *preserve*) ~ meat / bacon / ham / fish / leather / hides.

custom *n* (1) afternoon tea is a general / time-honoured / old ~ in England; ancestral / hereditary / oriental / *etc* ~s; it is his ~ to rise early; it is a ~ for a gentleman to raise his hat to a lady; most countries have different ~s; study the ~s of the natives; □ once a use and ever a ~ (2) don't be a slave to ~; ~ requires us to stand when the national anthem is played; the dictates / power of ~; a constitution rooted in ~ (3 *buying from a shop/ firm*) he gives most of his ~ to one shop; we hope that we shall continue to receive your ~; build up ~; I shall withdraw my ~ from that shop. (4) it took us an hour to get our luggage through the ~s; ~s formalities / regulations; a ~s declaration / examination (on the train) / inspection / officer; ~s duties are levied on imported goods; ~s is the next stop after passport control.

cut *n* (1) make a (deep) ~ in a tree; a ~ in one's finger / on the finger; she had minor ~s and bruises but no major injuries; ~s (and nicks) on the face (after shaving); a deep ~ through a hillside (for a road) (2) a steak is a ~ of beef; a nice ~ of meat; a ~ off the joint; this year's ~ of wool (3) a ~ of his whip; give a horse a ~ across the flank; make a ~ at an enemy with a sword (4) the ~ of a coat / dress; clothes of strange and ancient ~ (5) we took the short ~ *(direct path)* across the fields; there is no short ~ to learning. (6) a ~ in price(s); a wage / salary ~; a ~ in expenditure / production; a power ~ *(less electric current)*; where can we make a ~ in this long article? there were several ~s in the film. (7) give s.o. the ~ direct *(refuse to deal with him)* (8) that remark was a ~ at me *(meant to hurt me)*.

cut *vt/i* (1a) we ~ wood with a knife, paper and cloth with scissors; ~ a ribbon in two / three / pieces / half; ~ apples into halves; ~ one's finger; ~ o.s. with a knife; ~ one's face / o.s. when shaving; he fell and ~ his elbow; ~ a pack of playing cards *(divide it)*; this knife ~s badly; how this rope ~s *(hurts as if cutting)*; ~ting wind (1b *cut + adj*) he fell and ~ his knee open; ~ one's head open in falling; ~ a boat loose; ~ o.s. loose from one's family; ~ o.s. free from ropes; ~ short s.o.'s remarks (*interrupt him;* → 12); □ to ~ a long story / the matter short (I married her three weeks later); have one's career ~ short by illness; □ ~ it (rather) fine *(allow o.s. hardly any margin of time or money)* (1c *idiomatic uses*) □ ~ one's coat according to one's cloth *(spend within one's income)*; □ ~ one's own throat *(act against one's interests)*; □ ~ no ice *(have little effect)*: that ~s no / doesn't ~ much ice with me; it's all very well, but will it ~ any ice? □ ~ (an army, *etc*) to pieces *(utterly defeat)*; □ it ~ me to the heart *(keenly distressed me)*; □ (this argument / factor) ~s both ways *(serves both sides)*. (2) the frozen meat won't ~; this stone ~s easily. (3 *make by cutting*) ~ peat / firewood; ~ initials in / on a tree / steps in a rock; ~ a hole in the fence / a notch in wood / a figure in stone; ~ a trench / canal / tunnel / road (through a hill); ~ a pattern in(to) s.th.; ~ a diamond / jewel *(shape it)*; ~ a key *(make it); ~ a record (record s.th.)*; ~ the rotten part out of an apple; ~ an advertisement out of a paper; I'd better ~ plenty of sandwiches; she's in the kitchen ~ting the bread and butter (4 *cut short, cut off*) ~ the grass / hedge; ~ s.o.'s hair (short); ~ one's nails; ~ corn / flowers; I don't like to ~ flowers; please ~ a slice of cake for me / me a slice of cake; □ ~ the ground from under s.o. / from under / beneath s.o.'s feet *(leave the other disputant defenceless)* (5 *strike*) the sailor ~ at the pirate with his sword; ~ at nettles / a hedge with a stick (6) the storm ~ *(interrupted)* all telephone service; ~ into other people's conversation (7) this soap will ~ *(dissolve)* the grease. (8) ~ a tooth *(have it appear through the gum)*; the baby is ~ting its teeth; the last primary tooth is ~ at about two years of age; □ ~ one's wisdom-teeth / eye-teeth *(learn by experience)* (9) at which point does the line AB ~ *(cross)* the line CD? the path ~s through the wood; socially, cricket ~s across all barriers. (10 *reduce*) ~ prices / expenses / quality; ~ the working day from eight to seven hours; ~ a speech / article / *etc*; since the show was long, two songs were ~. (11 *not attend*) ~ a lecture / class / meeting; ~ school; □ ~ a loss / one's losses *(give up an unprofitable course of action)*: a successful business man is one who knows when to ~ his losses. (12 *not recognize*) no gentleman would ~ an old acquaintance, as you have done; ~ s.o. dead; ~ s.o. short *(interrupt abruptly and prevent him from speaking* → 1b); I have never known him ~ a date in my life. (13 *hurt*) her remark ~ me deeply; ~ting irony (14 *go, hurry*) I must ~ *(leave)*; our attack was so sudden that the enemy ~ and ran *(ran away quickly)*; they began to run and we ~ after them; don't ~ across the flower bed; we decided to ~ across the moor to the village. (15 *interfere*) does my suggestion ~ across anything you have in mind? he'll oppose anything that ~s across his own interests; that ~s at all my hopes *(makes it unlikely that they will be realized)*. (16) □ ~ a figure *(impress others by the extravagance of one's appearance)*; his chief ambition was to ~ a figure in the best social circles; ~ a grand / sorry / poor / ridiculous figure; □ ~ a dash (with the ladies) *(make a brilliant show)*; □ ~ a caper / capers *(jump about merrily, act foolishly)*. (17 *cut into: take away from, diminish*) she ~ heavily into the money left to her *(spent a lot)*; the U.S. will have to ~ into inventories to make up the deficit.

cut along when he saw the policeman he ~ ~ *(hurried off)*.

cut away (1) ~ ~ all the dead wood from the tree (2) he threw down his weapon and ~ ~ across the fields. (3) the actual story of Hamlet ~s cleanly ~ from the older-fashioned concept of heroism and villainy.

cut back (1) ~ ~ trees / rose-bushes (2) ~ ~ expenditure / production / *etc* (3) ~ ~ to a scene *(in a film)*.

cut down (1) ~ ~ a tree *(fell it)* (2) ~ ~ a father's coat *(make it smaller for the son)*; ~ ~ an article to make it fit the pages of a magazine (3) the epidemic ~ ~ *(killed)* many of our best men. (4) ~ ~ expenses / rations / the accident rate / s.o.'s monthly allowance; ~ ~ (one's) smoking; ~ ~ on luxuries; we must ~ ~ a lot (on entertainment).

cut in (1 *interrupt*) he ~ in with a facetious remark; he ~ in as I was explaining. (2) a motor-cycle suddenly ~ in *(overtook us and pulled in too soon)*.

cut off (1) ~ ~ a piece of cake / a branch from a tree; ~ ~ s.o.'s hair / leg; □ ~ ~ a corner *(go straight instead of round a corner)*; ~ ~ one's nose to spite one's face *(injure one's own interests in seeking to injure another's)* (2) the heavy snow ~ the farms ~ from all contact; I was ~ ~ in the middle of my phone call; he was ~ ~ from his supplies; ~ ~ s.o.'s retreat; a people ~ ~ from the sea (3) ~ ~ imports / the gas supply / the electricity; the exchange ~ ~ the phone because the bill was unpaid; ~ ~ a son's allowance (4) too many men are ~ ~ *(killed)* in the prime of life; death ~ him ~ in his prime. (5) ~ s.o. ~ *(disinherit him)* with a shilling / without a penny.

cut on we ~ on *(hurried)* in spite of the darkness.

cut out (1) ~ ~ a tumour / growth (2) ~ ~ figures / designs / a picture (out of a newspaper) (3) ~ ~ a path through undergrowth (4) ~ ~ the jokes from a speech; ~ ~ unimportant details (5) (I shall try) to ~ ~ smoking / drinking / tobacco / all starchy foods; ~ ~ the nonsense! he told the student to ~ ~ that sort of behaviour; the aircraft landed with one engine ~ ~ *(not in use)*. (6) he ~ ~ *(contrived)* a comfortable job for himself. (7 *outdo*) he ~ ~ all the other suitors for the lady's hand; he's trying to ~ me ~ with my girl; I don't want to be ~ ~ by my own daughter; they found they were ~ ~ by this newcomer. (8) he seems to be ~ ~ *(gifted)* for the job; she is obviously ~ ~ to be a nurse; she realized that she was not ~ ~ for teaching / to be a teacher. (9) suddenly the car ~ ~ *(left the line of traffic to overtake another car)*; let's ~ ~ (of here) *(inform: leave)*.

cut up (1) ~ up the meat for the baby / a slice of ham; she ~ the cake up and gave me a piece. (2) the enemy aircraft ~ up *(destroyed)* the entire village; ~ up the enemy's forces (3 *inform: upset*) the news of his brother's death ~ him up very badly; she is very ~ up about her failure; don't be so ~ up about it! (4) the turkey ~ up well *(there was plenty of meat on it)*; this piece of cloth will ~ up into several suits; □ ~ up well *(die leaving a large fortune)* (5) □ ~ up rough *(inform: become angry and menacing)*; he'll ~ up rough if you don't give him the money.

D

damage *n* (1) did your house suffer any ~ in the recent floods? the typhoon caused / did much ~ (to our house); the ~ to the car was slight; great / severe / irreparable / extensive / light / slight ~; ~ by fire / from careless handling; the ~ is estimated / computed at £150.
(2 *~s: money in compensation for damage*) be awarded a thousand dollars ~s (for an injury); claim ~s from a driver (for the loss of ...); sue s.o. for ~s.

damage *vt* (1) furniture / luggage (badly) ~d by fire; frost ~d the crops; slightly ~d goods; the pictures were ~d in transit; ~one's lungs by excessive smoking; he has a ~d finger; an eye ~d by strain under bad light; ~ a motor by overheating it; the goods arrived in a ~d condition. (2) his reputation was ~d; overzeal will ~ the cause. - *vi* (3) china ~s easily.

dance *n* (1) ballroom / social / classical ~s; modern / classical / expressionistic / primitive / traditional / interpretative ~; may I have the next ~ with you? the next ~ is reserved for you; □ lead s.o. a (pretty) ~ *(give him a lot of trouble)* (2 *a social event with dancing*) give a ~; go to a ~; invite s.o. to a ~.

dance *vt* (1) ~ a waltz / fox-trot / jig / *etc*; ~ a part / role (in a ballet); F. ~d a superb Giselle; a gala performance with N. and F. ~ing the Bluebird pas de deux (2) ~ a baby on one's knee; he ~d his partner across the floor; the dervish ~d himself into an ecstasy / trance. (3) □ ~ attendance on s.o. *(pay great attention to his wishes)*. - *vi* (4) ~ to jazz music; ~ (a)round s.o. / s.th.; ~ (a)round in a circle; □ ~ to s.o.'s tune / piping *(do what he says)*; ~ (about / around the room) for joy; the sudden pain made him ~ up and down. (5) raindrops / the hail ~d on the pavement; the leaves were ~ing in the wind; the boat is ~ing on the waves.

danger *n* (1) get into ~; put s.o. in / lead s.o. into ~; be in ~ of breaking / collapsing / dying / losing one's money / being dismissed / dismissal / arrest; → run *vt* 66; there is ~ threatening; the patient is now out of ~; the medicine soon put him out of ~; there is no ~ of our being late. (2) icebergs are a ~ to all ships; a ~ to national security; there is a / some ~ that he ...; warn s.o. of an imminent / impending / threatening ~; expose o.s. to a ~ / ~s; the ~ of war / the sea; ~s are (looming) ahead.

dare *vi* (1 *have the courage to*) anybody ~ do that; I ~ ask him; you ~ not ask him, ~ you? ~ he do it? he ~ not; I don't know whether he ~ try; ~ you jump from the roof? he does not ~ (to) ask the results of the examination; he would not ~ (to) approach the headmaster on this matter; my brother usually ~s to do anything; he ~d to come to you? oh no, he would never ~ to come. (2 *have the impudence*) he ~s to question my authority; he ~d to doubt my honesty of purpose; this guard has ~d to ask me for a pass; how ~ you take my car! how ~ you speak to me like that? - *vt* (3 *challenge*) I ~ you to jump over the stream; he ~d me to pull down the notice; he is always ~ing me to play a trick on someone; I ~ you to deny the truth of what I said. (4 *meet boldly*) Columbus ~d the peril of the sea; he will ~ any danger.

dark *adj* (1) a ~, moonless night / sky; a ~ (corner in a) room; it's growing / getting ~. (2) ~ blue / green / *etc*; a ~ colour; a ~ dress / suit / *etc*; ~ clouds; ~ beer; ~ meat *(of fowl)*; ~ hair / skin / eyes; a ~ complexion (3) the D~ Continent *(Africa)*; the D~ Ages *(early Middle Ages)* (4 *unhappy*) it was the ~est day of her life; a ~ hour / time; a ~ mood; ~ despair; □ look on the ~ side of things *(be without hope)* (5 *unpromising*) ~ prospects / premonitions / forebodings; the future looks ~. (6 *mysterious*) a ~ saying; the meaning of this word is ~ (to me); a ~ passage (in a text); ~ hints; a ~ secret; □ keep s.th. ~ *(a secret)*; the ~ subconscious (7) a ~ *(angry)* look; he looked at her ~ly. (8) ~ *(evil)* thoughts / designs / deeds.

dash *vt* (1) ~ a cup / vase / *etc* to the ground; ~ s.th. to pieces (2) she fainted, so we ~ed some water over her; ~ s.o. with water; ~ed with mud / blood (3 *destroy)* she ~ed all my hopes; his joy was ~ed. - *vi* (4 *move violently*) hearing the cry he ~ed outside / upstairs / out of the room; the waves ~ed against the shore / on the rocks / over the sides of the ship; the elephant ~ed through the bushes; a car ~ed by; he ~ed around trying to get ready in time.

dash off (1) the horse ~ed ~ down the street; I must ~ ~ now. (2 *write quickly*) ~ ~ a letter / composition / article; he ~ed ~ a note to his brother.

date *n* (1) what's the ~ today? what's today's ~? what's the ~ of the foundation of Rome? the most important ~s in history; bear a ~; (give) the exact ~ (of s.th.); fix / settle the ~ for a meeting (2 *period of time*) buildings of medieval ~; at that ~ electric light was unknown; it was at an early ~ that the wheel was invented; (go / be) out of ~ *(obsolete)*; up to ~ *(current, modern)*; bring a catalogue up to ~; keep up to ~ in (one's reading); all this machinery is up to ~; he is not up to ~ in his knowledge and methods; up-to-~ methods / ideas / *etc*; to ~ *(until now)*; we have collected just over £100 to ~. (3 *inform: appointment*) have a ~ with s.o.; make a ~ with one's girl (4 *inform: person dated*) who was his ~ at the school dance?

date *vt* (1) the letter is ~d May 3rd; we ~ letters in the heading. (2) historians ~ events as before or after the birth of Christ; can you ~ this old Greek statue? (3 *inform: have a date with*) have you ever ~d her? - *vi* ((4) these costumes ~ from the 16th century; a friendship ~ing from before the war; the gate ~s back to the late 17th century. (5 *become out of date*) this textbook is beginning to ~ .

day *n* (1) a light / bright / sunny / glorious / rainy / wet / calm / quiet / windy / stormy / clear / dull / foggy / cold / chilly / rough / cheerless ~; a big / red-letter *(fortunate)* / lively / lazy / sad / dreary / gloomy / (un)eventful / memorable / working / holy / *etc* ~; he played the guitar the livelong ~; an infamous ~ in history; s.th. is done in open ~ *(in full daylight)*; □ (money laid aside) for a rainy ~; travel by ~; work during the ~; travel ~ and night; he left the house before ~ *(before dawn)*; I've been writing letters all ~ (long) / all the ~; what brings you home at this time ot (the) ~? (2 *24 hours*) there are seven ~s in a week; I saw him three ~s ago; if today is 1 May, this ~ week will be 8 May and this ~ fortnight will be 15 May; what ~ of the week is it? the other ~ *(a few days ago)*; ~ after ~ *(for a long, wearisome period)*; ~ by ~ (the situation is improving); ~ in ~ out *(constantly)*; the weather changes from ~ to ~; no one knows what will happen from ~ to ~; live from ~ to ~ *(without planning ahead)*; the situation may alter from one ~ to the next; one (fine) ~ *(at some time past or future)*; one of these ~s *(at some time in the future)* (3 *working-day*) I've done a good ~'s work; the workers want a six-hour ~; be paid by the ~; he went swimming on his ~ off; □ call it a ~ (→ call *vt*1) (4 *days: period*) the ~s of Queen Victoria; in those ~s *(then)*; in these ~s *(now)*; in this ~ and age; in his boyhood ~s; in ~s to come; in ~s of old; in bygone ~s; he has seen better ~s; □ fall on evil ~s *(suffer misfortune)*; □ end one's ~s *(die)* (5 *his / its / etc + day: period of success*) colonialism has had its ~; I've had my ~; my ~ is done *(over)*; she was a beauty in her ~. (6 *the day: contest*) we've won / carried the ~; the ~ is ours; we've lost the ~.

dead *adj* (1) he has been ~ for three hours *(died three hours ago)*; shoot / strike s.o. ~; ~ leaves; I hate ~ flowers; rock or cosmic dust is ~ matter; I fired and the lion fell ~; ~ march *(for a funeral)*; more ~ than alive *(inform: exhausted)* (2 *without activity*) the ~ hours of the night; the ~ season of the year; be in a ~ sleep; a ~ volcano; ~ air ; a ~ fire *(one nearly out)*; a ~ tennis ball *(no longer springy)*; the train came to a ~ *(abrupt)* stop; motor-cars cannot stop ~. (3) ~ *(dull)* sounds; ~ *(not brilliant)* colours; a ~ surface (4 *unfeeling*) ~ fingers; my fingers have gone ~; he is ~ to all feelings of shame / remorse. (5 *not used*) Latin is a ~ language; a ~ letter (*law no longer obeyed;* → 6) (6 *not usable*) a ~ match *(one that has been struck)*; a ~ wire *(one without electric current)*; a ~ microphone; the telephone went ~; a ~ letter (*an undeliverable one;* → 5) (7 *complete*) ~ silence / calm; a ~ faint; be in ~ earnest; a ~ certainty / secret; a ~ loss *(one with no compensation)* (8 *exact*) at ~ centre; a ~ shot *(an exact shot; a man whose shots are exact)*; a ~ heat *(race in which winners finish exactly even)*.

dead *adv* (1 *completely*) ~ asleep / tired / drunk; ~ sure; ~ beat *(tired)*; be ~ against a plan / *etc*; the wind was ~ against us. (2 *exactly*) ~ on the target; coming ~ towards us; ~ ahead.

dead *n* (1) the ~ tell no tales; this noise could raise the ~; these horrors could make the ~ turn (over) in their graves. (2) (in) the ~ of winter / night.

deadly *adj* (1 *causing death*) (a) ~ poison; ~ weapons; a ~ disease / epidemic; a ~ drought plagued the whole area; the ~ bite / fangs of an asp; the eagle grasped the rabbit in its ~ talons; the ~ waves swept the sailor overboard. (2 *suggestive of death*) ~ white; a ~ pallor / paleness; a ~ calm / quiet / atmosphere (3 *implacable; mortal*) ~ enemies; enter into / be engaged in ~ battle / combat (4 *destructive in effect*) ~ sins; a ~ insult; a ~ attack; his review of the play included some very ~ criticism. (5 *extreme, abso-*

lute, unqualified) ~ accuracy / aim; ~ determination; ~ silence; with ~ gravity / seriousness; a ~ bore. - *adv* (6 *like that of death*) lie ~ still; be ~ quiet (7 *to an extreme*) ~ accurate / determined; ~ serious.

deal *vt* (1) ~ the cards (2) ~ a blow to s.o.; the boys were soon ~ing each other resounding blows. - *vi* (3) who ~s *(the cards)*? (4) ~ well / badly by s.o. *(treat him)*; he has always ~t well by me; you've been badly ~t by. (5) a shop ~s in goods; ~ in stocks and shares (6) ~ with a firm / tradesman; ~ at a shop; I've stopped ~ing at that shop - their prices are too high. (7) mathematics ~s with numbers; you will find that subject ~t with on page 62; history ~s with the past; ~ with a problem / matter / question / crisis (8) ~ (fairly) with a partner; ~ with s.o. leniently; he knows how to ~ with people; how should criminals be ~t with? he is difficult / impossible / easy to ~ with; policemen were sent there to ~ with the rioters.

deal out (1) ~ ~ things (to various people); ~ ~ cards / gifts / money; ~ ~ blows (2) ~ ~ equal justice to all.

death *n* (1) ~ comes to all men / knocks at the door; die a natural / hero's / violent / cruel ~; meet one's ~ *(die)*; face certain ~; put / do to ~ *(kill)*; be burnt / frozen / starved to ~; drink o.s. to ~; work o.s. to ~; sick / bored / tired / worried to ~ *(extremely)*; a fight to the ~; ~ from lung cancer / drowning / *etc*; in ~ he looked serene; lie still in ~; united in ~; life after ~ (2 *cause of death*) that dangerous ladder will be the ~ of you yet; drink will be the ~ of him; □ catch one's ~ (of cold) *(catch a very bad cold)* (3) the ~ of one's hopes / plans / ambitions; the ~ of the local mining industry.

debt *n* (1) an outstanding / unsettled ~; a bad ~ *(one unlikely to be paid)*; pay / settle / discharge a ~; collect / recover a ~; pay one's ~s; be (deep/ ly) in ~ (to s.o.); I am up to my ears / the eyes in ~ to him; get / run into ~; get out of ~; he went into ~ for £1,000; contract / incur ~s (2) I owe him a ~ of gratitude for ...; I shall always be in your ~ for the kindness you have shown me; in my brief discussion of this question I wish to acknowledge a ~ to Mr N.; the fact that you saved his life puts him in your ~.

decision *n* (1) come to / arrive at / make / take / reach a (firm) / *etc* ~; a just / fair / equitable / reasonable / grave / adverse / (un)favourable / (un)wise / unpopular / moral / rash / lightning / *etc* ~; announce a (final / irrevocable) ~; the ~ rests with you; his ~ was quickly made; his ~ is unshakable; falter in one's ~; reverse a ~; go back on a ~; bring a question to a ~; submit a matter to s.o.'s ~; give a ~ on a case; his ~ was in our favour. (2 *ability to decide*) a man of ~; show great ~ in s.th.; he lacks ~.

declare *vt* (1) ~ a session open / closed; ~ the results of an election; ~ war (on / against s.o.) / peace; the company ~d a dividend of 6 per cent. (2 *say clearly, solemnly*) the prisoner ~d his innocence / that he was / himself to be innocent; ~ an Act unconstitutional; ~ one's intention / willingness / readiness to do s.th.; ~ o.s. willing / ready / prepared to do s.th.; ~ o.s. a friend; ~ o.s. in favour of s.o./ s.th.; ~ s.o. a liar / s.th. a lie; ~ s.o. the winner; ~ (o.s.) for / against s.o./ s.th.; ~ on oath that ... (3 *make a statement of dutiable goods, taxes*) have you anything to ~? will you ~ the goods on this form, please; ~d profits.

decline *vt* (1) ~ an invitation / offer / challenge; ~ any responsibility / liability / obligation. - *vi* (2) when he was asked to help he ~d; ~ to answer / sign / *etc* (3 *slope down*) the road ~s; the sun ~s *(goes down)* (4) his health / strength / courage / energy (slowly) ~d; the prices began to ~; business ~d; the fever has ~d; he passed his ~ing years in the country; great nations rise and ~.

decorate *vt* (1) we ~d our Christmas tree; the streets were ~d with flags. (2) ~ a room / house *(paint or paper it)* (3) the general ~d the soldier (for bravery).

decrease *vt* (1) ~ friction by oiling the wheels; devices to ~ household drudgery. - *vi* (2) speed ~d as the car went uphill; the population of the village has ~d to 500; the birth-rate / death-rate / temperature / heat / cold / flood ~d; ~ in number / size / extent / quantity / importance; ~ gradually / by degrees / little by little / slightly / rapidly / slowly / *etc*; her fears ~d with the approach of dawn; his influence is ~ing.

deed *n* (1) a good / kind / illustrious / brave / daring / heroic / bad / evil / black / foul / mean / base / vile / villainous /

wicked / treacherous / *etc* ~; do / perform / carry out a ~; be responsible for one's ~s; there is no good ~ but bears some fruit; in word and ~ (2 *document*) draw up a ~.

deep *adj* (1) a ~ river / well / hole; a hole ten feet ~; a ~ wound; ankle-~ in mud; knee-~ / waist-~ in water; a ~ plunge; fry in ~ fat; minerals are often found ~ in the ground; with his hands ~ in his pockets; □ in ~ water(s) *(in difficulties)*; □ still waters run ~ *(s.th. unknown may be beneath calm)*; →go off 1. (2) a ~ shelf / drawer; a plot of land 100 feet ~; a ~ cave; the box is 10 inches long and six inches ~; a ~ formation / array; the soldiers were drawn up six ~ *(in six rows)*; a house ~ in the valley; lost ~ in the woods; ~ in industrial England (3 *low, of sounds*) in a ~ voice; the ~ notes of a cello; a ~ bell (4 *intense, of colours*) a ~ red; in ~ mourning (5) ~ feelings / sympathy / love / passion / sorrow / grief / gratitude / interest / influence; ~ sleep; ~ disgrace; a ~ impression; heave a ~ sigh; take a ~ breath; be ~ in love (6) a ~ mystery / secret / problem / subject; he's a ~ one *(conceals his feelings)*. (7 *absorbed*) be ~ in a book / map; ~ in thought / study; be ~ in debt / difficulties (8) a ~ thinker / theoretician / intellect; a ~ insight (into s.th.); ~ learning.

deep *adv* (1) dig ~ (to find water); drink ~ *(a great deal)* (2) the road led ~ into the forest. (3) work / study / read ~ into the night; go ~ into a subject; sink ~ into the mind.

deeply *adv* be ~ interested / moved / in love / offended; discuss ~; feel s.o.'s death ~; be ~ indebted to s.o.

defence *n* (1) the high walls round the town are a ~ against enemies; a warm overcoat is a good ~ against the cold; attack is the best ~. (2) fight in ~ of one's country / of liberty; there is no real ~ against air attacks; weapons of ~; spend money for national ~; I can find nothing to say in ~ of his action. (3) the accused made no ~; the lawyer / witness for the ~; what ~ did the accused offer?

defend *vt* (1) ~ o.s. against an enemy / dog / charge; I ~ed myself with a stick; ~ one's life / liberty / rights / interests / country (bravely / courageously / vigorously / heroically / stubbornly / *etc*); ~ o.s. against an accusation *(try to disprove one that has been raised)* (2 *keep free from attack, etc*) for over 900 years the sea has ~ed Britain from invasion; ~ the weak and helpless from harm; ~ o.s. from an accusation *(prevent one being brought against one)* (3) the accused had a lawyer to ~ him. (4) ~ an idea / righteous cause.

define *vt* (1) ~ (the meaning of) a word; ~ a term / concept; ~ s.o.'s duties; the powers of a judge are ~d by law. (2) the treaty ~s the borders of the two countries. (3) the hills were sharply ~d against the sky; a well-~d image.

defy *vt* (1) ~ public opinion / the law / an order / a threat; ~ the storm; ~ death; ~ s.o.'s wishes (2 *challenge*) this shop ~ies all others to beat its prices; I ~ you to repeat that word. (3) the window ~ies every attempt to open it; the problem ~ied solution *(could not be solved)*; ~ attempts at capture.

degree *n* (1) a right angle has 90 ~s; water boils at 212 ~s Fahrenheit; we had 12 ~s of frost last night; heat is unbearable at 40 ~s in the shade; the thermometer stands at / registers / reads 15 ~s centigrade; one ~ of latitude or longitude is about 69 miles. (2) climb a steep hill by easy ~s; improve by ~s; their friendship by ~s grew into love. (3 *amount, extent*) a high ~ of skill in (dancing / one's use of a tool); his work has reached a high ~ of excellence; the highest ~ of perfection / insolence / *etc*; he must accept some ~ of responsibility; (he is scrupulous) to a high / the last ~; be conscientious to the last / highest ~; he was not in the slightest ~ interested; to what ~ are you interested in this matter? to some / a certain ~; he suffers to such a ~ that he can't sleep. (4) ~s of relationship / kinship / consanguinity; they are realted in / relatives of the second ~. (5) a (mathematical) equation of the second ~; x^n is x to the nth ~. (6) a first- / second- / third-~ burn *(lowest to highest)* (7) lords and ladies of high ~ *(rank)* (8) an academic ~; a bachelor's / master's / doctor's ~; a candidate for a doctor's ~; an honorary ~; he has to have an engineering ~ for that job; study for a ~; gain / attain / obtain a ~; my son has taken his ~ at the university in law / history / *etc*; confer a ~ upon s.o.; grant a ~ to s.o.

delay *vt* (1) rain ~ed the game twenty minutes; frost can easily ~ fruiting; my work ~ed me at the office; I was ~ed on the way / by the traffic. (2) ~ one's journey; he ~s payment from day to day; I've ~ed writing to him till today; you mustn't ~ sending the message. - *vi* (3 *be slow*) don't ~; he didn't ~ an instant.

delight *n* (1) films give great ~ to millions of people; take / have ~ in (doing) s.th.; it was a ~ to the boys to go fishing with their father; to the children's great ~ / much to the ~ of the children, he ...; he noticed with ~ that he...; who can imagine my ~ when...; she went into raptures of ~ over the gift. (2 *cause of joy*) a bright sunny day is a ~; the garden was her great ~; the ~s of country life.

deliver *vt* (1) ~ letters / parcels / mail / goods / groceries / a message (to s.o.); □ ~ the goods *(inform: fulfil one's promises, do what is expected)* (2) ~ up stolen goods; ~ over one's property to one's son; ~ up charge of one's office to one's successor; ~ s.o. into s.o.'s hands; ~ s.o. up / over to s.o.; ~ o.s. up to justice (3) ~ a blow / attack / assault (4) a woman is ~ed of a child *(gives birth to it)*; the doctor / midwife ~ed her of the child; more women called the new doctor to ~ their babies. (5) ~ a speech / lecture (on s.th) / pronouncement; a badly ~ed sermon (6) ~ s.o. of an opinion; the speaker ~ed himself of a host of fine sentiments. (7) ~ s.o. / an animal from / out of captivity; ~ s.o. from his enemies; ~ us from evil; only education can ~ people from fear and superstition. - *vi* (8) I've just moved into this district - do you ~ there? (9 *inform: be diligent, productive*) this is a cut-throat business - if you don't ~ you get fired. (10 *give birth to offspring*) women that repeatedly ~ prematurely present special problems.

demand *n* (1 *authoritative request*) the workers' ~s for wage-increases; a ~ for an answer; (make) an exorbitant / excessive / unreasonable ~; meet / satisfy / grant / refuse / reject s.o.'s ~s; passengers must show their tickets on ~; payable on ~; he is in great ~ as an entertainer; Scott's novels are not much in ~ nowadays. (2 *claim*) make (great) ~s (up)on s.o.('s energy / resources / good nature); make excessive ~s (up)on s.o.'s patience; make considerable ~s (up)on one's employees; I have / people make many ~s on my time; have many ~s on one's purse; it's impossible to satisfy all ~s. (3) (the laws of) supply and ~; there is an (increasing) ~ for houses in the new area; a big ~ for mini-skirts; these goods are in great / not much in ~ just now; there is little ~ for these goods.

demand *vt* (1) ~ payment / satisfaction / money (from s.o.); ~ one's rights; she ~ed an apology / explanation (of his behaviour from him); he ~ed his release / that he should be released / to be released; he ~ed to be told everything; he / this letter ~s an immediate answer; the mind and body of a child ~ a great deal of play. (2) the situation ~s tact / patience; work that ~s great precision / special knowledge; do what the law ~s of one; I am willing to perform all the duties ~ed of me. (3 *inquire with authority)* "who are you?" he ~ed; the policeman ~ed the man's business / his name and address.

deprecate *vt* hasty action is to be ~d; the entire congregation ~d his outspoken sermon; ~ a practice / plan / *etc.*

depreciate *vt* (1 *lower in value*) ~ currency (2 *say that s.th. has little value*) he ~d our efforts to write good English; ~ ideals. - *vi* (3 *sink in value*) in recent weeks the value of the dollar has ~d; the purchasing power of money has ~d; perishable goods ~ rapidly.

depress *vt* (1) ~ the keys of a typewriter / piano; ~ a lever (2) this medicine ~es the action of the heart; ~ trade / a market; trading was ~ed by rumours. (3) bad news / wet weather ~es most people / makes most people feel ~ed; he has been ~ed since his failure; ~ing heat / news; a ~ing landscape.

deprive *vt* ~ s.o. of his property; I won't ~ you of your seat; ~ s.o. of sleep / pleasure / wealth; he was ~d of his employment; ~ s.o. of his rights as a citizen; he was ~d of all help; the accident ~d him of the use of his right arm; indignation had ~d him of speech; age ~d him of his sight; ~ s.th. of its substance/ glory.

depth *n* (1) the ~ of the pond was 10 feet; what is the ~ of the well? the sunken ship lies at a ~ of 50 feet; the immeasurable ~ of the sea; the snow is four feet in ~ *(4 ft deep)*; □ out of / beyond one's ~ *(in water too deep to stand in; beyond what one can understand)*; if you can't swim, don't go out of your ~; when people start talking about economics, I'm out of my ~. (2) the height, width and ~ of a box; in the ~s of the forest; in the ~ of the country; in the ~ of winter (3) the piano had great ~ of tone; the ~ *(intensity)* of a colour (4) a man of great ~; the book shows ~ of thought; she showed a ~ of feeling that surprised everyone; in the ~s of despair; in the ~ of one's heart; examine / study s.th. in ~ *(very thoroughly)*; here in ~ is a portrait of Spain as it was and is.

derive *vt* (1) ~ one's income from a farm; ~ great benefit from frequent exercise; ~ pleasure from (doing) s.th.; ~ much instruction from a lecture / one's knowledge from books; ~ one's character from one's father; governments are instituted among men ~ing their just powers from the consent of the governed. - *vi* (2) the word ~s / is ~d from Latin; this ceremony ~s from two old military manoeuvres; an awakening culture ~ing naturally from our own soil and past.

descend *vi* (1) the balloon ~ed in a field; the lift ~ed to the basement; ~ from a platform / to earth / to the bottom of a mine-shaft; ~ into a well; the sun slowly ~ed over the hills. (2) the hill gradually ~s to the lake; steps ~ing to the lower lawn (3) the estate ~s from father to son; she is ~ed from a noble family; the Welsh are ~ed from the Britons. (4) he ~ed from a long line of soldiers. (5) ~ to particulars / details (in a book / speech) *(pass on to them)* (6) would he ~ to such methods? she even ~ed to nagging / fraud; ~ from wealth to poverty (7) wolves ~ed on the flock; the fleet ~ed on the island, bombarding it fiercely; twenty guests ~ed upon us on Saturday afternoon. - *vt*(8) we ~ed two flights of stairs.

describe *vt* (1) ~ s.o./ s.th. (in detail / fully / accurately / vaguely / briefly / *etc*); ~ what you saw; please ~ it to me; words cannot ~ the scene; ~ one's purposes *(state them)* (2 *call, qualify*) ~ s.o. as a liar; he has been ~d as the most generous man of his age; I shouldn't ~ him as clever; he ~s himself as a doctor. (3 *draw*) ~ a circle / triangle / curve (4 *move along*) in the dense fog we had ~d a circle; the planets ~ their set paths; the arrow ~d a parabola.

design *n* (1) the ~ for clothes / furniture / book-bindings / a machine / a building; a dress ~; an aeroplane ~; a school of ~ (2 *plan*) a ~ for saving money; he has ambitious ~s for his son. (3 *pattern*) a flower ~; a pretty ~ for embroidery; the box was carved with an intricate ~; (fabrics) in a great number of ~s (4 *general arrangement, planning*) the building is poor in ~; a machine of faulty / excellent ~; the picture lacks ~. (5 *intention*) it is my ~ to leave on Monday; morality, like religion, is a product of human ~; he was there by ~, not by accident, as we had at first supposed; have ~s *(evil intentions)* against s.o. / (up)on s.o.'s life / money; he seems to have unfriendly ~s upon you.

design *vt* (1) ~ a building / home / machine / garden; ~ clothes / book-bindings / carpets / *etc*; a well-~ed machine; ~ a plan / project (2 *intend*) this room was ~ed for the children / as a nursery / to be a nursery; boats ~ed for river traffic; he ~s to be a lawyer; he ~ed his son to be an actor / for the theatre; the American people did not ~ to make their government dependent on the States.

desire *n* (1) a ~ for fame / wealth / power / knowledge; a ~ to succeed / become rich / travel / *etc*; feel a strong ~ to do s.th.; the ~ for freedom burned in their hearts; satisfy / fulfil / comply with s.o.'s ~ (2 *request*) at the ~ of the director (3 *thing desired*) I hope you will get all your ~s.

desire *vt* ~ happiness / freedom / peace; his behaviour leaves much to be ~d; our hotel rooms were all that could be ~d; all the pretty things (that) her heart ~d.

despair *n* (1) he was filled with ~ when...; ~ came upon them; the poor woman was in ~; he was in ~ of ever being able to pay off his debts; drive s.o. to ~; fall into ~; sink in ~; courage born of ~; in the depths of ~ (2 *cause of despair*) that son of mine is the ~ of my life; his recklessness is her ~; he was the ~ of his schoolmasters.

despair *vi* ~ of s.o. / success / finishing a task; the doctors ~ of saving her life; his life was ~ed of; ~ for s.o. *(feel deep sympathy, sorrow)*.

destine *vt* (1) ~ s.o. for the army / ministry; freight ~d for Israeli ports; old cars ~d for the scrap-yard; food ~d for human consumption (2) he was not ~d to live long; we were ~d never to meet again; ~d to decay / disappointment.

destroy *vt*(1) ~ a building / bridge / army / *etc*; the flood / enemy ~ed the village; ~ a document (by burning it); the forest was ~ed by fire; ~ s.o.'s / one's health (2) ~ s.o.'s hopes / dreams / illusions / plans / love / reputation; ~ a mood; ~ a friendship by deceit.

detail *n* I'll tell you all the ~s later; further ~s; full ~s; pass from ~s to the whole; leave out ~s; I cannot remember in ~; he answered the question in ~; go / enter into ~; go / enter into (all) the ~s (of s.th.); pay careful attention to ~(s); get lost in the ~s; this is a mere ~; this is only / but a ~.

determine *vt* (1 *fix, settle*) ~ the date for (a trip); ~ the time / place / price / value / penalty / terms of a contract / conditions / *etc*; this incident ~d his whole career; the ~ing factor; the circumference of a circle is ~d by the radius; eye colour is ~d by genes. (2 *regulate*) the pull of the moon ~s the tides on the earth; the sale of ice cream is partly ~d by the weather; demand ~s supply. (3 *find out*) ~ the extent of the damage; ~ a question; ~ an unknown quantity / the speed of light / *etc*; ~ (the meaning of) a word (4 *cause s.o. to resolve*) the accident ~d her to be more careful; the news ~d me to act at once; this fact ~d him against further delay. – *vt/i* (5) he ~d to go to college; we ~d on an early start / to start early; he ~d on becoming a painter; ~ on a course of action / plan; he is ~d to go / on going there.

develop *vt* (1 *cause to grow*) water, sunlight and air help to ~ plants; gymnastics ~s the muscles; fresh air and exercise ~ healthy bodies. (2) ~ one's personality / powers / faculties (fully); ~ one's memory / mind; a highly ~ed civilization; at this age the character is not yet fully ~ed. (3 *put to use*) ~ a country's natural resources; ~ an area / street *(build houses there)* (4 *bring into being*) you should try to ~ the reading habit; ~ a taste for s.th.; he ~ed unexpected courage / a strange habit; the car ~ed great speed / 70 horsepower. (5 *begin to have*) ~ a cough / fever / wobble / symptoms of TB (6 *expand*) ~ a business / railway network / organization / institution; ~ trade relations; the position / post isn't a very good one now, but it could be ~ed. (7 *work out in detail*) the candidate ~d his plan of campaign; the new process was ~ed from the inventions of two Germans; we want to ~ this model more fully; ~ a theory / doctrine / argument / idea; ~ a case / one's plans to an audience (8) ~ a film / plate / negative / print. – *vi* (9 *grow and mature*) buds ~ into blossoms; the fruit ~s from the flower; a chicken ~s in the egg; the child is ~ing slowly / rapidly; London ~ed into the general mart of Europe; we must let things ~; the fever / disease ~s normally. (10) the mind ~s from year to year; the story gradually ~ed in the author's mind; the situation might easily ~ into a general crisis; the quarrel grew hot, and finally ~ed into a lawsuit.

devil *n* (1a) the ~ is not so black as he is painted; sell one's soul to the ~; □ between the ~ and the deep (blue) sea *(in a dilemma)*; □ give the ~ his due *(be just even to s.o. one dislikes, or to s.o. who deserves only very little)*; □ play the ~ with *(ruin)*; □ talk of the ~ (and up he pops / and he will appear / and you'll see his horns); □ the ~ to pay *(trouble ahead)*: there's the ~ to pay – John has just broken a window. (1b *inform*) □ go to the ~ *(be ruined)*; (as far as I'm concerned you can) go to the ~ *(go to hell)*! (2 *inform: likeable person; term of endearment*) the old ~ refused to pay me; when I scolded him, the little ~ merely grinned; the poor ~'s starving; you lucky ~! (3) he's a ~ with the girls. (4) he's pleasant enough socially, but he's a ~ to those that work for him; I have never known such a ~ for work *(one extremely eager to work)* as you are. (5 ~ *of: very bad; inform*) a ~ of a mess / noise / journey / time; we had the ~ of a job to get the car going. (6 *the ~, used in questions; inform*) what the ~ is happening over there? where the ~ did I put my pen? I don't know when the ~ we're supposed to get this work done; who the ~ broke my typewriter? how the ~ am I supposed to read this handwriting? why the ~ didn't you tell me?

devise *vt* (1) ~ an appliance / engine / apparatus / new style in hats; ~ an expedient (2) ~ a plan (to escape from prison) / scheme (for making money) / plot (to overthrow the government); ~ new ways of doing s.th.; we must ~ means to check these abuses; she was not in the habit of ~ing falsehoods; ~ how to do s.th.

devote *vt* (1) ~ one's time / money / abilities / life to s.o. / s.th.; ~ o.s. to a task / work / problem; ~ o.s. to amusement; ~ all one's energies to s.th.; be ~d to one's studies / books / mother; be ~d to football / a doctrine / *etc* (2) they ~d part of the park to a playground; ~ a page to advertisements; this magazine is ~d to science.

devour *vt* (1) the lion ~ed its prey; ~ one's food / dinner (2) fire / flames ~ed the building. (3) ~ an adventure story / scene; ~ novel after novel; he ~ed every word; ~ s.o. with one's eyes / looks; she ~ed him with kisses. (4) she was ~ed by anxiety / curiosity / ambition / envy; I am ~ed with anxiety.

die *vi* (1) he ~d happy / young / poor / rich / a poor, rich man / a martyr / a hero / a beggar; ~ of cancer / malaria / (old) age / hunger / thirst / grief / sorrow / laughter / laughing / a shock; ~ from a wound; ~ in action / battle / harness *(while working)* / one's bed *(of age, illness)* / one's boots, shoes *(by violence; while still vigorous)*; ~ for one's country / faith; ~ for love / a friend; ~ by violence / pestilence / the sword / one's own hand; die a natural / violent / glorious death (→ death 1); ~ in poverty / through neglect / on the scaffold / at the stake; ~ with laughter / laughing / curiosity; I nearly ~d of boredom; □ never say ~ *(don't give in)*; □ ~ in the last ditch *(resist to the utmost)*; □ ~ hard *(be difficult to suppress, disappear slowly)*; malicious rumours / superstitions / distrust and suspicion / customs / opinions ~ hard. (2) these flowers will soon ~. (3) the breeze ~d towards evening; the sound ~d on the air; don't let the fire ~; the ~ing day (4) his fame ~d soon after him; the memory will never ~; the secret ~d with him; a ~ing custom; the smile ~d on her lips. (5) she was ~ing with curiosity to know whether ...; he's ~ing to go to sea; I am ~ing for a drink / for a sight of you / to see you.

die away the music / voices / noise ~d ~; the breeze ~d ~; the colours of the sunset ~d ~; his hopes ~d ~ at last.

die back the dahlias ~d ~ *(to the roots)* when the frosts came.

die down a storm / gale / wind / fire / noise / quarrel / controversy ~s ~; the waves / flames ~d ~.

die off (1) trees / plants / leaves / flowers ~ ~ (2) the family ~d ~.

die out (1) families / races / species / organizations ~ ~; many Red Indian tribes have now almost ~d ~. (2) beliefs / customs ~ ~; this practice is ~ing ~; religion will ~ ~.

diet *n* (1 *food*) the prisoner's ~ was coarse and dry; the Japanese ~ of rice, vegetables, and fish; a nutritious / rich / bland / meagre / varied / *etc* ~; (2 *a particular diet*) no cake for me - I'm on a ~; the doctor put him on a ~; a reducing / vegetarian / saltless / health / *etc* ~; keep to a strict ~.

differ *vi* (1) one thing / person ~s from the other (markedly / sharply / in size / shape / colour / *etc*); the two ~ only in price. (2) I ~ with / from you entirely; I'm sorry to ~ from you; I must ~ with you on that matter; I beg to ~ *(don't agree)*; men ~ in opinion about s.th.; □ they agreed to ~ *(gave up trying to convince each other)*; □ tastes ~ *(different people have different tastes)*.

difference *n* (1 *state of being different*) the ~ between summer and winter / day and night / *etc*; the ~ is in price only; he realized the wide ~ that existed between his aims and the result. (2) the ~ between 8 and 10 is 2; there are many ~s between German and Russian; a great / marked / considerable / essential / small / slight / *etc* ~; far-reaching ~s; make little / some / no / not any / not much / a (great) / a great deal of ~ *(be of little / some / etc importance)*; it makes no / won't make much ~ whether you ...; what ~ does it make? as if it made any ~! not that it makes any ~ to me, but ...; does that make much ~ to the price? I'll do it again, slowly - it makes all the ~; I advise you to make no ~ between them / in your treatment of them *(treat them alike)*; □ split the ~ *(come to a compromise, divide what is left over)* (3) a (serious) ~ of opinion; I have never had any ~ with him; the fatal ~s in the Cabinet; settle one's ~s and be friends again.

different *adj* (1 ~ + BE, AE *from*, BE also *to*, AE also *than*: *unlike*) two men could hardly be more ~; no thing is ~ from itself; these figures tell a very ~ story from that of only two years ago; I'm of an altogether ~ opinion from you; roller-skating is very ~ from / to ice-skating; a very ~ situation from / to the one under which we live; vastly ~ in size than it was 20 years ago; they behaved ~ly at school than they did at home.

(2 *separate, not the same*) that's quite a ~ matter; put on a ~ dress; study the behaviour of males in ~ age groups; many ~ kinds of food; ~ points of view; we go

to ~ butchers. (3 *several, various*) ~ people told us the same story; on ~ occasions; I've looked for the gloves in ~ places, but I can't find them. (4 *unusual*) she has a very ~ way of dressing; advertising that strives to be ~.

difficult *adj* (1) a ~ problem / task / passage / language / situation / *etc*; this question is ~ (to answer); the mountain was ~ to ascend; the roast looks rather a ~ piece to carve; an explanation ~ to follow; an object ~ to attain / of attainment; a task ~ of accomplishment; an aim ~ of achievement; a problem ~ of solution; the place is ~ of access / to reach. (2) a ~ child; he is a very ~ man to get on with / to argue with; he is ~ to please; the famous actress was being rather ~ *(was causing trouble)*.

difficulty *n* (1 *state of being difficult*) we were surprised at the ~ of tunnelling through the rock; have / experience ~ in doing s.th.; did you have any ~ (in) finding your way? he didn't grasp the ~ of the task; he did it, but with ~; without any / much / the slightest ~; if you are in ~, ask someone's advice; the swimmer appeared to be in ~; that puts me in a ~; get / run into ~ (2 *s.th. difficult to do, etc*) we were faced with the ~ of tunnelling through the rock; the text is full of ~ies; the ship got into ~ies near the coast; be working under ~ies; he's always in *(financial)* ~ies; face an (unexpected / unforeseen / considerable / *etc.)* ~; he managed to smooth out the ~ies between them; Dad made ~ies when I said I'd study abroad; please don't raise ~ies.

dig *vt* (1) ~ the ground / a field / a garden (2) ~ a grave / hole (in the ground) / mine / pit / trench / well; ~ a foundation; ~ one's way / a path through the snow (3 *get by digging; fig: get by stubborn persistence*) ~ clay / coal / peat / potatoes; ~ worms; ~ s.th. out of one's pocket(s); he dug the truth out of an unwilling witness; the police dug a confession out of the suspect. (4 *push*) he dug (his fork) into the pie; he dug his spurs into his horse's side / flank(s); he dug his horse with his spurs; ~ s.o. in the ribs; she dug her elbow into his stomach. (5 *search*) ~ facts from a book. - *vi* (6) ~ for coal / gold / water / buried treasure (7) the wheels of the tractor dug into the mud. (8 *make excavations*) next month we'll go ~ging at Delphi. (9 *search*) ~ for information; ~ through a pile of old letters; ~ into documents / a book; ~ into the history of mankind / the meaning of a text / the facts of a case; ~ (deep) into one's pockets / purse *(also fig: spend money)*; the lawyer dug under the testimony to reveal a hidden motive; we haven't found the answer yet but we're still ~ging.

dig down the roots ~ ~ into the ground.

dig in (1) the manure should be dug in well; the rider dug his spurs in. (2) soldiers / certain animals ~ themselves in; the soldiers dug in for the night.

dig out (1) ~ ~ a trench (2) he was buried under the avalanche and had to be dug ~. (3) ~ ~ secrets / old manuscripts / the truth.

dig up (1) ~ up one's garden / a field (2) ~ up roots / a plant / a bone / an old statue; ~ up treasure (3) ~ up old grievances; ~ up the (background) facts of a (legal / medical / *etc*) case.

digest *vt* (1) ~ food; some foods ~ / are ~ed more easily than others. (2) ~ a lesson / the facts / what one reads; ~ s.th. psychologically; he ~ed his father's advice. (3) ~ an insult / treatment; this is more than I can ~.

dignify *vt* (1 *add to prestige of*) choral chants and rich vestments ~ an otherwise plain church service; his unselfishness ~ied even his most insignificant act; a profound silence ~ied the mournful procession; a family crest ~ies his stationery. (2 *add an artificial air of dignity*) let us not ~ his crimes by calling them political necessity; I shall not ~ your question with an answer / that remark by commenting on it. - *adj* (3) a ~ied ceremony / ritual / dance / *etc*; a ~ied judge / old lady / *etc*; a ~ied carriage / way / manner (of speaking, bearing o.s.) / appearance.

dignity *n* (1) bear / carry o.s. with ~; there is ~ in even the lowest of God's creatures; honest labour carries a ~ of its own; his emotional outbreak was a shameful loss of ~. (2) invest a position with the ~ of an important title; though a base criminal she pretended a ~ which confused even the most sceptical investigators.

dinner *n* have you had ~ yet? they were having ~ / were at ~, so I couldn't see them; we're going to ~ at N's tonight; ask s.o. to ~; it's time for ~; what are we having for ~? do you change / dress for ~?

you can get a good ~ at this restaurant; a ~ of five courses; a five-course ~; a formal / ceremonial / light / substantial / *etc* ~.

direct *vt* (1 *tell s.o. where to go*) can you ~ me to the station? (2 *cause to move to a point*) ~ one's eyes to the door; ~ one's steps to a house; ~ a searchlight to a point; ~ a letter / parcel to s.o.'s home / business address; ~ radio waves to Asia; X-rays are ~ed through a portion of the body. (3) ~ one's / s.o.'s attention to s.th.; ~ one's efforts / energies / energy to s.th.; ~ one's remarks / criticism to s.o.; ~ o.s. to a task / one's work / the study of a problem (4 *manage*) ~ a business / campaign; ~ work / workmen; policemen ~ traffic; the film director ~s the film *(guides the actors, cameramen, etc)*; who ~ed (the orchestra) at yesterday's concert? (5) he ~ed his secretary to admit no callers; I was ~ed to go to England; the general ~ed the troops to retreat / an advance to be made.

disadvantage *n* (1) fear of water is a ~ in learning to swim; have the ~ of being small; being small, he was at a (great / serious) ~; have the ~ of another person *(be at a disadvantage, compared with him)*; put / place s.o. at a ~; feel at a ~; English spelling is a grave ~ to the language; study under ~s (2) rumours were spread to his ~ *(harm)*.

disagree *vi* (1) your statements about it ~ with those in my history books / with the facts. (2) s.o. ~s with s.o. / a plan / idea / proposal; I ~d with him about N's qualifications / on that matter / over the new proposals. (3) this damp weather ~s with my rheumatism; such food ~s with him.

disappoint *vt* (1) ~ s.o. bitterly / sorely / severely; I was ~ed to find you out; be ~ed with one's new house / the result of an exam / s.o.'s reply; be ~ed at the result of the election / not having been invited; I was ~ed at her lack of understanding; her lack of understanding ~ed me; be ~ed in love / one's hopes; be ~ed in the new assistant / one's eldest son / the Government; what are you looking so ~ed about? the performance / his work was ~ing; look at s.o. ~edly; □ be agreeably ~ed *(glad that the results are better than expected)* (2) ~ s.o.'s plans / hopes / expectations; ~ed ambition; commit suicide out of ~ed love; she had a very ~ed look when ...

discard *vt* (1) ~ one's winter clothing in spring; ~ an instrument (as useless); these are books ~ed from the library; ~ (a card) *(in playing)* (2) ~ old beliefs / habits / opinions; ~ obsolete terminology; ~ former friends; modern research ~s obsolete hypotheses without scruple or sentiment.

discharge *vt* (1) ~ s.o. from one's service / his employment; ~ s.o. from hospital / prison; ~ a servant / worker / patient / prisoner; ~ a soldier; ~ s.o. from the Service (2) ~ a ship; the ship ~d its cargo at Liverpool. (3) the factory ~s its waste into the river; chimneys ~ smoke into the atmosphere; the Nile ~s itself into the Mediterranean; lightning is caused by clouds ~ing their electricity; ~ an accumulator / battery / cell; an abscess ~s matter; ~ pus / hormones / *etc* (4) ~ an arrow / bullet / torpedo; ~ a gun (5) ~ one's duty / an obligation / a vow; I have a duty to ~. (6 *settle*) ~ a debt / one's liabilities. - *vi* (7) this pipe ~s into the sewer; the sewers ~ out at sea; the battery ~d. (8) suddenly the gun ~d.

discontinue *vt* (1) ~ payments / a correspondence / one's visits; ~ (taking in / a subscription to) a newspaper; a man quits work on the instance - he may ~ a practice gradually; those who ~d smoking cigarettes ran a steadily diminishing risk of dying from the effects. - *vi* (2) the publication will ~.

discourage *vt* (1) the teacher's criticism did not ~ the pupil; he easily gets ~d; don't let one failure ~ you. (2 *make s.th. seem not worth while*) highway patrols ~ speeding; inflation ~s saving; I ~d our customers from buying these articles.

discredit *n* (1 *loss of credit*) bring ~ on o.s. / the whole family / one's school; do s.th. to the ~ of one's family; bring o.s. / s.o. / s.th. into ~; fall / come into ~ (2 *disbelief*) his past lies throw / cast ~ on him / his evidence. (3) he is a ~ to his family / his school / himself.

discredit *vt* (1 *throw doubt on*) he ~ed the belief (that toads cause warts). (2 *not believe*) I ~ all those stories. (3) his conduct has ~ed him with the public; ~ o.s.

discretion *n* (1 *prudence, good judgement*) please handle this information with all possible ~; (the) utmost ~ is called for here; you can rely on his complete ~ if he takes up your case; act with / show ~ in buying a house (2 *freedom to make decisions*) he was given power to distribute the money at his ~; how the money is distributed is (with)in the ~ of the treasurer; you have full ~ to act; the law allows him a wide ~ in deciding whether ...; I shall act at / use my own ~; leave s.th. to s.o's ~ / to the ~ of the judge; that is a matter of ~; age / years of ~ *(age at which one is able to decide for o.s.).*

discriminate *vi* (1 *distinguish*) careful reading helps us to ~ between good writers and bad / good writers from bad; ~ red from scarlet; the law ~s between assassination, murder, and man-slaughter; the ~ing reader / audience / *etc* (2 *treat differently*) import duties which ~ against / in favour of certain goods / countries; I never realized how unpopular children are, how ~d against.

disease *n* (1) an acute / chronic / infectious / contagious / insidious / malignant / latent / incurable / mild / serious / *etc* ~; a hereditary / occupational / infantile / tropical / *etc* ~; a children's / deficiency / stomach / skin / eye / *etc* ~; a ~ of the brain / heart / liver / *etc*; contract / have a ~; suffer from a ~; be / fall / be taken ill with a ~ (2) in parts of Africa there is a lot of ~; the business of doctors is to cure ~. (3) materialism is a ~ of our time.

disgrace *n* (1) bring ~ on o.s. / s.o. / one's family / *etc* (2) he told a lie and is in ~ (with the others); get / fall into ~; get o.s. / s.o. into ~ (3) these dirty streets are a ~ to the town; he is a ~ to his family / his profession / the church / *etc.*

disguise *vt* (1) ~ s.o. / o.s. as a policeman / servant; ~ one's voice; ~ o.s. with a false beard; a bed ~d as a couch; horseflesh ~d as beef (2) he ~d his anger with a smile; ~ one's disappointment beneath a cheerful appearance; there is no ~ing the fact that we ...

dislike *n* have / conceive a (strong / violent / subconscious / *etc*) ~ of / for cats; take a ~ to s.o./ s.th.

dismiss *vt* (1 *allow to leave*) the teacher ~ed the class; ~ an assembly (2 *discharge*) ~ a clerk / servant (for being dishonest / without notice); ~ an officer from the army / Service; be ~ed (from) the Service (for cowardice) (3 *discard mentally*) she tried to ~ my explanation as mere evasion; ~ excuses / doubts / hesitations / all thoughts of revenge / a possibility; ~ a matter / idea from one's mind; a legend, which he summarily ~ed; ~ a subject in a few words; the judge ~ed the case *(refused to consider it further).*

disorder *n* (1) a room in ~; the enemy retreated in ~; throw troops into ~ (2) the ~ in the streets during the strike; troops were called out to deal with the ~s in the capital. (3) a ~ of the digestive system; suffer from mental ~; ~s of the mind; organic / circulatory / *etc* ~s.

dispatch *vt* (1) ~ a letter / message / telegram / parcel / goods; ~ a messenger / ambassador; the committee ~ed its chief counsel to Germany to make an on-the-spot check of the charges. (2) ~ business / a business deal; ~ one's lunch *(eat it quickly)* (3 *kill summarily*) ~ a criminal / prisoner.

dispense *vt* (1) ~ alms / charity / one's favour to s.o.; ~ justice (to s.o.); ~ clothing to the needy (2) ~ medicine / remedies (to the sick); ~ a prescription; a ~ing chemist. - *vi* (3 ~ *with: do without*) ~ with s.o.'s service / help; these men can be ~d with; it's so warm today - I can ~ with an overcoat; ~ with all formalities / an oath (4 ~ *with: make unnecessary*) machinery ~s with much labour; radio has not ~d with gramophone records. (5) ~ s.o. from an obligation / a duty / fasting.

displace *vt* (1) don't ~ anything on my desk; their cities were in ruins and numbers of families were ~d. (2) the jet-plane is ~ing the propeller-driven plane; machinery has ~d manual labour; his book has not yet been ~d by any other work; Tom has ~d Harry in Mary's affection; weeds ~d all other plants. (3) a ship ~ing 10,000 tons.

display *vt* (1) ~ a flag; ~ goods in a shop window / the new fabrics to the buyers; the peacock ~ed its fine tail feathers. (2) ~ courage / talent / fear / anxiety / *etc*; he ~ed great activity / all his eloquence / his ignorance / no sign of emotion / great intelligence; she was never able to ~ her full personality.

disposal *n* (1) the ~ of garbage; garbage / waste / sewage ~ is a problem. (2 *selling, giving away*) the ~ of the car / estate (3 *arrangement*) the ~ of objects in a window display / of furniture in a room (4 *settlement*) the ~ of business affairs; his final ~ of the matter (5 *power to use*) a car was placed / put at the ~ of the visitors; he placed / put £80 at my ~; my services are always at your ~; in time of war the government must have entire ~ of all material resources.

dispose *vt* (1 *arrange*) troops ~d for immediate withdrawal; God ~s all things according to His will. (2 *make inclined*) the news ~d me to believe that he ...; the remark ~d him to like the man immediately; feel ~d to help s.o. / go for a walk / *etc*; a dog ~d to bite; be well / ill ~d towards s.o. -*vi* (3) Man proposes, God ~s.

dispose of (1 *get rid of*) ~ of rubbish / sewage / *etc*; ~ of old clothes by burning them; recently I had to ~ of an attic full of valueless treasures. (2 *sell, give away*) will you ~ of these old books for me? ~ of public offices to one's political friends; the basic procedure is reading addresses and ~ing of the mail accordingly. (3 *finish*) I think we have ~d of all his arguments; the article ~d of the matter in two paragraphs; ~ of *(settle)* a quarrel; ~ of *(destroy)* enemy planes.

dispute *vi* (1) ~ with / against s.o. on / about a subject; some people are always ~ing; they ~d over politics for hours. - *vt* (2) ~ a question (3 *question the validity of*) ~ an idea / statement / decision / claim / right; the election (result) was ~d; seven towns ~d the honour of being Homer's native place; I don't ~ that he is clever. (4 *fight for*) the Marines ~d every inch of the beach when enemy boats landed; ~ the victory until the last minute of the game; ~ an advance by the enemy *(resist it)*.

dissipate *vt* (1) the sun ~d the fog / mist / clouds / darkness. (2) ~ fear / doubt / ignorance / gloomy thoughts / *etc* (3 *waste*) he ~d his money / fortune in almost no time; ~ one's energies / efforts. - *vi* (4) the mist ~d before the wind; the clouds ~.

dissolve *vt* (1) ~ a substance in a liquid (2) gasoline ~s wax; aqua regia is able to ~ gold and platinum. (3) ~ a marriage / friendship; ~ a company / society / assembly / parliament / firm. - *vi* (4) salt / sugar / soap / *etc* ~s in water; the snowman ~d into a puddle; the clouds / fog ~d into rain; she ~d in(to) tears. (5) the society / assembly / firm / *etc* ~d. (6) our dreams of success ~d when ...; her illusions ~d; the view ~d in mist.

distance *n* (1) a ~ between two places; the infinite ~s of the universe; the stopping ~ of a car; a short / long ~; the shops are a short ~ away; in London all ~s are so great; the station is no ~ (away) *(quite near)* / is a great ~ off; it's quite a ~ from here; the ~ covered / travelled was 50 miles; he lives within easy ~ of his work *(the distance to his place of work is not great)*; within walking ~ of the shops; at a ~ of 100 metres there was ...; follow s.o. at a (short) ~; the village looked beautiful at a ~; live at a ~ from one's work; the picture looks better at a ~; we heard the bells pealing in the (far) ~; clouds gathered / hills rose in the ~; we saw the car disappear in(to) the ~; look / see into the ~; approach s.th. to within a ~ of two metres; one can see nothing from that ~; look at / view s.th. from / at a ~; I've only seen the building from a ~; admire s.o. from / at a ~; □ keep one's ~ *(keep away from the vehicle in front; not be very friendly)*; □ keep s.o. at a ~ *(treat him with reserve)* (2) things look different at a ~ of 10 years; look back over a ~ of 30 years; at this ~ of time.

distinguish *vt* (1 *see, hear*) ~ distant objects; ~ s.th. through the fog; I cannot ~ the letters from this distance; he heard voices, but couldn't ~ the words. (2) ~ A from B / between A and B; it's difficult to ~ real pearls from culture pearls; can you ~ the twins apart? (3 *be a mark of difference*) speech ~es man from the animals; what ~es a boot from a shoe? (4 *give prominence to*) the geniality that ~es him; the king ~ed him by his friendship; his style is ~ed by a preference for short sentences; his reign was ~ed by a clever economic policy. (5) ~ o.s. by one's courage / good manners / talents; ~ o.s. at playing the piano.

distract *vt* (1) the noise ~ed my attention / me from my work; ~ s.o.'s thoughts / attention from s.th.; what can we do to ~ her mind from the sorrow caused by her child's death? -*vi* (2 *confuse*) he received so much different advice that he was almost ~ed; ~ed between love and duty; ~ed with grief / anxiety; drive s.o. ~ed *(mad)*.

distress *n* (1) she is in great ~ over the illness of her son; she cried out in ~; she could not conceal her ~; to his ~, his son has fallen in with bad company; his bad behaviour was a great ~ to his mother. (2 *great poverty*) the floods this year have caused great ~ in several areas; there is great ~ here among the poor; relieve ~ among the poor (3 *danger, difficulty*) ship in ~; be in great (financial) ~; get into ~.

distress *vt* news of the accident ~ed her; a cough ~es one when it is tight; I'm much ~ed to hear the news of his death; ~ing news; don't ~ yourself *(worry)*.

disturb *vt* (1 *upset the peace of*) Mr N. has given orders not to be ~ed; sorry to ~ you; ~ a sleeper / animal; ~ s.o.'s attention / equanimity; the noise ~ed my work; her life had never been ~ed by passions; ~ peace and order; a magnetic needle is ~ed by the presence of iron; the oars ~ed the smooth surface of the lake; the war ~ed all his plans; ~ an arrangement (2 *worry*) rumours of the plane crash ~ed her greatly. (3) don't ~ the books on that shelf; don't ~ my papers.

dive *vi* (1) ~ (from the bridge / off the pier) into the waves; ~ for coins / pearls; the submarine began to ~. (2 *move quickly*) ~ into one's pocket / handbag; ~ into a corridor / street; the rabbit ~d into its hole; the aircraft ~d steeply. (3) ~ into a book / subject / one's work.

divide *vt* (1) a high fence ~s their farm from ours; ~ sheep from goats; we must not ~ our forces; England used to be ~d up into a number of small kingdoms. (2) ~ a cake among ten guests; the money was ~d equally among the boys; ~ things out (among various people); ~ the work between them; how shall we ~ the work up? you may ~ the blame between you; ~ one's time between work and play (3 *arrange*) the books were ~d according to subjects; ~ people into groups / a book into chapters / a town into wards / a road into lanes (4) they were ~d on the question of borrowing money; opinions are ~d on that point; don't let such a small matter ~ us. (5) ~ 100 by 10; 6 ~d by 2 is / gives 3; ~ his figures by ten if you want a truer picture of the facts. - *vi* (6) the Nile ~s at its mouth and forms a delta. (7) the subject ~s into three branches. (8) 3 will not ~ into 10; 5 ~s into 20 four times; 7 will not ~ by 2; 15 ~s by 5.

divorce *n* (1) apply / plead / sue for (a) ~; obtain a ~ from one's wife / husband; she was granted a ~ from her husband; ground(s) for ~; a ~ suit / settlement (2) the ~ between religion and science / intentions and acts / ideas and practice; the ~ of ownership from management.

divorce *vt* (1) ~ one's wife / husband; be ~d from one's wife / husband; ~ o.s. from s.o.; the judge ~d Mr and Mrs N. (2 *separate*) when the second rocket ~s itself from the first, ...; we will ~ the two subjects entirely; what happens to the soul when it is ~d from the body? the horror finally ~d his mind from reality and he was sent to an asylum; justice should not be ~d from mercy; he proposed to ~ church and state. -*vi* (3) a month later they ~d.

do *vt* 1-9; *vi* 10-17

The patterns are grouped as follows: do + *dir obj: 4, 5, 6;* do + *indir obj* + *dir obj: 7;* do + superlatives as *obj: 1b;* do + *indefinite pron:* 1d; it + do + inf: 14; have / be done: 17; do + *adv*: 16; make s.th. do: 15b; will + do: 15a; do + *prepos:* → separate entries.

(1 *carry out; be engaged in*)

(1a *do + noun, pronoun*) ~ (some) work / housework / a job / one's duty / one's military service; you can't make a mistake if you ~ it in this way; what are you ~ing there? what shall I ~ next? it's easier said than done; □ no sooner said than done *(done at once)*; □ well begun is half done; he never ~es things by halves (→ half); my brother has lost all his money - I must ~ the decent thing and give him some; what is the decent / right / proper / correct thing to ~? ~ s.o.'s bidding *(what he commands)*; □ that (sort of thing) is not done *(not considered right)*; ~ business (→ business 1); ~ justice (→ justice 1) (1b *do + best, worst, or synonyms*) ~ one's best / the best one can; I'm ~ing my (level) best for you / to help you; although he did his best, he failed his examination; the doctor did his best / utmost / all he could / everything in his power, but the patient died; I shall take no notice of his threats - let him ~ his worst. (1c *do + good;* → 7) she's done a lot of good; we should try to ~ some good every day; I had my house painted last week, but it hasn't done much good; you can talk to him, but it won't ~ any good *(be any use)*; he could ~ better / worse. (1d *do + indefinite pronoun*) can I ~ anything for you? I have nothing to ~; are you ~ing anything tomorrow? there is nothing to ~ *(no work, no spare-time occupation)*; there is nothing to be done *(all is in vain)*; the doctor says he can ~ nothing; I'm sorry, but I can ~ nothing for you *(can't help)*; I shall ~ everything possible / you say.

(2 *cause*)
~ (great) damage / (much) harm / evil / wonders; ~ mischief (→ mischief 1); try what kindness will ~ *(effect)*; one of the fuses must have gone - I wonder what did it.

(3 *work at, have as occupation*)
what does he ~ for a living? he makes baskets; ~ dressmaking for a living; he graduated last March but hasn't got anything to ~ yet *(hasn't a position)*.

(4 *do + noun: the meaning of* do *is expressed by the noun*)
~ a lot of correspondence *(correspond, write letters)*; ~ the cooking; we did the journey in five hours; ~ a painting / portrait; he did a picture of her; ~ a play; he did (all) the talking; I'll ~ the translation for you / ~ you the translation; ~ the washing; he does the work of two men; ~ a weep *(inform)*.

(5 *do + noun: the meaning of* do *is suggested by the noun*)
(5a *clean, tidy*) ~ the beds *(arrange the coverings, etc; more commonly* make, → make 1); ~ *(wash)* the dishes; she had done her face *(applied cosmetics to it)* and fixed her hair; ~ one's hair; will you ~ *(arrange, water)* the flowers? ~ a room / the stairs / the windows; ~ the garden *(weed, dig, water it)*; the paper-hanger did the whole house in a week; ~ *(brush)* one's teeth (5b *cook*) ~ the steak lightly / to a turn *(perfectly)*; mind you ~ the beef well; how would you like your mutton chop done? the meat is not done enough - put it back in the oven and ~ it a little longer. (5c *busy o.s. with*) ~ needle-work / knitting / crocheting / woodwork / handicrafts; ~ gymnastics / sport (5d *study, learn, prepare*) are you ~ing history at school? I want to ~ medicine; he has been ~ing engineering at N. University; he's busy ~ing his lessons / homework for tomorrow; you must ~ this exercise / test / essay again; when will you ~ your exam? (5e *solve*) I showed him how to ~ this problem; I can't ~ this sum. (5f *travel*) the car ~es 60 miles an hour; it ~es 25 miles to the gallon *(a gallon of petrol is enough to drive 25 miles)*; we did 300 miles in a day. (5g *visit, tour*) have you done Paris yet? did you ~ the British Museum? foreigners in London ~ing the sights; you can't ~ England in a fortnight. (5h do *in individual cases*) I've done six copies of the letter *(written, made)*; ~ the pools *(gamble on them)*; ~ time *(inform: be in prison)*; he was ~ing two years for theft; he ~es *(entertains)* his guests well; ~ battle *(fight)*; in his room crates ~ duty as / for book shelves.

(6 *play the part of, perform*)
who is ~ing Ophelia? he ~es Hamlet very well; the group is ~ing *Macbeth*; are they ~ing any of Mozart's operas? he ~es the host admirably *(is an admirable host)*; □ (I suppose we must) ~ the polite (thing) *(be polite; inform)*; □ ~ the handsome (thing) by s.o. *(act generously towards; inform)*; □ ~ the dirty on s.o. *(play a mean trick on him)*.

(7 *do + indirect object + direct object*)
~ s.o. credit (→ credit *n* 3); ~ s.o. a disservice; ~ s.o. a favour; the medicine did him (no) good / didn't ~ him any good; it won't ~ you any good to stand out in the rain; his holiday has done him a world of good (→ 1c); ~ s.o. harm; ~ homage to s.o.; ~ s.o. honour / ~ honour to s.o.; ~ s.o. justice (→ do 1a, justice 1); the portrait ~es him great injustice; ~ s.o. a kindness / kindnesses; ~ reverence to s.o.; ~ s.o. a (dis)service; ~ s.o. a good / bad turn *(a service, disservice)*: ~ me a good turn and lend me some money; he has done me many good turns; ~ violence to s.o. / s.th.

(8 *inform: cheat*) that dealer did me over the sale of those pictures; be careful - he'll try to ~ you if he can; you feel rather a fool when you realize that you've been done.

(9 *inform: ruin*) now you've done it *(spoiled things)*; that has done me *(ruined my chances, hopes, etc)*.

(10 *act, behave*) ~ as I do; ~ as I tell you; □ when in Rome, ~ as the Romans (do).

(11 *make progress*) everything in the garden is ~ing splendidly; how is your son ~ing at school? business is ~ing badly / well; the patient has been ~ing well all day; he's much better today - I think he'll ~ now *(get well again)*.

(12 *manage*) I wonder how she ~es on so small an income.

(13 *be doing: be happening*) what's ~ing in town this week? there's nothing ~ing

in a small village like this; "Help you out? Nothing ~ing! I'm not ~ing your job and mine, too!"

(14 *do + infinitive: be advisable*)
it always ~es to keep on good terms with your rich relations; it doesn't ~ to let a child always have its own way; there's likely to be a rush for seats, so it won't ~ to be late; it doesn't ~ to work too hard / to complain; how would it ~ for me to write to him?

(15a *will do, will do for, do for: suffice, be satisfactory*) if you can't spare a dozen eggs, half a dozen will ~; that's not quite what I wanted, but I think it will ~; will it ~ if we let you have an answer by Friday? even if those plums are not ripe enough to eat, they will ~ to make jam with; this hotel will ~ (for) us; will this racket ~ you? take this piece of muslin - it will ~ you for a turban; this place would ~ for a gymnasium; don't throw those scraps away - they will ~ for the dog; these shoes won't ~ for mountain-climbing; this old suit is not fit to go to the office in, but it ~es for working in the garden; this log will ~ for a seat / for us to sit on. (15b *make s.th. do: make s.th. be sufficient*; → make 24a) can you make £5 ~? the soldier made the helmet ~ for a frying-pan.

(16 *do + adv*)
(16a *do + well, right, etc*) he's ~ing very well in business *(making money)*; he did quite well out of the sale of his house; I hear that the firms have done badly this year; how did you ~ in your examination? well done! you would ~ well to send for the doctor; you did well / quite right to refuse his offer; in behaving like that you did right / wrong; you would ~ wrong to make a change; you would ~ wisely to withdraw. (16b *do s.o. well: treat well, entertain liberally*) they ~ you very well at that hotel; Smith will certainly ~ you well; he ~es himself well *(provides well for his own comfort)*.

(17 *have done, be done: have, be finished*)
will the carpenters have done by 12 o'clock? have you done with *(finished using)* the ink? she has done sweeping the room; I've done talking - I'm going to act; when will the shoes be done for me to collect them? when day is done ...; his work is never done; will he ever have / be done? she keeps pestering me to go and see her, so I'll go now and have done with it; give him what he wants and have done with it.

do about we cannot ~ anything ~ it; you ought to ~ something ~ your cough; what shall we ~ ~ lunch: go to a restaurant, or have it at home?

do at "How is your book progressing?"-"I haven't done anything at it for the last fortnight."

do away with (1 *get rid of*) let's ~ ~ ~ these old newspapers; they did ~ ~ this law in 1949; mechanical appliances have done ~ ~ much of the drudgery of housework; we must ~ ~ ~ that practice as soon as possible. (2 *inform: kill*) the dog is sick - it's time he was done ~ ~ ; the gang threatened to ~ ~ ~ him if he informed the police.

do by when the terms of the will became known, several members of the family felt they had been badly done by *(treated)*; the firm did well by all its employees; she always thinks herself hard done by.

do down (1) ~ ~ the walls with a duster *(clean them)* (2) he did her ~ over the price of her car *(cheated; inform)*; I've been done ~ once, and I'm not risking it again.

do for (1) it's difficult for elderly people to find anyone who will ~ ~ them *(take care of the housework)*. Mrs N. ~es ~ the new teacher; he's old enough to ~ ~ himself. (2) how shall we ~ ~ food *(get meals)* during that long train journey? (3 *inform: finish off, ruin*) last night's gale has done ~ my fruit-trees; these old shoes are about done ~ *(completely worn out)*; let's take a rest - I'm done ~; brilliant play by our opponents did ~ us; it was this piece of evidence that did ~ him; the country's done ~; when the bullet hit him, he knew he was done ~. (4) → do 15a, 15b.

do in (1) all this work just ~es me in; she felt done in after the morning's work; I can't walk another step, I'm completely done in. (2 *inform: kill*) she was done in by a maniac.

do into ~ a fable ~ poetry / a story ~ verse / Horace ~ English.

do out (1 *BE clean; tidy)* we must ~ ~ the house / the drawers of my desk; that cupboard hasn't been done ~ for ages. (2 *BE paper and paint*) could you ~ ~ two rooms for me while the family are away on holiday? we shall have to have our meals in this room while the dining-room is being done ~ . (3 ~ ~ *of: cheat out of; inform*) he was done ~ of his inheritance; he has done me ~ of £500. (4) → do 16a.

do over when did you ~ the dining-room ~ (*paint, paper it*)? ~ ~ this wall before you begin on the other room; I should ~ it ~ with green paint if I were you.

do to what are you ~ing to that picture? he was ~ing something to his car; just look what the dog has done to our hyacinths.

do up (1) he buys second-hand furniture, ~es it up, and then sells it for new; quite a comfortable house if it's done up a bit; I'm having the outside of the house done up; ~ up *(decorate)* food (2) ~ up a parcel / bag; ~ up one's shoelace; a girl with her hair done up in curlers; please ~ up my suitcase; ~ up (the zip on) a dress; this dress ~es up at the side. (3 *inform: exhaust*) the long journey did us up; I can't go any farther - I'm done up.

do with (1 *need*) my car could ~ ~ a wash; that raincoat of yours could ~ ~ a clean; I could ~ ~ a cigarette / a drink / something to eat / *etc*; she said she could ~ ~ new shoes; after that long spell of cold weather we could ~ ~ some sunshine. (2 *make use of*) could you ~ ~ a few pounds of plums? make ~ ~ (→ make 23a) (3) what shall I ~ ~ this piece of cloth? I cannot remember what I did ~ my umbrella *(where I put, left it)*; what does he ~ ~ himself all day? the children didn't know what to ~ ~ themselves for joy / impatience. (4) he had a lot to ~ ~ that fellow / plan; he has to ~ ~ all sorts of people. (5 *to ~ ~: connected with*) how I spend my money is nothing to ~ ~ you; I am interested in anything (that has) to ~ ~ stamps; I don't know precisely what his business is, but I think it has to ~ ~ cutlery; what's that got to ~ ~ me? (6 *done ~: finished*) all the magazines in that pile are done ~ *(of no further use)*; all the Christmas celebrations are now over and done ~. (7) have done ~ (→ do 17) (8 *tolerate*) I can't ~ ~ her silliness; I can't ~ ~ a lot of noise when I am trying to work; don't you find him difficult to ~ ~?

do without (1) the survivors did ~ food and water for five days; we can ~ ~ luxuries; → make 23a (2) I can ~ ~ the car today if you need it; no-one can ~ ~ sleep for very long. (3) I can ~ ~ your advice *(inform: don't want it)*.

dog *n* (1) a female ~; this ~ bites; a fierce / vicious / *etc* ~; ~s must be kept on the lead / leash; no ~s (allowed); □ give / throw to the ~s *(throw away)*; □ go to the ~s *(be ruined)*; □ rain cats and ~s *(very heavily)*; □ lead a ~'s life (→ lead *vt* 6); □ lead s.o. a ~'s life (→ lead *vt* 6); □ lead a cat-and-~ life (→ lead *vt* 6); □ help a lame ~ over a stile *(help s.o. in difficulty)*; □ let sleeping ~s lie *(not raise issues that might cause trouble)*; □ ~ in the manger *(s.o. who prevents others from enjoying s.th. that is useless to himself)*; □ not even a ~'s chance *(no chance at all)* (2 *inform: fellow*) a lucky / gay / sly ~; I'm too old a ~ to learn new tricks.

dominate *vt* (1) he ~d his younger brother; a great man can ~ (over) others by force of character; the strong usually ~ (over) the weak; Goethe ~d his age. (2) ~ one's emotions / passions; love and duty struggled to ~ his mind; be ~d by fear (3) the mountain ~s the valley; the fort ~s the town.

door *n* (1) a front / back / oak / iron / massive / *etc* ~; who lives next ~ (to you)? □ next ~ to *(very nearly)* impossible; my brother lives two ~s off / away; it's a 10-minute journey from ~ to ~; go from ~ to ~ to sell s.th.; it's cold out of ~s; within ~s; (negotiate) behind closed ~s; open / shut / close / (un)lock a ~; knock at a ~; hammer at / on the ~; bang a ~; slam a ~ (to); the ~ (was) opened and . . .; the ~ flew open; the ~ banged shut / slammed (to); the ~ opens into the corridor / on to the garden; → answer *vt* 1; □ lay s.th. at s.o.'s ~ *(blame him for it)*; □ show s.o. the ~ *(send him out)*; □ be at death's ~ *(so ill as to be likely to die)*; □ get / have a foot in the ~ (→ foot *n* 1) (2) a ~ to success; open a / the ~ to (negotiations); close / shut the ~ upon (negotiations).

double *adj* (1 *twice as much, large, good, etc*) a ~ choir; a ~ chin; a ~ portion; this material is ~ width; two ~ whiskies, please; his income is now ~ what it was; ~ joy / pleasure; have ~ luck; pay ~ the price / ~ as much; bread costs ~ what it used to; ~ the number of people came; do ~ (the) work (2 *having two like parts, things, etc*) a gun with a ~ barrel; a ~ door / window; a box / trunk with a ~ bottom; a ~ -breasted suit; a knife / axe with a ~ edge; a ~ coat of paint; a ~-decker (bus); a ~ exposure *(two exposures on the same section of film)*; a ~ row (of trees); a ~ star; a ~ (railway) track; ~ vision; fold paper ~; ride ~ *(two on a horse)*; sit ~ *(two on a chair)*; sleep ~; see ~; ~-lock a door (3 *intended for two persons, things*) a ~ bed / room; this bed performs a ~ service / serves a ~ purpose - during the day it's a couch; ~ harness *(for two animals)*; a ~ murder; a ~ wedding (4 *combining two things, qualities*) a ~ advantage; a man with a ~ character; engage in ~-dealing *(dishonesty)*; a ~-dealer *(dishonest, deceitful person)*; wear a ~ face; live a ~ life *(one partly dishonest)*; play a ~ game; a ~ meaning *(one usually indecent)*; a ~-meaning joke; a ~ victory / winner.

double *vt* (1 *make twice as much, large*) ~ a sum; ~ one's income / stake (in a game) / offer; your savings will ~ themselves in time. (2 *play at the same time*) he's ~ing the parts of a servant and a country labourer. (3 *duplicate*) the soprano ~s the violin. (4 *fold, bend*) ~ (up) paper / material / a blanket; let me ~ the blanket round you; ~ one's fists *(close tight)* (5 *sail round*) the ship ~d the Cape. - *vi* (6 *take the place of*) Jane ~d for her sister waiting on customers. (7 *become twice as much, large*) the investment ~d in value in ten years; the population ~d in the meantime.

double up (1) → double *vt* 4; he ~d up his legs and kicked out (when swimming). (2) this carpet is too thick to ~ up. (3) he ~d up *(rolled up)* with pain / laughter; ~d up by a blow in the stomach; the blow ~d him up with pain.

doubt *n* he never felt a ~ of God's existence; I had never entertained the least / slightest ~ of / about his honesty; I have (my) ~s about it / as to this being true; have (grave / serious / gnawing) ~s about s.o.('s trustworthiness); I have no ~ about it (in my mind); be in ~ about s.th.; I'm in ~ (about) what to do; the authenticity of the document has for long been in ~; five minutes from the end, the outcome of the match was still in ~; he'll come without (a) ~ *(certainly)*; you've no ~ *(certainly)* heard the news; facts beyond ~; the truth of the story is beyond ~; → benefit *n* 1.

doubt *vt* ~ s.o.('s honesty) / his word / the truth of this story; I ~ whether I said that; I have never ~ed that he can work if he wants to; I do not ~ (but) that he will help you; it is not to be ~ed that he...

doubtless *(AE also ~ly. In BE ~ly is considered substandard or incorrect.) adv* (1 *certainly*) he was ~ guilty although there was no actual proof; he is ~ the best man for the job. (2 *probably*) she will ~ agree although she hasn't committed herself yet; he will ~ get well again - doctors are so good these days.

drain *vt* (1 *draw off*) they ~ed the water from the pond; ~ the pond of water; ~ the blood from a carcass (2 *draw liquid from*) ~ a wound; ~ a swamp / field / cask / water-tank / pipe; two rivers ~ this valley. (3) ~ *(empty)* a glass; ~ *(drink)* a pint of beer (4) the country was ~ed (of its manpower and wealth) by the war; ~ s.o. of his wealth and strength; be gradually ~ed of one's energy; ~ a subject of its meaning. - *vi* (5 *discharge water*) the street ~s into the sewer; this field ~s into a small river. (6 *become dry*) she left the dishes to ~ (on the ~ing-board).

drain away (1) dig trenches to ~ ~ the water (2) the water will soon ~ ~. (3) his fortune ~ed ~; his life was slowly ~ing ~.

draw *vt* (1) horses ~ carts; ~ a load; ~ one's belt tighter; he drew his hat over his face / eyes; she drew him to her by the sleeve; ~ your chair nearer to the table; the archer drew the bow slowly; □ ~ the long bow *(exaggerate)*; □ ~ it mild *(not exaggerate)*; ~ the curtain across the window / aside; ~ a curtain / blind / veil *(close it)*; □ ~ a / the veil over s.th. *(not describe it)*; ~ an injection *(fill a syringe)*; a face ~n with pain / anxiety (2 *pull out*) ~ a cork (out of a bottle); ~ nails (from a plank); he drew a letter from his pocket / a document from his wallet; suddenly he drew a pistol / knife; have a tooth ~n; □ ~ s.o.'s teeth *(make him harmless)* (3 *of breath: take in*) ~ a (deep) breath; stop to ~ breath *(to rest)*; ~ one's first / last breath *(be born; die)* (4 *get, obtain*) ~ water from a well; ~ beer from a barrel; ~ a bath *(let water run into it)*; ~ blood (from s.o. / a vein); ~ a card (from a pack) / trumps; ~ lots; ~ a winning ticket; ~ a prize *(win it by chance)*; ~ the winner *(~ a prize, etc)*; ~ a blank *(get nothing after hoping to win, etc)*; ~ sounds from a flute / trumpet / *etc*; ~ a / one's salary; ~ (one's) wages; ~ interest;

~ a regular income from / out of s.th.; ~ unemployment benefit: ~ money from the bank / a fund; I want to ~ some money out of my savings account; ~ facts from a book; I couldn't ~ any information from him; he ~s his inspiration from nature; ~ a moral from a story; ~ a conclusion / inference (from s.th.); this is an unpleasant conclusion to have to ~; her dancing drew great applause; his sad story drew tears / groans from all who heard it. (5 *try to get information from*) she refused to be ~n. (6 *remove what is inside*) a poultice ~s an abscess; ~ a fowl *(remove its entrails)* (7 *bring to an undecided conclusion*) ~ a game / match / contest / fight / battle (8 *attract*) the magnet ~s the needle; moths are ~n by light; flowers ~ bees; street accidents always ~ crowds; the play drew a full / big (*inform*) house; it drew a large audience; the ~ing power of a play; she didn't feel ~n to him at all; ~ attention to s.th.; if you have changed your address, please ~ the new address to our notice; ~ s.o. into a conspiracy; one day you will ~ ruin on yourself; ~ a reproof (9 → 12) ~ a straight line / circle / triangle / *etc* (with a pen / pencil / brush / *etc*); ~ a curve with compasses; ~ a diagram / plan / picture / figure; can you ~ a horse? ~ a portrait from life / memory; he drew his pen through the words; □ we must ~ the line *(set a limit)* somewhere / at (using violence). (10 *write out*) ~ a bill / cheque / order (on a banker / for a sum); ~ a will (11 *describe in words*) the book's characters are well ~n; ~ a comparison / contrast / distinction between A and B; he drew a parallel between the causes of the French and the Russian revolutions. – *vi* (12 → 9) in her leisure-time she ~s; an artist ~s with crayons. (13 *move, come*) Christmas is ~ing near; the two ships drew level (→ level *adj* 2); at last we drew level with them; in this race for supremacy, N. has ~n ahead; the speaker drew to a conclusion; the year ~s to a close. (14) the wagon ~s *(can be drawn)* easily. (15 *allow the passage of air*) the chimney / furnace ~s well; this cigar ~s badly. (16 *of tea, become stronger*) let the tea ~ for five minutes. (17 *of a ship, require a certain depth*) the boat ~s 15 feet. (18) the two teams drew (→ 7).

draw away (1) ~ s.o. / s.th. ~ (from s.o./ s.th.) (2) every year in spring, he is / feels ~n ~. (3) that ship was faster than ours and soon drew ~ from us.

draw back (1) ~ ~ a curtain (2) the natives drew ~ when the strangers approached. (3) he had promised to help me, but at the last moment he drew ~ .

draw down (1) ~ ~ a blind over a window; it's time to ~ ~ the curtain *(enough has been said)*. (2) ~ ~ s.o.'s anger on o.s.; the statesman drew a lot of opposition ~ when he introduced the new bill.

draw for ~ ~ a prize (in a lottery).

draw forth his skill drew ~ exclamations of wonder and praise.

draw in (1) the fishermen drew in their nets; a snail ~s in its horns; I advise you to ~ in your horns *(be more careful)*. (2) ~ in one's expenditure(s) *(spend money more carefully)* (3) he's ~ing *(calling)* in the loans he made last year. (4) the days were ~ing in *(getting shorter)*. (5) the train drew in at 8.23 a.m. (6) the lorry soon drew in and allowed us to overtake it. (7) I've only £2 left - I shall have to ~ in *(be careful in spending money)*.

draw into (1) ~ s.o. ~ an argument (→ draw 8) (2) we drew ~ a side road, where we stopped to have some lunch.

draw off (1) ~ ~ one's gloves (2) ~ ~ water from a cask; make ditches to ~ ~ the water; ~ ~ beer / wine; ~ ~ smoke / gas (3) when the enemy saw how strong we were they drew ~ .

draw on[1] (on *is adv*) (1) ~ on one's gloves (2) time ~s on; winter is ~ing on. (3) his promises drew me on *(attracted me)*; the girl's indifference drew him on all the more; the thieves drew the young boy on until he became one of them; ~ on an animal *(bring it into a trap)*.

draw on[2] (on *is prepos*) ~ on one's banking account *(get money from it)*; ~ on one's savings; you mustn't ~ on your capital, you must live on the interest; one cannot ~ only on past experience; if newspapermen cannot get facts for their stories, they sometimes ~ on their imagination.

draw out (1) heat metal and ~ it ~ into a long wire (2) ~ ~ one's sword; he put his hand in his pocket and drew ~ a diamond; he drew £50 ~ *(of his account)* to pay for his holiday. (3) ~ ~ the facts from a witness (4) ~ ~ a scheme *(set out the particulars in writing)* (5) ~ ~ a speech / one's remarks / the subject into three volumes; the battle was long (and) ~n ~; a long-~n-~ discussion (6) ~ ~ a shy girl *(make her speak)*; ~ ~ a minister in Parliament on / about an affair (7) the days began to ~ ~ *(get longer)* quite noticeably; the speeches drew ~ endlessly. (8) the train was ~ing ~ (of the station) just as we arrived on the platform. (9) the car suddenly drew ~ towards the middle of the road; a lorry drew ~ of a side street. (10) ~ ~ of an / one's engagement.

draw over she drew him ~ *(to her)* by the sleeve.

draw round well, ~ ~ (me) *(come close)* and I'll tell you the story.

draw together the ships drew ~ until they were able to exchange signals.

draw up (1) ~ up a bucket of water from a well; he drew himself up (to his full height) (2) ~ up troops ready for battle; a regiment ~n up in front of the palace (3) ~ up a document / declaration / agreement / lease / will / *etc*; ~ up a list of things required; ~ up a letter (stating our grievances) (4) they all drew up at / round the table *(moved nearer)*. (5) the troops drew up on the parade-ground. (6) a car drew up *(came to a stop)* at the door; he drew up the car opposite the Grand Hotel; the car drew up to the kerb *(stopped beside it)*.

dream *vt/ i* (1) ~ of / about home / an island / *etc*; he ~ed that he was at sea; he often ~s; I ~ed a dream. (2 *entertain an idea*) I should never ~ of doing such a thing; ~ of a better day; when I was young I ~ed of becoming a surgeon; he little ~ed that he would be chosen.

dream away ~ one's days / time / life / the hours ~.

dream up I wonder who ~ed up that idea - it's pretty absurd, anyhow.

dress *n* (1) a wool / silk / taffeta / green / blue / olive / *etc* ~; an ordinary / formal / evening / full-length / fancy / summer / wedding / ready-made / tailor-made / *etc* ~; a plain / simple / fashionable / becoming / low-cut / low-necked / décolleté / *etc* ~; the new ~ suits her well / sits well (on her) / fits exactly / fits her like a glove. (2) not care much about ~; evening ~ can be worn by men and women; he is very fastidious in his ~; all appeared in full ~.

dress *vt* (1) ~ a child / o.s. / a doll (2 *be ~ed: be wearing*) she was ~ed in white / green / the latest fashion / old-fashioned clothes / a woollen costume / *etc*; be properly ~ed for skiing; □ be ~ed (up) to the nines *(smartly, showily)*; □ be ~ed to kill *(inform: showily overdressed)* (3 *provide with clothes*) it costs a lot to ~ a wife and three daughters; she is expensive to ~.

(4 *prepare*) ~ meat / a chicken / *etc*; ~ a salad *(with oil, vinegar, etc)*; ~ a wound *(clean, bandage it)*; ~ a field *(with manure)*; ~ (the surface of) stone / leather / textiles; ~ one's hair *(comb, arrange it)* (5 *decorate*) ~ a shop window; ~ a ship / street with flags. *-vi* (6) it will take me five minutes to ~; ~ with taste / care; she knows how to ~; she always ~ed in perfect taste; guests are requested to ~ for dinner *(put on evening dress)*; he has to ~ well in his position.

dress down (1) ~ ~ a horse *(brush it)* (2 *reprimand*) he ~ed the office boy ~ for his insolence.

dress up (1) nowadays people don't ~ up on Sunday. (2) ~ the children up for the party (3) he ~ed up as Father Christmas / for the fancy-dress ball / in a period costume.

drink *vt/ i* (1) ~ water / milk / wine / poison / medicine / *etc*; ~ out of / from a cup / glass / bottle; ~ from one's cupped hand; ~ from the river; ~ a cup of (coffee / *etc*) (2 *wish well*) ~ s.o.'s health / success; ~ success to s.o. / an undertaking; ~ to s.o.('s health / success) (3 *of plant, soil*) → drink in 1, drink up 1. (4 *take alcoholic liquors*) he ~s moderately / heavily / far too much / like a fish; ~ o.s. to death; he ~s all his earnings; I don't ~; be / get (o.s.) / make s.o. drunk; ~ s.o. under the table *(get him drunk first)*; he was drunk on two glasses of beer; drunk with success.

drink down he drank ~ the bitter medicine without complaining.

drink in (1) the parched soil drank (in) the rain. (2) ~ in beautiful scenery / music; he drank in every word of the story.

drink up (1) ~ up one's wine; the plant drank (up) all the water. (2) ~ up so that we can go.

drive *vt* (1) ~ cattle (to market) / the cows out of the shed; ~ s.o. out of the house; ~ the enemy out of their positions; □ ~ s.o. into a corner / to the wall *(into a difficult position)* (2) the gale drove the ship on the rocks; the wind was ~ing the rain against the window-panes; ~ a golf ball; ~ a nail into s.th.; ~ a nail home *(hammer it in completely)*; □ ~ home a / the point *(explain it clearly and forcefully)*; ~ an argument home *(cause it to make a deep impression)* (3) the machine is ~n by steam; steam or water ~s the mill. (4) ~ a tunnel / road through a hill (5) ~ a car / taxi / train; he ~s his own car; he drove his car into a wall / to pieces; the car is easy to ~. (6) my brother will ~ me / the luggage to the station; ~ s.o. up to / into town; ~ s.o. back home / to his home (7) □ ~ a (good / hard) bargain *(effect it)*; □ ~ a roaring trade *(sell a lot very fast)*; ~ an idea out of s.o.'s mind.

(8 *force to work*) some employers ~ their workmen too hard; ~ pupils; he is driven by (an uncompromising) ambition; he ~s himself too / very hard. (9 *force into a certain state*) this noise is ~ing me mad / crazy; ambition drove him to success; ~ s.o. to distraction *(madden)*; domestic troubles drove him to suicide / drink / despair; his indifference to financial matters is going to ~ him to rack and ruin *(ruin him)*.

(10 *force to do s.th.*) ~ s.o. to do a task; hunger drove him to steal (food); they were driven by sheer necessity to sell some of the family plate.

– *vi* (11) can you ~ (a car)? do you ~ yourself / ~ (a car)? I have ~n 2,000 miles; I drove the distance in three hours / the whole way; ~ carefully / carelessly / recklessly / at a high, dangerous, *etc* speed / like mad / like a madman; ~ into a (one-way) street / round a bend / on a country road / through a town / *etc* (12) the ship drove on the rocks; the clouds drove across the sky; ~ing wind; he let ~ at me (with his right) *(aimed a blow at me)*. (13) what are you ~ing at (with that remark) *(what do you mean)*? tell us plainly what you are ~ing at.

drive away (1) ~ a dog / burglar ~ (2) ~ s.o. ~ / off (in a car) (3) she waved and drove ~ / off. (4) he was ~ing ~ at his dissertation *(working hard at it)*.

drive in (1) ~ in a nail (2) ~ in an idea.

drive off the policemen drove the crowd ~; → drive away.

drive on ten minutes later we were able to ~ on.

drive out (1) ~ ~ the sheep to the meadows (2) ~ ~ a nail (3) ~ ~ air / gas / water (4) ~ ~ the invaders; he was ~n ~ in disgrace.

drive over we'll ~ ~ *(come by car)*.

drive up he drove up *(arrived)* in a large American car.

drop *vt* (1) she ~ped a tear; he ~ped his medicine in his eyes; he ~ped the letter into the letter-box. (2 *allow to fall accidentally*) she ~ped the vase; don't ~ the baby; the printer has ~ped a letter here; □ ~ a brick *(say s.th. indiscreet)*; he ~ped *(gambled away)* 100 francs at the Casino last night. (3 *allow (o.s.) to fall on purpose*) he ~ped his hand; ~ anchor *(lower it)*; ~ supplies / troops by parachute; the Americans ~ the 'u' in 'colour' and write 'color'; unable to hold on any longer, he let himself ~ into the water. (4 *cause to fall; kill*) the hunter ~ped two geese with one shot; he ~ped the elephant in its tracks. (5 *allow to get off*) ~ s.o. (from a vehicle); I will ~ you (off) at your door; the ship ~ped the pilot outside the harbour.

(6 *cause to stop, give up*) ~ a discussion / inquiry / plan / idea / custom / habit / title; ~ a hobby / interest / friendship; let us ~ the subject / matter; ~ it! *(inform: stop talking about s.th.)* should our schools ~ Latin? he ~ped his attempt at ...; he has ~ped his intention of (doing s.th.); the two ~ped their quarrelling); if a fire alarm is given, ~ whatever you are doing and leave the building at once. (7) the police ~ped the charge of manslaughter; the prosecution ~ped the case against the secretary; Germany ~ped her demand for the return of her colonies; he ~ped his claim (against the firm). (8) ~ pretence / one's mask of disinterestedness / one's assumption of superiority / one's air of injured innocence / one's guard / *etc* (9) ~ s.o. / an acquaintance; we have ~ped John from the team; in off seasons, all part-time employees are ~ped *(dismissed)*. (10 *send*) ~ s.o. a note / card / letter; ~ s.o. a line / a few lines; she'll surely ~ us a word giving us the time of her arrival. (11 *express casually*) ~ a hint / suggestion / warning / remark. (12 *allow to become lower*) he ~ped his voice to a whisper; don't ~ your voice at the end of this sentence. – *vi* (13) a gentle rain ~ped; tears were ~ping from her eyes. (14) an apple ~ped to the ground; the book ~ped from / out of her hands; three bombs had

~ped there; there was not a sound - one could have heard a pin ~; the penny ~ped (→ penny 1); I'm ready to ~ *(very exhausted)*; ~ asleep; I haven't seen John for a long time - he has simply ~ped out of sight. (15 → 3) he ~ped into a chair; he ~ped out of the window (onto the lawn); he ~ped on one knee / his knees. (16 *move down*) our boat slowly ~ped downstream; the hinges on the door seem to have ~ped; our team ~ped to the 8th place among the Olympic teams; he suddenly ~ped into Russian. (17 *become lower, less strong*) his voice ~ped at the end of the sentence / to a whisper; her loud wailing ~ped to a moan; the wind ~ped at sunset.
(18 *of things that can be expressed in numbers: decrease, fall*) the price / production / sales of sugar ~ped 5 per cent last month; these articles have ~ped in price; the speed of the plane ~ped from 200 to 100 m.p.h. as it came in to land; the pressure / temperature / voltage / fever / pulse rate ~s; attendance is ~ping; standards in public examinations are ~ping every year; fluency in reading aloud has ~ped in this class.

drop away (1) at first there were thirty students, but ten have ~ped ~. (2) the mountains ~ped ~ to the south *(appeared to recede)*.

drop back (1) ~ ~ into a(n old) habit (2) → drop behind.

drop behind he ~ped ~ / back on the hike when he became too tired to keep up.

drop by ~ by sometime! John ~ ped by this morning to tell me . . .

drop down he ~ped ~ dead; he ~ped ~ behind the rocks and took cover.

drop in if you are over in this district, ~ in and see us; he ~ped in to dinner / to see me yesterday; I wish he wouldn't ~ in on me so often; ~ in on us again sometime.

drop off (1) in autum the leaves begin to ~ ~; fruit ~s ~ a tree. (2) his customers ~ped ~; the number of students ~s ~ at the end of term; their receipts were ~ping ~; business ~s ~. (3 *inform*) he ~ped ~ (to sleep). (4) → drop *vt* 5.

drop on (1) as I was looking through some books, I ~ped on just what I wanted. (2) why does he alsways ~ on me to answer the most difficult questions?

drop out (1) two cars won't hold fifteen people - five of us had better ~ ~ . (2) he used to be in this class but he ~ped ~ .

drop through that big scheme seems to have ~ped ~ *(come to nothing)*.

due *adj* (1 *payable*) this bill is now ~ / falls ~ next Friday; the rent is ~ on the first of the month; the amount ~ (2 *morally owing*) thanks are ~ to Mr N.; praise / respect / reverence is ~ to s.o.; first place is ~ to Homer; the share ~ to him (3 *expected to arrive*) the train is ~ (in) at 4.12 p.m.; when is the steamer ~? he is ~ at his office on Monday; Aunt Rose is ~ to come again. (4 ~ *+ on, + inf: scheduled to speak, perform*) Mr N. is ~ to speak twice tomorrow; he is ~ on in ten minutes. (5 *planned*) some buildings have become ~ for demolition under a slum-clearance scheme; be ~ for promotion (6 ~ *to: attributable to, caused by*) his absence is ~ to illness; death ~ to pneumonia (7 *proper, adequate*) after ~ consideration; with all ~ respect; with ~ care / caution; → course *n* 2.

dust *n* furniture covered in ~; a cloud of ~; the car raised a terrible ~ as it passed us; □ make / raise a ~ *(cause a disturbance)*; □ throw ~ in s.o.'s eyes *(mislead him)*; □ shake the ~ off one's feet *(leave in anger)*; □ bite the ~ (→ bite *vt* 1).

dust *vt* (1) ~ the furniture; □ ~ s.o.'s jacket *(beat him)* (2) sparrows ~ed themselves in the road; my clothes have got ~ed all over. (3) ~ a cake with icing-sugar; ~ sugar onto a cake; ~ a plant with insecticide.

dwell *vi* (1 *lit*) ~ abroad / at home / in a mansion / in the country; what fine houses they are, and how happy must those people be who ~ in them. (2 ~ *on: think, speak about s.th. for a long time*) his mind dwelt on unhappy memories; she is a person who ~s upon her griefs; we will not ~ on that matter any longer.

E

ear *n* (1) drooping / pointed / *etc* ~s; his quick ~s caught the sound of . . .; may I have a word in your ~ *(talk to you in private)*? □ be all ~s *(listen eagerly)*; □ in (at) one ~ and out (at) the other *(completely unheeded)*; I should think his

~s are burning *(he might feel that we are discussing him)*; were your ~s burning last night? □ be up to the / one's ~s in debt / work; □ over head and ~s (in debt); talk to deaf ~s; □ he turned a deaf ~ to (our requests). (2) have a good / nice / poor / no / not much ~ for music; play music by ~.

early *adj/ adv* (1 *near the beginning*) in the ~ morning / evening; ~ in the morning / evening; at an ~ hour / age; she died ~ in childhood; work from ~ in the morning till late at night; they danced till ~ morning / into the ~ hours. (2 *before the main period of development, history*) the ~ history of Egypt; the ~ Christians; ~ Gothic / baroque; an ~ civilization / document / example; ~ finds; the ~iest finds date from the fifth century; man learned ~ to use tools; an ~ model of a car; the project is still at an ~ stage. (3 *before the usual time*) it is still ~ in the day; an ~ breakfast; go to bed / rise ~; an ~ diagnosis / treatment / symptom; crocuses are ~ spring flowers; an ~ winter; ~ peaches / fruit; his ~ death; he died ~ in life; he is on ~ duty; in southern countries ~(ier) marriages are common; I shall come by / on an ~ train; the ~iest date for the meeting would be in April; the ~iest he can come is 9 o'clock; the shoes will be ready on Friday at the ~iest; please answer at your ~iest convenience *(as soon as it is convenient for you)*.

earn *vt* (1 *receive for work*) ~ money / a good wage; ~ one's living / livelihood / (daily) bread (2 *of money: bring in*) the investment should ~ you 6 per cent; the shares ~ a dividend of 9 per cent; risky securities naturally ~ a higher return. (3 *obtain by merit or wrongdoing*) he ~ed the office the hard way; ~ fame / glory / a good reputation; ~ s.o.'s favour / confidence / affection; you have ~ed our gratitude; the theft ~ed him two months in jail; his actions ~ed him the contempt of all his colleagues; a well-~ed rest.

ease *n* (1 *freedom from pain, toil, trouble, etc*) a life of ~; I enjoyed a lasting ~; a short ~ after the day's work; → take *vt* 17; a mild sedative brought a certain ~; □ at (one's) ~ *(free from anxiety, embarrassment, etc)*; feel (ill) at ~; seated at ~ in a comfortable chair; is she at ~ in the company of others? a comfortable couch, on which you can lie at your ~; his friendly manner soon put his visitors at their ~; → set *vt* 21b. (2 *freedom from difficulty*) the ~ with which he answered the questions surprised me; we shall be able to complete the work with (the greatest) ~ by the end of the month; shallow waters where she could swim with ~; ~ of access.

ease *vt* (1) ~ the burden of (a donkey / *etc*) (2) ~ pain / tension; ~ s.o.'s misery / burden / suffering; ~ one's conscience / mind; this will ~ her (mind of) anxiety; this method will greatly ~ your task; ~ a patient *(give him relief)*; he has been ~d *(robbed)* of his purse. (3 *make less tight, looser*) ~ a dress at the side seams; ~ a coat under the arms; ~ a door / drawer (that opens with difficulty) (4 *move slowly, carefully*) ~ a car into a garage; he ~d himself into his chair. (5) ~ (down) the speed of a boat. -*vi* (6) the situation has ~d (off).

ease down ~ the car ~ to 20 m.p.h. on this curve; ~ ~ an engine; → ease *vt* 5.

ease off (1) he ~d ~ the rope. (2) she lowered the flame and the boiling ~d ~; my headache has now ~d ~ a little; → ease *vi* 6.

ease up the men on the bench ~d up *(moved apart)* after two of them left; she promises that rich cake when sugar supplies ~ up *(become more plentiful)*.

easily *adv* he lifted the box quite ~; he is not ~ satisfied; you can ~ imagine my surprise; things may / could ~ turn out otherwise.

easy *adj / adv* (1) an ~ story / book / task; an ~ victory / victim; an ~ passage to translate; ~ of access; buy s.th. on ~ terms *(by instalments)*; it's ~ier said than done. (2 *not tight, comfortable*) the coat was an ~ fit; an ~ coat; an ~ chair; drive at an ~ pace (3 *free from worry, pain, etc*) be ~ in one's mind; lead an ~ life; make life ~ for o.s.; be in ~ circumstances; rest ~ (4 *pleasant, not awkward*) an ~ manner; ~ manners; he is ~ to get on with; □ take it ~ *(not work hard; not get excited)*; □ go ~ (→ go *vi* 20b) (5 *not strict*) an ~ teacher; very ~ parents (6 *inform: open-minded*) I'm ~ *(I agree to anything you say)*; I'm ~ whether we stay or go.

eat *vt* (1) ~ bread / soup / an apple / *etc*; she never ~s fat; cattle ~ grass / hay / grain / *etc*; the cat has ~en a mouse; the moths have ~en holes in the material; ~ one's lunch / dinner; ~ one's fill (of s.th.);

those children of mine have an appetite - they ~ me out of house and home; I'll ~ my hat if it does happen; □ ~ one's words *(take them back)*; □ ~ humble pie *(apologize humbly)*; □ ~ one's heart out *(worry unnecessarily)* ; she is ~ing her heart out because she can't go to that dance. (2 *consume, destroy*) an old car ~s oil; a stream ~s away land along its bank. - *vi* (3) we ~ at 7 o'clock; ~ at a restaurant; at weekends we often ~ out; ~ like a horse / wolf; we ~ to live; can you ~ with chop sticks? □ ~ out of s.o.'s hand *(be completely submissive)*. (4 → 2) rust ~s into iron; acids ~ (into) metal; he has ~en into most of his savings.

eat up (1) ~ up one's food; ~ up one's breakfast with enjoyment (2) the flames ate up the wood. (3) the car ate up the miles. (4) be ~en up with envy / pride (5) waiting for buses ~s up too much time.

edge *n* (1) the ~ of a table / sheet of paper / coin / wood / pond / cliff / river; sit on the ~ of a chair (2) a knife with a sharp ~; put an ~ on a knife *(sharpen it)*; take the ~ off s.th. *(make it blunt)*; chocolate before a meal takes the ~ off one's appetite; take the ~ off an argument *(spoil its effect)*; □ give s.o. the (sharp / rough) ~ of one's tongue *(speak roughly, scold)*; the scraping sound set my teeth / nerves on ~; be on ~ *(nervous, restless)*; why are you so on ~? he was all on ~ to get away.

edge *vt* (1) ~ a tablecloth with lace / a path with plants; reeds ~ the lake; a road ~d with poplars; writing-paper ~d with black (2) ~ a knife / chisel / *etc*; ~d tools (3 *move little by little*) ~ a cupboard into a corner / a piano through a door; ~ one's way into / through / out of a crowd. - *vi* (4) ~ along a cliff; ~ away (5) ~ (o.s.) into a conversation.

edition *n* (1) publish / issue a new / (un)abridged / condensed / revised and enlarged / school / library / bound / pocket / cheap / popular / two-volume / *etc* ~ (of a book); the work has already gone through ten ~s. (2) the morning / evening / Sunday / early / late / special / illustrated ~ (of a newspaper) (3) he is a smaller ~ of his brother; he is a second ~ of his father.

education *n* (1) (a) primary / secondary / higher / technical / commercial / art / physical / university / further / adult / vocational ~; college of ~; ~ college; further ~ comprises vocational and non-vocational courses outside the universities at all levels; adult ~ refers to non-vocational study outside the universities; give one's children a good ~; he has received / enjoyed a careful ~. (2) his ~ in the field of science is remarkable.

effect *n* (1) have / produce a (rapid / immediate / deep / profound / beneficial / useful / harmful / far-reaching / magical / *etc* ~ (on s.o./ s.th.); the acid had little / much / no ~ (on the metal); suffer from the ~s of (the) heat; tanning is the ~ of exposure to sunlight; the ~ of the typhoon was (to leave many families homeless); the ~ of his words was staggering; feel the full ~ of s.th.; my warning had the desired ~; be of (no / little / considerable) ~; carry / put one's threat into ~; give ~ to one's threat / *etc*; we tried again and again, but to no ~; take ~ *(produce the result intended; come into force)*: the remedy didn't take ~; the increase will take ~ from April 1st; in ~ *(really; in operation)* the fence, intended to prevent accident, in ~ increased it; the law is still in ~; this ruling has been changed with ~ from April 1 st. (2 *impression*) a pretty ~ (in a painting); sound ~s; the music created the ~ of a wild thunderstorm; a display of wealth calculated for ~ (3 *meaning*) a rumour was spread around to the ~ *(saying)* that the firm was in financial difficulties; he sent her a note to that ~. (4 *~s: property*) their household ~s were sold at auction; personal ~s.

effect *vt* ~ a change / cure / sale / compromise; he tried to ~ an end to the quarrel; ~ a meeting between two people; ~ one's purpose.

effort *n* (1) make a (serious / zealous / resolute / tireless / creditable / splendid / conscious / cooperative / desperate / vain / useless / wasted / *etc* ~; unremitting / untiring / *etc* ~s; it is a great ~ for me (to do that); the meeting meant a considerable ~ for me; if you don't make an ~ you'll never succeed; make / use every ~ (to do s.th.); all the doctors' ~s to save her were in vain; their ~s were rewarded with success. (2 *thing achieved*) his spurt was a magnificent ~; that's a pretty good ~.

egg *n* (1) a fresh / new-laid / rotten / soft-boiled / hard-boiled / *etc* ~; → lay *vt* 3a; → set *vt* 1b; the ~s of an insect; □ put /

have all one's ~s in one basket *(risk everything in a single venture)* (2 *inform*) he is a bad ~ *(wicked person)*; good ~ *(compatible fellow)*.

elaborate *vt* (1) ~ a plan / proposal / point / theory / system / technique; ~ an invention / machine; ~ a work of art; when he died he had roughed out the composition of the picture, but not yet ~d the details; he ~d this theme in his second book. - *vi* (2) he ~ed at great / some length about / on the plan; he ~ed further about the projected railway.

embark *vt* (1) the ship ~ed passengers and cargo / troops. (2) this is a kind of business in which I would not ~ my capital. - *vi* (3) ~ for France (4) ~ on a law career / new business undertaking / new course of policy.

embarrass *vt* (1) ask ~ing questions; his words made me feel ~ed; the teacher's praise ~ed the shy boy; the boy was ~ed by such praise; she was ~ed at such a request; keep an ~ed silence; lack of money ~ed him. (2) wearing a sword ~ed his movements; seeing he was ~ed with his luggage, I offered to help him; she was ~ed with offers of assistance.

emerge *vi* (1) ~ from water / a place of hiding; the submarine at last ~d; the car ~d from a side street; the cat cautiously ~d from behind the box. (2) ~ victorious from a battle; N. ~d from the competition as the best high jumper; the candidate ~d in a stronger position from the elections. (3) a new society is ~ing; he is one of the few outstanding conductors to ~ since the war; these ideas ~ again and again in his books; the impression that women ... ~s very strongly from the inquiry; snags are bound to ~ when we start production; two essential points ~d from the discussion.

employ *vt* (1) one thousand hands are ~ed at this factory; the tutor has been ~ed for years; he was ~ed on research into ...; we cannot ~ you for the time being. (2) ~ a tool / means / weapon; a crowbar had been ~ed to force the door open; a bulldozer was ~ed for excavating the foundations of the building; he ~ed his spare time to good advantage; ~ one's time in reading; ~ questionable methods in business (3) driving ~s much of a salesman's time.

empty *adj* (1) an ~ box / bottle / purse / room / house; your glass is half ~; ~ space; the medicine should be taken on an ~ stomach. (2 *without substance*) ~ prattle / words / promises / boasts / threats / hopes; arguments ~ of meaning (3) an ~ mind / head; an ~-headed person.

encounter *vt* (1) we ~ed bad weather on our trip; when sailing across the North Atlantic, vessels occasionally ~ floating masses of ice; ~ difficulties / dangers / obstacles / resistance / (a good deal of) opposition; ~ an old friend / surprise / adventure; ~ the enemy. - *vi* (2) the two armies ~ed (one another) at T.; the first time we ~ed we ...

encourage *vt* (1) ~ s.o. in his work / studies / idle ways / extravagance; ~ s.o. to work harder / take risks / try again; an example that ~d people to fight for liberty; she ~d him with a smile to continue his tale; ~ing news; I didn't find his reply very ~ing. (2) ~ a boy's interest in music; ~ s.o.'s personality; ~ a movement / development; sharp competition among newsmen tends to ~ sensationalism; the government should ~ the arts; the conversation was skilfully ~d by host and hostess; high wages ~ early marriage; his disappearance ~d the belief that he was guilty.

end *n* (1) the ~ of a line / stick / rope / piece of string / road / path; the ~s of a cask / barrel; the extreme ~; the upper / lower ~ (of s.th.); arrange the tables ~ to ~; at the (far) ~ of the road; at the opposite ~; sign one's name at the ~ of a letter; we walked the street from ~ to ~ / from ~ to ~ of the street; the two ships collided ~ on; the fashionable ~ *(part)* of town; the west / east ~ of a town; the ~s of the earth; the other ~ of the world; □ on ~ *(upright; consecutively)*; place / stand the box / barrel on (its) ~; it rained for three days on ~; □ make s.o.'s hair stand / set s.o.'s hair on ~ (→ hair); no ~ of *(very much / many; very great)*: he went to no ~ of trouble to help me; I've warned you no ~ of times not to touch that machine; there'll be no ~ of a row about this; he thinks no ~ of himself; she was no ~ disappointed; □ make both ~s meet (→ meet *vi* 8); □ go off the deep ~ (→ go off 1); □ be at a loose ~ / *(AE)* loose ~s *(have nothing interesting to do)*; □ begin / start s.th. at the wrong ~; □ get / have hold of the wrong ~ of the stick *(be completely mistaken)*

(2 *temporal completion, conclusion*) the ~ of the day / year / century / meeting / speech / work / lawsuit: the ~ of life; the ~ of the world / all things; towards the ~ of the twenties; at the ~ of the day / year / *etc*; the holidays are at an ~; from beginning to ~; the ~ of a book / chapter / story / letter; the ~ of a career / business connection; the year / his life is drawing to an ~; there is an ~ to everything / no ~ to it; arriving when the meeting was at an ~; the semester / war / *etc* came to an ~; he will come to a bad ~; a true friend is faithful to the ~; fight (s.th. out) to the bitter ~; make an ~ of / put an ~ to s.th. (→ put *vt* 11); □ in the ~ *(at last)*; in the ~ he said ...; in the ~ you will come to understand; in the ~ he gave up; turn out all right in the ~.

(3 *conclusion, non-local, non-temporal*) the supplies / money came to an ~; we are at the ~ of our petrol; be at the ~ of one's resources; ... until his money was at an ~; that's the ~ of the jam; my patience is at an ~; □ be at one's wits' ~ *(not know what to do)*; □ be at the ~ of one's tether *(have no more patience)*; we had trouble without ~; that's / this is the ~ *(inform: the limit, worst)*.

(4 *death*) he was nearing his ~; have a peaceful ~; an untimely ~; his ~ came suddenly.

(5 *aim, purpose*) gain / win / achieve / attain one's ~(s); to what ~ did he say that? to this ~; with this ~ in view; what is the ~ of life's journey? his family's happiness was the ~ for which he worked; he used the firm's money for his own ~s.

(6 *small piece that remains*) a cigarette ~; the stub ~ of a pencil; candle ~s; → odds 4.

end *vt* (1) ~ a speech / piece of work / quarrel / conflict; ~ one's career / life; he ~ed his days in exile / peace; he ~ed the music; his speech ~ed the ceremonies. – *vi* (2) the road ~s here / ~ed in a farmyard; the pyramid ~s in a point; the word 'pot' ~s in / with a consonant. (3) the play ~ed at 3 o'clock; the day ~ed in a glorious sunset; the evening ~ed with music; the golden age ~s with Ovid; he ~ed by saying ...; how does the story ~? the chapter ~s with a murder; Mr N. / her letter ~ed on a cheerful / gloomy / warning note; I don't know how things will ~; the discussion ~ed in the defeat of the government; the match ~ed in a victory for our opponents; it ~ed in the doctor being sent for; → end up 2.

end off → end up 1.

end up (1) ~ up / off a speech with a quotation; we started with soup and had ice cream to ~ up with. (2) how will it ~ (up)? even the most expensive cars ~ (up) as scrap metal; he joined the firm as an office boy and ~ed (up) as a director; if you go on doing that kind of thing, you'll ~ (up) in prison; he might ~ up by thinking (we did it); → smoke *n* 1.

enemy *n* (1) the common / a personal ~; the internal / external / foreign / alien ~; a bitter / deadly / mortal / fierce / sworn / avowed / declared ~; fog is the sailor's deadliest ~; polio is an ~ of humanity; care is the ~ of happiness; the best is the ~ of the good; jealousy is an ~ *(hostile)* to true friendship; they think he is an ~ to progress; make an ~ of s.o.; he made many ~ies by (doing) this; he is his own (worst) ~; rust is iron's worst ~. (2 *opposing military forces*) the ~ is at the gate; the ~ are in a strong position; the ~ were completely taken by surprise; fall into the hands of the ~ / ~ hands; face the ~; beat the ~ in battle; ~ aircraft / troops / ships / *etc*.

energy *n* (1) mental / physical / vital ~; have no / lack ~; be full of / have plenty of ~; possess / show / display ~; set about a task with great / tenacious ~; a man of boundless ~; he spoke with ~ and enthusiasm; waste / dissipate one's ~ / ~ies; apply / devote one's ~ies to a task (2) atomic / electrical / kinetic / potential ~; the relation of ~ to matter.

engage *vt* (1) ~ a room at a hotel; ~ seats at the theatre / in the train; ~ a taxi; *(esp AE)* he ~d passage to the U.S. (2) ~ (s.o. as) a servant / guide / teacher; she was ~d to play the leading role in the new opera. (3) the news / sports page ~d his attention; the landscape ~s the eye; tennis and golf ~d most of his time; an ~ing smile / manner (4) ~ s.o. in conversation (5 *begin fighting with*) we ~d the enemy at dawn.

(6 *bind by a promise to marry*) ~ o.s. to s.o.; Henry has got ~d; my niece has become ~d to a doctor; are they ~d yet? an ~d couple (7 *~d: occupied, busy*) the taxi is ~d; the line / number is ~d; s.o. is ~d in conversation / business / *etc*; be ~d in washing the car / writing a book / *etc*;

be ~d on research into plant diseases / the plans for the new library / *etc*; she can't see you - she is ~d with a visitor; my time is fully ~d (with my daily work). (8 *fit*) the notches of a key ~ the wards of a lock; ~ the clutch / first gear (of a car). - *vi* (9 → 5) our orders are to ~ at once. (10 ~ *in: busy o.s. with*) s.o. ~s in sports / business / gardening / politics / argument / controversy / battle (11 *promise, bind o.s.*) he ~d to make payments for his house; I will ~ to manage the business if you will ~ (yourself) to provide the capital; (*BE also with* that) can you ~ that all his statements are trustworthy? (12 → 8) the teeth in this cog-wheel ~ with those of the other; the two cog-wheels ~; the gears ~d with a terrible grinding sound.

enhance *vt* (1) ~ property values / prices; an estate ~d by careful management (2) ~ s.o.'s pleasure / the attraction of s.th.; ~ the guest's enjoyment of the pleasures of the table; flowering bushes ~d the beauty of the garden; the charm of this wild land is ~d by the presence of deer; a young girl should avoid trying to ~ her looks with heavy make-up.

enjoy *vt* (1) ~ life / fresh air and sunshine / the beauties of nature; ~ one's dinner / leisure / holidays; I shall ~ this book in peace this evening; we ~ed the picnic; I don't ~ modern music; I don't ~ sitting a dance out. (2 *have the benefit of*) ~ good health / rights / privileges; ~ a good income / high reputation; the novel ~ed an unheard-of popularity; he has ~ed a careful upbringing. (3) ~ o.s. *(be happy).*

ensure *vt (AE → insure)* (1 *make certain)* ~ peace / freedom / prosperity / success / the safety of the state; this medicine will ~ his recovery; this form of organization ~s close co-operation between the two firms; this measure ~s visitors quiet sleep; she did her best to ~ that we had a good time. (2 *make sure of getting, obtain*) ~ victory; ~ a good income for o.s. / o.s. of a good income; ~ a good harvest; ~ a favourable outcome to the negotiations; I cannot ~ you a post / a post for you; the new government ~d for its people the highest incomes in Asia outside Japan; the agreement ~s to the Continent a supply of valuable raw materials. (3) ~ s.o. against / from risks.
- *vi* (3 *make safe or secure*) ~ against s.th.; the pianist ~ed (himself) against loss of his hands; he ~ed against disturbances by sound-proofing his doors and walls.

enter *vt* (1) ~ a room / house / church / town; ~ harbour / the arena; the train ~ed a tunnel; where did the bullet ~ the body? the rain could not ~ the frozen earth; the place where the river ~s the plain (2) the idea never ~ed my head once; ideas ~ the mind through the senses; ~ s.o.'s consciousness (3 *become a member of*) ~ a school / college / club; ~ the army; ~ the Church *(become a priest)*; ~ Parliament / politics / a profession / a monastery / one's father's firm (4) ~ a contest / race; she ~ed the painting competition with a landscape called 'Dawn'; she ~ed her painting in the competition. (5 *enrol, register)* ~ a child in a / at school; ~ s.o. in a club; ~ a date in a diary / sums in an account-book / invoices in a ledger / items in a register / names on a list; ~ one's name on a list (for s.th.); the item was ~ed to your account; you should never have received this bill - the goods were ~ed to you by mistake; ~ one's name / o.s. for an examination / the high jump / *etc*; ~ a car for a race; ~ a protest against s.th. / claim for s.th. / plea of 'not guilty' (to this charge) / complaint (that . . .)
(6) ~ the 1960's / the age of space travel; when America ~ed the war; he ~ed life with many advantages; ~ a (new) phase / stage; with the break-up of the Roman Empire, Europe ~ed an era of barbarism. - *vi* (7) please ~ without knocking; ~ by a door / side entrance (8) ~ for the high jump / *etc*; ~ for a contest / competition / course / examination; ~ for a fair (9) ~ into details / particulars / a matter; ~ into a conversation / talk (with s.o.); ~ into competition / negotiations (with s.o.); they ~ed into a bitter argument about politics. (10) ~ into s.o.'s service; ~ into s.o.'s rights; ~ into an agreement (11 ~ *into: be a factor in*) the question of cost never ~ed into our calculations; the possible use of more up-to-date machinery ~ed into our plans / considerations. (12 ~ *into: share sympathetically*) ~ into s.o.'s feelings; ~ into the spirit of the game; ~ into all the fun of a children's party (13) he has ~ed upon his sixtieth year; we have ~ed upon a new period of history; ~ upon a new phase (14 ~ *upon: begin to deal with, take up*) ~

upon a task; ~ upon discussions / negotiations; ~ upon a (diplomatic / *etc*) career / another term of office / one's new appointment / one's duties; ~ upon an inheritance.

entertain *vt* (1) ~ friends at / to dinner (2) the magician has ~ed many audiences. (3 *take into consideration*) ~ an idea / opinion / thought; the chairman will ~ nominations; he refused to ~ her plea; he does not even ~ the possibility of failure; ~ an offer / proposal (4 *keep in the mind, harbour*) ~ a doubt about s.th. / suspicion; ~ hopes of a peaceful settlement; he ~s the friendliest sentiments towards him; I ~ no apprehension / fears for his safety; ~ no grievance against s.o. - *vi* (5→ 1) the Smiths ~ a great deal.

envy *n* (1) excite / provoke / cause / arouse / stir up (s.o.'s) ~; be filled with ~ at / of s.o.'s success; the sick child was filled with ~ of his healthy friend; his ~ of his brother soon turned to jealousy; words spoken in ~; turn green with ~; eye s.th. with ~ (2) pretty clothes make her the ~ of all her friends; my brother and I were the ~ of all our friends; our garden was the ~ of the neighbourhood.

envy *vt* I ~ you (your good food); he ~ies anyone who is happy / anyone's happiness; I don't ~ you that difficult task; you are to be ~ied; ~ s.o. (for) his good fortune; you are ~ied for that (reason) / on that account; they ~ied her on account of her good luck; he is a person much to be ~ied.

equal *adj* (1) divide s.th. into ~ parts; ~ pay for ~ work; all men are ~ before the law; ~ chances; the two cases are ~ly heavy; ~ in size / price; four plus four is ~ to eight; your share is ~ to his; in the sight of God the rich are ~ with the poor. (2 *adequate*) be ~ to the occasion / a situation; I believe we are ~ to that responsibility; be / feel ~ to performing a task / climbing that mountain / *etc.* (3 *calm*) keep an ~ mind in a time of anxiety.

erect *vt* (1) ~ a statue / monument / memorial (to s.o.); ~ a temple / house / tower / tomb (2 *put in an upright position*) ~ a flagstaff / mast / fence; ~ a perpendicular on a line (3) ~ a government; ~ emotional barriers.

error *n* (1) a grammatical / orthographic / typing / clerical ~; an ~ in grammar / spelling / reasoning; a few printers' ~s; make / commit an ~; fall into the ~ of believing ...; put right / correct / set right / rectify an ~; a serious / grave / fatal / fundamental / light / slight ~; several ~s have crept into this translation; ~s and omissions excepted (2 *moral offence*) repent the ~s of a sinful life (3 *condition of being wrong*) be in ~; do s.th. in ~; the letter was sent to you in ~; everyone is liable to ~; your solution of this problem is not free from ~; at last he saw the ~ of his ways; lead s.o. / fall into ~.

escape *vi* (1 *get free*) ~ from / out of jail / prison / a cell; ~ from control; an ~d prisoner; ~ (from) one's keepers / pursuers; the canary has ~d (from its cage); ~ from a burning building / a sinking ship / harassing social conditions; ~ narrowly / by the skin of one's teeth; the longing to ~ from everyday life (2) some gas ~d from the stove; let the water / steam ~. - *vt* (3 *be uttered involuntarily*) a cry of pain ~d him; no word ~d him / his lips. (4 *avoid, keep safe from*) he was lucky to ~ the storm; ~ an accident whole; ~ punishment / influenza / injury / death / disaster / danger / (one's) fate / (one's) destiny; where can we go to ~ the crowds? ~ responsibility; ~ one's original bias (5) this fact has ~d my attention; ~ notice / observation (6 *be forgotten, unnoticed by*) his name ~s me for the moment; this fact ~d me; nothing ~s him.

establish *vt* (1) ~ a new state / government / business / agency / newspaper; ~ a reign of terror; a firmly ~ed empire; ~ a school / university / new *(university)* chair (2 *settle s.o. in a position, place*) he ~ed his son in a business; N. was ~ed as governor of the new province; we are now comfortably ~ed in our new house.
(3 *win general recognition for, prove*) ~ a rule / custom / claim / charge / alibi; Newton ~ed the law of gravity. (4 *ascertain, determine*) ~ the (precise) facts; an ~ed fact; ~ s.o.'s guilt / innocence / identity / name / whereabouts; ~ the number (of those) present / the cause of death; it was ~ed in court that the defendant had not been in X; it has meanwhile been ~ed that the car had been stolen in Paris; how can one ~ the weight of a planet?
(5 *place on a firm basis*) ~ one's power; ~ (law and) order; this institution has become / is firmly ~ed; he ~ed his reputation as a surgeon; he ~ed himself in literature. (6 *bring into being*) ~ communica-

tion / peace / personal contact (between...); ~ a precedent / connection / relationship / friendly atmosphere / economic balance (between two countries).

esteem *n* have ~ for s.o.; I have the greatest ~ for his candour; his conduct deserves ~; this action won him the ~ of the public; his modesty acquired him the ~ of his colleagues; gain (s.o.'s) ~; *Treasure Island* has enjoyed the ~ of generations of readers; he / his name is held in (high) ~; go up / rise / go down / fall in s.o.'s ~; he lowered himself in our ~ by his foolish behaviour.

estimate *n* a (reasonable / precise / conservative) ~ of value / cost / *etc*; make an ~ of the costs; form a (true / false) ~ of (the value of) s.th.; at / on a rough ~; the carpenter gave an ~ of $65 for the job; did the builders exceed their ~?

estimate *vt* (1) ~ the costs; I ~d the cost at / to be nearly £100; ~ the value / size / weight / number of s.th.; his fortune is ~ed at £10,000; I ~ the distance at about 50 yards; we ~d that it would take him four hours to do the journey. (2) ~ the effect of a speech / a man's character; let us dispassionately consider Eliot's "The Waste Land" and try to ~ its position. - *vi* (3) ask a contractor to ~ for the repair of the building.

evade *vt* (1) ~ a blow / attack / danger / *etc*; ~ justice / punishment / one's enemies (2 *find a way of not doing*) ~ military service / income tax / the law / one's duty; ~ an obligation / discussion / opportunity; ~ responsibility; ~ a question; ~ paying one's debts / giving an answer (3 *be too difficult for*) the flavour ~s definition.

even *adj* (1) an ~ surface / ground / floor; an ~ coat of paint; apply paint ~ly; the child has ~ teeth; there were hedges as ~ as a brick-wall. (2 *regular*) ~ motion / stride; an ~ flow of work; a healthy person has an ~ pulse; ~ breathing; ~ distribution; an ~ly distributed load; the ~ wear of a tyre / mechanical part; his work is not very ~ *(varies in quality)*. (3 *exact*) an ~ ten seconds; an ~ quart has two pints. (4) 2,4,6,8 are ~ numbers. (5 *of amounts, distances, etc: equal*) these two horses were ~ at the finish; our scores are now ~. (6 *of equal height*) the river rose till it was ~ with the windows; he hung the picture ~ with his eye. (7 *of chances: equally balanced*) an ~ contest; it is ~ money that he will keep the title; □ break ~ *(be neither winner nor loser; make neither a profit nor a loss)*; □ get / be ~ with s.o. *(get revenge on him)* (8 *not easily excited*) an ~ temper / disposition.

event *n* (1) an everyday / historical / tragic / dramatic / unforeseen / unlikely / notable / imminent / *etc* ~; current / recent / *etc* ~s; in the normal / natural course of ~s (he will be head of the firm); the wedding was quite an ~. (2) an athletic / sporting ~; he was third in the javelin ~. (3) in the ~ of his death *(if he dies)*; in the ~ of war; in that ~ *(if that happens)*; in any ~ *(whatever may occur)*; in the ~ *(as things turned out)*: I had my doubts about the wisdom of the decision, but in the ~ it proved to be most advantageous; at all ~s *(anyhow)*; someone must have persuaded N. to come - at all ~s, he was there.

evidence *n* (1) there was some ~ of foul play but no clue; is there any ~ of the safe having been tampered with? the ~ of the footprints near the window; death from lung cancer, which some ~ correlates with excessive smoking; when the ship reached port, it gave / bore (abundant) ~ of the storm; give ~ of one's / s.o.'s goodwill / gratitude / intelligence; □ be in ~ *(notably present)*; she's the sort of woman who likes to be very much in ~; Smith was nowhere in ~. (2 *legal* ~) furnish / tender / produce / adduce / collect (documentary / written / (in)direct / *etc*) ~; massive / eloquent / sobering / contradictory / *etc* ~; a shred / scrap of ~; I have no ~ for it; the ~ was strongly against him; put in / submit as ~; s.o. is convicted on circumstantial ~; found a judgement / sentence / decision on (clear / conclusive / incontestable) ~; the ~ of the first witness / of my own eyes; the second witness was called on to give ~; the witness said in ~ that he ...; □ turn *(BE)* Queen's / Kings's / *(AE)* State's ~ *(testify for the prosecution and against one's former allies in a legal case)*
(3 *~s: traces*) ~s of the presence of prehistoric man have been found in the caves in southern France; ~s of volcanic action.

examination *n* (1) an entrance / intermediate / final / oral / viva-voce / written / state ~; an ~ in spelling and reading / botany / *etc*; hold a (severe / stiff / *etc*) ~; go in for / take / sit for / pass / fail (in) an ~; be exempted from an ~ (2)

an ~ of the teeth / lungs; an ~ of s.o.'s eyes / eyesight; a microscopic ~; an ~ of s.th. under the microscope; make an ~ of s.th.; a medical ~ (3) on ~ it was found that the signature was not genuine; under ~ the prisoner broke down.

examine *vt* (1) ~ pupils / students / candidates (in English / chemistry / *etc*); ~ s.o. on a text / the Elizabethan age / an author / his knowledge of English / *etc*; ~ a witness (in a court of law) (2 *reflect upon*) let us ~ ourselves / our consciences / our souls (in the light of God's Commandments); it is time to ~ past mistakes / attitudes with a view towards personal improvement. (3) ~ s.o.'s lungs / the pearls (with a magnifier) / old (Church) records; at the customs our luggage was ~d; have one's teeth / eyes ~d; ~ parcels for the presence of contraband; ~ a (new) theory / plan / proposal / problem.

example *n* (1) I'll give you a practical / concrete ~; please give an ~ of a metaphor / this rule. (2 *specimen, sample*) this embroidery is an ~ of her best work; that's without ~ *(precedent)*. (3 *model*) the boy is an ~ for all of us; take John as an ~; take an ~ from John; follow John's ~; set / give (s.o.) a (warning / good) ~; hold s.o. up as an ~; □ ~ is better than precept; □ bad ~s corrupt good manners. (4 *warning*) let this be an ~ to you; his devotion to duty was an ~ to others; make an ~ of s.o. *(punish him as a warning to others)*.

exceed *vt* (1) ~ the speed limit; the expense has ~ed our estimate; ~ one's instructions / commission; reality / their accomplishments ~ed all expectation(s); the task ~s his ability; ~ s.o. in skill / ability / strength / courage / height / *etc* (2) 30 ~s 13 by 17.

exchange *n* (1) an ~ of greetings / addresses / letters / remarks / information / views (between two people); we found the ~ of city life for a country vacation very restful; they meet for an ~ of ideas; I let him have my watch, and took his camera in ~; I took his watch in ~ for my camera. (2) ~ of money; the rate of ~ (3) foreign ~ *(currency)*; operations in foreign ~; foreign ~ dealings / business; ~ control (authorities).

exchange *vt* (1) the two ~d places; Mary ~d seats with Anne; would you like to ~ (places) with me? ~ greetings / confidences / glances / letters / books / addresses / goods / ideas / reminiscences/prisoners; ~s.th. with s.o. for s.th. equivalent; □ ~ blows / words *(quarrel)* (2) where can we ~ our dollars? – *vi* (3) dollars ~ at / for DM 2.00.

excite *vt* (1) this piece of news ~d us all very much / made us all very ~d; get ~d about s.th.; please don't get ~d; don't ~ yourself; you mustn't ~ the patient; I was very ~d to hear from you again; it was very ~ing to hear...; an ~ing book / film; ~ the mind / senses; the wine had ~d their minds; in an ~d voice (2) ~ curiosity / interest / attention / admiration / affection / pity / envy / jealousy / contempt (in s.o.); ~ thirst / the appetite / the imagination (3) ~ a riot / rebellion; ~ the people to rebellion / to rebel against the government (4) ~ an organ / nerve; ~ s.o. sexually (5) ~ a dynamo / magnetic field.

excuse *n* (1) make / give / offer a (credible / plausible / reasonable / valid / legitimate / glib / far-fetched / *etc*) ~; stammer / mutter a (poor / feeble / lame / threadbare / paltry / thin / slim / flimsy / shaky / silly / sorry / unworthy / insufficient / unsatisfactory / *etc*) ~; I cannot accept that ~; you always have a different ~; I am tired of these ~s; what is your ~ for failing to hand in your homework? she gave many ~s (for her behaviour) but...; in ~ of his late arrival, he pleaded that he...; where the law is concerned you cannot plead / offer ignorance in ~ of your conduct / as an ~ for your conduct; ignorance / his youth is no ~; there is nothing to be said in ~ for him; make / send one's ~s (for not coming) (2 *pretext*) his back-ache is only an ~ for not gardening; a poor / feeble / lame / *etc* ~ (→ 1).

excuse *vt* (1) ~ a fault / transgression; ~ s.o. ('s laziness / being lazy); ~ s.o. (for) his laziness; please ~ us / our calling you by your first name; I hope you will ~ me this time; please ~ me for coming late; ~ my contradicting you; if you will ~ the expression; ~ s.o. to the host / teacher; ~ o.s. on the ground that... (2 *be a reason for not blaming*) shyness ~s her awkwardness; his youth ~s him / his failure; nothing can ~ such carelessness. (3 *release from an obligation*) please ~ my son this afternoon; may I be ~d? I need not go there – the headmaster has ~d me; Mr

A. has ~d us our homework tonight; your ill health will ~ you from night duties; he is ~d night duty; I cannot ~ you from attending my classes; he asked to be ~d from attending the meeting. (4 *dismiss*) the manager gruffly ~d his visitor *(sent him out)*; the judge ~d the jury for the rest of the week; at the end of the trial the jury were ~d with the judge's thanks. (5 *AE: not demand; cancel, remit*) our teacher ~d the mathematics homework; the state has finally ~d the unpopular tax.

execute *vt* (1) ~ a plan / project / task / purpose / command / commission; ~ a warrant / sentence (on s.o.); an officer ~s the law when he proceeds against its violators; ~ legislation; I'm afraid he will ~ his threats; please ~ the *(trade)* order as soon as possible. (2 *fulfil*) ~ the duties of a chairman (3) he ~d the piano solo / the role of Hamlet perfectly; ~ complicated dance figures; a delicately ~d painting; a picture ~d in oil; design and ~ a statue (4) ~ a murderer / spy (5 *legal use*) ~ a deed / contract *(sign, make legal)*; ~ a will *(carry out the terms of)*.

exercise *n* (1) morning / (deep-)breathing / physical / gymnastic / rhythmic ~s; compulsory / voluntary / conditioning ~s (in sports); arithmetic ~s in addition; ~s in English grammar / *etc*; learning things by heart is a good mental ~; (do/ practise) (five-)finger ~s; ~s for the violin / flute (2 *practice of mental, physical powers*) swimming is good ~; walking, cycling, rowing are all healthy forms of ~; ~ of the mental faculties; fresh air and ~ will do you good; the doctor advised her to take more ~. (3 *use, employment*) the ~ of tact and patience is essential in diplomatic negotiations; his excuses showed considerable ~ of the imagination; he freed himself by the ~ of sheer strength; define the circumstances in which the ~ of power is good and bad; the ~ of a function / duty / right; the ~ of influence / parental authority (4) military ~s.

exercise *vt* (1) ~ the muscles / mind; he ~d his fingers daily to restore them; ~ a horse; he is ~ing himself in fencing; ~ children in mental arithmetic (2) ~ diligence / care / discretion / authority (over s.o.) / one's rights / the right (to vote); ~ an influence; ~ (all one's) self-control / patience; ~ one's gifts; ~ duties / a function (3 *make demands on*) ~ s.o.'s patience (4 *engage the attention of*) this problem has ~d the best brains in the industry. (5 *vex, worry)* was ever a generation so ~d about its education as ours? I am very much ~d about the shortcomings of my son. - *vi* (6) you must ~ every day; you don't ~ enough.

exhaust *vt* (1 *use up*) ~ (one's) supplies / provisions / stores / ammunition; my funds were ~ed by the trip; ~ s.o.'s / one's resources / means / patience / strength / energy; ~ the soil (2 *make empty*) ~ a well (3 *pump out*) ~ air / gas / water (from / out of s.th.) (4) he ~ed himself playing tennis; be / feel ~ed; the hare fell to the ground, ~ed; running the mile is ~ing. (5 *discuss thoroughly*) ~ a subject.

exhibit *vt* (1) he ~ed all the symptoms of a cold. (2) ~ articles for sale / flowers in a flower show / paintings in / at an art gallery (3) ~ courage / special gifts / one's qualities / a contempt of death. - *vi* (4) she ~s in several galleries; the ~ing firms / artists.

expand *vt* (1) heat ~s solids / gases; ~ a tube (2) some flowers ~ (their petals) in sunshine; the breeze ~ed the flag. (3) ~ trade (relations) / one's foreign trade; we want to ~ our business; the purpose of education should be to ~ the minds of children, not merely to fill their heads with facts. (4 *treat more fully*) ~ a topic; the author ~ed his short story into a novel. - *vi* (5) heat causes solids to ~; air ~s as it rises; a tyre ~s when you pump air into it; the theory of the ~ing universe (6) the valley ~s into a wide plain; the river ~s and forms a lake. (7) our business / foreign trade has ~ed still more; the society ~ed into a worldwide organization. (8) → 2; the flag ~ed in the breeze; his face ~ed in a smile of welcome.

expect *vt* (1 *think likely*) it is better than I had ~ed; I ~ the train will be late; it was to be ~ed that he ...; I ~ to go on a trip; I ~ to see him / him to come; I ~ (that) he will come; how am I ~ed to know that? I knew what to ~; you cannot ~ (to get) anything good from him; you cannot ~ any good of him; that's just what I ~ed of / from him; I have nothing more to ~ of / from life; I didn't ~ such behaviour of you. (2 *feel sure of the arrival of*) we're all ~ing you; I was ~ing a letter from her; I ~ visitors; ~ s.o. to dinner; when do you ~ him back? □ be ~ing *(inform: be* *pregnant)*; he ~ed a storm; he's ~ing the bill any day. (3 *hope for, look for as due*) you can't ~ any money; you can't ~ any more for the price; I ~ obedience / you to obey; I ~ that you shall obey. (4 *require s.th. of s.o., s.o. to do s.th.*) a speech will be ~ed of you; you're ~ing too much of her; you are ~ed to work late if need be / to do a good job; I ~ you to work hard; you surely don't ~ me to do all that work in one day, do you? (5 *inform: suppose*) I ~ it was the cat.

expectation *n* (1) he was proved correct in his ~; he ate a light lunch in ~ of a good dinner; live in constant / joyful ~; after weeks of ~ the big day came. (2 *reasonable chance*) is there any ~ of getting away early? (3 *s.th. expected*) his worst ~s did not materialize; the result disappointed their ~s; beyond ~(s); contrary to (all) ~(s); according to ~(s); come up to / answer / meet / fulfil s.o.'s ~s; surpass / exceed s.o.'s ~s; disappoint / fall short of s.o.'s ~s (4 *~: future prospects, esp of inheritance)* a man of / he has great ~s; we have great ~s of you *(expect you to be very successful)*. (5 *BE*) ~ of life (*AE* life expectancy).

expense *n* (1) the ~ of running a car has risen; a new car would be a great ~; that will entail a lot of ~; they spared neither effort nor ~; it is foolish to go to the ~ of taking music lessons if you never practise; go to great ~ over s.th. / on s.o.'s account; I don't want to put you to the ~ of engaging a private tutor for me; (live / be trained / *etc*) at public / the firm's / other people's ~; the town will meet / bear the ~; in this matter the question of ~ is of no importance / ~ is no object; he will go to any ~. (2) my ~s have been very heavy recently; we had big ~s; regular / recurrent / running / fixed / variable ~s; meet / defray ~s; witnesses have their ~s refunded; household / travelling ~s; I was offered a hundred dollars plus ~s; travel on an ~ account (3 *source of costs*) an old car can be a great ~ to run; illness, marriage, holidays and other ~s have made me very poor. (4 *spending of strength, etc*) speed at the ~ of accuracy; he became a brilliant scholar but only at the ~ of his health; have a good laugh / be funny at s.o.'s ~.

experience *n* (1) have little / (not) much / great / unusual / practical / *etc* ~ (in a field); have ~ in book-keeping / of teaching; only women with ~ of office work need apply for the position; does he have the necessary ~ for the job? he lacks ~; he's a man of ~; gather / get ~ (in one's youth); considerable ~ has been acquired in the teaching of English; learn by ~; from my own ~ I know...; know from bitter ~; I speak from ~; I can confirm that from personal ~; in my ~ this material has always been good; it is known / we know from previous ~ that frost is...; previous ~ has shown that frost is... (2 *event which has given one ~*) a memorable / rewarding / unusual / strange / singular / delightful / everyday / unpleasant / trying / agonizing / *etc* ~; the ~s of his childhood; the unforgettable ~ of first love; the trip abroad was a rich ~; studying French was a novel ~; I had two moving ~s.

expose *vt* (1) ~ one's back / o.s. to the sun / air (2 *leave unprotected*) ~ a new-born baby; ~ s.o. / o.s. to danger / cold / a risk; ~ o.s. to the enemy fire; he has ~d us to (universal) ridicule; ~ s.o. to blame / criticism / censure; the site is very remote and ~d. (3) ~ a film *(allow light to reach it)* (4 *bring to light*) excavations have ~d a Roman pavement; ~ roots (5) ~ goods in a shop window (6 *reveal, show up*) ~ a crime / secret / plot / plan; ~ corruption / abuse / the fallacy in an argument / one's ignorance; discover and ~ the awful truth; ~ a villain.

express *vt* (1) ~ one's feelings / thoughts / gratitude / thanks / condolences / opinion / willingness; ~ annoyance / anger / discontent / concern / appreciation (in words / a poem / *etc*); ~ a doubt / wish / opinion; ~ the desire to do s.th,; ~ one's meaning by gestures / glances; ~ o.s. (clearly / fluently / clumsily / correctly) in English; if I may so ~ myself (2) his attitude ~ed disdain; her face ~es strength of will. (3 *send fast*) ~ a package to Paris.

extend *vt* (1) ~ a wall / fence / road / railway; ~ one's journey to N.; ~ a garden / a school building / one's premises (2) ~ a visit for a few days / lunch break by 15 minutes; I should like to ~ my holidays into August. (3 *stretch out at full length*) ~ one's arms / legs; ~ one's hand to s.o. (4) ~ a cable between two posts (5) ~ trade relations / one's foreign trade (to South America) one's business / one's circle of acquaintances; at that time

France ~ed its power and influence into neighbouring countries; ~ one's interest to (include) s.th.; ~ a sphere of influence / one's range of knowledge / a concept / the meaning of a word (6 *offer*) ~ sympathy and kindness to one's neighbours; ~ a warm welcome / invitation to s.o.; ~ favour / hospitality to s.o.; ~ (financial) help to s.o.
- *vi* (7) these plains ~ for many miles; an estate that ~s to the sea (8) our experiments ~ed over several years. (9) our business / foreign trade has ~ed to South America; their sphere of influence has ~ed; his influence ~s far beyond the frontiers of his own country. (10) his knowledge of mathematics does not ~ to calculus.

extent *n* (1) from the roof we were able to see the ~ of the park; the whole ~ of the kingdom (2) no one knows the ~ of his debts; the ~ of a disaster; amazed at the ~ of his knowledge; the full ~ of his kindness; to a great / some / certain ~ he is himself to blame for his misfortunes; to a large / slight ~; to what ~ can he be trusted? he owed people money to the ~ of £5,000.

extract *vt* (1) ~ a cork from a bottle / a bullet from a wound / a splinter from one's finger / a letter from a file / a (wisdom-) tooth (2) ~ the juice from fruit / oil from olives / gold from ore (3) ~ information / a secret from s.o.; thus they have ~ed the maximum propaganda value from it. (4) ~ words / sentences from a book; ~ figures from a balance sheet (5) → root *n* 5.

eye *n* (1) weak / sharp / large / big / quick / dreamy / liquid *(clear)* / dull / deep-set / sunken / dry / watery ~s; thoughtful / pensive / watchful / searching ~s; have a practised / quick ~; ~s dim with tears; with downcast / wide ~s; see s.th. with the naked ~;give s.o. / get a black ~ *(hit / be hit hard in the eye)*; an artificial / glass ~; raise / lower / shut / close / open / roll / strain / blink one's ~s; half-close one's ~s (with tiredness); run / cast one's ~ over / through a letter / account; fix one's ~(s) on s.o./s.th.; turn one's ~s on s.o./s.th.; cast a covetous ~ / longing ~s on s.th.; wink an ~ at s.o. (to give him a hint); follow s.o. with one's ~s; look s.o. straight in the ~; it was so interesting that I couldn't take / keep my ~s off it; see / witness s.th. with one's own ~s; it happened before / in front of my ~s; the Eye of the Universe *(God)* (2 *idiomatic phrases containing verbs*) be all ~s *(watch intently)*; catch s.o.'s ~ *(capture his attention)*; close one's ~s to (faults / defects / *etc*); cry one's ~s out; give an ~ to s.o.; the children are playing in the garden - you might give an ~ to them now and again; if you had half an ~ *(were not so dull)* (you would see that it won't go through the doorway); have an ~ for (beauty / colour / a horse / a pretty girl / a bargain); have an ~ on s.o./ s.th.; have one's ~ on s.o.; have an ~ to business / one's own advantage / the main chance; he always has an ~ to his own interest; keep an ~ on (the baby); keep an ~ on the time or we'll be late; keep one's ~ on s.th. *(look steadily at it)*; keep one's ~s open / skinned / peeled *(watch carefully for s.o., s.th.)*; it leaps to the ~ *(is obvious); make ~s at s.o. (flirt with s.o.)*; make s.o.'s ~s open *(astonish him)*; open s.o.'s ~s to s.th. *(make him realize it)*; that incident opened my ~s to the true character of the man; see s.th. with half an ~ *(at a glance); see ~ to ~ (with s.o.) (agree perfectly)*: I think we see ~ to ~ on that subject; set ~s on s.o./ s.th. *(catch sight of)*: she wants everything she sets ~s on; I hope I shall never set ~s on him again; shut one's ~s to the truth; turn a / one's blind ~ to s.th. *(pretend not to see)*; use half an ~ *(have half an eye)* (3 *idiomatic phrases containing prepositions*) (see s.th.) in one's mind's ~; in the ~s of all (he is guilty); you're only a child in his ~s; John's work had little worth in the ~s of his teacher; in the ~(s) of the law (it is theft); under one's very ~s *(right in front of one)*; up to the / one's ~s in (work / reading proofs) *(very busy)*; up to the ~s in debt; (I look upon the problem) with a different ~; with an ~ to / for / on s.th. *(with s.th. in mind)*: designed with an ~ to comfort; all his investments were made with an ~ to the future; with one's ~s open *(with full understanding of what is involved)*.

F

face *n* (1) a round / oval / broad / chubby / thin / lean / rosy / ruddy / weather-beaten / rugged / rough / old / wrinkled / withered ~; a lovely / beautiful / pretty / ugly / (un)familiar / strange ~; it happened before my ~; he flushed / went red in the ~; the sun was shining in our ~s; it is hard to cycle with the wind in one's ~; she shut the door in his ~; strike s.o. in the ~; she'll only laugh in your ~ if you say that; the stone struck him on the ~. (2 *expression*) a smiling / cheerful / open / honest / solemn / sad / gloomy / sulky / angry ~; keep a straight ~ *(not smile)*; she's a good judge of ~s. (3 *impudence*) he had the ~ to (ask for more). (4) the ~ of a coin / clock / playing-card / crystal / building / dam; a cube has six ~s; the ~ of cloth; the Eigerwand is a notoriously dangerous ~; wipe them off the ~ of the earth; you misinterpret the ~ of such affairs. (5 *idiomatic phrases containing verbs*) lose ~ *(drop in prestige)*; make ~s / a ~ *(grimace)*; make a long ~; pull ~s / a ~; pull a long ~; put a bold / good ~ on a matter *(show courage in facing it)*; put a new ~ on s.th. *(make it look different)*; it is not easy to excuse his conduct, even if you put the best ~ on it *(represent it in the best light)*; Aunt Ann is coming to see you, so you had better put your best ~ on; save (one's) ~ *(avoid losing one's reputation)*; if he has once set his ~ against a thing *(resolved not to do it)*, nothing will persuade him to change his mind; he was ashamed to show his ~ *(let himself be seen)*. (6 *idiomatic phrases containing prepositions*) in the ~ of *(in spite of)*; courage in the ~ of danger; persevere in the ~ of all obstacles; in the ~ *(defiance)* of authority; what could he do in the ~ of all these difficulties? fly in the ~ of (*defy*; → *fly vi* 5) public disapproval / all the facts / truth; look s.o. in the ~ *(steadily)*; be unable to look s.o. in the ~ *(feel ashamed in his presence)*; he has looked death in the ~; death stared him in the ~; look facts in the ~; his argument appears quite convincing on the ~ of it *(judging by appearances)*; the story is absurd on the ~ of it; see / meet ~ to ~; come ~ to ~ with s.o.; bring two persons ~ to ~; he's a liar, and I don't mind telling him so to his ~ *(not behind his back)*; flatter s.o. to his ~; lie to s.o.'s ~.

face *vt* (1 *be opposite to*) he stood ~ing the window; the audience ~d the speaker; the picture ~s page 10; a large mirror ~d the door; our house ~s (on to) the park; how does your house ~? it ~s (to the) south; the kitchen ~s the street. (2 *turn, have one's face towards*) she ~d her partner in the square dance; he turned to ~ the orchestra; she dared not ~ me. (3 *confront*) find o.s. / be ~d with / by a difficulty; ~d with the evidence, he confessed; the conference will ~ the Western Powers with the biggest test of their own unity. (4 *be confronted with*) in that case the engineering industry would ~ extraordinary dislocations; thus the engineers ~d a stiff problem. (5 *meet without shrinking*) ~ trouble / reprimand / punishment / unpleasant consequences / ruin / disgrace / one's accusers / the facts / danger / death; ~ a danger boldly; now she had to ~ the world for herself; I can't bear to ~ your sister after what has happened; □ ~ the music *(meet the consequences without shirking)* (6 *be likely for, threaten*) death ~s everyone sooner or later; extermination ~s many of the larger mammals; our losses left us ~d with ruin; great issues that ~ the British (7) ~ a wall with stucco / marble.

face down *(AE)* he ~d his adversary ~ *(overcame him with a resolute stare)*.

face out *(BE)* despite all the evidence against him, for over an hour he ~d it ~ *(refused to admit his fault)*; he ~d me ~ that he knew nothing about the matter *(maintained to me)*; he used to ~ his lies ~.

face up to (1) ~ up to facts / the truth *(acknowledge)* (2) ~ up to the future *(meet it resolutely)*; he ~d up to all his troubles manfully; she couldn't ~ up to the prospect of living in reduced circumstances.

facilitate *vt* aeroplanes ~ travel; modern inventions ~ housework; this method will greatly ~ your task; this new detergent ~s washing clothes or dishes; that will ~ the spreading of the new doctrine; a no-parking regulation to ~ traffic movement.

fact *n* (1) a well-known / plain / (un)known / historic / accomplished / established / stubborn *(not to be ignored)* ~; the bare / naked / foregoing ~s; it's a (proved) ~ / an accepted ~; know s.th. for a ~ *(definitely)*; ~s speak louder than words; he got the ~s distorted; that fire burns is a ~. (2) the story is founded on ~; one must be able to tell ~ from fiction; → matter *n* 4; □ in ~ *(actually, in truth)*: there are chain store tobacconists, grocers, butchers - in ~, all kinds of shops; those people can afford to waste more material, and in ~ they do so; after the death of Chaucer we come to a barren period of our literature - in ~ in the intellectual life of the country generally; where, in ~, does English come from?

fade *vi* (1 *lose colour*) some colours ~ easily; my socks ~d in the wash; guaranteed not to ~; the colours ~d into one another. (2 *of sound: lose intensity*) the sound of drums ~d away; the music ~d in the distance. (3 *disappear*) the ship ~d from sight / our eyes; later on the coastline ~d into darkness; s.th. ~s from memory (4 *lose vigour, intensity)* the flowers ~ in autumn; the daylight ~d; her youth has ~d; summer ~s into autumn. - *vt* (5) the sun has ~d the curtains / wall-paper. (6) time had ~d her beauty.

fade away (1) → fade *vi 2*; the daylight / vision soon ~d ~. (2) she became ill and slowly ~d ~.

fade in ~ in a *(film, radio, TV)* scene / effect / melody; the camera ~s in onto the lovers in a park.

fade out ~ ~ a scene / effect / melody; the scene of the jungle ~d ~ to reveal in the next shot the interior of an office.

fail *vt/i* (1 *be unsuccessful*) ~ a test / examination; ~ in a course / examination; ~ in physics / English / *etc*; his uncle ~ed in business; the attempt / attack ~ed; all his plans ~ed. (2 *be not enough, come to an end*) our water supply has ~ed; our wheat crop ~ed *(was inadequate)* two years running; the wind ~ed (us) *(was not strong enough for our boat)*; the engine ~ed every 5 minutes; his courage ~ed him; words ~ me to describe the scene / express my pain; time would ~ me to tell all that happened during that day. (3 *become weak*) his sight / hearing / breath is beginning to ~ (him); his health is (fast) ~ing him; he is ~ing in health. (4 *become bankrupt*) several enterprises ~ed last year. (5 *not help*) ~ a friend; do not ~ me in my need. (6 *lack*) he ~s in perseverance. (7) he ~ed to pass the exam / report to the police / *etc*; she ~ed in persuading / to persuade him; he had ~ed to keep his promise; ~ to appear. (8) ~ a candidate *(decide that he has failed)*; I can't understand why they ~ed him.

failure *n* (1 *lack of success*) the ~ of the attack on the fort; the ~ of the candidate in the election; all his efforts ended in / met with ~. (2 *lack of performance*) engine / power ~; the ~ of electric power (3 *becoming weak*) heart ~; the ~ of his health (4 *financial crash*) a bank ~; the ~ of the company (5 *the fact of not doing*) his ~ to answer made the police suspect him; an accident due to the mechanic's ~ to adjust the brake; lapses are usually due not to deliberate choice of the worse, but to ~ to think of the better. (6 *a running short*) ~ of supplies; the ~ of this year's crops / crop ~s brought on near famine. (7 *unsuccessful person, thing*) he was a ~ in business / as a teacher; the play was a box-office ~; success came after many ~s.

fair *adj* (1) a ~ share; a ~ decision / distribution of profits / criticism / trial / verdict / settlement / law; by ~ means; I'm being ~ to both sides; this teacher is strict but ~; he always gives ~ judgement; charge ~ prices; ~ profits (2 *moderate, average*) his game / spelling is only ~; the goods arrived in ~ condition; a ~ chance of success; a ~ *(considerable)* inheritance; □ ~ to middling *(good enough but not very good)*; □ be in a ~ way *(likely)* (to win £100 / to succeed) (3 *according to the rules*) ~ play; a ~ fight / match / player / opponent; ~ competition (4) ~ *(favourable)* wind (5) in ~ weather *(no rain)* (6 *light-coloured*) ~ hair / skin; a ~ complexion (7 *form: beautiful*) a ~ maiden; this land so green and ~; the ~ sex (8 *clean*) make a ~ copy of (this letter); such behaviour will spoil your ~ name *(good reputation)* . (9) those are only ~ words / promises; put s.o. off with ~ words; the ~ speeches of the politicians (10 *inform: complete, thorough*) it was a ~ scramble getting away; it was a ~ treat to watch him outsnob the snobs; a ~ miracle.

fair *adv* (1 *according to the rules*) play / fight / hit ~ (and square) (2) write / copy s.th. out ~ (3 *squarely*) it caught him ~ between the eyes; he was struck / the ball hit him ~ on the chin. (3 *inform: completely*) the question ~ bowled him over;

it ~ beats me how he could say such a thing.

fairly *adv* (1 *just*) treat s.o. ~; distribute s.th. ~; let's fight the election ~ and cleanly; the games were judged ~; he did not act ~ towards me. (2 *completely, positively*) we were ~ in the trap; he was ~ beside himself with rage; his suggestion ~ took my breath away; he ~ bellowed across the hall; his hobby has ~ run away with him. (3 *moderately*) he plays ~ well; he's a ~ good player; a ~ good dinner but nothing special; I can see ~ well from here; it is ~ evident that he ...; you're ~ safe if you watch what you're doing.

faith *n* (1) have you (any) ~ in your doctor / his word / what he says? I haven't much ~ in this medicine; don't put your ~ in such a remedy; I've lost ~ in that fellow; lose one's ~ in humanity; we cannot prove that there is a life beyond death - we can only accept it in / on ~. (2 ~ *in God*) true / deep / abiding ~; a firm / steadfast / living *(active)* / childlike / mystic ~; change / lose / abjure one's ~; die for one's ~; find one's lost ~ again; come to a ~ in God; his ~ helped him through his misfortunes. (3) the Christian / Catholic / Protestant / Jewish / Muslim ~ (4) literature is his only ~; realism is his literary ~. (5) (do s.th. / act) in good ~ *(honestly)* / in bad ~ *(dishonestly)*; this action is a breach of good ~. (6 *promise*) keep / break ~ with s.o.; give / pledge one's ~ to s.o.; you cannot expect your friends to trust you if you do not keep ~ with them.

fall *n* (1) a (heavy) ~ of rain / snow (2) the ~ of a tree; I had a (nasty) ~ at tennis / when riding / from a horse; give s.o. a ~ *(make him fall)*; □ ride for a ~ *(act recklessly)* (3) the ~ of a dress / skirt (4) a ~ in purchasing power / prices; sales show a ~ of ten per cent. (5) the ~ of a city / stronghold / government / dynasty.

fall *vi* The patterns are grouped as follows: ~ + *adj*: 16; ~ + *n*: 16; idiomatic phrases: 1b; ~ + *prepos*: among 2a; at 9d, 9e; by 12; for 11; from 2e, 6; in 2d; into 2a, 2b, 5, 14; (up)on 2c, 5, 7, 8a, 14, 15; out of 2d; to 2f, 8b, 11, 12; under 2c, 14.

(1a) rain ~s from clouds; ~ing leaves / snow; newly ~en snow; many trees fell in the storm; let ~ (→ 6, let *vt* 2); ~ down the stairs / downstairs / headlong *(head first)*; ~ in(to) a pond / out of the window / over a box / off one's horse / on / to the floor / ground; ~ off / from a chair / a ladder / one's bicycle; ~ on one's feet / knees / head; he fell flat on the carpet; ~ on the fire; ~ over o.s. / one's own feet *(also fig;* → 1b); ~ overboard; she fell on his neck *(embraced him)*; they fell into one another's arms; exhausted, he fell into a chair; he took no hurt, he fell soft; he slipped and fell ten feet; he fell full length; he fell to his death *(died)*; the book fell from / out of her hands; s.th. ~s to bits / pieces; the building had ~en in ruins; many buildings fell in the earthquake.

(1b *idiomatic phrases*)
~ between two stools *(do two things unsuccessfully)*: you will probably ~ between two stools if you try to please your mother and your wife; ~ by the way *(drop out)*: we always expect a certain number of students to ~ by the way(side); ~ by the wayside *(be unable to continue)*; he tried to walk from London to Edinburgh but he soon fell by the wayside; he says he is going to live an honest life, but I think he'll ~ by the wayside; ~ on deaf ears *(be ignored)*; ~ on one's feet *(get out of a difficulty successfully)*: no matter what he does, he always seems to ~ on his feet; ~ on stony ground *(have no effect)*; ~ over o.s. *(be over-anxious)*: he almost fell over himself to offer his services to me; ~ over each / one another *(hasten to do before others)*: people were ~ing over each other to get tickets for the celebrity concert; (our plans) fell to the ground *(failed)*.

(2 *get, come; usu. of persons*)
(2a) he fell among thieves / evil companions; s.o./ s.th. ~s into the hands of (the enemy / a blackmailer / *etc*).
(2b) ~ into an ambush / trap; ~ into conversation with s.o.; ~ into a deep / heavy sleep / a trance; ~ into a habit / bad habits; ~ into line (with) *(accept a course of conduct)*; ~ into discredit / disgrace / error / temptation; the house / machinery has ~en into disuse; s.th. ~s into decay / oblivion.
(2c) he has ~en on bad / evil days / times *(is suffering misfortune)*; we never know when we may ~ on hard times; he has ~en under suspicion; ~ under s.o.'s notice / displeasure.
(2d) the two fell in love; they fell in love with each other; she fell in love with him / the beautiful dress; ~ out of love with s.o.

(2e) later on he fell from favour and was imprisoned in the Tower.
(2f ~ *to: start doing*) ~ to eating / working / fighting; Peter fell to dreaming; after a rest we fell to work; suddenly they fell to argument / blows; it was a mere accident that they fell to discussing this problem.
(3 *hang*) the curtains / skirts fell in thick folds; the dress ~s well; the skirt fell *(reached)* to the knee; her hair fell to / on her shoulders / across her face / in her eyes.
(4 *slope downwards*) the land ~s gently to the river / away from the house; here the ground ~s precipitously.
(5 *seem to come down*) the light / shadow fell on her face; night fell; darkness fell upon the scene; a silence fell on them; a hush fell on the audience; fear fell upon them; hardships ~ on s.o.; success fell into his lap.
(6 *be spoken*) he let ~ a remark; not a word fell from his lips.
(7 *reach*) strange sounds fell on our ears *(we heard them)*; my gaze / eye fell on a curious-looking object.
(8a *fall on: occur, come to*) Christmas ~s on a Monday; Easter ~s early this year; the choice fell on a woman; the lot fell (up)on me; all the expenses fell on me *(I had to pay);* responsibility / suspicion / the blame ~s on s.o.; the bulk of the work will ~ on you and me,
(8b *fall to: pass by right, obligation*) the inheritance fell to the nephew; an honour ~s to s.o.; it fell to his brother to do the job / break the news to the parents; it ~s to you to divide the money.
(9a *become less, lower*) prices ~; sales have ~en by ten per cent.
(9b) the temperature has ~en 10 degrees; the voltage / pressure / fever has ~en; the barometer / glass was ~ing most of yesterday.
(9c) the wind / water level is ~ing; his voice fell to a whisper.
(9d) his face / countenance / jaw fell at the news *(took on an expression of disappointment).*
(9e) his spirits fell at the bad news.
(10 *be captured*) the fortress / besieged city finally fell.
(11 *yield to temptation*) the woman tempted him and he fell; a ~en woman / angel; ~ to temptation; ~ for s.o./ s.th. *(inform: be attracted, deceived by)*; I fell for the picture as soon as I saw it; he was the kind of man any girl would ~ for; they met on a cruise, fell for *(in love with)* each other and were married six months later; his story sounds incredible but some people might. ~ for it; ~ for a trick.
(12 *die, be killed*) many people fell in the diphtheria epidemic; ~ in battle; Hector fell by Achilles' hand; ~ by the sword; seven lions fell to his rifle.
(13 *be voted out of office*) the Government has ~en again.
(14 *belong*) ~ under a category / class; ~ under s.o.'s jurisdiction / authority; the subject ~s under three heads; in 'abyss' the accent / stress ~s on the last syllable; s.th. ~s into three periods / five divisions / *etc.*
(15 *fall (up)on: attack*) ~ on one's enemy; robbers fell upon him; they fell on the food.
(16 *fall + adj, n: become*) when does the rent ~ due? (→ due *adj* 1); ~ ill (with a disease) (→ ill *adj* 2); his horse fell lame; ~ asleep / silent; I fired and the lion fell dead; ~ flat *(fail to have the intended effect)*; his speech / the scheme for ... fell flat; the best joke can ~ flat; ~ foul of *(displease)*; the students fell foul of their teacher; I threw the ball to my friend but it fell short (of him); our supplies fell short *(became inadequate)*; the measures proposed ~ (far) short of *(are inferior to)* what is required; the salary increases fell short of what the employees had expected; he ~s short in a number of respects: in punctuality, in courtesy, and ...; ~ short of one's duty; the house fell a prey to the flames; ~ a prey to s.o.'s plans; ~ a prey / victim to a disease; ~ (a) victim to the wrath of the tyrant; ~ heir to an estate,

fall away (1) here the ground ~s ~ *(~s precipitously)*; → fall *vi* 4. (2) his supporters began to ~ ~ *(desert him)*; ~ ~ from a party / cause (3) in this crisis, prejudices fell ~ *(disappeared).*

fall back (1) the attackers fell ~ *(retreated)* (from the city). (2) we fell ~ on the old ice-box *(used it as a substitute)* when the refrigerator was out of order; if all else fails, we can ~ ~ on going by bus.

fall behind (1) the wounded wolf fell ~ (the rest of the pack). (2) don't ~ ~ with *(paying)* your rent; ~ ~ with one's payments / correspondence / work.

fall down (1) he fell ~ senseless / dead. (2 *inform: fail*) it was on the oral exam that she fell ~; he ~s ~ on everything he is asked to do; the scheme will ~ ~ on the question of cost.

fall in (1) there was a big hole and she fell in. (2) the roof / bridge fell in during the storm. (3) while staying in Paris we fell in with *(met by chance)* a party of Swiss tourists; ~ in with bad company (4) ~ in with *(agree to)* a plan / scheme; make what arrangements you like, and I'll ~ in with them. (5) the soldiers fell in *(lined up)* for inspection.

fall off (1) my hat fell ~; a lot of apples have ~en ~. (2) the number of students often ~s ~ at the end of term; the output in the motor industry always tends to ~ ~ during the summer months; the demand for refrigerators fell ~. (3) the standard of her homework has ~en ~; support for the new plan quickly fell ~.

fall out (1) mind the baby doesn't ~ ~! his hair is ~ing ~. (2) one of the hikers had to ~ ~ as a result of a sprained ankle; several voluntary helpers had to ~ ~ because of domestic difficulties. (3) how have things ~en ~ with you? everything fell ~ as we had hoped. (4) it so fell ~ *(happened)* that we were in N. on that very day; it fell ~ that I could not be present. (5) they had been good friends, until they fell ~ *(quarrelled)* about some trivial matter; they fell ~ over a girl; she has ~en ~ with all her neighbours. (6) the soldiers fell ~ *(dissolved a formation)*.

fall over (1) the child fell ~ in the street; don't run or you will ~ ~. (2) ~ ~ backwards to do s.th. *(inform: be very eager)*.

fall through the plan fell ~ because no one supported it; a project / scheme / bargain ~s ~.

fall to (1) the door fell to. (2) after grace had been said they all fell to *(started eating)*.

false *adj* (1) make a ~ start *(in a race)*; a ~ alarm; play / sing a ~ note; take / make a ~ step *(stumble)*; ~ news; a ~ report / meaning / idea / notion / assumption / opinion / conclusion; ~ logic; this book gives a ~ picture of him; place s.o.'s conduct in a ~ light; be ~ly accused; ~ pride / piety; a ~ sense of shame / modesty / honour (2 *dishonest, deceitful*) ~ weights; make / give a ~ declaration to the customs; a ~ friend / person; make a ~ statement; give a ~ impression; be ~ to s.o. / a cause / one's promises; he is ~ of heart / mind; he is ~ in word and deed; a ~ promise / tax return; swear ~ly; → sail *vi* 1; → play *vi* 15, *vt* 15a. (3 *not genuine*) a ~ coin / cheque; under a ~ name; ~ hair / teeth; a ~ plait / beard; a ~ hem / door / window; ~ pearls; a ~ bottom *(secret compartment in a trunk)*; a ~ prophet; the ~ acacia.

falsify *vt* (1) ~ facts / records / accounts; ~ a passport / will; ~ a story / issue; produce ~ied champagne (2) my hopes / fears have been ~ied *(proved wrong)*. (3 *pervert*) ~ the course of justice.

familiar *adj* (1) this part of the country is not ~ to me; that name seems ~ to me; the ~ voice of an old friend; a ~ friend / quotation / expression / sight; be on ~ terms with s.o. (2) I am not ~ with this part of the country / every detail; I seem ~ with the name; make o.s. ~ with s.o./ s.th.; be(come) ~ with s.o. *(know, get to know, him)*; I felt he was becoming too ~ with me *(began to take undue liberties)*. (3 *informal*) write in a ~ style; ~ language.

familiarize *vt* ~ o.s. with a book / business / science / *etc*; ~ students with the use of dictionaries / *etc*.

family *n* (1) one's immediate ~ includes parents, brothers, and sisters; the father of the ~ is the head of the ~; they are a ~ of six; how are (all) your ~? you can't really blame him for it - it's in the ~ *(inherited)*; a respectable / noble / royal ~; a man of good ~; found / support a ~ (2 *children*) he has a large ~; has he any ~? bring up / rear a ~ (3) the ~ of nations; a ~ of animals / plants; a ~ of words.

fancy *n* (1) (he has / his tales show) a lively ~; vagabond ~ies; give way to a boyish ~; ~ colours the prospect of the future; our likes and dislikes often seem to be founded on ~ rather than reason; the loves of Zeus seem to have caught the ~ of many poets; → take *vt* 14, 17. (2) the ~ies of youth / a poet; a ~ has taken him just now to do that; did I really hear someone come in or was it only a ~? (3 *liking*) I had a sudden ~ for some mushrooms; she took a ~ to the house as soon as she saw it; how does this strike your ~? take / catch s.o.'s ~ *(please him)*.

fancy *vt* (1 *imagine*) I had such a scare - I ~ied the rock was a crouching wolf; ~ him wearing a pair of shorts; I can't ~ his doing such a thing; she ~ied him an artist; I ~ied myself to be a child once more; ~ (your) meeting him like that! ~ that, now! (2 *suppose*) she ~ies that everybody admires her; I ~ied I heard a knock; I ~ he is in town. (3 *like, want to have*) I ~ that green one; it's natural to ~ people who agree with us; I don't ~ his living with us for six months; does he really ~ riding? do you ~ a glass of beer? she ~ied some fruit. (4 ~ *o.s.: have a high opinion of o.s.*) he ~ies himself as a swimmer.

far *adj / adv* (1) ~ countries / shores; the ~ horizon; the Far East / West; he has travelled ~ and wide; search ~ and wide / near for s.o.; people came from ~ and near; the reason is not ~ to seek; the day is still ~ distant; □ go ~ (→ go *vi* 11b); don't carry the joke too ~; → carry *vt* 12, *vi* 18. (2) the ~ side of a room; a house on the ~ side of the lake; the ~ end of the street. (3 ~ + *adv*) ~ above the clouds; ~ ahead; the house lies ~ away; how ~ away from the sea is London? he is ~ and away our best swimmer; his idea is ~ and away better than mine; ~ back in the past; be ~ from home / one's native land / one's parents / *etc*; the problem is ~ from being solved; he is ~ from well / wealthy / a fool; ~ from relieving my cough, the medicine aggravated it; ~ from admiring him, she loathes him; I'm not dissatisfied, ~ from it, but ...; ~ be it from me to contend that he ...; ~ into the night; the holidays are not ~ off. (4 *adv* + ~) let's go as ~ as the river; as ~ back as 1900; as ~ as he is concerned, ...; he will help you as ~ as he can / is possible; by ~ (→ 5); how ~ is London from the sea? how ~ can you walk? how ~ can he be trusted? now that we have come so ~, we may as well go all the way; we have had no trouble with the car so ~ *(up to now)*; so ~ so good; so ~ as I know he will ...; it is all right thus ~. (5 ~ *before comparatives*) an elephant is ~ larger than a horse; this is ~ better / the best way / the most useful; this is by ~ the better way / best way / most useful; this is better by ~; this is the better / best way by ~; this way is (by) ~ the best.

fashion *n* (1) a current / feminine / exotic / *etc* ~; (dresses in) the latest ~; a type of dress is in / comes into / goes out of / is out of ~; follow the ~; set the ~; miniskirts were all the ~. (2) behave in a strange ~; be entertained in a magnificent ~; he has done the work after / in a ~ *(in a way, not well)*; a film after / in the ~ of Orson Welles.

fast *adj / adv* (1) a post ~ in the ground; make the door ~ *(lock it)*; make a boat ~ (to a post / the bank); make a ship ~ (to the quayside); make a rope ~: → make *vt / i* 21; hold ~ to the sled as we go downhill; the doors / her eyes were ~ shut; stand ~; stick ~ *(be unable to make progress)* (2 *steady*) a ~ friend / friendship (3) a ~ colour / dye *(resistant to fading)*; ~ to light; ~-dyed cotton; this blouse is ~ in colour. (4) a ~ horse / car / train / cruiser / journey / trip / race / walker / worker; a ~ racetrack *(allowing fast races)*; the night is ~ closing in; my watch is (ten minutes) ~ *(goes too fast)*; run / drive / fly / fall / breathe ~; please don't speak / talk / walk so ~; light travels ~er than sound; it was raining ~. (5 *dissipated*) lead a ~ life; a ~ woman / crowd; live ~; □ play ~ and loose (→ play *vi 15) (6 slang*) a ~ worker / guy (with women) *(s.o. who flouts conventions and moral standards)*; a ~ talker *(a glib and deceptive person)*; he's such a ~ talker that he can get out of any trouble you can imagine; □ pull a ~ one (on s.o.) *(be tricky or deceptive)*; he pulled a ~ one on his boss and told him he had got stuck in the elevator; he pulled a ~ one and arranged an extra week of vacation time.

fasten *vt* (1) ~ the lid of a box; ~ the door (with a strong lock); ~ s.th. to a wall (with paste / a nail) / to a dress (with a pin) (2) ~ one's eyes on s.o./ s.th. *(look fixedly at)*; ~ one's attention / thoughts / hopes on s.o./s.th. (3) ~ the responsibility / the blame / a fault / a crime / a nickname on s.o. *-vi* (4) the door won't ~; this dress ~s down the back. (5) the dog ~ed on the seat of the man's pants. (6) he ~ed *(fixed his attention)* on one particular point of my argument; if he has once ~ed upon an idea, there is no dissuading him from it. (7) ~ upon an excuse *(grasp it)*; looking round the room for someone to tell his tale of woe to, he ~ed upon me; he ~ed himself upon me for the rest of the evening. (8) world attention at the moment necessarily ~s on the disturbing news which ...

fate *n* (1) the eternal powers of ~; ~ stepped in and prevented our meeting; ...

but ~ has decided otherwise; the irony of ~; as sure as ~ *(quite certainly)* (2) a sad / relentless / inexorable / *etc.* ~; we wondered about the ~ of the missing pilot; leave / abandon s.o. to his ~; take one's ~ into one's own hands; bear one's ~ (with patience); resign o.s. / submit to one's ~; his ~ is sealed; it took the jury five minutes to settle his ~; no man can escape his ~; they met their various ~s. (3 *death*) go to / meet one's ~; decide s.o.'s ~ *(whether he shall be killed).*

fault *n* (1) we all have our ~s; overlook s.o.'s human ~s; love s.o. in spite of his ~s; with / for all his ~, he is a good fellow; his greatest ~ is unpunctuality; the book has one ~, it is too tedious; a hidden / latent / obvious / endearing / *etc* ~; commit a ~; count s.th. as a ~ against s.o.; know / see / recognize one's own ~s; admit / own / acknowledge a, one's ~ (frankly / reluctantly); □ find ~ with *(criticize)*; she is always finding ~ (with our work); I have no ~ to find with them; I can't find any ~ with it *(nothing to criticize)* / in it *(no specific defect)*; my memory was at ~ *(wrong)*; the calculation does not work out correctly, but I cannot see where it is at ~; you shouldn't have said that - that's where you were at ~; we are still at ~ *(at a loss)* to know which is the best course to take: (be generous / careful / critical) to a ~ *(excessively)* (2) the ~ lies with you, not with me; if we are late for the concert, it'll be your ~; it is not my ~ that we ...; the ~ is all mine; it is all my ~; whose ~ is it? it's his own ~. (3) a ~ in grammar / subtraction / *etc*; an essay with numerous ~s of syntax; we found a ~ in the electric system.

favour *n* (1) look on s.o. / a plan with ~; win / gain / have / enjoy / lose s.o.'s ~; find ~ in s.o.'s eyes / with s.o. *(please him)*; the ~ of the gods / stars / muses; be in ~ of s.o.'s plans / interests / proposals *(support them)*; be / stand high in s.o.'s ~; be in high ~ with s.o.; is she in / out of ~ with her employer? get into ~ with s.o.; a doctrine that was in ~ at the moment (2 *partiality*) show ~ towards s.o.; win a position by ~ more than by merit (3 *advantage*) evidence in our ~; the exchange rate is in our ~; balance in your ~ *(banking)* (4 *act of kindness*) do s.o. a ~ □ a ~ for s.o.; ask a ~ of s.o. / s.o. a ~; do me the ~ of coming tomorrow; you would be doing me a great ~ if ...; I would esteem it a great ~ if you would kindly ...; grant s.o. a ~ (willingly / reluctantly); confer a ~ on s.o.; bestow one's ~s on s.o.; request the ~ of s.o.'s company *(invite him)*; do me a ~ and leave me alone *(inform).*

favour *vt* (1) I ~ that idea; fortune ~s the brave. (2 *honour, oblige*) ~ s.o. with one's presence / visit; please ~ us with an early reply; ~ s.o. with one's advice / opinion on s.th.; Miss N. will now ~ us with a song. (3 *encourage*) ~ s.o.'s plans / interests (4 *be partial*) a coach should not ~ one player over another on his team. (5 *facilitate, help*) the damp climate ~ed the spread of the epidemic; be ~ed by circumstances / fortune (6 *suit*) yellow ~s her complexion.

fear *n* (1) a (great / bottomless / unfounded / groundless / imaginary / instinctive / indescribable / inexplicable / unutterable / nameless / secret / maddening / mortal / deadly / *etc*) ~ came over / assailed / overcame / seized / overwhelmed / numbed / paralysed / haunted him; cause / arouse / provoke ~; spread ~ and terror; the ~ of death / illness / isolation; lingering ~s; grave ~s were felt for the safety of the miners; I entertain no ~s for his safety; set s.o.'s ~s at rest (→ set *vt* 21b); he told a lie for ~ of being punished / of the consequences / (that) he would be robbed; knowing he had many enemies, he went about / was in ~ of *(losing)* his life; be in bodily ~ *(afraid of physical pain)*; all his children stood in ~ of him; put s.o. in ~ *(terrorize him)* (2) there is no ~ of that happening / of his escaping / that he will escape / of infection; no ~! *(inform: certainly not)* (3) the ~ of God / the Lord.

fear *vt* (1) cats ~ water; ~ s.o.('s anger) / death / disgrace; you have nothing to ~; some of them ~ to come out of their hiding-places; no people need ~ being exploited by us; he did not ~ to die. (2 *imagine in fear*) ~ the worst; I have long ~ed that this would happen. (3) I ~ I must go. (4) ~ God / the Lord. - *vi* (5 *be anxious about*) ~ for s.o. / his health / his safety; ~ for one's life.

feather *n* grow new ~s; lose / cast one's ~s; lose a few ~s (in an argument / *etc*); ruffle one's ~s; □ a ~ in one's cap *(s.th. to be proud of)*; □ fine ~s make fine birds; □ birds of a ~ *(people of the same sort)* (flock together); □ show the white ~ *(show fear)*; be in high / full / good / fine

~ (*be in a good mood; be very happy or healthy*).

feature *n* (1) a man of handsome ~s; she has even / regular / hard / sharp / coarse / *etc* ~s; an actor's mobile / massive / etc. ~s (2 *s.th. characteristic*) the tower clock is a ~ of the new school building; her eyes are her best ~; the geographical ~s of a district *(the lakes, rivers, mountains, etc)*; regular ~s of the journal are book reviews and the Question Box; the story has some unusual ~s. (3 *chief attraction*) the ballet was a ~ of the show. (4 *film*) the ~ began at 7.30 p.m.; a double-~ *(two movies for one price)*; short subjects precede the ~.

feature *vt* (1 *give prominence to*) ~ a story / picture in a newspaper; today's newspaper ~s a story on our mayor; the theatre was ~ing a mystery film; a new series of documentary programmes will ~ the theme of research in industry. (2) this film ~s Brigitte Bardot. (3 *have as a characteristic*) the string quartets ~ a style typical of the last century; dinner was in a restaurant which ~d steaks on the / its menu. (4 *AE, be characteristic of*) radicalism ~ed this period; industrial expansion ~ed the last century. - *vi* (5 *play a significant part*) he is one of the figures who ~ in the book.

feed *vt* (1) ~ the cat / birds / chickens / baby; he has a large family to ~; ~ the cattle on / with hay; his wife seems to ~ him well. (2) we fed the scraps to the pigs. (3) ~ paper / tape into a machine; ~ data into a computer; ~ an engine with water / a furnace with coal; ~ coal into a furnace; ~ a fire with fuel (4) springs ~ ponds; several small streams ~ the river. (5) ~ one's hopes on horoscopes; ~ propaganda to the people / the people with propaganda. - *vi* (6) the cows were ~ing in the meadows; cattle ~ chiefly on grass; we ~ at one o'clock each day *(inform)*; have you fed yet? □ ~ out of s.o.'s hand *(be willing to obey)* (7) Soviet influence in the Near East ~s on fear; his ego ~s on flattery.

feed up (1) those turkeys have been fed up specially for Christmas; a convalescent needs ~ing up. (2 *inform*) I'm fed up with (listening to) his constant complaints.

feel *vt* (1 *touch*) ~ s.th. with the hand / finger / stick; the blind recognize objects by ~ing them; he felt his foot cautiously; ~ s.o.'s pulse; just ~ how hot my forehead is; ~ the edge of a knife; ~ one's way towards an agreement (2 *realize through the senses*) ~ hunger / heat / cold / pain / a blow / the draught / *etc*; did you ~ the earthquake? I felt the earth shake / the ground trembling; he doesn't ~ the heat at all; I can ~ a nail in my shoe; the dead cannot ~; do fish ~ pain? (3 *realize in one's mind*) ~ joy / love / anger / sorrow / grief / despair / relief / repentance / remorse for s.th. / satisfaction / contempt for s.o. / pity for s.o.; ~ hope / strength / courage (within one); ~ a / the desire / urge to do s.th.; ~ an effect / the (full) effects of s.th.; the consequences were widely felt; ~ the force of an argument / an interest in s.th. / the beauty of a scene / the want of sympathy / *etc* (4 *be of the opinion half intuitively*) we ~ he is telling the truth; she felt things were about to go wrong; what do you ~ about the suggestion? we felt the plan to be / that the plan was unwise; she felt in her bones *(knew instinctively)* that the decision was wrong. - *vi* (5) he felt to see if his wallet was still in its place; ~ (to see) whether the water is warm enough yet (6 *search*) he felt along the wall until he found the door; he was ~ing about in the dark for the switch; he felt in his pocket for a penny. (7 → 2) the dead cannot ~. (8 *be consciously in a certain state*) ~ cold / warm / comfortable / happy / young / ten years younger / refreshed / tired / bored / sad / ill / sick / well / giddy / insulted / hurt / guilty / envious / (un-)kindly towards s.o. / off-colour / *etc*; ~ disposed / inclined to do s.th.; ~ coerced in opinion; ~ strong enough to speak; I felt full of pain after the accident; I ~ sure that you will ...; my fingers ~ dead; my leg felt painful; the sight makes me ~ rather sick; ~ at ease / a new man / a new woman / out of place / like a fish out of water; you will ~ at home here; she doesn't ~ (quite) herself today; ~ equal, up to a task / a long walk / doing s.th.; how are you ~ing today? I'm ~ing much better, thanks; □ ~ like *(feel inclined for)*: I don't ~ like cards / work; do you ~ like a game of tennis / a cup of tea? I ~ like some tea, don't you? ~ bad (*AE also* badly); Mary is ~ing rather bad today - she's had some bad news; she felt bad when she heard the news; don't ~ bad - I'll help you. (9 *have sympathy*) ~ for s.o. (in his sorrow / loss); ~ with s.o. (10)

velvet ~s smooth; the air ~s chilly; the wall felt hot.

feel out (*try to assess s.o.'s viewpoint*) I tried to ~ him ~ on the issue but he wouldn't tell me anything; ~ him ~ about the Smith Plan.

feeling *n* (1) he had lost all ~ in his left leg. (2 *sensation*) a ~ of hunger / cold / pain / discomfort; a prickly / creeping / *etc* ~ (3 *emotion*) a ~ of joy / happiness / anger / gratitude; speak / sing / play with (much) ~; the music is full of ~; have a ~ for music; a ~ of achievement; a warm / deep / uncontrollable / uncomfortable / *etc* ~ came / crept over him; a ~ not to be described (4) s.o.'s inner ~s; she's entirely ruled by her ~s; have you no ~s? show / display one's ~s (openly); have warm / kindly ~s towards s.o.; appeal to s.o.'s better ~s (5 *sympathy*) has he any ~ for the suffering of others? he's a man of ~; good ~ *(friendliness)*; ill ~ *(bitterness)* (6 *opinion, impression*) we had a / the ~ that (the story was too long); my ~ is that (he is unreliable); instinctive ~; your remark shows that my ~ was right. (7 *excitement*) there was a great deal of ~ over the elections; the speech aroused strong ~(s) on all sides; ~ had risen so high that a quarrel ... (8 *sensitive understanding*) he hasn't much ~ for natural beauty; ~ for language.

feign *vt* ~ illness / death / indifference / modesty / humility / piety / friendship / *etc*; ~ o.s. mad; her love is ~ed.

fetch *vt* (1) ~ water from the river; I have come to ~ the money; shall I ~ you your hat / your hat for you? ~ s.o. a glass of water; please ~ me the book from my desk; the new chair is in the garden - please ~ it in; he ~ed his camera out to show us. (2) ~ the doctor! please ~ the children from school; interrupt s.o. to ~ him to the telephone; he's ~ing me this afternoon because we are playing in a match. (3) the old Bible ~ed a record sum; ~ high prices (4) ~ a (deep) sigh; ~ a (dreadful) groan.

fetch up (1) we drove as far as we could and ~ed up *(came to a stop)* at Liverpool; ~ up in jail (2 *BE*) the girl ~ed everything up *(vomited)* soon after she had eaten. (3) ~ up a sigh.

fever *n* (1) have a (slight / high) ~; he hasn't much ~; he was running a ~; he was suddenly seized with a ~; shake with ~; an attack / bout of ~; the ~ dropped. (2) scarlet / typhoid / rheumatic / yellow / *etc* ~ (3) be in a ~ of activity / anxiety / impatience / expectation / anticipation / excitement.

few *adj* (1) please give me a ~ more minutes / examples / *etc*; ~ *(not many)* / a ~ *(some)* people came; (only) a ~ seats were left; we have only a ~ (more) miles to go; please move the table a ~ inches to the left; a man of ~ words; he has come up with very ~ genuinely new ideas; there are quite a ~ reasons why we shouldn't go; there were not a ~ *(many)* objections to his suggestions; how ~ of the applicants are really qualified? some ~ questions remain unanswerable; the report lists no ~er than 20 different examples; try to make ~er mistakes / express yourself in ~er words; ~er and ~er voters agree with his policies; every ~ minutes / days / years / *etc*; every ~ inches / feet / miles / *etc*; → many *adj* 1. (2 *predicative uses*) we are too ~ to be of any help; □ ~ and far between *(rare)*: his good moods are ~ and far between; they turned out to be ~er in number than had been supposed. - *pron* (3) a ~ of the guests stayed until after midnight; quite a ~ of the votes were invalid; most people usually tell the truth - ~ always do so; ~, perhaps none at all, have any hope of surviving the crash; not many of my friends have driver's licences - even ~er have cars; → many *pron* 3. - *n* (4) the (under)privileged ~ are not at issue here; true leaders are the ~est of the ~; the many and the ~ *(the masses and the elite)*; the discerning / a select ~.

field *n* (1) a ~ of wheat / potatoes / *etc*; a corn- / rice-~; a cultivated / tilled ~; work in the ~s; woods and ~s; roam over ~ and meadow; an open / smooth / level ~ (2) a ~ of ice / snow; an ice- / snow- / oil- / gold- / coal-~ (3) a cricket / hockey / baseball / rugby / football ~; a playing- / landing- / flying-~ (4) the ~ of battle; a battle-~; the regiment is in the ~; take the ~ (against s.o.) *(before a battle)*; hold / lose the ~; drive an enemy from the ~ (5 *range of operation, etc*) a ~ of vision / view; a visual ~; a magnetic ~; the earth's gravitational ~ (6) a ~ of knowledge / scholarship / science / research / art / literature / politics / *etc*; he decided to go into the ~ of medicine; there is still a wide ~ for exploration here; he saw a new ~ opening up before him; that is outside my ~. (7 *background*) a flower on a ~ of blue.

fight *n* (1) the quarrel led to a ~; a ~ between two dogs / armies; the boys had a ~; put up a good / poor ~ *(fight with / without courage)*; a hard / bitter / fierce / obstinate / stubborn / desperate / bloody / *etc* ~ (2) the ~ for life / against death; the ~ for liberty / against disease / *etc* (3 *fighting spirit*) be full of ~; give / show ~ *(be willing to fight)*; the bad news took all the ~ out of them.

fight *vi* (1) ~ against / with an enemy; ~ with an ally; ~ for a friend / a cause / one's faith; the sick man fought for his life for days; he fought against sleep in vain; he has many temptations to ~ against; ~ over an issue; □ ~ shy of *(be reluctant)*; being very reserved, she always fought shy of strangers / entering into a discussion; ~ bravely / heroically / stubbornly / obstinately / desperately / fair; ~ to the last breath / to the (bitter) end / to the death / to a finish *(decision)*; □ ~ with one's back to the wall *(desperately)* (2) he fought (on every front) in the last war. - *vt* (3) ~ a battle / duel / good fight (4) ~ the enemy / a fire; ~ a disease / epidemic / opinion / temptation / *etc*; ~ social distinctions / privileges / *etc*; she had to ~ her emotion; ~ one's way in life / the world *(make progress by overcoming difficulties)*.

fight back she had to ~ ~ her tears.

fight down ~ ~ a temptation / one's fear / *etc*.

fight off ~ ~ an attack / enemy / illness / fever / *etc*.

fight on they decided to ~ on *(continue fighting)*.

fight out he won't be able to ~ the duel ~ (to the end); let's ~ it ~ *(decide the matter by fighting or discussion)*.

figure *n* (1) write all the ~s legibly; double ~s *(from 10 to 99)*; an income of five ~s *(between £10,000 and £99,999)*; he has all the ~s right at his fingertips; be good at ~s *(arithmetic)* (2 *price*) buy / get / sell s.th. at a low / high ~ (3 *drawing*) geometrical / plane / rectilinear / *etc* ~s (4 *s.th. drawn, painted, cut in stone, etc*) painted / sculptured ~s; these ~s represent characters from Greek history. (5) ~s of a dance; skate / cut ~s (6 *appearance of a person*) the ~ of a man in the dark; he was a lofty, noble ~; he was a fine ~ of a man; the guard at the door was a gigantic ~; she's dieting to keep her ~; he has a good / bad / poor / handsome / lank / *etc* ~; a woman with a slender ~; cut a fine / poor / sorry / ridiculous ~ *(give such an impression)*; he cut a sorry ~ in this debate; he cuts a fine ~ in his uniform; look a ~ of fun (7 *person*) King Alfred was one of the noblest ~s of his age; the familiar ~ of the London policeman; in this play the ~ of the mother is less convincing. (8) a ~ of speech.

figure *vt* (1 *decorate*) a ~d glass window; ~d silk (2 *imagine*) ~ s.th. to o.s.; ~ o.s. a hero. - *vi* (3 *appear*) ~ in a play / on a list / in the news; ~ in history; his name ~d among the guests.

figure out (1) can you ~ ~ this arithmetic problem? ~ ~ the cost (2) the translation ~s ~ at £5. (3) I can't ~ ~ *(understand)* his purpose.

fill *vt* (1) ~ a hole with sand / a tank with petrol / a cushion with feathers; ~ a gap *(also fig)*; the dentist ~ed my tooth; ~ one's pockets / stomach; ~ one's head with useless knowledge; ~ a letter with news; go and ~ me a glass of water / a glass of water for me; an actor who ~s the house *(attracts an audience)* (2a *occupy the whole of, said of things, persons*) his books ~ed three boxes / several shelves; the report ~s three volumes; the mourners ~ed the little chapel; the hall was ~ed to the very last seat; the sound of singing ~ed the air; they ~ed the air with their cries; (the) smoke ~ed the room; (the) wind ~ed *(swelled)* the sails; she has the voice to ~ the theatre (2b *as 2a, said of activities, abstract things*) the preparations ~ed every minute of the day; my studies ~ (up) all my spare time; the news ~ed us with great sadness; the thought ~ed her mind; he / his heart was ~ed with gratitude; his eyes were ~ed with terror; his experiments ~ed us with admiration; he was ~ed with admiration / ambition. (3 *appoint s.o. to*) ~ a vacancy; they ~ed the post / job yesterday. (4 *fulfil*) the grocer will ~ the order; □ ~ the bill *(be satisfactory)*; the new book ~s a need / want. (5 *do the duties of*) he ~s the office / his post well; he ~s the position of president. - *vi* (6) the pit slowly ~ed (up) with water; the theatre began to ~ (up); the sails ~ed with wind; her eyes ~ed with tears.

fill in (1) ~ in a hole / ditch (2) ~ in a map / picture / piece of embroidery; the painter ~d in the smaller details later. (3) ~ in a (registration / application) form / cheque; ~ in one's name / sex / date of birth / *etc* (on a form).

fill out (1) eat plenty of cream - that'll ~ your cheeks ~. (2) her cheeks began to ~ ~; he has ~ed ~ since I last saw him. (3) ~ ~ a cheque / *etc* (→ fill in 3).

fill up (1) ~ up a glass / bucket / *etc*; ~ up a gap / the gaps in s.th.; ~ it / her right up *(with petrol)*; ~ o.s. up with food; → fill *vt* 2b. (2) first you must ~ up this form. (3) ~ up a post *(appoint s.o. to it)* (4) the channel of the river ~ed up with mud; → fill *vi* 6.

film *n* (1) a ~ of dust / wax / oil / mist / *etc*; an icy ~ around the fence; a ~ has formed on his left eye. (2) put in / insert / load a (photographic) ~; expose a ~ for a fiftieth of a second; develop a ~ (3) a silent / sound / colour / three-dimensional / feature / short / instructional / documentary ~; make / take / shoot a ~; the ~ is showing / is on at the Odeon; she wants to go / get into (the) ~s; a ~ actor / fan / star / festival / *etc.*

film *vt* (1) ~ one of Shakespeare's plays / a scene. - *vi* (2) he is ~ing in southern France. (3) this story ~s easily; she ~s well.

find *vt* (1 *discover by searching*) have you found the key? they found the documents on him; the missing girl has not been found yet; will you ~ Ann her spectacles / Ann's spectacles for her? they dug 20 feet and then found water; I know where / how to ~ him; can you ~ your way in / out / back / home? ~ a way of doing / to do s.th.; ~ ways and means; the statement found its way into print *(was printed)*; good craftsmen are difficult to ~ nowadays; ~ one's place (in a book) *(find the required page)*; I can ~ nothing new to say on the subject; □ ~ one's feet *(be able to walk, to act independently)*; □ ~ o.s. *(discover one's powers)*; □ ~ fault with s.o. (→ fault *n* 1) (2 *get, obtain by effort*) ~ work / a job / a wife / the capital for a house; ~ a friend (in s.o.); ~ me a taxi, please; we'll ~ you a chair; ~ the solution to a problem; ~ the unknown; he couldn't ~ the courage to do it; he always ~s (the) time / leisure to (read novels); he can ~ no peace; he cannot ~ peace of mind; the idea found acceptance; I can ~ no excuse for his behaviour. (3 *discover by chance, meet with*) I found the money in the street; ~ a mistake in a book; he was found dead / injured near his car; you don't often ~ such people; we found him at work / at home / asleep / napping; did you ~ her in / up / in bed / out? we hope this *(letter)* ~s you in good health; he found the house empty / the door closed; you will ~ some paper in the left drawer; you must take us as you ~ us; he found (a) difficulty in breathing. (4 *be given, obtain without effort*) ~ enjoyment / pleasure / satisfaction in (doing) s.th.; ~ favour with s.o. / in s.o.'s eyes (→ favour *n* 1) (5 *learn by experience, study, etc*) you will ~ it very interesting there; ~ s.th. easy / difficult / hard / a labour (to do); ~ it easy / difficult / impossible / *etc* to do s.th.; ~ s.th. beautiful / distasteful / *etc*; how do you ~ the house? ~ s.o. charming / shallow / dull / a burden / *etc*; don't you ~ it very hot here? he found his wife gone; he found himself surrounded by enemies; he woke to ~ himself in hospital; ~ o.s. outwitted; we found him (to be) / that he was dishonest; I ~ that I have been mistaken; I ~ it pays to (learn French); I found my attention wander / them to have left the room; the doctor found that he had cancer; ~ the cube root of 64; what do you ~ the total? please ~ (out) when the train starts / how to get there. (6 *be found: there is, are*) emus are found in Australia; this plant is / can be found everywhere. (7 *reach*) the bullet found its mark; water ~s its own level; rivers ~ their way to the sea. (8 *determine and declare*) ~ s.o. guilty / insane; no jury would ~ it murder / that he is ...; they found a verdict of guilty; ~ the case proven (9 *provide*) the employer ~s accommodation; an uncle found the money for his education; wages £12 a week, with board and lodging found; all found *(board, lodging and clothes provided free)*; while he was at the university, a relative found him in pocket money *(provided it for him)*; she earns scarcely enough to ~ herself in the necessaries of life. - *vi* (10 → 8) the jury found for / against the defendant.

find out (1) he was unable to ~ ~ the answer / where she lived / who broke the window; ~ ~ s.o.'s address / the precise facts; ~ ~ a plot / a crime / the truth; the 11th commandment: thou shalt not be found out; this damp weather ~s ~ my rheumatism; did you ~ ~ about the trains to B.? (2) I was disappointed to ~ you ~ *(not at home*; → find *vt* 3).

finger *n* the fore- / index / middle / ring / little ~; crook / cut / burn one's ~; pinch one's ~s in the door; get one's ~s jammed in the door; eat / point at s.th. / drum on the table with one's ~s; count s.th. on one's ~s; □ his ~s are all thumbs *(he is clumsy)*; my ~s are itching (with impatience); have facts / figures / *etc* at one's ~-tips / ~-ends *(know them well)*; □ have a ~ in the pie *(take part in s.th. in an undesirable way)*; she has a ~ in every pie; he has a ~ in this business; he'll burn his ~s in that enterprise; put / lay one's ~ to one's lip; lay / put a, one's ~ on s.th. (→ lay *vt* 2, put *vt* 7a); → spot *n* 3; □ turn / twist s.o. round one's (little) ~ *(dominate him)*; he wouldn't lift a ~ to help you.

finish *vt* (1) ~ one's work / a piece of work / a speech / a journey / *etc*; when will you have ~ed / be ~ed with your work? hand in a ~ed piece of work; I have ~ed (reading / using / writing) the book; the road is nearly ~ed; serve (up) the ~ed dish; I have ~ed the pie *(eaten it)*; ~ one's tea; we ~ed dinner with coffee; he ~ed his days in poverty; I have ~ed with this character once and for all. (2 *exhaust, exasperate*) that long climb almost ~ed me; the work in the garden ~ed him; his cynicism ~ed me completely. (3 *vanquish, destroy, kill; also fig*) after three glasses of beer he is (positively) ~ed *(inform, fig: drunk)*; the stock market crash ~ed him; the last battle ~ed the enemy; the court decision virtually ~ed all hope of further appeals. (4) ~ wood with varnish; the woodwork is beautifully ~ed *(polished)*; he gave the picture a few ~ing touches. - *vi* (5) it was noon and he still had not ~ed; he ~ed by reciting a sonnet / with a sonnet.

finish off (1) let me ~ this ~ before I leave. (2) the heavy blow ~ed him ~ *(knocked him out)*.

finish up (1) the meeting ~ed up with community singing; the car ~ed up in the ditch. (2) he ~ed up by becoming Mayor.

fire *n* (1) strike ~ with / from a stone; lay a ~ *(prepare it)*; light a ~; make a ~ *(lay and light it)*; light / kindle the ~; → take *vt* 10f; stir / poke the ~; the ~ is alight / has gone out; the ~ is burning brightly / blazes (up) / flares (up) / flickers (up) / spreads a pleasant warmth / dies down / goes out; cook on / over a good / fast / slow / low ~; turn on the electric ~ *(heater)*; □ play with ~; □ out of the frying-pan into the ~ *(from a bad position into one that is worse)*; □ add fuel to the ~ *(make passions stronger)*; □ go through ~ and water (for s.o. / a cause) *(endure severe hardship)*; he said he would go through ~ and water to win her hand. (2) set ~ to a house / a house on ~; (a) ~ broke out in the house next door / spread rapidly / raged for two days / reduced the town to ashes; catch / take ~ (easily); he noticed that the hut was on ~; □ set the world / Thames on ~ *(do s.th. spectacular)* (3) open / cease / ~; bring / put the enemy / a position under ~; be under ~ *(also fig)*; be exposed to (enemy) ~; come under ~ *(also fig)*; be caught between two ~s *(also fig)* (4) the ~ of love / hatred / enthusiasm / passion / youth; the audience was gripped by the ~ of his speech; she / the horse has ~.

firm *adj* (1) ~ flesh / muscles / calves / dough / fruit / fabrics; (build on) ~ ground; □ be on ~ ground *(sure of one's facts)*; a ~ chair; the table stands ~. (2 *not easily upset, removed*) a ~ foundation / structure; a ~ lock; the ~ position of a bandage / splint; gain a ~ footing / foothold; become ~ly settled / established (3 *strong, steady*) walk with ~ steps; a ~ voice; give s.o. a ~ glance; have one's eyes ~ly fixed on s.th.; stand ~ (4 *not easily influenced, strong*) a ~ belief / opinion / faith / hope / intention / decision / resolution / answer / will / principle / *etc*; he was polite but ~; I am ~ly resolved to do it; take ~ measures; be ~ with children *(not yield)*; be ~ of purpose / in one's resolution to do s.th. / in one's belief; hold ~ to one's beliefs; be ~ friends with s.o.; take a ~ attitude / stand in / on a matter (5 *not liable to cancellation, modification*) a ~ offer / order / sale / purchase / contract / agreement / promise; buy / sell s.th. on ~ account; ~ prices; a ~ stock market.

first *adj* (1) the ~ letter of the alphabet is 'a'; the ~ house in the road; the ~ two persons; the fastest runner comes in ~ in the race; arrive / leave / speak / finish ~; ~ come, ~ served; the ~ row; in the ~ place *(to begin with)*; ~ gear *(in a car,* *etc)* (2 *earliest*) the ~ edition of a book; the ~ snow; we caught the ~ train home; I shall call on you at the ~ opportunity; do it ~ thing tomorrow; → put *vt* 16. (3 *most important, leading*) he is the ~ surgeon in London; the ~ families of the town; that was a performance of the ~ order; ~ violin(ist) / soprano; he considered it is ~ duty. (4 *initial, rudimentary, fundamental*) he hasn't the ~ idea of drawing; he doesn't know the ~ thing about it; ~ principles; at ~ hand *(directly)*; he has gone to China to study conditions there at ~ hand; at ~ sight *(when seen for the first time)*; (fall in) love at ~ sight; a risky plan at ~ sight.

first *adv* (1 *for the first time*) when did you ~ see him / see him ~? we ~ went there last year; he ~ asked my name; work ~ and play afterwards; I shall have to think that over ~. (2 *before anything else*) I must finish this work ~. (3 *sooner, rather*) "Eat that food!" - "I'd starve ~"; he said he would resign ~.

first *n* (1) the ~ of January is a holiday; on the ~ of next month; who is the ~ of the speakers? he would be the ~ to *(readily)* (admit it); ~ of all, I must tell you ...; at ~ *(at the beginning)* we thought he was joking, but ...; she did not wish to go at ~ but changed her mind; it was evident from the ~ *(start)* that he never intended to carry out his promise; the scheme has been mismanaged from ~ to last *(from beginning to end)*. (2) put the car in ~ *(gear)*; shift into ~.

fit *adj* (1 *suitable, suited*) the food is not ~ (for a dog) to eat; the text isn't ~ for publication; a ship ~ for service; he is not ~ for the position / to return to work yet; the weather is not ~ for cricket / to go out in; his language is not ~ to be repeated. (2 *proper*) it is not ~ that you should be merry while your brother is dying; do what / as you think ~; he didn't see ~ to adopt my suggestion; he didn't even see ~ to say thanks; → see *vt* 21. (3 *in good health*) he keeps ~ by playing tennis; British people are becoming increasingly ~. (4 *ready, so much as*) she worked till she was ~ to drop; he was laughing ~ to burst himself; she felt ~ to cry; the engine bellowed ~ to deafen him; she sobbed ~ to break her heart; □ I'm (just about) ~ to be tied *(AE inform: very nervous, upset)*.

fit *vt* (1) this coat doesn't ~ me; does the key ~ the lock? (2 *be the right person, thing for*) a present to ~ the occasion; he ~s the description. (3 *make the right person, thing for*) his experience ~s him for the job; ~ o.s. for one's new duties; military training ~s men for long marches / to make long marches; ~ a policy to a new situation (4 *put into place*) ~ a new door; ~ the handle on; ~ s.th. into an opening; ~ a plank in a floor; ~ the bookcase in between the windows; can you ~ the lid on / this piece in? the text is too long, we can't ~ it into the programme. (5 *attach, install*) ~ shelves to a wall / number plates to the front and rear of a car; ~ fog lights (6 *adjust the size of s.th. so as to be right*) I had a new suit ~ted (on); ~ on a garment; ~ a garment on s.o. (7 *provide*) ~ a room with a carpet / a cupboard with shelves. - *vi* (8 → 1) these shoes ~ well; the door ~s badly; the lid ~s on that tin; a cork ~s into the neck of a bottle; this pane doesn't ~ into our window frame. (9 *correspond*) your theory does not ~ with the facts.

fit in (1) → fit *vt* 4; we can ~ you in at the corner table. (2) the new armchair ~s in nicely; some pieces of the puzzle do not ~ in. (3) ~ in a visit / appointment; I can ~ you in between 3 and 4 p.m. (4) how will my arrangements for the holidays ~ in with yours? this item doesn't ~ in with the rest of the programme; ~ in with s.o.'s plans (5) she didn't ~ in with the others; he ~ted in so well to our way of living.

fit on → fit *vt* 4, 6.

fit out ~ ~ a ship for a voyage; ~ ~ a shop / hotel / *etc*; a boy ~ted ~ for school; ~ s.o. ~ with his uniform / with all he needs; ~ workers ~ with tools; he ~ted himself ~ with a new suit.

fit up (1) ~ up a house (with modern furniture); they have ~ted the caravan up with all the latest gadgets; we ~ted up one of the bedrooms as a study; the cellar was ~ted up as a workshop. (2) a microphone was ~ted up in the pavilion to broadcast a commentary on the match; it took us about half an hour to ~ up the apparatus. (3) could you ~ me up with *(inform: give me)* a new bulb?

fit *n* (1) a ~ of coughing / madness / hysteria / *etc*; a fainting ~; she gave a moan and fell down in a ~; she almost had a ~ when she saw the bill; the bill gave her a

~. (2) a ~ of laughter / merriment / passion / enthusiasm / generosity / anger / pique / rage / melancholy / energy / *etc*; he did it in a ~ of temper; fly into a ~ of temper; burst into a ~ of laughter; by ~s and starts *(irregularly)*; traffic moved by ~s and starts; this watch of mine goes by ~s and starts; he does his homework by ~s and starts.

fix *vt* (1) ~ a shelf to a wall; ~ a stake / post in(to) the ground; ~ a loose tile / a wobbly chair-leg (in place) / a banging shutter (2) ~ a date / day / (meeting-) place / sum / price / quota / limit / frontier / boundary; ~ a tax at a certain amount; ~ the details of s.th.; ~ the time and place of / a time and place for the next meeting; ~ a meeting for 3 o'clock; ~ the route of a journey; nothing (final) has been ~ed yet; we have ~ed for the meeting to be held on Friday. (3 *inform: repair*) ~ a broken machine; the plumber ~ed the leaky pipe; a screw has come out - we can soon ~ that for you. (4 *inform: prepare*) mother ~ed lunch; ~ a salad (5 *inform: arrange*) ~ one's hair (6 *direct*) ~ one's eyes on s.o./s.th.; ~ one's mind / thoughts / hope on s.th.; ~ one's affections on a woman (7 *take and hold*) ~ facts / dates in one's mind; the unusual sight ~ed his attention / kept his attention ~ed; ~ s.o. with one's eye / an angry stare (8 *make permanent*) ~ a (photographic) negative / print; a ~ing-bath; a ~ing-agent; ~ colours (when dyeing (9) how are you ~ed for cigarettes - could you give me one? how are you ~ed for next Friday evening? how are we ~ed for time *(how much time have we)*? - *vi* (10 *choose*) he ~ed on a bungalow rather than a small house; ~ on a date for s.th. - *adj* (11 → 2) a ~ed income; sell goods at ~ed prices; have ~ed *(definite)* principles; a ~ed idea (12 → 6) look at s.o./ s.th. with a ~ed gaze; stare / gaze / look at s.o./ s.th. ~edly.

fix up (1) ~ up a tent / temporary platform / *etc*; he ~ed up the garage as a workshop. (2) they ~ed him up in the spare room / for the night; we phoned the hotel and were ~ed up without the slightest difficulty; we tried to get you ~ed up somewhere; I think we can ~ you up with what you want; ~ s.o. up with a job; can you ~ him up with a date for Saturday? (3) we ~ed up the quarrel / question of payment; I've ~ed up a visit to the theatre for next Friday; I have ~ed up for the decorator to come on Monday; I have ~ed up about the bus for next Saturday. (4) I've ~ed up to go to the theatre on Friday evening.

flash *n* (1) a ~ of lightning; did you see the ~? do s.th. in a ~ *(in a very short time)*; everything happened in a ~. (2) a ~ of hope / merriment / wit / genius / inspiration / anger; the ~ of your eyes (3) do you like this ~ (photo)? a ~ bulb / gun / exposure; up-to-date ~ equipment; an electronic ~ (attachment).

flash *vi* (1) a light ~ed on the dark shore; the lightning ~ed across the sky; a torch ~ed in his face. (2) the express train ~ed past; a figure ~ed across the screen; the idea ~ed into / through his mind; it ~ed upon me / across my mind that we ... (3) the angry woman's eye ~ed with rage; his face ~ed with joy / excitement / anger; ~ing anger / wit. - *vt* (4) ~ a light in s.o.'s eyes / face; ~ a signal; ~ news across / around the world (by radio); ~ a smile at s.o.; he ~ed a wad of banknotes at me. (5) her eyes ~ed fire / defiance.

flat *adj* (1) a ~ lid / table-top / floor / roof; a ~ forehead / nose / chest; a ~ region / coast (line); ~ ground / country; one of the tyres is ~ *(has no, little air)*; he hit it with his ~ hand. (2) fall / lie ~ (on the back / floor / ground); he knocked the man ~; he threw himself ~ on the bed; the earthquake laid the town ~. (3) a ~ plate / dish / pan / box / package; a ~(-heeled) shoe (4 *dull*) ~ beer; this drink tastes ~; life seemed ~ to him; a ~ joke; □ (a joke, story) falls ~ *(has no effect)*; a ~ tone of voice (5 *absolute*) ~ nonsense; give s.o. a ~ denial / refusal; that's ~ *(my last word)* (6 *uniform*) a ~ tint of red (7 *below the true pitch*) a ~ note.

flat *adv* (1 → flat *adj* 5) she told him ~ she wouldn't go; he went ~ against his promise; go ~ against orders; he told me ~ that he ... (2 → flat *adj* 7) sing ~.

flavour *n* (1) a delicate / strong / pleasant / nasty / *etc* ~; the ~ of the soup was spoilt by too much salt; sweets with different ~s; ice-cream with a chocolate ~ (2) a newspaper story with a ~ of romance; the ~ of adventure / irony; this word has a slightly old-fashioned ~; the book has a decadent ~. (3) condiments impart ~ to food; this fruit is something like a lemon in ~; when you have a bad cold, your food sometimes has very little ~.

flee *vi* (1) ~ from / before the enemy *(form)*; ~ from temptation; the enemy were defeated and fled in disorder. - *vt* (2) ~ a danger; he fled his father's wrath; he killed his enemy and fled the country.

flesh *n* (1) people of ~ and blood; put on / lose ~ (→ put on 3; lose *vt* 3); I have corresponded with him, but I have never met him in the ~ *(personally)*; the angry *(inflamed)* ~ of a wound; proud ~ *(growing in a wound)*; □ make s.o.'s ~ creep / crawl / *(frighten him)* (2) one's own ~ and blood *(near relations)* (3) go the way of all ~ *(die)*; □ the spirit is willing, but the ~ is weak; the sins of the ~ (4) the ~ of fruit.

flight[1] *n* (1) study the ~ of birds / insects / aircraft / missiles; the art of ~; shoot a bird in ~ *(while it is flying)* (2) a non-stop / intercontinental / continuous / scheduled / round-the-world / trial / *etc* ~; three ~s a week to Tokyo; I wish you a pleasant ~; ~ 239 to New York; a ~ from London to Paris takes about an hour; the spring and autumn ~s of birds; the ~ of an arrow / bullet / missile (3 *group*) a ~ of geese / birds / insects / locusts / arrows; a ~ of aircraft / bombers (4) a ~ of stairs / steps; my bedroom is two ~s up; we had to walk up four ~s. (5) the ~ of time; a ~ of thoughts / fancy / wit / ambition / the imagination.

flight[2] *n* seek safety in ~; be in ~ *(be fleeing)*; put to ~ *(cause to flee)*; take (to) ~ *(flee)*; the ~ of the middle-aged from the cities.

fling *vt* (1) ~ one's hat up (in the air); ~ one's arms out / up / round s.o.'s neck; ~ a stone at s.o./ s.th.; he was flung from his bicycle; he flung the man bleeding on the ground; ~ a door / window open / shut; ~ one's clothes on / off *(dress / undress)*; ~ off one's pursuers; ~ s.o. into prison; he flung himself into a chair; she flung herself into his arms / on his mercy. (2) ~ s.o. a scornful look; ~ abuse / a curse at s.o. (3) ~ caution / prudence to the winds; ~ down the gauntlet to s.o. *(challenge him)*; ~ certain facts / s.o.'s failures in his teeth *(reproach him with them)* (4) ~ o.s. into a job / undertaking *(take it up energetically)*. - *vi* (5) she flung out of the room; he flung away in a rage; ~ off without saying good-bye.

float *vi* (1) wood ~s on water; yellow leaves ~ing in a pool; dust ~s in the air; a balloon ~ed across the sky / in the air; a boat ~ed down the river; ~ on air *(fig: be overjoyed)*. - *vt* (2) ~ logs / a raft down a river; there isn't enough water to ~ the ship. (3 *launch*) ~ a business company / loan.

flood *vt* (1) ~ land with water (from a river); the fields / rivers were ~ed with heavy rains; a cellar ~ed with water (2) ~ a burning building with water; ~ a mechanism with oil; ~ the stage of a theatre with light (3) be ~ed with applications; his admirers ~ed him with letters. - *vi* (4) the water ~ed over the dikes into the town; bright light ~ed into the room; crowds ~ed over / into / onto s.th.

flourish *vi* (1) he is ~ing in his new job; I hope you are all ~ing; a ~ing industry; a business / country ~es; art and science began to ~; the spirit of liberty ~ed in this country. (2 *said of s.o.'s main artistic period*) he ~ed in the early 18th century. - *vt* (3 *wave*) ~ a sword; ~ a telegram with good news; he was ~ing his cane as he strolled along.

flow *vi* (1) liquids / gases ~; electric current / traffic ~s; the river ~ed into / down to the sea / over its banks; the tide ~s *(rises and falls)* twice a day; all the oil has ~ed out; blood ~s through the body; royal blood ~s in his veins; the tears ~ed from her eyes; the champagne ~ed like water; crowds ~ed down the avenue. (2) gold / the profits ~ed out of the country; capital ~ed in. (3) wealth ~s from industry and economy; wisdom ~s from experience; such poems ~ easily from his pen; the compliments ~ed from his lips; talk ~ed freely. (4 *hang down*) a ~ing robe; her golden hair ~ed down her back / over her shoulders.

fly *vi* (1) birds / insects / aircraft / pilots / bullets / arrows / sparks ~; ~ high (in the air / sky) / low; ~ over / across the ocean / round the world; ~ a thousand kilometres; □ as the crow ~ies *(straight)*; □ the bird is / has flown *(the person wanted has escaped)*; □ ~ high / at high(er) game *(aim high(er), be ambitious)*; fight till the feathers begin to ~; they quarrelled till the fur began to ~. (2 *float, wave*) flags / kites were ~ing everywhere; □ (pass an examination) with ~ing colours *(triumphantly)* (3 *move fast*) he flew down the road; she flew out of the room; it's getting late, we must ~; the bird flew out (of the cage); "Fire!" - and all the people flew out of the house; the wheels flew round; the door flew open; □ send s.o. ~ing (→ send *vt* 5); □ make the money ~ *(spend it fast)* (4) how time ~ies! (5 *attack*) the dog flew at the man's throat; the cat flew at the mouse; he flew at her like a madman; ... and now you ~ at me with bitter reproaches; ~ in the face / teeth of (discretion / providence / *etc*) *(act defiantly*; → face *n* 6); let ~ (→ let *vt* 6) (6 *be a pilot*) he has flown for years. (7) ~ into a rage / passion / temper. - *vt* (8 *flee*) ~ the country; □ ~ the coop *(slang: escape)* (9) have you ever flown the Atlantic? (10) have you flown this type of aircraft? (11) this plane ~ies passengers and freight. (12) ~ a kite / the (German) flag.

fly off (1) his hat flew ~ (his head); the birds flew ~; the tyre of one of the wheels flew ~; □ ~ ~ the handle *(inform: lose one's temper)*; ~ ~ at a tangent *(suddenly introduce an irrelevant topic).*

follow *vt* (1) please ~ me! I ~ed him to the door; ~ s.o. like a shadow; I tried to ~ the car on my bicycle; number 10 leads, ~ed by number 5; he entered, ~ed by his assistants; □ ~ one's nose *(keep straight on)*; □ ~ s.o. through thick and thin; the masses ~ed him blindly. (2) C ~s B, B ~s A; 4 is ~ed by 5; a juggling act ~ed the singer; he will ~ his father as chairman. (3) Monday ~s Sunday; night ~s day; calm ~ed the storm; violence ~ed the loud quarrelling; one disaster ~ed (on) another *(immediately).* (4) he ~ed the road over the pass; the railway ~ed the river for 5 miles; the mountains ~ the coast; I am ~ing this line with my finger and my eye is ~ing my finger. (5 *read, watch*) ~ closely the first paragraph as I read it; ~ the score of the music as you listen; ~ an eclipse of the moon; ~ s.o.'s progress (6 *listen to*) ~ a speech attentively / closely / carefully; he was ~ing the story with interest; ~ with close attention every note of the music / (every move in) the game / the evidence of the accused / *etc* (7 *conform to*) she is ~ing the fashion slavishly; ~ a pattern / s.o.'s example / the specifications; this wording ~s exactly that in the original; □ ~ suit *(do the same)* (8 *understand*) I can't ~ the argument / the speaker / what he is saying / your line of thought; he talks so quickly that I cannot ~ (him); I can ~ the logic of these remarks. (9 *take as a guide*) ~ s.o.'s advice / order / instruction; ~ a rule / principle / precedent / method / policy / course; we ~ed the directions on the label; ~ the customs and beliefs of one's forefathers; ~ one's inclination / bent; ~ the dictates of one's heart (10 *be a consequence*) ill health often ~s a poor diet; the vengeance that ~s crime. - *vi* (11 → 1) ~ close on s.o.'s heels; he went too fast for me to ~ (him); □ ~ in s.o.'s footsteps *(do as he did)* (12 → 2) a bibliography ~s at the end of the article; the missing articles will ~ in a few days; his arguments are as ~s: ... (13 → 10) it ~s from the evidence that (he is not guilty); that does not ~ at all; what ~s from this? - *adj* (14) spell the ~ing words: ...; the meeting was held on the ~ing day.

follow on please go ahead - we shall ~ on when we have rested.

follow out ~ ~ these instructions faithfully; ~ ~ a plan / enterprise *(carry it out to the end).*

follow through after the bombardment the infantry failed to ~ ~.

follow up (1) he ~ed up his first letter with a reminder. (2) the police have ~ed up a number of clues; ~ up an advantage / victory (3) the author soon ~ed up with another novel.

food *n* (1) (un)eatable / plain / simple / adequate / rich / nourishing / (un)wholesome / well-cooked / tasty / light / liquid / *etc* ~; buy some ~; there isn't much ~ in that part of the world; do you know a hotel where one can get good ~? I'm off my ~ *(have little appetite).* (2 *food that is being cooked*) shallow frying needs a hot pan and enough clear fat to keep ~ from sticking. (3 *kind of food*) baby ~s; new ~s are not always given an immediate welcome; Italy relies chiefly upon ~s from corn, such as macaroni. (4) mental / intellectual ~; ~ for thought / meditation.

fool *n* he's a silly old / awful ~; you silly ~! be no (body's) ~ *(be clever, shrewd)*; look like a damned ~; make a ~ of o.s. (→ make *vt* 1c); be a ~ for one's pains *(do s.th. without getting any reward, thanks)*; (go / be sent) on a ~'s errand *(a useless one)*; (live / be) in a ~'s paradise *(be happy without reason)*; play the ~ *(do* *silly things)*; no ~ like an old ~ *(of aged lover).*

fool *vi* (1) don't ~ around / about with that gun! stop ~ing (about)! - *vt* (2) ~ s.o. out of his money / into doing s.th.; ~ s.th. out of s.o.; you won't ~ me!

fool away ~ ~ one's money / health / chances / time.

foot *n* (1) person / animals / birds / snails / insects have feet; a slender / dainty / narrow / broad / clumsy ~; have big / small feet; from head to ~; have shoes on one's feet; with / in bare feet; (make a journey) on ~; a plan / scheme / enterprise is on ~ *(in progress)*; on one's feet *(standing; in good health; earning one's living)*; lift / lower / drag / shuffle / stamp one's feet; □ get cold feet *(also fig: get frightened)*; get sore feet from walking; make one's feet sore with walking; set ~ on land / in s.o.'s house (→ set *vt* 19); □ be / lie at s.o.'s feet *(also fig: admire)*; □ he had the whole world at his feet; □ lay one's heart / wealth at s.o.'s feet (→ lay *vt* 2); □ he always falls / lands on his feet (→ fall *vi* 1b, land *vi* 1); □ have a ~ in both camps *(play a double game)*; □ have one ~ in the grave *(be near death)*; □ get / have a ~ in the door *(make / have an opening which may lead to s.th. useful)*; □ carry s.o. off his feet (→ carry *vt* 12); □ put one's ~ down (→ put *vt* 7a); □ put one's best ~ forward (→ put forward 1); □ put one's ~ in it (→ put *vt* 7a); □ put one's ~ in one's mouth (→ put *vt* 7a); □ put a ~ wrong (→ put *vt* 7a); □ set s.o. / s.th. on his / its feet (→ set *v* 21b); □ set s.th. on ~ (→ set *v* 21b); □ stand on one's own (two) feet (→ stand *vi* 1) (2) the ~ of a cup / wineglass / vase / armchair / chest of drawers / bed / blanket / grave / column / tree / ladder / staircase / wall / mountain / hill; at the ~ of the page; the ~ of the list; the ~ of a stocking (3) the wall is 3 feet high; calculate in feet; four feet six inches; a man five ~ two; a floor 30 square feet in area (4 *step*) walk with a light ~; be light / swift of ~; have a light ~.

foot *vt* (1) ~ a stocking / sock (2) ~ the floor *(dance)*; we had to ~ it *(walk).* (3) ~ (up) a column of figures; ~ the bill *(inform: pay)*: John had come without any money so I had to ~ the bill (for two meals and the wine).

foot up (1) → foot *vt* 3; ~ up an account (2) the various items ~ up to £2.

force *n* (1) the ~ of fire / water / the wind; the destructive ~ of a bomb; the (elemental) ~ of a hurricane / the waves; exposed to the full ~ of the storm; killed by the ~ of the explosion; the (impersonal) ~s of nature; the ~ of steam / electricity; electric / magnetic ~s; ~ and mass; a ~ acts on / is exerted on / is applied to a body; we were compelled by ~ of circumstances to take the course we did; spiritual / supernatural / mysterious ~s; there are ~s in action here beyond the reach of human intellect. (2) the ~ of a blow / throw / jump / *etc*; use / employ / apply ~; resort to ~; try to achieve s.th. by / with / through ~; I shall only give way to ~; renounce the use of ~; brute / brutal / open / unconcealed ~; take s.th. from s.o. by ~; the window can only be opened by ~; the strength of the door resisted the ~ of the blow; the police used ~ to break up the fight. (3) ~ of character / mind; be overcome by the ~ of one's emotions; hatred is often an impulsive ~; that's ~ of habit. (4 *power to convince*) an argument without much ~; he tried to give ~ and emphasis to his words; the ~ of evidence (5 *person, thing that changes the minds of people*) the driving ~ behind a reform; this party developed into a third ~ in parliament; Christanity has been a ~ for good in many countries; there were adverse ~s at work to prevent his nomination; beware the ~(s) of evil. (6) the ~ of a law / agreement; a law / rule / regulation / new tax / *etc* is in ~ / comes into ~ / is put into ~ / remains in ~. (7) a labour / office ~; a police ~; the armed ~s; ground ~s; he was sent with a small British ~ to W.; an expeditionary ~; the *(armed)* ~s give good opportunity for general education; join ~s with s.o. *(unite)*; the members of the society turned up in ~ *(in great numbers)* at the Annual Meeting.

force *vt* (1) ~ one's way through a crowd; ~ a way in / out / through; ~ an entry into a building; a ~d landing; a ~d march *(one made rapidly)*; □ ~ s.o.'s hand *(make him act unwillingly)*; □ ~ the pace *(cause to speed up more than is reasonable)* (2 *obtain by force*) ~ a promise out of s.o. / a confession from s.o.; a ~d confession; ~d labour (camp) (3 *make s.o. do*) ~ s.o. to (work hard / sign a paper / *etc*); ~ s.o. into action; his conscience ~d him into repaying what he had stolen. (4 *produce* *with difficulty*) ~ a smile; a ~d laugh; (the song) ~d tears from his eyes. (5 *break open*) ~ a lock / (open) a door (6) ~ food (up)on a child; I have had this ~d upon me; the Allies ~d the Treaty of Versailles on the Weimar Republic; we ~ no doctrine down our students' throats. (7 *cause to grow more quickly; also fig*) he ~d the plants by bringing them into the warm house; ~ a pupil / a child's mind *(hurry on his mental development).*

forfeit *vt* ~ one's life / health / happiness; ~ respect by one's actions; ~ the good opinion of one's friends; ~ one's title by marrying; ~ one's estate by treason.

forgive *vt* (1) ~ a sin / insult / offence / unkindness / wrong / *etc*; nothing could ~ such rudeness. (2) ~ a wrongdoer; will you ~ me? Am I ~n? he was ~n for stealing the money; they forgave him his crimes. (3) ~ (s.o.) a debt. - *vi* (4) he doesn't ~ easily; let's ~ and forget.

forgo *vt* ~ a pleasure; ~ a holiday in order to finish a job; I shall have to ~ my visit to the theatre; she decided to ~ sweets to lose weight; profits on one item are forgone in order to attract trade to all the others.

form *n* (1) the ~ of a crystal / mountain / body / *etc*; the arena is in the ~ of a U; a well-proportioned ~ *(body)*; without shape or ~; have a sense of ~; take ~ (→ take *vt* 10 f); give s.th. shape and ~; the human ~; outward ~; appear in another / a different ~; s.th. shows itself in its true ~; his speech was in the ~ of a bitter attack; the thing is assuming concrete ~; a poem in the ~ of an ode; the content and ~ of a novel; a sculpture perfect in ~ and expression; the simplest ~s of life; ice, snow and steam are ~s of water. (2 *a being*) a ~ appeared in the distance; dim ~s passed him in the mist. (3 *kind, variety*) the lemon is a ~ of citrus fruit; ~s of animal and vegetable life; malaria appears in / takes various ~s; I had the disease in its most virulent ~; medicine in the ~ of powder / in powder ~; a prize in the ~ of free tickets; compensation in the ~ of additional days off; ~s of government; a ~ of living / worship / activity; tax evasion is a ~ of dishonesty. (4 *customary behaviour*) it's polite ~ to shake hands when meeting a person; good / bad ~; to say 'Good morning' is a mere matter of ~; do s.th. for the sake of ~ / for ~'s sake; she attaches great importance to ~; pay too much attention to ~(s) (5 *legal form*) the ~ of a contract / document / procedure / *etc*; in due / proper ~; the legal ~ of marriage (6 *condition of health, training*) the ~ of an athlete / horse / *etc*; be in (good) ~; be on ~ (at a performance / in a race / *etc*); be in top ~ / at the top of one's ~; be in capital / cracking ~; be off / out of ~; not be on ~; keep in ~; the team's ~ is improving. (7) the word 'cactus' has two plural ~s; 'cactuses' and 'cacti'; the past tense ~ of 'run' is 'ran'; the words 'plough' and 'plow' are different in ~ but identical in meaning. (8) fill up / in a (telegraph / tax / order / *etc*) ~.

form *vt* (1) ~ s.th. after / from / (up)on a model; he ~ed a small bowl from the clay; the artist ~ed the figure in wax; the baby is able to ~ short words but not sentences; ~ one's sentences with care; the rain had ~ed large puddles in the street; a liquid ~s bubbles; blood ~s clots. (2) ~ s.o.'s mind / character; ~ good habits (3) ~ the plural of a noun / the participle of a verb (by adding an ending) (4) some English words ~ the plural in '-en'; 'men' is ~ed from 'man'. (5 *organize*) ~ a committee / business company / political party / band of marauders / *etc*; invite s.o. to ~ a government; ~ a class for beginners in Russian; they ~ed themselves into a committee. (6 *constitute, be*) the cavalry ~ed the vanguard of the army; five colleges ~ed the university; s.th. ~s an obstacle; what ~s the basis of this compound? a river ~s the frontier / boundary; the Nile ~s a delta; s.th. ~s part of s.th. larger; the Tories ~ed the majority. (7) ~ an idea / plan / opinion / judgement / conclusion / resolution; ~ a friendship / attachment - *vi* (8) bubbles / blisters / crystals / buds ~ (under certain conditions); clouds began to ~; ice ~s at the temperature of 0° C; the idea ~ed in his mind.

fortune *n* (1 *chance, luck*) have good / bad ~; have ~ on one's side; I have had the good ~ to know this man; try one's ~; seek one's ~ in a new country; by good ~ I succeeded the first time; be favoured by ~; ~ smiled upon him; may ~ accompany your endeavours; the ~(s) of war (2 *destiny, future*) tell s.o.'s ~; tell s.o. his ~; did you have your ~ told? (3 *prosperity, great sum of money*) he went to America and soon made a ~; a man of

~; his brains are his ~; accumulate / lose / gamble away / squander a ~; come into / inherit a ~; she spent a small ~ on books; the reorganization cost the firm a ~.

foster *vt* (1) ~ the sick / a child (2 *encourage*) ~ foreign trade / nationalism / academic freedom; ~ friendship between two nations; ~ s.o.'s musical ability / artistic talent; ~ ideas / plans; Prohibition tended to ~ gangsterism. (3 *have in one's mind*) ~ a desire for revenge / hopes for success / ambitions / evil thoughts.

found *vt* (1) ~ a school / hospital / new city / Church / business / newspaper / empire / scholarship / new Chair / *etc*; ~ a family (2) ~ arguments / a theory / one's opinion (up)on facts; a story ~ed on facts; ~ a doctrine firmly / securely; our expectations are ~ed on the success we have had; ~ one's hopes on s.o. / s.th.

frame *n* (1) the skeleton is the ~ of the body; the ~ of a building / ship / aircraft / bicycle / *etc* (2 *human body*) he has a heavy ~; a large ~ to feed; his ~ was wasted by disease; a girl of slender / with a slender ~; s.o.'s meagre ~ (3) the ~ of a door / window / mirror; a door / window / picture / photograph ~ (4 *system*) a ~ of government; the ~ (work) of society (5) (in) a happy / sad / discontented ~ of mind; in the ~ of mind to welcome any diversion.

frame *vt* (1) ~ a picture / mirror / *etc*; ~ the page of a book with an ornamental border; have an oil-painting ~d (2) a structure ~d to resist the fiercest storms; a man not ~d for hardships (3) ~ a reply / answer / sentence / statement / rule / theory / system of philosophy; ~ a method / plan; he was unable to ~ his words properly; his part in the ~ing of the post-war world can be seen in the United Nations. (4 *inform: make appear guilty by falsifying the evidence*) the accused alleged that he had been ~d by his enemies; ~ a case against a neighbour to get rid of him. - *vi* (5 *give promise of success*) plans that ~ well / badly; the child is ~ing well.

free *adj* (1 *not in captivity, not prevented from moving*) the prisoners were ~ again; he had been chained - how did he manage to get ~? set s.o. / a bird ~; (grant s.o.) ~ passage; swing ~ly; suspended to allow ~ movement; ~ fall (2 *not reserved, occupied*) the room will be ~ in May; is this place ~? a ~ table / seat; a ~ telephone / typewriter; a ~ *(telephone)* line; ~ time; a ~ day; tomorrow is ~; he never has a minute ~ now; when can you arrange to be ~? he is ~ in the afternoons. (3 *not being used*) he grabbed it with his ~ hand; have one's hands ~ (*empty*; → 7) (4 *not busy*) are you ~ this evening? when would you be ~ to start? ~ personnel (5 *not fastened*) the ~ end of a rope / the reins; leave one end of the rope ~; one of the parts has worked ~ *(loose)*. (6 *not combined*) ~ oxygen (7 *not restricted, not confined*) a ~ flow of traffic; a ~ road; the ~ play of forces; ~ play of the imagination; thought is ~; you are ~ to do what you like; do s.th. of one's own ~ will; □ give / allow s.o.('s enterprise) ~ play / scope; □ give s.o. ('s enterprise) a ~ rein; □ give ~ rein to one's thoughts / emotions / imagination / pen / *etc*; □ give / leave / allow s.o. a ~ hand *(authority to act)*; □ have / get a ~ hand; □ have one's hands ~ *(be able to do as one likes;* → 3); make ~ use of s.th.; ~ exercises *(without apparatus)*; act / decide / express one's opinion on s.th. / speak out ~ly (8 *not subject to external domination, a despot, etc*) a ~ country / society / democracy / *etc*; slavery used to exist in America, but now all men are ~ there; a road built by ~ labour *(not slaves; not members of trade unions)*; ~ citizens / men / people; the F~ Hanseatic City of Bremen; the ~ world; a ~ press; (the right of) ~ speech; ~ expression of opinion; ~ elections (9 *without trade restrictions*) a ~ port; a ~ market; ~ imports; ~ economy / competition / enterprise / trade (10 *free from what is thought of as an assailant; free of what has been removed*) ~ from danger / troubles / pain / fear / care(s) / disease / anxiety / blame / restraint / error / faults / impurities / bacteria / alcohol / ice / fog; an area ~ from cholera; keep ~ from colds and flu; a day ~ from wind; ~ of charge / income tax / duty / work / prejudice / one's bad companions; all the main roads are now ~ of obstructions; ~ from / of punishment / debts / mistakes / deductions / suspicion; □ make s.o. ~ of one's house / library / *etc (give him the unrestricted use)* (11 *unrestrained in manners, morality*) ~ love; he was too ~ with his secretary; be (too) ~ in one's conversation / speech / behaviour; a ~ and easy behaviour; make ~ with s.th. (→ make *vt/i* 21) (12 *not hav-*

ing to be paid for) ~ tickets for the theatre; a ~ copy of a book; the refreshments are ~; ~ education; ~ admission; there's a ~ offer of a toothbrush with every tube of toothpaste you buy this week; a ~ pass (for rail travel); ~ accommodation; ~ on rail Munich; carriage ~; delivered ~; the price is quoted ~ German frontier; 'F.O.B.' means '~ on board'. (13 *generous*) he is ~ with his money; give ~ly; give things away with a ~ hand; be ~ with one's praise / advice; a ~ flow of water; ~ bloomers *(plants with many flowers)* (14 *spontaneous*) a ~ offer; ~ conversation / laughter (at a party) (15 *not faithful to the original*) a ~ translation; a ~ adaptation; ~ly adapted from Goethe; a ~ interpretation of the text; a ~ copy / likeness (16 *not consistent with rules*) ~ verse; a ~ fight.

free *adv* (→ free *adj* 12) children are admitted ~; get in ~; travel ~ (on the railways); he has / gets the accommodation ~.

free *vt* (1) the prisoners were ~d; ~ a man from prison / slavery / the wreckage of a train; ~ an animal from a trap; she tried to ~ herself from his embrace. (2) ~ s.o. from debt / anxiety / fear / an obligation; ~ the mind from prejudice (3 *relieve*) ~ s.o. of a task / a responsibility for s.th.; try to ~ o.s. of prejudices; ~ s.o. of a burden / worry.

freedom *n* (1 → liberty 1) take up arms for ~; give prisoners their ~; win / gain / lose / enjoy (religious / political / intellectual) ~; live in ~; the basic ~s; ~ of conscience / action / speech / thought / will; rob s.o. of his ~; the four ~s - ~ of speech, ~ of religion, ~ from fear, ~ from want; ~ from pain / disease / fear / hunger / blame / debt / tax / obstruction / oppressors / restrictions / controls / *etc*; ~ of speech / communication / the press / the air *(broadcasting)* / the seas; academic ~. (2) (give s.o.) the ~ to do s.th.; speak with ~; the question was discussed with great ~; treat s.o. with the ~ and familiarity of an equal; give a friend the ~ of the house / library *(allow him to use it freely)*; give s.o. / receive the ~ of a city *(honorary rights of citizenship)* (3 → liberty 2) take / use ~s with s.o.

freeze *vi* (1) put your overcoat on - it's ~ing outside; it was ~ing last night; ~ hard; it is going to ~ tonight. (2 *cover with ice*) the puddles are frozen; the roads were frozen; the waterpipes are frozen; the lake was frozen over. (3 *become ice, become covered with ice*) the lake froze over in January; all the window-panes froze over; the radiator froze (up); the pipes have frozen; water ~s at a temperature of 0° C; the oil is ~ing; the ground was frozen hard; *(fig)* a frozen smile; the smile froze on his lips / face. (4 *become very cold*) ~ to death; his hands froze to the oars; I'm ~ing *(inform)*. (5a *turn into s.th. like ice*) my fingers are quite frozen; we were frozen stiff (*inform*); the news made her blood ~ (in her veins) *(curdle)*. - *vt* (5b) the sight of the monster froze the blood in his veins. (6 *make into ice*) ~ ice-cream; frozen meat / vegetables (7) late frosts sometimes ~ the apple blossom. (8) ~ capital / assets / credits; ~ prices / wages.

friend *n* (1) he is a ~ of mine / of my brother's; ~s and relatives; ~ and foe; a close / fast / bosom / intimate / faithful / stalwart / unfailing / consistent / constant / dependable / desirable / familiar / discreet / invaluable / new / old / lost ~; a dubious / inconstant / fair-weather ~; they are inseparable / warm / near ~s; a common / mutual ~ of ours; he has shown himself / proved a true / loyal ~; we are old ~s of his family; we have been ~s with his family for years; I have been (great) ~s with him ever since our schooldays; make ~s with s.o.; they became ~s; they are ~s again; he is ~s with everyone; I have no ~s here; be a good ~ to s.o.; have a good ~ in s.o.; make a ~ of s.o.; this has made him many ~s; a soldier / actor / *etc* ~ of his; they parted good ~s. (2) the dog is man's best ~; a vacuum-cleaner is the housewife's best ~; night is the ~ of smugglers and thieves; who goes there - ~ or foe *(milit)*? (3) he was a ~ of the people; a ~ of / to the poor; he was a ~ to many charities / all good causes; a ~ to those in need.

friendship *n* a durable / lasting / lifelong / close / intimate / unstable / *etc* ~; a ~ of twenty years; bonds / ties of ~; form / strike up a ~ with s.o.; win s.o.'s ~; break off a ~; live together in ~; help s.o. out of ~; never forget old ~s; swear eternal ~; the two countries signed a ~ pact.

fright *n* (1) be filled with ~; die of ~; the deer took ~ at the shot; get / have a (sudden / terrible / mortal / deadly / *etc*) ~; the clock has just struck five - it gave me such a ~, because I had an appointment at half past four; scream / turn white with ~ (2 *inform*) what a ~ you look in that silly hat.

frighten *vt* did I / the noise ~ you? be (badly) ~ed by s.th. / s.o.; be ~ed at (seeing / hearing) s.th. / s.o.; would you be ~ed at / of a ghost? why are you ~ed of me? there's nothing to be ~ed of; he's ~ed of looking silly; she was nearly ~ed out of her life; ~ s.o. into / out of doing s.th.

front *n* (1) the (main / rear) ~ of a building; a ~ room; the ~ door / garden / seat / *etc*; the ~ wall needs paint; the ~ page of a newspaper; ~-page news; a picture in the ~ of a book; the ~ of the bus / train was empty; please go in ~; there is an oak in ~ of the house; only those in the ~ can see; □ come to the ~ *(become well known)*; □ be in the ~ rank *(be well known)*; a ~-rank scientist (2 *land facing a body of water*) the house was on the lake ~; have a walk along the (sea-)~. (3) send soldiers / go to the ~; at / behind the ~; fight on two ~s; he fought for two years at the ~; attack on a wide ~; □ change ~ *(alter abruptly the grounds of argument)* (4 *appearance*) put up / on a bold ~; show / present a bold ~; (5 *impudence*) have the ~ to do s.th.

fruit *n* (1) the ~ of the beech is called a beech-nut; the ~s of poppy are capsules; acorns and grains of wheat are ~s; the ~s of the earth *(grain, etc)* (2) apples, oranges, and grapes are ~s; dry / fleshy ~s; soft / stone / kernelled ~; (un)ripe / raw / green / mellow / juicy / delicious / dried / candied / bottled / tinned / canned ~; mangoes are exotic ~s; an exotic ~; do you like ~? have some ~; a diet mainly of salads and ~; □ forbidden ~s taste sweet. (3) I hope your work will bear ~; this book is the ~ of years of hard work; the ~s of labour / study / industry.

full *adj* (1 *filled completely*) the box is (half) ~; the room was ~ of people; drink a glass ~ of milk; fill your glass ~; a ~ stomach; a ~ *(well supplied)* cupboard; the cupboard was ~ (up) with rubbish; a ~ house *(theatre with no seats empty)*; s.th. is ~ to bursting / overflowing / the brim / the top; a ~ heart; my heart is too ~ for words; be ~ of work (2 *having plenty*) a purse ~ of money; cheese ~ of maggots; ice ~ of cracks; be ~ of ideas / ambition / one's subject / oneself / vitality; an essay ~ of mistakes; a ~ *(plump)* figure; ~ curtains *(having many folds)*; a ~ meal (3 *complete, maximum*) a ~ orchestra; a ~ moon; trees in ~ blossom; ~ *(expanded)* sails; a book bound in ~ leather; ~ binding; in ~ daylight; he fell ~ length on the ground; drive a car at ~ speed; sail a ship ~ speed ahead; a horse at ~ gallop; in ~ career; wait a ~ hour; ~ *(formal)* dress; ~y prepared / armed; items ~y described in the catalogue; ~y satisfied / convinced; I don't ~y understand. (4 *loose, of women's clothes*) a ~ sleeve; make the coat a little ~er across the back. (5 *not qualified, restricted*) ~ agreement / membership / pay; he gave us a ~ report; give ~ details; the army was in ~ retreat; he is very ~ on this point *(treats it thoroughly)*.

full *adv* (1 *exactly*) hit the target ~ in the centre / him ~ on the nose (2 *directly*) look s.o. ~ in the face.

full *n* (1) (the moon / tide) is at the ~ *(highest point)* (2) they played 'Hamlet' in ~ *(completely)*; write one's name / the date in ~; pay a sum in ~; the speech was reported in ~. (3) we enjoyed it to the ~ *(utterly)*; we have striven to the ~ to convince him, but ...; do s.th. to the ~ of one's ability / powers / desire.

fun *n* (1) be fond of ~; we had a lot of ~ at the picnic; we had great ~ with the model railway; sailing a boat is great ~; I don't see the ~ of (doing) it; I only did it for ~; do s.th. for the mere ~ of it; things said in ~ must not be taken seriously; because he stammered slightly, the boy made ~ of / poked ~ at him. (2) she is great ~ (at a party / to go out with / to be married to); the game was no ~.

function *n* (1 *special activity, definite task*) the ~ of a person / organization / machine part; the ~ of the heart; the ~s of the nerves; the appendix has no recognizable ~; the production of insulin is one of the ~s of the pancreas; each word has a particular ~ in a sentence; glass has an important ~ in modern architecture; what is the true ~ of education? this law has a double ~ (to fulfil). (2 *official duty*) perform / carry out one's daily ~s; exercise administrative ~s; the ~s of a judge; he fulfilled his ~ as interpreter very well;

he welcomed her in his ~ as mayor. (3) attend a great state ~; speak at a ~; see s.o. at a public / social ~.

function *vi* (1) the telephone was not ~ing; a machine / engine / clock ~s; does this typewriter ~ properly? her kidneys are ~ing normally. (2) he ~s as registrar; the government ~s through numerous divisions. (3 *serve*) some English adjectives ~ as adverbs; shivering ~s to maintain the heat of the body.

furnish *vt* (1) ~ a room with tables / chairs / *etc*; ~ a room in oak / walnut / *etc*; ~ a room sparsely / elegantly / in the latest style / with taste; a well- / ill-~ed room (2) ~ a library with books; ~ a camp with supplies / supplies to a camp; ~ information to s.o ; Jane will ~ the cakes for the party; one cow ~ed milk for all of them; democracy ~es its own checks and balances.

fuss *n* don't make so much / get into such a ~ about trifles; I'm the last person to make a ~; she made a lot of ~ about preparing dinner; there's nothing to make a ~ about; she made a loud ~ over the leaky tap; you will spoil Ann if you make such a ~ of her *(surround her with flattering attentions).*

fuss *vi* (1) she is inclined to ~ about / over trifles; she is always ~ing! don't ~ over the children so much; oh, don't ~ (so), Ann! - *vt* (2) don't ~ me *(make me nervous).*

G

gain *n* (1) a ~ in weight / health / knowledge; a ~ to knowledge / one's happiness; a ~ in prices (2) his ~s from his business; a thief's ill-gotten ~s; the love of ~; interested only in ~.

gain *vt* (1) ~ admission / admittance / currency / permission (to do s.th.) / possession of s.th. (2) ~ experience / knowledge / influence in s.th. / independence / one's liberty / favour / confidence / love / esteem / popularity / (a good) reputation / fame / s.o.'s support for s.th. / strength / power / promotion / impetus; ~ an impression; ~ a reward; ~ a(n academic) degree; ~ a victory; □ ~ the day (→ day 6); □ ~ the upper hand (over s.o.); ~ one's point (→ point *n* 11); ~ a case at law; the culprit hopes to ~ something from confessing; what ~ed him such a reputation?... ~ed him many friends / much praise (3 *win*) ~ a prize / the championship (4a) ~ a / one's living; he ~ed ten dollars by this deal. (4b) ~ land from the sea (5 *reach*) ~ one's destination; ~ the summit / top of the mountain / shore / harbour (6) a watch / clock ~s (five minutes a day) (7 *acquire as an increase*) ~ weight / speed; ~ ground *(advance)*; ~ time *(obtain a desired delay).* - *vi* (8) I have ~ed on that transaction. (9) ~ in weight / five pounds (in weight); ~ in knowledge / wisdom (10) ~ on the others in a race *(get closer to them)*; ~ on one's pursuers *(leave them further behind)* (11) the sea is ~ing on the land.

gale *n* (1) a stiff / strong / hard ~; a ~ was blowing (from the west); it was blowing a ~; a ~ rages. (2) a ~ / ~s of laughter.

gallop *n* go for a ~; ride at a / at full ~.

gallop *vi* (1) ~ across a field / off (at full speed) (2) ~ through one's work / one's homework / a book / a lecture. - *vt* (3) ~ a horse.

gamble *vt* (1) ~ at cards / with money / on horses / in shares / on football pools / on the Stock Exchange (2a) ~ one's wages / reputation. - *vi* (2b) ~ with one's life / future; ~ on a spell of fine weather / on the weather being fine.

gamble away ~ ~ one's fortune / savings.

game *n* (1) play / have a ~ of cards / chess / billiards / cricket / tennis / football; win / lose a ~; play (outdooor / indoor) ~s; he plays a good / poor ~ (of cards); the Olympic G~s; skittles has been a popular ~ for centuries; □ play the ~ *(be fair;* → play *vt* 2b); play a winning / losing ~; □ play a double ~; □ play s.o.'s ~ *(help him unintentionally)*; □ beat s.o. at his own ~; □ be off one's ~ *(not playing well)*; □ have the ~ in one's hands; □ the ~ is up *(lost)*; □ the ~ is not worth the candle. (2) the ~ of diplomacy; see through s.o.'s (clever) ~; I wish I knew what his ~ is; so that's your (little) ~; none of your little ~s! □ make ~ of s.o. *(make fun of)*: only boors make ~ of the weak and defenceless. (3) big / small ~ *(animals)*; fair ~; □ fly at high(er) ~ (→ fly *vi* 1) (3a) a dish of ~.

gang *n* a ~ of workmen / labourers / boys; a ~ of criminals / thieves / slaves; a slave ~; a railroad ~.

gang *vi* ~ up with a group of youths / round a cheerleader; a number of youths ~ed up and ...; ~ up on s.o. *(inform: attack in a group).*

gaol *n* → jail *n.*

gap *n* (1) a ~ in a hedge / fence / wall; leave a(n ugly) ~; make / tear a ~ (2) a ~ in a conversation / story; a ~ in one's knowledge / memory / education; a (wide) ~ between the views of two men / ideals and actions / expenses and income; fill / stop / supply a ~.

gather *vt* (1a) ~ a rose / flowers / fruit / honey (1b) he ~ed wood and made a fire; ~ sea-shells; ~ one's books and papers together; ~ your toys from the floor. (1c) ~ folds in a dress; ~ a skirt at the waist; ~ the brows; his brow was ~ed in thought. (1d) ~ a fortune / wealth (2) he ~ed his scarf round his neck and went out into the cold; she ~ed the crying child in her arms. (3a) ~ troops / an army; he ~ed a crowd round him; □ be ~ed to one's fathers *(form: die)* (3b) a good football game always ~s a crowd. (4) ~ information / impressions / experience / one's thoughts / one's breath; □ ~ o.s. together; ~ one's wits together (5) the books have ~ed dust; that tabletop ~s a great deal of dust. (6) a car ~s speed; a ship ~s way. (7) what did you ~ from his statement / from what he said? I ~ (from these facts / his remark) that he ... – *vi* (8) a crowd ~ed round him; clouds ~ed on the horizon. (9) ~ together, boys and girls, and let me tell you a story; some animals ~ together for warmth or protection.

gather in ~ in the harvest / corn.

gather up (1) ~ up those crumbs! ~ up the pieces of a broken dish (2) ~ up a child in one's arms (3) ~ up one's energies / strength (for the hard job).

gauge *vt* (1) ~ the rainfall / the strength of the wind / (the contents of) a barrel; ~ s.o.'s speed (2) ~ s.o.'s character / strength / conduct; I would not ~ the future on what I know of the past; ~ing the probable response of the electorate by sampling techniques.

gaze *n* look at s.o. with a bewildered / vacant / solemn / mournful / steadfast / *etc* ~; return s.o.'s ~; I met his cold ~ for a moment; she dropped her eyes before his ~.

gaze *vi* ~ at scenery / a scientific experiment / *etc* (with astonishment / attentively / intently / thoughtfully / furtively / stealthily / inquiringly / steadfastly / *etc*); ~ (up)on a scene (in bewilderment / with mute rapture); ~ in a shop window / mirror; ~ into s.o.'s face / eyes; ~ into the sky / water; ~ out of the window / through a telescope / over the hedge / across the road; ~ in wonder; stop ~ing round.

gear *n* (1 *tools, etc*) climbing ~; a sportsman's ~; tennis / *(AE)* football / fishing / riding / *etc* ~ (2) first (*also* low / bottom) / second / third / fourth / high / reverse ~; most motor-cars have three or four ~s; a car starts in low ~; change / shift into / engage (second / *etc*) ~; drive in / on top ~; a car cannot go unless it is in ~ / when it is out of ~; put / leave a car in ~; be out of ~; run in neutral ~; *(BE)* ~ lever; *(AE)* ~-shift; ~box (3 *fig*) s.th. is out of ~ *(is not workinq smoothly)*; the whole balance of payments was thrown seriously out of ~; let's get this business back in ~ and start showing some profits.

gear *vt* (1) ~ up / down a car; ~ up production (2) ~ production to demand / to seasonal demands; ~ one's efforts to an overall plan; we have ~ed our organization to this type of work; tourism here is ~ed to the native traveller.

generalize *vi* (1) ~ about life / on the need for s.th. - *vt* (2) ~ a conclusion from a number of facts / details (3) ~ the use of a new invention.

generate *vt* (1) ~ electricity / steam (power); current ~d by a dynamo; friction ~s heat; ~ a sentence (2) ~ hatred / a conflict / an opinion / a feeling / hope; he ~s ideas that we should all consider.

generation *n* (1) the present / past / postwar / coming / rising / future / unborn ~; parents, their children and their grandchildren make up three ~s; a ~ ago; in the third ~; the beat ~ (2) Detroit's ~ of cars with tailfins; a third-~ computer.

generous *adj* (1) be ~ to people in need / with one's money / with compliments; ~ in one's conduct / attitude / support of a good cause; ~ in giving help (2) a ~ gift; a ~ portion of pie; a ~ figure / bosom.

genius *n* (1) Mozart showed (great) ~ almost from infancy; men of ~ (2) Einstein was a (mathematical) ~. (3) have a ~ for languages / acting / making friends / making enemies / making up excuses; he is a ~ at diplomacy; she is a ~ with a frying-pan. (4) the ~ of Greek civilization / the British constitution / the Renaissance (period) (5) s.o.'s good / evil ~.

germ *n* (1) (milk / *etc*) free from ~s (2) the ~ of life / death / war / an idea / a plan.

gesture *n* (1) make a / answer with a / invite s.o. with a (friendly / welcoming / solemn) ~; a ~ of embarrassment / contempt / admiration / friendship (2) a ~ of friendship; you should at least make a ~; an empty / noble / handsome ~.

get *vt* 1a - 3, 4c, 5, 6b, 6c, 7, 12a, 12b; *vi* 4a, 4b, 6a, 8 - 11, 12c, 12d, 13 - 16.
The patterns are grouped as follows: ~ + *adj*: 4a; ~ + *adv phrase*: 8; ~ + *obj* + *adv phrase*: 7; ~ + *indir obj* + *dir obj*: 1b, 1d; ~ + *inf*: 5a, 5b; ~ + *obj* + *inf*: 5c; ~ + *present part*: 6a; ~ + *obj* + *present part*: 6b, 6c; ~ + *past part*: 4b; ~ + *obj* + *past part*: 4c; ~ + *prepos*: at 9; before 10; into 11; out of 12; over 13; round 14; through 15; to 16; with various *prepos in a local sense: 8.*
(1 get + object; not fig: receive, obtain)
(1a) ~ a letter / a telegram / some cigarettes / a present / a message / no reply / information; ~ a pension; □ ~ no change out of s.o. *(inform: no answer)* (1b) ~ me a few pencils; I'll ~ my hat; you must ~ *(buy)* some new shoes; where did you ~ that trouser suit? ~ a pound of meat from the butcher; will you ~ me a ticket / ~ a ticket for me? ~ oil by drilling; whatever money he has, has been got by hard work. (1c) ~ breakfast / lunch / dinner; ~ one's living; how does he ~ a living? ~ some money from s.o.; ~ a good price after bargaining; ~ a salary / £500 a year / a prize / one's share; I got the camera cheap; ~ results; he'll never ~ a wife that way; ~ one's remove (1d) ~ fame / credit; such conduct will ~ the club a bad name. (1e) ~ a disease / a fever / a cold / the measles / a wound / a bump on one's head / a blow on the head; ~ one's second teeth; he is already ~ting a beard. (1f) ~ a thief; ~ him before he escapes; ~ s.o. on the phone; you can always ~ me by phone; how many stations can you ~ on your new radio? (1g) if we divide 12 by 3 we ~ 4; ~ a good view; ~ permission from s.o.; ~ leave to go home; ~ admission / employment / wealth; ~ one's discharge; ~ possession of s.th. / a sight of s.o. / a glimpse of s.o.; ~ hold of s.th.; ~ a surprise / fright / shock / idea; ~ the worst of it; ~ satisfaction (for an insult) (1h *learn*) ~ a poem by heart / a lesson (1i) ~ six months (for stealing); they deserve the treatment they ~; you'll ~ it when mother comes home; □ ~ more *(punishment, bad results)* than one bargained for.
(2 *get + s.o., s.th.; fig, inform*)
(2a *understand*) I don't ~ you / your meaning; do you ~ what I mean? ~ the meaning of a story / the point of a joke; sorry, I didn't ~ your name; this is just between us, ~ it? (2b *puzzle*) this matter ~s me; I'm afraid I can't answer that question - you've got me there. (2c *slang: annoy*) people who chew gum all the time really ~ me; he really ~s me with his stupid questions. (2d *injure, kill*) the bullet got him in the arm; he got the tiger first shot; he has escaped my vengeance so far, but I'll ~ him one of these days; the frost got the azaleas this year.
(3 *idiomatic phrases*)
~ the better of one's opponent (→ better *n*); ~ the best of both / two worlds (→ best *n* 1); ~ big ideas *(inform)*; ~ quite a kick out of s.th. *(inform: be very satisfied)*; ~ a grip on o.s. *(control o.s.)*; ~ one's knife into s.o. *(inform: bear a grudge)*; ~ cold feet *(inform)*; ~ the jitters / jittery *(inform: get into a panic)*; ~ the wind up (→ wind *n* 1b); ~ the wrong end of the stick (→ end *n* 1); ~ it all wrong *(inform: misunterstand)*; ~ the sack / one's cards *(inform: be dismissed)*; ~ one's hand in (new work); ~ one's teeth into s.th. (→ tooth 1b); ~ the hang of (a story / argument / paragraph / *inform*); the police got wind of the burglary (→ wind *n* 3); ~ word to s.o. (→ word *n* 3); ~ one's (own) way (→ way 10); ~ the upper hand of s.o.
(4 *get + adjective, past participle*)
(4a *get + adjective, past participle used as adjective*) ~ cold / warm / hot / wet / dry / rich / dark / light / better / ill / worse / well again / hungry / seasick / tired / pale / happy / sentimental / melancholy / excited / ready (to do s.th.) / *etc*; ~ even with s.o.; the dog got loose; the dog doesn't let me ~ close to it; you can't ~ close to her *(fig)*; ~ rid of s.o. / s.th.; ~ acquainted; ~ used to s.th.; ~ married; ~ drunk.

(4b *get + past participle: passive action*) the pudding got burned; he got his arm broken in a fight; her dress got torn (on a nail); he got his hand caught in a machine; ~ dismissed for doing s.th.; ~ scared; Miss Jones, ~ this done right away.
(4c *get + past participle: causative*) ~ one's hair cut / one's shoes mended / the knives sharpened / one's season ticket renewed / this text printed / the work finished in time; ~ the laws obeyed / this policy changed; I never ~ anything done; his lazy ways soon got him fired; let's ~ done with it *(finish it)*; ~ a man drunk.
(5 *get + infinitive*)
(5a) ~ to like / know / see s.o. / s.th.; they soon got to be friends; he finally got to own the business / to be manager of the firm; what would he say if he got to hear of this affair? (5b) I must ~ to see the exhibition sometime this week; the windows are so high up that it is difficult to ~ to clean them. (5c) we could not ~ the car to start / the fire to burn / the lawn-mower to work; ~ him to keep quiet; I can't ~ him to get up early / her to talk; we'll ~ him to go with us; why don't you ~ someone to help you?
(6 *get + present participle*)
(6a) it's time we got going / moving; once he ~s going he can't stop; things haven't really got going yet; we got (to) talking and did not notice the time; she warned him not to ~ drinking or gambling. (6b) the lecturer soon got us thinking; we got him talking about his travels; he got the President nodding approval more than once; can you ~ the clock going again? (6c) you ~ it happening with any modern house; in those days you never got working men standing for Parliament; you won't ~ me inviting those people to my house again.
(7a *move, transport*) ~ s.th. somewhere; how am I to ~ this parcel home? ~ a dog out of the room; I can ~ a lot into the suitcase; we couldn't ~ the piano through the door. (7b *fig*) he tried to ~ his friend into the club; ~ s.o. through an examination; ~ a ship under way (→ way 6); ~ s.o. into trouble; ~ s.th. into s.o.'s head; ~ s.th. into one's head; he got it into his head that he . . .
(8 *get vi: move somewhere, reach*) I ~ home at 6 o'clock each day; did he ~ here? I got on board the ship; ~ from N. to P.; we tried hard but did not ~ anywhere *(fig)*; after all this work we've got nowhere; he'll ~ there *(inform: obtain success)*; ~ across a road / river / mountain; ~ into a building / the garden / the cinema / *etc*; ~ into a bus / coach / car / train / carriage; ~ into the boots; ~ off a train / plane / bus / ship / ladder; we ~ off the bus here; ~ off one's bicycle / horse; ~ off the rails; ~ off the grass / my toes! we ~ on the bus here; ~ on one's bicycle / horse; ~ on one's feet / legs *(also fig: rise to speak)*; he / that music ~s on my nerves *(fig)*; ~ out of bed / the train / prison (through the window); □ ~ out of bed on the wrong side (→ bed 1); ~ over a wall / gate / stile; the horse got over the distance in ten minutes; ~ round *(visit)* all the departments; can we ~ through that fence? when does the train ~ to London? they have got safe to land / shore; ~ to one's destination / England / *etc*; is N. an easy place to ~ to? ~ under the table / blanket; ~ under the skin; □ ~ under s.o.'s skin *(annoy him)*; the ship will ~ under way in a few minutes' time (→ way 6).
(9a) I can't ~ at the ceiling light without a ladder; he can't ~ at the money until he is 25. (9b) the job won't take long to do when we once ~ at it; ~ at the truth / the root of a problem (9c *get at: mean, imply*) I could not see what he was ~ting at; he mentioned no names, but everyone knew who he was ~ting at. (9d *get at: understand*) I can't ~ at what he means. (9e *get at: bribe*) one of the witnesses had been got at. (9f *get at: find fault with, criticize*) I have my faults, but that is no reason why he should be constantly ~ting at me.
(10) don't let the others ~ before you in learning.
(11a) ~ into debt / mischief / trouble / a habit / difficulties / a fix *(inform)* a mess *(inform)*; ~ into (dis)favour with s.o.; ~ into s.o.'s good graces; ~ into a temper / rage; ~ into conversation with s.o.; ~ in(to) touch with s.o.; ~ into bad ways / habits; ~ into the way of doing s.th.; ~ into bad company; □ ~ into hot / deep water (→ hot *adj* 1, deep *adj* 1) (11b *dress*) ~ into one's clothes; ~ into one's pyjamas / one's swimming trunks / a tuxedo / evening clothes / *etc.*
(12a) ~ an explanation / confession / piece of information out of s.o.; we could ~ nothing out of him. (12b) what do you

~ out of dancing? why do you drive so fast - what do you ~ out of it? what will you ~ out of being president? he won't do anything unless he ~s something out of it. (12c) ~ out of s.o.'s reach / (s.o.'s) sight; ~ out of here at once! ~ out of debt / the habit of doing s.th.; ~ out of hand *(break from control)*; his imagination is ~ting out of control. (12d) ~ out of an engagement / one's duties / military service; try to ~ out of doing (s.th. unpleasant); he is trading on his ill health in order to ~ out of all the work; there's no ~ting out of it - we shall have to go.
(13a) ~ over one's illness / disappointment / shock / s.o.'s rudeness; he never got over the death of his son; I can't ~ over his daring to say such a thing. (13b) ~ over a habit / one's shyness / all one's difficulties; you can't ~ over *(deny)* the fact that he knew he was doing wrong; ~ over *(forget)* a love affair; she's gradually ~ting over their break-up.
(14a) ~ round the regulations / law; ~ round a difficulty / problem (14b *get round: persuade by flattery, BE*) she got round her uncle to buy her a car; his wife knows how to ~ round him.
(15a) how am I to ~ through all this work / correspondence today? I've got through it / the exam; ~ through one's work slowly; ~ through a lesson (15b) he got through £3,000 in about a month; he soon got through his allowance; how did you ~ through all the money?
(16a) I've got to the end of the sixth chapter; when it ~s to ten o'clock I begin to feel tired; when you ~ to seventy you are not so active as you were at fifty; you should ~ to bed now. (16b) from arguing they finally got to fighting / blows; □ ~ to grips with a problem (16c) ~ to business / work; □ ~ to the bottom of s.th. (16d *get to: affect*) this music really ~s to you.

get about (1) ~ ~ by bicycle / car; ~ ~ on crutches; he's ~ting ~ again after his illness; nowadays people ~ ~ *(travel)* much more than they used to. (2) news / rumours / stories ~(s) ~ (that ...); it got ~ that she was secretly engaged.

get abroad → get about 2.

get across (1) the bridge is destroyed - we can't ~ ~ (the river); ~ the troops ~ (the river) (2) ~ one's ideas / meaning ~ (to s.o.); he found it difficult to ~ his jokes ~ to an English audience; his ideas never got ~ to the students. (3) he ~s ~ *(annoys)* everyone.

get ahead (1) he got ~ of the other students. (2) it needs a lot of work to ~ ~ (in business / *etc*).

get along (1) she said she had to ~ ~; we had better ~ ~ home before the fog ~s worse; ~ ~ with you *(go away; stop being silly)*! (2) he's not wealthy but he ~s ~ (all right); the patient is ~ting ~ well; how are you ~ting ~ (with your French)? they're ~ting ~ (together) quite well. (3 *get older*) grandfather's ~ting ~, you know, and doesn't hear so well as he used to.

get around (1) he ~s ~ a great deal *(travels)*. (2) he never got ~ to thanking them.

get away (1) the board was nailed to the wall and we couldn't ~ it ~; ~ s.o. ~ to the seaside (2) try to ~ ~ (from home); one of the men got ~. (3) the thief got ~ (with the jewels). (4) they don't let their children ~ ~ with everything; he ~s ~ with the most unlikely tales.

get back (1) he never got the money ~; I promise to ~ *(take)* you ~ before dark. (2) what time did you ~ ~ home? he got ~ from Rome yesterday. (3) ~ ~ to health (4) he'll ~ ~ at you in some way *(fig)*; □ ~ one's own ~ (on s.o.) *(have one's revenge)*; □ ~ ~ at s.o. (for s.th.).

get behind ~ ~ with one's rent; ~ ~ in business *(not succeed)*; ~ ~-hand with one's reading.

get by (1) please let me ~ by; a lorry blocked the road, so that we couldn't ~ by. (2) I can't ~ by without you(r help); I just (barely) got by on the test; the story sounds pretty fishy to me, but you may manage to ~ by with it.

get down (1) ~ ~ from a horse (2) I can't ~ these big tablets ~; ~ s.o.'s temperature ~ (3) ~ ~ a message / the text / what he said (4) the hot weather / bad news / hard winter ~s him ~ *(makes him feel bad)*. (5) ~ ~ to work / business / serious study / a task / (the) facts; I'm afraid the job will have to be got ~ to; □ ~ ~ to brass tacks *(the heart of a matter)*.

get forward I hope he'll be ~ting ~ with his education.

get in (1) ~ in the harvest / the crops / debts / taxes; he told me to ~ the car in; ~ in reports from ... / information of the enemy's movements; ~ in s.o. to repair s.th.; □ ~ one's hand in *(become practised)*; □ ~ in a word / a word in edgeways *(manage to say s.th.)* (2) he forgot his key and couldn't ~ in; the burglars had got in through the kitchen window. (3) what time did you ~ in last night? the train ~s in to London at 8.10 a.m. (4) he got in *(was elected)* with a good majority. (5) he's important - try to ~ in with him; he got in with a bad crowd.

get off (1) he can't ~ ~ his coat / his gloves / a ring from his fingers; ~ a nut ~; □ ~ s.th. ~ one's chest *(say it)* (2) ~ a letter / parcel ~ to s.o.; ~ the children ~ to school; ~ a baby ~ to sleep (3a *prevent s.o.'s being punished*) his lawyer always ~s him ~; his youth got him ~. (3b *escape punishment or evil*) ~ ~ with a warning / fine; ~ ~ cheap(ly) / lightly; he got ~ with only a scratch from the accident; ~ ~ scot-free (4) I'm ~ting ~ at the next station; □ tell s.o. where he ~s ~ *(where tolerance comes to an end)* (5) ~ ~ early from school; I can ~ ~ tomorrow; he got ~ after breakfast / by the evening train; he couldn't ~ ~ to sleep; □ ~ ~ to a flying start; ~ ~ on the wrong foot *(make mistakes)* (6) he got ~ with a French girl at the dance *(started an affair with her)*; she is trying to ~ ~ with John.

get on (1) ~ on one's boots / clothes; ~ your hat and coat on! I can't ~ the lid on. (2) he is good at ~ting his pupils on. (3) I'm afraid I must ~ on - I must be back at six. (4) ~ on in life; ~ on (well / ill) (at school / with one's work / in one's new job / in one's exam); how is your garden ~ting on? time is ~ting on; you can't ~ on without money in this world; it's the pushing type of person who ~s on; you'd better ~ on with the supper, or we shan't eat tonight; the builders couldn't ~ on for lack of materials; I'll ~ on with it straight away. (5) ~ on well with s.o. / together; he is a difficult person to ~ on with. (6 *be getting on: recover*) how are you ~ting on? he had an attack of bronchitis, but he's ~ting on fairly well now. (7 *getting on for: nearly*) it was ~ting on for noon / midnight when ...; he's ~ting on for 75; ~ting on for five hundred people were present; I paid ~ting on for ten pounds for it. (8 *get on to, inform: recognize*) ~ on to s.o.'s tricks / dishonesty (9 *get on to: communicate with, phone*) if we don't receive a reply by tomorrow morning, I shall have to ~ on to him. (10 *get on to: find fault with continually*) keep ~ting on to s.o. (about his speech / dress / drinking).

get out (1) ~ ~ a stain; I could not ~ the cork ~ (of the bottle). (2) ~ your dog ~ at once! he ordered his car to be got ~; she got ~ her passport / dictionary and ... (3 *publish*) ~ ~ a book; they got ~ a newspaper with only ten men. (4) tell s.o. to ~ ~ (5) somehow the secret / news got ~; we mustn't let this story ~ ~.

get over (1) ~ ~ facts / information *(make s.o. understand and accept)* (2) let's ~ the washing-up ~; we're hoping to ~ the meeting ~ fairly quickly.

get round (1) the story / it soon got ~ that he ... (2) we'll ~ ~ to building a proper garage one day; I never ~ ~ to doing any sport nowadays.

get through (1) we couldn't ~ the piano ~ (the door); ~ a Bill ~ (Parliament) (2) there was so much snow that the trains could not ~ ~; your message didn't ~ ~ (to me); operator, I can't ~ ~ to Western 84751; the Bill got ~ (Parliament). (3 *make s.o. understand; convince*) I talked to John for an hour, but I couldn't ~ ~ to him; I shouted into her ear until at last I got ~ to her. (4) ~ ~ *(an examination)*; he will ~ ~ *(recover)*; ~ ~ with a job / one's work.

get under they got the fire ~ in half an hour; the revolt was quickly got ~.

get up (1) he got up (from the chair) and locked the door; we ~ up at seven. (2) the wind / storm / sea / fire is ~ting up *(becoming violent)*. (3) we got up to page 12 last lesson; we soon got up to the others. (4) don't ~ up to any mischief; he ~s up to all sorts of tricks; go and see what the children are ~ting up to. (5) he got us up early; ~ the children up and dressed for school. (6) ~ up a party (for s.o.'s birthday) / a play / a dance (at the club) / a concert / a subscription; ~ up an article (for sale) / a book; we must ~ up a group to see that play. (7) the train was ~ting up speed; ~ up steam *(produce it for an engine; also fig: work o.s. into anger, energy)*; □ he's got the wind up *(inform: feels afraid)*. *(7 learn)* ~ up a subject / one's Latin; he got up enough English to pass the exam. (9) she got herself up for a dance / like a film star; she was beautifully got up; one of the rooms was got up to represent an English inn; have these shirts got up *(starched and ironed)* well; ~ o.s. up as a sailor; ~ a girl up as a gipsy.

gift *n* (1) a generous / splendid / gorgeous / lavish / divine / wonderful ~; a birthday / Christmas ~; such blessed ~s as peace and quiet; make a ~ of s.th. (2) have a ~ for art / music / poetry / languages / organization; □ have the ~ of the gab *(be good at speaking).*

girl *n* (1) a carefree little ~; a delightful / charming / fetching / sweet / attractive / pretty / beautiful / stunning ~; an artless / plain / sensitive / touchy / delicate / mild / meek ~; a quarrelsome / whimsical ~; a friendly / good-natured / nasty ~; a respectable / clever / intelligent / gifted / stupid / silly; ~ (2) shop / factory / office ~s (3) my wife and I have two ~s. (4) John and his ~(-friend).

give *vt* 1-9, *vi* 10-13. The patterns are grouped as follows: ~ + *abstract obj:* 3a, 3b, 6; idiomatic phrases *esp* 8; ~ + *prepos: on* 13; *to* 1-4, 6, 7, 9c, 9d, 10. For ~ + *noun obj* combinations not listed here see the nouns.
(1 *give s.th. as a present or like a present*)
(1a) ~ s.o. a present / money / a ring / a watch (as a present) / a piece of cake / a drink / *etc*; ~ s.o. a prize / a scholarship / a name / a title; ~ one's daughter('s hand) to s.o. in marriage; she gave him a beautiful baby boy; ~ s.o. credit / (a) discount; ~ little to charity; ~ s.o. one's telephone number; ~ freely / liberally / generously / readily / hesitatingly / reluctantly (1b) ~ s.o. work / homework / an assignment; ~ the porter your bags; ~ s.o. a message / information (1c) he gave the offender a stiff sentence / three months; □ ~ it him (hot) (→ hot *adj* 2); his father gave it to him for breaking another window. (1d) you've ~n me your cold; ~ s.o. the measles / *etc*; the dog has ~n them fleas.
(2 *pay, give in exchange for s.th.*)
I will ~ you 100 marks for the painting; I gave a good price for this suit; I'll ~ it you for £2 / ~ you £2 for it; I would ~ the world for it / to do it / if I ...; I would ~ a lot / anything to know where she is / what happened.
(3a *give + noun is synonymous with a verb identical with the noun; the 'give + noun' phrase refers to a single instance, specific occasion, is not general in meaning)*
~ an / one's account of s.th.; ~ (s.o.) advice (on s.th.); ~ the alarm; ~ (s.o.) an answer; ~ birth (to a son / an idea); ~ a cheer / three cheers (for s.o.); ~ a little / loud cry; ~ a command; ~ s.o. a cue; they will ~ their decision today; a decision was given for the defendant; ~ a demonstration (of s.th.) / a description of s.th. / an explanation; ~ a groan; ~ heed to (a warning); ~ (s.o.) help / a helping hand; ~ (s.o.) a hint; ~ s.o. an injection; ~ instruction (in s.th.); ~ (s.o.) an interview; ~ a jump; ~ s.o. a kiss; ~ s.o. a kick; ~ a lecture (on s.th.); can you ~ me a light (for my pipe, *etc*)? ~ (s.o.) a (quick) look / a (loud) laugh; ~ offence (to s.o.); ~ an order / orders that ...; ~ praise; ~ preference to s.o./s.th.; ~ (s.o.) a / one's promise; ~ s.o. a rap (on the knuckles); ~ (s.o.) a rebuke / a reply / a ring *(phone him)*; ~ me a ride on your shoulders, Daddy; ~ s.o. a scolding / a shock; ~ a shout; ~ a shrug (of one's shoulders) / a sigh / a smile; ~ the slip (to one's pursuers): he ran after me, but I gave him the slip; ~ a speech; ~ a start *(jump up)*; ~ support (to s.th.); ~ a talk (on s.th.); ~ s.o. a turn (→ turn *n* 12); ~ (s.o.) a warning / a (warm) welcome; ~ one's word (→ word *n* 9) (3b, *similar to 3a, but noun and synonymous verb are not identical*) ~ s.o. a blow; ~ s.o. a lift (in one's car); ~ instruction (in s.th.); ~ a lecture (on s.th.) / a lesson / lessons; ~ laws; ~ rise to *(cause)*: the industrial revolution gave rise to accelerated urbanization; ~ no sign of life / signs (of annoyance / exhaustion / *etc*); ~ tit for tat.
(4 *present, offer*)
~ s.o. one's hand / a lady one's arm; the book ~s a table of measures; our class is ~ing a play; ~ a ball / banquet (in s.o.'s honour) / concert / dinner / party; □ ~ s.o. a hand *(help)*; □ ~ s.o. a free hand; □ ~ him an inch and he will take an ell *(BE)* / a mile; ~ one's life to / for s.th. (5 *provide, furnish*) cows ~ milk; this land ~s a good yield; oil-lamps do not ~ a good light; the sun ~s us light and warmth; sugar ~s us energy; ~ (good / bad) results; 3 times 4 ~s 12; ~ security.
(6 *give + abstract nouns*: → 3)
~ authority (to s.th.); ~ one's attention to s.th.; ~ s.o. the benefit of the doubt; ~ cause / grounds for (complaint); ~ s.o. a

chance; ~ consent (to s.th.); □ silence ~s consent; ~ credence (to a story); ~ s.o. credit for s.th.; ~ s.o. all the details; ~ s.o. his due *(judge him fairly)*; ~ (all) one's energies to s.th.; ~ evidence against s.o.; ~ (abundant) evidence of (what happened); ~ (s.o.) a (good) example; ~ expression to s.th.; ~ the facts; ~ food for thought; ~ force to (an argument); ~ fun; ~ a (rough) idea of s.th.; ~ ground (→ ground *n* 2); he gave me the impression of (a worried man / that he was worried); ~ s.o. the lie (→ lie *n*); ~ him my love (→ love *n* 3); ~ momentum to (a campaign); ~ notice (→ notice *n* 2); ~ one's oath that ...; ~ s.o. occasion to / for s.th.; ~ one's opinion of (the new plan); ~ s.o. the opportunity of (doing s.th.); ~ s.o. pain (→ pain *n* 1); ~ (s.o.) permission (to do s.th.); ~ (s.o.) (much) pleasure; ~ precedence to (a car); he gave no reason for his lateness; ~ s.o. one's (kind/ kindest) regards; ~ thought to (a problem); ~ s.o. (a lot of) trouble; ~ unity to s.th.; ~ weight to (an argument); ~ way → separate entry.

(7 *give + expression of time*)
~ s.o. time to do s.th.; you'd better ~ yourself an hour to get there; ~ yourself plenty of time; ~ s.o. a holiday; ~ s.o. time / an hour / a week / the afternoon off; he ~s his free time to golf.

(8 *idiomatic phrases*)
~ s.o. / o.s. a pat on the back; ~ s.o. full marks; ~ s.o. good grades (for an achievement; AE) ~ s.o. a good telling-off / ticking-off / choking-off *(all inform)* / talking-to; ~ s.o. a piece of one's mind / the rough edge of one's tongue; ~ it s.o. straight from the shoulder (→ shoulder *n* 1); ~ s.o. the cold shoulder (→ shoulder *n* 1); ~ s.o. a dose of his own medicine; ~ s.o. the lowdown *(inform: full information)*; I hate snakes - they ~ me the creeps; not ~ a fig for s.o.; ~ a damn / *(BE)* a tinker's cuss / *(AE)* a tinker's dam(n) *(slang: not care at all)*; you have to ~ it to the French - they know how to make cars; they gave me to understand / I was ~n to understand that I ... (→ understand *vt* 5a).

(9a be ~n: *be presented as a basis of calculation*) these facts being ~n, the argument makes sense; ~n A and B, C follows. (9b ~n: *if ... is available, present*) ~n paper and pencil, could you write a short story? ~n the right atmosphere, he is relaxed, witty and stimulating. (9c) he is ~n to boasting / exaggerating his achievements / gaiety and revelry. (9d) it is not ~n to many people to become great musicians; it is ~n to few of us to live to be a hundred.

(10) ~ to the Red Cross; □ ~ and take *(compromise for cooperation; exchange ideas)*: a willingness to ~ and take is important for success in marriage; an informal meeting in which there would be opportunities to ~ and take (11a) the mattress does not ~ *(is not elastic)*. (11b *give in, collapse*) the floor / ice gave under my feet; the antique chair gave when she sat on it; at the height of the storm the bridge gave; the frost is ~ing. (12 *yield*) we can't negotiate until each side is willing to ~ on some points. (13) the window gave on (to) a beautiful garden / the sea; the house ~s on to a river; the exit ~s on to a busy road.

give away (1) ~ ~ s.th. free / all one's money; ~ ~ goods / possessions: property (2) ~ ~ one's daughter in marriage; the bride was ~n ~ by her father. (3) ~ ~ a secret / the answers to the questions / information; his accent / coughing gave him ~; □ ~ ~ the game *(make known a secret)*; □ ~ ~ the show *(spoil it by revelations)* (4) you've ~n ~ everything you stood for / a good chance of winning the match. (5) Mrs N. gave the prizes ~ at the Speech Day.

give back you haven't ~n ~ the books you borrowed from me.

give in (1) ~ in one's exercise books / manuscript / *etc*; these pound notes may be ~n in at any bank; ~ in one's resignation / one's notice (→ notice *n* 2); □ ~ in one's name *(announce one's willingness to do s.th.)* (2) the rebels were forced to ~ in; you've won - I ~ in! ~ in to s.o.'s demands / views / wishes; ~ in to a disease; children who are always ~n in to by their parents soon become spoiled.

give off ~ ~ heat / smell / vapour / a distinctive odour; boiling water ~s ~ steam; → give 7.

give out (1) ~ ~ vapour / smoke; the jasmine ~s ~ a sweet perfume. (2) ~ ~ books / leaflets / copies of a pamphlet / exam papers to the students (3) the news was ~n ~ on / over the radio; it was ~n ~ / the announcer gave ~ that the 3.30 train ...; he gave ~ that he was going to England. (4) he ~s himself ~ to be a doctor. (5) the car gave ~ *(failed)*; the horses gave ~ yesterday; our food supplies gave ~. (6) his strength / patience gave ~.

give over (1) he gave ~ charge of his office to his successor today; ~ the knife ~ here, please! (2 *inform*) ~ ~ teasing the cat; ~ ~ a habit / certain kind of conduct (3) the last hour of each meeting was always ~n ~ to discussion; the whole of the page was ~n ~ to an analysis of the book. (4) she gave herself ~ to tears.

give up (1) ~ up a habit / smoking / sweets / trying to help him; ~ up an attempt / all hope / one's claims to s.th. / the study of s.th.; ~ up one's flat / a post / one's job / a fortress; □ ~ up a game as lost; □ ~ s.o./ s.th. up for lost; □ ~ s.o./ s.th. up as a bad job (2) the doctors have ~n him up; why have you ~n Mary up – I thought you were going to be married! (3) he refused to ~ up the documents; don't ~ me up to the police; the bandit gave himself up; □ ~ up the ghost *(die)*; our car has ~n up the ghost *(fig: become useless)*. (4) his week-ends are ~n up to golfing; the students gave themselves up to demonstrations against the new ruling. (5) the swimmer gave up after 20 minutes.

give way (1) ~ ~ to traffic coming from the right; our army had to ~ ~. (2) the balcony gave ~ and fell into the street; the ground underneath / the ice / the bridge gave ~; the rope gave ~ *(broke)*. (3) winter ~s ~ to spring; the stormy weather gave ~ to sunshine; her jealousy gave ~ to admiration. (4) ~ ~ to despair / grief / s.o.'s persuasion / s.o.'s bullying / s.o.'s impudent demands / tears; ~ ~ to s.o. / one's feelings; stand firm – don't ~ ~!

glance *n* a quick / casual / covert / furtive / meaning(ful) / angry / disapproving / reproachful / suspicious / wistful / frightened / searching / significant ~; take a ~ at s.th.; give s.o. a (quick, *etc*) ~; give o.s. a ~ in the mirror; cast / throw / shoot a (shy, *etc*) ~ at s.o.; see s.th. at a ~.

glance *vi* ~ at the clock / (shyly) at s.o.; ~ over a book / a letter / a catalogue / some papers / *etc*; ~ through a letter / round a room; ~ at s.o. / s.th. quickly / hastily / searchingly / inquiringly / *etc*.

glass *n* (1) made of ~ (2) drink a ~ of milk; raise / put a ~ to one's lips; empty / drain a ~ (to the bottom); fill a ~ (to the brim); pour s.o. a ~; he has had a ~ too much. (3) the ~ *(barometer)* rises in fine weather; the ~ is falling; what does the ~ say? (4) look at yourself in the ~ (5) I can't read without ~es; a pair of ~es.

glean *vt* ~ a field; ~ corn; ~ bits of information / facts (from books) / news.

glide *vi* (1) a ship / train / skater ~s past; the bird ~d through the air; the snake ~d through the undergrowth; a skater ~d over / on the ice; the pianist's fingers ~d over the keys. (2) the nurse ~d about the sickroom. (3) the years ~d by. – *vt* (4) ~ the feet (in dancing).

glimpse *n* a fleeting / occasional ~; catch / get / have a ~ of s.o./s.th. (from the window of a train); he found no time for a ~ at / of the papers.

glove *n* throw down / take up / accept the ~; handle s.o. without ~s / with kid ~s; take the ~s off *(also fig)*.

glow *vi* (1) hot coal ~s; the numbers of a clock ~ in the dark; ~ing metal (2) the trees ~ed in the sunset / with autumn shades. (3) ~ with enthusiasm / excitement / pride / anger / health; ~ from embarrassment; ~ at good news; (describe s.th.) in ~ing colours.

gnaw *vt* (1) dogs ~ bones; the rats ~ed away the wood; ~ one's finger-nails (2) the lie he told ~ed his conscience; fear / anxiety ~s (at) s.o.'s heart; ~ing pains / grief.

go *vi*

The patterns are grouped as follows: go + *adj*: 8, 11b, 20; go + and + *v*: 5; go + *inf*: 4; go + *present part*: 3; go + *n* (in *adv* sense): 22; go with non-personal subjects: 7, 9, 10b, 11-19; personal or non-personal subjects: 20–22; go + *prepos* (in a non-local sense): against 9; at 1; by 1, 12, → go by 3-5; for 2, 14, 17, → go for 1-4; in 14, 16, → go in 1; into 16, → go into 1-5; on 1, 2, 14, 15, → go on 10, 11; through 7, → go through 1-8; to 2, 6b, 14, → go to 1-5. For other *prepos* → separate entries.

(1 *be in motion*)

~ along / down a road / street; ~ down / up the river; ~ down the stairs / downstairs / upstairs; ~ over a frontier; ~ past a building; ~ into the dining-room / the school *(building)*; ~ home; ~ to one's house; ~ to the door / window / one's room; ~ to town; we're ~ing to London tomorrow; ~ to Mr Smith (for instructions); ~ by bus / tram / car / train / rail / land / air / plane / sea / ship / boat / steamer; ~ on foot / all fours / horseback; ~ to the cinema / theatre / office / tax-office / welfare office / the post(-office) / *etc*; fast trains ~ (at) 80 m.p.h.; don't ~ far afield; ~ abroad; ~ on board (a ship); ~ aboard; ~ ashore; the horse went at a trot / gallop.

(2 *move with a specified purpose*)
~ to school / college / university / church / market; ~ to bed / work; ~ *(BE)* (in)to hospital / *(AE)* to the hospital (→ hospital); □ ~ to the bar *(become a barrister)*; ~ to sea *(become a sailor)*; ~ on an errand / on errands; ~ for a walk / ride / swim / stroll / mountain hike / trip (into the country); ~ on a journey / voyage / trip / excursion / outing; ~ on holiday; ~ on a / one's holiday; ~ on leave; □ ~ on the stage *(become an actor)*; ~ on the films; ~ on the streets *(become a prostitute)*; all my plans have gone west *(fig: failed)*; this engine has gone west.

(3 *go + present participle*)
(3a) ~ bathing / cycling / walking / hiking / rambling / riding / mountain-climbing / skating / swimming / fishing / shooting / hunting / collecting bird's eggs / birds' nesting / blackberrying / duck-shooting / hop-picking / nutting / shrimping / dancing / drinking / shopping / sight-seeing.
(3b) ~ farming / teaching / nursing / bricklaying / soldiering.
(3c) don't ~ doing that! he saw a rabbit and went rushing after it; her hat went floating gaily out to sea.

(4 *go + infinitive*)
(4a) ~ to buy s.th. / to ask s.o. for advice / to find s.th. / to see Mr Hill / to write a letter / *etc.*
(4b) it all / that ~es to show / prove that he ...; the money collected ~es to help our hospital; ... the sounds that ~ to make up the complicated system of a language.

(5 *go +* and *+ verb*)
~ and get your coat; let's ~ and dine; ~ and see if the post has come; don't ~ and make a fool of yourself.

(6 *pass; pass to a certain condition*)
(6a) an hour ~es quickly; there is an hour to ~ yet; there are only ten days to ~ before their arrival.
(6b) ~ to sleep *(fall asleep)*; my leg has gone to sleep; a person / a business ~es to pieces; a business / a school ~es to pot *(inform)*; the house has gone to rack and ruin *(inform)*; to ~ to seed *(of plants; fig: become old and useless)*.

(7 *move, be moved along, spread; of things*)
the knife / bullet went through his heart; the rain has gone through my coat; the car will not ~ through the gate; the water / steam ~es through a tube; ~ from hand to hand; all applications ~ through his hands; the story ~es that he was once ...

(8 *go + adj: live in a certain way. For 'go + adj'* → *also* go 20)
~ naked / barefoot(ed) / hungry / armed.

(9 *progress, develop*)
sales of the book are ~ing quite well; how are rehearsals for the play ~ing? things / everything went well at the meeting; things aren't ~ing very smoothly; how did the election ~ at Hull? the election went against him; the case went against him *(he lost it)*; the case went in his favour; promotion ~es by age / merit / favour (in this organization).

(10 *leave, disappear*)
(10a) are you coming or ~ing? we had better ~ now; I must be ~ing now; people / the years come and ~; the bus has already gone; the bus / train / boat for Bonn ~es at 7 o'clock; when does the next train ~? if he doesn't work harder, he will have to ~.
(10b) my pain has gone / will soon ~; his sight went early / is ~ing; I wish the cold weather would ~; she found that her diamond ring had gone; some papers have gone from my desk; compulsory Latin / these regulations must ~; the car must ~ *(be sold)*; my money is ~ing fast; all hope is gone; poor Smith is gone / has gone from us.

(11 *extend, reach*)
(11a) this road ~es to York / past the house / through the forest; does this railway ~ to the coast? ... where the bridge ~es over / across the river; the fence / wall ~es all round the garden; the property ~es to the river; the tunnel ~es straight through the mountain.
(11b) their difference of opinion ~es deep. (For *go + adj* → *also* go 8, 20); this will ~ far / a long way towards (overcoming our troubles); a pound note doesn't ~ far these days; a bottle of milk will not ~ far amongst all these people; if he works hard, he will certainly ~ far / a long way; he has brain, he'll ~ far / *(inform)* places;

the treaty is all right as far as it ~es; what he says is true as far as it ~es.
(12 *function*)
this machine / clock ~es by electricity; we couldn't get the car to ~; can you make this watch ~?
(13 *become broken, fail*)
that clock will not work - the spring has gone; the clutch has gone; my ankle's gone again; the light will not come on - the bulb has gone; the trousers have gone at the knees; the platform went *(collapsed)*; first the sails and then the masts went; the bank may ~ any day.
(14 *be given, be spent, be sold*)
first prize went to my friend; that money ~es to charity; honours do not always ~ to those who deserve them; this article ~es well / *(inform)* like hot cakes; these washing-machines are ~ing for a few pounds; the car went cheap; all his money ~es on, for books / women; half my salary ~es in / for rent, food and clothes.
(15 *fit, belong*)
coats ~ on the coatrack; the cups ~ on the top shelf; where do you want the bookcase to ~? this shoe ~es on the left foot; your left hand should ~ here.
(16 *find enough room*)
too big to ~ into the basket; my clothes won't ~ into this small suitcase; his luggage won't ~ in the car.
(17 *be accepted, be valid*)
American dollar notes ~ almost anywhere; what he says ~es; what my friend has just said ~es for me too; it ~es without saying that...
(18 *have certain words or notes*)
the song ~es like this; I forget how the chorus ~es; I'm not sure how the rhyme / tune ~es; this verse ~es to the tune of ...; the argument ~es more or less like this.
(19 *produce a certain sound*)
the bell has gone; a bell ~es at the end of each lesson; a cat ~es "miaow, miaow"; the firework / gun went bang; ~ phut / smash; the hooter went for the men to stop work.
(20 *go + adjective or adverb without -ly: become; act.* For *go + adjective see also go 8, 11b*).
(20a) ~ crazy / mad / insane; ~ berserk / balmy / dotty *(all inform)*; ~ pale / white / grey / red (with anger) / hungry / lame / deaf / blind; he went hot and cold; ~ bad / sour / wrong; the machine went dead; has your electric iron gone wrong? ~ free / unnoticed / unpunished / unchallenged; ~ bankrupt; ~ short (of s.th.) *(get less than one should)*; this country will ~ Liberal / Communist one day; America went dry after World War I.
(20b) ~ counter to orders; a shot / letter ~es astray; plans can ~ wrong; if you take this direction / keep to these principles, you can't ~ wrong; ~ easy with (the sugar / the oil can / the butter / *etc*); ~ easy here, the road is very rough; be ~ing strong *(of a person, organization)*.
(21) he is a good teacher as teachers ~; that's really dirt cheap as things ~ today; £4 for a pair of shoes is not dear as things ~.
(22 *go + noun, frequently with adverbial meaning*)
~ 80 miles *(the distance of 80 miles)*; ~ the short way; he went this way; □ ~ one's own way; □ ~ all the way with s.o. *(agree completely)*; these facts ~ some way to explain his behaviour, but not the whole way; it has just gone *(struck)* six; ~ *(bet)* £10 on a horse; ~ halves / shares with s.o. in s.th.; ~ fifty-fifty; □ ~ the whole hog *(do s.th. thoroughly)*; □ ~ one better (than s.o.) *(outdo him)*; ~ bail for s.o.; ~ it rather / a bit strong *(inform: exaggerate somewhat)*.

go about (1) she ~es ~ in black; he went ~ (the country) doing good; a story / rumour is ~ing ~ that... (2) I must ~ ~ my business; he went ~ his work very quietly; he went ~ repairing the car; how will you ~ ~ getting enough money for it?

go after (1) he went ~ the pigeons with a gun (2) ~ ~ a prize / a pretty girl.

go against it ~es ~ my principles / the rules / orders / s.o.'s wishes (to do s.th.); it ~es ~ my conscience / nature / principles (to do s.th.); □ it ~es ~ the grain (with s.o.) (to do s.th.)

go ahead (1) the black horse went ~; ~ ~ and ask her! may we start now? - Yes, ~ ~! (2) you can ~ ~ with the project next week; ~ ~ with your plans (3) he is ~ing ~ fast *(making progress)*.

go along (1) you can ~ ~ with him. (2) make up the story as you ~ ~ *(continue)*; ... but you'll find it easier as you ~ ~. (3) I'll ~ ~ with your plan; most of the committee went ~ with the managing director in his proposals.

go at (1) ~ at one's work with enthusiasm; □ ~ at it hammer and tongs / for all one is worth *(inform: energetically)* (2) they went at each other furiously; □ they went at it tooth and nail *(inform: fought fiercely).* (3) → go 1.

go away (1) he has gone ~, he doesn't live here now; they have gone ~ *(left home for a holiday, a weekend or on their honeymoon)*; are you ~ing ~ for a holiday this year / on holiday? he has gone ~ with my razor; □ ~ ~ with one's tail between one's legs (2) the epidemic is not likely to ~ ~ soon; trade has been ~ing ~ from Hamburg since 1945.

go back (1) ~ ~ (by train / *etc*); the steamer ~es ~ tomorrow; I must ~ ~ to my work. (2) our country is ~ing ~. (3) his family ~es ~ to the time of Charlemagne. (4) ~ ~ on one's word / on a promise / on a decision; ~ ~ on a friend *(betray him)* (5) s.th. ~es ~ to (fundamental principles / *etc*).

go before (1) pride ~es ~ a fall. (2) he ~es ~ me in seniority. (3) this will have to ~ ~ the president.

go behind ~ ~ a person's word *(search for a hidden meaning)*; ~ ~ a decision *(re-examine the grounds for it).*

go beyond ~ ~ the speed limit / one's orders / one's instructions; in the auction, many articles went ~ their value; your behaviour has gone ~ a joke.

go by (1) many years have gone by since we first met; time went by slowly; in times gone by; don't let this opportunity ~ by. (2) the car went by; we waited for the procession to ~ by. (3) a good rule to ~ by; he ~es by the rules / directions. (4) you can't always ~ by appearances; you can't ~ by that clock / what he says. (5) he ~es by the name of Charlie.

go down (1) a ship ~es ~; the sun has gone ~. (2) the price of s.th. has gone ~; s.th. has gone ~ in price; silk is ~ing ~. (3) this pill won't ~ ~. (4) she went ~ in her exam; Rome went ~ before the barbarians. (5) the wind has gone ~ a little; the river is ~ing ~ *(its water is falling).* (6) the new play / the speech went ~ well with the audience; that explanation / proposal will not ~ ~ with him; work doesn't ~ ~ well after a holiday; how did your speech / his funny story ~ ~? the new teacher doesn't ~ ~ well with the pupils. (7 *BE*) universities ~ ~ *(finish their work before a holiday)*; we ~ ~ *(leave the university)* on July 25th. (8) he'll ~ ~ in history (as a tyrant, *etc*); Nelson has gone ~ as an English hero. (9) his new history of France ~es ~ to 1970. (10) several boys went ~ with flu last term.

go for (1) can you please ~ ~ a doctor at once? (2) his hard work went for nothing / very little; in investing money one may ~ ~ a dividend or for capital increase. (3) the dog went ~ *(attacked)* the postman; furious, he went ~ her *(with words or his fists)*; they went ~ me in the newspaper. (4) ~ ~ a pretty girl; he doesn't ~ ~ serious music very much.

go forward (1) the army went ~ at a rapid speed; his work is ~ing ~ well. (2) what's ~ing ~ here?

go in (1) a door opened and we went in; the nail won't ~ in; the key won't ~ in the lock; ~ in to lunch / dinner (2) the sun has gone in *(hidden behind a cloud).* (3) ~ in for an examination / a competition / a scholarship (4) do you ~ in for sport? ~ in for golf / tennis / stamp-collecting / medicine / nursing / teaching / *etc* (5) he plans to ~ in with a new business firm.

go into (1) the whole family went ~ mourning on their uncle's death. (2) 2 ~es ~ 6 three times. (3) ~ ~ business *(become a business man)* / society / industry / politics / the Army / the Church / Parliament; ~ ~ retirement (4) ~ ~ a matter / problem / field *(study it)*; ~ ~ details / particulars / the reasons for s.th. / the cause of s.th.; □ ~ ~ a huddle *(discuss privately)* (5) ~ ~ hysterics / fits of laughter / fits of emotion.

go off (1) she went ~ without saying good-bye; he went ~ with his neighbour's wife / with my stamp albums; I saw him ~ing ~ on his bicycle; □ ~ ~ the beaten track *(do s.th. unusual)*; □ ~ ~ the deep end *(inform: BE, AE give way to strong emotion; AE act recklessly, go to extremes)* (2) a pain / ache / headache / *etc* ~es ~; she went ~ into a faint / trance; the lights / gas / water went ~. (3) a bomb / pistol / fire-cracker / firework ~es ~; s.th. ~es ~ 'bang' / 'pop'; □ ~ ~ into a passion (4) the goods went ~ rapidly. (5) the play / concert / party / *etc* went ~ well; everything went ~ according to plan; there seems to be a crowd over there - I wonder what's ~ing ~. (6) this meat / milk / fish / fruit has gone ~; his work has gone ~ very much lately; as an actor he's gone ~ a lot; her looks have gone ~ recently.

go on (1 *continue; often with noun or -ing-form*) the months went on and ...; we became good friends as the evening went on; how much longer will this hot weather ~ on? we must ~ on working / trying / *etc*; prices ~ on rising fast; ~ on with one's work / studies / story / *etc*; □ ~ on to the bitter end;□ ~ on forever (2 *do next, proceed; with inf or* to) he went on to say ... *(and then he said)*; I could also ~ on to point out ...; he went on to his second argument. (3 *go ahead*) you ~ on, I'll wait; I shall ~ on and book rooms in the next hotel. (4) these shoes / gloves won't ~ on. (5) the light / gas / water ~es on. (6) what's ~ing on next door? harvesting is ~ing on in the south; things are ~ing on much as usual. (7) how did you ~ on in your exam? I don't know how we should have gone on without your help. (8) ~ on at s.o. *(criticize)*; she went on about his being late; they ~ on like an old married couple *(argue)*; if you ~ on like this, you'll be expelled. (9 *BE ~ on + for; AE without prepos*) he was ~ing on for *(approaching)* sixty; we stood in the queue ~ing on for half an hour. (10) ~ on the parish / a relief fund / the dole; go on social security; ~ on half pay (11) ~ (up)on a principle; he went on the assumption that ...; have you some data / any facts / enough evidence to go (up)on?

go out (1) ~ ~ into the street / garden; ~ ~ by the back door; ~ ~ into the night (2) ~ ~ to dinner / a dance; Betty went ~ every night last week; he never ~es ~; did you ~ ~ last night? (3) ~ ~ to business / service / work / play; when she was eighteen she went ~ as a governess; ~ ~ shopping / riding / *etc* (4) the tide is ~ing / has gone ~. (5) Mark has gone ~ to Hong Kong; he went ~ to Australia to farm. (6) the Tories have gone ~; the left-wing party is ~ing out and soon there will be an election. (7) all the dockers went ~ (on strike) last week; are we likely to gain anything by ~ing ~? (8) a fire / flame / light / candle / match ~es ~ (9) the news went ~ that the strike was over; all the invitations for the party have now gone ~. (10) a fashion / method ~es ~; long dresses have gone ~ (of fashion) this year. (11) her heart went ~ to him *(she felt sympathy for him)*; our hearts ~ ~ to those poor war orphans. (12) □ ~ all ~ *(make one's utmost effort)*; □ ~ ~ of one's way (to help s.o.); □ ~ ~ of one's mind *(inform: go mad)*.

go over (1) ~ ~ to one's flat / place / *etc*; he went ~ to talk to his old friend. (2) ~ ~ to the Liberal Party / Communism / the enemy / *etc* (3) ~ ~ one's work / the details / a manuscript / (the terms of) a contract / the accounts (carefully); ~ ~ a house / car / *etc* before buying it (4) ~ ~ *(practise, rehearse)* a song / one's part in a play / the last scene / this chapter / this lesson / the main facts (again) (5) he went ~ *(dealt with)* a great many points in his speech. (6) the play went ~ well *(was accepted)*.

go round (1) the road is blocked, so we shall have to ~ (the long way) ~. (2) I'm ~ing ~ to see Mr Hill. (3) is there enough to ~ ~ *(for all of us)*? the cake would not ~ ~ the whole class.

go through (1) the nail went right ~; the wire ~es ~ / is too thick to ~ ~ this aperture; the crowd fell back to let him ~ ~; the bill must ~ ~ Parliament; □ ~ ~ fire and water (for s.o. / to do one's duty) (2) the train ~es right ~; if you ~ straight ~ to the station, you'll catch the train. (3) ~ ~ your breathing exercises once more; it took an hour to ~ ~ the whole programme; □ ~ ~ the motions *(pretend to do s.th.)* (4) ~ ~ a desk / a drawer / s.o.'s pockets (to find s.th.) (5) ~ ~ an illness / a very bad time / hardships; if you only knew what I had to ~ ~ with him! □ ~ ~ the mill / it *(inform: have a rough time)* (6) ~ ~ one's work / part in a play / the figures carefully; I can't ~ ~ these letters in an hour; please ~ ~ my essay. (7) the novel went ~ many editions. (8) ~ ~ a fortune *(spend it completely)*; they soon went ~ all their food / money. (9) the deal / our application went ~; his plans went ~. (10) he went ~ with his plans; ~ ~ with a plan / reforms / one's studies; you'll have to ~ ~ with it once you start.

go to (1) ~ to work / *etc*; a book / article ~es to press; ~ to war (with / against s.o. / a country); ~ to court / law (about s.th.); ~ to one's death; ~ to hell / the devil; □ ~ to the wall *(be defeated)* (2) ~ to any / all / great / extreme lengths (to help s.o.); ~ to great / enormous expense (to get s.th.); he even went to the expense of hiring a gardener; his success has gone to his head; the girl's beauty went to Jack's head; ~ to trouble (to achieve s.th.); ~ to the bad *(inform: become morally bad)*; ~ to the dogs *(slang; of persons, organizations: become useless)* (3) how much can you ~ to *(pay)*? (4) these apples ~ four to the pound; how many ounces ~ to the pound? 12 inches ~ to the foot. (5) what qualities ~ to the making of a statesman? years of work have gone to its making.

go together her hat and coat / these two colours / beer and cake just don't ~ ~ at all.

go under (1) the tiny vessel went ~. (2) his business went ~.

go up (1) we saw the mountaineers ~ing up; ~ up in a balloon; ~ up a ladder / wall / tree (2) the barometer / temperature went up. (3) yesterday the bridge went up; the whole building went up in flames; → smoke *n* 1; □ ~ up into the air *(explode with rage)* (4) prices / wages / rents / costs ~ up; cotton has gone up; the cost of living is ~ing up. (5) ~ up to s.o. and say ... (6) ~ up to town / to London; he is looking forward to ~ing up (to Cambridge) in September; ~ up to a higher class (7) I'll ~ up to *(offer)* £200. (8) new buildings / factories are ~ing up everywhere.

go with (1) he will ~ ~ Mary as far as the junction; *(fig)* ~ ~ a girl / boy; we let the boat ~ ~ the current. (2) a set of tools ~es ~ each car; the box ~es ~ the instruments; disease usually ~es ~ squalor. (3) I can't ~ ~ you on that; he always ~es ~ his party; □ ~ ~ the crowd *(follow the fashion)*; □ ~ ~ the tide / times *(do as others do)* (4) ham ~es ~ eggs; those shoes ~ ~ your handbag; purple ~es ~ yellow; I want a hat to ~ ~ this dress; a plural noun ~es ~ a plural verb.

go without (1) ~ ~ a hat / an overcoat / *etc* (2) ~ ~ food for three days; I can't ~ ~ sleep; we shall have to ~ ~ a holiday this year; my family was so poor that as a boy I often had to ~ ~; □ it ~es ~ saying that... (3) → go 17.

go *n* (1 *in games*) it's my ~ now; whose ~ is it next? (2) he passed his driving test (at the) first ~; each person is entitled to three ~es; I don't think I can, but I am willing to have a ~ (at it); the attempt was no ~ *(useless)*. (3) shoes like those are all the ~ this summer. (4) be on the ~ *(active)*; he still has plenty of ~ in him. (5) make a ~ *(success)* of s.th. (6) □ from the word ~ *(from the beginning)*; I knew he was dishonest from the word ~. - *adj* (7 *inform: ready*) all planes / systems *(in space technology)* are ~.

goal *n* (1) score / make / kick a ~; win by two (~s) to one; keep ~ (2) one's ~ in life; his ~ was to win back the property; set o.s. a (high) ~; the ~ of one's ambition / desires.

god *n* G~ (only) knows! thank G~! make a ~ of money / one's belly.

good *adj (in predic use)* (1) be ~ at a subject / a sport / doing s.th.; he's ~ at his job. (2) milk is ~ for children; oil is ~ for burns; s.o. is ~ for a task / for nothing; he is ~ for a subscription of £50 *(will give it)*. (3) it was ~ of you to come; he was ~ enough to do it. (4) be ~ to s.o. *(kind)* (5) be ~ with s.o. *(in dealing with s.o.)* (6) s.th. is as ~ as new / dead; the work is as ~ as done; he as ~ as told me that I was a liar; be as ~ as one's word *(keep one's promise)* (7) are all fruits ~ to eat? is this water ~ to drink? is the milk / meat still ~?

good *n* (1) there is some ~ in everyone; ~ and evil; do (more harm than) ~; (2) he did it / was punished for his own ~; I'm telling you this for your own ~; he will come to no ~; he's up to no ~. (3) what's the ~ of complaining? is it any ~ trying? it's no ~ (her) talking to him. (4) he's leaving the country for ~.

gossip *n* (1) believe all the ~; be fond of (inquisitive / insidious / malicious / scandalous) ~; unconfirmed ~ (2) have a good ~ with s.o.

govern *vi* (1) in Britain, the King reigns but does not ~. - *vt* (2) ~ a country / a people (mildly / wisely / tyrannically / *etc*) (3) ~ one's temper / passions (4) self-interest ~s all her actions; the metric system is ~ed uniformly by the factor of ten; principles ~ing a case.

government *n* (1) our country needs strong ~; the ~ of a country, state or city (2) a republican / democratic / liberal / representative / corrupt / *etc* ~; form / overthrow / rise against a ~.

grade *n* (1) a high ~ of milk / meat; ~ A milk; a high ~ of intelligence (2) □ on the up / down ~ *(rising, falling; also fig)*; □ make the ~ *(succeed)*.

graduate *vi* ~ from a university / in a subject; he ~d in 1958.

grain *n* (1) a cargo of ~; a few ~s of rice (2) (not) a ~ of truth / sense / ambition / hope / vanity; □ say s.th. with a ~ of salt; → go against.

grant *vt* (1) ~ a favour / request / petition; ~ s.o. permission / a request (to do s.th.); ~ a(n academic) degree to s.o. (2) ~ the truth of what s.o. says; I ~ his honesty / that he is honest; ~ a mistake / the force of an argument; ~ed that he is a genius - I still don't like him.

grasp *vt* (1) ~ a nail with the pincers; ~ s.o. by the hands / shoulders; ~ s.o.'s hand / arm (2) ~ a fact / an idea / a problem / a theory / the meaning / the truth; I didn't ~ his point. - *vi* (3) ~ at an object / an opportunity.

gratify *vt* (1) ~ s.o.'s curiosity / thirst for knowledge / whims; ~ (emotional / sexual / monetary) needs / desires (2) he was ~ied by his son's success / with the result / to learn that I was . . .

gratitude *n* show one's ~ to s.o. for s.th.; do s.th. out of / from (pure) ~; earn s.o.'s ~; express one's ~.

great *adj* (1 *of size, extent, volume*)
(1a *larger than other members of a class*) the ~ cats *(tigers, lions, etc)*; elephants and all the other ~ beasts; the G~ Lakes; the ~ bone *(sacrum)* (1b *large in number, quantity, etc*) a ~ company / throng / army; a ~ number of people / ideas / *etc*; a ~ amount of patience / wisdom / diligence / *etc* (1c *long in duration*) a ~ while (ago); (at) a ~ age; the artifacts could not be dated but were obviously of ~ age; he lived to a ~ old age.
(2 *high in quality or degree; above the average*)
(2a *high degree; intense*) a ~ light / pain / crisis / nervousness / agitation / *etc*; ~ poverty / wealth; the new opera was a ~ fiasco; the two are ~ friends; ~ intelligence / ignorance; a ~ degree of understanding (characterized their relationship); the scene made a ~ impression on his mind; a ~ influence; he was ~ly influenced by Schopenhauer; a ~ burden (2b *eminent; distinguished; illustrious; superior*) a ~ playwright; a ~ painting / work of art / book / piece of literature / composition / *etc*; Newton's ~ discovery; she was a ~ beauty (in her day); he is as ~ a leader as you will find anywhere; he belongs to the ~ men of all times; the sword-swallower was the fair's ~(est) attraction. (2c *powerful; influential*) a ~ political family / dynasty / house; the world's ~ religions / religious leaders / *etc* (2d *important*) one of the ~ moments in the history of the world; the ~ day arrived; the team's winning was a ~ event. (2e *impressive; imposing*) a ~ ceremony / parade; a ~ array of colours / banners / *etc*; the ~ outdoors (2f *showing nobility of mind, purpose, etc*) a ~ man; a man of ~ moral stature; ~ ideas; ~-hearted (2g *very much of a; acting much as*) he is a ~ reader / theatre-goer / *etc*; he's a ~ one for fishing / playing practical jokes.
(3 *important; highest in its class*) the ~ seal (*also* G~ Seal); the ~ house *(owner's house on an estate)*; the ~ hall / gate / portal / temple / *etc* (4 *in relationships*) (~-) ~-grandfather / -mother; (~-) ~-grandson / -daughter (5 *enthusiastic about*) ~ on s.th.; John is ~ on bullfights / dog-breeding; he is a ~ boxing fan; a ~ admirer of yours / Yeats / *etc* (6 *inform: clever; expert; skillful*) he is ~ at tennis / algebra / *etc*; a ~ hand at small house repairs (7 *AE inform: excellent; first-rate*) that is a ~ book; it was a really ~ movie; she bakes a ~ apple pie. (8) ~ with child *(form: pregnant)* (9a *intensifier: especially large, good, etc*) a ~ big surprise / present / *etc*; I'm going to buy you a ~ big ice cream cone; give Mommie a ~ big hug and kiss. (9b *modifier*) ~ deal; he is a ~ deal younger than I expected; ~ many; a ~ many of those invited failed to show up; a ~ many reasons why . . . (10 *in titles, names*) Charles the G~; Frederick the G~; the G~ Dane *(dog)*; the ~ auk; the G~ Bear (11 *exclamations*) G~ God / Scott / Caesar('s ghost) / *etc*; ~ heavens / guns / *etc* (12 *derisive uses*) the ~ unwashed / unpaid; you're a ~ help *(ironic: none at all)*! (13 *city and suburbs*) G~(er) London / New York / Atlanta / *etc*.

greet *vt* (1) ~ s.o. kindly / amiably / politely / formally / with a smile / with loud applause / with cheers / with (a hostile) silence; ~ one's guests; ~ s.o. with a shower of stones (2) castles ~ us from the heights; a magnificent view of the sea ~ed us; the strange smell ~ed him on the stairs; a loud noise ~ed our ears. (3) ~ a joke with laughter; the audience ~ed the magician's trick with awe.

grief *n* (1) have / feel / suffer (great / deep / agonizing / secret / hidden) ~ about, for, over s.o. / a loss / a disaster; to die of ~; □ come to ~ *(meet with disaster)* (2) his failures were a great ~ to his parents.

grind *vt* (1) ~ grain / meal / coffee (-beans); ~ corn into flour; ~ a metal into dust / to pieces; ~ s.th. to powder; ~ flour (2) ~ a knife / axe (to a sharp edge); ~ a lens / diamond; □ have an axe to ~ *(a personal interest to serve)* (3) ~ one's teeth (together); ~ one's heel into the ground; he ground his knee into his opponent's stomach. (4) ~ a handmill / coffee-mill / barrel-organ (5) ~ Latin into a boy's head; ~ a boy in Latin. - *vi* (6) the door ground on its hinges; a ship ~ing on the rocks (7) the truck slowly ground up the hill. (8) ~ for an examination.

grind away ~ ~ at one's studies *(work hard).*

grind down (1) the miller ground the corn ~. (2) ~ a bad tooth ~ (3) ~ ~ *(oppress)* the people / opposition; be ground ~ by poverty / taxation / tyranny.

grind out the barrel-organ ground ~ a tune; ~ ~ a tune on a barrel-organ; ~ ~ some verses *(produce them with difficulty).*

ground *n* (1) fertile / barren / stony / marshy / watery / frozen / *etc* ~; ~-to-air missile; the ~ rocked under his feet; *(fig)* plans / schemes / hopes fall to the ~; our hopes were dashed to the ~ *(were disappointed).* (2) hold / stand / keep one's ~ *(also fig)*; gain ~ (→ gain *vt* 7); give ~ *(move back)*; lose ~; cover (much, *etc*) ~ *(also fig, of a report, lecture, etc)*; cut the ~ from under s.o.'s feet; □ that suits me down to the ground *(inform: thoroughly).* (3) till the ~ *(soil)*; □ break fresh / new ~ *(cultivate new land; also fig)* (4) the ship hit / touched ~ *(bottom of the sea).* (5) have (good / sufficient / no) ~(s) for s.th. / doing s.th; there is no ~ for anxiety / alarm; you haven't much ~ / many ~s for complaint; on legal / moral / religious / personal ~s; on what ~s do you suspect him? (6) red flowers on a black ~.

grow *vi* (1a) fruit / grain / *etc* ~s (wild / in the fields / *etc*); daisies ~ in meadows; how quickly he is ~ing; he is ~ing an inch a day; she has decided to let her hair ~; skin / flesh ~s together; plants ~ from seed or from cuttings; he will ~ into the new jacket; *(fig)* ~ into a plant / man / fine boy; ~ out of one's clothes; *(fig)* ~ out of a bad habit / childish habits (1b) this firm grew from very small beginnings; the factory grew out of a small workshop; most prejudices ~ out of ignorance. *(fig).* (2) the volume of their shouts grew to a roar; support grew steadily for his policies; the city has ~n in size and importance; ~ in splendour / wisdom / popular esteem (3a) it is ~ing dark; ~ old / tired / ill / weary / impatient / thin / pale / rich / eloquent / sentimental / old-fashioned / wise / *etc*; you will ~ used to it; how tall you've ~n. (3b) his father was ~ing to be an old man; ~ to like s.th./ s.o. (4 ~ *on, upon: come to appeal to; become a habit*) his music grew (up)on me; you may not like this book at first, but it ~s (up)on you; you must be careful that smoking / the habit of taking drugs doesn't ~ (up)on you. - *vt* (5) ~ plants / cereals / sugar-cane / roses / *etc*; ~ a beard (6) he has ~n a habit of (twitching his nose).

grow up I want to be a pilot when I ~ up; ~ up in the country; she grew (up) into a beautiful girl; an intimacy / legend / *etc* ~s up.

guarantee *vt* (1) ~ a watch; a watch ~d for six months (2) ~ (to pay / the payment of) a debt; ~ success / s.o.'s good behaviour; I ~ that the sum will be paid / that it will never happen again / that these statements are correct; I ~ the correctness of these statements; we can't ~ our workers regular employment; ~d genuine (3) I can ~ that you will enjoy yourself; can you ~ me a job when I get there?

guard *vt* (1) a dog ~s s.o.; ~ a camp / prisoner / treasure / secret (carefully / jealously / *etc*); ~ one's life / reputation. - *vi* (2) ~ against disease / an accident / failure / bad habits / laziness / *etc* - *adj* (3) a ~ed *(cautious)* answer; speak in ~ed terms / use ~ed language.

guess *vt* (1) ~ a riddle / a secret / s.o.'s intention / what he intends to do / s.o.'s thoughts / what he is thinking; you've ~ed it / her age (right / wrong); ~ s.th. from s.o.'s manner (2) can you ~ my weight / how much I weigh / what my weight is? I should ~ his age at 60 / him to be 60. (3 *AE*) I ~ I'll stay / you're tired after your journey. - *vi* (4 → 2) ~ at a distance; it's no good ~ing at the answer - ask someone! can't you even ~ at her age? I don't really know, I'm just ~ing.

guide *vt* (1) ~ s.o. through the woods; ~ a boat towards the port; ~ a blind man / s.o.'s hand / the plough (2) let o.s. be ~d by God; I'll be ~d by you *(act as you suggest)*; be ~d by common sense; the book ~d us in the art of...

H

habit *n* good / bad / saving / possessive / unsteady / vulgar ~s; his drunken ~s; my horse has a ~ of kicking; acquire / fall into / get into the ~ of doing s.th.; fall / get into bad ~s; he is in the ~ of (rising early / *etc*); change one's ~s; do s.th. from force of ~.

hair *n* fair / flaxen / light / brown / red / auburn / copper-coloured / golden / grey / greying / white / dark ~; straight / lank / crisp / curled / curly / kinky / sleek / thick / thin / thinning / falling / unkempt / wild ~; do / tidy / arrange / comb / brush / wash / shampoo / dry / set / smooth (down) one's ~; cut / clip / trim one's ~; have one's ~ cut / washed / *etc*; □ keep your ~ on *(slang: keep control of o.s.)*; □ lose one's ~ *(also fig: lose one's temper)*; tear one's ~ (out) *(fig: be anguished about s.th.)*; he's tearing his ~ out over the new contract; □ the ghost story made his ~ stand on end / set his ~ on end *(terrified him)*; □ split hairs (over minor matters → split *vt* 1); he didn't turn a ~ *(kept absolutely calm)*; □ escape by a ~'s breadth / have a ~-breadth escape.

half *n* take ~ of s.th.; he gave me ~; cut / divide s.th. in ~ / into ~ves; what is ~ (of) twelve? he is not a man to do anything by ~ves; (a good) ~ of his employees are ill; my better ~ (*wife, sometimes husband*); □ go ~ves (with s.o. in s.th.); too clever by ~ *(very conceited)*.

half *adj/adv* ~ a minute / dozen / cup of tea / *etc*; a ~ bottle of wine; to stay up ~ the night; ~ the time he isn't here; every ~ hour; ~ as much again as one expects; ~ asleep / undressed / finished / *etc*; ~-baked *(also fig, inform: poorly thought out)*; ~-baked ideas / plans; I only ~ understood him; I had ~ promised it to him; do s.th. with ~ a heart / ~-heartedly *(not very energetically)*.

hand *n* (1) hold s.th. in one's ~; → put 1, 7a, 7b; take (→ take *vt* 22b) / lead s.o. by the ~; hold out one's ~ to s.o.; let one's ~ drop / fall; a sonata for four ~s; *(fig)* I have my ~s full / my ~s are full; *(fig)* lend me / let me have a ~ now; give me a ~ at (opening the window); *(fig)* he gave me his ~ *(pledge)* on it; give s.o. a free ~ (→ free *adj* 7); have one's ~s free (→ free *adj* 3, 7); *(fig)* he is the boss's right ~; he is my right-~ man. (2) he has a good ~ with horses; she has a light ~ at pastry; try one's ~ at doing s.th.; *(fig)* to be an old ~ at doing s.th.; he is a good ~ at cricket / at doing s.th. / with a gun. (3) have a ~ *(influence)* in doing s.th.; to keep a firm ~ on / keep one's ~s on s.o. / s.th. (4) he writes a good / fair / legible ~. (5 *prepos + ~*) he lives close at ~; I had no money at ~; if you need me, I'll be at ~; the exams are at ~; suffer at the ~s of (the police); get to know s.th. at first / second ~; a pullover knitted by ~; a letter delivered by ~; (pass) from ~ to ~; the matter is in your ~s; the children are in good ~s; leave s.th. in s.o.'s ~s *(control)*; he is in the ~s of some money-lenders; go / walk / stand ~ in ~; stupidity and conceit often go ~ in ~; I still have some money in ~; your plan is now in ~ *(receiving attention)*; have a piece of work in ~; these noisy children need to be taken in ~ (→ take *vt* 22b); have a situation well in ~; the situation is well in ~; I can't give you the exact figures off ~; on the right / left ~; on the one ~ ..., on the other ~; to have certain goods on ~ *(available, for sale)*; to have s.th. on one's ~s *(the troublesome responsibility of it)*; the boys have got out of ~; to deal with a situation out of ~; by conquest the land came under his ~; talk with one's ~s; (rule) with a firm ~; with a bold ~; (treat s.o.) with a high ~ / high-handedly *(arrogantly)*.

hand *vt* please, ~ me my hat; ~ s.o. into / out of the taxi; ~ s.o. across the street.

hand down ~ ~ a tradition; the secret / title / *etc* has been ~ed ~ since the 14th century.

hand in ~ in one's resignation / notice; ~ in an application / letter at an office / *etc*.

hand on ~ a message / pamphlet on to other people; ~ s.th. on from one generation to another.

hand out ~ ~ leaflets / exam papers to students; I ~ed them ~ five shillings.
hand over ~ ~ the money to the cashier / the fortress to the enemy / a criminal to the police.
hand round ~ ~ a letter.
handle *vt* (1) don't offer a biscuit if you've ~d it; wash your hands before you ~ my books; do not ~ the goods on display. (2) ~ an instrument / one's tools; too tired to ~ a car; ~ a baby; ~ s.th. carefully / in masterly fashion / with care (3) a grocer ~s foods, soaps, *etc*; does this shop ~ imported goods? (4) I don't know how to ~ her / this difficult boy; ~ a(n unruly) crowd; ~ s.o. gently / with great tact / with kid gloves / roughly / without gloves (5) this book ~s the problems of old age in a very sympathetic way. (6a *have responsibility for*) ~ a legal case; who's ~ing the Jones contract? you need a professional to ~ your investments; my lawyer ~s all my business affairs. (6b *treat, esp medically*) Dr. Smith does not ~ heart cases; the soccer team's masseur can ~ almost any kind of muscle problem. (6c *manage professionally*) ~ a boxer / wrestler / football team / *etc*. - *vi* (7 → 2) the new car ~s beautifully.
hang *vt* (1a) ~ a picture (askew) / curtains / tapestry / wall-paper (on a wall) / a lamp from the ceiling; ~ a wall / room with pictures / drapery / wall-paper; ~ a door / window (on its hinges); ~ meat / game; game needs to be well hung; ~ s.o. (on the gallows); to ~ o.s.; □ I'll be ~ed if (this is not true); the wardrobe is hung full with clothes; the streets were hung with flags. (1b *AE*) ~ one on s.o. *(inform: strike s.o.)* Jones hung (a good) one on Smith in the fourth round; ~ one on *(slang: get drunk)*: I hung one on last night and feel rotten today. (2) a huge lamp hung from the ceiling; the curtains are ~ing crooked / askew; the skirt just ~s loose around her; a door ~s on its hinges; ~ on s.o.'s neck *(also fig)*; hang on s.o.'s *(fig)* lips / words / answers; the baby hung on its mother's skirt *(also fig)*; much ~s on his decision; dark clouds / *(fig)* disaster hung over the town; a fearful danger ~s over his head; □ ~ in the balance *(be undecided)*; □ his life hung by a thread; the scheme has hung fire *(has not gone on)* for some months; □ let things go ~ *(take no interest in them)*; let an opportunity go ~.
hang about we hung ~ until the shops opened; we saw a suspicious-looking man ~ing ~ outside the bank; a thunderstorm / a cold / the flu may ~ ~.
hang back she hung ~ when they asked for volunteers *(did not offer herself)*.
hang on I'll ~ on till you arrive; please ~ on a minute *(on the phone)*; some of the guests hung on to the very end; it was hard work, but we hung on; → hang 1.
hang out (1) ~ ~ a flag / banner / sign / signal; ~ ~ the washing (to dry) (2) our supplies / resources won't ~ ~ for more than two days more. (3) the besieged garrison hung ~. (4) where does he ~ ~ *(slang: live)*?
hang over the discussion of this matter can easily ~ ~ till next morning.
hang round ~ ~ art galleries and museums; ~ ~ bars / street corners; do you mind if I just ~ ~ here until my bus comes? ~ ~ s.o.'s neck *(seek his company)*.
hang together (1) his arguments don't ~ ~. (2) if we all ~ ~ our plans will succeed.
hang up (1) ~ up a, one's coat / hat / *etc;* don't ~ up *(the receiver)*, please! he got cheeky, so I just hung up (on him). (2) bad weather ~s up *(delays)* work; the plan has been hung up; I was / got hung up in a traffic jam.
hard *adj/adv* (1) ~ as iron / a rock / nails; the bread has gone ~; frozen ~; an egg boiled ~; a ~-boiled egg; a ~ pencil / nib; the material feels ~; a ~ blow (on the chin); ~ water / light / sound; raining ~; the wind blows ~; training has made him ~; ~ currency; ~ prices *(tending to stay high)*; he is ~ of hearing *(rather deaf)*; pull / push ~; drink ~; swear ~; try ~ to do s.th.; work / study / think ~; a ~ worker (2) a ~ task / problem / translation / language / struggle / winter / frost / rain / lot / fate / punishment; □ a ~ nut to crack; □ it's ~ to take (→ take *vt* 10b); ~ times; have been through a ~ school; breathing ~ after a long run; ~ to understand; it's ~ to say which is better; to learn s.th. the ~ way; he is (a) ~ (man) to please; he is a ~ man to see. (3) he is ~ (up)on his son / his servants / his clothes; a ~ master; it's very ~ on him that he cannot go too; ~ luck (4) follow ~ after / behind / upon s.o.; be ~ on s.o.'s heels; ~ by *(near, at hand)*; we were ~ at

it *(very busy)* all the time; □ be ~ up (in life) *(in need, esp of money)*; □ be ~ up for (an excuse / for words to express one's feelings / for ideas); □ run s.o. ~ *(pursue closely)*.

harm *n* cause mental / bodily ~; come to no ~; it will do you no ~; there's no ~ (in) doing it / trying; I see no ~ in it; he meant no ~ (in doing it); out of ~'s way *(in safety)*.

haste *n* why all this ~? be / act / do s.th. in (great) ~ / in no ~; in blind ~; a note written in ~; in his ~ he forgot it; without ~; make ~ *(form)*.

hate *vt* she ~s the cold; ~ s.o./ s.th. like poison; I ~ crying / having to get up early / being contradicted; I ~ to disappoint you but ...; I should ~ you to have a fruitless journey.

have *vt*

The patterns are grouped as follows: ~ + *abstract obj:* 2c–g; ~ + it: 11; ~ + *inf with* to: 7; ~ + *obj* + *inf with* to: 8; ~ + *obj* + *inf without* to: 5b, 6a; ~ + *obj* + *past part:* 5d, 6c; ~ + *obj* + *present part:* 5c, 6b; can, will (not) ~ + *inf without* to: 9b; can, will (not) ~ + *obj*: 9a; can, will (not) ~ + *obj* + *past part:* 9d; can, will (not) ~ + *obj* + *present part*: 9c; idiomatic phrases: 12.

(1a *contain*) the house has five rooms / a garden / large windows / *etc*; the book has (beautiful) illustrations; how many days has a week? (1b *be in a relationship to*) ~ three children / brothers / few friends / several enemies.

(2 *possess*)

(2a) ~ a house / farm / car / riches / money (to burn) / *etc.*

(2b) ~ good / poor health / blue eyes / long legs / beauty / a neat figure / *etc*; ~ a cold / a (high) temperature / a fever / a headache / measles / gout / something wrong with (one's knee / chest / *etc*); do you often ~ colds? ~ you (got) a cold now? ~ a squint.

(2c) ~ abilities / talents / capacity / the ability (to do s.th.) / a taste for s.th.; ~ energy / patience / a kind heart / a good memory / a (good / bad) temper / tact / charm / respect / *etc*; he has something against me.

(2d) ~ authority / powers / influence / liberty / credit / the right to (do) s.th.

(2e *have* + *noun* is synonymous with *be* + an adjective derivable from the noun: *have mercy* = *be merciful*) ~ the kindness / goodness to do s.th.; ~ the impudence / cheek to do s.th.; ~ mercy / pity; ~ success; he had the curiosity to ask John if ...; ~ contempt for s.o.

(2f *have* + *noun* is synonymous with a verb derivable from the noun: *to have a swim* = *to swim*) ~ a wash / a bath / a swim / a walk / a dance / a talk / a joke / a drink / a smoke; ~ a laugh; ~ a look / a peep (at s.th.); ~ a lie-down; ~ a date (with s.o.); ~ a / another try; ~ a quarrel / a fight / a (nasty) row (with s.o.); ~ a desire / a wish; ~ a liking / a dislike for s.o.; do you ever ~ dreams? I ~n't much hope of (getting a ticket); ~ no choice / option (but to agree); he had a suspicion that he ...; his pride had a fall.

(2g *have* + *abstract object*) ~ a plan; I ~ a feeling / the proof that he ...; ~ an intuition / a presentiment / a notion; not ~ the faintest / slightest / least / *(inform)* foggiest idea; ~ you any idea what / who / *etc* ...? ~ no grasp of s.th.; what reason ~ you got for thinking that he ...? ~ (no) time (for s.o./ s th.); do you ~ much time for reading? ~ you (got) time to come with me? we ~ only five minutes (left); not ~ a minute to spare; ~ leisure; ~ a good command of (French); ~ bearing on s.th.; ~ a (wide) vogue.

(3 *get*) tea is not to be had here; there was nothing to be had; you can ~ it for the asking; she is going to ~ a baby; he had one child by his first wife; how often does your dog ~ puppies?

(4 *take, eat, etc*) ~ tea / coffee for breakfast; ~ breakfast / lunch / dinner; will you ~ a glass of milk? ~ a cigarette; we didn't ~ Latin at school; do we ~ translation every Friday?

(5 *experience*)

(5a *have* + *object*) ~ a party / concert / meeting / wedding / much social life (in this town); ~ good / difficult times; ~ adventures / a crisis / a disappointment / a surprise; we didn't ~ much difficulty / trouble (finding the house); did you ~ a good holiday / a pleasant journey / a smooth passage / a nice time / a good night last night? he doesn't ~ an easy time; ~ an operation; we have never had it so good *(inform)*.

(5b *have* + *object* + *infinitive without* to) one night he had a thief break into his shop; I cannot bear to ~ you think me impertinent.

(5c *have* + *object* + *present participle*) I

~ several problems troubling me; I ~ a cold coming; he has a friend waiting to see him; he has books lying everywhere.
(5d *have + object + past participle*) I had all my expenses paid by my father; he had his leg taken off; I had all my books stolen; I have never had my word doubted; I've had this forced upon me; ~ you any money / time left?
(6 *cause*)
(6a *have + object + infinitive without* to) please ~ the boy bring the box to my house; she had her father pay for it.
(6b *have + object + present participle*) the taste of the food had him asking for more; the doctor will soon ~ him walking again.
(6c *have + object + past participle*) I had my hair washed / a photograph taken / the text translated / *etc*; you'll ~ to ~ it seen to.
(7 *have +* to-*infinitive: must*) I have to / I've had to give up smoking; the door had to be forced open; do we ~ to change at Crewe if we go by this train? does one ~ to have a passport to go to Poland?
(8 *have + object +* to-*infinitive: there is s.th. which one can/ must do, would like to do*) I ~ no pen to write with; he has a family to be proud of; I ~ a request to make; we ~ some new photos to show you; he hasn't got much to complain of; we ~ little to eat / (much) work to do / nothing to lose / no time to lose; he still had a long way / far to go; do that once more and you'll ~ me to reckon with.
(9 *usu neg: want / not want definitely*)
(9a *can / will have + object*) I won't / can't ~ such conduct; I can't go there with you, my mother won't ~ it.
(9b *can/will have + object + infinitive without* to) I won't ~ you say such things; I will / would ~ you know that this ...; I can't ~ you borrow any more money from him.
(9c *can/will have + object + present participle*) I won't ~ you talking me over with John; we won't / cannot ~ anyone behaving in this manner.
(9d *can/will have + object + past participle*) we won't / cannot ~ these orders disobeyed; I won't ~ it said that I treated him unfairly.
(10 *inform: cheat, defeat*) there's nothing we can do about it, we've been had; mind he doesn't ~ you; he had me in that argument.
(11 *have +* it) let him ~ it *(inform: hurt him physically or with words)*; rumour has it that he did it; he will ~ it *(insists)* that our plan is impracticable; he won't ~ it *(admit)* that the conditions are unfair; I ~ it *(understand suddenly)*! he's so badly injured that I'm afraid he's had it *(inform: is dead)*; his bicycle looks as though it's had it; we realized that our team had had it *(been defeated)*.
(12 *idiomatic phrases*)
~ a bone to pick with s.o.; ~ a chip on one's shoulder *(take offence quickly)*; ~ one's cake and eat it; ~ it both ways; ~ s.th. one's own way; ~ a job *(difficulty)* doing s.th.; ~ a soft spot for s.o.; ~ guts *(inform: courage)*; ~ several irons in the fire; ~ a screw loose / bats in the belfry *(inform: be mad, crazy)*; I think I've had one too many / one over the eight *(inform: am drunk)*.
(13 *have down / in / over / round / up: have s.o. as guest / worker*) she had some friends in / round for tea / down for the week-end *(from town)* / up for the week-end *(from the country)*; she had some friends over for tea *(friends living in another part of the town)*; we shall ~ the decorators in next month.

have back let me ~ it ~ soon.

have in (1) ~ we enough coal in for the winter? (2) I didn't know he had it in him to go on alone. (3) since that mistake I made he's really had it in for me *(nurses a grudge against me)*. (4) → have 13.

have on (1) she had a red dress on; he hadn't any money on him; ~ you the time *(a watch)* on you? (2) ~ you anything on this evening? we've a very important piece of work on at the moment. (3) may we ~ the television on? (4 *BE; inform*) they had him on on April 1; don't believe him, he's having us on!

have out (1) I had to ~ that tooth / my tonsils ~. (2) let her ~ her sleep ~ *(sleep until she wakes up)*. (3) she had it ~ with him about forgetting her birthday.

have up (1) ~ s.th. up one's sleeve *(as a surprise)* (2 *BE; inform*) he was had up for speeding / burglary / slander. (3) → have 13.

head *n* (1) a bare / bald / curly *etc* ~; it cost him his ~ *(also fig)*; nod / shake / bend / turn / toss one's ~; carry / hold one's ~ high; put one's ~ in at the door / out of the window; my ~ is aching /

splitting / swimming (with so many dates) / nearly bursting; (dirty) from ~ to foot; fall / jump ~ first / foremost; he is / stands a ~ taller than she (is/does); he is taller than her by a ~; the wine / blood went to his head. (2 *of things*) a marble ~ of Caesar; the ~ of a hammer / axe / nail / pin; the ~ of a staircase / bed; a (fine) ~ of cabbage / lettuce; at the ~ of the page / parade / regiment / class / government; the ~ of a river / lake; who is the ~ of that firm / school? (3 *piece*) fifty ~ of cattle; a large ~ *(number)* of game; the charge is a pound a ~. (4 *mind*) have a clear / cool ~; a good ~ for figures / mathematics / business; have a bad / no ~ for heights; have a good ~ on one's shoulders *(common sense)*; an old ~ on young shoulders *(wisdom in the young)*; (he made the story up) out of his own ~. (5 *ripening boil*) the boil came to a ~ *(was about to burst)*; come to a ~ *(fig: reach a crisis)*; to bring s.th. to a ~ *(fig)* (6 ~ *used fig*) ~ over heels (in debt / in love); have a bad / *(inform)* thick ~ (from drinking); the successes have gone to his ~ / have turned his ~ *(made him conceited)*; have a swelled ~ *(be conceited)*; he isn't quite right in the ~ *(inform)*; he is out of / off his ~ *(inform: mad; very excited)*; he has his ~ screwed on the right way *(talks / acts sensibly)*; bite / snap s.o.'s ~ off (→ bite off, snap off); give s.o. his ~ *(allow him to do as he sees fit)*; give a horse his ~ *(give him free rein)*; act / go over s.o.'s ~ *(act without his consent)*; s.th. is over one's ~ *(too complicated for one to understand)*; it went completely out of his ~; put / set a price on s.o.'s ~ *(life)*; → get *vt* 7b, put *vt* 7a, b, take *vt* 22c, soft *adj* 7.

head *vt* (1) ~ a deputation / commission / parade / procession / revolt; ~ the firm; ~ a list; how will you ~ the chapter? - *vi* (2) ~ south / for home / for (a destination); *(fig)* he is ~ing for disaster. (3) ~ off a flock of sheep / the cattle / a criminal *(intercept)*; ~ off a collision / quarrel.

heal *vt* ~ s.o. of a disease *(more usual: cure)*; time ~s all wounds / sorrows; ~ a breach; the wound ~s slowly / is ~ing well; the cut soon ~ed up / over.

health *n* (1) physical / bodily / mental ~; be in good / sound / weak / poor / bad / ill ~; delicate / frail / precarious / shattered / ruined / broken ~; he is the picture of ~ / bursting with ~; how is your ~? for reasons of ~ (2) to drink (to) s.o.'s ~ / a ~ to s.o.; I drink to your ~.

hear *vt* (1) ~ a noise / sound / shout / whisper / voice / *etc* clearly, *etc*; I ~d a clock strike / striking; I have ~d it said that he ...; from all I ~ he is ...; God ~d my prayer. (2 *listen*) please ~ what I have to say; ~ Mass; go to ~ an opera; ~ a boy his lesson; ~ a complaint; ~ a case / a defendant / the evidence. - *vi* (3) Grandfather doesn't ~ well any more.

hear about I've ~d a lot ~ you; you will ~ ~ this later.

hear from we haven't ~d ~ him for a long time; let us ~ ~ you soon.

hear of I've never ~d of her; the explorers were never ~d of again; I've ~d nothing but good of him; you'll ~ of this further; he will not ~ of your doing it!

hear out don't make any decision yet: please ~ me ~.

heart *n* (1) a strong / sound / healthy / weak ~; my ~ stood still when I ...; with beating ~; the ~ beats / pulsates / palpitates / throbs (violently). (2) a light / gentle / kind / pure / sympathetic / yearning / soft / warm / cold / hard ~; with a heavy ~; die of a broken ~; have a ~ of gold / stone; his ~ jumped / skipped / leapt for joy; grief is gnawing at her ~; do s.th. with half a / with one's whole ~ (→ half *adj* 1, whole *adj* 1); he has no ~; how can you have the ~ to (drown the kittens)? □ have one's ~ in the right place; □ have one's ~ in one's work; □ have s.th. at ~ *(be deeply interested)*; □ have one's ~ in one's mouth *(be badly frightened)*; □ have one's ~ in one's boots *(be without hope)*; □ lay one's ~ at s.o.'s feet; □ set one's ~ on s.th. (→ set *vt* 19); □ set s.o.'s ~ at ease (→ set *vt* 21b); □ take ~ (→ take *vt* 17); □ take s.th. to ~ (→ take *vt* 22b); □ take s.o. to ~ (→ take *vt* 22b); □ wear one's ~ on one's sleeve (→ wear *vt* 1a); (he is a man) after my own ~; (I loathe him) at ~ / in my ~ of ~s; (get / learn / know s.th.) by heart *(from memory)* (3 *of things*) the ~ of the city / forest; (get to) the ~ of the matter / subject / mystery; the ~ of a lettuce / cabbage / tree.

heat *n* a gentle / intense / intolerable / fierce / infernal / merciless / scorching / oppressive ~; (bake) at an even / moderate / medium ~; in a ~ of 40° centigrade in the shade; in the ~ of the battle / debate / argument; words spoken in the ~ of the moment.

heavy *adj* (1) ~ metal; a ~ box / *etc* (*2 intense*) ~ rain / fog / storm; a ~ blow (on the head); a ~ fall; trees ~ with apples / fruit; ~ crops; a ~ *(dark)* sky; ~ sea *(with big waves)*; be ~ with sleep / wine; a ~ *(thick)* black line (3 *difficult to do / work / digest / etc*) ~ work / task / duty / reading; a ~ road *(difficult to travel over)*; ~ food / bread / pudding; ~ expenses / taxes (4) ~ features *(without grace)*; ~ manner / style *(tedious)*; ~ news / fate *(sad)*; her heart was ~ at parting from her home; a ~ bass voice; a ~ loss; a ~ drinker / smoker.

help *vt* (1) I ~ed her (to) lift the case / to her place / out of the car / on with her coat / off with her dress; ~ s.o. out (with s.th.) *(temporarily)*; ~ s.o. out of a difficulty; he cannot be ~ed; →dog *n* 1. (2) may I ~ you to some more rice? ~ yourself to the fruit; here's a spoon to ~ the gravy with. (3) that's not to be ~ed; it can't be ~ed; I can't ~ thinking that he ...; I can't ~ his being so silly; he cannot ~ the egoism.

hide *vt* (1) trees ~ the house; clouds ~ the sun; ~ o.s. / a fact / the truth from s.o.; ~ s.th. from view; ~ one's feelings (from s.o.); hide one's disappointment (2 *BE*) they found it hidden up behind a cushion – *vi* (3) he hid among the trees; quick, ~ in the wardrobe! (4 *BE* → 2) you ~ up and I'll try and find you. – *adj* (5) a hidden treasure; his words had a hidden meaning.

high *adj/ adv* (1) a ~ tree / hill / mountain / room / tower / building; a ~ jump / dive / kick / flight; the sun / plane is ~ in the sky; climb ~; aim ~ *(also fig)*; fly ~ *(also fig: have great ambitions)*; search ~ and low *(everywhere)* for s.th.; (he sailed) the ~ seas *(the open oceans)*; how ~ is it? it's ten feet / an inch ~. (2 *chief, important*) a ~ office / official; of ~ rank; a ~ altar; ~ and low *(all classes of society)*; ~ life *(that of the upper classes)*; live ~ *(luxuriously)*; ~ honours / esteem / praise; ~ hopes; be born for ~er things; ~ value / degree / quality (3 *of sounds*) ~ notes / tones; speak in a ~ voice; I can't sing so ~. (4 *intense*) ~ wind / (blood) pressure / temperature; he has / is running a ~ temperature; ~ speed; shift into ~ gear *(of a car)*; a ~ salary; ~ prices; at a ~ cost; pay ~ for s.th.; they charge very ~; £1,000 would be ~ for this car; a ~ offer / rate of interest; in ~ *(angry)* words; in ~ *(gay)* spirits; have a ~ old time (5 *of time, in science: more advanced*) ~ summer; at ~ noon; it's ~ time you went / (for you) to go; ~ er mathematics / arithmetic / mammals (6 *good, noble*) a man of ~ character; ~ aims / ideals / principles; a ~ *(courageous)* spirit; a ~ sense of duty.

highly *adv* ~ seasoned food; ~ amusing / interesting / annoying / fashionable / educated / cultivated; ~ paid; a ~ placed official; that's ~ improbable; to speak ~ of s.o.; to esteem s.o. ~; I was ~ astonished / surprised.

hint *n* drop / let fall / give s.o. a broad / strong / delicate / gentle / cautious / useful ~ (that this ...); know how to take a ~; act on a (mere) ~.

hire *vt* the user of a thing ~s it; the owner ~s it out; ~ a gardener / a charwoman / a taxi / a boat / a bus / a hall for a meeting; ~ out bicycles / boats (by the hour).

hit *vt* (1) ~ s.o. on the head; he was ~ by a stone; ~ s.o. a hard blow; ~ s.o. below the belt *(also fig)*; ~ the mark / target; ~ s.o. foul; the car ~ the wall; he ~ his head on / against the lamp-post; ~ s.o./ s.th. hard *(also fig)* (2 *used fig*) ~ the road *(start / resume travelling)*; ~ s.o.'s fancy / taste *(appeal to him)*; ~ the (right) nail on the head; you've ~ it *(said exactly the right thing)*; the bad news ~ him suddenly; be hard ~ (by s.o.'s death / *etc*) (3 ~ *+ prepos*) ~ at s.th. *(try to hit it)*; ~ off s.o./s.th. *(give a good derscription / imitation of it)*; Mary and I ~ it off at once *(got on well)*; ~ out (at s.o.) *(attack with fists or verbally)*; ~ (up)on an idea / method / plan / right answer.

hold *vt* 1-9, *vi* 10.
The patterns are grouped as follows: ~ + *adj*: 10; ~ + *obj* + *adj*: 1, 2, 5; ~ + *obj* + *adv phrase: 1, 2, 5;* ~ + *obj* + *inf*: 5; ~ + that-clause: 5; non-personal subjects: 3, 10; idiomatic phrases: 1, 3a.
(1 *keep fast with the hand(s), teeth, etc*) ~ s.th. fast / tight(ly) / firmly / gently (in one's hand); ~ s.o.'s hand; they held each other's hands; he held me by the sleeve; he held the knife between his teeth / the dog between his knees; he held his sides with laughter; ~ s.o. in prison; ~ s.o. prisoner / as (a) hostage; □ ~ one's head high *(face the world confidently; be proud)*; □ be left ~ing the baby *(having unwanted responsibility)*; □ he can't ~ a

candle to her *(is inferior to her).* (2 *keep in position*) the walls ~ the roof in position; the column ~s the weight of the roof; ~ o.s. well / badly / straight; ~ (yourself) still while I take your photo; ~ o.s. ready / in readiness (to do s.th.); ~ s.o.'s attention; the speaker held his listeners(' interest); ~ a note *(in singing)* (3a *contain*) this trunk won't ~ all your clothes; the barrel ~s / will ~ 20 litres; the room ~s twenty people; does this pan ~ water? sea-water ~s minute quantities of all metals; the acid ~s the sulphate in solution; □ his argument doesn't ~ water *(is not sound).* (3b *as 3a, abstract objects*) an artist needs the belief that life ~s some beauty and meaning; a closer look at the disaster may ~ lessons for the future; ~ promise / good prospects (of improving / *etc*) (4 *have in the mind*) ~ strange opinions / strong views (on a matter) / a mass of details in one's head; he ~s to the opinion / view that we ...; we ~ great hopes of (increasing production). (5 *consider*) ~ a man to be a fool; ~ the accused to be innocent; ~ s.o., o.s. responsible (for s.th.) / guilty / blameless; they ~ nothing sacred / life cheap; ~ s.o. in great / high esteem / in great respect / in high regard / in contempt; the judge held the lawyer in contempt of *(sentenced him for breaking the rules of court procedure)*; he ~s that this ... (6a *keep back*) he held his breath for 20 seconds; ~ one's tongue / peace *(be quiet)*; ~ one's temper; ~ one's hand *(not punish; delay action)*; there's no ~ing him now; I've tied him hand and foot - that ought to ~ him! (6b *detain*) ~ him until I call the police; the police were unable to ~ the surging crowd; the suspect was held for further questioning. (7 *have, own*) ~ property / land / 1,000 acres near N. / shares in a gas company; ~ the patents for this device / the copyright for the play / orders for six months' production; ~ a degree / the record for (swimming this distance); ~ a right / an option / the authority (to act) / the power (to call a meeting); the person who paid ~s the receipt; he ~s a copy of the contract. (8 *occupy*) ~ the position of (secretary) / the rank of (major) / the office of treasurer; the Governments ~s office for five years; ~ a fort(ress) / one's position / the town (against enemy forces); □ ~ one's ground / one's own *(not give way)*; a debater / team / sick person ~s his own. (9 *conduct*) ~ a meeting / debate / conference / conversation / course of lectures / examination / inquiry / a receiption (in honour of s.o.) / birthday party / church service; ~ court. - *vi* (10 *remain unbroken / unchanged*) when I stick these things together with glue, it ~s; will the rope / anchor ~? how long will the fine weather ~? if the arid conditions ~ in the area, many cattle will die; my offer / promise still ~s; evidence / a contract / a statement / an offer / the argument (still) ~s good; the same rule ~s *(is valid)* for everyone; if the theory is based on accurate data, it will ~; does the same percentage / prognosis / evaluation / hypothesis ~ in all cases? does that ~ true for males as well?

hold against ~ s.th. ~ s.o. *(blame him for it)*; ~ it ~ him *(bear a grudge).*

hold back (1) the police held ~ the crowds; he was so impatient that I couldn't ~ him ~; nothing can ~ me ~. (2) she held ~ the truth / some information ~ (from us); ~ ~ one's emotion. (3) we wanted them to join the others, but they held ~; buyers are ~ing ~ *(making no offers).*

hold by (1) ~ s.o. by the arm / hand / coat / *etc* (2) ~ by one's beliefs / convictions; ~ by one's father's advice.

hold down (1) ~ one's head ~ (in shame) (2) ~ a job ~ *(inform: keep it)* (3) ~ criticism ~ (by suppressive measures).

hold forth (1) ~ s.th. ~ *(offer)*; ~ ~ hopes of profit (2) he held ~ for two hours *(spoke at length to an audience; often neg).*

hold in ~ in one's temper; ~ o.s. in *(restrain one's feelings).*

hold off (1) ~ your dog ~; ~ ~ an attack; we held the enemy ~ until ...; his cold manner ~s people ~. (2) ~ ~ one's departure *(postpone)* (3) cotton is falling in price, and buyers ~ ~. (4) will the rain ~ ~ until evening? ~ ~ for a minute (until I finish what I'm doing).

hold on (1) the pin ~s the wheel on *(keeps it in position).* (2) the export of cotton held on *(continued)* for many years; the survivors cannot ~ on much longer. (3) ~ on (a minute) *(stop a moment).* (4) just (you) ~ on now *(inform: calm yourself)*! ~ on to the wall / the railings; they held on to each other; he held on to the bush until he was rescued; ~ on to one's shares *(not sell them)*; ~ on to one's hopes; I had to ~ on to myself so as not to shout.

hold out (1) she held ~ her hand for me to shake; ~ your arms ~. (2) ~ ~ some hope / promise / likelihood (to s.o.); the doctor did not ~ ~ much hope of the patient's recovery. (3) ~ ~ money / information on s.o. *(keep it from him)* (4) ~ ~ against attacks; the soldiers held ~ for ten days; she held ~ although the pain was terrible; I think the engine will ~ ~ till we get home; his supply of food held ~ for a week. (5) ~ ~ for *(insist uncompromisingly)*: the union is ~ing ~ for (better working conditions); the blackmailer held ~ for a full million dollars.

hold over (1) ~ s.th. ~ s.o. *(as a constant threat)* (2) the last two items on the agenda will be held ~ until the next meeting. (3) the film is being held ~ another week *(will be shown longer).* (4) if the fine weather ~s ~, we'll make our trip.

hold to (1) ~ him to the / our agreement *(force him to keep it)*; ~ him to his promise / oath / part of the bargain / the conditions of the contract (2) ~ to one's choice / course of action / convictions; ~ to an opinion; we decided to ~ to our original plan.

hold together (1) a leader who ~s the team ~ (2) the old coat hardly ~s ~ now.

hold up (1) ~ s.th. up (so everyone can see it); ~ your hand up; props ~ up a tunnel. (2) ~ s.o. up as a good / bad example; ~ s.o. up to ridicule (3) a policeman ~s up traffic; thick fog held up a number of trains; he held up our departure, because he got up late. (4) masked men held up a mail van *(stopped and robbed).* (5) if the weather ~s up, I shall be glad.

hold with I don't ~ ~ such behaviour / giving children a lot of pocket money / that view.

holiday *n* cheap ~s; a continuous / legal / national / paid / unpaid ~; ~s by the sea / at the seaside / in the country / in the mountains / in the sun / abroad; they are on ~ in Capri; go on ~ / on a ~ / on one's ~; go to N. for a ~; have / take a ~; take a month's ~ in summer; take your ~ during the off-peak season; spend one's ~ by the sea / in France; she is away on ~ this week. *(Note: Chiefly BE: a period of rest from work. AE* → vacation *n*).

home *n* (1) a quiet / peaceful / happy / humble / joyless ~; find a new / temporary / permanent ~; make one's ~ in the country; is there anybody at ~? make yourself at ~; I always feel at ~ with Mr N.; I'm never at ~ in a big city; he's quite at ~ with children / mathematics. - *adv* (2) is he ~ yet? they are ~ from their travels; be one one's way ~; go / get (back) / arrive ~; write ~; □ (her cooking) is nothing to write ~ about *(inform: not very good)*; → blow² *n* 1, bring home, drive *vt* 1, strike *vi* 18a.

hope *n* (1) (there is) little / not much ~ for him / a better future / *etc*; a gleam / glimmer / flash / ray of ~; a newborn / slight / faint / well-founded / well-grounded / reasonable / justified ~ (of success / *etc*); ruined ~s; have you any ~? place / put one's ~(s) in s.o./ s.th.; set one's ~s on s.th.; pin one's ~s on s.o. / s.th.; find new ~ (in); give up ~; give s.o. / awaken / raise (new) ~; destroy s.o.'s ~s; (he is) past / beyond ~. (2) you are my last / only ~; he is the ~ of the family.

hope *vi* I ~ to see him tomorrow; he firmly ~d to be elected; ~ for success / to succeed; we were all ~ing for good weather; let us ~ for the best / for better days; they are still ~ing; ~ against ~.

hospital *n* go into ~; be / lie in ~; send s.o. to ~; be admitted to ~ *(Note: AE the ~ in all the phrases).*

hospitality *n* (1) show ~ to s.o.; offer s.o. ~; return s.o.'s (kind / generous / lavish) ~; give s.o. ~ for the night (2) ~ *(free board and lodging)* will be provided.

hostility *n* (1) feelings of ~; receive s.o. with (fierce) ~; show ~ towards s.o.; treat s.o. with (marked) ~ (2) start / cease ~ies; at / with the outbreak / start of ~ies; with / after the cessation of ~.

hot *adj* (1) ~ water / fire / sun / stove; (bake s.th. in) a ~ oven; ~ fever; ~ weather / day / country / climate; blazing / burning / boiling / red ~; I like my food ~; I am / feel ~; ~ kisses / tears; I went ~ under the collar (with embarrassment); □ ~ air *(boasting)*; □ be in / get into ~ water *(inform: trouble)*; make it / a place too ~ for s.o.; give it him ~ *(BE, inform: scold, punish severely)* (2) ~ curry / mustard / pepper (3) a ~ temper; a ~ struggle / battle / chase; ~ war; get ~ over an argument; a ~ issue (4) a ~ trail / scent (of a hare); ~ news; this is ~ off the press(es) / from the press; □ be ~

on the trail (of a discovery); be ~ on s.o.'s tracks / heels; a ~ sales item; a ~ *(slang: fast)* (sports) car (5) ~ *(electric)* wire / rail; □ ~ *(slang: stolen)* money / goods.

hour *n* (1) pay / hire by the ~; walk for ~s (and ~s); the happiest ~s of my life; the small / wee ~s *(after midnight)*; the dead ~ of the night; □ at the eleventh ~ *(almost too late)* (2) strike the ~; come at an early ~; disturb s.o. at all ~s of the day and night (3) school / office / business / working ~s; lunch ~; the news is broadcast on the ~; keep early / good / regular / late / bad ~s; □ after ~s *(of business, etc)* (4) an ~ from here (5) questions of the ~ *(topical ones)*; in the ~ of danger / temptation; in a good / evil ~.

house *n* (1) a habitable / (un)inhabitable / (un)inhabited ~; a ~ inhabited / occupied by (workers / *etc*); a two-storied / five-roomed / pretty little / modest / large / big / enormous / huge / spacious / roomy / commodious ~; a detached / semi-detached / terrace / two-family / self-contained / prefabricated ~; a dilapidated / ramshackle / tumble-down ~; a ~ of worship / God; the H~ of Commons / Representatives; a parliament of two ~s; a ~ of cards *(also fig)*; a ruling ~; have a ~ (with a garden); the ~ is my own; he has a ~ of his own; go to / arrive at / be at one's ~; bring / deliver s.th. to s.o.'s ~; stay in the ~; leave the ~; drive s.o. from / turn s.o. out of ~ and home; keep the ~ *(BE: not go outdoors)* (2) keep ~ *(maintain a household)*; run the ~; keep open ~ *(be hospitable)*; □ set / put one's ~ in order *(put one's affairs straight)* (3) the whole ~ is ill. (4 *theatre*) play to a full / empty ~; bring down the ~ *(win approval)*; this play draws a big ~ *(inform)*. (5 *inn etc*) a speciality of the ~; the drinks are on the ~ *(free)*. (6 *firm*) the ~ of Rothschild; a publishing ~ (→ publish vi 4, 5).

house *vt* ~ a family / guests; ~ furniture / one's books (in an attic); ~ tools in a shed; ~ a yacht for the winter.

humour *n* (1) a story full of ~; good / ill / genuine / unsophisticated / irrepressible / dry ~; have a (good / no / not much) sense of ~; (be) lack(ing) ~; have wit and ~ (2) in a good / bad / ill ~; not in the ~ for work / fighting; in no ~ to be contradicted; (keep away from s.o. who is) out of ~ *(displeased)*; put s.o. in a good ~.

hunger *n* (1) gnawing / unsatisfied ~; feel / suffer (from) / die of ~; I'm dying of ~ *(inform)*; satisfy one's ~; ~ is the best sauce. (2) a ~ for adventure / excitement / money / praise / the Word of God.

hunger *vi* ~ for kindness / love / friends / praise / money; he ~s for her.

hungry *adj* (1) be / feel / get / go / remain ~; leave the table ~; be as ~ as a hunter; work makes one ~. (2) be ~ for love / praise / money / news (3) ~ years; ~ soil.

hunt *vt* (1) ~ (big) game / stags / deer / hares / *etc*; go (out) ~ing; wolves ~ in packs. (2) ~ down a criminal / an escaped prisoner; ~ out s.th. that has been put away; I shall ~ out my old photograph album to show you; ~ up old records / quotations; the police have ~ed up all the rioters (3) ~ a cat out of the garden; ~ s.o. from the village. - *vi* (4) ~ after wealth / happiness; ~ for s.th. lost.

hurl *vt* (1) he ~ed a stone at us / through a window; ~ a spear at a tiger (2) ~ insults / threats / abuse / an accusation at s.o. / into s.o.'s face (3) they ~ed themselves at / upon the enemy.

hurry *n* be (always) in a / in an indecent ~; I'm in a ~ (to leave); in my ~ I forgot it; I'm in no ~ for them to take this matter up; there's no ~ (about it); why all this ~?

hurry *vi* (1) don't ~; there's plenty of time; ~ to work / s.o.'s help; ~ home; ~ off to do s.th.; ~ over a task; ~ up, or we shall be late! - *vt* (2) don't ~ her; if we ~ the work, it may be spoiled; ~ soldiers to the front line; ~ s.o.'s departure; ~ him up!

hurt *vt* (1) tight shoes ~ (me) for weeks; ~ one's foot / back / *etc* (2) ~ a person('s feelings) (with spiteful words); ~ s.o.'s reputation; be deeply ~ (by a remark / criticism / *etc*); she was ~ to find that he had forgotten her birthday. (3) it won't ~ this watch to wear it in water; the bad weather ~ his trade. - *vi* (4 → 1) that bump / my head ~s; does your hand ~? (5 → 3) it won't ~ to postpone the matter for a few days.

husband *vt* ~ one's monthly allowance; ~ one's strength / resources / supplies / financial means.

hush *vt* (1) ~ the baby to sleep (2) ~ up an unpleasant fact / a scandal / *etc*. - *vi* (3) he asked me to ~ *(be silent)* during the music.

I

ice *n* the permanent ~ at the poles; ~ covers a lake / river; ~ drifts / floats downstream; the ~ doesn't bear yet; ~ melts / thaws / cracks / breaks; □ break the ~ *(overcome formality)*; □ cut no ~ *(have no effect)*; □ be / skate / tread on thin ~ *(be in a delicate situation)* (2) put food / drink on ~ (3) two (vanilla) ~s, please!

ice *vt* ~ drinks; ~ cakes; the pond was ~d over.

idea *n* (1) the realm of ~s; a general / special / old / new / precise / vague / common-sense / sound / magnificent / noble / bright / capital / excellent / productive / fancy / fanciful / crazy / mad / insane / lunatic / false / erroneous / silly / childish / muddy / peculiar / elusive ~; the main / central ~ (of a book / *etc*); be obsessed / possessed with a fixed / dismal / gloomy ~; have / form / conceive / hit upon / strike upon an ~; it was a good ~ of yours to (come here); I suddenly had the ~ that he ...; I don't want him to get the ~ that he ...; what gave you / how did you get that ~? the book gives you a good ~ of (life in Russia); put ~s into s.o.'s head; □ get ~s into one's head *(have unrealistic hopes)*; what's the big ~ *(inform: threatening request to justify one's words or actions)*? whose bright ~ was that *(inform: ironic)*? (2 *plan*) have you any ~s for the future? that man is full of new ~s. (3 *knowledge*) I have no ~ who is coming; I haven't the remotest / slightest / *(inform)* foggiest ~. (4 *opinion*) force one's ~s on other people.

idle *adj* (1) they are ~ because they haven't found employment; the machines in the factory are ~ at present; spend many ~ hours during the holidays (2 *useless*) ~ gossip / tales / talk / wishes / threats / fears; an ~ jest / rumour / protest; it's ~ to expect help from him.

ignore *vt* ~ s.o.('s existence); ~ s.o.'s advice / an objection / an order / *etc*; he ~d their presence; ~ those threats!

ill *adj/adv* (1) ~ health / omen / management / success; ~ will (to / towards s.o.); s.o.'s ~ advice; in an ~ temper / humour; have / meet with / experience ~ luck; do s.o. an ~ turn; take s.th. ~; you must not take it ~ of him; it ~ becomes him to criticize; speak ~ of s.o.; he can ~ afford (to do that); behave ~; □ ~ at ease *(uneasy)*; □ it's an ~ wind that blows nobody any good. (2) be / fall / look ~; be taken ~ with (a disease); he is ~ with fever / measles / age / worry / anxiety; he is lying ~ in bed / in bed ~; she was more ~ than we thought; be seriously / gravely / critically / dangerously ~; mentally ~.

illness *n* (1) he was suddenly seized with ~; be absent (from work) because of ~; there is not much ~ in the village this summer. (2) a long / short / slight / serious / fatal / terminal / physical / mental / *etc* ~; a children's ~; have / be suffering from an ~; he was suddenly seized with a (severe / *etc*) illness; recover from / get over an ~; inherit an ~ from s.o.

imagination *n* a fertile / creative / lively / vivid / strong / luxuriant / weak / poor / erratic ~; her illness is pure ~; see s.th. in one's ~; his ~ led him to believe he ...; give (free) rein to one's ~; the success surpasses all ~; with a little ~ you will find a way.

imagine *vt* (1) I can well ~ that; we had not ~d it to be so difficult; can you ~ their doing such a thing? he can't ~ why she ...; ~ his surprise! I ~ he will resign. (2) he ~s himself to be a millionaire; I ~d I heard a knock; do not ~ that I am satisfied.

immediate *adj* (1) an ~ answer / reply; the ~ cause of his trouble was (lack of money); take ~ action / steps; we have no ~ plans; in the ~ future (2) in ~ contact; has no ~ connection with; my ~ neighbour; one's ~ family includes parents, brothers and sisters; the / his / one's ~ successor (in an office / to the throne / *etc*).

imply *vt* (1) good drama ~ies conflict; great achievements ~ much effort. (2) his tone ~ied evil intentions; sometimes a mere gesture can ~ haughtiness; do you mean to ~ that I am not as good as you are? did he ~ anything interesting?

importance *n* the matter is of (great / prime / the utmost / little / not much) ~ (to us); it is of slight / no great ~ that he ...; a book of ~; speak with an air of ~; to attach ~ to s.th.; increase in ~.

impose *vt* (1) ~ duties (on goods) / a tax (on tobacco) / a fine (on s.o.); ~ a task / certain conditions / silence / obedience /

restrictions on s.o.; ~ (up)on s.o. the duty of doing s.th. (2) ~ o.s. / one's company on others; ~ one's advice on s.o. - *vi* (3) ~ (up)on s.o.'s good nature; I won't ~ on you by asking too many favours.

impression *n* (1) give a bad / unfavourable ~; make a good / bad ~ (on s.o.); the speech made a strong / deep / lasting ~ on us; he gave (us) the ~ of a very worried man; he doesn't make a very adult ~; what ~ did it make on him? what ~ did you have of her? be under a (right / wrong) ~ (that ...); leave an ~ on s.o.; leave s.o. with an ~ (2 *vague idea*) I have the ~ that he ...; it's my ~ that he ...

improve *vt* (1) ~ a situation / conditions / s.o.'s health / character / the soil; this is not good enough: I want to ~ it. - *vi* (2) business / the situation / his financial position is ~ing / has ~d; this year's sales have ~d 10% over last year's; his health is ~ing; he is ~ing in health; I found him much ~d (in health); ~ in (one's) Latin (3) you can ~ on *(do better than)* your last effort.

improvement *n* there has been a (gradual / marked / decided / distinct) ~; his condition continues to show ~; an ~ in the weather / in doing s.th. / in one's work / in health; this is an ~ on your previous efforts; the second edition of the dictionary is a great ~ over the first; the road is a (great) ~ on the old one; make ~s on one's house / property / *etc.*

impulse *n* (1) give an ~ to trade / education / *etc* (2) he bought the car on (an) ~; act on (an) ~; be ruled by ~; seized with / feel an (irresistible) ~ to do s.th.; give s.o / get / receive an ~; a man of ~.

inaugurate *vt* (1) ~ a professor / president / *etc* (2) ~ a new system / a new custom / a policy; the invention of the motor-car ~d a new era in travel. (3) ~ an exhibition / a new building / *etc.*

inch *n* 32 ~es of rain fell last year; convert ~es into centimetres; □ (the car missed me) by ~es; □ (advance) ~ by ~; □ (he) is every ~ (a gentleman / a soldier / *etc*); □ (they did) not yield / *(inform)* budge an ~; □ he came within an ~ of (succeeding / being struck by a stone); □ give him an ~ and he'll take an ell *(BE)* / a mile.

inclination *n* (1) an ~ of the head / body; the ~ of the roof (2) have / show / evince a (strong / great / decided) ~ for s.th. / to do s.th.; follow an ~ / one's own ~s; sacrifice ~ to duty; he has an ~ to stoutness / to grow fat; his present ~s are towards a singing career.

incline *vi* (1) italic type ~s to the right. (2) he ~s to leanness / towards s.o.'s view. - *vt* (3) ~ one's ear to s.o.; ~ the head in prayer (4) be ~d to agree with s.o. / believe that he ... / do s.th.; his letter ~s me to believe that he ...; he's ~d to be lazy; feel ~d for a walk.

include *vt* breakfast is not ~d in the price; price ~ing postage and package; does my work ~ running errands for the others? please ~ me on your list.

income *n* ~ and expenditure; source of ~; ~ from capital / work / investment; have a (good / large / big / enormous / huge / fair / small / slender / meagre / decent / moderate / medium / average) ~; real / settled / fixed / regular / steady ~; live within one's ~.

increase *vt* (1) ~ prices / taxes / the production / *etc*; ~ s.o.'s wages / salary; ~ s.o.'s pleasure / beauty / interest (in s.th.); ~ one's knowledge / efforts / power / influence; the driver ~d speed. - *vi* (2) prices / taxes / wages ~; production / speed ~s; s.o.'s skill ~s with practice; the population has ~d by 10,000 to 87,000; our difficulties are ~ing; ~ in number / quality / pricc / intensity / size / power.

incur *vt* ~ debts / great expense / a loss / heavy losses / an injury; ~ s.o.'s anger / displeasure / hatred; ~ blame / a great danger.

indicate *vt* (1) his symptoms ~ mumps; soft teeth ~ a lack of proper diet; all this ~s danger. (2) ~ s.th. on a map (with one's finger); he ~d a mistake to me; a signpost ~s the road. (3) ~ one's choice / consent / *etc*; ~ the reason why ...; ~ what you think about this. (4) a case in which the following treatment is ~d; strong measures were clearly ~d.

induce *vt* (1) what ~d you to do that? (2) illness ~d by overwork; ~ sleep / labour (by means of pills) (3) when you see a great man, you can ~ a great mother.

indulge *vt* (1) ~ a (sick) child; the family ~d the girl's every whim; ~ a liking for sweets; opportunities to ~ almost any taste of the visitors; ~ one's fancy; can lung cancer be cured so that smokers may ~ their habit without risks? is betting a pastime to be ~d? ~ o.s. with wine; he ~s (himself) in the luxury of a good cigar. - *vi* (2) ~ in a habit / hobby; he seldom ~ s in a holiday / a cigar / cycling / day-dreaming / strong language.

infer *vt* ~ an unknown fact from a known fact; from his appearance I ~ red he was poor; it can be ~ red from this assumption that ...

inflict *vt* (1) ~ a wound / blow on s.o.; ~ pain / suffering / cruelties on s.o.; ~ casualties; ~ a punishment / penalty / the death penalty on s.o. (2) ~ one's views on s.o.; he ~ s his troubles on everyone; ~ o.s. / one's company on s.o.

influence *n* (1) have / exercise a (good / favourable / beneficial / decisive / bad / dangerous) ~ on / over s.o., s.th.; exert an ~ over / on s.o.; bring (every) ~ to bear on s.o.; use one's ~ (in favour of / to the disadvantage of s.o.); be under the ~ of s.o.; be under the ~ of drink / alcohol; a man of ~; his ~ makes itself felt / prevails / dominates. (2) he is an ~ for good in the town. (3) the ~ of the moon (on the tides) / of climate (on vegetation).

information *n* fresh / first-hand / alarming / incredible / inside / confidential ~; (further) ~ on application; for (further) ~ apply to ...; according to the latest ~; seek ~ about s.th. (from s.o.); ask for (detailed) ~; get / gather / collect / pick up / give / furnish / impart / receive / obtain ~ (about s.th.); do you have any ~ on taxes?

infringe *vt/i* ~ (upon) a law / rule / copyright (regulations) / trade-mark / civil liberties; ~ upon s.o.'s rights.

ingratiate *vt* he ~ d himself with the boss by flattery; the little puppy quickly ~ d itself with Mary; with an ~ ing smile.

inhibit *vt* these early experiences ~ ed his adult development; she feels very ~ ed because of her stammer; she is an ~ ed person; ~ wrong desires and impulses.

initiate *vt* (1) ~ a plan / programme / reform / investigation / the proposed legislation (2) ~ s.o. into a secret society (3) ~ s.o. into a mystery / the mysteries of (grammar).

injure *vt* (1) ~ s.o.'s eye / face / leg / health / *etc*; be ~ d in an accident; fruit-trees ~ d by frost; houses ~ d by the storm; this tax will ~ local enterprise / all business. (2) ~ s.o.'s reputation / feelings / pride / chances / prospects / authority; ~ a friendship by resentment. - *adj* (3) in an ~ d voice; ~ d looks.

inquire *vt* (1) ~ s.o.'s name / the reason / what s.o. wants / where to go / how to do it (2) ~ about the price / s.o.'s health / progress / the train to N.; ~ after s.o.'s health / welfare; ~ for a letter at the post office / for a book in a shop / for the manager; ~ into (the cause of) a matter / the present conditions in Germany; ~ of s.o. the reason for s.th. / of s.o. which way one should take. - *adj* (3) an ~ ing look / glance; an ~ ing (turn of) mind.

insert *vt* ~ a key in a lock / a coin in a slot / the paper into the typewriter; ~ a new pane of glass; ~ an advertisement in a newspaper / a new paragraph in an essay / a clause in(to) a contract.

insight *n* get / gain a (new / deeper) ~ into a problem / human character / a mystery; give / afford / grant s.o. an ~ into s.th.; it gave us fresh ~ s into the difficulties to be faced; these tests have given scientists astonishing new ~ s into the mysteries of sleep; a man of (great) ~.

insist *vi* (1) ~ on the importance of (being punctual); if you ~, you will only make him angry. (2) ~ on one's innocence / the fact that one is innocent; he ~ s on driving her home. (3) ~ on one's rights / an immediate answer / being paid at once; I ~ on (his) being there / (on it) that he shall be there; don't agree unless he ~ s. - *vt* (4) he ~ s that he saw a flying saucer. (5) he ~ s that you apologize.

inspire *vt* (1) honesty ~ s respect / admiration (in us); ~ s.o. with a thought / a feeling / a principle / courage / hope / confidence / enthusiasm / fear; ~ a thought / a feeling / *etc* in(to) s.o.; the Scripture was ~ d by the Holy Ghost; the prophets were ~ d by God; his guardian angel must have ~ d him to stay at home that day. (2) the article was ~ d by a member of the government. - *adj* (3) an ~ d poet / artist / preacher; in an ~ d moment.

install *vt* (1) ~ plumbing / wiring / electricity / heating / a lighting system / a bath / a boiler / a machine / an engine (in a car / an aircraft) (2) ~ s.o. in an office; ~ a bishop / dean; ~ s.o. as president / bishop / dean (3) the cat ~ ed itself near the fire / he has got himself ~ ed in a nice little flat; be comfortably ~ ed in a new home.

institute *vt* (1) ~ an inquiry / a search for ... / legal proceedings against s.o. / an action at law; ~ an (entrance) examination / a new diploma / a law / a tax / an office; to secure these rights, governments are ~d among men. (2) ~ s.o. to / into a benefice.

instruct *vt* (1) ~ a class (in history / swimming) (2) ~ one's lawyer to make an inquiry; he ~ed the clerk to do it at once / when to leave / how to do it; the police have been ~ed to take measures. (3) the judge ~ed the jury (about procedure); I have been ~ed by my agent that you still owe me £20.

instruction *n* (1) give / receive ~ in (chemistry / foreign languages / *etc*); get one's ~ at home (2) the ~s are on the bottle; give s.o. / receive ~s to arrive early / how to use the device; read the ~s first; have (distinct / strict / precise / secret) ~s to do s.th.; take ~s from s.o.; await further ~s; under ~s from the Town Council.

insult *n* to call a brave man a coward is an ~; fling an ~ in s.o.'s face; take / swallow / suffer / put up with a (deliberate) ~; add ~ to injury; give s.o. / demand satisfaction for an ~.

insult *vt* (1) ~ s.o. with words; his impertinences ~ed his sister's guests. - *adj* (2) he became ~ing in his language; use ~ing language.

insure *vt/i* (1) ~ (one's home) against fire; ~ against theft / accident / *etc*; ~ o.s. / one's life for £2,000 (2) the insurance company ~d his property for £10,000. (3 *AE*) → ensure *vt, vi.*

integrate *vt* (1) ~ studies with athletics in the school day; the course of teaching at K. has been planned to ~ and relate subjects from each of three main groups; in our ~d society the prosperity of each group is dependent on that of every other; ~ the members of a team; an ~d personality (2) immigrants are quickly ~d into the community.

intend *vt* (1) what do you ~ doing / to do today? we ~ them to do it; he ~ed no harm; the ~ed effect (2) this gift is ~ed for you; his remark was ~ed for me; he has ~ed his son / his son is ~ed for the medical profession; is this sketch ~ed to be me? this money is ~ed for a new carpet; a boat ~ed for river traffic. - *vi* (3) what do you ~ by this word?

intense *adj* (1) ~ heat / pain / excitement / strain / desire / disgust; an ~ storm (2) an ~ person *(having strong feelings)* (3) an ~ life *(ardent, strenuous).*

intensive *adj* (1) an ~ programme / search; ~ preparations; an ~ development; make an ~ study of a subject (2) ~ bombardment; ~ (methods of) agriculture / horticulture.

intention *n* have good / honourable / serious ~s (of doing s.th.); have you any ~ of going there? what is the ~ behind this question? I had every ~ of writing, but ... ; I haven't the least / slightest ~ of coming; he has no ~ of marrying her; if I did it, it was quite without ~; his ~s are good, but he seldom carries them out.

interchange *vt* ~ gifts / letters / opinions / ideas / commodities; ~ front and rear car tyres.

interest *n* (1) have a (lively / passionate / warm / maternal / womanly / *etc*) ~ in s.th.; rouse / arouse / awaken (great / strong / keen / intense / *etc*) ~ for s.th. in s.o.; common ~s; secular ~s; feel / take no, not much, a great ~ in politics; rouse s.o.'s ~ in a plan (2) suspense / local colour adds ~ to a story / novel. (3) fashion is her main / chief ~; his two great ~s in life are music and painting; intellectual ~; golf is one of my father's outside ~s. (4 *importance*) a matter of (considerable / not much) ~ (to the community); problems of ~ to the public / of public ~; it has no ~ for me; a subject of perennial ~ (5 *advantage, profit*) act in s.o.'s / one's own ~(s); look after / protect / safeguard s.o.'s ~s; look after one's own ~s; work in the ~(s) of humanity; travel in Asia in the ~s of a British firm; it is to / in your ~ to do it; it is / lies in your own ~ to go there. (6) have an ~ in a firm / an estate.

interfere *vi* (1) the pillar ~s with the view; absence ~s with school work; allow pleasure to ~ with duty; ~ with a machine; a tight arm band will ~ with circulation of the blood. (2) this does not concern you, so don't ~; I don't like to be ~d with; ~ in other people's affairs; the police refused to ~ (in this matter); ~ in a debate; ~ between husband and wife.

interrupt *vt* (1) ~ a speaker / conversation / process / series; ~ s.o.'s sleep; the remark ~ed his flow of thought; don't ~ (me) when I'm busy; bad weather ~ed air travel for a few days; traffic was ~ed by floods. (2) that house ~s our view of the lake.

interval *n* (1) after a brief ~ the programme continued; (irregular) ~s of sanity; wake up at ~s through the night (2) the ~ between the two lawns was filled with flowers; buildings placed at wide ~s; camping grounds at ~s along the road.

intervene *vi* (1) the years that ~ between elementary school and university are very important; the ~ing days seemed years. (2) if nothing (unexpected) ~s, we shall go as planned. (3) ~ in a dispute / between people who are quarrelling; the argument continued until Father ~d; it is about time that the police ~d (in this matter).

introduce *vt* (1) I was ~d to Mr N. / (in)to his family / to society; he ~ed her to all his friends. (2) ~ new fashions / a new subject (for discussion) / a new custom / new books (into all the schools) (3) ~ s.o. to work / a process / a science / an office (4) a short overture ~d the opera; ~ a new epoch (5) ~ a catheter into the bladder.

intrude *vt* (1) ~ one's opinion / view upon others / into the conversation; a strange thought ~ed (itself) into my mind. (2) ~ (o.s.) into a meeting / s.o.'s. company. - *vi* (3) ~ upon s.o.'s privacy / time (4) a loud crash ~d on the silence of the night.

invade *vt* (1) ~ a country (and conquer it) (2) a town ~d by tourists; swarms of children ~d the swimming pool. (3) sounds / diseases / feelings ~ s.o.; a mind ~d by worry and anxiety (4) ~ s.o. else's rights / s.o.'s privacy. - *vi* (5) the enemy ~d from the north.

invent *vt* (1) Watt ~ed the steam engine; ~ a new device / method / machine / contrivance (2) ~ a story / an excuse / calumnies about s.o.; what explanation can we ~? it is an ~ed story.

invest *vt* (1) ~ capital / money in government stock; ~ one's savings in a firm (2) the new bishop will be ~ed tomorrow. (3) the bishop was ~ed with ring and staff; ~ s.o. with an office / a dignity / full authority / the right to vote (4) ~ed with an air of mystery / romance; he ~ed his hero with the virtues of a god. - *vi* (5 → 1) ~ in *(inform: buy)* a new hat.

investigate *vt* ~ terrain / a cave; ~ a case / crime / the cause of (an accident) / the state of public opinion; the FBI ~s every applicant for federal employment.

invite *vt* (1) ~ a friend to tea / lunch / dinner; ~ s.o. to one's house / a banquet; ~ s.o. to come closer / attend a meeting / say a few words (about s.th.); the cool water of the lake ~d us to swim. (2) ~ applications for a post; ~ (s.o.'s) comments / opinions / questions; your suggestions are ~d; a good performance ~s applause. (3) this unrestricted freedom ~s abuse; thus he ~d trouble / mockery / new difficulties. (4) he didn't ~ me in; we have been ~d out to John's house tonight.

invoke *vt* (1) ~ God's blessing / the gods; ~ a genie / evil spirits (2) ~ the power / protection of the law; ~ s.o.'s aid / s.th. as a proof; ~ vengeance on one's enemies; ~ emergency measures.

involve *vt* (1) success always ~s effort / hard work; this job ~s little work; a chance which ~s risk; metrication ~s the complete reorganization of British industry. (2) this problem ~s us all; be ~ed in one's work; be (deeply) ~d in a scandal / in a fight with s.o. / in debt; don't ~ yourself in unnecessary expense.

iron *n* (1a) malleable / wrought / cast ~ (1b) a waffle / soldering / electric ~ (2) a man of ~; rule with a rod of ~; have other / (too) many ~s in the fire; strike while the ~ is hot. - *adj* (3) an ~ will / hand / constitution; rule with an ~ hand.

iron *vt* (1) ~ clothes / a shirt / the washing; ~ out wrinkles (2) ~ out difficulties / misunderstandings / problems / points of disagreement.

irritate *vt* (1) soap can ~ a baby's skin; the smoke ~d my eyes; ~ the stomach / nerves (2) the noise / laughter ~d him; I'm very ~d about it / by the delay.

issue *n* (1) the point / place of ~; an ~ of blood from the nose / a wound; land buried under the ~ from a volcano (2) the ~ of a new coinage / a newspaper; buy new stamps on the day of (their) ~ (3) new ~s of bank-notes / stamps; the most recent ~ of a periodical; the ~ of *the Times* for Monday (4 *problem*) derbate an ~; raise a new ~; argue political / controversial ~s; the point / matter at ~ *(under discussion)*; those are the basic questions at ~; take / join ~ with s.o. on / over s.th. *(disagree, argue)* (5 *result*) what was the final ~ of the problem? bring a campaign to a successful ~; await the ~; a problem that involves important ~s.

issue *vt* (1) ~ (winter) clothing to troops; ~ ammunition to the police; ~ the police with ammunition (2) ~ bank-notes / stamps / shares / a book / a newspaper /

a magazine (every month) / a new coinage; ~ a ticket / passport / decree / regulation / proclamation / command. – *vi* (3) smoke ~s from the chimneys; blood ~s from a wound; water / steam / gas ~s (forth) (from a pipe).

J

jail *n* (1) go to ~; break ~ *(escape from it)* (2 *imprisonment*) he was sentenced to ~ for 30 days; be kept in ~ until...

jam *n* (1) a traffic ~ (2) *(inform)* be in / get into a ~; like most boys I used to get into ~s and then run to my mother for help.

jam *vt* (1) he ~med his finger in a car door; get one's fingers ~med in the door / between two logs; the drawer is ~med. (2) a thread ~med the sewing-machine; ~ the brakes on; the parade ~med traffic all over town. (3) she ~med all her clothes into a small suitcase; he ~med four apples in his pocket; the corridors were ~med by hordes of schoolchildren; 7 million refugees have been ~med into the overcrowded area; he ~med his hat on his head. (4) ~ the enemy's broadcasts / radio stations; a ~ming station. – *vi* (5 → 1) a ship ~med in the ice. (6 → 2) the brakes ~med and the car skidded badly; the rifle ~med when he tried to fire it.

jealous *adj* (1) be ~ of s.o. / of s.o.'s success; a ~ husband / wife; ~ acts / looks (2) keep a ~ eye on s.o.; be ~ of one's rights; guard one's rights ~ly.

jealousy *n* ~ seized him / took possession of him; feel / arouse (groundless / unfounded / wild) ~; his constant ~; tired of all these ~ies and quarrels; he killed her in a fit of ~; show great ~ of s.o.'s success.

jeer *vt* (1) only poor sports ~ the losing team; they ~ed the umpire's decision; he ~ed his opponent when he tried to speak; 'you're a coward', she ~ed. – *vi* (2) ~ at a defeated enemy / an idea.

jerk *vt* (1) don't try to ~ the tablecloth from under the dishes; he ~ed the fish out of the water. (2) don't ~ your words: try to recite more smoothly. – *vi* (3) the train ~ed along / ~ed to a (sudden) stop.

jingle *vi* (1) a small bell ~s; coins ~d in his trouser pocket. – *vt* (2) he ~d the bells; he ~d his keys / the money in his pocket.

job *n* (1) a vacant / temporary / spare-time / permanent / full-time / slavish / tedious / rush / plum ~; she has a ~ as a translator; be out of a ~; look out for / apply for / find / lose a ~; □ be on the ~ *(inform: be at one's work; pay attention to what one is supposed to do)*; keep on the ~ until you've finished; it's time to get back on the ~; □ lie down on the ~ *(inform: neglect one's duties)*: Jones got fired for always lying down on the ~. (2) you can wash my car: I'll give you fifty pence if you make a good ~ of it; your new car is a lovely ~; be paid by the ~; this is not my ~ to do. (3) □ a good / bad ~ *(fortunate / unfortunate state of affairs)*; → best *n* 1; give s.th. up as a bad ~. (4 *inform: difficult task*) it's a ~ for a poor man to keep his wife and children decently dressed; she was all wound up, and we had a ~ to get a coherent story out of her.

join *vt* (1) ~ one thing to another; ~ several things / pieces together; ~ two rivers by a canal; ~ an island to the mainland with a bridge; ~ two persons in marriage; which rivers ~ the Danube at Passau? □ ~ battle *(begin fighting)*; □ ~ forces (with s.o.); □ ~ hands *(also fig)* (2) the U.S.A. ~s Canada along an immense frontier. (3) ~ the Boy Scouts / a club / a party / the Army (4) will you ~ us / our party? ~ s.o. in a walk / on his way / for dinner; may I ~ (you) in the game? – *vi* (5) parallel lines never ~; the roads ~ here.

join in the organist plays well-known tunes and sometimes the audience ~s ~.

join in with I decided to ~ ~ ~ them when they said they were going to buy a yacht.

join up he wanted to ~ ~ and fight for his country.

join with will you ~ ~ me in buying a present for her?

joke *n* (1) make a (good / funny / standing / harmless / stale / threadbare / feeble / silly) ~ about s.o./s.th.; have a ~ with s.o.; play a ~ on s.o.; fail to see / miss (the point of) a ~; □ (it was said / done) only in ~; a practical ~ *(to make s.o. appear ridiculous)* (2) he treated the rule as a ~; paying for this will be no ~; it's beyond a ~ *(rather serious).*

journey *n* a pleasant / tiring / tiresome / monotonous / *etc* ~; a ~ home / abroad / there and back; a four days' ~; a ~ of four days; the ~ takes ten hours; how much is the ~? go / come / send s.o. on a ~; make a ~ (round the world/ through Europe / across Russia); we wish you a pleasant ~; a sentimental ~ *(reverie).*

joy *n* there was great ~ everywhere; heartfelt / exquisite / sincere / intense / unutterable / everlasting ~; passing ~s; feel / show ~; he found great ~ in his children; they danced / jumped / wept for ~; be beside o.s. with ~; in ~ and in sorrow; to my great ~ she consented; her thoughtfulness is a ~ to her mother; it was a real ~ to watch him work; the ~s of homelife.

judge *vt* (1) God will ~ all men; ~ a contest / competition; who is going to ~ the roses at the Flower Show? (2) we ~d his story to be true; we ~d it better to postpone the matter; I can't ~ whether he was right or wrong / how much longer that will last; it is for you to ~; ~ (s.o.'s) character; ~ distances (3) don't ~ people too harshly; ~ s.o., s.th. fairly / correctly / rightly / harshly / severely / *etc*; don't ~ him by his appearance, but by his actions; ~ing from her looks she isn't under forty.

judgement *n* (1) sit in ~ on s.o. / a case; give / pass / render ~ on s.o.; concerned with bringing the past to ~; error of ~; the ~ of a criminal (2 *decision*) the ~ was in John's favour; ~ was given for the plaintiff, who was awarded £2,000 damages; a deliberate / just / unjust / hard / lenient ~; a snap *(hasty)* ~; make hasty ~s (3 *ability to judge*) a man of ~; show good / excellent / unfailing / poor ~ in doing s.th.; use one's best ~; he acted with ~. (4 *punishment*) people often think their troubles are a ~ for their sins. (5 *opinion*) in my ~ he is wrong; I leave it to your ~; in the ~ of most people he is the best.

juggle *vt* (1) the clown ~d three oranges and a lemon; he ~d the figures to make the company seem prosperous; ~ s.o. out of his money. – *vi* (3) ~ with balls (4) ~ with words / facts / figures.

jump *n* (1) a high ~ off a diving board; the long / high ~; □ be one ~ ahead *(through cleverness)*; □ get / have a ~ on s.o. *(inform: have a head start on him)*: we'll never catch him, he's got a big ~ on us. (2) the baby gave a startled ~ at the loud noise; give s.o. a ~ *(frighten)*; □ be all of a ~ *(very nervous)*; □ on the ~ *(AE, inform: very busy; on the go)*: you'll never reach him on the phone - he's always on the ~; I can't stay long - I'm just here on the ~; her lively youngsters keep her on the ~. (3) a ~ in temperature / exports; prices went up with a ~.

jump *vi* (1) the dog ~ed at the car; ~ into / out of a taxi; ~ over a puddle / hurdle / fence; ~ out of one's chair; ~ up (from one's chair); ~ up and down in excitement; ~ ahead *(move rapidly ahead, passing others)*; ~ at an offer / chance / opportunity / suggestion *accept eagerly)*; □ ~ down s.o.'s throat *(reprimand severely)*; ~ into a situation / undertaking *(enter it rashly, enthusiastically)*; ~ on an inattentive pupil *(by suddenly asking a question)*; they ~ed on her every time s.th. went wrong; □ ~ out of one's skin *(with surprise)*; □ ~ to conclusions *(conclude rashly)*; □ ~ to the mind; these are names which ~ to the mind (2) she ~ed in fright at the strange sound; ~ for joy; my heart ~ed when I heard the news. (3) the conversation ~ed from one subject to another; the price of wheat just ~ed 3 cents on the bushel. - *vt* (4) ~ a ditch / gate / *etc*; ~ a horse over a hurdle; the train ~ed the rails / track; ~ a class / year (at school); □ ~ a train *(travel illegally)*; □ ~ the queue *(not wait for one's turn)*; □ ~ the gun *(inform: start too soon)* (5) ~ a claim (→ claim *n* 3).

justice *n* (1) divine ~; do / dispense / find / meet with ~; grant s.o. ~; treat s.o. with / do s.o. ~; use ~ even in dealing with one's enemies; he complained with ~ that he ...; to do him ~, we must admit that his intentions were good; no painting can do ~ to her beauty / her beauty ~; do ~ to an occasion / a meal *(show one's appreciation)*; you're not doing yourself ~ *(you could do much better if you tried).* (2) a court of ~; bring a criminal to ~; administer ~; legal / punitive / social ~; an act of ~; let ~ take its course.

justify *vt* (1) nothing can ~ such conduct; how do you ~ your absence? it would be difficult to ~ him; he ~ies sending his son to Eton on the ground that ... (2) the fact that you are my son doesn't ~ your taking my car without asking; this would ~ the Government doing what they are not ~ied in doing at the moment.

K

keen *adj* (1) (a knife with) a ~ edge; a ~ knife; ~ *(cold)* air; ~ *(cutting)* wind; ~ rays (of the sun) (2) ~ interest / feelings / pangs / hunger / appetite / desire / competition (3) ~ sight / eyes / hearing; a ~ mind / intellect / intelligence / wit / critic / sarcasm / irony (4) a ~ golfer / sportsman / pupil; he is very ~ to (see Paris); be ~ as mustard.

keen on be ~ on music / sport / camping; ~ on going abroad / money-making / *etc*; not ~ on cooking / going to this party; he is ~ on (Tom's marrying) her.

keep *vt* 1 - 11; *vi* 12, 13.
The patterns are grouped as follows: ~ + *adj*: 13; ~ + *obj* + *adj*: 8b; ~ + *obj* + *adv phrase*: 8a; ~ + *obj* + *past part:* 8a, 8b; ~ + *obj* + *present part:* 8c; ~ + *obj* + *predicative complement*: 8b; ~ + *present part*: 12; ~ + *prepos*: → separate entries.
(1 *continue to have in one's possession*)
you may ~ this - I don't want it back; he always ~s old letters; ~ records on file; we'll ~ that for the future / for later on / for a rainy day; may I ~ the money? ~ hold of s.th.; ~ goal / wicket.
(2 *continue to have in a certain place*)
~ one's hands in one's pockets; he kept his bicycle in the cellar; the cold weather kept us indoors.
(3 *prevent from leaving*)
~ s.o. in prison / custody; extra work kept me at the office until 10 o'clock; I won't ~ you long; don't let me ~ you.
(4 *remain in a place*)
~ one's bed / room / the house *(through illness)*; ~ one's feet *(not fall, e.g. on ice)*; ~ one's seat *(on a horse)*; ~ the saddle; ~ one's ground / footing *(against opposition)*; ~ the right side of him (and you will ~ clear of trouble).
(5 *provide what is necessary for; support*)
he earns enough to ~ him / his family; he has a wife and three children to ~; ~ a maid / servants; her father pays for her rent and board, but she ~s herself in clothes.
(6 *own and manage, raise, run, etc*)
~ a school / shop (→ shop 1) / inn; ~ sheep / poultry / bees / pets; ~ boarders / a mistress / a car; the shop doesn't ~ what we want; ~ a supply of (certain articles); ~ house; □ ~ open house *(entertain all comers)*; □ ~ a good table.
(7 *manage, make regular entries in*)
~ a diary; ~ an account; ~ the accounts / books.
(8 *maintain*)
(8a *chiefly keep + object + adverbial phrase*) ~ a house in good repair; ~ a, one's car / the streets in good condition, under control; ~ these things out of the way; ~ s.o. in steady employment; she kept her little brother out of mischief; ~ o.s. aloof; ~ s.th. within limits / bounds; ~ s.th. in one's head / in mind / in remembrance / in view; ~ s.th. under one's hat *(inform: hold it secret)*; ~ s.o. in a good mood; ~ s.o. abreast of the news; □ ~ s.o. in the dark (about s.th.); □ ~ body and soul together; □ ~ an eye on s.o.; □ ~ one's fingers crossed *(to bring good luck)*; □ ~ one's head above water *(stay out of debt)*; □ ~ one's mouth shut; □ ~ one's nose to the grindstone; □ ~ one's nose out of s.o. else's affairs; □ ~ fear at bay; □ ~ the wolf from the door *(ward off extreme poverty)*.
(8b *keep + object + adjective, past participle, noun*) ~ s.th. dry / clean / moist / *etc*; these goods must be kept cool and dry; woollens ~ one warm; ~ o.s. warm; ~ one's hair short; ~ the door open / shut / locked; ~ s.o. alive; ~ the children quiet / occupied; that will ~ you busy for some time; that ~s you young; ~ one's eyes open *(also fig)*; ~ one's eyes glued to the TV set; ~ s.o. informed (about s.th.); ~ s.th. (a strict) secret.
(8c *keep + object + present participle*) they kept me / I was kept waiting, standing in the rain; ~ the fire burning; try to ~ him working; will £20 ~ you going until payday? it has always been British policy to ~ the other powers guessing; □ ~ the ball rolling *(keep the conversation / work / etc going)*; □ ~ the pot boiling *(earn enough money to buy food)*
(8d *not lose, not give up; with abstract ob-*

ject) does the pot ~ heat well? ~ one's figure / looks; s.th. ~s its colour / shape; ~ a clear head; ~ one's balance / head / dignity / composure / countenance / temper; he kept his wits during the accident; ~ order (and discipline) / silence / the peace; ~ the upper hand; ~ one's illusions / innocence; ~ a straight face *(not smile)*; ~ good / bad / doubtful company; he stayed at home to ~ his wife company; he prefers to ~ company with foreign girls (→ company 1); ~ a tight / loose rein on s.o./s.th. (→ rein 2); ~ a good / sharp / pour look-out; ~ watch (→ watch *n* 1, 2).

(9 *continue to follow*)
~ one's way / course; while that big lorry ~s the middle of the road we can't get past it; □ ~ track of (current events).

(10 *fulfil, not break*)
~ a / one's promise / the law / a treaty / an appointment / one's word / a secret / faith; □ ~ one's counsel *(keep one's views, plans secret)*; ~ pace / step (with s.o.); ~ time *(of watch, music)*; my watch usually ~s very good time; he never ~s time when we play together; ~ good / bad / early / late hours.

(11 *observe, celebrate*)
~ Christmas / the Sabbath / one's birthday.

- *vi* (12 *keep + present participle: continue doing, do repeatedly*)
~ smiling / hoping / moving / pedalling; he kept coughing; s.o. ~s slamming the door; I ~ thinking I can hear someone in the next room; □ ~ going *(continue doing s.th.; continue to live)*; although ill and exhausted he kept going; the whisky helped him to ~ going.

(13 *keep + adjective, adverbial phrase or absolute: remain in a certain condition*)
~ quiet / calm / friendly / silent / mum / fit / well / cheerful / sober / young (by swimming) / in good health / *etc*; the weather will ~ fine; I could not ~ awake; ~ clear of (alcohol); the fruit is ripe now but it will ~ good until we want it *(will not be damaged)*; milk ~s well in a refrigerator; I hope you're ~ing well; this meat won't ~ (fresh) for two days; □ ~ cool *(fig)*; ~ up to date; that news will ~ *(can be told later)*; ~ right / left *(when driving)*; □ ~ in touch with (old friends); □ ~ on good terms with (one's rich relations).

keep apart let's ~ the two things ~.

keep at (1) he kept (hard) ~ his English until it was perfect. (2) they kept ~ him *(asking questions)* for over an hour. (3) we must ~ him ~ it *(not let him stop)*.

keep away I was kept ~ *(from coming)* by a cold; he kept ~ from them for months; an apple a day ~s the doctor ~ *(proverb)*.

keep back (1) the police kept ~ the crowds; ~ ~ money; try to ~ ~ the tears; inability to study kept him ~ in class. (2) she can ~ nothing (~) from her friends; he kept ~ some of the facts. (3) '~ ~!' he shouted; ~ ~ from the edge of the platform.

keep down (1) ~ that dog ~! he can't ~ any food ~. (2) ~ ~ the number of rabbits; ~ the price ~ (3) ~ one's voice ~ (4) you can't ~ a good man ~; a tyrant ~s ~ a nation.

keep from (1) ~ information ~ s.o.; they kept the bad news ~ him until the last moment. (2) what ~s you ~ joining us? bad weather kept them ~ going; we must ~ them ~ getting to know our plans; they tried to ~ the roof ~ falling (in).

keep in (1) we don't normally eat corned beef, but I always ~ a tin in as a stand-by; ~ the fire in until I return. (2) he kept the boys in for an hour after school. (3) ~ in one's feelings *(restrain)* (4) □ (he plays the violin every day) to ~ his hand in *(keep his skill)*. (5) because he was influential they advised her to ~ in with him.

keep off (1) ~ ~ all attacks with a stick; curtains intended to ~ ~ mosquitoes (2) the doctor told him to ~ ~ whisky. (3) let's ~ ~ the subject. (4) ~ ~ the grass! don't touch me, ~ ~! the farmer told me to ~ ~ his land.

keep on (1) ~ one's hat / coat on; □ ~ one's hair on *(inform: not lose one's temper)* (2) the firm kept him on *(did not dismiss him)*. (3) he kept on talking until he was told to stop; don't give up hope: ~ on trying. (4) turn to the left and ~ on till you come to the church; ~ straight on; ~ on until you succeed. (5) I wish she wouldn't ~ on about her ailments; he kept (going) on and on about his stamp collection. (6) ~ on at s.o. *(nag him)*.

keep out (1) ~ him ~ (of here)! they kept ~ the police by barricading the door; the rugs ~ ~ the draught; these shoes don't ~ the rain ~ any more. (2) ~ ~! can't you read the sign on the door? (3) I want to ~ ~ of this whole business.

keep to (1) the lorry kept to the middle of the road; traffic in Britain ~s to the left; visitors to the park must ~ to the paths. (2) ~ to a promise / one's word / a plan / a contract / a fixed date / an undertaking (3) ~ to the subject (in one's speech) / point / syllabus / regulation; ~ to a strict diet (4) she ~s (herself) (very much) to herself; ~ a fact / the news to o.s.; you may ~ your opinion / (silly) remarks to yourself; ~ one's thoughts to o.s.

keep together they agreed to ~ ~ during the evening; ~ one's thoughts ~.

keep under try to ~ one's passions ~; they kept him ~ by constant discipline; ~ a patient ~ with an anaesthetic.

keep up (1) props ~ up a tunnel; what ~s up a swimmer? (2) ~ up prices / the standard; ~ (a labour force) up to strength (3) I wanted to go to bed, but John kept me up; (a glass of brandy) to ~ up one's health / strength / spirits; ~ ~ your spirits / courage! (4) ~ ~ the house / the property / a road (5) ~ ~ acquaintance with s.o.; ~ ~ a friendship; ~ ~ an effort / an activity / your music; ~ ~ an attack / a correspondence / one's French; ~ ~ the payments for goods bought on H.P.; ~ ~ one's payments punctually (6) ~ ~ a reputation / tradition / custom; □ ~ up appearances (7) the noise / rain kept up all day.

keep up with (1) ~ up with s.o. walking / driving / swimming / *etc* (2) in mathematics she could not ~ up with the rest of the class; it's difficult to ~ up with the international situation; □ ~ up with the times *(not lag behind)*; □ ~ up with the Joneses *(maintain the same standard of living as one's neighbours)*.

key *n* (1) put the ~ in a lock; turn the ~; a ~ to open a can / wind a toy (2) a ~ to a problem / mystery (3) a ~ for the use of teachers; a ~ to a test; a colour ~ to a map (4) Gibraltar is the ~ to the Mediterranean. (5) the ~ of C major; speak in a high / low / sharp / plaintive ~; sing off-~; □ in a minor ~ *(sadly)*; □ all in the same ~ *(monotonously)*. - *adj* (6) a ~ man; s.o. in a ~ position; ~ personnel; ~ industries; the ~ word is not domination or segregation but partnership.

kick *n* (1) a bruise caused by a ~; give a ~ at the door; □ more ~s than halfpence *(more harshness than kindness)*; □ get the ~ *(slang: be dismissed)* (2 *inform*) get a good deal of / a big / quite a ~ out of (dancing) (3 *inform: strength*) he has no ~ left; a cocktail with not much ~ in it; that car still has a lot of ~ left in it. (4) he's a good / bad ~ *(football)* (5 *~s; slang: fun*) just for ~s; how about going bar-hopping (just) for ~s? the children got their ~s out of tying tin cans to cats' tails. (6 *slang: field of interest, usu temporary*) he's on a model aeroplane ~; he's on some (kind of a) ~ about snake farming.

kick *vt* (1) ~ a dog / a football / a goal / a door open; ~ a hole in s.th.; ~ a man when he's down; □ ~ one's heels *(BE: be kept waiting)*; ~ the bucket *(slang: die)*. - *vi* (2) the baby was ~ing (and screaming); this horse ~s; □ ~ over the traces *(become undisciplined)*; □ he ~ed when asked to work another hour.

kick against ~ ~ the treatment one receives; ~ ~ authority; □ ~ ~ the pricks *(hurt o.s. by useless resistance)*.

kick at ~ at the treatment one receives; why should we ~ at the arrangements?

kick around (1) ~ s.o. ~ *(treat roughly)* (2) ~ ~ *(lead a wandering life)*.

kick downstairs ~ s.o. ~ *(esp out of the house)*.

kick off (1) ~ ~ one's slippers (2) they ~ed ~ at 2 o'clock *(started the game)*.

kick out ~ s.o. ~ *(inform: dismiss, eject)*; they ~ed him ~ of office / the club / the bar.

kick up (1) ~ up the edge of a carpet (2) ~ up a row / a noise / a storm / a dust *(all inform: cause a row)*; ~ up one's heels *(enjoy o.s. after dull work)* (3) the motor began to ~ up *(make trouble)*.

kick upstairs ~ s.o. ~ *(get him out of the way by promoting him)*.

kill *vt* (1) ~ s.o. (cruelly / brutally / coward-like / treacherously) (with poison / a dagger / *etc*); he was ~ed in an accident / by lightning / in self-defence / in action / in battle; they were ~ed to the last man; the shock ~ed her; □ ~ two birds with one stone (2) the frost ~ed the flowers / crops / young plants and shoots. (3) ~ an engine / machine *(inform: cut off its power)* (4) ~ s.o. with kindness; the weather's ~ing me. (5) ~ s.o.'s hopes; we spent the whole morning just ~ing time; we ~ed an hour looking out of the window; ~ a proposal / a bill in Parliament (6) the new carpet ~s your curtains *(spoils their effect).*

kill off the new insecticide ~ed ~ all the pests; late frosts may ~ ~ the young plants.

kind *n* (1) a distinct / definite / *etc* ~; apples of several ~s; several ~s of apples; apples / people of all ~s; all ~s of apples / people; people of this ~; *(inform)* these ~ of people; what ~ of apple is that? what ~ of man is he? what ~ of a car is it *(good or bad)*? he is the ~ of man who will hit back; he is a financier of some ~ (or other); she is not the ~ (of person) to talk scandal; was it difficult? - nothing of the ~! two of a ~ *(of the same sort)*; we had coffee of a ~ *(of a very poor sort)*; *(inform)* I ~ of thought this would happen. (2) they differ in degree but not in ~ *(nature)*; pay / repay in ~ *(goods, not money)*; provide aid in ~ rather than in cash; reply to insults in ~ *(by insults)*; repay insolence in ~.

kindle *vt* (1) the spark ~d the dry wood; wood too wet to ~; ~ a flame; the setting sun ~d the sky. (2) ~ passions / enthusiasm / s.o.; he ~d the interest of his audience. - *vi* (3) the fire ~d. (4) he ~d at / to this idea; her eyes ~d with excitement.

knack *n* have a ~ for remembering names; it takes practice to get the ~ of serving in tennis; improvisation is his ~; adult emigrants to a new country eventually acquire the ~ of communicating inoffensively with the natives; it's quite easy when you have the ~ of it.

knife *n* a blunt / sharp ~; get / have one's ~ into s.o. *(dislike and attack whenever possible)*; before you can say ~ *(very suddenly).*

knit *vt* (1) ~ (s.o.) a pair of socks; ~ wool into a dress; ~ a dress out of wool; ~ting needles; (his shop specializes in) ~(ted) goods. (2) ~ one's / the brows; ~ one's forehead (3) a surgeon ~s broken bones (together); mortar is used to ~ bricks together. (4) the families were ~ together by common interests / a long friendship; the mystery story was closely ~; a closely ~ argument. - *vi* (5 → 2) his brows ~ with worry. (6 → 3) the broken bone ~ted quickly.

knock *vt* (1) ~ a nail into the wall / the bottom out of a box / one's head on, against the wall / *etc*; □ ~ one's head against a brick wall *(try to do the impossible)*; ~ s.o./s.th. on the head *(also fig. of plans)*; the car ~ed a hole in the fence; ~ s.o. unconscious (2) what ~s *(inform: impresses)* me is his impudence. (3 *slang*) don't ~ the car industry, it's not that bad. - *vi* (4) ~ (softly) on / at the door; ~ on the table *(to make o.s. heard)*; poverty / hunger ~ed at the door. (5) the engine of this old car is ~ing badly.

knock about (1 *inform*) he has ~ed ~ (Africa) for years; ~ ~ the streets (2 *inform*) ~ s.o. ~ *(beat with fists)*; when he's drunk, he ~s his wife ~ a lot; the small boat was ~ed ~ in the rough sea. (3) ~ furniture / decorations / *etc* ~ *(damage)* (4) have s.th. ~ing ~ *(lying somewhere)*; that book is ~ing ~ here somewhere.

knock against *(BE)* I ~ed ~ Mr N. in the park this morning.

knock down (1) ~ nuts ~ off a tree; ~ ~ the attacker's arm (2) ~ s.o. ~ accidentally; he was ~ed ~ by a bus; you could have ~ed me ~ (*also* over) with a feather *(I was so surprised).* (3) the furniture was ~ed ~ *(taken apart)* before shipment; ~ ~ an old house (4) I wanted £250 for my car, but he ~ed me ~ to £220; the cost of the painting was ~ed ~ to $5. (5) the auctioneer ~ed the camera ~ to me at 50p; a mahogany table was ~ed ~ for five pounds. (6 *AE, slang: earn*) he ~s ~ at least $200 a week; → knock up 5.

knock in ~ in a nail / wedge / post; ~ the top of a barrel in.

knock off (1) ~ the snow ~ one's clothes / the dust ~ one's coat (2) ~ ~ 20p from the list price; I got him to ~ a bit ~ (the price). (3 *inform*) come on, it's time we ~ed ~ (for tea); the workmen ~ed ~ at 5 o'clock; my health compels me to ~ ~ work; ~ it ~! *(slang: stop that noise!)* (4) ~ ~ an article / a novel (for a magazine); he ~ed the poem ~ in 10 minutes; he ~ed ~ two chops *(slang: ate, finished).*

knock on ~ ~ a window / door.

knock out (1) ~ ~ one's pipe; ~ ~ one of s.o.'s teeth (2) ~ s.o. ~ *(knock him unconscious)*; ~ ~ one's opponent *(also fig)* (3) I was almost ~ed ~ by the news. (4) ~ ~ a tune *(play unskilfully).*

knock over you nearly ~ed that bottle of glue ~; → knock down 2.

knock together (1) his knees ~ed ~ in fright; shall I ~ their heads ~ *(force them* *to stop quarrelling)*? (2) ~ boards ~ and make a bookcase; a dog-kennel was ~ed ~ in no time.

knock up (1) ~ his arm up! (2 *BE*) tell him to ~ me up at 6 o'clock! (3 *BE*) ~ up a meal; within 30 minutes he had ~ed up a bed out of some old pieces. (4 *BE*) he ~ed himself up by overwork; the hikers were ~ed up after their long walk. (5 *BE, slang: earn*) he ~s up £5,000 a year. (→ knock down 6) (6 *AE, slang: make pregnant*) ~ up a girl.

know *vt* (1) ~ s.th. slightly / clearly / for certain / inside out / in (its every) detail / from (bitter / personal) experience / from hearsay / by hearsay / from a reliable source; ~ s.o. well / slightly / through and through; ~ the answer / all the answers / one's subject / a lot of French / how to play chess / one's lines in a play / that N. is an honest man / *etc*; ~ (a poem) by heart; he ~s Berlin like the back of his hand; man will never ~ the origin of life; ~ one's way about (a place); do you ~ your way around Hamburg? I don't ~ the way from here; □ ~ one's business / what's what / the ropes / a thing or two *(have good judgement, practical experience)*; if he ~s what's good for him he will (do it); not ~ one's own mind *(not know how to decide s.th.)*; I don't ~ what to do; I ~ because he told me; ~ which side one's bread is buttered (on) *(know one's advantage)*; I always knew it would turn out badly; there's no ~ing when we shall meet again; how do you ~? nobody is to ~ *(be told)*. (2 *be informed*) do you ~ how old he is / whether he is here / what's going on / *etc*? who ~s where they went? what did you expect? he does not ~ any better; you ought to ~ better than to (go swimming after a big meal). (3 *be acquainted, familiar with*) do you ~ Athens / Mr N.? I should like to ~ Mr N.; he ~s the road / the circumstances; we ~ all our neighbours; I ~ him by sight / (only) by name; he doesn't ~ me any more; I have ~n him since I was a child; we have ~n one another for years / from our London days; he's ~n to the police; he's ~n as a successful composer; make o.s. ~n to s.o.; □ I don't ~ him from Adam / her from Eve *(inform: not at all)*; I would like to get to ~ her (better); this summer I really got to ~ Rome properly; we have only come / got to ~ one another properly in the last few months. (4 *recognize*) I don't think I would ~ him again; she knew him from afar; I would not ~ her in a crowd; I knew her at once by her voice / walk; I knew him for a German; he ~s good music when he hears it; ~ truth from falsehood / a pine from a fir; they're twins and it's impossible to ~ one from another / ~ them apart. (5 *experience*) she has ~n hardship / poverty and sorrow / hunger all her life; he has never ~n true love / a home; he has ~n better days; he ~s no fear; I have never ~n him cut a date in my life; have you ever ~n it (to) snow in July? I have never ~n you to arrive home at this time; her enthusiasm knew no bounds. - *vi* (6 → 2) I didn't ~ about that; I knew about that last week; I ~ of an excellent restaurant near here; everyone ~s of the accident; has he been ill? - not that I ~ of; I don't ~ him personally, but of course I ~ of him.

knowledge *n* (1) have (some / little / no great / not much / no exact) ~ (of s.th.); a baby has no ~ of good and evil; have a good (general) / thorough / substantial / intuitive / intimate / superficial / elementary / slight ~ of (a subject); have a reading / speaking ~ of (a language); acquire / obtain (profound / extensive / limited) ~; apply / use one's ~; widen / extend (the scope of) one's ~; add to one's (store of) ~; brush up one's ~ of (Latin) (2) ~ of the defeat soon spread; his ~ of the trails; it is common ~ that he ...; bring s.th. to s.o.'s ~; it has come to my ~ that he ...; he hasn't come in yet, to my ~; to the best of my ~; he had to my certain ~ been forced to act in that way; he married without the ~ of his parents.

L

labour *n* (1) physical / bodily / manual ~; the ~s in the field; earn one's living by manual ~; find it a ~ to (learn a long poem); a ~ of love *(task that gives pleasure)*; hard labour *(punishment)* (2) skilled and unskilled ~; capital and ~; the Ministry of L~; 6 per cent of the ~ force are out of work; in the United States ~ enjoys high wages. (3 *political party*) the L~ vote; vote L~; the constituency has gone L~. (4 *childbirth*) be in ~; ~ begins; ~ pains.

labour *vi* (1) ~ in the fields; they ~ed night and day on the new bridge; she ~ed over the composition; ~ at a task / to complete a task / for the happiness of mankind (2) the hikers / bus ~ed up the steep hill; the ship ~ed through the heavy seas. (3) ~ under a delusion / difficulty / disadvantage / misapprehension. - *vt* (4) there's no need to ~ the point *(express in unnecessary detail)*; ~ an argument.

lack *n* there is a ~ of fresh water/ young teachers / *etc*; she has no ~ of friends; he shows no ~ of courage; he couldn't make the trip for ~ of money; starve for ~ of fresh food; the plants died for ~ of water.

lack *vt* (1) he ~s the money for it; she does not ~ friends; she saw to it that her guests ~ed nothing; they ~ed the opportunity; the boy ~s a father's hand; he ~s the ability / (necessary) courage / experience; he ~s the nerve / courage to do it; he does not ~ / is not ~ing (in) courage; I ~ words to express my gratitude. (2) the story ~s imagination; the text ~s precision; all the team ~s is a goal-keeper. -*vi* (3) only one guest is ~ing; money was ~ing for the plan; humour is ~ing in his speeches.

lament *vt* (1) ~ (the death of) a friend / (over) one's misfortunes / for a dead person / for a loss / over s.o.'s death (2) ~ s.o.'s folly / absence. - *vi* (3) ~ing loudly they stood round the grave.

land *n* (1) travel over ~ and sea; come in sight of ~; he was glad to be on ~ / reach ~ / come to ~ again; are you going by ~ or by sea? (2) good / fertile / arable / cultivated / heavy / barren / dry / stony / swampy ~; good wheat ~; forest ~; go / work on the ~ (as a farm worker); building ~ (3) his ~ goes up to that wood; own houses and ~s (4) one's native ~; the ~ of the free; a strange / new / unknown / foreign / alien / remote / unsettled ~; visit distant / far-off ~s; the Promised L~; the L~ of Promise; a ~ of plenty.

land *vi* (1) ~ on water / the ground / at a destination; we ~ed in M. instead of L.; we ~ed home just after midnight; thus he ~ed in a strange city; the parcel ~ed on his head; he fell out of the window and ~ed on his feet; □ ~ on one's feet *(be fortunate)* (2) that fellow will ~ in prison / jail one of these days; ~ in great difficulties. - *vt* (3) the pilot ~ed the plane (safely). (4) we ~ed a three-pound trout. (5) this train will ~ you in New York; the taxi ~ed him at the station. (6) such behaviour will ~ you in jail; his extravagance ~ed him in debt; ~ o.s. in trouble / great difficulties; we have been ~ed in this difficulty through following your advice. (7) ~ a contract / order / appointment / prize / scholarship; I've just ~ed a job in a bank. (8 *slang*) ~ s.o. a blow / one (on the nose / in the eye / *etc*) (9) be ~ed with (a disagreeable responsibility); the reorganization has ~ed me with a great amount of additional work.

language *n* (1) animals do not possess ~. (2) one's native / a foreign / an alien ~; the ~s of Asia; dead / ancient / classical / living / modern / artificial ~s (3) s.o. with a great command / flow of ~ (4) the written / spoken / colloquial / literary ~; simple / fine *(elaborate)* / sublime / coarse / bad / offensive / vile / vulgar / strong *(angry)* ~; s.o.'s intemperate ~; speak the same ~ *(also fig)* (5) technical / legal / scientific ~; the ~ of science / poetry / diplomacy (6) mathematical / deaf-and-dumb / sign / finger / animal ~; the ~ of flowers / animals / love / the eyes.

languish *vi* (1) ~ in prison / poverty (2) the roses ~ed in the summer heat. (3) his interest ~ed *(became less)*. (4) the exiles ~ed for their native land. - *adj* (5) a ~ing illness / death; give s.o. a ~ing look / glance; give a ~ing sigh / moan / *etc*.

lapse *n* (1) a ~ of memory / taste / the tongue; have momentary ~s (2) a ~ into crime / into savagery / from virtue / from true belief (into heresy); a ~ of justice (3) the ~ of time; after the ~ of several hours; after a long ~ (of time); the ~ of a custom (4) the ~ of a right / privilege / lease; notify s.o. of the ~ of his driving licence.

lapse *vi* (1) he ~d into his native tongue; some Christians ~ from the practice of their faith; ~ from virtue into vice; ~ into bad habits / sin / despair / decay (2) time ~s; his attention ~d during the long speech. (3) the lease ~ed when he didn't pay the rent; privileges may ~ (to s.o. else) if they are not made use of. (4) this custom has ~d *(ceased to be).*

large *adj* (1) a ~ figure / size / diameter / dog / tree / shop / hall / hotel / town / empire / country / sum / profit / debt; a man with a ~ family needs a ~ house; she inherited a ~ fortune; ~ farmers; on a ~ scale; this was ~ly due to a misunderstanding. (2 *liberal, generous*) a ~ heart; ~ charity / tolerance / understanding; he gives ~ly to charity. (3 *not restricted*) give s.o. ~ powers / discretion; ~ ideas / views; hold a ~ view in the matter.

at large (1) he will soon be at ~ *(free)*; the escaped convict is still at ~. (2) he went into the question at ~ *(fully)*; talk / write at ~ *(with details)*; speak on a subject at ~ (3) popular with the nation at ~ *(as a whole)*; that's a matter of concern to the world at ~; a service to the public at ~; (an) ambassador at ~ *(not assigned to a particular country)* (4) he scatters accusations at ~ *(without definite aim).*

lash *vt* (1) formerly criminals were ~ed; ~ a horse across the back with a whip (2) the wind ~ed the trees; the rain was ~ing (against) the windows; the lion ~ed its tail (angrily). (3) they ~ed the poles together *(fastened)*; ~ one thing to another; ~ s.th. down (4) he ~ed me with a torrent of angry words; the speaker ~ed the crowd / audience into a fury / rage / state of excitement. - *vi* (5) ~ at s.o./ s.th. *(strike)*; he ~ed out in all directions as the thieves attacked him; the horse ~ed out (at me) (with its hoofs).

last *adj/ adv* (1) the ~ letter of the alphabet is z; the ~ house in the road; the ~ two / two ~ persons; he was ~ in the race; the slowest runner comes in ~ in the race. (2 *immediately before the present*) ~ night / week / month / summer / year; on Tuesday ~; ~ May; in May ~; in the ~ few days / weeks; this day ~ week *(a week ago)*; the ~ time I saw him was yesterday; I saw him ~ in Paris; when did you ~ go to the dentist? ~, we visited Naples; the ~ thing *(newest fashion)* (3 *only remaining*) the ~ biscuit in the jar; spend one's ~ shilling; her ~ hope; the ~ survivor (4 *least likely, least suitable*) he is the ~ man for such a job; that's the ~ thing I should do; the ~ person one would suspect (5 *final*) I've said my ~ word on the matter (→ word *n* 2a); the L~ Judgement; the L~ Supper; the ~ sacraments (6) the ~ word (in automobile safety) *(definitive statement about)*; the ~ word in fashions *(inform: the newest thing).*

last *n* (1) he is the ~ of his family; the ~ shall be the first *(Bible).* (2) he held out until the ~; thus saying, he breathed his ~ *(form: died).* (3) we shall never hear the ~ of this *(the talk will go on)*; I hope we've seen the ~ of him *(shall never see him again).*

at last he succeeded at ~; daylight came at (long) ~; (now) at ~ I understand you.

last *vi* (1) the rain ~ed three days; his illness ~ed a month; our love will ~ forever. (2) the bread ought to ~ for two days; I have enough tobacco to ~ (me) (for) three days. (3) stone buildings ~ longer than wooden ones. - *vt* (4) your suit will ~ you many years.

last out how long will our water supply ~ ~? have we enough oil to ~ ~ a long winter? we shall never ~ ~ the party without some more whisky.

late *adj/ adv* (1) I was ~ for school / work today; am I ~? arrive ~; a ~ arrival; go to bed / stay up ~; keep ~ hours; the crops are / spring came ~ this year; marry ~ in life; the train was ten minutes ~. (2) in the ~ afternoon; in ~ summer / autumn; in the ~ eighties; it survived ~ into the Middle Ages; ~ Latin / Middle English; I'll be seeing you ~r on. (3) the ~ floods / political troubles; his ~ illness; the ~st models / fashions / news; the ~st thing *(newest fashion)*; as ~ as last week; during the ~ war (4) her ~ husband; the ~ king (5) of ~ *(recently)*; (be here on Monday) at (the) ~st.

lately *adv* I haven't seen him ~; I saw her as ~ as last Sunday.

laugh *n* a contagious / infectious / mirthful / hearty / *etc* ~; she gave a little / a loud ~; they had a good ~ at my expense; raise / give rise to a ~; break into a ~;

join in the ~ ; a ~ of scorn; have the last ~ *(triumph)*; get / have the ~ of s.o. *(get the better of him).*

laugh *vi* (1) ~ heartily / loud(ly) / goodnaturedly / approvingly / *etc* (at a joke / for joy / with delight); burst out ~ ing; ~ in s.o.'s face *(defy openly)*; ~ on the wrong / the other side of one's mouth / face *(change from joy to sorrow)*; they ~ed me out of reading; we ~ed him out of his bad mood; ~ over a letter *(while reading it)*; ~ to o.s.; the speaker was ~ed to scorn; □ ~ up one's sleeve *(be secretly amused)*. - *vt* (2) ~ one's pleasure / thanks (3) ~ o.s. helpless / sick / into convulsions / to death.

laugh about (1 about *is prepos*) years later they ~ed ~ the fear they had felt before they discovered that the 'horrible beast' was only a hungry dachshund; what is he / are you ~ing ~? that's nothing to ~ ~; he can still ~ ~ the days when he was poor. (2 about *is adv*) we were ~ing ~ *(laughing spontaneously; more or less enjoying laughing for its own sake)* and generally having a good time; the boys were ~ing ~, doing nobody any harm at all.

laugh at (1) ~ at a funny story (2) ~ at s.o. who is in trouble; he won't be ~ed at; he is afraid of being ~ed at; they ~ed at him for carrying an umbrella; get o.s. ~ed at (3) ~ at difficulties.

laugh away ~ one's troubles / s.o.'s fears / doubts ~.

laugh down ~ ~ a speaker / proposal; when he stood up to object, the rest of the class ~ed him ~.

laugh off ~ ~ the accusations / the criticism / a difficult situation.

laughter *n* convulsive / derisive / scornful / *etc* ~; burst into (a peal of) ~; roar / shout / die with ~; double up with ~; → shake *vt* 1 a, *vi* 6.

launch *vt* (1) ~ a ship (2) ~ a spear / blows at / against s.o.; ~ a glider / rocket / missile (into orbit) (3) ~ a new business / a plan / a (news)paper / an attack; no drug was ever ~ed with more drama than penicillin; ~ s.o. / an enterprise on a course; ~ a young man into business (4) ~ censure / a threat against s.o. - *vi* (5) ~ into expense; ~ into strong language (6) ~ forth into an explanation *(begin a long one)* (7) ~ out on a voyage of discovery; ~ out into a new argument *(start it)*; ~ out into extravagance.

law *n* (1) a strict / harsh / oppressive / *etc* ~; a statutory / (un)written ~; common ~; bring in / enact / enforce a ~; put a ~ into force (2) the Constitution is the basic ~ of the United States; the ~ of the land; keep within / stick to / break the ~; put / place o.s. outside the ~; be above the ~; all men are equal before the ~; □ lay down the ~ *(be pompously dogmatic)* (3) study / *(BE)* read ~; follow / go in for the ~; choose ~ as a profession; moral ~; natural ~; civil / commercial / criminal / international / martial / military / *etc* ~; lynch ~; the ~ of nations (4) keep / maintain ~ and order; go to ~ against s.o.; get in(to) trouble with the ~; □ take the ~ into one's own hands (5) cleanliness is the first ~ of hygiene; the ~s of painting / harmony / perspective; the ~s of the jungle; □ be a ~ unto o.s. *(do what one thinks right)* (6) a ~ of nature; a natural ~; the ~ of gravity / motion / supply and demand / *etc.*

lay *vt* 1, 2, 3a, 4, 5a, 6-9; *vi* 3b, 5b.
(1) ~ him on the sofa / on his side / here; ~ linoleum / a floor / the foundation (stone) / a (submarine / telegraph) cable; a bricklayer ~s bricks; ~ rails / mines; ~ colours on canvas; he laid his hand on my shoulder; he laid his axe to the tree *(began to chop)*; ~ a burden (up)on s.o. *(also fig)*; ~ a wreath *(ceremonially)*; ~ a floor with tiles / carpet; ~ a yard with straw.
(2 *lay + parts of the body; fig*)
I forbid you to ~ a finger on the boy *(beat him)*; ~ one's finger on s.th. *(point out the trouble etc)*; he keeps everything he can ~ his hands on; how dare you ~ hands on me *(use force against me)*? he laid violent hands upon himself *(tried to commit suicide)*; I have it somewhere, but I can't ~ my hands on it *(find it)* just now; ~ heads together *(discuss, plan together)*; ~ s.th. to heart *(think about it seriously)*; ~ one's heart at s.o.'s feet (→ foot *n* 1) (3a) birds and insects ~ eggs. (3b *vi*) the hens are ~ing well this year.
(4 *cause to lie flat, to disappear*)
sprinkle water on a road to ~ the dust; ~ a storm; rainstorms laid the oats; ~ a ghost / spirit *(cause it to stop appearing)*; what can we do to ~ his doubts?
(5 *prepare, make ready*)
(5a) ~ the table (for dinner); ~ a place (at table); ~ another place; ~ the cloth; ~ a

fire *(prepare the wood etc)*; ~ a trap / snare / ambush; ~ siege to (a town) (5b *vi*; → 5a) ~ for three / for one more (6) the (scene of the story) is laid in Tahiti.

(7 *lay + object + adjective*)
~ s.th. crosswise; ~ bare roots / *(fig)* the roots of the matter / plans / secrets; ~ one's heart bare; ~ open a plot; the victory laid open the road to Rome; ~ one's cheek open (by falling); ~ o.s. open to attack / censure / a charge / an accusation / criticism; ~ s.o. low; the blow laid him low; I've been laid low by influenza; the army laid waste the whole countryside.

(8 *lay + person + adverbial phrase*)
he was laid to rest / sleep in the churchyard; ~ s.o. under an obligation to do s.th.; your conduct ~s me under the necessity of punishing you; ~ s.o. (fast) by the heels *(catch and jail).*

(9 *lay + abstract object*)
~ the facts before a committee / a law before Parliament; the advocate laid the case before the court; let's ~ this before the boss and see what he decides; ~ one's hopes on s.o./ s.th.; ~ great / little store upon s.o./ s.th. (→ store *n* 3); ~ stress / emphasis / weight / great importance on s.th.; ~ claim to (s.o.'s possessions); ~ the foundation(s) of / for (one's future success); ~ a wager (on the result of a race); I'll ~ you £5 (to 1) that he will not come; I'll ~ you a bet that he ...; ~ heavy taxes on tobacco and wine; ~ an embargo; ~ strict injunctions on s.o.; ~ an obligation / line on s.o.; ~ the blame (for s.th.) on s.o.; ~ on s.o. the duty of doing s.th.; don't ~ your misfortunes at my door *(blame me for them)*; ~ a charge against s.o.; ~ s.th. to s.o.'s charge.

lay about he laid ~ him fearlessly *(struck out in all directions)*; when he was surrounded he laid ~ him / them with his walking-stick.

lay aside (1) ~ a book ~ (to listen) (2) ~ money ~ (for one's old age); ~ ~ a few shillings every week (3) ~ ~ *(political)* party differences / old habits.

lay away (1) the department store will ~ ~ Christmas presents *(until paid for).* (2) ~ ~ money (3 *AE, inform: bury*) ~ ~ a dead person.

lay back the horse laid ~ its ears.

lay by (1) ~ by provisions (2) ~ by money (for a holiday); he has a tidy sum laid by.

lay down (1) ~ a baby ~ gently; she laid herself ~. (2) ~ ~ a ship *(start building it)*; ~ ~ a railway / road (3) ~ ~ one's arms / hopes; ~ ~ office; □ ~ ~ one's life for others / a great cause) (4) ~ ~ claret and port *(store in a cellar)* (5) ~ ~ certain conditions (to s.o.) / rules / a price; → law 2; ~ s.th. ~ as a maxim; prices laid ~ by the manufacturers; the Magna Carta was meant to ~ ~ the rights of men; the Act ~s it ~ that ... (6) ~ ~ a wager / bet; he laid ~ $5 on the horse to win, place or show.

lay in (1) ~ in the oars (2) ~ in food / provisions / supplies / a good stock of .../ stores for the winter.

lay into *(inform)* I jumped to my feet and laid ~ him; I let him have his say and then I laid ~ him.

lay off (1) ~ s.o. ~ *(discharge, esp temporarily)* (2) you'd better ~ ~ smoking for a while; the doctor told me to ~ ~ (work / alcohol / *etc*) for a few weeks. (3) ~ ~ a badminton court *(mark off).*

lay on (1) ~ on a coat of plaster; ~ the paint on thickly / in a thin coat; □ ~ it on thick / with a trowel *(give excessive praise) (2) ~ on a (special) train (add it)* (3) ~ on gas / electricity to a house; ~ the water on; this house has no electricity laid on. (4) the attackers laid on many blows until he fell to the ground. (5) ~ on taxes penalties (6) ~ on entertainment and food *(organize, provide)*; theatres and concerts were laid on for the visitors; ~ on a civic reception.

lay out (1) ~ ~ a rug / a cold meal ready for guests / articles *(for inspection)* / books *(for reading)*; ~ ~ a corpse *(make ready for burial)* (2) ~ ~ a garden / park / estate; ~ ~ the pages of a newspaper / magazine (3) ~ ~ money *(spend)*; ~ ~ one's money wisely / carefully (4) ~ o.s. ~ to do s.th. *(take pains)*; she laid herself ~ to make her guests comfortable. (5 *inform*) the blow laid him ~; she was laid ~ by the intense heat.

lay up (1) ~ up provisions / a supply of s.th.; ~ up trouble for o.s. (by doing or not doing s.th.) (2) a bad attack of influenza can ~ you up for several weeks; be laid up with a broken leg; my sister has been laid up with bronchitis for three weeks. (3) ~ up a ship / car (for repairs).

lead *vt* (1) ~ s.o. / an animal by the hand; ~ a horse by the bridle / reins; ~ s.o. to his room / a blind man across a road / a horse (to water) / the troops through the mountains; ~ the way (→ way 6); ~ a girl / a woman / the bride to the altar; □ ~ s.o. a (pretty) dance *(cause him a lot of trouble)*; □ ~ s.o. by the nose *(control him completely)*; □ ~ s.o. into evil ways; □ ~ s.o. up the garden path *(mislead him)* (2 *be the leader of*) ~ an army (into battle) / an expedition / a mutiny / s.o. to insurrection / a team (of experts) / a gang (of workers / thieves); ~ the country through a war; a conductor ~s an orchestra / band / choir / the singing / a group in the singing of a song; ~ the Liberal Party / a party into the election campaign; ~ the fashion (3 *be the first*) ~ a list / the world in literacy / a parade; a brass band led the regiment; ~ one's opponent by 100 votes / by 8 points (4 *influence*) she is easily led by her friends; he is easier led than driven; what led you to this conclusion / the conclusion that he ...? ~ s.o. into temptation (5 *cause to do*) they led me / I was led to believe that there was no danger; what led you to think so / to conclude that he ...? (6) ~ a life of luxury / crime / *etc*; ~ a good / happy / care-free / busy / quiet / peaceful / double / hard / happy married life; ~ a dog's life *(a very bad one)*; ~ a cat and dog life *(quarrel constantly)*; ~ one's life in one's own way; ~ s.o. a miserable / hard life; ~ s.o. a miserable existence; ~ s.o. a dog's life *(worry him constantly)*. - *vi* (7 → 1) you ~ and we'll follow. (8 *of roads, etc*) the road ~s to the river / through the forest / over the pass / across the pass; where does this road ~? the lights ~ to the mansion; the door ~s into the yard / into the kitchen / to the bedroom. (9) Paris ~s in fashion; the German team is ~ing (by) 2 to 1; (a boxer) is ~ing on points. (10 *fig*) (attempts / efforts) ~ to success / to nothing / nowhere; they have not led to any result; God knows what that will ~ to; facts that led to his death / the misunderstanding; → question n 1.

lead astray ~ s.o. ~ *(tempt him to do s.th. wrong)*.

lead away (1) the gangsters led the man ~ with them. (2) let no orator ~ you ~ from loyalty.

lead off (1) the captain led ~ *(away)* his team. (2) he led ~ by introducing himself; who is to ~ ~ in the debate? □ ~ s.o. ~ on a false track.

lead on (1) the moving star led the wise men on; he led on his forces in gallant style. (2) gambling often ~s on to other vices. (3) Mary led everyone on to think she was getting married.

lead out ~ ~ a horse *(from the stable)*; he led ~ the lady to the dance.

lead up to what I have just said ~s up to my next point; his arguments led up to a startling conclusion; then he led up to the question of money.

leaf (1) new / green / dead ~ves; the trees will soon be in ~ / come into ~. (2) a book of 100 pages has 50 ~ves; loose ~ves.

leak *n* a ~ in a roof / the gas-bag of a balloon / a ship; a ~ of information; a ~ in (national) security; the roof has a bad ~; the gas ~ is serious.

leak *vi* (1) water is ~ing from the bucket. (2) the boat ~s badly / like a sieve; the kettle / boiler / water-pipe is ~ing. (3) this pipe ~s gas. (4) the rain is ~ing in (through a crack in the roof). (5) the news / secret has ~ed out; the truth will ~out gradually. - *vt* (6) camera bellows which ~ light (7) the spy ~ed the secret to his superior; political plans are sometimes ~ed intentionally to grateful reporters.

lean *vi* (1) the Leaning Tower of Pisa; ~ over a fence / the table; ~ on a table / one's elbows; ~ on my arm! do not ~ out of the window; she was ~ing right out of the window. (2) she still ~s on her mother; ~ on a friend's advice / others for guidance (3) ~ towards Marxism; her interests ~ towards sports; ~ to the side of mercy (4 ~ + *adv*) ~ back against the wall; ~ backwards; ~ out; trees that ~ over in the wind; □ ~ over backward to do s.th. *(try very hard)*. - *vt* (5) ~ a ladder against the wall; ~ one's elbows on the table.

leap *vi* (1) he ~t on his enemy with a knife in his hand; the Indian ~t from the cliff; the salmon ~t up the falls; ~ over a fence; □ look before you ~. (2) ~ to one's feet; his heart ~t for joy. (3) he ~t at the opportunity; ~ into action (4) s.th. ~s to the eye. - *vt* (5) the runner ~t a ditch / a wall; swollen rivers ~ed their banks. (6) ~ a horse over a hedge.

learn *vt* (1) ~ a lesson / a poem (by heart) / a language / French / a science / a trade / a craft / a game / the way to do a thing / tricks; he is ~ing to swim / how to ride a horse. (2) ~ a piece of news / the truth / the full results; did you ~ something about him? I was unable to ~ any details; at the station we ~ed that the train would be (three hours) late; I was sorry to ~ the sad news of his death / that he had died; (there is no means of) ~ing what is happening. - *vi* (3) he used to be intolerant but he has ~ed with maturity; some people never ~; ~ by experience (4) ~ of / about an accident (in the newspapers); I only ~ed of their elopement yesterday.

leave *n* (1) when is your next home ~ *(holiday in government or military service)*? where are you going on your next ~? ~ of absence; sick-~ (2) take one's ~ *(go away)*; take ~ of one's friends; □ take French ~ *(go away without saying good-bye)*; □ take ~ of one's senses *(behave as if mad)* (3 *permission*) you have my ~ to stay away from the office tomorrow; the soldier asked for ~ (to visit his family).

leave *vt* (1 *go away*) ~ the room; I left home / the house at 8 o'clock; when did you ~ Rome? the train left the track. (2 *go away finally*) ~ home / school / college / a job / a country; the cook has threatened to ~ us; my husband / typist has left me; he left medicine for the law *(changed to the legal profession)*; □ ~ s.o. in the lurch *(desert in difficulties)* (3 *go away without taking s.th., doing s.th.*) ~ the cake where it is; I left my books upstairs / at home / at John's house; he left his hat in / on the train; he left half his work until the next day; ~ your hat and coat in the hall; ~ important documents with a friend (4 *not interfere*) ~ a decision / the choice to s.o.; ~ s.o. to himself / his own devices; ~ the wounded to their fate; ~ him to it *(leave him to do it alone)*; ~ a matter to chance (5 *allow to remain in a certain state*) she left the flat in good condition / in disorder; ~ things as they are; let's ~ it at that. (6 ~ + *object* + *adjective, participle*: *allow to be in a certain state)* ~ a door open / the windows firmly fastened / a section of a form blank; his illness has left him weak; his words left her calm / unconcerned; ~ s.o. free to do s.th.; are you going to ~ me alone? ~ that box / the matches alone! ~ her alone *(don't tease, worry her)*; I would not trust him to ~ the money alone; why alter the present system? it is best / my advice is to ~ well alone *(not to improve what is already good)*; ~ s.o. / s.th. standing *inform: be far superior)*: this is the best photo we have received, it ~s all the others standing; we left him painting the gate; the news left me wondering (what would happen next); he left his listeners wondering (what the future would bring); the question was left hanging; it is better left unsaid; it ~s much to be desired; ~ no stone unturned *(try everything)* (7 *allow to remain*) two from five ~s three; don't ~ any of your dinner *(eat it)*; ~ a margin; when I have paid all my debts, there will be nothing left / I shall have nothing left; his interpretation ~s room for argument; ~ a blank for the question you cannot answer. (8 *hand over before going away, deposit; also fig*) ~ a tip; did the postman ~ anything for me? ~ a message / one's (telephone) number with s.o. (saying that ...); did he ~ a message for me? please, ~ word for me with my secretary if you get a reply; he went off without ~ing his address; ~ a good impression / a trace / an unpleasant taste; the wound left a scar. (9 *entrust, hand over*) I'll ~ the matter in your hands / you to attend to the matter; he left his wife to deal with the creditors; he left his friend in charge of the house / the house in his friend's charge; we left him to paint the gate. (10 *leave behind at one's death, give to s.o. at one's death*) he ~s a wife and two children; he left Mary all his money / all his money to Mary; he has left his wife nothing but debts; he left her poor. (11 *give up, cease*) ~ hold of s.th.; don't ~ go until I tell you; make that dog ~ go of my coat; you must not ~ go of my hand. (12 *in giving directions: pass*) we left the town on our right; ~ the church on your left and go up the hill. - *vi* (13 → 1) all the guests left by ten o'clock; we're ~ing for Paris next week; it's time for us to ~ / we left.

leave about he is always ~ing his papers ~.

leave behind (1) I left my bathing-suit ~ so I can't go swimming. (2) the fast runner left all the others ~. (3) ~ no traces / an unpleasant taste / a good name ~.

leave off (1) ~ ~ one's winter clothing (2) ~ ~ work at two o'clock; we left ~ at the end of Chapter Two; has the rain left ~ yet? ~ ~ raining / biting one's nails / teasing the cat.

leave out (1) ~ ~ a letter / word (2) you might find it easier to ~ me ~ altogether. (3) he left the key ~ for you.

leave over (1) ~ a matter ~ until tomorrow; we shall now ~ the meeting ~ until next week. (2) how much money was left ~ when you had paid all the debts?

leg *n* (1) short / long / straight / crooked / fat / thin / skinny ~s; have a stout pair of ~s; your ~s are younger than mine; stand firm / be steady on one's ~s; be on one's ~s; be all ~s *(tall and thin)*; keep one's ~s *(not fall)*; □ be on one's last ~s *(exhausted; near death)*; □ not have a ~ to stand on *(no excuse, good argument)*; □ put one's best ~ forward (→ put forward 1); □ stand on one's own ~s (→ stand *vi* 1); □ pull s.o.'s ~ (→ pull *vt* 1b); □ shake a ~ (→ shake *vt* 1a) (2) a trouser ~; the ~ of a stocking; a table ~; a stool with three ~s.

lend *vt* (1) ~ s.o. a book (to read) / a bicycle / an umbrella / *etc*; ~ s.o. money (at interest) / £10 (2) ~ s.o. a (helping) hand (with s.th./ in doing s.th.); ~ s.o. assistance / support; ~ s.o. an ear / one's ear(s); ~ one's name / support / influence to a project; I refuse to ~ my name to such a questionable enterprise; a lake ~s beauty to the countryside; distance ~s enchantment to the view; ~ colour to s.th. (3) this tool ~s itself to many uses; deep-focus photography ~s itself to shots of extreme beauty; this peaceful garden ~s itself to meditation; don't ~ yourself to such dishonest schemes.

length *n* (1) the ~ of a road / river / field / stick / board / *etc*; the carpet is 9 feet in width and 12 feet in ~; the boat won by a ~; be ready to go (to) all ~s / any ~(s) *(do anything necessary)*; go to great ~(s) *(make great efforts)* to do s.th. (2) what was the ~ of your stay in Rome? make a stay in Rome of some ~ (3) a ~ of rope / pipe / tubing; a dress ~.

at length (1) speak at (some / great) ~ (2) explain s.th. at ~; treat a subject at ~ (3) at ~ he came to understand it.

less *adj* (1 *smaller*) the area of Mexico is ~ than that of the United States; in a ~ degree; of ~ importance / value / magnitude; ~ size means ~ weight; of two evils choose the ~; no ~ a person than the Prime Minister; the remark was something / somewhat ~ than polite; it is nothing ~ than robbery to ask such a high price. (2 *fewer*) ten is ~ than a dozen; ~ than 20 of them remain; no ~ than three people have offered to buy the castle; had ~ men killed but more wounded; France consumes ~ potatoes per person than England. (3 *not so much*) (make) ~ noise, please! he has ~ strength than I have. (4 *shorter*) we'll get home in ~ time if we fly; of ~ duration; the ~ time it takes, the better. (5 *more limited in quantity*) pay ~ money for the house; eat ~ butter; have ~ difficulty with one's work; this will cost (you) £100 more or ~ *(about £100)*.

less *adv* I was ~ scared than surprised; my head aches ~ now; he is ~ clever than his brother; try to be ~ impatient; this subject is more or ~ difficult; I don't suspect him of robbery, even / still / much ~ of robbery with violence.

less *n* (1) of two evils choose the ~; people have been hanged for ~. (2 *shorter period* → less *adj* 4) in ~ than an hour; □ in ~ than no time *(very quickly; very soon)*; I expect to see ~ of her in future. (3 *a smaller quantity* → less *adj* 5) I had ~ than a dollar to spend; some gave little, others ~, others still ~; he paid no ~ than £1,000 for it.

less *prepos (minus)* a year ~ two days; £20 a week ~ 90p. for National Insurance contribution.

lesson *n* (1) an English / arithmetic / piano ~; a ~ in music / English / geography; sports are important, but so are ~s; have ~s with s.o.; give / take ~s (in English / *etc*); he is busy doing / learning / going over his ~s for tomorrow. (2) a bitter / tough ~; that was a ~ to us; teach s.o. a ~ (he won't forget); the ~ bore fruit.

let *vt* (1 *allow*) ~ him go / do it; ~ me help you; ~ him have it; ~ him be here by ten o'clock; ~ me know what happens; ~ him say what he likes, I still believe . . .; . . . but mother wouldn't ~ us; the police ~ no one enter the building; I won't ~ it be said that I . . .; shall we ~ the matter drop? □ ~ s.o. have his say / way; □ ~ s.o. have it straight from the shoulder *(say it firmly)*; □ ~ things take their course; □ ~ s.o. stew in his own juice; they ~ themselves go and cheered wildly; he ~ himself go on the subject; he got tired and ~ the sack go / ~ go of the sack; I don't agree with all you say but we'll ~ it go at that; ~ him try; ~ them do their worst; ~ come what may; he doesn't need your help, ~ him be; ~ the poor dog be; (it is best to) ~

sleeping dogs lie (→ dog 1); ~ me catch you doing that again! (2 *allow through neglect*) don't ~ the fire go out; he ~ the book fall from his hand; they ~ the prisoner escape. (3 *allow to escape, flow out, etc*) ~ (the) air out of a balloon; ~ blood from s.o.; ~ the hens out of the coop; ~ s.o. out of hospital; ~ one's dog loose at night; he ~ loose at her *(spoke harshly)*; □ ~ the cat out of the bag *(inform, fig)* (4 ~ + *inf: imperative*) ~'s listen to her; ~'s have a drink, shall we? ~ us both have a try! don't ~'s talk about it; ~ AB be equal to CD; ~ X be smaller than Y. (5 *insert*) ~ a stone block into the floor / a slab into the wall / a pole in the concrete (6 ~ + *inf following immediately*) it should be ~ die; he ~ drive with his left fist; he ~ drive at me with a stone; ~ drop a hint; ~ fall a hint / remark; he ~ fall that he would be coming; he picked up a stone and ~ fly at my dog; I ~ fly at him *(attacked him verbally)*; he ~ fly impetuously with "Why do you stand for it?"; don't ~ go the rope; do ~ go of my coat! live and ~ live; ~ slip an opportunity / project; the opportunity was ~ slip. (7a *rent*) ~ a room to lodgers; she ~s rooms by the week; have you a room to ~? ~ land for grazing / for a year; ~ a house furnished. – *vi* (7b) how much does the house ~ for? the room ~s well.

let alone (1) ~ me ~ - I'm finishing my essay; ~ him ~ to do it (2) ~ this useless scheme ~; please, ~ the record player ~, or you'll break it. (3 *BE*) ~ me ~ for spending money if I get the chance; you can ~ him ~ *(rely on him)* for knowing where to get a bargain. (4) he can't juggle two balls, ~ ~ six.

let by please, ~ me by.

let down (1) ~ ~ a window / the bucket into the well; ~ ~ a skirt / hem; she ~ ~ her hair *(also fig: throw off restraint when on holiday / at a party / etc)*. (2) ~ s.o. ~ gently / easily *(criticize mildly)* (3) ~ s.o. ~ *(disappoint)*; this is the second time I have been ~ ~ by him; he will never ~ you ~. (4) if he had any self-respect he would realize he was ~ting himself ~ *(losing his reputation)*. (5) don't ~ ~ *(stop making an effort)* till the job is finished.

let in (1) ... crying "Let me in!"; he ~ himself in with my key. (2) the curtains ~ the light in; my coat ~s in the rain; these shoes are ~ting in water badly. (3) ~ o.s. in for a lot of work / a debt / an obligation / a task; I didn't know what I was ~ting myself in for when I promised to do that job; by an incautious remark I ~ myself in for a speech. (4) ~ s.o. in on a secret; unknowingly he ~ the spy in on the secret weapon.

let into (1) they would not ~ him ~ the meeting / building. (2) ~ s.o. ~ a secret (3) he rose to his feet and ~ ~ *(attacked)* the last speaker.

let off (1) the boiler ~s ~ water / steam; s.o. ~s ~ steam *(uses strong language)* (2) ~ ~ fireworks / a firecracker / an arrow / a gun / a shot (3) ~ s.o. (without punishment / with a warning / with a fine instead of sending him to prison) (4) ~ s.o. ~ his homework / a fine / from doing s.th.

let on (1) don't ~ on what we are buying Dad for Christmas / (that) I told you. (2) he ~s on *(pretends)* he is healthy; he ~ on that he was a police inspector.

let out (1) ~ the cat / sheep ~; the dog was barking to be ~ ~; ~ ~ water / air; ~ the water ~ (of the bath-tub); don't bother to come to the door, I can ~ myself ~; she wouldn't ~ him ~ on such a cold day. (2) ~ ~ a garment / the seams / the folds / the sleeves (of a garment) / the trousers round the waist (3) ~ the fire (go) ~ (4) ~ ~ a secret (5) he ~s ~ his car on hire; ~ ~ caravans at 12 francs a day (6) that mule has a habit of ~ting ~ at people *(kicking)*; accused of dishonesty, she ~ ~ at her employer.

let through (1) they ~ me ~ when I showed my passport; the police ~ the doctor ~ (the barrier). (2 *inform*) ~ s.o. ~ an exam (3) the curtains ~ the light ~; my coat ~s the rain ~.

let up (1) the wind / rain ~s up; the pain has ~ up. (2) we mustn't ~ up now; ~ up on a task; in the six years we sat under him learning mathematics, he never once ~ up on us.

letter *n* (1) capital / small ~s; the ~ of the law; in ~ and spirit; (carry out an order) to the ~ (2) a private / informal / love / poison-pen / official / business ~; a ~ of recommendation; a prepaid / stamped / registered / express / airmail / surface / pneumatic / tubular / returned / poste-restante / dead *(undeliverable)* / inland / foreign ~; a ~ to be called for; inform s.o. by ~; write s.o. a ~ / a ~ to s.o.; sign /

seal / close / post / mail / stamp / register a ~; have a ~ registered; the ~ weighs 20 gram(me)s / is overweight / reaches the addressee / bears a wrong address / is (duly) delivered / miscarries / is misdirected / is kept till called for / is returned to the sender; our ~s have crossed in the post; my ~ crossed yours; ~s to the editor.

level *n* (1) 100 ft. above sea ~; water seeks / finds its own ~; □ find one's own ~ *(the people with whom one is socially etc equal)* (2) a high ~ of intelligence; an intellectual / social / moral ~; she is on a higher ~ than he; the general ~ of the class is high; rise to higher ~s *(of civilization)*; responsibility at the highest ~; prices at inflated ~s (3) a high fat / sugar ~ (in the blood); the blood-alcohol ~ (4 *inform*) on the ~ *(without deception)*; I don't think he's on the ~ (with us / about his taxes); on the ~, now, tell me how it really was.

level *adj* (1) a ball rolls when laid on a floor that is not ~; a ~ ground / field; make a surface ~ (2 *equal*) a ~ race *(in which the competitors keep close together)*; a ~ crossing; the shelf is ~ with my chin; → draw *vi* 13. (3 *well-balanced; steady*) ~ temperature; ~ tones; a ~ look; have a ~ head; be ~-headed; do one's ~ best *(everything possible)*.

level *vt* (1) ~ an area / site / road (up / down); carpenters ~led the sunken floor; death ~s all men. (2) ~ a building (to / with the ground) (for a car-park); the buildings were ~led by the earthquake. (3) ~ a / one's gun (at a tiger); ~ an accusation against / at s.o.

level off (1) ~ ~ a surface (2) the plane climbed to 7,000 feet and then ~led ~; the upward surge of German industrial production has ~led ~ this year.

level out education ~s ~ differences of class; all social distinctions were ~led ~ / away.

liable *adj* (1) if the car is damaged, I will consider you ~; be ~ for one's wife's debts / all the expenses (2) ~ to charges / fees / taxes / (customs) duty / a (heavy) fine / imprisonment; if you disobey the law, you are ~ to arrest / prosecution. (3) he is ~ to fits of depression / malaria / seasickness; s.o. is ~ to fly into a temper at any time / to catch cold / to get an infection; all men are ~ to make mistakes (occasionally); we are ~ to be overheard; matinee hat wearers are ~ to be insulted (→ apt 3); he is ~ to promise more than he can perform *(the evil suggested is the shame he feels;* → apt 3).

liberty *n* (1 (→ freedom) personal / political / intellectual ~; basic / civil ~ies; ~ of conscience / action / speech / the press; rob s.o. of his ~; give s.o. back his ~; take up arms for ~; ~ is the right of all men; ~, equality, fraternity; life, ~ and the pursuit of happiness; give me ~ or give me death; the Statue of L~ (2) have ~ of choice; allow o.s. the ~ of doing s.th.; may I take the ~ of drawing your attention to a mistake? make a stand for civil rights and ~ies *(privileges)*; don't take ~ies with her *(be too familiar)*; he could not take such outrageous ~ies with me.

at liberty (1) the escaped prisoner is still at ~; set prisoners / slaves at ~ (2) when will you be at ~ *(not busy)*? (3) I am not at ~ to tell you; you are at ~ to go when you wish; you are quite at ~ to print any of my remarks.

lick *vt* (1) ~ (at) a lollipop; a cat ~s its paws / wounds; ~ed the spoon clean; ~ one's lips *(also fig)*; □ ~ one's chops *(anticipate s.th. with relish)*: the lion ~ed his chops at the sight of the helpless rabbit *(also fig)*; ~ one's wounds *(also fig)*; the flames / fire / waves ~ed the roof; □ ~ s.o.'s shoes / boots *(be servile)*; I'll make him ~ my shoes; □ ~ s.o./ s.th. into shape; he'll get ~ed into shape at his new school. (2) ~ a team / an opponent *(inform)*; well, that ~s everything! then if you can't ~ that perplexing job, try sleeping on it. - *vi* (3) the flames ~ed at our feet; the waves ~ed (away) at the crumbling river bank.

lick off the boy ~ed the jam ~ (his lips).

lick up ~ up (spilt) milk.

lie *n* a deliberate / obvious / downright / outright / malicious / brazen / barefaced / transparent / white *(harmless)* ~; it is all a ~; what a pack of ~s; tell (s.o.) ~s; deceive s.o. by ~s; act a ~ *(deceive without using words)*; give s.o. the ~ *(accuse him of lying)*; give the ~ to s.th. *(show that it is false)*.

lie[1] *vi* you are lying! he ~d to me; if you do something wrong, don't ~ about it; ~ to s.o.'s face.

lie[2] *vi* (1 *be in a horizontal, resting position*) a pen is lying on the desk; the book lay open on the table; don't ~ in bed all

morning; ~ face downwards / on one's back, side; ~ on the sofa (and rest); ~ asleep / stretched out / sick / ill / dying / dead / helpless / idle; ~ at s.o.'s feet *(also fig: admire)*; → oar; fields ~ barren / waste; a field / mind ~s fallow; we'll let the matter ~; her body / his wife ~s *(is buried)* in the village churchyard.
(2 *be situated*) Canada ~s north of the United States; the town ~s near the river; the village lay (spread out) before us; a pall of smoke ~s over the town; □ find out how the land ~s *(see how matters are)*.
(3 *be, remain in a certain condition*)
(3a ~ + *adj*) the snow lay thick on the ground; money lying idle in the bank; cars / vehicles ~ idle; → anchor *n* 1; don't let your talent ~ idle; ~ low *(avoid being seen)*; the coast lay open to attack; the lobster lay heavy on his stomach; this matter / the crime / the loss of the money ~s heavy on his conscience (3b ~ + *adverbial phrase*) ~ in ambush / in wait (for s.th.); (your) life still ~s in front of you; jealousy ~s at the root of her actions; the town lay in ruins after the earthquake.
(4 ~ + *adverbial phrase: be; of abstract things*) the blame ~s at your door; conspiracies lay behind the disorders; the trouble ~s in the engine; it ~s within your power to do good or evil; he will do what ~s in his power; as far as in me ~s *(form: to the best of my power)*; success ~s in diligence and vigilance; you know where your interest ~s; it / the decision ~s with you (to accept the proposal); the author's sympathies do not ~ with Napoleon; the book's chief value ~s in its pictures.

lie back ~ ~ in an armchair; ~ ~ and enjoy life.

lie down (1) I think I'll ~ ~ (on the couch) and have a rest; 'go and ~ ~' suggests a rest on (not in) the bed. (2) ~ ~ under an insult / injustice *(accept it without protest)*; take an insult / *etc* lying ~ (3) ~ ~ on the job *(not do one's best; be lazy)*: I'll fire anybody I catch lying ~ on the job.

lie in (1) we shall be able to ~ in on Sunday morning. (2) I have not visited her at all while she has been lying in *(been in bed to give birth to a child)*.

lie over (1) let a matter ~ ~ for a few days (2) a bill / account ~s ~ *(remains unpaid)*.

lie up (1) after his nervous breakdown the doctor ordered him to ~ up for a few weeks *(stay in bed, in his room)*. (2) a motor-car / ship ~s up *(stays unused)*.

life *n* (1) how did ~ begin? (2) is there any ~ on the planet Mars? animal / plant ~ (3) ~ is sweet; it is a matter of ~ and death; the struggle for ~; he gave his ~ for his country; he gave all his ~ to (the study of languages); devote / sacrifice one's ~ to charity; risk / do s.th. at the risk of one's ~; run for dear / one's (very) ~; lose / save one's ~; I can't for the ~ of me (remember what happened / eat such things / *etc*); come / bring to ~; this ~ *(life on earth)*; the ~ beyond; the other / future / eternal / everlasting ~ (4) three ~ves were saved; how many ~ves were lost? take s.o.'s ~ *(kill him)*; take one's own ~; put an end to one's (wretched) ~ (5 *period between birth and death*) he lived all his ~ in Rome; spend one's ~ in idleness; marry early / late in ~; sentence to imprisonment for ~; □ have the time of one's ~ *(enjoy o.s. very much)* (6 *social activities, pleasures*) there's not much ~ in a small village; sailors do see ~. (7 *way of living*) a ~ of ease / luxury / toil and trouble / sin; social / public / high *(upper-class)* / private / married / family / country / town / city ~; (lead / live) a decent / good / blameless / clean / noble / religious / holy / secluded / quiet / peaceful / full / devout / easy / prosaic / idle / busy / wild / troublesome / corrupt / sinful / (un)happy / miserable / vicious ~; s.o.'s inner ~; his ~ was a success / failure; some people have easy ~ves; I wonder wether ~ in the Navy has changed Henry very much. (8 *vitality, energy*) he is full of ~; put more ~ into your work; he was the ~ (and soul) of the party *(was merry and caused others to be merry)* (9) a portrait / picture taken from (the) ~; draw / portray / imitate s.o. to the ~.

lift *vt* (1) ~ a box (off / from the ground) / a weight / a stone; ~ a car; a crane to ~ 20 tons; ~ a child out of bed / onto the chair; ~ one's hand (to strike / against s.o.) / one's eyes / one's face; ~ one's hat; □ not ~ a hand *(do nothing)*; □ he is fond of ~ing his elbow *(likes a drink)*; ~ the waist / shoulder of a dress / a dress at the waist / shoulder (2) ~ potatoes *(dig up)* (3 *inform: steal*) ~ cattle / jewels / *etc*; his book is not original - long passages in it have been ~ed from other authors. (4) hard work ~ed him out of poverty; the good news ~ed my spirits. (5) ~ a restriction / prohibition / embargo / ban. - *vi* (6) the fog / mist / clouds / darkness ~ed. (7) the window won't ~ *(cannot be raised).*

lift out ~ an injured person ~ (of a car).

lift up ~ s.o./ s.th. up (from the ground); ~ up one's arm(s) / eyes (to heaven); ~ up one's feet; ~ up one's voice in praise *(speak, sing loud).*

light *n* (1) open the blinds and let in the ~; the ~ *(daylight)* began to fail; by the ~ of the moon; a feeble / pale / faint / diffuse / mysterious / bright / clear / dazzling / glaring ~; hang the picture in a good ~; stand in s.o.'s ~ *(also fig)*; stand in one's own ~ *(also fig)* (2) shine your ~ on the keyhole; ~s were burning in every room; traffic ~s; turn / switch on / off a ~; the ~s went out. (3 *spark, flame*) have you got a ~ for my cigarette? put a ~ to the fire; strike / blow out a ~ (4 *fig uses*) the ~ in her eyes; the ~ died out of her eyes; put s.o./ s.th. in a favourable / good ~; he put me in a bad ~; in the ~ of (new discoveries / these changes / *etc*) we must revise our plan; see s.th. in a different / (un)favourable / rosy ~; I have never looked upon it in that ~; cast / throw / shed (a new) ~ on (a problem); the ~ of knowledge / reason; many new facts have come to ~ / been brought to ~; (act) according to one's ~s *(beliefs, degree of wisdom).*

light[1] *adj* a ~ room / day / sky / complexion / colour / blue / red / *etc*; ~ (-coloured) hair; a ~-coloured dress; it is already ~; it is growing / getting ~.

light *vt* (1) ~ a (bon)fire / match / candle / torch / lamp / cigarette; ~ the streets of a town; holding a ~ed / unlit candle (2) our houses are ~ed by electricity; the room is lit by gas; a ~ed road; a poorly lit road / room; brightly / festively lit; the vehicle must be lit at night according to the regulations; ~ the town (3 *guide with a light*) ~ the way / s.o. on his way; he ~ed me down the steps with a torch. - *vi* (4) the match lit as soon as I struck it.

light up (1) a fire / a sudden flash of lightning / hundreds of fairy-lamps lit up the sky / the whole street; he lit up the stairs with his torch; the streets were brightly lit up. (2) a smile lit up her face; her face / eyes lit up with pleasure. (3) in winter we have to ~ up about four o'clock. (4) ~ up one's cigarette / pipe; he lit up and said . . .

light[2] *adj / adv* (1 *not heavy*) a ~ box / burden / load; a pair of ~ shoes; a ~ pair of shoes; ~ clothing; ~ architecture; a ~ building / pillar / bridge / railway / cruiser; ~ snow; travel ~ *(with little luggage)* (2 *not violent; gentle*) a ~ tap / touch on the shoulder; a ~ blow; ~ (foot)-steps / movements; a ~ wind / breeze; the wind was blowing ~ly; she is ~ on her feet; a ~ sleep / sleeper; sleep / tread / fall ~; have a ~ hand (in making pastry / in managing affairs / *etc*) (3 *less than usual in degreee, amount, etc*) ~ beer / wine / food / bread / pastry; a ~ diet / meal; a ~ attack of illness; ~ soil; a ~ coin; ~ money / weight / traffic (4 *not serious*) ~ comedy / reading / entertainment / literature / music / remarks; a ~ writer / comedian / programme; this is no ~ matter; make ~ of *(treat as of little importance)* (5 *thoughtless*) ~ conduct; a ~ woman; a man of ~ character; treat s.th. in a ~ way (6 *happy, care-free*) a ~ heart; in a ~ mood (7 *easy to do, bear*) a ~ task / job / affliction / punishment; ~ taxation; your work / duties will be ~; too complex to be answered ~ly; get off ~(ly) *(without heavy punishment).*

like *vt* (1 *find pleasing, attractive; enjoy*) do you ~ sports / fish / *etc*? all his classmates ~ him; there's nothing I ~ better than strawberries / travelling / *etc*; she ~s him but she doesn't love him; I ~ sitting in the sun; I didn't ~ going there *(I went there, but didn't enjoy it)*; do you ~ learning Chinese? I ~ you for telling the truth. (2a *choose, prefer*) I will go when I ~; how do you ~ your tea? I ~ it rather strong; I ~ people to tell the truth; do you ~ tea or coffee *(not an invitation* → 4)? history is the subject I ~ most / the most; he likes to think he never makes a mistake. (2b *implies prudence*) I ~ to go to the dentist twice a year; I ~ to check his work as he is often inaccurate. (3 *neg + ~ + inf: not do s.th.*) I didn't ~ to go there *(so I didn't do it)*; I don't ~ to contradict him; I didn't ~ to drink it as I didn't know what it was. (4 ~ *in conditional constructions: want to have; with inf: wish*) he would ~ a cup of tea / time to consider it / *etc*; would you ~ tea or coffee *(an invitation* → 2a)? he'd ~ to help; I should ~ you to go there / to know that I . . .; what would you ~ to do when (you leave school)? would you ~ to join us at tennis / to come for a walk / to learn Chinese? (5 *how + ~: find, feel about*) how do you ~ his new play / this wine? (6 *of food*) I ~ lobster but it doesn't ~ me *(gives me indigestion)*. (7 *ironical uses*) I ~ his impudence! Well! I ~ that! I should ~ to know / see (how he . . .).

limit *n* a ~ of growth / stress / period of time; a ~ of s.o.'s power / authority / patience; ~s of knowledge; a speed ~; (outside) the city ~s; a time ~ for speeches; an extreme / superior / upper / inferior / lower ~; narrow ~s; learn the ~s of one's abilities; I have reached the ~ of my patience; exceed a ~; (his greed) knows no ~s; put / set a ~ / ~s to (the expense of . . .); keep (s.th.) within ~s; you can trust him within ~s; within the ~s of legality; (supply s.th.) without ~; □ there is a ~ to everything; that's the ~! off ~s *(AE esp military: prohibited area)*: this building is off ~s (to unauthorized personnel).

limit *vt* (1) ~ the expense to (the essential / what one can afford); I should ~ him to 5,000 words for his article; ~ o.s. to (one piece of candy a day / the essentials); I shall ~ myself to three aspects of the problem. - *adj* (2) his knowledge / intelligence is very ~ed; our freedom is ~ed in this respect; a ~ed number of seats / seating capacity / number of persons; have a ~ed horizon / intelligence; have only ~ed resources.

line *n* (1) (draw) a straight / bent / curved / continuous / wavy ~; wind drove the rain in oblique ~s; a car with clean ~s; the goal ~; did the ball cross the ~? the pure ~ of his profile; the classic ~s of the town hall; a dividing ~ / ~ of division; the fine ~ between neurosis and psychosis (2) a ~ of cars / trees / chairs / people; a waiting ~; *(AE)* stand in ~ ; a long ~ of low hills; fly in a straight ~ (across the sky) (3) hold the *(telephone)* ~, he's just coming; he'll be on the ~ himself in a moment; ~ engaged! (4) deep ~s of care in s.o.'s face (5) an air / bus / steamship ~ (6) a railway / a branch / the main ~; cross the ~ by the bridge; fall from a train on to the ~ (7 *course of action, way of thinking*) the ~ of march of an army; choose / follow the ~ of least resistance; take a strong ~ *(act energetically)*; what ~ do you expect to take? study a subject on sound / the wrong ~s *(by good / bad methods)*; keep to / take one's own ~ *(be independent)*; the story will be written along the following ~(s); be in / out of ~ with *(agree / disagree with)*; bring into ~ *(make agree)*; come / fall into ~ (with) *(agree with)*; toe the (party) ~ *(accept the ideas etc)* (8a) a descendant of Bach in a direct / the male ~; the last of his ~; he comes of, from a good / royal ~. (8b) he is in ~ for the presidency / promotion / throne / *etc* (9) read the first ~; □ read between the lines; the actor forgot his ~s; I hope these few ~s *(brief letter)* will reach you; drop / send me a few ~s. (10) what's his ~? his ~ is banking / stockbroking / *etc*; he's in the building / drapery ~; oil painting isn't really (much in) my ~. (11) the salesman showed his ~ to the shopkeeper; we have a cheap ~ in felt hats; he stocks the best-selling ~ in woollen underwear; we don't deal in that ~. (12) *(inform: information)* get / have / give s.o. a ~ on s.o./ s.th. (13 *inform*) on the ~ *(in jeopardy)*; you are putting your reputation on the ~ with such questionable actions.

line *vt* (1) ~ the paper before writing; ~ s.th. out on paper (2) ~ a box with felt (3) cars / crowds of people ~d the kerb; a road ~d with trees / police (4) a ~d face; a face ~d with anxiety.

line up (1) he ~d up the children (to get on the bus); ~ up the wheels of a car (2) ~ up workers for a cause; his father had him ~d up for a career in the ministry. (3) the children quickly ~d up in the playground; the soldiers ~d up for inspection. (4) the editorial said that the Government is ~ing up with the United States against Russia.

link *vt* (1) ~ things together; ~ one's arm in / through another person's arm; she ~ed the bracelet round her wrist. (2) this road ~s York with London; two towns ~ed by a canal; gossip ~ed their names; in recent years the Geiger counter has ~ed hands with the atom to fight disease; ~ one's fortune with s.o./ s.th.

link up ~ up one question with another; this question ~s up / is ~ed up with another; where do they ~ up? this proposal ~ed up with the idea . . .

lip *n* lower / upper ~; trembling / compressed ~s; his ~s tightened a little; she refused to open her ~s *(say anything)*; curl one's ~ *(show scorn)*; bite one's ~; hang on s.o.'s ~s; keep a stiff upper ~ *(be* *brave, obstinate)*; that word never passed his ~s; escape s.o.'s ~s *(be said thoughtlessly)*.

listen *vi* (1) ~ to a person / a sound / a story / music / distant voices / s.o.'s speech / the church bells / approaching footsteps; ~ to s.o., s.th. intently / attentively / appreciatively / calmly / breathlessly / patiently / willingly / with half an ear; just ~ to the shouting! ~ for *(expect)* a certain sound; please ~ carefully for the telephone bell while I'm upstairs; ~ to the wireless / the radio / a station; did you ~ in *(listen to the radio)* last night? do you ever ~ to the radio / in to any of the B.B.C.'s programmes? (2) ~ to advice / counsel / reason / temptation; don't ~ to him, he knows nothing about it.

little¹ *adj* (1 *small*) a ~ dog followed me home; what a pretty ~ house; those nasty ~ children; a nice / nasty / horrid ~ room; how are the ~ ones? the ~ Smiths *(the Smith children)*; ~ but nice / mine; the ~ finger / toe; the L~ Bear / *(AE)* Dipper; you ~ rascal / scamp! she is expecting a ~ stranger *(a baby)* (2 *not long*) shall I go a ~ way with you? stay a ~ while; let's take a ~ trip. (3 *not tall*) he is very stout for such a ~ man; she is a nice ~ thing. (4 *narrow, petty*) your generosity seemed foolish to his ~ mind. (5 *fig*) he grumbled at her in spite of her poor ~ efforts to please; why do you come to me with every ~ difficulty? don't worry about (such) ~ things; it is no ~ thing that he is asking; Labour - the ~ man's party; so that's your ~ game *(of deception)*.

little² *adj* (1) he has (very) ~ knowledge of the matter / influence on it; ~ value / importance; she got ~ thanks for her trouble; my ~ bit of money (2 *a + ~: some*) give me a ~ sugar and a ~ cream; will you have a ~ cake; he knows a ~ English; stay with me a ~ while; the problem has given us not a ~ *(very much)* trouble.

little *adv* (1) he slept (very) ~ last night; I see him very ~; he talks ~ with other students; that is ~ short of *(is almost)* madness; you are ~ better than a thief; we waited ~ more than an hour. (2 *form: ~ placed before such verbs as* imagine, guess, think, realize, suspect, know) when I first came to this country, I ~ thought that I should stay so long; they ~ suspect that their plot has been discovered; he ~ knows / ~ does he know that we ... (3 *a + ~*) the skirt is just a ~ too short; stay with me a ~ longer (→ little² *adj* 2, little *n* 2); you must trust him a ~ ; he was not a / more than a ~ embarrassed.

little *n* (1 *small amount*) she gives ~ to charity; → less *n* 3; buy / sell s.th. for very ~; we must keep what ~ we have; he did what ~ he could; *(BE)* every ~ helps; ~ by ~ (gradually) (2 *a + ~: a short time*) stay with me a ~ (→ little² *adj* 2, little *adv* 3); after a ~ she glanced at him; he stepped out into the garden for a ~. (3 *a + ~: a certain amount*) she spent a lot of money but still has a ~ in the bank; I saw only a ~ of his work.

live *vi* (1) fish cannot ~ out of water; he still ~s (*commoner*: is still alive); ~ to be old / to a great age / to be a hundred; we may ~ to see another world war; I shall not / never ~ to see it; he will hardly ~ to see another day. (2 *dwell*) ~ in a house / hotel / town / country; the house has not been ~d in for many years; ~ at an address / 29 Euston Road; on a farm / abroad / among people / with one's friend / with a relative (3 *lead a life;* → life 7) ~ happily / honestly / simply / peacefully / poorly / from hand to mouth / beyond one's income / within one's income / in comfort / in prosperity / in abundance / in a fool's paradise / in great style / in reduced circumstances / the way the Germans do / together in unity (4 *fig*) his memory will always ~; he ~s in the memory of his family. - *vt* (5 → 3) ~ a life of luxury / a happy life / a (very un)healthy life; life was ~d by the Smiths on a fabulous scale; ~ one's faith.

live by ~ by hard honest labour / one's loyalties.

live down (1) ~ ~ a blunder / misdemeanour / shame / scandal; the Government can never ~ ~ the dishonest nature of its ultimatum. (2) she has ~d ~ all suspicion of her character; ~ ~ opposition to o.s. / an evil rumour about o.s.

live for ~ ~ one's work / golf / children / *etc.*

live off ~ ~ one's parents; farmers ~ ~ the land they cultivate; ~ ~ the fat of the land.

live on (1) the old people died but the young ones ~d on. (2 *of food, money; also fig*) ~ on bread and water / candy and ice-cream / fruit / a milk diet; ~ on one's earnings / a small pension / £20 a week; ~ on air *(appear to eat very little)*; ~ on one's wits *(get money dishonestly)*; ~ on one's name / reputation; she ~s on her memories.

live out (1) he won't ~ ~ the night / another week. (2) servants and soldiers ~ ~ *(not where they work)*.

live through can he ~ ~ the night? ~ ~ good times / difficult times / adventures / changes / two wars / many a storm / serious illness / poverty.

live up to (1) ~ up to the principles of Christianity / one's faith / one's reputation *(put into practice)*; ~ up to one's opportunities / the hopes of one's parents (2) ~ up to one's income *(spend it completely)*.

load *vt* (1) ~ (up) a cart / lorry / truck / boat / donkey / *etc* with s.th.; ~ a ship with grain; the table was ~ed with food; the lorry was ~ed with bricks; ~ s.o. (down) with parcels; ~ one's stomach with food; a heart ~ed with sorrows (2) ~ a bag on to a lorry; ~ goods on to a vehicle / into a ship; ~ a film *(put it into a camera)* (3) ~ s.o. with work / presents / honours / favours / praise / insults / abuse; he is ~ed with money. (4) ~ a gun / pistol / camera; are you ~ed *(is your pistol loaded)*? (5) he ~ed his arguments with facts that could not be challenged.

lock *vt* (1) ~ a door / box / trunk / cupboard; the door was ~ed fast. (2) ~ papers (away) in a drawer; have a secret safely ~ed (away) in one's breast (3) ~ arms / fingers (together); she ~ed her arms round his neck; they where ~ed in each other's arms; they were ~ed together in a fierce struggle; his jaws were tightly ~ed. (4 *stop revolving*) he ~ed the wheels of the car to prevent its being stolen. - *vi* (5) does this trunk ~? the box ~s easily / automatically. (6 → 4) the wheels ~ed when he braked.

lock in ~ o.s. in; she is ~ed in and nobody knows where the key is; he ~ed himself in his room.

lock out (1) ~ s.o. ~; I got home late last night and found myself ~ed ~. (2) ~ ~ workers *(prevent them working)*.

lock up (1) ~ up a house / room; ~ up before you leave. (2) ~ up a child / dog in a room; ~ the money / these papers up; ~ s.o. up *(imprison)* (3) his money is all ~ed up in land / long-term securities.

lodge *vt* (1) ~ flood victims in the schoolhouse (2) can you board and ~ me? (3) he ~d a bullet in the tree; ~ a blow on s.o.'s jaw / a knife in s.o.'s chest (4) ~ one's money and valuables in the bank (5) ~ a complaint / protest with (the director) against (a colleague). - *vi* (6) where are you ~ing now? I am ~ing at Mrs N's. (7) a fish-bone ~d in his throat; the bullet ~d in his arm.

long *adj / adv* (1) this room is 10 feet ~; how ~ is the river Nile? we had to walk two ~ *(tedious)* miles; a ~ list; a ~ dozen *(13)*; □ ~ in the tooth *(aged)* (2) a ~ visit / illness / war / life / friendship / memory; the ~ vacation; don't be ~ (about it); he / the chance was a ~ time (in) coming; the ~ last sleep; one's ~ home *(grave)*; were you waiting ~? I was waiting a ~ time; the work won't take ~; we have ~ thought so / been of that opinion; I can wait only three days at (the) ~est; I can't wait any ~er; he's no ~er living here; stay as ~ as you like; that happened ~ ago / ~ before the war / ~ after her death; all day / night / week ~; all his life ~. - *n* (3) the ~ and the short of it, he won't come; before ~.

look *vi* (1) ~ who it is; ~ who's here! we ~ed but saw nothing; he ~ed straight in front of him; he ~ed my way; ~ what time the clock says; ~ at s.o./ s.th. in astonishment / in surprise / in utter bewilderment / attentively / closely / fixedly / steadfastly / reflectively / searchingly / coldly / mildly / curiously / questioningly / inquiringly / inquisitively / doubtfully / furtively / casually / hastily / vacantly / pleadingly; ~ sharp *(make haste)*; ~ before you leap *(first think, then act)*; □ ~ a gift horse in the mouth *(critize a present)*; ~ s.o. in the eye / face (→ face *n* 6); look facts / death in the face (→ face *n* 6) (2) this house ~s south (→ look on / out / to) (3 ~ + *adj*) he ~ed cheerful / happy / glad / puzzled / warned / sad / tired / frail / ill / excited / angry / serious / grave / stern / solemn; the sky ~s rainy; the crops ~ well; she ~s well *(healthy)*; does this hat ~ well / good on me? he ~s well / good in uniform; the patient ~s much better; he tries to ~ big *(impress others)*; ~ alive *(hurry up)*! things are ~ing black / grim for him; ~ black (at s.o.) *(angry)*; ~ blue *(sad)*; we made him ~ small *(insignificant)*. (4 ~ + *like / as if*) he ~s like a big dog; he is only thirty but he ~s like an old man; what does she think she ~s like in those clothes? it ~s like rain / as if it's going to rain; John ~s like winning / as if he will win the race; it ~s like being / it will be a fine day; you ~ as if you slept badly. (5 ~ *+ n / to be*) he ~s every inch a king; he ~s the picture of health; she ~s sadness itself; he doesn't ~ his age / years; he's only 40 but he ~s 50; she ~ed a perfect dream *(very beautiful)*; she ~s her best in tweeds; she ~ed to be in good health; he ~ed to be stronger than he really was; you don't ~ yourself today; ~ one's thanks / consent *(express it by one's appearance)*; ~ daggers at s.o. *(fiercely)* (6 *imperative: pay attention*) just ~ what you're doing! ~ (and see) whether the postman has been yet; ~ where you're going! (7 ~ *+ inf: expect*) he is ~ing to be promoted.

look about (1) John ~ed ~ but saw no one; he ~ed ~ the room; we passed the afternoon ~ing ~ the town; we hardly had time to ~ ~ us before we had to continue our journey. (2) are you still ~ing ~ for a job? I ~ed ~ for you but ...; they ~ed ~ for help for a long time.

look after (1) they ~ed ~ the train as it left the station. (2) ~ ~ the baby / the cat / one's old mother; he's well able to ~ ~ himself / his own interests.

look ahead he said he had been ~ing (far) ~ when he suggested manufacturing synthetic fibres.

look around → look about 1.

look at (1) (→look *vi* 1) ~ at the ceiling / sky / floor; ~ at o.s. in the mirror; ~ at television / the blackboard; ~ at me! ~ askance at s.o.; ~ at the world through rose-tinted spectacles; s.o. is fair / good to ~ at; to ~ at him one might think he was angry / one should say he is very young. (2 *will / would not + ~ at: reject*) probably he will not ~ at the offer. (3 *examine*) a man has come to ~ at the drains; ~ at a question from all sides; he ~ed at the problem another way.

look back (1) ~ ~ in anger / with sorrow; ~ ~ upon the days of one's youth; Edison is a good man to ~ ~ upon. (2) I'll ~ ~ later *(visit again)*. (3) once the refugee had arrived in England, he never ~ed ~ *(made constant progress)*; you can't ~ ~ at this stage of the work *(must be willing to persevere)*.

look down (1) ~ ~ at the floor; ~ ~ a microscope; □ ~ ~ one's nose at s.o. *(contemptuously)* (2) she ~ed ~ (up)on all her neighbours.

look for (1) ~ ~ s.th. (lost); □ ~ ~ a needle in a haystack; if you are ~ing ~ trouble *(want a fight, argument)*, I'll give it to you. (2) I'll ~ ~ you about 3 o'clock; I'm ~ing ~ a cheap coat. (3) ~ ~ politeness from all one's employees; ~ ~ a better result next time; what are you ~ing ~ in life? ~ ~ amusement / understanding.

look forward ~ ~ to a party / the summer holidays; I'm ~ing ~ to seeing you again / your next visit.

look in (1) ~ in at the window (2) won't you ~ in (on me) on your way home? several friends ~ed in on the sick man that day.

look into (1) ~ ~ a box / the mirror / her eyes (2) ~ ~ a question / subject / record; I will ~ ~ your complaint about ...; something is wrong and he wants me to come along and ~ ~ it.

look on (1) my windows ~ on (to) the garden. (2) you two play and I'll ~ on; ~ on passively at s.th.; may I ~ on with you *(read from your book together with you)*? ~ on the bright / dark side (of things) *(be optimistic / pessimistic)* (3) ~ (up)on s.o. as an authority / as one's friend / *etc*; he ~s on her as a child; she ~s on him with awe / distrust; I ~ upon the problem with a different eye.

look out (1) ~ ~ and see if the rain has stopped yet; he stood at the window and ~ed ~ (at the view). (2) the house ~s ~ on fields / over the valley; my windows ~ ~ on (to) the garden. (3) ~ ~, there's a car coming! ~ ~ he doesn't cheat you! he ~ed ~ as he crossed the road; when you're eating fish, ~ ~ for bones; the eagle was ~ing ~ for prey; I'm ~ing ~ for a cheap coat; I ~ed ~ for you at the station but ... (4 *BE*) she ~ed ~ his address in the directory; ~ ~ a suitable design for a dress; he'll ~ ~ some new stamps for me / me ~ some new stamps.

look over (1) he ~ed ~ to(wards) her; we ~ed ~ the fence; ~ ~ here / there! (2) ~ ~ the account books / the house / one's papers *(inspect briefly)* (3) ~ ~ an error *(overlook)*.

look round (1) when I ~ed ~ for her she was leaving the hall. (2) have we time to ~ ~ (the town) before lunch? don't make a hasty decision, ~ ~ well first.

look through (1) he ~ed right ~ me *(ignored).* (2) ~ ~ the account books; have you ~ed the exam papers ~ yet? ~ ~ a photo-album (3) his greed ~ed ~ his eyes.

look to (1) a building that ~s to the south (2 *pay attention*) ~ to it that this never happens again / that the children are ready; and who will ~ to the baby? the country must ~ to its defences; ~ to your manners *(don't be so rude).* (3 *expect*) he ~s to a quiet old age; ~ to s.o. for help / advice / leadership; the principle that the old should ~ for support to the rest of the community; wives ~ to their jobs to provide a higher standard of living for their families; I ~ to you to help me / give me advice / *etc.*

look up (1) ~ up at the ceiling / sky; hearing a shout, he ~ed up (from his book). (2) ~ up a word in a dictionary; ~ up the time (of the next train) / a fast train to L. (3) you ought to ~ him up; ~ me up when you come to Rome. (4) she ~ed us up and down as though we were men from Mars. (5) every boy in the school ~ed up to *(respected)* the headmaster. (6 *improve)* things will ~ up again (with the Smiths); trade / the price of cotton is ~ ing / beginning to ~ up this year.

look *n* (1) have / take a ~ at s.th.; I had a good ~ at it this morning; give s.o. a kind / gentle / sympathetic / expectant / keen / interested / interrogative / inquiring / longing / yearning / pleading / frank / faraway / funny / sidelong / blank / knowing / wary / sharp / fierce / withering / significant / sly / arch / forbidding / glacial / glum / sad / sullen / grim / reproachful / disapproving / angry / cold / stern / scornful ~; give s.o. a black ~ / black ~s; she gave him a long, searching ~; she threw an angry ~ at me; let's have a ~ round. (2) the town has a European ~; do you notice any changes in the ~ of the country? he hasn't the ~ of a journalist; she had a very disappointed ~ when I said she must stay at home; have a frank / blank ~ in one's eyes; I don't like the ~ of him / things; she has her mother's ~s; good ~s are more important than intelligence; his good ~s impressed everybody; have good ~s (but no money); by the ~s of him he is ...; they aren't rich by the ~ of them.

loose *adj* (1) a ~ board / window / door / tooth / knot / thread / end of rope; ~ papers in a box / pages in a book; □ be at a ~ end / ~ ends *(have nothing to do)* (2) the dog got / broke ~ and ran away; the dog can't be left ~; the sheep roamed ~ on the hills; she wore her hair ~; carry one's change ~ in one's pocket; my shoelace has come ~; a nail / bolt / screw works ~; □ have a screw ~ *(inform: be a little mad)*; there's a screw ~ somewhere *(s.th. is wrong).* (3) ~ sand; (trample down) the ~ soil (4) a ~ collar / coat / boot; a ~ weave; ~-fitting clothes; ~ reins; □ ride with a ~ rein *(also fig: manage s.o. indulgently)* (5) his ~ talk / conduct / morals; bad punctuation is a sign of ~ thinking; a ~ thinker; a ~ argument; (have) a ~ tongue; lead a ~ life; a ~ woman; rules ~ly enforced; he let ~ his indignation; □ be on the ~ *(immoral)* (6) a ~ definition / translation / count; talk rather ~ly about s.th.; employ words ~ly.

loosen *vt* (1) ~ a screw / one's belt; one's grasp / hold of s.th. (2) ~ the soil (before planting) (3) this medicine may ~ your cough / the bowels; wine ~ed his tongue. (4) ~ regulations / discipline. - *vi* (5) the screw / knot has ~ed; the lid ~s when you heat it. (6) the sign of the Commonwealth's ~ing are unmistakable.

loosen up (1) ~ up one's muscles (2) the muscles are ~ing up.

lose *vt* (1) ~ s.th. of which one has had possession: a glove / pencil / coin / watch / umbrella; he lost his son (in a car accident) / his wife (to tuberculosis); you will ~ nothing by waiting. (2) ~ a / one's key; we've lost the / our way; ~ o.s. / be lost *(lose the way)*; we've lost our bearings *(the way; also fig)*; he lost himself in the crowd; he's lost all track of her since they left school; ~ one's place in a book; we lost sight of him in the crowd; the ship was lost sight of; we must not ~ sight of the fact that ... (3 *get rid of*) I've lost my cold; ~ weight / flesh; he has lost that terrified look. (4a *fail to keep*) ~ one's hair / health / life / good looks / balance; ~ one's job / work / friends / customers (to a rival shop); the cloth has lost its colour; the car lost speed; he lost himself *(was absorbed)* in his book. (4b ~ + *abstract object*) ~ one's chance; he will ~ his chance of success unless he works harder; ~ connection (with s.o./ s.th.) / consciousness / courage / credit / face (with one's class) / faith / favour with s.o. / ground / one's head / heart *(courage)* / one's heart to s.o., s.th. / hope; s.th. ~s its importance; he lost interest in the matter; the film / book soon lost interest; ~ one's patience / one's memory / rank / one's reputation / one's reason *(become mad, excited)* / self-control / self-respect / one's sense of proportion / one's senses *(reason)* / one's temper (over a little thing like that) / touch with s.o., s.th.; it was so cold that we lost the use of our hands. (5 *not catch; miss*) the thief was lost in the crowd; he lost his companion in the crowd; we lost the bus / the post / an opportunity; we lost the / our train (by about a minute); I lost your last few sentences; we lost the point of his argument; I lost most of the sermon; his words were lost in the applause. (6a *waste*) we lost time because of heavy traffic; ~ no time (in) doing s.th.; there is not a moment to ~; □ be lost upon *(fail to impress)*; my hints were lost upon him; its truth is lost upon less subtle observers. (6b *of watches*) my watch ~s / is ~ing two minutes a day. (7 *not win*) ~ a game / a match / a prize / a battle / a war / a (case in a) lawsuit / a motion (in a debate); a lost cause (8 *cause the loss of*) his mean remarks ~ him many friends / our sympathy; her rudeness lost her the, her job / position / situation. (9 *be lost: disappear, die*) the ship and all the crew were lost; conversation is a lost art; s.o. is lost to honour / duty / (all sense of) decency / shame *(is insensible to it)*; be lost in thought / wonder / admiration. - *vi* (10 → 1) you won't ~ on that deal *(suffer a loss)*; will the publisher ~ by it *(publishing the book)*? how much did he ~ on the transaction? the story did not ~ in the telling *(became bigger, was exaggerated)*. (11 → 7) ~ at a game; my horse lost in the second race; ~ to s.o. *(be defeated by him)*; play a ~ing game.

loss *n* (1) have a ~ (instead of a profit); a (gradual) ~ of health / wealth; ~ of / in weight (2)... is a serious ~ for (the town); he is a born actor and certainly a ~ to the stage and screen; (bear / suffer) a slight / considerable / incalculable / irreparable / outright / dead *(complete)* ~; realize the extent of a ~; share a ~ with s.o.; (sell s.th. at) a ~ of £100; a ~ of blood / time / opportunities; without any ~ of time; such a man is no great ~. (3) the ~ of the race / contest / battle / contract; this game is their first ~. (4) both sides suffered heavy ~es (in the battle).

lot *n* (1) draw / cast ~s for s.th.; the ~ came to / fell upon me. (2) they chose their representative by ~. (3) poverty is his ~; his ~ has been a hard one; it is / falls to my ~ to do it; throw / cast in one's ~ with s.o. *(join up with him)*; he is a bad ~ *(inform: wicked person)*. (4) a new ~ of shoes has just arrived in the shop. (5) the house and the ~ it stands on; a neighbouring / empty / vacant / bushy ~ (6) we have a ~ of work to do / of money to spend; what a ~ of rabbits; all this must come to an awful ~ of money; I want a ~ more; he works a ~ at home; think a ~ *(highly)* of s.o.; □ I have a ~ on / a ~ of work on my hands; you'll need ~s of patience; ~s of people came; there's ~s of cocoa in this cake. (7 *the ~: the whole quantity*) we had a fine show of dahlias but frost spoilt the ~; take the (whole) ~, I don't want any; that's the ~ *(everything)*.

love *n* (1) a mother's ~ for her children; ~ between husband and wife; ~ at first sight; parental / married / conjugal ~; great / deep / sincere / true / unrequited ~; fall in ~ (with s.o.); fall out of ~; be in ~ (with s.o.); make ~ to s.o. (2) a ~ of books / learning / adventure; to show ~ towards one's neighbours; she fell in ~ with the cottage at once; □ there's no ~ lost between them *(they heartily dislike each other)*; a ticket was not to be had / you could not get a ticket for ~ or money; I wouldn't kiss him for ~ (n)or money *(under any circumstances)*; he works in the garden just for the ~ of it. (3 *greetings*) give my ~ to Jane; send s.o. one's ~ (4) play a game for ~ *(not for money)*.

love *vt* (1) ~ one's wife / parents / children dearly / deeply / with all one's heart (2) ~ God / one's country / all men / a pet (animal) (3) ~ music / painting / golf / playing tennis / sea-bathing / *etc*; will you come with me? I should ~ to; I would ~ to hear that orchestra play; children ~ listening to fairy tales.

low *adj* (1) a ~ wall / table / mountain / range of hills / forehead; a room with a ~ ceiling; the shelf is too ~ on the wall; the picture hangs ~; the glass *(barometer)* is ~; the clouds hung ~; the moon was ~ in the sky; ~ tide / water; □ be in ~ water *(short of money)*; wear a ~(-necked, -cut) dress / a dress with a ~ neck; the dress was cut ~ at the back. (2) ~ classes; ~ life *(that of the lower classes)*;

have a ~ station in life; a man of ~ birth; ~ value / quality; ~-quality goods (3 *of sounds*) speak in a ~ voice; the ~ notes of a cello; a ~ whisper (4 *less than usual, near the bottom of a scale*) ~ content / height / weight / temperature / pressure / speed / intelligence; a ~ diet *(simple)*; our water supply is (getting) ~; name a ~ number; the ~est bid; ~ wages / prices; the river is ~ *(has little water)*; a very ~ oil consumption (5 *vulgar*) ~ manners / tastes / ideas / conduct / conversation / language; a ~ fellow / company / trick / remark; a ~ comedian / comedy; I never fell so ~ as that *(degraded myself so much)*; he wouldn't sink as ~ as that. (6 *unfavourable*) have a ~ opinion of (liars) (7 *little advanced*) a ~ form of life; ~er tribes / races; animals of ~ organization (8 *weak, depressed*) ~ vitality / state / condition; (be in) ~ spirits / in a ~ state of health; be feeling ~; a ~ pulse; the patient is very ~, but the new drug will help him; the fever left him feeling ~; a ~ fever.

low *adv* (1 → low *adj* 1) bend / bow / fly / aim / shoot / burn ~ ; the shot went too ~. (2 → low *adj* 3) speak ~(er) (so they won't hear us); talk ~; I can't sing any ~er.

lower *vt* (1) ~ a boat into water; ~ a flag / a window / the blinds / the ceiling of a room; ~ o.s. / s.o. on a rope (2) ~ the price of milk / the rent of a house; ~ the rates / taxes / duties / tariffs; ~ the water in a canal / the light beam of a car (3) ~ one's voice (to a whisper) (4) his conduct has ~ed him greatly in public opinion; his arrogance ~ed him in her estimation / esteem; ~ s.o.'s pride (5) poor diet ~s resistance to illness; ~ the value / quality of s.th. (6) ~ o.s. (to do such a thing) / in the world's esteem; you would not ~ yourself in the least by doing this job.

luck *n* (1) have good / bad ~ (in one's affairs); have more ~ than judgement; have hard ~; wish s.o. (good) ~ for, in an examination / enterprise; good ~! I wish you ~! best of ~ *(wishes)*! rotten ~! bad ~! your ~ was out ! better ~ next time *(commiseration for a failure)*! no such / worse / just my ~ *(disappointment)*. (2 *good luck*) what a stroke / great piece of ~! some people have all the ~ *(said enviously)*; he's got the ~ of the devil / the devil's own ~; as ~ would have it; I had the ~ to (find him at home); with varying ~; trust to ~; keep s.th. for ~ *(as a talisman)*; try / help one's ~; be out of/ in ~ *(un/ fortunate)*; my ~ has run out; ~ has turned against me; be down on one's ~ *(be poor, unemployed, etc)*; I never have any ~!

M

mad *adj* (1) drive / send s.o. ~; ~ ravings; a ~ laughter; be ~ with pain / rage / fear; he has a ~ look in his eye; you must be ~! (2 *foolish*) a ~ idea / enterprise / undertaking; what a ~ thing to do! it was ~ of him to do it; a ~ rush towards the exit; drive at a ~ speed; drive / talk / run / work / *etc* like ~ *(inform)*; why did he act so ~ly? she rushed ~ly down the stairs. (3 *eager to have*) the dog was ~ for water; he was ~ for / after a new car. (4 *wildly enthusiastic*) he is ~ on, about football / ballet; he was quite ~ with joy; be ~ly in love (5 *inform: angry*) he was ~ about / at losing the money / missing the train; she was ~ with me for spilling the ink; don't be ~ at me! (6 *in love*) she is ~ about John. (7 *exceedingly merry*) we had a ~ time at the party.

mail *n* (*chiefly AE; BE* → post[2]*n*) (1) could you put this letter in the ~ for me? the ~ must go through; please remit by ~; simply drop this application card in the ~ and ...; this answer came by (return) ~; send a letter by air (~) / surface (~) (2) has the ~ come yet? when is the next / first / last ~-delivery? this letter just came / arrived in the ~; private ~; first- / second-class ~ (3 the ~s: *system of mail transportation*) Mr G. has taken charge of the ~s; the suspect was convicted for using the ~s to defraud; misuse of the ~s is punishable by heavy fines.

mail *vt* (*chiefly AE; BE* → post[1] *vt*) please ~ this letter / package for me; stamp your letter before you ~ it; applications must be ~ed before Sept 1st if ...

maintain *vt* (1) ~ a speed of 50 miles an hour / the temperature / an even temperature; ~ one's health / one's strength / a (good) reputation / a situation / a high standard of morals; a good student ~s his marks by regular study; ~ an open mind on a question; ~ one's rights (2) to ~ our schools and roads we must spend a great deal of money; ~ a bridge / the streets in good condition (3) ~ quiet (in the library) / (the) (social) peace / law and order / the relationship with s.o. / (good / friendly) relations with s.o. / one's composure (4) ~ one's view / one's opinion / an assertion / an argument / a fact; he ~ed that he had told the truth; it is, as some people ~, a bad mistake. (5) he ~ed his innocence when accused of breaking the window. (6) ~ a family / a large household / a son at the university.

make *vt* 1-20, 22, 23a, 24-33; *vi* 23b; *vt/ i* 21.

The patterns are grouped as follows: ~ + *adj*: 11; ~ + as if: 23b; ~ + believe, do: 23a; ~ + *inf with* to: 23b; ~ + it + *indef article* + *n* + *inf*: 20; ~ + *obj* + *adj*: 22a; ~ + *obj* + from + *n*: 1b; ~ + *obj (esp abstract)* + *indef article* + *n*: 19; ~ + *obj* + *inf without* to: 24; ~ + *obj* + of + *n*: 1b–1e, 30; ~ + *obj* + out of + *n*: 1c; ~ + *obj* + *past part*: 22a; ~ + oneself + *adj*: 22b; ~ + oneself + *past part*: 22b; ~ + *personal obj* + *indef article* + *n*: 18; ~ + *personal obj* + *n without article*: 17; ~ + *prepos*: → separate entries.

Patterns 1–5: ~ + *n of basically concrete meaning*; 6 (partly 4, 5) - 16: ~ + *n corresponds to a verb more or less identical with the n;* 25-33: ~ + *n of basically abstract meaning.*

(1a *construct, produce with one's hands, industrially*)

~ bread; ~ a cake / desk / coat / new suit / kite / cart / plough; this cake is made with self-raising flour; she made herself a dress (out) of an old curtain (→ 1b); she made the material into a dress; ~ a film / a book / a sonnet / verses; ~ her a bouquet / a bouquet for her; ~ an aeroplane out of this sheet of paper; we ~ paper into many things; ~ goods / articles / bricks / paper / *etc* (by machine); ~ a road / railway / canal; our firm ~s 10,000 machines every year; all articles made by us are guaranteed for one year; made to order; custom-made; she made coffee / tea / cocoa / chocolate / grog / punch (for all of us); I made myself a cup of tea; ~ the breakfast / dinner / meal (→ 29); ~ one's toilet / a bed / one's bed; ~ a fire; ~ hay (while the sun shines); □ ~ hay of *(put into disorder)*; whose turn is it to ~ / ~ the cards *(shuffle them)*? ~ water (→ water *n* 1b, 6); ~ a hole / slit / tear / incision / fold / corrugation (in this paper); ~ a depression (in the rubber) / an impression (on the soap / on s.o.); ~ an impact on s.th/ s.o.

(1b *made from, of*)

wine is made from grapes; he made a boat from a tree-trunk; the jug is made of the finest china; a table made of wood; a bridge made of steel; a blouse made of silk; □ be made of money *(very rich).*

(1c *make* + *noun* + of/ out of + *noun / person*)

~ a friend / ally / supporter / enemy / opponent of s.o.; we shall never ~ a scholar of that boy; ~ a dancer / artist / actor / soldier / liar / *etc* out of s.o. (→ 18); we must ~ an example of him *(punish him as a warning to others)*; let them see what you are made of; ~ a fool / mock / laughing-stock of s.o. (→ 18); ~ fun / game / sport of s.o.; she rarely ~s game of her sister; □ ~ mincemeat of s.o. *(beat him severely)*: the fighter made mincemeat of his opponent.

(1d *make* + *noun* + of + *o.s.*)

~ a fool / an object of ridicule / a laughing-stock of o.s.; ~ an ass / beast / nuisance of o.s.

(1e *make* + *noun* + of + *noun*)

~ a business of politics *(~ politics one's profession)*; ~ a success of s.th.; ~ a good job of s.th.; ~ the best of things / one's time; ~ a mess of a job; ~ a mess / hash / muddle of s.th.; ~ a joke / jest of (s.o.'s inability to do it); ~ a point / issue / failure / reality of s.th.; he ~s a point of reading a fresh book every month; don't ~ a habit of (taking pot); ~ a practice of (rising early); he is ~ing hard work of the job by (not using a computer); he ~s no secret / mystery of (his attitude); ~ a clean breast of (the whole matter); they made a clean sweep of (their old furniture) *(got rid of it)*; the locusts made short work of the ripe standing corn; the lawyer will make short work of John's arguments; the unruly crowd made a shambles *(state of disorder, ruin)* of the bar; □ ~ a mountain out of a molehill; □ ~ a virtue of necessity; ~ something of o.s. / one's life; something could be made of that subject; do you want to ~ something of it *(argue about it)*? ~ much of: the report made much of the firm's efficiency; I couldn't ~ much of his lecture / all this scribble (→30); he made much of her carelessness (*made a fuss of;* →25b); the Prime Minister had made little of the Party's achievements in his speech.

(2a *create*)
God made man / the world; you are made for this job.

(2b *have as a grammatical form*)
'write' ~s in the past tense 'wrote'; 'child' ~s 'children' in the plural.

(3 *make + noun: make room, progress*)
~ room for him at your desk; ~ accommodation available at your desk for him; ~ a place / space for this in the cupboard; ~ a gap between the two desks; ~ head (-way) (against s.th.); ~ (a) way through the crowd to the car; ~ way for s.o.; ~ one's way in business / in the world; ~ (good/ slow) progress; science has made great advances; ~ advances to s.o.; ~ a retreat / withdrawal.

(4 *make + noun: make what one sees or hears*)
~ a face / a grimace / faces / grimaces (at s.o.); ~ eyes at her; ~ an expression of sorrow / joy / relief / displeasure; ~ a sound (like a bee) / a rustling sound / a noise (with s.th.) / a tapping noise / an explosion with a paper bag / an exclamation (of surprise) / an ejaculation (of pain); ~ music.

(5 *make + noun: make what one writes, draws, etc*)
~ a stroke / a cross / angle / mark / spot (on the blackboard); ~ a (rough) draft (of a letter); ~ a plan / sketch / outline / drawing / diagram / design of (the house *etc*); ~ a portrait / caricature (of him); ~ a note / copy / record / list / inventory (of s.th.); ~ an entry (in the book); ~ an order (for a set of tools) / a (written) application / a (written) offer / a bid for s.th.; ~ an extract / summary / précis / review / revision / résumé (of this article); ~ a survey of this question; ~ an appreciation of (the position); ~ a report (on s.th.).

(6a *make + noun: verb of motion*)
~ a motion / movement (with one's right hand); ~ a gesture (with one's hand / of delight / of impatience / *etc*); ~ a bow / curtsey / jump / leap / somersault; ~ a rush / dash / dive for the door; ~ haste; ~ a turn round the table / tour of the village; ~ a move *(also fig: in foreign policy)*; it's time we made a move; ~ one's entrance / exit / farewell / escape; ~ing our entrance we joined the throng.

(6b *make + noun: verb of pretence*)
~ a threat (to hit him); ~ a feint (of hitting / to hit him); ~ a pretence / show / demonstration (of hitting him) (→ 23b).

(6c *make + noun: verb of travelling*)
~ a journey to Rome / trip to town / tour of Ireland / voyage to India / excursion to the lake / visit to the museum / detour; I have several calls to ~ .

(7 *make + noun: verb of saying*)
~ a remark / reply / response / statement / assertion / allegation / announcement / oration / pronouncement (about s.th.); ~ a speech (on/ about s.th.); ~ (no) answer; ~ a few criticisms; ~ mention of s.th.; ~ a (brief) reference (to s.th.) / an allusion (to s.th.) / intimation (of s.th.) / only a passing observation of the fact that . . .; ~ an acknowledgement of (s.o.'s contribution); ~ due acknowledgement to those who . . .; ~ a proposal / suggestion / recommendation (to s.o.) (that it . . .); ~ an appeal / plea / petition for help; ~ a request (to s.o. for s.th.); I have a request to ~; ~ a joke / jest / crack (about s.th.); ~ an explanation (for failure); ~ an accusation / charge (of favouritism / against s.o.) / claim (for damages) / demand (for reducing work); ~ pretensions (to s.th. / to be s.th); ~ a protest (about s.th.); ~ a (full) confession (of guilt) / admission (of failure) / disclaimer (of one's liability); the accused have made an avowal / disavowal of complicity; ~ a disclosure / revelation (about one's action); ~ a rebuttal / denial (of lateness) / (flat) contradiction (to a statement) / objection (to a proposal).

(8 *make + noun: verb of suppositon*)
~ the assumption / supposition / surmise / hypothesis / postulate / deduction / conclusion that . . .; ~ a (wild) guess (at s.th.) / approximation of s.th. / (precise) estimate of s.th. / (accurate) assessment of s.th. / judgement / valuation / evaluation of s.th.

(9 *make + noun: verb of giving*)
~ a present / gift / contribution / donation / payment (of £2 to a fund); ~ s.o. a present (of a necklace); ~ him a donation (of £2 for the fund); ~ a payoff *(AE inform: bribe)*; ~ (a) delivery; the firm made delivery the same day (we bought the goods); they made immediate delivery.

(10 *make + noun: verb of deciding*)
~ a choice / selection / resolution.
(11 *make + noun: verb of ordering; various synonyms*)
~ a rule / ruling / regulation / order / law; the committee made a rule that clubrooms close at 10 p.m.; they made an order for his arrest; Congress ~s the nation's laws; ~ a contract / agreement / settlement / pact / treaty / alliance; ~ terms with s.o.; ~ an arrangement / arrangements (with s.o. for s.th.); ~ a will; ~ a bargain (with s.o. / about s.th. / to sell s.th.); ~ a policy; ~ war (on a country); ~ peace; ~ a date / rendezvous / meeting with s.o.; ~ an appointment with s.o. (for s.th./ to do s.th.); ~ the acquaintance of s.o.; ~ friends with s.o.; this had made him many friends.
(12 *make + noun: verb of endeavouring*)
~ an attempt (to do s.th.) / a try / an effort (to do s.th.); ~ every endeavour (to be here early).
(13 *make + noun: verb of testing*)
~ an examination (of s.th.) / an inspection (of s.th.) / an inquiry / inquiries (about s.o./ s.th., as to whether ...) / investigations / a study (of s.th.); ~ an experiment (to find out ...) / a test / the discovery (of s.th.) / an analysis of s.th./ a synthesis of s.th.; ~ a / one's diagnosis; ~ a prognosis / prediction / prophecy (that it ...) / forecast.
(14 *make + noun: verb of restricting*)
~ a qualification / reservation / restriction / limitation; I must ~ the qualification that the use of the drug is beneficial in very small doses; the regulation ~s limitations on the age of entry; ~ the condition / proviso / stipulation / prerequisite that ... (→ 20).
(15 *make + noun: verb of compensating*)
~ compensation (for s.th.) / restitution of s.th. (to s.o. / for damages done) / reparation (by doing s.th.); ~ amends to s.o. for (an injury / damages done); ~ amends by apologizing; ~ a substitution (of A for B).
(16 *make + noun = verb; examples similar to 6-15 but grouped alphabetically*)
~ an acquisition (of s.th.); ~ addition (of some milk); ~ allowance(s) (for his youth); ~ an alteration / apology; ~ one's appearance; ~ an attack (on favouritism) / a beginning (to do s.th.) / a bid for freedom / a bid to do s.th. (for a certain price) / a book *(take bets* → book *n* 3) / a break with s.o./ an (exact) calculation (of s.th.) / a cancellation (of s.th.) / a change (in s.th.) / a classification (of things) / a collection (of things) / a commitment (on doing / to do s.th.) / a complaint (about s.th.); ~ contact with s.o.; ~ a correction; ~ (great) demands upon (s.o.'s energy / time); ~ a deletion / division (of s.th. into s.th) / end (of/ to s.th.) / engagement (to do s.th.) / exception (in a case) / excuse (for lateness); he is always ~ing excuses; ~ a clear getaway / halt / (good) impression / increase (in s.th.) / insertion / (emergency) landing / mixture (of sand and clay) / modification (in s.th.) / oath (to do s.th.) / offer (to do s.th.) / omission / pause; ~ preparations (for s.th.); ~ a promise (to do s.th.); ~ provision for (one's old age) / against (losses); ~ a purchase / reduction (in s.th.) / sacrifice / search (for s.o./s.th.) / start (to do s.th.) / stand for (one's principles) / stand against (the enemy); ~ an undertaking (to do s.th.); ~ use of s.th.; ~ a vow (to do s.th.).

(17 *make + noun + (no article) noun; of persons*)
let's ~ him captain / chairman / secretary / *etc*; ~ s.o. king; he made her his wife.

(18 *make + noun + indefinite article + noun; of persons*)
she made him a good husband (→ 27); they made him a member of the committee / a clerk / an engineer / a librarian / a peer / a general; ~ s.o. a dancer / artist / actor / soldier / liar (→ 1c); ~ s.o. / o.s. a fool / laughing-stock (in the whole village); ~ s.o. / o.s. the laughing-stock of the whole village / office / *etc*; → 1c, 1d).

(19 *make + noun + indefinite article + noun; of things, chiefly abstract*)
he made that a habit; the telegram ~s his return a certainty; the new discovery ~s positive results a likelihood / (im)probability / (im)possibility (→ 22); we should ~ this a matter for the committee to decide; we must ~ the solution of our production problems a matter of urgency; a good purpose ~s hard work a pleasure.

(20 *make +* it *+ indefinite article + noun + to + infinitive*)
he made it a habit to rise early; she ~s it a rule to be late; he ~s it a custom / practice / routine to drink milk for breakfast; they ~ it a condition / proviso / stipulation / prerequisite that we ... (→ 14); the Railway Act ~s it an offence to travel

without a ticket; these reactions ~ it a mistake to repeat the treatment
(21 *make + adjective*)
~ certain / sure (of a fact / of the time of arrival / that she... / whether he...); there's a train at 9.10 but you ought to ~ certain / sure; I'll go to the theatre and ~ certain / sure of our seats *(reserve them)*; I made certain he was going to hit me *(inform: felt sure)*; ~ bold with s.th. *(take the liberty of using it)*; I ~ bold to say that he...; she made so bold as to bring the prisoner refreshments; the ship made fast; he seems to have made free with my whisky while I was away; ~ good: one seldom ~s good without hard work; that boy will never ~ good; the man who ruined my car must ~ good *(compensate)* my loss; let me ~ good your loss; ~ good *(fulfil)* a promise / boast; ~ good one's escape; ~ good a statement; ~ the best of one's qualities / an event / an opportunity; the situation is difficult but we must ~ the best of it; ~ the best of a bad job / bargain; he wants to ~ the best of both worlds *(avoid a compromise)*; ~ light of s.o. / s.o.'s qualities / troubles; ~ light of a situation / illness; ~ merry; ~ the most of s.th.; he ~s the most of the little he has.
(22a *make + noun + adjective / participle*)
this ~s me tired / sick / sleepy / *etc*; ~ s.o. content / happy / sad / *etc*; ~ the pace big(ger) / the slices thick(er); cleaning ~s the surface bright; water ~s them rusty; oiling ~s the screws looser; ~ the rope fast (to the post); the telegram ~s his return certain; the new discovery made positive results (un)likely / (im)probable / (im)possible (→ 19); ~ s.th. impossible for s.o.; when I arrived in the new district everybody made me welcome; he made his meaning clear; I'll ~ it worth your while *(will reward you)*; this medicine has made me well *(healthy)* / better; ~ s.th. known; ~ one's influence felt; it will ~ you liked by everyone; the report / president made it clear that reforms are overdue.
(22b *make + o.s. + adjective / participle*)
~ o.s. tall(er) / useful / the smartest / elegant / scarce / (un)popular; he ~s himself familiar with (the regulations) / cognisant of (the facts) / (fully) aware of (all the circumstances) / competent in (all fields); ~ o.s. understood / heard (above the noise) / liked / respected and obeyed.

(23a *make +* do / believe)
I don't know how she ~s do *(manages)* on so small an income; we had to ~ do with 50 marks a week / with half the amount / without a dictionary; the children made believe that they were pirates / to be pirates.
(23b *make + infinitive / as if*)
he made as if (he were going) to strike me; he made to reply and then stopped (→ 6b).
(24a *make + noun + infinitive*)
they made her cry / hurry / hesitate / *etc*; it made us laugh (to watch them) / smile (to think of those days / realize our good fortune); ~ s.th. fit / fly / jump; here is a toy, ~ it go / work; that dress ~s her seem young(er); it ~s the room seem smaller; she made him look silly; (the weather) made her feel fine / blue; the book ~s the reader think; ~ the child behave! there isn't much of it but we'll ~ it do *(be sufficient)*; I shall have to ~ this old overcoat do for a bit longer; that made him sit up *(inform: was a great surprise)*.
(24b *make + o.s. + infinitive*)
(you must) ~ yourself hold your breath / do your duty / face the facts; she ~s herself appear young by wearing that dress; one ~s oneself feel ridiculous by appearing without shoes.
(25a *make + mistake and synonyms*)
~ a mistake / error / blunder / howler / mess (of things, one's life, *etc*) / faux-pas / slip (of the tongue, pen) / miscalculation / oversight
(25b *make + fuss and synonyms*)
~ a fuss / row / scene / outcry / confusion / disturbance / a song and dance *(inform)* / a lot of ado (about s.th.).
(25c *make + trouble and synonyms*)
~ trouble / mischief / difficulties.
(26 *make + difference and synonyms*)
~ a / no difference between things; ~ a contrast / comparison / distinction / analogy / parallel between A and B; s.th. ~s all the difference.
(27 *make + noun: become, turn out to be)*
he would ~ a good actor / officer / *etc*; John and Ann ~ a handsome couple; she made (him) a good wife (→ 18); the site would ~ a good playground; this length of cloth will ~ me a suit; grey walls ~ the best background for paintings; this story ~s excellent / lively / very depressing reading; □ one swallow does not ~ a summer; one high note does not ~ a singer; that ~s the fifth roe I've seen today; this ~s

the third time you have failed this examination; those plants will not ~ much, the soil is too poor; I don't think he will ever ~ much, he hasn't the brain; your dance will ~ the show *(~ it successful)*; that performance will ~ him.

(28 *make used for distance, destination, time*)
if we hurry we can ~ home by sundown; you can ~ it if you hurry; she is tired out already, she'll never ~ the summit; we made Rome in three days by driving all the time; we made land at sunset; the ship was only just able to ~ port; we've made 80 miles since noon; the ship was ~ing only nine knots; don't ~ it any later than eleven o'clock, will you?

(29 *make + noun:* reach; achieve)
~ good marks at school; ~ one's mark *(do s.th. noteworthy)*; he will ~ his mark in the world *(become famous)*; he had made a name (for himself) / reputation (as a stamp-collector); this decision of our government will ~ history; he is ~ing a good score under difficult conditions; ~ five points in a game / a trick (in a card game); *(fig)* ~ a point (→ point *n* 11); will they ~ the finals? ~ a good dinner / meal *(eat well*; → 1a).

(30 *make + pronoun /* sense + of *+ noun: understand*)
he (can't) ~ sense of this; I can ~ nothing / can't ~ anything of this telegram / all this scribble (→ nothing *pron*); what are we to ~ of his behaviour? what do you ~ of the new assistant? → ~ much of 1e.

(31 *make used of figures, parts that constitute a total, a whole*)
two and two ~ four; two pints ~ a quart; a hundred pence ~ a pound; twelve inches ~ a foot; 90 degrees ~ a right angle; oxygen and hydrogen ~ water; these two gloves don't ~ a pair; rice and bacon ~ a fine dish.

(32 *make + noun + a figure: calculate; estimate*)
I ~ the answer / total / addition / amount / result £787; I ~ the distance (about) 20 yards / the weight 4 ounces / the height 10 feet; how large do you ~ the audience? what time do you ~ it? what do you ~ the time / total / *etc*?

(33 *earn, gain; used of money, time*; → money)
he ~s £800 a year / a good salary; he is ~ing 10p per dozen / a handsome profit / a loss of £5 on the deal; ~ a / one's living by (giving lessons / from one's writing); ~ a fortune (by doing s.th.); ~ a / one's pile *(earn and save a lot of money)*; I've made *(a profit)* on the shares; he made handsomely on the bargain; the firm is willing to ~ you an advance of £50; ~ capital (out) of (s.o.'s mistakes); we made 20 minutes by coming this way (instead of following the road); the train made good time.

make after the constable made ~ the thief *(not common)*.

make against these dissipations ~ ~ your chances of success.

make at several men made ~ *(attacked)* me as I left the restaurant.

make away while the others were arguing I made ~ on my bicycle.

make away with (1) the unhappy woman tried to ~ ~ ~ herself *(commit suicide)*. (2) the tiger made ~ ~ all the meat; he has made ~ ~ five thousand pounds.

make for (1) he made ~ the exit as fast as he could; ~ ~ the shore / home / the nearest town; what are you ~ing ~? (2) when I was halfway across the field the bull made ~ me and I had to run; the dog made ~ me. (3) economic independence made ~ later marriages and more frequent divorces; a happy marriage ~s ~ contentment; ~ for understanding / good relations between ...

make from (1) → make 1b (2) I can ~ nothing ~ these scribblings (→ make 30).

make of (1) made of → make *vt* 1b (2) ~ much / little of → make *vt* 1e (3) ~ something / nothing of *(understand*: → make *vt* 30) (4) ~ fun / *etc* of → make *vt* 1c (5) ~ a fool / *etc* of → make *vt* 1d (6) ~ a habit / *etc* of doing → make *vt* 1e.

make off he made ~ in the opposite direction; the thief made ~.

make off with the thief made ~ ~ the jewellery; the puppy made ~ ~ a beefsteak; someone has made ~ ~ my umbrella.

make out (1) I can't ~ ~ what you're saying / the meaning of this passage; someone is coming down the mountain but I can't ~ ~ who it is / ~ him ~ ; can you ~ Mr Smith ~ *(what kind of a man he is)*? (2) ~ ~ a list / cheque (for s.o. to the amount of $50) / bill / receipt / account (of all the sums paid) / income tax return / document in triplicate; when I buy something I always have a bill made ~ for it. (3) the testimonial ~s him ~ *(shows him as)* a person of the highest character; the barrister made ~ his case very clearly. (4) you tear along like a madman and then you try to ~ ~ it's my fault; you can't ~ ~ that we haven't tried to help you; he ~s me ~ a fool; are you trying to ~ ~ that I am a liar? things aren't as bad as you ~ ~. (5) let's ~ ~ *(pretend)* that we are foreigners; he made ~ to be ill/ poor; he made ~ that he hadn't done it. (6) I think he will ~ ~ *(inform: get along, succeed)* all right; how is he / are things ~ing ~? how did the children ~ ~ while their parents were absent? ~ ~ in a race.

make out of (1) → make *vt* 1a. (2) → make *vt* 30. (3) → make *vt* 1c.

make over (1) ~ ~ a dress (2) ~ ~ *(transfer formally)* all one's property to s.o.; I have made ~ the house into your name / to the National Trust.

make towards the swimmer made ~ the right bank of the river.

make up (1a) I made up a book from the loose pages; she made up the material into a dress; she made up the suit from old material; this material is too narrow to ~ up well. (1 b) ~ up a parcel (of disused clothes); ~ up goods into parcels / bundles; the grocer was ~ing up the butter into half-pounds packages. (1 c) ~ up a page of type *(arrange it technically)* (1 d) ~ up (a bottle of) medicine / a prescription.
(2) water ~s up most of the earth's surface; the book is made up of long and boring dialogues. (3) let's ~ up a good story; ~ up a poem / an excuse; that's not true, you've just made it up. (4) we need one more player to ~ up *(complete)* a team; a few pounds are still wanting to ~ up the requisite sum. (5) the grocer made up my account; the teacher will ~ up the report cards today. (6) students should ~ up the work they miss; we must ~ the loss up next week. (7) ought girls to ~ up at the age of 12? actors ~ up before the performance; ~ up one's face; isn't she badly made up! (8) ~ up a / one's quarrel; they won't ~ up since they quarrelled; they soon made it up after their quarrel; why don't you ~ (it) up with her? the differences were soon made up. (9) □ ~ up one's mind *(decide)*; at last he has made up his mind (to do it); I can't ~ up my mind to anything; the war is already lost - we must ~ up our minds to that *(accept it as unavoidable)*. (10) he must ~ up for the damage he caused; the Government won't ~ up your loss; how can we ~ up to you for what you have suffered? (11) it is hard to ~ up for lost time; you don't think her beauty could ~ up for her stupidity? let's try to ~ up for what we have missed. (12) some people ~ up to *(flatter)* rich or influential persons.

make *n* (1) he knows all the ~s of French cars; what ~ of car have you? what ~ are those cigarettes? (2) she liked the cloth but not the ~ *(style)* of the coat. (3) □ be on the ~ *(inform: try to make money out of everything)*.

making *n* (1) it seems like a difficulty of your own ~; a mistake of his ~ (2) he has the ~s of a leader. (3) military service was the ~ of him *(caused him to develop well)*. (4) s.o.'s ~s *(earnings)*.

man *n* (1) ~ is mortal; ~ today faces / men today face a struggle for survival; the busy hum of men; no ~ can tell what...; the inner ~ *(soul; stomach)*; the outer ~ *(body; appearance)* (2) a big / tall / huge / short / healthy / sick ~; a young / old / aged / handsome / ugly ~; a holy / honest / honourable / respectable / determined / able / enterprising / solid / matter-of-fact / outstanding / independent ~; a cultivated / intellectual / learned / professional / medical ~; a contrary / credulous / canny / sinful / wretched / drunken / fast *(extravagant)* ~; a ~ of high culture / intellect / great learning / principles / high principle / stature / decision / substance *(money)* / few words / wide interests / many talents *etc*; a ~ of letters *(writer and scholar)* / arts *(gifted)* / spirit *(courageous)* / the world *(experienced)*; a / one ~ in a thousand *(unequalled)*; the ~ in the street *(average person)*; a ~ about town *(cosmopolitan society idler)*; be one's own ~ *(free to act; possess one's senses)*; (he is spoken of as) the coming ~. (3) ~ and wife (4) masters / officers and men; the major led his men into battle; the electricity company sent a ~ to fix our lights. (5) stop crying and act like a ~; be a / play the ~! are you a ~ or a mouse? (6) if you want to sell, I'm your ~ *(I accept your offer)*; if you want a good music teacher, I'm your / here's your ~ *(s.o. suitable)*.

manage *vt* (1) ~ a horse / sailing-boat / oar / rifle; ~ a (naughty) child / a fool / one's wife; it is a long time since I had much to do with small children, but I'm sure I could ~ Susan all right. (2) ~ a team / business / firm / shop / factory / undertaking / household; ~ (the affairs of) a State; ~ a (difficult) situation; Granny is much better now, I think she can ~ everything herself; so you ~d it after all; ~ one's resources (3) he ~d to swim across the river / get what he wanted / be in time; he didn't ~ to catch the train; he ~d to make a mess of it / make matters worse. (4) can you ~ another piece / slice *etc (eat)*? (5) there are some sectors where national monopolies mean that the market will inevitably be ~d; outside the ~d sectors of the economy, too, competition is imperfect. - *vi* (6) can you ~ on your own? but you're surely not taking the children with you, are you? there's nothing else I can do, but I shall ~; I can ~ without you; we can't ~ with these poor tools; if I can't borrow the money, I shall have to ~ without; we have no blue ones, would a grey one do? yes, I could ~ with a grey one.

manifest *vt* ~ the truth of a statement; he ~ed an interest in music even as a child; ~ displeasure / contentment / joy / grief / *etc*; here is the true line of division between the two parties which will ~ itself in any new orientation of Labour policy; a symptom / disease / ghost ~s itself.

manner *n* (1) do it in this ~; solve the problem in the usual ~; genetics deals with the ~ in which traits are transmitted; (she is lazy) in a ~ *(to a certain extent)*; what ~ *(kind)* of man is he? if you are not to the ~ born *(accustomed to that practice from birth)*, you'll never learn it; in the lab he has all ~ of scientific instruments around him; our towns are crammed with all ~ of rubbish. (2) he has an easy, natural ~ in reading the news; have a breezy / easygoing / cavalier / grand / homespun / winning / dry / coarse / crisp / abrupt / absent / cold / downright / contentious / suspicious / uncivilized / infamous / awkward / unfortunate / bold / businesslike / democratic ~ (3) this book tells about the ~s and morals of the ancient Romans; his new novel is a study in the ~s of a class. (4) s.o.'s good / excellent / fine / engaging / gentle / precise / grown-up / uncouth / rustic / slipshod / unfinished / crude / barbarous / intolerable / beastly / rough / common ~s; the gracious ~s of the kind old lady; he's (got) no ~s; it is bad ~s to interrupt / stare at people. (5) a picture done in van Gogh's early ~ (6) □ by all / no ~ of means *(of course, surely / in no way whatever)*; □ in a ~ of speaking *(so to say / speak)*; □ to the ~ born *(born to high position)*; the general was to the ~ born; he was a general to the ~ born; though born a pauper, his bearing showed him to the ~ born.

manoeuvre *vt* (1) ~ a fleet / an army / troops (2) ~ one's car into the garage / a difficult parking-space; ~ a friend into a good job; ~ an opponent into doing s.th. / out of office (3) they ~d his resignation. -*vi* (4) the fleet is ~ing off the east coast; the ships ~d so that they were in a position to attack. (5) the debater's arguments left his opponent no room in which to ~.

manufacture *vt* (1) ~ goods / furniture / plastics / shoes / *etc*; ~ wool into yarn (2) ~ an excuse / story; ~ novels / verse *(write badly)*.

many *adj/pron* (1) I have a few stamps, but not ~; he made six mistakes in as ~ lines; you gave me two too ~; I wish he'd go away, he's one too ~ here; he was one too ~ for *(cleverer than)* you that time. (2) I've been here ~ a time; ~ a man would welcome this; ~ another day would pass before ...; ~'s the time I've *(I've often)* seen him do it. (3) ~ are called but few are chosen; there are ~ who think so; I did not find ~. (4) I have a good ~ things to do today; a great ~ stayed away; there were a great ~ abstentions; in most countries the ~ have to labour for the few.

map *n* a political / population / cultural / historical / relief / tourist / traveller's / city / astronomical / heavenly / oceanographic / nautical ~; a ~ of the world / the oceans / North American waterways / ancient Carthage; a large-/ small-scale ~; □ put (a town) on the ~ *(make famous)*; space travel put Cape Canaveral on the ~; □ wipe off the ~ *(destroy completely)*: the earthquake / battle virtually wiped N. off the ~.

map *vt* (1) ~ a region / river / *etc*; they ~ped the dangerous gusts. (2) ~ out one's time; the city ~ped out a campaign to get rid of slums.

march *n* (1) soldiers on the ~; a ~ of ten miles; a day's ~ back to camp; □ steal a ~ on s.o. *(get an advantage by clever action)* (2) the ~ of time / events / civilization; the onward ~ of science.

march *vi* (1) ~ 30 miles a day; the troops ~ed in(to the town) / by / past / away / off / out; he ~ed up and down the platform impatiently (2) time ~es on. - *vt* (3) ~ a prisoner off / away (to prison); the sergeant ~ed his men through a swamp; the boy was ~ed off to bed by his father at ten o'clock.

margin *n* (1) a wide / broad / narrow ~; don't write in the ~ of the page; leave a ~ on the left (side of the page) (2 *BE*) along the ~ of the river / pool; sit on the ~ of a lake / road (3) he escaped punishment / defeat by a narrow ~; behaviour beyond the ~ of decency (4) he gave himself a ~ of ten minutes to catch the train; we of American labor are justly proud that our members have, by an immense ~, the highest productivity per man-hour in the world; America may prove unable to counterbalance this technological lead by greater speed on the assembly line: for the first time, Russia has a ~ over the US.

mark *n* (1) dirty ~s on the new book; a strawberry ~ on the shirt; the tyres left ~s on the road. (2) a horse with a white ~ on its head; a birth-~ (3) ~s of old age / suffering; a gift as a ~ of one's esteem; his business shows all the ~s of success; a distinguishing / identifying ~; patience is the ~ of a good teacher. (4) punctuation ~s; a question / exclamation ~; price-~s on goods (5) he got 70 ~s out of 100 for physics; get / gain / obtain full / good / poor ~s for French (6) he hit the ~ nine times; shoot wide of the ~ *(also fig)*; your guess / calculation is beside the ~; hit / miss the ~ *(succeed / fail)*; he is an easy ~ *(is easily cheated)*. (7) a man of ~ *(fame)*; make one's ~ *(attain distinction)* (8) get off the ~ *(athletics: start)*; be quick / slow off the ~ *(be a quick / slow beginner)* (9) (s.o.'s work is) up to the ~ *(as good as usual)* / below the ~ *(inferior)*; he doesn't feel quite up to the ~ *(is not in his usual good health)*.

mark *vt* (1) the wet vase ~ed the table with a ring. (2) the architect ~ed the spot where the living room was to be; ~ goods / parcels; ~ (the prices of) articles; the prices of these goods are all clearly ~ed on them; ~ linen / one's clothes with one's name; ~ one's name on one's clothes; a zebra is ~ed with stripes; his face was ~ed with smallpox. (3) the circle on the map ~s the place where the treasure is buried. (4) his record ~s him as a promising candidate; what are the qualities that ~ a great leader? his style is ~ed by a predilection for metaphors; a predilection for metaphors ~s his style. (5) they ~ed him for early promotion. (6) □ (you) ~ my word(s); ~ carefully how it is done / how to do it *(form)* (7) ~ a test / essay / exam paper; ~ s.th. leniently / strictly; □ ~ time *(wait until one can make further progress)*.

mark down all our articles have been ~ed ~ for the sales; ~ ~ prices.

mark off (1) ~ ~ a distance on a map (2) the members of upper-class society have a behaviour and way of speaking that ~s them ~ from the rest of the community.

mark out (1) is the ground ~ed ~ for our game? ~ ~ a site / boundaries (2) he was ~ed ~ for promotion.

mark up ~ up goods / prices.

market *n* (1) go to (the) ~ to buy food; the next ~ is on Friday (2) the coffee / beef / wool ~; the stock ~; the ~ is dull / calm / lively / active / bullish; the ~ rose / fell *(prices rose / fell)*. (3) his house is put on / is on / will come into the ~ *(is / will be sold)*; the used-car ~ is very active when new models come out. (4) the U.S.A. is Brazil's best ~ for coffee; teenagers are the chief ~ for blue jeans; open a foreign ~ for cars (5) there is a ~ in the U.S.A. for British cutlery; there is no ~ for these goods.

marriage *n* (1) make a proposal / offer of ~; a ~ has been arranged between A and B; contract a ~ with s.o.; make a good / wealthy ~; annul / dissolve a ~; give / take s.o. in ~; related by ~; there were three children by the ~; a child by / from a previous ~; a happy / unhappy / left-handed / invalid / broken ~; ~s are made in heaven. (2) our ~ took place on Dec. 2; in Germany the civil ~ takes place before the church wedding. (3) Balanchine's ballet 'Serenade' is the perfect ~ of choreographic patterning and symphonic music.

married *adj* (1) a ~ woman / couple (2) ~ life / state.

marry *vt* (1) she ~ied a Frenchman; he ~ied his childhood sweetheart; be happily

~ied. (2) he ~ed his daughter to a writer; she has ~ed off all her daughters; she is ~ed to a doctor; they are going to get ~ed. (3) a minister ~ed them; they were ~ed in a Registry Office / in London. (4) this book ~es a sketchy text to a fine collection of illustrations; in the film "Hamlet" we wished to achieve the poetic truth ordained by Shakespeare by ~ing a sensitive intimacy in the acting to a significant austerity of the background. - *vi* (5) ~ for love / money; ~ early / late in life; ~ again / a second time / well; old enough to ~; ~ beneath one *(one's social level)*; when he ~ied into money he broke with his former friends; ~ in haste, repent in leisure.

mask *vt* (1) clouds ~ed the moon. (2) ~ one's feelings / passions; ~ one's enmity under an appearance of friendliness. - *adj* (3) a ~ed woman; a ~ed ball.

mass *n* (1) the baker shaped the ~ of dough into a loaf. (2) a ~ of stone / rock / water / snow / leaves / correspondence / red; ~es of clouds in the sky; a ~ of people in the courtroom; I have ~es of work to do; the (great) ~ of *(most of)* voters want a new school; the ~es *(lower classes of society)* (3) the huge ~ of the pyramid amazed me.

master *n* (1) ~ and man *(servant)*; no man can serve two ~s; be one's own ~; be ~ in one's own house; be ~ of oneself; be ~ of the situation; be ~ of a subject *(know it well)*; he has made himself ~ of the language *(can use it freely)*; one cannot be ~ of one's fate; be ~ of a large fortune; at last he met his ~ *(s.o. stronger etc)*. - *adj* (2) the work of a ~ hand; a ~ mind; there may even be a positive advantage today in having a team rather than a single ~ mind in charge; his ~ passion is stamp-collecting.

master *vt* (1) the animal trainer ~ed the lions and taught them tricks; ~ unruly children; ~ one's temper / feelings / fear (2) ~ a foreign language / the saxophone / the craft of navigation.

match *n* (1) I'm looking for a ~ for this paint; have you got a ~ for this ribbon? (2) the coat and trousers are a ~ *(go together well)*; the two kinds of cloth are a good / bad ~; tan shoes are a good ~ for a brown dress; those colours are a poor ~. (3) she is not yet a ~ for her mother in cooking; she will be (more than) a ~ for him; he has met / found his ~; we shall never see his ~ *(s.o. like him)*. (4) make a ~ of it *(marry)*; they are an excellent ~ *(pair)*. (5) he is a good ~ (for any girl) *(a desirable husband)*. (6) a boxing / wrestling / cricket / football / badminton / tennis ~ took place yesterday; win / lose a ~ (by two goals / points).

match *vt* (1) the two candlesticks ~ each other exactly. (2) her skirt doesn't ~ her blouse; I want some ribbon to ~ this blue material; a shirt with a tie to ~; that red ~es (with) that; the ribbons don't ~. (3) there are so many socks that it is difficult to ~ them *(sort them in pairs)*. (4) ~ one's strength with / against s.o. else's; ~ one's wits against s.o.else's; ~ one's wits against another's; these intuitive doctors note many faint clues and ~ them with relevant information accumulated over a lifetime of experience. (5) the promoters ~ed the two fighters *(put one against the other in a contest)*. (6) as hard as I try, I can't ~ him in tennis / in archery / at ping pong; can any country ~ France for wine? can you ~ that joke *(tell one equally good)*? (7) can you ~ (me) this silk *(find exactly the same)*? (8) you should ~ him with *(marry him to)* a rich heiress.

matter *n* (1) solid / liquid / gaseous ~; purulent ~ *(see 7)*; some of the ~ in an atom bomb is changed to energy; the antithesis between ~ and mind; dead ~; waste ~; dirt is ~ in the wrong place. (2) the ~ of the lecture was good, but the delivery was bad; the ~ of an essay book (3) advertising ~; printed ~; postal ~ *(everything sent by post)* (4) money / financial / legal / business ~s; burglary is a ~ for the police to handle; I have come on a private ~ / on a ~ of business; American usage differs from British on this ~; it is a ~ of regret / for congratulation that he...; rising early is a ~ of habit; these ~s are too high for me; you take ~s too seriously; don't do that, it will only make ~s worse; it is a ~ of life and death; □ as a ~ of fact *(in reality; although you may not know it)*; would you mind taking them along to the shoemaker? no, not at all - as a ~ of fact, I must take my shoes, too; □ a ~ of course *(s.th. expected as natural)*; a late breakfast was with him a ~ of course; □ for that ~ / for the ~ of that *(if that were now in question)*: youngsters do not greet each other on the phone the way their elders do, or for that ~, the way their elders would like them to; in the ~ of *(as regards)*; he is strict in the ~ of discipline; □ (this is) no laughing ~. (5) an idea of little ~ *(importance)*; no ~ how hard he works he ...; it is no ~ / it makes no ~ whether you get there early or late. (6) is there something / anything the ~ *(wrong)* with you? is anything the ~ with your pipe? (7) ~ *(pus)* forms in a dirty wound. (8) (not more than) a ~ of 10 days / 10 miles / £20 *(about 10 days etc).*

matter *vi* it doesn't ~ (to me) (at all) whether ...; what ~s is that he is interested in it; long holidays ~ more to him than a high salary; I'd give my consent - a lot that would probably ~! - to her marrying anybody except a man who drank every day; ... and that's what ~s now; what does it ~? it hardly ~s at all; What about me? Of course, I don't ~.

meagre *adj* (1) a ~ face / frame (2) a ~ diet / fare / meal; ~ clothing; ~ information / attendance at a conference / style; the help he gave us was ~.

meal *n* breakfast: this ~ is eaten before starting for work; there are people who take their ~s according to a prescribed diet; have a (very) light / heavy ~; a cooked ~; a ~ à la carte; all ~s en route; ~s served in the compartment; a nice / hearty / substantial / plain / frugal / one-course / miserable / sketchy ~; eat s.th. between ~s.

mean *vt* (1 ~ + *obj: signify, denote*) the Russian word 'dom' ~s 'house'; it ~s nothing *(is meaningless; → 2)* (2 ~ + *obj, gerund, clause: have as a consequence, be a sign of*) this frontier incident probably ~s war; rearmament ~s postponing any projected programme of further social reform; the accident ~s more expense; those black clouds ~ rain; four-leaf clovers ~ luck; his refusal ~s my ruin; does that mean that he won't come? that can ~ only one thing - he has given it up; it ~s nothing *(does not matter*; → 1) (3 ~ + *obj, clause: have in mind, want to say*) try to say what you ~ as clearly as possible; do you ~ Smith junior or senior? you don't ~ the Minister himself is coming? I ~ that you are a liar; I didn't ~ you; when I say 'no' I ~ 'no'; what does he ~ by that remark? (4 ~ + *obj, inf: plan; intend*) he ~s mischief / no harm / us no good; do you ~ business (→ business 3)? do you ~ to say (that) you won't come? do you ~ us to understand that you ...? I did not ~ you to hear it; she didn't ~ to hurt you; he ~s (his son) to succeed; is this picture ~t for me *(to be a gift; to be a picture of me)*? ~ well / ill by s.o. *(have good / bad intentions)*; he ~t it for a joke; what do you ~ by such behaviour / making all this noise / coming so late? (5 ~ + *obj, to-obj, clause, inf: be of importance, value to*) your friendship ~s a great deal to me; it ~s a lot to have good friends when you are in trouble; I cannot tell you what he has ~t to me; if you knew what it ~s to live alone; that doesn't ~ much; it ~s something if even he is against it. (6 ~ + *obj*, for-*obj, inf*: *destine*) I ~t this purse for you; I ~ this house for my son; he was obviously ~t for a / to be a lawyer *(by his parents; by Providence).*

mean *n* (1) the / a happy / golden ~ *(a moderate course of action)* (2) the ~ of 5 + 6 + 10 is 7. (3) ~, *always in the plural,* → means.

mean[1] *adj* (1) a ~ house in a ~ street; this handsome park was once a ~ slum area; clothes of ~ quality (2) that was a ~ trick / swindle! a ~ action / conduct / character / remark; a ~ person / creature / rascal; don't be so ~ (to her)! that was ~ of you; you were ~ to laugh at his mistakes; he took a ~ advantage of me; behave / treat s.o. ~ly (3) people of ~ birth; men of the ~er sort; many great men have risen from ~ beginnings to positions of importance. (4) this should be clear even to the ~est intelligence; he is no ~ *(a good)* scholar / orator; that was no ~ achievement for him. (5) he is rather ~ over money matters; he is as ~ as a miser.

mean[2] *adj* what is the ~ annual temperature here? the ~ temperature for the day was 70°.

meaning *n* the ~ of a word / phrase / symbol / sign / gesture / notion; the word 'ball' has more than one ~; an original / ordinary / literal / figurative / superficial / double ~; in the full ~ of the word (2) when I said, "Put it out" he misunderstood my ~ and put out the cat instead of the light; he looked at me with ~; what is the ~ of this / all this noise? *(expresses indignation).*

means *n* (1) find (new) ways and ~; attain / reach one's end / aim by fair / foul ~; this may prove a ~ to an end; if a ~

to extending the trade is to be found, we shall have to compromise; the end justifies the ~; the ~ do / does not justify the end; any ~ to an end; secret ~ were / a secret ~ was found; there is / are no ~ of knowing that; there seem(s) to be no ~ of getting there; every ~ has / all ~ have been tried; he won by ~ of a clever trick; thoughts are expressed by ~ of words; could you by any ~ *(possibly)* lend me some money? we are by no ~ *(not at all)* satisfied; you should by all ~ *(certainly)* see that film. (2) he is a man of ~ *(is rich);* he has private ~; his ~ are not up to his needs; his family had only modest ~; he lives within / beyond his ~ *(spends less / more than he earns).*

measure *n* (1) (the suit is) made to ~; take s.o.'s ~ *(also fig)*; take the ~ of a situation / of what one does; I gave him some sweets for good ~ *(more than required).* (2) an inch is a ~ of length, a gallon a ~ of capacity; linear / square / cubic / liquid / dry ~; ~ of length / area / volume / capacity (3) we all seek a ~ *(certain amount)* of security for ourselves; hard work and a ~ of luck pulled the Finns through; in such ideas there is a ~ of truth and a ~ of nonsense; her joy was beyond ~ *(very great)*; his failure is in a large / great ~ due to his laziness; there was joy without ~; give him his ~ of praise. (4) popularity is a bad ~ *(criterion)* of merit; deeds are a better ~ of character than words; a test providing a ~ of ability (5) take ~s for / against s.th. / to ensure victory / to prevent floods; effective / forcible / drastic / stern / severe / harsh / rigorous ~s; preliminary / precautionary / provisional / final / legal / illegal / legislative ~s; a wise / foolish / *etc* ~; suggest / propose / carry out / execute / enforce a ~.

measure *vt* (1) ~ dimensions / a quantity; ~ the length / size / speed / strength of s.th.; the tailor ~ed me for a suit; □ ~ one's length *(fall flat on the ground)*; □ ~ o.s. / one's strength with / against s.o.; □ ~ others' corn by one's own bushel *(judge others by o.s.)* (2) the table ~s 3 feet across; when fully grown the male can ~ 6 ft. high at the shoulders.

measure off ~ ~ enough material (for four curtains) / a hundred-metre course.

measure out ~ ~ corn / milk / cloth / a dose of medicine / enough flour for a cake; ~ ~ a tennis court.

measure up (1) ~ up wood / land (2) some men failed to ~ up to the Army's physical requirements.

meat *n* lean / fat / streaked / tough / tender / minced / pickled / smoked / chilled / frozen / raw / cooked ~; different kinds of ~; baked ~s and frozen ~s; pork is the ~ from a pig; there's not much ~ on a duck; dark / light ~ *(of fowl)*; one can buy ~ all of a piece / on the bone / cut up / sliced; cook / boil / stew / braise / fry / roast / grill / broil ~; preserve / dry/ salt / cure / smoke / souse / pickle / corn / tin / can ~; □ one man's ~ is another man's poison. (2) the ~ of a walnut / coconut (3) the ~ *(substance)* of a book; there's not much ~ in this argument.

medicine *n* (1) study / *(BE)* read ~; general / internal / curative / preventive ~; practise ~ (2) take a bitter / nasty / distasteful / tasteless / harmless / effective / efficacious ~; a good ~ for colds; □ take one's ~ *(submit to what is unwelcome).*

medium *n* (1) a happy ~ between want and wealth; stick to a happy ~ *(avoid extremes)* (2) the telephone is a ~ of communication; the newspaper is an advertising ~ / a ~ of advertisement / a ~ for advertising; the space advertisers buy in trade journals and other media; freedom of speech, freedom of information in any ~ - these are the beginning and the foundation of good human communications. (3) paint is pigment in an oil ~ *(substance)*; air is the ~ of sound; these viruses cannot be grown on artificial media, but require living tissue. (4) all three sisters claim to be ~s; that ~s have access to knowledge beyond the ordinary is certain, but ...

meet *vt* (1) ~ s.o. in the street / on the stairs; we met each other quite unexpectedly; he'll ~ *(sports: fight with)* him in the semifinals; when John and Bill wrestle, John ~s his match in Bill; ~ one's death / doom (2 *get to know, become acquainted with*) come along and ~ my wife; pleased to ~ you; have you met the new headmaster yet? my husband would like to ~ you; you know her? yes, we met yesterday; he met his future wife in a train; I have met a lot of interesting people while travelling. (3 *come together, assemble*) the finalists ~ tomorrow; the two trains ~ *(pass each other)* at Crewe; this class ~s daily; the council will ~ in the li-

brary. (4 *be present at the time of arrival*) the hotel bus ~s all the trains; I'll ~ the late bus; guests will be met at the station; she met the train from London.
(5 *react, in an active way;* → meet with)
(5a *react to s.th.*) ~ success and failure with a grin / the ups and downs of life with calm; ~ good luck / good fortune / misfortune / disaster (with equanimity); he met his fate bravely; ~ a suggestion with a counter-suggestion / an argument with a counter-argument / a measure with a counter-measure / a challenge with a counter-challenge; ~ a (difficult) situation / an emergency with energetic measures; ~ force with / by force; ~ a danger with circumspection / s.o.'s obstinacy with kindness; how can we ~ this competition? he met these questions / the constant questioning / the cross-examination calmly / with equanimity. (5b *experience*) they met only danger, hunger and privation on the journey; the liberators of Paris met a delirious welcome from the citizens; I'm used to ~ing smiles and cheers at one meeting and a hostile reception at the next; ~ a difficulty / difficulties / (unexpected) opposition / disbelief / criticism(s) / objections / apathy / support / approval; the Minister met one rebuff after another on tariff reform; the tariff reform met one rebuff after another; he met opposition to his proposals from all directions; his proposals met opposition from all directions. (5c *satisfy*) ~ s.o.'s wishes / a request / a demand / an enquiry; will this ~ your requirements? ~ the demands for a product / a company's needs for electric power; ~ every condition of / stipulation in this contract; this timber will ~ all requirements / specifications as to hardness; will this ~ the case? ~ s.o. half-way *(compromise)*; our firm will ~ your orders promptly. (5d *satisfy, pay*) have you enough money to ~ the bill? ~ one's obligations / the cost of s.th. / the charges / one's debts / the monthly premium on an insurance policy; the firm must first ~ this claim for £500; I cannot ~ your price / your figure for the repairs; I need cash: I'll ~ the market (price) and sell.
(6 *come into contact, touch*) this lane ~s the main road a mile from here; his bat met the ball with a crack; his hand met hers; ~ the eye / ear *(be visible / audible)*; a fine view ~s the eye from this window; what a sight met her eyes; the sound of laughter from the playground met the ear; she was afraid to ~ my eye / his glance; there's more in it / to this question than ~s the eye *(s.th. is hidden)*; she met her friend's greeting with a smile.
- *vi* (7 → 1) we met quite unexpectedly; good-bye till we ~ again; we arranged to ~ at the corner; when can we ~? (8 → 6); the letter L consists of two lines that ~ at the lower left; the rivers ~ below the city; he has grown so fat that his clothes won't ~; their hands met; their eyes met; □ make both ends ~ *(make income and expenditure equal).*

meet with C1 *come upon by chance*) ~ ~ an old friend at a dinner party; such men are not often met ~; this mistake is met ~ everywhere. (2 *experience; the person or thing that meets with s.th. is the victim, not the agent;* → meet 5) ~ ~ misfortune / an accident / great kindness / (much/ massive) opposition / (many) obstacles; ~ ~ discouragement / resistance / difficulties / a rebuff; our efforts met ~ success; our suggestions met ~ (his) (dis)approval; the proposal met ~ an objection.

meeting *n* (1) a chance ~ with a friend in the street; a casual / genial / fortuitous / unforgettable ~; she is shy at a first ~. (2) a public / official / informal / political / protest / election / committee / sports / *etc* ~; an annual / orderly / extraordinary general ~; call / convene / summon / hold / arrange / postpone / cancel / call off a ~; he had a ~ *(attended it)*; who addressed the ~? (3) the town ~ voted to increase taxes. (4) a large fortress was built at the ~ of the two rivers.

melt *vt* (1) a temperature above 32° ~s ice; ~ butter in a pan (2) pity ~ed her heart; his pleading ~ed her; this tale would ~ the hardest heart. - *vi* (3) snow and ice ~ in spring; sugar ~s in tea; this cake ~s in the mouth. (4) her heart ~ed with pity / at the baby's smile; she ~ed into tears; in the rainbow one colour ~s into another.

melt away (1) the snow / fog soon ~ed ~. (2) my money ~ed ~.

melt down ~ ~ gold / silver articles to reuse the metal.

memory *n* (1) speak / draw / recite s.th. from ~; commit (a poem) to ~ (2) a good / bad ~ (for names / dates); have a tenacious / wonderful / unfailing photographic / weak / poor / misty / short ~; have no / a distinct ~ of s.th.; □ he has a ~ like a sieve; his ~ never fails him / is often at fault; some people have better ~ies than others; I write this to the best of my ~; he is ..., if my ~ serves me (al)right; have s.th. fresh in one's ~; keep / retain s.th. in one's ~; lose one's ~; it has escaped / slipped / gone out of my ~; refresh / trust / search one's ~ (3 *that which is remembered*) I have a wonderful ~ of these days; it brought back to me ~ies of my schooldays; a (hazy) ~ of (one's) childhood; call up / bring back old ~ies; retain a clear ~ of s.th.; cherish s.o.'s ~; keep s.o.'s ~ green / alive; lose all ~ of (the war); he has a very pleasant ~ of you; she lives on her ~ies; his ~ is dear / sacred to us; ... is but a ~ *(no longer exists)*; the church is only a ~ now. (4) Christmas is celebrated in ~ of Christ's birth; a monument to the ~ of s.o.; honour / stain the ~ of a deceased colleague; he never did anything worthy of ~. (5) never before within the ~ of man had there been such a storm; within living ~.

mend *vt* (1) ~ shoes / clothes / china / a coat / a broken window / a road; ~ a hole / tear / break (2) the thief promised to ~ his ways if given another chance; that won't ~ *(improve)* matters; ~ one's pace *(go faster)*; ~ the fire *(add fuel)*. – *vi* (3) things are ~ing; under his mother's care the sick child ~ed quickly.

mention *vt* I only just ~ed it to him; don't ~ our plans to anybody; I don't want you to ~ my arriving late; ~ s.th. in passing / incidentally; he ~ed no names; it isn't worth ~ing (that...); ~ s.o. in one's will; as ~ed above; there were three of us, not to ~ / without ~ing the child; ...not to ~ the extra cost; "Thank you!" – "Don't ~ it."

mention *n* shortage of space forbids the ~ of further examples; the first ~ of this custom is found in Tacitus; make ~ of s.th.; make honourable ~ of s.o.; there was no ~ of it in the newspaper.

mercy *n* (1) God showed him ~; God in his (great / infinite) ~ healed him; have ~ on s.o.; show ~ to / on s.o.; ask / beg (s.o.) for ~; appeal to s.o. for ~ / to s.o.'s ~; throw o.s. on s.o.'s ~; the king was / treated them without ~; be at s.o.'s ~; the damaged ship was at the ~ of the sea / waves. (2) it is a ~ that no one was hurt; that's a ~! we must be thankful for small ~ies.

merit *n* (1) a man of (great) ~; there isn't much ~ in giving away things that you don't want. (2) what are the ~s of this plan? decide a case / judge s.th. on its ~s; whatever they propose is viewed in Washington, not on its ~s, but in relation to the problem of Russia; the honest endeavour to see the ~ of each proposal; □ make a ~ of (one's actions, behaviour) *(expect credit for them).*

merit *vt* s.th. ~s praise / a reward / censure / punishment.

merry *adj* (1) a ~ boy / face / voice / mood / laugh / song; ~ laughter / life; she is always ~; make ~ over s.o./ s.th.; it is not fit that you should make ~ while the country is fighting a war. (2) a ~ evening / meal / twinkle in his eye; (wish s.o. a) M~ Christmas.

mess *n* (1) the burglars left the room in a ~; (things are in) an awful / complete / nasty / terrible ~; wipe up the ~ *(spilt liquid)*; the workmen cleaned up the ~ before they left. (2) make a ~ of s.th. *(spoil it)*; a nice ~ you've made of it! (3) how did you get into such a ~ *(difficult situation)*?

mess about / around *(inform)* (1 *tinker with*) John is here somewhere. He's ~ing ~ with his fishing equipment; he likes to spend the day ~ing ~ (at the boat docks / doing nothing in particular) (2 *get involved with*) you'll get into trouble with the law if you ~ ~ with that motorcycle gang; stop ~ing ~ with my sister!

mess up (1) don't ~ up the living room / new dress (2) the rain ~ed up our plans to camp out; ~ up arrangements / the situation / a scheme; ~ up an examination *(fail it)* (3 *slang*) the kidnappers ~ed up *(beat)* their victim before they released him.

message *n* (1) deliver / send / receive a ~ (by post / mail / phone / wireless); convey / take a ~ to s.o.; can I take a ~? his secretary will give him the ~; leave a ~ for s.o. / with s.o. (saying that ...); a farewell ~ *(speech)* (2) the ~ of an angel; a film with a ~ for modern youth.

method *n* (1) have / use / employ a (sound / sensible / practical / (in)efficient / proved / proven / antiquated) ~ (of doing s.th.); modern teaching ~s (2) the book lacks ~; a man of ~; there's ~ in his madness *(his behaviour is not so unreasonable as it seems).*

mill *n* (1) water-~; wind~; the ~s of God grind slowly; □ go through the ~ *(undergo hard training / experience)*; □ put s.o. through the ~ (2) a cotton / paper / silk / spinning / weaving / rolling / steel ~; a saw~.

mill *vt* (1) ~ grain / flour / ore *(crush it)* / steel *(make into bars).* - *vi* (2) cattle / crowds ~ about / around; the police had no difficulty controlling the ~ing crowd.

mince *vt* (1) ~ meat / onions / parsley (2) □ not ~ matters / one's words *(speak bluntly)* (3 *do in an affected way*) ~ one's steps. - *vi* (4) ~ across the room / down the corridor *(walk with affectedly short steps).*

mind *n* (1 *memory*) bear / keep s.th. in ~; you must always bear in ~ that he ...; have s.th. fresh in one's ~; I cannot call to ~ when I saw him; recall s.th. to s.o.'s ~; he / that put me in ~ of his father / of my promise / of a very funny story; put s.th. into s.o.'s ~ *(suggest it to him)*; put s.th. from / out of one's ~ *(force o.s. to forget)*; search one's ~ (for a name); pass / go out of s.o.'s ~
(2a *feeling and thinking*) ~ is the mysterious something which feels and thinks; a hot summer day inclines neither the ~ nor the body to activity; body and ~; ~ and matter; a triumph of ~ over matter; the freedom of ~; he has a good ~ if he would only use it; have a great / noble / lively / sprightly / sparkling / alert / acute / active / powerful ~; have a childlike / slow / sluggish / sick / petty / little / base / narrow ~; an (un)trained / mature / judicious / original / productive / inquisitive / penetrating / literal *(matter-of-fact)* / subtle / literary / tranquil ~; have an open ~ *(be not yet decided)*; have a one-track ~ *(persist in nothing but one idea)*; an agile ~ solves problems quickly; cultivate / improve one's ~ *(for further examples 'verb + ~' →* 2c); a frame / state of ~ *(mood)*; absence of ~ (→ absence); presence of ~ (→ presence)
(2b *phrases with prepos + ~*) it's easy enough to see what is at the back of his ~; what have you in ~ *(what is your idea/ plan)*? I really had a larger table in ~; conceive s.th. in one's ~; this news made him uneasy in his ~; be unsettled in one's ~; with these aims (well) in ~, we have tried to ...; in his childlike innocence of ~ he believed that he ...; not in one's right ~ *(mad)*; I'm in two ~s whether to go or not; be in two ~s about s.th.; I see my home town in my ~'s eye; we are (all) of one ~ (on the subject); if you're all of my ~ *(agree)*; you and I are of the same ~; is he still of the same ~ ? be of an upright / petty / *etc* turn of ~; I've got a weight off my ~; the letter has taken a weight off my ~; the exam will be on my ~ till I know I passed it; the accident weighed heavily on his ~; have a weight on one's ~; have s.th. on one's ~ *(be worried by it)*; be out of one's (right) ~ *(mad)*; he has gone / is out of his ~; → sight *n* 2; the best vacation, to my ~, is a month by the sea.
(2c *phrases with verb + ~*) apply / put one's ~ to (a problem / one's work *(concentrate on it)*; change one's ~ *(opinion)*; close one's ~ to s.th.; give s.o. a piece / bit of one's ~ *(tell him frankly what one thinks of him)*; give your ~ *(attention)* to what you're doing; keep your ~ on what you're doing; someone who knows his own ~ never changes it; not know one's own ~ *(be full of doubts)*; lose one's ~ *(become insane)*; make up one's ~ (→ make up 9); occupy one's ~ with s.th.; occur to s.o.'s ~; put / set s.o.'s ~ at rest *(calm him*; → set *vt* 21b); set one's ~ to a task (→ set *vt* 19); read s.o.'s ~ *(thoughts)*; he has set his ~ on becoming an engineer; once he sets his ~ on something he works tirelessly for it; he must speak his ~ at all times *(say plainly what one thinks)*; take one's ~ off s.th.; take s.o.'s ~ off s.th. *(help him stop worrying about it)*; tell s.o. one's ~ *(tell him frankly what one thinks about him)*
(3 *desire*) have a good / great ~ to do it / not to go; I have half a ~ to (go to bed); you may come along with us if you have a ~ to; I have a ~ to ask her to the dance; he had no ~ to put up with any nonsense. (4 *intellectually gifted person*) the leading ~s of the nation; one of the great / noblest ~s of the century; he is not a great ~; Freud was a seminal ~.

mind *vt* (1 *be careful*) ~ the step! ~ your head (on that low ceiling)! ~ you don't fall! ~ this basket, it's got eggs in it; you'd better ~ what you're doing; now ~ what I tell you; he warned us to ~ no one saw us. (2 *look after, take care of*) during the war his wife had to ~ the shop; ~ a ma-

chine; ~ the baby / children / neighbour's dog; □ ~ your own business / affairs *(don't interfere)*; □ ~ one's P's and Q's *(one's behaviour)* (3 *object*) I don't ~ the cold / rain / heat; do you ~ draughts? I don't ~ a joke, but this is going too far; would you ~ waiting *(please wait)* for a few moments? do you ~ staying a little longer *(please stay)*; do you ~ my staying a little longer *(please allow me to stay)*; I shouldn't ~ *(I'd like)* living in a house like that. (4 *care, worry*) I don't ~ whether I go or not; never ~ your headache, come out for a walk, it'll do you good. (5 *obey*) that dog won't ~ anyone; ~ you, I don't ~ ~ing the children as long as they ~ *(obey)* me.
- *vi* (6 → 1) ~ out! there's a car coming; if you don't ~, you'll be hurt; ~ and lock the door after you (7 → 3); if nobody ~s, I'll open the window; do you ~ if I...? (8 → 4) don't ~ about the gossip; never ~ *(don't worry)*!

mingle *vt* (1) ~ guests. - *vi* (2) the waters of the two rivers ~ near our town; their voices ~d in song. (3) the soldiers were forbidden to ~ with their prisoners; ~ in / with the crowds. - *adj* (4) with ~d pride and sorrow; truth ~d with falsehood; with ~d feelings.

minister *vi* (1) doctors ~ to the sick; ~ to s.o.'s needs / requirements (2) ~ to a congregation. - *vt* (3) ~ the sacraments.

minute *n* (1) five ~s to six; be ten ~s late; arrive twenty ~s early; some ~s behind schedule (2) wait a ~; I shan't be a ~; lunch will be ready in a ~; just a ~; I expect him any ~; the weather is so changeable that you don't know what to expect from one ~ to the next; we reckon to have lunch at one o'clock, but we're not to the minute *(punctual)*. (3) the ~ *(as soon as)* he opened the door he knew what was wrong. (4) up to the ~ *(most recent)*; her wardrobe is always up to the ~; an up-to-the-~ report / fashion; up-to-the-~ news.

mischief *n* (1) a storm that did much ~ to shipping; such wild speeches may work great ~; people who carry tales about others can do great ~; do s.o. a ~ *(hurt him)* (2) those children are always (getting) into ~; he's up to ~ again; he just did it for ~; keep s.o. out of ~; (3) she is full of ~ and the life of every party; her eyes were full of ~. (4) that child is a little ~.

miss *n* (1) his first shot was a ~; ten hits and one ~ ; a lucky ~ *(fortunate escape)* (2) I'll give the party a ~ *(not go there)*; I'll give the prunes a ~ *(not order, eat them)*; let's give York a ~ this year *(not visit it)*.

miss *vt* (1) ~ the target / mark; he ~ed me by a hair's breadth; □ ~ one's mark *(fail in what one tries to do; be not good enough)* (2) I ~ed the bus and had to walk; he ~ed the ball *(did not catch it)*; ~ one's aim / vocation; ~ a chance / opportunity; he is a lawyer, but he has ~ed his true profession: he ought to have been an actor; □ ~ the boat / bus *(fail to grasp an opportunity)* (3) how many lessons have you ~ed? he ~ed school for a week; ~ a meeting / an appointment / the beginning of a concert; we ~ed seeing that film; she didn't ~ a dance. (4) she ~ed the point of (the joke) (5) you can't ~ my house / the way. (6) I ~ed you very much while you were away; I ~ my dog *(am longing for it)*; we ~ our friends when they go away. (7) I ~ed my purse when I went to buy a ticket; I ~ my watch; he's so rich he wouldn't ~ £100 if he lost it; you were ~ed *(your absence was noticed)*. (8) he ~ed (death) by inches; he barely ~ed getting hurt in the accident; I narrowly ~ed being run down. (9) she ~ed some notes in her song; the cleaning woman ~ed some dust in the corner. - *vi* (10 → 1) the boxer's punch ~ed; that's the third time you've ~ed; try again, but don't ~ this time. (11) my watch / dog is ~ing; you were ~ing from *(not present at)* the meeting; only one guest is ~ing; several pages are ~ing (from the book); he has two teeth ~ing. (12) one of the valves *(in an engine)* is ~ing *(failing to function properly)*.

miss out (1) the printers have ~ed ~ a word; please ~ ~ the sixth verse; on Sundays we ~ ~ lunch. (2) he ~ed ~ on (getting) the promotion; he ~ed ~ on his first bet, but his second brought him 10 to 1.

mistake *n* a bad / serious / clumsy / fatal / grievous / glaring / common / costly / light / slight / foolish / silly / ridiculous ~; a grammatical / spelling ~; a ~ in spelling; make / commit a ~; we should be making a grave ~ if we...; he made a ~ in (announcing the names); correct / rectify / set right a ~; repair / remedy one's ~s; several ~s have crept into the text; it was a ~ to think he could do it; I took his umbrella by ~; we've had a wretched summer this year, and no ~ *(inform: certainly)*; let there be no ~ about it this time.

mistake *vt* (1) ~ s.o.'s joking / identity / meaning; I mistook you for your sister; there is no ~ing (his sincerity / what ought to be done). (2) you have ~n the road / door / time; we've ~n the house *(come to the wrong one)*. - *adj* (3) he was ~n about the speed of the car / this matter / her age; I thought he was honest, but it appears that I was ~n in him; I was ~n in what I told you yesterday; a ~n opinion / idea; in the ~n belief that he ...; if I'm not (greatly) ~n; I might be ~n; that's just where you are ~n.

mix *vt* (1) ~ ingredients; ~ flour with water (to make paste); ~ flour and water together (2) ~ (s.o.) a drink; ~ concrete (3) ~ business with pleasure (4) her party ~ed old and young together. - *vi* (5) oil doesn't ~ with water. (6) ~ with (other) people; ~ in society / the crowd / the highest circles; I've ~ed among all classes of people. - *adj* (7) ~ed biscuits / pickles; ~ed feelings; a ~ed company (8) a ~ed school (for boys and girls); ~ed bathing; a ~ed marriage.

mix up (1) ~ up ingredients / the flour with the water (2) people often ~ him up with his brother; ~ up the soda and the flour (3) ~ s.o. up by asking irrelevant questions; she ~ed up the times of the trains; she got the times of the trains ~ed up; be all ~ed up *(confused)* (4) many famous people were ~ed up in the case; I don't want to be ~ed up in the affair.

moan *vi* (1) ~ with pain / in one's sleep (2) ~ about one's misfortune / one's difficulties. - *vt* (3) ~ (out) a plea for help.

model *n* (1) use the business letter in the book as a ~; choose s.o. as one's ~; he is a ~ of industry / modesty. (2) she's the ~ / a perfect ~ of her mother *(exactly like her)*; an aeroplane ~; a ~ of an ocean liner; the ~ of a school to be built (3) that car is the latest ~; a sports ~; the latest Paris ~s *(dresses, etc)* (4) she sits as a ~ to painters. (5) she is a fashion ~.

model *vt* (1) Ruth ~led herself after / on / upon her mother; you should ~ your behaviour on Tom's. (2) ~ a dog / s.o.'s head in / out of clay; delicately ~led features (3) (this mannequin certainly knows how to) ~ a dress. - *vi* (4) she prefers to ~ in wax. (5) this clay ~s well.

model *adj* a ~ wife / husband / child; ~ behaviour.

moderate *vt* (1) ~ one's anger / enthusiasm / demands; even though you are angry, try to ~ your voice; exercise a ~ing influence upon s.o. (2) ~ a public meeting / debate / discussion. - *vi* (3) the wind is ~ing; fury ~s.

moderate *adj* (1) sell s.th. at a ~ price; I'd like a ~-priced room; have a ~ appetite; a ~ly large audience (2) show only ~ enthusiasm; a man of ~ views / opinions; he is ~ in his requests / demands; a ~ drinker; (have only) ~ skill; a ~ climate.

moderation *n* advise more ~ in eating and drinking; a gradual ~ of s.th.; eat with ~; drink in ~ can act as a stimulant.

modest *adj* (1) be ~ about one's achievements; ~ behaviour; a ~ man / hero; young girls are often ~ in speech, dress and behaviour. (2) ~ prices / means / desires; a ~ salary / fortune; a ~ success; be ~ in one's requirements; his demands are ~.

modify *v* (1) now that you know the facts, will you ~ your opinion? ~ one's plans (2) you'd better ~ your tone *(be less rude)*; I think he'll ~ his demands in the end. (3) in 'he ate a large apple' 'large' ~ies 'apple'; adverbs ~ verbs, adjectives, or adverbs.

moment *n* (1) wait a ~; just a ~; one ~; *(inform)* half a ~; I'll be back in a ~; he won't be a ~; can I have the book for a ~? I stood listening (for) a ~; we didn't get a ~'s peace; he has his (brighter) ~s; she said it in an unguarded ~; it was all over in a ~ / in a few ~s. (2) the decisive / critical / psychological ~; the ~ of decision; a historic ~; wait for a favourable / an opportune / the right ~; the finest ~s of his life; I'm busy at the ~; I expect him at any ~; at the first ~; (he arrived) at the (very) last ~; this is not the ~ to discuss it; he is the man of the ~ *(important)*; the ~ *(as soon as)* I saw him I recognized him; I'll tell him the ~ he gets in. (3) an event / affair of great ~; a matter of ~; s.th. is of great / little / no ~.

money *n* (1) plenty of / little ~; (make) heaps / piles / stacks / pots of ~; a nice / tidy bit of ~; ready ~ *(cash)*; counterfeit / bad ~; foreign ~; easy / hard-earned ~;

~ easily earned; haven't you got the right ~? please have the exact ~ ready; have you any ~ on / with you? pay in German ~; pay ~ down *(cash)*; come into ~; lose (a lot of) ~ over a transaction / on this deal; □ make ~ *(obtain wealth*; → make *vt* 33); □ be coining ~ *(obtain wealth quickly)*; marry s.o. for money; □ have ~ to burn *(very much ~)*; □ put ~ before morals; be well off for ~; if it weren't for ~ (we could do that); ~ cannot buy it; his ~ is all in hotels; □ get one's ~'s worth; □ get little / poor value for one's ~ ; □ it's ~ for jam *(easily earned)*.
(2 *currency*) what are the differences between a hard and a soft ~? few European ~s are as stable as the Swiss franc.

mood *n* his ~s often change / vary from day to day; (be in) a good / pleasant / cheerful / militant / bad / dark / dismal / grave / melancholy / earnest / dreamy / light / pensive ~; I'm not in the ~ for joking / for serious music / for work / to work; he's a man of ~s *(his ~s vary)*; → put *vt* 7b.

moon *n* (1) the new / half / full / waxing / crescent / waning / old ~ ; a pale / silvery / bright ~; the ~ is in its first / last quarter; the ~ has a ring / halo; is it a new or a full ~? is there a ~ tonight? □ promise s.o. the ~ (2) once in a blue ~ *(very rarely)*.

mop *v* (1) ~ the floor; □ ~ the floor with s.o. *(defeat him completely)* (2) ~ one's brow; please ~ up this mess / this pool of water; ~ up the last resistance (of troops) (3) ~ up arrears of work; ~ up food *(inform: eat)*.

moral *n* (1) the ~ of a story; there is a ~ to the story; draw the ~ from a story / an experience (2) (a person of) lax / loose ~s; deplore s.o.'s lack of ~s; his ~s are excellent; maintain a high standard of ~s.

moral *adj* (1) ~ standards / rights / obligations / law / philosophy; a ~ question / problem; a man of strict ~ principles; man is a ~ being; it is ~ly good to do such a thing. (2) a ~ act; live a ~ life; a ~ man (3) a ~ book / story / tale / talk (4) a ~ victory; give s.o. ~ support; ~ courage; □ a ~ certainty *(s.th. highly probable)*.

morale *n* the ~ of the troops / the people / a nation / a country; fewer men have left their jobs - the ~ of the working force has improved.

morning *n* a bright / sunny / fair / misty / cloudy / gloomy / rainy ~; ~ breaks / dawns; I met him this ~ / yesterday ~ / on Monday ~ / on the ~ of the 21st / every ~ / one ~ last week; when he woke up it was ~; I will phone her in the ~ *(tomorrow ~)*; "You don't look very happy!" - "I'm afraid it's the ~ after the night before" *(headache etc after drinking etc)*.

mortify *vt* (1) it ~ies me to forget the name of a person I'm introducing; feel ~ied at one's failure to pass the examination; be / feel ~ied at / by s.o.'s rudeness; we were ~ied to realize how little we had done; a ~ing defeat (2) ~ the flesh (by self-denial).

motion *n* (1) if a thing is in ~, it is not at rest; the ~ of the planets around the sun; never get off a bus while it is in ~; set / put / keep s.th. in ~ (2) a circular / swinging / jerky ~; he made a commanding ~ for silence; all her ~s are clumsy / graceful; impart ~ to a body; the regular ~ (of a machine); the smooth ~ (of a carriage) (3) propose / bring forward a ~; the ~ was adopted / carried / rejected / lost by a majority of ten; on the ~ of Mr N. (for adjournment).

motion *vt* (1) ~ s.o. in / away / to a seat; he ~ed me to come nearer. - *vi* (2) the host ~ed for the visitor to be seated; he ~ed to him to take a seat.

motive *n* do s.th. / act from low / selfish / base / mean / noble ~s; do s.th. from ~s of kindness; her ~ for taking the blame was to shield her brother.

mould *n* (1) a pudding ~; make jelly in a ~ (2) a man of honest/ heroic ~ *(character)*; cast in the same ~ *(of the same character)*.

mould *vt* (1) ~ glass / wax / clay / plastic; ~ a clay figure; ~ a head out of / in clay (2) ~ s.o.'s character / mind; our early experiences ~ our lives; ~ young people for future tasks; he ~ed his character on his father's. (3) a dress / corset that ~s the figure.

mount *vt* (1) ~ a hill / a ladder / a horse / a bicycle / the pulpit / the throne; the speaker ~ed the platform. (2) the captain ~ed his men on the captured horses; ~ed police (3) ~ a gun; cannon were ~ed on the hill top; ~ a jewel (in gold) / a picture *(frame it)*; ~ stamps in an album; ~ insects / slides (for a microscope); ~ an exhibition *(prepare it)* (4) ~ an assault / campaign / operation / war *(prepare and* *start it)*; ~ a successful trade offensive; ~ guard (over s.o./ s.th.) *(act as guard for)*. - *vi* (5) he ~ed to the top of the steps; he ~ed *(his horse)* and rode away. (6) ~ing debts; bills soon ~ up at a hotel; the alternative will be chaos in view of the ~ing output of cars; tension ~s. (6) a blush ~ed to her face; the blood ~ed to his head.

mountain *n* (1) volcanic / folded ~s; a high / steep / towering / tremendous / majestic ~; climb (up) a ~; go / climb down a ~; go (up) into the ~s; take a holiday / live in the ~s; at the foot of a ~ (2) a ~ of potatoes; a ~ of work / debts / difficulties; a ~ of a man; the waves were ~ high.

mourn *vt* (1) ~ the loss of s.o. / s.th.; we're all inclined to ~ the passing of old institutions; his death was ~ed throughout the country; ~ one's dead. - *vi* (2) ~ for a child / a friend / the dead; ~ over a loss / frustrated hopes / one's misfortunes.

mourning *n* a house of ~; go into / put on / be in / go out of / wear ~; the widow was in deep ~; put s.o. into ~.

mouth *n* (1) open / wash / rinse / wipe one's ~; keep one's ~ shut; the news passed from ~ to ~; the news spread by word of ~; this sounds strange in your ~; he stood there with open ~ *(astonished)*; put words into s.o.'s ~ *(suggest that he has said them; tell him what to say)*; take the words out of s.o.'s ~ *(say what he was going to say)*; laugh on the wrong side of one's ~ *(lament)*; be down in the ~ *(sad)* (2) the ~ of a cave / tunnel / river / bag / bottle / pitcher; N. is at the ~ of the river T.

move *n* (1) the ~s in chess; it's your ~. (2) a ~ towards settling the strike; what will your next ~ be? a lightning *(very fast)* ~; shall we make a ~ now *(to a different place)*? the thief made a ~ towards the door; don't make a ~ or I'll shoot; unless we make a ~ *(begin to act)* soon, we shall be in a hopelessly weak position. (3) we plan a ~ *(change of residence)* in the spring; □ (he's always) on the ~; you'd better get a ~ on *(inform: hurry up)* or you'll be late.

move *vt* (1) ~ your chair nearer to the fire; the wind gently ~d the leaves; ~ s.th. to and fro / from the spot / from its place; I cannot ~ my arm; ~ one's bowels *(empty them)*; □ ~ heaven and earth (to do s.th.) (2) the story of their sufferings ~d us to tears / deeply; tears will not ~ him (to pity); be ~d with pity / compassion; ~d by hatred / fear; he was much ~d by the news. (3) her advice ~d him to action; nothing I said ~d him to offer his help; his pride ~d him to try the high dive. (4) ~ a vote of thanks / an amendment / for a new trial; I ~ that we take a vote on that next week. - *vi* (5) the train started to ~; a few leaves ~d in the wind; it's your turn to ~ *(in chess, etc)*; when you press a button, the wheels begin to ~; ~ forwards / backwards / sidewards / up and down; ~ on / onwards / northeast / *etc*; lights were ~ing about in the darkness; the earth ~s round the sun; the procession ~d through the streets; '~ along, please', said the conductor; the police tried to ~ on the crowd; we're ~ing (*BE* house) next week; we ~d out on Monday and the new tenants ~d in(to the flat) on Tuesday. (6) the work (on the new building) ~s slowly; time ~s on; many African peoples are ~ing into independent nationhood / towards independence; ~ from success to success (7) we must ~ *(take action)* at once in this matter; the police ~ quickly whenever a crime is committed. (8) they ~ in high / the best society; ~ in literary circles; this child ~s in a world all his own; the discussion ~d on an elevated plane. - *adj* (9) a (very) ~ing sight / scene / tale / speech; one of the (most) ~ing ideas of our century.

move up (1) ~ up in a queue (2) be ~d up (in)to a higher form; ~ up *(to a higher form)*.

movement *n* (1) (watch) the ~ of the dancer's feet; the ~ of a broken limb is painful; a graceful / impatient / wooden / *etc* ~; make a ~ of impatience; the thief made a ~ towards the door; have one's ~ *(empty the bowels)* at the same time of day; there was a general ~ in the hall. (2) the detectives watched every ~ *(action)* of the gang. (3) the antislavery ~; a social / political / religious ~ (4) the first ~ of a sonata / symphony (5) the ~ *(rhythm)* of the dance music; the quick ~ *(progress)* of the plot.

much *adj/pron* he never eats ~ breakfast; did it cost ~? did you have ~ difficulty (in) finding the house? our country owes ~ to freedom from war; ~ of what he says is true; ~ was said but little done; we have ~ to be thankful for; you have given me too ~; I have too ~; she's got a bit of a cold, but it's nothing ~; she isn't ~ to look at; the old building doesn't seem like ~, but it has a famous history; how ~ (flour *etc*) do you want? how ~ (money) do you earn? how ~ *(what price)* are the eggs? you can have as ~ as you like; too ~ will be bad for you; it's a bit ~ *(inform: rather unpleasant)* if we ...; (his work) isn't up to ~ *(not very good)*; his efforts didn't amount to ~; he's not ~ of a translator / scholar / tennis-player / cinema-goer; it wasn't ~ of a dinner; can you let me have this ~? I have only done that ~ so far; I'll say this ~ in his favour; he is too ~ for *(superior to)* me; that book was too ~ *(difficult)* for me; I didn't make ~ of *(understand)* that lecture; we mustn't make too ~ of *(consider important)* this incident; we don't think ~ of him *(have a poor opinion of him)*; he thinks too ~ of himself; he left without so ~ as saying 'good-bye'; he had not so ~ as his fare home; many doctors had not so ~ as *(even)* heard of it.

much *adv* (1 *before adj*) there's nothing ~ wrong with him; he is ~ better today; I'm ~ taller than you; work ~ harder; this is ~ the best. (2 *before past part*) was the car ~ damaged? you seem ~ annoyed; we should be ~ surprised if he succeeded. (3 *with v*) he doesn't swim ~; I don't think ~ about it; it doesn't ~ matter / matter (very) ~; how ~ do you really want to go there? I don't go there ~. (4) the patient's condition is ~ the same; ~ to his surprise / regret he ...

muddle *vt* (1) his brain was ~d by too many questions; two drinks ~ him; don't ~ things up; his papers are dreadfully ~d; you've ~d the scheme completely. – *vi* (2) he's still ~ing on/ along; she ~d through (the exam paper) and somehow passed.

murder *vt* (1) ~ s.o. cruelly / brutally / in a cowardly manner / in cold blood / in broad daylight; the ~ed man was a rich merchant; the bombing ~ed most of the civilian population. (2) ~ a song *(sing very badly)* / a sonata / the English language; ~ one's opponent *(slang: defeat him soundly)*; we ~ed them 20 to 0.

music *n* (1) vocal / instrumental / electronic / chamber / sacred / secular / classical / modern / contemporary / popular / dance / martial / oriental / incidental ~; gay / lovely / luscious / sublime ~; compose / write / play / make ~; have a gift / an ear for ~; set / put (a poem) to ~; □ face the ~ *(face one's critics, not shirk)* (2 *the written notes*) he could read ~ with ease; the ~ for the Chopin sonata; I brought my flute but left my ~ at home. (3) the ~ of the waves / wind / birds / spheres.

muster *vt* (1) they managed to ~ a hundred signatures; go and ~ all the men you can find. (2) ~ (up) (all) one's courage; he could not ~ the strength to do it; cannot ~ up much sympathy for it; ~ sufficient public support for the plan; the Common Market seems to have an appeal for Americans which the Free Trade Area cannot ~.

mutual *adj* (1) we looked at each other with ~ suspicion; ~ enemies / well-wishers; ~ friendships / love / hatred / aid / consent / trust / dependence / concessions (2 *common*; considered incorrect by some) their ~ friend John; ~ travels / interests.

mystery *n* (1) (its origin) is surrounded by / wrapped in / shrouded in / lost in (impenetrable) ~; with a real note of ~ in his voice; an air of ~; he makes no ~ of his attitude. (2) a religious / deep / profound / unfathomable ~; the murder remained an unsolved ~; do tell me – I hate ~ies; this ~ has never been fathomed.

N

nail *n* knock / hammer / drive in a ~; drive home a ~; hit the (right) ~ on the head *(say, do the right thing)*; the shock was another ~ in his coffin *(s.th. to ruin him)*; (pay) on the ~ *(at once)*.

nail *vt* (1) ~ s.th. on the wall *(indicates place)*; ~ s.th. to the wall *(indicates attachment)*; ~ a board down / on; they ~ed up the box by ~ing down the lid; ~ up a notice / picture; □ stand ~ed to the spot (2) ~ *(secure)* an order for goods / a contract (3 *inform*) ~ a lie *(prove it to be false)* (4 *inform*) the police ~ed *(caught)* the thief; the hunter ~ed *(shot)* a pheasant in flight.

nail down (1) → nail *vt* 1. (2) ~ s.o. ~ (to a promise); ~ s.o. ~ to a particular date for completing the work.

naked *adj* (1) ~ savages (2) ~ trees / rock; ~ rooms; a ~ sword; fight with ~ fists; see s.th. with / be visible to the ~ eye (3) the ~ truth / facts; a ~ *(unsupported)* assertion.

name *n* (1) Christian / first / given / family / maiden / pet ~; a sacred ~; a friend of yours. Wren by ~; do you know a person by / of the ~ of Wren? no one of / by that ~ lives here; what's your ~ ? tell / give me your ~; call s.o. by his ~; know s.o. by ~; sign s.th. with one's ~; he writes under the ~ of Smith; (live) under a fictitious ~; □ call s.o. *(insulting)* ~s; (I arrest you) in the ~ of the law; he hasn't a penny / a decent pair of shoes to his ~; he is boss in ~ only; it is a democracy in ~, but a dictatorship in fact. (2 *reputation*) win a ~ for o.s.; the firm has a good ~ for workmanship; lose one's good ~; have a bad ~; a good ~ is better than great riches; he is a big ~ in the theatre *(inform).*

name *vt* (1) ~ a baby; ~ a child John; the child was ~d after its father. (2) can you ~ all the flowers in the garden? ~ the capital of Eire; ~ the day for (our picnic); ~ one's price; the criminal refused to ~ his accomplices. (3) ~ s.o. chancellor / for the directorship / to an office / to a post; ~ one's successor; ~ s.o. a coward.

narrow *adj* (1) a ~ staircase / passage / road / bridge / river / valley; ~ space; a ~ skirt; ~ trousers / sleeves; within ~ limits / bounds (2) a ~ choice; live in ~ circumstances; a ~ circle of friends (3 *with a small margin*) a ~ escape / victory / majority / lead; win a race by a ~ margin (4 *strict*) a ~ examination of the facts / questioning / search; a ~ definition; in the ~est sense (of the word) (5 *not tolerant*) a ~ mind; have ~ views / principles.

narrow *vi* (1) this road ~s to one lane. – *vt* (2) ~ a definition; we ~ed the possibilities (down) to one answer; this ~ing of our social lives; ~ down one's research to a smaller field.

natural *adj* (1) ~ phenomena / forces; ~ flowers / rock formation / weapons *(teeth, fists, etc)* / gas / selection; a ~ *(illegitimate)* child; a ~ spring; ~ enemies; ~ resources *(coal, oil, etc)*; ~ science; a ~ law (2) ~ gifts / abilities / courage; ~ teeth; a ~ blonde; her hair curls ~ly; she is ~ly musical. (3) he is a ~ orator / linguist; that sort of thing comes ~ to her *(she does not have to learn it).* (4) die a ~ death; it is ~ for dogs to fight; fighting is ~ to dogs. (5) speak in a ~ voice; a ~ attitude; behave ~ly; try to be ~ before the microphone.

nature *n* (1) man has a struggle against (the forces of) ~; miracles are contrary to ~; □ pay the debt of / one's debt to ~ *(die)*; in the course of ~ (2) ~ is at its best in spring; the beauties of ~; people used to worship ~ *(trees, winds, etc)*; animate ~ *(plants, animals)*; ~ study; paint / draw from ~ (3 *simple life*) a return to ~ (4 *qualities; character*) different breeds of dogs have different ~s; John has a very different ~ from his sister; be selfish / proud / shy / friendly by ~; have a shy / *etc* ~; it is only human ~ to want the material things of life; (take advantage of) s.o.'s good ~; s.o. is of a placid / quarrelsome / *etc* ~; it's against ~; it's not in her ~ to lie; it's in the ~ of things that man seeks ... / for man to seek ... (5) the substance had a hard, brittle ~; scientists study the ~ of the atom; it's the ~ of liquids to be fluid. (6) soup of a watery ~; things of this ~ don't interest me; this trip is in the ~ of work; the flower was in the ~ of a daffodil.

naught *n* bring (plans) to ~ *(ruin)*; come to ~ *(fail)*; set s.o. at ~ *(defy)*; care ~ for *(consider worthless).*

necessary *adj* (1) a ~ condition / requirement; the ~ capital / means; (take) the ~ measures / steps; I shall do everything ~; food is ~ to life; sleep is ~ to health; are all these books really ~ (to you)? hard work is ~ for success in life; great patience is ~ for a teacher; a licence is ~ to drive a car; it is not ~ for you to go. (2) a ~ evil / consequence / conclusion; his illness was the ~ result of overwork.

necessitate *vt* these new facts ~ a further inquiry; the riot ~d prompt action by the police; that ~d translating all the documents into French; the skill required ~s years of training.

necessity *n* (1) ~ compelled him to steal; be driven by ~; he was under the ironical ~ of having to rest from his vacation; submit to the ~ imposed by the laws of the universe; □ ~ knows no law; □ ~ is the mother of invention; □ make a virtue of ~ (→ virtue 1); bow to ~ *(do what is necessary)*; in case of ~ you can call on me. (2) food and warmth are ~ies; the bare ~ies of life (3) be in ~ *(poverty)* (4) a logical ~ .

neck *n* (1) up to one's ~ in water / in difficulties; be in it up to the ~ *(in trouble)*; the dress has been cut too wide at the ~; he could have broken his ~ doing that; he broke his ~ *(inform: tried very hard)* to get her a job; the horses came in ~ and ~ *(together)*; □ stick one's (own) ~ out *(slang: disregard obvious dangers or risks)*; hang on s.o.'s ~; save one's ~ *(escape hanging / the results of being foolish)*; get it in the ~ *(inform: be severely criticized; have a painful experience)* (2) the ~ of a violin / an axle / a tooth / a dress / land; knock the ~ off a bottle (3) have the / a ~ *(inform: impudence)* to ask for another loan; that fellow's got ~ enough for anything.

need *n* (1 *lack of s.th. necessary*) are you in ~ of advice / help? I stand in great ~ of his assistance; he felt the ~ of money; I have ~ of you *(I want you)*; we have no ~ of your advice; your ~ is greater than mine; our tour had to be given up through ~ of money. (2 *compelling circumstances*) there's no ~ for alarm; is there any ~ for all this hurry / (for us) to hurry? there is no ~ to write and thank him; I will come it ~ be; "He'll come and fetch you." - "Oh, there's no ~ for that." (3 *requirement*) personal / physical ~s; my ~s are few; supply s.o.'s ~s; attend / minister to s.o.'s ~s; my ~s are supplied; he earns enough to satisfy his ~s; there's a growing ~ for (qualified teachers); there was a ~ for caution; there is a real ~ today for this sort of book. (4 *poverty*) be in ~; she kept her ~ secret; □ a friend in ~ is a friend indeed.

need *vt* (1) he ~s money urgently; ~ correction / rest / consolation / *etc*; the soil ~s rain; plants ~ sunlight and water to grow; does anybody ~ this pen? have you everything you ~ for the journey? this is a book I have been ~ing a long time; it ~ed the horrors of war to open their eyes; I ~ you; we ~ time; what he ~s is a good whipping. (2) he doesn't ~ to be told *(he already knows it)*; you don't ~ to return the book today; no more ~s to be said about it; I did not ~ to be reminded of it; we didn't ~ to wait for her, because she sent us a telegram; it ~s to be done carefully; it ~ed doing / mending; this ~s looking into; the plants ~ watering every day; he ~s no urging. (3) he ~n't be told *(let's keep it secret)*; you ~n't be afraid; he need not trouble himself; why ~ it be today? you ~n't complete this essay tonight; "~ you go so soon?" - "No, I ~n't"; ~ anybody know? I don't think that ~ be considered; I ~ hardly say that I ...; you only ~ say so; no one ~ know this; one ~ only consider the facts.

needle *n* (1) ~ and cotton / thread; thread a ~; pass a thread through the eye of a ~; □ a ~ in a haystack / bundle of hay *(s.th. impossible to find)* (2) a magnetic / hypodermic / gramophone / pine / fir ~.

negative *adj* (1) give a ~ answer (2) ~ criticism; ~ virtue *(doing neither wrong nor good)*; ~ praise *("that work is not done badly")*; ~ personality; the test gave a ~ reaction; minus ten is a ~ quantity; a ~ statement *(in logic)* (3) ~ly charged particles.

neglect *vt* (1) don't ~ your homework; ~ one's duty / studies / health / family / children (2) he ~ed to tell us that he ...; don't ~ having your teeth attended to.

negotiate *vt* (1) ~ peace; ~ a treaty / agreement / settlement / terms / sale of property / loan (2) the old car could hardly ~ the hill; a difficult corner for a large car to ~; my horse ~d the fence well. - *vi* (3) ~ with s.o. for s.th.; ~ with s.o. on an issue / about one's wage claims; if only the two nations would begin to ~; no one can ~ in an atmosphere of distrust.

negotiation *n* enter into ~ with s.o. for an agreement / about a problem; open / start / carry on / break off / resume ~s; be in ~ with s.o.; price is a matter of ~; the ~s came to a standstill / were successful / failed / resulted in a deadlock.

neighbour *n* (1) a ~ of mine / my sister's; they have been good ~s to us; we're next-door ~s; my next-door-~ often comes in for a cup of coffee; we were ~s at dinner. (2) the new building dwarfs its ~; the falling tree brought down its ~.

nerve *n* (1) the ~s conduct nervous impulses; the ~ of a tooth (2) he is suffering from ~s *(becomes easily excited)*; he doesn't know what ~s are *(is not troubled by fear, etc)*; have ~s of iron / steel *(be never afraid, worried)*; have a fit of ~s *(be unable to control o.s.)*; that noise gets on my ~s; → edge *n* 2. (3 *courage,* *impudence*) it took ~ to be cheerful in the leaking boat; he hadn't the ~ to speak; he had the ~ to talk to his boss about it; lose / regain one's ~; he never lacked ~; I used to do a lot of climbing, but I haven't the ~ for it now; you have a ~! (4 *sinew*) □ strain every ~ *(make great efforts).*

nervous *adj* (1) the ~ system; a ~ breakdown (2) she is ~ on the stage / in the dark; a ~ person gets upset often; what are you so ~ about? you make me ~. (3 *vigorous*) full of ~ energy; a ~ style of writing.

new *adj* (1) a ~ building / school / grave; a ~ idea / experience / kind of motor / *etc* (2) discover a ~ star / plant / insect / land; that word is ~ to me. (3) ~ and second-hand books; ~ shoes; is the bicycle ~? ~ bread / cheese / milk / wine / hay / potatoes; a ~ car; a ~ page; tap a ~ barrel; she wears a ~ dress every day; a ~ director / teacher / friend; ~ hope / courage / strength; a ~ start; after a rest I felt a ~ man / woman; the holiday made a ~ man of him. (4) a ~ moon; lead a ~ life (*give up old habits*;→ life *n*7); a ~ year; New Year's Eve / Day (5) I am ~ to the work; the work is ~ to me; this district is ~ to me; I am ~ to this district. (6 *the + ~: modern*) the ~ age / journalism / aristocracy / woman.

news *n* have you had any ~ of / from Tom? there has been a lot of ~ from France; the latest / local / foreign / sports / *etc* ~ (is just beginning); in Britain, broadcast ~ is no longer the sole responsibility of the B.B.C.; the more important ~ is printed on the front page; the incident made front-page ~; (Mr N.'s visit is) most welcome ~; the ~ today is very hopeful; this is good / glad / ugly ~; what good ~! what's the ~? what's in the ~? what's on the ~ *(on radio, TV)*? I heard it on the ~ last night; an interesting item of ~; a piece of (good) ~; □ no ~ is good ~; that's ~ to me *(I did not know it)*; □ break the ~ to s.o. *(tell s.o. bad news).*

next *adj/adv* (1) the ~ house; the house ~ to ours; the ~ street / turning to the right; a seat ~ (to) the fire; sit ~ to me; the ~ person you meet; the first, the ~ and the last; what are you going to do ~ ? what's the ~ thing to do? Ann was the ~ (person) to arrive; he lives ~ door (to us) (→ neighbour 1); it is ~ door to impossible / madness / dishonesty; my name comes ~ on the list; after Tom, John is the ~ oldest boy in the class; the ~ world *(life after death)*; New York is the largest city ~ to London; she eats ~ to *(almost)* nothing; I can do that in ~ to no time; ~ to knowing when to seize an opportunity, the most important thing is to know when to forgo an advantage. (2) the ~ bus / train / day; (he'll go there) ~ Friday / week / month / summer / *etc*; we shall be in Rome by this time ~ week.

nice *adj* (1) a ~ day / car / dog / meal; ~ weather; a ~ little girl; ~ clothes; it's ~ and warm here; that'll suit me ~ly; you did it very ~ly; don't do that - it's not ~; that wasn't very ~ of you; you have made a ~ mess of it; that's a ~ *(nasty)* thing to say to your aunt! (2 *subtle*) ~ shades of meaning; a ~ distinction / point of law; he has a ~ ear for music. (3 *particular*) he is not too ~ in his business methods; she is very ~ in her dress.

night *n* (1) have / pass a good / bad / wakeful / sleepless / restless ~; we sleep at ~; burglars work by ~; the owl sleeps by day and hunts by ~; to avoid heavy traffic some people prefer to travel by ~; sleep during the ~ (and work during the day); ~ after ~ she sat by the child's bed; travel over ~; an over~ journey; we stayed over~ at a hotel; have a ~ out / off *(spend it in pleasure away from home)*; make a ~ of it *(spend it in merry-making)*; turn ~ into day *(do at night what is usually done in the day)* (2 *darkness; also fig*) before we were out of the woods, ~ caught us; he went out into the ~; the ~ of the soul; the ~ of ignorance (3) a first ~ *(première).*

nimble *adj* (1) a ~ person; ~ fingers / movements; be ~ of foot / hand; be ~ on one's feet / with one's fingers / with one's hands; squirrels are ~ in climbing trees. (2) a ~ mind; a ~ answer.

nod *vi* (1) he ~ded when asked if he had lost something; he ~ded to me as he passed; ~ded to show that he understood; have a ~ding acquaintance with s.o.; be on ~ding terms with s.o. (2) the lilies were ~ding in the breeze. (3) she sat ~ding *(half asleep)* by the fire / over her work; the teacher caught him ~ding. - *vt* (4) ~ the head; ~ a greeting / one's farewell; ~ approval / assent; he ~ded me a welcome.

noise *n* make / produce a constant / continual / continuous / loud / shrill / confused / frightful / weird / sudden / deafening ~; don't make so much / such a loud / a ~ (or you'll wake him up); what's that ~? what are those strange ~s? the ~ of traffic; the ~ grows louder / swells into a roar / nearly deafens me / drives me mad / dies away; make a ~ (about s.th.) *(complain)*; make a ~ in the world *(become much talked about)*; he is a big ~ *(inform: an important person)* in the shipping world.

nominate *vt* (1) ~ s.o. (as a candidate) for a position / appointment / employment; ~ s.o. for the presidency / for president (2) ~ s.o. to an office / post *(appoint)*.

nonsense *n* that's pure / sheer / downright ~; talk ~; stand no ~; I want no more of your ~.

nose *n* (1) hit s.o. on the ~; blow / wipe one's ~; speak through one's ~ *(in a nasal manner)*; □ count / tell ~s *(the number of supporters)*; □ poke / push / thrust one's ~ into s.o.'s affairs / business *(interfere)*; □ turn up one's ~ at *(scorn)*; bite / snap s.o.'s ~ off *(speak angrily to him)*; □ put s.o.'s ~ out of joint *(disconcert him, spoil his plans)*; → cut off 1, follow *vt* 1, keep *vt* 8a, lead *vt* 1, look down 1, pay *vi* 6; (right) under s.o.'s (very) ~ *(immediately in front of him)*; as plain as the ~ on your face *(obvious)* (2) a dog with a good / keen / sharp ~; have a ~ for scandal / news (3) the ~ of an aeroplane / ship.

nose *vt* (1) the dog ~d the grass in search of a trail. (2) to ~ her safely all this distance the ship was equipped with unusual guidance gear. (3) the ship ~d (its way) slowly through the fog. (4) the dog ~d out a rat; she ~d out an old scandal. - *vt* (5) he's always ~ing into other people's affairs; she has been ~ing about / around in my cupboard again.

note *n* (1) speak for an hour without a ~ / ~s; take / make a ~ of s.th.; take ~s on a lecture; the ~s in the book make the meaning of the text clear. (2) a ~ *(short letter)* of thanks; a hurried ~; an exchange of ~s between governments (3) strike / hit a ~ on the piano; a whole / half / quarter / eighth ~; strike the right ~ *(say, do what is appropriate)*; strike / sound a false ~; this book strikes a new ~ in (sociology). (4) a ~ of exclamation (!); a ~ of interrogation (?) (5) a ~ of sadness in her voice; a ~ of self-satisfaction in his speech (6) Jones is a man of (some/ no) ~. (7) a matter worthy of ~ *(attention)*; take ~ of what he says.

note *vt* (1) ~ (down) s.o.'s address (2) he ~d that the door was open. (3) ~ this carefully; ~ how to do it / I did it.

nothing *pron* he has ~ to say *(nothing worth mentioning)*; there's ~ on television tonight; I got it for ~; all our work has gone for ~ *(was in vain)*; they quarrelled for ~ *(no good reason)*; ~ but desert for miles; it's ~ but impudence on his part; London is ~ if not *(is very)* up to date; English counties are ~ if not *(are very)* individual; there's ~ like *(so good as)* leather for shoes; he has ~ in him *(is worthless)*; there's ~ in it *(it's untrue)*; that's ~ to *(compared with)* what followed; she's ~ to him *(he's not interested in her)*; come to ~ *(fail completely)*; make ~ of (*not understand*; → make *vt* 30); he makes ~ of *(considers unimportant)* a few mistakes; he made ~ of *(failed to use)* his opportunities; he made ~ of doing all the work himself.

nothing *n* (1) ~ cannot become an object of consciousness. (2) they were having drinks and saying sweet ~s; a little ~ of a dress; she felt like a mere ~ in his presence.

notice *n* (1) put up a ~; a ~ of forthcoming concerts; ~s of births, marriages and deaths in the newspapers; (flights are cancelled) till further ~. (2) give a tenant ~ to quit / leave his flat; give him ~ to leave; give an employee / servant a month's ~ *(tell him that he must leave after a month)*; I have given / handed in my ~ (for the first of May); I've given ~ that I am leaving my flat on the first of next month; give ~ to terminate an agreement / contract / *etc*; the event was cancelled at / on short ~; a loan at / on short ~ (3) bring s.th. to s.o.'s ~; take (no) ~ of what he says; it escaped (my) ~; his remarks should be beneath / not worth (your) ~; worthy of ~; the rumour received no particular ~; it has come to my ~ that he ...; bring o.s. into ~.

notice *vt* I ~d that Jane was wearing a new dress; I ~d Jane's new dress; by chance I ~d him in the crowd; a mistake that was ~d at once; they ~d him hesitate to sign the agreement. - *vi* (2 *BE*) I wasn't ~ing *(paying attention)*.

notify *vt* (1 *inform*) he ~ied the post office of his change of address; ~ the police of a loss; please ~ me of the times of your broadcasts. (2 *report officially*) ~ a birth; ~ the police of an accident / an accident to the police; 4000 cases of the disease are ~ied each year; three new cases of polio were ~ied in Manchester yesterday.

notion *n* (1) the ~ of my doing it is absurd; I have no / not the haziest ~ (of) what he means / of the meaning of these words; I haven't the ghost of a ~; a foggy / cloudy / sudden ~; his head is full of silly / strange ~s; his ~ of a good film is not hers; the ~ is not fully worked out in his mind; he has a ~ that I'm cheating him; we sometimes have strange ~s about other countries. (2 *understanding*) he has a good / no ~ of Greek / economy. (3 *intention*) have no ~ of resigning / obeying / letting himself be put upon (4 *whim*) we got a sudden ~ to go fishing.

nourish *vt* (1) babies are ~ed with milk; ~ one's family / children (2) ~ the soil *(with manure)* / animals / plants (3) ~ hope / high hopes / hatred / discontent / ambition / illusions. – *adj* (4) ~ing food.

novel *adj* ~ devices / gadgets; ~ ideas / problems; holiday-makers who like ~ activities can go treasure-hunting; studying Russian was a ~ experience.

nucleus *n* (1) the ~ of a cell / a crystal / condensation / an atom / a comet; atomic / fissionable / radioactive nuclei; cancer cells differ from normal cells in the appearance of their nuclei. (2) the ~ of a party / army / team; this splinter group formed the ~ of the new party.

nuisance *n* s.o./ s.th. is a ~ *(causes trouble, annoys)*; flies are a (beastly) ~; this boy is a ~ in class; what a ~! make a ~ of o.s.; commit no ~ *(notice: do not leave rubbish here, etc)*; create a public ~.

numb *adj* fingers ~ with cold; the sound made us ~ with fear; a mind ~ to grief.

number *n* (1) a (large / small / limited / *etc*) ~ of books / boxes / rooms / accidents / people / *etc*; a (small) ~ of the students are still here; there were a large ~ of people at the meeting; the ~ of students is not so great this year as last; they have a ~ of things to do; ~s of people came to see the exhibition; they came in great ~s; they won by (force of) ~s; the enemy exceeds us in ~; they were twelve in ~; (I have done it) ~s of time / times without ~. (2) one, three, forty are ~s; 1, 3, 40 are ~s; a cardinal / ordinal / even / odd / whole / fraction(al) / total ~; consecutive ~s; an (un)lucky ~; he is not good at ~s *(arithmetic)*. (3) live at No. 6; dial s.o.'s ~; the ~ is engaged; □ look after / take care of ~ one *(inform: look after one's own interests)* (4) the current / the May / a back ~ of 'Punch'; he is a back ~ *(old-fashioned)*. (5) for her next ~ Jane will sing a folk song. (6) 'men' is plural in ~.

number *vt* (1) ~ the seats; we ~ ed the tickets 1 to 500. (2) I ~ the people in this group to be 32; □ the days of his life / his days are ~ed *(there are few left)*. (3) ~ s.o. among one's (closest) friends (4) the school's library ~s about 5,000 books; the population of the island ~s 15,000; we ~ed twenty in all; the team ~ed ten.

nurse *vt* (1) ~ a baby *(give milk to)*; ~ing mothers (2) ~ sick people / wounded soldiers / an invalid; ~ a weak ankle; ~ a cold *(stay at home, keep warm, etc)*; unless properly ~d, scarlet fever may produce dangerous complications. (3) ~ (young) plants (4) ~ hopes / feelings of revenge / a grudge / a grievance (5) ~ a glass of (vermouth) *(drink it very slowly for full enjoyment)*.

nut *n* (1) mixed ~s; □ a hard ~ to crack *(fig)* (2 *slang: head*) be off one's ~ *(slang: insane)*; be ~s *(slang: mad)*. (3) oh, ~s! *(mild interjection)*.

O

oar *n* pull a good ~ *(row well)*; □ put / shove / stick one's ~ in (*intrude*; → put in 1); □ rest / lie on one's ~s *(stop work for a time out of contentment with what has been done)*.

oat *n* ~ straw; summer / winter ~s; rolled ~s; ~meal; □ sow one's wild ~s *(lead an immoral life while young)*.

oath *n* (1) take / make / swear a (solemn) oath; swear a false ~; put s.o. on (his) ~ *(make him take an oath)*; administer the / an ~ to s.o.; release / relieve s.o. from his ~; declare / state s.th. on ~; on my ~ it happened as I am telling you; bound by (an) ~; ~-bound; under ~ (2) utter / let out an ~ *(swear-word)*.

obedience *n* strict / implicit / unquestioning / blind / passive / *etc* ~; (act) in ~ to one's parents / the law / the authorities / instructions / orders; get ~ *(get o.s. obeyed)*; compel / exact ~ from s.o.; enforce ~ (up)on s.o.; refuse ~; ~ training *(of dogs)*.

obey *vt* ~ s.o. (instantly / implicitly / willingly / reluctantly / hesitatingly / mechanically); ~ orders / commands / the law / a principle / a rule / one's conscience; get o.s. ~ed; I wish my orders ~ed at once. (2) all bodies ~ the law of gravitation. - *vi* (3) you can't train animals that can't or won't ~.

object *n* (1) material / concrete / physical / inanimate ~s; an ~ of art (2) (s.o. is) an ~ of pity / general mirth / admiration / pleasure / praise; they had become ~s of universal hatred; be the ~ of severe criticism (3) Bill's one ~ in life is to become a famous surgeon; he's a proper ~ of, for charity / ridicule; a man with no ~ in life; work with the ~ of (earning fame); fail / succeed in one's ~; the ~ of the game is to ...

object *vi* (1) mother always ~s when we do that; he stood up and ~ed in strong language. (2) ~ to s.o.'s plans / being treated like a child; why do you ~ to him? - *vt* (3) he ~ed that nobody would have time for so much extra work.

objection *n* make / raise an ~ (to s.th.); he made the ~ that he ...; refute an ~; my ~s (to the project) no longer have any foundation / are no longer valid; I have no ~ (to make) to your proposal / to him.

obligation *n* (1) have an / no ~ to do s.th.; your first ~ is to learn all you can; the ~s of conscience / good citizenship; she feels an ~ to everyone who helps her; repay an ~; be under (an) ~ to s.o. for his help; put s.o. under an ~ (2) he meets all his ~s *(debts)* promptly.

oblige *vt* (1) ill health ~d him to retire at the age of 58; the law ~s everyone to pay his taxes; we ~d ourselves / were ~d to settle our father's bills. (2) he's always seeking to ~ his friends; could you ~ me with a match? please ~ me by shutting the door; he has greatly ~d us by (undertaking the business). - *vi* (3) the singer ~ed with an encore.

obscure *adj* (1) an ~ corner / view; increasing darkness made the road signs ~. (2) the ~ meaning of his words; an ~ passage in the text; it is ~ to me; a man of ~ origins; the ~ workings of nature; the ~ beginnings (of a famous man); his ~ beginnings; ~ feelings (3) an ~ little village; an ~ island; an ~ poet / country lawyer.

obscure *vt* (1) the moon was ~d by clouds; a heavy fog ~d the street lamps; ~ s.th. from s.o. / view (2) all those long words ~ his meaning; ~ a fact / truth; there is always a price to pay when passions have ~d interests.

observance *n* (1) the ~ of rules / religious festivals / customs / duties; insist on strict ~ of the rules; a nationwide ~ of two minutes' silence (2) a religious ~ *(ceremony)*.

observation *n* (1) the ~ of experiments / natural phenomena / heavenly bodies / landscapes; the experiment needed careful ~; come under ~; keep s.th. / be under (constant) ~ (2) a man of no ~; a detective must develop his ~. (3) escape ~ *(being seen)* (4) write your ~s of the experiment in your notebooks; publish one's ~s on American bird life (5) my aunt made an ~ about how much I had changed.

observe *vt* (1) ~ the growth of plants / the movement of clouds / the stars / the enemy (closely / carefully / attentively / *etc*); I ~d him go(ing) out; by chance I ~ him in the crowd; three unidentified aircraft were ~d. (2) ~ Christmas / the Sabbath / an anniversary / s.o.'s birthday / a feast / a festival (3) ~ the doctor's instructions / laws / regulations / proprieties; ~ a method / principle / command; ~ silence / neutrality (4) "You are wrong," he ~d; he ~d that we ... - *vi* (5) he is a man who ~s very keenly.

obsess *v* the idea that he might lose his position ~ed him; be ~ed by/ with an idea / fear.

obstacle *n* natural / artificial ~s *(in a race)*; meet / get rid of / avoid / overcome numerous / innumerable ~s; come across unsuspected / unexpected / formidable / insuperable ~s; a fence is no ~ to him / jumping.

obstruct *vt* (1) a fallen tree ~ed the road; a tumour ~s the duodenum; ~ traffic / the circulation of the blood / the working of the bowels; ~ an opponent (2) the high trees ~ed our view. (3) stony ground and rain ~ed the building of the tennis court; ~ the progress of a Bill through Parliament; be ~ed in the execution of one's duty; ~ justice by refusing to testify.

obtain *vt* (1) ~ the post one desires; the picture ~ed a high price at the auction; ~ an interview with s.o.; he ~ed enough money to establish a small business; ~ results / rights / information / evidence / the copyright (of a book); ~ knowledge (through study); ~ one's liberty (by force); ~ exemption (from s.th.); ~ permission (from s.o.) to do s.th.; ~ promotion. - *vi* (2) shaking hands upon meeting is a custom that ~s in many countries; the men are paid lower wages than ~ elsewhere; this system is based on the conditions ~ing immediately after the First World War.

occasion *n* (1) on this ~ I would like to say ...; it was on that ~ that I first met my wife; on such / similar / comparable / different ~s; on the ~ of the centenary / our silver wedding (I received the medal); a formal / festive / much celebrated / momentous / historic ~; Christmas is always an ~ for merrymaking; the families celebrate together all special ~s, such as birthdays and holidays, and ...; we still visit each other on ~(s); □ be up to / equal to the ~ *(able to do what is necessary)* (2) I have often had ~ to complain of his coming late; there is no ~ to be angry; I had no ~ to see him; that may perhaps give ~ for scandal; give ~ to an outburst of popular indignation; give s.o. ~ to do s.th.; take (the) ~ to do s.th.; if good ~ offers.

occasion *vt* a violent storm ~ed a new delay of two weeks; the boy's behaviour ~ed his parents much anxiety; ~ protests / criticism / a riot.

occupation *n* (1) he is by ~ a teacher / editor / driver / shoemaker; we should choose an ~ according to our ability; in our country there is no ~ that a worker need feel ashamed of; a gainful / remunerative / profitable / rewarding / dull / tiresome / dangerous / *etc* ~; follow an ~ (2) painting is a pleasant ~; leisure(-time) / spare-time ~; ~(al) therapy (3) quick ~ of these new houses is expected; the ~ of a house by a family; the house was finished a month ago, but the owner is not yet in ~; no one is yet in ~ of the house. (4) the ~ of the capital forced the enemy to surrender; ~ of enemy territory / a fort / a height; ~ troops; an army of ~.

occupy *vt* (1) ~ a seat / table / car / room / flat; he is waiting to ~ the new house he has just bought. (2) the dinner ~ied two hours; stamp-collecting ~ies his spare time. (3) ~ enemy / the enemy's territory; ~ a position / town / fort / height (4) ~ an important position in a ministry (5) ~ o.s. with one's stamps / the children / a novel / studying plants; ~ one's time by reading and knitting; the children must be kept ~ied; I am ~ied at the moment; he is ~ied in translating / with the translation of a French novel. (6) many anxieties ~ied his mind; he is too much ~ied by his worries.

occur *vi* (1) an event / incident / opportunity / wonder / crime ~s; this case actually ~red; when did it ~? it ~s every day; I hope no accident has ~red to them. (2) several misprints ~ on the first page; these plants ~ in this country. (3) an idea suddenly ~red to me; has it ever ~red to you that I ...? his name doesn't ~ to me.

occurrence *n* (1) an everyday / rare / singular / peculiar / odd / unfortunate / happy ~ (2) frequent ~ of floods led to the building of dams along the river; every unusual ~ of a common word is registered; the ~ of events; the fish is of regular ~ along this coast; s.th. is of daily / frequent / rare ~.

odd *adj* (1) 1, 3, 5, 7 are ~ numbers; the ~ pages of a book (2) an ~ shoe / boot / glove / stocking; two ~ volumes of an encyclopedia; the ~ player *(one more than needed)* can keep score or substitute; □ ~ man out *(person left when the others have been paired; person who cannot fit himself into a community)*; □ ~ man over *(one in excess of a fixed number)* (3 *occasional, miscellaneous*) at ~ moments; ~ jobs; a few ~ possessions (4) two hundred ~ *(200 + a little extra)*; it cost twelve pounds ~; I had 40 ~ dollars in my pocket; here's a pound: pay the bill and keep the ~ money; there are 1006 - what shall we do with the ~ six? (5) his behaviour was very ~; she was ~ in her behaviour / appearance / dress; he's an ~(-looking) old man; how ~ (that he should have forgotten it)!

odds *n* (1) in a tug of war the ~ are with the heavier team; be fighting against great / heavy / fearful ~ (2) the ~ are just about even between the two teams; the ~ are in our favour / against us; give

~(of 10 to 1) on a racehorse / fighter / *etc*; the ~ on the champion are only 5 to 4; if we have a red sunset, the ~ are that tomorrow will be fair; what are the ~ on his getting the post? the ~ are that he will come; it makes no ~ whether he comes or not; what ~ does it make whether ...? what's the ~ *(likelihood)* that they don't come after all? the pay is good - and even if the hours are irregular and uncertain, what's the ~ *(what does it matter)*? (3) be at ~ (with s.o.) (on a question); the two are always at ~ with each other; they are always at ~ as to who drives the car. (4) ~ and ends; get s.th. second-hand at an ~-and-ends sale.

odour *n* (1) a disagreeable / musty / obnoxious / repulsive / vile ~; the ~ of animals of prey; lilacs have a pleasant ~; a faint ~ of suspicion (2) be in good / bad / ill ~ with (the authorities).

offence *n* (1) stealing is a criminal ~; minor / major / culpable ~s (2) an ~ against good taste / manners; that was an ~ to his pride / the ear / the eye / her sense of beauty; the loud discords were an ~ to his sense of harmony. (3) weapons of ~; the most effective defence is ~. (4) give / cause ~ (to s.o.); no ~ was meant; take ~ (at s.th.); she is too quick to take ~; if I may say so without giving ~.

offend *vt* (1) I'm sorry if I've ~ed you; be ~ed at/ by a remark; he ~ed me with his insults; such a personal question might ~ some people. (2) colours that don't match ~ the eyes; ~ the ear / palate; ~ed pride. - *vi* (3) ~ against custom / decency / good manners / the law / good morals; the verdict ~s against one's ideas / sense of justice; that sentence ~s against English usage. (4) those who ~ *(break the law)* are often punished.

offer *n* an inviting / kind / liberal / favourable / advantageous / definite / spontaneous ~; make s.o. an ~ for s.th.; make an ~ (of marriage) to a lady; that is the best ~ I can make; I am open to an ~ *(willing to consider one)*; goods on ~ *(for sale)*.

offer *vt* (1) ~ one's arm to a lady / one's lips (for a kiss); ~ a reward / a plan / one's services; he was ~ed a post / job; ~ one's hand *(for s.o. to shake)*; ~ one's hand in friendship; ~ a helping hand; ~ an opinion / suggestion; the book ~s a fund of sound advice; have you any excuse to ~? many ~ed to help; he ~ed to drive. (2) the house was ~ed at a low price; ~ goods (for sale); ~ a price (3) ~ (stout) resistance (to the enemy) / violence (4) ~ (up) prayers to God; ~ up a sacrifice. - *vi* (5) take the first opportunity that ~s; ... when the possibility ~s.

office *n* (1) a public / ecclesiastical / government ~; the ~ of secretary / bishop / Minister of Finance / *etc*; enter upon / accept / seek / hold ~; put s.o. into ~; take / come into / leave / resign ~; the Labour Party is in / out of ~; a post / telegraph / tax ~ (2) work in an ~; an architect's / lawyer's ~; our London ~ (3) she performs the ~ of hostess very graciously; the ~ of host / chairman; through the good ~s *(kindness)* of a friend; ask for s.o.'s good ~s *(intervention, recommendation)*; perform the last ~s for s.o. *(conduct the burial service for him)*.

offset *vt* ~ losses by profits; the gains have been more than ~ by losses; we must increase the price of flour to ~ the increased cost; his good qualities ~ his shortcomings.

oil *n* (1) crude / essential / volatile ~s; vegetable / animal / mineral ~s; whale / olive / coconut ~; □ burn the midnight ~ *(study at night)*; □ pour ~ on the flame(s) *(make a quarrel more bitter)*; □ pour ~ on troubled waters *(smooth matters over)*; strike ~ *(find oil; fig: become very prosperous, successful)* (2) paint / painting / painter in ~(s) (3) an exhibition of ~s.

oil *vt* ~ a hinge / lock / bicycle; one of the (sparking-)plugs is ~ed up; □ ~ the wheels / works *(make things go smoothly by being tactful)*; □ ~ s.o.'s palm *(bribe him)*; □ ~ so up *(inform: flatter him)*.

old *adj* (1) a child nine months / ten years ~; a ten-year-~ child; how ~ is he? (2 *not young*) sixty - that's not ~! he is saving for his ~ age; live to an ~ / a ripe ~ age; an ~ man / woman; an ~ maid *(elderly unmarried woman)*; ~ people / folk(s); one's ~ man *(inform: father; husband)*; the Old Man *(boss)*; one's ~ woman *(inform: wife)*; twelve years is ~ for a dog; a young man with an ~ face; too ~ to work; ~ for such work / his years; ~ in years / one's ways / appearance; what will he do when he grows / gets / is ~? love never grows ~; ~ in body, young in mind; one is as ~ as one feels; in his ~ age / ~er days; ~ Mrs Smith said ...; there's no fool like an ~

fool; ~ wives' tale *(superstition)* (3 *not new, modern*) ~ bread / clothes; an ~ book / song / picture / car / tree / house; an ~ master *(painter; painting)*; ~ customs / fashions / families / names / civilizations; ~ wine / brandy; the ~ year; an ~ *(out-of-date)* timetable; of the ~ school *(conservative)*; of ~ standing; O~ English / French / High German / London; the O~ Testament / World (4 *long known, long-lasting*) an ~ friend / acquaintance; the same ~ faces; ~ love endures; an ~ friendship / story / debt (5 *former*) my ~ Latin teacher; in our ~ flat we ...; the ~ course of the river; he visited his ~ home, where he had lived as a boy; in the (good) ~ days; the good ~ times; call up ~ memories; an ~ boy / girl *(former member of a school)* (6 *having much experience*) an ~ soldier / salt *(sailor)*; an ~ hand at s.th.; ~ offenders; he is ~ enough to know better; □ an ~ head on young shoulders (7) good ~ Joe; ~ chap / fellow / man / boy / pal! well, ~ dear! (8 *inform: ~ as intensifier*) a good ~ row; he'll eat any ~ thing; any ~ thing will do; a stupid ~ fool.

omit *vt* (1) ~ a letter / word (from a sentence) / sentence / name / line / passage (in copying / by mistake) (2) don't ~ doing your homework; don't ~ to do this week's homework; 'to neglect' means to carelessly ~ doing something that should be done; he wished his parents had ~ted to have him baptized; he ~ted to give me the full information.

once *adv* (1) I've been there ~; sing the song through just ~; go to the cinema ~ a week / fortnight; ~ nought is nought; ~ five is five; he's late ~ again; I should like to see her ~ again / more before she leaves; say it ~ more; (I've seen that) more than ~; (he visited us) ~ or twice / ~ and again; (I don't mind a glass of wine) ~ in a way / while; I tell you ~ (and) for all that I (will not allow such conduct); settle a matter ~ (and) for all; not ~ *(never)* have you done what I asked! he didn't ~ offer / never ~ offered to help; if she ~ starts talking, she is hard to stop. (2 *formerly*) we ~ lived in Wales; he must have been young ~; there ~ was / lived a giant who ...; ~ upon a time. – *conj* (3) ~ he hesitates we have him; ~ it goes, it goes well; I never wake before eight o'clock, ~ I get to sleep. – *n* (4 ~ *used as a noun*) ~ is enough; ~ won't hurt; please do it this ~; I think we might relax the regulations for this ~; do let me stay up later tonight, mummy – just for this ~.

at once (1) come here at ~! I will do it at ~ (2) you can't do two things at ~; don't all talk at ~; drink the whole bottle at ~ (3) the story is at ~ amusing and instructive; in a manner at ~ dogged and half-hearted; she is at ~ a great actress and a great singer.

for once the train was punctual ~ ~ *(as an isolated exception)*; he is behaving himself ~ ~; he is right ~ ~ *(this time, though usually wrong)*.

open *adj* (1) an ~ door / gate / window / box / drawer / passage / church / mouth / letter; the door flew ~; at last I had the box ~; with ~ eyes *(also fig)*; ~ ears *(keen attention)*; an ~ shop; ~ for the sale of ...; we are *(the shop is)* ~ till 7 today; the exhibition is now ~; the museum is ~ for three hours a day / ~ to the public; ~ for inspection; *(fig)* only one course is ~ to us; leave the door ~ for discussion (2 *not enclosed, obstructed*) ~ country; the ~ sea; an ~ river *(not barred by ice, mud)*; an ~ harbour; ~ water; an ~ view; an ~ winter *(free from frost, snow)*; ~ weather; our garden is ~ to the road; an ~ weave *(not close)*; ~ ranks; his bowels are ~ *(not constipated)*. (3 *not covered*) an ~ boat / car / carriage; an ~ drain / sewer / well / grave; an ~ sore / wound / rupture; an ~ plain / field; one side of the shed is ~ to the weather; in the ~ air; an ~-air theatre (4 *spread out, unfolded*) an ~ umbrella; the flowers were all ~; these buds will be ~ soon; leave the book ~ at the right page; *(fig)* his mind was an ~ book *(one could easily read his thoughts)*; with ~ hands *(generously)*; (receive s.o.) with ~ arms; have an ~ mind about s.th. *(be free to decide)*; be ~ to suggestions / evil influences / an offer (5 *free to all*) ~ spaces *(parks, etc)*; a road ~ to traffic; an ~ port *(one for all ships)*; an ~ competition / scholarship; □ keep ~ house *(offer hospitality to all comers)* (6 *not settled*) an ~ question; leave a matter ~; an ~ invitation *(one for no specified time)* (7) s.th. is ~ to abuse (by unscrupulous people); ~ to injuries / temptation; his conduct is ~ to criticism *(invites it)*; your words were ~ to misconstruction; lay o.s. ~ to attack / criticism / ridicule / suspicion / censure / a charge of corruption (8 *known to all, not disguised*) an ~ secret / scandal / quarrel; an ~ character / countenance / face; ~ contempt / hatred / hostilities; an ~ letter (to a newspaper); he looked with ~ curiosity; he was quite ~ with me. (9 *not occupied*) is the position still ~? we have a waiter's job ~; I have an ~ evening next Monday; the ~ season *(free for legal hunting).*

open *vt* (1) ~ a door / gate / window (wide); ~ a box / drawer / bottle / wound; ~ the shop; we ~ at nine; ~ a new road / new bridge (to traffic) / outlets for trade; ~ a *(new)* shop / business; the school is to be ~ed tomorrow; ~ the door to *(give opportunity for)* (2) ~ a road (through a forest) / mine / well; the thaw ~ed the river. (3) ~ an umbrella / book / newspaper / road map / parcel / letter; ~ one's hand / mouth / eyes; he half ~ed the door; he never ~ed his lips *(said nothing)*; ~ the book to page 9; I ~ed (the book) at page 9. (4) ~ one's mind / one's heart / oneself to s.o.; the science exhibition really ~ed my eyes; ~ the eyes of s.o. to s.th. *(explain how he has been deceived, etc)*; books ~ a world of enjoyment and knowledge. (5) ~ a debate / conference / public meeting / campaign / ceremony / conversation; ~ an account (at a bank); ~ the ball / season / proceedings; ~ negotiations / Parliament; ~ fire (at / on s.o.). - *vi* (6) the door ~ed and ...; this door ~s into the dining-room / on to the terrace; these shops do not ~ on Mondays; the drawer / bottle / door won't ~; the seam ~ed; the wound ~ed again; during the earthquake cracks ~ed in the earth. (7) the flowers / buds are ~ing; the view / scene ~ed before our eyes. (8) a (whole) new world ~ed before his eyes. (9) the season ~ed with "Aida"; the session (was) ~ed with a short address; the book ~s with a quotation; the story ~s with a murder.

open out (1) ~ ~ a folding map / a table-cloth (2) the district has been ~ed ~ considerably *(developed).* (3) the view ~ed ~ before our eyes. (4) after some time he began to ~ ~ and told us ...

open up (1) ~ up a wound; the surgeon ~ed up his thigh and removed the bullet. (2) ~ up a new shop / branch (3) the aeroplane ~s up many remote places; ~ up a mine / path; ~ up a region to the tourist trade / undeveloped land / a new market (4) this discovery ~s up completely new methods of treatment to doctors; ~ up new prospects / possibilities / opportunities / the possibility of doing s.th. (5) Woolworths are ~ing up in Reading. (6) trade is ~ing up again*(becoming active).*

operate *vi* (1) the tractor ~s on diesel oil; the engine ~s smoothly; this machine doesn't ~ properly; it ~s day and night; (the bus / steamer) ~s daily / all the year round. (2) ~ on s.o. / a limb / an organ for a disease / growth; the surgeon who ~d on the boy said ...; he was ~d on for appendicitis; the doctor ~s from 8 to 10. (3) several causes ~d to bring on the war; this new law / tax ~s to our disadvantage; is the drug ~ing yet? the medicine ~d quickly on him. (4) an army ~ing on a large scale; the troops ~d most skilfully; ships / planes ~ from a base. - *vt* (5) ~ a machine / crane (electrically); can he ~ that car? (6) ~ a shop / railway line / coal-mine / *etc*; the bank ~s a new savings scheme. (7 → 2) not all surgeons will ~ malignant growth; the ~d limb regained strength slowly. (8) time has ~d a change in him.

opinion *n* (1) a candid / decided / unyielding / (un)biased / personal / golden / favourable ~; a minority / lay ~; religious / political ~s; contrary / varying ~s; ~s differ about that; there is more than one ~ about that; this is a matter of ~; he told me his ~ about the matter; what is your ~ of John? I have no ~ on that question; give / advance / express / put forward an ~; form an ~ on s.th.; I am of (the) ~ that we ...; I am entirely of your ~. (2) public ~ (is against him); (this proposal) offends local ~; in my ~; in the ~ of most people (3) have a good / high / low / poor ~ of s.o./ s.th.; have far too big an ~ of o.s.; have quite an ~ of o.s.; have no ~ of s.th. *(think badly of it)* (4) get a lawyer's ~ on a question; counsel's ~; call in / procure an expert ~; give an expert ~ (on s.th.); you had better have another ~ (before one kidney is taken out).

opportunity *n* a good / delightful / golden / (un)favourable / unforeseen / unexpected ~; a lost ~; a good ~ presented itself / arose / offered to do s.th.; ~ makes the thief; socialists believe in equality of ~; this is a good ~ to tell him;

there will be an ~ (for you) to see him later; there is no ~ for research; I have an ~ of going to England next year; will you have an ~ to see him? have no / not much / little / not any ~ for doing / to do s.th.; this may give me an ~ to study abroad; give s.o. an ~ for criticism / to criticize / of criticizing; it gives him an ~ of developing his powers; take / seize / grasp / avail o.s. of the ~ to do / of doing s.th.; seek an ~ to do s.th.; I saw an ~ to make money; lose the ~ of / an ~ for doing s.th.; miss / let slip the, one's ~.

oppose *vt* (1) ~ s.o. / a scheme / suggestion / proposal / tax (vigorously); ~ a dictator (in open rebellion); I won't ~ your wishes; be ~d to (a plan / your going abroad) (2) ~ a dike to the fury of the waves (3) ~ reason to / against prejudice; ~ prejudice with reason; ~ anger with good nature; ~ s.th. to s.th. else; ~ two things to one another; ~ sunlight and shadow in a picture.

opposite *n* darkness and daylight are ~s; ~s attract one another; ~s come together; she says one thing but means the ~; she is the exact / complete / very ~ of her sister; he did just the ~; reconcile ~s.

opposite *adj* (1) he ran across to the ~ house; in the ~ direction; in ~ directions; the ~ sides of a building (2) a member of the ~ faction; the ~ camp (3) his tastes are completely ~ to hers; in the ~ sense / meaning; have the ~ effect; hold ~ opinions / views.

opposition *n* (1) the enemy met with (fierce) ~; the proposal was dropped owing to the ~ of some delegates; his ~ to raising taxes; he won praise for his ~ to the new law. (2) the white figures are placed in ~ to the black; I have always condemned the ~ of force with force; place o.s. in ~ to the prevailing opinion (3) the socialist party is in ~; we need a stronger ~; the leader of Her Majesty's O~.

oppress *vt* (1) the peasants were ruthlessly ~ed by the nobles; the American colonists felt that England was ~ing them by/ with unfair taxes; ~ed by a tyrant / the law; an ~ed nation (2) (feel) ~ed with the heat; the heat ~es me; ~ed with debts / anxiety; he looks as if all the cares of the world ~ him.

option *n* (1) I haven't much ~ in the matter; I had no ~ (but to accept it); he was given three months' imprisonment without the ~ of a fine. (2) none of the ~s is satisfactory; have the ~ of French or Russian; have an ~ between French and Russian (3) if I decide to sell the house, you shall have first ~ on it.

orbit *n* (1) the ~ of a planet / artificial satellite / electron; put a satellite into ~; go into ~; how many satellites are now in ~? (2) keep a country in the Western ~; within the ~ of my influence; such matters are outside my ~.

orbit *vt* (1) a satellite ~ing the earth / moon (2) when did the USSR ~ the first sputnik? today we can ~ an amazing payload. (3) surrounded by ~ing artificial moons. - *vi* (4) a plane ~ing *(travelling in circles)* over a landing-field.

order *n* (1) (in) alphabetical / numerical / chronological / apple-pie ~; I will answer your three questions in ~; (arranged) in ~ of size / importance / merit; put a room in ~; keep ~ in a cupboard; put / set one's affairs in ~; he has a great love of ~; the ~ of *(religious)* service / church worship / confirmation; the ~ of nature / things; the question whether there is a moral ~ or not; the social ~ *(of a state)* (2) the machine / car is now in (good working) ~; s.th. is in complete / perfect ~; my stomach is out of ~; my work is in good ~. (3) the police restored ~ after the riots. (4) he / the meeting was called to ~ by the chairman; (raise) a point of ~; the chairman ruled that the question was in / out of ~. (5) follow / evade / ignore an ~; (dis)obey ~s; act on / under ~s; do s.th. on s.o.'s ~s; he is under ~s to do it; I have ~s to remain here; take ~s from s.o.; execute / carry out an ~; he gave ~s for the guests to be well looked after; by ~ of the (Town Council); ~s are ~s. (6) give a tradesman an ~ for goods; put goods on ~; fill an ~ *(supply the goods)*; ~s are / will be accepted here; a suit made to ~; we are sold out of that dictionary, but we have some more copies on ~. (7) send this ~ *(these goods)* to 17, High Street; the chef prepared four ~s of fried chicken; has the girl brought your ~? (8) a money / postal ~ (for 20 p.); an ~ on a bank (9) in ~ to hear better, he sat in the front row; he worked hard in ~ that he might leave earlier. (10) the general wore all his ~s and decorations; the O~ of Merit / the Garter (11) a religious ~; the Masonic O~ (12 *sort, degree)* his work is usually of a high ~; sentiments of a noble ~; in style and in editorial attitude the Star Press belongs to a dying ~; his fortune is on the ~ of *(approximately)* 3 million pounds; in short ~ *(quickly; immediately)*; the diplomat was dispatched to the troubled area in short ~.

order *vt* (1) ~ an attack / retreat; the captain ~ed the passengers to abandon ship; he ~ed her to maintain the strictest secrecy; the chairman ~ed silence; he was ~ed (to go) to Spain; the boy was ~ed out of the room; the doctor ~ed him complete rest / a mustard plaster / to (stay in) bed; the director ~ed the cargo *(AE)* sent / *(BE)* to be sent by rail; the judge ~ed the prisoner *(AE)* removed / *(BE)* to be removed from the courtroom. (2) ~ goods (from Paris) / a taxi / a suit (of clothes) / a duck from the butcher / lunch for 1.30; ~ tickets for tonight / in advance / by subscription; I have ~ed the car for 4 o'clock. - *vi* (3) have you ~ed (yet)? have you already ~ed? - yes, I've ~ed a bottle of wine.

organization *n* (1) an international ~; the Red Cross ~ (2) the good ~ of the colonel's troops helped him win many battles; the human body has a very complex ~. (3) he is engaged in the ~ of a new club; who planned the general ~ of our government?

organize *vt* (1) ~ an army / team by much drilling; ~ a government / political party / club / company (2) ~ an expedition / collection / exhibition / attack / strike; ~ games and entertainment among the passengers; ~ summer courses for teachers; ~ oneself / one's thoughts; a scientist must ~ his work carefully. (3) ~ the farmers into a cooperative. - *vi* (4) workers have a right to ~ into unions.

origin *n* follow a river to its ~; a place / country of ~; a word of Greek ~; a man of low / humble / noble / French ~; the family is Irish by ~; there are a number of words in English which were French in ~; nobody knows the ~ of that rumour; the ~ of a quarrel / dispute; the ~(s) of civilization; folktales are of popular ~.

original *adj* (1) the ~ inhabitants of a country; the ~ manuscript; what does the ~ Greek say? the ~ plan was afterwards changed; the Institute was ~ly quite small. (2 *creative*) an ~ writer / thinker / composer; he has an ~ mind. (3) ~ ideas; an ~ design; he made a very ~ remark; speak / think / write ~ly.

originate *vi* (1) the fire ~d in the engine room/ under the floor; fireworks ~ed with the Chinese; the strike ~d in the demand for (higher wages); their friendship ~d in a chance meeting; adult fears often ~ in childhood insecurity. - *vt* (2) the Chinese ~d fireworks; ~ a new fashion / dance step.

ounce *n* it weighs less than an ~; he hasn't an ~ of common sense / courage / sympathy; □ an ~ of practice is worth a pound of theory.

oust *vt* the umpire ~ed him from the game; ~ s.o. from a position; coloured slides virtually ~ed black-and-white; in America a new set of officials ~s the old ones whenever the Opposition ~s the Government.

outbreak *n* (1) an ~ of fire / war / hostilities / a volcano; an ~ of temper / anger; at the ~ of war; an ~ of fever / measles / smallpox / an epidemic (2) put down an ~ *(riot)*.

outburst *n* (1) ~s of flame; an ~ of steam / lava from a volcano (2) an ~ of anger / violence / laughter / energy.

outgrow *vt* (1) ~ a shirt / one's clothes; he has ~n his elder brother; □ ~ one's strength *(grow too quickly during childhood)* (2) she outgrew her shy habits; ~ childish interests / opinions (3) weeds will soon ~ the flowers in this garden.

outlet *n* (1) the ~ of the fish tank / a water-pipe / a lake; an electrical ~ *(AE: socket)*; Gdansk is Poland's ~ to the sea. (2) he wants an ~ for his energy / feelings.

outline *n* (1) the ~ of a triangle / tree; the ~ of this drawing is scratchy and broken; a sharp / hazy ~ (2) draw an ~ of Cape Cod; fill in the ~ in red (3) he wrote an ~ of his history lesson; he gave the class an ~ of the points he intended to cover; I shall trace in ~ the development of English on English soil. (4) they agreed on the broad ~s of a wage settlement; I shall sketch only the ~s of the problem.

outline *vt* (1) ~ the figures in a picture (2) ~ a plan / scheme / five-point programme for s.th. / idea; he tried to ~ a catastrophe that no reliable witness had actually seen.

outlook *n* (1) it is a nice flat, but I don't like the ~; the house has a pleasant / wonderful ~ (over the harbour). (2) he has a narrow ~ (on life); my political ~ is very gloomy. (3) it is a poor ~ for me if John has failed the exam - he is much better than I am; the ~ is gloomy / not promising / *etc*; further ~ / the ~ for tomorrow: dry and sunny (4) the ~ for steel demand in the U.S.; the business ~ for next year is favourable.

output *n* the coal-mine's daily ~ is 1,000 tons; the factory has a daily ~ of 200 pairs; the average / total ~; the literary ~ of a year *(books, etc)*.

outrage *n* (1) during a war many acts of ~ are committed; do ~ (2) a lynching is an ~ in a democracy; ~s committed by a drunken mob; the use of H-bombs is an ~ against humanity; an ~ against / upon decency.

outrage *vt* (1) they seized and brutally ~d her. (2) the daring train robbery ~d everybody; ~ public opinion / one's sense of justice / all decency.

outright *adj* (1 *frank*) he has an ~ manner. (2 *thorough*) s.o.'s ~ wickedness; an ~ denial / refusal; catch s.o. in an ~ lie.

outright *adv* (1) say ~ what one thinks; I told him ~. (2 *at once*) he responded ~ to the appeal; he was killed ~ by the blow. (3 *once and for all*) refuse s.th. ~; destroy s.th. ~ (4) pay for a car ~ *(not in instalments)*; buy / sell s.th. ~.

outstanding *adj* (1) an ~ landmark; an ~ feature of the landscape (2) an ~ achievement; be ~ in courage / scholarship / ability; be ~(ly good) at Latin; a painter ~ for his landscapes; an ~ly intelligent / beautiful woman; he has rendered ~ services to the cause of sport. (3) ~ debts / liabilities (4) a good deal of work still ~.

overcome *vt* (1) ~ the enemy; ~ by liquor / gas fumes / the enemy (2) ~ difficulties / obstacles / bad habits / a temptation / discouragement / reserve; it took him a long time to ~ his fear of the dark; sleep overcame him; be ~ by grief / fear; be ~ with loneliness / emotion / fatigue.

overdo *vt* (1) you're ~ing the story by bringing in so many details; such generalizations can easily be ~ne; he rather overdid his gratitude; ~ one's part in a play; don't ~ it *(be moderate)*. (2) ~ne beef. - *vi* (3) you must be careful of ~ing *(wearing yourself out)*.

overflow *vt* (1) the river sometimes ~s its banks / the surrounding countryside. (2) the crowd ~ed the main room / into the halls. - *vi* (3) a man ~ing with kindness (4) their generosity ~s.

overhaul *vt* (1) ~ an engine / machine / organization; the system has been ~ed since then; be ~ed by a doctor *(inform)* (2) the fast cruiser soon ~ed the slow cargo boat.

overlook *vt* (1) ~ a name on a list / a mistake / several errors (2) ~ s.o.'s carelessness; the offence will be ~ed if the culprit will own up; I'll ~ that mistake if you'll be more careful next time. (3) this room ~s / from my window I ~ the park; Belfast is ~ed by a range of hills.

overpower *vt* (1) a sentry ~ed by the attackers; the police quickly ~ed the thieves; ~ed by the heat (2) ~ed by the show of wealth around him. - *adj* (3) ~ing smell; ~ing grief.

oversee *vt* ~ work / workmen / proofs / the export department.

oversight *n* (1) the omission of your name from the list was an ~. (2) under the ~ of a nurse; have (the) ~ of children; he has general ~ of the works.

overstep *vt* ~ one's authority; ~ the limits of good taste; ~ the mark *(take a thing too far)*.

overtake *vt* (1 *BE*) we got behind a lorry and could not ~ it for miles. (2) he overtook me and we had a long talk; a storm overtook them two hours later. (3) misfortunes overtook him; be ~n by / with fear / surprise (4) exports have already ~n last year's figure. - *vi* (5 *BE*) never attempt to ~ on the crest of a hill.

overthrow *vt* (1) ~ the images in churches (2) ~ an enemy / a democratic system / a government; ~ the established order; all my plans were ~n.

overtime *n* father put in ten hours of ~ this week; work ~; be on ~ *(work overtime)*; he is earning ~; be paid extra for ~.

overturn *vt* (1) ~ a chair by hitting against it; he ~ed the boat. (2) ~ a government. - *vi* (3) the tractor / boat ~ed.

overwhelm *vt* (1) a high wave ~ed the boat; the village was ~ed when the floods came. (2) the enemy were / the defence was ~d by superior forces. (3) your kindness / generosity ~s me; a series of misfortunes ~ed him; be ~ed with grief / gratitude. - *adj* (4) ~ing grief / sorrow; an ~ing victory.

owe *vt* (1) ~ s.o. money; he ~d money to every tradesman in the town. (2) I still ~

nearly a hundred pounds on that car *(the car has been partially paid for).* (3) ~ s.o. gratitude / loyalty; ~ obedience to one's father; I ~ him an apology; I ~ him a debt for showing me ... (4) ~ one's life to the doctors; ~ one's success to good luck / one's own efforts; I ~ him much; we ~ to Fleming the discovery of penicillin; we ~ Fleming this discovery; never in the field of human conflict has so much been ~d by so many to so few. - *vi* (4 → 2) he paid all that was ~ing; there are large sums still ~ing; he still ~s for his piano *(has not paid for it).*

own *vt* (1) ~ a house / two cars / *etc* (2 *acknowledge as one's own*) ~ a hat / pamphlet / child; s.th. that nobody will ~ (3 *admit as existent, true*) ~ one's deficiencies / a mistake / oneself indebted; he ~ed himself at fault; I have to ~ my ignorance; he ~ed (that) he didn't know / was wrong; I ~ that I am somewhat disappointed. - *vi* (4 ~ + to: *confess*) he ~ed to being at fault / a sense of shame / having done it.

own up at last the man ~ed ~ *(confessed frankly)*; he ~ed ~ to breaking the window; he ~ed ~ that he had taken the book without permission.

own *adj* my ~ brother / father / *etc*; one of my ~ children; his ~ flesh and blood; he brought his ~ lunch; this is my ~ house; it has a flavour / delicate quality all its ~; he did it by his ~ efforts; she bakes her ~ bread / makes her ~ clothes; I saw it with my ~ eyes; stand on one's ~ (two) feet; be one's ~ man / master; those were his ~ words; mind your ~ business! do s.th. on one's ~ account / responsibility; do s.th. of one's ~ accord / free will; do s.th. at one's ~ risk / expense; act in one's ~ name; act for / in one's ~ interest; I speak from my ~ experience.

own *n* the house is my ~; □ a small thing, but mine / my ~; call s.th. one's ~; have s.th. for one's ~; give s.o. s.th. for his (very) ~; make s.th. one's ~; → come into 6, get back 4, hold *vt* 9; I have decided to go on holiday on my ~ *(alone)*; can you do it / finish on your ~ *(without help)*? he is (working) on his ~ *(not for an employer)*; they have a house of their own; I have no resources of my ~; he has no will / ideas of his ~; for reasons of his ~ he refused to join the club.

P

pace *n* (1) walk ten ~s to the north; the runner lengthened his ~; the military ~ is about 2 1/ 2 feet. (2 *speed*) a ~ of three miles an hour; start / go / walk / ride / drive at a good / great / rapid / sharp / brisk / deliberate *(unhurried)* / slow / *etc* ~; (advance) at a snail's ~; quicken / slacken one's ~; set the ~ (→ set *vt* 14a); keep ~ with s.o. *(also fig)*; keep ~ with the times; □ go the ~ *(go very fast; lead a gay life)*; □ put a horse / plane / person / *etc* through its / his ~s (→ put *vt* 4a, 9).

pace *vt* (1) ~ (up and down) a room; ~ the floor anxiously (2) ~ (off / out) a distance (of 20 yards); he ~d out the length of the garden. (3 *set the pace for s.o.*) he ~d the runner on his bicycle; an (un)~d race.

pack *n* (1 *bundle*) a hiker's ~; a mule ~; a ~ of books / cigarettes (*AE*; *BE* packet) (2) a ~ of hounds / beagles / wolves / baboons / tunas / grouse / *etc*; a ~ of thieves / hoodlums / fools (3) a ~ of cards *(a complete set)* (4) a ~ of lies / nonsense (5) a medicinal ~; an ice ~ *(medicine)*; a mud ~ *(cosmetics).*

pack *vt* (1) ~ goods in shavings / a case / *etc*; ~ clothes into a trunk / a trunk with clothes; I've forgotten to ~ my shoes; have you ~ed (up) your things? (2 *make into a parcel*) ~ a lunch; take a ~ed lunch to work every day (3 *fill tightly*) a train ~ed with people; the cafés were ~ed to capacity; the audience ~ed the theatre; the harbour was ~ed with craft; the book is ~ed with facts; a passage ~ed with meaning (4 *press*) ~ people into an already overcrowded bus; people were ~ed (up) like sardines. (5) ~ a leaky joint in a pipe. - *vi* (6) please excuse me while I ~; have you ~ed yet? don't plan on taking too much with you: just ~ for a short trip; □ send s.o. ~ing (→ send *vt* 5) (7 → 4) crowds ~ing into the cinemas on a wet day; the audience ~ed into the auditorium. (8) these books ~ easily; this suit will ~ without wrinkling.

pack off she ~ed the children ~ to their aunt's *(inform)*; I wish you'd ~ yourself ~ *(go away).*

pack up (1 → pack *vt* 1) ~ up a parcel / one's belongings; spend an evening ~ing up (2) → pack *vt* 4. (3) it's getting dark, so we had better ~ up *(inform: stop working)*; I shall have to ~ up gardening until we get some better weather.

pain *n* (1) the child looks as though it is in (great / awful) ~; feel some / not much / no ~; I couldn't sleep / walk for ~; cry / scream with ~; she felt sure she had given / caused him great ~; his face twisted with ~; → put *vt* 9; do fish feel ~? (2a *localized pain*) (I've got) a ~ in the knee / ear / *etc*; ~s in the back / stomach / *etc*; stomach / abdominal / *etc* ~s; a dull / intense / exquisite / sharp / severe / (un)bearable / violent / shooting / gnawing / *etc* ~ (2b *fig, inform: nuisance*) he gives me a ~ (in the neck) *(is bothersome, unpleasant)*; he's a (real) ~ in the neck. (3 *punishment*) a person who is banished from his country on ~ of death is under threat of death if he returns. (4 *~s: effort*) take (great) ~s to be accurate / with one's work; go to / be at great ~s to do s.th.; one achieves nothing without ~s; the table was beautiful - no ~s were spared in the workmanship.

paint *vt* (1) ~ a wall / house / fence (green / white / *etc*); ~ one's face / fingernails; □ ~ the town red *(inform: go out and celebrate on a grand scale)* (2) ~ a landscape / flowers (from nature / life); ~ s.th. on the wall; ~ on a name; ~ (s.th.) in oil(s) / water-colours; ~ s.th. in bright / dark / gloomy / *etc* colours *(also fig)* (3) ~ a cut with iodine; ~ the throat (4) he is not so black as he is ~ed; ~ a bright / gloomy picture (of the future); the ads ~ed the resort as a winter wonderland. – *vi* (5) does his wife ~ too (in her spare time)?

pair *n* (1) a ~ of shoes / gloves / laces / ear-rings / socks / stockings / book-ends / oars (2) a ~ of spectacles / binoculars / scissors / shears / pliers / pincers / tweezers / tongs / trousers / pants / pyjamas / slacks / shorts / suspenders / braces / scales; a ~ of semi-detached houses (3) a ~ of twins / crooks / birds / *etc*; the waltzing ~s; the horse and rider made a fine ~. (4) a happy ~; they were a devoted ~.

paper *n* (1) this is poor quality ~; sheets / pieces of ~; writing- / wrapping-~; typewriter ~ (2 *examination paper*) we got a rather stiff ~; our history ~s are due tomorrow; was it a hard ~? ~s for the G.C.E. are set a ordinary and advanced level. (3 *learned article*) he is working on / writing a ~ on Marx. (4 *newspaper*) a morning / evening / Sunday / quality / popular / national / provincial / local / illustrated / *etc* ~; which ~ do you take? (5 *~s: documents*) the sentry asked for our ~s; official / legal / citizenship ~s; send in one's ~s (→ send in 1) (6 *printed money*) only silver, please, no ~.

parcel *n* (1) he gave me a ~ containing two dresses; a postal ~; send s.th. by ~ post; the ~ rate to N. is 20p.; an air / (un)-insured ~; ~ delivery; a ~ office / counter (3) part and ~ (→ part *n* 5).

pardon *n* ask for ~; he begged my ~ for his clumsiness; I beg your ~, but I think not; I beg your ~ *(what did you say)*?

pardon *vt* ~ s.o. for doing wrong; ~ s.o. an offence; I know you will ~ my / me saying so, but ...; ~ me for / my contradicting you.

part *n* (1) ~s of the building are falling down; the central ~ of the city; the rear ~ of the house; the inmost ~ of the jungle (2 *~s: region*) I am a stranger in these ~s; an ocean journey to foreign ~s (3) the ~s of a machine / clock; the interior ~s of a telephone; spare ~s of a machine (4) the job took the best *(largest)* ~ of a week to finish; I shall be going shopping the latter ~ of the week. (5) the whole is equal to the sum of all its ~s; walk ~ of the way home; ~ of the work has already been completed; he did the lesser ~ of the work; each student volunteered to write a ~ *(section)* of the magazine; only (a) ~ of his story is true; ~s of the book are interesting; □ ~ and parcel *(an essential part or function)*; the essential / integral ~ of s.th.; the house is furnished in ~ *(not completely)*; the story is in ~ autobiographical and in ~ fictitious; the land is marshy in ~s; the story is well written in ~s; the audience consisted for the most ~ *(mainly)* of women; this region is for the most ~ uncultivated. (6 *equal portion*) fifteen minutes is a fourth ~ of an hour; use two ~s sugar to one ~ cocoa. (7 *role*) play a (major / minor) ~; he spoke / acted his ~ very well; who takes the ~ of the queen? a speaking ~; □ play a ~ *(act deceitfully)* (8 *share*) take (a) ~ in an activity; play a large / active ~ in an undertaking; I had only a small ~ in these events; he wants no ~ in this affair; everyone can take ~ in this game. (9 *side in a dispute, transaction, etc*) she always takes her husband's ~ *(supports him)*; for my ~ *(so far as I am concerned)* you can do whatever you please; it was a lapse on my ~; the bill was sent you owing to a mistake on the ~ of a secretary. (10) take teasing / a joke / *etc* in good ~ *(without offence)* (11) sing the bass ~; sing in three ~s; the trumpet ~; orchestra ~s.

part *vt* (1) ~ one's hair at the side / in the middle; ~ a log with one blow of the axe (2) the policeman ~ed the crowd / two fighters; a fool and his money are soon ~ed; a strait ~s the island from the mainland; □ ~ company *(dissolve a connection; disagree)*: she ~ed company with her sisters; the friends ~ed company over politics; on that question I'm afraid I must ~ company with you. - *vi* (3) the rope ~ed in the middle; the curtains ~ed. (4) they ~ed at the crossroads; let us ~ (as) friends; he ~ed with her on bad terms. (5) ~ with one's possessions; he hated ~ing with his piano.

pass *vt* 1-17; *vi* 18-27. The patterns are grouped as follows: ~ + *indir obj* + *dir obj*: 5; ~ + *obj* + *adv phrase*: 4; it + ~ + *obj* + how, that: 16; *non-personal subjects*: 2, 8, 14, 16, 19-22, 27; *personal or non-personal subjects*: 1, 12, 18, 23, 25; ~ + *prepos*: for 25, 26; from 23, 24; into 23; on 26; through 19; to 23, 24.
(1) we ~ed his house / a monument / Mr Smith on the way; we ~ed (each other) in the street; the second runner ~ed the first; no complaints ever ~ his lips. (2) the ship ~ed the channel; the main road ~es our school; the railway ~es Timtown (→ 19); the River Thames ~es Windsor. (3) ~ the preface and go on to the text. (4) he was ~ing his hand across his forehead / over the surface; ~ a comb through one's hair / the string (a)round the parcel / the liquid through a sieve / a rope through a hole; he ~ed his sword through his enemy's body; ~ your eye over this and see if there are any mistakes. (5 *give*) ~ (me) the salt, please; ~ this message to Bill; I ~ed the cases out of the train window; the letter was ~ed round the table; □ ~ the buck (to s.o.) *(inform: shift the responsibility to him)* (6) ~ rumours all over a village; arrested for ~ing counterfeit banknotes. (7) they ~ed the time playing cards; the patient ~ed a good night; they ~ed ten minutes admiring the view. (8) hobbies ~ the time; playing cards ~ed the hours. (9) the guard checked the papers, then ~ed the visitor; the sentry ~ed the returning soldier; ~ troops in review; *(fig)* ~ events in review (10) the examiner ~ed him (in physics) (but failed him in botany). (11) he ~ed his examination / diploma / oral test (with flying colours). (12) the engine will ~ inspection / scrutiny / all tests; (the recruits / devices / *etc*) ~ed muster *(were considered satisfactory)*. (13) he has ~ed the stage where / when building up new interests is easy; this car has ~ed the stage where / when repair is possible; we have ~ed (through) the initial stages; the country ~ed (through) a stage of reconstruction. (14 *be accepted, approved by*) the bill ~ed the House of Commons / the first reading; that will not ~ the Customs. (15) Parliament ~es a law (against s.th.) / an amendment / legislation / *etc*; the meeting ~ed a resolution / vote of thanks / motion (by a large majority). (16 *surpass*) it ~es my understanding / knowledge how he could have escaped; it ~es comprehension how quickly science progresses; a story that ~es belief. (17 *utter, give*) she ~ed a remark about every passer-by; ~ the time of day with s.o. *(exchange greetings; have a short chat)*; ~ one's word of honour to remain loyal; the critic ~ed judgement on the play; the judge ~ed sentence after the verdict / on the accused; he ~ed the opinion that Jim would win. - *vi* (18) your papers are in order, you may ~; he ~ed by / behind / in front of me; the funeral procession ~ed slowly; the road was too narrow for cars to ~; the teacher was ~ing to and fro before the class; we ~ed through several villages. (19) the railway ~es through Timtown (→ 2); the current ~es through this wire; angry letters / sharp words ~ed between them; strange thoughts ~ed through his mind. (20) time ~es, never to return; the night ~ed quietly without incident; the first ten minutes ~ quickly; two weeks have ~ed since I ... (21 *happen, take place*) what ~ed while I was on holiday? did you see / hear what was ~ing? come to ~ *(happen)*: strange things came to ~; bring to ~ *(cause to happen)*: his wife's death brought a change to ~ in his attitude towards religion; his rude behaviour ~ed without rebuke; his remark / his escape / this development ~ed unno-

ticed. (22) this state of affairs will soon ~; the fit of nausea ~ed; the molten state of metal ~es as the temperature falls; this state of mind / indecision will ~; his infatuation / feeling of ingratitude ~ed; the old customs are ~ing; the pain soon ~ed; wait till the danger ~es. (23) his estate ~ed to his heirs; the child ~es to adulthood through the difficult teen years; man ~ed from a nomadic to an agricultural state before written history began; at about 100° C. paraffin ~es to gas; when water boils it ~es into steam; ~ from youth to age; ~ through a crisis (→ 13) (24) in this chapter he ~es from the facts to their implications from the internal situation to external affairs; she ~ed from tears to laughter / from confidence to despair. (25 *be accepted, approved*) the bill ~ed and became law; that won't ~; he ~ed in French / the examination; my son has just ~ed for a doctor *(passed that exam)*; he would never ~ for an Englishman; material that ~es for silk; the facsimile isn't good, but it will ~. (26 *AE; express an opinion*) a judge ~es on questions of law; will you ~ on the authenticity of this drawing? (27) judgement ~ed *(was given)* for the defendant. (28 *be unable to give an opinion*) I must ~ on that question.

pass away (1) all this trouble will ~ ~. (2) he ~ed ~ during the night.

pass by (1) they ~ed by. (2) I cannot ~ the matter by without making a protest.

pass off (1) a pain / a headache / fatigue / *etc* ~es ~ *(decreases)* (2) the meeting / gathering / hour / *etc* ~ed ~ without an incident; it was an awkward situation, but it ~ed ~ all right. (3) he tried to ~ himself ~ as a Member of Parliament; he cribbed the calculation and ~ed it ~ as his own. (4) ~ new things ~ as antiques; ~ ~ counterfeit coins on shopkeepers (5) ~ ~ s.th. unpleasant / embarrassing (with a joke / easily); he ~ed ~ the accusation with a laugh.

pass on (1) he bowed to her and ~ed on. (2) ~ s.th. on to others; after the death of her parents she was ~ed on from one relative to another; ~ news on by word of mouth (3) her childhood friends had all ~ed on *(died)*.

pass out (1) at the sight of the letter she ~ed ~ *(inform: fainted)*. (2) the accident victim ~ed ~ in the ambulance on the way to the hospital *(inform: died)*. (3) he ~ed ~ *(left college)* with a degree in chemistry.

pass over (1) would you ~ the book ~ to me, please? (2) they ~ed him ~ for promotion; boys ~ed her ~ in favour of her prettier sister. (3) ~ ~ a fault / offence / breach of regulations / *etc* (4) ~ ~ the details of s.th. / some important aspects of the subject.

pass round he ~ed ~ the cigarettes.

pass through we are merely ~ing ~; I know L. very little, for I just ~ed ~ once in the bus.

pass up ~ up an invitation to dinner; ~ up a good opportunity for promotion.

passion *n* (1) a deep / violent / fierce / burning / secret / *etc* ~ seized / inflamed him; ~s were running high; have / feel / develop a ~; yield to / master / conquer / subdue / suppress / conceal a ~; with fanatical ~ he attacked Calvinism; the ruling ~ *(dominating motive in s.o.'s life)*; a ~ for fame / glory / music / chess / swimming / cleanliness (2 *anger*) get / fall / fly into a ~; be in a ~; choking with ~; a towering ~ *(violent rage)* (3 *love*) conceive a ~ for s.o.; be filled with ~ for s.o. (4 *outburst*) a ~ of anger / grief; she suddenly broke into a ~ of tears; he jumped up in a ~ of alarm. (5) accuracy became a ~ with him; fishing is his present ~; she is his ~ of the moment.

patience *n* (1) have (little / no / much / endless) ~ (with s.o.) (to do s.th.); work with ~; he has not sufficient ~ for this work; lose (one's / all) ~; be / get out of (all) ~ with s.o. *(no longer able to endure)*; his ~ was severely put to the test / tried / taxed; what put him out of / exhausted his ~? my ~ is at an end / gave out; there is a limit to ~; it takes ~ to (sew well); her ~ was rewarded. (2 *BE*) a game of ~ (*AE* solitaire).

pattern *n* (1) rugs with a rose ~; geometrical carpet ~s; a checkered / lacy / *etc* ~; ~s of frost / frost ~s on the window; the jugs come in several ~s. (2 *sample of cloth*) a bunch of ~s from the tailor (3) a paper ~ for a dress; cut a dress according to a ~; knit a jumper from a ~ (4 *distinctive type*) a bicycle of an old ~; a new ~ of army rifle (5 *model*) the U. S. constitution has been a ~ for those of many new republics; she is a ~ of virtue. (6) the behaviour ~s of teenagers; the characteristic sentence ~s of a language; Tom's whole class were of a ~: restless, noisy, and troublesome.

pattern *vt* (1) mother ~ed her new curtains after the ones she saw in the shop. (2) he ~ed his life after his father's; ~ yourself on him; a new organization ~ed on the Jesuits.

pay *vt* 1-5, 10; *vi* 6-9. (1) ~ workmen / the tailor / the doctor / *etc*; please buy me an eraser - I'll ~ you / ~ for it when you come home (→ 7); ~ s.o. for his services; be paid monthly; we were paid only half our salary; paid labour / assassins (2) ~ money (into an account / bank / fund); I paid you the money last week; ~ an amount in full / the full fare; I paid (him) £20 for it; how much did you ~ for it? ~ a high price / too much (for s.th.); ~ cash (→ 6); ~ (s.o.) a deposit / first instalment; ~ a fee / salary; ~ dues / taxes / wages; ~ 6 per cent interest on a loan (3) the investment paid 5 per cent last year; your training will ~ you well in the future. (4) ~ a bill / a debt (to the last penny) / a fine / one's subscription / the cost; have you paid your account? ~ damages (→ damage *n* 2); □ ~ one's way *(not get into debt; pay one's share of expenses)*; *(fig)* she paid his sarcasm in kind. (5) will you please ~ the taxi; paid work / employment; a well- / badly paid job / situation (6) buy now - pay later; have you paid (for it) yet? ~ forthwith / on the nail *(inform: at once)*; ~ (in) cash (→ 2) / (in) ready money / by cheque; ~ in / by instalments; he paid for me at the pictures; let me ~; I'll ~; □ ~ through the nose *(inform: much too high a price)*; the murderer paid with his life. (7 *pay + for*; → 1, 2, 6) you may buy goods at one counter and ~ for them at another by ~ing the cashier; the meat has been paid for; ~ for s.th. in advance / on delivery; *(fig)* money will not ~ for the loss of happiness. (8 *pay + for: suffer the consequences of*) the thief paid for his crime with a heavy jail sentence; he paid dearly for his kind-heartedness; he paid for his folly with his life; he shall / I'll make him ~ for this! (9) this work / dishonesty does not ~; it ~s to advertise. (10) ~ attention to s.o./ s.th.; ~ one's attention to s.o.; ~ attention! ~ heed to s.th.; ~ a call on s.o.; ~ (s.o.) a visit; ~ s.o. a compliment (on his work); ~ a compliment to a lady; that's the greatest compliment that I have ever been paid; ~ s.o. honour; ~ the last honours / one's last respects to s.o.; ~ respect to s.o./ s.th.; → court *n* 3.

pay back (1) ~ ~ money one owes (2) he paid her ~ for her unkindness; → coin *n*.

pay in she paid in $100 at / to the bank.

pay off (1) twenty men were paid ~ *(paid their wages and discharged)*. (2) the new machinery should ~ ~ in the long run; it was a risk, but it paid ~. (3) ~ ~ a creditor / a debt / the mortgage on the property; he paid a pound a week ~ the debt. (4 *inform: bribe*) the report proved that the police had been paid ~ by organized criminals.

pay out (1) ~ ~ a sum of money / wages (to s.o.); ~ ~ his shares / inheritance to s.o. (2) ~ ~ one's partner (in a firm) (3) I've paid him ~ for the trick he played on me; wrong-doers are usually paid ~ in the end; so he's swindled you, has he? that ~s you ~ for the way you cheated me.

peace *n* (1) bring about / restore ~; bring ~ to a country; belligerents make / conclude ~; break / disturb / maintain / keep the ~; after a brief (period of) ~ war broke out again; a stable / lasting / long-desired / *etc* ~ (2) a peace was signed between the two countries. (3) ~ of mind; inner ~; find ~; the ~ of a place / an evening / the woods; deep ~ lay over the land. (4) live together in ~ and harmony / friendship; live at ~ with one's neighbours; he felt at ~ with all the world; make one's ~ with s.o.; leave s.o. in ~; I just want (my) ~ and quiet.

peak *n* (1) the (highest) ~ of a montain; the ~ of a gable / cap / beard / curve (2) the ~ of his career; at the ~ of the epidemic; the ~ (hours) of traffic; tourism is at its ~ in August; traffic reaches its ~ on this road about 5 o'clock.

pen *n* (1) dip a ~ into ink; with a stroke of the ~; the ~ raced over the paper; put (one's) ~ to paper; set ~ to paper; he took up / reached for his ~; give free rein to one's ~ (2 *writing*) make a / one's living with / by one's ~; that is from the ~ of Heine; the ~ is mightier than the sword; a master of the ~ (3 *style of writing*) have a ready ~ *(write easily)*; he knows how to wield a skilful / fluent ~; have a scathing ~; he writes with a witty, incisive ~.

penalty *n* (1) spitting forbidden - ~ £5; no smoking under ~ of instant dismissal; trespassing forbidden under ~ of imprisonment; pay the ~ of one's follies / misdeeds / crimes; the ~ for theft / non-performance of contract / *etc* is heavy; his hangover was a ~ for drinking too much; incur a ~ by omitting to do s.th.; impose a ~ on s.o. (2 *in sports: disadvantage*) a ~ kick / point / area.

penetrate *vt* (1 → 9) a knife / a foreign body / poison ~s (into) s.th.; the bullet ~d the wall / (deep into) the thigh; the foglights ~d the mist. (2 *enter the interior of* → 8) ~ a forest (→ 8) (3 *permeate* → 9) the water ~d my shoes; the light ~d the darkness of the room; bad smells ~d (through) the building; *(fig)* the whole poem is ~d with religion. (4 *obtain a share of*) our firm succeeded in ~ing the Canadian coffee market. (5 *affect deeply*) ~ the mind; be ~d with a desire for s.th. (6 *comprehend* → 10) ~ the meaning of s.o.'s words; scientists try to ~ the mysteries of nature; we soon ~d his disguise / his designs / the secret. (7) new ideas ~d the country; the propaganda ~d the remotest corners of the land. – *vi* (8) ~ into a house / town / forest / country (9 → 1,3) water / light ~s into s.th.; the water had ~d everywhere; the water ~d through my shoes; the cold gradually ~d through the whole house (10 → 6); ~ into a field of learning; his discovery enabled scientists to ~ into the secrets of genetic determination. (11) the army has ~d to Berlin / through the enemy lines; the rumour has not ~d to us. – *adj* (12 *acute; sharp-witted*) a ~ing observation; a ~ing mind (13 *loud; fear-inspiring*) a ~ing cry / shriek / glance.

penny *n* (1) the unit of currency is the pound sterling divided into 100 (new) pence (p); pay a debt to the last ~ (→ pay *vt* 4); that will cost a pretty ~ *(a good sum of money)*; □ in for a ~, in for a pound *(what has been begun must be finished)*; □ turn an honest ~ *(earn some money by real work)*; □ be ~-wise and pound-foolish *(careful in small, wasteful in large matters)*; □ a ~ for your thoughts *(what are you thinking about so abstractedly?)*; □ spend a ~ (→ spend *vt* 1); □ the ~ dropped *(s.th. was understood)*. (2) in the U.S.A. a ~ is a cent.

pension *n* be entitled to / have / get an old-age / retirement / war / widow's / *etc* ~; nowadays people on a ~ find it difficult to live; retire on (a) ~; place s.o. on ~; be on a ~; draw one's ~ at the post office.

people *n* (1) the streets were crowded with ~; ~ may say what they please; what will ~ say? several ~ were hurt; prominent / decent / nice / disreputable / *etc* ~; village / country ~; towns~; the ~ of a parish / in this village; shut-in ~; the dictator was a cruel man in ~'s opinion *(~ in general)* / in the ~'s opinion *(the opinion of that country's citizens)*. (2 *relatives*) my ~; John's ~; he took me to meet his ~. (3) the ancient Greeks were a wise and cultured ~; the ~ of Australia; the Jewish ~; the ~s of the world / Africa; the king and his ~; a brave / warlike / united / *etc* ~ (4 the ~: *the electorate*) representatives chosen by the ~; government of the ~, by the ~, for the ~ (5 the ~: *the working classes*) a man of the ~.

perceive *vt* (1) I ~d an object looming through the mist; ~ a dim light / a faint sound / a slight change in temperature; stars too remote to be ~d by the eye; we do not ~ things as they really are. (2) I ~d that he would refuse; he failed to ~ the meaning of the poem; I ~ a note of sarcasm in your voice; this is a nice idea, but I ~ difficulties in putting it into practice.

perform *vt* (1 *carry out*) ~ a task / surgical operation; I have a duty to ~; ~ one's duties / a social function / miracles / what you promise / a promise; she ~s the office of hostess very graciously. (2 *execute in the established manner*) ~ the marriage ceremony (3) ~ a play / dance / ballet / opera / role / part; ~ (a piece of) music; ~ a juggling act; ~ gymnastics (with / without special apparatus). – *vi* (4) the soloist ~ed poorly; while the band played, the clowns ~ed; the Philharmonic Orchestra ~s to many audiences; ~ in the role of Romeo; ~ing dogs / seals / *etc* (5) the engine ~s well in cold weather.

peril *n* (1) we faced the ~ of falling rocks; be in ~ of drowning; in ~ of (losing) one's life; these rights / liberties are in ~; the ~s of war / the sea (2 *risk*) if you disobey these regulations, you do so at your own ~.

permission *n* give / grant s.o. ~ (to do s.th.); get / obtain (s.o.'s) ~; he has her ~ to park in the drive; ask for ~; without even asking ~; with your (kind) ~ I would like to ...; by whose ~ did you enter the park?

permit *vt* (1) ~ s.o. (to do) s.th.; the librarian does not ~ talking / us to talk here; ~ me to say that I ...; I am ~ted wine; the law ~s the sale of such drugs. (2) how can you ~ such insolence? (3 *make possible*) the addition of a window ~s better air circulation; his condition would not ~ his going / him to go out. - *vi* (4 → 3) I will come if my health ~s; drop in when time ~s; I was to have gone tomorrow, weather ~ting; in a tone which ~ted of no reply; a decision that ~s of no delay; the sentence is so worded that it ~s of two interpretations; there were too many present to ~ of any intimacy.

persevere *vi* (1) ~ no matter how difficult the task; he ~d in his efforts / his studies / studying French; you may not find it easy, but if you ~ with it you will master it in time; encourage s.o. to ~ with his own educational development. - *adj* (2) a ~ing student.

persist *vi* (1) ~ in one's opinion / claims / folly; he ~ed in this lie; he ~s in doing what he shouldn't / mispronouncing that word. (2) I ~ that you made a mistake when ... (3) the fog is likely to ~ in most areas; the belief in witchcraft still ~s amongst some people; the tradition has ~ed to this day.

person *n* (1) four ~s saw him; who is this ~? there's a strange ~ to see you; some people are quite different ~s amongst their friends from what they are in their business relations; applicants are requested to apply in ~; please send a substitute if you cannot come in ~; he is a ~ of high calibre / of consequence / of moral consistency / *etc*; he is a bountiful / designing / cheerful / contented / deceitful / (ir)resolute / inquisitive / intense / negative / nervous / noble / obnoxious / orderly / pitiless / superficial / timid / *etc* ~; he is the ~ in question. (2 ~s: *people, officially*) six ~s are allowed to stand *(a notice in a bus)*; the dish will provide enough for four ~s *(recipe)*. (3 *living body*) offences against the ~ *(bodily attacks)*; she found a good friend in the ~ of her landlady; we should keep our ~s clean.

persuade *vt* (1 *cause to do s.th. by reasoning, urging*) ~ a sick man to stay in bed; we could not ~ him to wait; I am glad you ~d me to change my mind; I couldn't ~ him to my way of thinking; can you ~ her out of her foolish plans? (2 *cause to believe s.th. by reasoning*) she ~d him that she was telling the truth; can I not ~ you that this is so? it will take a lot to ~ me of the advisability of such a course; ~ s.o. of the truth of a report / that the report is true; I am almost ~d of his honesty / that he is honest.

pertain *vi* (1) the mansion and the lands ~ing to it; privileges that ~ed only to the wealthier class; the documents ~ing to the case; the enormous stress women lay on everything ~ing to clothes. (2) the enthusiasm ~ing to youth; the destruction and havoc ~ing to war; responsibilities that ~ to fatherhood; in matters ~ing to man and his environment.

photograph *n* a black and white / colour / clear / blurred / *etc* ~; take a ~ (of s.o./ s.th.); do you take ~s?

photograph *vt* (1) ~ s.o./ s.th. - *vi* (2) I always ~ in black and white. (3) she ~s badly *(is not photogenic)*; the children ~ed very attractively.

piano *n* an upright / cottage / grand / baby grand / player ~; a concerto for ~ and orchestra; play the ~; tune a ~; the ~ is out of tune; practise a piece on the ~; accompany s.o. on the ~.

pick *vt* (1) ~ flowers / berries / mushrooms; ~ fruit / a pear / *etc* from a tree; ~ a thread from / off one's coat (2 *separate*) ~ rags; ~ s.th. to pieces / apart (3 *empty*) ~ s.o.'s pocket *(steal s.th. from it)*; ~ s.o.'s brains *(get ideas, information from him)* (4 *using s.th. pointed, remove extraneous matter from*) ~ one's teeth *(get food from the spaces between them)*; ~ (meat from) a bone; □ have a bone to ~ with s.o. (→ bone *n* 2); □ ~ a lock *(unlock it with a wire, etc)*; ~ a fowl / chicken / *etc (AE; remove its feathers)* (5 *make with s.th. pointed*) ~ a hole in s.th.; □ ~ holes in an argument *(find its weak points)*; ~ ice *(make holes in it)* (6) birds ~ grain; a girl ~s food *(eats it in small amounts)*. (7 *choose*) we ~d a good day for the picnic; we tried to ~ the shortest route; ~ the largest / best ones; can you ~ the winning horse in a race? ~ a contestant from the audience; ~ one's way / steps along a muddy road; ~ one's words *(choose them carefully)*; ~ a quarrel / fight (with s.o.) *(provoke it)*. - *vi* (8 → 1) fruit ripe for ~ing; the ~ing season (9 →

6) as he was ill, he only ~ed at his food *(ate without appetite)*. (10 ~ + *on: choose, with neg. undertone*) the professor always ~s on me to translate long passages; we had ~ed on a most unsuitable spot for a camping site; why do you always ~ on me to do the unpleasant jobs? he is always ~ing on *(criticizing)* me; he always ~s on small points to criticize.

pick off the hunter ~ed ~ *(singled out and shot)* a duck rising from the marsh.

pick out (1) ~ ~ a well-known face in a crowd; after much searching she ~ed ~ this ring; ~ ~ one's successor (2) ~ ~ a tune on the piano *(play it by ear)* (3) ~ ~ the meaning of a text *(by careful study)*.

pick over ~ ~ a basket of strawberries *(examine and throw out the bad ones)*; eager shoppers were ~ing ~ the shirts on the bargain table.

pick up (1) ~ up ground (with a pickaxe) (2) ~ up a stone / handkerchief / pin / *etc*; ~ up one's hat (3 *AE tidy*) ~ up a room (4) he fell but at once ~ed himself up. (5) the train stopped to ~ up passengers; ~ up a hitchhiker (6) ~ s.th. up cheaply at an auction sale; there are still bargains to be ~ed up. (7) he ~ed up a girl at the cinema last night. (8) yesterday I ~ed up Moscow on my radio. (9 *get, learn by chance, casually*) she ~ed up knitting very quickly; ~ up words / idioms / the rudiments of a subject; ~ up a habit / some useful information (10) ~ up *(increase)* speed (11) the train ~ed up *(increased speed)* after the slope. (12) ~ up *(regain)* one's health / courage (13) she is ~ing up *(regaining her health)* wonderfully since she came out of hospital. (14) trade is ~ing up *(improving)*; the weather may ~ up very soon.

picture *n* (1) draw / paint a ~ (of s.th.; *also fig*; → draw *vt* 9, paint *vt* 4); copy / frame / restore a ~ (2) on entering the hut we saw a ~ of misery; she is a perfect ~ of a girl. (3) he is the ~ of his father; he looks the ~ of health. (4) a verbal ~; Mommsen's ~ of ancient Rome; give (s.o.) a clear / true / realistic / accurate / false / *etc* ~ of s.th.; form a (true / *etc*) ~ of s.th. in one's mind; → put *vt* 9 (5) the roses were a ~ this year; she was a ~ in her new blue dress. (6 *film*) did you like the ~ last night? go to the ~s *(cinema)*; I saw that story on the ~s.

piece *n* (1) a ~ of chalk / paper / wood / glass / ivory / cloth / (broken) china / cake / chocolate / land / *etc*; s.th. comes / falls / breaks to ~s; break / pull / smash / tear s.th. to ~s; cut s.th. in(to) ~s *(in the form of ~s)*; *(fig)* his plans are now in ~s; □ go to ~s *(suffer a nervous collapse)*; his actions and principles are all of a ~ *(consistent)*; his conduct in this matter is of a ~ with his other actions. (2 *a single unit belonging to a set*) a dinner service of 48 ~s; 32 ~s in a chess set (3 *coin*) a five-cent ~ (4 *unit, quantity in which goods are sold*) muslin comes at 12 yards to the ~; a ~ of wallpaper *(12 yards)*; cloth sold by the ~ (5 *amount of work*) work by the ~; pay a workman by the ~ (6 *instance*) a fine ~ of workmanship; a careful / wretched / *etc* ~ of work (7) a ~ of advice / luck / news / information / evidence / nonsense; a classical ~ of furniture; □ give s.o. a ~ of one's mind (→ mind *n* 2c) (8 *composition*) a fine / excellent / *etc* ~ of music / poetry / work; play that ~ again; what is your favourite piano ~?

pile *n* a ~ of books / papers / hats / bricks / stones / wood / sand / lumber; make ~s of sand; put things in a ~; a ~ of correspondence was awaiting her; □ make a ~ *(slang: earn a lot of money)*; □ make ~s of money; a ~ of things to do *(inform)*; a ~ of work *(inform)*.

pile *vt* (1) ~ (up) books / logs (on each other) / leaves / sand / coal (on a fire) / earth / *etc*; ~ more coal on; *(fig)* ~ work on (to) s.o. (2) ~ a table with dishes; the wagon was ~d high with hay. (3) ~ up money / a fortune; ~ up food against the winter (4) the snow is ~ing up on the roofs. (5) work ~ing up; his debts are ~ing up; don't let bills ~ up. (6 *get somewhere in a disorderly group*) they ~d into his car / into the restaurant / off the train / down from a ledge.

pill *n* (1) take ~s (regularly); □ (ingratitude) is a bitter ~ (to swallow); □ gild / sugar a ~ (2) the ~ *(oral contraceptive)*: prescribe s.o. the ~; take / go on / be on the ~; she forgot (to take) her ~ and then it happened; so far there is no ~ for men.

pin *vt* (1) ~ up a notice (with drawing-pins); ~ a flower to a dress; ~ papers / cloth together (2) ~ one's faith on s.o./ s.th.; ~ a crime / affair on an innocent person (3 *immobilize*) the wrestler ~ned his opponent to the mat; the driver was ~ned under the wreckage.

pin down (1) the victims were ~ned ~ by a fallen tree; the debris ~ned him ~ (2) ~ s.o. ~ to a promise / agreement; they ~ned him ~ to giving a definite time; the judge tried to ~ him ~ with skilfully posed questions. (3) I cannot ~ the quotation ~ to its author.

pinch *n* (1) he gave her a playful / spiteful ~; the ~ of new shoes (2) a ~ of salt / snuff; □ (take s.th.) with a ~ of salt *(with reservations)* (2 *stress*) feel the ~ of poverty / hunger; at a ~ / if it comes to the ~ *(if there is need)*; there's the ~ *(difficulty)*.

pinch *vt* (1) ~ one's finger in the door; ~ s.o.'s cheek / arm / leg (2) the elastic / shoe ~es (me); the biting wind ~ed the child's face; be ~ed with *(suffer from)* cold / hunger (3) be ~ed for *(short of)* money / cash; be in ~ed circumstances; he was ~ed by the fall of prices; they were severely ~ed by the drought; the builders were ~ed by the shortage of timber. (4 *take without permission*) who's ~ed my fountain-pen? (5) this collar ~es; *(fig)* that's where the shoe ~es *(that's the difficulty)*. (6 *economize unduly*) when short of money we are forced to ~; they ~ed and scraped for years to save money. - *adj* (7) ~ing cold; be in ~ed circumstances.

pitch *vt* (1 *set up*) ~ camp / a tent; *(fig)* ~ one's tent *(settle)* (2 *throw*) he tends to ~ the ball too high; let's ~ the drunkard out; the men ~ed the hay into the loft; □ ~ a yarn *(tell a story)* (3 *set in a musical key*) he ~ed the violin a little higher; ~ the piano; ~ the voice high; *(fig)* he ~ed his hopes too high. (4 *fall heavily*) the painter suddenly ~ed forward off the ladder; he ~ed on his head. (5 *move up and down lengthwise, of ships*) the ship ~ed in the heavy seas. (6 *make camp*) we ~ed near a stream. (7 ~ into: *attack*) why did the man ~ into Jim? a man rose to his feet and ~ed into the speaker. (8 ~ into: *get busy with)* we ~ed into the work; the boy ~ed into the food. (9 ~ upon: *choose casually, arbitrarily*) we ~ed on a day for our picnic; when he needs a volunteer, he always ~es on me.

pitch in if I really ~ in *(work vigorously)*, I may be able to finish before supper.

pity *n* (1) her ~ was unbounded; be full of / filled with / feel ~ (for s.o.); I have no ~ for people who suffer through their own folly; the bully had no ~ on his victims; we took ~ on the hungry cat and gave it some milk; weep from ~; give a beggar s.th. out of ~ (2) it is a (great) ~ (that) he ...; what a ~ you can't come with us; the ~ is that he ...

place *n* (1 *space in general*) time and ~; an adverb of ~ (2 *particular location*) a ~ to hang a picture; this is the ~ where they first met; lose one's ~ in a queue; → *take vt* 10d; the vase is in its ~; some of the books are out of ~; I like everything to be in ~; I can't be in two ~s at once; a tidy person likes to have a ~ for everything and everything in its ~; a restaurant is not the ~ for an argument; *(fig)* this is no ~ for such an outburst; *(fig)* I'd take the job if I were in your ~; put yourself in my ~; □ in ~ *(appropriate)*: the proposal is not quite in ~; his way of doing it is not in / is out of ~; that remark was quite out of ~; he felt out of ~ in their company; use water in ~ of milk; in the first / second ~ *(firstly / secondly)* (we must define our terms); all over the ~ *(everywhere)*: the papers were scattered all over the ~; I have been all over the ~ to find you; the nurse takes the ~ of *(is substitute for)* the mother; astronomy took the ~ of astrology; the battle of Hastings took ~ *(happened)* in 1066; the ceremony will take ~ outdoors. (3 *spot on the body, a surface*) a sore ~ on the back; a decayed ~ in a tooth; a worn ~ on the carpet / in a coat; there is a wet ~ on the floor. (4 *seat*) occupy / secure / reserve / book a ~; take your ~s! take one's usual ~ (at table); change ~s with s.o.; please save my ~ for me; go back to your ~; she resumed her ~ on the sofa; lay ~s *(set the table)* for three (5 *dwelling*) they have a ~ in town and a ~ in the country; please come and have dinner at my ~; I called at Jack's ~ on my way home; there's no ~ like home. (6 *building, area used for a special purpose*) a nightclub is a ~ of entertainment; a ~ of amusement / business / assembly / worship / departure / *etc*; an eating / market-~; a ~ of interest; a(n) (un)healthy / objectionable / convenient / *etc* ~; a stupid ~ to park a car; he will soon need a larger ~ for his expanding business; the easiest ~ to buy good British cloth is in Canada. (7 *village, town*) his family and mine come from the same ~; trains rarely stop in that ~ any more; go to ~s and see things; the holy ~s; I'm a stranger in this ~ myself. (8 *~s: region*) travel to distant ~s; faraway ~s (9 *passage*) find the ~ where one left off reading; I've lost my ~; she always cries at the sad ~s. (10 *rank*) aristocrats of power and ~; Shakespeare's ~ in literature; you must keep him in his ~ *(not allow too much familiarity)*; servants must know their ~; put s.o. in his ~ (11 *job*) he lost his ~ at the bank; several ~s that have not been filled; persons in high ~s in government; a ~ on the board (of managers); he's the right man in the right ~. (12 *responsibility*) it's your ~ to look after your guests / to see that the office staff get here early; it's not your ~ to offer criticism. (13 *position of a figure*) calculate a fraction to 4 ~s.

place *vt* (1 *put in a certain place*) warm rugs were ~d beside the beds; she ~d the child in the cradle; the waitress ~d the glasses in front of us; ~ them in the right order; ~ an advertisement in the newspaper; ~ a garrison in a city; → disposal 5. (2 *appoint, etc*) the President ~d him in the Department of Agriculture; the agency ~d him with a good firm; ~ s.o. in a job (3) ~ a sum to s.o.'s credit; ~ £100 in bonds (4) ~ an order for goods with a firm (5 *sell*) how can we ~ all this stock? he ~ed his novel with a famous publishing house. (6) ~ (one's) confidence / trust in s.o.; ~ reliance / importance on s.th.; ~ restrictions on s.th. (7 *recognize*) I know his face, but I can't ~ *(identify)* him; he's a difficult man to ~; ~ an accent (8 *make*) ~ a telephone call; ~ a bet (9 *determine the place of s.o. in a race*) the judges' sole duty is to ~ the horses; be ~d *(BE be among the first three)*: my friend's horse wasn't ~d. – *vi* (10 *AE come in second in a horse race*) he bet on the horse to win, ~, or show *(1st, 2nd, 3rd)*.

plain *adj* (1 *clear*) ~ English; in ~ speech; ~ talk; this is the ~ truth; it is ~ that he is lying; make one's meaning ~; he made it ~ that he ...; speak / write ~ (2 *simple*) a ~ meal / diet / living; ~ food; ~ drawings *(not coloured)*; a ~ style; dressed in ~ clothes *(not in uniform)*; ~ people / country-folk (3 *of one colour, without design*) a ~ dress / wallpaper (4 *frank*) a man of ~, blunt speech; will you give me a ~ answer to a straight question? ~ dealing *(honesty)*; □ to be ~ with you *(to speak openly)* (5 *BE not beautiful*) a ~ girl; crying is the refuge of ~ women, but the ruin of pretty ones. (6 *complete*) ~ madness / folly / stupidity.

plan *vt* (1) ~ a house / garden / new suburb / *etc*; ~ned economy (2) ~ a journey / campaign / day; a ~ned tour (3 *intend*) we ~ to go there next year; the boys are ~ning to build a hut; we ~ned reorganizing the entire system but ...

plant *n* (1) a tree is a ~. (2 *one smaller than bush, shrub*) a garden / exotic / fertile / prickly / dead / *etc* ~; an annual / biennial / perennial ~; grow / raise ~s; a ~ takes root / springs up / grows / flourishes / is in full bloom / withers / dies (3) a manufacturing / industrial / automobile / ice-cream / *etc* ~; almost every type of industrial ~ is manufactured in Britain, including iron and steelworks ~, chemical and refining ~ and nuclear power station ~. (4) the heating ~ for a home; the power ~ of a submarine (5 *AE the buildings, equipment of an institution*) the sprawling ~ of the university; this school has a fine ~ but not enough teachers. (6 *inform: s.o. or s.th. placed so as to mislead, deceive*) the magician used a ~ in the audience to assure the success of his trick; the accused man claimed that the money in his suitcase was a ~ put there by his enemies.

plant *vt* (1) ~ a tree / flower / vegetable; ~ cabbages in a field; ~ out pansies / strawberry runners (2) ~ a lawn; ~ a garden (with seeds) / a field with cabbages (3 *fix in position*) he ~ed his feet and wouldn't move; he ~ed himself in front of me / the door; ~ posts along a road (4) ~ a colony / community; ~ settlers in a colony (5 *inform*) ~ a blow on s.o.'s ear (6) ~ a love for learning in growing children (7 *inform*) ~ (secretly) documents / money / incriminating evidence on s.o.; ~ a(n electronic) bug; secret microphones were ~ed all over the diplomat's office. (8 *inform: hide*) ~ stolen goods (9 *inform: place as a trap*) they ~ed marked notes to prove the man's guilt.

play *n* (1) the children are at ~; children are fond of ~; the love of ~ is an old English characteristic; □ that's just child's ~ *(very easy)*; he meant it in ~ *(not seriously)*; a ~ on words *(a pun)* (2 *gamble*) he lost a fortune in an hour's

~. (3 *drama*) the (collected) ~s of G.B. Shaw; a historical / problem / character / drawing-room / stage / *etc* ~; let's go to the ~ *(theatre)* this evening. (4 *manner of playing, also fig*) we admired his fine ~; a lot of rough ~ in the football match yesterday; that was pretty ~! defensive / offensive ~; fair ~; foul ~ *(unfairness; criminal action)*; do the police suspect foul ~? (5) it's your ~ *(next move)*. (6) the ~ of sunlight on water / of a searchlight against the night sky; the ~ of shadows on a wall (7) give the rope more ~; a joint with too much ~ *(not tight enough)* (8) give free ~ to one's fancy / emotions (→ free *adj* 7); allow full ~ to one's imagination / curiosity; the (free) ~ of forces (→ free *adj* 7); new evidence has been brought into ~ in this trial; bring all one's knowledge into ~ in solving a problem; come into ~.

play *vi* 1, 2a, 10–16, 18, 19; *vt* 2b–9, 10a, 15a, 17. The patterns are grouped as follows: *idiomatic phrases*: 2b, 7, 11; ~ + *prepos*: at 2a, 15; by 2a; for 10, 15; into 15; on 2a, 16, 19; to 11; with 1, 15.
(1) the children are ~ing in the garden; he is ~ing with Jim; she has no one to ~ with; ~ indoors / out of doors; ~ with a toy / doll / top / kitten / *etc*; ~ with one's watch-chain; they ~ed at soldiers / Red Indians / keeping shop / forfeits. (2a) ~ at ninepins / skittles; the sound of someone ~ing on a violin / flute / *etc*; he ~s by ear *(not from notes)*; ~ fair / foul (2b) children ~ing games; the children were ~ing shop; let's ~ (that we are) pirates; ~ football / cricket / tennis / golf / chess / *(BE)* draughts / *(AE)* checkers / cards / *etc*; ~ ninepins / skittles; ~ the violin / flute / piano / *etc*; ~ first violin in an orchestra; □ ~ second fiddle (to s.o.) *(be less important)*; □ ~ the game (→ game *n* 1); ~ a game for love (→ love *n* 4); *fig)* he ~ed the documents into the hands of (the enemy) (→ 15). (3) ~ (a) Chopin (sonata); ~ me some Chopin / some Chopin for me; ~ a piece on the violin / flute / piano; ~ a waltz; record s.th. on tape and ~ it back (4) ~ (the role / part of) Lady Macbeth; ~ a comedy / 'Hamlet' / *etc* (to a full house); he ~ed his part well; ~ the principal part *(also fig)* (5 *perform in*) they ~ed Brighton for a month; ~ the leading theatres (6 *accompany with music*) a band ~ed the procession into the arena; the organist ~ed the congregation out (of the church) / in(to the church). (7 *include in a team*) shall we ~ Smith in the next match? who(m) shall we ~ as goalkeeper? *(fig)* he ~ed his brothers against each other; children often try to ~ one parent against the other (→ play off); ~ a pawn / card / trump; ~ one's ace of spades; □ ~ one's cards well / badly *(make good / bad use of opportunities)* (8 *have as partner*) will you ~ me at chess / dominoes / *etc*? we used to ~ your school at football; ~ another team / club; England is ~ing Australia. (9) ~ a joke / mean trick on s.o.; he has ~ed me a trick; who's been ~ing tricks with my tools? (10a *gamble*) ~ for high stakes; ~ high / low; he went on ~ing until he had lost everything. (10b) he ~ed his last dollar. (11 *perform*) they ~ed every night (to a full house); □ ~ to the gallery *(try to win popularity by appealing to the masses)*; the strings are ~ing well this evening. (12) what's ~ing tonight *(what is being performed, shown)*?
(13) we hope this scene will ~ well. (14) the lawn / cricket pitch ~s well; the court ~s slowly after rain; the piano ~s better now. (15a *not act seriously*) they are only ~ing; you must not ~ with a woman('s affections); he ~ed with the idea of going to Canada; ~ fast and loose *(trifle)* with a girl's affections; he's merely ~ing at being a student; ~ at gardening; what does he think he is ~ing at *(what's he up to)*? he asked her what she was ~ing at; ~ false (with a friend); if you act that way, you will be ~ing right into his hands; let's ~ for safety rather than take a risk. – (15b) ~ s.o. false on s.th. *(cheat him)*; (16 ~ + *on*) ~ on an instrument (→ 2a); ~ on words *(make puns)*; ~ on s.o.'s fears / credulity / sympathies *(take advantage of it)*; ~ on an illness / one's popularity. (17) ~ a hose, water on a lawn / on a fire / into the flames; ~ a searchlight on an object in the sky; ~ one's guns on the enemy's lines (18) the fountains ~ daily; the water of the fountain ~ed in the air; the searchlight ~ed along the road. (19) the moonlight ~ed on the water; shadows ~ed on the ceiling; a smile ~ed on her lips; his fancy ~ed round the idea of proposing to Ann.

play about don't ~ ~ with that razor; students ~ ~ in class.

play down ~ ~ the seriousness of the situation / one's part in the discovery.

play off she ~ed ~ one boy-friend against the other.
play out (1) they decided to ~ the match ~ until a goal had been scored; the actors ~ed the comedy ~ in spite of the mishap. (2) the old type of family party is ~ed ~ *(finished)*. (3) ~ ~ *(exhaust)* one's supplies (4) be ~ed ~ *(exhausted)* after a strenuous walk.
play up (1) come on! ~ up! *(vigorously)* (2) the class ~ed the new teacher up *(teased him)*; those children do ~ their parents up. (3) my rheumatism does ~ me up during this damp weather *(is a nuisance)*; the engine of this car is ~ing me up again. (4) the newspaper ~ed up *(emphasized unduly)* the issue; for several months the film has been ~ed up in our town. (5) he constantly ~ed up to *(tried to please)* his boss.
plead *vi* (1 *beg earnestly*) the prisoner ~ed for his liberty; ~ with s.o. for mercy; she ~ed with him not to go away. (2 *argue*) he ~ed for / against the defendant; Jim ~ed (not) guilty (to the offence / to having done it). (3) that lawyer has ~ed before many judges. - *vt* (4 → 2) he ~ed his case well; get a lawyer to ~ one's case / cause (5 *offer as an excuse*) she ~ed ignorance of the law / poverty / *etc*; ~ one's youth / old age.
please *vt* (1) it's difficult to ~ everybody; she was easily ~d by flattery; ~ yourself *(do as you like)*; you can ~ yourself; ~ the ear / eye. - *vi* (2) manners that ~; the chief object of a play should be to ~ and entertain. (3 *choose; prefer*) he does as he ~s without thinking about other people; I shall do as I ~; take as many as you ~; go where you ~. - *adj* (4) it is ~ing to the eye; the ~ing taste of homemade bread. (5 *~d: glad*) I am ~d that you are well; we would be very ~d if you could visit us; we are very ~d with our new house; I am very ~d with him - he passed his exam yesterday; he was ~d at being chosen to captain the team; he was ~d about his success; I shall be ~d to go with you; I am ~d to be home again; ~d to meet you!
pleasure *n* (1) the present gave him great / much ~; it gives me no ~ / is no ~ to me to go to the theatre by myself; find ~ in (listening to) music; it would give / afford us great ~ if you could visit us; express one's ~ at s.th. to s.o.; she showed no ~; the sight of ... filled her with ~; spoil s.o.'s ~ ; he seems to take ~ in (teasing his sister); could you help me please? - with ~! live a life of ~; he is a man of ~; hedonists pursue ~ and avoid pain. (2) the ~s of friendship; worldly / sensual ~s; an unexpected / perverse / harmless / doubtful / *etc* ~; deny / allow o.s. a ~; may I have the ~ of dancing with you? will you do me the ~ to come to see me? take a ~ in contradicting.
pledge *n* (1 *s.th. given as security*) I'm holding his car as a ~ for the loan; accept / redeem a ~ (2) goods lying in ~; put / hold s.th. in ~; take goods out of ~ (3 *token*) a ~ of friendship (4 *promise*) under ~ of secrecy; all the members signed a ~ to keep their meeting secret; take / sign the ~ *(promise to abstain from alcohol)*; Christian marriage involves a solemn ~ of lifelong faithfulness.
pledge *vt* (1) he ~d his wife's pearl necklace. (2) ~ one's word / honour / life; ~ allegiance (to the flag); I ~ you my word that (he is innocent); be ~d to secrecy; my government will go forward with the policies to which they are ~d.
pluck *vt* (1) ~ feathers from a fowl (2) ~ flowers / fruit (3) ~ a harp string / *etc* (4) ~ a fowl *(pull out its feathers)* (5) ~ a child from a fire. - *vi* (6) ~ at s.o.'s sleeve.
pluck up (1) ~ up weeds (2) ~ up (one's) courage *(overcome fear)* (3) he always ~ed up *(his courage)* at the approach of danger.
plunge *vt* (1) ~ one's hand into cold water / a hole; ~ a knife into s.o.'s heart (2) ~ a room into darkness (3) attitudes liable to ~ us into war; he has no money and is ~d into debt; ~d in business; he was ~d deep in despair / sorrow; be ~d into grief. - *vi* (4) the swimmer ~d into the pool; he ~d in head first. (5) he ~d into the thicket / through the crowd. (6) ~ into a discussion / argument; ~ into debt.
point *n* (1) the ~ of a needle / pin / thorn / pen / tool / knife / stick / weapon; *(AE)* the ~s of the fingers; a pen / pencil ~; give a ~ to / put a ~ on a pencil *(sharpen it)*; at the ~ of the sword *(under threat of violence)*; stand on the ~s of one's toes; she dances well on her ~s; □ not to put too fine a ~ on it *(to speak bluntly)* (2) a ~ of land juts into the bay. (3 *dot, mark*) a (full) ~ *(a full stop)*; a decimal ~: 2·3 (*read*: two ~ three); a ~ on the map (4) northwest is a ~ of the

compass; the four cardinal ~s (5) the ~ of intersection of two lines; a ~ where two lines cross (6 *mark on a scale*) the freezing-~ of water is 0° C.; the boiling-~; the melting-~ of metal; the cost of living went up several ~s last month; □ possession is nine ~s of the law *(strong evidence in one's favour).* (7) win / be defeated on ~s; he scored ten ~s; our team leads by two ~s. (8 *definite place*) a ~ of departure; at this ~; the ~ of no return *(also fig)*; a ~ of contact; ~s of interest (on a route); we're leaving for Chicago and ~s west; view-~ *(also fig)*; *(fig)* ~ of view *(aspect)*: he sees things from a different ~ of view. (9 *definite, decisive moment in time*) a turning-~ (in his career); at this ~ (he paused a few seconds); when it came to the ~ (he refused to help); be on the ~ of (leaving / phoning / *etc*); be at the ~ of death / war; his health / patience / temper was at breaking-~. (10 *item in a speech, argument, etc*) there were four main ~s in his proposal; the speaker carefully listed each ~ of his plan; a ~ of order *(question of debating procedure)*; a ~ of conscience / honour *(s.th. that affects one's honour, etc)*; a major / minor / moot *(undecided)* / sore / *etc* ~. (11 *the essential thing)* I don't see your ~; you've missed the whole ~; the ~ of a story / joke; don't get away from the ~; (I wish he would) come to the ~ *(stop talking about unessential things)*; his reply was short and to the ~; keep to the ~ when you answer; that remark was not to the ~; what you say is beside the ~ *(has nothing to do with the matter)*; he got low marks for his essay, because much of it was off the ~ *(irrelevant)*; carry / gain one's ~ *(establish an argument, achieve a purpose by persuasion)*; make / score a ~ *(prove that a statement is true)*; make a ~ of doing / it a ~ to do *(do deliberately)*: he makes a ~ of answering / it a ~ to answer letters at once; in ~ of fact *(as a matter of fact)*; in ~ *(pertinent, suitable)*: let me give you a case in ~. (12 *feature*) everyone has both good and bad ~s; (generosity) is his strong ~ / not one of his strong ~s; what are her best ~s as a secretary? (13 *purpose*) what's your ~ in coming? there's not much / no ~ in doing that; do you think there's any ~ in (repairing these shoes)? (14 *fig: stage*) he reached the ~ when (he could no longer control his anger); frankness to the ~ of insult; morale had reached a low ~.

point *vt* (1) ~ the way (2) ~ a gun / rifle at s.o. / a stag; she was ~ing her finger at me; ~ the hose at the car; ~ a telescope at a deer on the hillside (3) he ~ed *(directed)* the car south. (4 *sharpen*) ~ a pencil / tool (5 *give force to*) ~ a speech with jokes; ~ an argument with facts; all the teacher's stories ~ a moral. (6 ~ + at *implies direction;* ~ + to + *noun emphasizes the noun, not direction;* ~ + to + left, north, *etc implies direction*) it is rude to ~ at people, but not rude to ~ to them; what's he ~ing at? they'll ~ at you in the street and whisper ...; one of the boys was ~ing at something in the garden; 'look at this', he said, ~ing to a blood stain on the carpet; he ~ed to the door; the gardener ~ed proudly to his dahlias; the weather-vane ~s (to / towards the) North; the arrow ~ed to the left / south; the hands of the clock ~ed to half-past six. (7) fever ~s to some disturbance in the blood; all the evidence ~s to robbery as the motive of the crime; everything ~s to his being the culprit / to a bright future for her; their policy ~s in the same direction as ours.

point out (1) ~ ~ an object in the sky; ~ ~ to visitors all the objects of interest; ~ me ~ the ones you would like. (2) ~ ~ a mistake to s.o.; ~ ~ the difficulties of a matter / the advantages of a proposal / the necessity of a step (3) his intelligence ~ed him ~ for very high office. (4) he ~ed ~ that it was not his fault.

police *n* (1) the ~ are after him; send for / phone for / call in the ~; ... but the ~ refuse to believe her; the ~ of Great Britain are absolutely free of political pressures; women ~ were first used when ...; the ~ are not only concerned with crime - it is their duty to see ... (2 ~ *force*) in Germany a secret State P~, known as ..., was set up; this organization also acted as a political ~. (3 *members of a* ~ *force*) several ~ are patrolling the neighbourhood; it was a real dictatorship and there were ~ everywhere; ... where 17 border ~ were killed.

policy *n* (1) adopt / pursue a (sound / wise / prudent / cautious / disastrous / foolish / *etc*) ~; we have a new company ~; a firm's advertising ~; our nation's foreign / social / economic / *etc* ~ (2) it was good ~ to consent; honesty is the best ~; ~ demands occasional compromise.

polish *vt* (1) ~ metal / floors / furniture; a ~ed surface (2) his speech needs ~ing; a ~ed gentleman. - *vi* (3) this wood won't ~; a flooring that ~es easily.

polish off the boy ~ed ~ the meal in next to no time *(inform)*; ~ ~ an opponent *(inform: dispose of him completely)*; ~ ~ a job.

polish up ~ up one's French; the style of the translation needs to be ~ed up.

politics *n* (1 *art of political government*) he divided his early years between soldiering and ~; to Gandhi ~ is not too big and peanuts are not too small; ~ is the art of government. (2 *practice of conducting political affairs*) our future depends on world ~; Britain's loyalty to NATO ~; ~ attract many ambitious men; ~ has no attraction for me as a career; the adoption of the policy outlined in the memorandum was a decision of high ~. (3 *political affairs*) American ~ are not easily understood by the average Englishman; be active in local ~; the O'Dwyer administration ends its first year with the town's respect: ~ have not dominated its appointments or policies nearly as much as was feared; ... times when ~ have been conducted in the grand style (4 *political manoeuvres*) we could not approve of his ~ in winning passage of the bill. (5 *political principles, opinions*) a person's ~ are his own affair; the same ~ were followed by his successors; his ~ are rather unorthodox; what are his ~?

ponder *vt* (1) ~ a problem / question; we ~ed many things; he ~ed his next words thoroughly; ~ the advantages of doing s.th. - *vi* (2) give me a few days to ~ over it (over *emphasizes prolonged thinking*); ~ over an incident; what are you ~ing over?

poor *adj* (1) he's been very ~ since his business failed; ~ people living in a ~ house; be ~ and yet contented; I am the ~er by £10. (2 *bad*) he is a ~ speller / speaker / cook / *etc*; a ~ crop / harvest; this is ~ cloth / food; a ~ dinner; ~ land / soil *(not fertile)*; goods of ~ quality; a ~ supply of materials; a ~ attendance *(few people)*; a country ~ in minerals; be ~ in health / ideas / spirit / quality / *etc*; ~ work(manship); business was ~ this year; that is a ~ consolation; he made a ~ excuse; a ~ speech; a ~ appearance; I have a very ~ opinion of him. (3 *feeble, miserable*) he's a ~ devil; he tells lies because he's a ~, worthless creature. (4 *needing sympathy*) the ~ child cried all night; ~ chap! ~ girl! ~ you! ~ thing!

pop *vt* (1) ~ a cork out of a champagne bottle (2) he ~ped his head in at the door; will you ~ this letter in the post for me? I'll ~ the kettle on and we'll have a cup of tea; she ~ped a peanut into her mouth / a cake into the oven; ~ one's head out of a window (3) ~ the question *(inform: propose marriage)*. - *vi* (4) the cork ~ped. (5) his eyes ~ped (out) with amazement / in surprise. (6) ~ round to a shop; ~ in and see me some evening; the children were always ~ping in and out; will you ~ across to Mrs Jones for me? he ~ped off last week for a few days' holiday.

pop up this question has ~ped up again; we were discussing it when Mr Short's name ~ped up.

pose *vt* (1) ~ a group for a photograph; the artist ~d his model carefully. (2) ~ a difficult problem; the great questions that a peace conference would ~; an extra guest ~s a problem because we haven't enough beds. - *vi* (3) she ~d for the photographer. (4 ~ + as: *claim to be*) he ~d as an expert on stamps; he likes to ~ as a judge of literature. (5 *present o.s. insincerely*) he seems to be ~ing in all his behaviour; I wish she would not ~ so much.

position *n* (1) I was in a good ~ to see the whole stage; he took up his ~ in front of the door; the director told all the players to take their ~s; the pilot radioed the control tower for his ~; the relative ~ of the hands of a clock; the ~ of a river is often marked by a mist; the players were in ~ *(normally placed)*; be out of ~ (2) attack / storm the enemy's ~; a fortified ~ (3 *advantageous* ~) manoeuvre for ~ (in war / at chess) (4) sit / lie in a comfortable ~; be in a sitting ~ (5) he has a good ~ at the bank; hold / occupy a (temporary / permanent) ~ (as teacher / in the Civil Service / *etc*); apply for a (vacant) ~; find / get / obtain / lose / give up / resign a ~; applications are invited for the ~ of clerk / typist / office-boy / driver / *etc*; a ~ as housemaid; rise to a ~ of responsibility (6 *social standing*) s.o.'s social ~; he has a ~ to maintain in the community; he occupies a high ~ in his town;

a person of (wealth and) ~ (7 *situation; condition*) be in a good ~ (financially); the economic ~ of the town; be in an unenviable / awkward / ridiculous / false / *etc* ~; you have placed him / yourself in a critical ~; put s.o. in a difficult / dangerous / *etc* ~; bargain from a ~ of strength; what's the ~ of affairs? is he in a ~ to marry? I am not in a ~ either to contradict or affirm this statement; what would you do if you were in my ~? put yourself in my ~. (8 *attitude, viewpoint*) what is your ~ on the question of ...? define / state one's ~; he took up the ~ that we ...

possess *vt* (1) that's all I ~; he ~es a house and a car; ~ property / wealth; ~ certain rights (2) ~ courage / (endless) patience / graciousness / *etc* (3) they ~ed themselves of her money by illegal means. (4 *be ~ed of: have*) he is ~ed of health, wealth and good sense; be ~ed of money / land / intelligence / *etc* (5 *get control over*) what ~ed him to act so? fear ~ed him. (6 *keep o.s. under control*) ~ o.s. / one's soul in patience *(be patient)* (7 *dominate*) be ~ed by / with fear / terror / greed / envy / ambition / an idea; be ~ed by / with the devil / an evil spirit.

possessed *adj* (1 *dominated by an evil spirit, mad*) you are surely ~; these ~ fools; he is a man ~; behave / scream like one ~ (2 *calm*) she remained ~ despite the trying circumstances.

possession *n* (1) be in ~ of a passport / large fortune / *etc*; have s.th. in one's ~; the deeds are in the ~ of my solicitor; take / get / regain / resume ~ of s.th.; the stolen articles were (found) in his ~; he came into ~ of the book; the book came into his ~; the painting passed into the ~ of Mr D.; this clever move put him in ~ of the estate; illegal ~ of fire-arms; □ ~ is nine points of the law (→ point *n* 6); is he in full ~ of his senses? (2) his most precious ~ is a ...; a man of great ~s; he lost all his ~s; domestic and foreign ~s of the Crown (3 *self-control*) his ~ in the emergency was absolute.

post[1] *n* the ~ of clerk / typist / stenographer / office-boy / driver / *etc*; be appointed to a diplomatic ~; hold a ~ in a bank; how do you like your new ~? what is your official ~ in the school? be offered a teaching ~ abroad; be given a ~ as director.

post[2] *n (chiefly BE; AE →* mail *n)* (1) I'll send the book by ~; it came to me by ~; answer by return of ~; the letter crossed in the ~ with the one I sent you; secrecy of the ~ (2) has the ~ come yet? this parcel has come with this morning's ~; you'll get it in tomorrow's ~; catch / miss the ~ *(be / not be in time for the clearance of letters)*; letter / newspaper / parcel ~ *(also AE)* (3 *post office*) will you take this letter to the ~ (*AE* to the post office)?

post[1] *v* (1 *BE; AE →* mail *vt*) will you ~ this letter for me? many of the letters ~ed in London for Europe are delivered the following day. (2 *inform*) he is well ~ed; keep me ~ed (about / on his activities).

post[2] *v* (1) ~ s.th. on a notice-board; ~ (up) a bill / placard on a wall; ~ no bills! the police ~ed a no-parking sign in our street. (2 *AE put a notice on*) it is forbidden to ~ the building; ~ a wall (over) with placards (3 *make known*) ~ students marks; ~ up a sale / entertainment / speaker / *etc*; ~ a ship as missing.

post[3] *vt* (1) ~ soldiers along a road / sentries round a camp; ~ a look-out (2) ~ an officer to a unit; after that training we'll be ~ed to a ship; he was ~ed to duty with the Air Force.

pot *n* (1) a milk- / tea- / coffee- / jam- / flower-~; an earthenware / china / aluminium ~; the ~ holds / contains tea; the ~ holds a pint / six cups; □ put a quart into a pint ~ *(try to do the impossible)*; □ make the ~ boil *(earn one's living)*; □ keep the ~ boiling (→ keep *vt* 8c); □ the ~ calls the kettle black *(the accuser has the same fault as the accused).* (2) I've made a ~ of tea; a ~ of tea for two, please! a ~ of stew / soup / *etc* (3) make a ~ / ~s of money (4) a big ~ *(inform: important person)* (5) □ go to ~ *(inform: become ruined)*: with no one to care for it, the old garden went to ~.

pound *n* (1) the ~ is the unit of mass equal to 16 oz. avoirdupois or to 12 oz. troy; exact / demand one's ~ of flesh *(every part of a debt)* (2) the British unit of currency is the ~ sterling (→ penny *n* 1); □ in for a penny, in for a ~ (→ penny *n* 1).

pour *vt* (1) ~ tea into a cup / wine into a glass / boiling water on to the tea / the soup through a sieve / a bucket of water over s.o.'s head / water over the flowers / molten metal into a mould; ~ out a cup of tea for me / me out a cup of tea; □ ~ oil on the flame(s) (→ oil *n* 1); □ ~ oil on troubled waters (→ oil *n* 1); □ ~ cold water on s.o.'s schemes / enthusiasm / *etc (discourage him)* (2) the river ~ed its waters through the breach. (3) the Underground stations ~ thousands of workers into the streets each morning. (4) ~ out one's feelings / troubles (to a friend); the lost boy ~ed out his story to the policeman. - *vi* (5) the river ~s into the sea; the waters ~ed over the fertile fields; blood ~ed out of the wound; the sweat was ~ing off him; it's ~ing (with rain); it was absolutely ~ing down; it was a ~ing wet day; □ it never rains but it ~s *(events, esp misfortunes, come many together).* (6) many people ~ed into / out of the hall; more people came ~ing in; soldiers ~ into a country; letters of complaint ~ed in. (7) the words / a song ~ed from her lips.

poverty *n* (1) extreme / utmost / abject / dire / wretched / *etc* ~; fall into / be reduced to ~; live in ~; ~ is no disgrace / sin / vice / crime. (2) ~ of the soil (in phosphates) (3) ~ of language / vocabulary; a ~ of intellect; the essay shows ~ of ideas; be hampered by a ~ of supplies.

power *n* (1 *ability to act*) the chameleon has the ~ of changing its colour; the ~ of motion; I will do everything (that lies with) in my ~; it is not within / is out of my ~ to do that / accept the offer / *etc*; it is beyond my ~ to tell how I suffered. (2 *faculty*) his ~s are failing; he is losing his ~s; ~ of speech; a man of great intellectual ~s; mental / poetic / creative ~s; the latent ~s in a human being; this work was beyond her ~s; the healing / curative ~(s) of a plant / drug (3 *strength, force*) the ~ of, in s.o.'s arms / legs / voice; the ~ of an acid to corrode metal; the healing ~ of herbs; the destructive ~ of a bomb; the ~ of a blow; s.o.'s jumping ~; anthracite has a high heating ~; the purchasing ~ (of the dollar); do s.th. to the best of one's ~; more ~ to your elbow! *(said to encourage s.o.)*; the ~ of s.o.'s argument(s) / words / love / hate; knowledge is ~; will-~ (4 *energy, force used to do work)* the machines of the factory are running at full / half ~; the ~ of an engine / machine / magnet; the ~ of the wind / elements; a loom driven by ~; a ~ loom / lathe / drill / saw; steam / water / electric / mechanical / motive ~; an engine of 40 horse-~ (5 *control, authority*) political ~; a king's temporal / absolute ~; imperial / royal ~; the ~ of the law / of Parliament; the legislative / judicial / executive ~; the balance of ~ in Europe; put s.o. into ~; come into / rise to ~; attain ~ by overthrowing the government; the Bolsheviks seized ~ in 1917; s.o., a party in ~ / out of ~; be in / fall into s.o.'s ~; have ~ over s.o. / life and death; have the ~ of life and death over s.o.; have s.o. in one's ~ (6 *right*) the ~ to sign a document; ~ of attorney *(a written authorization)*; have (full) ~s to do s.th. / act; the ~s of the president; presidential / congressional ~; use / abuse / exceed one's ~s (7 *state*) the Great P~s; the lesser ~s; belligerent ~s; the U.S.A. is a great naval ~; at one time the Roman Empire was a world ~. (8 *person, organization having great influence*) the press is a great ~ in Britain; the ~s that be *(those in ~)*; the Armada was a mighty ~ *(military force)* (9 *fig: moving force*) ~s of good / evil / heaven / hell / *etc*; the heavenly ~s; there are ~s in play here beyond the reach of human intellect; preserve us from the ~s of darkness. (10) 10 to the ~ of 3 is 1,000 *(10^3 = 1,000)*; the fifth ~ of 2 is 32. (11 *magnifying capacity of a lens*) the ~ of a lens / microscope; a telescope of high ~ (12 *inform: large number, amount*) we saw a ~ of people; he does a ~ of work; this stout does me a ~ of good.

practice *n* (1) put a plan / scheme into ~; it looks all right, but it will not work in ~. (2 *common way of doing s.th.*) the ~ of closing (shops) at 6 p.m / of going to bed late / *etc*; it is not the ~ here for women to appear in the streets in shorts; the shameful ~s of a blackmailer; the unwholesome ~s of folk medicine; make a ~ of daily exercise / cheating at exams / boasting of one's abilities / dining early; make it a ~ to rise early (3 *repeated exercise*) don't be late for the choir ~ / the ~ match; ~ makes perfect; it takes years of ~ to acquire the skill of an expert; have / need / want (regular / daily / an hour's) ~; she refused to play the piano, because she was out of / not in ~. (4) he plans to set up ~ in his home town; his son will take over his ~; Mr D. is (no longer) in ~ as a doctor; Dr. N. has retired from ~. (5 *clients*) a lawyer / doctor with a large ~; sell one's ~.

practise *vt* (1) ~ a profession / art; ~ medicine / (the) law / music (2) ~ the / one's violin; ~ (a new piece on) the piano;

she ~d writing with her left hand. (3) ~ a class in French pronunciation; ~ a dog in s.th. (4) ~ what you preach; ~ early rising; ~ thrift; he ~d charity towards all; ~ democracy / one's democracy / one's religion. - *vi* (5)Does Dr. D. still ~? he ~ed (successfully) for four decades / in a small village. (6) you must ~ daily; if you don't ~ you'll never learn the scales. (7) ~ on the flute / at shooting.

preach *vt* (1) ~ the gospel / Buddhism / *etc*; ~ Christianity to the heathen; who ~ed the sermon? (2 *urge*) ~ moderation and prudence; ~ reform / revolution; he ~ed the need for new ambulances; → practise 4 (3 *give advice in a tiresome way*) don't ~ me a sermon about laziness. - *vi* (4 → 1) ~ on a text / subject; he ~ed for two hours. (5 → 3) it's hard to talk with him because he always ~es; he does nothing but ~ at his children.

precaution *n* take (necessary / extra / special / *etc*) ~s (against s.th.); take an umbrella as a ~; wrap up well as a ~ against cold; safety ~s.

precipitate *vt* (1) he ~d himself into the struggle for the ball. (2) what ~d the country into war / the crisis? (3) ~ a crisis / s.o.'s ruin; the decision of the umpire almost ~d a riot; the loss of his wife ~d his neglecting his duties at the office; this incident ~d her departure; the employer's refusal to talk to the union ~d a strike. (4) silt is ~d at the mouth of the river. (5) the surplus moisture is ~d as mist, rain, dew or snow; we were able to ~ the crystals.

predict *vt* ~ rain / a good harvest / an earthquake / the weather; ~ the future / fall of a civilization; he ~ed the results of the election with amazing accuracy; he ~ed that he would be miserable without her.

prefer *vt* (1) I ~ this house to that one; I ~ beef to mutton *(general preference)*; I think I should ~ beef rather than mutton *(specific occasion)*; where cricket is concerned, I ~ to watch rather than to play; I ~ skating to skiing; I ~ (my daughter / your) travelling by train - it's safer; I ~ not to think about it. (2 *legal use: present for consideration*) ~ a charge / complaint against s.o.

preference *n* (1) have a ~ for Swiss chocolate; choose one thing in ~ to another; he was given ~ over everyone else; the undue ~ given to his brother made him jealous. (2 *right to choose*) he was allowed no ~. (3 *that which is preferred*) his ~ is for simple cooking; what are your ~s? the purple dress is my ~.

prejudice *n* (1) have a (deep-rooted / inveterate) ~ in favour of / against s.th.; listen to modern music without ~; the war against ~ is never-ending. (2 *disadvantage)* this law operates to the ~ of the majority; be careful that you say nothing that may be to the ~ of your case; this concession is made without ~ to any future decision of the committee.

prejudice *vt* (1) her red hair ~d him against / in favour of her; these considerations ~d me against the plan; his honesty ~d us in his favour. (2 *weaken; injure*) he ~d his claim by asking too much; lack of education ~d his chances for success.

prepare *vt* (1) ~ a medicine / vaccine / meal / *etc*; ~ a bath for s.o.; ~ a speech / sermon / balance-sheet / *etc*; ~ a lesson / one's lessons at home (2) ~ the ground for seeds / *(fig)* negotiations; ~ pupils for an examination / a patient for surgery (3) ~ s.o. for bad news / a shock; ~ s.o. to hear s.th. - *vi* (4) ~ for a trip / examination; ~ for an attack *(get ready to repel it)*; the enemy ~d to attack *(got ready to attack)*. (5) ~ for the worst / bad news / *etc* (6 *be ~d: be willing*) be ~d to do / say / admit s.th. / for things to go wrong; are you ~d to keep silent? they are not ~d to discuss the matter with us.

prescribe *vt* (1) ~ regular hours of study; the law ~s a penalty for doing that; the law ~s the use of special forms for income tax returns; fill up the ~d form; the ~d curriculum of the university (2) a doctor ~s a remedy / treatment (for a patient); he ~d plenty of fresh air and rest for the invalid.

presence *n* (1) his ~ embarrasses me; his ~ was not noticed; during his ~ in London he ...; he said it in my ~ / the ~ of his friend / his friend's ~; I was to have done it, but in the ~ of Mr D. *(since he is here)* I think I should ask him to do it; be calm in the ~ of danger; □ have / show (great) ~ of mind *(ability to act quickly in case of danger, etc)*; your ~ is requested *(you are invited)*; parcels may be examined for the ~ of contraband; establish the ~ of radioactive particles in s.th. (2 *appearance*) a man of fine / noble ~; a man of heavy, uninspiring ~ but considerable eloquence.

present[1] *n* past and ~; live for the ~ (moment); Mr N. is not at home at ~ *(now)*; there are at ~ only two applications for the post; that is enough for the ~ *(now and a little longer)*.

present[2] *n* a birthday / wedding / Christmas ~; give s.o. (s.th. as) a ~; buy a ~ for s.o.; make s.o. a ~ of money / a book / a ring / *etc*; I have brought you a small ~ from ...; accept / refuse a ~; thank (s.o.) for a ~.

present *vt* (1) certificates and prizes are ~ed at a school speech day; ~ a valuable watch to an old employee who is retiring; the firm ~ed him with a cheque; the cheque was ~ed to him by the director. (2) ~ a petition / complaint (to s.o.); ~ a cheque (at a bank for payment); the grocer ~ed his monthly bill; the waiter ~ed our bill for lunch; ~ one's compliments / greetings / thanks to s.o. (3 *introduce*) Mrs Smith, may I ~ Mr Jones? the teacher ~ed the visitor to the class. (4) a theatre manager ~s a play / a certain actor in a play; this theatre ~s films on a wide screen. (5) ~ o.s. at a friend's house; ~ o.s. for trial examination (6) he ~ed a ragged appearance; in spite of all her troubles, Helen managed to ~ a gay appearance at the party; ~ a bold front (→ front 4) (7) ~ an alternative plan; ~ an argument convincingly (8) taking a trip always ~s the problem of what to do with the pets; this case ~s some interesting features / no difficulty; a subject that ~s no difficulties; in his lecture he ~ed several vulnerable points; other sections of the book ~ big question marks.

present *adj* (1 *now existing, occurring, etc*) the ~ moment / day / month / time / state of affairs; German literature of the ~ day; ~-day literature; crowded schools are a ~ problem; in the ~ case; the ~ writer *(I who am writing)*; the ~ volume *(the one under review)*; the ~ document; the ~ topic; ~ company excepted *(those present are not meant)*. (2) many people were ~ (at the wedding); all ~ assented; you are always ~ in my thoughts. (3) carbon is ~ in many minerals.

preserve *vt* (1) ~ fruit / vegetables / eggs / meat / fish / *etc*; a solution to ~ wood from / against dry rot; ~ furniture / a building / a monument / the countryside (2) ~ one's eyesight / health / strength; careful driving helps to ~ lives; a well-~d man of sixty; ~ s.o. from harm / danger / death; ~ one's dignity / composure / honour; ~ appearances; small gifts ~ friendship; ~ peace / silence / a tradition; few of his early poems are ~d; ~ the memory of a benefactor (3 *protect game, fish for private use*) the fishing in this river is strictly ~d. (4) God ~ us! Heaven ~ me from that / false friends.

press *n* (1) a ~ of the hand; give s.th. a light ~ (2) a cider- / wine- / trouser- / *etc* ~ (3) a printing-~; the book is in the ~ *(being printed)* now; get a book / manuscript ready for the ~; send a book to the ~; the book / newspaper has gone to ~; see a book through the ~ (→ see 16) (4) the daily / periodical / religious / Conservative / *etc* ~; the liberty / freedom of the ~; the ~ has great political influence; a ~ campaign / cutting / conference / gallery / *etc* (5 *critical commentaries*) the book / play had, received a good / bad ~. (6 *pressure*) the ~ of modern life; there is a great ~ of business; the ~ of work kept Father late at the office; the ~ of the crowd drove them on.

press *vt* 1 - 7a; *vi* 7b - 10; *adj* 11. The patterns are grouped as follows: ~ + *obj* + *inf*: 7a; ~ + *prepos*: be ~ed by 4a; ~ for 7b; ~ s.o. for s.th. 7a; be ~ed for s.th. 4a; ~ on 10; ~ s.th. on s.o. 5.

(1) ~ trousers / a suit / a shirt / flowers / *etc*; ~ grapes; ~ butter into a dish; ~ one's pencil on the paper; she ~ed the child to her breast / heart; ~ s.o. against the wall / into a corner; his face was ~ed close to the window; ~ s.o.'s hand; he ~ed a kiss on her forehead / lips; he ~ed her in his arms. (2) ~ wine from grapes / juice out of / from fruit (3) ~ a lever / a button / the trigger of a gun; ~ the door-handle down; ~ (down) the accelerator (pedal) (4a) ~ s.o. hard / closely; ~ the enemy *(give him no rest)*; they were hard / close ~ed on all sides by the enemy; ~ed to the utmost, they had to surrender; his creditors are ~ing him hard; he was ~ed by problems on all sides / by poverty. (4b be ~ed for: *be desperately short of*) we were (hard) ~ed for time / money / space. (5) ~ a gift / money / one's opinion / one's advice on s.o.; ~ on s.o. the urgency of the matter; (he refrained from) ~ing his views. (6 *put for-*

ward with insistence) ~ a / one's claim; ~ a point (7a ~ for: *demand insistently*) they ~ed (the minister) for a reply; we ~ed her to stay; they ~ed him for payment of the debt / to pay the debt. – *vi* (7b) ~ for higher wages / an inquiry into s.th. / extra staff / *etc* (8 → 1) don't ~ so hard! a bone was ~ing on the nerve; ~ on one's pen; the crowd ~ed against the barriers / upon the filmstar. (9 *require immediate action*) the matter does not ~; time ~es; let me know if anything ~es. (10) worries / debts ~ed on him / on his mind. – *adj* (11) the matter is ~ing; time is ~ing; her entreaties grew more ~ing; ~ing business / demands for payment.

press down (1) → press *vt* 3. (2) these taxes ~ ~ heavily on the people.

press in (1) ~ in a window-pane (2) the room was full, but five more people managed to ~ in.

press on ~ on with one's work; they ~ed on to reach the village before dark.

pressure *n* (1) a ~ of five pounds to the square inch; the ~ of the atmosphere; atmospheric ~; the tyre ~ of a car; the ~ of the vaulting on the piers; have a sensation of ~ in the pit of one's stomach (2) the light ~ of his hand reassured her; the ~ of a bone on a nerve (3 *compelling influence*) put ~ on s.o.; bring ~ to bear on s.o.; do s.th. / work under ~; sign a document under ~; yield to the ~ of public opinion; he is under ~ from his creditors. (4 *s.th. that weighs down*) the ~ of worries / debts; the ~s of city life; under the ~ of necessity / poverty / taxation / work; I'm always under ~ of work; with us the ~ of business is greatest in December. (5) live / work at high ~ *(with great energy and speed).*

presume *vt* (1 *take for granted*) I ~ you will be at the meeting; they ~d him (to be) dead; he is ~d dead; I ~ this decision to be final; you are Dr. Miller, I ~? no one, I ~, denies it; never ~ that a man is guilty until he is proved so; you had better ~ no such thing. (2 *venture*) the young lawyer ~d to tell the judge he was wrong; I won't ~ to disturb you; I wouldn't ~ to contradict a person of your knowledge and experience; he ~d to compare himself with you. – *vi* (3 ~ (up)on: *take advantage of*) she ~d on her friend's hospitality and wore out her welcome; ~ing upon an acquaintance of a few hours, he asked to borrow five pounds; do not ~ upon his tolerance; ~ on s.o.'s good nature.

pretence *n* (1) don't believe his story – it's all ~; his pious words were mere ~; my sleepiness was all ~; do s.th. under the ~ of friendship / religion / patriotism / ignorance / *etc*; he got a lot of money under the ~ of collecting for the blind; I wonder how long he will keep up the ~ of being unable to understand our language. (2) excuse s.o. from s.th. on a ~ of urgent business; he is constantly absent on the slightest ~; he used the slightest ~ to get out of doing any work; he was prosecuted for taking money under false ~s. (3) a ~ to knowledge; he was destitute of any ~ to wit. (4) he is a person without ~ *(is natural, sincere).*

pretend *vt* (1) ~ illness / to be ill / that one is ill; ~ ignorance; ~ to go to sleep; he ~s to have forgotten the letter; the trapeze artist ~ed to fall just to thrill the audience; I don't ~ to know all the answers. (2) let's ~ (that) we're astronauts; the boys ~ed to be Robin Hood and Little John; they ~ed to have their arms and legs tied. – *vi* (3) he is a man who ~s to great knowledge / learning / an honour / generosity; I do not ~ to be learned; the scheming nobleman ~ed to the throne. (4) the children are only ~ing; play the game of 'let's ~'; let's ~ *(children's game).* – *adj* (5) ~ed kindness; a ~ed interest in art; his ~ed wealth was proved to be non-existent.

pretension *n* (1) the princess had ~s to the throne; his ~s to the money were acknowledged to be right; I have no ~s to learning; he makes no ~s to being an expert at the game; her ~s to superior judgement have no basis in fact. (2) he is a person without ~ *(is natural, sincere)*; he has little ~: even in London he dresses without much obvious interest in the result.

pretty *adj* (1) a ~ girl / child / face / picture / garden / cottage / *etc*; a ~ song / scene / story / piece of music; he writes ~ little stories; □ sitting ~ (→ sit *vi* 1 d) (2 *ironical*) here's a ~ mess; a ~ kettle of fish *(awkward state of affairs)* (3 *inform: considerable*) it'll cost him a ~ sum / penny.

pretty *adv* (1 *moderately*) it's ~ good; I am ~ well, thanks; a ~ good score; a ~ wealthy man (2 *very*) it's ~ hot / awful / late; a ~ nasty trick; the wind blew ~

hard; you had better do it ~ quick; that is ~ much the same thing.

prevail *vi* (1 ~ (up)on: *use persuasion successfully*) he ~ed upon us to accompany him; she can hardly ~ upon him to eat; try as I would, I could not ~ upon him to follow my advice. (2 *triumph*) they ~ed over their enemies in the battle; right will ~ (over wrong) in the long run; truth will ~ (over falsehood); we cannot hope to ~ against such overwhelming odds; reason will never ~ with some people. (3 *be common*) strong winds ~ in those regions; the ~ing wind (is a westerly); strange customs ~ among the inhabitants; superstition ~s among ignorant people. (4 *be predominant*) green tints ~ed in the upholstery.

prevent *vt* ~ war / an accident / a quarrel / *etc*; a severe cold ~ed his attending / him (from) attending the meeting; we did that to ~ the rain coming in; glass must be packed carefully to ~ it (from) breaking; only a miracle could have ~ed such a thing / that happening; that doesn't ~ him from / his being a damned fool; that must be ~ed at all costs.

prey *n* (1) the lion pursued his ~ / went in search of ~; a bird / beast of ~; the deer fell (a) ~ to the lion. (2) confidence tricksters and their ~; the banker turned out to be the swindler's easy ~; the poor are often the ~ of money-lenders; away from home the young man soon fell (a) ~ to those more cunning than himself; the ignorant are easy ~ *(potential victims)* for the unscrupulous; fall a ~ to a disease (3) he sat there, a ~ to gloom and despair; be a ~ to fear / anxiety / melancholy.

price *n* (1) buy / sell s.th. at a low / high ~; ask / charge a moderate / adequate / (un)reasonable / fancy / extravagant / exorbitant / excessive / *etc* ~; regular / normal / favourable / popular / ruinous / fixed / reduced ~s; what is the ~ of that watch? ~s are cheap here; his ~s are too high; ~ on request; ~s per day and person (at a hotel, *etc*); ~s subject to alteration; ~s rise / go up / drop / fall / remain stable / *etc*; → fetch 3; it must be done at any ~; □ every man has his ~ *(can be won over by a bribe, etc)*; put / set a ~ on s.th./ s.o.'s head (→ head *n* 6) (2) loss of health is a high ~ for success; his freedom was the ~ he paid for security; he gained the victory, but at a heavy ~; the ~ of fame (3 *value*) jewels of great ~; beyond / without ~ *(priceless)*: the crown jewels are beyond ~.

price *vt* (1 *find out the price of*) we spent the day ~ing furniture at various shops; we ~d several cars before buying. (2 *mark the price on*) all our goods are (clearly) ~d; a ~d catalogue *(one with prices)* (3 *fix the price of*) ~ the new stock; he ~s his goods very high; the rent was ~d too high for our family; low- / high-~d articles (4) ~ o.s. / one's goods out of the market *(fix prices so high that sales decline)*.

pride *n (1 feeling of satisfaction*) feel a natural ~ in one's success; we feel civic ~ in the new museum; take (a) ~ in one's work / achievement / appearance / *etc*; he told me with ~ that he ... (2 *proper self-respect*) his ~ kept him from asking for money; don't say anything that may wound his ~; false ~ *(tendency to avoid as degrading what is not so)*. (3) she is her mother's ~; the new school is the ~ of the district; this stamp is the ~ of his collection (4 the pride: *the best of a group*) this bull is the ~ of the herd. (5 *excessive self-esteem*) □ ~ goes / goeth before a fall; his ~ was his downfall; ~ took possession of him; ~ filled / blinded him (6 *most flourishing period*) in the ~ of manhood / youth.

principle *n* (1 *law of nature*) Archimedes' ~; the ~ of gravity / natural selection / *etc* (2 *essential truth on which other truths are based*) the ~s of political economy / modern physics / *etc*; scientific ~s; establish a ~ (3 *fundamental doctrine, tenet*) the ~s of the Stoics (4 *basic method of operation; essential characteristic*) the ~s of multiplication; he objects to the ~ of the thing, not to the method; a working ~ for general use; the ~ of the internal-combustion engine; a kindergarten run on modern ~s; a community organized on the patriarchal ~; in ~ *(as regards essentials)*: I agree in ~, but I dislike his methods; in ~ I have nothing against it, but ...; accept a plan in ~ (5 *actuating agency, force*) the interacting ~s of Good and Evil; the ~s of human behaviour (6 *basic rule of conduct*) abide by / have firm / sound / strict / cast-iron / no ~s; a guiding ~; a man of liberal ~s; live on the ~ of brotherly love; live up to / adhere to one's ~s; it's against my ~s; a man with ~s; faithful to the ~ that (the end justifies the means) (7 *guiding sense of what right conduct requires*) a man of (no) ~; he shows great concern for ~ in business affairs; I have made it a matter of ~ never to run into debt; on ~ *(as a matter of moral ~)*: an opponent on ~ of the death penalty; he never gambles, on ~; reject s.th. on ~; on ~ / as a matter of ~ he does not go to the cinema. (8 *constituent of a substance giving it some distinctive quality*) this bark contains a bitter ~ used in medicine; the active ~ of a drug; the fatty ~ of a substance.

print *n* (1) that ~ is too small to read; clear / illegible / large / small ~ (2 *act of printing*) rush an article / book into ~ *(hasten to publish it)* (3 *state of being printed*) dialect words rarely seen in ~; is the book still in ~ *(printed and on sale)*? be out of ~; he likes to see himself / his name in ~; I have never seen this tale in ~. (4 *picture, design made by printing*) a collection of old ~s (5 *photograph*) I want six ~s of that snapshot; contact / over-size ~s (6 *printed textile material*) she chose a pretty cotton ~ for her new dress; a coloured / floral / *etc* ~; a ~ dress (7 *letters like those used in* ~) write the address in ~. (8) the ~ of a human foot (in the sand); a finger- / foot-~ (9) her face bore the ~ of many hardships; the ~ of the age.

print *vt* (1) ~ a text / picture / design / pattern; ~ a manuscript; ~ visiting cards / (3,000 copies of) a book / an engraving / *etc*; ~ a word in capitals (2 *cause to be published*) do you intend to ~ your stories? (3 *produce a design on*) ~ a fabric (4 *produce a photograph from a negative*) you used too much light when you ~ed that picture; ~ (off) ten copies from a negative (5 *write in letters like those used in print*) ~ your name on these forms. (6) the mark of a foot was ~ed on the sand; the horses ~ed their hoofs on the wet grass. (7) the incident ~ed itself on her memory. - *vi* (9 → 5) please ~. (8) this film / plate / picture hasn't ~ed very well; the photograph has ~ed badly.

prison *n* (1) go to ~; send s.o. to ~ (for ten years); put s.o. in ~; throw / (*form*) cast s.o. into ~; be in ~; break out of ~; escape from ~; release / discharge s.o. from ~; a ~ sentence; a ~ cell (2) the body is the ~ of the soul; his office was a ~ to him on fine spring days; any cage is a ~ to the bird living in it. (3 *imprisonment*) ~ is no cure for first offenders.

prize *n* (1) compete for a ~; award s.o. a ~ for s.th.; win / gain a ~; take / carry off (the) first ~; draw a ~(-winning ticket) in a lottery / raffle; a consolation ~; a booby ~ *(given to s.o. who is last)* (2) this puppy is the ~ of the litter. (3 *thing worth struggling for*) the ~s of life; the ~s of the profession *(high posts, etc)*.

prize *vt* ~ s.o.'s friendship; ~ liberty more than life; my most ~d possessions.

problem *n* raise / discuss / tackle / attack / deal with / solve a (difficult / thorny / knotty / complicated / intricate / involved / serious / grave / *etc*) ~; moral social / present / *etc* ~s; the housing ~; a mathematical ~; the ~ is to find a suitable man.

proceed *vi* (1 *go on*) the trial is ~ing; the story ~s as follows; I now ~ to some further instances / the next item on the agenda; ~ with one's work / a speech; he ~ed to take off his coat / to inform me that I ... (2) ~ against s.o. *(take legal measures)* (3) the whole trouble ~ed from a misunderstanding; my criticism of your work ~s from a wish to help you; certain diseases ~ from dirt; strange sounds ~ from the chimney.

process *n* (1) the ~ of digestion; a natural / evolutionary / psychological ~; the ~ of water becoming ice; the ~ of growth is helped by proper nourishment (2) a new ~ for making steel; a chemical ~; this is a wasteful ~. (3) training to become a doctor is a lengthy ~; a house still in ~ of construction; be in the ~ of moving to a new neighbourhood; be in ~ of completion; in ~ of time *(as time goes on)*.

process *vt* ~ raw material; ~ milk / cheese / grain (in making cereals) / leather / *etc*; he now ~es 20 tons of potatoes a day; recent improvements in ~ing yeast by debittering have made it more palatable.

procure *vt* please ~ me a copy; I will ~ it for you; I must try to ~ one; I must ~ the money by tonight; this book is difficult to ~.

produce *n* wheat, potatoes, rice, grapes, oranges are all ~; agricultural / farm / dairy / garden ~; horticultural ~ is perishable.

produce *vt* (1) ~ one's passport / ticket (at the gate); the lawyer ~d the evidence during the trial; ~ proofs of a statement; ~ witnesses; after some searching she ~ed an old photograph from the drawer; the magician reached in his hat and ~d a rabbit. (2a) ~ a sound / note (2b) a tree that ~s good fruit; this soil / field ~s heavy crops; a mine ~ing silver; Australia ~s wool and meat. (2c) ~ electricity / steam / a vacuum / a (chemical) reaction; electric current ~d by a dynamo; friction ~s heat; bacteria that ~ fermentation (2d) ~ foodstuffs / meat / industrial products / chemicals; Germany ~d more wine this year than last; the leather-goods industry ~d less than expected. (2e) money invested ~s interest / dividends. (2f) ~ progeny / a litter of puppies / eggs / *etc*; it was a great thrill to both of them to have ~d a boy. (2g) this family / country has ~d a great artist / outstanding sportsman / *etc*; that century ~d few great men. (3) success ~d by hard work; ~ an effect / desire / conclusion; ~ hatred; the morphine ~d a feeling of contentment in him; his arrival ~d a sensation; statements calculated to ~ action (4) ~ a work of art; Dickens ~d many books; this author has ~d little in the last few years; has he ever ~d a novel? (5) ~ a play / film; 'Carmen', ~d by A.N. (6 *print; bind; design*) a well-~d book; these books are tastefully ~d.

product *n* (1) the ~s of a country; this medicine is a German ~; industrial ~s; staple ~s; the factory seeks a market for its ~s. (2) these evils were the ~ of laissez-faire; he is a true ~ of his time; his failure was a ~ of laziness. (3) a ~ of the imagination; the ~ of his thought. (4) the ~ of three times four is twelve.

production *n* (1) the ~ of industrial products / chemicals / agricultural produce; the ~ of electricity / steam / heat; mass ~; this firm specializes in the ~ of microscopes. (2 *quantity produced*) this year's ~ is higher than consumption; ~ has dropped in the last few months; a fall / increase in ~ (3) the show is now in ~; the ~ of literary work (4) he is famous for his imaginative Shakespeare ~s; an amateurish ~; this opera was an expensive ~; that film is one of the best ~s of last year. (5) the finest ~s of Michelangelo; the noblest ~s of literary genius; his early ~ as a writer; skilful artisans, whose choice ~s could secure a ready sale. (6 *designing, making, of books*) the ~ of the book, with its many coloured plates, photographs and drawings, is magnificent. (7) on ~ of the passport *(when the passport is shown)*; he demanded the ~ of evidence in support of the allegation.

profess *vt* (1 *declare openly that one has*) ~ principles / beliefs / interests / ignorance / *etc*; ~ a distaste for playing cards; they ~ed great admiration for his scholarship. (2 *claim*) he doesn't ~ to be an expert; he ~ed himself satisfied. (3 *declare falsely*) he ~es to be sorry but he doesn't look it; he ~ed extreme regret. (4) ~ Christianity / communism / a doctrine; he ~es a Protestant faith. (5a *follow as one's profession*) ~ law / medicine / sculpture (5b *teach as a professor*) he ~es history / modern languages / fencing.

professed *adj* (1 *admitted*) he is a ~ atheist; he is ~ly an authority on the subject. (2 *declared falsely*) ~ friendship; he is only ~ly poor. (3 *avowed*) a ~ nun.

profession *n* (1) the ~s of law, medicine, architecture and teaching are the learned ~s; the medical / legal / teaching ~; he is a lawyer / doctor / engineer / teacher / clergyman by ~; journalism is an overcrowded ~; take up / practise / exercise / pursue / carry on a ~; what ~ do you intend to follow? he has no fixed / settled ~; the question is whether to enter a ~ or seek a career in industry. (2 *any vocation, occupation*) a carpenter / dancer / *etc* by ~; the military ~ (3 *members of a ~ collectively*) an insult to the ~; it is against the etiquette of the ~; this healer is respected by the medical ~. (4 *statement of belief, feeling, etc*) a ~ of faith / loyalty / *etc*; ~s of regard; insincere ~s; in practice if not in ~ (5) the ~ of Christianity.

profit *n* (1) the net ~ is the actual gain; imaginary / hoped-for ~; ~ made; a firm's ~; the ~ of a firm / of a corporation / from a transaction; a firm makes a (handsome) ~ (on goods / the sale of goods); a transaction yields a ~; rake in huge ~s; have a share in the ~s; sell s.th. at a ~; the firm is working at a ~; do s.th. for ~; derive little ~ from a transaction; he writes for ~, not for pleasure. (2) having such an excellent teacher is to your ~; I have read that book to my ~; pursue graduate studies with ~; he gained a lot of ~ from his visit; there is no ~ in such counter-accusations.

profit *vi* he will not ~ much by doing that; we shall not ~ by such action; we ~ed by his good advice; her health ~ed from her stay at the seaside; I ~ed from reading that book / that experience; he ~s from the weaknesses of others.

progress *n* (1) we made no ~ through the heavy traffic; they made good / slow ~ up the mountain; the ~ of the planets (2) make good / great / fast / rapid / remarkable / astonishing / steady / slow/ *etc* ~; the ~ of man(kind) / civilization / science / etc; the cultural / economic / technological ~ of a country; ~ in medicine / technology / the mastery of a subject / *etc*; my work is making good ~; good ~ is being made on the electrification of ...; they are making good / satisfactory ~; we can notice Ted's ~ on the piano; the meeting was already in ~ *(going on)*; inquiries / preparations are in ~; there is some ~ towards a solution of the problem / a settlement of the dispute.

progress *vi* (1) ~ on a trip (2) a melody / a narrative / time ~es (3) the building operations (are) ~(ing) slowly; my work / research is ~ing (well); civilization ~es slowly; the disease has ~ed so far that an operation is unavoidable. (4) he ~ed in his studies / knowledge; ~ in mastery of a language; she has ~ed under (the / a) doctor's care; how are you ~ing with your driving lessons?

prolong *vt* (1) ~ a visit / one's stay / a journey; ~ a conversation / discussion; ~ a contract / armistice; ~ the term of payment; ~ life; a ~ed *(long)* visit / peace / period; ~ed questioning / negotiations; a succession of heavy and ~ed storms (2) ~ a line / wall.

promise *n* (1) make / give / keep / fulfil / carry out / break a (sacred / solemn) ~; a ~ to return soon; a ~ of a toy; a false ~; a ~ to marry (2 *firm expectation*) the fields give fair ~ of a good harvest; there's not much ~ of good weather. (3) a new writer of great ~; the land of ~.

promise *vt* (1) they ~d John a new bicycle for his birthday; ~ s.o. a warm welcome; she ~d help / to go tomorrow; ~ me that you will come. (2) early mist ~s a fine day; the sky ~d a storm. – *vi* (3 *assure*) it was not so easy, I ~ you; I won't go there again, I ~ you that! (4) did he ~? (5 *give cause to expect good results*) the crops ~ well; he ~s well as a mathematician; his forthcoming novel ~s well. – *adj* (6) a ~ing young man / situation / start.

promote *vt* (1) he was ~d (to be) captain; he was ~d to a captaincy / the rank of captain. (2) rain ~s the growth of plants; exercise ~s good health; a drug that ~s circulation; the government should ~ the arts; ~ science / research / (world) peace; ~ a scheme / a bill in Parliament; most countries ~ their foreign trade; ~ the development of the resources of backward countries; ~ friendship / good feelings / understanding between the nations; ~ s.o. in his career (3 *push the sales of s.th. by advertising*) a sales campaign to ~ a new product; American industry knows quite a bit about ~ing its wares. (4 *organize and start*) ~ a new business company (5 *organize, esp. financially, and present*) ~ a boxing match.

pronounce *vt* (1) ~ a word correctly / wrongly; ~ every syllable with care; she ~s (English) abominably. (2 *declare formally, authoritatively*) the judge ~d the man guilty; ~ sentence (of death) (on s.o.); the minister ~d them man and wife; the doctor ~d him free from infection; four days after the operation the boy was ~d out of danger; he ~d the meeting adjourned. (3 *declare as one's opinion*) the wine was tasted and ~d excellent; he ~d himself in favour of / against the candidate. – *vi* (4 *give judgement*) I can't ~ on a matter I know nothing of; the court of inquiry ~d for / against the employers; the country has ~d against any more nationalization.

pronounced *adj* (1 *strongly marked*) a ~ taste of peppermint (2 *very distinct*) a ~ contrast / tendency; a ~ success; she has ~ly Slav features; a ~ change in the weather (3 *decided*) have very ~ views; my opinion is a very ~ one; have a ~ dislike of s.th.

proof *n* (1) there was much evidence against the accused, but it did not amount to ~ of guilt; that is an absolute ~; clear / positive / conclusive / convincing / cogent / striking / cast-iron ~; documentary ~; give / produce /

adduce / provide ~ of s.th.; offer ~ that ...; this is ~ that he is lying; I want some ~ of what he says; his fingerprints were a ~ of his guilt; if ~ is needed for these statements; I have no ~ of it; he hesitated – a ~ that he was not very sure of himself. (2 *establishing the truth of*) the ~ of his client's innocence is up to the lawyer; this is not susceptible / capable of ~; here is a letter in ~ of his statement; the burden of ~ lies with the plaintiff. (3 *sign, token*) give / show ~ of one's gratitude / goodwill / intelligence *etc*; ~ of one's friendship; he has given us many ~s of his loyalty; show ~ of one's cowardice. (4 *test*) put a new invention to the ~; it must be brought to the ~; it has stood the ~; laboratory ~ of the presence of gold in the sample; □ the ~ of the pudding is in the eating *(quality is tested in practice)*. (5 *impression taken from type to make corrections, etc*) read / correct ~s; pass the ~s for press *(agree that printing may be begun)*.

proper *adj* (1) ~ behaviour; behave ~ly; is it quite a ~ book? it is not ~ for a young girl to go there; that is not the ~ thing for a schoolgirl; ~ people don't do that; a ~ young lady (2 *fitting, suitable*) water is the ~ element for fish; the meat was well done and ~ly seasoned; now is the ~ time to (plant strawberries); find the ~ (meaning of a) word; when a child has mastered a difficulty, praise is a ~ reward; give s.o. a ~ *(thorough)* tongue-lashing / whipping / *etc*; what is the ~ course to take? it must be done at the ~ time and in the ~ way; do as you think ~. (3 *accurate*) in the ~ sense of the word; the ~ name of these birds is Pinguin – it has been corrupted to Penguin; he is not ~ly speaking a chemist. (4 *belonging to*) the books ~ to this subject; festivities ~ to the occasion; privileges and duties ~ to an archbishop; diseases ~ to tropical climates (5 *strictly so called*) we didn't live in the hotel ~, but in an annex; shellfish do not belong to the fishes ~; Greece ~ *(not the islands)*.

property *n* (1) these books are my ~; whose ~ is this? he has a small ~ *(land and a house)* in the country. (2 *possessions*) he lost all his ~ in the fire; he is a man of ~ *(is wealthy)*; the secret of the invention became common ~; personal ~ *(movable things)*; real ~ *(land, buildings)*; private / public / enemy / other people's ~; literary ~ (3 *right to possess*) is private ~ in itself wrong? he had ~ in land. (4 *characteristic, quality*) the ~ies of water / a gas / a magnet / *etc*; the soothing ~ of an ointment; the natural ~ies of coal; plants with healing ~ies; it has the ~ of dissolving grease.

proportion *n* (1) payment in ~ to work done; the ~ of deaths to births / of men to women in a country; the ~ of sugar to flour in a cake (2 *satisfactory relation*) the door is out of ~ with the windows; a room of good ~s; your expensive tastes and your financial means are out of ~; a model village in which everything is in ~ / in the correct / right / wrong ~; his expenditure on luxuries is high in ~ to his income / to what he earns; the salary offered is out of (all) ~ / bears no ~ *(is far too high, low)* to the work involved; her anger was out of ~ to the offence; if only he could see things in ~, he would not make such a fuss about trivialities. (3 *~s: size*) a rock of gigantic ~s; a desert of vast ~s; a room of generous ~s (4 *a part in its relation to the whole*) a large ~ of the debt remains; a small ~ of the students are still here; a large ~ of the population is illiterate; we hope to pass a greater ~ of our candidates next year.

propose *vt* (1 *suggest*) ~ a plan / motion / new method; what salary do you ~? ~ a toast / s.o.'s health *(ask people to drink s.o.'s health)*; he ~d driving to London on the following day; I ~ stopping now; I ~ waiting till the police get here; he ~ed that a messenger (should) be sent; we ~d to our friends that we should all go to the theatre. (2) ~ s.o. for chairman / an office / (membership of) a club (3) has he ~d (marriage) to you? (4 *intend*) she ~s to catch the early train; the subject I ~ to discuss tonight is ...; what do you ~ to do when your funds run out? I ~ to stop now.

prosecute *vt* (1) the city ~d the man for stealing; ~ s.o. for libel / slander / theft / exceeding the speed limit; trespassers will be ~d. (2) the city ~d a claim against the man for stealing. (3 *carry on*) he ~d his trade in spite of all the difficulties that confronted him; ~ an inquiry / an investigation / one's studies; King John established a free port from which to ~ his war with Ireland.

prospect *n* (1) a house with a superb ~; a splendid ~ over the bay; they admired the ~ beneath them. (2 *mental view*) this book has opened a new ~ to my mind. (3) there is a ~ of a change in the weather; the ~(s) for the harvest; the future offers a gloomy / cheerful ~; the ~s of achieving the pact are not good; we have been given the ~ of various large orders; they held out to him the ~ of a new flat; that's a sad ~. (4 *~s: chance for success*) his is a job with good ~s; the scandal has greatly injured his ~s. (5) I see no / little / not much ~ of his recovery; is there any ~ of a meeting? I have little ~ of success; he has the ~ of an excellent job; he has an excellent job in ~. (6 *possible customer*) our salesmen have found a number of new ~s.

protect *vt* (1) ~ s.o. from the cold / rain / *etc*; ~ s.o. against the (inclemency of the) weather; they put up dikes to ~ the land (from being flooded); ~ s.o. from his enemies; ~ s.o. against his own rashness; effect an insurance policy to ~ o.s. against loss by fire. - *vi* (2) a floor wax that ~s as well as shines.

prove *vt* (1) ~ a fact / assertion / the truth of s.th.; ~ s.o.'s / one's identity / innocence; his innocence is not yet / has not yet been ~d; experience has ~d his theory; ~ one's claim; ~ a will *(establish its authenticity)*: when he died his will was ~d at over half a million; that remains to be ~d; the exception ~s the rule; he was ~d to be the person in question; ~ s.o.'s statements wrong / exaggerated; ~ s.o. wrong; I shall ~ to you (beyond doubt / conclusively / convincingly) that he ... (2 *show*) ~ one's goodwill / courage / worth (in adversity / as a friend) / ability / usefulness / *etc*; his action ~s his good heart / his good, bad taste / him to be a coward; he has ~d his loyalty over and over again; he ~d himself a true friend; the book has ~d its worth as an introduction to the English language; the device has ~ed (itself) a valuable aid on all occasions. (3 *turn out to be*) the story ~d (to be) quite false; should the news ~ true, ...; the document ~d to be a forgery; he ~d (to be) reliable; he ~ed (to be) a reliable friend; the mechanic ~ed satisfactory for the work; his pessimism ~ed justified; the new machine has ~ed a failure. (4 *test by experiment*) ~ an aircraft / gun / tank / rifle; ~ ore; tests are used to ~ things in laboratories; the new airliner made a successful ~ing flight from N. to D.; ~ a man's worth / courage.

proven *adj* (1 *verified*) N. is a ~ aggressor; that is a ~ fact / case of mumps / *etc.* (2 *esp AE tested*) a ~ (*also* proved) remedy for influenza.

provide *vt* (1) the trees ~ shade; ~ a plan / mechanism (for co-ordination); ~ food / clothing / a home / *etc* for s.o.; 20 beds have been ~d for the injured. (2) his mother ~d him with the necessary money; he ~d himself with what was necessary; his firm ~s him with a car; the book is ~d with an index. (3 *stipulate, state*) the lease ~s that the tenant shall ...; the law ~s that these buildings may not be demolished. - *vi* (4) ~ for / against contingencies; ~ for one's old age / family / *etc*; we must ~ against a bad harvest / for the future; in cutting material for a dress, you should ~ for shrinkage in the wash; he ~d for his children in his will; is he able to ~ for a wife?

provoke *vt* (1 *anger, enrage*) her rude answer ~d John; ~ s.o. to anger / fury; enough to ~ a saint; ~d beyond endurance; don't ~ the dog. (2 *stir up, arouse*) the mishap ~d a hearty laugh; ~ anger / indignation / curiosity / *etc*; the article ~d much criticism; ~ a smile / answer / reaction; ~ comment / comparison / retaliation (3 *stimulate to action*) he was at last ~d to read some poetry; his impudence ~d her into slapping him on the face. (4 *bring about*) what could have ~d such an incident / riot? their arrival ~d an international crisis; he did his best to ~ an argument; ~ appetite; ~ fermentation.

publish *vt* (1 *make known*) ~ scientific discoveries / a will / a decree / the banns of marriage; in this book several important finds are ~ed for the first time; a ~ed price *(fixed price of a book)* (2) ~ a book / periodical / map / piece of music / engraving / record; what year was this book ~ed? The Manchester Guardian Weekly will continue to be ~ed from Manchester. (3 *~ the books of*) Random House ~es Faulkner and other writers. - *vi* (4) we ~ every day except Sunday; the new house will start to ~ next month. (5) he has decided to ~ with another house.

pull *n* (1) the puppy gave my trousers a ~; give a ~ at a rope (2) it was a hard ~ (climb) up the hill. (3) the ~ of the moon on the tides; the ~ of the tide / a magnet / a heavenly body (4 *rowing*) he went for a short ~ on the lake. (5) he took a ~ at the bottle / a long ~ on his pipe. (6 *inform: advantage over*) he has a strong / not much ~ with the manager; get a job through ~ (7 *inform: power of attraction*) an advertising slogan with tremendous ~; an actress with great box-office ~.

pull *vt* 1-6, 7a, 8; *vi* 7b; 9-15. The patterns are grouped as follows: ~ + *obj* + *adj*: 1a; ~ + *obj* + *adv phrase*: 1a, 3, 8; ~ + *prepos*: at 9, 11; for 15.
(1a) horses ~ carts / wagons; ~ a sled up a hill; ~ the door open / shut; he ~ed me into the room; ~ s.th. closer / nearer; ~ s.th. towards one; ~ one's hat over one's eyes; ~ your chair to the table; they ~ed the rope round the tree several times; ~ s.o./ s.th. round a corner / obstacle; ~ s.th. apart / to pieces; we ~ed the old sheet to pieces for rags; *(fig)* I never get into conversation with her but she starts ~ing someone or other to pieces; *(fig)* he felt ~ed this way and that way by duty and by ambition. (1b *idioms*) ~ a fast one over / on s.o. *(inform: gain an advantage by a trick)*; ~ s.o.'s leg *(inform: try to make him believe what is not true)*; ~ one's punches *(attack less vigorously than one is able to; also fig)*; ~ one's socks up *(inform: make a greater effort)*; ~ strings *(exert one's personal influence)* ~ one's weight *(take one's full share of work, responsibility)*; ~ wires *(use influence to secure some advantage)*: it is he who ~s the wires; ~ the wool over s.o.'s eyes *(inform: deceive)* (2 ~ *out*) ~ a cork / nail / tooth; ~ weeds / turnips / *etc* (3 *tug at*) ~ s.o.'s hair; he ~ed my ears / sleeve; he ~ed me by the ears / sleeve. (4 *strain*) ~ a muscle / ligament / tendon; ~ a (wry) face / grimace; ~ faces; ~ a long face *(show signs of dislike)* (5 *draw out a small weapon ready for use*) do you know what to do when someone ~s a knife on you? (6) ~ a print *(take a proof from type)* (7 a row) ~ a boat; ~ a good oar *(row well)* (7b *vi*, → 7a) we ~ed ashore. (8) an engine which ~s such extraordinary performance and mileage out of so little petrol; great efforts will be needed to ~ the country through her present difficulties (→ pull through 2). – *vi* (9 → 1,3) the horse ~s well; be careful with this car – the brakes ~ to(wards) the left; the horseman ~ed at the reins; ~ at a rope; the rope ~ed apart. (10 *be capable of being ~ed*) the drawer won't ~ – it has got stuck. (11 *inhale, etc*) ~ at a pipe / cigar; ~ at a bottle (12) my pipe is ~ing very badly today. (13 *drive, run*) an old car ~ed into the drive; the ship ~ed out of the harbour; → pull out 2, pull over. (14 *fig: move*) we can't ~ out of the agreement now; → pull out 3. (15 *AE*) the spectators ~ed loudly for *(cheered)* the home team; I'll be ~ing *(hoping)* for you!

pull away (1) together they ~d the cart ~. (2) the dress has ~ed ~ at the seams; the sleeve is ~ing ~ from the armhole. (3) it was hard for him to ~ ~ from the ties of home.

pull back (1) the troops ~ed ~ beyond / to the line of fire. (2) suddenly the man ~ed ~ his fist and slammed it into the mirror.

pull down (1) she ~ed the blinds ~. (2) ~ ~ a house (and rebuild it) (3) an attack of fever soon ~s you ~.

pull in (1) I would have fallen out had he not ~ed me in; ~ s.th. in through the window; the fishermen ~ in their nets. (2) has the train from A. ~ed in yet? the driver ~ed in at a roadside café; the boat ~ed in to the shore. (3) you will have to ~ in (your expenses) if you want to escape bankruptcy; □ ~ in one's belt *(inform: live frugally)*.

pull off (1) who ~ed the handle ~? ~ ~ one's hat / shoes / gloves; ~ ~ a ring (from one's finger) (2) I'm hoping that I may ~ ~ *(succeed in getting)* a scholarship to Oxford; did you manage to ~ the bargain ~? it was a difficult feat, but he ~ed it ~.

pull on (1) ~ one's gloves / stockings on (2) let's ~ *(row)* on.

pull out (1) ~ ~ hair / feathers; ~ ~ a tooth; ~ ~ a drawer; he ~ed ~ a big wallet. (2) ... only to see the train just ~ing ~ (of the station; → pull *vi* 13); the boat ~ed ~ into midstream. (3) we are so deeply committed that we can't ~ ~ now (→ pull *vi* 14).

pull over the car ~ed ~ when I blew my horn; suddenly the car in front of us ~ed ~ *(moved across the road)*.

pull round (1) ...; but she is ~ing ~ nicely now *(inform: recovering from illness)*; under the new management the firm should ~ ~. (2) ~ s.o. ~ by careful nursing; ~ a firm ~.

pull through (1) with careful nursing the patient should ~ ~; our firm has always ~ed ~. (2) the doctor will ~him ~; he was determined to ~ the firm ~ (→ pull *vt* 8).

pull together (1) if we all ~ ~ we may succeed (2) ~ a team / organization ~ (3) ~ yourself ~, man!

pull up (1) ~ up the blind; he ~ed himself up on the wall; ~ one's socks up (→ pull *vt* 1b) (2) he ~ed up a daisy on the lawn; □ ~ up trees *(inform: achieve good results)*: he isn't the kind of person who is likely to ~ up many trees. (3) ~ up a chair (→ pull *vt* 1a) and sit down. (4 *come to a stop*) the car ~ed up outside the Town Hall; ~ up at the 'George' for lunch / the traffic lights; ~ up sharp / short *(stop suddenly)* (5 *bring to a stop*) the policeman ~ed up the motorist and ... (6 *reprimand*) ~ s.o. up (sharp) about / for his bad behaviour / laziness / carelessness / *etc* (7) ~ up *(improve)* one's French / knowledge / *etc* (8) the racehorse ~ed up from last to third / fourth to first (position).

punish *vt* (1) ~ s.o. (heavily / severely / *etc*) for a crime / a fault / misconduct / cheating / *etc*; ~ s.o. with / by a fine (2) how would you ~ theft / lying / *etc*? crimes are ~ed by the law; the crime was ~ed by death. (3 *inform: handle roughly*) ~ an opponent / an engine (4 *inform: use up; eat; drink*) ~ one's food *(eat much)*; ~ a quart of whisky *(drink it)*; ~ the cold beef. - *adj* (5) a ~ing *(exhausting)* race / defeat.

punishment *n* (1) the ~ of crime / an offence / an offender; ~ of / for illegal possession of firearms (2) the ~ was a fine; make the ~ fit the crime; inflict a ~ on s.o. for s.th.; deserve / receive / get / undergo / suffer a ~; a light / heavy / harsh / severe / (un)just / (un)deserved ~.

purchase *n* (1) make / effect / negotiate a (good / advantageous / *etc*) ~; acquire s.th. by ~; ~ on approval / as per sample; ~ and sale; contract / deed of ~ (2 *thing bought*) I brought my ~ home to show you; this clock is a recent ~ of mine. (3 *firm hold, grip*) secure a ~ on s.th.; I cannot get a ~ on it.

purchase *vt* (1) ~ an estate / valuable picture / diamond ring / *etc*; (2) ~ one's life at the expense of one's honour; ~ independence / freedom with one's blood; a dearly ~d victory (3) expert flattery may ~ an honest man. (4) the ~ing power of money.

purport *n* (1 *meaning*) the main ~ of his letter; he gave the ~ of their talk in a few words. (2 *purpose*) the main ~ of his visit to France.

purport *vt (profess, often falsely; seem to mean; imply)* a document ~ing to be official; the book ~s to be a translation; a law that ~s to be in the interest of morality; men ~ing to be citizens; a society which ~s to be classless, but is ...; the message ~ed to come from the president; what do his actions ~?

purpose *n* (1) for what ~ is this instrument? collect money for a charitable ~; use tax money for legitimate ~s; for practical ~s; what is the ~ of this law? answer / serve one's / the ~; serve a dual ~; this suits / answers my ~ (very well); there was a ~ behind his remark; a novel with a certain ~ (2) have a ~ in life; what was your ~ in doing that? it was certainly not my ~ to offend you; I came here for the ~ of seeing you; carry out one's ~s with tenacity; attain / achieve one's ~; he never did anything without a ~; do s.th. with honesty of ~; men of honest ~; □ of set ~ *(deliberately)*: the insult was made of set ~; do s.th. on ~ *(intentionally)*: how could he do such a thing on ~? he has left the book here on ~ for you to read; be wanting in ~ (3 *result*) he works hard, but to no ~; it would be to no ~ (to speak to him); to act to good ~ *(with great success)*; to the ~ *(relevant)*: none of her objections were to the ~.

pursue *vt* (1) ~ a thief / a fugitive / the enemy / one's prey (2 *move along*) he ~d the river to its source; *(fig)* he felt their eyes ~ing him. (3 *fig: follow close upon*) bad luck ~d him; be ~d by misfortune (4 *seek to attain*) ~ an end / a purpose; ~ an / one's / the same object; ~ pleasure (5 *proceed in accordance with*) ~ a method / plan (6 *continue*) ~ a journey / course of action / train of thought / inquiry / policy; ~ one's studies / way; ~ a topic / subject; she ~d her struggle to gain fame. (7 *practise*) ~ a profession / occupation / hobby / pastime; ~ law as a profession; determined to be a great actress, she ~d the theatre with such intensity ...

push *n* (1) give s.o. a (playful) ~; give the door a hard ~; he opened the gate with /

at one ~; □ at a ~ *(if absolutely necessary)*: we can sleep eight people in the house at a ~; □ when / until it comes to the ~ *(critical moment)*: when it came to the ~ I found I had forgotten everything. (2 *strong effort*) make a ~ to finish the job (3 *determination*) he hasn't enough ~ to succeed; a man of ~ and go (4 *influence*) use ~ (to get s.th.) (5) give s.o. the ~ *(inform: dismiss him)*; get the ~.

push *vt* 1 - 9; *vi* 10 - 14.
(1) we ~ed the desk, but it was too heavy to move. (2) ~ a bicycle uphill; you ~ (the cart) and I'll pull (it); she ~ed the pram into / out of the room; he ~ed him off the wall; ~ a cork into a bottle; ~ a button; ~ a door open / shut / to; ~ him out of the way; ~ o.s. forward *(also fig: get attention)* (3) ~ one's way through the crowd; □ ~ one's way *(make one's way by being forceful)*; □ ~ one's fortune *(utilize every chance of advancing it)* (4 *urge*) they ~ed him into doing it; we ~ed him to do his homework / make a speech; ~ s.o. for payment; I don't want to ~ you *(inconvenience by urging)*; be ~ed for *(short of)* money / time / room / help (5 *force towards the limits of capacity*) they ~ed the child too hard at school. (6 *use influence to help*) ~ a friend; haven't you got someone who can ~ you? (7 *get accepted*) ~ a bill through Congress; ~ a claim / one's claims; ~ one's wares; the shop is ~ing *(trying hard to sell)* toys because the Christmas rush is over; the salesman tried to ~ inferior merchandise on his customers; all the unpleasant jobs are ~ed on to me. (8 *develop, esp to an extreme degree*) ~ an idea; he ~ed the argument one step further; ~ a doctrine to extremes; ~ an analysis too far (9 *inform: approach in age or number*) he's ~ing 60 (years) / 200 pounds. - *vi* (10) he ~ed at the door, but it wouldn't open; you ~ *(the cart)* and I'll pull (→ 2); please do not ~. (11) he ~ed through the crowd; the rude fellow ~ed past (me). (12 *move*) ~ing still further south we come to Australia. (13 *be capable of being ~ed*) a swinging door that ~es easily (14 *make a strong effort*) ~ for more pay / higher wages.

push along (1) the men were ~ing a heavy cart ~ in front of them. (2) I must ~ ~ now, it's nearly 8 o'clock; we shall have to ~ ~ if we want to reach the village before evening.

push around he seems to think that his task in life is to ~ others ~; I am not going to be ~ed ~ by him.

push aside ~ ~ all obstacles; ~ s.o. ~.

push away she ~ed ~ her plate; he ~ed her ~ angrily.

push back he ~ed ~ his chair; the police ~ed ~ the crowd.

push down he ~ed him ~ off the wall; the bullock ~ed the boy ~.

push off (1) then we ~ed ~ (from the land) *(in boating)*. (2 *inform*) it's ten o'clock - it's time we were ~ing ~.

push on (1) we shall have to ~ on if we wish to reach the village before evening; the army ~ed on through the snow; we are ~ing on with the work as fast as circumstances will permit. (2) ~ on s.o. to do s.th.; ~ on a pupil; ~ things on.

push out (1) who ~ed the pram ~? reporters were immediately ~ed ~; she ~ed ~ her lower lip; plants ~ ~ new roots. (2) the cape ~es ~ into the sea.

push over (1) he ~ed the chest ~ to me. (2) don't ~ me ~! he ~ed the chair ~.

push through (1) the chest was wide, but we managed to ~ it ~. (2) the pressure from the crowd ~ed the shop window ~. (3) ~ a matter ~ *(bring it to a conclusion)*; the government wanted to ~ the Bill ~ (Parliament).

push up (1) ~ up a window; he ~ed up his spectacles; □ ~ up (the) daisies *(be dead)*: another year of this and I'll be ~ing up daisies. (2) the wage increase ~ed up prices; ~ up sales.

put *vt* 1-17; *vi* 18.
The patterns are grouped as follows: ~ + *obj* + *adj*: 16; ~ + *obj* + *prepos* + *n*: 1-13, 15, 17; ~ + *obj* + *prepos* + *n*: at 6a, 12; in, into 4b, 6, 13; on 4c; out of 6; to 5, 6, 13b, 15; ~ + *obj (abstract n)* + *prepos* + *n*: 11; ~ + *obj* + *prepos* + *abstract n*: 9; ~ + *obj* + *prepos* + *n* (idiomatic meaning): 10; ~ + *obj* (part of the body) + *prepos* or *adv*: 7a; ~ + *obj* + *prepos* + *n* (part of the body): 7b; ~ + *prepos*: into 18; on, upon 14; to 18.
(1 *place, set in the basic local sense*)
~ the books / one's elbows on the table; he ~ his hands in(to) his pockets / to his ears; he ~ his arm round her; ~ a leaf into a file; ~ a screw in the wood; ~ the plug in the socket; ~ a cupboard closer to the

wall; ~ a wire / string / bandage round s.th.; ~ coal on the fire; ~ a match to the kindling wood / documents / leaves / *etc (ignite and burn)*; ~ a thing in(to) its proper place; ~ the car in the garage; ~ plants in the ground; ~ an arrow to the bow; ~ *(sew)* a patch on a dress; ~ spurs to a horse; ~ milk in the tea / a little more salt in the soup; ~ a child / sick person to bed; he is going to ~ a new engine in his car; ~ a dog on the chain; ~ s.o. in fetters / irons / chains; ~ a horse to the cart; ~ a new handle to a knife; ~ an obstacle in s.o.'s way *(also fig)*; he was ~ out of the room for being impudent; ~ one's pen to paper *(start writing)*; I didn't know where to ~ myself *(because of embarrassment)*; ~ a child to school *(have it taught there)*; ~ a child in a special school; ~ s.o. in prison / jail.

(2 *thrust; send*)

~ a knife into s.o. *(inform: stab him)*; ~ a bullet through s.o.('s head) *(inform: shoot him)*; ~ a satellite into orbit (round the earth); ~ a man on the moon; ~ the shot / weight *(in athletics)*.

(3 *write*)

I ~ a mark against his name; ~ s.th. in black and white; ~ the prices on articles; ~ one's signature to a document; ~ s.th. on paper.

(4a *similar to* put 1 *but fig*)

~ a tax on beer; ~ an advertisement in a paper (for s.th.); he ~s Keats above Byron; the experts refused to ~ a price on the Rubens painting; ~ competition in a strait-jacket; ~ one's feelings into a song; ~ power into the hands of s.o.; ~ s.th. on the market *(offer for sale)*; ~ a play on the stage; ~ a bus on the road *(start operating it)*; ~ one's pen through a word *(strike it out)* ~ a horse through its paces *(test it)*; ~ a man on a job *(assign him to work at it)*: I don't think I've a man I can ~ on that job this morning; I wouldn't ~ it past him (to cheat his own mother) *(think him capable of doing, esp of undesirable things)*.

(4b *put in, into: invest*)

~ one's money in real estate; ~ one's savings into securities; ~ money into the lottery.

(4c *put on: gamble*)

he ~ his last penny / a pound on that horse.

(5 *submit*)

~ a proposal / question before / to s.o. / a committee / *etc*; ~ s.o. a question; ~ a suggestion / one's views to a meeting / board / *etc*; ~ a question to the vote; ~ a motion / resolution (to a meeting) *(to be voted on)*; one member of the committee wished to ~ an amendment; □ ~ the question *(ask those present to vote)*.

(6a *put + s.o./s.th. + preposition + noun: cause to do, this verb being more or less identical with the noun*)

~ s.th. at the service of s.o.; ~ a machine / plant in action / operation; ~ s.th. into force (→ force *n* 6); ~ s.th. in motion; ~ books / work / affairs / a room in order; ~ names in alphabetical order (→ order *n* 1); ~ a ladder / *etc* in position; ~ s.o. in possession of the facts / *etc*; ~ s.th. into reality; ~ a machine / pump / *etc* out of action / order; ~ a gun / a ship / a tank out of action; ~ birds / an outlaw / an army to flight; ~ a dog / cat to sleep *(kill it)*; ~ a prisoner to death; ~ s.o. to (great) expense; ~ s.o. to the blush.

(6b *put + s.o./ s.th. + preposition + noun: cause to be done, this verb being more or less identical with the noun*)

~ s.th. in(to) practice; ~ s.th. into production; ~ ideas / *etc* into shape *(arrange them)*; ~ s.th. into / out of use; ~ a knife / *etc* out of (a child's) reach; ~ a sum to s.o.'s credit (→ credit *n* 5); ~ s.o. to (great) inconvenience; ~ s.o. to ransom *(cause him to pay ransom)*; ~ s.th. to the test; ~ s.o.('s loyalty / courage) to the test; ~ s.o. to trial; ~ s.o. to torture; ~ s.o. to trouble (→ trouble *n* 1); ~ s.th. to good use; give me your old bicycle, I can ~ it to good use; ~ one's knowledge to practical use; ~ s.th. to (a) bad use; □ be (hard) ~ to it *(have great difficulty; AE also* be hard put*)*: we were ~ to it to find the missing notebook; I was hard ~ to it to find the money to pay my debts; he was hard ~ to it to satisfy his creditors; you would be hard ~ to it to find a pleasanter place than this.

(7a *put + n [part of the body] + preposition or adverb; idiomatic*)

~ one's back into s.th. *(work with all one's energy)*; ~ s.o.'s back up *(inform: annoy, anger him)*; ~ a bold / good / *etc* face on s.th. (→ face *n* 5); ~ one's finger on (the cause of the trouble); ~ one's foot down *(show strong determination, be firm)*; ~ one's best foot foremost *(walk very fast;* → put forward 1*)*; ~ one's foot in it *(inform: make a tactless remark)*; ~ one's foot in one's mouth *(AE say/ do s.th. indis-*

creet); when he ~s a foot wrong *(makes the smallest mistake)* the manager is down on him; ~ one's hand in(to) one's pocket *(spend, give money)*; ~ one's hands in one's pockets *(leave action to others)*; ~ one's hand to a task / *etc (start working at it)*; the three of you must ~ your heads together and come up with an idea; ~ s.o.'s mind at rest (→ mind *n* 2c); ~ s.o.'s nose out of joint (→ nose *n* 1); ~ one's shoulder to the wheel (→ shoulder *n* 1).

(7b *put + s.o./s.th. + preposition + noun [part of the body]*)
~ s.o. out of countenance *(disconcert him)*; ~ o.s. in(to) s.o.'s hands *(give him power to decide for one)*; will you ~ the matter in(to) my hands? ~ s.th. into s.o.'s head / mind *(suggest it to him)*; ~ s.th. out of s.o.'s head *(cause him to forget)*; ~ the idea out of your head *(give it up)*; ~ s.th. from / out of one's mind (→ mind *n* 1); ~ s.th. into s.o.'s mind (→ mind *n* 1); ~ s.o. in mind of s.o./ s.th. (→ mind *n* 1).

(8 *put s.o. + preposition + noun expressing emotion*)
~ s.o. at his ease (→ ease *n* 1); ~ s.o. in fear (→ fear *n* 1); ~ s.o. in a good humour; ~ s.o. in a rage; ~ s.o. in a state of anxiety; ~ s.o. in(to) a good / bad mood; → temper *n* 1a.

(9 *put s.o. + preposition + abstract noun*)
~ s.o. in charge of s.o./ s.th. (→ charge *n* 6); ~ s.o. in / out of danger (→ danger 1); ~ s.o. in a difficulty (→ difficulty 1); ~ s.o. in a difficult / dangerous / *etc* position (→ position *n* 7); ~ s.o. in the picture *(inform: give him full information)*: I don't know precisely what the position is - please ~ me in the picture; ~ o.s. in s.o.'s place (→ place *n* 2) / position (→ position *n* 7); ~ s.o. in his place (→ place *n* 10); ~ s.o. in the wrong (→ wrong *n* 1); ~ s.o. into power (→ power *n* 5) ~ s.o. off his guard *(make him incautious)*; ~ s.o. on his guard *(warn him)*; ~ s.o. off his stroke *(interfere with what he is doing)*: your interruption has ~ me off my stroke; ~ s.o. off the scent (→ scent *n* 2); ~ s.o. on his honour (not) to do s.th.; ~ s.o. on (his) oath (→ oath 1); ~ s.o. on (to) the right path; ~ s.o. on the wrong track; the dying dog was shot to ~ him out of pain / his misery; ~ s.o. out of the way *(kill, imprison him)*; the police ~ him through a severe examination *(examined him severely)*; ~ s.o. through an ordeal; □ ~ s.o. through it *(inform: test thoroughly; inflict suffering to make him confess)*; ~ s.o. through his paces *(test his abilities)*; ~ s.o. to shame *(shame him by doing better)*: when Mary sings she ~s me to shame - her voice is so much better than mine.

(10 *put + concrete noun + preposition + noun; idiomatic*)
~ (all) one's cards on the table (→ card 2); ~ the cart before the horse *(reverse right order)*; ~ all one's eggs in one basket (→ egg 1); ~ the lid on s.th. *(inform: outdo all earlier examples of; put an end to)*; these latest regulations have ~ the lid on our plans; ~ money before morals (→ money 1); ~ a spoke in s.o.'s wheel *(inform: obstruct his designs)*; you can ~ that in your pipe and smoke it *(inform: you can say nothing against it)*; ~ the wind up s.o. (→ wind *n* 1a).

(11 *put + abstract noun + preposition + noun*)
~ the blame on s.o. (→ blame *n* 1); ~ an end / stop to a discussion / nuisance / practice / *etc*; he ~ an end to himself / his life (→ end *n* 2); ~ one's faith in s.th. (→ faith 1); ~ a (false) interpretation on (events / *etc)*; ~ life into s.th. (→ life 8); ~ a limit to one's outlay / *etc* (→ limit *n*); ~ one's mind to a problem / one's work (→ mind *n* 2c); ~ pressure on s.o. (→ pressure *n* 3); ~ the responsibility on s.o.; ~ a restraint on s.o.; ~ spirit into one's work / *etc* (→ spirit 5); ~ a high value on s.o.'s service / *etc* (→ value *n* 1); ~ one's / a veto on s.th.

(12 *put at: estimate*)
I ~ her fur coat at £200; he ~s the distance at five miles; ~ s.o.'s age at sixty.

(13a *put in, into, or + adverb: formulate*)
~ s.th. into words; ~ s.th. in writing; the speaker ~ his case plainly; he ~ his arguments very well / clearly ; how well you ~ it! ~ s.th. bluntly; □ to ~ it in a nutshell *(say it briefly)*.

(13b *put in, into, to: translate; adapt*)
~ a text into Russian; how would you ~ it in French? ~ a poem to music; ~ prose into verse.

(14 *put on, upon: take advantage of s.o.'s good nature*)
some of the employees felt ~ upon when they were asked to work late; rather than do anything for herself she will ~ upon others; I don't mind obliging other people,

but I do object to being ~ upon; don't let yourself be ~ on.
(15 *put + to + [usually]-ing: set to work*)
~ the troops to digging trenches; ~ her to setting the table; ~ a boy to shoemaking / a trade.
(16 *put + noun + adjective*)
~ the price too high; we must ~ the room shipshape / straight before our guests come; the servants ~ everything shipshape in the kitchen; □ ~ first things first *(do things in order of importance)*; ~ right a mistake / pupil; what's the time - I want to ~ my watch right; the light wouldn't work yesterday, but it has been ~ right now; can you ~ this machine right? if I am / something is wrong, please ~ me / it right.
(17 *take, transport by boat*) can you ~ me across the river *(in a ferry-boat)*?
vi (18 *move, of ships*)
the steamer ~ (out) to sea; the yacht ~ into Malta for stores;→ put back 4, put in 7, put off 9, put out 14.

put about (1) ~ ~ *(spread)* a story / rumour; who has ~ ~ this wicked lie? (2) the guest did not wish to ~ his hostess ~ *(inconvenience her)*. (3) she was very ~ ~ *(worried)* by his long absence / when she heard that he ... (4) ~ ~ a boat *(change its course)*; there's a storm coming, we must ~ ~.

put across (1) ~ s.th. ~ to an audience *(convey its meaning effectively)*; he understands his subject well, but can he ~ it ~? children should be taught by someone who understands them and knows how to ~ a subject ~ (to them) in a classroom; ~ ~ a song *(sing it effectively)*: N. doesn't have much of a voice but he knows how to ~ a song ~ anyway. (2) let's ~ something ~ Jack *(inform: deceive him)* - he will believe anything; don't think you're going to ~ that story ~ us. (3) ~ a business deal ~ *(inform: make a success of it)*.

put aside (1) ~ this ~ for me; he ~ his work ~ when I entered his office. (2) I ~ ~ ten shillings every week; we must ~ some of this food ~ for tomorrow.

put away (1) ~ ~ the dishes / toys / *etc*; ~ the car ~ *(in the garage)* (2) ~ ~ money *(save it)* (for a trip / one's old age) (3) when he became a man, he ~ ~ childish thoughts; ~ ~ care (4) ~ ~ food / drink *(inform: consume)* *(5 place in confinement, in a mental home)* he acted so strangely that he had to be ~ ~.

put back (1) ~ things ~ (where they belong); ~ a book ~ on the shelf (2) he ~ his watch ~ an hour; ~ the clock ~ *(also fig.: reverse progress)* (3) he was progressing well after his illness, but the cold weather has ~ him ~; cloudy weather often ~s ~ the ripening of the grain; the strike ~ ~ production badly. (4) the boat ~ ~ *(returned)* (to harbour); the small boat ~ ~ to shore.

put by (1) ~ by *(save)* money; he's got a few hundred pounds ~ by; □ ~ s.th. by for a rainy day (2) ~ by *(ignore)* a problem / a suggestion / difficulties; he ~ the idea by and then forgot about it; Smith was ~ by in favour of Miller.

put down (1) ~ ~ a load; ~ ~ the tray; ~ the tray ~ on the table; ~ that knife / gun / *etc* ~! □ ~ one's foot ~ (→ put *vt* 7a) (2) the bus stopped to ~ ~ passengers. (3 *BE*) ~ ~ *(preserve)* eggs; ~ ~ wine *(store it in a cellar)*; he has ~ ~ a good cellar of wine. (4) ~ ~ *(write)* an address; ~ s.th. ~ on paper; ~ s.th. ~ in black and white; ~ the particulars ~ in one's notebook; ~ the shoes ~ to my account *(charge them to me in your books)*; you can ~ the drinks ~ to me; ~ me ~ for £2 *(as willing to give to charity, etc)*; ~ my name ~ for the competition / trip to B. / *etc.* (5) ~ ~ an amount of money *(pay in a lump sum)* (6) ~ ~ an animal *(kill painlessly)* (7) ~ ~ a rising / a rebellion / resistance; the rebels were soon ~ ~; ~ ~ pilfering / gambling; ~ ~ *(silence)* a heckler at a meeting (8) I should ~ him ~ *(consider)* as, for a teacher / fool / etc. (9) I ~ his failure ~ to laziness / carelessness / *etc*; ~ a remark ~ to bad humour.

put forth (1) ~ ~ buds / shoots / leaves / blossoms / fruit / roots; deer ~ ~ antlers. (2) no one has ~ ~ a workable solution. (3) ~ ~ *(exert)* all one's strength; we will have to ~ ~ our best efforts to win; she had to ~ ~ all her charm in order to ...

put forward (1) he ~ his watch ~ an hour; □ ~ one's best foot ~ (*walk / work as fast as one can;*→ put *vt* 7 a) (2) ~ s.o. / o.s. ~ (as candidate); he ~ himself ~ as the only man who could save the country; we ~ him ~ for treasurer.

put in (1) he ~ his head in at the window; he has bought his furniture before he has a house to ~ it in; □ ~ one's oar in *(in-*

form: interfere): who told you to ~ your oar in? ~ in a cartridge / film; ~ in a new pane of glass / a part of a machine; ~ the car in *(the garage)*; ~ in a screw; ~ the dirty washing in (to soak); ~ in electricity / gas / the telephone (2)" ~ in your stomach!" cried the sergeant. (3) ~ in an appearance (at the meeting) *(be present for a short time)* (4) ~ in *(do)* two hours' weeding ; how much time does he ~ in at the office? ~ in an hour's piano practice (5) ~ in *(insert)* a pause / extra lesson; he talked so fast that I could not ~ in a single word; ~ in one's word *(make a remark)*; ~ in a (good) word (with s.o.) for s.o.; ~ in a claim for s.th. (to an insurance company); I have ~ in a request for a telephone / a complaint at the police station. (6) how many candidates did your school ~ in for the G.C.E. examination this year? ~ in a caretaker / bailiff *(install in office)* (7) let's ~ in at that restaurant and have some lunch; when does the liner ~ in at London? (8) "Why are you going there?" John ~ in. (9) did you ~ in for that post in the library? the engineers are ~ting in for an increase in wages; he ~ in for a week's holiday / a transfer to London.

put off (1) a bus / the conductor ~s ~ the passenger; where do you want to be ~ ~? (2) ~ ~ doubts / fears / childish fancies (3) ~ ~ the light / wireless / gramophone / central heating; ~ ~ a gas fire / electric radiator (4) ~ s.th. ~ to a later date; ~ ~ one's departure; ~ ~ a meeting / match; ~ ~ going to the doctor / doing s.th. unpleasant; ~ s.o. ~ *(postpone an engagement made with him)* (5) he ~ me ~ with a couple of words; she tried to ~ ~ the landlord with many hard-luck stories; ~ s.o. ~ by promising s.th. / by giving an excuse / with fine words / with an excuse (6) a difficulty ~s s.o. ~; that will not ~ me ~ from doing what I think right; they had intended going into the country for the day, but were ~ ~ by reports of traffic jams; don't let Jack ~ you ~ going to L.; Tom ~ me ~ my trip to Japan by telling me... (7) when I saw the maggot in the cheese I was rather ~ ~ having another slice; the bad smell has ~ me ~ my food; his manners are enough to ~ anyone ~ completely. (8) I don't like people talking when I am writing a letter - it ~s me ~ *(inform: distracts)*; his coughing ~ me ~. (9) the boat ~ ~ earlier this morning; they got into a boat and ~ ~ at once.

put on (1) ~ on paint / a coating of fat / a table-cloth / a gramophone record / the kettle; ~ water / the soup / the vegetables on (to boil); ~ the meal on (to cook) (2) ~ on a dress / winter clothes / make-up / all one's decorations / one's spectacles (3) she has ~ on pounds living here; ~ on flesh / weight (4) ~ on *(increase)* speed / pace / pressure / a spurt; □ ~ it on *(overcharge)*: some of the hotels ~ it on during the holiday season. (5) ~ the light / wireless / gas-fire / night-latch on (6) ~ on the brakes / a brake *(also fig)* (7) ~ ~ *(operate additionally)* an extra train / relief bus (8) ~ting on a play takes up a lot of time and energy. (9 *assume an attitude, often deceptively*) ~ on an act; ~ on airs *(show conceit)*; ~ it on *(behave deceptively)*: he looked very sad but it was all ~ on; ~ on a grave expression / an aggrieved look / an air of joviality / innocence / *etc*; ~ one's best face on (→face *n* 5); →front 4 (10) he ~ his watch ~ an hour.

put out (1) have you ~ the cat ~? ~ a chair ~ on the balcony; don't get drunk or they'll ~ you ~. (2) he ~ ~ his hand for me to shake; ~ one's tongue ~ (for the doctor / at a person); the bush ~ ~ buds. (3) the teacher ~ ~ books and pencils for his pupils; ~ ~ clean clothes (4) ~ ~ a joint *(dislocate)*: he fell and ~ his shoulder ~. (5) ~ ~ a fire / candle / coal fire; ~ ~ the light / gas (-fire); the light will be ~ ~ soon. (6) ~ ~ s.th. *(produce industrially)*: the firm ~s ~ 1,000 bales of cotton sheeting every week. (7) ~ ~ a book / pamphlet *(publish)* (8) ~ ~ work *(to be done off the premises)*; all repairs are done on the premises and not ~ ~; ~ one's girls ~ to service *(cause one's daughters to work as maids)*; we ~ ~ the washing. (9) ~ ~ money *(invest)* (at interest); he has £1,000 ~ ~ at 5 per cent. (10) you've ~ our whole plan ~ by arriving late. (11) the stranger did not want to ~ us ~ *(inconvenience us)* by accepting our invitation; he ~ himself ~ to help me. (12) be very ~ ~ *(upset)* by s.o.'s behaviour / long absence; the least thing ~s him ~. (13) ~ ~ *(exert)* all one's strength; they were ~ting ~ their best efforts; Uncle ~ himself ~ to give us a good time. (14) the ship ~ ~ to sea; the ship ~ ~ from harbour.

put over (1) he always ~s ~ his ideas very well; she has a talent for ~ting ~ any good song; ~ ~ a film / play / policy *(secure appreciation for it)*; ~ o.s. ~ on an audience *(impress one's personality on it)* (2) ~ one ~ s.o. *(win by doubtful means)*; be careful or he'll ~ something ~ you; nobody ~s anything ~ me - I'm much too clever; ~ s.th. / one ~ on s.o.

put through (1) operator, can you ~ me ~ now? please ~ me ~ to extension 104; I want to ~ a call ~ to Mr N. / Hamburg. (2) ~ ~ a business deal; the new plan has been ~ ~ successfully.

put to ~ a door to *(almost close it)*.

put together (1) ~ a machine ~; □ ~ your / our / their heads ~ (→ put *vt* 7a) (2) planned states have been ~ ~ before. (3) I must ~ my thoughts / ideas ~ before I go on to the platform; □ ~ two and two ~ *(infer things from what one sees, etc)*.

put up (1) ~ up one's hand (to catch a ball / to get the teacher's attention); ~ your hands up! ~ up one's feet *(rest with the legs horizontal)*; ~ one's hair up; help me ~ the ladder up; he stopped reading and ~ up *(laid aside)* the paper; □ ~ s.o.'s back up (→ put *vt* 7 a) (2) ~ up a picture / notice / sign / name-plate; ~ up storm warnings (for ships) / a flag / a sail (3) ~ up *(build)* a fence / shed / tent (in the garden) / building / bridge (4) the shopkeeper has ~ up the goods in two parcels; ~ herrings up in barrels; the hotel will ~ us up some sandwiches; the deck chairs have been ~ up for the winter. (5) ~ up a partridge / fox *(cause it to leave cover)* (6) ~ up *(raise)* a price; ~ ~ the rent by £3 (7) ~ ~ a prayer to God (for s.o.'s safety) (8) ~ up goods for sale / auction; why are you ~ting your house up for sale? (9) ~ up *(offer)* a good / poor fight / (stout) resistance (→ fight *n* 1); ~ up a good show *(come near success)*; → front 4. (10) ~ up *(provide)* money: Jack and I are building a house - I'm doing the work and he's ~ting up the money; his father ~s up the money for his dental clinic. (11) ~ s.o. up as a / one's candidate; we ~ him up for the position of secretary. (12) are you going to ~ up for the secretaryship? my brother is ~ting up as the Liberal candidate at B. (13) could you ~ me up for a night? (14) ~ up at a hotel / boarding house / *etc* (15) please ~ the new office-boy up to his duties *(inform him)*; that's a brilliant idea - who ~ you up to it? (16 put up to: *persuade to do s.th. wrong*) he said he never intended stealing the money, but some friends had ~ him up to it; "who ~ you up to this?" asked the policeman. (17) the robbery never took place - someone ~ the police up to it *(warned them)*; ~ s.o. up to a trick (18) ~ up with *(endure without complaint)* nonsense / insolence / bad conditions / *etc*.

puzzle *vt* (1 *confuse, perplex*) you ~ me; the problem ~d him; ~ s.o. with a question; he was (quite) ~d how to act / to know what to do. (2 *exercise hard*) he ~d his brains / head to find the answer / over the problem / about the problem. - *vi* (3 *make a great mental effort to find a solution, meaning*) ~ over a problem.

puzzle out I was unable to ~ ~ the message; ~ ~ a mystery / the truth.

Q

qualified *adj* (1) a ~ doctor / translator / accountant / *etc*; be ~ in several languages / as an interpreter / for a better post / to practise medicine; do you know a man ~ for that job? I didn't consider myself ~ to express an opinion on the matter. (2 *entitled*) a man ~ to vote (3 *limited, restricted*) the daring plan had the ~ support of his team-mates; (un)~ praise.

qualify *vt* (1) his training ~ies him to take up various careers / for the job; ~ o.s. in law; he spent many years in ~ing himself as a surgeon. (2 *make s.o. eligible, entitle*) the degree of his injury ~ies him for assistance; the conditions that ~ one for unemployment benefit; you have training and experience that should ~ you for a higher post; residence ~ies you for membership; his long experience ~ies him to speak with authority on this matter. (3 *describe*) could you ~ his behaviour as offensive? the audience ~ied the speaker as a bore. (4 *modify, restrict*) ~ a statement / endorsement / *etc*; ~ the terms of a contract / will; a ~ing clause (5 *make less severe*) ~ a criticism; ~ justice with mercy; the jury ~ied the conviction with a recommendation of mercy. (6 *limit the meaning of*) adjectives ~ nouns. (7 *alter the flavour, strength of*) ~ brandy with water; he ~ied his coffee with a few drops of whisky. – *vi* (8 *become trained*) ~ in law / medicine / pharmacy / *etc*; ~ as, for a doctor / lawyer / teacher / *etc*; ~ for a post / position / the bar / *etc*; he ~ied for the football team by hard training. (9 *become entitled, eligible*) ~ for unemployment benefit / tax relief / *etc*; he searched the regulations to see how he could ~ and demand relief as a right.

quality *n* (1) goods of high and low ~; clothes of mean ~; s.th. is of poor / inferior / fair / good / excellent ~; silks of fine ~; goods of the first ~; manufacture goods in various ~ies; ~ matters more than quantity. (2 *high ~, excellence*) a tobacco of ~; s.th. has ~ *(is good)*; the restaurant earned its fine reputation by the ~ of its food. (3) the acid ~ of a lemon; the chemical ~ies of alcohol; the melodious ~ of her voice; ability to think is man's outstanding ~; honesty is the cardinal ~ of his character; he has many good ~ies; he has all the ~ies of a great ruler; she has the ~ of inspiring confidence.

quantity *n* (1) I prefer quality to ~; mathematics is the science of pure ~; expressed in terms of ~ (2) a large / great / enormous / huge ~; he has an impressive ~ of books; the ~ of flour called for in the recipe is 1 lb. (3 *large amount*) we were dismayed to see the ~ of food wasted on the picnic; extract ore in ~; he buys things in large ~ies; a ~ of jewellery was missing; we had ~ies of rain this summer; the cyclamen is found here in ~ies. (4) x denotes an unknown ~; a physical ~ (5) he is still an unknown ~ in political circles.

quarrel *n* (1) a (bitter / violent / sordid / *etc*) ~ arose / followed / ensued / *etc*; a drunken ~; begin / start / raise a ~ with s.o. about s.th.; → pick *vt* 7; settle / make up / compose a ~ (2 *reason for complaint*) I have no ~ with / against Mr N., but I dislike his brother; the / my real ~ with him is the way he treats dogs; he has no ~ with his present salary. (3 *reason for disagreement*) what is your ~ with this definition? I have no ~ with your arrangements for the trip.

quarrel *vi* (1) A ~s with B; A and B ~ with each other; several persons ~ amongst themselves; ~ about / over s.th. (2 *find fault*) ~ with a proposal; a bad workman ~s with his tools; □ (it's no use) ~ling with one's bread and butter *(express dislike of, give up the employment one lives by)*.

quarter *n* (1 *one fourth*) a ~ of a mile *(440 yards)* / of an hour / of 28 *(7)* / *etc*; the first ~ of this century; □ a bad ~ of an hour *(short unpleasant experience)*; a ~ mile / yard / circle; I can get it for a ~ (of) the price / for ~ the price. (2 *point of time 15 minutes before, after an hour*) the clock has just struck the ~; it's a ~ to / past two; it isn't the ~ yet. (3 *three months*) we showed a fine profit the second ~; the bank sends out a statement each ~; pay one's rent at the end of each ~; owe several ~s' rent (4 *one of the moon's phases*) the moon at the first / in its last ~ (5 *direction, region*) from what ~ does the wind blow? the wind is moving round to the opposite ~; people came from all ~s (of the globe / earth); he has travelled in every ~ of the globe; men running from all ~s / every ~ (6 *person(s) from whom, place from which help, information may come*) the news came in from several ~s of the community; he got some support from other ~s; he received secret information from a high ~; don't look for sympathy in that ~. (7 *district*) the Italian ~ of New York; the residential / manufacturing / industrial / working-class ~; an artist's ~ (8 *quarters: lodgings*) take up one's ~s with s.o. / at an inn / in a house; come to my ~s; they lived in close ~s *(crowded space)* at the barracks; we found excellent ~s at an inn; the army went into winter ~s; □ at close ~s *(close together)*: she looks much older when you see her at close ~s. (9 *mercy*) give / receive ~; ask for / cry ~; give no ~ to s.o. *(fig: attack relentlessly)*; no ~ asked or given.

question *n* (1) ask s.o. a ~; ask a ~ of s.o.; put / address a ~ to s.o. (→ put *vt* 5); have a ~ (to ask s.o. / to put to s.o.); don't ask so many ~s; you should do that without ~; I accept his explanation without ~; what a ~! a simple / difficult / theoretical / academic / ingenuous / intelligent / silly / suspicious / embarrassing / ambiguous / tricky / *etc* ~; a leading ~ *(suggesting the desired answer)* (2 *doubt*) there is some ~ about his qualifications; there is no ~ but that he (will succeed); his honesty has never been called in(to) ~ *(doubted)*; his honesty is beyond (all) ~; there is no ~ about that; that is very much in ~ *(doubtful)*. (3 *subject of discussion*) that is the / another ~; an open ~; the ~ is whether we . . .; that is out of the ~ *(impossible)*; what you say is beside the ~ *(irrevelant)*; is he the man in ~? that is not the subject in ~; □ come into ~ *(become of practical importance)*: if sending me to Moscow ever comes into ~, I shall refuse at once. (4 *problem, matter; examples under 1 may have this meaning*) the social ~; a political / economic / *etc* ~; a ~ of grammar / etiquette; that is only a ~ of time; it's (all) a ~ of (money); bring up / raise a ~; → pose *vt* 3; an open / unsolved / unsettled / controversial / vexed / knotty / tricky / burning / *etc* ~.

question *vt* (1) the judge proceeded to ~ the witness; the prisoner was ~ed for three hours; I shall ~ him about that matter; the pupils ~ed the teacher about the results of the test. (2 *doubt*) ~ the accuracy of the statistics / the truth of s.th. / s.o.'s right to s.th.; he ~ed her sincerity; I ~ whether he is right; ~ s.o.'s sanity (3 *challenge; dispute*) ~ a decision; she ~ed the judge's authority in the case.

quick *adj/ adv* (1) a ~ fox / train; a ~ walk / trot / movement / flick of the wrist / pulse; walk at a ~ pace; I ran as ~ as I could; you are walking too ~ for me; he ran / did it ~ly; he wants to get rich ~; ~ growth; a ~ succession of events; ~ gestures (2 *of persons*) she is very ~ at (in) her work / decisions; a ~ worker; work ~ly; he is ~ at noticing mistakes *(general)*; he was ~ to notice the mistake *(particular)*; be ~ (about it)! (3 *prompt*) ~ action / vengeance; a ~ response; a ~ retort; ~ understanding / wits; a person with a ~ mind could have avoided the accident; a ~ eye / ear; ~ sight; give ~ answers; a man of ~ observation; be ~-eyed / -sighted / -witted; be ~ to take offence / to grasp a point / to answer / in answering (4 *of human faculties*) a ~ student / child; be ~ of hearing / understanding / foot *(agile)*; be ~ at learning / picking up a language / figures (5 *easily aroused*) a ~ temper; be ~-tempered (6 *not lasting long*) a ~ shower / journey / lunch; a ~ look / glance; what about some curried rice, Ann? that's ~ to make. (7 *burning strongly*) a ~ fire / heat; ~ flames (8 *consisting of living plants*) a ~ hedge; a ~ pot of plants.

quiet *adj* (1 *without motion*) a ~ sea; ~ waters (2 *without sound*) ~ footsteps; a ~ street / village; the machine room was ~ for once. (3 *not speaking*) keep ~; be ~! the baby was ~ all night. (4 *not active*) a very ~ man; ~ neighbours (5 *free from excitement, calm*) ~ times; a ~ life / old age; a ~ mind / conscience; she has a ~ disposition and seldom loses her temper. (6 *having a reserved manner*) a ~ person (7 *done in a restrained way*) a ~ reproach; a ~ admonition (8 *free from activity*) a ~ Sunday afternoon; spend a ~ evening at home reading; a ~ walk in the garden / smoke (9 *of colour: not loud, not showy*) ~ colours; pale blue is a ~ colour; he favours ~ neckties. (10 *not revealed*) harbour ~ resentment; a mood of ~ happiness; ~ irony; keep s.th. ~.

R

race[1] *n* (1) the human ~; nuclear weapons pose a threat to the (human) ~. (2) the black / white / Mongolian / Caucasian / Nordic / Jewish / Anglo-Saxon / *etc* ~; ~ hatred / prejudice / conflict (3 *zoological, botanical division*) the four-footed / winged ~; the ~ of fishes; produce a new ~ of potatoes (4a *posterity of*) the ~ of Adam (4b *descent*) a man of noble / Oriental / *etc* ~; these peoples are separate in language and ~. (5 *any group*) journalists are an interesting ~; the ~ of poets; a long ~ of seafaring men.

race[2] *n* (1) a horse- / boat- / cycle- / motor- / dog- / greyhound-~; a pursuit / endurance ~; a 100-metre / hurdle / relay ~; a close *(almost equal)* ~; a cross-country ~; they spent a day at the ~s *(a series of horse / dog ~s)*; run a ~ (with s.o.); win / lose a ~; a ~-horse / -course / -crew / *etc* (2) a ~ for a train; it was a ~ for (one's) life; □ a ~ against time *(an effort to do s.th. before a certain time)* (3) an armament / arms ~; ~ for the presidency / governorship / *etc*; a ~ for power / wealth (4 *course of life*) run one's ~; his ~ is nearly run *(he is near the end of his* *life).* (5 *swift current*) a ~ of water in a stream.

race *vi* (1) you'll have to ~ to catch the bus; boys ~ing home from school; they ~d to see what was happening; they ~d along; their pens ~d over the paper; the stream ~d down the valley; □ ~ against time (→ race[2] *n* 2) (2 *compete*) ~ with s.o. (for a prize) (3 *engage in horse- / etc racing*) he ~s at all the big meetings. (4a *run at high speed with little, no work to do*) don't let the engine ~; the ship's screw is ~ing. - *vt* (4b *cause to run as in 4a*) he ~d the motor of his car. (5 *cause to go at full speed*) he ~d me along at 5 miles an hour; he ~d me to the station in his car; *(fig)* ~ a Bill through (Parliament) (6 *cause to have a race with*) I'll ~ you to the corner; he ~d his bicycle against a motorcar; if a vehicle you are overtaking accelerates, do not ~ it but fall behind. (7 *cause to compete*) which horse is he going to ~? - *adj* (8) the ~ing world; ~ing car / yacht / boat; ~ing season.

radio *n* (1) speeches broadcast by ~; ~ and television; ~ engineering / industry / astronomy / studio / broadcast / play / receiver / set / advertising / dealer / operator / amateur / *etc*; the play was written / adapted for ~. (2) I heard it on the ~; listen to the ~; I bought a new ~ yesterday; switch / turn / put on the ~; switch / turn off the ~; tune (in) the ~ to a wavelength (3) send / transmit a message by ~; the pilot receives directions over the ~; the two ships are in ~ contact with one another; ~ location / patrol car / taxi / *etc*; ~ frequency / wave / beam / beacon.

radio *vt* (1) ~ a message; the ship ~ed its time of arrival; the flier ~ed that he... (2) ~ s.o.; ~ the ship that help is coming. - *vi* (3) the ship ~ed for help.

rage *n* (1) a speechless / violent / towering / *etc* ~; fly / get / fall into a ~; when opposed he often went into a ~; be boiling / choking / blazing / foaming / blind / mad with ~; be in a (fit of) ~; kill s.o. in a ~; put s.o. in(to) a ~ (2) the ~ of the sea; the ~ of a storm / fire / epidemic (3 *formal: strong desire*) have a ~ for notoriety / hunting / horses / stamps; the ~ for conquest (4 *s.th. very popular*) big hats were (all) the ~ (that summer).

rage *vi* (1) he ~d against / at fate; he never ceased ~ing against his enemy; she ~d at him for his carelessness. (2) the wind ~d round the house; the waves / sea ~d; the storm ~d all night / itself out *(came to an end)*; the epidemic ~d many weeks. (3) the battle ~d ten days; the debate ~d for a long time. - *adj* (4) the ~ing sea / wind / *etc*; a ~ing toothache / fever.

raid *n* (1) Caesar made his two ~s on Britain in 55 and 54 B.C.; we must expect new ~s by the enemy; (be killed in) an air ~; a police ~ (on a gambling ring) (2) a ~ on a bank; a bank ~.

raid *vt* (1) the police ~ed the gangsters' headquarters. (2) boys have been ~ing my orchard; somebody has ~ed the refrigerator (of all the milk).

rain *n* (1) a (nice / gentle / continuous / *etc*) ~ fell steadily; a (heavy / pouring / pelting / torrential / *etc*) ~ was beating / was lashing / splashed / pattered against the window panes; a drizzling / refreshing / persistent / *etc* ~; a heavy patter of ~; a shower / fall of ~; it has turned to ~; ~ set in / started; the ~ is pouring down (→ pour *vi* 5); a water shortage caused by lack of ~; the villagers had to wait until the next ~s *(in tropical countries)*; ~ or shine: we'll be there come ~ or (come) shine *(regardless of the weather; fig: under all circumstances)* (2 *rainy weather*) we had ~ most of last summer. (3) a ~ of arrows pierced his armour; a ~ of ashes / rice / fire; a ~ of invitations / congratulations / kisses / blows / telegrams; a ~ of vituperation.

rain *vi* (1) it's just come on to ~; it started ~ing hard / fast; → pour *vi* 5; it ~ed off and on. (2) tears ~ed from her eyes / down her cheeks. (3) invitations ~ed down on us; bullets ~ed down on us. - *vt* (4) it was ~ing buckets / cats and dogs *(violently)*; it ~ed large drops; it has ~ed itself out. (5) they ~ed presents on the bride and groom; it ~ed blood; it ~ed invitations; they ~ed confetti / blows on us; ~ benefits / favours on s.o.; they ~ed bombs down on us.

raise *vt* (1) ~ a window / the curtain; ~ a weight; I can't ~ the trunk; ~ a sunken ship; ~ one's hat (to s.o.) / one's hand (in a salute / against s.o.) / one's arm / head / skirt; □ ~ the elbow *(drink much)*; ~ one's eyes; ~ one's eyebrows *(also fig)*; ~

one's glass to one's lips / to s.o.; ~ (a cloud of) dust; □ ~ a dust (→ dust n.); ~ game birds *(cause them to fly away)* (2 *cause to be upright*) ~ a flagpole; the chair fell over so he ~d it again; ~ an overturned motorcar; ~ s.o. from a sitting / lying / kneeling position; the sound of the bugle ~d him from his bed. (3a *erect*) ~ a house / palace / monument (3b *make higher*) ~ a wall; ~ a house two stories (3c *as in 3b, of musical notes*) ~ a note a semitone (4 *grow; bring up*) ~ crops / wheat / one's own vegetables / *etc*; ~ terriers / horses (on grass) / sheep / *etc*; ~ a (large) family; ~ a child (5 *make rise according to a scale*) ~ the temperature (to 100°); hard physical work will ~ anybody's temperature; ~ the heat of a furnace; ~ the school leaving age (to 16); ~ a standard; *(fig)* ~ one's / s.o.'s reputation; it will ~ his reputation if he ... (6a *cause to rise; of dough*) ~ dough / bread; self-~ing flour *(BE,* → rise *vi* 4b) (6b) ~ cloth *(give it a nap)* (7 *increase*) ~ prices / taxes / the rent / a salary / wages; ~ the standard / cost of living; ~ the literacy rate; ~ a bid / wager / bet (8 *promote*) ~ s.o. to corporal / the rank of colonel; ~ a soldier from the ranks *(make him an officer)*; ~ s.o. to noble rank / to the peerage; ~ s.o. to power (9) ~ a number to the third power; 3^4 is three ~d to the fourth power (→ power *n* 10). (10a *increase in pitch, strength*) ~ the voice; speak with ~d / in a ~d voice; ~ the volume of a radio; ~ one's voice (in opposition / protest); he ~d his voice against the corrupt conditions in his town. (10b) ~ a colour *(make it brighter)* (11 *utter in a loud voice*) ~ a loud cry / shout; the crowd ~d an outcry at the umpire's decision; ~ the alarm (12) the news / danger ~d his spirits; ~ (s.o.'s) hope(s) / expectation; ~ false hopes in s.o.

(13) ~ (s.o. from) the dead; ~ the spirit of a deceased person (14) ~ trouble; ~ a disturbance / revolt; ~ a rebellion with stirring speeches; ~ a controversy / prejudice; ~ (a storm of) protest; ~ Cain / hell / the devil *(inform: start a big row)*: he would ~ Cain about the slightest mistake. (15 *cause to appear*) ~ a laugh (among the audience) / a smile; a story that might ~ a blush on the cheeks of a young girl; a long walk that ~d a good thirst; not the brown shoes - they ~ blisters on my feet; ~ fears / suspicion / resentment (16 *bring up*) I should like to ~ the following point; ~ comment / criticism; ~ a subject / question / objection (to s.th.) / complaint / claim / demand; ~ doubts about s.th.; ~ an accusation against s.o.; he ~d the issue of his opponent's eligibility; ~ a difficulty / problem (17 *collect*) ~ money / £100 / a loan / a mortgage on a house / a tax / a subscription; ~ an army / a fleet / troops (18a) ~ a blockade / siege *(abandon it; force the enemy to abandon it)* (18b *remove*) ~ an embargo / injunction.

rally *n* (1) a political / peace ~; a boy scouts' ~; a car ~: the Monte Carlo R~ (2 *a return of strength*) a ~ in prices.

rally *vt* (1) ~ troops after a battle; ~ one's supporters; ~ support for s.o. (2) ~ one's spirits / strength; they ~ied their energies for the counterattack. - *vi* (3) the troops ~ied after the retreat; ~ round the flag; my supporters are ~ing round me again. (4 *come together for a common purpose*) ~ to a cause / the support of the Prime Minister (5) ~ after a fever / from an illness.

range *n* (1a) a ~ (of mountains); a ~ of cliffs; a ~ of buildings / attics; pupils in a ~ (1b *area*) a wide ~ of meadows (2 *the region over which a plant, animal is distributed*) what is the ~ of deer in this country? the book gives the ~s of all species. (3 *area with targets for shooting at*) a rifle ~ (4 *distance to which a gun will shoot, etc*) the ~ of a gun / telescope; at a ~ of 5 miles; at close ~; (the enemy are) in / within / out of / beyond ~; fire at short / long ~; the missile has a ~ of 2,000 miles; the flying ~ of an aircraft; the enemy have found the ~ of *(distance to)* our camp. (5 *class, order*) the upper / higher ~s of society (6 *distance between limits, extent*) the annual ~ of temperature; the ~ of the flute / her voice *(between top and bottom notes)*; within the income ~ of £4-5,000; a wide ~ of prices; a wide ~ of man-made fibres are used in textile manufacture; beyond the ~ of his vision; it is within the ~ of possibility that he ...; the book covers a wide ~ of subjects; a wide ~ of friends; a wide ~ of interests; the ~ of knowledge / duty; the thorniest question in the whole ~ of politics; his reading is of very wide ~. (7 *scope of knowledge, etc*) that subject is outside my ~; Hebrew is out of my ~.

range *vt* (1) trees were ~d along the roadside; ~ books on a shelf according to size; they ~d themselves on each side; the members of the cast were ~d in their proper places on stage. (2a *wander through*) ~ the countryside / forests / hills / seas (2b *as* in *2a, fig*) a talk ~ing the widest horizons (3 *put in a class, etc*) he ~d himself with the opposition; the American Government ~d itself solidly behind the Common Market; they were ~d against us / among the rebels / on the side of the enemy / with the enemy. (4) ~ a telescope on an object; ~ a gun on an enemy ship. - *vi* (5 *stretch in a line*) the peaks ~d as far as he could see; the mountains ~ north and south; the shabby houses ~d along the road. (6a *move freely*) these animals ~ through the desert; cattle ~ing over the plains; ~ through the town on the last night of carnival (6b *as in 6a, fig*) the talk ~d over a variety of matters; his studies ~ over many languages; a speaker who ~d far and wide; his thoughts always ~d far afield. (7 *occur over an area*) a plant that ~s from Canada to Mexico (8 *vary*) prices ~d from $5 to $10; the temperature ~s between 0° and 30° C; the children ~d in age from two to five.

rank *n* (1) a ~ of soldiers; orchestra players arranged in ~s; a cab- / taxi-~ (2) (promote s.o. to/ raise s.o. to / hold) the ~ of captain; he is above a major in ~; the ~ of bishop; he belongs to the highest ~s of society. (3a) a churchman of high ~; an artist of the first ~; a second-~ dancer (3b *high social standing*) a man of ~; pride of ~; → take *vt* 10d. (4a *~s: body of private soldiers*) the general had risen from the ~s; → raise *vt* 8; non-commissioned officers and other ~s; ~ and file *(ordinary soldiers)*; the ~ and file of Labour voters; ~-and-file Union members (4b *~s: common people*) the president of the firm had come up from the ~s; the ~s of the working class (5 *slang*) pull ~ *(use one's authority to gain an advantage)*; although the sergeant's suggestion was better, the young lieutenant pulled ~ on him and insisted on his own poorer plan.

rank *vt* (1) ~ men according to their height; he ~ed the chessmen on the board. (2 *place in a category*) she was ~ed among the best-dressed women; ~ s.th. very highly; I ~ed her with the better students; his achievement was ~ed with that of Prometheus; some of our present-day Sunday painters may one day be ~ed among the great artists. - *vi* (3 *belong to a category*) he ~s with our finest poets; ~ above / next to / among s.o.; she ~s first / low in her class; will my shares ~ for the next dividend?

rate *n* (1 *fixed ratio*) what is the ~ of exchange for the dollar? a ~ of exchange of 50 francs to the dollar (2 *charge, wage, price fixed according to a scale or standard*) hotel ~s varying with the number of rooms in the suite; the publisher's usual ~ for short stories; the high ~s charged by the railways; the letter / parcel / telegram ~; the British Commonwealth ~; the Foreign R~; printed papers at reduced ~; the ~s for trunk calls have been raised; drapery fabrics bought at the ~ of a dollar a yard; articles sold at cut ~s; the ~ for picking hop has gone up; an electric ~ of 7 cents per kilowatt-hour; gas- / water-~(s); no one but the council can decide the ~ of taxation. (3) our ~ of speed was ten miles per hour; an absentee ~ of 5 men per 1,000 employees; Britain's share rose by 8 per cent - nearly three times the ~ of increase in the world as a whole; the death-~ is 1.7 per 1,000 (per year); birth / marriage ~; the ~ of progress over the past century; the ~ of interest per annum; fighter planes of very high speeds and prodigious ~s of climb (4 *speed*) at the / a ~ of 50 miles per hour; go / drive / travel at a good / moderate / fast / great / terrible / rapid / dangerous / *etc* ~; work at a rapid / *etc* ~; at the ~ you're going you'll never finish the job / you'll be finished in an hour or two; a method by which wind ~s in the ionosphere can be calculated. (5 *local tax*) local / parish ~s; ~s and taxes, the church- / poor-~ (6 *class, grade*) this teacher is first ~; he is a first-~ teacher; most of these dictionaries are second ~. (7) at any ~ *(at least)*: at any ~ he didn't forget; it was a mediocre film, but at any ~ there was one outstanding performance; at this / that ~ *(given the present, those conditions)*: we can't afford to go on living at this / that ~ for long; it's foolish to live up to the last penny of your income - you'll always be hard up at that ~.

rate *vt* (1) what do you ~ his fortune at? each offence is ~d at a fixed sum. (2) ~ a student's class performance; he ~d her low on reading skills; he was ~d one of the rich men of the city; they ~ him as a public menace; I do not ~ his merits high; I ~ him among my benefactors. (3) the house is ~d at £100 a year (→ rate *n* 5) - *vi* (4 *be considered*) he ~d high on the team; he ~s as a fine workman.

raw *adj* (1) ~ meat / fish / carrots / eggs / *etc*; eat an apple ~ (2 *unprocessed*) ~ material / silk / hides / timber / ore / sugar; ~ spirit *(undiluted alcohol)*; ~ whisky; ~ data (3 *untrained*) a ~ recruit / beginner / youth / hand (4 *with the skin removed*) a ~ wound / sore; ~ flesh; the soles of his feet were ~ with / from walking. (5 *damp, chilly*) a ~, foggy day at the beach; a ~ November morning; ~ wind(s) (6 *crude*) ~ style; his manners are ~; a ~ *(outspoken)* portrayal of truth / the facts (7 *inform: harsh, unjust*) he received a ~ treatment from his friends; get a ~ deal *(slang: be treated unfairly)*.

reach *n* (1 *act of reaching*) make a ~ for a gun; get s.th. by a long ~; it was a long ~ from the bed to the light switch. (2 *extent of reaching*) the ~ of a gun; I want a cottage within ~ of London *(from which L. can be reached, which can be reached from L.)*; in those days L. was not within the ~ of most people living as far north as Manchester; I have my dictionaries within my ~ / within easy ~; within easy ~ of Oxford are the Cotswolds; the box on the cupboard is out of my ~ *(I'm too small)*; knives should be out of the ~ of children / out of the children's ~ / out of ~ of the children. (3 *as in 2, fig*) luxuries are not within the ~ of the poor; he was beyond ~ of human aid; no help was within ~; an idea not within his ~; no area of this earth compares with Switzerland in variety and ~ of beauty. (4 *straight part of a river*) ... on one of the loveliest and gayest ~es of the River Thames is Maidenhead. (5) a ~ of woodland.

reach *vt* (1) ~ out one's hand (for s.th.); the tree ~ed (out) its branches. (2) please ~ me that book / the sugar *(inform)*; he ~ed down his hat; ~ s.th. with one's hand (3) the rubber plant ~es the ceiling; this road ~es the river; this ladder won't ~ the window. (4 *arrive at*) ~ the other shore / the summit of the mountain / the end of one's journey; we ~ed France in May; we shall ~ Paris in the evening; the place is easily ~ed by car; this news / your letter ~ed me today; you can ~ him at this phone number; the number 236538 will ~ me at any time of the day; we tried to ~ them by cable; sorry, Mr M. can't be ~ed (at the moment). (5) distant stars the eye cannot ~; I called, but couldn't ~ you; not a sound ~ed our ears. (6 *come to*) he has ~ed the age of 60 / end of his life; a puppy that has ~ed full size / maturity is called a dog; the car ~ed a high speed; last year's record was not ~ed this year; ~ a phase / stage; I have ~ed the limit of my patience; ~ certainty / a goal / the object of one's desires / success early in life / a position (7 *amount to*) the cost of the building has ~ed a million dollars; the cost will ~ millions; the price of apples ~ed a new low. (8 *succeed in interesting, affecting, etc*) advertising used as a means of ~ing an audience; ~ s.o.'s conscience; her words failed to ~ him; men who cannot be ~ed by reason (9) he finally ~ed a decision; ~ an agreement with s.o./ a conclusion.
- *vi* (10) he ~ed (out) for the revolver; you must ~ out further; I cannot ~ down to it / so high; a hand ~ed out and held me. (11) the coat ~ed (down) to his feet; the bookcase ~ed (up) to the ceiling; the carpet ~es under the counter; a tower ~ing to the skies; the road doesn't ~ as far as my house; as far as the eye can ~ *(fig, to the horizon)*; the speaker's voice did not ~ to the back of the hall. (12) sums ~ing to a considerable total (13) his influence ~es far beyond the frontiers of his own country; the law cannot ~ him.

reach back an old man's memory ~es ~ over many years; annals that ~ ~ to ancient times.

reach down → reach *vt* 2, *vi* 10, 11.

reach out → reach *vt* 1, *vi* 10.

react *vi* (1 *respond*) ~ to an idea / suggestion / drug / *etc*; ~ to a shock by jumping; how did the audience ~ to his remarks? the patient ~ed favourably to the treatment. (2 *act in opposition*) people will not endure oppression for ever - sooner or later they will ~ against it; he ~ed against my suggestion. (3 *have an effect*) tyranny ~s upon the tyrant; applause ~s upon a speaker; John's bad manners will ~ against him in time. (4) nitrous oxide ~s upon the metal; the ways in which molecules ~ one with another are largely understood; the new medicine ~s adversely upon the liver; from all over France poured in ghastly accounts of how the drug ~ed – fiery headaches, blackouts, . . .

read *vt* (1a) ~ a book / paper / map / piece of music / lot of fiction; ~ a French book in the original; ~ the clock / time / directions / instructions / minutes; ~ s.o.'s writing / shorthand (notes); ~ French / music / Braille / traffic signs; □ ~ the riot act to s.o. *(fig, inform: give a warning that bad behaviour must stop)* (1b *correct*) ~ printer's proofs (→ proof *n* 5) (2) ~ s.th. aloud / silently / in silence / fluently / hesitatingly / (in)distinctly / to o.s. / *etc*; please ~ me the letter; ~ a story to the children; he ~ me a lesson / (severe) lecture *(reproved me)*; ~ a speech / sermon *(not speak extempore)* (3 *BE study*) ~ law / physics / English / *etc*; what are you ~ing? politics, philosophy and economics.
(4) ~ a barometer / gas-meter / precision instrument / *etc*; ~ (off) values from a precision instrument (5) the thermometer ~s 30 degrees; the watch ~s 3.45; the speedometer ~s 90 miles. (6) for 'one thousand' another version ~s 'ten thousand'. (7 *substitute*) ~ 'marry' for 'merry'. (8) ~ s.o.'s thoughts / intentions / expressions; ~ s.o. like a book *(understand him perfectly)*; she ~ in his eyes an earnest appeal.
(9a *interpret*) she ~ his letter to mean that he didn't intend to come; ~ into a poem a deeper meaning; ~ s.th. into a sentence / statement / situation / set of facts; he ~ an underlying sarcasm into her letter; silence must not always be ~ as consent. (9b *explain; interpret*) ~ a riddle / dream / magic symbols / s.o.'s hand / s.o.'s palm; ~ the writing on the wall *(fig)* (10 *predict*) ~ the future / s.o.'s fortune (in tea leaves) (11) ~ o.s. to sleep; ~ o.s. hoarse / stupid. – *vi* (12) ~ in a book; he ~s with difficulty; I have no time to ~ / for ~ing; □ ~ between the lines *(understand what is implied)*: from her letter I could ~ between the lines that she was homesick. (13) he is ~ing to the children; does he preach extempore or ~? (14 *learn*) I ~ it in the newspaper; I ~ of his death in The Times; did you ~ about *(learn the details of)* that accident in the High Street? he likes ~ing about ancient people. (15 *BE ~ + for = study*) ~ for an examination / Honours / the first degree / the Bar *(to become a barrister)* (16) the contract ~s as follows: . . .; a rule that ~s two different ways. (17 *make an impression when read*) these talks ~ better in The Listener than they sound on the air; this play ~s better than it acts; his letter ~s well; her letter ~s as if she doesn't intend to come; it ~s like a lie / threat / translation.

read off (1) → read *vt* 4 (2) ~ ~ an announcement / list / poem.

read on please ~ on; ~ on and see what happens.

read out all the class listened as he ~ his essay ~; ~ ~ an announcement / list / poem.

read over ~ ~ a text *(examine it)*.

read through (1) ~ it ~ six times. (2 *examine*) would you mind ~ing ~ this report? ~ s.th. ~ to the end.

read up ~ up a subject *(study it specially)*.

read up on *(acquire knowledge by reading)* I'm going to have to ~ up on Cromwell – I don't know much about how he came to power.

ready *adj* (1) dinner is ~; your dress is ~; the mechanic called to say that the car is ~; when will you be ~? he was ~ on time; troops ~ for battle; are you ~ for dinner / the theatre? make (everything) / get ~ for a journey; make / get s.th. ~; ~ for the fight / to fight; ~ to start / receive the guests; the guide had a torch ~; hold a room ~ for s.o.; hold o.s. ~; keep your tickets ~; ~-to-serve soups; *(in sporting events)* (get) ~, set, go! (2a *immediately available*) a ~ source of supplies; (pay) ~ cash / money (2b *likely to do*) a tree ~ to fall; a bud just ~ to burst (3 *willing*) she is ~ to suffer in order to stay slim; she is ~ to forgive. (4 *on the point of*) I was so tired that I was ~ to drop; she felt ~ to cry. (5 *prompt*) be ~ with a reply / suggestion / explanation; he gave a ~ consent; the students gave ~ answers; the idea found ~ acceptance; a keen mind and ~ wit; he is always ~ with an answer / excuse; he always has an answer / excuse ~; he is too ~ to suspect others; he is very ~ with his criticism / at excuses. (6 ~ *+ past part*) the cases are ~ packed / packed ~; buy a suit ~-made / a ~-made suit; buy food ~ cooked; *(fig)* ~-made *(unoriginal)* ideas.

real *adj / adv* (1 *having objective existence*) sunshine and rain are ~; was the figure you saw last night ~ or imaginary? a story taken from ~ life; the events you will see in the film are ~ and not just made up. (2 *genuine*) ~ gold / pearls; ~ silk, not rayon; this stone is not ~; a ~ diamond / antique; the ~ thing *(not an inferior article)*: the simulation sapphire mink furs appeared even more luxurious than the ~ thing; that's not his ~ name; ~ cream (3 *true, not merely apparent or socalled*) the ~ reason for an act; a ~ victory; a ~ friend; ~ sympathy; the ~ value of things (4) ~ estate *(property consisting of land, houses)* (5 *inform: really*) it was ~ hard work; this is ~ good coffee; we had a ~ good time; you did a ~ nice job painting the house.

reality *n* (1) belief in the ~ of miracles; the search after God and ~; put s.th. into ~; in ~ *(really)*: he was brave in appearance, but in ~ a coward. (2) the grim ~ies of bombing cities; we must stick to the ~ies. (3 *lifelike resemblance*) the scene was reproduced with startling ~.

realize *vt* (1 *understand, be conscious of*) ~ one's mistake / error; ~ a danger / difference; ~ the importance / value of s.th.; she suddenly ~d the significance of his remark; he ~d that she was in danger / how it was done; he hardly ~d what was happening; I fully / quite ~ the fact that he ... (2 *usually pass: make real*) all his hopes / ambitions / fears / plans were ~d; her wish was ~d at last; sales management sees to it that the sales forecast is ~d. (3 *make realistic*) these details help to ~ the scene. (4 *sell for money*) ~ securities / investments (5 *bring as the result of selling, etc*) the goods ~d $800; the sale of the house ~d a large profit; ~ a certain price; he knows how to ~ profits; he ~d *(made)* a fortune.

reap *vt* (1) ~ a field (of wheat) (2) ~ corn / wheat / a crop / a harvest; *(fig)* we ~ as we (have) sow(n) / what we have sown; ~ where one has not sown (3) ~ praise / glory / laurels; ~ large profits; ~ the fruits of one's labour; John did the work, so he should ~ the benefits.

rear *n* (1) the ~ of the drawer; the kitchen is in the ~ of the house; a room at the ~ of a building; please move to the ~ (of the bus). (2) he was at the ~ of *(behind)* the building; to the ~ of the house there is a piece of woodland; take two paces to the ~; the ones at the ~ could not see anything. (3) the enemy attacked us in / from the ~; a mounted policeman rode at the ~ of the procession; □ bring up the ~ *(be the last in a line)*.

rear *adj* the ~ lamps / wheels of a car; leave the bus by the ~ entrance; a ~ room / row / bench.

rear *vt* (1) ~ one's head; ~ a ladder / pillar / mast (2) ~ a castle / cathedral / monument (3) ~ poultry / cattle / dogs; the hen ~s her brood; ~ a crop (4) ~ a child (on milk / the best of food); ~ a family. - *vi* (5) suddenly the horse ~ed *(rose up on its hind legs)*. (6) the mountain ~ed above the village; the skyscraper ~s high over the neighbouring buildings.

reason *n* (1 *power to think, etc*) only man has ~; his ~ has shown him the right course; he has lost his ~ *(is mad)*; regain one's ~ (2 *common sense*) why don't you listen to ~? it is contrary to ~; bring s.o. to ~ *(make him act reasonably)*; I can't see the ~ of it; □ it stands to ~ *(is obvious to reasonable people)* that (a person's health suffers if he smokes); (with)in ~ *(reasonable)*: I would do anything (with)in ~ to help a good cause; she tried to keep her demands (with)in ~; it is not (with)in ~ to expect a person to work for 12 hours a day; □ out of (all) ~ *(unreasonable)*: to ask for £15,000 for a small house like that is out of all ~. (3) there is (no) ~ to assume that he ...; I saw ~ to believe that ...; I have (every) ~ to suppose that she ...; I have no ~ to complain / for complaint; have sufficient ~ to do s.th.; he has his own ~s for it; is there any ~ why we should not start? there is a (good) ~ / are (good) ~s for that; what is the ~ for the delay? what is your ~ for doing that? the ~ was that / *(inform)* because I was very tired; that certainly is a ~ to celebrate; he complains with ~ (that he has been treated unfairly); I said so with good ~; a plausible / solid / apparent / obvious / convincing / compelling / compulsive / cogent / dominant / inexplicable / important / comprehensible / feeble / cold / *etc* ~; give / state the ~s for / against (doing) s.th.; state / indicate s.th. as the ~; adduce / bring forward / allege / advance (good / *etc*) ~s; for this ~ I can't ...; do s.th. for personal / economic / technical / practical ~s; do s.th. for ~s of economy / policy / security / *etc*; he is retiring for ~s of health; by ~ of *(because* *of)*: he was consulted regarding such problems by ~ of his long experience; for the (simple) ~ that *(because)*: we decided against installing new heating apparatus for the ~ that it would be too costly.

reason *vi* (1) the ability to ~ makes man different from the animals; I ~ from these premises that our will cannot be free; I ~ from experience; ~ rightly / wrongly (about / upon s.th.) (2 *argue*) it is no good trying to ~ with him about / on the matter; he is someone you simply can't ~ with; there is no ~ing against those who will misunderstand. – *vt* (3 *say as an argument*) he ~ed that if we started at dawn, we could arrive before noon. (4 *think through logically*) ~ a problem out; ~ out the answer to a question; a (well-)~ed statement / exposition / amendment / *etc*; ~ed criticism is what we want; ~ what is to be done / why s.th. was done / *etc*; he ~s so clearly that anyone can follow him. (5 *persuade by argument*) I tried to ~ him out of his fears / plan; ~ s.o. into obedience / accepting a proposal.

reason away you cannot ~ ~ my arguments / the facts.

recall *vt* (1) ~ a diplomat (from his post, to his country); an order to ~ all officials from leave; the edition was ~d from the booksellers. (2) he ~ed his mind from pleasant daydreams to the dull task at hand. (3) ~ an order / decision; ~ a promise (4) I can't ~ his name for the moment; can't you ~ telling me that story last week? can you ~ what she said? (5) everything here ~s my youth to me; legends that ~ the past.

receipt *n* (1) the ~ of a letter / order / goods; acknowledge ~ of a letter / consignment; (up)on ~ of the news I sent a telegram; payable on ~; I am in ~ of your letter of 8th May; I was not yet in ~ of a salary; those in ~ of a pension (2) a ~ for payment; ~s are usually written on special ~ forms. (3) the ~s of the football match; ~s from travel have increased greatly since 1950; the current account is that which most people keep for their day-to-day ~s and expenses.

receive *vt* (1a) ~ a letter (through the post) / present / invitation / answer / salary (from s.o.) / wages / money / rent / compensation (for time lost) / *etc*; ~ news (→ ~ 5); ~ a name / (honorary) degree; ~ orders / instructions (from s.o.); we have not yet ~d the outstanding amount; she ~d the third prize / an award (1b *be given; ~ + noun = passive verb, identical with the noun*) ~ admission *(be admitted)*; ~ acceptance; ~ an education *(be educated)*; ~ warning; a man in public office often ~s much censure from all sides; ~ a (hearty) welcome / reward / rebuke / punishment; ~ an insult; ~ support; American manners have ~d much unfavourable comment. (1c) she ~d much attention; ~ sympathy (from s.o.); your letter will ~ our immediate attention; ~ an idea / impression; I have ~d the impression that he ... (2a) ~ an ambassador / delegation / *etc* (2b) ~ a guest / visitor; ~ s.o. with open arms / cordially / coldly / frostily / *etc*; they ~d us at the front door; the conductor was ~d with enthusiastic applause; he has to ~ the visits of many people; ~ s.o.'s attentions (3 *be at home to*) they ~d their neighbours on Sunday. (4) ~ s.o. into a club / an association / the Church (5 *accept*) all the critics ~d the play favourably; how did she ~ his offer? he ~d the news very calmly (→ ~ 1a). (6a) a priest ~d his confession; ~ an oath (6b) ~ a blessing / sacrament (7) ~ stolen goods *(in order to resell them)*; he was convicted of ~ing *(stolen goods)* and sentenced ... (8 *be subjected to, experience*) ~ a broken arm / black eye / shock / serious wound; ~ bad advice; ~ a severe beating; ~ 30 days *(imprisonment)* (9) a barrel to ~ rain water; this pit ~s the juice from the grapes. (10) this pillar ~s a heavy load; the arches ~ the full weight of the roof. (11) ~ a (radio / TV) station / signal; a ~ing set / station. – *vi* (12) it is more blessed to give than to ~ (Bible). (13 *be at home to visitors*; → 3) my grandmother always ~d on Wednesdays. (14) this antenna is built to ~ but not to transmit.

reception *n* (1) meet with / give s.o. a kind / friendly / warm / hearty / cool / cold / icy / hot / hostile / *etc* ~ (→ receive *vt* 2b); ~ hall / room (2) the critics gave the play a favourable ~ (→ receive *vt* 5); the audience gave his speech a very hostile ~. (3) hold / give a ~ (for s.o. / in honour of s.o.); there was a ~ after the wedding ceremony. (4) radio ~ from Britain was good / poor last night; wireless ~ (5 ~ *desk, at a hotel, etc*) please go to ~.

reckon *vt* (1) ~ a bill / a price / the cost / a ship's position / how much one has spent; he ~s that he does 8 hours' work a day; he ~s 400 persons attended. (2 *be of the opinion, think*) I ~ you are lucky to have got the house so cheaply; this place is ~ed one of the best hotels in the town; it was ~ed a great play by the critics; this book is ~ed as the best of the year; she ~s him among her best friends; they ~ him to be the best worker; what do you ~ of the Joneses' new house? I didn't ~ much of the sermon. (3 *inform: assert*) he ~s that he can do it / to be able to do it. (4 *inform: do as a general rule*) I always ~ to go to my son's for Christmas; we never ~ to go to bed before midnight; I ~ to start work at 9 a.m.; what train do you ~ to catch each morning? - *vi* (5) he can't ~ yet; children ~ on their fingers. (6 ~ *with: take into account*) he's a person to ~ with; he hadn't ~ed with so many obstacles. (7 ~ *with: settle accounts with*) they will ~ with him later; when the fighting is over, we'll ~ with the enemy's sympathizers. (8 ~ *without: not count*) you had better ~ without me, as I am not sure whether I shall be able to be present; there were fifty people present, ~ing without the officials; □ ~ without one's host *(make plans without consulting the chief person concerned)* (9 ~ *on: rely on*) I hope I can ~ on you(r support) / you to support me (in this matter); my investments in that company can no longer be ~ed on as a source of income; I should think we can ~ upon at least twenty people turning up. (10 ~ *on: expect, provide for*) he didn't ~ on his opponent's strength; we are ~ing on a devaluation of the franc.

recognize *vt* (1) ~ a distant object (2 *identify as s.th. previously known, etc*) ~ the / s.o.'s handwriting; she ~d him from afar (by his walk); I ~d him as a German; ~ s.o.('s voice); I ~d him from the description; he ~d her as a fraud. (3) ~ a fact / danger / difference; ~ the importance / value of s.th. (4) ~ s.o. as heir / a country as a sovereign state; the U.S.A. has ~d Red China. (5 *admit to be valid*) ~ a debt / obligation / error / claim / authority / truth; ~ s.o.; refuse to ~ a doctrine; ~ s.o.'s claim as valid (6 *admit acquaintance with*) he ~d us with a wave; the Browns no longer ~ the Smiths. (7) ~ an achievement / merit / service; ~ a work to be excellent.

recommend *vt* (1) ~ s.th. unreservedly / wholeheartedly; I can ~ this candidate to you / for the job; can you ~ me a book? the book is not ~ed for young people; this hotel is to be ~ed for its good cuisine. (2 *advise*) ~ caution / a long rest / *etc*; the doctor ~ed special exercises for her; he ~ed going / her to go to Spain for a cure; the physician ~ed the treatment of bruises with applications. (3 *make acceptable*) a plan that has little to ~ it; his careful workmanship ~s him.

recommendation *n* (1) speak in ~ of s.o./ s.th.; buy s.th. on the ~ of a friend; a letter of ~ (2) the committee submitted its ~s; make ~s (3 *quality that recommends s.o., s.th.*) ease of access is a strong ~ for the site; his personal ~s for the post appear to be of the slightest.

reconcile *vt* (1) all efforts to ~ him with his brother proved vain; become ~d with s.o. (2) it is difficult to ~ his action with the principles he professes; ~ individual liberty with social welfare; ~ two extremes (3) ~ o.s. / become ~d to one's fate; he ~d himself to his recent bad luck; I cannot ~ myself to having no say in the matter. (4) ~ a quarrel; they ~d their differences of opinion.

record *n* (1) public ~s; a court / congressional / *etc* ~; a ~ of road accidents / a meeting / a telephone conversation / *etc* (2) make / write a ~ of s.th.; he keeps an exact ~ of everything he does; who keeps the ~s of the society's proceedings? I can find no ~ of it. (3) a matter of ~ *(s.th. proved by being recorded)*; on ~ *(recorded so far)*: last summer was the wettest on ~; the worst year on ~ for polio was 1946; there was no birth certificate on ~ to reveal her age; he went on ~ *(made a public statement)* as advocating immediate integration; I don't want to go on ~ / to put myself on ~ / you to put me on ~ as saying that he ...; off the ~ *(confidentially)*: please understand that what I am telling you now is strictly off the ~; he spoke off the ~; □ bear ~ to *(give proof of)*: I can bear ~ to his previous good conduct. (4a *facts, achievements known about s.o., s.th.*) his ~ is good / is against him; he made a good ~ in college; he has / shows a good / clean / bad / criminal ~; the ship has a fine sailing ~; London Underground has a high safety ~: only 14 have been killed since 1938. (4b *criminal* ~) they discovered that the suspect had a ~. (5 *s.th. kept as a reminder*) he gave it to her as a ~ of her visit. (6) achieve / hold a ~; the world / European ~ in s.th.; beat / break a ~; equal a ~; N. cut C.'s ~ by two minutes (flat); two world ~s fell; a ~ run; a ~ crop / attendance / year for motor-car sales / *etc*.

record *vt* (1) ~ the events as they occur; ~ one's thoughts in a diary; ~ a / one's vote; he is ~ed to have built the church in 1270. (2) ~ a speech / piece of music (on tape); the orchestra ~ed the symphony. (3a) clocks ~ time, thermometers ~ temperature; no seismograph ~ed the earthquake. (3b) this stone ~s a famous battle; this document ~s that the event ... (4 *serve as evidence*) this gift will serve to ~ our appreciation. (5 *be able to be ~ed*) the piano does not ~ well.

recover *vt* (1a) ~ one's losses / a lost purse / a stolen watch / *etc*; ~ land from the sea; he ~ed his kingdom; ~ one's expenses from s.o.; although they caught the thief, the police were unable to ~ the stolen goods; recently some lost articles were ~ed from the Titanic. (1b) he ~ed his health / sight / hearing / breath / voice/ appetite; ~ (one's) consciousness *(after fainting)*; I'm ~ing my strength (after an illness); ~ one's courage / peace of mind / composure; ~ s.o.'s love / affection / favour / respect (1c) he almost fell, but quickly ~ed (himself); ~ one's balance; ~ one's senses / spirits; ~ one's feet / legs *(stand up after a fall)* (2) a stay in the country will ~ you; I'm quite / fully ~ed (from my cold); a corpse cannot be ~ed to life. - *vi* (3) he ~ed slowly from pneumonia; he has not quite ~ed yet; I haven't yet ~ed from my astonishment / the shock / the financial failure; ~ from a defeat / a disaster / the effects of an earthquake (4) prices / shares have ~ed.

recovery *n* (1) the ~ of a lost article (2) the ~ from influenza; make a quick ~; he made a rapid ~ from his losses; wish s.o. a speedy ~ (3) the cotton industry has made a good ~.

red *adj* (1) ~ colour / dye / stains / *etc*; ~ hair / cheeks / eyes; eyes ~ with weeping; be ~ with anger; become / go ~ in the face; ~-hot; □ see ~ *(get suddenly very angry)*; □ paint the town ~ (→ paint *vt* 1) (2 *having to do with bloodshed, violence, etc)* with ~ hands; a ~ battle; ~ ruin / vengeance; a ~ republican / radical (3 *Soviet; communist*) the R~ Army; ~ ideas; this organization becomes more and more ~.

red *n* (1) the ~s and browns of autumn (2) she was dressed in ~. (3) be in the ~ *(in debt)*; come out of the ~; the newspaper strike put many businesses in the ~.

reduce *vt* (1 *make smaller*) this ointment will ~ the swelling; ~ that passage to half the number of words (2 *make less*) ~ the price; at a ~d price / rate; ~ wages / salaries / taxes / costs / one's expenses; ~ fares for tourist parties; a tablet to ~ temperature; ~ the weight / distance; ~ overweight / one's weight (by ten pounds); working time has been ~d by four hours a week; ~ the speed of a car; ~ pressure; ~ the value / quality of s.th. (2b *lower the price of*) ~ an article; these goods have been greatly ~d (in price). (3 *weaken*) ~ health; that drug ~s a person's hearing / taste / *etc*; ~ pain (4 *change to a simpler form*) ~ a fraction (to lower terms); ~ 6/ 8 by 2 to 3/ 4 ; ~ shillings to pence / yards to inches; ~ s.th. to ashes / dust / a powder; ~ wood logs to pulp; ~ s.th. to its elements / components (5 ~ *to: change to a different form*) ~ s.th. to (an) order(ly arrangement) / classes / a system; ~ a statement / argument / equation to its simplest form; ~ one's ideas to writing; a contract may be unenforceable because the parties have failed to ~ the agreement to writing; ~ a theory / rule to practice; ~ facts to headings; ~ anomalies to a rule; ~ a plan to an absurdity *(show its absurdity)*; the whole problem ~s itself to the question whether ... (6 ~ *to: bring to a certain state*) ~ noisy children to silence / order; ~ an officer to the ranks; □ (live in) ~d circumstances *(comparative poverty)* (7 *bring under control*) his task was to ~ that fortress / town; ~ the rebels (to submission) (8 ~ *to: compel*) alcohol ~d him to poverty / begging; the news ~d her to tears; she was ~d to despair / submission / borrowing / *etc* (9 *dilute*) ~ paint with oil (10 *restore to normal condition*) ~ a dislocated / fractured bone (11a *decrease weight of*) exercise can help to ~ stout people. - *vi* (11b *lose weight by dieting*) she has been ~ing for the last few weeks; a ~ing diet.

refer *vt* (1a) if he needs any information, ~ him to me; ~ a patient to a specialist; I was ~red to the Inquiry Office; he ~red

me to books on linguistics; the asterisk ~s the reader to a footnote; the reader is ~red to . . . (1b *submit for consideration*) we ~red the argument to arbitration; ~ a dispute to the U.N. (2a *attribute*) he ~red his depression to his childhood illness; ~ ill temper to indigestion / miraculous tales to ignorance (2b *assign to a place, period, etc*) historians ~ the fall of Rome to 410 A.D.; minute organisms which some ~ to animals, others to plants.
- *vi* (3 *speak of, allude to*) ~ to s.o./ an event in one's speech / letters / books; he several times ~red to the modern increase in expenditure (4 *turn to for information*) ~ to a dictionary / map; the speaker often ~red to his notes; can you complete a day's marketing without once ~ring to your shopping list? he ~red to his watch for the exact time. (5 *relate, apply to*) these questions ~ to a different subject; this description can only ~ to the battle of X; this remark ~s to you; this pronoun ~s to the object of the clause. (6 *quote as proof*) ~ to s.o.('s evidence); in this matter I can ~ to my colleagues / to other similar cases; ~ to a former employer for a recommendation.

reflect *vt* (1) a mirror ~s light / heat / sound; the sunlight was ~ed from the water; the moon shines with ~ed light. (2) the mirror ~ed her face; they gazed at the stars ~ed in the lake. (3 *show, reveal*) his face ~ed his emotions; his behaviour ~ed his upbringing. (4 ~ *on: bring*) his success ~s credit on his trainer; his conduct ~s dishonour upon him; what he did ~ed glory / discredit on his country. - *vi* (5 ~*on: think*) ~ (up)on one's good fortune / what one has heard / one's past / a problem / *etc*; I want time to ~; ~ twice before you act; when we are feeling sorry for ourselves we should ~ that there are others less fortunate than we are. (6 ~ *on: bring discredit*) much of what he said ~ed (adversely) upon his truthfulness; such conduct ~s upon the sincerity of his professions; his crimes ~ed on the whole community; his poor speeches ~ed unfavourably on his desirability as a candidate.

refute *vt* ~ an argument / statement / assertion; ~ an opponent.

regard *n* (1) the tyrant had little ~ for human rights; he thinks only of himself - he has no ~ for others; more ~ must be paid to safety on the roads; ~ must be had to public opinion; having ~ to all the circumstances, I think we may be satisfied with the results; out of ~ for *(considering)*: I declined to make the matter public, out of ~ for his parents; act without ~ to decency; do s.th. without ~ to expense / consequences (2 *esteem*) he stands high in their ~; be held in high ~ (by s.o.); show (high) ~ for s.o.; have a (great / high / low) ~ for s.o.('s judgement) (3 ~*s: kindly thoughts; good wishes*) please give my ~s to your parents; give him my best ~s; With kind(est) ~s, Yours sincerely *(at the end of a letter)* (4) with ~ to *(concerning)*: err with ~ to facts; with ~ to this matter I should like to say . . .; in this ~ the book is quite satisfactory.

regard *vt* (1) ~ s.o. as a friend / genius / fool / *etc*; ~ s.th. as wrong / absurd / discreditable / *etc*; they ~ed him as (being) fit for promotion; I ~ it as madness / my duty to do it (2 *fig: look upon*) I ~ his behaviour with suspicion; I still ~ him kindly; ~ s.o. with favour / reverence / horror / *etc* (3 *pay attention to*) now ~ what I have to say; he doesn't ~ my advice. (4 *esteem*) she ~s scholarship highly. (5 *concern*) this does not ~ me at all; my decision ~s your happiness; as ~s his suggestion, I was non-committal.

register *vt* (1) ~ a name / item (on a list / in a register); ~ a patent / deed / new trade-mark; ~ one's car; ~ a birth / marriage / death; ~ (one's) luggage; ~ a letter / parcel; ~ s.o. for voting (on the voting rolls); ~ a student (in a school); ~ (s.o. / o.s.) at a university; have you ~ed for the summer term? (2) yesterday the thermometer ~ed (the heat as) 97°. (3) her face ~ed surprise. (4) you must ~ with the police; ~ at a motel (5 *have some effects*) my plea didn't ~ on him at all; he heard, but did it ~? - *adj* (6) a ~ed company; send a letter by ~ed post *(AE:* mail); a ~ed letter; ~ed bonds (7 *having the pedigree recorded*) a ~ed poodle / Siamese cat / thoroughbred (horse) / *etc* (8 *officially examined*) a ~ed nurse.

regulate *vt* (1 *govern, direct according to rule*) laws which ~ the succession of seasons; ~ the traffic (2 *reduce to order, uniformity*) ~ one's habits / conduct; ~ the industries of a country / one's expenditure(s) (3 *adjust to some standard, re-*

quirement) ~ a watch / (the speed of) a machine / the pressure of a tyre; ~ the temperature; the furnace smokes so much that it needs to be ~d; they ~ the flow of water by the sluice gate; she ~s her hours to fit in with his.

reign *vi* (1 *to be monarch*) he ~ed (over the country), but he did not rule or govern. (2) confusion ~ed; silence ~ed in the deserted streets; cholera ~s in India throughout the year; terror ~ed under Robespierre.

rein *n* (1) hold / pull / drop the ~s; draw ~ / in the ~s *(go slow, stop; also fig)*; give a horse the ~s / a free ~ (2) assume / drop the ~s of government *(enter upon / give up office)*; hold the ~s of government; his wife holds the ~s; give ~ / the ~(s) to one's imagination / anger / feelings / passsions *(allow them full freedom)*; keep a loose / tight ~ on s.o./ s.th. (→ keep *vt* 8d).

relate *vt* (1 ~ *with, to: establish a connection*) it is difficult to ~ the findings of Dr. A. with those of Professor B.; ~ events to probable causes; many experts ~ crime to slums; scientists cannot ~ the phenomena with / to anything we know, to each other; ~ theory and practice. (2) ~ one's adventure (to s.o.); horrible to ~, he was killed last night; strange to ~, I met him in India. - *vi* (3 ~ *to: concern*) these regulations ~ only to people under the age of 21; he showed me all the correspondence ~ing to the matter; many experts think that crime ~s to slums; he notices nothing but what ~s to himself. - *adj* (4 *be ~d to: be connected with*) the Dutch language is closely ~d to German; reading and writing are ~d subjects; be ~d to s.o. by blood / marriage; closely / distantly ~d; ~d in the first degree; are they ~d? he is ~d to him by blood.

relation *n* (1) the ~ between cause and effect; the ~ between wages and costs / of wages to costs; man's ~(ship) to his environment; I see no ~ between the two events; the outlay bears no / is out of all ~ to the object aimed at; plan with / in ~ to the future; the report has ~ to a state of things now past. (2) the ~ of the findings of Dr. A. with those of Professor B. is the next step to be taken (→ relate *vt* 1). (3) we are anxious to maintain good ~s between our neighbours and ourselves / good ~s with our neighbours; have / entertain (close / friendly) ~s with s.o.; human / social / marital ~s; public ~s (officer / firm / campaign); business / foreign ~s; mutual ~s between two countries; enter into / establish ~s with s.o.; establish / break off / re-establish diplomatic ~s; good / friendly / strained ~s with France (4) all his ~s are coming to see him; he can't stand his wife's ~s; he is a distant ~ of our family; what ~ is he to you? is he any ~ to you? (5 *narration*) the ~ of his adventures / an anecdote / *etc*; I didn't like his ~ *(how he related it; what he related)*.

relationship *n* (1) → relation 1; the ~ between teachers and students; bring different activities into close ~ (2) his ~ to a noble family; degrees of ~; blood ~.

release *vt* (1) ~ one's hold of s.th.; she tried to ~ her hand from his grasp; ~ the brakes of a car; ~ a mechanical part / a mechanism / the shutter of a camera; ~ bombs; activities that ~ one's stored-up energy; ~ heat (2a) ~ a prisoner / bird / trapped animal; ~ a dog from the chain / its lead; ~ s.o. from captivity / from imprisonment / on bail (2b) ~ s.o. from a promise; ~ one's fiancé (from his promise); ~ s.o. from a debt / obligation / duty; ~ houses from rent control; ~ s.o. from pain / his suffering; ~ s.o. from doing s.th.; nobody can ~ you from your responsibility. (3) ~ an article / bulletin / news item; ~ pictures / documents (for publication); ~ a film; details of the scheme have not yet been ~d to the public.

relief *n* (1) the medicine brought him some ~; the tablet will bring you (instant / temporary / *etc*) ~; you will get ~ from this medicine; get ~ from pain / anxiety / the burden of taxation; the ~ of suffering; heave / breathe a sigh of ~; to his ~ he heard that he ...; it was a (great) ~ to me to find the children safe; the warm sun was a ~ after days of rain. (2 *s.th. that relieves*) I wish I knew of a ~ for neuralgia. (3 *variety, change from monotony*) we crossed wide stretches of moorland without ~; the trees were a ~ to the eye; a black dress without ~ (4 *release from duty*) the rescuers worked in eight-hour shifts with two hours' ~; the ~ of troops / a sentry (5 *one who replaces another*) I am waiting for my ~. (6 *freeing from a siege*) he sent out an army for the ~ of the town; a ~ army (7 *food, money, etc, given*) the Red Cross sent ~

to the flood victims; provide ~ for refugees; live on ~ *(state assistance)*; ~ work; a ~ fund; a ~ organization for refugees.

relieve *vt* (1a *lessen, remove*) remove the lid of a pot to ~ steam pressure; add a column to ~ the stress on the others; opium derivatives ~ pain but do not ~ the spastic state; ~ distress / want / need; ~ s.o.'s suffering / anxiety; ~ one's conscience; ~ one's feeling (by shedding tears, using strong language, *etc*); ~ o.s. / nature *(empty the bladder, bowels)* (1b *bring help*) ~ the poor / distressed / sick (2a) ~ s.o. of a burden / task / obligation; let me ~ you of your suitcase; ~ s.o. of worry / doubts; ~ s.o. of the necessity of doing s.th.; nobody can ~ you of your responsibility; this medicine will ~ you; tears ~d her; I was much ~d to hear it; feel ~d of a great weight (2b *discharge*) ~ s.o. of his post / office / duties (2c *deprive*) ~ s.o. of his watch / his wealth / a tidy sum (2d *free from what afflicts one*) ~ s.o. from indigestion / anxiety / fear / sorrow(s) (3 *free from a siege*) he sent out an army to ~ the town; a ~ing army (4 *make less monotonous*) a black bodice ~d with white lace; ~ the tension of a drama with comic episodes (5 *replace s.o. on duty*) ~ troops / a sentry; ~ the guard / watch; you shall be ~d at 10.30.

relish *n* (1 *enjoyment*) he eats with great ~; she finds no ~ in eating oysters; he used to tell the story with ~. (2 *flavour*) lemon gives this dish quite an exquisite ~; a ~ of nutmeg / garlic / *etc*; a ~ of the sea (3 *liking*) have no ~ for one's food; he had a decided ~ for modern painting; he has no ~ for hard work / that task. (4 *s.th. that stimulates*) Yorkshire ~ is a kind of sauce; olives and sardines are ~es; hunger is the best ~; danger gives ~ to adventure; some pastimes lose their ~ when one grows old.

relish *vt* (1 *make pleasing to the taste*) ~ a dish with sauce; excellent coffee ~ed with hot cakes (2 *enjoy*) I don't ~ my food as I used to; I do not ~ the task / prospect; ~ one's dancing lessons / a good joke / the beauties of a poem; she ~ed staying / her stay in Rome; do you ~ being admired by your listeners? - *vi* (3 *fig: have a flavour*) a sentiment which ~es of cynicism; a literary style which ~es of the Bible.

remark *n* (1) make / pass a ~ about s.th.; I will not repeat his ~s on the subject; I have a few ~s to add; make a ~ / some ~s / a few ~s *(give a short talk)*; he dropped / let fall a ~; an introductory / explanatory / complimentary / acid / sharp / biting / cutting / hurtful / wounding / nasty / unfriendly / unhappy / unfortunate / hasty / offhand / careless / incidental / naive / playful / facetious / innocuous / inoffensive / irrelevant / witless / trite / inane / imbecile / enigmatic / ironical / satirical / sarcastic / derogatory / prophetic / bold / cheeky / witty / apt / critical / concise / classic / choice / *etc* ~. (2 *noticing*) s.th. worthy of ~ ; escape ~ *(pass unnoticed)*.

remark *vt* (1 *say casually*) someone ~ed that tomorrow would be a warm day; 'you are wrong', he ~ed;... as he so aptly ~ed. (2 *notice*) I ~ed a slight accent in her speech; it passed un~ed. - *vi* (3 *make comment*) he ~ed on her lack of intelligence; several people ~ed upon the fine quality of the work.

remedy *n* (1) a ~ for a cold / the gout / *etc*; a headache ~; herbal ~ies; an efficacious / drastic / universal / *etc* ~ (2) the ~ of abuses / social evils; this fault is beyond ~ / all ~ies (3) a ~ for unemployment; there is no ~ but lying.

remedy *vt* (1) codliver oil is used to ~ improper nutrition. (2 *put right*) ~ a matter / evil / abuse; he ~ied the rattle in the refrigerator.

remember *vt* (1) I have just ~ed that it's your birthday today; I can't ~ his name for the moment; I ~ the occasion of our first meeting; don't you ~ me? I ~ it accurately / dimly / only vaguely / *etc*; I ~ going to the post office; I distinctly ~ paying him - I gave him £2; I can't ~ dates; history will ~ Churchill as the man who ...; I ~ the village as a place of very narrow streets; we shall always ~ him for his generosity. (2 *not forget*) I must ~ to go to the post office; please ~ to wipe your feet before coming in; I'll try to ~ the exact date; ~ your appointment with the dentist. (3 *give a present; tip*) ~ a friend on his birthday; the company always ~s us at Christmas; don't forget to ~ the doorman; he ~ed me in his will. (4 *convey greetings from s.o.*) please ~ me to your family; my wife wishes to be ~ed to you. - *vi* (5) if I ~ right(ly), he ...; as far as I (can) ~.

remind *vt* (1 *cause s.o. to remember*) ~ me to phone him tomorrow; it is a good thing that you have ~ed me of it; did you ~ him about that book he borrowed? (2 *bring to mind*) he ~s me of his brother; that story ~s me of an experience I once had; this family scene suddenly ~ed me of my father coming home one day and announcing...

remove *vt* (1a) ~ a book from a shelf / the lid from a pot; ~ the film (from a camera); ~ the dishes / napkins / cloth from the table; ~ a bandage; ~ one's coat / hat / jacket (1b *move to another place*) she ~d the painting to another wall; Peter the Great ~d the seat of government from Moscow to St. Petersburg; □ ~ mountains *(perform miracles)* (2a *do away with*) ~ dandruff / wrinkles / corns; ~ grease / a stain from a garment; ~ the bark / rind; ~ rubble / debris; ~ one's name from a list (2b *as in 2a, fig*) he ~d all traces of having been there; ~ obstacles / difficulties / mistakes / inequalities / doubts / *etc*; ~ the cause of a quarrel / a cause of worry; ~ the source of trouble / a disease (3a *send away; dismiss*) ~ a tenant; ~ a boy from school for misbehaviour; ~ a man from office (for embezzling) / an officer from the army; ~ a rival (3b *kill*) he was ~d by poison. – *vi* (4 *change one's residence*) we ~ to Paris early in July; ~ into the country.

render *vt* (1a *give, furnish, esp s.th. due*) ~ aid / help (to those in need); ~ praise; ~ thanks to God (1b *submit for payment*) ~ a bill / account (1c *pay*) ~ a tax; ~ tribute; ~ good for evil (1d *do*) ~ s.o. a service / kindness; ~ obedience / attention (1e *deliver formally*) ~ a verdict / judgement / decision; ~ an account / report. (2 ~ + *n* + *adj: make*) the surprise ~ed him speechless; the blow ~ed him unconscious; her desire to ~ everyone happy; this ~s it probable; the tone ~ed it an insult. (3 *perform; express artistically*) the sonata was admirably ~ed; his way of ~ing Hamlet; he knows how to ~ perspective; he ~s landscapes with great skill and artistry. (4 *translate*) ~ a text / poem / idiom into English; you have ~ed my meaning accurately. (5 *melt, clarify*) ~ fat / butter / lard.

render up ~ up a city to the enemy.

renounce *vt* (1 *cease to acknowledge*) ~ one's own son / an heir / a friend(ship); ~ principles / s.o.'s authority / a treaty (2a *give up*) ~ a design / attempt / plan; ~ all thought of doing s.th.; ~ all worldly pleasures / the world (2b *give up formally*) ~ a right / claim / possession.

rent *vt* (1a) ~ land / a house / a flat; do you own your house or ~ it? ~ a flat by the month (1b) ~ a television set / washing machine / *etc* (2) Mr Hill ~s this house / land to us at £60 a month. (3) the premises ~ at £700 a year; this house ~s at a high sum / cheaply.

repair *n* (1) traffic will be diverted while the road is under ~; your bicycle / boot / house / health needs ~. (2) the ~ of a flat tyre; it's time we had some ~s done; this old house needs a lot of ~s; the shop is closed during ~s; ~s done while you wait. (3 *condition*) the plumbing is in bad ~; the house is (kept) in good ~; put a machine / boat / *etc* in ~; the machine / car is in / out of ~; it is ruined beyond ~.

repair *vt* (1) ~ a flat tyre / machine / boat / building / bridge; ~ clothes / shoes (2) ~ a wrong / loss / deficiency; ~ damage.

replace *vt* (1) she ~d the book on the shelf; '~ your receiver, caller, I'll ring you back.' (2) the saw rapidly ~d the axe; silk is being ~d more and more by manmade fibres; Smith ~d Brown; nobody can ~ a mother. (3) he ~d Brown by Smith; ~ coal with / by oil; all the damaged parts were removed and ~d with new. (4 *return, give the equivalent of*) ~ a broken vase; ~ a sum of money borrowed; the broken window-pane must be ~d; he promised to ~ the money he had stolen.

report *n* (1) an exact / accurate / detailed / full / comprehensive / true / false / (un)favourable / adverse / confidential / *etc* ~; a classified ~ on rocket research; an annual ~ is necessary; the ~ of an eyewitness / by-stander; the ~ of a speech / lecture; an unconfirmed ~ of an earthquake in Chile; he gave a ~ on the situation; a ~ from abroad; as ~s from Peru indicate,...; draw up / compose a ~; make a ~ for s.o. / on s.th. to s.o.; he is, by ~, a most able scientist. (2 *rumour*) mere ~ is not enough to go upon; the ~ goes / ~ has it that he...; don't listen to idle ~s. (3 *BE*) a school(boy's) ~; the ~s conference.

report *vt* (1) ~ (on) s.th. in detail / fully / faithfully / accurately / vaguely / briefly / *etc*; ~ a speech / accident / event / *etc*; ~

a burglary to the police; □ ~ progress (to s.o.) *(state what has been done so far)*; his words were ~ed to the President; he is well / badly ~ed on; he ~ed the Pole to be accessible; the firm ~ed selling three times as many bicycles as last year; it is ~ed that he... (2 *make a complaint against*) I intend to ~ him to the Dean for cheating; I shall have to ~ (you for) your unpunctuality. - *vi* (3) we had to ~ to the headmaster / at 10.30 / for duty (at the office); when you have finished this work, ~ (yourself) to the manager. (4) he ~s for the evening paper.

represent *vt* (1 *present an image of*) the picture ~s a hunting scene; this statue ~s Lincoln as a young man; the stage setting ~s a hotel lobby (2 *describe*) the article ~ed the dictator as a benevolent despot; the candidate ~ed himself as a friend of the people; he is the person he ~s himself to be; he ~s his father as (being) a monster; they ~ed the matter as though I were to blame for everything; I am not what you ~ me to be. (3 *form: point out, explain*) he ~ed to them the folly of such a move; ~ the theory of relativity to an audience; I can only ~ it to you by metaphors; ~ one's urgent needs to the authorities; he ~s that he has / to have seen service; such excuses ~ nothing to me. (4 *act on behalf of*) a lawyer ~s his client; he ~s our company in Chicago; ~ one's government in a foreign country; many countries were ~ed by their ambassadors at the birthday celebrations. (5 *be the delegate of*) he will continue to ~ us in Congress; how is our town ~ed in Parliament? he ~s us on the council / committee; he ~ed us at the reception / wedding / meeting. (6 *be, constitute*) his work ~s an important contribution to science. (6a *be an example of*) a genus ~ed in Europe by two species (7a *be a symbol of*) ∞ ~s infinity; the letters of the alphabet ~ sounds; in this painting the cat ~s evil and the bird, good. (7b *express by a symbol*) ~ musical sounds by notes (8 *play, act*) ~ a play / character; the actor ~ed Hamlet as too heroic a character. (9 *correspond to*) these notes ~ eight hours' work; the llama of the New World ~s the camel of the Old World; an inch of rain ~s 100 tons to the acre.

reproach *n* (1) a term of ~; a look of ~; he is beyond / above ~. (2) she heaped ~es on him. (3) he acted in such a way as to bring ~ upon his family; a life without ~ (4) such conduct on the part of an officer is a ~ to the regiment; environmental pollution is a ~ to civilization.

reproach *vt* (1) ~ s.o. with dishonesty / bad conduct / extravagance / *etc*; I have nothing to ~ myself with; ~ s.o. for being late / his lack of attention / *etc* (2) his eyes ~ me.

reputation *n* (1) this firm has an unrivalled ~; he had a poor ~ as a lawyer; he has the ~ of being a great scholar / rich man; he is a man of good / high / honourable ~; enjoy a high ~; acquire / make / gain a ~ (for o.s.) (as a teacher / *etc*) (2 *good* ~) he lost / ruined his ~ when he started to gamble; in the world of society, ~s are quickly made and quickly lost; build up a ~; → live up to 1.

request *n* (1) an (untimely / (un)reasonable / *etc*) ~ for information / help / money / *etc*; we have received multiple ~s for this book. (2 *thing asked for*) obtain one's ~; all my ~s were granted. (3) do s.th. at the (urgent) ~ of s.o.; the orchestra played numbers at / by ~; catalogues will be sent on ~ (to this office). (4) he is much in ~ as a lecturer; articles imported from India are in great ~.

request *vt* he ~ed permission to speak; we ~ the honour of your company at dinner; I must urgently ~ you to stop; visitors are ~ed not to touch any objects; an answer is ~ed; I have a favour to ~ of you.

require *vt* (1 *need*) I ~ seven hours sleep a night; he ~s medical care; do you ~ any more information from me? a candidate ~s to hold a certificate; does this machine ~ much attention? (2 *demand*) ~ s.o. to account for money spent; they ~d me to keep silent; what do you ~ of me? ~ cooperation; do all the law ~s / that is ~d by (the) law; good taste ~s that he should make an apology immediately; the law ~s annual income-tax returns; this article should be made ~d reading in all the colleges. (3 *make necessary*) this work ~s infinite patience / great skill / unusual concentration / great precision / *etc*; this matter will ~ a great deal of money / time; the situation ~s tact / patience / immediate action; it ~d all his strength to hold them back; his wound ~s little care; how often do these carpets ~

cleaning / to be cleaned? all the data in this article ~ careful checking.

research *n* pure / fundamental / applied / scientific / scholarly / academic ~; be engaged in ~ (to discover the cause of s.th.); do ~ (into s.th.); most pure ~ is conducted in the universities; the ability to carry out independent ~; ~ in a field / into a problem; cybernetics can be used for ~ on the human body or on the workings of an inanimate machine; recent ~es on the thyroid gland; Darwin's ~es made it clear that ...; ~ into ancestry; ~ over a period of years has established that we...; years of ~ / ~es over a period of years have established...; his ~es have been fruitful.

research *vt* (1) ~ a matter thoroughly. - *vi* (2) ~ into a problem.

reservation *n* (1) mental ~; accept s.th. without ~ / with two small ~s; I can recommend him for the post without ~. (2) ~ of seats / rooms in advance; write for ~s; it is advisable to make an early ~; make your ~s well in advance.

reserve *vt* (1) ~ some money for an emergency; ~ part of profit for reinvestment; we must ~ our energies for the tasks that lie ahead. (2a) ~ a (train) seat / table / room; seats should be ~d in advance; a ~d seat ticket (2b) the hotel ~d a room for us. (3) we ~ Saturday evenings for entertaining friends; ground ~d for gardening; this room is ~d for chess players; the use of this room is ~d to staff members; a great future is ~d for you. (4) he ~s all rights in his inventions; author's rights ~d (5) the judge ~d his decision; I will ~ judgement until I hear your side of the story.

resign *vt* (1) ~ an office / position / post / seat / claim / agreement / *etc*; ~ the chairmanship / secretaryship / editorship; he ~ed his rights under the patent; the doctor has ~ed all hope. (2) she ~ed her child to an adoption agency; I ~ my children to your care. (3) ~ o.s. to sleep / rest / death / meditation / s.o.'s guidance; he ~ed himself to a long wait; ~ o.s. / be ~ed to one's fate / the inevitable / living in reduced circumstances. - *vi* (4) he ~ed from the committee / board of directors / Cabinet; he has ~ed from three of the many offices he held; he ~ed as chairman a week ago.

resist *vt* (1) ~ an invasion / attack / disease; ~ aggression / old age / infection; ~ the enemy / the police; she firmly ~ed his (immoral) advances; few women manage to ~ M.'s charms (for long). (2) this glass ~s heat; a watch-case that ~s water (3) ~ (the) temptation (to do s.th.); she can't ~ cigarettes / chocolates; who can ~ the intoxication of the first spring day? he won't ~ the right kind of approach; it was so ludicrous, she could scarcely ~ a smile; he can't ~ teasing children; she finds it hard to ~ buying anything attractive.

resolution *n* (1) a man of ~; his lack of ~; show (great) ~ in a crisis (2) what ~s have you made (for) this year - are you going to give up smoking and go on a diet? New Year's ~s (are made to be broken); make good ~s (3) he has made a (firm) ~ to give up his job; pass / take a ~; strengthen s.o.'s ~ (4) a committee can pass / carry / adopt / reject a ~ (in favour of / for / against s.th.) (5) the ~ of a mystery / question / doubt / discord / conflict / *etc.*

resolve *vt* (1) he ~d to work hard / that nothing should induce him / that he would do it; the committee ~d to authorize this step; be it ~d that... *(parliamentary formula)* (2) ~ a mystery / question / problem / equation / difficulty / doubt / conflict / dispute / *etc* (3) ~ a mixture into its constituents; a compound is ~d / ~s (itself) into its elements; a powerful telescope ~s a nebula into stars. - *vi* (4 *reach a decision*) they ~d on a less violent course of action; the committee ~d on N.'s proposal. - *adj* (5) he was ~d on going there.

resort *vi* (1) if other means fail, we must ~ to force / drastic measures; ~ to crime / violence / bribery / lies (2 *go*) ~ to a place of entertainment; a beach to which many people ~.

respect *n* (1) I have great ~ for your work; he has little / no ~ for anyone; youth should show ~ to old age; we can show ~ to a person only in his presence; we can show ~ for him whether he is present or not; hold s.o. in (high) ~; earn / win (s.o.'s) ~; gain s.o.'s ~; command ~; treat s.o. with (due) ~; do s.th. out of ~ for s.o.; I say it with all (due) ~ to you. (2 *consideration*) in fixing the salary we shall have ~ to the work entailed and the qualifications of the person appointed; we must have / pay ~ to the needs of the general reader; a policy without ~ to race, colour or creed; justice should be administered without ~ of persons. (3 *~s: greetings*) give him my ~s; he sends his ~s; my ~s to your dear parents; we called on the new neighbours to pay our ~s. (4) they resemble each other in all / some / a few ~s; the plan is faulty in every / one / this ~; in some / certain / a number of ~s; the company made its plans with ~ to future needs; there are difficulties with ~ to the wording; I can say nothing with ~ to his competence as a workman; he is superior in ~ of intelligence.

respect *vt* (1) children should ~ their teachers; I ~ his judgement; I ~ him, but I could never be fond of him; he knows how to make himself ~ed. (2) ~ the law; ~ s.o.'s rights / wishes / privacy.

respond *vi* (1) ~ briefly to a question; ~ to a suggestion / invitation / appeal; he ~ed to my remarks with a sneer. (2) nerves ~ to a stimulus; the disease did not ~ to the treatment. (3) the canoe's ~ing to the paddle astonishes one at first; the aircraft ~s to the controls.

responsibility *n* (1) have / accept / take / assume (full) ~ for s.th.; he declines all ~ for it; do s.th. on one's own ~; he is not afraid of ~; a post of great ~ (2) the president has great / heavy ~ies; a family is a great ~; he asked to be relieved of his ~ / ~ies; feel the ~ies of one's position.

responsible *adj* (1) be ~ to s.o. for s.th.; are you ~ for breaking this window? don't blame me for the mistake - I'm not ~ for it; he is not ~ *(capable of acting rationally).* (2 *be ~: be the cause*) termites are often ~ for the collapse of wooden foundations; the rain was ~ for the poor attendance; two things are chiefly ~ for this lack of interest; the amateur movement is ~ for most of the best playwriting of America; research is ~ for most of that improvement. (3) give a task to a ~ man; a ~ boy should be chosen to collect the club dues. (4) a ~ job / post / position; he is too young for such ~ work.

rest[1] *n* (1) did you have a good night's ~? he needs ~ after the long journey; I have not had a moment's ~ all day; let's sit down and take / have a ~; give s.o. a ~; we had several ~s on our way up the mountain; the wheels of the mill are at ~ *(not moving)*; the poor man is now at ~ *(dead)*; → set *vt* 21b; the pendulum comes to ~ when the clock runs down; go to ~ *(to bed)*; → lay *vt* 8; bring a machine to ~ (2) an arm / back / neck / foot ~.

rest *vi* (1) ~ after the day's labours; ~ on a couch / seat / *etc*; his arm ~ed on the table; □ ~ on one's laurels; → oar *n* (1a) the ball ~ed at the edge of the hole; clouds ~ing on the mountain tops (2 *lie buried*) ~ in a cemetery; ~ in peace (3) his glance ~ed for a moment on her face; his eyes ~ed on the ceiling; a sunbeam ~ed on the altar. (4) the statue ~s on a pedestal; the roof ~ed on arches. (5) his theory ~s on false tenets; science ~s on phenomena; success or failure ~s on your efforts; the charge ~s on the evidence of one witness; all the difficulty ~s in the fact that he ...; the final decision ~s with the headmaster; the blame ~s with them; let us let the matter ~ *(as it is)* (for the time being); I shall not let it ~ at that; the matter cannot ~ here *(must be carried further)*; → assure *adj* 4. - *vt* (6a) ~ one's head on a pillow; ~ one's eyes; ~ one's feet after a march; he ~ed his back against the tree. (6b) he ~ed a ladder against the wall. (7→3) he ~ed his gaze on the ceiling. (8) ~ one's defence on a plea of insanity.

rest[2] *n* some of us stayed, the ~ went home; the ~ of the students are in the corridor; the ~ of the essay is unfinished; the ~ of the essays have been collected; the ~ of the evening was rather dull; eat what you want and put the ~ in the fridge.

restore *vt* (1) ~ stolen jewels to the owner; ~ a book to the shelf; ~ an employee to his old post (2) ~ (law and) order / an old custom; after a war we should dismiss all thought of revenge and think only of ~ing friendship; ~ a monarch / the monarchy; ~ the king to his throne (3) ~ a painting / text / ruin; ~ an ancient building / extinct animal; ~ s.th. (to its original beauty / form) (4) ~ s.o. to health; ~ s.o.'s health / strength; feel completely ~d; ~ vital functions; ~ s.o.'s reputation.

restrict *vt* (1) the trees ~ our vision. (2) ~ one's expenditure / expenses; ~ s.o.'s movement / freedom (of choice) / power / authority; my time is ~ed; I am ~ed to advising; his authority is ~ed within narrow limits; he ~ed himself to four cigarettes a day. - *adj* (3) this rule has a very ~ed application. (4 *esp AE exclusive of certain minorities*) they live in a

~ed neighbourhood; the club fought in vain to keep its membership ~ed.

result *n* (1) a natural / necessary / (in)direct / (un)favourable / surprising / brilliant / meagre / poor / *etc* ~; achieve / obtain (good / bad) ~s; announce / give out the ~s of a competition; his infirmity is the ~ of an accident; he appealed against the decision with the ~ that he now has to pay even more; he refused to have medical attention; and as a ~ he became seriously ill; you took a great risk, though in the ~ it did not turn out so badly as it might have done. (2) the ~ of a mathematical problem / physical experiment; the calculation gave / yielded / showed the following ~; did the experiment establish a ~?

result *vi* (1) his death ~ed from an overdose of drugs; a flood ~ed from the heavy rain. (2) the accident ~ed in the death of two people; this matter will ~ in unpleasantness; your effort should ~ in success; ~ badly / in failure / in a victory.

resume *vt* (1) ~ one's seat; ~ one's hat *(put it on again)* (2) she ~d her maiden name; ~ possession of property; ~ control (3) ~ one's courage / good spirits / strength (4) ~ a subject / discussion / a story / play; ~ one's work / studies (5 *sum up*) ~ the main points of an argument; a book which ~s all his views. – *vi* (6 *continue after interruption*) summer services ~ next week (→ service *n* 7).

retain *vt* (1) this vessel won't ~ water; some metals ~ heat for a long time; we built a wall to ~ the earth behind our house. (2) this cloth ~s its colour; this paint ~s its lustre. (3) ~ an old custom; ~ control of one's car (4) he ~ed his vitality to the end; ~ one's sense of humour; I shall always ~ an agreeable memory of it. (5) have difficulty in ~ing names; ~ s.th. in one's head / memory / mind.

return *vi* (1) ~ home (exhausted) / the way one came / from abroad / to work / to public office / *etc*; a ~ed emigrant (2) ~ to one's old habits; then he ~ed to his original theme; her thoughts constantly ~ed to childhood; her mind ~ed to that happy day when... (3 *occur again*) summer ~s; these fits ~ at intervals. (4 *answer*) "...," he ~ed; she attacked him, but he ~ed with a witty remark. – *vt* (5) ~ a book to a shelf / the library; ~ the pipe to its owner; ~ the fish to the water; ~ a child to her mother; ~ a door to its closed position (6) ~ a call / visit; he ~ed the salutation with a polite bow; ~ a favour / compliment / insult / blow; my love is not ~ed; ~ a service; ~ evil for good (7 *reflect*) ~ light / sound (8 *repay*) ~ a loan (9 *yield*) this investment ~s a good profit; ~ an income / a revenue / dividends (10 *(re)elect*) ~ s.o. to Parliament; the voters ~ed him by a landslide.

revenge *n* (1) a thirst for ~; do s.th. in ~; his ~ was to set the papers on fire; have / take (one's) ~ on s.o.; get / take / have (one's) ~ for s.th.; ~ is sweet. (2) be full of ~ (3) we'll have another game to give you your ~.

revenge *vt* ~ an insult / s.o.'s death / one's dead brother; ~ o.s. on s.o. for s.th.; we shall ~ ourselves for our defeat.

review *vt* (1a) we ~ed (the events of) the past; ~ the situation; they ~ed their lessons for the test. (1b *consider again*) ~ a manuscript in the light of criticism (2) the general ~ed the troops. (3) ~ books for a newspaper; The Times ~ed her book favourably. – *vi* (4) he ~s for some local newspaper.

revoke *vt* ~ a permission / consent / promise / driving licence / decree / grant; he ~d his will; a judge may ~ a sentence; I have made a promise and will not ~ it.

revolt *vi* (1) ~ against the government; ~ against parental authority (2) ~ at coarse language; human nature ~s at the mistreatment of children; he ~s from eating meat. – *vt* (3) such low behaviour ~s me; cruelty ~s decent people.

rich *adj* (1) ~ persons / states / nations (2 *expensive, costly*) ~ furniture / carving / jewels; a ~ fabric / garment / dress; a ~ banquet / feast; a ~ gift / reward (3 *fertile, abundant*) a ~ soil / land / country; a land ~ in minerals / natural resources; a ~ mine; rivers ~ in fish; a ~ harvest; a ~ supply; a diet ~ in proteins; a confection ~ with sugar and spice (3b) a country ~ in traditions; a countryside ~ in beauty; a design ~ with colours; a man ~ in kindness (4 *full; strong*) ~ colours / sounds / smells; a ~ odour; a ~ voice; ~ purple (5 *of food*) a ~ cake (*containing much fat*); a ~ gravy *(spicy)* (6 *inform: highly amusing*) a ~ joke / incident.

ride *vi* (1) he ~s well; they like to ~ for pleasure; he jumped on his horse and rode away / off. (2a) ~ in a car / bus / taxi / tram / train; ~ bareback; ~ on horseback / mule-back / donkey-back / camelback; ~ on s.o.'s back; some birds ~ (on) the wind; the ship rode on the (crest of the) waves; a boat ~ing (on) the waves; the ship rode at anchor in the harbour (→ anchor *n* 1); ~ a good pace; we have ridden for an hour - let's walk for a change; he rode 60 miles before he found a petrol station; □ ~ for a fall *(court danger, disaster; usu. fig)*; let a problem / an issue ~ *(take no action on it)* (2b) a blood-red moon rode in the cloudless sky; the moon was ~ing high. (3a) the car ~s smoothly (over bumps in the road) (3b) the ground ~s hard; the rain made the ground ~ soft. (4 *fig: move along*) he's ~ing along on his friend's success; he rode into office on a tide of discontent; distress is ~ing among the people. (5 *depend on*) all his hopes are ~ing on getting that promotion; his future success ~s on this merger going through. - *vt* (6a) he ~s a good horse; ~ a donkey / camel / *etc*; ~ a horse to death; ~ a hobby / principle / joke to death; ~ a hobby(-horse) *(concern o.s. with one's favourite occupation* (6b) ~ a motor-cycle / bicycle (7) ~ a road / region / ford; ~ the country / desert / prairies (8a) ~ a baby on one's back; he rode her on his knees. (8b *cause to ride or be carried*) the crowd rode the athlete triumphantly through the streets on their shoulders; ~ s.o. out of town on a rail *(also fig: expel; censure severely)*: if the mayor's staff try to impose new taxes the voters will ~ them out of town on a rail. (9) ~ a race (10 *dominate; usu. as part*) a nightmare ~s the sleeper; a man ridden by fears / prejudices; fear-ridden; a country ridden by a power-mad dictator (11) □ ~ herd on *(AE keep watch, control on)*: you'll have to ~ herd on those school-children or they'll be up to mischief.

ride down (1) ~ ~ a fugitive *(catch him)* (2) the police rode the demonstrators ~. (3) ~ ~ a minority.

ride out

ride out (1) next Sunday we want to ~ ~; the cavalry rode ~. (2) the ship rode ~ the gale; ~ ~ a storm *(also fig)* / crisis.

ride up her skirt rode up above her knees; trousers that tend to ~ up.

right *n* (1) fight for the ~; know the difference between ~ and wrong; he was taught to do ~; I will never give up the struggle, for I know I am in the ~; it is difficult to decide which of the two is in the ~. (2) basic / fundamental / civil / kingly ~s; the constitutional ~s of a citizen; an inalienable ~; the ~ to vote; he has a / no / not much ~ to do that; claim / demand / defend one's ~s; stand on / assert one's ~s *(insist on them)*; freedom of speech is a ~ of all Americans; □ by ~(s) *(according to what is right)*: the property should belong to me by ~; the people should by ~s have been given a voice in their government. (3 *ownership*) he has a 50-percent ~ in a silver mine; the author controls the screen ~s for the book. (4 *~s: true state*) set / put things to ~s; set a room to ~s. (5) turn to the ~; on the ~ you see ...; the seat on my ~ is reserved; to the ~ lay a large field; you will find quite a good café to the ~ of the post office. (6 *a right turn*) we made a ~ at the top of the hill. (7 *right half, wing*) we attacked the enemy's ~; our ~ crumbled. (8 *right hand*) he hit him with his ~. (9 *right-hand blow*) a ~ to the jaw.

right *vt* (1) ~ a fallen lamp; ~ a capsized boat; ~ o.s. after stumbling; the boat ~ed (herself) on the next wave. (2) ~ a crookedly hung picture (3) ~ one's point of view (4) ~ a wrong / injustice; a fault that will ~ itself (5) he was ~ed in court.

right *adj* (1) in the circumstances his conduct was ~; it is only ~ to tell you ... / that you should know ...; it is not ~ for children to sit up so late; it was quite ~ of you to ask; telling the truth was the ~ thing to do. (2) the ~ answer / solution / conclusion; your opinions are ~ enough; he was ~ in his opinions; what's the ~ time? is your watch ~? ~ you are *(I agree)*. (3 *appropriate*) the ~ time to act; say the ~ thing at the ~ time; he is the ~ man in the ~ place; the ~ people were invited; see that you take the ~ train; are we on the ~ road? be on the ~ side of *(younger than)* forty (4 *sound, normal*) she wasn't ~ in the head when she made the will; be in one's ~ mind *(not mad)* (5 *in good health*) he is all ~ again; do you feel all ~? this medicine will soon put you ~. (6 *in good order*) put things ~; put a watch ~; if anything is wrong, please set it ~. (7 *front, upper*) spread the tablecloth with the ~ side up (8 *authentic*) who is the ~ owner? (9) the ~ side / wheel / eye / *etc*; we made a ~ turn at the corner. (10) a ~ angle.

right *adv* (1) behave ~; obey one's conscience and live ~ (2) add a column of figures ~; do a job ~ the first time; decide / judge / remember / guess ~; nothing goes ~ (with me). (3 *completely*) ~ on to the end; his hat was knocked ~ off. (4 *of time: immediately*) ~ after breakfast; you must come ~ away *(at once)*. (5 *of position: immediately*) ~ by the church; ~ here; ~ round the house; ~ in the middle; he was standing ~ behind me. (6 *straight*) come ~ home; ~ to the bottom; go ~ to the heart of the matter; he looked him ~ in the eye; the apple was rotten ~ through. (7) keep ~; turn ~; look neither ~ nor left.

ring *vi* (1) the bell rang twice; metal objects / glasses ~; the sound of hunting-horns rang through the forest. (2a *sound*) the coin ~s true *(genuine)* / false; his words ~ true; his cry / curse is still ~ing in my ears. (2b) my ears are ~ing. (3a) just ~ if you need anything; ~ for a servant (3b) if you ~ at 5.30 I shall probably be in. (4) the playground rang with happy shouts; the room rang with laughter; the hall rang with applause. – *vt* (5) ~ a bell *(also fig: sound familiar)*; ~ a chime / peal / alarm; □ ~ the changes: you can ~ the changes on the same old sweater by using different jewellery. (6) the bell rang a low tone. (7) the bell ~s the hours. (8 *test by sound*) ~ a coin on the counter (9) ~ me tomorrow; can you ~ this number for me, please? who could I ~?

ring back I'll ~ you ~ in half an hour.

ring in ~ in the New Year / Sunday / a festival.

ring off he suddenly rang ~ in the middle of the conversation.

ring out (1) ~ ~ the old year (2) their songs rang ~ merrily; the church bells rang ~; his brave words rang ~; let a song / one's voice ~ ~; suddenly a shot rang ~.

ring up (1) ~ me up at six o'clock. (2 *register on a cash register*) the cashier rang up our bills.

rise *vi* (1a) ~ to one's feet (from a sitting / lying / kneeling position); ~ from the table (after dinner, *etc*) / one's sickbed; the committee rose *(finished work)* at 7; when Parliament ~s for the summer recess, . . . (1b *get up after sleeping*) ~ early / late (1c) Christ rose from the dead; the ~n Lord (1d) ~ from misery (2a) a bird / the balloon / the airship rose in the air; smoke ~s; the fog is ~ing at last; before the curtain ~s, we . . .; a blush rose to her cheeks; fear caused his hair to ~; my gorge / stomach ~s *(disgust is felt)*. (2b) the moon ~s; the sun is ~ing in the sky; the ~n sun (3) the river / lake rose and spread over the fields; the temperature / thermometer rose above normal; the barometer / glass ~s in fine weather; the fever rose. (4a *grow*) a blister rose on his hand; weeds rose overnight. (4b *become larger*) the bread / cake is ~ing; the yeast causes the loaf to ~; self-~ing flour *(AE.* → *raise vt* 6a) (5) a storm rose; if a wind should ~, . . .; a quarrel rose between them. (6) the mountain ~s abruptly; a castle ~s in the distance; the tower ~s to a height of 60 feet; the Empire State Building ~s above the other skyscrapers; ~ing ground; the path ~s as it approaches the woods. (7 *be built*) a skyscraper is ~ing in the river area; the new building ~s higher each day. (8) the prices ~ continually; sugar has ~n 5 pfennigs a pound; our exports have ~n by six per cent. (9) ~ (high) in a profession / organization / hierarchy; ~ in society / the world; you will ~ in your job if you have ability; ~ to high honours / to power; a man likely to ~; a ~ing young politician / lawyer; the ~ing generation *(young people)* (10 *become more intensive*) her voice rose in indignation / to a shriek; her colour rose. (11) indignation rose in him; feel one's temper ~ing; the desire rose in him to see her again; his spirits rose *(he became more cheerful)* when he heard the news. (12) the idea rose from my knowledge of him. (13) the whole country rose against the tyrant; the slaves rose against their masters; ~ in revolt / rebellion / arms (14 ~ *above: become superior to*) ~ above the commonplace; this film does not ~ above the ordinary; ~ above one's misfortunes; ~ above temptation / petty jealousies (15 ~ *to: prove o.s. equal to*) ~ to the occasion / emergency / requirements; ~ to one's responsibilities; Fred ~s to the demands of his school work. (16) the river ~s *(begins)* in the mountains / from this spring; the Nile ~s near the equator.

rise up (1) the mountains rose up before us. (2) ~ up against the invaders; ~ up in arms (against s.o.) *(get ready to fight; also fig)*.

risk *n* take a ~ *(knowingly)*; run a ~ *(trust to luck)*; he must run the ~ of being arrested; take foolish ~s; expose o.s. to / incur a ~ ; I think it's a ~ worth running; do s.th. at the ~ of one's life / at one's own ~ ; send s.th. at owner's ~ ; I must tell him the truth at the ~ of hurting his feelings.

risk *vt* (1) ~ one's life (to no purpose); ~ one's neck (2 *take the chance of*) ~ one's health / money / fortune / reputation; ~ a fall in climbing / sprained ankle; ~ a battle; you must ~ the jump / surgical operation; he ~s being arrested; you must ~ losing a little; it's silly to ~ getting your feet wet.

rival *n* (1) they are ~s in business / trade / love; A. is the ~ of B.; they are both ~s for Ann's hand. (2) he has no ~ in Shakespearean roles; in the Elizabethan age there is no ~ to Shakespeare as a tragic dramatist; (a stadium) without a ~; she is without ~ in the field of genetic studies.

rival *vt* (1) the department stores ~ one another in special sales. (2) ~ s.o. in intelligence / beauty / *etc*; he soon ~led the others in skill; the Hudson ~s any European river in beauty; the potteries which Wedgwood established soon ~led those of Holland.

road *n* (1) a trunk / principal / non-principal ~; an arterial / country / mountain / alpine / zigzag / switchback / (un)paved / (un)surfaced ~; a straight / winding / crooked / muddy / dusty / icy / rough / impassable / *etc* ~ ; ~ closed (to all vehicles); no through ~; design / construct / maintain a ~; this ~ goes / leads to Eton; this ~ goes / leads / runs through the forest / across the mountain / over the mountain; the ~ broadens / widens / narrows / bends / makes a bend / rises / ascends / slopes up / winds steeply upwards / descends / slopes down; get on the pavement - don't stand in the ~; we found an injured man lying in the ~; there was ice on the ~; there are lots of cars on the ~ today; in 1970, 7,501 people were killed on the ~s; how long were you on the ~ *(travelling)*? he's on the ~ *(as a travelling salesman)* for one of the major dress manufacturers; be / go on the ~ *(touring as a theatrical company)* (2) the ~ to peace; he's on the ~ to recovery / bankruptcy; there are many ~s to Rome; the ~ to Hell is paved with good intentions; there is no infallible / royal ~ to success, fame.

roll *vt* (1a) ~ a marble across the floor; ~ a barrel / hoop / ball; the waves ~ed the bathers toward the shore; the river ~ed its waters to the sea; ~ tree-trunks down a hill; ~ o.s. on one's face (1b) ~ a wheelbarrow down the road (1c) ~ one's eyes (at s.o.) (2a) ~ a cigarette / spill; ~ wool into a ball (2b) ~ a baby in a blanket (3) ~ a lawn / tennis court; ~ s.th. flat; ~ metal in a ~ing-mill; ~ dough for pastry; ~ed oats; ~ed gold (4a) ~ one's r's (4b) ~ a drum - *vi* (5a) the ball / marble ~ed across the floor; the coin ~ed under the table; the tree-trunks ~ed down the hill; the tears were ~ing down her cheeks; he ~ed over in bed; □ be ~ing in money / luxury *(have a great deal of it)* (5b) the car ~ed down the slope; the wagon train ~ed westward. (5c) planets ~ on their courses. (5d) the smoke ~ed across the sky; the mist ~s away; the waves ~ed towards the shore. (6) this dough ~s well *(is easy to ~)*. (7) ~ing country; a ~ing plain; away to the westward ~ed a range of mountains; hills that ~ to the sea (8) the thunder / echo / organ ~ed; drums were ~ing. (9) the ship ~ed on the stormy sea.

roll by the years ~ed by uneventfully.

roll in (1) subscriptions are ~ing in *(arriving in large quantities)*. (2) they would ~ in *(come home)* later and later every night.

roll on → roll by.

roll out (1) ~ ~ a map (on the table) (2) ~ ~ dough / pastry.

roll round spring ~ed ~ again.

roll up (1) ~ up a map / carpet / umbrella / piece of paper; ~ up wool / one's sleeves (→ sleeve 1); he ~ed himself up in a blanket. (2) paper sometimes ~s up; the kitten / hedgehog ~ed (itself) up in a ball. (3) ~ up the enemy front (4 *AE*) ~ up *(accumulate)* many debts; ~ up a huge fortune (5) a big coach ~ed up to the inn. (6) his debts were ~ing up.

room *n* (1a) a small / nice little / large / spacious / cheerful / light / airy / dark / noisy / (barely) furnished / empty / *etc* ~; a dining- / sitting- / living- / breakfast / reception / drawing- / front / back ~; a bath~ / bed~ / guest~; a ~ at the back; an assembly / hotel / single / double / spare ~; connecting ~s; a ~ facing south / the street; ~s to let / vacant; a ~ with private bath or shower / with a view of the sea; let / rent / take a ~; live in / occupy a ~ (1b *~s: lodgings*) he sells his house and takes ~s in the city; I expect you at my ~s. (2) make some ~ on the shelf; this table takes up too much ~; is there ~ for me in the back seat? there was scarcely ~ to breathe / no ~ to turn in (3 *opportunity*) there is ~ for improvement *(things might be better)* / hope / mistrust / doubt / difference of opinion; ~ to expand; there is ~ to argue whether... (4 *people in a ~*) the ~ became silent when Jack sat down at the piano; the whole ~ laughed / was hushed.

root *n* (1a) the ~ of a plant; the carrot is cultivated for its orange-red ~; pull up a plant by the ~s; take / strike ~ *(grow ~s; also fig: become established)*: the idea gradually began to take ~. (1b) such ~s / ~ vegetables, as carrots, turnips, *etc* (2) the ~ of a tooth / hair / finger-nail; the ~ of the tongue (3) the ~ of a problem; → strike *vi* 18a; the spiritual ~s of an author / theory; the scientific / social ~s of a phenomenon (4) his selfishness was the ~ of the trouble; get to / at the ~ of the trouble / matter (5) the square ~ of 4 is 2, the cube ~ of 27 is 3; extract the ~ of a number.

rough *adj* (1) a ~ surface; ~ paper / skin / hands / cloth; a ~ board; a dog with a ~ coat; ~ hair; a ~, unshaven face; a ~ road; ~ country (2) a ~ sea; a ~ *(windy)* day; ~ water / weather; a ~ crossing; the plane had a ~ flight in the storm. (3a *coarse*) ~ food (3b *acid*) ~ wine / claret / cider (4 *harsh*) a ~ sound / voice; a ~ temper (5 *requiring strength rather than intelligence*) ~ work (6 *violent*) boxing is a ~ sport; a ~ fight; ~ behaviour ; a ~ temper (7 *unpolished*) a ~ gem / diamond; □ a ~ diamond *(a good-hearted, but uncultured fellow; also: a diamond in the rough)* (8 *unrefined; rude*) ~ workmanship; a ~ manner / treatment; ~ handling; ~ language / style; they exchanged ~ words; he has a ~ tongue; a ~ (but hearty) welcome; ~ kindness; a ~ man / fellow / customer / soldier; don't be so ~ with the child. (9 *incomplete, crude*) a ~ sketch / drawing / draft / translation; ~ notes; a ~ copy; a ~ly made table; a ~ly hewn stone; ~ garden furniture (10 *lacking comfort*) a ~ camping holiday; lead a ~ life away from civilization; ~ accommodation at a country inn (11 *inform: very trying*) a ~ time; it was ~ on her having to work on Saturdays. (12 *not exact*) a ~ estimate / guess / calculation / analysis / classification / outline; a ~ circle; ~ly speaking, it's about 6 miles to her house from here; the costs amount ~ly to £100.

rouse *vt* (1a) ~ s.o. from sleep; ~ a sleeper; the fire-alarm ~d the household. (1b) ~ pheasants / foxes / red deer / *etc*; strong winds ~d the sea. (2) he is too phlegmatic to be ~d to action; nothing can ~ him (from his lethargy); he stood like one ~d from a dream; she made an effort to ~ herself from sorrow; the news of the Boston Tea Party ~d all the American colonists; the sight ~d him to anger. (3) ~ s.o.'s energies / spirits / imagination / enthusiasm / suspicion / anger / indignation / resentment; he is terrible when ~d. - *adj* (4) a ~ing speech / sermon / song / cheer; a ~ing *(vigorous)* campaign / trade / welcome; a ~ing *(extraordinary)* lie.

row *n* (1) have a ~ with s.o. (over / about s.th.); kick up / make a ~; he is always ready for a ~ *(is quarrelsome)*; what's the ~ *(matter)*? (2) I shall get into a ~ for this *(be reprimanded)*.

rub *vt* (1a) ~ oil / ointment into one's skin / on one's leg; ~ wax polish over a table-top; ~ salt / pepper into meat; ~ the dirt out of clothes; ~ the skin off one's knee; ~ the corners off s.o. *(make him socially adjusted)*; ~ the sleep from one's eyes; ~ a substance to powder; ~ s.th. through a sieve (1b) ~ one's hands together; □ ~ shoulders with s.o. *(have a casual acquaintance with s.o.)* (2) ~ o.s. / one's leg with ointment; ~ a table-top with wax polish; ~ one's feet sore; she ~bed the baby with a towel; ~ the glasses with this cloth; the dog ~bed its head / itself against my leg; ~ a surface dry / smooth (3 *make sore*) ~ one's shin on a rail; my shoe is ~bing my heel. (4) what's the door ~bing on? the wheel is ~bing on / against something.

rub along (1 *BE manage to exist somehow*) "How are you getting on nowadays?" - "Oh, just ~bing ~ ." (2 *BE live without quarrelling*) we manage to ~ ~ together.

rub down (1) ~ a chair ~ with sandpaper; ~ ~ the paint / a wall (2) ~

~ a horse; ~ o.s. ~ after a bath; please ~ me ~ *(give me a massage).*

rub in (1) ~ oil / ointment in (2) the lesson needs to be well ~bed in. (3 *emphasize s.th. unpleasant*) everyone has his failings, but no-one likes them to be ~bed in; the situation was embarrassing enough without having you ~ it in.

rub off n (1) ~ dirt / rust / chalk ~ ; ~ ~ the skin (2) a colour that easily ~s ~.

rub out (1) ~ dirt / a stain ~ (2) the stain won't ~ ~.

rub up (1) ~ up the chromium on a car / silver spoons / *etc*; □ ~ s.o. (up) the wrong way *(inform: offend him by tactlessness)* (2) ~ up one's German / physics / memory / *etc* (3) ~ up against a newly painted door (4) ~ up against people *(meet them by accident).*

ruin *n* (1) the ~ of our hope; the ~ of property in a fire; this flood will be the ~ of the harvest; gambling led to / was his ~; she was the ~ of him; plan s.o.'s ~ (2 *state of being destroyed*) the house fell into / to ~(s); everything has gone to ~; bring to ~; be in ~s (3) the old castle is now only a ~; the ~s of an Egyptian temple; he is but the ~ of what he was.

ruin *vt* (1a) the frost ~ed the crops; an earthquake ~ed the city; churches ~ed by bombs; a car ~ed by neglect; don't read in such bad light - you'll ~ your eyesight; beauty ~ed by dissipation; the inflation ~ed him *(financially).* (1b *inform: spoil*) the rain ~ed her hair. (2) ~ s.o.'s career / chances of success.

rule *n* (1) Roman ~ extended over the entire Mediterranean; before 1775, America was under the ~ of Britain; people suffering under the malign ~ of a tyrant; during the ~ of George III; absolute ~; establish / strengthen one's ~ (2) ~s of conduct; the ~s of arithmetic / chess / *etc*; keep / observe / obey / break a ~; he does everything by ~ *(according to regulations)*; ~ of thumb *(a rough, practical method)*: all his calculations were done by ~ of thumb. (3) it is John's ~ to take a walk before breakfast; in country churches it is the ~ for men and women to sit apart; rainy weather is the ~ here during the summer months; the ~ rather than the exception; he makes it a ~ to go / makes a ~ of going for a walk every day; as a ~ *(usually)*: as a ~ I don't go to the office on Saturday morning.

rule *vt* (1) the king ~d his country wisely; ~ over people / a country; for centuries, England ~d the seas; ~ a household; she ~s her husband; □ ~ the roost *(be dominating, esp in a household)*; one should not be ~d by hatred / one's passions. (2) the court ~d *(decided)* that the information had nothing to do with the case; ~ on a case (3) ~ lines on paper; ~ paper.

rule out how can we ~ ~ the possibility of error; the possibility that he ... cannot be ~d ~; candidacies ~d ~ by the election laws; ~ ~ all chance of a misunderstanding.

run *vi* 1-39; *vt* 40a-67.

The patterns are grouped as follows: concrete subjects 1-20; time is involved 21-23; language 24, 25; ~ + *adj* 1a, 2, 4, 13a, 38, 39; ~ + *obj* + *adj* 46, 47; ~ + *prepos*: across 10; after 11; for 1a, 1e, 36; from 30; in 27; into 10, 18b, 19, 21, 29, 31, 51, 65; on 8a, 41d; out of 32; over 1d, 33; through 18b, 33, 34, 51; to 29, 35a-d, 43; with 14. The following *vi/ vt* patterns are semantically identical or closely related: 1c, 44; 1d, 50a; 3, 48; 5a, 41a; 6, 42; 7, 41b; 8a, 41d; 12, 54; 13a, 57a; 18a, 55; 28b, 60; 31, 65; 36, 64; 37, 58.

(1a) you must ~, not walk; she ran to meet us; we ran to his aid; the dog ran after the burglar; ~ fast / hard; ~ for the doctor; ~ upstairs and get the iodine; he took a ~ning jump; dogs were found ~ning in the streets; the lions ran loose in the streets. (1b *go a short distance*) would you ~ to the post-box with this letter for me? ~ round to the shop; ~ round to a neighbour's (1c, *of animals*) the fox ran to earth / ground; the hare ran to ground; ~ from cover; the salmon are ~ning *(migrating, esp prior to spawning; → 39).* (1d) her eyes ran over the room; Mary's eyes ran critically over her friend's new hat and dress. (1e *run away*) he grabbed the gun and ran; ~ from danger; ~ for your lives! ~ for it: you had better ~ for it before anyone else arrives.

(2 *move, roll, be driven*) the ball ran over the kerb and into the street; the sea is / the waves are ~ning high; the tide is ~ning strong. (3) did you ~ (in the race)? he used to ~ when he was at college; is he ~ning in the 100 metres? (4) who ran third? his horse ran second.

(5a *move on or as if on wheels*) the car ran along the road; trams ~ on rails; sledges ~ well over frozen snow; the train was

~ning at 60 miles an hour. (5b *move rapidly or on an indicated course*) the ship was ~ning before the wind; we ran into port for supplies.

(6 *go regularly*) the ferry ~s every three hours; this bus ~s between N. and L.; a coach ~s between these two towns; the 8.10 train isn't ~ning today. (7) the ship ran aground / on a rock; the bus ran into a wall; she was so sleepy that she ran into a lamp-post.

(8a *function*) how does your new watch ~? cars ~ on petrol or diesel oil; this plant ~s on steam / electricity; this car won't ~; the sewing-machine doesn't ~ properly. (8b *be in operation*) the motor is still ~ning; the mills are ~ning full time; the works have ceased ~ning; the furnace ~s most of the day. (9 *run up / down: make a quick trip*) ~ up to London for a day; shall we ~ down to N. to take in a play this weekend? (10 *run across / into: meet accidentally*) he ran across an old friend in Paris; you never know who you'll ~ into at a big party; he ran across her name in the telephone directory. (11 *run after: inform: pursue amorously*) he ran after her for years, but she wasn't interested in him.

(12 *move freely*) the rope ~s in the pulley. (13a *flow*) water ran down the pipe; the water ran over the dam; the rapids ran over the rocks; the river ran into the sea; the perfume ran down the side of the bottle; tears ran down her cheeks; who has left the tap / water ~ning? let the water ~ before you drink it; my blood ran cold *(I was filled with horror)*. (13b *melt and flow*) the ice-cream is starting to ~; wax ran down the burning candle. (14 *be covered with a flow*) the gutters are ~ning with water; the bathroom floor was ~ning with water; her eyes were ~ning with tears.

(15 *discharge pus, mucus*) a ~ning sore / nose; your nose is ~ning. (16a) ink ~s on porous paper; a drop of oil ~s on paper; fresh paint ran over the window moulding on to the pane. (16b *come out*) some colours ~ in washing; will the colour ~ in this cloth? the dyes in this fabric are guaranteed not to ~ in washing. (16c *lose colour, dye*) don't buy materials which ~ when washed. (17 *creep, grow*) the vines ran along the wall; the ivy ran up the side of the house.

(18a *extend*) book shelves ran from floor to ceiling; a fence ~s round the entire site; dry rot ran all through the roof; a scar ~s across his left cheek; this street ~s east and west; the road ran around the park / north to Litchfield; the road ~s through mountains / straight for several miles; a range of mountains ~s parallel to the Pacific. (18b) the story ~s through four instalments in the magazine / for eight pages; the book ~s to just over 300 pages; his most popular novel ran into / through ten impressions; the book has ~ into six editions; his speech ran over the time limit. (18c *running: successive*) we have had a wet summer three years ~ning; it happened several days ~ning; win four times ~ning.

(19 *run into: merge*) the two towns ~ into one another. (20 *pass rapidly*) fire ran through the stubbles; fire will ~ along a street of wooden houses. (21 *run into: extend in time*) the weeks ran into months; one year ran into the next, and still there was no change; the holiday ran into a third week.

(22 *be presented*) the play ran for six months / a hundred nights; the film ~s for two hours. (23 *be in effect*) the contract has two more years to ~; the bill has 20 days to ~ *(before payment can be claimed)*. (24 *be worded*) the poem ~s like this; I forget how the next verse ~s; the letter ran as follows; this poem ~s smoothly.

(25 *spread rapidly*) a whisper / rumours ran through the crowd; the news of his promotion ran all over town. (26a) a shudder ran through him; a shiver ran down his spine; the pain ran up my arm.

(26b) the idea / song kept ~ning through his mind; his thoughts were ~ning upon the past; in her mind she ran through / over all the conversations they had had together; our talk ran on recent events; the speaker ran from one topic to another; the motif of jealousy ~s through the whole play.

(27 *run in: be hereditary in*) insanity ~s in the family; this talent ~s in our family.

(28a *be printed*) two thousand copies ran before the typographical error was

discovered. (28b *be published*) the account ran in all the papers; the political cartoon always ~s on the editorial page. (29 *run to / into: amount to*) the bill ran to £52; it ran into hundreds of pounds; losses that ran into millions of dollars; his income ~s into five figures *(is £10,000 or more)*. (30 *run from... to: vary*) the tickets ~ from $1.50 to $5.00; new cars ~ from a ten-passenger limousine to a three-wheeled runabout with room for one; your work ~s from fair to bad.
(31 *run into: get into*) he will ~ into trouble / debt if he is not careful about his spending; the project ran into difficulty. (32 *run out of: exhaust a supply of, have no more*) after three weeks we ran out of provisions (→ run out 4); she couldn't bake a cake, because she had ~ out of sugar; he ran out of time and could not finish his examination.
(33 *run over / through: deal with rapidly*) ~ over some notes; we'll ~ over *(repeat)* that song again; ~ through one's mail during breakfast; ~ through the main points of a subject / a list of names; ~ through the accounts (34 *run through: spend quickly*) ~ through a fortune / amount of money. (35a *run to: come to; produce*) her sister is fat too, but the family ~s to being overweight; all the water ran to waste *(was wasted)*; ~ to ruin; these plants ~ to seed *(cease flowering as seed comes)*; he / his talents / his abilities ran to seed *(grew shabby)*. (35b *run to: tend to have*) this author ~s to sentiment; this novel ~s to long descriptions. (35c *run to: be sufficient for*) his income won't ~ to two holidays a year; the house needs redecorating, but my money won't ~ to it; will the coffee ~ to two cups for each person? (35d *run to: BE afford*) we can't ~ to a new car this year.
(36 *esp AE, be a candidate*) ~ for office / Parliament / the Presidency (37 *develop a ladder*) silk stockings ~ more easily than nylons; her stocking ran.
(38 *run + adj: become*) the well / river ran dry; we ran short of money / tea / *etc* (→ short *adj* 4,5); money was ~ning low; feelings / passions ran high *(became violent)*; the plants in my garden / the children are ~ning wild *(have got out of control)*; the engine ran wild; it's tragic when a poet ~s dry *(ceases to have ideas)*.
(39 *run + adj: have a certain size, be at a certain level*) trout / potatoes are ~ning large this year; our apples ~ rather small this year; casualties are ~ning high; sales are ~ning just above last year's figures; prices for fruit are ~ning high this season.
- *vt* (40a) he ran the full length of the room; every morning he ran the path round the reservoir to keep in condition; he ran the mile in four minutes. (40b *roam about in*) why do you permit the children to ~ (in) the streets? (40c) the disease must ~ its course; we can do nothing except let matters ~ their course (→ course *n* 2).
(41a) can you ~ a tractor? do you ~ a car? I don't ~ my car during the winter; who ran the car into the garage? can I ~ my sewing-machine off the light circuit? (41b) ~ a car into a ditch / tree; she ran the car up on the kerb; he ran the ship aground. (41c *allow to run idle*) don't ~ the engine in the garage with the doors closed. (41d) ~ a machine / plant / train on oil / steam / *etc* (42 *operate*) who ~s the ferry between the two villages? ~ a regular steamboat service; ~ extra trains before Christmas; they ~ the presses 24 hours a day.
(43 *drive*) ~ a herd of cattle (44) ~ a fox to cover / earth; ~ deer on foot; *(fig)* ~ a quotation to earth *(find it after a long search)*.
(45a) I'll ~ you home in my car; a neighbour offered to ~ us to the station. (45b *smuggle*) ~ liquor / guns / arms (across the border) (46) ~ o.s. to death; he ran himself out of breath trying to keep pace; ~ s.o. off his feet / legs *(inform: tire him out)*; she ran him ragged with her petty requests. (47 *compete against s.o. in a race*) I ran him to the corner and beat him by three steps; ~ s.o. hard / close *(press him severely in a race, competition)* (48 *enter*) ~ a horse in a race; he ran his best filly in the Florida Derby. (49) ~ a race; ~ an errand / message; ~ errands / messages.
(50a) ~ one's fingers over a shelf / through one's hair / over the keys of a piano; she ran a quick brush over the carpet *(inform)*; he ran his eyes over the letter. (50b) ~ one's head into / against

a wall (in a dark corridor) (51) ~ a needle into / through one's finger; ~ a splinter into one's hand (52) ~ a nail into a board; ~ a comb through one's hair; ~ one's hand into one's pocket; the soldier ran a sword through his adversary. (53 *run, force one's way through*) ~ a blockade; while attempting to ~ the rapids John lost control of his canoe and...; □ ~ the gauntlet *(suffer severe criticism)*
(54 *cause to extend*) ~ a rope in a pulley; ~ the rope between those two trees. (55) ~ a wall / ditch round the town; ~ a telephone cable from A. to B.; ~ a partition across a room (56) ~ a line over a surface / through a word.
(57a *cause to flow*) ~ the water into that ditch; ~ the water for a bath / into the sink; ~ some hot water into the bowl (57b) she ran a hot tub for him; when do you want me to ~ the bath?
(58) ~ a stocking on a nail *(cause it to have a ladder)* (59 *sew rapidly*) ~ a hem round the cuff; ~ a seam.
(60 *publish*) did your paper ~ this story? the newspapers ran the story on page one. (61) ~ an account / bill *(allow it to accumulate before paying)* (62) ~ a temperature *(have a fever).*
(63 *manage, control*) ~ a business / factory / hotel / private school / night-class / home / concert / dance / competition / *etc*; □ ~ the show *(inform: be boss in s.th.)*; modern Britain is ~ by the Establishment; Mr N. is ~ by his secretary; ~ one's own life (64) ~ a candidate for Parliament; our party is ~ning John Smith in this election. (65) ~ s.o. into debt; my wife never ~s me into unnecessary expense. (66 *expose o.s. to*) ~ a risk (→risk *n*); through his habitual lateness he ran the danger of being fired; if you do that you ~ the chance of being suspected of theft. (67) □ ~ riot *(act without restraint; grow in wild profusion)*: his imagination ran riot; our roses ~ riot.

run about he ran ~ in the park.

run away (1) the boys ran ~ after they had broken the window; don't ~ ~, I have something to say to you. (2) she ran ~ and left her family; he ran ~ to sea; ~ ~ from school (3) the maid ran ~ with *(stole)* some valuable jewellery. (4) he ran ~ with his neighbour's wife. (5) smoking ~s ~ with your money. (6) don't let your car / horse ~ ~ with you. (7) don't let your enthusiasm / imagination / temper ~ ~ with you. (8) don't ~ ~ with the idea *(think wrongly)* that the examination will be easy.

run back shall we ~ ~ over *(review in the mind)* the events of the past few days?

run by the years ran by.

run down (1) the clock has ~ ~; the battery is / has ~ ~ - it needs recharging. (2) the careless driver ran ~ the two cyclists. (3 *find*) I managed to ~ ~ the manuscript; ~ ~ information (4 *capture*) ~ ~ a criminal / an escaped prisoner (5 *defame*) Jones was constantly ~ning ~ his boss; don't ~ the man ~ like that! she was always ~ning her husband ~ at parties. - *adj* (6) he is ~ ~ and should take a holiday; look / feel ~ ~.

run in (1 *BE*) I am still ~ning this car in; the car isn't ~ in yet. (2 *inform: arrest*) ~ s.o. in for speeding / shoplifting / *etc* (3 *visit casually*) if I'm in the neighbourhood, I may ~ in for a few minutes.

run off (1) he snatched the package and ran ~. (2) ~ the water ~ when you have had your bath; she ran ~ the fat on the top of the meat. (3) ~ one's legs ~ trying to get something (4) ~ ~ *(print)* 3,000 of these posters (5) ~ ~ *(write)* an article for the local paper; ~ ~ a new song.

run on (1) ~ on letters *(not write them separately)* (2) the account he gave ran on at some length. (3) he will ~ on for an hour if you don't stop him; his tongue ran on as if it would never stop. (4) time ran on.

run out (1) ~ ~ to see what is happening (2) the tide is ~ning ~. (3) the water must be ~ning ~ somewhere on this side; the sand was ~ning ~. (4 *come to an end*) after three weeks our provisions / supplies ran ~; my subscription ran ~ last month; time / money is ~ning ~, and we must hurry; his patience has ~ ~. (5) a pier ~ning ~ into the sea; the building ~s ~ into the road at this point. (6) he had ~ her ~ in his little car to the hotel for lunch. (7) ~ o.s. ~ *(exhaust o.s.).*

run over (1) I will ~ ~ to see you after dinner. (2) the pot, brought too quickly to a boil, began to ~ ~; someone must have left the tap on, for the water was ~ning ~ and flooding the bathroom. (3) ~ ~ a child / animal / *etc*; be careful or you'll get ~ ~ .

run round (1) ~ ~ in a circle (2) ~ ~ to a neighbour's house (→ run *vi* 1b).

run through (1) the pipe is blocked, so that the water cannot ~ ~ . (2) ~ s.o. ~ with a sword; he ran the tiger ~ with a spear.

run up (1) he came ~ning up (towards me); ~ up for the jump (2) prices ran up to 80p a pound; the sales of the book ran up overnight. (3) ~ up against difficulties; the firm has ~ up against great competition. (4) ~ up a flag on the mast (5) please ~ up the two columns of figures and see if they balance. (6 *construct hastily*) ~ up a shed in the garden (7 *sew rapidly*) ~ up a skirt in an afternoon; his wife soon ran up the small tear in his coat. (8) ~ up a bill (at the grocer's); ~ up an account; ~ up costs unnecessarily; I soon ran up a bill for £50 at this hotel; he ran up huge debts. (9) his debts ran up over the years.

run *n* (1a) the pace he sets is more like a ~ than a walk; let's have a ~ to see who'll pay for the ice-cream; he set off at a ~; a quick ~ around the block (1b) it's a three-minutes' ~ to, from the bus-stop / between the underground and the railway station. (1c *quick trip*) have / take a (short / quick / fast) ~; a ~ into town / to the office / up, down to Bridgeport (1d *regular route, of ships, trains, etc*) the New York-Philadelphia / Dover-Calais / *etc* ~; the accident happened on the ~ to Lancaster; how long does the ferry ~ take? (2a *AE baseball*) a ~ to first / second / third / home (plate); a ~ around the bases; a home-~; three ~s, one out, no errors (2b *BE cricket*) he scored 62 ~s before being caught by Knott. (2c *AE football; BE soccer*) a great / long / short / *etc* ~; N. tried a ~ around left end / through the middle. (3a *of sports grounds*) a ski / slalom / *etc* ~; an artificial / (poorly / well) prepared ~ (3b *attempt during a sporting event*) this is J.'s last ~ - let's see if he can beat his first one! P. missed a turn during his first ~ and was forced to drop out of the competition. (4 *of fish*) a salmon / shad / *etc* ~ *(where they migrate)*; the shad ~ runs along the east coast; a ~ of salmon *(school of migrating salmon)*; the ~ of leaping, struggling salmon up the rapids is a breathtaking sight. (5 *track; enclosure*) a chicken / rabbit / dog ~; the tracks indicated we had found a rabbit ~; the dog was kept in a long, high-fenced ~. (6a *military*) a bombing ~; three bombing ~s were flown over the area; during the bombing ~ on N. the plane was hit by a ground-to-air missile. (6b *smuggling*) a whisky / weapons / contraband / *etc* ~; the informer told the police they could catch the smugglers on a gun ~ through a mountain pass; during Prohibition the St. Clair River was the scene of several whiskey ~s from Canada to Michigan. (7 *free access*) he gave them the ~ of the library. (8a *progression; sequence*) the ~ of events has shown that...; there has been a ~ of bad winters; the ~ of cold summers has been going on now for 3 years. (8b *unbroken series*) the play had / enjoyed a ~ of 5 seasons / a long ~ on Broadway; during a ~ of good luck he won three lotteries and two horse-races. (9 *in banking; brokerage*) a ~ *(customers' demands for their money)* on a bank; there was a ~ on the bank which liquidated its cash reserves; the ~ on AP stocks sent prices skyrocketing. (10 *AE tear, esp in knit materials*) these nylons have a ~ in them; she caught a ~ (in her stocking) on a rough chair leg; she felt a ~ creeping slowly up her leg / stocking. (11 *kind, class, type*) the ordinary ~ of skiboots; a hotel out of the common ~ *(better than others)* (12a *phrases*) a ~ for one's money *(strong competition)*: we may not win but we can give them a (good) ~ for their money; in the long ~ *(ultimately)*: you may be able to cover up the deceit now, but in the long ~ you'll be discovered. (12b *on the run: in retreat, hiding*) the thief was caught on the ~; he broke into a bank and is now on the ~ (towards the border). (12c *on the run: in a hurry from place to place*) J. dropped in to see us, but he was on the ~ and only stayed a couple of minutes; the doctor was so busy that he could only manage to eat a sandwich on the ~; why are you always on the ~ ?

rush *vi* (1) he ~ed to the door / down the corridor; he ~ed to help her; they ~ed out of the room; the bull ~ed at him; don't

~ blindly into this dangerous situation. (2) tears ~ed to her eyes; blood ~ed to his face; the idea ~ed into his mind. (3) don't ~ through your work; don't ~ into divorce; ~ into print *(publish s.th. after too little preparation)*; he is always ~ing into things - he never stops to think about the consequences; ~ to conclusions *(form them hastily)*.
- *vt* (4) he ~ed the work *(did it too fast)*. (5) they ~ed the child to the doctor; please ~ this package to the post office; they ~ed troops to the battlefield. (6) he ~ed his wife to get to the party on time; I refuse to be ~ed - I must think it over. (7) ~ s.o. into marriage; ~ a bill through Congress; □ ~ s.o. off his feet *(force him into hasty action)* . (9 *inform: charge a very high price*) how much did they ~ you for that?

S

sacrifice *n* (1) the ~ of a lamb / of fruit to the gods; the ~ of happiness / one's life; make a ~ to the gods; you will gain nothing by the ~ of your principles. (2) a noble / heroic / useless / *etc* ~; his health was the ~ demanded of him for his success; Christ gave his life as a ~ for sinners. (3) he made many / great ~s for his son's education. (4 *loss*) be sold at a ~.

sacrifice *vt* (1) ~ (a slave) to a deity; ~ sheep / oxen / fruit (2) all his life he has ~d himself for his family; he ~d his whole life to the cause of revolution. (3) ~ comfort to convenience; she ~d her leisure to work for the hospital; he ~d a promising career for a momentary fancy; ~ accuracy for vividness (4 *sell at a loss*) I had to ~ my car.

safe *adj* (1) a ~ place; the ship is ~ in port; be ~ from pursuit / infection / one's enemies; render a house ~ against fire / tempests / floods / *etc*; render a city ~ from attack *(ensure that no one will attack it)* / against attack *(make it safe if anyone should attack it)* (2 *free from injury, etc*) my brothers have returned ~ (and sound) from the war; the car crashed, but they were ~; the parcel came ~. (3 *involving no risk*) a ~ policy; a ~ estimate / guess; 50 miles an hour is ~ on a wide road; is this beach ~ for bathing? is the bathing ~ here? is it ~ to leave him? your secret is ~ with me. (4a *giving security*) a bridge not ~ for heavy trucks; this rope is not ~; □ be on the ~ side *(take no risk)*: although the sun was shining he took his umbrella to be on the ~ side. (4b *trustworthy, cautious*) a ~ guide / statesman / critic; a ~ method; a ~ player / play (5 *unable to do harm*) a criminal ~ in jail; is your dog ~ (to touch)? these toys are ~ for small children. (6 *certain*) he is ~ to win the election; a ~ seat in Parliament; that's a ~ bet.

sail *n* (1) hoist (up) / haul (up) / lower / shorten / strike the ~s; under ~ *(moving with ~s spread)*; in (full) ~ *(with (all) ~s spread)*; set the ~s of a ship; □ set / make ~ *(hoist the ~s; begin a voyage)*: he / the ship set ~ for Tahiti; □ take in ~ *(reduce the amount of ~ spread; become less ambitious)*; □ take the wind out of s.o.'s ~s (→ wind *n* 1b) (2 *sailing-ship*) not a ~ in sight; a fleet of 30 ~ (3 *voyage*) a five-day ~; we went for a ~ in his new boat; the island is 10 days' ~ from this port.

sail *vi* (1) go ~ing; ~ before the wind; □ ~ against the wind *(also fig: act under opposition)*; □ ~ close to / near the wind *(sail almost against it; come close to breaking a law)*; he ~s for America tomorrow; when did you ~ to Norway? □ ~ under false colours *(also fig)* (2 *start a voyage*) the liner ~s tomorrow; we are ~ing at dawn. (3) the airship ~ed slowly over the city; gulls ~ing in the blue; the duchess ~ed into the room *(walked in a stately manner)*; he would ~ into *(scold)* his wife when work was going badly. - *vt* (4) ~ the seven seas; he ~ed the Pacific on a raft. (5) ~ a yacht; can you ~ a boat?

sale *n* (1) arrange for the ~ of one's books; the law prohibits the ~ of alcoholic liquor to anyone under the age of 18; is this house for ~? all the pictures in this exhibition are for ~; offer s.th. for ~; copies of the book are on ~ at all the principal booksellers; tickets on ~ a week in advance.
(2 *instance of selling*) ~s of wine have gone up; ~s are down this year; find a

quick ~ for an article (3 *demand*) there is little ~ for these goods; goods with a ready ~; there is no ~ for watches of that kind nowadays. (4 *selling at reduced prices*) a winter / summer / clearance / pre-season / end-of-the-month / *etc* ~; get s.th. at ~ price / at, in the ~s; a ~s day.

satisfaction *n* (1) find (complete) ~ in s.th.; he found great ~ in painting the picture; get ~ out of s.th.; a life of leisure cannot give him ~; he finished the exercise to the ~ of his teacher; he has proved his case to my ~; to our great ~ we heard ...; there was general ~ with / at the result; express one's ~ at / with s.th.; it was a great ~ to his mother when he passed the examination; have the ~ of knowing one has done one's best; I note with ~ that you ...; I heard it with great ~. (2) the ~ of a creditor; the ~ of s.o.'s needs / request / demands / *etc* (3 *compensation for an injury, insult*) demand ~ (for an insult); give s.o. ~ (for an insult); obtain / receive / refuse ~.

satisfy *vt* (1) ~ a need / obligation / standard / demand / request / debt / doubt / objection / expectation / *etc*; ~ the minimum requirements; you will never ~ the examiners with work like that; did he ~ the examiners *(pass the exam at the lowest level)*? ~ (the claims of) one's creditors; the conditions were ~ied by only five of the candidates.
(2) we ~ied our hunger with some bread; ~ one's appetite / thirst (3) ~ an offended person; ~ a wrong (4 *convince*) he ~ied the police that he was innocent; before he engaged me, I had to ~ him of my ability to do the work; I am ~ied of the truth of his story; it was obvious that he was not ~ied by my story. (5) $x = 2$ ~ies the equation $3x = 6$. - *adj* (6) with a ~ied smile; he is never ~ied with anything for long.

save *vt* (1) ~ s.o. / o.s. from drowning / falling / injury / disgrace / humiliation / a danger / one's enemies; ~ a life; the gifts ~d many from starvation; ~ (one's) face (→ face *n* 5); ~ one's skin *(avoid loss, injury, etc)*; ~ the situation *(deal with it successfully)*: his humorous remark ~d the situation. (2a *keep from wear*) ~ a dress by wearing an apron; ~ one's eyes by reading under proper light (2b *keep unhurt*) God ~ our gracious queen.
(3 *make unnecessary, avoidable*) you ~ a mile by taking this short cut; the tunnel ~s a distance of 200 kilometres; □ a stitch in time ~s nine; machines ~ labour; a labour- / time-~ing device; it will ~ trouble if we start early; most people are only too glad to be ~d the trouble of thinking for themselves.
(4 *avoid the waste of*) ~ fuel with this new stove; that will ~ you 50p a week; we can ~ money and time by careful organization / cutting down on some items; ~ material by economical layout; I'd rather ~ my strength for s.th. more worthwhile; ~ o.s. for s.th.; what we ~ on one thing we spend on another.
(5 *lay aside for future use*) ~ (up) money / material (for future use / a holiday / *etc*); ~ s.th. up for a rainy day *(time when one needs money)*; ~ a postage stamp for one's collection; I have ~d these cherries for you; I'm ~ing this last chapter for tomorrow. - *vi* (6) housewives are frequently better able to ~ than their husbands; we've got to start ~ing (for a rainy day) soon; ~ for one's old age; there are better ways to ~ than by not eating; the equipment is rather expensive, but you ~ on running-costs; ~ with us *(bank advertisement)*. (7) Jesus ~s! (8 *AE, able to be preserved*) lettuce doesn't ~ well - it must be served fresh; potatoes ~ well in cool, dry cellars.

say *vt* (1a) 'So much the better,' he said; he said he was sorry / he would come today; he said (that) he had not seen her; I said to him that I ...; I have something to ~ to you; ~ your name again, please; ~ the wrong thing; ~ what you think / mean; I can't ~ it any plainer; don't believe everything people ~; □ ~ a good word for s.o. *(praise, excuse him)*; that's what I've always said / been ~ing all the time; there's a lot to be said for that / on both sides; nations are said to have the governments they deserve. ~ s.th. seriously / in fun / in joke / in jest / in plain words / in plain English; □ that's easier said than done; □ no sooner said than done; that's well said; I cannot ~ what I feel. (1b *phrases with to say, saying*) needless to ~, he came late as usual; strange to ~, I liked her; the place is full of insects, to ~ nothing of the snakes; he is acting, to ~ the least, rather rashly; that is to ~ *(in other words)*: the whole family, that is to ~ four persons, were there; it goes without ~ing *(is obvious)* that you will be invited. (1c *say used adverbially*) ~ *(approximately)*: I want some pens, ~ a dozen; a third of the population, ~, is illiterate; I will probably get there in, ~, 10 minutes; let us ~ *(for example)*: any country, let us ~ Sweden, might do the same; I ~ *(used to open a conversation, express surprise)*: 'I could find out a bit more about it if you like'. - 'I ~ , that's awfully decent of you.'; and - I ~ , John, don't tell your Mother or ... (2 *rumour*) they ~ / people ~ / it is said that war is imminent; he is said to be the best swimmer in the town; I have heard ~ that she ... (3 *recite*) ~ a poem / prayer / lesson; ~ one's prayers; can you ~ your lesson? (4 *say + non-personal subjects*) the clock ~s 11:10; → glass 3; the papers ~ exports are down; it ~s in the Bible / Guardian that we ... (5a *judge; decide*) it is hard to ~ what is wrong; I cannot ~ *(don't know)*; there is no ~ing who it was; perhaps you'll be a pilot yourself one day - there's no ~ing. (5b *say to: think of*) what do you ~ to a walk in the park / a fortnight on the Continent somewhere ? I wouldn't ~ no to a glass of beer *(would accept it willingly)*.

scale[1] *n* (1) the ~ of a ruler / thermometer; this tape measure has a ~ in inches. (2) the ~ of taxation / salaries / *etc*; a wage ~; professors are high in the social ~; sink in the ~ (3) a model on a ~ of one inch to one foot; a map to the ~ of one inch to the mile; a map / diagram drawn to ~ (4) we have no ~ by which to judge his achievements. (5 *relative magnitude*) business on a large / small ~; they built a residence on a yet more magnificent ~. (6) the major / minor ~ of F sharp; play / sing (the) ~s; practise (one's) ~s on the piano (7) the decimal ~ goes by tens, the binary ~ by twos.

scale[2] *n* put the weight on the left and the meat on the right ~; a pair of ~s; a set of kitchen ~s; bathroom / household / letter ~s; he tipped / turned the ~s at 80 kilograms *(weighed 80 kg)*; □ tip / turn the ~s *(decide an issue)*: his past record turned the ~s in his favour; the present crisis should tip the ~s for our candidate.

scan *vt* (1 *examine minutely*) the shipwrecked sailor anxiously ~ned the horizon; she ~ned his face anxiously to see why he was angry; ~ proposals (2 *glance at hastily*) ~ the headlines; I ~ned the classified advertisements; the girls leisurely ~ned the goods in the window; he read several and ~ned the rest.

scare *vt* (1) the dog ~d me to death; the birds were ~d by the sudden barking of the dog; the idea ~s her; the noise ~d them off; the dogs ~d the thief away; the man had a ~d look; I was ~d stiff *(inform)*; I am ~d of crossing the road, with all this traffic about *(feel fright)*; she was ~d to cross the road *(did not want to)*. - *vi* (2) Joan ~s easily *(is easily frightened)*; she ~s at the slightest noise.

scene *n* (1a *place where an event occurs*) Oxford was the ~ of the boat race; he returned to the ~ of the murder; the ~ of the disaster was the North Sea; the world is a ~ of strife; □ quit the ~ *(die)*; the political ~ (1b *place where the action of a play, novel occurs*) the ~ of the story is New Orleans during the Civil War; the ~ of the novel is laid in India.
(2) the second ~ of the third act; an act of four ~s; the ~ between Romeo and Juliet; this play has many memorable ~s; a comic / tragic ~; the mob ~ in a film (3 *scenery*) the opening ~ in this opera is a garden; the ~s are changed / shifted during the intervals; behind the ~s *(also fig)*; he needs a change of ~ *(to get out of his usual surroundings)*. (4 *view; picture*) the sunset was a beautiful ~. (5) please don't make a ~ in such a public place; distressing ~s occurred during the earthquake.

scent *n* (1) these roses have a delightful ~; the ~ of hay (2) the hounds picked up the ~ of a fox; put the dogs on the ~; follow / lose / be thrown off the ~; be on the (right) ~ *(also fig)*: we are on the ~ of an important discovery; the ~ was strong / hot / cold / poor; they tried to throw / put the police off the ~. (3) hounds hunt by (their keen) ~. (4) a bottle of ~; she put some ~ on her handkerchief.

scent *vt* (1) the hounds ~ed a fox; the buffalo ~ed our approach. (2) ~ a mystery; the reporter ~ed a story in the man's suspicious behaviour; finding blood stains, the police ~ed a crime. (3 *give scent to*) ~ed soap / cigarettes; the lilacs ~ed the air; ~ed flowers.

schedule *n* (1) the ~ allows three weeks for this stage; he always has a full ~; (leave / arrive / everything goes) according to ~; be ahead of / behind ~; despite setbacks we shall manage to complete the work on ~. (2) trains / buses / *etc* are ahead of / behind / on ~ *(early, late, punctual).*

schedule *vt* the journey is ~d for five days; we have ~d publication for June; the house is ~d for demolition; their departure was ~d for 5 p.m.; the mayor is ~d to make a speech.

scheme *n* (1 *plan; project*) a business ~; a ~ for rural electrification / building a new motorway / lodging the extra guests; the development of pension ~s; a man full of literary and other ~s; a clever / artful / wild / lunatic / impractical / visionary / rascally / *etc* ~ (2 *arrangement; system*) a colour ~ for a room; the ~ of our living-room is restful to the eyes; the ~ of a sonata; the place of man in the ~ of things; a ~ of philosophy (3 *plot, intrigue*) his ~ to overthrow the / for the overthrow of the government was discovered in time; shady / crooked / dishonest / *etc* ~s.

school *n* (1) a boys' / girls' / co-educational ~; a private / municipal / public / State(-aided) / voluntary / independent / grant-aided / county ~; a nursery / infant / junior / primary / elementary / secondary (modern / grammar / technical) / comprehensive ~; a boarding / day / evening / night / Sunday / vocational / dramatic / continuation / (non-)denominational / special ~; a ~ for the blind (and deaf) / for the mentally subnormal; Father went to the / called at the ~ to see the headmaster; be accepted by a ~; enter a ~ (→ 3).
(2 *school building*) the ~ stands near the church; the ~ was destroyed by bombs. (3 *process of being educated, training*) go to / be at / leave ~; put a child to ~ (→ put *vt* 1); send a child to ~ (for the first time); John is not at ~ *(attending ~)* today; is Susan still at ~ or has she left? I was at ~ *(on the ~ premises)* until half past five; I have left my textbook at ~; pupils are not allowed in ~ *(in the ~ building)* before 8.30 a.m.; we did the first part of the exercise in ~ *(in lesson time)*, and the rest for homework. (4 *lessons*) there will be no ~ today; ~ begins / is over at 1 p.m.; why was he kept (in) after ~? → break up 6. (5 *pupils*) the ~ will assemble in the hall; the entire ~ rose when the headmaster entered. (6 *part of a university*) the Medical S~; the Law S~; the London S~ of Economics; the S ~ of Dentistry.
(7 *conditions of gaining experience*) he was brought up in a hard ~; the hard ~ of experience (8) painters of the Impressionist ~; the Florentine / modern ~; the Platonic ~ of philosophy.

scope *n* (1 *area covered by an activity, plan*) the ~ of his travels includes America and Africa; such subjects are not within the ~ of this book; an investigation / undertaking / study of wide / considerable ~ (2 *room for free activity*) he needs more ~ for displaying his gifts; give one's fancy full ~; he seeks ~ for his energies; free ~ to individual enterprise (3 *limit of capacity*) algebra is beyond the ~ of a small child; beyond the ~ of his imagination / his ~; all matters within the ~ of your understanding.

score *n* (1) the ~s of the lash on a slave's back; the ~s of tribal markings (2 *number of points gained*) the ~ is 20 to 5 in our favour; what was the final ~ in the football game? keep the ~ *(record it during play)* (3 *money owing*) run up a ~ *(get into debt)*; pay / wipe off ~s *(pay debts)*; pay off / settle a ~ *(avenge a wrong)*: in the old West they paid off a ~ with bullets; have an old ~ to settle / wipe out (with s.o.) (4 *reason*) complain on the ~ of low pay; he stayed away on the ~ of ill health; be rejected on the ~ of age; I have no doubts on that ~. (5a *twenty*) about a ~ of years ago; a few ~ years ago; three ~ and ten *(length of human life)*; in a limit of a few ~ words it is not possible to give more than a general impression. (5b *scores: many*) ~s of people were at the dance. (6 *copy of orchestral music*) we've got the ~ but not the individual parts; a full / orchestral / piano ~; follow the ~ while listening to the symphony.

score *vt* (1) ~ a tally-stick; ~ meat before cooking; rocks ~d by glacial action (2 *keep a score*) he ~d the points in the game on a special card. (3a) ~ a goal / points / tricks / *etc*; I ~d five points over my opponent; he ~d 98 on the test; *(fig)* ~ a point (→point *n* 11); the play ~d a great success; ~ an advantage (3b *count*) an ace ~s ten. (4a) this music is ~d for a small orchestra; ~d for piano and cello (4b *compose the music for*) ~ a film / play / *etc*. - *vi* (5 → 2) who's going to ~? I've taken up bridge, but I still don't know how to ~. (6a *win*) ~ over a rival; he was winning the argument but I finally ~d when I brought out some facts he didn't know. (6b *be a hit*) an actor who ~s every time; despite his charms he never was able to ~ with her *(inform : win her favours)*. (7 *in sports: make a point or points*) the home team ~d in the second half; neither team has managed to ~ as yet.

score off ~ ~ an opponent *(defeat in an argument)*; he ~d ~ his rival by proving him wrong.

score out the name and date have been ~d ~ *(crossed out)*.

score up (1) ~ up points / runs / *etc* (2) he will ~ up that remark against you *(make you pay for it)*.

scorn *n* (1) his face showed the ~ he felt; eyes full of ~; hold s.o./ s.th. in ~; hold s.o./ s.th. up to ~ *(of others)*; have ~ for s.o./ s.th.; dismiss a suggestion with ~ ; □ laugh to ~ *(treat contemptuously)*: her good advice was laughed to ~ ; think ~ of *(despise)* (2) he was the ~ of / a ~ to the village.

scorn *vt* (1) he ~ed the old beggar; she ~ed his underhanded attempt to blame her for what he had done. (2) she ~ed my help; I ~ed his attempts to make friends with me; she ~s lying / telling lies / to (tell a) lie; I should ~ rubbing / to rub shoulders with such a person as that. - *vi* (3 *AE*) she ~ed at his awkward attempt to ice-skate; the teacher ~ed at the pupil's answers.

scrape *vt* (1a) ~ the paint off the door / from the floor / *etc*; ~ the butter (on to the bread) (1b) ~ a hide / wall; ~ the floor before applying the varnish; don't ~ the floor with your shoes! ~ one's chin *(shave)*; ~ one's plate *(leave nothing on it)*; ~ your shoes on the doormat before you come in. (1c) ~ a hole; he ~d his initials on the rock. (2) he fell and ~d his knee / the skin off his knee; ~ one's arm on a rough wall; ~ a mudguard (3 *move scraping*) ~ furniture across the floor; he ~d (his feet) along the corridor. (4) he ~d up old parts from the junkyard to rebuild his car; she ~d together a meal from leftovers; ~ up a team *(gather with difficulty)*; ~ *(AE* out) a living *(with difficulty earn enough money)*; he ~d a living out of re-selling old newpapers: he ~d out a living by doing odd jobs. (5a) ~ out music / a tune (on a stringed instrument); ~ out a tune from a fiddle.
- *vi* (5b) he ~d on his violin; the orchestra was ~ing through *The Blue Danube*. (6) his chalk ~d on the blackboard. (7 *pass along (almost) touching*) the two cars managed to ~ by without touching; the car ~d along the wall; the aeroplane ~d over the housetops; ~ through a hedge (8 *economize*) by careful ~ing they managed to survive. (9) he just ~d through his examination; he barely ~d through on the test.

scrape along he can just ~ ~ *(manage to live, with difficulty)*.

scrape down ~ ~ a wall / *etc*.

scrape off ~ ~ mud / paint / *etc*.

scrape out (1) ~ ~ a hole (2) ~ ~ a pipe / greasy saucepan (3) → scrape *vt* 5.

scrape through (1) we shall ~ ~ somehow. (2) → scrape *vi* 9.

scrape together after years of sacrificing they had ~d enough money ~ to buy a small automobile.

scrape up → scrape *vt* 4.

scratch *vt* (1a) ~ a surface; the kitten ~ed (me); he ~ed his ear / his head *(also fig)* / himself behind the ear; ~ mosquito bites; don't ~ (yourself)! the speaker / inquiry has only ~ed the surface of the problem. (1b) he ~ed himself / his hands on the brambles / a nail; ~ a polished table (1c) ~ a match on a wall.
(2a) he ~ed his name on the wall; ~ his name from the list; ~ the burs off one's coat (2b) ~ a hole in the ground (3 *write hurriedly*) ~ a few lines to a friend.

(4 *cancel*) ~ a match / race; ~ a horse / competitor. - *vi* (5) the chickens are ~ing in the sand; the dog ~ed at the door. (6) the pen ~es (badly); the needle is ~ing on the record; chalk ~es on the blackboard.

scratch along we ~ed ~ that year on very little money.

scratch off ~ a word / name ~.

scratch out (1) ~ ~ a hole (2) ~ a word / name ~ (with a penknife); ~ my name ~ - I don't want to participate; ~ s.o.'s eyes ~.

scratch through ~ a word / name ~.

scratch together → scratch up 2.

scratch up (1) the dog ~ed up a bone; Rover ~ed up the lawn to bury his bones. (2) ~ up a few pounds / a meal.

scream *vi* (1) eagles / hawks / vultures / sea-gulls / owls / parrots / pea-fowl ~; the sirens and whistles ~ed. (2) she ~ed when she saw the mouse; ~ in anger (3a) ~ with laughter; the comedian had the audience ~ing. (3b) ~ing fun; ~ingly funny (4 *be conspicuous*) that red dress really ~s; posters ~ed outside the theatre; in the slums houses ~ for repair. - *vt* (5) the baby ~ed itself to sleep; ~ o.s. hoarse.

screen *n* (1) a fire-~; a folding / Japanese ~; a window ~; a tall Oriental ~ separating the living-room from the dining-room (2 *anything that conceals*) a ~ of trees; a smoke ~; a ~ of fog prevented our seeing the ship; a ~ of secrecy (3) a projection / television ~ (4 *cinema*) stars of stage and ~; the celebrities of the ~; a ~ fan / hero / actor / play / test; the ~ rights.

screen *vt* (1a) ~ one's eyes with an eye-shade; ~ s.th. from the wind; the sun was ~ed by clouds; ~ the windows to keep out mosquitoes (1b *as 1a, fig*) ~ s.o. from hardships / suspicion / blame; I'm not willing to ~ your faults. (2 *project on a screen*) ~ slides / a film (3 *make into a film*) ~ a story / play (4 *sift*) growers ~ oranges to keep the same sizes together. (5 *test thoroughly, select*) ~ candidates; the manager ~ed the boys looking for the job; his secretary ~s his visitors so that salesmen never get to see him; the FBI ~ed possible traitors out of the organization; they carefully ~ed all visa applications. - *vi* (6) this book / actor will ~ well / badly.

sea *n* (1a) the ~ covers most of the earth's surface; the calm / smooth / serene / rolling / choppy / restless / sleepless / tumultuous / heavy / rough / wild / stormy ~; the ~ raged / thundered against the rocks / swallowed ship and crew; the high ~s *(open ocean)*; the Seven Seas *(all the oceans of the world)*; swim in the ~; sail on the ~; Brighton is on the ~; most boys at one time or another dream of following the ~ *(being a sailor)*. (1b *phrases with sea, without article*) a ship at ~; praying for those at ~; he was buried at ~; he has two sons in the army and a third at ~ *(being a sailor)*; □ be (all) at ~ *(puzzled)*: when it comes to mathematics, I'm completely at ~; go / travel by ~ (and land); the crew refused to go to ~ *(set out on a voyage)* in such an unseaworthy vessel; as a boy his great ambition was to go to ~ *(become a sailor)*; the expedition is nearly ready to put (out) to ~ *(embark on a voyage)*. (2 *big wave*) the vessel shipped a ~; a high ~ swept the sailor overboard; the heavy ~s almost drowned us. (3 *fig*) a ~ of upturned faces / flame(s) / fire / trouble(s); ~s of blood.

search *vt* (1) he ~ed his desk for the letter / the records for their address / the woods for the missing child; ~ a room / s.o.'s suitcases / s.o.'s pockets; luggage is ~ed at the custom-house; he ~ed the vase for the slightest scratch; the police ~ed the suspect for the missing gems; ~ (through) a drawer; he ~ed his heart many days before making a decision; ~ one's conscience; he ~ed his memory / mind for the man's name. (2 *penetrate*) the sunlight ~ed the room's dark corner; the cold wind ~ed every part of the city. - *vi* (3) ~ for s.th. (high and low).

search out ~ ~ *(find)* all the facts / an old friend.

season *n* (1) the four ~s; the dry / rainy ~ (2) the nesting ~ *(of birds)*; the harvest / holiday / theatrical / opera / football / *etc* ~; Easter is a glad ~; Christmas is a ~ of merry-making; the New Year is a ~ for making good resolutions; a dead / dull ~ (in trade / tourism); during the off (-peak) ~; travel in low ~; asparagus is in / out of ~ now; a word in ~ *(advice when it is* *useful)*; in ~ and out (of ~) *(at all times)*: misfortunes plague this family in ~ and out of ~. (3 *BE*) a weekly ~ (-ticket) to London, please.

seat *n* (1a) a comfortable / cushioned ~; you'll have to use that box for a ~; take a ~ *(sit down)*; take one's ~ at a table / in a theatre; keep one's ~ *(remain sitting)*; resume one's ~; that is the old man's *(habitual)* ~. (1b) the bus has 60 ~s; a numbered / vacant / reserved ~; ~ taken; (secure) a corner ~ (for o.s.); ~s should be reserved / booked in advance; I have taken ~s for tonight's concert (→ take *vt* 3). (2) a chair with a cane ~; the ~ of the sofa is torn. (3) he had to have the ~ of his trousers mended; put a new ~ in a pair of trousers (4 *buttocks*) she is big around the ~. (5 *posture on horseback*) he has a good / poor ~. (6 *country mansion*) as a result of heavy taxation many country ~s are being sold. (7 *centre of activity*) a ~ of learning; Washington is the ~ of the U.S. government. (8 *right to sit because of membership*) a ~ in Parliament / in Congress / on the stock exchange; win a / lose one's ~; he was elected to a ~ in the senate. (9) the ~ of the trouble; the heart is the ~ of passion.

seat *vt* (1) the teacher ~ed the pupils at nine o'clock. (2) the theatre ~s 1,200 people. (3 *allot a seat to*) the usher ~ed us in the front row; where shall we ~ the guests / new pupil? (4) ~ a chair; ~ a pair of trousers.

second *adj* (1a) our club meets the ~ day of every month; the ~ house from the corner; I have my hair cut every ~ week; Osaka is the ~ (largest) city in Japan; the first, ~ and third prize; who is the ~ in command here? our swimmer came in ~; they offer service ~ to none *(unsurpassed)*. (1b *in music*) the ~ violin / trombone / alto; → play *vt* 2b. (2 *other*) you will need a ~ pair of shoes; we were so hungry that we all had ~ helpings; he thinks he is a ~ Einstein; → sight *n* 1.

secret *n* (1) a strict / dead / dark / open ~ (→ dead *adj* 7; dark *adj* 6; open *adj* 8); keep a ~; keep s.th. a ~ from s.o.; betray / let out / blab out a ~; we have no ~s from one another; entrust s.o. with a ~; let s.o. into a ~ (→ let into 2); hold a meeting / conduct negotiations in ~; he makes no ~ of his attitude.
(2) hard work was the ~ of his success; the ~ of health is temperance. (3 *s.th. hard to understand*) science will never solve all the ~s of nature.

secret *adj* (1 *hidden*) a ~ door / compartment / drawer / room / pocket / *etc*; our most ~ thoughts; a ~ motive; ~ grief (2 *kept from the knowledge of others*) ~ information / diplomacy / orders / documents / funds; a ~ marriage / ballot / session / treaty / remedy / sign / weapon; a ~ agent / society / meeting / doctrine; ~ police; have a ~ understanding / agreement with s.o.; keep s.th. ~ from s.o.

secure *adj* (1) a ~ harbour / hideout; ~ from attack / fear / interruption / the cold / one's enemies; here in the vault the necklace is ~; make a house ~ against burglars / fire / the weather; make one's investments ~; the best way to be safe is never to feel too ~.
(2 *firmly fastened, dependable*) is this ladder ~? a ~ foundation / structure; s.th. more ~ than this old padlock; a ~ knot / fastening; ~ly locked (3 *free from anxiety*) feel ~ among close friends; be emotionally ~ (4 *certain*) a ~ life / hope of salvation; our victory is ~; they are ~ of victory; a ~ belief; she was ~ of her religious belief; he earned a ~ place among the baseball immortals.

secure *vt* (1a *fasten tightly*) ~ the doors and windows; ~ a buckle; ~ your seat belts! he ~d the prisoner (with ropes); ~ a boat (1b) ~ a rope / fastening (2 *make safe, protect*) ~ a town with a wall; ~ valuables; ~ a house from / against burglars; the sandbags ~d the town during the flood; lock the door to ~ us from interruption; ~ o.s. against loss.
(3 *make certain*) the first Amendment to the Constitution ~d for the Americans freedom of speech, press and religon; the novel ~d his reputation; ~ *(guarantee)* a loan; a loan ~d on landed property (4 *obtain*) ~ materials / good seats at the theatre / a ticket for a concert / a bargain; ~ a high government post; I have ~d my object. (5 *capture*) no one is safe until the murderer is ~d.

see *vt* 1 - 16; *vi* 17 - 26.
The patterns are grouped as follows: ~ + *obj* + *inf*: 1, 10; ~ + *obj* + *past part*: 1, 5; ~ + *obj* + *present part*: 1; ~ + *question word* + *inf* or *clause*: 1, 2, 4, 13; ~ +

that-clause: 1, 2, 5, 10, 13; be ~n + *inf*: 1; be ~n + *present part*: 1; *non-personal subjects*: 15; ~ + *prepos*: about 22, into 23, over 24, through 16, 25, to 5, 26.

(1) I can ~ the sky from where I sit; can you ~ that church over there? have you ever ~n (a white mouse / *etc*)? the moment he saw us he ran away; did you ~ that film / the Fred Astaire show last night? ~ p. 15 / § 24 / below / above *etc*; how many people did you ~ come? I saw the thief running away; the airman was ~n to land / landing; I have often ~n it done; I saw him arrested; I saw it advertised in the newspapers; I can't ~ how to do it; I can't ~ where the wire is attached to the motor; I saw how it happened; I must ~ what can be done; I ~ today's the fifth / it's already ten o'clock; he must have got over his flu, for I saw him out yesterday *(walking out of doors)*; → age *n* 5; back *n* 1; double *adj* 2; eye *n* 2; last *n* 3; life 6; red *adj* 1; sight *n* 3b; way 2b.

(2a *read*) I ~ in today's paper that our team won; we saw in the last chapter how (steam can be converted into movement). (2b *hear; learn*) we shall ~ in the next lecture the causes of ...; we have already ~n what Churchill did when ...

(3 *view as a spectator*) ~ a play / football match; I just don't understand how he could ~ that going on without doing something about it; we intend to ~ the castle tomorrow; fly N. Air Lines and ~ the world. (4 *find out*) ~ who is at the door; go and ~ what he wants; ~ if there's any paper left / if you can translate this; look over my work and ~ what I'm doing wrong; go and ~ for yourself (if you don't believe me); can you ~ where the mistake is?

(5 *see + that-clause, see + part: make sure*) I'll ~ (to it) that the work is done (→ 26); ~ you don't trip; the inspector will ~ (to it) (that) each part is made to specification ; if you go out, ~ that you lock the door; I'll ~ the luggage put in myself; I was there myself and saw it done; I'll ~ justice done to you.

(6a *meet*) are you ~ing him at lunch today? I'll ~ you at the races; I wish to ~ the manager, please. (6b *date*) she's ~ing too much of the same boy. (7 *receive*) the ambassador finally saw him; the doctor will ~ you now; the doctor saw ten cases today; the Board cannot ~ all applicants this morning; he's too ill to ~ anyone. (8 *visit*) I'll ~ you at your house tonight; he finally saw the ambassador; you must ~ your dentist.

(9 *escort*) ~ s.o. home / to the station / to the door; I'll ~ you downstairs / across the road / off the premises / as far as the corner; I'll stay and ~ you on the bus.

(10 *recognize*) ~ a mistake / error / flaw; I saw that it was / it to be a mistake; they saw the possibility / certainty of success in following the new plan; he saw the chance of helping us / an occasion to do it / an opportunity / *etc*; ~ from s.o.'s appearance that he has a bad conscience; you can ~ (at once) that he is a German; he saw that he was wrong; I ~ no difficulty / danger / risk in diving; ~ (the) fear in s.o.'s eyes.

(11 *imagine*) I can't ~ him as an actor; he could ~ war ahead. (12 *judge*) I ~ the matter differently; I've come to ~ the problem in another light; ~ s.th. in a false / the worst light (→ light *n* 4) (13 *understand*) I fail to ~ what you mean; from your letter I saw that you ...; ~ the point (→ point *n* 11) / joke / meaning of the remark / importance of the proposal / implications of his statement; I can't / don't ~ the good of being early / use of this delay / purpose of this step / advantage of doing it; I can't ~ what good being early does / what use this delay will serve / *etc*; now I can ~ the causes of this condition; I can't ~ your reasons for taking such a step / any point in arguing about it (→ point *n* 13). (14 *experience*) he has ~n a good deal in his / a lot of life; I never saw such rudeness; he has ~n fifteen years' service; this coat of mine has ~n hard wear; → better *adj* 1.

(15 *be a witness of; non-personal subjects*) the 19th century saw the rise of the second German empire; each year has ~n the disappearance of important newspapers; this week ~s the beginning of a new year for listeners of "English by Radio"; he did not win a Grand Prix race until the year 1962, which saw him world champion; London has ~n British, Roman, Saxon, Danish and Norman conquerors; the Abbey has ~n the crowning of English monarchs since A.D. 1000. (16 *see through: help get through*) ~ a book through the press (→ press *n* 3); he's

~ing his brother through college *(providing money, encouragement)*; he promised to ~ his client through the law-suit; we have enough bread to ~ us through the week-end.
-*vi* (17) cats can ~ in the dark; a blind man cannot ~; ~ing is believing *(if I see, I'll believe it).* (18 → 4) go and ~ for yourself (if you don't believe me). (19 → 12) as far as I can ~ (he's in the wrong). (20 → 13) now do you ~? yes, I ~; (oh,) I ~! "I see," he said with a knowing smile. (21 *think*) now, then, let's ~; let me ~, where did I put those letters / how does that song go? they did things as they saw fit (→ fit *adj* 2). (22 *see about: attend to*) he promised to ~ about the matter; we must ~ about getting the house repainted; ~ about *(getting)* lunch / a new coat / *etc*; ~ about *(finding)* a hotel; it's time you children were ~ing about *(going to)* bed. (23 *see into: investigate*) ~ into a matter / complaint / *etc* (24 *see over: inspect*) ~ over a house / factory / *etc*; I should not think of making an offer for the house until I had ~n over it. (25 *see through: not be deceived by*) ~ through a scheme / trick / story / plan; ~ through s.o.; I immediately saw through his (cheap) attempt to gain my confidence. (26 *see to: take care of, attend to*) I'll ~ to it that the work is done (→ 5); would you mind ~ing to the seats? something has gone wrong with my electric iron - could you ~ to it for me? you had better ~ to getting the dinner; I shall have to have my eyes ~n to; Dr. N. has a lot of patients to ~ to; she saw to all his needs; you won't be put to this trouble again - I'll ~ to that.

see off (1 *accompany to the place of departure*) they had come to ~ their friends ~; I am much obliged to you for ~ing me ~. (2) if you want to go out, I'll ~ the children ~ to bed; after she had ~n the children ~ to school, she ...

see out (1 *stay until s.th. is finished*) we decided to ~ the match ~. (2 *live, last to the end of a period*) the patient will not ~ the week ~; I hope to ~ a few more years ~ yet; I'll ~ the term ~ before I retire; we have enough fuel to ~ the winter ~; ~ the Old Year ~ (and the New Year in) (3a) ~ s.o. ~ *(accompany him to the door)* (3b) the gateway is rather narrow, so I had better ~ you ~ *(help you get the car through).*

see over *(inspect)* we saw the property ~ before we bought it; ~ this ~ before you approve the contract.

see through (1 *stick to s.th. until completion*) never start on a project unless you are prepared to ~ it ~; I am determined to ~ this affair ~; you must ~ the task ~ once you start. (2 *help get through*) we have enough bread to ~ us ~; will five pounds ~ you ~? he trusted to God to ~ him ~ (the difficulties).

seek *vt* (1) we are ~ing the lost climbers; ~ shelter (from the rain) / (a place to) rest / adventures / the truth / the solution of a problem; are you ~ing a quarrel *(trying to start it)*? → far *adj* 1. (2 *ask for*) ~ (s.o.'s) advice (on s.th.) (3 *try to obtain*) ~ approval for s.th. / fame / promotion / redress; ~ an opportunity / nomination; he ~s recognition of his work; he went to America to ~ his fortune. (4 *seek + inf: try*) ~ to establish a fact / convince s.o.; modern methods of instruction ~ to make us penetrate the spirit of the language. -*vi* (5 ~ *for: try to find, emphasizing persistence*) ~ for information; he went from village to village, ~ing for work. (6 *be sought after: be in demand*) early editions of Shakespeare's plays are much sought after by collectors; a sought-after speaker.

seize *vt* (1) in her fright she ~d his arm / him by the arm; ~ s.o. by the hands / shoulders; ~ s.th. with one's hand; he ~d his sister's toy; ~ a weapon; he ~d hold of the first weapon that came to hand. (2 *capture, conquer*) ~ a thief; ~ a fortress (by storm) / a bridge (3 *take possession of by law*) ~ real estate / property / goods / contraband / enemy ships; the police ~d the opium found in the flat; the property was ~d by the State.
(4) ~ an opportunity; try to ~ the power / crown (5 *understand clearly, quickly*) ~ an idea / distinction; he was quick to ~ a point; naturally he ~d the suggestion that we should be friends again. (6) she was ~d with fear; panic ~d the crowd. -*vi* (7 *make instant use of*) he would ~ upon any excuse to justify himself; ~ upon a chance / occasion / opportunity; he was quick to ~ upon a point.

seize up one of the ship's generators had ~d up *(become stuck through heat).*

sell *vt* (1a) ~ goods / property / rights to s.o.; he sold his house to us; *(fig)* ~ one's soul for political power; the defenders of the fort sold their lives dearly. (1b *effect* *a sale*) he sold their house for them. (2a *offer for sale*) he ~s antiques; we ~ only shoes in this shop. (2b *help to* ~) advertising sold a million copies; his name in the cover sold the book. (3a *cause to be accepted*) ~ an idea to the public (3b *persuade to accept; convince*) ~ the voters on a candidate; he sold me on the idea of continuing school and now I'm grateful. (4 *betray*) he sold them to the police; ~ one's country / honour / chastity (5 *inform: cheat*) he was sold over the deal; I think that America was sold in 1917-19. - *vi*(6) ~ dear / cheap / by auction / wholesale / retail / at a profit / at a loss; ~ short *(under s.th.'s true value)*; you can imagine J.'s chagrin when prices went up after he had sold short to finance another project; ~ under price *(at a loss; below usual market value)*; we are ~ing (these goods) under price to introduce you to the luxury of owning ... *(advertisement)*; I like this house - will he ~? → buy *vi* 6. (7a *be offered for sale*) eggs ~ at 40p a dozen; this shirt ~s for $10. (7b *find a buyer*) umbrellas ~ best on a rainy day; his first book sold like hot cakes *(rapidly)*; these goods ~ quickly. (8 *win acceptance*) here's an idea that'll ~.

sell off ~ ~ surplus stock *(sell what remains at a reduced price)*; the city is ~ing ~ a large number of small lots at public auction.

sell out (1) ~ ~ one's whole stock of s.th.; ~ ~ before the market falls; the novel sold ~ within a week of publication; eggs are sold ~; we are sold ~ of eggs; every shop she went to was sold ~. (2 *slang: betray*) he sold the gang ~ (to the police / to another gang) to revenge himself; Blackie sold ~ when he heard that he was not to be included in the next job; I've been sold ~!

sell up he sold up *(sold everything)* and emigrated to Canada; the bankrupt man was sold up by his creditors.

send *vt* (1a) ~ a letter / a parcel / goods by post / mail / air (mail); ~ s.th. express / by return of post; ~ a telegram / message; ~ baggage in advance; → word *n* 3; I must find out some way to get my money sent me from London; ~ (s.o.) one's love / compliments; John ~s his excuses, but he has been delayed at the office; ~ aid / help / relief to s.o.; they sent their son to college; we sent a delegation to the convention. (1b *ask to come, be brought*) ~ for the doctor / police; the snake-bite serum had to be sent for by special messenger; ~ for some bread / a prospectus; ~ for *(order)* a dozen copies of the book (1c *direct*) ~ a punch to the jaw (2 *give, cause to happen, of God, fate*) trials sent from above; a prophet sent to lead his people; ~ rain / pestilence / *etc.*
(3 *transmit by radio*) ~ the message in code (4 *emit, utter*) the lion sent a roar through the jungle. (5 *cause to be, become*) the blow sent him flying to the ground / spinning / reeling; he sent an empty pickle jar whizzing after them; the noise sent him crazy; □ ~ s.o. packing / about his business *(dismiss unceremoniously)*. - *vi* (6 → 3) the ship's radio ~s on a special band of frequencies; these antennas are designed to ~ only - they cannot be used to receive.

send away (1) she sent her son ~ for a holiday in the country. (2 *dismiss*) they sent him ~ for misconduct. (3 ~ ~ *for: send to a distance for*) when we lived in the country we had to ~ ~ for many things that we needed.

send down (1) this remedy will ~ the temperature ~; ~ prices ~ (2 *BE expel from the university*) ~ a student ~ (for the rest of the term); he was sent ~ for misbehaviour. (3 *BE inform: put in jail*) the judge sent him ~ for 3 years.

send forth the flowers ~ ~ a sweet odour; plants ~ ~ roots / leaves / a stem; ~ ~ steam.

send in (1) ~ in an application / letter / bill; ~ in an article to a newspaper; ~ in money; ~ in one's resignation; ~ in one's papers *(of officers: resign)* (2 *enter for a competition*) he sent in several poems and a short story for the competition.

send off (1) ~ ~ a letter / parcel; get these books sent ~, please. (2 *accompany to the point of departure*) we all went to the airport to ~ him ~. (3) ~ ~ fumes.

send out (1) ~ ~ a messenger / spy; ~ ~ an order / invitations; the circulars have all been sent ~. (2) ~ ~ rays / electric waves / heat / light / steam (3) flowers ~ ~ leaves / shoots / fragrance.

send up (1) his request for leave was sent up to the head office for approval; ~ up money / a bill / an application (2) the remedy sent his temperature up; ~ up prices (3 *AE inform: put in jail*) he was sent up for 5 years; the judge sent him up for armed robbery.

sensation *n* (1a) (have / experience) a ~ of cold / heat / roughness / pain; it does not hurt, it is merely an unpleasant ~. (1b) a ~ of dread / fear / weariness / giddiness / comfort / *etc* (2a) it was quite a ~ to see the Queen at close hand; melodrama deals largely in ~. (2b) the scandal was a ten-day ~; her bright red dress was a ~ at the party; make / create / cause a ~.

sense *n* (1) the five ~s are sight, hearing, smell, taste and touch; have a keen / acute ~ of hearing (2 *sensation*) a (pleasant) ~ of warmth; a ~ of cold / pain (3 *understanding, appreciation*) have a ~ of honour / duty / responsibility / (personal) dignity / gratitude / triumph / shame; a ~ of direction / locality; a(n intuitive) ~ of danger / security; have no ~ of right and wrong; he was overtaken by a ~ of discomfort; the moral ~ (4 *practical wisdom*) he shows a great deal of ~ in going home early; there's a lot of ~ in what he says; have the ~ to do s.th. *(be wise enough to do)*; what is the ~ of talking like that? sound / good ~; common ~ *(sound practical judgement)*: he doesn't have ~ enough to come in out of the rain. (5 *meaning*) the ~ of s.o.'s remarks; he was using the word in a different ~; in the narrow / full / ordinary / strict / literal / figurative ~ of the word; in a general ~; his attitude / statement does not make ~ *(is not intelligible)*; → make *vt* 30. (6 *~s: normal state of mind*) bring s.o. to his ~s; come to one's ~s; he has taken leave of / is out of his ~s *(is mad)*; she was frightened out of her ~s; be in one's (right) ~s.

serve *vt* (1) ~ the state / Church; ~ one's country / king / employer / master; □ no man can ~ two masters; ~ God; ~ one's time *(term of office; → 7b)*; I wish I could ~ you in this matter; discoveries in the cure of disease ~ all mankind; if my memory ~s me right *(if I remember right)* (2a) ~ a customer (with an article); are you being ~d? we were ~d by three waiters. (2b) ~ goods (to customers) (3 *satisfy the needs of*) his old car has ~d him well; my raincoat has ~d me for years; two libraries ~ the town; this railway line ~s a large district; we are well ~d with gas / electricity / *etc* in this town; this will ~ our needs for the moment. (4a → *11a; fulfil a requirement, be useful*) any heavy object will ~ the purpose; a tool that ~s many purposes (4b) this ~d him as a pretext; this should ~ you as an example; that excuse will not ~ you. (5a) ~ food / drink to s.o.; lunch is ~d; ~ the vegetables; ~ fine food; these cakes must be ~d hot. (5b) ~ one's guests (with food and drink); I was ~d with tea and cake; may I ~ you some tea and cake? (6 *deliver; legal*) ~ a writ / warrant / summons (to appear in court) on s.o.; ~ s.o. with a summons / *etc* (7a *work through*) ~ a term of apprenticeship (7b) ~ a term of imprisonment / a prison sentence; ~ one's time *(imprisonment; → 1)* (8 *treat*) fate ~d her badly; that ~d him ill; he ~d her shamefully / ill / generously / tenderly; that ~s him right *(is the punishment he deserves)*. - *vi* (9a → 1a) he ~s as gardener and chauffeur (to Mr N.); ~ as president / juror / *etc*; ~ on a committee / jury / *etc* (9b) ~ in the army / air force / ranks; ~ afloat; a soldier ~s with a regiment, a sailor ~s in a vessel. (10 *be a shop-assistant, waiter, etc*) she ~s in a shop / a bar / the kitchen; ~ at table / a counter (11a → 4a) the settee ~s as a bed; a box ~d (them) for a table. (11b *be sufficient*) this cushion will ~. (11c → 4b) may this ~ as a warning to you; that will ~ to explain my actions.

serve out ~ ~ rations; the Red Cross ~d ~ tins of food to the earthquake victims.

serve round ~ ~ food.

serve up ~ up dinner; she ~d up an excellent lunch.

service *n* (1a *employ*) be in royal / papal ~; be in the king's / Pope's ~; enter s.o.'s ~; take s.o. into one's ~(s); in the ~ of a company; he was presented with a cheque in recognition of forty years' ~ with the firm. (1b *being a servant*) she is in ~ (with the Smiths); go out to / go into ~; send a girl out to ~; he was in ~ as chauffeur with Mr N. (2 *branch of government, etc*) officials and employees of the public ~; the civil ~ *(branches of government outside the armed ~s)*; (enter) the diplomatic / consular ~; the armed / fighting ~s; be on active ~ *(in the army, etc)*; which ~ *(army, navy, etc)* were you in during the war? grow old in (the) ~ (of the state); he has seen fifteen years' ~ (→ see *vt* 14). (3a *assistance, benefit given to others*) he did me a ~; he has not done her a ~ by (publishing the letter); render s.o. a ~; can I be of ~ to you? his professional knowledge has been of great ~ to us; I

am at your ~ whenever you should need my advice; you will have an English-speaking guide at your ~ at all times; put / place s.th. at s.o.'s ~; a man of great ~ to the community (3b *of things*) my car is at your ~; what good ~ this fountain pen has done me! I cannot wear this coat any longer - it has done its ~; put a horse to good ~ in hauling logs.
(4a *work etc done for s.o.,s.th.*) he devoted himself / his life / all his strength to the ~ of God / others / a good cause / the Church; in the ~ of a good cause; ~ to the nation / the people / one's fellow men; certain books are published at a loss as a public ~. (4b) military / regular ~; ~ with the colours; have you done your military ~? he saw ~ on several fronts (→ 2). (4c *maintenance provided by a dealer for items bought*) the manufacturer guarantees ~ and parts; send the car in for ~ every 5,000 miles (4d) ~ at the altar / in the temple (5 *~s: s.o.'s helpful, esp professional activities*) he is not yet well enough to dispense with the doctor's ~s; do you need the ~s of a lawyer / doctor / interpreter / *etc*? legal / medical ~s; s.o.'s valuable / eminent / voluntary / *etc* ~s; for ~s rendered; your ~s to the firm are much appreciated. (6 *use*) the old buses are still in ~. (7 *system of public communication, transportation*) an hourly bus ~; postal / telephone / train ~; put a railway carriage / bus / ship into ~; summer ~s resume next week. (8) the ~ in this restaurant / shop is very poor; you get very good / fast ~ in this restaurant / shop; in some restaurants the ~ of the food is not as hygienic as it might be; ~ à la carte; ~ on board; ten percent for ~; ~ and taxes included (9) celebrate / perform / conduct / take Divine S~; hold a (morning / evening / baptismal / marriage / funeral / burial) ~; take part in / attend a ~; a ~ of thanksgiving / intercession / *etc* (10 *in law: delivery*) the ~ of a writ / summons (11 *cups, plates, dishes,etc*) a breakfast / dinner / dessert / tea ~ (of twenty pieces); modern table ~s are usually simple in design.

set *n* (1) a ~ of china; a breakfast / coffee / tea / fruit ~; a ~ of tools / carving-knives / golf clubs / cards / books / chairs / stools / studs; a ~ of (false) teeth; a chess ~; a ~ of postage stamps; a ~ of pencils; a (pen and) pencil ~ (2 *apparatus*) a receiving / wireless / television / all-mains ~; a chemistry ~; a carpentry ~ (3a *group of persons*) a ~ of thieves; the racing / golfing / smart / jet / jazz ~; the fast ~ *(persons who gamble, etc)* (3b) a ~ of social institutions; a ~ of principles / ideas (4 *posture, arrangement*) the ~ of his shoulders; the ~ of her features / head (5 *fixed direction*) the ~ of his mind was obvious; the ~ of public opinion (6 *fit*) the ~ of his coat; the ~ of the drapery.

set *vt* 1a - 21; *vi* 22 - 32.
The patterns are grouped as follows: ~ + *inf*: 15a; ~ + *part*: 15b; ~ + *n* + *adj*: 21a; ~ + *n* + *adv phrase*: 21b; ~ + *prepos*: about 29,30; against 16; on 16, 31. The following transitive / intransitive patterns are semantically identical or closely related: 1a, 22; 5, 23; 6, 25; 7a, 26a; 7b, 26b; 7c, 26c; 8, 27b.
(1a *place*) he ~ the table beside my chair; ~ a vase on a table; ~ the bowl in the centre; we ~ food and drink before the travellers; he ~ the stake in the ground; he ~ the chair back on its legs; she ~ the baby on its feet; ~ glass in a window; ~ seedlings / bulbs / plants; a house ~ in a beautiful garden; lamps ~ in the walls; blue eyes ~ deep in a white face. (1b *place somewhere for a specific purpose*) ~ a glass to one's lips / one's lips to a glass; ~ a wind instrument to one's lips; ~ the axe to a tree *(cut it down)*; ~ the axe to the root of an evil; ~ one's seal / signature / name / hand to a document; ~ pen to paper; ~ spurs to a horse; ~ dough *(AE put it aside to rise)*; ~ milk with rennet; ~ sail (→ sail *n* 1); ~ a bloodhound on a trail; ~ a fowl *(on eggs)*; ~ eggs; we ~ a supervisor over the new workers; ~ sentries at the gate (1c *set + abstract object: place*) he ~s honour before glory; our teacher ~s a high value on neatness; she ~s neatness at a high value; she ~s great / little / no / not much store by him *(considers of great, etc value)*; I don't ~ much store by what the neighbours think; the advantages must be ~ against the disadvantages.
(2 *make ready for use*) ~ a chair; ~ a trap / snare (for s.o./ s.th.); ~ a table for coffee / for five people; ~ a blade / knife / razor *(sharpen it)*; ~ a saw *(adjust its teeth)* (3) diamonds ~ in platinum; a ring ~ with rubies; a

bracelet ~ with pearls; ~ gems in rings / on bracelets; panes ~ in lead.

(4) ~ a match / light to the leaves; ~ fire to a house (→fire *n* 2); ~ leaves on fire; ~ some paper alight (5 *bring together the parts of*) ~ a broken bone / limb / joint; ~ a fracture (6) ~ one's / s.o.'s hair *(fix it when damp so that it dries in waves)*; ~ s.o.'s hair on end (→hair).

(7a *cause to become firm*) pectin ~s jelly; ~ glue / mortar / cement; rust has ~ the weathercock. (7b) ~ a colour / dye *(make it fast)* (7c *put into a rigid state*) he ~ his shoulders squarely; too much exercise ~s a boy's muscles prematurely; his lips were firmly ~; he was sitting there his face ~; □ ~ one's face against s.th. (→face *n* 5); →tooth 1b. (8 *direct*) they ~ their horses towards home; ~ one's course to the south; the current ~ them eastwards; ~ one's face towards home (9 *regulate*) ~ a clock (by the time-signal on the radio); he ~ the alarm for seven o'clock; ~ the dial on an oven; ~ a gramophone at / to 45 r.p.m.; ~ a thermostat at 70 (10) ~ type *(for printing)*; ~ a manuscript / article (→set up 11). (11) ~ words / a poem to music; ~ piano music for the violin / orchestra.

(12 *fix a time*) ~ a date for s.th. / the wedding-date; they ~ midnight for the escape; ~ a term for a project / a (time) limit; ~ Friday as the deadline; we ~ the meeting for 3 o'clock; ~ a limit / limits to s.o.'s ambition / authority (13) ~ a standard / norm / record (14a) ~ (s.o.) a (good) example; ~ a precedent / fast pace; ~ the pace *(in a race; also fig)*: the Joneses ~ the pace and their neighbours try to keep up with them; ~ the fashion; ~ an exercise / task / (examination) paper / problem / puzzle; what questions were ~ in the examination? a list of ~ *(prescribed)* books; ~ a law / order / punishment (14b) ~ a pupil / an employee / o.s. / one's wits / one's hand to a task; he ~ himself to his chores; she ~ the children to raking the leaves; ~ s.o. homework / a lesson / a task / *etc*; we haven't been ~ any homework; the teacher has ~ us a lot of homework today.

(15a *set + infinitive: cause to do*) he ~ the man to chop wood; I ~ myself to study the problem; ~ s.o. to work on a project / at mowing the lawn; ~ a thief to catch a thief. (15b *set + participle: cause to be in a state*; → 21) his remark ~ me thinking; I was ~ wondering by this remark; he ~ the engine going; he wound the clock and ~ it running; one juicy murder in a town will ~ a police chief's phone ringing for a week; no-one seems inclined to ask a question, so I'll ~ the ball rolling *(take the first step; →ball[1] n* 1). (16 *set +on, against: incite to attack*) let me catch those boys again and I'll ~ the dogs on them; ~ spies on a person; ~ people against one another (17 *fix an amount, price*) the club ~ £10 as the membership fee; he ~ $100 as the right amount for the car; ~ a price on s.th./ s.o.'s head (→head *n* 6) (18 *value*) he ~ the car at $500; the damage has been ~ at £100.

(19) ~ one's heart / hopes / mind on s.th. (→mind *n* 2c); you won't find the work difficult, if only you ~ your mind to it; she had ~ her heart on having a pearl necklace for her birthday; ~ eyes on s.th./ s.o. (→ eye *n* 2); ~ foot on land / American soil; she vowed never to ~ foot in his house again. (20a) ~ the scenery / stage *(build the scenes)*; the assistant stagemanager is responsible for ~ting and clearing the stage; the scene is ~ for the tragedy *(in a drama, novel)*. (20b) ~ a play / novel in a certain locality; the second act is ~ in a street.

(21 *cause to be in a state;* →15b)

(21a *set + noun + adjective*) ~ your hat straight; ~ things right (→right *adj* 6); ~ a pupil right *(correct him)*; a good night's rest will ~ you right; ~ a prisoner free (21b *set + noun + adverbial phrase*) ~ one's affairs / house in order; ~ a prisoner at liberty; ~ s.th. in motion; ~ s.o. / s.th. on his, its feet *(make him / it self-supporting)*; ~ a rumour / *etc* on foot *(start it)*; a chance action may sometimes ~ on foot a whole train of events; how can we ~ her heart / mind at ease? we must ~ her (mind / fears / doubts) at rest; a considerate host seeks to ~ his guests at ease; my jokes ~ the whole table in a roar; ~ people by the ears / at variance / at loggerheads *(cause them to argue, quarrel)*; ~ the law / judge at defiance *(defy the law, etc)*; ~ s.o.'s teeth / nerves on edge (→ edge *n* 2).

- *vi* (22 *sit on eggs*) when the hens ~ they ... (23 *become whole again*) the broken bone ~. (24 *form fruit*) the pears / tomatoes / *etc* have ~ well. (25) long hair ~s more easily than short hair. (26a *become firm*) the jelly has / is ~; continue boiling the jam till the first signs of ~ting; cement ~s after several hours. (26b *become fast*) the dye has ~. (26c *assume a rigid state*) his face ~ *(he had a hard look)*; his eyes ~ *(when dying, fainting)*; his body has / is ~ *(is fully developed)*; his character has / is ~ *(no longer easily formed)*.

(27a) the moon is ~ting; the sun has / is ~; *(fig)* his star has ~. (27b *go in a specified direction*) the current ~s to the north; the wind ~s from the west; *(fig)* public opinion is ~ting against the proposal; the tide has ~ in his favour. (28 *fit, hang*) the jacket ~s badly; a well-tailored suit ought to ~ well.

(29 *set + about: start doing*) ~ about a task / a job / one's work; any task can be irksome if it is not ~ about in the right spirit; immediately she arrived home she ~ about preparing a meal. (30 *set + about: attack*) the dogs ~ about the man; in a very forceful speech he ~ about his critics. (31 *set + on: attack suddenly*) as he turned the corner a gang of ruffians ~ on him; the dog ~ (up)on me and bit me. (32 *set to work: start working*) they ~ to work as soon as they arrived; he ~ to work on the project / to dig the garden.

set about who ~ this rumour ~ *(spread it)*?

set apart ~ ~ some of one's money for old age.

set aside (1) she ~ ~ her winter clothes and took out her summer frocks. (2 *reserve*) the hotel manager ~ two pleasant rooms ~ for us; a nearby field was ~ ~ for parking space. (3) let's ~ ~ all formality; I can't ~ ~ my personal feelings completely. (4 *disregard*) the committee ~ ~ all the director's objections; he ~ ~ all their offers; ~ a claim / will ~ (5 *in law: declare invalid*) the judge ~ ~ the lower court's decision; the court of appeal ~ the conviction ~.

set back (1) the house is well ~ ~ from the road. (2 *stop the progress of*) the news of her brother's death ~ Kitty ~ and caused the doctors great concern. (3) ~ ~ one's watch two hours (4 *inform: cost*) this new pen ~ me ~ £5.

set down (1) he ~ ~ the heavy sack and rested. (2) the taxi ~ ~ a passenger at the hotel; the plane ~ us ~ in Miami at midnight. (3) ~ s.th. ~ in writing / in the form of a contract; the police sergeant ~ ~ the charges made against the prisoner. (4 ~ ~ *as: consider*) they ~ him ~ as unfit / a fool. (5 ~ ~ *to = attribute to*) ~ a failure ~ to bad planning; ~ ~ one's success to hard work (6) we ~ ~ *(landed)* in heavy fog.

set forth (1) Columbus ~ ~ with three small ships; we ~ ~ at dawn. (2) ~ ~ one's political views; the principles of the American government are ~ ~ in the Declaration of Independence. (3 *display*) she ~ ~ all her new ornaments on the shelves.

set forward (1) ~ one's watch ~ one hour (2) ~ ~ one's opinions.

set in (1) winter ~ in early this year; ..., before the thaw / bad weather ~s in; darkness / dry rot / a bitter cold had ~ in. (2) the tide is ~ting in *(flowing towards the shore)*.

set off (1 *depart*) they ~ ~ for home / for Japan / in brilliant sunshine / in silence. (2) ~ ~ a clause by a comma (3a) ~ ~ a firework / gun / mine / rocket (3b) ~ ~ a mechanism / fire-alarm / *etc* (4) my friend's enthusiasm ~ me ~ collecting stamps; ~ s.o. ~ laughing; ~ ~ a strike; the unpopular law ~ ~ a series of protests; if you can ~ him ~ on his pet subject, he will go on for hours. (5a *enhance by contrast*) the pink wall helps to ~ ~ the bright green curtains; the red scarf ~ ~ the dark tweed; ~ ~ a red dress with white; we must take care to get the right kind of frame to ~ ~ the picture. (5b) ~ ~ gains against losses.

set on (1) in order to complete the contrast in time the firm ~ on *(engaged)* twenty more men. (2 ~ *on: urge to do s.th. wrong*) he isn't really mischievous - his brother ~s him on; agitators tried to ~ the crowd on to acts of violence.

set out (1) ~ ~ seedlings / bulbs / plants; they debated whether to ~ ~ petunias or pansies. (2 *prepare; arrange*) it took them an hour to ~ ~ the room ready for the reception; deduct marks for work that is ~ ~ untidily; all the goods were ~ ~ on a stall; □ ~ ~ one's stall *(display one's qualifications)* (3) ~ ~ *(design)* a pattern (4 *state*) ~ ~ the reasons for one's decision / the case for s.th. / the arguments against s.th.; the letter is clear and well ~ ~. (5 *adorn*) she ~ herself ~ very attractively for the ball. (6a ~ ~ + *infinitive: undertake*) he ~ ~ to prove his point; the booklet ~s ~ to answer that argument; Lincoln ~ ~ to abolish slavery in the United States. (6b) she ~ herself ~ *(made a great effort)* to give the children a good time. (7) it was raining when we ~ ~; ~ ~ for home / for Japan / on foot.

set to (1 *make a vigorous effort*) the men ~ to and worked with great determination; he did not care for the task, but he ~ to and did it. (2a) the two boys ~ to *(started fighting)*. (2b) they were all hungry and at once ~ to.

set up (1a *erect, make ready for use*) ~ up a ladder / post / statue / stall / platform; ~ up the ninepins again; ~ men up on a chessboard; ~ up a sewing-machine; the scouts quickly ~ the tents up. (1b) ~ nuts well up *(tighten them)* (2) ~ up a record; ~ s.th. up as a norm; ~ up a theory (3) ~ up a business / newspaper / organization / committee / hospital / school / religious order / fund / colony (4) ~ up a candidate; ~ s.o. up as a candidate (5) ... where he ~ up as a schoolmaster / grocer / *etc*; ~ up in business (for o.s.); ~ up shop (6a) his father ~ him up in business as a greengrocer; the inheritance ~ him up for life. (6b) it is pretty costly nowadays to ~ a boy up with clothes when he is going away to school; all the pupils are now ~ up with the necessary textbooks; be well ~ up with clothes / reading-matter / *etc* (7) ~ up a shout / yell; someone in the crowd ~ up a cry that the police were coming. (8) I don't ~ up *(claim)* to be an authority on this subject; I don't ~ myself up as an authority on English grammar; that man ~s up for a doctor, but I think he has no qualifications; I have no wish to ~ myself up as an example to others. (9 *make healthy, happy*) her holiday has ~ her up again; ~ting-up exercises; the compliment ~ her up for the day. (10 *cause, esp a disease*) the cold foggy air ~ up an irritation in his throat; what has ~ up the rash on his face? (11) ~ up a manuscript (in type); ~ up type.

set *adj* (1 *firm*) (well-)~ jelly; ~ fair *(of weather: fine, with no signs of change)* (2 *fixed*) a ~ date; at a ~ time; ~ rules; a ~ wage / price; a ~ hand *(way of writing)*; the hall holds a ~ number of people. (3 *rigid*) a ~ smile / stare / look (4 *customary*) a ~ practice / formula; ~ phrases / terms; ~ forms of prayer (5 *determined*) a ~ purpose; ~ opinions; s.o.'s ~ ways; be ~ in one's opinions / ways; be ~ on becoming an actress / having that fur coat; he's dead ~ on winning this race; once he is ~ on an idea, there's no talking him out of it; she seems ~ against having electric light in the house. (6 *prepared beforehand*) a ~ answer / speech (7 ~ *for: ready*) is everyone ~? we are now (all) ~ for the seaside / journey; ~ for trouble (8 ~ *for: likely to experience*) at last we seem ~ for a period of prosperity; he was all ~ for a brilliant career. (9 ~ + *infinitive: ready and keen*) be all ~ to go; they were all ~ to begin.

settle *vi* (1 *come quietly to rest*) a bird ~d on the bough; our parakeet will often ~ on my finger. (2 *take up permanent residence*) on retiring he ~d in a village; the Normans ~d in England. (3a) a sediment ~d at the bottom of the bottle; dust ~d on the piano. (3b) fog ~d on the moors; it's snowing, but the snow isn't ~ing. (4 *become clear*) an hour later the liquid had ~d. (5 *of a building, etc: sink slowly*) a new house ~s after a few years; the roadbed ~d; the ship is ~ing *(sinking)*. (6) silence ~d on the group. (7 *of disease: become localized*) a cold ~s in one's head; the cold has ~d on my chest. (8 *of ground: become firm, esp after rain*) the ground has ~d at last.

(9 *end a dispute*) they ~d out of court. (10a *adjust accounts*) we will ~ with you later; ~ with one's creditors (10b *pay what is owing*) will you ~ for me? (11 *become calm*) I'll wait until the class ~s before starting the lesson; the weather has ~d at last; things will soon ~ into shape.

(12 *settle + on, for: agree on*) ~ on a plan of action / spot for picnic; after a good deal of discussion about what they should have for breakfast, they ~d for bacon and eggs. (13 *get accustomed to*) ~ into a job; he cannot ~ to work; I can't ~ to

anything *(I'm restless).* - *vt* (14a → 1) he ~d himself in a chair; she ~d herself (down) comfortably / snugly with the new novel. (14b *cause to come quietly to rest*) the nurse ~d her patient for the night; then she ~ herself in an armchair in the next room. (15 *cause to take up permanent residence*) the ~d immigrants in urban areas. (16 *provide a region with settlers*) the French ~d this colony with army veterans; ~ a district with people (17 *take up residence in*) ~ an area / territory / *etc*; the pilgrims ~d Plymouth. (18a *clarify*) ~ a liquid (18b) ~ dregs / a sediment; the rain ~d the dust. (19a *pay*) ~ a debt / bill / account / obligation (19b *settle + on: make over legally*) ~ money / property / an annuity / an estate on s.o. (20 *end by reaching a decision*) ~ an argument / doubt / conflict / dispute / controversy / quarrel / clash; there were too many problems to ~; the lawsuit was ~d out of court / amicably. (21 *fix definitely by agreement*) ~ a price / result / day / date; ~ conditions / the terms of a contract; ~ the time and place of a meeting (22a *put in order*) ~ one's affairs (22b) he ~d his son in business *(found a position for him).* (23 *make calm*) ~ the nerves / stomach / mind; the thunderstorm might ~ the weather; ~d weather *(continuously fine)* (24 *stop from annoying*) a sharp word will ~ that youngster ; if he gives you any further trouble, let me know - I'll ~ him.

shake *vt* (1a) ~ a bottle of milk; ~ a pillow / mattress / door-mat / carpet / table-cloth; we shook the plum-tree; the wind shook the windows; the earthquake has ~n the foundations of the house; a heavy sea shook the boat; detonations shook the air; sobs shook her frail body; ~ one's sides with laughter; ~ a leg *(inform: dance)*; ~ hands with s.o. / s.o. by the hand *(as a greeting)* (1b *of parts of the body, etc, ~ as a gesture*) ~ one's head (at / over s.th.) *disapprovingly)*; ~ one's fist at s.o. *(threateningly)*; ~ one's finger at s.o. *(as a warning)*; ~ a stick at s.o. (1c *obtain by shaking*) ~ fruit / nuts from a tree; he took the bottle and shook two aspirins into his hand. (1d *get rid of by ~ing*) ~ the dust out of / off s.th.; ~ leaves from a tree; □ ~ the dust off one's feet (→ dust *n*) (2 *mix*) she shook the milk before pouring it; ~ dice (3 *get rid of*) it seemed that they would never ~ their pursuers; he shook his pursuers from the trail. (4 *weaken*) the physical strain has ~n his health; ~ s.o.'s belief / confidence / self-esteem; his lying shook my faith in him; ~ a witness's evidence (5 *shock*) the fall shook me; the experience shook him badly; she was much ~n by / at the news; he was ~n by his father's harsh scolding; ~ the very foundations of society. - *vi* (6) my hand shook so badly that I almost dropped the cup; his hand / voice shook with emotion; his sides were ~ing with laughter. (7) ~ before using. (8 ~ *hands*) let's ~ hands and be friends again.

shake down (1) ~ ~ fruit (2) ~ ~ a litter (3 *BE inform: sleep on an improvised bed*) let's spread the blankets on the floor - we can ~ ~ on those for the night. (4a *AE inform: extort money from*) he was charged with ~ing ~ a number of influential politicians. (4b *AE search thoroughly*) Captain Q. ordered the mate to ~ ~ all the crew's lockers for the lost key. (5 *test the performance of*) the crew shook the boat ~ after even minor changes in the design; the pilot refused to ~ ~ the controversial new aeroplane.

shake off (1) ~ ~ dust (2) sand ~s ~ easily. (3 *get rid of*) ~ ~ a pursuer / undesirable acquaintances / anxiety / a bad habit / a cold.

shake out (1) ~ ~ dust (2) ~ ~ a vessel / box (3) ~ ~ a table-cloth / sail.

shake up (1) ~ up a pillow / mattress / *etc* (→ shake 1); ~ up a bottle of medicine (2) I feel pretty ~n up after that fall; the collision shook the passengers up pretty badly. (3 *inform: rouse to activity*) the teacher gave the pupil a severe report in the hope that it would ~ him up.

shame *n* (1a) feel ~ at having done s.th. wrong / being caught in a lie; be filled with / overcome with ~; blush for / go red with ~ (1b *susceptibility to ~*) he is without / is lost to / has no ~. (2 *disgrace*) a life of ~; his actions brought ~ upon his parents; to my ~ I must confess that I ...; ~ on you! put s.o. to ~ (→ put *vt* 9) (3a *s.th. to be ashamed of*) the bankruptcy of his business was a ~; the poor condition of our streets is a ~ and a disgrace; a crying / burning / great / *etc* ~ (3b *inform: s.th. regrettable*) it was a ~ that the rain spoiled your holiday; it's a ~ you can't come home for Christmas.

shame *vt* (1 *cause to feel shame*) his cowardice ~d him. (2 *force by shame*) we ~d him into doing his share of the work / apologizing for it.

shape *n* (1a) the ~ of a crystal / building / ship / mountain / *etc*; the rock has a round / angular / peculiar / *etc* ~; the mountain has the / is in the ~ of a cone; a piece of land in the ~ of a triangle; a quince is something like a pear in ~; the tree took the ~ of a ghost in the fog (→ take *vt* 10f); the (noble) ~ of his head (1b *dimly perceived form*) the ~ of a ghost; weird ~s in the fog (2 *proper* ~) the hat has lost its / has gone out of / is out of ~; give s.th. ~ (and form); this jersey keeps its ~ even when it is washed; that hat of yours doesn't seem to be in ~. (3 *figure, body, esp of a woman*) she's not pretty, but she's got a great ~. (4 *form; embodiment*) a paper-weight in the ~ of a lizard; a reward in the ~ of an extra holiday; a troublemaker in the ~ of a friend; an angel in the ~ of a woman; a monster in human ~; the clay gradually took ~ under / in the hands of the potter; the house / plan is beginning to take ~; our plans are taking (on) a definite ~. (5 *state of repair, physical condition*) the old house was in bad / poor ~; he was sick last year, but is in good ~ now; he is the best player we have when he is really in (good) ~; swimming keeps a person in good ~.

shape *vt* (1) ~ clay / wood / metal (into figures); ~ (a mass of) dough (into loaves); the mountain is ~d like a cone; ~ s.th. after / from / on a model; beautifully ~d hands (2a) ~ figures out of clay (2b) ~ a reply (3) ~ a boy for his career; ~ one's future.
- *vi* (4) clouds ~ing on the horizon (5) our plans are ~ing well; the way things are ~ing we can hope that ...

share *n* (1) have a ~ in the profits / in a business; each of the children had his ~ of the cake; pay one's ~ of the bill; I took / bore my ~ of the cost; she did more than her ~ of the work; □ (get) the lion's ~; let me go ~s with you in the taxi fare. (2) ordinary / preference / fully paid-up ~s; hold ~s in a company.

share *vt* (1) ~ a room / burden; may she ~ your umbrella? we'll ~ the cost of the bill between (the three of) us. (2) please ~ your lunch with your sister; he will ~ the winnings with you. (3) ~ s.o.'s enthusiasm / joy / hope / opinion / fate / danger / sorrows / sufferings; ~ responsibility (4 *distribute*) ~ things out among various people. - *vi* (5) ~ in an activity / the profits; he ~d in the planning of it; we asked our neighbour to ~ in the Thanksgiving dinner; ~ in a friend's joy / experiences.

sharp *adj* (1) a ~ knife / razor / blade / pair of scissors; a ~ pin / needle; a pin with a ~ point; ~ brambles / thorns; the table had ~ corners. (2) a ~ ridge / hill / peak / summit (3) a ~ bend / curve in the road; the car made a ~ turn; a ~ slope / incline (4a *as if cut with a knife*) a ~ outline; a ~ *(not blurred)* photographic image; a ~ nose; he had a ~ face. (4b *distinct, marked*) ~ differences of opinion; a ~ distinction / contrast / impression (5) a ~ pain / pang; a ~, biting wind; ~ frost / air (6 *acid*) ~ taste / flavour; a ~ cheese; ~ wine; this sauce is too ~ for me. (7 *shrill*) a ~ sound / note / whistle / cry / voice (8 *harsh*) a ~ remark / retort / reproof / scolding / satire / criticism; ~ words (9 *quick*) a ~ run / walk; we must be ~ if we are to catch the train. (10 *keen*) ~ vision / sight / hearing / eyes / ears; a ~ sense of smell; a ~ nose; ~ wits / intelligence (11a *quick-witted*) a ~ child; be ~ at arithmetic; a ~ lad who will be an asset to the firm. (11b *shrewd*) he is ~ at making a bargain; a ~ bargain (11c *shrewd to the point of dishonesty*) he was too ~ for me; ~ practices; a ~ lawyer / gambler (12 *alert, attentive*) a ~ look-out; they kept a ~ watch for the enemy. (13 *violent*) a ~ fight / struggle / contest; a ~ temper; a ~ attack of illness.

shed *vt* (1) ~ tears; ~ the blood of an enemy *(kill him)*; ~ one's blood for one's country; the war ~ the blood of thousands. (2a) trees ~ their leaves; snakes ~ their skins; a crab ~s its shell; ~ hair / feathers; how often do stags ~ their antlers / horns? (2b) ~ one's (wet) clothes; we ~ our overcoats in the spring. (2c) he ~ his troubles as a duck ~s water. (3) this cloth ~s water; an umbrella ~s rain. (4 *spread*) the lamp ~ a soft light; a fire ~s warmth; ~ fragrance / perfume / sound; the Christmas tree ~ joy among the children; *(fig)* ~ light on a problem / mystery; ~ favours / misery; ~ love / kindness / radiance around one. - *vi* (5) the cat is ~ding (its hair); the dog is ~ding badly. (6) all the leaves have ~.

shift *vt* (1) ~ a bundle from one hand to another; ~ one's weight to the other foot; will you help me to ~ the furniture about / round? (2) ~ scenery / the scenes (on a stage) (3) ~ the location of a factory; *(fig)* ~ the blame / responsibility (on) to s.o. else (4 *accomplish*) ~ a job / task (5 *change*) ~ friends; ~ ideas. - *vi* (6 *move*) ~ from one foot to another; ~ in one's chair *(move nervously)*; the scene ~s to a cave; the wind ~ed to the north; they ~ed about *(moved to various places)* for several years. (7 *get along; manage as best one can*) he ~ed through life; she had to ~ for herself after her parents died.

ship *vt* (1 *put in a ship*) ~ goods / passengers / sailors (2 *take on*) ~ a new crew (3 *send; transport*) ~ goods from London to New York; ~ goods by express train / lorry (4 *have water enter over the side of the ship*) ~ water / a wave / a sea (→ sea 2). - *vi* (5 *serve on a ship*) he ~ped as a steward.

shock *n* (1) the ~ of an earthquake / explosion; the ~ of a blow / fall (2) (get) an (electric) ~ (when one touches a live wire) (3a *violent disturbance of the mind*) the burglary was a ~ to her sense of security; the book provided a ~, nothing more; (get / have) a mental / emotional ~ (3b *collapse of circulatory functions*) he is suffering from ~; he died of ~ following an operation on the brain. (4 *the cause of such a disturbance*) the rebuke came as a ~; the news was a terrible ~ to me.

shock *vt* (1) he enjoyed ~ing people; I am ~ed to hear that he ... / at his cruelty; nothing will ~ him into a change of conviction. - *vi* (2) he doesn't ~ easily.

shoe *n* brush / black / polish / shine (a pair of) ~s; put on / take off / lace (up) / unlace one's ~s; get / have ~s mended / soled; my ~s are too loose / too tight / worn out / waterproof / *etc*; my ~s need mending / stretching / *etc*; my ~ pinches at the toe / heel (→ pinch *vi* 5); □ I should not like to be in your ~s.

shoot *vt* (1) ~ a bullet (from a gun) / arrow (from a bow); ~ a gun; he shot a pistol / arrow at me. (2) ~ a rabbit; he shot him in / through the leg; ~ s.o. dead; ~ o.s.; he was shot *(executed)* at dawn. (3a *hunt*) ~ game / partridges / grouse / hares / *etc* (3b *hunt the game on*) ~ land / an estate (4 *go rapidly over*) ~ rapids / a fall (5 *fling, direct swiftly*) the volcano shot lava high into the air; as a result, the driver was shot out of the car; ~ the spotlight on the doorway (6a) ~ a ball / puck (6b) ~ a goal (7) ~ dice / marbles (8) in the spring, plants ~ buds. (9) ~ questions at s.o.; ~ a look / glance (at s.o.); she shot him an angry look; he shot a smile at his wife. (10) ~ a film / picture / scene (11 *streak with different colours*) the sky was shot with many colours; hair shot with grey. - *vi* (12a) can you ~? does this gun ~ straight? will that gun ~? ~ wide *(far from the mark aimed at)* (12b → 2) ~ at s.o. / a target (with a revolver / bow and arrow / *etc* (13 *hunt*) go ~ing; he fishes, but he doesn't ~; ~ing-season; ~ing-licence; ~ over an area / preserve (14a *move rapidly*) he shot past me on his bicycle; he came ~ing along; he shot out of the door; the car shot ahead and was soon out of sight; the missile left its pad and shot thousands of miles into space; the meteor shot across the sky; a ~ing star *(meteor)* (14b) pain shot through his injured arm; chills shot up and down her spine. (14c) an idea shot across / into his mind. (15) rose-bushes ~ again after being cut back.

shoot away (1) he had a foot shot ~. (2) ~ ~ one's ammunition (3) on the command 'go' the runners shot ~ from their marks.

shoot down (1) we shot ~ several ducks; ~ ~ an aeroplane (2) ~ ~ a man; he was shot ~ in cold blood / like a dog.

shoot off he had a foot shot ~.

shoot out (1) he shot ~ his arm and grabbed the ball; the snake shot its tongue ~. (2) the volcano ~s ~ flame and rocks. (3) a rabbit shot ~ and disappeared ... (4) the cape ~s ~ into the sea.

shoot up (1) several hands shot up as soon as the teacher asked the question; flames ~ up. (2) the boy has shot up during this year; the warm weather made the plants ~ up. (3) prices / rents ~ up *(rise suddenly)*.

shop *n* (1) a butcher's / chemist's / fruit / antique / *etc* ~; open / manage / close down a ~; keep a ~ *(be a shopkeeper)*; keep ~ *(run it)*: she kept ~ for him while he went to his wife's funeral; when do the ~s open / close? □ set up / open ~ *(open a business)*: she saved her money and set up ~ as a milliner; □ shut up ~ *(cease trading, functioning)*: if we cannot recruit new members to the society, we shall soon have to shut up ~; □ talk ~ *(discuss one's trade, profession, etc)*; □ come / go to the wrong ~ *(wrong person for help, information, etc)* (2 *workshop*) an engineering / fitting / machine / carpenter's / *etc* ~.

short *adj* (1) a ~ distance / path; I live a ~ way off; a ~ skirt / thread / piece of string; he has rather ~ legs; be ~ in the arm / leg / sleeves; a dress with ~ sleeves / ~-sleeved dress; ~ grass / hair; she wears her hair ~; she has had her hair cut ~; these buses are used on ~ runs; he took the ~est way home; a ~ article / text / speech / report / poem; he made ~ notes; → cut *n* 5. (2 *not lasting long*) a ~ wait / visit / stay / journey / holiday / rest / nap; we were together for one ~ hour; a ~ life; a ~ time ago; a ~ time before / after that day; the days are getting ~er; ~-term loans; → cut *vt* 1b, notice *n* 2; please make it ~, I haven't got much time; the factory is on ~ time *(working fewer hours than usual)*; ~-time work(er) (3 *not tall*) a ~ man; he is ~ and fat; he is ~ of stature. (4 *less than a correct, sufficient amount, etc*) give a customer ~ weight / measure; a ~ dozen; a ~ supply; potatoes are ~ / in ~ supply this year; our supplies ran ~; the ice cream ran ~ at the picnic; my patience is running ~; a ~ mile; a ~ throw; ~ views (5 *lacking the correct, sufficient amount, etc*) be ~ of money / funds / sugar / petrol / *etc*; when he counted his money he found he was 40 pence ~; he was a dollar ~ of the train fare; keep s.o. ~ (of money / food); be ~ in one's payments; the collection amounted to a few pence ~ of ten pounds *(e.g. £9.80)*; I have run / am ~ of coffee; I ran ~ of money / tea / patience / *etc*; I was ~ of breath; he was ~ in experience; Texas alone is 5,000 teachers ~ this year; → go *vi* 20a. (6 ~ of: not reaching) we are still a mile ~ of our destination; little / nothing ~ of *(little / nothing less than)*: her performance was nothing ~ of marvellous; the essay is decidedly ~ of satisfactory. (7 *of memory, not retentive*) have a ~ memory (8a *saying little, said in few words*) he / his answer was ~ and to the point. (8b *not friendly*) a ~ manner; ~ behaviour; he was very ~ with me; he gave me a ~ answer; his answer was a ~ "No". (8c) for ~ *(by way of abbreviation)*: he is called Ben for ~; cello is ~ for violoncello; in ~ *(in a few words)*: in ~ / to cut a long story ~, we arrived too late (→ cut *vt* 1b). (9 *easily aroused*) a ~ temper; be ~-tempered (10 *of pastry, crumbly*) how does one make pastry ~? ~ crust is suitable for pies and tarts; biscuit eats ~ *(crumbles in the mouth)*.

short *adv* (1 *suddenly*) stop ~; → cut *vt* 12, pull up 4, take up 2a (2 *curtly*) he talked ~ with everyone. (3 *before a particular point*) the arrow landed ~; he jumped ~; it lies somewhere ~ of London; → fall *vi* 16, come *vi* 9, sell *vi* 6 (4 ~ *of: without going as far as*) ~ of lying I will say what I can for you; this is the only thing to do, ~ of scrapping the whole project.

shot *n* (1) fire a ~; the ~ echoed through the woods; a random ~ *(also fig, → 7)*; have / take / try a ~ at s.th. *(also fig, → 7)*; like a ~ *(without delay)*: he was off like a ~; he came out like a ~ with the answer; □ a ~ in the dark *(a random guess)* (2 *cannon-ball*) a round ~ of some pounds (2a) → put *vt* 2. (3 *a leaden pellet for a shotgun*) the hare was riddled with ~; three ~ were extracted from his head. (4 *s.o. who shoots*) he is a good / poor / crack / dead ~. (5 *injection*) have you had your polio ~? □ a ~ in the arm *(s.th. that stimulates)*: a reduction in taxation would be a ~ in the arm for industry. (6 *critical remark*) that was a ~ at you. (7 *attempt*) → 1; I am doubtful whether I can do it, but I don't mind having a ~; the answer is not correct, but it's a good ~; (make) a bad ~ *(wrong guess)* (8) the exterior ~s of this film were taken in Britain, the indoor ~s were done in our studio.

shoulder *n* (1) broad / narrow / square / round / sloping / high / *etc* ~s; a ~ of mutton; stand ~ to ~ *(also fig)*; have broad ~s (*be able to bear much*): if you want to tell me your troubles, I have broad ~s; □ give s.o. the cold ~ / turn a cold ~ on s.o. *(treat with hostility)*; □ put one's ~ to the wheel *(make an effort)*; → rub *vt* 1b; □ straight from the ~ *(of criticism: frank)*: the lawyer told him straight from the ~ that his case was weak. (2) the ~ of a tool / bottle / mountain.

shoulder *vt* (1) ~ a gun / bundle / burden (2) ~ one's way through a crowd; ~ people aside (3) ~ responsibilities / debts / a task; ~ the blame.

shout *vi* (1) he ~ed to warn me; he ~ed with joy / pain / for help; he ~ed to / for me to come. (2 *speak very loudly*) she had to ~ because he was deaf. - *vt* (3) ~ oaths in anger; he ~ed a warning; ~ (out) one's orders.

shout down they ~ed the speaker / chairman ~.

show *n* (1 *exhibition*) a flower / horse / cattle / motor ~ (2 *display*) vote by (a) ~ of hands; a fine ~ of cherry-blossom; some of her paintings are on ~ in the local art gallery; put goods on ~; a ~ of determination / strength / grief; an ostentatious ~ of knowledge; this china is only for ~ and not for use; he did it for ~; he is fond of ~. (3 *visible trace*) no ~ of fatigue (4a *appearance*) a ~ of health in her rosy cheeks; a claim with some ~ of justice / reason; one must pierce beneath the ~s of things. (4b *pretence*) his boasting was only a ~ of courage; he made a ~ of not hearing me. (5 *performance*) I see the ~ *(opera, musical, etc)* begins at 7; after four months, when I could make a crude ~ of talking the language, I sailed to ...; □ put up a good ~ (→ put up 9) (6 *inform: undertaking*) he wrecked the whole ~; → give away 3, run *vt* 63. (7 *chance of showing one's powers*) give him a fair ~; it got no sort of ~.

show vt (1a) he ~ed his books to me / me his books; I was ~n some patterns; a clock ~s the time; you must ~ your ticket at the barrier; the window ~s the interior; that dress ~s your underwear; → face *n* 5; must we ~ ourselves at the meeting? his disappointment ~ed itself in his looks; → colour *n* 6, door 1, fight *n* 3, front *n* 4; □ ~ one's hand / cards *(reveal one's plans)*; □ ~ one's teeth *(look angry)*; □ ~ a clean pair of heels *(escape)* (1b *exhibit*) ~ goods in a shop; ~ a house; he ~s his dogs for prizes. (2 *guide*) she ~ed me to my seat; she ~ed me over / through / round the house; he ~ed us all over / round the town; ~ a visitor into a room; shall I ~ her in? who ~ed you round? (3) they are ~ing a new film (at the Odeon). (4 *explain*) his letter ~s why he did not come; he ~ed her why she ought to do it; I'll ~ you what I mean; ~ the solution of s.th.; he ~ed (me) the way (to the village); he ~ed me how to do it. (5 *prove*) the evidence ~ed that he was sane at the time; I can ~ that it is so; he will ~ you the absurdity of it; his experiment ~ed the theory to be false / that the theory is false / the falsity of the theory. (6a *give evidence of*) ~ ability / talent / genius; that article ~s a bias against the Socialists; he / his attempt ~s (no lack of) courage; ~ dexterity in doing s.th.; she ~ed great discretion about the secret; he ~s high intelligence for a boy of his age; ~ an interest in sports; she has never ~n us anything but kindness; the garden ~ed neglect; ~ mercy to a defeated enemy; he ~ed no pity; he can ~ no results / has no results to ~; s.th. ~s signs of damage / improvement / *etc*; he ~ed little willingness to work. (6b) the thermometer ~ed 10 below zero; the account ~s him as a scoundrel; the farm ~ed a profit. - *vi* (7a *be, become visible*) did her slip ~? the buds are just ~ing; s.th. ~s to advantage. (7b) her embarrassment ~ed when she blushed; his fear ~ed in his eyes. (7c) he said he would be there, but he didn't ~. (8) ... is a nice film which is now ~ing in London (→ film *n* 3).

show off (1) ~ ~ one's goods in a shop window; ~ ~ exhibits; the parade was designed to ~ ~ all the latest weapons of war. (2) she went to church to ~ ~ her new clothes; a swim-suit that ~s ~ her figure well (3 *boast*) don't ~ ~ so much - try to be modest; she was always ~ing ~ in public.

show up (1) the bright sunlight ~ed up the faded patches in the carpet. (2) her wrinkles ~ed up in the strong light; blue will not ~ up on a black background. (3) his skill ~ed up their incompetence; they ~ed her up as a liar; ~ up an impostor / fraud (4) if he fails to ~ up, let me know.

shut *vt* (1a) ~ a door / gate / window / lid; → door 1; ~ a drawer; ~ a letter; ~ one's mouth / eyes / lips; → eye *n* 2; he ~s his ears to all appeals for help / my arguments. (1b *fold up, etc*) he ~ the screen and put it away; ~ a knife / telescope / book / hand (1c ~ *the door(s) of*) ~ a room / house / shop / *etc* (2) ~ the dog in the kitchen; she ~ the child in his room until he stopped crying; ~ a bird into a cage (3) ~ a road to all traffic (4) they ~ her out of the building; they ~ him from their circle. (5 *stop the operation of*) he will have to ~ the shop; we are ~ting the office for two weeks in June. (6) she ~ her finger / dress in the door. - *vi* (7) the gate ~ in the wind; the lid ~s automatically; a door that ~s easily / close; the door won't ~; the box / knife / flower ~s.

shut down (1) ~ ~ a factory (2) ~ ~ steam (3) the factory ~ ~; the summer resort ~ ~ during the winter. (4) the fog ~ ~ rapidly.

shut in (1) why was he ~ in? ~ o.s. in; she broke her leg in a fall and has been ~ in for several weeks. (2) the house is ~ in by trees; we are ~ in by hills here.

shut off (1) ~ ~ water / gas / steam (2) ~ ~ the radio (3) he is ~ting himself ~ from society; ~ ~ from the outside world; this country has ~ itself ~ from all western influences.

shut out (1) don't let the door bang to or I shall be ~ ~; ~ ~ immigrants / imports; ~ ~ sunlight; these trees ~ ~ the view. (2) this ~s ~ any danger of fire.

shut to ~ the door to!

shut up (1) ~ up jewels in a safe; ~ up a puppy in a pen; ~ a child up in a room (2 *close the doors and windows of*) they ~ up the house when they went on holiday; don't forget to ~ up when you leave the shop; ~ up shop for the night / permanently (→ shop *n* 1) (3 *inform: stop talking*) ~ up and listen to your father! I wish he would ~ up complaining. (4) he started complaining, but I soon ~ him up; when he starts on that subject he is not easily ~ up.

sick *adj* (1) a ~ person / animal; ~ game; do dogs often fall ~? he has been a ~ man all his life; look after one's ~ mother; report (o.s.) ~; the (mentally / chronic) ~ (2a *likely to vomit*) feel ~ (from / with overeating); bus rides make her ~; I am easily sea- / air- / car-~. (2b *suffering an attack of vomiting*) I was ~ three times; I was ~ yesterday. (3 *showing that s.o. is ill*) a ~ look / smile / pallor; the ~ smell of disinfectant in the corridors (4 *mentally, emotionally deranged*) it makes me ~ to think of what he has done; be ~ with anger / envy; his manners make me ~; she was ~ at heart *(sad)*; a ~ mind; wild statements that made him seem ~; ~ fancies; laugh o.s. ~ (5 ~ *of: disgusted by*) be ~ (and tired) of complaints; ~ of parties / rice pudding / this constant rain; be heartily ~ / ~ to death of s.th. (6 ~ *for: longing for*) ~ for home / a change of scene (7 *sadistic, morbid*) ~ jokes / humour; a ~ comedian (8 *inform: weak, poor*) his painting looks pretty ~ by comparison with yours; that used to be quite a flourishing business, but it's been looking rather ~ for the last year or two; *(AE inform)* prices nowadays can sure(ly) make $20 look ~!

side *n* (1a) a cube has six ~s. (1b *vertical ~, not top, bottom*) the ~s of a box; the ~ of a hill (1c *as in 1a, but not front, back*) there was a path / garden at the ~ of the house; the shed was leaning to one ~; come and sit by / at my ~; I have a pain in my (left) ~; □ at the ~ *(compared with)*: she is quite clever at the ~ of the other girls; my suit looks quite shabby at the ~ of yours; □ on the ~ *(confidentially; in addition to one's regular activity)*: I'm telling you this on the ~; in addition to my wages I make a few pounds more on the ~; he dates another girl on the ~; ~ by ~ *(close together; also fig)*; □ split / shake / burst one's ~s (with laughter) *(laugh heartily)* (1d) a ~ of beef / bacon (1e *part of s.th. away from the centre*) the ~s of a room; he crossed to the far ~ of the room; the east ~ of a city (2) write on both ~s of the paper; the right ~ of the cloth (3) the 3 ~s of a triangle; the 4 ~s of a rhombus (4 *one of two halves*) the right / left / north / sunny ~ of the road; only one ~ of the moon is visible to us; the debit ~ of an account (5 *direction*) arrows came at him from all ~s / every ~; look on all ~s *(in every direction)* (6 *space near a dividing line*) stay on this ~ of the hedge; on this ~ of the Alps; which ~ of the river are we? □ on the wrong / right ~ of 50 *(above / below 50 years of age)*; on the dear / heavy / small / short / *etc* ~ *(dearer, etc than expected)*: it's good material, but it's on the dear ~; these shoes are on the large ~ *(too large)*; prices for ... were on the high ~; this cake is a little on the sweet ~. (7 *aspect*) study all ~s of the question; consider all ~s of a problem; he has many ~s to his character; his character has many ~s; look on the bright / dark / gloomy ~ of life / things; see life only on its pleasant ~; life presented only its tragic ~ to him; err on the ~ of leniency; the sunny ~ of her nature (8 *one of two groups of opponents*) they divided into two ~s to play the game; our ~ won the baseball game; the ~s in a battle. (9 *one of two opposing positions*) be on the winning / losing ~; change ~s in a dispute; whose ~ are you on? Italy entered the Great War on the ~ of Germany; I am on your ~ in this issue; there are always two ~s to an argument; hear both ~s of a dispute; take ~s with / against s.o. in a dispute / on an issue; take s.o.'s ~ (10 *line of descent*) a cousin on his father's ~; grandparents on one's maternal ~; his / her ~ of the family.

sight *n* (1 *power of seeing*) his ~ was restored by an operation on his eyes; have good / bad / poor ~; lose one's ~ *(become blind)*; have long / short / near ~; small print ruins one's ~; □ second ~ *(ability to look into the future)* (2 *act of seeing*) the first ~ of the sea was a thrill to the boy from the Middle West; the very ~ of him makes me tremble; he stopped at the ~ of the picture; at / on ~ *(immediately when seen)*: translate s.th. at ~; ~ translation; shoot s.o. at / on ~; at the ~ of us he ran away; a draft payable at ~; sing / play music at / from ~; have / catch / get / gain / lose ~ of s.o./ s.th.; I would recognize him at (first) ~ / on ~; it was love at first ~; I know her by ~, but not to speak to; it was done in my ~ *(before my eyes)*; do s.th. in ~ of everybody; we are (with)in ~ of land; in ~ of the enemy *(seeing the enemy; → 4)*; out of ~, out of mind (3a *s.th. seen, visible*) she was a lovely ~ in her wedding-dress; a beautiful / pitiful / sorrowful / melancholy / lamentable / comical / *etc* ~; ~ unseen *(without seeing s.th. beforehand)*: we bought the car ~ unseen. (3b *thing worth seeing*) poppies make a fine ~; □ a ~ for sore eyes *(s.o., s.th. very welcome)*; the ~s of London; a sightseer is one who goes to see / visit the ~s. (3c *s.th. ugly, etc to look at*) what a ~ you look in those slacks! the car was a ~ after the accident; she does look a ~! (4 *range of vision*) land is in ~; in ~ of the enemy *(being seen by the enemy; → 2)*; keep s.o./ s.th. in ~; keep out of my ~ in future! he didn't let her out of his ~; the plane was still in / soon out of ~; victory is not yet in / still out of ~. (5 *opinion, judgement*) he can do no wrong in her ~; do what is right in your own ~; all men are equal in the ~ of God. (6 *sights: viewing device*) the ~s of a rifle / telescope / *etc*; adjust the ~s (of a rifle); raise / lower one's ~s *(also fig: goals, aims)* (7 *observation taken with a sight*) take a careful ~ before firing; take a ~ with a compass; take a ~ at the sun.

sign *n* (1a) mathematical ~s; the plus and minus ~s (+ ,–); the circle as a ~ of infinity; deaf-mutes converse by ~s; £ is a ~ that means 'pound'; (make) the ~ of the cross (over s.o.) (1b *gesture*) he nodded as a ~ of agreement; the policeman gave a ~ to the driver to stop the car. (2) a traffic / road / danger ~; a shop ~; the butcher's ~ ; the ~(board) of an inn (3 *evidence*) a sudden fall in the barometer is a ~ of a storm; dark clouds are a ~ of rain / that it will rain; those are ~s of a bad character; the first ~s of a disease; there is every ~ of a speedy recovery; his trembling was a ~ of fright; she saw no ~ that he would change his mind; ~s and wonders (4 *trace*) there was no ~ of life anywhere; there wasn't a ~ of them.

sign *vt* (1a) ~ a letter / document / cheque / confession / *etc* (1b *write*) ~ one's name (1c *approve; ratify*) ~ a bill into law (2 *engage*) ~ a new player; → sign on 1, sign up (3 *indicate by gestures*) he ~ed his wish to leave; the policeman ~ed (for) them to stop; ~ one's consent (4 *fig: indicate*) this treaty ~s a new era in international relations. – *vi* (5 *write one's signature*) please ~ in full; ~ in s.o. else's name; did you ~ for the package? (6 *make a sign*) he ~ed to me to come.

sign away ~ ~ *(give up)* rights / property.

sign off at 11 p.m. the radio station ~ed ~ *(stopped broadcasting)*.

sign on (1 *engage*) ~ on a seaman / twenty more workers; the sports club ~ed on a new manager / player for the football team. (2) how many seamen have ~ed on so far? (3) when does the TV station ~ on?

sign over she ~ed ~ *(~ed away)* her mansion to the church for use as a school.

sign up (1) the recruiting officer ~ed up my brother for a four-year period. (2) the soldier ~ed up for another three years.

simple *adj* (1 *easy to understand, use*) a ~ matter / problem / task; ~ rules / instructions; written in ~ English; ~ tools (2 *not complicated*) a ~ device / machine / design / organism; a ~ head cold; ~ forms of life; it will be ~st if you go there yourself. (3 *consisting of only one kind, part*) a ~ substance; a ~ fracture; a ~ sentence / tense; ~ interest *(on capital only)* (4 *ordinary, humble*) a ~ soldier / workman; a ~ household; ~ affairs / tastes; ~ folk; his neighbours are ~

people. (5 *not elaborate, unadorned*) ~ beauty; a ~ style; ~ architecture; speak ~y; ~ food / cooking; a ~ meal / diet; a ~ gown; dress ~y; nothing is more ~ than greatness. (6 *unpretentious, modest*) a ~ way of life; lead a ~ life; live ~y; he is a ~ man and a great scholar; the great man had a ~ manner; ~ charm (7 *sincere*) a frank, ~ answer; she was ~ and trustful. (8 *lacking mental acuteness*) he is ~ about money matters; a dangerously ~ way of thinking; I am not so ~ as to believe him.

sing *vt* (1a) ~ a melody / song / tune; ~ the praises of s.o./ s.th.; □ ~ another tune / song *(become humbler)* (1b) ~ a baby to sleep. - *vi* (2 → 1) ~ in chorus; she promised to ~ for us; ~ to the guitar; ~ in / out of tune *(the right / wrong notes)*; □ ~ small *(cease boasting)* (3a) birds / insects / brooks ~ ; the kettle / wind was ~ing. (3b) bullets sang past our ears. (4 *be filled with ~ing*) the woods / my ears were ~ing. (5 *admit of being sung*) this lyric ~s well. (6 *slang: confess one's own or s.o. else's guilt in a crime*) I'll make him ~ if it's the last thing I ever do; if M. ~s we'll all be convicted.

sink *vi* (1) he sank into a chair / on one knee; he sank to / on the ground; his head sank on his breast; they sank into each other's arms. (2) the moon / sun is ~ing; the clouds are ~ing lower. (3) the ship sank slowly. (4 *come to a lower level*) the foundations have sunk; the river sank two feet during the dry spell; the tower is ~ing on one side. (5 *penetrate*) the knife sank into his flesh; his foot sank in the mud; she relaxed and let her head ~ into the pillows; the cart had sunk deep into the morass; the rain sank into the dry ground; dye / water ~s into a fabric. (6 *slope downwards*) the hills sank to the sea's edge; the field ~s towards the road. (7 *die down*) the storm is beginning to ~ ; I watched the flames ~. (8 *drop to a lower pitch*) his voice sank to a whisper. (9 *become hollow*) his eyes / cheeks had sunk (in). (10 *fall*) the temperature sank to 30° at noon; the barometer is ~ing; the price of eggs sank during the summer; the population sank from 20 million to 9; her opinion of him sank; he sank in their estimation. (11a *sink into: gradually enter a state*) ~ into sleep / silence / despair / vice / poverty / oblivion / insignificance / disuse; he sank into a gentle slumber; he sank easily into a new way of life; he's sunk in thought. (11b) the facts don't seem to ~ into his head; let this warning ~ well into your mind. (12 *become weak*) the patient is ~ing (fast) *(getting worse)*; his spirits / courage sank; his heart sank *(he lost hope, courage)*. (13 *degenerate*) the level of service at the hotel had sunk; after losing his job he sank until he was almost a bum; the old aristocracy sank in wealth and prestige.
- *vt* (14) the submarine sank the destroyer. (15 *lower the level of*) they sank the roadway by five feet; ~ a lake / river (16 *cause to penetrate*) the lion sank his teeth in the antelope's neck; he sank the dagger up to its hilt. (17 *dig, bore, lay*) ~ a hole / well / mineshaft; ~ a foundation; ~ a post in the ground; ~ a pipe / conduit (18) she sank her voice to a whisper. (19 *ruin*) drinking and gambling sank him completely; if they see us, we are sunk; ~ a plan (20 *conceal, ignore*) he has a habit of ~ing unpleasant truths; they sank their differences (in the face of the common enemy). (21 *invest*) he sank all his money into house-building / a new undertaking; ~ *(pay off)* a debt.

sink down (1) he sank ~ on the bench and waited for the next bus; he sank ~ in the pillows. (2) ~ ~ in the fen.

sink in (1) we had sunk in to above our knees. (2) his cheeks have sunk in. (3) he said it four times before the words really sank in.

sit *vi* (1a) sit on a chair / in an armchair / on the floor / at a table / close together / silent / withdrawn; it was the rule for men and women to ~ apart; they sat long over their whisky and their pipes. (1b *~ on eggs*) a ~ting hen; the hen wants to ~; my old hen isn't ~ting this year. (1c) ~ for an examination / degree (externally); ~ for one's finals; ~ for a portrait / to an artist (1d *fig*) the lookers-on were ~ting on their hands *(did not applaud)*; ~ on the fence *(refuse to commit o.s.)*; ~ting pretty *(inform: in a very favourable situation)*: he's been ~ting pretty ever since he got that new job; ~ tight *(take no action)*: I'm going to ~ tight till I hear what they're going to do. (2) go and ~ with / by her for a while. (3 *be situated*) the cottage ~s in a hollow; the house ~s well up on the slope; the island ~s in the harbour. (4) the jacket ~s well / badly (on / across your shoulders). (5 *remain inactive*) the food ~s heavy on my stomach; the scooter is ~ting *(standing unused)* by the roadside; they let the matter ~. (6a *be in session*) how often does Parliament / the committee ~? the court will ~ next week. (6b *sit on: deliberate over*) a coroner's jury was called to ~ on the case; the board of directors is ~ting on that issue at this moment. (7 *be a member of*) he ~s on the board / committee / jury. (8 *fig: lie, weigh*) his new authority ~s heavily on him; his dignity ~s well on him; your duties ~ lightly on your shoulders; an aura of greatness ~s easily upon him; the crime ~s heavy on his conscience. (9 *sit on: repress*) that young fellow has far too much to say - it's about time someone sat on him; I'll ~ on him if he tries to interrupt me; ~ on a proposal / a suggestion / bad news (10 *of wind: blow*) the wind ~s in the west tonight; in what quarter ~s the wind? - *vt* (11 *cause to sit*) ~ him on her left; the waiter couldn't ~ us for half an hour; he lifted the child and sat her at a little table. (12) she ~s her horse gracefully / very badly; he could hardly ~ his mule. (13) our dining-room table only ~s six (people).

sit down (1) ~ ~ on a chair / to work / to read (2) ~ a child ~ (there) (3) ~ ~ to an insult / an affront / a remark / objectionable behaviour.

sit in (1) I'd like you to ~ in on this conference. (2) have you got someone to ~ in *(act as baby-sitter)*?

sit out (1) the weather is too cold for us to ~ ~. (2) I don't enjoy ~ting a dance ~; a few preferred to ~ ~ *(not to dance)*. (3) though bored, they sat ~ the concert / lecture / sermon / play; we sat ~ the storm. (4 *stay longer than*) we sat ~ the other guests.

sit up (1a) ~ up straight! (1b) when I entered he sat up (in bed). (2) we sat up till two o'clock in the morning; she sat up all night (with the sick child); we let the children ~ up on Christmas Eve. (3) when I mentioned the Smiths she sat up *(inform: took notice)*; here's piece of news that will make you ~ up; our patient is beginning to ~ up and take notice *(is getting better)*.

size *n* (1) the ~ of a room / farm / amount / country / *etc*; measure the ~ of an object; this book is twice the ~ of that; nobody can afford a house that ~ nowadays; what ~ box do you want? a crowd of considerable ~; bears of some ~ *(fairly large)*; it is small in ~; take the ~ of s.th. *(measure it)* (2 *considerable size*) seek ~ rather than quality; notice the ~ of that spider. (3) children's ~s of shoes; ~ 9 shoes; ~s in shoes / stockings / gloves / hats; what ~ do you take (in gloves)? what ~ are you? I take / am ~ forty; what ~ hat do you wear? I need a smaller ~; it is several ~s too small; I think we have the suede shoe in your ~; we sell this machine in three ~s. (4 *total quantity*) the ~ of that shipment was only a dozen; the ~ of an order (5 *intellectual capacity*) it is not a job for a man of his ~. (6 *inform: state of affairs*) that's about the ~ of it.

skill *n* (1 *ability coming from practice, etc*) the ~ of a workman / surgeon; acquire / practice / develop ~ (in doing s.th.); this hairdresser shows a certain ~ in cutting hair; the driver showed great ~ in keeping the damaged car under control; embroidery takes painstaking ~; Ellen has a natural ~ on the piano; play the violin / billiards with great ~; the work calls for various ~s; domestic ~s; teach arithmetic ~s (2 *excellence, expertness*) the dancers performed with ~; our detectives show varying ~ and thoroughness in the detection of crime; do s.th. with accomplished ~; manage a person with ~ (3 *a craft, job requiring manual dexterity, experience*) what ~s do you have other than typing and shorthand?

skin *n* (1a) (have) a fine / delicate / fair / brown / leathery / greasy / oily / *etc* ~; wear s.th. next (to) one's ~; be soaked to the ~; ~ tissue; outer / inner / true ~ (1b *fig*) he's (all) ~ and bone(s) *(very thin)*; there was nothing left of the poor thing after her illness but ~ and bones; have a thick ~ *(be insensitive)*: working at the complaint desk of a shop is a good job for someone who has a thick ~; have a thin ~ *(be very sensitive)*: be careful what you say to her, she has a thin ~; risk one's ~; → save *vt* 1; by the ~ of one's teeth *(just barely)*: → escape *vi* 1; we made the last train by the ~ of our teeth; I shouldn't like to be in your ~; get under s.o.'s ~ *(inform: irritate; impress deeply)*: his laugh really gets under my ~; that sort of music always gets under my ~. (2) the ~ of snakes / fish / pigs / *etc*; raw ~s (3) the ~ of fruit / bananas (4) the ~ on (hot) milk; a ~ of thin ice (5) the aluminium ~ of an aircraft / wing.

sky *n* (1) a clear / brilliant / blue / cloudless / milky / leaden / cloudy / grey / overcast / stormy / sombre / ugly / dull ~; the night ~ / ~ at night; the ~ clouded over / was clearing / was brightening; sleep under the open ~; praise / extol / laud s.o. to the skies (2 *heaven*) they prayed to the ~ for help. (3 *climate*) the sunny skies of Italy; under a Greek ~; these fruits ripened under gentler / warmer skies.

sleep *n* get enough ~; I had only an hour's ~ last night; (be unable to) go to ~; go off / get to ~; have a ~; a deep / light / restful / (un)sound / dead *(deep)* ~; the ~ of death; the long / last / eternal ~; he talks / walks in his ~; my foot / leg has gone to ~.

sleep *vi* (1) he ~s well / badly / deeply / peacefully; you can ~ late tomorrow morning; ~ on / over a matter / question; □ let ~ing dogs lie (→ dog *n* 1) (2) the town slept; while England slept, Germany prepared the war. - *vt* (3) ~ a deep sleep; he slept the sleep of the innocent / just; she slept the night in the attic / ten hours (4) this hotel ~s 50 guests; this room can ~ four.

sleep away (1) ~ the day ~ (2) ~ ~ one's cares / a headache.

sleep in I'm sorry I'm late for work this morning - I slept in *(too long)*; don't set the alarm clock - I want to ~ in tomorrow.

sleep off ~ ~ a headache / hangover; ~ ~ one's fatigue / drunkenness.

sleep on she slept on after the bell had rung.

sleep out how often do you ~ ~ *(not at home)*?

sleep through ~ the night ~; the child ~s ~ now from ten o'clock.

sleeve *n* (1) the ~s of a dress / coat / *etc*; ladies sometimes put a handkerchief up their ~; roll / turn up one's ~s *(also fig: prepare for fight or work)*; roll / turn down one's ~s; pluck s.o.'s ~s; have a weapon / plan / *etc* up one's ~ *(concealed but ready)*; → card 2; → laugh *vi* 1; wear *vt* 1. (2 *BE*) where are the ~s of these two records?

slide *vi* (1) children ~ on ice; ~ down a snow-covered hill; boys like to ~ down banisters; ~ing surfaces / machine parts; a ~ing door / seat (2 *slip and fall*) he slid on the icy road; her foot slid away (from under her); the bottle slid from his hand. (3 *move quietly and easily*) she slid across the stage; the rider slid from the saddle; the plate slid through my hands; his pen slid across the paper; the drawers of this desk ~ in and out easily; *(fig)* ~ over a delicate matter (4a *move unnoticed*) he slid into the room / out of sight; □ let things ~ *(be negligent)*; he let his studies ~ to go to football practice. (4b) the years ~ past / by. (5 *change into a condition*) ~ into bad habits / sin / error. - *vt* (6) he slid the letter into her hand; he slid the book across the table / the coin into his pocket. (7) he slid a saving clause into the contract.

slip *vi* (1) his hand ~ped over the window-sill; water ~s off a smooth surface; the sleigh ~ped along over the snow; the ship ~ped through the waters; the bus ~ped by while they were engrossed in conversation. (2 *slide and fall*) he ~ped on a banana peel; her foot ~ped away (from under her); the car ~ped sideways on the icy road; the jug ~ped to the floor; the vase ~ped out of / from her hand; the fur coat ~ped from her shoulders; the fish ~ped through / out of my fingers. (3 *move quickly and easily*) the rider ~ped from the saddle; suddenly she turned pale and ~ped to the ground; *(fig)* he ~ped over the most important part. (4a *move unnoticed*) he ~ped from / out of the room; he heard someone coming and ~ped behind the curtain; money ~s through his fingers; this deal has ~ped through my fingers; several errors have ~ped into the text. (4b) the time / years ~ped by; let an opportunity ~. (5 *change into a condition*) ~ into a new way of life (5a *sink from a standard*) he used to be efficient but has been ~ping lately; his work ~ped last year. (6 *put on, take off*) ~ into a jacket / out of a dress; please excuse me while I ~ into something comfortable (7) his name has ~ped from my memory / mind. (8 *make a mistake*) as far as I know, he has never ~ped once; he often ~s in his grammar. (9 *inform: go a short distance*) I shan't be long, I'm just ~ping round to the shop. - *vt* (10) he ~ped a ring on her finger; he ~ped the shirt over his head; ~ a coin into the porter's hand; he ~ped me a note; ~ a key into a lock (11a *escape from*) he ~ped his pursuers; the dog ~ped his chain. (11b) it has ~ped my memory / mind / attention. (12 *let loose*) ~ a hound / hawk (13 *release*) ~ a catch; he ~ped the lock and the door creaked open; ~ *(undo)* a knot (14 *dislocate*) I ~ped a disk in my back and couldn't move for a month.

slip away an hour later he ~ped ~ *(left unnoticed).*

slip in a mistake has ~ped in.

slip off ~ ~ a blouse / *etc.*

slip on ~ on a dress / *etc.*

slip out (1) she ~ped ~ a minute ago. (2) she didn't mean it seriously, it just ~ped ~; the words ~ped ~ before he could stop himself.

slip up could you check these figures and see where I have ~ped up *(made a mistake)*? she ~ped up and put the letters in the wrong envelopes; she ~ped up badly on / over that answer.

slow *adj/adv* (1) the ~ progress of a snail; a ~ runner / worker / gait / march / train / trip / recovery; ~ growth / combustion; a ~ fire; a ~ response to a stimulus; be ~ in one's movements; be ~ at doing s.th. / paying / learning a language; tell the driver to go ~er; □ go ~ *(work slowly as a protest; be less active)*; how ~(ly) the time passes! how ~ you read! do speak ~er. (2) the clock is ten minutes ~ *(behind time).* (3 *not active*) ~ trade; a ~ market. (4 *needing more time than is usual to understand*) a ~ boy; ~ to grasp an opportunity / point; be ~ of mind / understanding; how ~ you are! (5 *not easily roused*) a ~ audience; she is ~ to (show) anger; be ~ to take offence / make up one's mind / believe / *etc* (6 *uninteresting*) a ~ afternoon / party; the party was a ~ affair; a ~ game / town (7 *causing slowness*) a ~ cricket pitch / track / billiard-table.

slow *vi* (1) the train ~ed down / up at the junction. - *vt* (2) he ~ed his step; ~ up a machine (3) his illness ~ed him at school.

small *adj/adv* (1) a ~ box / garden / room / flat / building; a ~ animal / stone / hole / size in shoes; ~ hands / feet; a ~ town / area / country / format / sheet of paper / dictionary; the dress is / he made the dress too ~ for me; the child is ~ for his age; a ~ waist; ~ but nice / mine; ~ but it works / goes; print s.th. in ~ print; slice the cake ~; → game *n* 3, letter *n* 1. (2 *not tall*) a ~ child / boy / man / tree / mountain; he is ~ and fat / weak; when I was ~ I ... (3 *not long*) a ~ step; we had to make a ~ detour. (4 *not great numerically*) a ~ family / household / dinner-party / group / class (of pupils) / audience / army / number of people; the firm has only a ~ staff. (5 *not great in amount*) a ~ amount / sum of money / salary / profit / loss / bill / expenditure / difference / reduction; ~ expenses; suited to the ~ purse; an ounce is a ~ weight; → change *n* 4; I'm afraid I haven't anything ~er; a ~ spoonful; a ~ beer *(also fig,* → *beer)* (6 *not great in duration*) a ~ delay / break; → hour 1. (7 *of little strength*) a ~ effort to improve is often worse than none; have a ~ effect on s.th.; do / render s.o. a ~ service; a ~ voice; that was not just a wind, that was a ~ hurricane. (8 *of little importance*) a ~ problem / mistake; that's a ~ matter; it is no ~ matter to do that; he only had a ~ part in the play; he only played a ~ part in the affair; → part *n* 8; ~ beginnings; □ feel ~ *(be ashamed)*: such unselfishness made us feel ~; I feel quite ~ in his presence; → sing *vi* 2, talk *n* 1. (9 *acting on a limited scale*) a ~ businessman / investor / farmer / manufacturer / saver; a ~ farm / enterprise / business; start (in a) ~ (way); live / carry on business in a ~ way; they talked big but lived ~. (10 *abstract uses*) the hope of finding the missing child is becoming ever ~er; the world is getting ever ~er; have ~ cause for gratitude; have ~ sympathy with s.o. (11 *mean, petty*) he has a ~ soul / mind; it is ~ of you to remind me of it.

smash *vt* (1) ~ an egg / window; ~ the china; he ~ed the vase against the wall; ~ a door open (2 *damage badly*) he ~ed his hand in the door. (3 *destroy*) they ~ed the drug racket; the depression ~ed him / his business; ~ s.o.'s prospects; ~ a record *(set up a far better one)*; ~ an organization (4 *defeat*) ~ an attack / a revolt / the enemy; ~ a theory (5 *hit violently*) he ~ed him on the head with a hammer. (6 *throw violently*) he ~ed a brick through the window. - *vi* (7 *break to pieces*) the glass ~ed on the floor; the jug fell and ~ed. (8 *come into violent collision*) his car ~ed into the bridge.

smash down ~ ~ a fence; the firemen ~ed ~ the door.

smash in the firemen ~ed in the door.

smash up (1) the youths ~ed up the furniture. (2) ~ up an organization / monopoly (3) his firm ~ed up during the slump.

smell *n* (1) breathe forth / give off / send forth a (pleasant / delightful / nasty) ~; a faint / strong / disgusting / peculiar / penetrating / *etc* ~; onions have an offensive ~; sulphur has a pungent ~; there is a ~ of gas here; the characteristic ~ of garlic; flowers with a sweet(ish) ~; these flowers have no ~. (2) have a ~ at this egg – is it fresh? (3) a ~ of corruption lingers about the name; the ~ of money.

smell *vi* (1) can fish ~? (2) the pastry ~s good; s.th. ~s (un)pleasant / nice / delicious / bad / nasty / *etc*; a rose that does not ~; this egg ~s *(bad)*. (3) the old man ~s of whisky. – *vt* (4) I ~ sulphur / something burning; you must ~ it to see what it is. (5) the puppy smelt all the corners of his new home; the dog was ~ing (at) the lamp-post. (6) the detective smelt foul play.

smell out (1) the dogs were successful in ~ing ~ the fugitive; ~ ~ game (2) ~ ~ *(discover)* a secret / enemy spies.

smile *n* an angelic / cheery / happy / sunny / winning ~; the gracious ~ of the king; a habitual / incredulous / complacent / demure / rueful / enigmatic / sarcastic / frosty / roguish / sickly / forced / wintry / wooden / grim / wry / *etc* ~; she gave a faint ~; he gave her his charming ~; my words brought a timid ~ to her face; he was all ~s.

smile *vi* (1) ~ happily / faintly / wryly / *etc*; ~ at s.o. ('s remark / behaviour / *etc*); ~ at a joke; say s.th. ~ingly (2) fortune / the gods ~d on them; luck ~ed on us that night. (3 *look welcoming*) the landscape ~d in the sunlight. – *vt* (4) ~ a welcome; she ~d a warm and friendly smile; ~ approval (5) ~ s.o. back into good spirits; ~ one's tears away.

smoke *n* (1) clouds / a column of (thick black) ~; the acrid ~ of petrol; ~ issued / was pouring from the chimney; ~ makes the eyes smart; the ~ nearly choked / suffocated me; □ end up in ~ *(come to nothing)*; the old house went up in ~; all our dreams went up in ~. (2) let's have a ~. (3 *inform: cigar, cirgarette*) this is the best ~ on the market; pass the ~s round (4) their hopes and dreams proved to be ~.

smoke *vt* (1a) ~ a cigar / cigarette / pipe (1b) ~ o.s. sick / to death (2) ~ meat / bacon / fish (3 *darken by smoke*) ~ glass; a ~d ceiling (4) ~ plants / insects (in a greenhouse); ~ furniture / a room. – *vi* (5) do you ~? he ~s like a chimney. (6) the chimney ~s. (7) the fire is ~ing badly; the lamp is ~ing. (8 → 1a) this pipe ~s well; a good cigar will ~ for at least half an hour.

smoke out (1) ~ ~ bees / a wasps' nest / a fox (2) ~ ~ enemy troops / a dug-out.

smooth *adj* (1) a ~ table-top / piece of wood / stone / tree-trunk / *etc*; a ~ surface / texture; ~ leather / paper / silk; a ~ road / pavement; the sea was as ~ as glass / a millpond; a ~ skin / cheek / chin; a ~ shave; ~ hair; grind metal / glass ~; a ~ tyre; s.th. is ~ to the touch. (2 *free from lumps*) a ~ batter / sauce; blend the ingredients ~ly with the milk; mix flour and milk to a ~ paste (3 *not sharp*) ~ cheese / wine (4 *not harsh*) a ~ voice; the ~ music of a ballroom dance-band (5) ~ driving; you will have ~ travelling once you reach the main road; a ~ crossing; the plane made a ~ landing; the journey went off ~ly. (6 *free from difficulties*) a ~ day at the office; ensure the ~ settlement of a matter (7 *tranquil*) a ~ temper / disposition (8 *suave*) I mistrust his ~ talk / manner / words; a ~ flatterer / hypocrite / talker; a ~ face *(suggesting hypocrisy)*; a ~ *(inform: shrewd; unscrupulous)* operator: don't do business with J. – he's too ~ an operator; he's a ~ operator with women. (9 *easy, elegant*) a ~ style / speech / speaker; ~ verse; the translation reads ~ly.

smooth *vt* (1) ~ cloth / fabric; ~ one's hair / dress; ~ wood by planing or sanding; ~ the sheets on the bed (2) ~ a bad temper; his manners were ~ed at boarding-school. (3) his friendship with the manager ~ed his way in the firm.

smooth away → smooth out.

smooth down ~ ~ an animal's fur.

smooth out (1) ~ ~ / away creases; ~ ~ irregularities in a surface (2) ~ ~ differences / difficulties; he ~ed ~ all the obstacles that had hindered us.

smooth over ~ ~ differences.

snap *vt* (1 *close, open rapidly*) ~ a clasp; he ~ped the lock shut; he ~ped the top from the bottle. (2 *seize (as if) with the jaws*) the dog ~ped the meat from the table; the wind ~ped the scarf from her hand. (3 *break with a sharp sound*) ~ a

twig in two; ~ a stick in half; ~ a thread; the blow ~ped the bone. (4 *cause to make a sudden sound*) ~ one's fingers *(also fig: be contemptuous of)*: it's no use telling them the dangers of smoking, because they'll just ~ their fingers at well-meant advice; ~ a whip (5 *speak sharply*) ~ a command; he ~ped them a sharp reply. (6 *take a snapshot of*) this is our son ~ped with his first trout.
- *vi* (7 *close, open rapidly*) the dog's jaws ~ped on the meat; the clasp / lock ~ped; the suitcase ~ped open. (8 *break suddenly*) the branch ~ped in the strong wind; he stretched the rubber band till it ~ped; the chain ~ped; the panes ~ped one after another. (9 *take quick bites*) the fish ~ped at the bait; the dog ~ped at the stranger('s heels). (10 *snap at: seize eagerly*) he ~ped at the chance to go; ~ at an opportunity / offer (11 *move quickly*) ~ to attention (12 *speak sharply*) don't ~ at the boy; "where have you been?" she ~ped (at him). (13 *give way*) after hours of waiting his patience ~ped. (14 *inform: recover quickly from illness or depression*) ~ out of it; he seemed a hopeless case, but he suddenly ~ped out of it and sat up in bed smiling; ~ out of it now and stop crying.

snap back he ~ped ~ a retort.

snap down (1) ~ a lid ~; ~ ~ the top of a trunk (2) his whip ~ped ~ on the pony's back.

snap off □ ~ s.o.'s head / nose ~ *(speak angrily to)*: I must have said the wrong thing to make him ~ my head ~ like that.

snap on ~ a lid on.

snap out ~ ~ orders; the irate customer ~ped ~ his complaints.

snap to the lock ~ped to.

snap up (1) I ~ped up a quick breakfast and dashed to the station; all the best bargains were ~ped up in the first hour of the sale; I should certainly ~ up such an opportunity. (2 *interrupt and retort sharply*) I had scarcely said three words by way of protest when he ~ped me up as though I'd no right to speak.

snow *n* (1) a heavy fall of ~; the ~ falls in large / small / tiny flakes; the ~ fell thickly; the ~ melts / thaws in spring. (2) a light ~; the heavy ~s of last winter; we shall have ~ soon. (3) a ~ of confetti; there was a ~ of soap-flakes on the floor.

snow *vt/i* (1) it is ~ing hard. (2) it was ~ing invitations. (3) we were ~ed up / in for three days; the car was / got ~ed up on the way to the town. (4) presents ~ed in on my birthday. (5) be ~ed under with things to do / correspondence / invitations to parties.

soak *vt* (1) ~ the wash in cold water; ~ bread in milk; ~ prunes / biscuits; ~ a rag in petrol; before planting the bushes ~ the ground with water. (2) the rain ~ed him to the skin; the rain ~ed my clothes; we came back ~ed to the skin; phew, I'm ~ed! (3 *remove by ~ing*) ~ a stain out of a napkin (4 *inform*) ~ o.s. in history; ~ yourself in art; a drama ~ed in blood and rape; he ~ed himself in the sunshine. (5 *slang: overcharge; tax heavily*) he was ~ed by the waiter; that firm ~ed me for the few repairs they did to the house; ~ing the tourist is a popular sport; ~ the rich. - *vi* (6) let the clothes ~ for a few hours in soapy water; he likes to get in the tub and ~. (7) the rain had ~ed through the roof / his overcoat; rain ~s into the ground; blood was ~ing through the bandage. (8) her clothes were ~ing from the rain; we came back ~ing. (9 *inform*) the idea hasn't ~ed into his head; I let it ~ into my subconscious. (10 *inform: drink immoderately*) they were ~ing at the bar.

soak in the lesson didn't ~ in.

soak out ~ ~ *(remove by ~ing)* stains; apply a poultice to ~ ~ the poison.

soak through (1) her clothes had been ~ed ~ by the rain; we came back ~ed ~. (2) the bandage must be replaced as the blood from the wound has ~ed ~.

soak up (1) cotton wool ~s ~ moisture; the big sponge ~ed ~ all the water on the floor; blotting-paper ~s ~ ink. (2) he needs to ~ ~ more facts.

soft *adj/adv* (1a) a ~ bed / pillow / fabric / fur; ~ goods *(textiles)*; ~ butter / clay; a ~-boiled egg; an egg boiled ~; ~ hair / skin; a ~ pencil; lie ~ *(on a soft bed)*; fall ~ *(taking no hurt)* (1b *relatively non-hard*) ~ wood / metal; ~ *(muddy)* ground; ~ soil / mud; ~ *(semiliquid)* soap *(also fig: flattery)* (2) a ~ climate / breeze; ~ air; ~ summer nights; a ~ rain; it was raining ~ly. (3 *not harsh, sharp, etc*) a ~ light / colour; a ~ voice; ~ music; play ~er, please; ~ murmurs / whispers; ~ contours; ~ wine (4 *not robust*) he was too ~ for the Marines; his muscles were ~ from lack of exercise. (5 *gentle, quiet*) a ~, grandmotherly woman; the ~(er)sex; ~ words; ~ meaningless talk; a ~ answer; she has a ~ tongue; a ~ touch / tread; ~ sleep / slumber; sleep ~; have a ~ heart (6 *inform: foolishly sentimental*) ~ glances; he is ~ on / about her; he has a ~ spot for dogs and babies. (7 *inform: feeble-minded*) be ~ in the head; he's a bit ~; she is ~ enough to believe anything; that's a ~ idea. (8 *inform: not requiring much effort*) a ~ job; a ~ thing *(a deal with easily-earned money)* (9 *non-alcoholic*) ~ drinks (10 *giving an immediate lather*) ~ water.

solution *n* (1 *act of solving*) the ~ of the problem took him ten minutes; the situation is approaching ~; this piece of evidence may help us in the ~ of the problem. (2 *being solved*) a problem capable of ~; problems that defy ~ (3) the ~ is as good as any other; he found the ~ of / to the problem in ten minutes; we are no nearer a ~ of the problem than we were when we started; a practical / theoretical ~; find / hit upon a ~; the ~ of / to the problem on page 10 will be published next week; there seems to be no ~ to the problem; economy is often the ~ to / of someone's financial troubles. (4) the ~ of sugar is faster in hot water than in cold; ~ in water is the best method. (5) a sugar-and-water ~; a strong / weak ~.

sorrow *n* (1) the ~ caused by the death of a friend; s.o.'s profound / agonizing / tormenting / bitter / secret / *etc* ~; look at s.o. in / with ~; be bowed / weighed down with ~; comfort those in ~; in ~ and in joy; express ~ for having done wrong; I am writing to express my ~ at the death of your father; to his ~ his son has fallen in with bad company; drown one's ~s in wine / drink (2 *cause of grief, etc*) Ann's late hours were a ~ to her parents; his first ~ was the bank failure. (3 *the expression of grief*) muffled ~; one feels uneasy in the presence of family ~.

sorry *adj* (1 *feeling pity*) he was ~ for the poor man / someone in trouble / *etc* (2 *feeling sympathy*) I am ~ that it hurts you; I am ~ to hear that sad news; I felt ~ for her when I saw how unhappy she looked. (3 *feeling regret*) I am ~ that I troubled you; I am ~ to differ from you; I am ~ to say that Mr. S. cannot see you now; I was ~ to hear that (you have been seriously ill); be ~ for a remark / what one has done; we are ~ to arrive late but...; I should be ~ for you to think that (I dislike you); he would be ~ to offend you; I am ~ about your misfortune / your wife *(her illness).* (4 *pitiful, sad*) come to a ~ end; a ~ sight; in a ~ state / plight; it was a ~ day when our team lost. (5 *worthless; inferior*) he is a ~ excuse for a football player; that was a really ~ art exhibit; he made a ~ attempt at (an) apology; a ~ bargain.

sort *n* (1) different ~s of flowers; this a new ~ of bicycle; that ~ of person; people of that ~; those ~ of people; all ~s of people; men of this ~ are...; what ~ of musician is he *(a violinist, member of a band, etc)*? what ~ of a musician is he *(is he good)*? he is some ~ of financier (→ 2); nice people, of course, but not really our ~; he is the ~ of man who will hit back; he is not the ~ to complain; I felt a ~ of numbing pain in my leg; the trees formed a ~ of arch; he is a solicitor or something of the ~; "you said you ..." – "I said nothing of the ~!" □ out of ~s *(unwell)*: I am feeling out of ~s today. (2 *an example of s.th. barely adequate*) he is a ~ of poet; he is a financier of ~s (→ 1); they served coffee of a ~ / a ~ of coffee / coffee of ~s; (*inform*) I ~ of thought this would happen; their conversation was ~ of tiresome. (3 *manner*) we spoke in this ~ for several minutes; after / in a ~ *(to a certain extent)* (4 *kind, type of person*) she's a good / decent / not a bad ~.

soul *n* (1) (they argued) the immortality of the ~; commit / commend one's ~ to God; → body 1; he has no ~ *(is cruel, selfish)*; a little man with a great ~ (2) he put his heart and ~ into the work. (3) the leader was the ~ of the expedition; she was the (life and) ~ of the party. (4) the ~ of the music was lost through careless playing; his performance lacks ~. (5 *embodiment*) he was the very ~ of tact; he is the ~ of honesty. (6 *person*) there was not a ~ in the house; the ship sank with 200 ~s on board; be a good ~ and help me; not a ~ must be told.

sound *n* (1) ~ travels slower than light; the clear / full / low / sweet / *etc* ~ of s.th.; a sharp / shrill / harsh / grating / hissing / hollow / strange / queer / melancholy / mournful / cheerful / almost imperceptible / unintelligible / dead *(not echoing)* / *etc* ~; the metallic ~ of a bell; m, ng are nasal ~s; there was not the slightest ~ to be heard; the ~ of a voice / word / instrument; the ~ of music / trumpets / gnawing / hail (2) this report has a bad ~; the news has a sinister ~; the plan has no very inviting ~; the entire work bears a ~ of pessimism. (3 *earshot*) soon we were within ~ of rushing water; within ~ and sight of the enemy.

sound *vi* (1) this black (piano) key won't ~; his hammering ~ed through the whole house; the music ~ed loud / softly through the night. (2) how sweet / gay / sad / solemn the music ~s; his words ~ed sweet in her ears; it ~s silly; the plan doesn't ~ reasonable; he ~s strange; his explanation ~s all right; it ~s true, but...; he ~ed calm / pleasant / hoarse / excited; his cough ~s suspicious; that ~ed like a shot; this sentence ~s wrong / does not ~ English; the whole business ~s rather fishy to me; it ~s too good to be true; her letter ~ed quite cheerful; she ~ed quite cheerful from her letter; he ~s very nice / a very nice man from her description; that doesn't ~ bad at all! that ~s a good idea. - *vt* (3a) ~ a trumpet / bell / *etc*; the oboe ~ed an A; ~ a high note / a note of alarm (3b *articulate*) ~ your consonants clearly; you must ~ each letter. (4) ~ the retreat; his speech ~ed a warning to aggressor nations; ~ the praise of God (5) ~ s.o.'s lungs / chest / heart; ~ the wheels of a railway carriage.

sound off *(slang: boast, complain loudly)* he's always ~ing ~ about how fast his sports car is; the football player ~ed ~ once too often to the referee about a decision and was expelled from the game.

sound *adj / adv* (1) a ~ body / heart / organ / limb / mind; be ~ in wind and limb; a ~ mind in a ~ body; he has ~ lungs / teeth / only one ~ kidney; he returned safe and ~. (2) ~ timber / boots / fruit / wine; a ~ machine (3) a ~ instinct / doctrine / principle / argument; ~ judgement; have / hold ~ views about s.th.; ~ moral values; ~ reasoning (4) a ~ business; an economically ~ branch of industry; a ~ investment (5) ~ advice; a ~ character (6 *thorough*) a ~ thrashing; be ~ly beaten at tennis; ~ sleep; sleep ~; be ~ asleep; be a ~ sleeper; a ~ grounding in mathematics.

space *n* (1a) the universe exists in ~; interstellar ~; the relations of things in ~ and time; infinite ~s (1b) man's determination to travel through ~; outer ~ *(the universe beyond the earth's atmosphere)*; ~ travel / flight; a ~ walk; a walk in / through (outer) ~; a ~ ship / station / suit (2 *extent in 3 dimensions*) the ~ occupied by a body; a thing's bulk is the ~ it fills. (3 *extent in 2 dimensions: distance, area*) trees set at equal ~s apart; two houses with (a / some) ~ between them; the waste ~s of the moon; open ~s *(ground not built on)*; the ~ is insufficient for a piano; have you enough ~ to work in? (4 *time interval*) within the ~ of half an hour; she worked for the ~ of an hour; in the short ~ of human life; after a ~ he continued his story. (5) write your name in the blank ~.

spare *vt* (1 *leave unhurt*) the prisoner was ~d; ~ one's enemy; ~ s.o.'s life; ~ s.o. his life; was he ~d (by fate) only to be ruined now? (2 *refrain from injuring*) she ~d his feelings; we must ~ her feelings and not criticize her. (3 *refrain from making great demands on*) he ~s neither himself nor his employees. (4 *conserve*) ~ one's strength / energy; ~ land for a garden (5 *use economically*) ~ the butter or we shall run short; don't ~ the wine; a walnut sundae, please, and don't ~ the whipped cream! (6 *give away without inconvenience*) can you ~ £20? can you ~ a cup of sugar? can you ~ me ten dollars till payday? we can't ~ the car tonight; we can't ~ a single worker during the rush hour; I can ~ you for tomorrow; can you ~ the time to help me? can you ~ me an hour? I have time to ~. (7 *have left over as a surplus*) the shelves fitted tightly with no room to ~; we arrived with no time to ~; he had two days to ~ before leaving Rome; have you got a room to ~? we can make the curtains and have a yard to ~; we have enough and to ~. (8 *save s.o. from s.th. unpleasant*) we wanted to ~ him embarrassment / the bother; ~ us the gory details; he was ~d nothing; ~ yourself the trouble; I was ~d that humiliation; he was ~d answering; I'll ~ myself the trip and send a telegram instead. (9 *omit, not use*) ~ the details; nothing was ~d for his comfort; ~ the rod (and spoil the child); he ~d neither time nor money to attain his end; ~ no pains / effort / expense (to make s.th.).

speak *vi* (1a) the child is just learning to ~; he ~s very little; he ~s clearly / plain(ly) / (in)coherently / fluently / boastfully / personally / officially / *etc*; ~ gently / frankly / amiably / rudely / *etc* (to s.o.); he was too upset to ~; ~ from one's heart *(sincerely)*; ~ to / with s.o. *(to is usual*; with *emphasizes an exchange of views, etc)*: may I ~ with you for a moment? I have never spoken to him; ~ in earnest / joke / jest; ~ in a whisper / mutter / threatening tone / quiet voice / *etc*; ~ in chorus; □ so to ~ *(if I may say so)*: we still don't have our heads above water, so to ~; → book *n* 1. (1b *speak about: discuss, relate; reprimand*) we spoke about the need for economy; we couldn't get him to ~ about his war experiences; will you ~ to him about his laziness? I'll see that he is spoken to about it. (1c ~ *of: mention; refer to*) he rarely spoke of his war experiences; he ~s of retiring at the end of the year; were you ~ing of me when you made that remark? ~ well / highly / ill of s.o. *(praise, etc*; → ill *adj/adv* 1); it ~s well of her good nature that she took no offence. (1d *to ~ of: worth mentioning*) Switzerland has no ore to ~ of; I got a few bruises, but they are nothing to ~ of; we have had no rain to ~ of for the last three weeks. (2 *make a speech*) I don't like ~ing in public; ~ at a debate / meeting; ~ on a subject / topic; she will ~ to the motion 'That women have greater intelligence than men'; next week I shall ~ to the title 'Education for Leisure'; you must ~ to the subject. (3 *speak for: speak on behalf of; recommend*) that is my opinion, but I can only ~ for myself; I will ~ for you; there is no need for me to commend his action - it ~s for itself; it spoke well for the boy that he owned up to his mistake. (4 *speaking + adv*) generally ~ing, long books are bad books; honestly ~ing, I pity him; that is, properly ~ing, a fraud; roughly ~ing, they are identical; strictly ~ing, it's a lie. - *vt* (5) the actor spoke his part badly; once the words were spoken, she was sorry; ~ (obvious) nonsense; □ ~ one's mind (→ mind *n* 2c); he spoke the truth; □ ~ volumes *(be significant)*: his silence spoke volumes. (6) he can read French but not ~ it; ~ (French) with(out) an accent; is English spoken here? (7 *be expressive*) actions ~ louder than words; the portrait ~s / is a ~ing likeness; ~ing eyes; a ~ing glance; his eyes and smile spoke a warm welcome; his face spoke of suffering.

speak out (1) ~ ~, we can't hear you. (2) Lincoln spoke ~ against slavery; you must ~ ~ if we are to remain friends.

speak up (1) the audience told the actor to ~ up; please ~ up! (2) the newcomer spoke up and opposed our plan.

speech *n* (1 *ability to speak*) ~ distinguishes man from the animals; he lost his ~. (2 *act of speaking*) he expresses himself better in ~ than in writing; he broke into ~; an outburst of violent ~; he is slow of ~; freedom / liberty of ~; ~ is silver, silence is gold. (3) (make / deliver / improvise) a lengthy / able / cultivated / convincing / effective / fiery / stirring / monumental / sonorous but meaningless / tedious / boring / tiresome / diffuse / wordy / pompous / unprepared / ordinary / *etc* ~ (on / about s.th., to an audience); an opening / debating / after-dinner ~ (4 *manner of speaking*) country / rustic / clear / (in)distinct / rapid / harsh / *etc* ~; 'slumber' is not used in ordinary ~; a metaphor is a figure of ~. (5 *language used*) he couldn't understand the ~ of the natives because it was in a foreign language; the Normans abandoned their native ~ and adopted the French language.

speed *n* (1) the ~ of light / sound / a vehicle / the wind; go / drive at a ~ of 50 miles per hour; he rode his bicycle at breakneck ~; average / high / excessive / (super)sonic / *etc* ~; it's dangerous to corner at *(a high)* ~; we drove down the motorway at full / top ~; on the straight the car builds up / works up / reaches a ~ of 110 mph; increase / maintain / reduce / slacken ~; work at full ~; his ~ in the test was two problems per minute; the ~ of thought (2) the ~ of a lens / film.

speed *vi* (1a) the plane sped through the air; bullets sped only a few feet over our heads; he sped down the street. (1b) his heart ~ed a little as he neared the house. (2 *go at too great a speed*) he was ~ing on the icy road and the car skidded; he ~ed for a while but slowed down when he saw a police car; he was fined for ~ing. - *vt* (3) he sped his horse over the fields; ~ an arrow from the bow; he sped his pen to complete the treatise; we sped our craft forward. (4) two other things happened that sped the process; factors ~ing the inflationary trend.

speed up (1a) ~ up a car / engine (1b) ~ up industrial production / delivery / proceedings / developments / the work in a factory / the growth of a plant (2a) the train soon ~ed up; he ~ed up when he saw that he was being followed. (2b) then the heart ~s up and the blood pressure rises.

spend *vt* (1) ~ (all one's) money (on s.th.); he ~s little on books; ~ one's wealth / resources; the ~ing habits of people; they spent freely; □ ~ a penny *(BE, visit a W.C.)* (2) we spent a very pleasant day by the sea yesterday; where do you intend ~ing your holidays this year? I ~ all my spare moments darning socks; I'll just have to ~ the evening being bored; she ~s too much time in dressing well; don't ~ too long over this problem; a well-spent life (3) ~ (all) one's strength; he has spent all his energy / has entirely spent himself in this matter; ~ one's life / blood for a cause; the storm has spent its fury / is spent; the rage / fever has spent itself; his fury spent itself in curses. – *adj* (4) a spent *(exhausted)* swimmer; spent ideas / dreams / visions.

spirit *n* (1) God is pure ~ / a ~; the S~ *(Holy Ghost)*; the S~ of God / the Lord; the world of ~ (2 *the immaterial part of man*) body, soul and ~; I shall be with you in (the) ~; render up / yield up one's ~ (3 *ghost*) the realm / world / abode of ~s; celestial / blessed / pure / evil ~s; ~s of the air / woods; be possessed by a ~; see ~s; there are ~s in the castle; conjure (up) / raise / summon / call up / invoke ~s; exorcise / lay ~s (→ lay *vt* 4) (4) what a noble / generous ~ he is! he was one of the leading ~s of the American Revolution / of the enterprise; Goethe is one of the greatest ~s of mankind. (5 *vigour, etc*) put a little more ~ into your work; fight with ~; be full of ~; a boy of ~; a man of broken ~; that's the ~! (6 *mental, moral attitude*) done in a ~ of mischief / mockery / enterprise / *etc*; in the ~ of reconciliation; he took the remark in (the) wrong ~; the poor in ~; be meek in ~; have a manful / martial / elastic / romantic / *etc* ~; she said it in a forgiving ~; the ~ of revenge / contradiction / Christian charity / wisdom; incompatible with the Christian ~ (7 *~s: state of mind*) in high / great / good ~s *(cheerful)*; in low / poor ~s *(depressed)*; be out of ~s; his ~s were low / at a low ebb; revive / restore (some)one's drooping ~s; the team's leaden ~s after defeat; animal ~s *(vivacity)* (8 *real meaning*) obey the ~, not the letter, of the law; act in accordance with the ~ of the constitution; carry out the ~ of the regulations; the ~ of Potsdam; enter into / understand the ~ of a poet (9 *frame of mind characteristic of a group*) the ~ of the times / age; team ~; the German / Greek ~; the (real) ~ of Spain / Christianity / 1848 / reform (10 *solution in alcohol*) ~(s) of camphor / nitre / turpentine / wine (11 *alcohol*) a glas of ~(s) and water, raw *(undiluted)* ~(s).

split *vt* (1a) ~ a log (in two); ~ a piece from a block; the lightning ~ the tree; the wind ~ the sail; □ ~ hairs *(make subtle distinctions)*; a ~ting *(violent)* headache; the audience ~ their sides *(laughed violently)* at the comedian's jokes; □ ~ the difference *(agree upon a price halfway between two suggested amounts)* (1b) ~ a compound / molecule / atom (2a) please ~ the ice cream so there will be enough for everyone; they ~ the profit between them; ~ up a class into several groups (2b *share*) we ~ a bottle of wine; let's ~ the cost. (3) the abdication of the king ~ the country; such a proposal would ~ the party. – *vi* (4) the extreme cold makes the rocks ~; the board ~ in half; fruit falls to the ground and ~s open; the jar ~ when the water froze; I felt as if I should ~ with laughter / curiosity / envy (5) this kind of wood ~s easily. (6) the party ~ (up) into small groups. (7 *split on: inform: betray*) the thief would never have been discovered if one of his companions had not ~ on him. – *adj* (8 → 1a) a ~ second *(extremely short period of time)* (9 → 1b) a ~ personality / mind *(lay term for schizophrenic condition)* (10 → 3) a ~ opinion / vote.

sport *n* (1a) hunting, fishing, shooting, horse-racing are (country) ~s; running, jumping, throwing the javelin are (athletic) ~s; swimming, rowing, water ski-ing, boxing, weight-lifting, wrestling, fencing, climbing, *etc* are ~s; indoor / outdoor ~s; a competitive ~; tennis / golf / football / *etc* is my favourite ~; what facilities for ~ are there? all kinds of ~ are played in the park; go in for / indulge in ~ (1b *pleasure derived from sport*) it was good ~. (2 *sports: meeting for athletic contests*) the school / inter-university ~s; the ~s were postponed. (3 *amusement*) the children thought it great ~ to dress up as pirates; find ~ in s.o.'s deep embarrassment (4 *fun*) say s.th. in

~; make ~ of *(deride)* s.o./ s.th.; we often do things just for the ~ of it; Mother teased us in ~. (5 *good fellow*) be a ~ (and treat me to a dinner); John is a ~ and always ready for a lark; a good / bad ~ *(s.o. who accepts defeat in good / bad humour).*

spot *n* (1 *dirty mark*) a grease / gravy / paint ~; a ~ of rust on the car; ~s of mud on her stockings; make a ~ / ~s on s.th. (2 *decorative, distinctive, etc mark*) ~s on animals, plants, diseased fruit; the leopard's ~s; a blue tie with pink ~s; he saw ~s before his eyes; sun-~s (3 *place*) the ~ where the crash occurred; a lovely ~ near the village; we can picnic in this ~; you could see him sitting for hours on end in the same ~; our car came to a dead stop and would not budge from the ~; □ in a ~ *(difficult situation)*; □ on the ~ *(where one is needed; immediately)*: if needed, engineers are on the ~ to help with ...; engage / arrest s.o. on the ~; we closed the bargain on the ~; he was run over and killed on the ~; a soft ~ (→ soft 6, heart 2); a tender ~ *(a subject that irritates s.o.)*; □ find s.o.'s weak ~; □ put one's finger on s.o.'s weak ~; □ touch the ~ (→ touch *vt* 1a) (4 *BE drop*) a few ~s of rain (5 *BE inform: small amount*) a ~ of lunch / supper; a ~ of leave; what about doing a ~ of work? I'm afraid we are in for a ~ of trouble; he's having a ~ of bother with his brother.

spread *vt* (1a) ~ a sheet / carpet / sail / tent; she ~ the blanket on the bed / over her knees; she ~ the clothes to dry; ~ a cloth on a table / over a chest of drawers; ~ papers out on the table; he ~ out the newspaper / map; ~ (out) one's arms; the bird ~ (out) its wings; ~ out hay (1b) the trees ~ (out) their branches. (1c) the potter ~ his wares; ~ out one's goods for sale (1d) he ~ varnish on the wood; ~ butter / jam on bread (2a) she ~ the floor with rugs / the table with a cloth; □ ~ the table *(place dishes, food on it for a meal)*; a meadow ~ with daisies (2b) ~ a slice of bread with butter / jam (3a *distribute*) ~ the pamphlets through the town; ~ manure on a field; flies ~ disease. (3b) ~ happiness (4) ~ knowledge / news / fame / rumours; ~ the word of the gospel; his name ~ fear in every quarter. (5 *extend in time*) a course of studies ~ over three years; instalments ~ out over twelve months; the adoption by the U.K. of the metric system, the change to be ~ over some twenty years; ~ work *(allow it to last longer than normal).* - *vi* (6a) the water ~ on the floor; the treacle ~ over the table; the damp ~ into the next room; the town has ~ greatly during the last few years; weeds ~ all over the garden. (6b) the plain ~ / lay ~ out before us; the woods ~ out as far as the eye could see; the scene / collection ~ before us; ~ing branches (7) the disease / fire / news / rumour ~ quickly through the village; ~ like wildfire; the panic is ~ing. (8) margarine ~s easily; it will ~ better if it is warmed.

spring *vi* (1a) a tiger about to ~; he sprang up from his seat / out of his bed / forward to help me; ~ to one's feet / into the air (1b) a branch sprang back and hit his face; the bolt sprang back into position; a trap ~s; the door sprang open and in he walked. (1c) memories ~ to life; new words ~ing into popularity; he sprang into fame; his anger ~s to the surface easily. (2) a sharp breeze had sprung up; tears sprang to her eyes; blood sprang to my cheeks. (3a) flowers ~ from seed / the soil; weeds were ~ing up everywhere; the winter wheat is ~ing *(begins to grow).* (3b) many new houses have sprung up in this district; industries sprang up in the suburbs. (3c *rise from a base*) the arch ~s from that slender pillar. (4 *originate*) the region where Rhine and Danube ~; out of their union sprang ten children; it is from the middle class that writers ~; courage ~ing from conviction; a suspicion sprang up in her mind; the quarrel sprang from a casual remark. (5 *split, crack*) my cricket bat has sprung; the board sprang from the fence during the storm. - *vt* (6) the dog sprang the gate. (7 *cause to operate*) ~ a lock / trap / mine (8 *cause to split, crack*) I've sprung my tennis racket; the ship sprang its keel on a rock; moisture sprang the board from the fence. (9 *develop suddenly*) the roof / ship has sprung a leak; a pipe sprang a leak and cream spurted in all directions. (10 *produce unexpectedly*) ~ a surprise / new proposal / question (on s.o.); ~ a joke *(make one suddenly)* (11 *cause to leave cover*) ~ a bevy of quail (12 *provide with springs*) this mattress is well sprung; the Vespa, sprung to ride smoothly and corner safely.

stage *n* (1) a revolving / sliding / sinking ~; appear on / come on to / go on to the ~; go off / quit the ~ (2 *theatre; acting*) write for the ~; suitable for the ~; go on the ~ *(become an actor*); the German / English / *etc* ~; he plans to make the ~ his career; he is very fond of the ~. (3 *scene of action*) Dunkirk was the ~ for spectacular troop withdrawal in World War II; the ~ of politics (4 *step, phase*) the caterpillar ~ in the life of a butterfly; the early / initial / intermediate / final ~ of s.th.; the ~s of fever; a ~ in the progress of society; he passed a long ~ of inactivity; at this ~ an interruption occurred. (5 *distance between two stopping-places*) travel by easy ~s *(unhurriedly)*; all the neighbours pitched in, and the barn was rebuilt by easy ~s.

stage *vt* (1) ~ a play / pageant / exhibition / conference; they ~d huge protest demonstrations; □ ~ a comeback *(return successfully to one's former position)* - *vi* (2) the play didn't ~ well.

stamp *vt* (1) ~ one's foot (2) ~ the floor / ground (3) ~ weights; ~ a document (with a seal) / passport; ~ the postmark on a letter; ~ one's address on an envelope; ~ an envelope with one's address; ~ patterns on cloth; *(fig)* age ~ed his face with lines (4 *put a postage-stamp on*) ~ a letter / envelope (5 *reveal*) his manners ~ him as a man of breeding; his ingenuity with words ~ed him as a potential poet. - *vi* (6) ~ about the room / upstairs / on a spider; he ~ed out of the room in anger.

stand *vi* 1 - 14; *vt* 15a - 20.
The patterns are grouped as follows:
~ + *adj*: 1, 5; ~ + *indir obj*: 20; ~ + *inf*: 19a; ~ + *past part*: 5; ~ + *prepos*: against 6b; by 6c; behind 6d; for 9, 11a, 11b, 12, 13; on 1, 3; over 6e; to 14; cannot ~: 17
(1) I am too tired to ~; ~ erect / upright / straight; ~ still / motionless; he stood withdrawn from the crowd; ~ clear from / of the gates (→ clear *adj* 4); soldiers ~ at attention (→ attention 5) / ease (→ ease *n* 1); ~ on one foot; □ ~ on one's own (two) feet / legs *(be independent)*; ~ aside / by the fire / at the door / on the doorstep / *etc*; his house ~s on a hill / by the bridge / at the corner; we stood at the corner, not knowing which street to take; the vase is ~ing on the table; the bicycle stood in the basement all winter; let the dough ~ for an hour before baking it; the house still stood after the earthquake; he stood up to his waist in the swirling waters; the rainwater stood *(did not run off)* in the basement; the fields stood under water (after the flood). (2 *be tall*) he ~s six feet (tall). (3a *have as one's place*) these dishes ~ on the top shelf; a beautiful oak once stood here. (3b as 3a, *fig*) where does Tom ~ in his class *(according to his ability, etc)*? how does he ~ on this question? (3c *stand on: insist on*) □ ~ on ceremony *(insist on formal politeness)*; it is not easy to get on to friendly terms with a man who always ~s on his dignity. (4) the temperature ~s at 25°C.; the dividend ~s at 7%; the score stood 18 to 14 at the half. (5 *stand + adj: fig: be as indicated*) ~ fast / ready (to run / for action) / aloof; ~ firm, don't give way! the statement / contract ~s good *(is true, valid)*; I ~ prepared to dispute it; he ~s convicted of treachery; ~ corrected *(admit the justice of reproof)* (6a *be in a certain position, situation*) ~ in danger of one's life; he stood in jeopardy of losing his licence; we ~ in need of help; I ~ third in line for promotion / on the list; will you ~ godmother to the child? ~ as sponsor for s.o.; I ~ to her in a peculiar relation; he ~s well with all his neighbours; the matter ~s thus: ...; as affairs now ~, we can ...; ~ alone *(be isolated; have no equal)*; the case ~s *(rests)* on his testimony. (6b *stand against: resist*) that fence will not ~ against the wind; his case would not ~ against the weight of evidence to the contrary. (6c *stand by: remain loyal to*) ~ by one's friends; a true friend will ~ by you; ~ by a promise / resolution / declaration / guarantee; ~ by what one has said / one's word (6d *stand behind: support*) we ~ behind our candidate. (6e *stand over: supervise closely*) he won't work unless someone ~s over him; unless I ~ over him he makes all sorts of foolish mistakes. (7 *remain unaltered, valid*) old as they are these rules still ~; the agreement ~s as signed; let the word ~; my offer ~s; a ~ing offer. (8 *esp AE be a candidate*) I should like to nominate Mr N. for the position if he is willing to ~; in 1950 he stood as Conservative candidate (in a by-election); he is ~ing for the council.
(9 *rise*) will volunteers please ~; everyone stood for the National Anthem / the Lord Mayor / the benediction; at the first note

all stood. (10 *halt*) ~ where you are; ~ or I fire! (11a *stand for: represent*) G. B. S. ~s for George Bernard Shaw. (11b) dictatorship ~s for the denial of individual freedom. (12 *stand for: advocate*) you have given away everything you stood for; the Conservatives ~ for free enterprise - Labour ~s for nationalization and state control of industry; ~ for pragmatism / the opposite (13 *stand for: inform: tolerate*) unpunctuality is something employers won't ~ for; he won't ~ for such nonsense; the way he treats you is shameful - I wonder you ~ for it. (14 *stand to: adhere to*) ~ to one's post / principles / statement; ~ to a promise / the terms; ~ to an allegation; I ~ to it that he never ...; □ it ~s to reason *(can be reasonably exptected)* that (he will be angry when we ignore his advice / you will be unwell if you don't eat sufficient food).

- *vt* (15a *place*) ~ the table in the corner / the chair by the lamp; if you're naughty again, you'll be stood in the corner; ~ them in a row; □ ~ s.o. in good stead *(prove useful to him in need)*: your experience will ~ you in good stead. (15b *place erect*) he stood the box on end / the ladder against the wall. (16 *face, encounter*) ~ an assault / a barrage of questions; he must ~ (his) trial (for murder. (17 *endure*) his eyes were strong enough to ~ the glare; the pottery will ~ firing up to 1300°; this furniture will have to ~ a lot of hard use; he cannot ~ pain / criticism / pupils who are late; this plan will not ~ (critical / further) discussion / study / analysis; how can you ~ that woman? he ~s no nonsense; she can't ~ his getting / him to get ahead of her. (18 *fig: go through successfully*) the theory / invention has stood the test; his loyalty has fully stood the test of adversity; □ ~ fire *(be under fire without giving way)*; □ ~ one's ground *(not yield)* (19a *be likely*) he ~s to win a fortune on this race; if this deal goes through, the company ~s to make a handsome profit; no-one ~s to gain by these proposals; Britain ~s to *gain / lose by the treaty. (19b be likely to experience*) he ~s a good / poor chance of succeeding in the examination; he ~s no chance / doesn't ~ a chance, against you. (20 *inform: give at one's expense*) ~ s.o. a drink / dinner at the Red Lion; if I manage to land the job, I'll ~ you all a free drink; he offered to ~ treat to all the company.

stand about several of the strikers were ~ing ~ at the street corner; the people stood ~ in small groups.

stand around we stood ~ all the morning without anything happening; the dirty dishes are still ~ing ~ from yesterday.

stand aside (1) he's a man who never ~s ~ when there's something that needs doing. (2) he stood ~ to let her pass.

stand back the policemen ordered us to ~ ~.

stand by (1) and did you just ~ by and do nothing? he stood by and did not even offer to help me; please ~ by while I fix this antenna. (2) several policemen were ~ing by *(ready to act)* in case of trouble; six fire-engines from the next town stood by in case of a further outbreak of fire.

stand down the Conservative candidate offered to ~ ~ *(withdraw)* in favour of the Liberal; he stood ~ and let his friend be nominated for the post; some weeks ago, when Fischer-Dieskau had to ~ ~ on the morning of one of its concerts, the Society was able to conjure up an alternative lieder singer.

stand in (1) you may have an hour off to go shopping if you can get anyone to ~ in *(substitute)* for you; Joyce got her big chance when she stood in for the famous actress. (2) let me ~ in *(share)* with you if it's expensive. (3) the detective was sure that the jeweller was ~ing in *(in conspiracy)* with the thieves.

stand out (1) his eyes appeared to ~ ~ from his head; the piers ~ ~ from the harbour wall. (2) the church tower stood ~ clearly against the sky; his mistake ~s ~ a mile in the report; he stood ~ by reason of his ability. (3) we've got thirteen people, and we only need twelve for the game, so someone will have to ~ ~. (4 *refuse to yield*) he stood ~ against her demands for years; once he had made up his mind there was no moving him - he stood ~ against all persuasion, arguments, threats or abuse; six workers still stood ~ even after an agreement had been reached with their union. (5 *stand out for: insist on*) the union leader stood ~ for an increase in pay.

stand over the debate will ~ ~ *(be postponed)* until next week; we let the project ~ ~ until the following year.

stand to + to *(wait in readiness)* for action.

stand up (1) I stood up to see better; ~ up for / in deference to s.o. (2 *resist decay*) the old building stood up well; wool ~s up better than silk. (3 *remain strong*) the case will never ~ up in court. (4) the traitor was stood up against a wall and shot. (5 *stand up for: support*) ~ up for a cause / the oppressed / one's friend; if you don't ~ up for yourself, you'll never get very far in this world. (6 *stand up for: fight for*) the speaker urged the workers to ~ up for their rights. (7 *stand up to: resist*) if you once ~ up to him / if he's once stood up to all his courage and bravado ooze away; the man stood up to all attempts at bribery. (8) these tyres will ~ up to even the roughest wear and tear; the new machine has not stood up to the test; my wife's health will not ~ up to this cold, damp climate.

start *n* (1) the ~ of the race; the race began after several false ~s; the work / everything is difficult at the ~; you will work here for a ~; make a (late / early / fresh / new) ~; he has made a good ~ in his career / on his novel; (he opposed us) from the (very) ~; from ~ to finish; a rich uncle gave him a ~ in life; he had a good ~ in life; the bride's parents gave the couple a ~ by buying them a house. (2 *an advantage at the beginning of a race*) the small boys were given / had a (head-) ~ of ten yards / seconds; they didn't give me much / any ~; *(fig)* he got the ~ of *(an advantage over)* his rivals. (3a *sudden movement*) a ~ of surprise; give a (sudden) ~; wake up with a ~; he sprang up with a ~; □ by fits and ~s *(with frequent pauses)*; traffic moved by fits and ~s. (3b *surprise; shock*) you gave me a ~; the sudden movement of the curtains gave her quite a ~.

start *vi* (1a) we must ~ early; when do we ~? we ~ed at six / at dawn / before noon / *etc*; ~ for a destination / on a journey / on one's way; we ~ for Paris in an hour; the train / ship ~s at ten; the train ~ed with a jolt; the car will not ~; let me ~ first *(in a race)*. (1b) ~ on a task / project; they haven't ~ed on the job yet; the decorators are ~ing on the kitchen tomorrow; when he ~s on that subject, he ...; last week we ~ed on Dickens, so ... (1c) the alphabet ~s with A; we ~ed (the meal) with soup; the school ~ed with 300 pupils - now there are 700; the meeting ~ed with a speech; they ~ed the meeting with cocktails; his illness ~ed with a slight cough; □ to ~ with *(at the beginning)*: to ~ with, the day was fine, but then it turned showery; I object on several grounds: to ~ with, you had no reason for arriving so late; he had $100 to ~ with, but ... (2) the party ~s at 9:00; school / term ~s tomorrow; how did the war ~? the fire ~ed in the kitchen; ~ in business; ~ from nothing / scratch; ~ again / afresh; the heath ~s at the end of this road.
(3 *move suddenly*) ~ out of one's sleep; the sudden clap of thunder caused everyone to ~; he ~ed back as if he had seen a ghost; he ~ed at the noise / exclamation / sound of my voice; the rabbit ~ed from the bush. (4 *become loosened*) some timbers in the hull have ~ed; a nail / one of the planks has ~ed. (5 *protrude*) eyes seeming to ~ from their sockets; his eyes nearly ~ed out of his head; tears ~ed to / from her eyes; blood ~ed from the wound.
- *vt* (6a) ~ one's work; we must ~ work at once; ~ the race now; we ~ school at 8 o'clock; ~ a business / enterprise / newspaper; ~ negotiations / a war; ~ a quarrel (with s.o.) / discussion / rumour; who ~ed it *(the quarrelling, etc)*? ~ a fire; he ~ed life in poverty. (6b *start + gerund, inf*) look, it's ~ed raining; it ~ed raining / to rain as we left the house; it ~s to get / getting dark early now; the barometer ~ed to fall / falling last night; the chocolate in my pocket has ~ed to melt / melting; my watch suddenly ~ed to gain two hours a day; I was surprised to hear that he had ~ed smoking; they have ~ed building the new school; we ~ed to laugh when he entered the room; we shall not ~ to learn / learning Spanish until next year; she ~ed to feel / feeling ill just after dessert. (6c *start + obj + part*) ~ the clock going / the engine running; → ball[1] *n* 1 this news ~ed me thinking; the smoke ~ed him coughing; I want to ~ him learning Latin next year. (6d) he ~ed his son in a small business; when can I ~ the baby on solid food? the record ~ed the young singer on the road to stardom. (7) who is going to ~ the runners? (8 *drive from a hiding-place*) ~ a hare (9 *cause to become loosened*) damp has ~ed the timbers.

start off (1) the summer ~ed ~ with a heat-wave. (2) ~ ~ on a journey; the horse ~ed ~ at a steady trot; let's ~ ~ with the zoo *(visit it first).*

start out (1) what else do I want? I made a list before I ~ed ~, but... (2) he ~ed ~ to reform the world / write a novel; he ~ed ~ to write his report on the accident.

start up (1a) the Russian course ~s up next week. (1b) numerous difficulties have ~ed up. (1c) next I press the self-starter and the car ~s up. (2a) ~ up a car / engine / generator / *etc* (2b) he has ~ed up a little business of his own. (3 *move suddenly*) ~ up from one's chair.

state *n* (1a) the ~ of s.o.'s health; his ~ of health is delicate; the patient's ~ is critical; a ~ of happiness; a ~ of disorder in the kitchen; the larval ~ of insects; the bridge is in a ~ of disrepair; in a natural / primitive ~; in a ~ of depression; some bachelors enjoy the single ~. (1b) the solid / liquid / gaseous ~ of matter (2 *condition of emotional agitation*) work o.s. up into a ~; what a ~ you are in *(how anxious, untidy, etc you are)*! (3 *status, rank*) he dresses in a manner befitting his ~; people in that ~ of life. (4 *luxury, splendour*) live in ~; the king drove in ~ through London; the President received the ambassador in ~; □ lie in ~ *(be exhibited publicly before burial).*
(5) a sovereign / federal / autonomous / republican / monarchical / imperial ~; a border / buffer / satellite / feudatory / welfare ~; the Irish Free S~ ; the S~ of Arizona ; the fifty States of the United States; the States *(the U.S.A.)*; ~ papers / documents; a ~ bank; new ~ legislation; bring industries under ~ control; railways ought to be managed by the S ~ / to be S~ property; Church and S~; ~ education / schools; affairs of ~.

stay *vi* (1a) please ~ here until I return; they ~ed at home; ~ indoors (on cold winter evenings); she ~ed by me until help arrived; he ~ed in the army for ten years. (1b) ~ calm / clean / single / sober / closed / *etc*; you must ~ still while I'm cutting your hair; the weather ~ed cold for more than a week; I can't get this door to ~ put *(in its place).* (2 *reside for a while*) I will ~ at mother's for the weekend; ~ at / in a hotel; ~ abroad / in a foreign country / in the country; our guest ~ed with us for a week. (3 *stop*) ~ where you are. (4 *wait*) won't you ~ till he comes / for supper?
- *vt* (5 *form: appease temporarily*) ~ one's hunger / thirst / appetite / stomach (6 *endure the demands of*) I don't think he will ~ the race / course; the horse can't ~ that distance; he cannot ~ the pace (*fig*); ~ing-power (7 *postpone*) the judge ~ed judgement until he could gather more facts.

stay in (1) I'm ~ing in this evening - I have a lot of work to do; the doctor advised me to ~ in for a few days. (2) will the trouser creases ~ in?

stay on (1) he ~ed on longer than the others. (2) the arms and shoulders are quite bare - how does that dress ~ on?

stay out (1) she made her father very anxious by ~ing ~ until midnight. (2) he decided to ~ the month ~.

stay up she ~ed up all night reading a book; we ~ed up for the late, late show (on TV); we usually let the children ~ up New Year's Day.

steal *vt* (1) ~ a car / *etc*; sixty marks were stolen from him; I have had my watch stolen; ~ time from a job (2 *obtain without asking permission*) ~ a kiss (from s.o.); ~ s.o.'s heart *(gain his love before he is aware)* □ ~ the limelight *(attract the most attention)*; □ ~ a march on s.o. *(secretly gain an advantage over s.o.)* (3 *do without being seen*) she stole a glance at him. - *vi* (4 *move quietly, secretly*) let's ~ out of the room on tiptoe; a tear stole down her cheek; the years ~ by; as ever, Christmas ~s up unawares upon us.

step *n* (1) walk with firm / light / heavy / quick / slow ~s; take / make a ~ (forward / backward); → false 1; advance ~ by ~ *(also fig)*; quicken / hasten / slacken one's ~s; direct / turn one's ~s homeward; retrace one's ~s *(go back)*; a waltz / tango / *etc* ~ (2) our house is only a few ~s from the beach; he couldn't walk a ~ further; we have made a long ~ *(much progress)* towards success; □ watch one's ~ *(behave prudently)*: if she doesn't watch her ~ she will be fired from her job. (3) we could hear his ~s in the hall; that's Jim - I know / recognize his ~; know s.o. by his ~s (4 *footprint*) we followed his ~s in the snow. (5 *manner of walking*) his ~ was fast and light; be in ~ with *(have the same pace as)* the others / the times; she's in ~ with today's fashion; the marchers did not keep / were out of ~ with the band; be out of ~ with the times (6) a ~ of a ladder; a staircase of 14 ~s (7 *degree*) a major is one ~ above a captain; go up a ~ in s.o.'s estimation; keep a ~ ahead of s.o.; she always manages to keep a ~ ahead of the latest fashions. (8 *action, measure*) collecting all the facts is the first ~ in making a decision; the five ~s to success; take a (necessary / decisive / prudent / bold / critical / rash / fatal / *etc*) ~; what's the next ~?

step *vi* (1) please ~ forward / backward / in / out; ~ across a pool of water / into a boat / on an object / on s.o.'s foot; ~ on to / off the platform; □ ~ on the gas / ~ on it *(inform: drive faster; also fig)* (2 *walk a little way*) ~ across the street; ~ down to the tobacconist's; ~ over to the bar; ~ this way / upstairs / in here please (3 *fig: enter into*) ~ into a fortune / good business opportunity. - *vt* (4) ~ three paces (5) ~ a dance / minuet / *etc.*

step by she ~ped by without even speaking.

step down (1) he ~ped ~ *(retired)* to give his brother a chance. (2) ~ ~ *(reduce the voltage of)* an electric current.

step in (1) ~ in and have some tea. (2) the two men were just about to quarrel when Mr N. / the police ~ped in.

step off ~ ~ *(measure)* ten feet.

step out (1) ~ ~ a moment and I'll show you my new car. (2) we began to ~ ~ *(walk more quickly)* when we realized how late it was. (3) ~ ~ *(measure)* ten feet (4) many shareholders ~ped ~ *(withdrew)* when the business was at a low ebb.

step up (1) he ~ped up to me and said ...; ~ up to Mr N's office on the next floor. (2) ~ up income tax / production / sales / s.o.'s salary (by a pound) (3) ~ up *(increase the voltage of)* an electric current.

stick *vt* 1 - 6; *vi* 7 - 18.
The patterns are grouped as follows: be, get stuck: 4; be stuck + for, on, with: 4; ~ + *obj* + *adv (prepos) phrase*: 1 - 3; ~ + *adv (prepos) phrase*: 7 - 18; ~ + *obj* + *prepos (non-local)*: with 2b; ~ + *prepos*: at 14, 15; by 13; in 8, 9; to 7, 16 - 18.
(1a) ~ a stamp on an envelope / a photo in an album / a bill on a wall / a notice on a bulletin-board; a notice stuck to the door said ... (1b) ~ a painting on the wall (with glue, tape) (2a) she stuck a pin into the cloth; he stuck a flower in his buttonhole; she stuck a needle in her finger / the blister; ~ a fork into a potato / a potato on a fork (2b) ~ a pin-cushion with pins; the nurse stuck me with a needle; a pudding stuck with almonds (3a *put casually*) he stuck the letter in his pocket; please ~ this book in the drawer; ~ the chair in the corner; ~ one's head out of the window (3b *place here and there*) ~ knick-knacks all over the room (4 *bring to a standstill*) the car was stuck in the mud (→ 9); the door / window has got stuck; □ get / be stuck in a rut *(make no progress)*; as far as you can, try and do the calculation yourself, but if you're stuck (with it) ask me; I'm stuck on this problem; we have completed half on the project, but now we're stuck for money; be stuck for the right word / materials; if we don't sell this car soon, we shall be stuck with it *(unable to get rid of it)*. (5 *BE inform: endure)* I can't ~ people who are always boasting of their own merits; the atmosphere is so close in this room that I can't ~ it any longer. (6 *BE* ~ it *(don't give in)*: go on, ~ it, don't let him get ahead of you!
- *vi* (7) the stamp won't ~ (to the envelope) any more; his tongue was ~ing to his palate; his wet clothes stuck to his body; a notice ~ing to the door said ... (8) the splinter stuck in his arm for a week; I found the nail ~ing in the tyre. (9 *become fixed*) the car stuck in the mud (→ 4); the key stuck in the lock *(could not be turned or withdrawn)*; her zip stuck halfway up. (10 *become motionless*) the car stuck on the hill; the door / window ~s; the wheels have stuck; ~ where you are. (11) your health is likely to suffer if you ~ indoors all day; fancy having to ~ in an office on a day like this; can you ~ on a horse? (12 *fig: remain permanently*) it's a nickname that will ~; a fact that ~s in the mind; □ ~ in one's throat *(be difficult to accept or utter)*: it is his treatment of his aged mother that really ~s in my throat; the words stuck in my throat. (13 *stick by: remain loyal*) ~ by a friend / decision / promise (14 *inform*) you are bound to succeed if you ~ at your work / books; ~ at a task / job (15 *inform*) he is the kind of person who wouldn't ~ at murder if it would serve his purpose; is there anything a person like that would ~ at? he'll ~ at nothing *(is quite unscrupulous)* to gain his ends. (16) ~ to a job

(until it is finished) / plan / schedule; ~ to the point - don't bring in irrelevant things; ~ to the letter *(fig)* / facts; if you ~ to the truth, you've nothing to fear; ~ too closely to the text; ~ *(drive)* very close behind a car / to the white guideline (17) get a few good friends and ~ to them; ~ to one's word / a promise / a resolution; a politician should ~ to his colours. (18 *stick to; keep dishonestly*) ~ to s.th. one finds / that is entrusted to one.

stick out (1) ~ ~ one's tongue; how he ~s ~ his chest! the beggar stuck ~ a grimy hand towards us. (2) a wad of papers stuck ~ of his pocket; his nose stuck ~ like a cliff. (3 *inform: insist*) ~ ~ for one's rights / a reduction in working hours; he stuck ~ for his price; the witness stuck (it) ~ that his story was true; it was a long journey, but we managed to ~ it ~ by playing cards; I had intended resigning my post in June, but I think I shall ~ it ~ till the end of the year. (4 *be obvious*) spelling mistakes often ~ ~ more than mistakes of construction; it's ~ing ~ that she's very clever; ~ ~ a mile *(be very obvious)*: that bright tie will ~ ~ a mile at the reception; his conceit ~s ~ a mile - even to strangers.

stick up (1) I saw a rifle ~ing up; his shirt collar was ~ing up. (2) she stuck her head up and laughed. (3) he stuck up for his friend who was accused; ~ up for one's rights / one's principles / a political party; ~ up for oneself *(refuse to allow o.s. to be treated unfairly)* (4) she's very stuck up *(haughty)*.

stir *vt* (1) ~ one's tea / a cup of coffee / a pudding (with a spoon) / the fire; ~ pigment into paint (2 *move, often slightly*) he would not ~ a finger (to help them); □ not ~ an eyelid *(remain unmoved)*; □ ~ one's stumps *(inform: walk faster)*; the storm ~red the sea to fury; the breeze ~red the leaves. (3) the news ~red him to action; obstacles only ~red him to greater efforts; ~ the imagination / s.o.'s interest; ~ pity / s.o.'s heart; the audience was deeply ~red; who ~red the crew to mutiny? ~ s.o.'s blood *(rouse him to excitement, enthusiasm)*.
- *vi* (4 *move, often slightly*) nobody ~red before daybreak; he is not ~ring yet *(is still in bed)*; he ~red slightly in his sleep; everyone in the house was ~ring; during the Christmas holidays things are really ~ring at our house; he never ~s out of the house. (5) the mixture does not ~ easily. (6) discontent is ~ring among the farmers; pity ~red in his heart.
- *adj* (7 *exciting; thrilling*) a ~ring performance by the orchestra; ~ring events; these are ~ring times.

stir up (1) his dive ~red up some mud; ~ up mud *(bring to light unpleasant facts)*; ~ up dregs (2) he wants ~ring up *(is indolent)*; ~ up envy / curiosity / passion / trouble / old troubles / old scandal; ~ up public opinion / sedition; ~ up a people / the country to rebellion; ~ up a hornet's nest *(arouse the fierce anger of a number of people)*.

stock *n* (1) the shop has a large ~ of goods; dead *(unsalable)* ~; a ~ of provisions; I am at the end of my ~ of wine; our ~s of food are very low; replenish one's ~s (of coal / *etc*); he has a good ~ of information; have / keep an article in ~ *(have ready for sale)*; this book is in / out of ~; □ take ~ *(make a list of one's ~)*; □ take ~ of *(estimate)* s.o. / a situation / one's position; □ take / put ~ in s.th. *(believe)*: I take little ~ in his story. (2 *ancestors*) he comes of Puritan / Irish / farming / good ~ (3 *shares*) my uncle owns most of the company's ~; his ~ is going up / down *(also fig: his estimation)*; his fortune is tied up in ~s and bonds. (4 *raw material*) a ham bone is ~ for soup; paper ~ *(e.g. rags to be made into paper)* (5 *broth prepared by boiling meat)* vegetable / bone / soup ~; vegetable water should be used as ~ for soups. (6 *s.th. lifeless)* ~s and stones *(also fig: stupid people)*; (7 *base, handle of s.th.*) the ~ of a rifle / plough / plane / whip (8 *farm animals*) a farm to be sold with the ~; grazing ~; live ~.

stop *n* (1) this train goes from London to Crewe with only two ~s; the train made a brief ~; bring a vehicle to a ~; the train came to a (dead / sudden) ~; he came to a ~ when he saw me; a scheduled ~; a ~ en route; *(fig)* put a ~ to s.th. (→ put *vt* 11); bring s.th. to a ~ (→ bring *vt* 9) (2) tram- / bus- / request ~ (3 *plug*) there must be a ~ in this pipe (4 *BE*) common ~s are the comma, the semicolon and the full ~.

stop *vt* (1a) he ~ped his car at the crossroads; ~ a horse / machine / train / clock; ~ the traffic; ~ a thief / fugitive; ~ your work just a minute; I shall now ~ my visits; ~ that nonsense / noise; ~ the enemy / war; *(fig)* he ~s at nothing (to gain his ends). (1b) he ~ped running / smoking / *etc*; the motorist ~ped looking at his map and drove on (→7a); do ~ grumbling! (2) he won't ~ me from / my going; what is there to ~ me telling him what I think of him? (3 *cut off*) ~ supplies; ~ s.o.'s wages; he has had his leave / beer / *etc* ~ped; the cost of the broken pane was ~ped *(deducted)* out of / from my pay. (4a) ~ (up) a hole / crack / gap / leak / pipe; ~ one's ears *(also fig)*; have a tooth ~ped *(BE filled)*; ~ a bottle / tube / *etc* with a cork / plug / *etc*; □ ~ the way *(prevent progress)* (4b) leaves ~ped (up) the drain. (5) the bank ~ped payment *(was unable to pay)*; ~ (payment of) a cheque (6 *BE punctuate*) a badly spelt and ~ped letter. - *vi* (7a) the car ~ped suddenly for a red light; ~ dead / short (→ dead *adj* 2, short *adv* 1); the train does not ~ here; can't we ~ for another coffee? no ~ping! the watch / speaker / *etc* ~ped; he ~ped (working, reading, *etc*, in order) to look at her; the motorist ~ped *(driving)* to look at the map (→ 1b); he never ~s to think; (7b) the pain ~s when I rest my leg. (8a *stay; visit*) we are ~ping at my sister's house overnight; I shall ~ here a few days; won't you ~ to dinner? (8b *BE*) I like to ~ in bed till the last moment; I shall ~ at home tonight; are you ~ping at this hotel?

stop up (1) → stop 4a, 4b. (2 *BE*) he used to ~ up (late) *(not go to bed until late)*; can I ~ up till Uncle Ted arrives?

store *n* (1) a ~ of food; lay in a ~ of fuel; do we have a ~ of canned goods for the next few weeks? have / keep s.th. in ~; I have a surprise in ~ for you; there is a great deal of trouble in ~ for them if they... (2) an ammunition ~; put furniture into ~ / in a ~ / in the ~s (3 *value*) set great / *etc* ~ by s.th. (→ set *vt* 1c); lay great / *etc* ~ (up)on s.th. (→ lay *vt* 9).

store *vt* (1) ~ food; they ~d up a good supply of coal for the winter; squirrels ~ (up) nuts for the winter; ~ s.th. away (for a long time) (2) ~ furniture (in a warehouse) (3) ~ one's mind with information / knowledge; she ~d her furs away for the winter; he ~d his old uniform away and forgot all about it. - *vi* (4) some foods won't ~; flour ~s well.

storm *n* (1a) a rain~ / snow~ / thunder ~; suddenly a ~ broke (→ break *vi* 23); a ~ was coming / was brewing / gathered / arose / burst; an intense / violent / furious ~ raged / swept over the country / uprooted trees / *etc*; □ a ~ in a teacup *(great excitement over a small matter)* (1b) a ~ of missiles / bullets (2) a ~ of tears / applause / hisses / cheers; a ~ of protests / criticism; a ~ in parliament (3) take a fortress by ~ *(also fig)*.

straight *adj / adv* (1a) a ~ line is the shortest distance between two points; a ~ edge / course / road; a ~ nose / back; ~ legs / shoulders; ~ hair; □ keep a ~ face *(refrain from laughing)*; walk ~; hold o.s. up ~; he looked ~ in front of him; he came ~ towards me; shoot ~ *(accurately)*; □ ~ from the shoulder (→ shoulder *n* 1) (1b) hang a picture ~; put a hat on ~.
(2 *tidy*) put / keep a room ~; ... a bit tired after the move, but the house is / we are nearly ~ now; keep records ~ (3 *reliable*) a ~ piece of information; a ~ tip (4a *honest*) a ~ character; you must try to keep ~; live ~; a ~ answer; tell me ~ what you think. (4b *go straight: give up crime and lead a reformed life*) when he left prison he resolved to go ~ but ...; I'm going ~ now - I didn't have anything to do with that robbery; it's hard to go ~ when everybody knows you're an ex-convict. (5 *correct*) ~ reasoning; a ~ thinker; he can think ~; let's get the facts ~. (6 *unmixed*) ~ whisky; *(fig)* it was ~ farce. (7 *by a direct route, without delay*) go ~ home; I must go ~ in because he's waiting; I want to come ~ to the point; I told him ~ away / off what I thought about the matter.

strain[1] *n* (1 *manner of speaking*) speak / write in a cheerful / angry / dismal ~; speak in lofty ~s; there was a ~ of sadness in her voice; a story with a ~ of satire; and much more in the same ~ (2 *music, songs*) the ~s of the nightingale; stirring / melancholy / martial ~s; the ~s of the organ / harp; the ~s of the ancient poets (3 *line of descent*) a horse of Arabian ~; a dog of good ~ (4 *persistent trait*) a ~ of insanity in his family; there is a ~ of mysticism / Irish blood in him; his character is marred by a ~ of fanaticism.

strain[2] *n* (1) the rope broke under the ~; will the cable stand the ~? (2 *severe demand on s.o.'s strength, etc*) the ~ of sleepless nights / running business / hard work / modern life; Aunt Ann's visit is a ~ on my hospitality; a ~ on one's resources; it is a severe ~ on me to do that; this lecture is / puts a great ~ on my attention; housework is a real ~; no one can give his best when he is working under ~ / a great ~; she became ill under the ~ of overwork; the ~ of the change-over period (to the metric system) must inevitably prove very severe. (3 *exhaustion*) suffer from mental ~ (4 *great effort*) he did it without (any) ~.

strain *vt* (1 *stretch to the utmost*) the weight of the piano ~ed the ropes almost to breaking / the breaking-point; ~ a parchment across an aperture; ~ a muscle / tendon (2a *make the greatest possible use of*) ~ one's eyes (to read s.th.) / one's ears (to catch a sound / overhear a conversation) / one's voice; ~ every nerve *(do one's utmost)* (to do s.th.); with ~ed attention / senses (2b) she ~ed herself to finish in time. (3a *injure by over-use, etc*) ~ one's eyes / ears / voice; I fear I have ~ed my heart; he ~ed his back lifting the box; fall and ~ one's ankle / wrist / shoulder; this print ~s one's eyes. (3b) she ~ed herself getting the work finished in time. (4 *clasp tightly*) the mother ~ed her child close to her breast; he ~ed me in his arms. (5 *make excessive demands on*) ~ s.o.'s generosity / patience; ~ one's resources; *(fig)* ~ one's luck (6 *subject to tension*) ~ a relationship; ~ed relations *(mutual distrust)*; a ~ed atmosphere; with ~ed *(forced) cordiality; a ~ed manner / laugh (7 force a meaning not intended*) a very ~ed interpretation; ~ the meaning of a word; he ~ed the truth to justify himself; ~ the law *(make it do what it was not meant to)*; ~ one's authority / powers / rights (8a *filter*) ~ a liquid / gravy / soup / *etc* (8b *draw off*) ~ water from spinach; ~ broth (8c *hold back by filtering*) ~ seeds from orange juice; ~ rice; ~ out impurities. - *vi* (9 *pull forcibly*) the dog ~ed at the leash. (10 *strain one's muscles, faculties*) do your best without ~ing. (11 *come near breaking*) the masts of the ship ~ed and groaned; the rope / tree ~ed. (12 *strain after: strive hard*) ~ (too much) after effect; ~ after a goal / an object (13 *strain at: resist forcefully*) ~ at accepting an unpleasant fact; there are people who ~ at the truth, yet accept every wild rumour without question; anyone would ~ at such an interpretation; □ ~ at a gnat *(be over-scrupulous)* (14 *filter*) the juice ~ed slowly through the sieve; sap ~ed from the bark.

stream *n* (1) a river or a brook is a ~; a clear / muddy / turbid / deep / shallow / wide / narrow / brisk / lively / sluggish ~; go up / down ~; □ go with the ~ *(do as most people do)* (2) ~s of blood / air / gas / light / tears; a ~ of sand trickled out; a ~ / ~s of lava; blood flowed in ~s. (3 *current*) row / swim against / with the ~; the Gulf S~; there is a strong ~ in the river. (4) a ~ of people / animals / cars / *etc*; a constant ~ of visitors came; a ~ of words (5) the ~ of history / opinion / one's experience / consciousness.

stream *vi* (1) the rain ~ed down; tears ~ed from her eyes / down her face; I have a ~ing cold. (2) her eyes were ~ing; the athlete ~ed with perspiration; a ~ing umbrella (3) the flag / her hair ~ed in the wind. (4) sunlight ~ed in through the windows. (5) workmen ~ed from the factory; the crowd ~ed out of the stadium. - *vt* (6) her eyes ~ed tears; the wound ~ed blood. (7) the wind ~ed the flags.

street *n* (1) a broad / wide / narrow / straight / winding / quiet / noisy / crowded / busy / empty / lonely ~; (off) the main ~; a by- / side-~; Selfridge's is in Oxford S~; he lived in Baker S~ / at 14 Bottle S~; ~ closed (to all vehicles); ~s thick with people / congested with traffic; □ be ~s *(very far)* ahead of (in attainment, progress, amenities, *etc*); □ be on easy ~ *(inform: well off)*; be on queer ~ *(inform: in financial difficulties)*; as a scholar he is not in the same ~ *(not to be compared)* with his predecessor; the man in the ~ *(the ordinary man)*; I was rather fortunate in the essay - it was right up my ~ *(inform: within my competence)*; on the ~s *(living by prostitution)* (2) the whole ~ knew about it / gossiped about the new neighbours.

strength *n* (1) the ~ of a man / horse / athlete / fleet / argument; the ~ of will / memory / judgement / mind; s.o.'s physical / muscular / Herculean / brute / unimpaired / spiritual / moral / latent / *etc* ~; he has the ~ of a horse / not the ~ of a cat; he hasn't the ~ to do it / walk / work; she still has all her ~; in old age one's ~ dwindles / declines; his ~ grew / increased / doubled / decreased / was flagging; his ~ was undermined / sapped by illness; his ~ failed / left him; build up (one's) ~; summon up / use all one's ~; recover / try / test / *etc* one's ~; this work was beyond her ~; with his last ounce of ~ he reached the shore; he began his work with fresh / renewed ~; □ on the ~ of *(relying on)*: I bought this car on the ~ of his recommendation / a one-year guarantee. (2 *ability to resist*) the ~ of a rope; the ~ of a fortress (3 *effectiveness, intensity*) the ~ of a drug; the alcoholic ~ of brandy far exceeds that of wine; coffee of normal ~; *(fig)* the ~ of his plea / argument / logic (4 *source of power*) knowledge is his ~; the Bible was her ~ and joy. (5 *force in numbers*) the squadron is at full / half ~; a regiment with a ~ of 3,000; what is your ~ *(how many are there of you)*? our police force is up to / below ~ *(up to / below the full number)*; the opposing team's supporters appeared in ~ *(great numbers)*. (6 *strong point*) make it clear what you consider are the ~s and weaknesses of the book; children exhibit special gifts and ~s relatively early.

stretch *n* (1) the cat woke and gave a ~; he woke up with a ~ and a yawn. (2 *length, area*) a ~ of rope / road; a ~ of grass / meadow / water (3 *period*) a ~ of time; for a ~ of ten years; a ~ in the army; work five hours at a ~ *(continuously)* (4 *excessive use*) by a ~ of authority / language / the imagination (5 *slang: prison term*) he did / was sent up for a five-year ~ (for armed robbery).

stretch *vt* (1) ~ elastic / linen / leather / gloves / shoes; ~ a rope (tight); ~ one's shoes by use; ~ a rubber band until it breaks; they ~ed the wires across the valley. (2) ~ a limb; he woke up and ~ed himself; ~ a tendon / one's muscles; ~ one's neck (to see better); ~ (out) one's hand(s) / arm(s) ; ~ one's legs *(go for a walk after sitting for a long time)* (3a *make appear to go further*) ~ food to feed extra guests; ~ money to keep within a budget (3b *make more by adding s.th.*) they caught the bartender ~ing the gin with water. (4 *make s.th. go beyond its proper limits*) ~ facts / rights; ~ the law / truth; ~ a point *(go beyond what is legitimate)*; ~ the intelligence / imagination. - *vi* (5a) he ~ed and yawned; can you ~ *(reach out)* for it? (5b) this elastic ~es easily; rubber will ~, but wood won't ~. (6) the road ~ed as far as the eye could see; the plain ~ed / lay ~ed out before us; the forest ~ed to the sea. (7) the war ~ed over four years. (8) will your generosity ~ that far?

stretch out (1) → stretch *vt* 1; ~ ~ one's hand to s.o.; he ~ed himself ~ on the ground; they were ~ed ~ on the lawn. (2) he ~ed ~ on the couch. (3) → stretch *vt* 6.

strike *vt* 1 - 17; *vi* 18 - 25.

The patterns are grouped as follows: ~ + *adj*: 18e; ~ + *indirect obj* + *direct obj*: 1a; ~ + *obj* + *adj*: 1a, 1d, 12b; ~ + *obj* + *adv (prepos) phrase*: 1a, 1c, 1e, 6, 10a, 16; ~ + *obj* + as + *adj*: 10a; it + ~ + *clause*: 10a; ~ + *prepos*: at 18a, on 24.

(1a) ~ s.o. (in the face / on the chin); ~ s.o. blind / dumb / deaf / senseless / dead; ~ one's forehead (1b) ~ s.o. a (violent) blow; who struck the first blow? (1c) he struck his fist on the table / a stick against the door; ~ the waters with a paddle; he struck a dagger into the dying man. (1d) these trees ~ their roots deep; do you think the plant has struck a root? (1e *strike into s.o.: fill s.o. suddenly with*) ~ fear into s.o.; Attila struck terror into the people of Europe. (2 *stamp*) ~ a medal / coin (in commemoration of s.th.) (3 *hit*) ~ a ball; ~ *(harpoon)* a whale; suddenly the snake struck the rabbit (→ 19a). (4 *attack*) ~ a target / the enemy (→ 19b) (5a) ~ the keys of a piano; ~ a string (on a guitar); ~ a bell (5b) ~ a note / sound *(by ~ing keys)* on a piano; ~ a chord; *(fig)* ~ a warning / *etc* note (→ note *n* 3) (6) the car struck the wall; the ship struck a rock; she struck her foot on a stone; his head struck the kerb; he struck his head against the kerb; the house was struck by lightning. (7) ~ a match; ~ sparks (from a stone) / fire / light (8) the clock is ~ing the hour; the clock struck ten; has it struck six yet? (9) an epidemic of measles / disaster / death struck the town; be stricken with fever / polio (10a) an idea struck me; ~ s.o. as desirable / impossible / absurd / *etc*; it struck me that he...; it ~s me you are afraid; how does it ~ *(impress)* you? ~ the imagination; a picture that ~s my fancy; the news struck him to the quick; be struck with horror / by the beauty of the scenery (10b *become visible to*) the first object that ~s my eye (10c) the sound struck them; a shrill peal of bells struck their ears. (11 *illuminate brightly*) the sun struck the weathercock. (12a *reach in travelling*) we struck Rome before dark. (12b *come across unexpectedly*) the next day we struck the river / a mountain range / the right path; the miner struck gold; ~ oil *(also fig: make one's fortune)*; they struck various difficulties; he struck the name of a friend in the newspaper. □ ~ it rich *(gain sudden wealth)*: he surely struck it rich when he married into the F. family. (13 *arrive at*) ~ a bargain (with s.o.) / compromise / agreement / balance / average (14 *assume*) ~ an attitude; he likes to ~ a noble pose. (15 *take down*) ~ sails / a flag / a tent; ~ camp *(vacate its site)*; □ ~ one's flag *(as a sign of surrender)*; ~ *(dismantle)* theatre scenery / a set (16) his remarks were struck from the minutes of the meeting; ~ a passage out of a book; → strike out 2. (17 *AE cease in order to put pressure on an employer, → 25*) ~ work.

- *vi* (18a) he seized a stick and struck at me; □ ~ while the iron's hot; □ ~ at the root of an evil; ~ home *(of a blow, remark: be very effective)*: the sermon on Christian charity struck home. (18b) all the news plants have struck *(taken root)*. (18c) about midnight the ship struck *(ran aground)*. (18d) the sun's rays struck *(penetrated)* through the fog. (18e *strike + adj: be noticeable*) the air / mist struck cold / raw; the sunshine struck warm; the room ~s warm and comfortable as you come in; the prison cell struck cold and damp. (19a → 3) then the snake struck. (19b→ 4) at dawn the enemy struck *(attacked)*. (19c) why did the trout not ~ *(grab at the bait)*? (20) the storm struck at dawn. (21) the match didn't ~. (22) the clock ~s; one o'clock struck; the hour has struck; *(fig)* the hour has struck for (a momentous decision). (23 *proceed in a specified direction*) he struck south; if you ~ through the woods you will come to the farm; they struck towards a new town. (24 *strike on: arrive at*) ~ on a solution / idea / plan; then he struck on a new way of doing it. (25 → 17) the union threatened to ~ to get their demands; ~ for higher wages / over some issue / against bad working conditions.

strike down (1) with one blow he struck ~ his opponent. (2) several men were struck ~ with cholera; the plague struck ~ more than half the population.

strike in "Where are you going?" Ann struck in; I struck in with a suggestion.

strike off (1) he struck ~ the beast's head with one blow of his sword; the butcher struck ~ a chop. (2) who struck ~ my name? he was struck ~ the medical register. (3) illness struck him ~ from social contacts. (4 *type, print*) she struck ~ several letters and had no more work to do; they struck ~ 300 copies of the book.

strike out (1) he struck ~ at his assailant. (2) I struck ~ the last two names / items in the list. (3 *make towards by walking, swimming, etc*) the explorers struck ~ for the high plateau; they struck ~ at dawn. (4) ~ ~ on one's own *(start a new enterprise alone)*.

strike through ~ a word ~.

strike up (1) ~ up a friendship / conversation *(begin it with s.o. met casually)* (2) ~ up a song! a popular waltz was struck up on a rather antiquated piano. (3) the band struck up just as I entered the pavilion.

string *n* (1a) some paper and ~ for a parcel; a ball of ~; get a long ~ for the kite; □ have two ~s / more than one ~ to one's bow *(several plans, alternatives available)*; pull ~s (→ pull *vt* 1b); □ (a generous offer) with no ~s attached / without ~s *(no limitations)*; □ have s.o. on a ~ *(inform: under control)* (1b) the ~s of an apron / bonnet (1c) the ~s of beans (1d) the ~ of glue / rubber; the cheese formed ~s. (2a) a ~ of beads / pearls / onions / *etc* (2b) a ~ of cars; a ~ of islands / lakes; a ~ of sausages / mules; she has a whole ~ of admirers. (2c) a ~ of questions / lies / curses / events (2d *business concerns owned by one person*) a ~ of hotels / retail shops (3) a piano / guitar / *etc* ~; the ~s of an instrument are plucked, bowed or struck; □ harp on one / on the same ~ *(keep talking on one subject)*; a ~ orchestra; ~(ed) instruments; the ~s *(stringed instruments)* are excellent.

stroke *n* (1) he dealt him a mortal ~; the woodcutter lopped off the branch with one ~ of his axe; the ~ of a hammer; aim a ~ at s.o.; □ little ~s fell great oaks. (2) a ~ of lightning (3a *regular movement*) the ~ of a swimmer / oars / skates; row a fast / quick / slow ~; the ~ of a piston (3b *method of swimming*) the crawl is a rapid ~. (4a *a single mark made by a pencil, brush, etc*) thin / thick ~s; portray s.th. with a few ~s; with one / a ~ of the pen (4b *distinctive feature*) his style revealed the ~ of a master. (5) on the ~ of ten / midnight the doors opened; arrive on the ~ (of time) *(punctually)* (6) a paralytic / apoplectic ~; a ~ of paralysis; a sun-~; he has had a ~. (7 *vigorous attempt*) a bold ~ for liberty (8 *achievement*) a ~ of genius; a fine ~ of policy / business / humour (9 *sudden happening*) a ~ of luck / fortune (10 *minimum of work*) not a ~ was done; we passed the summer without a ~ of work; he refused to do a ~ of work.

strong *adj/ adv* (1a) a ~ boy / man / horse; she is ~ for a girl; a ~ plant / tree; a ~ voice / wrist / memory / intellect (1b *healthy*) a ~ constitution; have ~ nerves; ~ eyes; feel ~ again; are you ~er now? → go *vi* 20b, go *vi* 22, come *vi* 11. (2) a ~ handshake; with one ~ blow the machine stamped out a mudguard. (3) a ~ wind / breeze / gale (4a *able to resist*) a ~ fortress; a ~ defence (4b) ~ cloth / walls; a ~ table / stick / bicycle / fabric / thread; ~ hair; a pair of ~ / a ~ pair of shoes; a ~ foundation (4c) a ~ stomach; a ~ head *(unaffected by alcohol)* (5 *competent in a field*) he's ~ in spelling / history / *etc*; he's no good at bat, but he's a ~ fielder; s.o.'s ~ point (→ point *n* 12) (6 *morally firm*) a ~ character / will; ~ determination; give ~ support to s.o./ s.th.; he has a ~ sense of duty; be ~ under temptation (7a *powerful in authority, resources*) a ~ nation / State / economy (7b *powerful in numbers*) a ~ contingent of men; a contingent a hundred ~ (8a) ~ tea / coffee / cigarettes / medicine / acid / poison; a ~ solution (8b) ~ whisky; ~ drink *(e.g. rum, gin)*; the fruitcake was too ~. (9a *having a high degree of flavour, odour*) ~ cheese; ~ perfume; a ~ aftershave lotion (9b *having an offensive flavour, odour*) ~ butter / bacon / cheese; his breath is rather ~. (10 *of high magnifying power*) a ~ lens / microscope (11 *intense*) ~ light / colour; a ~ smell (of gas) / odour / flavour; ~ heat; smell ~ (12 *marked*) a ~ family likeness; he bears a ~ resemblance to his grandfather; a ~ French accent (13 *vigorous*) ~ efforts; offer ~ resistance; resist ~ly; speak up for s.o. ~ly (14 *firmly grounded*) ~ faith / conviction; a ~ opinion / inclination / suspicion; she has ~ views about the U.N.; a man of ~ religious beliefs (15 *fervent*) he's a ~ Conservative; a ~ partisan; ~ supporters; ~ devotion; a ~ protest; a man of ~ affections and ~(er) dislikes (16 *very forceful*) ~ language / words / expressions; express one's indignation in the ~est terms.

study *n* (1a) be fond of ~; give one's time to ~ (1b) the ~ of law / finance / Greek / *etc* (2 *branch of learning*) English ~ies *(literature, philology, etc)*; writing and spelling are kindred ~ies; pursue special medical ~ies; *(fig)* his face was a ~ *(s.th. worth examining)*. (3 *studies: effort to gain knowledge*) pursue / continue / finish / stop one's ~ies (4a) Darwin made a ~ of certain finches; a comparative ~ (of two things); a ~ on the slum problem (4b) he published a ~ of foreign trade / Milton's poetry (5 *sketch, etc*) the artist made several ~ies of his subject before he began the portrait; a painter's methods are best revealed in his ~ies. (6) he was in deep ~ and didn't hear a thing; he was lost in (a brown) ~. (7) Mr N. is in the / his ~.

study *vt* (1a) ~ Latin / geometry / medicine / typing / the violin / *etc* (1b *memorize*) ~ a part (for a play) (2) ~ a problem / map / puzzle; ~ foreign trade / the political situation; ~ s.o.'s face (3 *give attention to*) ~ s.o.'s comfort; they ~ied nothing but revenge; ~ the wishes of one's friends / only one's own interests. - *vi* (4) ~ for the ministry / for the medical profession / to be a doctor; he had to ~ for two hours every evening.

stuff *n* (1 *material of which s.th. is made*) it's a hard, crystalline ~; wood, steel and other ~ for building; a cushion filled with some soft ~ (2 *personal belongings*) leave your ~ in the hall; put all your ~ away. (3 *thing, things*) we eat a lot of ~ from our own garden; green / garden ~ *(vegetables)*; do you call this ~ butter / beer / *etc*? clean the ~ out of a cupboard; the publishers have produced a lot of new ~ this year; this whisky / book / bowling is good / poor ~; there's been some good / dreadful ~ on TV lately; Bach composed some splendid ~; □ do one's ~ *(what is required)*; □ know one's ~ *(know a particular field well)*; □ ~ and nonsense *(foolishness)* (4 *essential quality*) courage and obedience are the very ~ of good soldiers; he has good ~ in him.

subject *n* (1) a loyal ~ (of the Queen); a British ~ (2a) an abstract ~ like philosophy; a deep / interesting / dull / delicate / ticklish / *etc* ~; what ~ is under discussion? a ~ of interest / derision / *etc*; wander from / return to the ~; let's change the ~; a ~ for laughter / compassion / discussion (2b) the ~ of a book / poem / drama / speech; his past has been the ~ of rumour. (2c) a short ~ *(short film)* (3) history is one ~ he is taking at school; botany and allied ~s; obligatory / compulsory / optional / subsidiary / basic / academic ~s; he has good marks in all ~s; history is my ~. (4 *s.o., s.th. experimented on*) the ~ of an experiment; he is a good hypnotic ~. (5 *s.o. suffering from a complaint*) an asthma ~; a hysterical ~ (6 *motive, cause*) a ~ for complaint / pity / ridicule / congratulation.

subject *adj/adv* (1) be ~ to the crown (1a) a ~ nation *(one under external rule)* (2 *apt to suffer frequently*) be ~ to fits / moods of depression / headaches / rheumatism / *etc*; the child is ~ to colds; the trains are ~ to delays when there is fog. (3 *exposed*) ~ to typhoons / damage / ridicule; all men are ~ to death. (4) the plan is ~ to your approval; ~ to variation / revision; ~ to charges / fees; the times of all trains are ~ to alterations; he is ~ to his father's will; life is ~ to change; this expression is ~ to misinterpretation; the cycles to which all civilizations are ~; ~ to the harvest being normal, I guarantee ...; ~ to correction, these are the facts.

subject *vt* (1) Alexander ~ed a great part of Asia to his power; Napoleon aimed at ~ing all Europe to his sway. (2) ~ s.o. to cross-examination / investigation / close questioning / *etc*; ~ o.s./s.o. to ridicule; the book was ~ed to severe criticism. (3) clay must be ~ed to great heat to be turned into bricks; these shoes will be ~ed to hard wear.

suffer *vi* (1) he ~s during the hayfever season; the patient is still ~ing. (2) ~ from toothache / backache / *etc*; your health is likely to ~ from overwork; the business ~s from lack of capital; your reputation will ~. (3a *be the victim of*) ~ injury/ an (irreparable) loss / attacks / a setback; the house ~ed some damage (in the recent floods). (3b *be made to bear*) ~ punishment / want / discomfort; ~ the consequences / pangs of conscience; he ~ed weakness after the accident. (4 *form: tolerate*) I do not ~ fools gladly; he ~s no one to contradict him.

suggest *vt* (1a *put forward for consideration or possible action*) ~ an alternative route / a visit to the zoo / *etc*; the subject of the thesis was ~ed by professor N.; I ~ (your friend's) going to the film tonight; the architect ~ed that the building be restored; he ~s that we meet at the station; a German musicologist ~ed that it would be more appropriate to call the 'age of Bach' the 'age of Telemann'. (1b *propose as a possibility*) we ~ed him for president. (2a *make one think of*) the symphony ~s a sunrise; this weather ~s spring; the scene inside ~s a combination of factory, office and railway station; the glove ~s that she was at the scene of the crime. (2b *serve as an inspiration for*) a drama ~ed by Harlem race riots (3 *bring before s.o.'s mind without plain expression*) I didn't tell him to leave, I only ~ed it; his look ~s that he would like us to leave.

sun *n* (1a) the noonday / midnight / radiant / glaring / *etc* ~; the ~ was blazing hot; rise with the ~ *(early)*; his ~ is set *(time of prosperity is over)*; under the ~ *(on earth)*: the most beautiful city under the ~ (1b) lie in the ~; be exposed to the ~; have the ~ in one's eyes; let in / shut out the ~; a place in the ~ *(favourable conditions)*.

supply *n* (1) last week our office began the ~ of household help; engaged in the ~ of raw materials to industry; a continual ~ of goods (2) an inexhaustible ~ of fish / coal / *etc*; a good / ample / generous / scanty ~ of s.th.; (in)adequate ~ / ~ies of s.th.; apples are in short ~ *(scarce)* this winter; the storm cut off our water ~; we still have a big ~ of bicycles; did you see our new ~ of shirts? our ~ies are running low / nearly exhausted.

supply *vt* (1) who ~ies the necessary tools? the farmer ~ied shelter for the hikers; ~ a town with electricity / electricity to a town; some shops were badly ~ied during the strike; could you ~ me with a notebook? (2) can you ~ the demand for coffee? the new power station will ~ the need for cheap electricity; ~ a deficiency / loss.

support *vt* (1) s.th. ~s a mass / load / structure; s.th. ~s pressure / weight /

strain; the foundation ~s the house; the buttress ~s the wall; be ~ed by a life-belt (2) a glass of brandy ~ed him / his strength; a good conscience / your approval / hope ~ed him; she ~ed him in his struggle; her kindness always ~s me in time of trouble; ~ed by hope; not enough food to ~ life (3) ~ a cause / resolution; the mayor hopes the voters will ~ his plan to build a new school. (4) this ~s his theory; an accusation not ~ed by proofs; these papers ~ his claim to the property. (5) I can ~ the fatigue / her insolence / life no longer; ~ extremes of climate (6) can he ~ a family? the Society now ~s 50 hospitals.

suppose *vt* (1) ~ you won a thousand pounds, what would you do with it? ~ the distance to be a mile; ~ we wait until tomorrow; just ~ing you could travel, where would you go first? the girl liked to ~ that she was a princess in disguise. (2a *think likely*) I ~ he may come today; I ~ you know what to do; what do you ~ he will do? I ~ I'll see you at the party; poor Ann, I don't ~ you get much time for relaxation; most people ~ him (to be) innocent; it is ~d that the occurrence was an accident; cats are ~d to have nine lives; strong coffee drunk before going to bed is ~d to keep you awake. (2b *believe without firm cause*) I ~d him to be away from home; I ~d that you had gone. (3 *be supposed: be expected*) what time are you ~d to be at work in the morning? a motorist is ~d to stop at a zebra crossing; the office staff are not ~d to use that door. (4 *be supposed: be claimed*) central heating by this system is ~d to be quite cheap; this chewing gum is ~d to clean your teeth. (5) what are you doing here? I thought you were ~d to be ill *(it was a fact that you are ill)*; who is ~d to be organizing this trip - you or me? (6 *presuppose*) this theory ~s the existence of life on Mars; the evidence ~s his presence near the scene.

sure *adj* (1) a ~ sign of rain; a ~ friend / guide / messenger; a ~ bet / winner / profit / cure; death is ~ *(inevitable)*; his death is ~; hard and honest work is the ~st way to success. (2 *safe*) to make a rope ~; a ~ foothold; stand on ~ ground (3) I am ~ it will rain / you will succeed / *etc*; I felt for a time ~ of his innocence - I am now certain of his guilt; he was ~ of ultimate success; he is ~ to come; they are ~ to accept it; there is ~ to be a garage there; be ~ to write to me as soon as you get there; be ~ and remember what I told you; make ~ (→ make *vi* 21); I shall certainly be present, but I am not ~ about my wife; to be ~ *(certainly; admittedly)*: 'you are going to vote for the proposal, aren't you?' - 'to be ~ I am'; she sings well, to be ~, but she can't act; ~ enough *(as might have been expected)*: I said he would fail his exam, and ~ enough he did; ~ enough, the picnic was rained out; for ~ *(certainly)*: we leave tomorrow for ~; I don't know for ~.

surely *adv* (1 *certainly*) he will ~ fail; you ~ can't be serious; the results are ~ encouraging. (2 *I'm confident, but not certain*) ~ you are not going out in this rain; ~ you are mistaken; ~ they will try their best; but, John, ~ it will be terribly expensive in any case. (3 *inevitably*) slowly but ~ summer turns into autumn. (4 *firmly, unerringly*) the expert skier glided ~ down the slope.

surprise *n* (1) cause great / complete / (un)pleasant / *etc* ~; the president's speech was a ~ to his advisers; he gave her a pearl ring as a ~; the new car was a ~ for Mother; truth must be elicited by ~; I have a ~ for you; the enemy took us by ~ *(came upon us suddenly)*; a fort must be taken by ~; the amount of the donation took us completely by ~ *(astonished us)*. (2) imagine Mother's ~ when she saw the new car! his ~ was visible; to my (great) ~; look at s.o. in ~; hear / see / notice s.th. with ~.

surprise *vt* (1) his generosity / her beauty / his behaviour / *etc* ~d me; he ~d me by his visit; she ~d me with a birthday-cake / her knowledge of the locality; it's nothing to be ~d about; I am ~d at you! he was ~d at receiving a telegram; I am ~d to find you here; he looked greatly ~d. (2) the burglar was ~d by the police; our night raid ~d the enemy. (3) ~ a secret out of s.o.; ~ the facts from a witness; ~ a witness into telling the truth.

surrender *vt* (1) he ~ed the stolen typewriter to the police; ~ one's watch to a robber; ~ a town / ship / army (to the enemy); ~ o.s. to the police (2) ~ o.s. to an emotion / habit / life of hardship (3) ~ freedom / one's liberty; the doctors ~ed all hope of his recovery. - *vi* (4) the Germans ~ed to the Allies; ~ on terms / unconditionally.

survey *vt* (1) ~ an estate / the coast / the country; the surveyor ~ed the farm before we bought it. (2) ~ a house / car before buying it (3) they sadly ~ed the scene before them; we ~ed the scene from the hill. (4) ~ a problem / situation / state of affairs; the last chapters ~ the closing years of her reign.

suspend *vt* (1) ~ a lamp / wreath from the ceiling; ~ a door on a hinge (2) a pall of smoke was ~ed over the city; the balloons appeared to be ~ed in mid-air; ~ solid particles in a liquid (3 *temporarily remove from office, membership, etc*) ~ a member of a club / teacher / football player / *etc* (4a) ~ (one's) judgement; shall I ~ final decision until I have further evidence? (4b) ~ sentence on a convicted man; he was given a ~ed jail sentence of six months. (5) ~ parking rules / ferry service / work / proceedings; ~ payment (6 *keep in a mood of expectation*) finish the story - don't ~ us in mid-air.

suspicion *n* (1) a faint / strong / grave / unfounded / *etc* ~; with mutual ~; a stranger regarded with ~, if not actual hostility; I have a ~ that he ...; have / entertain / harbour ~s about s.o./ s.th.; arouse ~ / s.o.'s ~s; dispel ~; look upon s.o. with ~; a look of ~; arrest s.o. on ~; be under ~ (of having stolen s.th.); remain under ~; be above (all) ~; our worst ~s were confirmed / justified. (2 *slightest notion*) he hadn't a ~ of the truth. (3 *a very small amount*) a ~ of garlic; tea with a ~ of brandy; just a ~ of sarcastic humour; a ~ of sadness in her voice; a ~ of a smile.

sustain *vt* (1) the foundation ~s the house; the buttress ~s the wall; be ~ed by a lifebelt; can this light shelf ~ (the weight of) all these books? ~ a burden (2) food ~s life; ~ing food; a glass of brandy ~ed him / his strength; a good conscience / hope / your approval ~ed him; religion ~ed them through dark times; he has been ~ed through life by his belief that ... (3) s.th. does not ~ comparison with s.th. else; ~ a defeat / severe contusion / shock / great loss; ~ criticism; die from injuries ~ed in the kitchen (4) ~ an argument / statement / charge / theory; the judge ~ed the lawyer's objection; the court ~ed his claim / him in his claim; further investigation ~ed my suspicions; face vigorous and ~ed opposition; hold debates or ~ed discussion (5 *keep up*) ~ an effort; make a ~ed effort; ~ a conversation; ~ *(act)* a role; ~ a note *(in singing)*.

swallow *vt* (1) ~ food / drink (1a) the ocean ~ed the ship; ~ed up by the shadows; the crowd ~ed him up. (2) he will ~ any story you tell him; ~ an insult (3a) ~ (one's) anger / pride / tears / laughter (3b) ~ one's words (4) expenses ~ up earnings.

swear *vt* (1a) he swore (eternal) friendship / fidelity; ~ an oath; I ~ by Almighty God that I ...; he swore he didn't know the man; he swore it on the witness stand; I would ~ to it; we could have sworn (to it that) we heard cries; I could not ~ to it that it was he / him. (1b) ~ a charge / accusation against s.o.; sworn evidence / statements (2) she swore not to be late. (3) ~ s.o. to secrecy; ~ a witness; sworn enemies / friends - *vi* (4) ~ to / before God; I couldn't ~ to the colour of his eyes. (5 *swear by: have great confidence in*) he ~s by his doctor / this mixture as a cure for a cold / that firm (6 *curse*) he started ~ing at the policeman; I feel I could ~ about this wretched weather; 'damn!' he swore.

swear in ~ in a jury; a new president will be sworn in today.

swear off ~ ~ smoking; he has sworn ~ drinking for Lent.

sweep *vt* (1a) ~ a room / floor / street / chimney / *etc* (1b) her beautiful dress swept the ground. (1c) ~ the dirt (up) into the corner; with a violent gesture he swept the papers from the table; the wind swept the leaves across the lawn / the snow into drifts; the waves swept me off the raft. (1d) ~ a way through snow / a path through fallen leaves (2 *pass over a surface*) the painter swept a brush over his canvas. (3a *clear*) ~ the sea of pirates; ~ the seas *(drive all enemies from them)* (3b) sandstorms swept the plains; a hurricane swept the Florida coast. (3c) ~ all obstacles from one's path; ~ s.o. out of power; □ ~ s.o. off his feet *(carry away by fascination, etc)*: the dashing Spaniard swept her off her feet; □ he wanted to ~ it under the carpet *(hide s.th. unpleasant)*. (4) he swept the valley with his binoculars; ~ the horizon; his gaze swept the countryside; his eyes swept the faces in the room. (5a) she swept her fingers over the strings; he swept his eyes over the countryside. (5b) he / his fingers swept the keys of the piano / the strings of the guitar / the lute. (6 *win a complete victory in s.th.*) Johnson swept the presidential election of 1964; ~ a constituency *(secure a large majority)*. - *vi* (7) a new broom ~s clean *(also fig)*. (8a) a big wave swept across the deck; the wind swept along the street; a procession was ~ing along the street; the settlements swept across the entire continent of North America. (8b) fear swept over Europe. (9) proudly, she swept from the room; she swept off the stage; the bride swept up the aisle. (10) his glance swept around the room. (11 *extend in a continuous or curving stretch*) the road ~s round the lake / by the dunes; the hills ~ down to the sea; the current ~s along the coast.

sweep along she waved to us as she swept ~ in her new car.

sweep away (1) ~ ~ dust; the pier was swept ~ by the flood; he was swept ~ by an avalanche. (2) ~ ~ slavery.

sweep by = sweep along.

sweep off (1) ~ ~ the snow; the wind swept my hat ~. (2) the plague swept ~ thousands.

sweep out ~ ~ a room; ~ ~ dirt.

sweep up (1) the gardener is ~ing up the dead leaves in the drive; → sweep *vt* 1c (2) the bird swept up.

swell *vi* (1a) the boil began to ~; his arm is ~ing (up); his face began to ~ (out); her ankles ~ed from standing; his cheek is swollen; he has a swollen cheek; *(fig)* ~ / be swollen with pride; □ have / suffer from (a) ~ed head *(conceit)* (1b) the sails ~ed out. (1c) the river is ~ing / swollen. (1d *curve upward*) the cask ~s in the middle. (2) the population has swollen to over a million; expenses / difficulties ~; swollen estimates; in time, Ann's savings will ~ into a substantial amount. (3) the noise ~ed; a ~ing note; the sounds ~ed and faded away. - *vi* (4a) the rain has swollen the river. (4b) the wind ~ed (out) the sails. (5) ~ a note (6) s.th. ~s the difficulties / expenses.

swing *vi* (1) a pendulum ~s; a door ~s on hinges; the door swung shut / to. (2) she swung round on her heel; the car swung round the corner. (3) the children went ~ing along singing a song; ~ merrily along (4) later on, the road ~s to the east. (5) his moods ~ from happy to sad without any apparent cause; he suddenly swung (over) to his opponent's point of view. (6 *slang: be executed by hanging*) I'll see to it that the man who shot the policeman ~s; let him ~ from the highest tree. - *vt* (7) ~ a club / bat / *etc*; ~ one's arms in walking; he swung the heavy sack on to his back; the big ape swung (itself) from branch to branch; ~ o.s. into the saddle; □ no room to ~ a cat in *(very little space)* (8) the driver swung the car into the drive; he swung the door open. (9) ~ s.o. round to one's point of view. (10 *slang: manage successfully*) can you ~ this deal? the advertising campaign swung the election.

T

table *n* (1) a circular / round / square / rectangular / oval / *etc* ~; a tea / dinner / dining / dressing / writing / extension / *etc* ~; sit at the ~; → lay *vt* 5, set *vt* 1a, 2; □ turn the ~s (on s.o.) *(cause a reversal; retaliate)*: fortune turned the ~s and we won; after a bad beginning, Joe turned the ~s on his opponent and won the game; drink s.o. under the ~; she gave money under the ~ *(as a bribe)* to get the flat. (2 *meal, food*) at ~ *(having a meal)*: be / sit / be seated at ~; rise from ~; serve / wait at ~; a hotel noted for its good ~; she sets / keeps a good / poor ~. (3) a ~ of contents (in a book); multiplication / logarithmic ~s.

take *vt* 1 - 14, 15a, 16 - 17, 19 - 22, 24; *vi* 15b, 18, 23, 25, 26.

The patterns are grouped as follows: ~ + *obj* + *inf*: 20; ~ + it + *obj* + *inf*: 21b; ~ + it + *adv phrase*: 22c; ~ + it + *clause*: 19; ~ + it + *past part*: 19; ~ + *obj* + *gerund*: 21c; ~ + *obj* + *prepos*: at 22b; by 1, 2, 14, 22a, 22b; for 5a, 10a, 22b; from 10a, 10b, 10f, 11; in 22a, 22b; into 22b, 22c; off 11, 22a; on 22b; out of 11, 22a, 22c; through 5b; to 5a, 5b, 22a, 22b; under 22b; upon 22c; with 14; ~ + *prepos*: after 23; for 24; from 26; to 26. For abstract *obj* see *esp* 17; idiomatic uses *esp* 22.

(1 *grasp, get a hold on a concrete object, esp with the hand(s) or arms; also of per-*

sons) ~ a pen (and begin to write) / brush / hat / sheet of paper; ~ it between your finger and the thumb; he took her arm; ~ s.o. in one's arms / to one's breast; ~ s.o. by the throat; ~ s.o.'s hand (while crossing the road); ~ a child / old man by the hand (→ 22b); ~ 2 oz. of butter *(recipe)*; ~ arms; ~ the reins; □ give him an inch and he will ~ an ell.

(2 *seize; capture; surprise*) ~ a town / fortress (by storm); ~ a prisoner; ~ s.o. prisoner / captive; he took 20 prisoners; the thief was ~n by the police; a rabbit ~n in a trap; ~ a dozen trout on a good afternoon; ~ a trick / opponent's card; he took my pawn; *(fig)* she took all hearts (by storm); ~ s.o. unprepared / unawares.

(3 *assume possession of; occupy; also fig*) ~ a seat (→ seat *n* 1b) / chair; he took his stand near the window (→ 17); ~ one's place at table (→ place *n* 1); ~ the place of s.o./ s.th. (→ place *n* 2); ~ a box at the opera / seats in advance (→ seat *n* 1b); we'll ~ the flat / house if you paint it; ~ a house by the sea; ~ lodgings; the couple took the floor *(began dancing)*; he ~s whatever he can lay his hand(s) on; you may ~ whichever candy you want; ~ what you can get; ~ whichever you wish; □ ~ a back seat *(occupy an inferior position)*: after being Chairman for so long, it was not a pleasant thought that he would now have to ~ a back seat; his writing has ~n a back seat because of other demands on his time.

(4 *use*) ~ the car / the 8.43 / early morning train; ~ a taxi / bus / train / ship / plane; ~ the lift - it's quicker; do not hurry, ~ your time; he took the time to finish it properly (→ 21a).

(5a *carry, lead to another place; personal subjects*) ~ the box in / out / away / back; ~ the letters to the post; please ~ the tea-tray indoors; I will ~ your trunk to the attic; ~ s.o. a present / glass of water / *etc*; may I ~ this book home? ~ a guest home; ~ s.o. to hospital / the doctor('s); he was ~n to prison; ~ it / your brother with you; ~ s.o. to a party / the theatre; next time I shall ~ my fiancée there with me; ~ your lunch with you! are you ~ing an umbrella? ~ a girl dancing / to a dance; ~ the dog for a walk; we took them for a ride in the country (→ 22b); do you ~ your dog to England? we don't want to ~ our car into France; the bus driver took his bus to the wrong depot; the captain took this ship alongside; the pilot took the plane above the weather; the children took their woes to their mother; the officer took the information to his superior; the old man took his secret to the grave. (5b *as 5a, non-personal subjects*) this road ~s you to town; the blue bus ~s you to the station; what took him to Rome *(why did he go there)*? the fine weather took many people to the sea; this film ~s us to 16th-century Venice; in this new book the author ~s his readers to Roman Britain; his ambition and perseverance took him quickly to the top of his field; his faith took him through this period of stress. (5c *of road, wall, fence: extend it*) ~ a wall / fence to a certain height / round a place / *etc*; the road will be ~n through our valley.

(6 *do, carry out an action appropriate to the dir obj*) ~ two steps, then jump! ~ steps to do s.th.; I had to ~ the step I took (→ step *n* 8); ~ measures (→ measure *n* 5) / precautions (→ precaution); ~ work for a friend; ~ a photo(graph) / flash photo; ~ dictation / a letter (in shorthand); ~ notes (→ note *n* 1); the class is ~ing a note of the date of the sports (→ 17); ~ s.o.'s measurements; ~ a census; ~ a role (in a play) / the part of the hero (→ part *n* 7); ~ the (steering) wheel / controls (of an aeroplane / boat / *etc*); ~ the reins (→ 22a); the horse will not ~ the fence; he took the corner at top speed / the hill in top gear.

(7 *take + noun: phrase definable in terms of noun*)

(7a *take + noun: phrase synonymous with verb derivable from noun: to ~ a look: to look*) ~ a look (at s.o./ s.th.); ~ a glance round you! ~ (a deep) breath / a breath of fresh air (→ breath *n* 1); ~ a bath; ~ a walk / drive / ride; let's ~ a run (to the beach / in the car to Oxford); ~ (to) flight *(flee, run away)*; he took a sudden leap; ~ the lead; ~ action; ~ no action until I see you (→ action *n* 1); ~ aim at s.th. (→ aim *n* 1); one's leave (→ 17, leave *n* 2); the weather / my sister has ~n a turn for the better; ~ an unexpected turn (→ turn *n* 3); ~ a vow (7b *take + noun: phrase synonymous with verb not derivable from noun: to take an oath: to swear*) ~ an oath; ~ a nap; ~ the air *(go out of doors, breathe fresh air)*; ~ a trip / excursion /

voyage; ~ a turn in the garden *(go for a stroll)*; ~ wing *(start flying)*.
(8a *choose and obtain against payment*) I'll ~ *(buy)* two pounds; we ~ two pints of milk daily; ~ a ticket; when did they ~ that house? (8b *choose and make use of, follow*) ~ a road / another road / a route / a direction; ~ the path to(wards) the village / the way to ...; ~ the shortest way / a wrong turning / a short cut (across the fields); we'll ~ the left fork at the crossroads; he kept to the road once he had ~n it; □ ~ the path of least resistance; ~ a / one's own course; his life took a course which ...; we can do nothing except let matters ~ their course (→ course *n* 2); ~ s.th. as an example; ~ any example you wish (→ example *n* 3); ~ World War II *(as an instance)* - what do we see? ~ these figures - they show a rise in taxation; ~ the way he drives his car. (8c *choose and do what is required*) ~ lodgers / pupils; who is ~ing *(teaching)* this class today? he ~s French with seven-year-olds; ~ lessons; she is ~ing classes in cookery; he ~s French at the university; he took a course in higher mathematics; ~ a (postgraduate / Honours / foreign-language) course; she took dancing lessons / ballet; if she can't drive, she'll ~ instruction.
(9 *enter into relation with*) ~ a wife / lover; ~ s.o. in marriage; ~ a partner / one's brother into the business; ~ s.o. into partnership.
(10a *accept*)
please ~ this gift; ~ a compliment with a smile; ~ an offer / bet / bribe / dare; don't ~ lifts from strangers; ~ employment / a job; ~ orders (from customers); ~ *(adopt)* a name / pseudonym; some people ~ my help as a matter of course; ~ it or leave it *(kind of ultimatum)*; our club ~s new members once a year; do you ~ summer visitors? ~ the chair *(become chairman)*; he took the Chair of Economics at B. *(became professor)*; the mayor took office last month; ~ the throne; ~ s.o. as he is; you must ~ us as you find us; he will not ~ a hint; ~ s.o.'s advice; ~ legal / medical advice (→ advice *n*); I'll ~ your word for it *(having no other proof)*; (you may) ~ my word for it! ~ it from me that he ...; if you are determined to act so foolishly, you must ~ the consequences; ~ a remark (in the wrong spirit); ~ an insult / humiliation / rebuke; ~ s.o.'s insolence; ~ an insult / defeat lying down; he took (the) defeat with equanimity; ~ your medicine *(defeat)* like a man; when failure comes your way, be a man and show that you can ~ it; he took it like a lamb; □ ~ the good with the bad; □ ~ the rough with the smooth.
(10b *react to, tolerate*)
~ things coolly / cheerfully; ~ the bad news very calmly; I should ~ it kindly of you if you would answer my letter; ~ s.th. ill *(resent it)*; he took it ill that I ... (→ ill *adj/adv* 1); ~ it / things easy (→ easy *adj/adv* 4); ~ s.o. / a remark / a suggestion / one's work seriously; he took it hard *(was intensely hurt)* that, when he had done so much for his uncle, he received nothing under his will; although she kept calm, she took his death hard; I won't ~ it *(such treatment)* from you; he will ~ no nonsense; he will not ~ this treatment; he can't ~ a joke; ~ criticism / punishment.
(10c *undergo*) ~ a heat treatment; ~ an examination (at the age of 15); ~ a / one's degree; ~ one's doctor's degree / a doctorate (→ degree *n* 8).
(10d *be given, granted*) ~ (the) first prize; ~ third place in a competition / race; ~ (holy) orders *(become a priest)*; ~ the veil *(become a nun)*; he ~s £40 a week; he ~s little by this move; ~ precedence of / over s.o.; he soon took rank as a leading attorney (→ rank *n* 3b).
(10e *subscribe to*) ~ a newspaper / magazine; do you ~ Punch?
(10f *of things; assume; accept*)
~ (definite) shape / form; the plans for the expedition are now ~ing shape / form; the problem now ~s the form of a quadratic equation; the sandwich ~s its name from an earl who invented it; the book ~s its title from Dante; s.th. ~s its colour / quality from s.th.; cotton does not ~ dyes well; parchment will not ~ ink; this table won't ~ a polish; this table could ~ *(needs)* a polish; ~ fire *(be ignited)*; the car ~s six people comfortably; ~ water (→ water *n* 1b).
(11 *take away, often with* from, off, out of) ~ 13 from 20; who has ~n my book? he took an apple from his pocket / money from the till / the baby out of the pram; ~ the book from a shelf; who has ~n the book from the library? I wish you wouldn't ~ my bicycle; a thief took the money; the flood took many families; ~ s.o.'s life; he took his own life; the sunlight

has ~n the colour from the material; he's always ~n other people's ideas; this line is ~n from Virgil; he has ~n all his motifs from Shakespeare; ~ one's material direct from life; he took whole passages straight from Dickens; ~ a picture off the wall / the washing off the line / the lid off the pot / the cream off the milk; they took his money off him *(robbed him)*; the crew were ~n off the wrecked ship; he was ~n off the night shift; ~ 10 per cent off the list price; I wonder what ~s his mind / attention off his work; ~ s.o.'s mind off his worries; he never took his eyes off me; ~ the pins out of one's hair; ~ (all) the fun out of (a story / *etc*); □ ~ the biscuit / cake *(surpass all others; of bad qualities)*: for sheer impudence he ~s the cake; his arrogance ~s the cake / biscuit.

(12 *eat, drink*)
~ breakfast / a meal; they always ~ a late dinner; a heavy meal should not be ~n just before going to bed; will you ~ soup? do you ~ tea or coffee? ~ a glass of milk; some people ~ sugar with porridge, others salt; ~ sugar in one's coffee; he ~s too much alcohol; ~ a medicine / tonic; ~ drugs / stimulants / poison / ether before an operation / snuff; ~ one pill three times a day *(prescription)*.

(13 *contract, suffer*)
~ a (bad) cold / (a) fever; be careful not to ~ cold; I took cold over the weekend; I took a chill; he took no hurt - he fell soft; he was ~n ill / *(inform)* bad (with malaria); he took ill *(inform)* on Thursday and by Sunday he was dead (→ 10b); be ~n with a violent pain / a fit of coughing; □ ~ a knock *(suffer a setback)*: the economy of the country has certainly ~n a knock this year; the team took a beating; he took a beating on the stock market.

(14 *attract, captivate*) your hat ~s my fancy (→ 17); the pretty ribbon took her eye; the urgent voice took his attention; he was much ~n with / by her manners / naïveté; she was ~n with the house on sight; ~ one's readers with one.

(15 a *photograph*) the photographer took us sitting down; he took a film of the children; ~ him in cap and gown. (15b *be a subject for photography*) she does not ~ well; she ~s badly.

(16 *measure, record*) ~ s.o.'s height / pulse / temperature; ~ soundings / a seismographic reading; the constable took the number of the car.

(17 *take + abstract obj, in alphabetical order according to noun object*)
~ account of s.th. (→ account *n* 4); ~ (a mean) advantage of s.o.; don't ~ advantage of his youth (→ advantage 2); I hope you didn't ~ alarm at the news; ~ the blame for s.th. one didn't do; she took the blame for his failure (→ blame *n* 1, 2); ~ care (with one's work / when crossing the road / that one ...; (→ care *n* 1); ~ care of s.o./ s.th. (→ care *n* 1); ~ one's chance of (losing the money; → chance *n* 4); ~ charge of s.o./ s.th. (→ charge *n* 6); you can ~ comfort in the fact that you aren't the only one to fail (→ comfort *n* 1); the sergeant took command of the company when its commander was killed (→ command *n* 2); he took consolation in the fact that he ...; ~ control of the situation; the co-pilot took control of the plane when the first pilot collapsed; ~ counsel (before doing s.th.); we took courage from the improvement in the patient's condition (→ courage); ~ cover (→ cover *n* 4); ~ credit for s.th. one / s.o. else has done; ~ a decision; the child ~s delight in being naughty; he took the direction of the organization on the death of Mr N.; ~ a (firm) dislike to s.o.; ~ one's ease *(relaxation)*: she took her ease on Sunday; ~ effect (→ effect *n* 1); ~ exception to s.th. *(object to it)*; they have ~n a fancy to their young niece / doing their own weaving (→ 14; → fancy *n* 3); ~ fright at s.th. (→ fright *n* 1); ~ heart *(gain confidence, courage)*: she took heart from the improvement in the child's health; ~ no heed of what people say; ~ hold of (s.o.'s hand / *etc*); ~ the initiative; ~ (an) interest in s.th. (→ interest *n* 1); ~ leave of one's senses (→ 7; → leave *n* 2); I must ~ leave to differ; another matter on which I ~ leave to have my doubts (→ leave *n* 3); ~ the liberty of doing s.th. (→ liberty 2); ~ a liking to s.o./ s.th.; ~ note of (a warning / *etc*); ~ note that we ...; ~ note of how he does it; he took little / careful note of what was going on; ~ (no) notice of (s.o.'s remarks / the instructions / the fire alarm / *etc*; small children like to be ~n notice of; a baby begins to ~ notice at quite an early age (→ notice *n* 3); ~ offence (→ offence *n* 4); ~ the opportunity to do s.th.; ~ every / an / the opportunity of doing s.th. (→ opportunity); ~ one's origin from s.th.; ~ pains (→ pain *n* 4); ~ part in s.th. (→ part *n* 8); he took his bro-

ther's part / part with his brother (in the argument) (→ part *n* 9); ~ pity on s.o. (→ pity *n* 1); ~ place (→ place *n* 2) ~ (a) pleasure in (contradicting / keeping one's house clean / *etc*; (→ pleasure 1,2); ~ possession of s.th.; I ~ pride in my work (→ pride *n* 1); ~ refuge / shelter (from the rain); ~ responsibility (→ responsibility 1); ~ revenge on s.o. for s.th. (→ revenge 1); ~ a risk / risks (→ risk *n*); where does this river ~ rise *(begin)*? plants / principles ~ root (→ root *n* 1); ~ satisfaction in doing s.th.; ~ sides / s.o.'s side (→ side *n* 9); I ~ my stand upon sound precedents; ~ stock (→ stock *n* 1); ~ trouble (→ trouble *n* 5); ~ one's turn; ~ turns (→ turn *n* 6); ~ umbrage *(offence)* (at the slightest provocation / *etc*); ~ a different / poor / *etc* view of s.o./ s.th. (→ view *n* 6); it's a ridiculous viewpoint to ~; he took the easy way out of the difficulty; you should ~ a warning from what happened to me.

(18 *be effective*)
the vaccine / my vaccination didn't ~ the first time; a plant ~s *(germinates)*; a graft ~s; paint will not ~ on a greasy surface; the fire took with only one match; the play didn't ~ well *(wasn't liked by the audience)* in the provinces; do you think this play will ~? watch the people to see how my speech ~s; there's one actor who took with the public; the novel / exhibition did not ~.

(19 *understand, interpret*)
I don't ~ you - could you explain again, please? how do you ~ that remark? you must not ~ his remark as an insult; I ~ your meaning; do you ~ my meaning, sir? how would you ~ this passage / word? I ~ it (that) (we are to wait here / you hold a similar view / *etc*); we can ~ it as agreed that you ...; if we ~ him correctly; I ~ it from your silence (that) you agree with us.

(20 *take + obj + inf: consider*)
I took the figure to be an 8; we took him to be intelligent / him to be a fool; I ~ this to be ironical / right / *etc*; how old would you ~ him to be? can I ~ that news to be official? he took that remark to be a high compliment / to mean he wasn't wanted.

(21a *require*)
the machine ~s a lot of room; this car ~s a great deal of oil; the climb took all our strength; s.th. ~s a great deal of courage; his hobby ~s most of his spare time; this work will ~ time *(much time)*; don't ~ too long *(hurry up)*; □ ~ s.o. all one's time *(be only just possible for one)*: it ~s me all my time to pay the rent; it took him all his time to keep his temper; what size (of shoes / *etc*) do you ~? I ~ size forty; this verb ~s an object / the dative / the following construction.

(21b *take + obj + inf: require*)
it took two men to lift the bed; how much cloth will it ~ to make an overcroat? it ~s three eggs to make this cake; it ~s time to do such a translation; he took only ten minutes to solve the problem; it'll only ~ me twenty minutes to dress; it'll ~ you longer to dress than me; it ~s skill / ability / courage to do that; it took nerve to be cheerful in that situation; it ~s two to make a quarrel; it ~s a brave man to do that; it ~s a poet to translate Homer.

(21c *take + gerund: require*)
his story ~s a lot of believing *(is difficult to believe)*; that record ~s some beating; this document ~s some understanding; he took a lot of convincing; this translation ~s a lot of doing.

(22 *idioms with adv phrases*)
(22a *take + obj + adv phrase*) ~ the bull by the horns; ~ time by the forelock; ~ a warning / s.o.'s words to heart; ~ one's misfortunes / small troubles to heart *(worry about them)*; ~ a leaf out of s.o.'s book *(follow his example)*; ~ a leap in the dark; ~ one's life in one's hand(s) *(go alone into great danger)*; ~ the mickey out of s.o. *(inform: make him look foolish)*; ~ the reins in one's hands; ~ a burden / responsibility off s.o.'s shoulders; ~ the wind out of s.o.'s sails (→ wind *n* 1b); as soon as we go on a holiday, our money seems to ~ wings (to itself); ~ the word(s) out of s.o.'s mouth (→ mouth *n* 1); ~ a joke too far.

(22b *take ~ s.o./ s.th. + adv phrase*) ~ s.th. into account (→ account *n* 4); ~ s.o. in the act; ~ s.th. on the chin *(bravely)*; ~ s.o. into one's confidence; ~ s.th. into consideration (→ consideration 1); ~ s.o. at a disadvantage; ~ s.o. by the hand *(help, encourage)*; ~ o.s. in hand *(pull o.s. together)*; ~ s.th. in hand *(start dealing with s.th.)*; ~ s.o. in hand *(start reforming)*; that boy wants ~ing in hand; ~ s.o. to heart *(become very fond of him)*; ~ s.th. to heart *(be much affected by it)*; ~ s.th. in good / bad part (→ part *n* 10); ~ s.o. for a ride *(deceive him)*; ~ s.th. in one's stride *(without special exertion)*; ~ s.o./ s.th. by surprise (→ surprise *n* 1); ~ to pieces *(dismantle)*: how do I ~ this machine / clock / rifle / *etc* to pieces? ~ s.o. to task (for doing s.th.; → task); ~ s.th. on trust; ~ s.o. under one's wing; ~ s.o. at his word (→ word *n* 2a).

(22c *take + it + adv phrase*)

~ it into one's head *(inform: get an idea)*: she suddenly took it into her head to go and see her aunt; he took it into his head that I was secretly opposing him; ~ it out of s.o. *(exhaust; take revenge on the undeserving)*: this hot weather ~s it out of me; a long illness ~s it out of you; he can't tell the manager off, so he ~s it out of/on the office boy; ~ it upon oneself *(without proper authorization)* to do s.th.

(23 *take after: resemble*) the younger child took after her mother; he is very frugal - he ~s after his father in that respect.

(24 *take for: assume (falsely) to be*) I ~ him for an experienced administrator; I took it for the truth; I took you for my cousin; ~ s.o. for a fool; what do you ~ me for? we saw something dash across the road - at first we took it for a dog; ~ opinion for fact; □ ~ for granted *(as a fact)*: all particulars should be carefully checked - nothing should be ~n for granted; I ~ it for granted that you will be coming to the meeting; we in Britain tend to ~ our liberties for granted.

(25 *take from: diminish*) Shelley may not have lived a blameless life, but that does not ~ from his achievement as a poet.

(26a *take to: go*) we are ~ing to the woods for peace and quiet; then we all took to the boats; ~ to one's bed (at the slightest indisposition); □ ~ to one's legs / heels *(inform: run away)* (26b *take to: form a bad habit, etc*) ~ to drink / gambling / theft / (a life of) crime; he has recently ~n to staying in bed of a Sunday morning; she took to nagging to get her own way. (26c *take to: embark on an activity*) after a few years he abandoned journalism and took to writing novels.

(26d *take to: develop a fondness, have a talent for*) he took to mathematics as a duck ~s to water; she took to French as though it had been her native language. (26e *take to: get to like*) I don't think I could ever ~ to what is called 'modern' poetry; I took to him immediately we met; men who do not ~ kindly to controls of any sort.

take aback they were ~n ~ *(unpleasantly surprised)* by what they saw / at seeing him now; the revelation of the real extent of the company's losses took the meeting ~.

take along I took my sister ~ to the dance.

take amiss ~ ~ *(resent)* criticism / advice / remarks / conduct; his joke was ~n ~ by some of the company.

take apart (1) he took me ~ in order to speak to me alone. (2) this crib ~s ~ for easy storage. (3 *inform: scold, thrash severely*) he virtually took his chauffeur ~ for not washing the car; the cat almost took that mangy dog ~.

take away (1) they took the rubbish ~; he has locked the room and ~n the key ~. (2) the general had his command ~n ~.

take back (1 *get back*) ~ ~ one's lawn-mower / *etc* (2 *return*) it was defective, and so she took it ~ to the shop; □ ~ the can ~ *(inform: answer for others' misdeeds)* (3) she said she would never ~ him ~ again; shopkeepers will not usually ~ ~ goods after they have been paid for. (4) he took ~ his accusation against her; ~ ~ one's statement (5) the book ~s us ~ to the old days.

take down (1) ~ ~ a building / a crane / the scaffolding round a building (2) he reached up to the third shelf of the bookcase and took ~ a dictionary; ~ ~ the curtains (3) ~ s.th. ~ (from dictation) (4) he took me ~ *(inform: cheated)* over that bargain. (5) a person who is always trying to ~ other people ~ *(humiliate)* gets himself disliked; this conceited fellow wants ~ing ~ a peg or two.

take in (1) ~ a lady in to dinner (2) do you ~ in summer visitors (→ take *vt* 10a)? after the death of her husband she had to ~ in boarders; they took in a hungry cat / a refugee; she ~s in washing / sewing. (3) ~ in a newspaper / magazine (→ take *vt* 10e) (4) ~ the trousers in a bit; it will be a perfect fit if it is ~n in slightly.

(5) Outer London now ~s in parts of several counties; the survey ~s in all the schools in this district. (5a *include in a visit, go to*) he is ~ing in the sights of ...; ~ in a film / play; we took in the Louvre on our weekend in Paris. (6 *understand*) he seemed unable to ~ in what I was saying; she could not ~ in all she was taught; his mind could not ~ in so many details; at first he didn't ~ in the seriousness of the accident. (7 *deceive*) we were completely ~n in by his story; she took them

in with her lies; he'll ~ you in if he gets the chance.

take off (1a) ~ ~ one's coat; ~ one's hat ~ *(greet)*; ~ ~ one's moustache; ~ ~ *(lift)* the receiver; *(fig)* ~ ~ one's hat to s.o. (1b) he had his leg ~n ~. (1c) a little vinegar will ~ ~ the oily taste. (2) the play was ~n ~ last week; the early morning train will be ~n ~ next month; the shopkeeper took several dollars ~ as he knew I was a good customer. (3) the child was ~n ~ by kidnappers; he was ~n ~ to prison; she took me ~ to see her garden; ~ o.s. ~ *(go away; anger is suggested)*: with this final remark, he took himself ~ in a fit of temper.
(4) millions were ~n ~ by the Black Plague. (5a) the plane took ~ / we took ~ from Gatwick at 10.30. (5b) he took ~ *(left)* for California. (6 *imitate*) several of the masters were ~n ~ by the pupils in their end-of-term show; the comedian took ~ several well-known people.

take on (1) the bus stopped to ~ on some children. (2a) ~ on an applicant / piece of work / task / job / bet; ~ s.o. on as an assistant (2b *accept as opponent*) I'm not going to ~ on a beginner; I can ~ him on any time at swimming; he's ready to ~ on all comers. (3) the chameleon can ~ on the colours of its background; ~ on appearance / patina / an attitude / a tone / *etc*; the trees ~ on autumn tints; this disease took on an epidemic character; his eyes took on a glazed expression; his voice took on a tender tone; ~ on importance (4) if this idea ~s on we shall make quite a lot of money out of it; the new style in men's suits did not ~ on. (5a *give expression to anger*) the indignant passenger took on about the rudeness of bus conductors till he was almost red in the face; there's no need to ~ on so. (5b *give expression to grief*) we all sympathize with your loss, but don't ~ on so - that won't help matters.

take out (1a) ~ ~ a handkerchief / *etc*; the whole motor can be ~n ~ for cleaning. (1b) ~ s.o.'s tonsils / appendix ~; how many teeth did the dentist ~ ~? (2) ~ ~ an ink-stain from a dress; the colour was ~n ~ of the curtains by the strong sunlight. (3) ~ the cows ~ to pasture; she has ~n the dog ~ for a walk; ~ a girl ~ (for / to dinner) (4 *set out*) they took ~ for the nearest beach. (5) ~ ~ an insurance policy / patent / licence / summons against s.o. (6) ~ a debt ~ in goods / services *(accept the latter in payment of the debt)*.

take over (1) he took me ~ to the island in his boat. (2) ~ ~ the chairmanship / responsibility / *etc*; many small firms have recently been ~n ~ by larger ones; ~ ~ a debt / lease (3) the new headmaster ~s ~ on September 1st.

take up (1) blotting-paper ~s up ink. (2a) ~ up a dropped stitch; he took up the fallen leaves with a rake; ~ it up with the tongs; ~ up floorboards / a carpet; taxis may ~ up passengers anywhere; ~ up a child in one's arms; he was ~n up *(arrested)* by the police for drunkenness last night; ~ s.o. up short *(interrupt abruptly)*; ~ up arms (against s.o.) *(get ready to fight; also fig)*; ~ up one's pen (to write); ~ up a collection (during a meeting) *(carry it out)* (2b) ~ up *(make shorter)* a dress / *etc* (2c) ~ up the reins of government; ~ up the cause of the homeless (3) this sideboard ~s up too much room; all the time of the meeting was ~n up with the discussion of three items. (4 *resume*) I took up (the story) where I had left off. (5a) ~ up a position / office / profession; ~ up one's residence at York; I ~ up my new post on March 1st; when he left school he took up journalism; ~ up a hobby / the study of Russian / fencing; ~ up work / a discussion (5b) ~ up a suggestion / proposal / idea (5c *adopt as protégé*) he used to ~ up any promising young writer. (6a) ~ up a threatening attitude; ~ up a challenge / a quarrel / the gauntlet (6b) ~ s.o. up on s.th. *(challenge him)*; I should like to ~ you up on the matter of overtime payment; ~ s.o. up on his remark; the author ~s up his critics in the preface of his latest book. (6c) he took the matter up *(pursued it)* with the director. (7 *take up with: keep company with*) she took up with the boy after he had saved her life; he took up with a girl of whom his family disapproved.

talk *n* (1a) have a little ~; have a ~ on / about s.th.; have a ~ to / with s.o.; I want a ~ with you; turn the ~ to another subject; informal / idle / dull / rambling / dirty / small *(trivial)* / tall *(boastful)* / instructive / *etc* ~ (1b *way of talking*) s.o.'s loose / tall (→ 1) / *etc* ~; use low *(vulgar)* ~; *a halting, lisping* ~ (2 *informal lecture*) he gave a ~ to the club on his travels; he broadcasts a weekly ~ called ... (3 *conference*) they held a series of ~s in an attempt to solve the problem; round-table / high-level / summit ~s; the ministers met for ~s on the government crisis. (4 *rumour*) there is a lot of ~ going around about her; there is ~ that you are going to sell your house; there is ~ of difficulties. (5 *the subject of conversation*) s.o./ s.th. is the ~ of the town; the wedding was the ~ of the day / neighbourhood. (6 *empty words*) that's just a lot of ~; it will end in ~; there's too much ~ and not enough work.

talk *vi* (1a) this parrot can ~; learn to ~; they are still ~ing in the conference room. (1b *gossip*) people will ~; if you do that, you will get ~ed about. (2a) ~ to / *(less common)* with s.o.; I might as well ~ to myself *(nobody is listening)*; ~ about / *(less common)* of s.th.; ~ing of *(being on the subject of)* test matches, who won the last? ~ very softly / convincingly / sensibly / *etc*; ~ big *(inform: boastfully)*; he ~s large but works not at all; ~ into a microphone; ~ over s.o.'s head / over the heads of one's audience (2b *give a lecture*) the professor ~ed on a difficult subject. (2c *talk of: mention as a possible course*) he ~s of retiring / a holiday / legal proceedings (2d *talk to: admonish*) I'll ~ to him. - *vt* (3a) ~ business / football / politics / philosophy / *etc*; ~ shop (→ shop *n* 1); ~ war (3b) ~ sense / nonsense (3c) ~ French / *etc*; ~ the way the English do (4 *bring into a condition by talking*) ~ o.s. hoarse; ~ s.o. into / out of doing s.th.; he can ~ me to sleep. (5 *idioms*) ~ nineteen to the dozen / one's head off / the leg off an iron pot / the hind leg off a donkey / a donkey's hind leg off *(go on ~ing for a long time)*; not ~ the same language; ~ o.s. out of s.th. *(argue one's way out of an awkward situation)*; ~ through / out of one's hat *(inform: talk nonsense)*.

talk back (1 *reply impertinently*) don't ~ ~ to your elders; he was punished for ~ing ~ to his mother. (2 *fig: respond belligerently*) the big guns ~ed ~ to the machine gun fire.

talk down (1) ~ s.o. ~ *(reduce to silence by speaking loudly)* (2) ~ ~ to s.o. *(speak condescendingly to)*: juvenile audiences do not like to feel that they are being ~ed ~ to.

talk over (1) ~ s.th. ~ *(discuss it)*: let's talk the matter ~; I won't have you ~ing me ~ with John. (2) ~ s.o. ~ *(persuade to change his mind)*: he is an expert at ~ing people ~ to his views.

talk round she sounded adamant over the phone, but I may still be able to ~ her ~ *(persuade her)*.

talk up (1 *AE speak favourably of; promote*) he has been ~ing up his proposals for a month now; ~ up a candidate (for election) (2 *speak loudly and clearly*) you are going to have to learn to ~ up without shouting; ~ up so that the examiner won't think you're afraid or unsure.

task *n* a light / difficult / burdensome / laborious / gigantic / herculean / monumental / thankless / ugly / irksome / *etc* ~; perform / carry out / fulfil / complete a / one's ~; set s.o. a ~; be equal to / able to cope with one's ~; it is the ~ of parents to help ...; the historical ~ of the white races; □ take s.o. to ~ (for / about s.th.) *(scold)*: the teacher took them to ~ for being noisy in her absence; he has been taken to ~ more than once about his carelessness.

taste *n* (1) the food has a fine / pleasant / nice / bad / nasty / acid / foul / mouldy / pungent / medicinal / not much / *etc* ~; the white of an egg has no ~; I don't like the ~ of game; it has a ~ of lemon / salt / fish / *etc*; □ leave a bad / nasty ~ in the mouth *(make one feel disgusted)* (2 *sense by which flavour is known*) a cold dulls one's ~; good cooks have a keen sense of ~. (3) won't you have a ~ of this cake / brandy / *etc*? *(fig)* give him a ~ of the whip! (4 *liking, preference*) add pepper / salt to ~ *(recipe)*; he has a ~ for good food / music / French literature / adventure; he has a ~ for sweet things / a sweet ~; an unnatural ~ for violence; he is gradually acquiring a ~ for it; he got into the ~ of it *(began to like it)*; satisfy the most discriminating ~; ~s differ; there is no accounting for ~(s); that is not (at all) to my ~; it is quite to my ~. (5 *ability to enjoy, judge beauty, etc*) she shows (great / good / bad / no) ~; he has good ~ in clothes / furniture / art; his ~ in women is poor; a cultivated ~ in poetry; a nice / morbid ~; artistic / sophisticated / ultramodern ~; he has exquisite ~; he is a man of ~; he is a critic without ~; it is composed in admirable ~; the remark / his behaviour was in good / in bad / in the worst possible ~; she was dressed with / in good ~.

taste *vt* (1) ~ this cheese - it's delicious; do ~ this wine! (2) can you ~ anything strange in this soup? I ~ garlic in it; you could ~ the rum in the cake; I have a bad cold and cannot ~ (anything). (3 *eat a little of*) he hadn't ~d food for three days; she barely ~d her dinner. (4 *experience*) ~ (the joys of) freedom; he has never ~d success; ~ the rigours of an Arctic winter; these young men who had only begun to ~ life. - *vi* (5) this milk ~s sour; the soup ~s good / sweet / bitter / too much of onions. (6a) Susan ~d slyly of the cake. (6b) the story ~s of treason.

teach *vt* (1) ~ s.o. / a class / a school; ~ dogs (2) ~ a subject / lesson; he ~es English / geometry / writing / *etc*; he ~es (the boys) French / French to the boys; he ~es the boys (how) to swim / swimming; he was taught French / (how) to ride / riding; ~ o.s. / s.th. (3a) ~ s.o. manners / obedience / a lesson *(fig) / etc*; I'll ~ you what's what! I'll ~ you to steal my apples *(thrash you so you won't steal them).* (3b) will nothing ~ you to be careful? the accident taught me to drive slowly ; suffering has taught me / ~es patience. - *vi* (4) she taught for many years in our local school.

tear *vt* (1a) ~ a piece of cloth; the hungry dog tore the meat with its teeth; ~ s.th. in two / pieces; ~ s.th. to pieces *(also fig: criticize sharply)*; she tore her dress on a nail. (1b) ~ a hole in s.th.; the loose nail tore a bad gash in his leg. (1c *remove by ~ing*) ~ a page out of a book / a sheet of a pad / a letter from its envelope; the wind tore his cap off / from his head; he tore the book from his hands. (2 *injure*) the teeth of the saw tore his leg; he tore his hand on a nail. (3) the grief ~s his heart; she was torn as to what she ought to do; it tore his heart to leave the children. (4 *divide into opposing groups*) the nation was torn by dissension; a country torn by civil war (5) he was unable to ~ himself from the place. - *vi* (6a) the paper tore when the parcel fell; her dress tore on a nail; the cobweb ~s at a touch. (6b) paper ~s easily. (7) he tore at the knot / the rope which bound him; the wind tore at the newly planted saplings. (8a *inform: move with great haste*) the two boys tore down the street; the children tore out of school; the car tore up the road; he tore up the stairs two steps at a time. (8b *tear into: attack physically or verbally*) he tore into the food with a will; she tore into him for being late for dinner.

tear apart (1) ~ a book / *etc* ~ (2) industrial conflict will ~ society ~.

tear away (1) the flood / avalanche has torn ~ everything. (2) she could not ~ herself ~ from the scene.

tear down (1) ~ a notice ~; he tore the picture ~ off / from the wall (2) ~ ~ a building.

tear off ~ ~ buttons / one's clothes.

tear out ~ ~ hair / a page / *etc.*

tear up (1) ~ a tree up; ~ up a plant (by the roots) (2) ~ a letter up (3) ~ up a contract / treaty *(fig).*

tell *vt* (1a) ~ me your name / where you live / what happened / why you ...; ~ a secret / lie / fib / falsehood; ~ the facts; ~ s.o. his fortune / future; I will ~ you my opinion; □ ~ me another (one) / that to the Marines *(I don't believe it)*; ~ s.o. straight that he ...; ~ s.o. to his face what one thinks; she told him flat(ly) that she wouldn't go; to ~ the truth, he isn't here; to ~ you the honest truth, this is all I know; ~ s.o. some home *(unpleasant)* truths; you're ~ing me *(inform: I know what you say is true; I don't believe you are serious).* (1b *assure*) I won't, I ~ you! it's pretty hard work, I can ~ you; I'm ~ing you *(inform: what I say is correct)* (1c *say positively*) there's no ~ing what may happen; who can ~ what tomorrow will bring? (2) ~ a story (to a child); I could ~ a tale of it; ~ s.th. in detail / convincingly / briefly / skilfully / *etc*; ~ us about your youth; I shall ~ you all about it later; I could probably have helped you, if only you had told me of it; the old house could ~ a great deal; the book / picture ~s how ...; don't ~ me tales / stories! ~ tales behind s.o.'s back; ~ tales (out of school) (3 *order*) ~ him to stop / leave / *etc*; do as you are told; don't ~ me what to do. (4 *distinguish, decide*) can you ~ who that is over there? one cannot ~ whether this manuscript is genuine or not; she can't ~ which is best; she could not ~ him by his voice; it is difficult to ~ them apart; ~ the time (5 *count*) ~ the cattle in a herd; a monk ~ing his beads; □ all told *(altogether)*: all told, 400 guests came.
- *vi* (6) he told of his many misfortunes. (7 *say positively*) you never can ~ *(appear-*

ances often deceive us) (8 *reveal*) your actions ~ more than your words; the ruined temples told of an ancient culture. (8a *reveal s.th. secret*) you won't ~, will you? the boy told on his naughty sister. (9 *be effective*) my scolding must have told because he has been good ever since; a contest in which every stroke ~s; every blow told; there are signs that the strain ~s and liver troubles occur; the boxer's experience told in his favour; age is beginning to ~ upon me; the strain was ~ing on his health; a ~ing argument.

tell off (1) several men were told ~ *(separated from the others and assigned)* for this task / to do this work. (2 *inform: scold*) it is about time that someone told him ~ (for his rudeness).

temper *n* (1 a) be in / have a gay / cheerful / serene / conciliatory / even / calm / sweet / fiery / inflammable / hot / wild / ugly / violent / *etc* ~; lose one's ~ *(become angry)*; keep / control one's ~; be out of ~ *(angry)* with s.o.; put s.o. in a bad / put s.o. out of ~ *(irritate him)* (1b *temper without adj: bad temper, rage*) a fit of ~; she has a ~; John is in a ~! she flies / gets into a ~ when she is contradicted. (2 *degree of hardness, etc*) the ~ of the steel in a blade.

term *n* (1a *period of time*) a ~ of ten years; a ~ of office / imprisonment; sign a contract for a three-year ~ (1 b *part of the academic year*) spring / summer / Michaelmas / *etc* ~ (1c *end of a period*) s.th. comes to its ~; he was born before ~. (2 *terms: requirements as to conditions, price, etc*) the ~s of surrender; the ~s of an agreement / sale; inquire about the ~s *(prices)* for a stay at a hotel; reasonable ~s; □ bring s.o. to ~s *(persuade him to enter into an agreement)*; □ come to / make ~s (with s.o) *(arrive at an agreement)*.
(3 *terms: relations*) be on good / bad ~s with s.o.; we are not on speaking ~s with him. (4 *expression*) a technical / medical / scientific / *etc* ~; the legal ~s in a document; law / golf / sports / *etc* ~s (5 *terms: language of a specified sort*) he spoke to me in ~s of reproach / endearment; in vague / injurious / the most flattering / *etc* ~s; in ~s of *(with reference to)*: our holiday was expensive in ~s of money, but in ~s of pleasure it was a bargain.

test *n* (1) misfortune is often a ~ of a man's character; success is not always a fair ~; s.th. has (with)stood the ~ of time; the race was an endurance ~ for both driver and car; the battery is on ~ at the moment; these steep hills will certainly put our car to the ~; put s.o.'s courage / loyalty to the ~ (2) a written / oral ~; a placement / aptitude / efficiency / intelligence ~; an eye ~; take a driving ~.

test *vt* (1) misfortunes ~ a person's character. (2a) ~ a student('s abilities / skill / knowledge) / s.o.'s hearing / *etc* (2b) ~ a substance chemically ; ~ ore for gold; have one's eyesight ~ed; a machine / bridge / weight / measure / *etc* must be ~ed before being actually used; a well-~ed remedy.

thick *adj/ adv* (1a) a ~ slice of bread / thread / book / carpet / coat / board / branch / tree-trunk / log / wall; ~ paper / china / lips / legs / snow-flakes / raindrops; put paint on ~ly; don't spread the butter too ~(ly); □ lay it on ~ (→ lay on 1); □ have a ~ skin / hide *(be insensitive)*; be ~-skinned; □ a bit ~ *(inform: hard to bear; unreasonable)*: three weeks of rain is a bit ~; they thought it a bit ~ when he called himself a genius. (1b) a board two inches ~; how ~ is the ice? (1c *broad*) a ~ line; ~ print (2 *not watery*) ~ syrup / condensed milk / ink / sauce / soup / blood (→ blood *n* 4); ~ , muddy water; the juice ran ~ly. (3 *close togehter; dense*) ~ hair / underbrush; the ~ woods; a ~ crowd; the roses grew ~ along the path; blows came / fell ~ and fast; the questions came ~ on one another; a ~ly populated region (4 *of vapour, gas, etc: dense*) ~ fog / mist / darkness; a ~ cloud; the weather was ~ *(foggy)* and drizzly; the air was so ~ we could scarcely breathe. (5 *thick with: filled, covered*) the floor was ~ with dust; we walked through a field ~ with daisies; the air was ~ with dust / smoke / snow (6a *hoarse*) a ~ voice (6b *indistinct*) the patient's speech is still quite ~; he has a ~ *(marked)* German accent. (7 *inform: intimate*) your son seems very ~ with that ginger-headed boy; you two are very ~; they are as ~ as thieves. (8 *inform: stupid*) he can handle routine tasks, but he's rather ~.

thin *adj* (1a) a ~ slice of bread / sheet of paper / thread / book / skin / board / wall; ~ ice; ~ clothes; a ~ wire / rope; the ~ places in a dress; spread the butter ~;

slice the ham ~ (1b *narrow*) a ~ line; ~ print (2) a ~ man; ~ legs / fingers; she was very ~ (in the face) after her illness; he's as ~ as a rake / lath. (3 *watery*) a ~ liquid / soup; ~ oil / blood.
(4 *not close together, not dense*) ~ vegetation / population; a ~ beard; his hair is ~ on top; a ~ly populated region; a ~ audience / house (5 *of vapour, gas, etc: not dense*) ~ mist / air (6 *lacking substance, strength*) ~ tea / beer / wine; a ~ voice; the ~ sound of the violins; a ~ smile; a ~ plot / excuse / story / disguise; I find this essay a bit ~; ~ humour; □ have a ~ time *(characterized by lack of money, pleasures, etc)*.

thing *n* (1 *material object*) there was not a ~ in the room; take those ~s off the table; she loves chocolate ~s; a ~ of beauty is a joy for ever; the ~ in itself; □ see ~s *(have hallucinations)*. (2 *s.th. not specified*) what's that ~ he's carrying? the stick had a brass ~ on it; all those ~s on the mantelpiece (3a *things: belongings, utensils, etc: usu pl*) he left his ~s at the station; she didn't have a ~ to wear; I've got my ~s *(clothes)* wet; take off your ~s; I'll wash the breakfast ~s. (4 *things: circumstances in general*) ~s will get better / are going badly; as ~s are, he will ...; that only makes ~s worse; I must think ~s over. (5 *fact, state of affairs*) it is a curious ~; we've got to end this ~ before it gets out of hand; it is a common ~ for a family to have a TV set; a little learning is a dangerous ~; this ~ is none of your business; there's another ~ I want to ask you about; honesty / wine / his death / *etc* is a good ~; □ make a good ~ of *(profit financially by)*: she made a good ~ of her spare-time hobbies; □ taking one ~ with another *(considering the various circumstances)*, I must say ...; □ for one ~ *(one reason is)* I haven't the money, for another I ...; I am / he doesn't look / feel quite the ~ *(quite well)* today.
(6 *things + adj: all that can be so described*) (be interested in) all ~s political / feminine / Russian / foreign / *etc* (7a *action*) what would be the best ~ to do next? do great ~s; we will not do ~s by halves; the proper ~ to do is to apologize for your mistake; do it first ~ *(as early as possible)* in the morning; does the cat have to be let out last ~ at night? he wouldn't do a ~ to help us; the ~ to do in that case is rush to the hospital; it is hardly the *(polite)* ~ to leave an invitation unanswered; that café is the *(fashionable)* ~ now; short skirts are now the ~; it's not quite the ~ to wear such a shirt to a formal dinner. (7b *task, chore*) I've got a lot of ~s to do today. (8 *event*) his death was a horrible ~; all good ~s come in / by threes; with God all ~s are possible; → close *adj* 6; a near ~ *(a narrow escape, of accidents, trains nearly missed, etc)* (9 *s.th. uttered, thought)* the president said some good ~s in his speech; I have just one ~ to say to you. (10 *person, creature*) she's a sweet ~; his daughter's a pretty little ~; poor ~! you silly ~; he's a wicked old ~; dumb ~s *(animals)*; we have a parakeet, but the poor ~ won't make a sound. (11 *the important point*) the ~ is to reach this line with the ball; the ~ is, can we get there in time? (12 *s.th. non-material*) spiritual ~s; ~s of the spirit / mind.

think *vt* 3 - 10; *vi* 1, 2.
The patterns are grouped as follows: ~ + *adj*: 4; ~ + *clause*: 4a, 5-7; ~ + *inf*: 10; ~ + *obj* + *adj, n*: 4b; ~ + *obj* + to be + *adj, n*: 4b; cannot + ~: 6; ~ + prepos: about 8, of 9, to 5.
- *vi* (1 *reason, use the intellect*) I ~, therefore I am; he does not say much, but he ~s a lot; do you ~ in English? ~ logically / independently (2 *turn over in the mind, consider advantages and disadvantages of s.th.*) ~ carefully before you begin; ~ before you speak; act without ~ing; ~ hard; her strange behaviour set me ~ing; ~ aloud *(speak one's ideas as they occur)*; ~ twice *(hesitate)*: I should ~ twice before I entrusted my money to him. - *vt* (3 *conceive*) ~ great / strange / evil thoughts; he says what he ~s; what made you ~ that? the child thought *(meant)* no harm in doing it. (4a *have as a firm conviction*) I ~ she is lying; → 5. (4b *thing + adj, noun*) I ~ him foolish; he ~s himself clever; ~ s.th. necessary / useful / *etc*; he didn't mind washing dishes, but thought it an indignity that he had to wear an apron; ~ o.s. somebody; we have always thought him (to be) a friend; from his photographs you would have thought him extremely handsome; ~ fit *(consider advisable)*: by all means, take a holiday if you ~ fit (→ fit *adj* 2). (5 *have as a tentative opinion, suppose*) I ~ she might refuse; I thought to myself that she ...; she was ~ing (to herself) how strange the

children were; I ~ it is true; "is he here already?" - "I (don't) ~ so"; "do you ~ you could do it?" - "I (should) ~ so"; how old do you ~ he is? I know what you are ~ing, but I am sure you are wrong; you might almost ~ you were in Scotland; I thought I should find her at home; I little thought I should see him again; I ~ I'll go for a swim. (6 *work out by reasoning*) I can't ~ how the story will end / what is best to do / what it could mean (7 *imagine*) I thought I heard a knock; who would have thought it! I had thought I could make money by it; only ~ what might have happened; I thought I wasn't seeing aright; I just can't ~ what to give her for Christmas; I can't ~ what you mean; you can't ~ how glad I am.
(8a *think about: consider*) this matter needs to be thought about most carefully; we shall soon have to ~ about our summer holidays; he thought about taking her to dinner and then the theatre; ~ about s.o.'s suggestion (8b *think about: have an opinion about*) read this letter and tell me what you ~ about it; I don't care what other people ~ about me. (8c *think about: be interested in*) these young girls ~ about nothing but clothes and hairstyles. (8d *think about: reflect upon*) she ~s too much about her troubles; he ~s too much about himself *(worries over his health, etc, too much)* whatever are you ~ing about? (9a *think of: call to mind*) I know the person you mean, but I cannot ~ of his name; the old man thought of his youth. (9b *think of: entertain, form an idea of*) I wouldn't ~ of allowing my children to stay out until this late hour; that's not to be thought of; at one time working-class people would never have thought of the possibility of their sons entering one of the professions; ~ of a number, add 3,...; in those days the Welfare State had not been thought of; John thought of it first; we shall have to ~ of some excuse to give them; you should have thought of that before; what might have happened does not bear ~ing of. (9c *think of: plan vaguely*) we are ~ing of going to Spain for our holiday this year; we are ~ing of moving to another house; ~ of retiring (9d *think of: have an opinion of*) what do you ~ of my new dress? ~ highly of s.o.('s abilities); I don't ~ much of this plan / idea; ~ a lot / little / nothing of s.o./ s.th.; I don't ~ much of him as a teacher; he thought of her as a friend; she thought of golf as a waste of time; he ~s too much of himself *(has too high an opinion of himself)*; he ~s of himself too much *(is too self-centred)*; ~ better of it *(change one's mind)*: he considered emigrating to Canada, but thought better of it; ~ nothing of *(consider lightly)* a 20-mile walk (9e *think of: consider)* I have my wife and family to ~ of; you must ~ of the future; ~ of others first; she ~s of no one but herself; there are a number of things to be thought of before we come to a decision. (10a *think + inf: have the idea of*) I didn't ~ to note down the number of the house; did you ~ to inquire whether there is a dining-car on the train? I never thought to look for the book under the cushions. (10b *think + inf: expect*) I did not ~ / never thought to see you here; he ~s to deceive us. (10c *think + inf: remember*) did you ~ to post that letter? he didn't ~ to lock the door.

think out ~ ~ a plan / scheme (carefully); he has already thought ~ all the details of his speech.

think over ~ ~ a suggestion / proposal / matter.

think up ~ up a (suitable) excuse / scheme / *etc*; can you ~ up an arrangement of furniture for this room? most of his after-dinner stories were thought up on the spur of the moment.

throw *vt* (1a) ~ a ball / rope to s.o.; ~ it to me please; ~ stones at a dog; ~ me an apple; she threw the letter into the stove / her hat on the desk; she threw herself into a chair; ~ s.th. out of the window; the ship was ~n on the coast / rocks; ~ open *(open wide suddenly; also fig)*: ~ open the windows; ~ open a competition; the subject was ~n open for discussion. (1b *put hurriedly*) he threw a log on the fire; she threw some clothes on the boy / a shawl over her shoulders. (1c) the horse threw its rider twice; he easily ~s his antagonists in wrestling; the horse threw a shoe; a snake ~s its skin. (1d) the hose ~s a 20-foot jet; a fire-engine ~s water on a burning building; a cannon ~s a shell. (1e *idioms*) ~ dust in s.o.'s eyes (→ dust); ~ *(BE)* a spanner / *(AE)* a monkey-wrench in(to) the works (→ work *n* 9); ~ a veil over s.th.; ~ cold

water on (a plan, *etc*) *(discourage)*: there would always be someone to ~ cold water on our ambitions; ~ o.s. at s.o.('s head) *(strive to win s.o.'s love)*: she ~s herself at any man who will look at her; ~ o.s. on s.o. *(commit o.s. to s.o.'s generosity, etc)*: he threw himself on the mercy of the court; the members of his wife's family have all ~n themselves on him.
(2) the general threw his reserves into the battle; ~ troops into action; the FBI threw every available agent into the case. (3 *build quickly*) ~ a bridge across a river (4 *shape on a potter's wheel*) he threw (the clay into) a vase. (5 *play*) ~ a card / an ace / three sixes; ~ dice (6 *of animals: give birth to*) ~ young (7) ~ *(inform: give)* a party (8) ~ *(inform: have)* a fit (of anger) (9) that lamp ~s a poor light; ~ a shadow (on s.th.; *also fig*); he threw an angry look at me; ~ a glance at s.th.; *(fig)* this discovery ~s new light on the matter (→ light[1] *n* 4) (10 *bring to bear*) ~ all your energy into your work; ~ o.s. into s.th. *(engage in with energy)*: she threw herself into making costumes for her daughter's party. (11 *put in a particular state, etc*) ~ things / a room into disorder; ~ everything into (complete) confusion; the party threw the household into a turmoil; ~ a man into prison / out of work; he threw his son out of the house; the pupil was ~n out of (the) school; ~ s.o. (*AE* for a loss) *(cause a setback)*: he was thrown (for a loss) by the difficult examination questions; it really threw me (for a loss) when I heard that she had married secretly. (12 *put into operation*) ~ a(n electric) switch; he threw a switch and flooded the stage with light; ~ a car into gear; he threw the car into first / reverse (gear) and raced out of the garage. (13 *inform: lose on purpose*) he was accused of ~ing the fight; he threw the fight in the fifth round.

throw about (1) the children were ~ing cushions ~; ~ paper ~; ~ one's arms ~ (2) ~ one's money ~ (3) ~ one's weight ~ (→ weight *n* 6).

throw away (1) ~ paper / *etc* ~ (2) you must not ~ ~ your money like this. (3 *fail to use*) ~ ~ a chance / advantage / opportunity; he threw ~ a college education and a professional career.

throw back (1) ~ ~ a ball; he threw his head ~. (2 *reflect*) ~ ~ light / heat (3) his illness threw him ~ a year at school.

throw down he threw ~ the book in disgust; ~ s.o. ~; ~ s.th. ~ to s.o.; he threw himself ~ on the ground when he saw that the man had a gun; ~ o.s. ~ before / in front of the altar; □ ~ ~ the gauntlet / glove to s.o. *(challenge to fight)*.

throw in (1) ~ in (the ball) *(football)*; she switched on the washing-machine and threw the dirty clothes in □ ~ in the sponge (→ throw up 1); ~ in the towel *(inform: admit failure; give up)* (2) ~ in the clutch of a car (3) the greengrocer threw in two extra apples; they ~ in breakfast with the room. (4) ~ in a remark; the chairman threw in an amusing anecdote to relieve the tension; □ ~ in one's lot with (a party / group) *(decide to share the fortunes of)*.

throw off (1a) ~ ~ the mask / one's overcoat (1b) ~ ~ a pursuer (2) ~ ~ undesirable acquaintances; ~ ~ a vice; ~ ~ fear; ~ ~ a / one's cold; ~ ~ one's mask (3 *say, write, perform with ease*) he threw ~ an article for me; ~ ~ lines of verse; the entertainer threw ~ a few songs and jokes to begin the show. (4 *mislead, confuse*) his air of innocence threw them ~; ~n ~ by jeers, she forgot her lines.

throw out (1) he threw his chest ~. (2) ~ ~ useless equipment; ~ ~ a customer; he has been ~n ~ for incompetence; he was ~n ~ (of the club); □ ~ ~ the baby with the bath water *(reject the essential along with the non-essential)* (3 *build as an addition*) ~ ~ a new wing (to a hospital) (4) that fire ~s ~ great heat. (5 *suggest casually, vaguely*) ~ ~ a hint / suggestion; the chairman threw ~ several good ideas. (6) the interruption threw me ~, so that I had to start again. (7 *reject*) we can ~ ~ that scheme; ~ ~ a Bill *(in Parliament)*.

throw over (1) ~ ~ a lever / steering-wheel (hard) (2 *abandon*) he threw ~ the study of Latin for engineering; when he came into a fortune he threw ~ most of his old acquaintances; she threw ~ her first husband for a richer man.

throw together (1 *make hastily*) ~ ~ a book (2) chance had ~n us ~ at a skiing resort; many races and nationalities have been ~n ~ in the American melting pot.

throw up (1) ~ up a ball / one's arms; he threw up his hands in utter amazement; ~ up the sponge *(inform: admit failure; give up)* (2) the patient ~s up everything he eats; ~ up one's dinner (3) ~ up a career / profession / task; he threw up his previous plan of going abroad for his holidays; if I don't get more money I shall ~ everything up and go.

thrust *vt* (1) he ~ the dagger into his side; she ~ the needle through the cloth; ~ open a door; he ~ his hands into his pockets; he ~ his fist in front of my face. (2) he ~ a dollar into the waiter's hand; he ~ the chair forward; she ~ me suddenly from her; they ~ themselves into the bus / forward; □ ~ o.s. forward *(be very self-assertive)* (3) he ~ his weight against the crowd; ~ one's way through a crowd (4) ~ o.s. into s.o.'s society / a conversation between others; the obligation / job was ~ upon him; ~ a present / one's opinion / o.s. on s.o.; don't ~ your opinion down other people's throats *(force them to accept them)*; he ~ aside all precautionary advice. (5) the tree ~ out many branches; a poplar ~s its rootlets far and wide; prosperous cities had ~ out suburbs. – *vi* (6) he ~ through the crowd. (7) he ~ at her with a knife; strike and ~ (8) railroads began to ~ into the buffalo country.

tie *vt* (1a) ~ a cord / string; ~ a rope round s.th.; ~ a scarf round one's neck / over s.o.'s eyes; ~ a horse to a tree; ~ two things together; ~ a rope in a knot; ~ on a label; *(fig)* my tongue is ~d *(I may not speak)*; be tongue-tied *(unable to speak)*; *(fig)* my hands were ~d so I could not do anything for you. (1b) ~ a bow / knot (in one's handkerchief); ~ a knot in a rope; ~ a bow in a ribbon (1c *make a knot, bow in*) ~ a scarf; ~ a bundle tight; ~ one's shoelaces / shoes (2a) great affection ~d them. (2b) be ~d to the house / one's bed by illness; we were ~d to home because of the baby; the weather ~d him to the house. (3 *put under some conditional relationship*) the house is ~d to the job. (4 *be equal with in a contest*) the home team ~d the visitors. – *vi* (5) does this sash ~ in front or at the back? (6 → 4) ~ with a competitor for a place / prize; the two teams ~d (for first place in the league).

tie down (1) he finds that a desk job ~s him ~. (2) ~ ~ capital (3) ~ s.o. ~ to his promise / what he has said; ~ o.s. ~.

tie in (1) ~ in your holiday plans with theirs. (2) his story ~s in with the facts; the statements do not ~ in.

tie off ~ ~ a blood vessel.

tie round they ~d the box ~ with a piece of ribbon.

tie up (1) ~ up a dog / boat / ship; ~ up a blood vessel / trailing plants; ~ up a parcel (2) capital ~d up in property (3) this firm is ~d up with Siemens; grammar has always been too much ~d up with logic. (4) I can't come along this evening – I'm (all) ~d up.

tight *adj/ adv* (1) a ~ knot (was made in the rope); the prisoner was ~ly bound and gagged; they bound his wound up ~; tie the string ~/ more ~ly on that parcel; hold on ~(ly) to s.th.; don't hold me so ~ly – you're hurting me; a ~ embrace; screw the nuts up ~; □ sit ~ (→ sit *vi* 1d); □ keep a ~ rein on s.o. / a ~ hand on / over s.o. (2) a ~ rope / belt / drum / tyre; draw a rope ~; ~ lips; keep your mouth ~ shut / shut ~. (3 *fitting (too) closely*) a ~ collar / coat; ~ shoes; a ~ cork / drawer; the dress is ~ across the chest / at the shoulders; a coat made to fit ~ round the waist (4 *impervious*) a ~ barrel / pot cover / water-tap; a good ~ roof; an air-~ tin; water-~ shoes; make a ship ~; the shutters are ~ly shut. (5a *completely filled, etc*) fill the bags so that they are ~; the stands were ~ly packed for the important match; the stands were packed ~ with spectators. (5b *inform: drunk*) he gets ~ every payday; he was as ~ as a lord. (6 *fig: packed closely*) a ~ schedule / arrangement (7 *strict, rigid*) his ~ control of the company; ~ restrictions (8 *concise*) a ~ style of writing (9a *difficult to manage*) be in a ~ situation / place / corner *(fig)* (9b *difficult to obtain*) a ~ commodity; ~ money; money is getting ~(er). (9c *characterized by scarcity*) a ~ market (10 *with opponents evenly matched*) a ~ race / game (11 *inform: stingy*) she is very ~ with her money.

tighten *vt* (1) ~ one's belt *(also fig)*; ~ a rope / spring / violin string; the baby ~ed his grasp on his mother's thumb; ~ (up) screws; ~ a nut up / down (hard). - *vi* (2) the rope ~ed; his muscles ~ed into steel bands.

time *n* (1) the world exists in space and time; past / present / future ~; until the end of ~; in (the) course of ~ (→ course *n* 2) (2 *the passing of days, years, etc*) ~ will show who is right; two o'clock is a point of / in ~; two hours is a period of ~. (3a *a portion of time*) a long / short ~ (→ long *adj* 2, short *adj* 2); what a (long) ~ you have been! how much ~ do you need? the train takes too much ~, so I'll take a plane; I shouldn't care to live here for any length of ~; the ~ of the football game was two hours and ten minutes; is youth the best ~ of life? at your ~ of life you must be careful not to overdo things; there are ~s when we ...; I like to take my ~ over my breakfast / a piece of work (→ take *vt* 4); he has been away all the ~; he says it all the ~ *(very often)*; half the ~ (→ half *adj*); the building was completed ahead of ~; be ahead of one's ~(s) *(have ideas in advance of the period in which one lives)*; ... but after a ~ I got to like it; at ~s *(occasionally)* the city becomes intolerable; at one ~ *(formerly)* (we were all animals); behind the ~s *(not up to date)*: the little town was / you are / such attitudes are behind the ~s; I didn't know what to say for a *(short)*~, then ...; for the ~ being *(for the present)*: let's forget about it for the ~ being; we will stay here for the ~ being; in ~ *(early enough)*: we came in (good) ~ for dinner; in ~ *(sooner or later)*: in ~ he'll see what is right; in ~(s) to come *(in future)* people may be taking holidays on the moon; students are pampered nowadays - it was very different in my ~ *(when I was a student)*; (they polished off all the cake) in (next to) no ~ *(very fast)*; gain ~ (→ gain *vt* 7); lose ~ (→ lose *vt* 6a); make ~ (→ make *vt* 33); kill ~ (→ kill *vt* 5); mark ~ (→ mark *vt* 7); be pressed for ~ (→ press *vt* 8). (3b *period appropriate for s.th.*) the ~ for sowing; there is a ~ for everything; what is the cooking ~ for a boiled egg? she has no ~ for bridge; I'll do it if I have (the) ~ (→ have *vi* 2g); serve one's ~ (→ serve *vt* 1, 7b); do ~ (→ do *vt* 5h); the ~ is up *(the ~ allowed is ended)*. (3c *part of the year, day*) harvest / carnival / Christmas ~; lunch / dinner ~ (3d *time(s): conditions of life, period characterized by s.th.*) how ~s have changed! we have had a good / grand ~ *(enjoyed ourselves)*; give s.o. a good ~; □ have the ~ of one's life (→ life 5); he's having a bad / hard ~; you've had a hard ~ of it, I know; exciting / stirring / hard / *etc* ~s; s.o.'s spare / leisure ~ (3e *time(s): period of ~ (associated with events, persons)* in ancient / biblical / prehistorical / former / modern ~s; the good old ~s; in Lincoln's ~; the ~ of Persia's supremacy; election ~s.

(4a *point of ~*) we agreed to meet at a convenient / given ~; at the ~ of the explosion nobody was around; at that ~ he was away from home; at a ~ *(in one operation)*: give me two books at a ~ / the books two / several at a ~; they would be away for a fortnight at a ~; the two visitors arrived at the same ~; I like it, (but) at the same ~ *(nevertheless)* it frightens me; I still see him from ~ to ~ *(occasionally)*; from ~ immemorial (4b *point of ~ appropriate for s.th.*) the ~ of arrival / departure / sailing; now it's the ~ to buy; it's ~ we went; it's ~ to make a change; it's high ~ to get up; we cannot wait for anyone who arrives after ~; against ~ *(with the greatest speed)*: we worked against ~ to get out the newspaper; arrive before ~; on ~ *(at the scheduled ~)*: the train arrived / left on ~; he rarely gets to work on ~; the buses on this route seldom run to ~; his ~ *(end of life)* has come; when her ~ came, she was delivered of a boy; watch one's ~ (→ watch *vt* 4).

(5 *time stated in hours, minutes*) what ~ is it? what is the ~? have you the ~ *(inform)*? can the boy tell the ~ *(read the clock)*? (6a *time measured in units*) the winner's ~ was 10.2 seconds; run a mile in poor / record ~; a clock / watch keeps good / bad ~ (→ keep *vt* 10) (6b *time-measuring system*) Greenwich / Central European / standard / mean / apparent ~; summer / daylight saving ~ (7a *an occasion*) this / that / next ~; that's the third ~ you have told me; he failed three ~s; I telephoned a number of ~s; there were ~s when he proved to be a friend in need; (I have warned him) ~ after ~ / ~ and again *(repeatedly)*; ~ and ~ again *(tiresomely often)*; I have told you that ~s out of number *(very often)*. (7b *times:*

multiplied by) three ~s four is / are / equals twelve; it is five ~s higher; yours is four ~s the size of mine. (8 *rhythm of a composition*) common / four-four / three-four / waltz ~; there was always one child who was not / could not keep in ~ with the music; some of the singers are out of ~; keep ~ (→ keep *vt* 10).

tip[1] *n* (1) a shoelace with a metal ~; a cane with a rubber ~; cigarettes with filter ~s / filter-~(ped) cigarettes (2) the ~ of one's nose / tongue; have s.th. / be on the ~ of one's tongue *(intention to say; almost remembered)*: it was on the ~ of my tongue to ask the same question; his name is on the ~ of my tongue; the ~s of one's fingers; she is an artist to her finger-~s; stand / walk on the ~s of one's toes / on ~toe (3) the ~ of a mountain.

tip[2] *n* (1) he gave the waiter a handsome ~ / a dollar as a ~. (2) a ~ to buy shares / from a bookie; acting on a ~ they had received, the police raided the club. (3) give s.o. ~s on painting / *etc.*

tip *vt* (1) I ~ped the waiter 10p.; I ~ped him for carrying my luggage; my father always ~ped lavishly. (2) several people have been ~ped *(considered; nominated)* for the vacant post.

tip off when the police arrived, the suspects had disappeared - they had been ~ped ~ by someone.

tire *vt* (1) this work / all the talking had ~d her (out); an invalid is ~d by the slightest exertion; they were all ~d out. (2) your stories ~ me. - *vi* (3) children ~ easily; the horses were ~ing. (4) he soon ~d of playing billiards; I shall never ~ of your company.

tired *adj* (1) this work makes one very ~; the patient gets ~ very easily; be dreadfully / dead ~; I am ~ with climbing that steep hill; I seem to get ~ from the least exertion. (2) I am ~ of listening to his complaints; I am ~ of rice pudding / life. (3) a ~ joke / phrase.

tolerate *vt* (1 *permit*) ~ a religion / political party; criticism of the government is ~d in democratic countries. (2) ~ pain / a nuisance / the heat / the strain of waiting (3 *respect without condemning*) ~ the conduct / opinions / beliefs of others; ~ s.o.'s moods with patience; we should learn to ~ one another. (4 *put up with*) are you going to ~ this injustice? he does not ~ lateness; bad behaviour is not ~d here; he won't ~ contradiction / reproach / such impudence; how can you ~ that woman? (5) most people can ~ very small quantities of arsenic taken internally; ~ poison / a drug.

tone *n* (1) harsh / shrill / loud / quiet / soft / *etc* ~s; the sweet ~s of a violin; the deep ~s of a bell; this bell has an unusually liquid ~; the mellow ~ of a cello; heart ~s (2) a carpet in ~s of brown; grey with a blue ~; soft ~s; a light / dull / *etc* ~ (3a) speak in an angry ~ / angry ~s; speak in a low / impatient / arrogant / lively / cheerful / kind / suspicious / *etc* ~; in a ~ of entreaty / command; a soft / clear / high / masterful / matter-of-fact ~; the doctor's ~ was serious. (3b) the ~ of a letter; the macabre ~ of Poe's stories (4 *spirit*) the liberal ~ of the 1930's; the ~ of the meeting was set by the president's friendly welcoming speech; a school with a good, healthy ~; the house has a conservative ~. (5 *normal healthy condition of the body*) good muscular ~; an athlete keeps his body in ~; lose / regain / restore ~.

tone *vt* (1) ~ a painting / drawing; ~ a *(photographic)* print *(chemically)* (2) the painting ~s (in) with the rest of the room; these curtains ~ (in) well with your rugs.

tone down (1) ~ ~ a colour *(make it less intense)*; ~ ~ a shade of blue (2) ~ ~ a voice (3) she ~d ~ the angry words in the letter; ~ ~ s.o.'s anger; the newspaper ~d ~ its attack. (4) the excitement ~d ~.

tone in → tone *vt* 3

tone up (1) ~ up a colour (2) exercise ~s up muscles.

tongue *n* (1a) he has a furred / dirty ~ *(symptom of illness)*; put out one's ~ (→ put out 2); → tip[1] *n* 2; □ say / do s.th. with (one's) ~ in (one's) cheek *(insincerely; ironically)*; have one's ~ in one's cheek (1b *as food*) will you take some ~? tinned ~ (2) s.o.'s mother / native ~; a foreign ~; the vulgar *(common)* ~ (3 *manner of speech*) (have) a sharp / bitter / spiteful / lying / venomous / foul / smooth / oily / flattering ~; have a ready ~ *(be quick to answer)* (4 *power of speech*) have you lost your ~? she wanted to say something, but couldn't find her ~; she never has the sense to hold her ~ at the right time.

tooth *n* (1a) an adult human has 32 teeth; a milk- / wisdom-~; a canine / eye- /

molar ~; clean / brush one's teeth; have a hollow / a cavity in a ~; drill / stop / fill / draw / extract / pull out a ~; wear false teeth (1b *idioms*) armed to the teeth *(heavily)*; by the skin of one's teeth (→ skin 1b); in the teeth of *(fully exposed to; in opposition to)*: in the teeth of the wind / storm; in the teeth of circumstances / criticism / public opinion; a bit long in the ~ *(elderly)*: she's a bit long in the ~ to play the part of a young girl; have a sweet ~ *(be fond of sweets)*; cast s.th. in s.o.'s teeth (→ cast *vt* 1b); cut one's teeth on s.th. *(begin to get experience)*: the hunter boasted of having cut his teeth on tigers; fly in the teeth of (→ fly *vi* 5); get one's teeth into a difficulty *(cope with it)* / a matter *(begin to grasp it)*; put teeth into *(make more effective)*: the proposed amendment will put teeth into the law; set one's teeth *(close the jaws tightly; be firmly determined)*; that noise sets my teeth on edge (→ edge *n* 2). (2) the teeth of a saw / rake / gear / comb / leaf.

top *n* (1 a) the ~ of a mountain / hill / tree / building; she laid her hand on the ~ of his head; the ~ of a table / car; at the ~ of the page; line 6 from the ~; from ~ to toe; from ~ to bottom; at the ~ *(upper end)* of the table / street; the red book is on ~ (of the pile); he gets commission on ~ of *(in addition to)* his salary; gale winds came on ~ of the floods; the sea and the warm sun made us feel on ~ of the world *(very happy)*. (1b *on top of: inform: in control of; informed about*) you've got to keep on ~ of your subordinates; his clever manipulations put him on ~ of his rivals and kept him there; he is always on ~ of the subject / matter / current events / the latest developments. (1c) the ~s of carrots / radishes / turnips (2 *highest degree*) (shout / bellow / talk) at the ~ of one's voice; the ~ of one's desires; is man the ~ of all creation? (3 *highest position*) there is room at the ~ in his profession; he is at the ~ of the class; come to the ~ *(be successful)*; (reach / be at) the ~ of the ladder / tree *(the highest position in a career)* (4 *AE inform: beginning*) the ~ of the inning / fifth (inning) *(in baseball)*; let's take it / start again from the ~ *(in rehearsing music)*.

top *adj* (1) the ~ shelf / drawer / landing / peg / right-hand corner (2) at ~ speed; ~ gear; pay ~ prices; ~ priority / quality; win ~ honours in a competition; he was in the ~ half of his class; the ~ boy; □ ~ man on the totem pole *(AE most important person)* (3 *inform: first-class*) a ~ performance.

top *vt* (1a) ~ a bottle / jar (1b) hills / a wall ~ped with snow; ~ a sundae with whipped cream; a church ~s the hill. (2 *go over the top of*) we ~ped the hill; the sun had ~ped the horizon. (3 *remove the upper part of*) ~ a plant / tall tree (4) he ~s his history class / the list of candidates (5) he ~ped last year's record / all rivals; ~ expectation; that ~s everything; he ~s *(is taller than)* 6 ft; can you ~ this one *(tell a better joke, story)*?

top up *(BE)* let me ~ up *(fill completely)* your glass; ~ up the radiator, please; the battery should be ~ped up every week.

toss *vt* (1) ~ a piece of paper into the waste-paper basket; ~ a ball (to s.o.); he ~ed the beggar a penny / a penny to the beggar. (2) a tree ~es its branches in the wind; the ship was ~ed by the waves; the flowers ~ed their heads in the wind. (3a *throw up, often suggesting impatience, contempt*) he was ~ed by the bull; the horse ~ed its rider; the horse ~ed its head; she ~ed her head disdainfully / back / up; □ ~ (up) a coin *(thereby deciding an issue)*: who's to pay for the drinks? let's ~ (up) a coin. (3b *mix gently*) ~ salad; ~ed salad; ~ carrots in butter; ~ hay (3c *agree with s.o. to decide s.th. by ~ing a coin*) I'll ~ you for who goes first. – *vi* (4 *move restlessly about*) he ~ed in his sleep; the clothes on the line ~ed in the wind; ~ing branches / plumes (5 *decide s.th. by ~ing a coin*) as there was only one ticket left they decided to ~ (up) for it. (6 *go with violent movements*) she ~ed out of the room in a fit of anger.

toss about (1) the ship (was) ~ed ~ on the stormy sea; ~ hay ~; *(fig)* be ~ed ~ in the storms of life (2) the sick child ~ed ~ in its sleep all night.

toss aside he ~ed ~ the argument that he ...

toss down → toss off 1.

toss off (1) he generally ~es off / down a cocktail or two before dinner. (2 *compose without effort*) ~ ~ a sonnet / newspaper article (3 *enumerate casually*) he ~ed ~ a few names.

toss up (1) → toss *vt* 3, *vi* 5. (2) suddenly she ~ed up *(inform: vomited)*.

touch *n* (1) I felt a (soft / light) ~ on my arm; a soap bubble breaks at the first / slightest ~. (2a *manner of playing an instrument, etc*) he has a light / firm / masterly ~ (on the piano); she plays the piano with a light ~; a violinist's first ~ of the bow (2b *manner of responding to a player*) this piano has not got a good ~. (3 *sense of contact*) cloth that is soft / rough to the ~; know s.th. by ~; the highly developed ~ of the blind; she revels in the ~ of fur. (4 *effect cuased by touching s.th.*) an object with a slimy ~; the cold ~ of marble.
(5 *sensitivity, understanding*) the dean has a marvellous ~ in dealing with the students. (6 *a light mark made with a brush, pencil, etc*) (add) a few finishing ~es (to a drawing / any piece of work); he was putting the finishing ~es to a major speech; *(fig)* his referring to the social aspect of the problem was a clever ~. (7 *distinctive trait, quality*) he has the ~ of a master; a sculptor with a bold ~; you can see his ~ in all these paintings.
(8a *a small quantity*) a ~ of salt / garlic / brandy / *etc*; a ~ of red; there was a ~ of colour in her cheeks; a ~ of frost in the air; the first ~es of autumn; a ~ of irony in his remarks; a ~ of sarcasm / impatience in his voice (8b *a small degree*) he fired a ~ too high. (8c *a mild attack*) he had a ~ of flu / rheumatism / lumbago / *etc*. (9 *communication*) get / be / keep in ~ with s.o. / s.th.; is he in / out of ~ with public opinion? it's difficult to keep in ~ with all the recent developments in science; lose ~ with s.o./ s.th.

touch *vt* (1a) ~ s.th. with one's finger / a stick; she ~ed the wet paint; ~ s.o. on the shoulder; do not ~ the poison cactus; he ~ed his hat (to me) *(as a salutation)*; □ ~ the spot *(be effectual)*: a glass of iced beer ~es the spot on a hot day; □ I would not ~ him with a barge-pole / pair of tongs *(have a strong aversion to him)*. (1b *set in motion, operate*) she ~ed the bell; ~ the ball with your cue; ~ the keys of the piano; ~ an electric switch (1c *apply lightly and briefly*) he ~ed his hand to his hat; ~ a match to the fire; he ~ed the stick to the ground.
(2 *be in contact with*) the point where the tangent ~es the circle; one of the branches is ~ing the water; the wheels of the car ~ed the kerb; the sun ~ed the horizon; here the road ~es the railway line. (3 *reach*) I can just ~ the ceiling (with my outstretched arm); he ~es 6 ft. *(measures just that)*; the water is not deep - I can just ~ (the) bottom; the ship ~ed bottom; □ ~ bottom (→ bottom *n* 6) (4 *go to; of roads, trains, etc*) does the train ~ *(go through)* Milan? the main road does not ~ this place; the ship will ~ (at) the following ports; the ship ~ed shore several times during the cruise.
(5 *not touch: not interfere with, etc*) don't ~ the papers on my desk; he would never have ~ed your bicycle. (6a *not touch: not eat, drink*) he did not ~ his lunch; I never ~ wine; she can't ~ a thing today. (6b *not touch: not use*) she never ~es the typewriter any more. (7 *relate to*) anything ~ing that subject interests me; what you say does not ~ the point at issue; ~ing that matter I can only tell you ... (8 *begin to deal with*) we didn't ~ the last item on the agenda; I didn't dare ~ the subject of a rise in salary; he could not ~ the algebra paper.
(9 *not touch: not compare with*) she can't ~ him as a pianist; nobody can ~ him for speed; there's not another woman there to ~ her; my skill at chess doesn't ~ yours; a style that cannot ~ that of Shaw (10a *affect, impress*) this grave decision ~es all of us; the question ~es you nearly; how does this ~ me? our conversation does not ~ you; his years in prison appear not to have ~ed him; a country un~ed by modern civilization (10b *injure, do harm to*) he was hardly ~ed by the fall; don't you dare ~ that child; he can't ~ you; this plant has been ~ed by / is ~ed with frost; he seems to be slightly / a bit ~ed *(mad)*. (10c *not touch: not be able to deal with, remove, etc*) water won't ~ that stain.
(11a *arouse a response in*) the story ~ed us all; the scene ~ed him / his heart; your kindness ~es me; we were all ~ed with pity when we heard that. (11b *cause pain, anger in*) her husband's rages no longer ~ her; the remark ~ed him to the quick; I ~ed his self-esteem; you've ~ed him on a tender place. (12 *touch with: tint slightly with*) (a) grey (dress) ~ed with rose; *(fig)* morality ~ed with emotion (13 *inform: obtain a gift, loan, etc from*) he ~ed us for 50p.
- *vi* (14) don't ~! (15) now they were so close to each other that they almost ~ed; their two heads ~ed as they whispered;

the two wires must not ~; the circles ~ at one point; *(fig)* there are several points at which our fields of activity ~. (16 *touch at: make a stop at*) our ship ~ed at Naples (→ touch *vt* 4) (17 *touch on: mention briefly, casually*) ~ on a subject / point / topic; I have already ~ed (up)on these questions (→ touch *vt* 8).

touch down we ~ed ~ at London Airport at 6.15.

touch off the activities of the stomach are ~ed ~ by the nervous system; a trivial incident may ~ ~ an argument / quarrel / dispute.

touch over → touch up 2.

touch up (1) ~ up a door / scratches; if you ~ the car up with a fresh coat of paint, it will look like new. (2) ~ up / over a picture / drawing / photograph / article.

town *n* (1 a) a small / near-by / neighbouring / inland / manufacturing / historic / flourishing / *etc* ~; live in a ~; □ paint the ~ red (→ paint *vt* 1) (1b *chief near-by ~, London*) be in / go up to ~; spend the week-end in ~; live on the outskirts of ~; he is the richest man in ~; the mayor is out of / not in ~ at the moment. (1c *business, shopping centre*) go to / work in ~; I shall be in ~ next week. (2) the whole ~ was discussing the news / knows it; be the toast of the ~ *(be famous, celebrated, esp temporarily)*: the victorious team was the toast of the ~; overnight the unknown starlet became the toast of the ~. (3 *urban way of life*) he prefers the ~ to the country.

trace *vt* (1 *follow*) ~ a path / track; ~ a river to its source (2a *follow the footprints of*) ~ game to its lair; ~ a deer through the forest (2b *discern by touch the outlines of*) ~ an object in the darkness (2c *see with difficulty*) in spite of the mist the sailors could ~ the outlines of an island. (3a *discover*) ~ a missing person (to a place); the police ~d the thief; be unable to ~ a lost letter (3b → 8) ~ one's ancestry / lineage (to a king); ~ a family back to the "Mayflower"; the rumour was ~d back to a journalist; ~ an infection to s.th.; ~ the cause of an epidemic; ~ a likeness / difference / evolution / causal connection / *etc* (4a *draw, make*) ~ a line / outline / figure / circle / pattern / map (4b *write laboriously*) ~ words / characters (5 *record in linear form*) the electrocardiograph ~s the heart action. (6 *copy a drawing by means of transparent paper*) ~ a design / map / *etc* (7) the commander ~d the plan of attack; he ~d out the plan of the house. - *vi* (8) his family ~s to the Norman Conquest; his fear of animals ~s back to an experience in his childhood.

track *n* (1a *path*) a ~ through a forest; □ the beaten ~ *(the usual way of doing things)*: England off the beaten ~; get / venture off the beaten ~; he never leaves the beaten ~. (1b *a pair of rails*) run on a / go on to another ~; run off / leave the ~ (2 *tracks: footprints*) a lion's ~s; follow the ~s left by an animal; □ in one's ~s *(just where one is)*: stop in one's ~s; modern man often goes on working till he drops in his ~s; such epidemics are now stopped in their ~s by a new drug; leave one's ~s everywhere *(also fig)*; □ cover up one's ~s (→ cover up 2); make ~s *(inform: run away)*; make ~s for *(inform: go in a hurry to)*; make ~s for the shop before closing time.
(3 *what shows that an animal, thing has passed*) car ~s; the ~ of a wheel / wagon / *etc*; they followed his ~ through the snow; □ off the ~ *(not pertinent; wrong)*: what you say is right, but off the ~; you will never work it out by that method - you are (getting) off the ~ altogether; on the ~ of *(successfully occupied in pursuing)*: the police are on the ~ of the man; he is on the ~ of a solution to the problem; be on the right / wrong ~; keep / lose ~ of *(keep in / lose touch with)*: keep / lose ~ of one's friends; he reads the newspapers to keep ~ of current events; he soon lost ~ of how much money he had spent. (4 *course*) the ~ of a meteor / storm / *etc*; follow the ~ of a murderer (5 *a course for races*) a running / race / cinder ~; ~ and field events.

track *vt* (1) the hounds ~ed the fox to its den. (2) ~ the course of an ancient wall.

track down (1) ~ ~ an animal; ~ s.o. ~ to / in a place (2) the engineers ~ed ~ the fault to a defect in a cable.

trade *n* (1) domestic / home / foreign / export / retail / wholesale / free ~; a town with a large ~; a ~ in cattle / grain / coal / *etc*; make one's money by ~; ~ was good last year; he wants to go into ~. (2) the grocery / furniture / woollen / *etc* ~; he sells only to the ~ *(retailers)*.

(3a *a craft, etc*) learn / carry on / pursue a ~; he is a baker / butcher / shoemaker / tailor / carpenter / bricklayer / mason / plumber / *etc* by ~; an honest / shady ~; soldiering is a dangerous ~. (3b) the tourist ~; the catering / printing / building / *etc* ~.

trade *vi* (1) ~ in goods / wares / commodities; ~ with a shopkeeper / firm / country (2 *trade on: take an unfair advantage of*) idle and unscrupulous people ~d on the vicar's generosity; he ~d on her helping him. - *vt* (3 *exchange*) ~ a watch for a camera; ~ seats with s.o.

trade in ~ one's old car in for a new one.

trail *n* (1) the wounded animal left a ~ of blood behind; the slimy ~ of a slug; the dog followed a false ~; get on / hit the ~; a hot ~; be hot on the ~ of s.o./ s.th. *(also fig)*; get off the ~; throw s.o. off the ~ (2) it had snowed so hard we couldn't find the ~; stamp a ~ through the deep snow; tortuous mountain ~s; wagon ~s; an Indian ~; blaze a ~ *(mark a path through a forest; be a pioneer)*; a ~ of destruction, left by a violent storm (3) the train left a ~ of smoke; the car raised a ~ of dust; the ~ of a meteor; ~s of mud on a carpet.

trail *v* (1a) the boy ~ed a wagon (behind him). (1b) she ~ed her long skirt; □ ~ one's coat *(inform: try to provoke)* (2 *hunt by following the tracks, etc*) ~ an animal; some dogs can ~ a man for many miles; ~ a fugitive to his hiding-place; we ~ed the car in front of us; they ~ed the stolen jewels to a shop in Rome. (3 *shadow*) ~ a suspicious person (4) ~ one's fingers in the water (5 *leave traces of s.th.*) ~ sand all over the floor; ~ dirt into the house; a racing car ~ing clouds of dust. - *vi* (5 *be drawn along*) her coat ~ed in the mud / along (on) the floor; the toy cart ~ed along the ground. (7) smoke ~ed from the chimney; a cloud of dust ~ed behind the car. (8 *walk slowly because of weariness, etc*) the tired children ~ed along behind their father; the old horse just ~s along. (9) the roses ~ed over the cottage door; creepers ~ed over roofs and walls.

trail off her voice ~ed ~ *(dwindled into silence)*; the train whistle ~ed ~ into the distance.

train *n* (1) a slow / express / fast / special / relief / local / suburban / passenger / goods / freight ~; the ~ for Paris; take the midnight / early morning / 6.20 a.m. ~ (to town); a direct / through ~ (to Rome); go / travel by ~; have lunch on the ~; I don't often see you on this ~; get into / out of a ~; get on / off a ~; when does your ~ leave? the ~ is due at 8.15; catch a / one's ~; miss the / one's ~; the ~ from N. is probably 20 minutes late. (2) a ~ of loaded camels; a mule ~; a wagon ~; a ~ of covered wagons; a long ~ of sightseers (3) by an unlucky ~ of events; the photo suggested a whole ~ of ideas; lose one's ~ of thought; a ~ of reactions (4 *what follows an event*) disease came in the ~ of war; the tornado brought havoc in its ~.

train *vt* (1a) ~ children (to be punctual / to punctuality); ~ an unruly boy (1b) ~ s.o. in a subject / skill / accomplishment; ~ soldiers / radio operators / *etc*; ~ s.o. for a profession / to business; ~ o.s. for s.th. / to do s.th.; ~ one's ear to distinguish various sounds; have one's voice ~ed; ~ a dog (to do tricks) (2 *train on: direct*) ~ a camera / telescope / gun on s.o. / s.th. (3 *make grow in a desired direction*) she ~ed the vines against the wall / to climb up the wall. - *vi* (4) ~ for a race / a post of responsibility / a teacher / *etc*; ~ as a doctor / lawyer / teacher; ~ in a subject.

transfer *vt* (1) ~ papers from one file to another; he ~red the package from one hand to the other; the manager was ~red to a different branch. (2) ~ one's affection to s.o. else; ~ (total) power to s.o. (3 *pass ownership to s.o.*) he ~red the shares to a nephew; ~ a title to land (to s.o.) (4 *convey to another surface*) ~ a design to an Easter egg; ~ a pattern / design / drawing (to a lithographic stone / to canvas / *etc*). - *vi* (5) he took the tram and ~red to the bus. (6) he ~red from the navy to the air force / from sales to advertising; the entire military unit will ~ to overseas duty.

travel *n* (1a) the difficulties of ~ in midwinter; discuss future ~ to Mars; interplanetary ~; information about ~ to Britain can be obtained in the major cities of the world from ~ agents; this agent specializes in ~ in Belgium; ~ agency / document / information / time / trade / *etc* (1b) set out on one's ~s; have you ever come across him in your ~s? if you happen to meet him on your ~s, you might remember me to him; is he back from his ~s yet? write a book about one's

~s; Gulliver's ~s; the ~s of Marco Polo (1c) a book of ~s (2 *traffic*) an increase in ~ on state roads.

travel *vi* (1) ~ by bus / coach / tram / car / train / ship / steamer / sleigh / sledge; ~ by air / road / sea; ~ through space / time; ships that ~ round the world; ~ inland / abroad / round the country; we ~led together; she ~s for pleasure; ~ first / second class; children up to ten years ~ free; ~ light *(with little luggage)*; ~ with one's back to the engine (2) sound waves will not ~ through a vacuum; light ~s faster than sound; the pain ~led down his arm. (3) her glance / eye ~led over the crowd; thoughts ~ fast; his mind ~led over recent events. (4 *work as a commercial traveller*) he ~s for a paint firm / in vacuum cleaners. - *vt* (5a) ~ a distance / region / road; he has ~led (all over) the world; a train that ~s 180 km an hour; I have ~led 8,000 miles. (5b) ~ (in) a region *(as a commercial traveller)*.

tread *vi* (1) ~ lightly across the room; she trod softly / lightly so as not to wake the baby; please ~ softly! ~ on s.o.'s feet *(not fig)* / on a cigarette stub / in a puddle; ~ on the accelerator; ~ on grapes; □ ~ on s.o.'s corns / toes *(offend him)*; I'm sorry if I'm ~ing on anyone's toes, but I thought it was an awful book; □ ~ on air *(be happy)* (2) ~ cautiously in your dealings with him; □ ~ warily *(act cautiously)*. - *vt* (3) ~ a path (through a forest); a well-trodden path; the path was soon trodden hard; □ ~ a dangerous path; he trod the moors all night; ~ a hole in the carpet; ~ the juice out of grapes; ~ soil round newly planted seedlings; (4 *crush*) in Europe, peasants still ~ grapes to make wine.

tread down (1) ~ ~ ground / a path; ~ ~ earth around a plant; ~ ~ flowers (2 *oppress*) the masses were a good deal trodden ~.

tread in let it lie - it'll ~ in sooner or later.

tread out (1) ~ ~ a fire (2) ~ ~ wheat; ~ ~ (the juice from) grapes.

treat *vt* (1a) ~ s.o. well / kindly / politely / (un)justly / (un)fairly / badly / roughly / ill / *etc*; ~ s.o. with (dis)respect / disdain / severity / courtesy / consideration / *etc*; ~ s.o. as a child / friend / enemy / fool / equal; ~ s.o. like dirt; I don't like the way he ~s his dog. (1b) ~ tools / machines / *etc* with care (2) ~ s.th. as a joke / a serious matter; ~ a matter as unimportant; he ~ed the matter far too seriously. (3a) ~ a patient (with a medicine / lotion / *etc*); be ~ed for cancer / arthritis / *etc*; which doctor is ~ing you? (3b) ~ a disease; has a doctor ~ed your cold? how would you ~ a sprained ankle? (4) ~ a metal with an acid; obstinate stains must be ~ed with special care in washing. (5 *pay for the food, etc*) ~ s.o. to a meal / drink / holiday / *etc*; his father ~ed him to the movies; when he ~ed her to dinner he ~ed himself to an entertaining evening. (6) the book ~s two main topics; a work which ~s of the caste system in India; that problem has been ~ed of in the previous chapter; ~ a subject scientifically / exhaustingly / superficially / *etc*; ~ a theme realistically; the lecturer ~ed his subject in great detail; the painter is famous for ~ing sporting scenes. - *vi* (7 *negotiate*) we cannot ~ with a person whose good faith is in doubt; he will never ~ for peace with them. (8 *bear the expense of food, etc*) is it my turn to ~?

trial *n* (1 *test*) give s.o./ s.th. a ~; put s.th. to ~; have a ~ of strength / wits with s.o.; the ~ of the new car showed up its flaws; learn by ~ and error; articles sent for ten days' free ~; on ~ *(when tested; to test s.th.)*: the gadget proved excellent on ~; he took it for a month on ~. (2 *examination before a judge*) he is on ~ for murder; his ~ for theft started today; the ~ lasted a week; conduct a ~; bring s.o. to / put s.o. on ~; stand one's ~ *(be tried at law)* (3 *trouble, hardship, etc*) his deafness is a great ~ to him; in his youth he was a great ~ to his parents; comfort in the hour of ~; the long winter was a ~ for the pioneers; life is full of ~s.

trick *n* (1 *s.th. done to cheat*) his illness was only a ~ to avoid school; a subtle ~ to outwit s.o. (2 *foolish, mean act*) the ~ of putting salt in the sugar-bowl; play a dirty / low / mean / shabby / contemptible / *etc* ~ on s.o. (3 *practical joke*) a boyish ~; he played a ~ on his mother; the children are always up to amusing ~s. (4 *the art of doing s.th. skilfully*) you seem to have mastered the ~ of making others laugh; by some ~ of memory (5 *a clever device, technique*) a card ~; a ~ in balancing; conjuring ~s; a rhetorical ~; learn the ~ of tossing a pancake; he taught his dog some amazing ~s; can your dog do ~s? □ the ~s of the trade *(ways of getting advantages, etc)*; □ do / turn the ~ *(produce the desired effect)*: another turn of the pliers should do the ~; □ know a ~ worth two of that *(have a much better plan)*; he had a ~ of winning *(somehow usually won)*. (6 *peculiar habit*) he had an annoying ~ of cracking his knuckles; she had a ~ of half closing her eyes. (7 *cards played in one round of a game*) she took the ~ with her king.

trick *vt* (1) he ~ed him out of his winnings / into revealing the secret; he was ~ed into buying a worthless ring; we've been ~ed. (2) considering the occasion a very special one, she ~ed herself out in all her finery; the two sisters were ~ed out in costly jewellery.

trouble *n* (1a *difficulty, annoyance*) I had much / a great deal of ~ with my landlord; I'm having ~ with my teeth; I have ~ in using the following words; he has a lot of family ~; I hope that this will not cause you too much ~; the problem has given us not a little ~; financial ~ may threaten security; life today is all ~ and annoyance; □ ask / look for ~ *(show lack of caution)*; be in ~ (with the police); get into ~ (with the manager); keep out of ~; get out of ~; I don't like putting you to so much ~; you won't be put to this ~ again - I'll see to that. (1b *s.th.,s.o. that is a cause of distress, etc*) the ~ with you is that you don't try; he has a lot of family ~s; for years the boy has been a ~ to his parents; I find it a great ~ to get up at six; would it be a ~ to you to post this letter for me? her greatest ~ is oversensitivity; what's the ~ *(what has happened)*? (2a *mental distress, worry*) ~ and woe were her lot in life; her heart was heavy with ~; this escapade will get you into ~ (→ 1a). (2b *an instance of worry*) some secret ~ weighing on his mind; a wife who shares all her husband's ~s; he is having money ~s (→ 1b). (3 *civil disorder*) political ~ in the new republic; there is ~ in many parts of the world; labour ~(s); the police rushed to the scene of (the) ~. (4 *physical disorder*) heart / stomach / mental / digestive / *etc* ~ (5 *effort*) thank you for all the ~ you have taken; the results were worth the ~ it took; he takes ~ with his work; he took the ~ to check every detail; it is disappointing that the project has turned out a failure after so much ~ has been taken over / with it; please don't go to any ~ for me; why did you go to so much ~?

trouble *vt* (1 *worry*) I'm rather ~d about my wife's health; he is ~d by debt; his ~d look told me that something was wrong. (2) may I ~ you for a match / to shut the window? could I ~ you for the newspaper, please? let me ~ you with one more question only; he is always ~ing me with some complaint or another; I am sorry to keep ~ing you about that letter; but ...; you need not ~ yourself about it any more; we are never ~d by beggars in this district. (3) her arthritis ~s her greatly; be ~d by rheumatism; be ~d with a nasty cough; that tooth which was ~ing me is quite all right now. (4 *annoy*) don't ~ her with petty complaints. (5) a heavy gale ~d the ocean waters; → water *n* 1b. (6) don't ~ to meet me at the station; don't ~ to dress / *etc*; please do not ~ getting me another cup of tea. - *vi* (7) just call and see me when you feel inclined - don't ~ about writing / to write first; I have a good breakfast and good meal in the evening, and never ~ with lunch; a person who asks your advice and then ignores it is not worth ~ing with. (8) she always ~d over her son's solitariness; if you ~ about every little thing that goes wrong, you will never have any peace of mind.

true *adj / adv* (1) his statement is ~; a ~ story; is it ~ that you...? a hope / dream / prophecy comes ~; his words ring ~. (2 *genuine*) ~ gold; ~ joy / feelings; a ~ gentleman / Christian; ~ friendship should last for years; he told me the ~ reason why he ...; a ~ interest in s.o.'s welfare; the ~ value of things (3 *rightful*) the ~ heir (to the throne) (4a) a ~ friend; be ~ to one's friends; be ~ to one's word / promise / principles; ~ to o.s. (4b *reliable, sure*) a ~ sign (5a *accurate*) a ~ balance / pair of scales / copy; a ~ aim; a ~ colour; ~ to a thousandth of an inch; be ~ to nature / life / form / type; aim ~ (5b *proper*) arrange things in their ~ order (6 *accurately shaped, fitted, etc*) these boards are not ~; the wheel / post / beam is ~. (7 *properly so called*) the whale is a ~ mammal; the lion is a ~ cat; ~ statesmanship (8 *in conformity with the characteristics of the type*) breed ~.

trust *n* (1a) we place / put our ~ in God / s.o. / s.th.; put no ~ in the future; there is no proof of his story - we can only take it on ~; I don't have any ~ in what he says; a breach of ~ (1b) God is my ~. (2) sell merchandise on ~ *(credit)*; he got the car on ~. (3 *charge; care*) leave valuables in s.o.'s ~; hold / have s.th. in ~ (4 *responsibility*) he considered his office a sacred ~; the child's care was to her a sacred ~; I have fulfilled my ~; he has a position of ~; carry out / violate the public ~.

trust *vt* (1) she ~s him implicitly; mother ~s the children's nurse; ~ s.o.'s word; if one can ~ the report in the papers (2 *expect confidently*) he ~ed the job would soon be finished; he ~ed to find oil on the land; can I ~ you to post this letter? I ~ you and yours are keeping well; I would not ~ that man to leave the money alone; you can ~ him to do something foolish. (3a) I would not ~ my money to a person like him; ~ one's affairs to a lawyer (3b) I shouldn't care to ~ him with a large sum of money; I ~ed him with my new pen - I hope he doesn't lose it; can I ~ you with a secret? (4 *permit to do without fear of consequences*) she does not ~ her children out of her sight; do you ~ your daughters to go out alone at night? (5 *give credit*) will you ~ us till payday? - *vi* (6) things work out if one only ~s; ~ in God / s.o.('s ability / honesty / *etc*); ~ to luck / chance / Providence.

try *vt* (1) ~ it before you say it's simple; ~ one's hardest *(make every effort)* to do s.th.; ~ to complete the examination; he tried very hard not to sneeze; he tried to clean the coat; ~ cleaning it with petrol; I couldn't tear it or break it, so I tried cutting it; ~ cooking them if you don't like them uncooked; he tried skiing but never liked it. (2a) ~ the brakes / this wine / our liver pills; ~ twice the quantity; ~ a new machine / remedy; the strength of a rope must be tried before it is used; you may ~ this appliance before you buy it; I could not get him to ~ (at) a somersault; he tried how far he could jump; ~ a new field / book (2b) ~ all the doors and windows before leaving. (2c) ~ s.o.'s courage / honesty / patience (→ 3); ~ one's luck / fortune; men of tried courage; he's a friend tried in many dangerous situations.
(3 *strain*) this print tries one's eyes / is ~ing to the eyes; this boy tries my patience (→ 2c); it tried her that he gave her no encouragement. (4) the man was tried for theft and found guilty; ~ s.o. on a charge of murder; Judge N. will ~ that case. (5) I have tried till I am tired; you must ~ harder; the liberty to ~ and err; do ~ and stop coughing; ~ and come, won't you? ~ for a scholarship / prize / post with the Air Ministry; he has tried everywhere for work.

trying *adj* I found the meeting very ~; proof-reading is ~ work; I have had a ~ day at work - everything has gone wrong.

try on ~ on new shoes / a coat / a dress / *etc*; ~ this on for size.

try out (1) ~ ~ an engine / boat / *etc*; ~ ~ a new remedy; ~ ~ a plan / idea / *etc*; ~ ~ a play *(perform it first in small towns)*; ~ ~ *(audition)* for a part *(in a play, etc)* (2 *melt down*) ~ ~ fat / oil / metals.

tune *n* (1) he was humming an old / lively / popular / *etc* ~; sing / play / set / arrange s.th. to the ~ of 'Auld Lang Syne'; □ to the ~ of *(to the, often unreasonable, amount of)*: I received a bill to the ~ of £500; □ change one's / sing another / a different ~ *(change one's attitude)*: she changed her ~ about children when she married and had her own; he will sing a different ~ when he has to earn his own money; □ call the ~ *(direct proceedings)*: I'm calling the ~ here, so do what I say. (2) some of this modern music has not much ~ in it. (3) the piano is in / out of ~; the piano and the violin are not in ~; sing in / out of ~ (4 *fig: harmony*) be in ~ with current ideas / the times / the crowd; the speech was out of ~ with the solemnity of the occasion.

tune *vt* (1) ~ one's / an instrument; ~ instruments to each other; a ~ing-fork (2) ~ a radio set to a given station; a ~ing control / knob / scale. - *vi* (3) listeners in Central Europe should ~ to 31.67 metres for that transmission.

tune in ~ in a radio set (to a given station); ~ in (to) Radio Luxembourg; what have you ~d in? you are not properly ~d in.

tune out ~ ~ that horrible music; see if you can ~ ~ the atmospherics.

tune up (1) ~ up a violin / piano / *etc*; *(fig)* the child ~d up *(began to cry)*. (2) the orchestra ~d up. (3 *adjust motor, engine*) before starting on our trip we should have the car ~d up.

turn *n* (1a) a slight ~ of the handle (1b) a ~ of the head / wrist; the ~ of a wheel; the wheel made three ~s and stopped;

make a ~ to the right; □ a hand's ~ *(work)*: he didn't do a hand's ~; it won't be necessary for you to do a hand's ~ yourself, but rather to supervise. (2) about a mile ahead, you'll come to a ~ in the road; a sharp / left-hand ~; take the second ~ to the right; □ at every ~ *(constantly)*: be held up at every ~; she met with kindness at every ~. (3 *direction, change*) the conversation took an interesting ~; take a ~ for the better / worse (→ take *vt* 7a); he gave the story a new ~; a new ~ of affairs; a ~ in the weather; at the ~ of the century; a ~ of luck / Fortune's wheel; □ on the ~ *(changing; going bad)*: the tide is on the ~; at last the condition of the patient seems to be on the ~; the milk is on the ~; □ done / cooked / roasted to a ~ *(just right)*: the steak is done to a ~.

(4a *sequence*) all did it in ~; I will see you all in ~ / you, each in your ~; □ out of ~ *(not in proper sequence; imprudently)*: he spoke out of ~ and destroyed the cordial atmosphere of the meeting. (4b) it's my ~ to pay the bill; it's your ~ to deal; □ by ~s *(alternately)*: she was grave and gay by ~s; they did their shopping and cleaning by ~s; my ~ will come. (5 *short walk, drive*) a ~ in the park / round the town; let's go for / take a ~ in the car (6 *a period of duty, activity*) a ~ of work; a ~ at the helm / oars; take a ~ at mowing the lawn / driving the car / washing up; I don't mind taking a ~ with the lawn-mower / the washing-up *(dishes)*; he takes ~s with the others in sitting up; I'll take ~s with you at cutting the hedge; they take it in ~s to go on duty *(do it alternately)*. (7 *service*) do s.o. a good / bad ~ (→ do *vt* 7); she repaid it with a bad ~; one good ~ deserves another. (8 *form, shape*) the ~ of her neck / ankle.

(9 *distinctive form, style*) a happy ~ of expression; an ugly ~ of phrase; I don't like the ~ of that sentence. (10 *natural inclination*) the ~ of his mind; he has a serious / gloomy / inquiring / mechanical / *etc* ~ of mind; be of a scientific / mechanical / humorous / *etc* ~; he has a ~ for mechanics. (11 *need*) this will serve your ~. (12 *small unpleasant shock*) it gave him a ~ to hear her voice; the shriek in the night gave us quite a ~.

turn *vt* 1-14; *vi* 15-24.

The patterns are grouped as follows: turn + *adj*: 22; turn + *predic noun*: 22; turn + *noun* + *adj*: 12; turn + *prepos*: against 9e, 19a; from 19b; into 11, 21; on 15a, 15b, 19e, 24; to 9f, 10, 11, 19c, 19d, 20, 21. The following *vt / vi* patterns are semantically identical or closely related: 1a, 15a + 16; 1b, 15b; 3, 17; 9e, 19a; 9f, 19d; 11, 21; 12,22; 13,23.

(1a) ~ a wheel; □ ~ s.o. round one's (little) finger *(dominate him)* (1b) ~ a doorhandle; ~ the key in the lock; ~ a tap / a switch / the knobs of a wireless set; □ ~ an honest penny (→ penny 1); □ ~ the scale(s) (→ scale[2] *n*); ~ the heating higher / low; ~ the radio / lamp / music / light / heat low; no sooner had I ~ed my back than I ...; ~ one's head / body / eyes (to the door); when he writes on the blackboard, the teacher ~s his back on the class / to the audience; □ ~ one's back on s.o. *(~ away impolitely)*; □ ~ one's back (up)on the world; → shoulder *n* 1; → ear *n* 1; → eye *n* 2; he can ~ his hand to anything *(is versatile)*; → head *n* 6. (1c) he ~ed his ankle. (1d) ~ your chair to the table; ~ s.th. upwards / on its side / inside out / upside down / best side outwards; ~ the rough / coarse side of s.th. outwards; I shall have this overcoat ~ed; □ ~ one's coat *(change one's principles)*; □ ~ the tables on s.o. *(change possible defeat into victory)* (2) ~ a somersault / cartwheel / handspring (3) ~ s.th. on a lathe / potter's wheel; ~ wood / ivory / a table-leg; the handle is of ~ed beechwood; ~ a lathe *(cause it to work)*; *(fig)* a well-~ed ankle. (4a) ~ a page *(to read it, write on it)* (4b) ~ the soil *(dig, plough it)*; ~ the sod / turf (4c) ~ a collar *(sew it on inside out)*; his wife ~s his shirt collars when they get frayed. (5 *go round*) ~ a corner; our company ~ed the enemy's flank; □ ~ the corner *(master a crisis)* (6 *go beyond*) he has ~ed *(is older than)* fifty; it has just ~ed half past two. (7 *drive*) ~ s.o. from one's door; ~ sheep into a pen / the cattle from the road; ~ the children out of the garden / room; ~ s.o. out of one's house for non-payment of rent (8 *direct*) ~ the hose on the fire; ~ a ship from her course / a car towards the centre of town; she ~ed her face / eyes *(another way)* (9a *divert, resist*) he ~ed the blow with his arm; this metal is thick enough to ~ a bullet. (9b *cause to change direction*) the police ~ed the advancing rioters by firing over their heads; *(fig)* nothing will ever ~ him from his purpose. (9c) he ~ed the conversation to more cheerful topics. (9d *make s.o. change his life*) what has ~ed him? (9e) she has ~ed him against his father. (9f) ~ the, one's mind / attention / thoughts to s.th.; he ~ed his mind to practical matters; he ~ed the resources of his energy and experience to the Socialist cause.

(10) ~ information / events / handicaps / *etc* to use / account (→ account *n* 4) / advantage (→ advantage 2); the team ~ed the defeat to advantage by overhauling its tactics; we ~ed the figures to use in the discussion.

(11 *turn to, into: change*) we decided to ~ the house into flats; the alchemists believed they would be able to ~ metals into gold; he ~ed the play into a farce; ~ s.o. into a hero; their friendship was ~ed to enmity through idle gossip; can you ~ the text into good English? ~ French into German; ~ prose into verse / sense into nonsense / ideas into deeds / good into evil (12 *cause to be*) boiling ~s water gaseous; heat ~s tar liquid; these processes ~ the metal hard; cold ~ed their ears pink; prison ~ed him bitter; ~ an animal loose *(allow it to roam free)*; you can ~ him loose in the library; the speech ~ed the crowd in our favour. (13 *make bad*) the heat ~ed the milk / butter; frost ~ed the leaves early; *(fig)* that smell ~ed my stomach. (14 *construct gracefully*) ~ a phrase (well); Shakespeare is the man to ~ the telling phrase; the ~ing of witty verse was Dryden's forte. – *vi* (15a) the wheel ~ed slowly (on the axle); the earth ~s (on its axis); *(fig)* that will make him ~ (over) in his grave. (15b) the door ~s on its hinges. (15c) my head is ~ing *(seems to spin)*. (16) this tap ~s easily *(can easily be ~ed)*. (17) wood that ~s well *(on a lathe)* (18a *change direction*) he ~ed when I called him; they ~ed and ran; ~ right here; the wind has ~ed. (18b) the tide has ~ed *(has started to ebb or flow)*; *(fig)* the tide of success ~ed and this great enterprise slowly declined; finally his bad luck ~ed and his third attempt was successful. (18c) the path ~s into the field and crosses the ditch; the road / lane / railway / *etc* ~s to the left / into the village / sharply / *etc.* (18d) he ~ed (to the) right / into a small street / down a narrow road / into the pub at the corner; she ~ed from the sight; he does not know where to ~ *(who to apply to)*; he does not know which way to ~ *(how to start dealing with an unpleasant matter)*.

(19a) ~ against s.o.; ~ in favour of s.o. (19b) he ~ed from the Democrats and joined the Republicans; she ~ed from him in disgust. (19c) ~ to s.o. for advice / assistance; I have no one but you to ~ to; ~ to a book for help; ~ to page 25 / chapter III (19d) having failed as a journalist he ~ed to acting; he ~ed to Christianity in his old age; ~ to crime / drink; the lecturer ~ed from the causes to the effects of the Great War; his thoughts ~ed homeward / to his family. (19e) don't tease that dog – it may ~ on you; he ~ed angrily upon the speaker.

(20) it may ~ to rain before long. (21 *turn to, into: become*) the wine ~ed to vinegar; water by freezing ~s to ice; sorrow ~ed to joy; a tadpole ultimately ~s into a frog; it ~ed into a nice day; he has ~ed into a very pleasant fellow. (22) water ~s gaseous when boiled; tar ~s liquid when heated; the milk ~ed sour; she ~ed pale at the sight of the lion; his hair is ~ing grey; the animal ~ed nasty; he has ~ed Moslem / Catholic / Liberal / Communist; ~ traitor; a lawyer *(who has)* ~ed poet; the little craft finally ~ed turtle *(capsized)*. (23 *become bad*) the milk / butter has ~ed; the leaves have ~ed *(changed colour)*; *(fig)* her stomach ~s at the sight of blood. (24 *turn on: depend on*) the value of the experiment ~s on the accuracy of the measurements; the decision ~s on the amount of time and money available; whether he goes or not ~s on whether he can afford it.

turn away (1) the football stadium was full and many people had to be ~ed ~. (2) ~ ~ one's face / eyes / gaze (from s.th.) (3) ~ ~ s.o.'s wrath; she skilfully ~ed the conversation ~ from so unpleasant a subject. (4) he ~ed ~ from me; she ~ed ~ from him in disgust; the aircraft / ship ~ed ~ from the target / enemy ship.

turn back (1) the police ~ed them ~ at the barrier. (2) we ~ed ~ when we saw the deep snowdrifts on both sides of the road.

turn down (1) ~ ~ one's sleeves / the collar of one's coat; ~ ~ the sheets / bed *(make the bed ready to occupy)*; ~

~ the pages of a book *(fold a corner)* (2 *lower*) ~ ~ the gas / heating; she ~ed ~ the radio when the telephone rang; ~ ~ the heat / the brightness of s.th. (3 *inform*) ~ ~ a proposal / scheme / application / offer; ~ ~ an applicant; ~ s.th. ~ flat *(absolutely)* (4) this line ~s ~(wards) and that line up(wards).

turn in (1) ~ in one's toes / feet (2) the agent ~ed in a confidential report; ~ in a resignation; he ~ed in his revolver to the police. (3) ~ in an old car for a new (4) his toes / feet / eyes ~ in. (5 *inform: go to bed*) it was midnight before we ~ed in.

turn off (1) ~ ~ the gas / water / tap; ~ ~ the light / radio / switch (2) is this where the road to N. ~s ~ / we ~ ~ to N.? (3 *inform: stop listening*) you could see him ~ ~ as she kept up her chatter.

turn on (1) ~ on the gas / water / tap; ~ the heating full on; ~ the heating on low; ~ the headlights on; ~ on the radio / television / switch (2) she ~ed on the charm and won him over. (3 *slang: affect with pleasure*) that music really ~s me on.

turn out (1) ~ ~ one's toes (2a) we ~ed ~ the cat for the night. (2b) he ~ed the boys ~ because they were creating a disturbance. (3) ~ ~ the gas / light (4a *empty*) ~ ~ a cupboard / drawer / handbag / *etc*; ~ ~ one's pockets (4b *BE clean*) ~ ~ a room (5 *produce*) she ~ed ~ four tapestries a year; the factory ~s ~ 20 cars each day; that school has ~ed ~ a number of well-known scholars. (6 *dress*) she was ~ed ~ in her best clothes; she always ~s her children ~ well. (7a *go out and assemble*) the whole village ~ed ~ to welcome the visitor; everyone ~ed ~ for the wedding. (7b *go out to face bad weather*) do we have to ~ ~ on such a night? (8 *inform: get up*) he did not want to ~ ~ on such a cold morning. (9) the day ~ed ~ fine; the eldest son ~ed ~ a rogue; the letter ~ed ~ to be a forgery; it will ~ ~ all right in the end; it ~ed ~ that the driver of the vehicle was drunk. (10 *of foods: be successful*) we were to have had a cheesecake but it didn't ~ ~; the pies and tarts ~ed ~ nicely.

turn over (1) she ~s the mattresses ~ every day; how does one ~ a pancake ~? (2) ~ a page ~; ~ the record ~ and see what is on the other side; ~ ~ the pages of a book *(read them cursorily)*; □ ~ ~ a new leaf *(inform: make a new start)* (3) he ~ed the money ~ to me; he ~ed the office work ~ to his assistant and left on a business trip; he ~ed ~ the business to his son; the thief was ~ed ~ to the police. (4) ~ ~ commodities *(buy and sell them)*; they ~ed ~ a million last year *(did business to that amount)*; turnover is the amount of money ~ed ~ by a firm in a year. (5) he ~ed the idea ~ a couple of times before acting on it; ~ ~ a problem (6a *start*) he ~ed ~ the car engine. (6b) the motor ~ed ~ without any trouble. (7) he ~ed ~ on to his other side; ~ ~ in bed; → turn *vi* 15a. (8) the canoe ~ed ~ as soon as it reached the rapids; why did the car ~ ~? (9) at the sight of it my stomach ~ed ~.

turn round (1) he ~ed his chair ~ to the window. (2) ~ ~ and let me see your face.

turn to in these days the husband often has to ~ to *(get to work)* and help with the housework; we all ~ed to and soon had the house tidy.

turn up (1) ~ up one's sleeves *(also fig, → sleeve n, 1)*; ~ up a collar *(make it stand up)*; ~ up the ends of one's trousers; → nose *n* 1 (2) ~ up a shovelful of earth; the plough ~ed up the earth; the farmer ~ed up some Roman coins. (3 *turn up: shorten*) ~ up a dress; ~ up a hem *(fold and stitch it so as to shorten a garment)* (4) ~ up the heating / lamp / radio; ~ up the heat / music / brightness of s.th. (5) I think I can ~ up his letter if I look through the files; you can ~ up the facts in any encyclopedia; ~ up a dictionary for a word (6) the stink ~ed her up *(made her vomit)*. (7) that line ~s up(wards) (→ turn down 4); s.o. 's eyes / nose / mouth / toes / shoes ~(s) up. (8a if he doesn't ~ up soon, we shall have to go without him; ... it was presumed that he was dead - then one day he ~ed up at a hotel in Paris. (8b) he was waiting for a job to ~ up; I'm sure your watch will ~ up eventually.

U

understand *vt* (1a *grasp the (full) meaning of*) I don't ~ this book; he does not ~ what you say; ~ a poem; the professor said he could not ~ Kant; he does not ~ responsibility; to ~ the present institutions, we must comprehend something of their history; he ~s English (→ 3) and he can make himself understood. (1b *make out clearly the speech of*) he spoke in such a thick accent no one could ~ him; the noise prevented my ~ing the telephone operator; make o.s. understood (2 *be thoroughly familiar with*) ~ machinery / a trade; she thoroughly ~s children; he doesn't ~ driving a car; being well informed about science is not the same thing as ~ing science; I could never ~ mathematics; I liked him better when I came to ~ him better. (3 *possess a passive knowledge of*) ~ Russian; ~ shorthand / a message in code (4 *explain successfully to o.s.*) ~ the meaning of s.th. / the point of his remark; I can ~ why he was disappointed; his behaviour is hard to ~; I quite ~ your difficulties; he must be made to ~ the importance of this step; I cannot ~ his / him behaving like that; can you ~ (anyone) wanting to climb Mount Everest? I can quite ~ your readers asking questions about... (5a *infer from information received, know from hearsay, etc*) I ~ that the doors open at 7.30; I ~ that you are going to the country; I ~ him to be / that he is a distant relation; I ~ that you are taking music lessons; no one could ~ that from my words; what do you ~ will happen? what did you ~ him to say *(infer from his words)*? I certainly understood him to say so; he was understood to have lost his fortune / to be in favour of the plan; I ~ him to be satisfied; I ~ the message to mean they aren't coming; he understood her suggestion as a complaint; "... the number of vacancies is limited." – "Yes, so I've always understood."; "Oh, the jug's gone! I'm sure I left it here." "Do I ~ that you left this poisonous solution in my jug?"; he gave me / I was given to ~ that it was done. (5b *accept as a fact*) I ~ that I shall be repaid; it is understood you will pay me next week; I ~ that you are trying to be truthful, but you are wrong; am I to ~ that your refusal is final? (6 *be understood: be supplied mentally*) in 'Ann likes tennis; Bill, golf' the word 'likes' is understood after 'Bill'.
– *vi* (7 *grasp what is meant*) he told them about it in simple words, hoping they would ~; as often as I've explained, you still don't ~; he can repeat every rule in the book, but he just doesn't ~. (8 *accept tolerantly*) if you cannot do it, I will ~; she relied on him to ~ and sympathize. (9 *have knowledge on a particular subject*) he ~s about boats; I doubt if they can really ~ about politics. (10 *believe*) your offer, I ~, is still open.

undertake *vt* (1 *attempt, carry out*) ~ a journey / task / project; ~ an analysis of s.th.; the ambassador undertook the mission to make peace; the butler undertook the duty of cooking. (2 *undertake + inf: promise*) John will ~ to bring the food for the picnic; the magician undertook to make rain; the government have ~n to rearm within a year. (3 *undertake + that: guarantee*) I will ~ that you shall be no loser / that he has not heard a word; the sponsors ~ that the candidate they propose meets all the requirements. (4 *accept as a charge engage to attend to*) ~ a patient; the lawyer undertook the case without a fee.

undo *vt* (1) ~ a knot / rope / piece of string; please ~ the package; she could not wait to ~ the glittering paper that hid her present; the knot / my shoelace has come ~ne. (2) ~ a button / zip fastener / garment / lock / barred door (3 *cause to be as if never done*) one cannot ~ the past; murder once done can never be ~ne; it will take years of Spartan living to ~ what the dictator did to the country; whatever the government now does, it cannot ~ its air attacks on Egypt. (4 *do away with*) we can't ~ the damage now; the survivors set to work to ~ the havoc done by the storm. (5 *destroy*) he did wrong, and in the end his wrongs undid him; technological advances had taken away his markets and undone him; he is already conceited and this sudden fame will surely ~ him.

unite *vt* (1) England and Scotland (were) ~d in 1706; the United Kingdom; the United Nations is not a reformatory for bad governments; in those days Scotland was not ~d to England. (2) ~ two pieces of wood with glue; one ~s layers of veneer sheets to form a plywood. (3 *join in marriage*) they were ~d in a civil ceremony. (4) he ~s generosity and forgiveness; his style ~s the severe with the ludicrous. - *vi* (5) oil and water will not ~. (6) the quarrelling groups ~d against the common enemy; the Liberals ~d with the Conservatives to oppose the measure; ~ in an attempt to do s.th.; → 1.

upset *vt* (1) the baby ~ the teapot; ~ a glass of milk / table / *etc*; an ~ milk pail; don't ~ the boat. (2a) ~ one's stomach; she had an ~ stomach; he ate something that ~ him. (2b) if anything ~ her, she cried; the news quite ~ me; she was very ~ by her mother's death. (3 *disturb completely, etc*) ~ a mechanism / system / *etc*; ~ s.o.'s plans; ~ a flat. (4) the boat ~. - *adj* (5) she had an ~ stomach. (6) he is emotionally ~; your parents are very ~ about the way you are carrying on. (7 → 3) the house is ~.

urge *vt* (1) ~ dogs on with shouts; the jockey ~d his horse forward with a whip. (2 *impel with vigour, push*) ~ the cause along; ~ one's flight (3) ~ s.o. to action / greater caution; his friends ~d him to accept the job; he ~d himself to study harder; ~d by necessity; I ~d his taking the pills at once *(said to his wife)*; I ~d him to take the pills at once *(said to him)*. (4) ~ the need of haste; ~ reform / a plan of action; he ~d exercise to maintain good health; let me ~ this thought upon you.

use *n* (1a) the ~ of tools; the ~ of fireworks is forbidden in the city; a thrifty ~ of time; the correct ~ of a word; it's for my personal ~; for immediate ~; she always kept a small stock of tinned foods for ~ in an emergency; when not in ~ *(being used)*, the apparatus should be kept in the case provided; these methods were not in ~ ten years ago; s.th. is in general ~; the soap is economical in ~; that method has only recently come into ~; that word / custom has now gone / fallen / dropped out of ~; could you make ~ of a pound of cooking apples? make good / bad ~ of s.th.; charitable organizations will make ~ of your old furniture; it is a pity to throw anything away if it can be put to ~; put s.th. to good / bad / unaccustomed / *etc* ~ (→ put *vt* 6b); put an article into ~ (1b *way of using*) learn the proper ~ of a tool; this ~ of the word is rare; the painter's ~ of colour; I taught him the ~ of maps. (2 *power of using*) he lost the ~ of his right arm. (3 *right to use*) the firm gave us the ~ of its name; room to let - ~ of piano included; he was denied the ~ of a library card. (4 *possibility of using*) have you any ~ for another calendar? I have the ~ of my brother's car whenever I need it; he allowed us to have the ~ of his tennis court; the Society would be glad of any clothing that you have no ~ for; *(fig)* she appears to have no ~ for the city; he has no ~ for *(dislikes strongly)* dictators; she had no ~ for *(patience with)* John; the instrument has different ~s; find a ~ for s.th.

(5 *usefulness*) you may have this dictionary, if it is of any ~ to you; it's of no ~ to look for that missing ear-ring; of what ~ is a knowledge of Latin in the modern world? if I can be of any ~ to you, I am at your disposal; he was of temporary ~. (6 *resulting good, profit*) what's the ~ ? I don't think it's any ~ offering to help them; it's no ~ trying to advise him; what ~ is it trying to help him? what ~ is there in attempting to do it? what is the ~ of sitting down after so short a way?

(7 *custom, practice*) we followed the prevailing ~ of such occasions; in such matters ~ is everything; once a ~ and ever a custom; the polite ~s of society.

use *vt* (1a) ~ a knife / plough / chair / book / *etc*; ~ s.th. for a purpose; ~ one's hands / arms; ~ one's fists *(fight)*; ~ flour for bread / potatoes for food / water for irrigation / paper for printing / *etc*; she ~s a lot of garlic in her salads; I have only ~d the towel once; we don't ~ this room in the winter; I did not ~ the return ticket; I ~ the tram every morning; only residents may ~ this footpath; may I ~ your name *(quote you as a reference)*? I ~d the time (to look round the town); ~ a word wrongly; a commonly ~d word; ~ every / all possible means to do s.th.; ~ one's money (to buy books); he ~d him as a tool to accomplish his plans. (1b *use + fig obj*) you should ~ caution before crossing busy streets / in doing it; ~ your common sense; the general ~d craft to mislead the enemy; he ~d cunning to avoid capture; you must ~ your discretion; ~ every effort to do s.th.; ~ force; ~ one's influence; ~ one's ingenuity (to invent s.th.); which method would you ~? ~ method in one's studies; ~ precautions (2 *consume*) they ~ half a ton of coal every week. (3 *deal with*) he considers himself unfairly ~d; he did not ~ his employees with much consideration; he has ~d me like a dog / ill; ~ an animal cruelly.

use up ~ up provisions / ammunition / *etc*; someone has ~d up all the ink; he went on spending his money until it was ~d up; ~ up one's strength; by the end of the war he felt ~d up and sick of life.

V

vacation *n (chiefly AE;* → *holiday n)* a three-week / month's ~; a (long) ~ from work; take a / go on (a) ~; spend one's ~ at home / at the sea(side) / at the beach / in the mountains / in Europe / hiking / camping / *etc*; a hunting / fishing / *etc* ~; where are you going on / during your ~? *(also BE)* the *(university)* summer ~s.

value *n* (1) the ~ of a college education; he learnt the ~ of discipline; the great ~ of a queen in chess; this ring is not gold, but it has a sentimental ~; moral / ethical ~s; put a high ~ on s.o.'s service / *etc*; what ~ do you put on her advice? set a high / low ~ on s.th. (→ set *vt* 1c) (2 *material worth*) this piece of land has greatly increased in ~; a house with a ~ of $25,000; sell s.th. below its ~; nothing of ~ *(valuable)* was stolen; goods which are no longer of any ~ to their owner; the stolen goods amount to about £5,000 in ~.
(3a *equivalent worth, return*) give ~ for ~ received; get good ~ for one's money; this car was good ~ for money; property to the ~ of £1,000; the winner may select any book he wishes to the ~ of £5. (3b *purchasing power*) the depreciated ~ of the dollar (4 *denomination*) the ~ of a coin / postage stamp (5) the ~ of a sum / an angle / x; the ~ of x^3 at 2 is 8.

value *vt* (1) he ~d the car at £300; I'll see to having her jewellery ~d. (2a *consider s.th. to have value*) the cowboy ~s his horse. (2b) ~ s.o.'s friendship / advice; from his parents he learned to ~ education; do you ~ her as a secretary?

vary *vt* (1 *change in form, character, etc*) a good doctor ~ies the treatment according to circumstances; he never ~ies his style; ~ one's methods (2 *cause to be different*) she ~ied the appearance of the room by rearranging the furniture; the orchestra ~ied last night's programme with one new selection; can you ~ the pressure of the gas? (3 *relieve from uniformity*) ~ one's diet. - *vi* (4 *be different*) weather ~ies from day to day; ~ in size / shape / price; ~ in colour (from yellow to brown); colours ~ in different lights; parents ~ greatly in the degree of their strictness. (5 *become different*) the landscape begins to ~ as one drives south; prices are continually ~ing; with ~ing success (6 *deviate*) ~ from a rule / a standard / the norm.

vengeance *n* (1) I will avenge the death of my brother: such ~ will be glorious; have you the right to ~? divine ~; the injuries you have done demand not only redress, but ~; wreak ~ (2 *act of vengeance*) a terrible ~; he was plagued with petty spites and ~s; take (one's) ~ (on s.o.); seek / inflict ~ on s.o.; □ with a ~ *(to an extreme degree)*: the wind blew with a ~; this was understatement with a ~; he attacked the job with a ~.

venture *n* (1) his latest mountain-climbing ~ has been unsuccessful; a ~ into a wilderness; a new business ~; a mining ~; one lucky ~ made his fortune; be ready for any ~; he declined the ~; □ at a ~ *(without real calculation)*: a successor was chosen at a ~. (2 *money risked*) my ~ is quite a small one.

venture *vt* (1 *expose to hazard, loss*) the explorer ~d his life in a trip through the jungle; ~ one's fortune; all war is a venture, and the brave man is he who ~s

most; I will ~ 50p on it; nothing ~, nothing have. (2 *take the risk of*) ~ a voyage into uncharted seas (3) ~ an opinion / remark / question; I ~d several guesses, but they all proved wrong. (4 *be bold enough*) I ~ to disagree; may I ~ to ask for an explanation? I ~ to say that (you are behaving foolishly); a somewhat nervous woman, she would never have ~d to address a stranger; men who have ~d to defeat their inhibitions have been surprised by the results.
- *vi* (5) he travelled deeper into the country than any explorer before him had dared to ~; don't ~ too far away from the coast; he seldom ~s into society; there seems to be no reason one can't walk freely about town, and I've ~d about. (6) ~ on a new task / risky undertaking / ambitious programme of reform; will you ~ on a slice of my home-made cake?

vibrate *vi* (1) the windows ~d with every passing lorry; bells / stretched strings / a bee's wings ~. (2) a voice ~ing with passion / happiness.

view *n* (1 *range of vision*) there is a wide / spacious / open / broad / extensive / clear / breathtaking / confined / *etc* ~ from this window; you get a good ~ from here; a lorry blocked the ~; she disappeared from ~; there was not a house in ~ *(to be seen)*; keep s.o./ s.th. in ~; the ship was soon beyond ~; the train came into ~ round the bend; in full ~ *(completely visible)*: the robbery was perpetrated in full ~ of the public; we had a distant ~ of Mt Everest; on ~ *(on display)*: the goods will be on ~ next Thursday; the house and its collections are on ~ to the public. (2) a room with a (superb / magnificent) ~ (of the mountains / *etc*): the house has a wonderful ~ of / over the harbour; her flat affords a ~ of the park; it was the finest ~ I ever saw. (3 *photograph, etc*) postcards with ~s of the town; an album of ~s (4 *act of seeing*) our first ~ of the ocean was in March; we came in ~ of the lake; a private ~ (of paintings before an exhibition is opened, *etc*) (5 *inspection*) they asked for a ~ of the house and grounds. (6 *way of regarding s.th., aspect*) take a poor / gloomy / *(inform)* dim / cheerful / *etc* ~ of s.o./ s.th.; take long ~s *(show foresight)*; take a different ~ (from yours); form / get a clear ~ of the facts; a critical ~ of postwar literature; as seen from a practical ~, the situation presents several problems; in ~ of *(considering)*: in ~ of the circumstances, it seems best to wait until tomorrow. (7 *opinion*) s.o.'s ~s of / on art; what are your ~s / is your ~ of the matter? sound / sane / sober / one-sided / diverse / dissonant / common / *etc* ~s; hold (strong) ~s on / about a matter; change one's ~s; state one's ~s clearly; fall in with s.o.'s ~s; ~s differ about that; in my ~; in the ~ of the magistrate, the offence was not a serious one. (8 *intention*) I have other ~s for my child's future; will this meet your ~s? the cat has ~s on the larder; with a ~ to *(with the aim, expectation of)*: he has bought land with a ~ to building a house; they saved their way with a ~ to being able to buy a car some day. (9 *prospect*) have some pleasure in ~; he resigned his post, though he had nothing else in ~; she went over the material with the scholarship examination in ~.

view *vt* (1 *look at*) ~ pictures in an art gallery; we had hired a window from which to ~ the spectacle. (2 *inspect*) ~ evidence / records; permission to ~ the house; ~ the construction of a road (3) he ~s the situation with alarm; ~ s.th. with disfavour; I ~ the matter differently; ~ a plan from every angle; ~ s.th. impartially; ~ the repercussions of a decision; she ~s every minor setback as a disaster.

violate *vt* (1) ~ a law / rule / promise / oath / principle / instruction / agreement / treaty; ~ one's conscience (2) ~ the silence (of a reading-room); ~ s.o.'s privacy / seclusion / feelings; ~ the calm (3) ~ a frontier (4 *treat disrespectfully*) ~ a church / shrine / sanctuary; ~ a human right (5 *rape*) ~ a woman.

virtue *n* (1) the Christian ~s of faith, hope, charity; mercy and justice are co-ordinate ~s; □ make a ~ of necessity *(do willingly what one has to do; make the best of a bad situation)* (2 *chastity*) a woman of ~; a woman of easy ~ *(an unchaste one)*; a woman who has lost her ~ (3 *good quality, advantage*) he has the ~ of knowing his weaknesses; the plan has the ~ of committing us to nothing; the ~ of this car is that it runs on very little fuel; this finish has the ~ of durability as well as beauty; by ~ of *(by means of)*: he succeeded by ~ of hard work; in / by ~ of *(because of)*: he holds the title merely in

~ of seniority; he was given the job by ~ of his great experience; he was able to do it by ~ of his office. (4 *efficacy*) the ~ of medicinal herbs; this medicine has very little ~ for curing headaches.

visit *n* (1a) make a ~; pay s.o. a (short / formal / courtesy) ~ (→ pay *vt* 8); go on a ~; receive / have a ~ from s.o.; return s.o.'s ~; we shall be honoured to receive a ~ from you; be on a ~ to friends; I do not live here - I am only here on a ~; Aunt D. is coming for a ~. (1b) a ~ to a museum / theatre; a ~ to the seaside; we prolonged our ~ to Rome. (1c) a ~ by a doctor; a ~ from / by a representative.

visit *vt* (1) we ~ our grandparents every Christmas; have you ~ed him lately? (2 *go to, look at as a sightseer, etc*) ~ a museum / monument / theatre / foreign country / *etc*; we intend to ~ Paris / the castle next week; I ~ed the places of my childhood; a spot ~ed by few; please ~ our showrooms. (3 *inspect*) a general ~s his troops; the bishop ~ed his diocese; ~ the scene of a crime (4 *go to s.o. to help*) ~ the sick / poor (5a) a doctor ~s a patient; ~ a client (5b) yesterday my brother ~ed his doctor. (6) ~ a church (for a few minutes of prayer) (7 *form*) be ~ed with afflictions / illness; famine often ~s this area. (8) he is not on my ~ing list *(he is no friend of mine)*; be on ~ing terms with s.o. *(exchange visits)*.

voice *n* (1) did you hear a ~? (have) a clear / fine / firm / gentle / soft / feminine / masculine / golden / harmonious / melodious / resonant / round / sonorous / monotonous / harsh / shrill / piping / raucous / familiar / (un)trained / *etc* ~; speak in a high / loud / low / deep / cheerful / plaintive / tragic / trembling / *etc* ~; shout / talk at the top of one's ~; his ~ trembled / faltered as he tried to speak; his ~ sank to a whisper / failed him; raise the ~; raise one's ~ against s.th. (→ raise *vt* 10a); the congregation lifted their ~s in song; → lift up; I recognized your ~ at once. (2 *vocal organs*) he strained his ~. (3 *the condition of the voice*) the soprano is in good / poor ~ tonight; be in ~ *(good voice)* (4 *a sound compared to the voice*) the ~ of the wind; the ~s of the birds / frogs in spring / the night (5 *speech*) lose one's ~ (6 *s.th. compared to speech*) the ~ of nature / hope / love; be obedient to the ~ of God; the still, small ~ *(conscience)* (7 *expression*) give ~ to one's misgivings / disapproval (by a letter) / indignation / anger / *etc*; give ~ to the general sentiment (8 *expressed opinion*) his ~ was for compromise; the people's ~ is the ~ of God; with one ~ *(unanimously)* (9 *right to express an opinion)* we were given no ~ in the election of officers; I have no ~ in the matter. (10 *singer*) music for one ~ / several ~s; a composition for ~ and orchestra; a piece for alto and tenor ~s.

voice *vt* (1) ~ an opinion (2) ~ one's feelings / discontent / protest / desire / hope / *etc*; ~ the general sentiment / opposition; the editorial ~d the universal longing for peace.

vote *n* (1) cast a ~ (→ cast *vt* 1b); give one's ~ for / to s.o.; the candidate polled 370 ~s; be elected by a narrow majority of ~s; win / lose ~s (2 *act of voting*) take a ~ on a question; put a question to the ~; a secret / open ~ (3 *ballot paper*) cast one's ~ into the urn; there were 12 spoilt ~s; the ~s were still coming in at midnight. (4 *the right to vote*) give women the ~; he is too young to have a ~; they have the ~ but don't exercise it. (5 *collective noun*) was the ~ for or against the resolution? the ~ was 560 / unanimous; a majority ~; he gained the ~ against D. (6 *a collective expression of will*) the farm / labour / Irish ~; the Conservative / Labour ~ (7 *an expression of approval*) give s.o. a ~ of confidence; a ~ of no-confidence / censure; move / propose / return a ~ of thanks; this action constituted a ~ for increased aid to education.

vote *vt* (1) ~ a measure / compromise / *etc*; the town council ~d funds for a new library; ~ s.o. into a committee / the chair; ~ an incompetent mayor out of office; ... would be needed to ~ a Popular Front into power and France out of Nato. (2 *inform*) the picnic was ~d a success / failure; they ~d the idea a good one; he was ~d rather a bore. (3 *inform: suggest*) I ~ we stop for lunch / for stopping. - *vi* (4) ~ for / against s.th.; ~ on a question; ~ by (a) show of hands / acclamation / name / ballot; ~ing age / participation; the Council ~d to call a conference of ...

vote down ~ ~ a proposal / plan / person.

vote through the Bill has been ~d ~.

W

wage *n* his ~s are £20 a weeck; to main tain and improve his ~s a worker joins a trade union; war against Napoleon made labour scarce and ~s high; find a job at a reasonable ~; earn a good ~; all I expect is a living ~ *(sufficient according to minimum standards)* a miner's / labourer's / *etc*~; a daily / weekly ~; a fair day's ~ for a fair day's work.

wait *n* (1) a ~ at the border; it was a long ~ before Fred found a taxi; □ lie in ~ (for s.o.) *(remain in hiding to attack)* (2) there will be a long ~ between trains; how long is the ~ here?

wait *vi* (1) ~ for s.o. (to do s.th.); she ~s for me every evening; ~ for the train / a nod / an occurrence / a reply to one's last letter / *etc*; I can hardly ~ for the day; we ~ed till ten; he was ~ing to see his rival lose; keep s.o. ~ing; we'll have to ~ and see. (2) your dinner / a letter is ~ing for you; I have a lot of work / a sick child ~ing for me at home. (3) that decision can't ~; it is a matter that can ~. - *vt* (4) ~ one's opportunity / turn; ~ a better time to ask for a rise; they are ~ing the signal. (5 *delay*) mother ~s supper until the whole family is home; don't ~ dinner for me. (6a *wait on: act as waiter*) ~ on s.o. at table / on s.o.'s table (6b *wait on: perform services for*) he expects all the family to ~ on him; he likes being ~ed on.

wait up (1) I was ~ing up for Ann *(stayed out of bed to await her arrival)*; he ~ed up for news of his son. (2) don't go so fast - ~ up for me *(stop and allow me to join you)*.

wake *vi* (1) what time did you ~ (up)? I woke early; ~ up, it's already nine o'clock! has the baby ~d / woken yet? we woke to a bright, sunny morning / to the sound of music; I woke (up) with a start / a headache. (2 *be awake*) whether I ~ or sleep, I think of you; I will ~ until you return; in our ~ing hours (3) he woke to the beauty of his surroundings / the true situation / the danger; ~ from one's daydreams. - *vt* (4) what time shall we ~ him (up)? something woke me (up); you will ~ the baby; I should like to be ~d at 7.30; please ~ me up in time for school; don't ~ me for breakfast. (5) the music ~d sad memories; ~ passions (6) he woke his audience to the need for concerted action.

wake up → wake *vi* 1, *vt* 4.

waken *vt* (1) what time shall we ~ him? the noise ~ed her; I was ~ed by his call. (2) ~ the reader's interest. - *vi* (3) it is pleasant to ~(up) in that bed; he ~ed to the smell of coffee.

walk *n* (1a *route taken*) this is my favourite ~; a milkman's ~ (1b *path*) a gravelled ~ in a garden; keep to the ~s; □ ~ of life *(occupation, position in society)*: he would have been happier in another ~ of life; there are honest and dishonest people in all ~s / every ~ of life; they found every ~ of life closed against them. (2) go for a ~ (with s.o.); take a (short) ~ in the garden; take s.o. for a ~; take one's last ~ *(die)*; we were on a ~ in the country when...; a pleasant / leisurely / long / *etc* ~ (in the woods / round a castle / *etc*) (3 *a distance walked*) a hour's ~; it is a long ~ to the shop; it is only a half-mile / ten-minute ~ (from town). (4 *manner of walking*) she has a mannish ~ / a ~ like a duck; know s.o. by his ~ (5 *a slow pace*) go at a ~.

walk *v* (1) I would rather ~ than run / ride; are you going by tram or are you ~ing? ~ faster! ~ at an easy / comfortable / leisurely / *etc* pace (→ pace *n* 2); ~ barefoot; the child can already ~; ~ along / down the street / into a room / out of the garden / downhill / *etc*; ~ into a lamp-post / trap; ~ in step; ~ on all fours / one's hands / tiptoe / crutches; ~ with a limp / stoop; we ~ed the whole way; he ~s an hour / four miles every day; within ~ing distance of the town (2) he typed so hard that the lamp ~ed right off the desk. (3 *walk into: inform: eat greedily*) the children soon ~ed into that apple pie. (4a *walk over; inform: defeat easily*) we just ~ed over the opposing team. (4b *walk over: completely disregard the rights of, etc*) he would ~ over other people if it served his purpose. - *vt* (5) we ~ed the Lake District; I've ~ed this path before; a policeman ~s his beat; ~ the floor all night; □ ~ the streets *(be a prostitute)*; □ ~ the boards *(be an actor)*; □ ~ the hospitals *(be a medical student)* (6 *cause to walk*) a policeman ~ed him out of the room; ~ s.o.

off his feet / legs *(tire him out)*; they were ~ing him round the room soon after his operation. (7 *lead, drive, ride at a walk*) he ~ed his horse through the village. (8 *accompany*) I'll ~ you home; please ~ Mr N. to the gate; I must ~ the dog before bed; he ~ed them about the park. (9 *push*) ~ a bicycle / motorcycle.

walk away (1) then she ~ed ~. (2) we ~ed the morning ~ along the beach. (3 ~ ~ *from: beat easily*) he ~ed ~ from his competitors. (4a ~ ~ *with: win*) Ann ~ed ~ with the first prize. (4b ~ ~ *with: steal*) someone has ~ed ~ with my umbrella.

walk off (1) she was annoyed with him and ~ed ~. (2a ~ ~ *with: win*) he ~ed ~ with the silver medal. (2b ~ ~ *with: steal*) someone has ~ed ~ with my umbrella. (2c ~ ~ *with: be outstanding in*) he ~ed ~ with the fight. (3) ~ ~ excess fat / a cramp / a headache (4) he put his arm round me and ~ed me ~. (5) ~ one's legs ~ (trying to get s.th. / looking for s.th.).

walk out (1) he ~ed ~ into the night. (2) nearly a hundred employees ~ed out (of an engineering works today) *(went on strike)*. (3 ~ ~ *on: leave in the lurch*) he ~ed ~ on his wife and children.

walk up (1) you needn't ~ up - there's a lift somewhere. (2) he ~ed up to me and said ...

want *n* (1 *lack*) plants dying for ~ of rain; he died for ~ of medical care; ~ of phosphates in the soil; a ~ of tact; if we did not succeed it was not for ~ of trying; it is not for ~ of money that they live so wretchedly. (2 *state of being without s.th., need*) be in ~ of a haircut / medical care; he is in ~ of an assistant; the house is in ~ of repair; this book fills / meets a longfelt ~. (3 *poverty*) a country where ~ is virtually unknown; freedom from ~; there is ~ in even the richest cities; be living in ~; come to ~; there are still many thousands of people in ~. (4 *wants: desires, requirements*) a man of few ~s; he has remarkably few ~s; culture increases human ~s; we can supply all your ~s; attend to / minister to s.o.'s ~s; provide for s.o.'s ~s.

want *vt* (1) he ~s his dinner; I ~ some sugar; she ~s everything she sees; she is always ~ing something new; all I ~ is privacy; I urgently ~ his help; when I ~ your opinion I'll ask for it; he's ~ed by the police (for murder). (2) I ~ to see you / to stay here / you to do it / her to be happy; he ~s to be notified; I ~ this parcel registered, please; I ~ these things changed. (3 *lack*) a box ~ing a lid; the statue ~s the head; she sings well, but she ~s confidence; he ~s judgement / knowledge / courage / *etc*; he ~s the power to carry out his ideas. (4a *BE: require, need*) this soup ~s a little more salt; we don't ~ a fire on such a warm day; he ~s rest; what you ~ to put you right is a good holiday; you don't ~ to work so hard; the house ~s painting; my boots ~ mending; it ~s careful handling / to be done with care; you ~ to watch that fellow, or he'll cheat you; you think you've got some fine roses, but you ~ to see mine. (4b *BE form: it wants s.th.: s.th. is lacking*) it ~s ten minutes to two; it ~s half an hour to the appointed time; it ~s one inch of the regulation length.
(5) we can stay home if you ~. (6 *want for, in: be deficient in*) he does not ~ for money; he did not ~ for abilities / courage; she saw to it that her guests ~ed for nothing; let him ~ for nothing; he is not ~ing in courage; he is ~ing in common sense / courtesy. (7 *be in poverty*) he must not be allowed to ~; he would never allow his parents to ~. (8 *be lacking*) a motor with some of the parts ~ing; there is something ~ing; all that ~s is his signature; only one guest is ~ing; I shall not be ~ing for my part; he was found ~ing (to the occasion / his duty); I hope you will not be found ~ing then.

war *n* (1) a civil / defensive / offensive / hot / shooting / bloody ~; a ~ of conquest / aggression; the biblical ~s; the ~s of religion; the ~ on land / at sea; in ~ and peace; no more ~! prepare for / arm for / plan a ~; start / begin a ~; declare / make ~ on a country; wage ~ against / on a country; go to ~ against a country; the two nations were at ~ with each other; carry the ~ into the enemy's country / camp *(also fig)*; go off to the war; prove o.s. in ~; return home from the war.
(2 *science of war*) be skilled in / trained for ~; ~ is the soldier's business; the art of ~ (3 *state of hostility*) cold ~; ~ of nerves / words (4 *fight*) the ~ against disease / on locusts; declare ~ on crime / poverty / drunkenness; the ~s of the elements *(storms, etc)*.

warm *adj* (1) ~ water; a ~ bath; drink ~ milk at bedtime; a ~ climate / summer / day; ~ weather; be ~ to the touch (2) ~ clothes; a ~ blanket; is this sweater ~ enough? ~ly dressed (3) a ~ fire / stove (4 *slightly overheated*) be ~ from fast walking (5 *full of feeling, cordial, etc*) a ~ reception / welcome / greeting; a ~ heart; ~ thanks; thank ~ly; ~ friends; a ~ supporter (6 *excited, slightly angry*) become ~ when contradicted; the debate aroused ~ interest. (7) yellow, orange, red are ~ colours; her dress was a ~ shade of brown. (8 *fresh*) a ~ trail / scent (9) be ~ *(of a player: near the hidden object)* (10 *inform: unpleasant*) he left when things began to get ~; make it / things ~ for s.o. *(excite feelings against him).*

warm *vt* (1) ~ (up) milk; ~ (up) a room; ~ o.s. at / by the fire; ~ one's cold hands before the fire (2) the thought of seeing the family again ~ed my heart. - *vi* (3) the milk is ~ing (up) on the stove. (4) ~ to one's work / a plan / an idea; my heart didn't ~ to(wards) him.

warm up (1) → warm *vt* 1; ~ up supper; ~ up a liquid to 80^0; after I had got ~ed up I settled down to work. (2) → warm *vi* 3; as the engine ~s up it will run more smoothly; it will ~ up as the day goes on; the land ~s up more easily than the sea; the air ~ed up by 10^0. (3) ~ up to a subject; the party began to ~ up after he came; he ~ed up as he went on with his speech.

warn *vt* (1) ~ ships of a hurricane; ~ s.o. of the consequences of his action; ~ s.o. of / against pickpockets; ~ s.o. against eating a toadstool / trusting s.o.; ~ s.o. against drink; he was ~ed that his life was in danger. (2 *inform: beforehand*) he ~ed them that he intended to leave in two weeks; ~ s.o. of an intended visit; a dinnerbell is rung to ~ people that dinner will soon be served. (3 *admonish*) ~ a careless driver; I ~ed him not to be late; he warned his employees to be on time; the author ~s us to remember that England ...; her look ~ed us it was time to leave. (4 *rebuke mildly*) ~ s.o. about smoking (5 *warn away, off: give notice to keep away*) a sign warns trespassers off private grounds / ~s boats away from the docks.

warn off the guard ~ed the intruder ~.

warrant *vt* (1 *justify*) the circumstances ~ such measures; the crime ~ed a severe punishment; he found that the case ~ed something being done; the importance of adverbials certainly ~s the subject being included in this grammar. (2 *give one's word for*) it will never happen again, I ~ you; I'll ~ he did! I'll ~ he's as good a gentleman as any. (3 *guarantee*) ~ s.o. honourable treatment; ~ an article / product / payment / safe delivery; these pills are ~ed to cure headaches; this material is ~ed (to be) pure silk; we ~ the diamond genuine; I ~ that the sum will be paid.

wash *n* (1) let me have a ~; give the car a ~(-down); that boy could stand a good ~; the stain will come out in the next ~ (→ come out 8); □ come out in the ~ *(come to light; have a good result)*: ... is unknown, but it will all come out in the ~; the situation may look hopeless now, but it will all come out in the ~. (2) we had a big / large / heavy ~ today; the blue shirt is in / at the ~; put s.th. in the ~; hang the ~ on the line (3) send the linen to the ~ (4 *flow, etc of water*) the ~ of the waves on the beach; the ~ of the waves had drenched us; he was listening to the ~ of the ocean; the ~ of the incoming tide; banks undermined by the ~ (5 *the rough water left behind a moving ship*) the little boats tossed about in the ~ from the liner's propellers. (6 *matter deposited by water*) the channel was blocked by ~ from the river. (7 *liquid with which s.th. is washed, coloured, etc*) he gave the building a ~ of pale blue; white~ (8 *cosmetic liquid, lotion*) a hair- / mouth- / eye-~; apply ~ to a skinned knee (9a *weak liquid*) the tea / soup is a mere ~; I never tasted such ~. (9b *dull writing*) I never read such ~.

wash *vt* (1a) ~ one's hands / face / *etc*; ~ the floor; please ~ this dish; go and ~ yourself; □ ~ one's hands of s.th. *(refuse to have anything to do with)*: if you won't follow my advice, I ~ my hands of the business; □ ~ (one's) dirty linen in public (1b *make wet*) her eyes were ~ed with tears; roses ~ed with dew (2) ~ dirt / grime out of clothing; ~ the dirt from s.th.; ~ dirty marks off a wall; ~ the dirt off your face! ~ the residue out of a glass (3 *be suitable as a washing agent*) this powder will not ~ woollens. (4) the waves ~ed the raft; heavy seas ~ed the lighthouse; a cliff / shore ~ed by waves (5 *carry, deposit, etc by means of water*) a sailor was ~ed overboard; the flood ~ed the bridge downstream. (6) the flood had ~ed a new channel in the sand / through the bottom lands. (7 *cover with a thin coating of colour, metal*) ~ a wall blue; ~ brass with gold (8 *free from sin, etc*) ~ the soul; be ~ed whiter than the snow. - *vi* (9) you should ~ before dinner; he never ~es in cold water. (10 *wash clothes*) Monday is the day we ~. (11 *undergo washing without injury*) fabrics guaranteed to ~; this sweater ~es beautifully; will this material ~? (12 *be driven by water*) the boat had ~ed ashore in the night. (13 *go sweeping*) water ~ing into the cellars / over the pier / *etc*; waves ~ing against the sides of our boat. (14 *be found true, bear investigation*) that argument / excuse won't ~; his honesty won't ~.

wash away (1) the rain had ~ed ~ the lettering on the stone; the river ~es ~ all the soil. (2) much of the topsoil ~es ~ each spring.

wash down (1) ~ ~ a car / the decks of a ship (2) ~ the chicken ~ with a little white wine; ~ ~ a pill.

wash out (1a) ~ ~ clothes (1b) ~ ~ a glass / bottle; ~ ~ a wound (1c) ~ ~ dirt / a stain / a mark; the colour has been quite ~ed ~. (2) that stain will ~ ~. (3 *damage by means of water*) the embankment was ~ed ~ by the storm. (4 *inform: cancel*) there seems very little support for the proposed excursion, so we had better ~ it ~; ~ ~ an arrangement / event (5) those children need more sleep - they look ~ed ~; the producer was / felt ~ed ~ after the final performance of the play.

wash up (1 *wash one's face and hands*) aren't you going to ~ up - dinner is almost ready. (2 *wash dishes*) who is ~ing up tonight? I'll ~ up the dishes, don't bother. (3) the storm ~ed the boat up on the shore; this timber has been ~ed up by the waves. (4 *be washed up: end disgracefully*) after that performance, he's all ~ed up as a singer.

waste *n* (1a) the project was a ~ of material, money, time and energy; it is (a) ~ of money / time / speech to do that; a wilful ~ of food / fuel; □ go to ~ *(be wasted)*: she hates to see good food go to ~. (1b *failure to use*) ~ of opportunity (2) factory ~ pollutes the rivers; a fortune made in salvaging factory ~s; burn up all the ~ (3) nothing grows in those desolate ~s; the forest fire left a blackened ~; a ~ of sand / snow / waters; the ~s of the Sahara (4 *gradual decay*) the ~ of disease; the ~ and repair of bodily tissue (5) bodily / body / natural ~(s).

waste *adj* (1 *not used*) ~ energy / water / steam; ~ talents; the land / fields lay ~ *(uninhabited; uncultivated)*. (2) (salvage) ~ products of manufacture; ~ matter / paper (3 *serving to hold refuse*) a ~ bin / pipe.

waste *vt* (1a) ~ money / one's allowance (on s.th. useless); I must not ~ any time; ~ one's breath / words *(talk uselessly)*; all your good advice is ~d on him. (1b *neglect to use*) ~ an opportunity / chance (2 *destroy, consume gradually*) the waves ~ the rock of the shore; the forest was ~ed by fire; a country ~d by a long and futile war (3 *reduce in health*) a man whom desire, disease and prison ~d; his frame was ~d by hunger / long illness; she has a ~ing disease. - *vi* (4) turn that tap off - the water is ~ing. (5) a candle ~s in burning; his resources were rapidly ~ing. (6) she is ~ing (away) for lack of food. (7) the might of England is ~ing. (8) time ~s too fast.

watch *n* (1) their ~ for the birds was unrewarding; the police kept a ~ on the house; keep ~ over one's flock / a treasure; on the ~ *(watching continuously)*: the customs officials were on the ~ for smuggled whisky; always be on the ~ against any attempts to cheat you. (2) keep ~ for pickpockets; if you keep careful ~, you may see a falling star. (3 *keeping awake*) a mother's ~ over a sick child / beside a sickbed (4) the sailor's ~ was from midnight to four o'clock. (5) the ~ reported a ship on the horizon; a ~ was posted at sunset; call out the ~.

watch *vt* (1 *observe attentively*) ~ s.o.'s reaction / a patient's progress; I ~ed him at it; I am ~ing you! *(a warning to a child)*; ~ a substance for its reaction; ~ the course of current events (2 *be a spectator at*) ~ a play / game / parade (on television); we ~ television every evening; did you ~ television last night? "~ me dive", she cried; I ~ed you playing football last night; have you ever ~ed people try(ing) to catch fish? (3 *look after*) ~ sheep; ~ the baby (4 *pay attention to*) ~ your manners; please ~ what you're doing; I ~ my figure very carefully; □ ~ one's step

(→ step *n* 2); □ ~ one's time (→ time *n* 4b). - *vi* (5) ~ while an experiment is being performed; if you ~, you may see how I do this trick; he ~ed to see what would happen. (6 *be careful*) ~ when you cross the street. (7 *stay awake*) ~ through the night / with a sick person (8 *be a spectator*) are you going to play or only ~? (9 *keep guard*) he was assigned to ~ at the door. (10 *watch for: wait for expectantly*) ~ for the postman; ~ for a signal / opportunity; ~ for symptoms of a disease (11 *watch over: guard for protection*) she ~ed over us like a mother hen over her brood.

watch out ~ ~ for cars when you cross the road; five frauds to ~ ~ for.

water *n* (1a) ~ freezes to ice at 0^0C or 32^0F and boils / evaporates at 100^0C or 212^0F; ~ falls (from the sky) as rain / issues from (the ground in) springs / forms seas / rivers and lakes, *etc*; ~ flows / bubbles (up through the sand) / gurgles / ripples / foams (along the beach) / gushes forth / drains into the gutter; fetch ~ from the river / a ~-tap; draw ~ from a well; → pour *vt* 1; sprinkle ~ on a path / a path with ~; purify (dirty) ~; fish live in (the) ~; the roads were under ~ after the heavy rain; on the ~ *(of ship, at sea; of s.o., on a ship at sea; in a boat)*: let's go on the ~ this warm afternoon; our steamer ships ~ (→ ship *vt* 4); (im)pure / (crystal-)clear ~; the lucid ~s of a mountain lake; hard / soft / heavy / stagnant ~; a body of flowing / running ~; shallow / deep ~; high / low ~; (a room with) running hot and cold ~.
(1b *idiomatic uses*) in deep ~(s) (→ deep *adj* 1); in smooth ~ *(making easy progress)*; in hot ~ (→ hot *adj* 1); in low ~ (→ low 1); like ~ *(extravagantly)*: spend money like ~; the champagne flowed like ~; like a fish out of ~ *(feeling uncomfortable)*; fish in troubled ~s *(try to profit from the difficulties of others)*; go through fire and ~ (for s.o. / a cause) (→ fire *n* 1); hold ~ (→ hold *vt* 3); keep one's head above ~ (→ keep *vt* 8a); make / take ~ *(of ship: leak, ship ~)*; pour oil on troubled ~s (→ oil *n* 1); throw / pour / dash cold ~ on a plan / *etc* (→ throw *vt* 1e, pour *vt* 1); still ~s run deep (→ deep *adj* 1).
(2 *body of water*) we crossed the ~ by ferry; a stretch of still ~; by ~ *(by ship)*: it was much less expensive to send the goods by ~. (3 *the surface of water*) above / below / on the ~ (4 *waters: part of the ocean*) in Icelandic ~s; we sailed south for Mexican ~s. (5 *natural mineral water*) last year we went to Marienbad for the ~s; drink / take the ~s *(go to a spa, etc)*; table / mineral ~s (6 *tears, sweat, urine*) a blow that brought the ~ to his eyes; the smell of fresh bread brought the ~ to his mouth; make ~ *(pass urine)* (7) toilet / lavender / rose / soda / *etc* ~ (8 *quality, of diamonds; also fig*) a diamond of the first ~; a pianist of the first ~; a fool of the purest ~.

water *vt* (1) ~ the flowers / street / lawn (2) ~ a horse / the pigs; ~ a ship (3) Egypt is ~ed by the Nile. (4 *add water to*) ~ soup / milk. - *vi* (5) his eyes ~ed in the smoke; □ make s.o.'s mouth ~ *(excite his appetite)*: the roasting turkey made my mouth ~. (6) the cattle ~ at the creek. (7) our ship will ~ at Hamburg.

water down (1) this drink is too strong - please ~ it ~ a little. (2 *weaken*) ~ ~ an unfavourable report / the details; Labour has a better chance of winning the next election by ~ing ~ its Socialist policy.

way *n* (1 a) the ~ to the beach is rocky; the ~ was muddy after the rain; he lives over / across the ~ *(on the other side of the road)*; the permanent ~ *(railway track)* (1b *space for passing, advancing*) clear / prepare a ~; make / work / force / push one's ~ through a crowd; clear the ~ (through the crowd); *(fig)* pave / prepare / clear the ~ for s.o. / reforms / *etc*; make a ~ for o.s.; blaze a ~ through dense woods; make ~ for the fire-engine; get out of my ~!
(2a *route from A. to B.*) the ~ home / to Munich; is this the right / quickest / shortest / best ~ to town? the nearest ~ to the station; which is the ~ in / out? *(fig)* the only ~ out was authoritarian rule for a time; ask / take / find / lose / know the ~ / one's ~ (to a place); know one's ~ about (a place); do you know your ~ around Hamburg / here? (take) a roundabout ~; I don't know which ~ to turn *(am confused)*.
(2b *idioms with verbs*) fall by the ~ (→ fall *vi* 1b); give ~ (→ give way); go one's ~(s) *(depart)*; go / take one's own ~ *(act independently, contrary to advice;→ go vi 22)*; go on one's ~ *(resume a journey)*; go out of one's ~ *(make an unusual effort)*: he went out of his ~ to amuse the

children / to be rude to me; make ~ *(withdraw;→* make *vt* 3): he made ~ for a younger man; pay one's (own) ~ *(meet one's expenses;→* pay *vt* 4); pay its ~ *(of business: be self-supporting)* ; put s.o. in the ~ of s.th. *(BE show him how to do it; help him to obtain it)*: you don't seem to have got hold of the idea yet - let me put you in the ~ of it; a friend put him in the ~ of earning a living; could you put me in the ~ of a good second-hand car? put s.o. out of the ~ (→ put *vt* 9); put o.s. out of the ~ (to do s.th.) *(inconvenience o.s. to help)*; see one's ~ (clear) to doing / do s.th. *(feel disposed to doing)*: I can't see my ~ (clear) to taking that trip; we couldn't see our ~ (clear) to spending so much money at once.
(2c *idioms: prepos + way*) by ~ of *(via)*: we went to Cairo by ~ of Rome; he drove home by ~ of the mountains; by ~ of *(for the purpose of; as a means of)*: he held out his hand by ~ of (an) apology; I ask these questions by ~ of finding out the true circumstances of the accident; I should like to say a few words by ~ of introduction / explanation / illustration; I only said it by ~ of a joke;... but we thought we would go to Scotland this year, by ~ of a change; he gave me this cheque by ~ of payment for the car; to number articles by ~ of distinguishing them; perhaps the best we can do by ~ of approaching a definition of the term is to raise a number of questions; by ~ of (doing) *(in the state of; in the habit of)*: she is by ~ of being a fine actress; he is by ~ of being an authority on the subject; he is by ~ of doing better work now than formerly; he was by ~ of being particular about his appearance; by the ~ *(during a journey)*; by the ~ *(incidentally)*: by the ~, have you received that letter yet? in the ~ of *(forming an obstacle)*; stand / be / get in the ~ of s.o. / s.o.'s ~; I cannot get the door open - that chair is in the ~; he is always in my ~; he might have succeeded, had not circumstances been in his ~; in the ~ of *(in the course of; usable as, resembling)* do s.th. in the ~ of business; what have we in the ~ of food? I've never seen a man fitted with anything but wooden stumps in the ~ of artificial legs; it would be very difficult to organize anything in the ~ of a successful rebellion against him; I'm afraid I cannot do much in the ~ of helping you; on the ~ *(in transit)*: the package is on its ~; on the ~ *(during the journey)*: it happened on the ~ to Rome; when I saw him he was on his ~ home; they are on the ~ *(coming, going)*; our car broke down on the ~ to B.; better weather is on the ~; out of the ~: the village is out of the ~ *(remote)* and hasn't even a station; I'll stand this box in the corner - it will be out of the ~ *(no hindrance)* there; I'll move this chair out of your ~; keep poisons somewhere where they are out of the ~ of children *(inaccessible)*; I feel better now that problem is out of the ~ *(dealt with)*; there was something decidedly out of the ~ *(improper)* about his perfunctory apology; such behaviour was out of the ~ *(unusual)* for him; I cannot help it if that question was out of the ~ - I did not set the examination paper.
(3 *distance*) a long ~ to Rome; she lives a long ~ from here; they've come a long ~; you were a long ~ away when it happened; I can't swim far, but she can swim a long ~; the station was a good ~ up the river; I will go a little ~ with you; *(fig)* your work is still a long ~ off perfection; this will go a long ~ towards / in overcoming the difficulty *(help a great deal;→ go vi 22)*.
(4 *direction*) look / come this ~; everybody face this ~! which ~ is he going / looking?
(5 *inform: district*) down our ~; we are having a drought out our ~; the crops are looking well (out) our ~; he lives somewhere London ~.
(6 *passage; progress*) make one's ~ on foot; make the best of one's ~ *(go as fast as one can)*; the ship / motor car / skater has hardly any ~ on; lead the ~ *(go in front; show how s.th. is done)*; push / fight / feel one's ~ forward / home / back; the boat slowly gathered / lost ~; make ~ *(also fig)*; make one's ~ *(go forward; achieve success;→* make *vt* 3): make one's ~ through the mud / in the world; make one's own ~ *(prosper by one's own resources)*; under ~ *(of ship: making headway; of enterprise, etc: making progress)*: all the preparations are well under ~.
(7 *manner*) where there's a will there's a ~; the right / wrong / best ~ of doing / to do s.th.; a childish ~ of talking; a luminous ~ of writing; an orthodox ~ of doing s.th.; she has a very different ~ of dressing; a new ~ of looking / to look at

a matter; answer in a polite ~ ; he behaved in a manly ~ for one so young; a modest / the cheapest ~ of living; his way of acting / thinking / speaking; the ~ he acts / thinks / speaks; that's the ~ to do it; there's only one sure ~ to succeed; what a mannish ~ to stitch on a button; the ~ to tie a knot; you will never manage it that ~ ; I don't like the ~ he smiles; the most surprising thing is the ~ people are prepared to answer such questions; in a big ~ *(on a big scale)*; a fruit-grower in a big ~ ; in a big ~ of business; in a small ~ *(on a small scale)* : a printer in a small ~ ; live in a small ~ ; in some ~ ; (the work must be finished) in one ~ or another; in every possible ~ ; the book is good in its ~ ; he is a nice fellow in his ~ ; you will find the work quite easy, once you get into the ~ of it; take care not to get into the ~ of living beyond your income; □ to my ~ of thinking *(in my opinion)*, (to do that would be dishonest); □ ~s and means *(methods of providing money)*.
(8 *characteristic trait of behaviour, habit*) the child has winning ~s; he has many strange ~s; I don't like his ~s at all; it's not his ~ to be mean; John, as was his ~, tipped the porter generously; don't take offence - it is his ~ / that's his ~ / that's the ~ he is; the grandmother lived by the ~s of the old country; the ~s of another country are different from our own; □ the ~s of the world *(how people behave)*.
(9 *inform: physical, etc condition*) things are / the old dog is in a bad / poor ~ ; she was in a terrible ~ *(very excited)*; she was in such a / a great ~ about it *(agitated)*.
(10 *one's course of procedure*) she always has her own ~ ; it is childish to want your own ~ all the time; have / get one's ~ *(do / be allowed to do what one wishes)*; Ann's mother always lets her have her ~.
(11 *scope of experience*) the best device that ever came in my ~ ; such matters never come / fall (in) my ~ ; a bit of good fortune came my ~ (→ come *vi* 3).
(12 *respect, particular*) the plan is defective in several ~s; in some ~s you are mistaken; in many ~s she is like her father; in a ~ *(to some extent)*: in a ~, she is the nicest person I know; I like the work in a ~ ; he is in every ~ a very competent doctor; can I help you in any ~ ? he is in no ~ to blame; □ once in a ~ *(occasionally)*.

weak *adj* (1) a ~ man / plant / tree; be ~ from hunger / after an attack of fever; too ~ to climb higher; ~ eyes / muscles / nerves; he has a ~ heart / bladder / voice / stomach; ~ health; a ~ constitution / imagination; the ~er sex *(women)* (2 *lacking force*) a ~ blow; a ~ wind; ~ sunlight; ~ defence / resistance; a ~ team / eleven / army (3 *hardly able to resist*) a ~ link in a chain; a ~ rope / bridge / fortress; *(fig)* s.o.'s ~ spot (→ spot *n* 3) / side (→ side *n* 7) / point (→ point *n* 12); the ~ point of a plan / argument (4 *low in intensity*) ~ sight / hearing; a ~ cry / pulse; a ~ current of electricity; the ~ vibrations (5) ~ tea / coffee / wine / brandy; a ~ infusion (6) a ~ mind / intellect; he means well, but has ~ judgement; he is (a bit) ~ in the head *(not very intelligent)*. (7 *morally feeble*) a ~ will / character; prove ~ under temptation; ~ compliance; ~ in faith / spirit; in a ~ moment (8) a ~ government / leader / ruler / nation (9 *ineffective*) a ~ argument / joke / attempt / excuse; a ~ reply to the charges; a ~ reasoner; it is one of the author's ~est novels; ~ logic / evidence (10 *lacking knowledge, etc*) be ~ in history / spelling / *etc*; a ~ set of answers (11 *tending towards lower prices*) a ~ market; a ~ demand for goods; prices are ~.

wear *n* (1) children's / men's / beach / travel ~ ; sports ~ ; foot ~ ; under ~ ; outer ~ (2 *durability*) this material is famous for long ~ ; there is plenty of ~ in it yet. (3 *using, being used*) these shoes have seen a lot of ~ ; articles for everyday / spring / winter ~ ; I've had a lot of ~ out of this coat. (4 *damage due to use*) show signs of ~ ; the coat is the worse for ~ *(rather worn)*; ~ and tear; the carpet shows ~.

wear *vt* (1a) ~ a dress / coat / fur / hat; ~ a watch / ring / necklace; ~ a beard / a wig / spectacles / a cane; ~ a disguise; he ~s size eleven shoes; she likes to ~ green; ~ mourning; *(fig)* the great man wore his honours with modesty; □ his wife ~s the trousers / pants (in the family); □ ~ one's heart on one's sleeve *(allow one's feelings to be seen)*; □ ~ (one's years) well *(look younger than one is)* (1b) ~ one's hair short / long / parted in the middle; ~ one's dresses short (1c) ~ one's shirt to tatters / clothes to rags (2) ~ a smile / broad grin / air of triumph /

very affronted look / sullen face (3) hard use has worn these gloves; the rough road wore the soles of my shoes; I have worn my socks into holes; a worn blade / doorstep; a well-worn volume; rocks worn by the waves; the swift stream wore the stones smooth; □ constant dropping ~s the stone. (4) ~ a hole in the carpet; water wore a channel in the rock. (5 *exhaust*) toil and care soon ~ the spirit; a ~ing experience; the worn look in her eyes.

- *vi* (6 *decay through use*) the heels of his boots were ~ing unevenly; the carpet ~s thin; this coat is ~ing. (7) a strong material that will ~ (well); colours that ~ well; these curtains have worn badly. (8) my patience is ~ing thin; my hopes wore thin. (9 *be easy to tolerate*) it's hard to get to know him, but he ~s well; that idea won't ~.

wear away (1) the soles of his shoes were worn ~. (2 *pass gradually, tediously*) we wore the afternoon ~ in arguing. (3) the inscription has worn ~. (4) his patience began to ~ ~.

wear down (1) the heels of her shoes are worn ~; mountains worn ~ to low hills (2) ~ ~ (s.o.'s) opposition / resistance (3) the hectic rush of my daily work is ~ing me ~; he returned from the tropics worn ~ by fever. (4) the heels are ~ing ~.

wear off (1) these rough roads soon ~ the tread of motor tyres ~. (2) where the paint had worn ~, the bare wood was exposed. (3) the effect of the drug / his headache wore ~ at last; s.o.'s shyness / the novelty of s.th. ~s ~.

wear on it grew colder as the day wore on; as the evening wore on, a few more visitors dropped in.

wear out (1 *render useless*) children ~ ~ their shoes very quickly; ~ ~ coins; □ ~ ~ one's welcome *(stay longer than one is welcome)* (2) it ~s me ~ to look after those children for a whole day; his work was so exacting that by the end of the day he was worn out; I am worn ~ with all this work; I felt worn ~ after the long journey; his patience was worn ~. (3) clothing seems to ~ ~ in no time nowadays; cheap shoes soon ~ ~. (4) the few creases in the jacket will ~ ~. (5) his patience wore ~.

wear through a coat worn ~ at the elbows.

week *n* (1) a ~ has seven days; in the Christian calendar, a ~ begins with Sunday; Christmas / Easter ~; this (coming) ~; last / next ~; what day of the ~ is it? □ a ~ of Sundays *(a very long time)*; □ ~ after ~; □ ~ in, ~ out (2) we work a 40-hour ~; my father is in town all ~ but spends ~-ends in the country. (3a *any seven days*) a ~'s holiday / vacation; be away about a ~; he left a ~ ago today; a ~ ago yesterday / last Saturday / *etc*; I shall come a ~ from now / today / tomorrow / (next) Tuesday / *etc*; they meet once a ~ / every ~. (3b *BE*) yesterday ~ *(8 days ago)*; last Saturday ~; I shall come today ~ / this day ~ *(if today is Monday: next Monday)*; tomorrow ~; (next) Tuesday ~.

weigh *vt* (1) ~ a parcel / baby / o.s. / potatoes / *etc*; ~ s.th. in one's hand (2) ~ anchor *(raise it to start a voyage)* (3 *AE make heavy*) we ~ed the curtains to make them hang properly. (4 *consider carefully*) ~ a proposal; ~ the facts / advantages of s.th. / evidence / consequences of s.th.; ~ one thing against another; □ ~ the pros and cons of s.th.; □ ~ one's words *(choose them carefully)*.

- *vi* (5) s.th. ~s a pound / ton / less / *etc* (6) your recommendation ~s heavily in his favour; his lack of experience ~ed heavily against his chances of promotion; his opinion doesn't ~ with me at all. (7) responsibility ~ed upon him; his lie ~ed on his conscience; these troubles ~ upon his mind. (8 *consider carefully*) ~ well before deciding s.th.

weigh down (1) trees ~ed ~ by snow and ice (2) be ~ed ~ with cares / by grief.

weigh out the grocer ~ed ~ 2 pounds of sugar; she ~ed ~ flour, sugar, and fat for a cake.

weigh up he ~ed up his chances of promotion before resigning; ~ a matter up in one's mind.

weight *n* (1a) air has not much ~; my ~ is 140 pounds; put on / lose ~; be under / over ~ *(weigh too little / much)*: he is twice my ~; buy / sell s.th. by ~; postage rates are determined by ~; s.th. is light / heavy in ~; two ounces in ~ (1b) these pillars have a great ~ to bear. (2) I need two ounce ~s; a clock worked by ~s; a ~ held the door open; put down that ~ and rest your arms. (3 *unit of weight*) the ounce, pound, ton, *etc* are ~s; a table of ~s and measures (4 *system of weights*) avoirdupois / troy / apothecaries' ~ (5 *fig: burden*) the ~ of cares; knowing you are safe takes a ~ off my mind; that's a great ~ off my mind; the ~ of evidence against him; he seemed enfeebled by the ~ of years; he feels the ~ of his responsibility; he broke down under the ~ of accusation. (6 *importance*) an opinion of great ~; this is an argument of great ~; his expertness in the field lends ~ to his conclusions; the judge gave great ~ to the testimony of the accused; □ carry ~ (→ carry *vt* 16); □ pull one's ~ (→ pull *vt* 1b); □ throw one's ~ about / around *(use one's influence for self-advantage)* : after the boss started throwing his ~ around, he managed to get a new car from the company.

while *n* she stayed only for a short ~; he arrived a short ~ ago; wait a long ~; in / after a little ~; where have you been all this ~? (he comes) once in a ~ *(occasionally)*; worth (one's) ~ *(one's time, expenses, trouble)*: the art exhibition that opened yesterday isn't worth your ~; it is worth ~ bearing in mind that he ...; it's not worth your ~ applying for a job in that firm; it is hardly worth (my) ~ troubling him; it will be worth your ~ to go and see him; he knew all the right people too because it was worth their ~ to know him; it is worth the ~ of a healthy male to take aesthetic matters seriously.

white *adj* (1) ~ colour; a ~ dress / flag; a ~ bear; ~ hair *(grey; very blond)*; ~ coffee *(with milk)* / bread / meat *(poultry; pork; veal)* / wine; ~ heat; she went ~ with terror; he turned ~ with rage; as ~ as a sheet (2 *snow-covered*) ~ trees; a ~ Christmas (3) the ~ race / man; a ~ club / school / civilization (4 *not printed upon*) leave the rest of the page ~; fill in the ~ space below. (5) a (little) ~ *(harmless)* lie.

white *n* (1) I don't like the ~ *(colour)* in this picture. (2) dressed in ~ (3 *s.th. white*) the ~ of an egg; the ~ of the eye; I prefer the ~ *(wine)*. (4) several ~s and negroes.

whole *adj* (1 *comprising the full quantity, without diminution*) he ate the ~ pie? they ran the ~ distance; a ~ loaf of bread; roast an ox ~; wait the ~ day; the rain lasted three ~ days; do you want a half or a ~ one? a fire destroyed nearly the ~ village; the ~ world; the ~ thing was a swindle; ~ families died of it; tell me the ~ truth; the ~ sum / amount; the ~ problem; give s.o. one's ~ attention; summon up one's ~ strength; do s.th. with one's ~ heart *(with concentrated efforts)*; he devoted his ~ energy to the task. (2 *containing all the elements properly belonging, complete*) she has a ~ set of antique china; ~ milk; ~ meal / wheat; *(fig)* education for the ~ man (3 *undivided*) swallow a thing ~ (4 *unimpaired, intact*) he was surprised to find himself ~ after the accident; although I dropped the vase, it's still ~; there's not a plate left ~; not a single window remained ~. (5 *fully related*) a ~ brother / sister.

whole *n* (1 *s.th. which lacks none of its parts*) an organic ~; the ~ is equal to the sum of its parts; if you will give me the ~, I will divide it fairly between us; regard a work as a ~; an indivisible ~; nature is a ~. (2 *all that there is of s.th.*) he accepted some of the parts but rejected the ~; the ~ of my money was stolen; he has read the ~ of Goethe; the fire did not damage the ~ of the house; the ~ of Europe; this incident determined the ~ of his career; we can't learn the ~ of a language, but only a selection of it; ... but the season as a ~ has been a successful one for us; the essay is a model of style; whether considered in ~ or in part; we have had quite a good summer on the ~; on the ~ our stay there was quite enjoyable.

wide *adj/adv* (1) a ~ door(way) / road / gauge / brim / margin *(also fig*: we allow a ~margin for extras*)*; a ~ table; make a board half a metre ~; a ~ plank; a ~ river; the river runs ~; ~ fields / seas; a ~ area; this paper is 8 inches ~; a road twelve ft. ~; ~ cloth; a ~ screen *(cinema)*; ~ sleeves / trousers / knickerbockers; a ~ gulf / gap / opening / wound; at ~ intervals; ~ly separated (2 *fully opened*) (stare at s.o.) with ~ eyes; a ~ mouth; open your mouth ~; greet s.o. with arms ~; ~ nostrils; he yawned ~; the window was ~ open; ~ apart; be ~ awake; a ~ grin (3 *extensive*) a ~ range; the ~ world / Atlantic; he has travelled ~ly; ~ly scattered; scattered far and ~; search far and ~; a ~ly distributed plant; the firm advertises ~ly. (4 *fig: extensive, comprehensive*) a ~ field of studies / view; (a man with) ~ interests; ~ influence / experience / favour; ~ reading; he is ~ly read; ~ publicity; he / it is ~ly known; a ~ selection of goods; a ~ assortment; ~ distribution / reputation / fame / appeal / acceptance / knowledge; a ~ generalization / discussion / range of subjects *(covering many particulars)*; a ~ distinction / difference *(things are far from identical)*; differ ~ly in opinions; be ~ly different; two ~ly differing accounts of an incident; a ~ culture; it will satisfy his ~st ambition; take ~ views *(free from bigotry, etc)*; hazard a ~ guess *(allowing for errors)* (5 *distant*) the ball went ~; a ~ ball; shoot / aim ~; a shot falls ~; the arrow fell ~ of the mark / target; (your answer was) ~ of the mark / truth / purpose; a solution ~ of the mark; the remark went ~ *(far from the aim, truth)*; □ give s.o. a ~ berth *(avoid him)* (6 *fluctuating greatly*) ~ prices (7 *BE slang: sharp-witted but dishonest*) a ~ boy.

will *n* (1a) the freedom of the ~ (1b) he has a strong / tenacious / (cast-)iron / weak ~; a man with an inflexible ~ to succeed; ~ can conquer habit. (2 *strong wish, determination*) has the patient the ~ to live? my hands are obedient to my ~; □ where there's a ~ there's a way; do s.th. against one's ~; □ at ~ *(as one pleases)*: you are free to come and go at ~; wander at ~ through the countryside; □ of one's own (free) ~ *(voluntarily)*: he did it of his own free ~; □ with a ~ *(vigorously)*: we set to work with a ~; have one's ~ *(get the thing desired)*; work one's ~ *(do the thing desired)* (3 *disposition towards others*) s.o.'s good / ill ~; with the best of ~ in the world I can't help him; s.o. shows good / ill ~; a person of good ~ trusts his fellow men. (4) s.o.'s last ~ and testament; under his father's ~ he can't have his money until he is 24.

will *vt* (1) he can walk if he ~s it; if he ~s success, he can find it; the separation was ~ed, not forced. (2 *influence, compel*) she was ~ed to walk the tightrope by the hypnotist; although he was sleepy, he ~ed himself to stay / into staying awake; ~ o.s. into contentment; the psychotherapist ~ed the patient to think himself well. (3) ~ money to charity (4) to ~ is not enough - one must do; many wish, but few ~ to be good. - *vi* (5 *decide*) others debate, but the king ~s.

win *vt* (1) ~ a fight / battle / war / argument / contest / competition / game / race; he won the race (in a new record time) / high jump; ~ a case (2) they won the shore through a violent storm; ~ the summit (3a) he won his post after years of striving; our firm won two contracts for the new road; ~ s.o.'s hand / one's wife (3b) ~ (s.o.'s) favour / affection / confidence / consent / friendship / heart / love; she ~s all hearts; ~ s.o.'s support for a plan; ~ respect / popularity / fame / glory / an honour; this action won him public esteem; ~ a friend; he has a ~ning smile / look. (4) ~ a prize (at shooting / in the lottery); his design won the first prize; he won the first prize with his design; he won 10 marks from me in a bet; ~ a point / goal; they won the victory cheaply; ~ a scholarship / promotion (5) ~ metal from ore (6) ~ (agricultural) land. - *vi* (7) we've won! ~ easily / hands down *(easily)* / by a length; ~ in a race / competition; ~ at cards / in the lottery; the boxer won on points; the home team won; you can't ~ all the time. (8) he applied for a scholarship and won.
(9 *with adj*) ~ *(struggle)* loose *(from constraints; also fig)*: he won loose and escaped (from captivity / his father's narrow-mindedness); ~ free from prejudice.

win out his finer nature won ~ *(was successful by effort)*.

win over ~ s.o. ~ to a point of view / to a plan / as an ally; he won her ~ by his kindness; ~ the audience ~.

win through despite all the hardships he eventually won ~ *(survived)*.

wind *n* (1a) the ~ is rising / falling; a cold ~ is getting up / springing up / blowing from the north; there isn't much ~ today; a brisk / friendly / high *(boisterous)* / fair *(favourable)* / contrary / adverse / perverse / inconstant / impetuous / tempestuous / wayward / icy / cutting / biting / chilly / *etc* ~; a west / east / offshore / *etc* ~ (1b *idioms*) in the ~ *(about to occur)*: there's good news in the ~; cast / fling / throw prudence / an agreement / *etc* to the ~s *(abandon it)*; get / have the ~ up *(inform: become frightened)*; (see / find out) how / which way the ~ blows / lies *(the state of affairs)*; put the ~ up s.o. *(BE inform: scare him)*; sail / be close to / near the ~ *(practise economy in one's affairs; be on the border of indecency, dishonesty; escape detection by a narrow margin)*; take the wind out of s.o.'s sails *(frustrate him by doing what he was about to do)* (2 *breath*) the horse was fairly old, but his ~ was sound; catch / lose / get back / recover one's ~; have a long ~ *(be able to run a long way, talk at great length)* (3 *airborne scent*) the deer caught our ~; □ get ~ of s.th. *(get to know s.th. secret)* (4 *wind instruments*) the ~ is / ~s are too loud for the strings.

wind *vt* (1) ~ electric wire with tape; ~ a baby in a shawl (2) ~ string into a ball / thread on to a reel / spool; ~ a string about one's finger; he wound a bandage round his arm; ~ a shawl round a baby / one's arms round a child; she wound the thread off the bobbin; □ ~ o.s. into s.o.'s affections *(win them by clever ways)*; □ ~ s.o. round one's (little) finger *(make him do anything)* (3 *twist together*) ~ the strands of a rope; ~ yarn (4) ~ a clock / watch / spring-driven toy; ~ a handle (5) the stream ~s its way through the woods. - *vi* (6) the river ~s through the forest; the road wound among the hills; a ~ing path / staircase (7) the ivy ~s round the house.

wind down the clock (slowly) wound ~ and stopped for ever. (2 *inform: calm down*) ~ ~ and try to tell me exactly what happened.

wind up (1) ~ up a bucket / an anchor / ore from a mine (2) ~ up wool into a ball (3a) ~ up a clock / watch (3b *get wound up: inform: become engrossed in s.th., esp in story-telling*) when he gets wound up there's no stopping him; once he gets wound up he can tell jokes for hours. (4) the path ~s its way up between the vineyards. (5) ~ up a speech with quotations; they wound up the evening with a song; ~ up one's affairs; the company was wound up two years ago. (6) we started with soup and wound up with dessert; the meeting will ~ up with a few songs; he wound up by shooting himself. (7) be wound up *(excited)*: when she arrived she was all wound up; his wound-up feelings; she was wound up to a fury. (8 *inform*) he wound up and began an interminable story.

wipe *vt* (1) ~ furniture with a damp cloth; ~ the teacups / windscreen; ~ your boots on the mat; ~ s.th. clean / dry (with a rag); ~ one's hands on a towel; ~ one's eyes (after crying) / mouth / nose (2) ~ the dirt off your shoes / from the pictures / out of a drawer (3) ~ a thought from one's mind (4) a plate which ~s clean in a few moments.

wipe away (1) ~ ~ a stain / *etc* (2) ~ ~ one's tears.

wipe off (1) ~ ~ words (from the black-board); ~ ~ the dust (from a chair) / oil / mud (2) that money enabled him to ~ ~ the debt on his house.

wipe out (1) ~ ~ a drawer / jug (2) can you ~ this blot ~? (3a) the tanks ~d ~ all resistance; the plague ~d ~ almost half the population; ~ ~ corruption / a debt / the arrears of rent; the failure of the crops ~d ~ the farmer's savings. (3b *inform: murder*) the gangster boss ~d ~ anyone who opposed him; he had the leaders of the rival gang ruthlessly ~d ~. (4) ~ ~ an insult (by vengeance) / a disgrace / old scores *(quarrels)*.

wipe up she ~d up the pool of coffee on the floor; ~ up dust.

wire *n* (1) copper ~; flexible / twisted / barbed / insulated ~; telegraph / telephone / electric ~s; a live ~ *(also fig: vigorous person)*; □ pull ~s (→ pull *vt* 1b) (2a) send a message by ~ (2b) send s.o a ~; send a ~ home (2c *telephone*) there's someone on the ~ for you.

wire *vt* (1) ~ bales of hay; ~ the halves together (2) ~ beads / pearls *(put them on wire)* (3) ~ a house (for electricity) (4a) please ~ the money at once. (4b) if I have any further information, I will ~ you; she ~d him to come at once. - *vi* (5) don't write - ~!

wish *n* (1) fulfil / disregard s.o.'s ~es; grant / refuse / deny s.o. a ~; I have no ~ for fame or position; ready to comply with every ~ of his master; carry out s.o.'s ~es; disobey s.o.'s express ~es; is it your ~ that I should go? if my ~es had all come true, I would be rich today; a person's last ~; a dying ~ (2) (send s.o.) best ~es for (the forthcoming examination) (3 *thing wished for*) you will get your ~.

wit *n* (1) s.o.'s ready ~; a subtle / dazzling ~; he has nimble / quick / slow ~s; he hadn't the ~s / ~ enough to know what to do in the emergency / to come in out of the rain; he hasn't the ~s for the task; □ have / keep one's ~s about one *(be mentally alert)*; □ live by one's ~s *(live by clever methods)*; □ be at one's wits' end (→ end *n* 3); out of one's ~s *(mad)* (2 *wits: mental abilities*) he kept his ~s during the accident; use one's ~s to get ahead (3) Ted's ~ kept us smiling in spite of our troubles; pages sparkling with ~; be possessed of both ~ and humour (4) he was one of the great ~s of his age.

withdraw *vt* (1) she withdrew her hand from his / from the hot iron; ~ a curtain (2) ~ unkind words / a remark / an untrue charge / an objection / one's objections; ~ an application / offer / subscription / privilege; ~ coins from circulation; ~ one's support; ~ a boy from school / a horse from a race (3) ~ money / one's savings (from the bank). - *vi* (4) they withdrew to an inner room / into a corner; the others tactfully withdrew; the army withdrew under fire; ~ into o.s. *(become unsociable)* (6) he withdrew before I could nominate him; ~ from society / an undertaking / reality.

woman *n* (1) men and women; a young / old / beautiful / pretty / comely / ugly / dowdy / *etc* ~; an unmarried / single / married ~; a ~ doctor / teacher / driver / friend; a ~ of the world *(experienced)* / with a past *(a scandal attaching to her)* / of the street(s) *(prostitute)* (2 *women in general*) ~ is the helpmate of man; ~'s work is never done; ~ is fickle. (3 *the woman: feminine nature*) the ~ in her was roused; there's not much of the ~ about her.

wonder *n* (1) we gazed on the scene in ~; we received the news of their arrival with ~; he felt ~ mingled with awe at the Grand Canyon; be lost in ~ at s.th.; be filled with ~ (2) the seven ~s of the world; signs and ~s *(miracles)*; do / work ~s; the ~ is that she survived it; it was a ~ she came at all; this old chest is a ~ of delicate workmanship; □ for a ~ *(surprisingly)*: she came on time, for a ~, and worked hard all day; he refused to help, and no ~; no ~ you were so late.

wonder *vt/i* (1) I ~ed why you went so soon / what she would do next / who he was; I ~ where he has gone / what the time is / whether it is time / if she'll really get here; I ~ if I could see Mr N. *(polite request)*; I have ~ed about your progress. (2) I ~ he wasn't killed / you have the nerve to do it / at your allowing him to do such a thing / at her annoyance / you allow him to do such a thing / she was annoyed; that's not to be ~ed at. (3) they ~ed with open mouths as the magician performed his tricks.

word *n* (1) abstract / concrete / everyday / household / archaic / obsolete / old(-fashioned) / new / modern / synonymous / antonymous / elegant / stylish / vogue / *etc* ~s; 'begin, stop' are working ~s, 'commence, cease' are formal ~s; this ~ occurs rarely / frequently; this ~ has fallen into disuse / is derived from Latin / is borrowed from French; I find it difficult to put my thoughts into ~s; I have no ~s to express my gratitude; she had no ~s for the sights she had witnessed; ~s failed her (→ fail *vt/ i* 2); □ ~ for ~ *(without omitting any; disregarding the meaning)*: repeat a statement ~ for ~; translate a text ~ for ~; in a / one ~ *(to sum up briefly)*: in a ~, there was no comparison; in so many ~s *(explicitly; bluntly)*: he didn't say that in so many ~, but that's what he meant; he told them in so many ~s to get out; a man / woman of few ~s *(laconic)*; she is a woman of many ~s but little wit; speak in plain / simple / high-sounding / stilted / *etc* ~s; big *(boasting)* / fair (→ fair *adj* 9) / hard / high *(angry)* / sympathetic ~s; hollow ~s of praise; exchange (a few) ~s (with s.o.); pass bitter ~s; use ~s sparingly; weigh one's ~s (→ weigh *vt* 4); Shakespeare's immortal / deathless ~s; understand not a single ~; miss a ~; fail to grasp the meaning of a ~; a play of / on ~s (→ play *n* 1); I couldn't get a ~ in edgeways (→ get in 1) / put in a ~ (→ put in 5).

(2a *things said*) his ~s went unheeded; I don't believe a ~ of the story; don't say a ~ about it; Mr N. will say a few ~s *(make a short speech)*; □ a ~ in season (→ season *n* 2); have the last ~ *(say s.th.*

final to which there is no answer); the last ~ on s.th. *(final word; final decision*; → last *adj* 5); the last ~ in s.th. *(latest model, best example, etc)*; the last ~ in sports cars; □ eat one's ~s (→ eat 1); □ put in a (good) ~ (with s.o.) for s.o. (→ put in 5); put ~s into s.o.'s mouth (→ mouth 1); he said a good ~ *(recommendation)* on your behalf; □ suit the action to the ~s *(do at once what one has said one will do, esp of threats)*; □ take s.o.'s ~ for it (→ take *vt* 10a); □ take s.o. at his ~ *(take a statement to be true)*; □ take the ~s out of s.o.'s mouth (→ mouth 1) (2b *words: text of a song, play, etc*) set ~s to music; the actor forgot his ~s.

(3 *message, information*) ~ came that he was still alive; we received ~ of his death; get / send ~ to s.o.; leave ~ for s.o. (at his office); get / have ~ of s.th. *(hear unexpectedly)*; □ by ~ of mouth *(orally)* (4 *utterance*) a ~ of praise / greeting / advice / warning

(5 *short talk*) Miller, I'd like (to have) a ~ with you; if you can spare me a few moments, I should like a ~ in your ear *(say s.th. confidentially)*; he had a ~ with *(admonished)* her about her continual lateness. (6 *words: empty talk*) ~s, ~s, ~s! ~s mean little when action is called for. (7 *command*) he gave the ~ to attack; □ his ~ is law *(his orders must be obeyed)*. (8 *words: a dispute*) they had ~s on the matter; we had ~s and she walked out on me; I understand he had ~s with the manager, and soon after that received his dismissal. (9 *possess pronoun + word: promise*) give / keep / break one's ~; you have my ~; he was as good as his ~ *(was dependable)*; a man / woman of one's ~ *(reliable person)*: as a woman of her ~, she pledged to come to our assistance if we needed her.

word *vt* ~ a question / sentence / contract / regulation carefully / precisely / *etc*; he ~s his thoughts badly; a well-~ed letter; the letter was ~ed in such a way as to suggest ...

work *n* (1a) physical / intellectual / mental ~; light / easy / heavy / uphill / tiring / exhausting ~; a stiff piece of ~; conscientious / worthwhile / (un)satisfactory / careless / slipshod / sloppy ~; dry / thirsty ~ *(~ causing thirst)*; do good / perform useful ~; be (hard) at ~; be busy with one's ~; come, there's ~ to do; set / get to ~ *(start working)* (on a task); set s.o. to ~ (on a task); start ~ on s.th.; checking the entries will be a week's ~; ~ first and play afterwards; ~ (is what) makes life enjoyable; take pleasure in ~; □ make short / quick ~ of *(deal with quickly, effortlessly)*: the children made short ~ of the cake.

(1b *activities relating to a person, situation, etc*) a mother's ~ is never done; her sick aunt made a lot of extra ~. (2 *what one does to earn money*) → 1; his ~ takes him abroad a lot; what is your ~? what ~ do you do? is your husband not at ~ today? he had an accident at ~; there are more people in ~ this month than last; be off ~ *(not working owing to illness)*; be out of / without ~ *(unemployed)*; he went about looking for ~; go to ~ (3 *the purpose of one's work*) he made the abolition of slavery his life's ~. (4 *output of a writer, artist, etc*) the ~s of Shaw / Bach / *etc*; poetic / literary / musical / artistic ~s; a ~ of art; this statue is a ~ of Rodin; this drama is a hard ~ to understand; we advise our readers not to waste their money on a useless ~ *(book)*; Goethe's scientific ~; the cabinet-maker was proud of his ~. (5 *result of natural events*) the tree's bent form is the ~ of wind and rain; *(fig)* this is vandals' ~. (6 *needlework*) after dinner she got out her ~. (7 *operation*) we were taken to the factory to see the machines at ~. (8 *works: factory, etc*) an iron / cement / glass / gas / water ~s; the Margam steel ~s mark a big step forward; our printing ~s is housed in a basement; when it is in full production, this ~s will be employing sixteen hundred people. (9 *works: moving parts*) the ~s of a watch are delicate. □ gum up the ~s *(slang: cause confusion, complications)*: his untimely arrival really gummed up the ~s; □ throw a *(AE)* monkey wrench / *(BE)* spanner in(to) the ~s *(inform: complicate, sabotage a situation)*: the committee threw a monkey wrench / spanner into the ~s by withdrawing all financial support at the last moment.

work *vi* 1-8; *vt* 9-20.

The patterns are grouped as follows: ~ + *adj* 4a, 16; ~ + *abstr obj*: 20; ~ + *prepos*: into 10, 19; on 8; wrought: 10, 19, 20.

(1) ~ hard / like a horse / without interruption / to death / into the next day; he's ~ing at a new invention / at Russian / on

a new novel; you can't expect to master a subject if you don't ~ at it; ~ for the pleasure of it / nothing / the abolition of slavery / promotion; he ~s in oils / water-colours; you can't expect a person to ~ all day on a bun and a glass of milk; the police are ~ing on the assumption that robbery was the motive of the crime; ~ from false assumptions; I ~ed through the book with difficulty; ~ with one's hands / a tool; she gets on very well with the people she ~s with. (2 *earn a living, etc*) → 1; she's too young to ~ and is still at school; he's ~ing in the printing trade / as a carpenter / in a new school (as a teacher); how do you like ~ing in a bank? he hasn't ~ed for six weeks; ~ overtime; he ~s at the Town Hall / for an employer / for a firm / for his family / for £30 a week / for his / a living / in town / with a firm; ~ in shifts; □ ~ to rule *(in strict accordance with regulations instead of striking)* (3 *operate, function*) the pump will not ~; the door ~s on a spring; the hinges ~ stiffly; the ~ing parts of a machine; the kidneys are ~ing normally. (4a *attain a condition*) the nail / nut / screw / knot ~ed loose; one of the parts has ~ed free (→ free *adj* 5); the shirt ~ed up his back; your blouse has ~ed out *(of the skirt)*. (4b *move very slowly*) the foundations show signs of ~ing; the rain ~ed through the roof; the wind has ~ed round to the south; he ~ed slowly along the ledge. (5 *ferment*) cider ~s and produces vinegar; the yeast is too old to ~; yeast makes beer ~; *(fig)* the idea ~ed like madness in his mind. (6 *move involuntarily under strong emotion*) you could tell by the way his face / features ~ed that it was bad news; her hands were ~ing in her lap as she talked. (7 *be successful, have a result*) the plan / system ~s; I don't think that method will ~; did the medicine ~? I'd like to see my money ~; *(fig)* flattery will not ~ with him. (8 *work on: influence, persuade*) she says she will never date him, but I'll ~ on her, and perhaps she'll change her mind; ~ on your father until he agrees; ~ on s.o.'s feelings / sympathy; the defence counsel ~ed on the jury's doubts.

- *vt* (9a *operate*) she can ~ many business machines; how do you ~ this pump? a mill ~ed by water / electricity; *(fig)* ~ a phrase to death *(use it too often)* (9b) ~ a (coal-)mine / farm; ~ land (10 *treat by labour, manipulate*) ~ butter / dough (thoroughly); ~ wood / iron; wrought iron; ~ clay into a vase; wrought in brass / stone; ~ a tight cork into a bottle; he ~ed the knife into the crack; ~ the oil into the mixture drop by drop; the pattern is ~ed into the material; *(fig)* ~ new facts into a treatise; ~ Shakespeare quotations into one's speech (11 *make by needlework*) she ~ed a cushion cover; can you ~ buttonholes? ~ initials on a handkerchief (12 *solve*) ~ an equation; you have ~ed your sum wrong. (13 *move very slowly*) he ~ed the heavy stone into place; he ~ed his way / himself along the ledge; he ~ed his way through the mud. (14 *carry on operations in*) ~ a district / region; this salesman ~s the East Coast. (15 *pay for by doing work*) ~ one's passage to America; ~ one's way through college (16 *keep s.o. at work*) she ~s her employees hard; ~ o.s. / an animal to death; ~ o.s. ill (17 *bring into condition*) he was able to ~ himself out of / himself from his fetters; can you ~ the screw / nut loose? (18 *influence insidiously, use trickery on*) ~ men to one's will; see if you can ~ your uncle for a new car; the swindler ~ed the whole town. (19 *excite the emotions of*) she ~ed herself into a panic / temper; he wrought his audience into enthusiasm. (20 *bring about*) the storm ~ed / wrought great ruin; the destruction wrought by the fire was appalling; time has ~ed / wrought many changes; the doctor ~ed / wrought wonders / miracles; this belief has wrought much evil; □ ~ one's will upon s.o. *(accomplish one's purpose)*.

work in (1) he managed to ~ the knife in(to the crack). (2) the tailor ~ed in the patch skilfully; *(fig)* can't you ~ in a few jokes *(into your lecture, etc)*? (3) the dentist was very busy but he said he would be able to ~ me in late in the afternoon. (4) the dust ~s in everywhere. (5) his ideas did not ~ in with those of his colleagues; a difficult task can be made easier if people will ~ in with one another.

work off (1) ~ ~ surplus weight / energy (2) ~ ~ arrears of correspondence (3) ~ ~ a debt (by doing odd jobs) (4) ~ ~ anger on s.o.; if anything upset him he ~ed his annoyance ~ on the rest of the family; ~ ~ one's bad temper on s.o. (5)

as I got about, the stiffness in my left leg gradually ~ed ~.

work out (1) ~ ~ an amount / area / *etc*; ~ ~ a puzzle / problem; they ~ed ~ that it would cost £80. (2) ~ ~ a debt (→ work off 3) (3) ~ ~ a plan / scheme / compromise / solution; you haven't ~ed the essay ~ carefully enough. (4) → work *vi* 4a (5) the bill ~s ~ at 70p.; a suit made of that material ~s ~ at 24 guineas; the total ~s ~ to 1,200; I cannot get the sum to ~ ~. (6) everything has ~ed ~ according to plan; things did not ~ ~ as we had expected; their plan did not ~ ~.

work over (1) for my term paper I ~ed ~ *(studied thoroughly)* 20 volumes of Roman history. (2 *slang: thrash, beat physically*) the gangster had the shopkeeper ~ed ~ so that he would cooperate; he ~ed him ~ with a rubber hose.

work up (1) ~ ~ the flour and butter into a paste; *(fig)* ~ ~ a collection of facts into an article (2) ~ up a portrait from a sketch; ~ up a sketch into a portrait (3) the business was almost bankrupt when he took it over, but within a few years he had ~ed it up to be a prosperous concern; ~ up a reputation for one's goods; she ~ed up her typing speed to seventy words a minute; she will have to ~ up the last movement before the concert. (4) ~ up some plans; the teacher told the class to ~ up the Industrial Revolution for the examination. (5) ~ o.s. up in a profession; he ~ed himself up to be head of the firm. (6a) ~ up enthusiasm for s.th. / the public's interest: ~ up a friendly feeling / rebellion (6b) they ~ed the crowd up; ~ o.s. up about trivial things / into a rage; she was all ~ed up when she arrived; the audience began to get ~ed up. (7) he ~ed up to the presidency. (8) the story ~ed up to a thrilling climax.

world *n* (1a *the earth*) travel round the ~ (1b *idiomatic phrases*) (I wouldn't be without my dog) for the ~; for all the ~ *(for any consideration; precisely)*; she wouldn't come to visit us for all the ~; you look for all the ~ like my Aunt Mary; it sounded for all the ~ as if he meant it; I thought for all the ~ that the car would plunge headlong down the bank; in the ~ *(used as intensifier)*: I never in the ~ would have believed such an obvious lie; where in the ~ did you find that hat? how in the ~ can they get there on time? what in the ~ are you doing that for? on top of the ~ (→ top *n* 1a); out of this / the ~ *(excellent)*: she bakes an apple pie that is out of this ~; he's out of this ~ *(far away from reality)*; we liked the house, but the price they asked for it was out of this ~ *(unrealistic)*; set the ~ on fire (→ fire *n* 2); think the ~ of *(admire greatly)*: his co-workers think the ~ of him.
(2 *universe*) space travel will teach us more of the ~. (3 *planet, star*) are there other ~s like ours? the starry ~s (4 *mankind*) the ~ lives in fear of nuclear warfare. (5 *part of mankind, of the world*) the Roman / ancient ~; the fashionable ~; the English-speaking ~; the Old W~ *(Europe)* (6 *life on this earth*) he has departed from this ~; bring into the ~ *(give birth to; assist in this)*: she / this doctor brought many children into the ~; come into the ~ *(be born)*; in this ~ and the ~ to come; the next / other ~.
(7 *social, secular life*) he is a man of the ~; he withdrew from the ~ to practise his art; come / go down in the ~; rise in the ~; he knows / has seen the ~; begin the ~ *(start one's career)*; □ how goes the ~ with you *(are your affairs)*? □ make the best of both ~s *(reconcile secular and spiritual interests)* (8 *all things of which one has experience*) his ~ is rather limited. (9 *everybody*) the ~ honours power / worships success; all the ~ / the whole ~ knows it; all the ~ came to the fair.
(10 *the whole of a domain, etc*) the animal / vegetable / plant / mineral ~; the insect ~; the ~ of art / books / music / sport / dreams / *etc*; woman's ~ (11 *great amount*) there is a ~ of difference between them; he gets a ~ of pleasure from music; a ~ of patience / trouble / anxiety; the medicine did me a ~ of good.

worry *n* (1) I don't want the ~ of a larger business; the ~ of her husband's illness has undermined her health; she shows signs of ~; cause / give s.o. a lot of ~; be consumed / eaten up with ~; lines of ~ (in s.o.'s face) (2) the chance of fire in this wooden house is a ~ to me; their son's illness has been a great ~ to them; her freckles are her greatest ~; an oppressive / undue ~; s.o.'s only ~; other people's ~ies don't bother him.

worry *vt* (1) his debts / her illness ~ied him; is something ~ing you? it ~ies me that the child makes no progress; I am

~ied about his health / by his long absence; with a ~ied face (2) he is always ~ing me about that money I owe him; don't come ~ing me with your complaints; the girl ~ied her parents with questions; the artillery ~ied the enemy. (3 *seize by the throat, etc*) the wolves ~ the sheep; the cat ~ied the mouse. (4 *harass by chasing, snapping at, etc*) the puppy ~ied the edge of the carpet; the dog is ~ing a bone. - *vi* (5) ~ about one's health; don't ~ about / over him; he ~ies over the least thing that goes wrong. (6) his condition is extremely ~ing.

worry along → worry through.

worry out ~ ~ a problem (by constantly attacking it).

worry through to others the situation seemed intolerable, but with luck and persistence she ~ied ~.

worse *adj* (1) we have had ~ weather than usual; I can't imagine a ~ piece of news; you are making things ~; my shoes are the ~ for wear (→ wear *n* 4); he is ~ off now than before. (2 *more ill*) she was ~ before she took this medicine; I'm glad you don't feel any ~.

worse *adv* you're playing ~ than ever; if he treated him ill, he treated me ~; I shall like you none the ~ *(not less)* if you speak frankly.

worse *n* ~ was to follow; there is ~ to tell; ~ cannot happen; a change to the ~; things are going from bad to ~; the patient took a turn for the ~.

worst *adj* the ~ headache I've ever had; the ~ boy in the class; the ~ house on the block; it's the ~ paper submitted.

worst *adv* she sings ~ when she is nervous; Tom played ~.

worst *n* I've had to deal with the ~ in sickness and poverty; be prepared for the ~; the ~ of it is that he ...; □ if the ~ comes to the ~ *(if the worst happens)*; □ get the ~ of it *(be defeated)*; □ at (the) ~ *(under the worst conditions)*: he will be expelled from school at (the) ~.

worth *n* (1) my jewelry would have little ~ if I tried to sell it; determine the ~ *(value)* of a diamond bracelet (2 *degree of excellence, etc*) do not underestimate his ~; her poems are of little ~ compared with her novels; she has little ~ as a student; a book of great / not much ~; a man of *(high)* ~ (3) buy sixpence ~ of nails; a shilling's ~ of sweets; he always gets his money's ~. (4 *s.o.'s material wealth*) what would you estimate his ~ at?

worth *adj* (1) this vase is ~ £10 / a great deal of money / nothing / little. (2 *deserving*) a visit to ... is ~ the effort; it's not ~ consideration; this is advice ~ taking; a place ~ visiting; three points are ~ quoting for our purpose; an opinion ~ having is ~ defending; □ for all one is ~ *(with all the power one has)*: he ran for all he was ~; □ for what it is ~ *(without any guarantee)*: take a story for what it is ~; ~ while (→ while *n*) (3 *rich to the extent of*): he is / died ~ millions.

wound *n* (1) he still feels the effects of his war ~s; a bullet / knife ~; a gaping / wide / serious / bloody / injurious / mortal / vital / angry *(inflamed)* / septic ~ (2) a ~ to his pride / vanity.

wound *vt* (1) he was ~ed in the war; ~ed by a bullet; several men were ~ed in the brawl. (2) ~ s.o.'s reputation / pride; he felt ~ed in his honour / affections; her sharp words ~ed him deeply.

wrap *vt* (1a) ~ (up) a package / parcel (in brown paper, *etc*); she ~ped her head in a scarf; ~ o.s. (up) in a blanket (1b) clouds ~ped the mountain's peak; a landscape ~ped in mist; the fog ~ped the streets in darkness. (2) ~ a scarf round one's neck; he ~ped his blanket closely round / about him. (3) an affair ~ped in mystery; why does he ~ (up) his meaning in such obscure language? - *vi* (4) ivy ~ping round a tree trunk (5) a sari ~s twice round the waist.

wrap up (1) → wrap *vt* 1a; he ~ped the child / himself up warm(ly); be all ~ped up in furs (2) → wrap *vt* 3. (3) you'd better ~ up well before you go out. (4) be ~ped up in one's work / studies; since he became ~ped up in politics I have lost touch with him; she is so ~ped up in her children that she has no time for anything else; be ~ped up in oneself; they are ~ped up in each other *(deeply interested in each other only)*.

wreck *v* (1) the collision ~ed the car beyond repair; the ship was ~ed; buildings ~ed by an earthquake; a crop ~ed by frost; you'll ~ your digestion if you swallow your food in that way; (ship)-~ed sailors (2) ~ s.o.'s hopes; plans ~ed by bad luck; if private educational institutions were ~ed it would be a disaster to the country. - *vi* (3) the trains

~ed at the crossing. (4) that is the rock your hopes will ~ on.

wring *vt* (1) ~ (out) wet sheets; he caught the chicken and wrung its neck; my clothes were ~ing wet. (2) ~ water out of wet sheets (3) ~ s.o.'s hand; ~ one's hands in despair / pain (4) ~ a confession from a thief; ~ money / consent / a promise from / out of s.o. (5) the account of the tragedy wrung our hearts.

write *vt* (1) ~ letters / figures / symbols on s.th.; ~ shorthand; ~ your name and address here; ~ a formula on the blackboard; it's written in ink / pencil. (2) ~ three pages; ~ a cheque (3) ~ a letter to a friend / certificate / application; he wrote me an account of his visit; ~ a poem / article / book / sonata; he ~s English better than he speaks it. (4) he wrote them the latest news; she has written twice that she is having a wonderful time; ~ him to return directly. (5) despair was written on every face; Tim's guilt was written all over his face.
- *vi* (6) Lucy could ~ when she was five; you must ~ legibly; he ~s a good / legible hand; ~ from dictation; ~ large / small / plain; ~ with a pen; what shall I ~ about? (7 *write a letter*) did he ~ to you? ~ home; ~ if you get work; he wrote to me for money; I wrote there / to them and received no reply. (8) he ~s for the Daily News; I ~ a little for the papers. (9) this pen ~s well.

write down (1) ~ ~ the following words; please ~ ~ your name at the bottom. (2 *judge*) I should ~ him ~ a fool; she wrote him ~ as a nonentity; whenever I hear a person protesting his sincerity I ~ him ~ a hypocrite.

write off (1) I'll ~ ~ for the application form; no sooner did he see the advertisement than he wrote ~ for particulars of the post. (2a) ~ ~ a debt / a sum of money / the arrears of rent (2b) when the car is a year old you can ~ two hundred pounds ~ its initial value. (2c) lending libraries have to ~ ~ a certain amount of their stock each year; 300 volumes have been written ~. (3 *dismiss from consideration*) of the five candidates, two can be written ~ straight away; I have written John ~ as a friend; the invention had to be written ~ as a failure. (4 *compose easily*) he wrote ~ the essay in ten minutes.

write out (1) ~ ~ a name in full / a number in words; ~ s.th. ~ in longhand; the witness wrote ~ his account of the accident; ~ ~ a cheque; ~ ~ a passage / a poem / one's part (from a book) (2) she has written herself ~ *(exhausted her ability)*; some say that the novel has been written ~.

write up (1 *put into writing, esp in full detail*) ~ up a report; the lecturer went to the blackboard and wrote up a formula; the students were asked to ~ up an account of what had been told them during the lesson; I have the minutes of the meeting in note form, but they have yet to be written up. (2 *describe in detail*) for homework, you are to ~ up the experiment you saw today. (3 *bring up to date*) she wrote up her diary every evening. (4 *praise*) the critics wrote up the production of the play.

wrong *adj/ adv* (1 *not morally right*) it is ~ to steal or tell lies; a ~ deed; you were ~ / it was ~ of you to contradict the boss; □ go ~ *(behave immorally)*: it is sad that one so young should go ~. (2 *not correct*) a ~ answer; that idea is certainly ~; dial a ~ number; a ~ expression / usage / use of words / date / *etc*; give s.o. (the) ~ information; first impressions can be ~; the ~ way to hold a golf club; he did his sum ~; a ~ly done sum; you did it ~ again; you've got the answer ~; don't get me ~ *(misunderstand me)*; my watch is ~ (→ 5); I think you are ~; I can prove you ~; do s.th. / aim / guess ~; lead s.o. ~; we were ~ly informed; he directed me ~ly; the man told me ~ and I got lost in the forest; that is completely ~ / as ~ as can be.
(3 *mistaken*) you are ~ in thinking him intelligent; he was ~ in what he said; you are ~ to blame him. (4 *not proper*) they chose the ~ time to drop in; do / say the ~ thing; economize on the ~ thing / in the ~ place; he put his hat on the ~ way round; a ~ interpretation / conjecture; □ on the ~ side of 50 (→ side *n* 6); □ get out of bed on the ~ side (→ bed *n* 1) (5 *out of order*) what's ~ with the pump? there's something ~ with my watch (→ 2); □ what's ~ with (that thing) *(it's quite satisfactory)*?
(6 *not the one wanted, expected*) that's the ~ house / person; go ~ *(take the ~ road)*; get into the ~ train; this is the ~

book – I wanted the red one; □ go ~ *(fail)*: everything is going ~ today; □ get / have hold of the ~ end of the stick (→ end *n* 1); begin / start s.th. at the ~ end (→ end *n* 1) (7 *not meant to be seen*) the ~ side of cloth; this sweater is ~ side out.

wrong *n* (1 *what is morally not right*) choose between right and ~; do ~ *(sin)*; put s.o. in the ~ *(make the guilt seem his)* (2 *act of injustice*) a grievous ~; two ~s never make a right; he committed many ~s; the ~s they suffered aged them; he has done me a great ~; do s.o. ~ *(judge his motives unfairly)* (3 *what is not correct*) he knew he was in the ~, but refused to concede the point.

Y

year *n* (1) there are 365 days in a ~; in what ~ were you born? a whole / full / round ~; half a ~; throughout / during the whole ~; all the ~ round; in the ~ of our Lord (1520); in the ~ 1950; (five) ~s ago; this / next / last ~; the current / next / following ~; the ~ after next / before last; in the coming ~; a ~ later / after; the success of this measure will be apparent in ~s to come; in a few ~s' time; we have been to that place for a holiday ~ after ~; ~ by ~ we grow a little older; there she lay ~ in ~ out, with no hope of recovery; once / twice a ~; a good / bad ~; the old / new ~. (2 *any period of 12 months*) I began work on August 14, two ~s ago today; it will be a ~ in December since we ...; it will be many ~s before he ...; today I met someone whom I had not seen for (several / many) ~s; it's ~s since I saw him; the astronomical / solar / lunar / calender / common *(not leap ~)* / academic / school / ecclesiastical / Church / financial / fiscal ~ (3 *year of age*) be ten ~s old; he is still young in ~s; he is tall / young for his ~s; in his tenth ~ *(at the age of 9)*; the ~s have not passed him by. (4a *year of studies, etc*) he is a student / apprentice in his third ~; serve one's ~ in the Forces (4b *year of imprisonment*) he got 12 ~s.

yield *n* (1) a good ~ from this farm; a good ~ of wheat; an increased ~ per acre; the ~ of a field / fruit-tree / mine (2) the ~ of an investment; the ~s on his shares have decreased this year.

yield *vt* (1) these trees will ~ good timber; this ground ~s a good / heavy crop. (2) bank deposits ~ interest; an investment ~ing 10% / a handsome return; the business does not ~ much profit; the research ~ed no result. (3) ~ ground to one's opponent; ~ a fort (to the enemy); he ~ed himself to temptation. (4 *give as due*) ~ precedence to s.o.; ~ a point in an argument; ~ the palm to s.o. *(be surpassed by him)*; ~ obedience / thanks; ~ the right of way to an ambulance. – *vi* (5) these fruit-trees ~ well. (6a) the willow ~s to the wind; the door suddenly ~ed to her hand. (6b) ~ at the first assault / to the rebels (7) ~ to s.o.'s demands / request; ~ to persuasion / pressure / force / temptation; the great principle in a contest with a child is: do not ~ but do not punish; the disease ~ed to treatment; his courage never ~s.

young *adj* (1a) a ~ child / boy / girl / man / woman / lady; a ~ animal / plant; ~ grass / foliage / green peas; she is a real ~ woman / proper ~ lady now; the ~ people of today; be too ~ for s.th. / to do s.th.; the ~(er) generation; a ~ nation / country / civilization; we are only ~ once; his legs are still ~. (1b *relating to youth*) in one's ~ days; in one's ~er years (1c *having the vigour, etc of youth*) he is ~ for his age / years; feel ~; be ~ in mind / heart / spirit; how do you stay so ~? a man of ~ ideas; the dress makes her look very ~; I am not as ~ as I was / used to be *(am losing vigour)*. (1d) ~ Mr Brown *(not the father)*; the ~ Joneses *(the children)* (2) a ~ enterprise / company / science (3) the ~ day; the night / year is still ~.

young *n* (1) this book is written for the ~; a game for ~ and old; the educated ~ of today (2) the tiger's ~; a mother hen protecting her ~; with ~ *(usu of animals: pregnant)*.

youth *n* (1a) his ~ was spent at a farm; be in the prime of one's ~; be past one's first ~; in his / my ~; keep one's ~; eternal ~; his ~ excuses him; gilded ~ (1b) the business, even in its ~, showed great potentiality; life was very different in our country's ~. (2) a number of ~s *(young men)* standing at the corner; a promising ~ (3) the ~ of the country / nation; the ~ of today; modern ~.